Studies on Korea:
A Scholar's Guide

Published with the support of the Joint Committee on Korean Studies of the American Council of Learned Societies and the Social Science Research Council.

Studies on Korea: A Scholar's Guide

edited by
HAN-KYO KIM
with the assistance of
HONG KYOO PARK

A Study from the Center for Korean Studies
UNIVERSITY OF HAWAII

THE UNIVERSITY PRESS OF HAWAII, HONOLULU

Library of Congress Catalog Card Number 79-26491
ISBN 0-8248-0673-5

Manufactured in the United States of America

To my colleagues in Korean studies
and to On Ja, Dorothy, and Annette

Contents

Chapter Editors   xv
Special Contributors   xvi
Preface   xvii
Editorial Format   xxi

CHAPTER 1. Bibliographies, Handbooks, Journals, and Other Publications/ *Han-Kyo Kim*   1
    Introduction   1
    Bibliography   4
       Bibliographies and Studies Guides   4
       Handbooks and General Surveys   9
       Journals and Monograph Series   10
       News Publications   11
       Reference Works   11
          Yearbooks   11
          Statistics   12
          Biographical Materials   12

CHAPTER 2. Archaeology/*Richard Pearson*   13
    Introduction   13
    Radiocarbon Dates from Korea (table)   19
    References Cited   22
    Bibliography   23

CHAPTER 3. History/*Yŏng-ho Ch'oe*   27
    I. General/*Yŏng-ho Ch'oe*   27
       Introduction   27
       Bibliography   41
          General Historical Surveys   41
          Politics and Society   44

          Religion and Education   45
          Foreign Relations   45
          Koreans Abroad   46
          Historiography   47
    II. Ancient Chosŏn, Three Kingdoms, and Koryŏ/*Hugh H. W. Kang and Michael E. Macmillan*   48
       Introduction   48
       Bibliography   52
          Politics and Society   52
             Ancient and Three Kingdoms Periods   52
             Silla   54
             Koryŏ   55
             Others   56
          Religion and Education   56
          Foreign Relations   58
             Korean-Chinese Relations   58
             Korean-Japanese Relations   58
             Korean-Mongol Relations   59
             Others   60
          Historiography   60
    III. The Yi (Chosŏn) Dynasty before 1876/ *Yŏng-ho Ch'oe*   61
       Introduction   61
       Bibliography   66
          Politics and Society   66
             Politics   66
             Law   69
             Economy   70
             The Taewŏn'gun   71
             Society   71

Religion and Education   73
   Confucianism and Catholicism   73
   Education   74
   The Sirhak *School*   74
   The Tonghak Movement   75
Foreign Relations   76
   Korean-Chinese Relations   76
   Korean-Japanese Relations   77
   Korea and the West   78
Historiography   79
IV. The Late Yi (Chosŏn) Dynasty: 1876–1910/
Young Ick Lew   80
 Introduction   81
 Bibliography   83
  Primary Sources   83
   Archival Sources   83
   Private Papers   84
   Official Government Publications   85
   Contemporary Periodicals   85
   International Agreements   86
   Memoirs, Travel Accounts, and
    Contemporary Treatises   86
  General   88
  Politics and Society   89
  Religion and Education   92
  Foreign Relations   93
   Multinational Relations   93
   Korean-American Relations   94
   Korean-Chinese Relations   98
   Korean-Japanese Relations   98
   Korea's Relations with Britain, France, Italy,
    and Russia   100
  Biographical Studies   101
V. The Japanese Colonial Period/
Yŏng-ho Ch'oe   102
 Introduction   102
 Bibliography   103
  Politics and Society   103
   Colonial Rule and Institution   103
   Korean Nationalism   106
   The March First Movement   107
   Communism   108
   Economy   109
   Society   110
   Koreans in Japan   111

Religion and Education   111
   Religion   111
   Education   111
  International Relations   112
  Biographies   112
VI. The History of Science/*Seong Rae Park* 113
 Introduction   113
 Bibliography   115
  General   115
  Mathematics, Physics, and Astronomy   115
  Medicine and Biology   117
  Geography and Geomancy   117
  Technology   118

CHAPTER 4. Philosophy and Religion/
Kah-Kyung Cho   120
 Introduction   120
 Bibliography   125
  General Works   125
  Primitive and Native Religions   126
  Confucianism   126
  Buddhism   127
   General Bibliography   127
   Books and Articles   127
  Tonghak (Eastern Learning) and Ch'ŏndogyo
   (Religion of the Heavenly Way)   128
  Philosophy   129
  Christianity   129
   General Bibliographies   129
   General Reports   129
   General Books and Articles   130
   Catholicism   132
   Protestantism   132

CHAPTER 5. Language and Linguistics/
Chin-W. Kim   134
 Introduction   134
  The Korean Language   134
  Origins of the Korean Language   136
  Korean Linguistics in the West   140
 Bibliography   141
  Bibliographies and Anthologies   142
   Bibliographies   142
   Anthologies and Festschrifts   142

Contents   ix

General Studies   143
  General Descriptions   143
  History of the Korean Language   143
  History of Korean Linguistics   143
The Sound System   144
  Phonetics   144
  Phonology   145
Lexical Structures   147
  Etymology   147
  Morphology and Word Formation   148
  Loanwords   149
Grammars (Syntax and Semantics)   149
  Pre-1967   150
  Post-1967   151
Historical and Comparative Studies   156
  Genealogy   157
  Historical Studies   157
  Comparative Studies   158
Dialectology and Sociolinguistics   159
  Dialectology   159
  Language Standardization   159
  Sociolinguistics   159
Writing Systems   160
  The Korean Alphabet (han'gŭl)   160
  Romanization   161
  Chinese Characters (hantcha *and* idu)   161
Dictionaries   162
  Korean and English   162
  Korean and Russian   162
  Others   162
Pedagogical Materials   163
  Learners and Readers   163
  Contrastive Studies   164

CHAPTER 6. Literature and Folklore/
Peter H. Lee   165
Introduction   165
  Poetry   165
  Folklore   166
  Fiction   168
  Drama   170
Bibliography   172
  General   172
  Poetry   172
  Folklore   173

Fiction   174
Drama   175
PhD Dissertations   175

CHAPTER 7. Art, Music, and Drama/
Lena Kim Lee   176
Introduction   176
  Art/*Lena Kim Lee*   176
    Aesthetic Characteristics   176
    A Brief Outline   178
    Three Kingdoms Period: Koguryŏ; Paekche;
    Silla 178; Unified Silla Period 181; Koryŏ Dynasty
    182; Yi Dynasty 184; Modern Period 186
  Music/*Bang-song Song*   187
    Court Music   187
    Ritual Music 187; Banquet Music and Military
    Music 188
    Folk Music   189
    Instrumental Music 189; Vocal Music 190
    Religious Music   191
    Buddhist Music 191; Shamanistic Music 192
  Drama and Dance/*Du-Hyun Lee*   192
    A Brief Outline   192
    Representative Plays   192
    The Ancient Period 192; Three Kingdoms and
    Unified Silla 193; Koryŏ Dynasty 193; Yi Dynasty
    193; The Modern Period 194
Bibliography   194
  Art/*Lena Kim Lee*   194
    General Works   194
    Books 194; Catalogs 195
    Architecture   196
    Book 196; Articles 196
    Sculpture   196
    Catalog 196; Articles 196; Unpublished
    Dissertation 197
    Painting   197
    Books 197; Articles 197; Unpublished Disserta-
    tion 198
    Ceramics   198
    Books 198; Catalogs 199; Articles 200
    Applied Arts   200
    Folk Art   201
    Books 201; Articles 201; Catalogs 201
  Music/*Bang-song Song*   202
    Books   202
    Articles   203
    Unpublished Dissertations   204

Selected Discography	205
Korean Music and Dance on Film	206
Drama and Dance/*Du-Hyun Lee*	207
Books	207
Articles	208
Unpublished Dissertations	208

CHAPTER 8. Education/*Don Adams* — 209
Introduction	209
Historical Survey	209
The Period of Chinese Influence	209
Initial Western Contacts	210
Japanese Rule	210
The Postwar Period	211
Contemporary Systems	211
Education in the South	211
Changing Goals in the South	212
Education in the North	212
Changing Goals in the North	213
Future Prospects	213
Bibliography	214
Bibliographies, Source Materials, and Periodicals	214
Bibliographies	214
Source Materials: Yearbooks, Statistics, and Annual Surveys	214
Periodicals	214
General and Historical	215
Primary, Secondary, and Higher Education	216
Administration, Policy, and Planning	218
Schooling and Society	220
Content and Methods	221
Doctoral Dissertations	222

CHAPTER 9. Geography and Natural Environment/*Shannon McCune* — 227
Introduction	227
Geography and Natural Environment	227
The Two Koreas	227
The Korean Peninsula and Its Surrounding Seas	228
Early Korean Descriptions	228
Early Western Descriptions	229
Geology and Physiography	230
Climate	231

Natural Vegetation	232
Natural Resources	232
Water Resources	233
Mineral Resources	233
Human Geography	234
Cartography	235
Early Korean Maps	235
European Maps	236
Modern Japanese Maps	236
American Maps	236
Modern Korean Maps	237
Bibliography	237
Geography and Natural Environment	237
Bibliographies, Journals and Accounts of Geographical Studies	237
Studies on Old Korean Geographical Works	238
General Geographical Studies	239
Descriptions and Travel Accounts	240
Government Publications	241
Recent Guidebooks and Descriptive Studies	242
Geology and Physiography	242
Mineral Resources	243
River and River Basin Studies	243
Weather and Climate	243
Natural Vegetation and Forestry	244
Land Use and Agricultural Regions	244
Population	245
Economic Development, Manufacturing, and Urbanization	245
Political Geography	246
The Maps of Korea	247
Early Maps and Atlases	247
Gazetteers	247
Map Series	248
Thematic Maps	248

CHAPTER 10. People, Family, and Society/*Vincent Brandt and Yun Shik Chang* — 249
Introduction	249
Traditional Patterns	250
Population	251
Values	254
Family and Kinship	254
Rural Society	256
Urbanization	257

Class and Subculture   259
Social Change   260
Bibliography   262
  General   262
    Books and Monographs   262
    Articles   262
    Unpublished Dissertation   263
  Values, Attitudes, Psychology, and Folk
  Religion   263
    Books, Monographs, and Articles   263
    Unpublished Dissertations   265
  Family and Kinship   265
    Books and Monographs   265
    Articles   265
    Unpublished Dissertations   266
  Rural Society and Agricultural Development 266
    Books and Monographs   266
    Articles   267
    Unpublished Dissertations   268
    Documents   269
  Urbanization and Migration   269
    Books and Monographs   269
    Articles   269
    Unpublished Dissertations   270
    Documents   270
  Social Change, Class, and Subcultures   270
    Books and Monographs   270
    Articles   271
    Unpublished Dissertations   272
    Document   273
  Research in Progress   273
    Dissertations in Progress   273
    Postdoctoral Research   273

CHAPTER 11. The Economic System / *Joseph Sang-hoon Chung*

                                             274
  Introduction   274
    Significance of the Economic System   274
    The Korean Economy in 1945   275
    The South Korean Economy   276
    Economic Development of South Korea   277
    The North Korean Economy   279
    Economic Development of North Korea   280
    Evaluation of the Two Economies   284
    Korean Economy Studies in the US   286

  Bibliography   288
    Yearbook and Annual Reports   288
      South Korea   288
      North Korea   288
    Documents and General Reference Works   288
      All Korea   288
      South Korea   288
      North Korea   288
    Statistics   289
      South Korea   289
      North Korea   289
    Pre-1945 Korean Economy   289
    The Economic System   290
    Economic Planning   291
      South Korea   291
      North Korea   292
    Agriculture, Collectivization, and Peasantry 292
      All Korea   292
      South Korea   292
      North Korea   293
    Industry   293
      South Korea   293
      North Korea   294
    Foreign Trade and Assistance   295
      South Korea   295
      North Korea   295
    Finance, Money, and Banking   296
    Economic Development   297
      All Korea   297
      South Korea   297
      North Korea   298
    Labor   299

CHAPTER 12. Government and Politics / *C. I. Eugene Kim*

                                             301
  Introduction   301
    The Republic of Korea   301
      General   301
      Political Culture, Ideology, and Political
        Socialization   302
      Political Leaders, Leadership Style, and
        Decision-making   302
      Political Participation, Political Parties, and
        Elections   303

Constitutional Development and Govern-
    mental Structure   305
Public Administration, Bureaucracy, and
    Government Performance   306
The Democratic People's Republic of Korea   306
    General   306
    Political Culture, Ideology, and Political
        Socialization   307
    Political Leaders, Leadership Style, and
        Decision-making   308
    Political Participation, Political Parties, and
        Elections   308
    Constitutional Development and Govern-
        ment Structure   309
    Public Administration, Bureaucracy, and
        Government Performance   309
Bibliography   310
    The Republic of Korea   310
    General   310
    Political Culture, Ideology, and Political
        Socialization   313
    Political Leaders, Leadership Style, and
        Decision-making   316
    Political Participation, Political Parties, and
        Elections   319
    Constitutional Development and Govern-
        ment Structure   324
    Public Administration, Bureaucracy, and
        Government Performance   325
    The Democratic People's Republic of Korea   328
    General   328
    Political Culture, Ideology, and Political
        Socialization   331
    Political Leaders, Leadership Style, and
        Decision-making   332
    Political Participation, Political Parties, and
        Elections   334
    Constitutional Development and Govern-
        ment Structure   335
    Public Administration, Bureaucracy, and
        Government Performance   336

CHAPTER 13. The Legal System / Chin Kim   338
    Introduction   338
        History of Korean Law   338

Sources and Structure of Law in South Korea   339
Judicial Administration in South Korea   341
    Organization of Courts   341
    Judicial Proceedings   341
    Judges, Prosecutors, Lawyers, and Auxiliary
        Personnel   342
Courts and Procuracy in North Korea   343
    Courts   343
    Procuracy   345
Bibliography   346
    Introduction   346
    History of Korean Law   346
    Sources and Structure of Law in South Korea   348
        Constitutional Law   348
        Administrative Law   348
        Labor Law   350
        Criminal Law   350
        Public International Law   351
        Civil Law   351
        Commercial Law   352
        Private International Law   353
        Laws Governing Industrial Property Rights
            and Copyright   354
    Judicial Administration in South Korea   354
    Courts and Procuracy in North Korea   355

CHAPTER 14. International Relations and
National Reunification / B. C. Koh   358
    Introduction   358
        International Relations   358
        National Reunification   359
        An Overview of Major Developments   360
        Foreign Policy Goals of the Two Koreas   363
        An Overview of the Literature   364
    Bibliography   365
        General and Theoretical   365
        Korea and the United States   368
            The Korean War   368
            Other Aspects of Korean-American Relations   370
        Korea and Japan   373
        Korea and the Communist World   374
            General   374
            Korea and the Soviet Union   375
            Korea and the People's Republic of China   376
        Korea and the Third World   377

Korea and the United Nations   378
Miscellaneous   379
National Reunification   379
General and Theoretical   379
General 379; Theoretical 381
The Pre-Dialogue Period: 1945–1970   382
The Post-Dialogue Period: 1971–1975   383

CHAPTER 15. North Korea/*Dae-Sook Suh*   386
Introduction   386
Bibliography and Reference Materials   387
Bibliography   387
Reference   387
Periodicals and Newspapers   388
Korean Communism   389
The Movement   389
The Development in the North   390
Kim Il Sung   391
Works by Kim   391
Works on Kim   392
The Workers' Party of Korea   392
The State System   393
The Political Process   393
Foreign Policy   394
The Economic System   395
Bibliography   395
Bibliography and Reference Materials   395
Bibliography   395
Reference   396
Periodicals and Newspapers   396
Korean Communism   397
The Movement   397
The Development in the North   398
Kim Il Sung   399
Works by Kim   399
Works on Kim   400
The Workers' Party of Korea   400
The State System   401
The Political Process   401

Foreign Policy   402
The Economic System   402

CHAPTER 16. Russian-Language Materials/
George Ginsburgs   404
Introduction   404
Bibliographic Guides and Surveys   405
General   406
Geography   407
History   408
Economics   409
Politics   410
Law   411
International Relations   412
Bibliography   413
Bibliographic Guides and Surveys   413
General   414
Geography   414
History   414
Economics   415
General   415
Agriculture   415
Industry   415
Foreign Trade and Aid   415
South Korea   416
Politics   416
Law   416
International Relations   416
Korean War   417
Militaria   417
Arts   417
Culture and Education   418
The Press   418
Linguistics   418
Literature   418
Natural Sciences   419

Appendix: Major Korean Dynasties and Rulers   421
Author Index   425

Chapter Editors

CHAPTER 1: Han-Kyo Kim, *University of Cincinnati*

CHAPTER 2: Richard Pearson, *University of British Columbia*

CHAPTER 3: Yŏng-ho Ch'oe, *University of Hawaii*

CHAPTER 4: Kah-Kyung Cho, *State University of New York, Buffalo*

CHAPTER 5: Chin-W. Kim, *University of Illinois*

CHAPTER 6: Peter H. Lee, *University of Hawaii*

CHAPTER 7: Lena Kim Lee, formerly *Seoul National University*

CHAPTER 8: Don Adams, *University of Pittsburgh*

CHAPTER 9: Shannon McCune, *University of Florida*

CHAPTER 10: Vincent Brandt, formerly *Harvard University,* and Yun Shik Chang, *University of British Columbia*

CHAPTER 11: Joseph Sang-hoon Chung, *Illinois Institute of Technology*

CHAPTER 12: C. I. Eugene Kim, *Western Michigan University*

CHAPTER 13: Chin Kim, *California Western School of Law*

CHAPTER 14: Byung Chul Koh, *University of Illinois at Chicago Circle*

CHAPTER 15: Dae-Sook Suh, *University of Hawaii*

CHAPTER 16: George Ginsburgs, *Rutgers University*

Special Contributors

CHAPTER 3: Ogg Li, *University of Paris,* compiled and annotated many non-English materials published in Europe with the assistance of Jennifer Strom, *University of Hawaii.*

Section II: Hugh H. W. Kang, *University of Hawaii.*

Section III: Michael E. Macmillan, *University of Hawaii,* prepared the bibliographic entries.

Section IV: Young Ick Lew, *University of Houston.*

Section VI: Seong Rae Park, *Hankuk University of Foreign Studies,* Seoul.

CHAPTER 5, Bibliography: Seok Choong Song, *Michigan State University,* prepared an overview of the development of grammatical descriptions of Korean for the section on "Grammars."

CHAPTER 7, "Music": Bang-song Song, *National Classical Music Institute,* Seoul.

"Drama and Dance": Du-Hyun Lee, *Seoul National University.*

CHAPTER 14: Young Whan Kihl, *Iowa State University,* compiled and annotated most of the bibliographic entries on the topic of "National Reunification."

Preface

THIS is a studies guide for those who are interested in various academic disciplines and topics relating to Korea. Its primary aim is to provide basic bibliographic information for college-level readers and others in the United States and elsewhere who may not have much background knowledge in Korean studies but who wish to read materials available in English or other Western languages on Korea. Its comprehensive coverage and the scholarly expertise of its contributors should also make this guide useful to serious researchers and specialists in Korean studies and to professional librarians.

Korean studies is yet a young field. Long after Asia, more specifically East Asia, had won recognition as an important area of academic and intellectual concern in the United States and other Western countries, Korean studies remained underdeveloped and virtually ignored. Korea as a field of study did not have a separate identity of its own; rather, it was treated as an appendage to the more preeminent Chinese or Japanese studies.

A set of interrelated factors that are largely historical and intellectual in nature may explain such neglect of Korean studies in the West. Historically, Korea's loss of political independence in the early twentieth century reduced the peninsular nation to a position of minor intellectual as well as political significance in the eyes of the Western nations. As Western scholarship in East Asia developed during the ensuing decades, it paid scant attention to Korea—which was left largely to the scholarly inquiry, as well as the political domination, of

the Japanese. At the same time, it must be added, modern scholarship among the Koreans themselves was slow to develop under adverse conditions created by foreign rule.

Liberation from Japanese rule in 1945 led eventually to the establishment of independent governments in Korea; but the development of scholarship in Korea-related subjects was a slower process in Korea, and even more so outside Korea. American involvement in postwar Korean problems stimulated publication of a limited number of serious works on Korea in the United States, but little original scholarship was evident. Scarcity, if not unavailability, of usable source materials and unfavorable conditions for research activities were responsible, at least in part.

More crucial, perhaps, were the paucity of interested scholars and the lack of recognition of Korean studies as a meaningful field of study with its own distinct identity. The shortage of scholarly manpower was a direct outcome of the past neglect, but it was also a reflection of the low level of esteem accorded Korean studies by the academic world. Amid an academic boom in area studies, especially in East Asian studies, beginning in the late 1950s, Korea was at best a peripheral topic to merit only passing attention by students of China or Japan. The close cultural as well as political linkage between Korea and China in the premodern period attracted a small number of students in Chinese history and culture to investigate related Korean topics, but mostly as a minor, albeit interesting, variant of the Chinese prototype. Similarly, students of modern Japanese history and politics might include Korea in their study of Japanese expansionism or colonial policies. For these students, the intellectual point of reference was either China or Japan, and their primary linguistic tool was either Chinese or Japanese. Intellectually Korea remained subjugated.

The influx of Korean students into American universities beginning in the mid-1950s had a totally unplanned yet significant impact on Korean studies in the United States. On a much reduced scale similar phenomena could be observed in other Western nations. Many among these Korean students were in the humanities and social sciences, chose Korean topics for their graduate theses, and, upon graduation, moved into the academic profession in the United States. Their research and publication activities began to inject new life into Korean studies. Even a casual reader of this guide will notice that a number of doctoral dissertations and later scholarly publications are the works of scholars bearing Korean names. In an interesting contrast to the fields of Chinese or Japanese studies, the great majority of scholars in Korean studies in the United States are ethnic Koreans.

The steady increase in the number of Koreanists, or scholars in Korean studies, was accompanied by corresponding growth in quantity and quality of their scholarly activities and roughly coincided with the rapid expansion of Asian studies programs across the United States made possible with funds provided by governmental and private sources. Temporary opulence and optimism reinforced academic and intellectual sophistication that began to recognize the intrinsic merits of Korean studies as a field within Asian studies. Courses devoted exclusively to Korean subjects were introduced into college and university curricula. A significant number of scholarly works came off the press. Seminars, conferences, and workshops on aspects of Korean studies have become more frequent than before. Sizable private foundation grants were given to several larger universities in the United States for the specific purpose of developing Korean studies. Centers for Korean studies came to be established at a couple of universities. A few profesisonal organizations of Koreanists have been created, some within the frameworks of well-established academic societies, among them the Committee on Korean Studies (CKS) within the Association for Asian Studies (AAS) and the Joint Committee on Korean Studies, SSRC-ACLS.

In the course of the 1970s, however, a new trend toward academic retrenchment has come to require critical reexamination of the rationale for area studies. As of this writing (1979) it appears beyond doubt that the era of rapid growth of Asian studies is at an end for the moment, as far as the American academic community is concerned. If special grants and research funds become scarce for the better entrenched fields of Chinese or Japanese studies, Korean studies faces even more difficult times ahead. It is no longer intellectual provincialism per se that threatens the fledgling field of Korean studies; it is no more difficult to argue for the need to identify as Korean studies those scholarly endeavors focusing on Korea using diverse methodological tools common to all area studies than it is to defend Chinese or Japanese studies. Korea's long and unique cultural heritage is clearly distinguishable from that of China or Japan; and the persistence and resilience of the Korean people in maintaining their ethnic and political identity despite repeated foreign incursions throughout their history can no longer be gainsaid. Few would challenge the significance of Korea's role in international affairs in East Asia in the past, the present, or the future. Clearly Korea, as a field of intellectual inquiry, no longer need be defended.

It remains difficult, however, to assert that Korean studies today represents as solid a body of scholarly knowledge, resources, and talents as do Chinese and Japanese studies. In terms of quantity and quality of scholarly publications, availability of research and instructional materials, or the academic stature and reputation of its practitioners, Korean studies is a generation or more behind Chinese and Japanese studies. Despite the remarkable progress of recent decades, Korean studies has merely reached its first plateau. A lot needs to be done.

In the pages of this guide, the reader will be able to see evidence of the long journey of Korean studies in the West, especially in the United States. It has been a journey marked by an uneven rate of progress. As

Korean studies struggles to reach a new height of academic stature and substance, it is indeed a fit time to take stock of past achievements and to consider future options. As one looks into the future, it is to be hoped that quality rather than quantity will be the primary concern of Koreanists—both in terms of new recruits into the profession and also of new research and publications. Taking a closer look at the substantive contents of Korean studies one might also wish for greater efforts in laying a solid foundation for the edifice of Korean studies rather than in pursuit of intellectual fads. Much needs to be done in collecting and making available basic research source materials in Korean studies and in synthesizing the fruits of past scholarship. There is also a continuing need to refine research methodology and to promote more rigorous standards of scholarship that are free of preconceived biases or a priori value judgments.

The present volume is at best a preliminary step in the new direction. Early planning for the guide took place under the sponsorship of the Committee for Korean Studies, Association for Asian Studies. The project was endorsed by the Northeast Asia Regional Council and the board of directors of the same association and was subsequently funded by the US Department of Health, Education, and Welfare under the provision of Title VI, Section 602, NDEA (Contract OEC-0-74-3056). The original version of this guide was completed in 1974–1975, but it has now been extensively revised and the various parts updated by the original authors.

The sixteen chapters in this guide correspond, for the most part, to customary academic disciplines: archaeology, history, philosophy and religion, language and linguistics, literature and folklore, art-music-drama, education, geography, sociology and anthropology, economics, political science, law, and international relations. In addition, Chapter 1 contains general bibliographic information and Chapters 15 and 16 deal respectively with North Korean studies and Russian-language materials on Korea. Political division of Korea since 1945 has created certain unique problems and topical interests for the study of North Korea warranting separate treatment. Russian-language materials are mostly unfamiliar even to many specialists in Korean studies despite their scholarly significance; hence a separate chapter was considered useful. It must be further noted that there are areas of overlapping coverage resulting from the nature of the subject as well as the interest and familiarity of individual authors. For example, discussions on and bibliographic references to North Korea appear in many chapters of this guide, especially those on education, the economic system, government and politics, law, and international relations, while the chapter on language and linguistics contains several references to Russian-language materials.

With a few exceptions, each chapter of this guide is the work of an individual scholar who has special competence in a given disciplinary area. For the sake of greater expertise, however, more than one author contributed to the chapters on history, art-music-drama, sociology and anthropology, and international relations.

Each chapter consists of two parts: an introductory essay and a bibliography. The essay is of moderate length and attempts to present an outline, a summary, or an overview of the subject area along with an assessment of the scholarly endeavors of the past, present, and future. Each bibliography is subdivided by categories that vary from chapter to chapter: topics, periods, or types of publications and materials. Our intention is to provide in each chapter, depending on the nature of the academic discipline or the current state of scholarship, the most appropriate and convenient, yet manageable, classificatory format for the reader. Bibliographic entries are annotated by the authors of the chapters except for certain cases: where adequate annotative references are made in the introductory essays, where the titles or other customary bibliographic information are self-explanatory, where works of relatively minor significance are involved, or where adequate annotations are available elsewhere in the guide as indicated through a system of cross-references. Wherever necessary, we listed a bibliographic item in more than one chapter, or under different subject headings even within the same chapter, for the reader's convenience as well as for comprehensive coverage of the subject area.

The chapter on history is the sole exception to the general organizational format. Due to the great scope of historical scholarship and the abundance of relevant materials, the chapter opens with a general survey and historiography that is followed by four chronological sections, each of which contains a narrative essay and bibliography. The current status of scholarship was the primary reason for the periodization scheme, while the need to link an author's narrative text directly to his bibliography led to the six more or less self-contained sections of the chapter. Another special feature of the history chapter is the section on the history of science, a largely neglected area within Korean history.

The appendix to this guide contains a chronological list of the rulers of various Korean dynasties and other ruling entities. There is, moreover, an author index comprising all the bibliographic entries arranged by author.

Romanization of Korean names and words has long been in a state of near anarchy. Despite wide acceptance of the McCune-Reischauer system among the writers of scholarly pieces in the United States, rival systems exist: the "Yale system" used by linguists in North America and two different systems devised by the governments of South and North Korea. Throughout this guide, the McCune-Reischauer system is used, even in the chapter on language and linguistics written by a linguist who prefers the Yale system—with exceptions as cited in the notes on editorial format that immediately follow this preface.

The list of acknowledgment for this work is long. The inception of the project in 1973–1974 owes a great deal to two members of the Northeast Asia Regional Council (NEARC) of the Association for Asian Studies (AAS), Professors H. W. Kang and A. Burks, and to Professors A. C. Nahm and E. Wagner who joined Professor Kang and myself in the initial planning sessions. Successive chairpersons of the AAS Committee on Korean Studies (C. I. E. Kim, J. K. C. Oh, B. C. Koh, G. Ledyard, Joseph S. Chung) and the members of NEARC in 1974–1975 gave their blessing and support for the project. Mrs. J. Petrov, Department of Health, Education, and Welfare, was most helpful and gracious

for the duration of the HEW contract. At the University of Cincinnati, appropriate administrative offices and the Department of Political Science provided logistical support.

Hong Kyoo Park, a graduate student at the University of Cincinnati, deserves special recognition for his faithful assistance throughout the entire duration of the project; he has been a resourceful and dedicated assistant without whom I would not have been able to complete the project. Other graduate students at UC, Ky Moon Oum and Ungjin Kim, lent additional helping hands at different stages of the project. K. P. Yang and T. H. Kang at the Library of Congress gave me and others on this project valuable bibliographic assistance as they have done for so many other Koreanists.

In the process of revision, two anonymous readers for The University Press of Hawaii and Professor G. Ledyard, a member of the Joint Committee for Korean Studies (SSRC-ACLS), provided most valuable and detailed commentaries which were instrumental in producing many of the substantive and editorial improvements in the manuscript.

Publication of the guide was made possible by a generous grant from the Joint Committee on Korean Studies (SSRC-ACLS). Additional financial contribution from the Center for Korean Studies, University of Hawaii, and the agreement of the Korean National Commission for UNESCO to become a copublisher in Korea further facilitated publication.

To all of these individuals and organizations, I owe deep gratitude. It is, however, to the more than twenty contributors who wrote essays and prepared bibliographies for the present work that I feel most indebted. It was their dedication to the field of Korean studies, their scholarship, their goodwill and cooperative spirit, and their sacrifice of time and energy that produced this guide. Whatever merit this work may possess is due solely to their hard work.

H. K.

Editorial Format

IN TRANSCRIBING Korean names and words, the McCune-Reischauer system is used, and, in the case of personal names, the customary Korean practice of placing the last (family) name ahead of the first (personal) name is followed. Two important exceptions to these general rules must be noted. First, the names of Korean authors who have written in English or in other Western languages, or whose writings have been translated into these languages prior to publication are spelled as they appear in their publications; frequently these Korean names also appear in the order of the first (personal) names followed by the last (family) names. In order to minimize any confusion concerning Korean names, capital letters are used for all last (family) names in the bibliographies and in the author index. Second, certain well-known proper nouns are given the way they are usually spelled. Examples: Syngman Rhee (rather than Yi Sŭng-man), Seoul (rather than Sŏul), Kim Il Sung (rather than Kim Il-sŏng), Pyongyang (rather than P'yŏng'yang).

The bibliography section of each chapter is arranged by subject areas, chronological periods, and, in certain chapters, the type of publication (books, articles, dissertations, and so forth). Within each of these subdivisions, the entries are arranged in alphabetical order.

English translations of bibliographic information—the names of organizations that have authored or compiled publications, the titles of publications, and so on—are given in brackets [ ] if the editors of this guide have translated them. If the English translations are given in the publications themselves, they are put in parentheses ( ).

In cases where a single issue of a journal is a combined issue bearing more than one volume or issue number for more than one publication date, these numbers are shown with a slash. For example: *Journal of Korean Studies* 10(4)/11(1) (Winter 1974/Spring 1975).

The listing of doctoral dissertations in the bibliography section includes wherever possible the *DA* (until 1968) or *DAI* (after 1969) and the UM numbers. They may be ordered from Xerox University Microfilms, PO Box 1764, Ann Arbor, MI 48106. For dissertations that are not available from Xerox University Microfilms, orders may be addressed directly to the degree-granting institution. (For full instructions for ordering the dissertations see Frank Joseph Shulman (comp. and ed.), *Doctoral Dissertations on Asia: An Annotated Bibliographical Journal of Current International Research*, 1(1) (Winter 1975), published for the Association for Asian Studies by Xerox University Microfilms.)

CHAPTER 1
Bibliographies, Handbooks, Journals, and Other Publications

Han-Kyo Kim

INTRODUCTION

WESTERN-LANGUAGE BIBLIOGRAPHIES on Korea date from the late nineteenth century and, considering the relative underdevelopment of Korean studies in the West, there has been a surprisingly large number of bibliographic publications on Korea. Some of these bibliographies are the products of serious scholarship and are useful today, even with the passage of time, for many types of research work on Korea. In this chapter, a partial listing of these bibliographies is presented.

Reviewing the record of publication of these bibliographies, there is a discernible pattern of fluctuation, and one is tempted to surmise that each of the high points in this pattern follows a rise in the Western readers' interest in Korean topics. Following the "opening" of Korea in the late nineteenth century, the first Western-language bibliography that dealt exclusively with Korea was published. Maurice Courant produced, in French, a four-volume bibliography of 3200 Korean books in 1894–1901. This impressive work, reprinted in 1966, remains a valuable research guide for students of Korean history and traditional culture (01-009).

The first attempt to compile an extensive bibliography of Western-language publications on Korea was made in the early 1930s. Horace H. Underwood, an American missionary in Korea, took stock of the first wave of Western-language publications on Korea, most of which had been written by Western travelers and residents in Korea (01-053); this work has since been updated by G. St. G. M. Gompertz (01-014).

As the Korean problem unfolded as an international issue in the post–World War II years, another series of bibliographic works was produced. A three-volume annotated bibliography was prepared by the US Library of Congress in 1950 in response to the urgent research needs of various US government agencies: 01-019 for Western-language materials, 01-042 for Russian-language materials, and 01-057 for materials in "Far Eastern languages." They are somewhat limited in coverage and clearly out-of-date today but are still of much value.

A reflection of the emerging scholarly interest in Korean studies that went beyond immediate concerns with contemporary events was the publication of the first Korean studies guide in 1954 by the Institute of East Asiatic Studies, University of California (01-136). Its coverage includes materials in Korean and other Oriental languages as well as those in Western languages. (Russian materials are covered in a supplementary volume published in 1958; see 01-001.) Introductory essays and annotations, especially those on primary sources for historical research, exemplify one of the best scholarly endeavors in Korean studies available in the West at that time. It is a prototype for the present volume.

In the 1960s, as Korean studies began to attract a growing number of specialists, many of them natives of

Korea, bibliographic output also increased steadily and substantially. Korean students of library science prepared bibliographies of more recent publications on Korea; Key P. Yang's valuable work for publications in 1945–1959 (01-060) and other works (01-007, 01-032) are examples. Thomas H. Kang's recent bibliographic essay also deserves mention here (01-022).

More significant is the appearance of specialized bibliographies in the last dozen or so years—a clear indication of the growing maturity of the field. They cover such diverse topics or disciplinary areas as the Korean War (01-003, 01-031, 01-041), social sciences (01-028, 01-054, 01-055), economy (01-061), history (01-017), the late Yi dynasty period (01-034), Japanese archives on Korea (01-037), public administration (01-002), legal history (01-025), anthropology (01-026), literature (01-059), traditional-style novels (01-050), music (01-051), North Korea (01-030, 01-054, 01-056), European works on Korea (01-035), Soviet works on Korea (01-013), and Korean collections held in leading American university libraries (01-011, 01-016). The quality and the usefulness of these works vary as much as the topics under their coverage. Nevertheless, these bibliographies, in addition to those appended to many scholarly publications on Korea (for an excellent example see the bibliography in *Communism in Korea*, 01-044), constitute an impressive variety and scope of bibliographic aids available in recent years.

Deserving of special mention are the works of Hesung Chun Koh and Frank Joseph Shulman. Koh's guide to Korean bibliographies, a seminal work designed to utilize a computerized system of information retrieval, is a most comprehensive bibliography of bibliographies in Korean studies (01-027). Shulman's compilations of doctoral dissertations written in Western languages on Korean topics cover the period since 1877 and bear testimony to the growth of Koreanists in recent years as well as to the trend of dissertation research on Korea (01-046, 01-047, 01-048).

Another noteworthy development in the recent period is the publication in Korea of English-language bibliographies on Korea (01-006, 01-014, 01-026, 01-033, 01-035). An especially important contribution to Korean studies is Lee Sung-nyong's *Korean Studies Today* (01-033); it covers a wide range of topics with em-

phasis on such areas as religion, history, literature, and art. The essay in each chapter attempts to assess what has been accomplished in each of these areas of Korean studies. The production of these bibliographies in Korea is undoubtedly due, in part, to the rapid growth in the number of English-language materials published in Korea. But it also reflects the recognition of the need to build an intellectual bridge between scholars in Korea and those in foreign countries.

Bibliographies on Korea are not confined to volumes that are exclusively concerned with Korean topics. Quite frequently Korean bibliographies are incorporated as part of bibliographic works on Asia or East Asia. Although the space limitation does not permit listing these general Asian bibliographies in this guide, a few of them merit a brief description. The most comprehensive and widely available bibliography for Asian studies is the annual September issue of the *Journal of Asian Studies* (01-020). Although the entries are not annotated, they are arranged by topic and type of publication (book, article, and so on). In the two issues for 1970 and 1971, Korean entries were further grouped in two sections: the Democratic People's Republic of Korea (North Korea) and the Republic of Korea (South Korea). In recent years, hundreds of Western and non-Western materials on Korea have been included annually. The *Journal of Asian Studies* superseded the *Far Eastern Quarterly,* which had regularly published separate volumes of *Far Eastern Bibliography* (1941–1956; published as the *Bulletin of Far Eastern Bibliography* in 1936–1940) (see 01-004, 01-012).

Other Asian bibliographies useful for Korean studies include Henri Cordier's monumental *Biblioteca Sinica* published in 1904–1907 (01-008), an annotated and still very useful volume on Japan and Korea by Bernard S. Silberman (01-049), and a more recent annotated guide to research in Asia by Raymond Nunn (01-038).

It should be evident from this cursory review of Korean bibliographies that a general, comprehensive, annotated, and up-to-date bibliography for Korean studies is greatly needed today, despite all those past efforts that have been mentioned. This guide is an attempt to meet this need and itself marks another milestone in the development of Korean bibliographies.

Listed under "Handbooks and General Surveys" in

the bibliography section of this chapter are titles that attempt to provide, with varying degrees of sophistication, a general introduction to diverse aspects of Korean society, culture, and current problems. Included are four examples of official or quasi-official publications by government agencies in Korea that are designed for casual foreign readers (01-065, 01-066, 01-067, 01-069). A highly commendable general survey for serious readers is the *UNESCO Korean Survey;* it is encyclopedic in coverage and contains articles written by established Korean scholars on history, art, literature, and other topics (01-068). An earlier effort to present general discussions on Korean history and culture was undertaken by an American anthropologist, Cornelius Osgood (01-070). Attention to contemporary political and socioeconomic conditions in North and South Korea is evident in a series of *Area Handbooks* prepared for the US Army (01-062, 01-063, 01-071, 01-072, 01-073). Although they are prepared under the auspices of the military bureaucracy, they are not pocket guides for US servicemen in Korea; rather, they represent scholarly endeavors for providing useful general background information.

The twenty-eight titles listed under ''Journals and Monograph Series'' are part of a much larger number of English-language publications produced in Korea, the United States, and elsewhere. Among the pre-1945 publications, *The Korea Review* (01-087) and *The Korean Repository* (01-092) are widely known. Published in Seoul by Western residents around the turn of the century, they contain interesting and informative articles on contemporary events and also on the history and the traditional culture of Korea. Another worthy publication of this era which resumed publication in 1948 is the *Transactions of the Korea Branch of the Royal Asiatic Society* (01-101); many scholarly and semischolarly studies by first and second-generation Western residents in Korea are preserved in the pages of the *Transactions.* A foreign missionary organization shared in these early efforts at periodical publication by issuing *The Korean Mission Field* beginning in 1904 (01-091).

More recently, there has been a remarkable growth of English-language journals in South Korea. Some of them are official or semiofficial publications that provide informative discussions and documentary materials on current political and international problems facing Korea (01-077, 01-083, 01-086). Less obviously partisan and more academic in orientation are several journals cited frequently in various chapters of this guide. The better known among them are *Journal of Asiatic Studies* (01-079), *Journal of Social Sciences and Humanities* (01-082), *Korea Journal* (01-084), *Korea Observer* (01-085), and *Koreana Quarterly* (01-096).

The absence of English-language journals from North Korea is partially, although not satisfactorily, compensated by a translation series that carries selected items from North Korean periodicals; the *Joint Publications Research Service* (JPRS) series prepared by an agency of the US Department of Commerce are invaluable despite occasional flaws in translation and the potentially more serious problems arising from their selective nature (01-078).

In the United States, there have been a few attempts to publish a scholarly journal in Korean studies but they have been largely ephemeral and attracted only limited attention from the scholarly community. This is perhaps a reflection of the state of Korean studies in the United States. *Asian Forum,* which includes pieces on non-Korean topics (01-075), and the *Journal of Korean Affairs,* which lasted five years till late 1976 (01-080), are the more durable among them. Promising more longevity, perhaps, are the two monograph series edited at the University of Hawaii (01-098) and the University of Washington (01-099).

There are of course a number of American journals devoted to general Asian studies or to various academic disciplines, and articles on Korea are occasionally printed in their pages. Enjoying wide recognition among the Asian studies journals are the *Journal of Asian Studies, Asian Survey,* and *Pacific Affairs.* These and other scholarly journals are not listed in the following bibliography. Standard reader's guides to periodicals should be consulted.

A selected list of sixteen items appears in ''News Publications'' in my bibliography. Undoubtedly there are many others, but the more widely circulated or the more accessible ones in the United States are presented here. Official or semiofficial North Korean publications dealing with current affairs include magazines (01-102, 01-109, 01-115) and newspapers (01-106, 01-116). Five entries have been published under official South Korean auspices: two in the United States (01-112, 01-113) and the others in Korea (01-107, 01-111), including one on North Korea (01-114). Two independent English-language daily papers are published in Seoul (01-105, 01-108).

The Washington-based *Korea Week* was, until early 1978 when it ceased publication, a professedly non-partisan weekly newsletter that was useful for Korea-related developments in the United States, especially in the US Congress (01-110). More obviously partisan are two pro–North Korean newsletters published in San Francisco and New York (01-103, 01-104). A unique publication in this category is *The Voice of Korea* published by a Korean emigré in Washington, D.C., for nearly two decades beginning in 1943 in order to bring the Korean cause to public attention in the United States (01-117).

South Korea produces a fair number of yearbooks, but *Korea Annual* by Hapdong News Agency is the only English-language publication that is widely available and handy (01-119). Its utility is enhanced by the inclusion of a Who's Who section which is the only biographical directory of prominent persons in South Korea available in English. From North Korea, no comparable yearbook or biographical directory is available in English, but selections from *Chosŏn chung'ang yŏn'gam* [Korean central yearbook] are translated in the JPRS series (01-078).

The paucity of North Korean sources is equally evident in publications of statistical data. Some economic data for the years 1946–1960, however, have been published (01-123). Several major statistical compilations from South Korean sources are listed in the bibliography; the Bank of Korea and the Economic Planning Board (a cabinet-level government agency) are the chief sources (01-120, 01-121, 01-124, 01-125). In addition, most governmental agencies and financial institutions frequently publish statistical information and many of them are in both Korean and English (for examples, see 01-126 and 01-127).

In general, not many reference works in English or any other Western language are readily available for Korean studies. It is an obvious handicap but also a challenge for those who toil in this field of inquiry.

BIBLIOGRAPHY

BIBLIOGRAPHIES AND STUDIES GUIDES

01-001. BACKUS, Robert L. *Russian Supplement to the Korean Studies Guide.* Berkeley: Institute of International Studies, University of California, 1958. Outdated but still useful guide to Russian-language materials on Korea prepared as a supplement to the *Korean Studies Guide* (01-036).

01-002. BARK, Dong-Suh and Jai-Poong YOON. *Bibliography of Korean Public Administration, September 1945–April 1966.* Seoul: 1966. Reproduced by US Operations Mission to Korea. 174 pp. Entries include 99 books and government publications, 1355 articles arranged by topic and publication date, and 513 master's theses. Valuable.

01-003. BLANCHARD, Carroll H. *Korean War Bibliography and Maps of Korea.* Albany, N.Y.: Korean Conflict Research Foundation, [1964?]. 181 pp. Comprehensive coverage including over 10,000 entries, some of which are news magazine articles or items of limited interest to students of Korea. No annotation. Maps illustrate military situation during the war.

01-004. *Bulletin of Far Eastern Bibliography.* Vols. 1–5. Washington: American Council of Learned Societies, 1936–1940. Entries include books on Korea published during these years. Superseded by *Far Eastern Bibliography* (01-012).

01-005. BUTLER, Lucius A. and Chaesoon T. YOUNGS (comps.). *Films for Korean Studies.* Occasional Papers of the Center for Korean Studies, no. 8. Honolulu: Center for Korean Studies, University of Hawaii, 1977. 167 pp. Lists more than three hundred English-language, 16-millimeter films dealing with the history, politics, culture, arts, and society of Korea. Includes a summary of contents for each film and information for borrowing, renting, or purchasing the film.

01-006. CHON, Munam (comp.). *An Index to English Periodical Literature Published in Korea, 1945–1966.* Seoul: Korea Research Center, 1967. 152 pp. Mimeographed. Contains some 220 subject and author entries that appeared in six periodicals. Includes an author and subject index, but no annotation.

01-007. CHUNG, Yong Sun. *Korea: A Selected Bibliography, 1959–63.* Kalamazoo: Korea Research and Publications, 1965. 117 pp. Mimeographed. Contains 967 entries, most of which are Korean-language publications, but includes a significant number of English-language materials as well. Entries are conveniently arranged by topic, but lack annotation.

01-008. CORDIER, Henri. *Biblioteca Sinica, dictionnaire bibliographique des ouvrages relatifs à l'empire chinois.* 5 vols. 2nd ed. Paris: 1904–1907. Also *Supplément et Index.* Paris: 1924. Reprinted by B. Franklin (New York), 1968. Entries on Korea, most of which are Western works (English, French, German, Russian) published before 1900, appear in vol. 4, pp. 2979–3007, 3235, and vol. 5, pp. 4406–4427. Extensive coverage but no annotation. Not very easy to use.

01-009. COURANT, Maurice. *Bibliographie Coréene.* Paris: E. Leroux, 1894–1896. *Supplément,* 1901. Reprinted by B. Franklin (New York), 1966. Contains about 3200 entries—Korean books from earliest times—and carefully annotated wherever possible. Includes an introductory essay on Korean literature, libraries, and so forth. A valuable bibliographic guide for any serious student of Korean studies.

01-010. ELROD, J. McRee. *An Index to English Language Periodical Literature Published in Korea, 1890–1940.* Seoul: Yonsei University, 1960. 198 pp. Covers articles in ten periodicals. A helpful guide to such periodicals as *Korea Review* (01-087), *Korean Repository* (01-092), and *Transactions of the Korea Branch of the Royal Asiatic Society* (01-101).

01-011. FANG, Chaoying. *The Asami Library: A Descriptive Catalogue.* Edited by E. Huff. Berkeley: University of California Press, 1969. 424 pp. Unquestionably the most valuable guide in English to the works of traditional Korean scholarship and literature. Full annotations for more than 900 titles of Korean printed books, manuscripts, and rubbings in about 4000 fascicles and sheets, about one-third of which are documents relating to law and government from private collections of Asami Rintarō (1869–1943), a Japanese jurist and bibliophile who was in Korea in 1906–1918. The Asami collection is now housed in the East Asiatic Library of the University of California, Berkeley.

01-012. *Far Eastern Bibliography.* Published annually as a separate volume of *Far Eastern Quarterly,* 1941–1956, by the Far Eastern Association. Covers scholarly works on Korea published during the year. Earl H. Pritchard edited "Bulletin of Far Eastern Bibliography, 1941–1945," *Far Eastern Quarterly;* Gussie Gaskill et al. edited "Far Eastern Bibliography 1946–1953," *Far Eastern Quarterly;* and Howard P. Linton edited "Far Eastern Bibliography, 1954–1955," *Far Eastern Quarterly. Far Eastern Quarterly* is the predecessor of *Journal of Asian Studies,* which has been issuing an annual bibliography since 1957 (01-020). Prior to May 1947 Korean materials appeared under various titles, "Manchuria and Korea," or "Central and Northeast Asia."

01-013. GINSBURGS, George. *Soviet Works on Korea, 1945–1970.* Los Angeles: University of Southern California Press, 1973. 179 pp. Lists 1126 items arranged by topic but no individual annotation. A comprehensive survey of Soviet studies on Korea precedes bibliographic listings. Chapter 16 of the present guide by the same author updates this earlier work of his.

01-014. GOMPERTZ, G. St. G. M. "Bibliography of Western Literature on Korea from the Earliest Times until 1950." *Transactions of the Korea Branch of the Royal Asiatic Society* 15(1963):1–263. Lists 2276 books and articles arranged by topic. No index. This is a revision of H. H. Underwood, "A Partial Bibliography of Occidental Literature on Korea from Earliest Times to 1930," *Transactions of the Korea Branch of the Royal Asiatic Society,* 20(1931):17–185, 1–17 (01-053), and G. St. G. M. Gompertz, "Supplement to 'A Partial Bibliography of Occidental Literature on Korea,' " ibid., 24(1935). Comprehensive and useful.

01-015. Harvard University. Library. *China, Japan, and Korea: Classification Schedule, Classified Listing by Call Number, Alphabetical Listing by Author, or Title, Chronological Listing.* Cambridge, Mass.: Harvard University, 1968. 494 pp. Korean entries are listed under "Japan and Korea" and appear on pp. 223–236. No annotation but arranged by topic. Covers English and Western-language materials, most of which are on Korean history.

01-016. _____. Harvard-Yenching Institute. Library. *A Classified Catalogue of Korean Books in the Harvard-Yenching Institute Library at Harvard University.* Cambridge, Mass.: 1962. Includes many basic reference works for the study of Korea before 1910.

01-017. HENTHORN, William E. *A Guide to Reference and Research Materials on Korean History: An Annotated Bibliography.* Honolulu: East-West Center, 1968. 152 pp. Lists 612 items arranged in three major sections for bibliography, modern reference works, and selected source materials for traditional Korean history. Annotations are helpful for students' use.

01-018. _____. *Korean Views of America, 1954–64: An Annotated Bibliography.* Honolulu: Center for Cultural and Technical Interchange between East and West, University of Hawaii, 1965. 66 pp. Mimeographed. Covers 183 articles that appeared in major South Korean periodicals in 1954–1964. These Korean articles discuss various aspects of American life and action from a Korean point of view; many of them appeared in *Sasangge* [World of thought], an influential magazine widely read by Korean intellectuals which has since ceased publication. Detailed and very useful commentaries for each item.

01-019. JONES, Helen D. and Robin L. WINKLER (comps.). *Korea: An Annotated Bibliography of Publications in Western Languages.* Washington: Library of Congress, 1950. 155 pp. Mimeographed. Lists 753 items arranged by subject area and adequately annotated. Emphasis is on publications issued since 1930 although many items are from pre-1930 works. Covers items held in major library collections in the United States. Still very useful. This is part of a three-volume bibliography on Korea; see 01-042 and 01-057.

01-020. *Journal of Asian Studies: Bibliography.* Published annually since 1957 as a separate volume of *Journal of Asian Studies* by the Association for Asian Studies. Covers scholarly works, official publications, and other materials on Korea published during the year. Arranged by subject matter in alphabetical order. Although the items are not annotated, comprehensive coverage makes this bibliography indispensable for any serious student. In the 1970 and 1971 issues, Korean entries were grouped into two sections: the Democratic People's Republic of Korea (North Korea) and the Republic of Korea (South Korea).

01-021. KANG, Sangwoon. *A List of Articles on Korea in the Western Languages, 1800–1964.* Seoul: Tamgu Dang, 1967.

01-022. KANG, Thomas Hosuck. "Korean Literature and Bibliography." In Allen Kent (ed.), *Encyclopedia of Library and Information Science.* Vol. 2l. New York: Marcel Dekker, 1977. Pp. 176-240. A scholarly treatise divided into sections: History of Publishing in Korea; Survey of Korean Scholarship; Bibliographical Control and Bibliographies; Korean Libraries and Information Systems; and Current Status of Korean Publication and Problems. Includes discussions on the Korean language, writing system, and religion, among other topics. Selective lists of relevant publications, most of them published in Korean in Korea, are appended to bibliographic essays on diverse topics.

01-023. KAZAKEVICH, I. S. "Korean Studies." In USSR Academy of Sciences, Institute of the Peoples of Asia, *Fifty Years of Soviet Oriental Studies.* Moscow: Nauka, 1968.

01-024. KERNER, Robert Joseph. *Northeastern Asia: A Selected Bibliography.* Vol. 2. Berkeley: University of California Press, 1939. Pp. 230–270. Reprinted by B. Franklin (New York), 1968. Out of date and of limited value.

01-025. KIM, Chin. "Korea." In John Gilissen (ed.), *Biblio-*

graphical Introduction to Legal History and Ethnology. 8 vols. Brussels: Université Libre de Bruxelles. Vol. E (6th vol.). 24 pp. Lists 130 entries arranged by topic with occasional annotations and brief bibliographic commentaries interspersed throughout the bibliography. Headings include: Bibliographies; General Works on History and Ethnology; Encyclopedias and Dictionaries; Periodicals; General Works on Legal History; Collected Sources of Law; Works (Public Law; Criminal Law; Private Law; Procedure; Legal Education and Profession). Unique and useful for students of Korean law and legal history.

01-026. KNEZ, Eugene I. and Chang-su SWANSON. *A Selected and Annotated Bibliography of Korean Anthropology.* Seoul: Taehan Min'guk Kukhoe Tosŏgwan, 1968. Includes 262 items in Korean and Japanese; some items are published in Pyongyang. Useful annotations.

01-027. KOH, Hesung Chun. *Korea: An Analytical Guide to Bibliographies.* New Haven: Human Relations Area Files, 1971. 334 pp. According to the preface, this work attempts "to serve social science researchers and to present the most comprehensive bibliography of bibliographies on Korean studies." Section 1: "Abbreviated Citation by Major Subjects"; Section 2: "Analytical Indexes." A seminal attempt to utilize a computerized system of information retrieval and a comprehensive bibliography of bibliographies.

01-028. _____. *Social Science Resources on Korea: A Preliminary Computerized Bibliography.* New Haven: Human Relations Area Files, 1968.

01-029. *Korean Books in Foreign Languages.* Pyongyang: Kukche Sŏjŏm, 1957–. Biennial publication in English. A catalog of books published in Chinese, English, Japanese, and Russian in various fields. Includes a brief description of each book and standard bibliographic data.

01-030. KYRIAK, Theodore E. (comp.). *North Korea, 1957–1961: A Bibliography and Guide to Contents of a Collection of U.S. JPRS Translations on Microfilm.* Annapolis: Research and Microfilm Publications, [1964?]. A useful guide to the Joint Publications Research Service series on North Korea for 1957–1961. Microfilmed articles are on topics of North Korean economy, politics, and society.

01-031. LEE, Chong-Sik. "Korea and the Korean War." In Thomas T. Hammond (ed.), *Soviet Foreign Relations and World Communism: A Selected and Annotated Bibliography.* Princeton: Princeton University Press, 1965. Pp. 787–806.

01-032. LEE, Soon Hi. "Korea: A Selected Bibliography in Western Languages, 1950–1958." Master's thesis (Library Science), Catholic University of America, 1959.

01-033. LEE, Sung-nyong (ed.). *Korean Studies Today:*

Development and State of the Field. Seoul: Institute of Asian Studies, Seoul National University, 1970. 350 pp. Contains chapters on religion, philosophy, linguistics, classical literature, modern literature, ancient arts, traditional music, dramatic arts, custom and folklore, history, traditional political and legal systems, economy, sociology, and science. Each chapter, prepared by a recognized Korean specialist, begins with a scholarly survey of the subject and the state of scholarship, followed by a short list of relevant publications. Very valuable, particularly for a study of traditional culture and history of Korea, but weak on social science fields for the contemporary period.

01-034. LEW, Young Ick. *Korea on the Eve of Japanese Annexation.* Seoul: 1967. 194 pp. Covers 1938 books, articles, theses, and archival sources in Chinese, Japanese, Korean, and English for the period 1904–1910 listed under 59 subjects.

01-035. LI, Ogg (ed.). "Catalogue of the Books and Articles on Korea Published in European Languages Except for Russian until 1950." In *Minjok munhwa yŏn'gu* [Studies of national culture]. Seoul: Koryŏ Taehakkyo, 1974. A comprehensive listing of the European works on Korea, especially for the late Yi dynasty period.

01-036. MARCUS, Richard (ed.). *Korean Studies Guide.* Compiled for the Institute of East Asiatic Studies, University of California, by Benjamin H. Hazard, Jr., and others. Berkeley: University of California Press, 1954. 220 pp. Contains seventeen chapters under these headings: Libraries, General Bibliography, and Periodicals; Reference Materials; Geography; Art and Archaeology; General History; Ancient Korea; Three Kingdoms and Unified Silla, Koryŏ; Yi Dynasty; Government, Economics, and Recent History; Sociology; Religion and Philosophy; Music; Language; Literature; Education; Special Reference Materials and Addenda. Each chapter has a brief survey followed by a carefully annotated bibliography. Appendixes include a chronological list of "Rulers and Dynasties," publishing houses and societies, and a brief glossary. Also includes eight maps of Korea for different historical periods. An index of titles and authors is provided. Although it is obviously out of date now, this volume remains the most useful and readily available studies guide. A supplement listing Russian-language materials on Korea was published in 1958 (01-001).

01-037. NAHM, Andrew C. (comp.). *Japanese Penetration of Korea, 1894–1910: A Checklist of Japanese Archives in the Hoover Institution.* Hoover Institution Bibliographical Series, no. 5. Stanford: Hoover Institution, Stanford University, 1959. 103 pp. A useful checklist of Japanese archives dealing with Japanese policy and activity in Korea in 1894–1910 that had been stored in the Archives and Documents Section of the Japanese Government-General in Seoul and were subsequently microfilmed and placed in the Hoover Institution library. Descriptive summaries of each folder and the analytical and language indexes are very helpful. Appendixes include lists of high Japanese and Korean officials of the period and a chronology of events in 1876–1910.

01-038. NUNN, G. Raymond. *Asia: A Selected and Annotated Guide to Reference Works.* Cambridge, Mass.: MIT Press, 1971. 223 pp. The section on Korea (pp. 182–195) contains sixty-eight items that are well annotated. Includes reference works, encyclopedias and handbooks, yearbooks, geographical dictionaries and gazetteers, chronological tables, censuses, statistical sources, bibliographies, periodicals, and newspapers.

01-039. PAIGE, Glenn D. "The Korean Collection of the Division of Oriental Manuscripts, Institute of Oriental Studies, Academy of Sciences of the U.S.S.R.: A Bibliographical Note." *Harvard Journal of Asiatic Studies* 19(December 1956):409–411. A brief discussion of a descriptive catalog of Korean holdings of the Soviet Institute of Oriental Studies prepared by O. P. Petrova in his *Opisanie pismennykh pamyatnikov koreikoi kultury* [A description of the literary monuments of Korean culture] (Moscow-Leningrad: Izd. Akademii nauk SSSR, 1956).

01-040. _____. "A Survey of Soviet Publications on Korea, 1950–56." *Journal of Asian Studies* 17(August 1958):579–594. Surveys the growing number of Soviet publications on Korea and attempts to present "a tentative report on the present state of Korean studies in the Soviet Union."

01-041. PARK, Hong-Kyu. *The Korean War: An Annotated Bibliography.* Marshall, Texas: Demmer Co., 1971. 29 pp. Lists 120 items, most of them in English, with very brief annotations.

01-042. PARRY, Albert et al. (comps.). *Korea: An Annotated Bibliography of Publications in the Russian Language.* Washington: Library of Congress, 1950. 84 pp. Mimeographed. Lists 436 items arranged by topic with brief annotations. These items are available in leading Russian-language research collections in the United States. See also 01-019 and 01-057.

01-043. Public Relations Association of Korea. *A Selection of Periodicals Published in Korea.* Part 1: *Periodicals in Foreign Languages.* Seoul: Public Relations Association of Korea, 1973.

01-044. SCALAPINO, Robert A. and Chong-sik LEE. *Communism in Korea.* 2 vols. Berkeley: University of California Press, 1972. "Bibliography" in pt. 2: *The Society,* pp.

1418–1491. Contains an extensive list of publications in Korean, Japanese, English, Russian, and Chinese that are relevant for study of Korean communism and North Korea. Succinct annotations for most items. Highly recommended.

01-045. SCHROEDER, Peter Brett. *Korean Publications in the National Agricultural Library.* Washington: National Agricultural Library, Department of Agriculture, 1963. 25 pp. Lists 79 periodicals and 110 monographs in English and Korean, most of which are published in South Korea.

01-046. SHULMAN, Frank Joseph. *Doctoral Dissertations on Asia: An Annotated Bibliographical Journal of Current International Research.* Vol. 1, no. 1(Winter 1975), published for the Association for Asian Studies (Ann Arbor: Xerox University Microfilms, 1975). Vol. 1, no. 2(Summer 1975–), published by the Association for Asian Studies. Semiannual journal that lists recent doctoral dissertations on Asia including Korea.

01-047. _____. *Doctoral Dissertations on Japan and Korea, 1969–1974: A Classified Bibliographical Listing of International Research.* Ann Arbor: University Microfilms International, 1976. 78 pp. Includes 314 dissertations on Korea and 88 on both Japan and Korea, a large majority of which were prepared at American institutions of higher learning. One-line annotations are given for some entries. Entries are arranged in an alphabetized topical order. This is a sequel to the entry listed below. This and the other unique contributions of Shulman should be consulted by all doctoral candidates in Korean studies.

01-048. _____. *Japan and Korea: An Annotated Bibliography of Doctoral Dissertations in Western Languages, 1877–1969.* Chicago: American Library Association, 1970. 340 pp. Includes 509 dissertations on Korea written in English, French, German, Russian, and other European languages; 331 of the Korean dissertations were prepared in the United States. For most entries, summaries of contents are provided. Valuable reference.

01-049. SILBERMAN, Bernard S. *Japan and Korea: A Critical Bibliography.* Tucson: University of Arizona, 1962. 120 pp. Lists 318 entries on Korea (pp. 92–114). Each entry is annotated. The table of contents is very detailed and helpful and each of nine subject areas (Land and People; Language; History; Philosophy and Religion; Art and Music; Literature; Government; Social Patterns; Economic Patterns) has a brief introduction. Despite its age, this work is still of great value, especially for students.

01-050. SKILLEND, W. E. *Kodae Sosŏl: A Survey of Korean Traditional Style Popular Novels.* London: School of Oriental and African Studies, University of London, 1968. 268 pp. Each of 531 entries is carefully annotated. Korean names, titles, and so forth are given in *han'gŭl* and Chinese characters as well as in roman alphabets. An impressive work.

01-051. SONG, Bang-song. *An Annotated Bibliography of Korean Music.* Providence, R.I.: Asian Music Publications, Brown University, 1971. 251 pp. Lists 1319 entries of which 792 are in Korean. Emphasis is on Korean traditional music but studies on traditional dances, drama, and related subjects are also included. Many items are annotated. Indexes of names and subjects enhance the usefulness of this work.

01-052. TSURUTANI, Taketsugu. *Rural Development in Japan, Korea, and the Philippines: A Bibliographical Aid.* Cambridge, Mass.: Center for Rural Development, 1969.

01-053. UNDERWOOD, Horace H. "A Partial Bibliography of Occidental Literature on Korea from Earliest Times to 1930." *Transactions of the Korea Branch of the Royal Asiatic Society* 20(1931):17–185, 1–17. The first comprehensive bibliography of Western publications on Korea; it has since been supplemented and superseded by Gompertz' bibliography (01-014).

01-054. United States. Bureau of the Census. *Bibliography of Social Science Periodicals and Monograph Series: North Korea, 1945–61.* Washington: Foreign Manpower Research Office, Bureau of the Census, 1962. 12 pp. Lists thirty-eight periodicals and three monograph series classified under: General Social Science; Cultural Anthropology; Economics; Education; History; Human Geography; Linguistics; Political Science; Public Health; Bibliography; and Statistics. Well annotated and useful.

01-055. _____. _____. *Bibliography of Social Science Periodicals and Monograph Series: Republic of Korea, 1945–61.* Washington: Foreign Manpower Research Office, Bureau of the Census, 1962. 48 pp. Lists 127 periodicals and 134 monograph series classified under: General Social Science; Cultural Anthropology; Economics; Education; History; Human Geography; Law; Linguistics; Political Science; Public Health; Social Philosophy; Social Psychology; Sociology; Statistics; and Bibliography. Well annotated and useful.

01-056. _____. Department of the Army. *Communist North Korea: A Bibliographical Survey.* DA Pamphlet 550-11. Washington: 1971. 130 pp. The first sixty-five pages contain an annotated but selective bibliography on North Korea with emphasis on those materials covering the period of 1965–1970, but older materials dealing with the history of Korea and the Korean War are also included.

Appendixes provide information on North Korean military posture, military structure, demographic estimates, Workers' Party organization, trade statistics, and a text of the Korean armistice agreement of 27 July 1953. Useful.

01-057. _____. Library of Congress. Reference Department. *Korea: An Annotated Bibliography of Publications in Far Eastern Languages.* Compiled under the direction of Edwin G. Beal, Jr., with the assistance of Robin L. Winkler. Washington: 1950. 167 pp. Mimeographed. Lists 528 entries arranged by subject area and adequately annotated. With a few exceptions, all items listed are available in the Library of Congress. This work is part of a three-volume bibliography on Korea prepared by the Library of Congress in 1950 in response to urgent research needs of various US government agencies shortly after the outbreak of the Korean War. A great majority of entries are in Japanese but included also are some Korean and still fewer Chinese-language materials. See 01-019 and 01-042.

01-058. _____. _____. *Union Card File of Oriental Vernacular Serials, Chinese, Japanese and Korean. Korean File.* Washington: 1966. 2 reels. Contains 3037 holdings cards from leading American academic institutions for Korean-language periodicals.

01-059. WOOD, Robert S. "Korean Literature: A Comprehensive Bibliography in English." *Korea Journal* 8(March 1968):30–34.

01-060. YANG, Key Paik. "Reference Guide to Korean Materials, 1945–1959." Master's thesis (Library Science), Catholic University of America, 1960.

01-061. YOO, Young Hyun. "A Selected Bibliography of Materials on Korean Economy." In Joseph S. Chung (ed.), *Korea: Patterns of Economic Development.* Kalamazoo: Korea Research and Publications, 1966. Pp. 201–241. Lists 393 items without annotation but arranged by topic. Mostly Korean-language publications with some Japanese and English materials.

HANDBOOKS AND GENERAL SURVEYS

01-062. American University. Foreign Area Studies Division. *U.S. Army Area Handbook for Korea.* DA Pamphlet 550-41. Washington: Government Printing Office, 1964. 595 pp. Updates US Army *Area Handbook for Korea* published in 1958. Divided into four sections: Social Background (including Historical Setting; Languages; and Artistic and Intellectual Expression among others); Political Background; Economic Background; and National Security. Selective bibliographies appear at the end of each section. Wherever appropriate, discussions of North and South Korea are separately treated within topical head-

ings. Subsequently revised; see 01-063, 01-071, 01-072, 01-073.

01-063. CLARE, Kenneth G. et al. *Area Handbook for the Republic of Korea.* Prepared for the American University by Westwood Research Incorporated. DA Pamphlet 550-41. Washington: Government Printing Office, 1969. An updated and revised version of the preceding entry (01-062). In this 1969 edition, North Korea is separately treated (01-071). Subsequently revised again in .1975 (01-072).

01-064. Hakwon-sa Ltd. *Korea: Its People and Culture.* Seoul: Hakwon-sa, ca. 1970. Third edition of *Korea: Its Land, People and Culture of All Ages,* published in 1960 and 1963. Covers a wide range of topics. Useful reference.

01-065. Korea, Democratic People's Republic of. *Facts about Korea.* Pyongyang: Foreign Languages Publishing House, 1961. 240 pp. Emphasis on North Korean economy and culture. Some statistical information included. Not to be confused with a South Korean publication with the same title (01-066).

01-066. Korea, Republic of. Ministry of Culture and Information. *Facts about Korea.* Seoul: 1971. A pamphlet, periodically revised, containing brief simplified information on South Korea including a directory of South Korean agencies overseas.

01-067. _____. _____. Korean Overseas Information Service. *A Handbook of Korea.* Edited by Kim Young-Kwon. Seoul: 1978. 825 pp. Lavishly illustrated work covering many topics of history, politics, society, and culture. A chart of the McCune-Reischauer romanization system side by side with the Ministry of Education system of romanization is helpful. Some rare historical photographs from "old" Korea.

01-068. Korean National Commission for UNESCO. *UNESCO Korean Survey.* Seoul: Dong-a Publishing Co., 1960. One of the best of its kind. Comprehensive coverage with emphasis on culture and history.

01-069. OH, Chae-gyong. *Handbook of Korea.* Rev. ed. New York: Pageant Press, 1958. One of the most widely available of its kind in American libraries.

01-070. OSGOOD, Cornelius. *The Koreans and Their Culture.* New York: Ronald Press, 1951. 387 pp. This pioneering study of a Korean village by an American cultural anthropologist contains general discussions of Korean history and culture as well. Still useful as an introduction to Korean culture and society.

01-071. SHINN, Rinn-Sup et al. *Area Handbook for North Korea.* DA Pamphlet 550-81. Washington: Government Printing Office, 1969. 481 pp. An updated and revised version of discussions on North Korea that were contained in the 1964 *U.S. Army Area Handbook for Korea* (01-062). Subsequently revised in 1976 (01-073). Includes an extensive bibliography on North Korea.

01-072. VREELAND, Nena et al. *Area Handbook for South Korea.* DA Pamphlet 550-41. Washington: Government Printing Office, 1975. Revision of earlier works with similar titles.

01-073. VREELAND, Nena, Rinn-Sup SHINN et al. *Area Handbook for North Korea.* DA Pamphlet 550-81. Washington: Government Printing Office, 1976. Revision of earlier handbooks on North Korea (01-071).

JOURNALS AND MONOGRAPH SERIES

01-074. *Asian Economies.* Quarterly since June 1971. Published by Research Institute of Asian Economies, Seoul. Includes many scholarly articles on Korean economy. English.

01-075. *Asian Forum.* Quarterly since 1969. Published by Institute for Asian Studies, Washington. Many articles on Korea written by Korean scholars in the United States.

01-076. *Bulletin of the Korean Research Center: A Journal of Social Sciences and Humanities.* Semiannual since 1960. Published by Korean Research Center, Seoul. Articles written mostly by Korean scholars in Korea. English. Superseded by *Journal of Social Sciences and Humanities* (01-082).

01-077. *East Asian Review.* Quarterly since 1974. Published by Institute for East Asian Studies, Seoul. Most articles deal with issues of Korea's international relations and national reunification. English.

01-078. Joint Publications Research Service (JPRS). Serialized publications of selected items from North Korean newspapers and periodicals, translated and published by Joint Publications Research Service, National Technical Information Service, US Department of Commerce, Springfield, Va., since 1961. Indispensable English-language sources for research on North Korea.

01-079. *Journal of Asiatic Studies.* Semiannual, 1958–1963; quarterly, 1964–1972; semiannual since 1972. Published by Asiatic Research Center, Korea University, Seoul. Mostly in Korean but contains a significant number of articles in English written by Korean and non-Korean scholars.

01-080. *Journal of Korean Affairs.* Quarterly, 1971–1976. Published by Research Institute on Korean Affairs, Silver Spring, Md. Emphasis on North Korean developments.

01-081. *Journal of Korean Studies.* Vol. 1 appeared in 1969, followed by only one more issue. Published by Korean Studies Society, Seattle.

01-082. *Journal of Social Sciences and Humanities.* Quarterly. Formerly *Bulletin of the Korean Research Center: A Journal of Social Sciences and Humanities* (01-076). English.

01-083. *Korea and World Affairs: A Quarterly Review.* Vol. l, no. 1, appeared in Spring 1977. Published by Research Center for Peace and Unification, Seoul. Carries articles on international relations, Korean unification problem, and North Korea, mostly written by Korean scholars in Korea or overseas. English.

01-084. *Korea Journal.* Monthly since 1961. Published by Korean National Commission for UNESCO, Seoul. One of the few enduring English-language journals published in Korea and a valuable sample of contemporary Korean scholarship in a wide range of academic disciplines available in English.

01-085. *Korea Observer.* Quarterly (irregular) since 1968. Published by Academy of Korean Studies, Seoul. Articles on humanities and social sciences. English.

01-086. *Korea: Policy Series.* Irregular. Published by Korean Overseas Information Service, Seoul. A government publication containing texts of official documents and relevant commentaries.

01-087. *The Korea Review.* Monthly (January 1901–December 1906), Published by Methodist Publishing House, Seoul. Articles by foreign residents in Korea, edited by Homer B. Hulbert. Provides valuable insight into the problems facing the Korean society at the turn of the century.

01-088. *Korea Review.* Monthly (March 1919–July 1922). Published by Korean Information Bureau, Philadelphia. Not to be confused with the preceding entry (01-087).

01-089. *The Korean Economist.* Irregular. Published by Korean Economic Society, Arlington, Va.

01-090. *The Korean Journal of International Studies.* Quarterly. Published by Korean Institute of International Studies. English.

01-091. *The Korean Mission Field.* Vol. 1 published in November 1904; monthly until 1941. Published by General Council of Evangelical Missions in Korea. Includes articles on Korean life and history.

01-092. *The Korean Repository.* Monthly, 1892, 1895–1898. Published by Trilingual Press, Seoul. Edited by Franklin Ohlinger and, later, by Henry G. Appenzeller and George H. Jones. Similar in content and format to *The Korea Review* (01-087). Photoduplicate edition was published by Paragon Book Reprint Press in 5 vols., 1964.

01-093. *Korean Research Bulletin.* Vols. 1–2, no. l/2, January 1943–May 1945. Berkeley: Korean Research Council.

01-094. *Korean Review.* Vols. 1–2, no. 1, June 1948–September 1949. Published by Korean-American Cultural Association, Seattle.

01-095. *Korean Studies Forum: An Interdisciplinary Journal of Research on Korea.* Semiannual; no. 1 for Autumn–Winter 1976/1977. Published by Korean-American Educational Commission and the University Center for International Studies, University of Pittsburgh.

01-096. *Koreana Quarterly.* Quarterly since 1959. Published by International Research Center, Seoul. Articles on social sciences and humanities. English.

01-097. *North Korea Quarterly.* Quarterly since 1974. Published by Institute of Asian Affairs, Hamburg.

01-098. *Occasional Papers of the Center for Korean Studies.* Serialized publication since March 1973 by the Center for Korean Studies, University of Hawaii, Honolulu.

01-099. *Occasional Papers on Korea.* Serial publication since April 1974 under the auspices of the Joint Committee on Korean Studies, SSRC-ACLS. Edited by James B. Palais and Margery D. Lang, University of Washington, Seattle.

01-100. *Social Science Journal.* Annual since 1973. Published by Korean National Commission for UNESCO, Seoul. English.

01-101. *Transactions of the Korea Branch of the Royal Asiatic Society.* Published in 1900–1941 and since 1948 by the Korea Branch of the Royal Asiatic Society, Seoul. The English-language journal in Korea with the longest record of continuous publication except for the World War II years. A valuable source for the study of twentieth-century Korea.

NEWS PUBLICATIONS

01-102. *The Democratic People's Republic of Korea.* Monthly since 1957. Published by Foreign Languages Publishing House, Pyongyang. A general magazine with illustrations.

01-103. *Korea Bulletin.* Monthly newsletter published by Committee for Solidarity with the Korean People, San Francisco. Pro–North Korean publication.

01-104. *Korea Focus.* Monthly since 1971. Published by American-Korean Friendship and Information Center, New York. Pro–North Korean news pamphlet.

01-105. *The Korea Herald.* English-language daily newspaper published in Seoul. Published as *The Korean Republic* in the early years.

01-106. *Korea News.* Three times a month; first appeared in 1958. Published by Korean Central News Agency, Pyongyang. Superseded by *Pyongyang Times* (01-116).

01-107. *Korea Newsreview.* Weekly; first appeared in 1972. Published by Public Relations Association of Korea, Seoul. English. Illustrated.

01-108. *Korea Times.* English-language daily newspaper published in Seoul since 1956.

01-109. *Korea Today.* Monthly, available since 1959. Published by Foreign Languages Publishing House, Pyongyang. Formerly *New Korea* (1947–1958).

01-110. *Korea Week.* Semimonthly, 1968–1978. Edited and published by Po Sung Philip Kim, Washington. Good coverage of Washington events concerning Korea.

01-111. *Korean Frontier.* Monthly pamphlet published by Korean Information Service, Seoul. General news coverage.

01-112. *Korean Report.* Irregular, April 1961– July/September 1969. Published by Korean Information Office, Washington. A South Korean government publication. Supersedes *Korean Survey* published September 1952–February 1961 (01-113).

01-113. *Korean Survey.* Monthly, October–May; bimonthly, June–September; September 1952–February 1961. Published by Korean Pacific Press, 1952–November 1958; by Korean Research and Information Office (later renamed Korean Information Office), December 1958–February 1961.

01-114. *North Korea Newsletter.* Weekly English-language newsletter published since 1976 by Naewoe Press, Seoul. Current events and weekly chronology of events in North Korea. Occasionally includes biographical data on North Korean leaders. Mirrors South Korea's official views on the North.

01-115. *The People's Korea.* Weekly since 1961. Published by Chōsen Shimpōsha, Tokyo. English.

01-116. *Pyongyang Times.* Weekly English-language newspaper since May 1962. Published in Pyongyang.

01-117. *The Voice of Korea.* Bimonthly, 1943–1961. Edited by Yongjeung Kim and published by Korean Affairs Institute, Washington. A newsletter on current events concerning Korea especially useful for the years preceding and following 1945.

REFERENCE WORKS
Yearbooks

01-118. Chosŏn Chung'ang T'ongsinsa (Korean Central News Agency). *Chosŏn chung'ang yŏn'gam* [Korean central yearbook]. Pyongyang. Selections from this yearbook, beginning with its 1958 issue, have been translated into English and published by the Joint Publications Research Service. (See 01-078.)

01-119. Hapdong News Agency. *Korea Annual.* Seoul: Hapdong News Agency. The only English-language yearbook regularly published in Korea. Available since 1964.

Statistics

01-120. Bank of Korea. *Economic Statistics Yearbook.* Seoul: annual. The mainstay of Korean economic statistics for many years.

01-121. _____. *Monthly Economic Statistics.* Seoul: monthly. Superseded *Monthly Statistical Review* in April 1969.

01-122. BELIAEV, Iu N. (comp.). *Development of the National Economy and Culture of People's Democratic Republic of Korea (1946–1959): Statistical Handbook.* Originally prepared in Russian and published by Gosplanizdat, Moscow, 1959. An English translation appeared in JPRS (1960).

01-123. Korea, Democratic People's Republic of. Central Statistical Board. *Statistical Returns of National Economy of the Democratic People's Republic of Korea, 1946–1960.* Pyongyang: Foreign Languages Publishing House, 1961.

01-124. Korea, Republic of. Economic Planning Board. *Korea Statistical Yearbook.* Seoul: annual. Formerly published by Ministry of Home Affairs.

01-125. _____. _____. *Statistical Handbook of Korea, 1969.* Seoul: 1970.

01-126. _____. Ministry of Agriculture and Fisheries. *Yearbook of Agriculture and Fisheries Statistics.* Seoul: annual.

01-127. _____. Ministry of Home Affairs. *The Municipal Yearbook of Korea.* Seoul: annual.

01-128. _____. Office of Public Information. *Statistics of Damage Suffered during the Korean War, June 25, 1950–July 27, 1953.* Seoul: 1954.

Biographical Materials

01-129. Hapdong News Agency. *Korea Annual.* (See 01-119.) Contains a Who's Who section for persons in the Republic of Korea. Inadequate and selective, but the only readily available biographical reference in English.

01-130. SOHN, Pow-Key. *Biographical Tables of the Koryo Period.* Berkeley: East Asian Studies, Institute of International Studies, University of California, 1958. Unique aid for students of Koryŏ history.

CHAPTER 2
Archaeology

Richard Pearson

INTRODUCTION

KOREAN ARCHAEOLOGY has traditionally been divided into the cultural periods of Paleolithic, Comb Pattern Pottery or Neolithic, Plain Coarse Pottery or Bronze Age, Kimhae Pottery or Iron Age, and Three Kingdoms. Many issues are implied by the use of the terms Neolithic, Bronze Age, and Iron Age. As applied to other parts of the world, these terms imply general forms of social organization, levels of social and political integration, and patterns of subsistence. In the Korean case, we know relatively little as yet about the plants or animals which may have been domesticated or the degree of the technological development in the Neolithic period. The term Bronze Age has generally come to imply tribal chiefdoms or small states with monumental architecture, writing, markets, and social stratification in addition to the production of bronze artifacts. While indigenous bronze production at an early date is known to have taken place in Korea, we do not know much about social organization and economy from the scanty data at hand.

As will be discussed below, Paleolithic manifestations in Korea have been dated to about 30,000 and 20,000 years BP (before 1950). Comb Pattern Pottery is thought to have been produced from the fifth to second millennia BC, while Plain Coarse Pottery appears in the last millennium BC. The Kimhae period covers the first three centuries AD and is followed by the Three Kingdoms period, which lasts from about AD 300 to 668.

Early work in Korea, undertaken by the Japanese, concentrated upon the later periods which had produced impressive art objects. Archaeological survey, enumeration of various antiquities, and many small excavations did, however, provide a basic outline of prehistory which has been revised and expanded by the current generation of Korean specialists. Museums were established, but few local people were trained. The relationship between Comb Pattern Pottery and Plain Coarse Pottery was pondered, and it was assumed that bronze objects were late in the time sequence and resulted totally from trade with China and thus were not representative indigenous expressions.

At present, Korean archaeologists place strong emphasis on the Liaoning-Liaotung-Manchuria area as a source of bronze technology, and the correspondences are easily seen in bronze dagger, knife, and mirror forms. (Much of the material from this area has only been available for about twenty years, through excavations by the People's Republic of China.) The ultimate origins of Korean bronze technology in the Karasuk area are harder to trace in detail. Other archaeologists have emphasized the role of Siberia and the trans-Ural area in the development of Comb Pattern Pottery; certainly the northern connections for this pottery are the most obvious ones. As yet, however, no study can point to specific sites and local sequences in the regions adjacent to Korea, partly because there is not a great deal of good excavation data from this area. I think the North Korean archaeologists may be closer to the mark in playing down diffusion and stressing the processes, both technological and social, of local cultural evolution.

The problem here is that the ideological component of their studies does not allow enough flexibility to test alternative hypotheses.

Japan was seen by some archaeologists as the center from which ideas diffused to Korea—an idea strikingly similar to the view, commonly held by Western prehistorians in the past, that culture diffused from western Asia to China and Southeast Asia. These views of diffusion are the products of the cultural imperialism which follows hand in hand with colonial domination. In contrast to the past view, at present it appears that many basic elements of early Japanese culture, such as ceramics, tomb forms, and metal tool forms, were introduced from Korea but soon developed along distinctively Japanese lines. Much more work needs to be done in the field of comparative ethnography before the full picture of Korean-Japanese cultural similarities is clear. Important Japanese excavations include those of Lolang, the Silla tombs of Kyŏngju, Unggi in northeastern Korea, and Tongsam-dong and Kimhae in the south. Important contributions to the interpretation of Korean archaeology are still being made by the Japanese, although the Korean archaeologists have moved rapidly to the fore. Some Koreans are quick to criticize the techniques used by the Japanese; however, more than twenty-five years after liberation, the majority of excavators continue to use these same methods, which are now considered obsolete by a substantial group in Japan.

Within the last ten years a radiocarbon chronology has begun to emerge (see Table 1). (I have attempted to organize the dates in a rough chronological sequence.) The Paleolithic has been recognized in both the north and the south at sites such as Kulp'o-ri and Sŏkchang-ni, and the sequent relationship of Comb Pattern Pottery to Plain Coarse Pottery has become clear. A great deal of work remains to be done on the internal chronology of both of these periods, since at present it rests on impressionistic comparisons of pottery styles, using samples that may be far from representative. Two American researchers, Alexander Townsend of the University of Hawaii (see 02-033) and Sarah Nelson of the University of Michigan, have attempted to use new techniques for establishing the internal sequence of sites from ceramic data. Research by Kim Sin-gyu on faunal remains from Korean archaeological sites has also

added a new dimension (Kim 1974). New work on bronze technology, including some metallurgical analysis (Ch'oe 1975:23), has been undertaken. Modern museums are being established in many centers, and publications from the Republic of Korea have increased at a rapid rate. Few libraries in the West have systematic holdings of Korean archaeological publications; however, annual bibliographies in the English publication *Archaeology in Korea: An Annual Review of Korean Archaeology,* edited by Kim Wŏn-yong, and in Japanese in *Chōsen kōkogaku nempō,* edited by Nishitani Tadashi, have made it much easier to keep up from abroad.

SUMMARY

The first human population which we know of inhabited the Korean peninsula in the latter part of the Pleistocene epoch. A lava tube, Billemot Cave on Cheju Island, has recently yielded animal bones and flake tools which are thought to date from the early Würm glaciation when Cheju was joined to the mainland (02-015:9). It is important to remember that at various times during the glacial maxima of the Würm, sea levels dropped and the extent of land in the Korean peninsula was considerably larger. The Pohai Gulf and the Yellow Sea may have been reduced to river valleys, and the Tsushima Strait is now thought to have been closed throughout the Pleistocene by a land bridge (Ichikawa, Fujita, and Shimazu 1970:164).

The evidence from the Kulp'o-ri site in the northeast of the peninsula and Sŏkchang-ni in the Kŭm River valley suggests that small hunting bands occupied seasonal camps in a variety of locations. The lower layers of Sŏkchang-ni, dating to roughly thirty thousand years ago, have yielded a range of stone tools which show similarities with contemporary technologies in Japan and China.

The upper layers of Sŏkchang-ni have produced evidence of a well-defined Upper Paleolithic settlement with the remains of a shelter. Some studies of the local environment at the time of occupation have been attempted by using ancient pollen grains found in the site deposit; a great deal more work needs to be done before this kind of study can be considered conclusive.

Following the Upper Paleolithic habitation of

Sŏkchang-ni there is a hiatus of at least fifteen thousand years. This means that we do not have any idea of the relationship between the Pleistocene population of Korea and those whose remains we find much later. From at least 4000 BC, and possibly earlier, pottery and flaked and polished stone tools have been found in virtually every corner of Korea with the exception of the higher elevations. The ceramics are termed Comb Pattern, or Geometric, since many of them have been incised or punctuated with decorations in zones or bands.

The appearance of ceramics in Korea is comparatively late for East Asia. In China and Japan, pottery is dated by radiocarbon to at least the ninth millennium BC—by far and away the oldest in the world. It has been estimated that the oldest ceramics in Korea may be contemporary with the Early Jōmon of Japan. It has also been suggested that the very earliest ceramics in Korea might be undecorated, plain forms which later developed into linear decorated types. Vessel forms change from pointed bottom to flat bottom as a general rule, from the Early Comb Pattern Pottery to the Late. In some sites, such as Kungsan, Chit'am-ni, and Tongsam-dong, large numbers of bone tools have been found. Tongsam-dong, in Pusan, yielded bone and antler awls, spatulate tools, gorges for fishing, barbed and unbarbed composite hooks, and ornaments. On the other hand, the shell mound of Shido, on a small island off the central western coast, yielded no bone tools and only stone net sinkers, an axe, a pebble celt possibly used for opening shellfish, stone flake knives, arrowheads, and grinding stones (B. S. Han 1970:32). Soil conditions were presumably favorable for the preservation of bone. Tongsam-dong yielded flake choppers, cobble scrapers, side scrapers, stone fishhook shanks, obsidian points (rare), celts, abrading stones, "hoes" (in the later periods), and a semilunar knife.

Analysis of animal bones from eight archaeological sites of this period in the Democratic People's Republic of Korea by Kim Sin-gyu (1974) suggests that ungulates were the main animal resource in the western plains of the north while carnivores were more important in the eastern mountainous areas. The particular importance of deer in the western area suggests that there may have been grassy areas with browse or grazing plants available. Burning may have been used as a hunting practice

or for swidden farming. Wild pig was another major resource.

In Korea it has been the custom to use the term *Neolithic* for these sites, in keeping with the older definition used in Siberian archaeology wherein polished stone tools and pottery are considered the hallmarks of the Neolithic. In other parts of the world, however, Neolithic is used for human groups who practice cultivation as a predominant means of producing their food. Although some progress has been made in the study of the subsistence patterns of these early cultures, particularly by the North Korean archaeologists, many problems remain.

A number of authors have suggested that cultivation may have begun as early as 4000 BC in Korea. Later sites such as Chit'am-ni, which could be assigned to the middle of the Comb Pattern Pottery period, have yielded carbonized millet. The earliest portion of the Comb Pattern Pottery period probably coincides with, or immediately follows, the period of highest water levels in the post-Pleistocene. The high water levels had the effect of reducing available land, particularly along the west coast where the gradient is gradual. Increased population density and impingement have been suggested as possible factors in the development of plant and animal domestication in other parts of the world; they might also be applicable in the Korean case. During the period from 6000 BC to about 2000 BC, it is believed that worldwide temperatures may have been warmer than at present and local precipitation patterns may have differed somewhat; however, specific data on this topic are not yet available for Korea. There is a hint that the climate may have been warmer, since water buffalo bones have been found in a number of North Korean sites. It is my understanding, however, that it is very difficult to distinguish the bones of various bovids, and I am somewhat hesitant to accept the identification outright. It has been argued, on the basis of the distribution and characteristics of Comb Pattern Pottery sites in the Middle Han River area, that cultivation of native plants such as millet, turnip, Chinese cabbage, grain sorghum, hemp, and soybeans was a major element in the subsistence base. In addition, riverine resources were important. North and South Chŏlla provinces, about which very little is known, may have been areas of early rice cultivation. Dr. Ch'oe Mong-yong of Chŏnnam University, Kwangju, is carrying out surveys in this area (Ch'oe 1974), and the shell-mound sites of the southeast coast are also becoming well known.

Comb Pattern Pottery sites are often found on slopes or low terraces in river valleys or seacoast locations. Houses are relatively large, semisubterranean structures. Circular and rectangular forms are known, and average dimensions range up to about 6 meters in diameter or about 4 meters to a side. Excavation at Amsa-ri in 1973 yielded a circular house 6.6 meters in diameter with a central stone-lined hearth (02-015:9). Excavations thus far have yielded little evidence of the internal distribution of tools within the houses, although some work on this topic has been done by Kim Chong-gi (02-009). It is still difficult to discuss the locations of various activities carried out within the settlements at this time. One might hypothesize that the larger Comb Pattern Pottery sites constitute base camps, each house within the camp containing an extended family. Virtually no burials are known. The Comb Pattern Pottery culture, if one can speak of such an entity, shares characteristics with contemporary "cultures" of the Liaoning–Liaotung area, the Soviet maritime provinces, and possibly the northern parts of Japan. Northwestern Korea in particular seems to have been in contact with the Liaotung and Shantung Peninsulas, judging from the presence of perforated stone celts, lenticular and quadrangular celts, and polished black pottery, in sites dating to the end of the Comb Pattern Pottery period and the Early Plain Coarse Pottery period.

At the beginning of the first millennium BC, pronounced changes are evident in Korean prehistory, and the period from 1000 BC to the first centuries AD is one of the most complex for archaeologists. New forms of ceramics and stone tools appear first, followed by new burial forms and bronze artifacts. Korean archaeologists attribute these changes to the arrival of new populations in the peninsula, possibly from the Liaoning area. Clearly there is a sharp distinction between Korean communities at this time and those of the North China Plain. It has been contended by North Korean archaeologists that the period of bronze production began early in the second millennium BC. On the other extreme, there are still Japanese scholars who contend that most

bronze objects found in Korea are trade pieces from the Warring States period of China and that indigenous production was very late—not much earlier than that of Japan. In my opinion, neither position can be supported on the basis of new finds from all over Korea, which have been cataloged in Kim Jeong-hak's Japanese publication *The Prehistory of Korea* (02-010) and in Kim Jung-bae's review article (02-024). Jar burials, which are thought to have diffused from Korea to Japan, have been found in such sites as Sinch'ang-ni in South Chŏlla province near the city of Kwangju (W. Y. Kim 1964).

The new pottery can be described as undecorated, coarse orange in color, with a narrow base. In northwestern Korea, painted and burnished red ceramics have also been recovered. The relationship of these new forms to the previous ones and the exact nature of the transition are difficult to document, since undisturbed, stratified sites are very rare. It is also thought that new linguistic groups may have entered Korea at this time.

Large imposing dolmens are also known from the end of the second millennium and the early first millennium BC. These have been classified into two types: a "table" form, with stone slabs for sides and a lid, termed the northern style; and a type consisting of a large boulder supported by small cobbles, the southern style. The distribution of the northern and southern types has been found to overlap in many regions, and the significance of the two forms is not clear at this point. A tribal society, living in relatively permanent villages with a well-developed agricultural base, possibly cultivating rice in the southern areas of the peninsula, must have produced these heavy monuments. There also appears to have been an increase in the range of domesticated animals at the time of Plain Coarse Pottery. Dogs, pigs, and cattle are found more often than at Comb Pattern Pottery sites. It is thought that some draft animals may have been used in the northwest in the Comb Pattern Pottery period, while in the northeast their utilization begins with the Plain Coarse Pottery. Horses are rarely found in what has been termed the Iron Age by Kim Sin-gyu (1974). From the Iron Age layers of the Musan site, 1.17 percent of the total number of individuals found were horses. From the Hoeryŏng Odong site, cows comprise 8.2 percent of the total number of individuals. Dogs were domesticated by hunters and gatherers. The second step, according to Kim Sin-gyu, was the domestication of pigs, which occurred along with further selection of dogs. Third, draft animals (horses and cows) were domesticated.

A site at Hunam-ni, Yŏju, thought to be from the Plain Coarse Pottery period, excavated in 1973 by the Department of Archaeology and Anthropology of Seoul National University, yielded two rectangular pit dwellings with floors covered with a hard-packed, limy material. It is not known what proportion of the entire site was excavated.

Polished stone daggers and ceramics have been found in some of the dolmens. Bronze artifacts, developed from Liaoning prototypes, have been found as early as the seventh century at sites such as Taegong-ni. Daggers, knives, buttons, small bells, mirrors with fine-line geometric decoration on the back, belt hooks, and other small ornaments have been found in burials of various forms throughout the peninsula. Their internal chronology and typological variations are being worked on at present.

The Ch'odo site, near Pusan, gives some idea of the sequence of development of one area during this general time period. Of the three strata uncovered, the lowest contained sherds of Plain Coarse Pottery. The middle layer of shells produced an extended human burial with an iron dagger and a necklace of tubular perforated green stones. From this layer, triangular stone arrowheads were recovered in association with reddish and grayish pottery of the Kimhae type, which is found from about 200 BC to the first centuries AD. The beginning date has cross-dating with Japanese Yayoi ceramics. The top layer produced later pottery from the Silla.

The period of Kimhae Pottery in the south of the peninsula might be termed protohistoric and has also been termed Iron Age. It is a complicated period during which the Chinese Han dynasty established a colony in the north which must have had a great effect in fostering the resistance of tribal groups in the south.

The colony in the north (known in Korean as Nangnang and as Lolang in Chinese) was established in 108 BC after the fall of the state of Chosŏn to the Han emperor Wu-ti. Four provinces or commanderies, said to comprise two-thirds of the peninsula, were set up, but they lasted only about twenty-five years. After a re-

trenchment, only the single colony of Lolang, near the present site of Pyongyang on the Taedong River, remained, lasting until the fourth century. Trade to a wide hinterland, including Japan and all parts of the peninsula, was of great importance. It is thought that iron figured foremost in this trade. The burials from Lolang have provided outstanding examples of the art and culture of the Han dynasty. Several good accounts are available in English and Japanese (02-019:38–60).

In 1973, a tomb of rectangular form with stone lining, originally covered with wooden boards, was found at Pŏpch'on-ni, Wŏnsŏng County, Central Korea (02-015: 12). It contained a fourth-century Chinese celadon sheep identical to finds from the Nanking area, as well as three grayish pottery vessels, one of which is said to possess Lolang characteristics. The celadon trade vessel, and perhaps at least one of the other vessels, may have been traded through Lolang. This tomb might serve as an example of Lolang influence, which extended some distance from the actual garrison on the banks of the Taedong.

Iron production is thought to have begun in the first few centuries AD, and the Han states in the south of the peninsula, Mahan, Pyŏnhan, and Chinhan, were probably particularly active in this endeavor. Southern Korea comprised a number of small states of thalassocracies (Ledyard 1976) which were in constant intercourse, due to ethnic similarities and trade ties, with the populations of the Japanese islands. It should be noted that contact between the Korean peninsula and the Japanese islands goes back to the times of Tongsam-dong (02-027:228–230, 247).

Some archaeological research is now being carried out on the small states of later periods, including the problematic "Japanese colony" of Mimana.

On the Three Kingdoms in Korea—Paekche, Silla, and Koguryŏ—a great deal of research has been carried out. It has not been very systematically published, and the emphasis has been on burials—a kind of sophisticated treasure hunt rather than the integrated study of the whole cultures. As a result, we can say virtually nothing about the everyday life of the people of these time periods. The economic systems, subsistence patterns, demographic aspects, and trade networks are virtually unexplored archaeologically.

Paekche pit graves yielding some small doubled iron slabs and paddle-impressed globular vessels were found at Namsan-ni, Kongju-gun, and were excavated by the Kongju Museum (Nishitani 1975:59–83). Excavations of the fortified Paekche site, Pungnap-ri, on the south bank of the Han River near Seoul, were undertaken by Kim Wŏn-yong in 1964 (Kim 1967). The site was built in the mid-third century AD and was overrun by the Koguryŏ in AD 475. In 1971, the tomb of the Paekche king Muryŏng, who ruled from AD 501 to 523, was found and excavated. The vaulted chamber, decorated in an immense variety of impressed tiles, contained the remains of the king and his queen, accompanied by a variety of grave goods which display the range of Paekche's cultural connections. The tomb itself is of central or southern Chinese form, as are some of the burial ceramics. The gold finials for attachment to horsehair caps are dramatically different from those of Silla. Other grave goods include carved jade earrings and a carved silver bracelet (National Museum of Korea 1971).

Dramatic discoveries of treasures were made at the Silla capital of Kyŏngju in 1973 and 1974 with the excavation of large numbers of tombs, some of which have been salvaged because of construction. More than seventy tombs of the Old Silla (ca. AD 300–668) were dug by teams from various institutions (02-015:12). Tomb 155, the first major Silla excavation since the Japanese work, contained an aboveground burial chamber covered with an inner mound of cobbles. Burial offerings were found on top of the chamber and accompanying the deceased—a king buried in extended position, head oriented to the east, with a gold crown, earrings, girdle, bracelets, and rings on all fingers. In a wooden chest at one end of the burial chamber a large number of important art objects were found, including a painted saddle mudguard made of many layers of birch bark. The motif is that of a galloping white horse in the center, surrounded by a band of arabesque design. The tomb is dated to the beginning of the sixth century, and the painting is the first substantial example of painting from Old Silla (02-015:13).

Earlier tombs of Old Silla, stone-lined pits datable to the second or third centuries AD (02-015:13), were excavated in 1973. They are considered by the excavators to be descendants of a type found in the late first millennium BC.

From other recent excavations in Kyŏngju, a number of artifacts, such as glass mosaic beads and a gold inlaid dagger sheath, resemble objects from Persia and Central Asia.

It would be particularly valuable not only to study the cultural geography of the Kyŏngju Basin at the time of the Silla but also to examine the cultural dynamics leading to the wide distribution of Silla ceramics—from areas such as Kangnŭng in Kangwŏn province to Cheju Island.

In the north, both in the valley of the Yalu and the Taedong, important finds of the Koguryŏ have been made (02-004). When archaeologists from Pyongyang visited Japan to attend symposia on the Takamatsu tomb, they mentioned that important tombs with painted motifs similar to Takamatsuzuka have been excavated in the area of Susŏng-ni. These have not yet been published in detail.

Finally it should be noted that some surface collection and test excavations have been carried out on the kilns which produced the famous Koryŏ celadons in the southwest of Korea. It is to be hoped that further detailed research will be undertaken on these kilns in the future.

The accomplishments of Korean archaeology have been substantial. The peninsula has a rich past and the problems to be studied through archaeology are profound and varied. My own view is that more rigor in choosing explanations, more attention to dwelling sites and their distribution over the landscape, and more concentration on subsistence patterns—more interest in the variations in patterns within each site, that is, and their meanings—will bring rewards in the future. These trends are being followed by archaeologists in many parts of the world.

TABLE I
Radiocarbon Dates from Korea

Number	Site and Provenience	Date BP	Date Christian Era	Recalibrated*	Cultural Affiliation
AERIK-5	Sŏkchang-ni VI lower layers (charcoal)(02-034)	30,690±3000	28,740±3000 BC		Paleolithic site, lower layers; see description by Sohn in Pearson (02-024)
AERIK-8	Sŏkchang-ni Locality I upper layers YM-4 (charcoal) (02-035: 274)	20,830±1880	18,880±1950 BC		Upper Paleolithic; see Sohn (02-031)
GX-0379	Tongsam-dong, 3 fragments; stratum C, pit 10-43; 125 cm length	4945±125	2995±125 BC	3630±125 BC	See Sample (02-027:318)
GX-0378	Tongsam-dong, Mokto period, charcoal from stratum E, pit 15-29; 163 cm deep (02-027:318)	5890±140	3940±140 BC	4580±140 BC	
GX-0492	Tongsam-dong (charcoal), Yŏngdo, stratum B, pit 11-43; 40–45 cm deep	3400±215	1450±215 BC	1660–1680±215 BC	
GX-0493	Tongsam-dong, Tudo period (early), stratum C, pit 12-43; depth 130 cm (charcoal)	3400±120	1450±120 BC	1660–1680±120 BC	
AERIK-22	Tongsam-dong, layer 2 (02-035: 278)	4170±100	2220±100 BC	2650–2780±100 BC	Charcoal, pit GX-11, ca. 140 cm below surface
AERIK-23	Tongsam-dong, layer 3, no. 1	4020±100	2070±100 BC	2490–2540±100 BC	Charcoal, pit GX-11, ca. 140 cm below surface
AERIK-24	Tongsam-dong, layer 3, no. 2 (02-035:278)	3980±100	2030±100 BC	2350–2460±100 BC	Charcoal, pit HX-11, ca. 140 cm below surface
AERIK-25	Tongsam-dong, layer 3, no. 3 (02-035:278)	3930±100	1980±100 BC	2190–2310±100 BC	Charcoal from pit HX-111, ca. 160 cm below surface
AERIK-26	Tongsam-dong, layer 3, no. 4 (02-035:278)	3880±100	1930±100 BC	2180±100 BC	Charcoal from pit HX-111, ca. 170 cm below surface
AERIK-27	Tongsam-dong, layer 3, no. 5 (02-035:278)	4400±90	2450±90 BC	2970–2990±90 BC	Charcoal from pit HX-VII, ca. 150 cm below surface
	Ch'odo Site, Pusan	4190±120	2240±120 BC	2690–2800±120 BC	
AERIK-7	South Tongmyŏng-ni, Kosŏng-gun, Kyŏngsang (02-034) (charcoal)	3573±48	1623±48 BC	1920–1950±48 BC	Polished stone tools found with slightly carbonized wood
AERIK-3	Tongnae, Pusan (02-034) (charcoal)	3469±78	1519±78 BC	1710–1750±78 BC	
	Taehŭksan Island, shell mound	3420±120	1470±120 BC	1690±120 BC	"Middle Neolithic" shell mound
AERIK-11	Shido I, bottom layer (02-035: 276)	3040±60	1090±60 BC	1240–1270±60 BC	Lower layer, undisturbed context
AERIK-10	Shido, middle layer (02-035:276)	2470±60	520±60 BC	500–640±60 BC	Plain Pottery culture
AERIK-9	Shido, top layer. B. S. Han, *The Shido Shell Mounds,* National Museum Report of Antiquities Investigation no. VIII (02-035:276)	1980±60	30±60 BC	AD 60±60 BC	

TABLE I *(continued)*
Radiocarbon Dates from Korea

Number	Site and Provenience	Date BP	Date Christian Era	Recalibrated*	Cultural Affiliation
AERIK-12	Shido, locality II, no. 1 (02-035: 276)	2870±60	920±60 BC	1010±60 BC	Charcoal from stone layer of cairn with Comb Pattern Pottery
AERIK-13	Shido, locality II, no. 2 (02-035: 276)	3100±60	1150±60 BC	1300–1360±60 BC	Charcoal from base of cairn with Comb Pattern Pottery
AERIK-14	Shido, locality II, no. 3 (02-035: 276)	3040±60	1090±60 BC	1240–1270±60 BC	Charcoal from base of cairn with Comb Pattern Pottery
AERIK-15	Kosŏng site, Tongwae-dong, Kosŏng-ŭp, South Kyŏngsang (02-035:276)	1730±70	220±70 BC	170–200±70 BC	Associated with Kimhae Pottery, bone implements, earthenware
AERIK-16	Songwŏn-ni, Kŭm River, Chang-gi myŏn, Kongju-gun, South Ch'ungch'ŏng (Yang 1972:277)	2880±120	930±120 BC	1020±120 BC	Associated with Plain Coarse Pottery, polished stone artifacts; thought to be too late by the collector, P. K. Sohn
AERIK-17	Songp'a-dong, YM-6, south bank of Han River, Sŏngdong-ku, Seoul	1920±130	AD 30±130	AD 110–90±130	Associated with elaborate wooden structure, several tens of meters long
AERIK-21	Songp'a-dong (see AERIK-17) (02-035:278)	1440±70	AD 510±70	AD 590±70	Part of roof construction
GX-0554	Osŏngni, Kyŏnggi-do (Kim 1969:4; 02-008)	2590±105	640±60 BC	780±60 BC	Group of dolmens, burial B1, northern-type dolmen, polished stone dagger, arrowheads, plain pottery
	Musan, northeastern Korea (Kim 1969:5)	2430±120	480±120 BC	440–470±120 BC	House site 15, containing polished semilunar knives, arrowheads, pottery
AERIK-28	Ch'ungsŏng, no. 1, Naepyŏng-ni, Puksan-myŏn, Kangwŏn (02-035:278)	2290±60	340±60 BC	400±60 BC	Charcoal, ca. 40 cm below surface
AERIK-29	Ch'ungsŏng, no. 2 (02-035:278)	2930±60	980±60 BC	1100±60 BC	Charcoal, ca. 70 cm below surface
AERIK-30	Ch'ungsŏng, no. 3 (02-035:278)	2590±60	640±60 BC	780±60 BC	Charcoal, ca. 70 cm below surface
KAERI-81	Yanggun-ni, YM-9 (02-021: 194–195)	2760±70	810±70 BC	900±70 BC	Plain Pottery site
KAERI-91	Sangjap'o-ri, Kaegun-myŏn, Kyŏnggi; human bone from southern-style dolmen (02-021: 196)	2170±60	220±60 BC	170–200±60 BC	Date thought to be accurate by excavators
KAERI-95	Yangsu-ri, charcoal from dolmen, Yangsu-myŏn, Yangp'yŏn-gun, Kyŏnggi (02-021:196)	3900±200	1950±200 BC	2190–2290±200 BC	Date thought to be too old by excavators
GX-0555	Hwangsŏng-ni, central Korea (02-008:124)	2360±370	410±370 BC	420±370 BC	Collagen from human bones in cist coffin, dolmen 13
AERIK-4	Yangsan site	1731±122	219±122 BC	AD 280±122	

TABLE I *(continued)*
Radiocarbon Dates from Korea

Number	Site and Provenience	Date BP	Date Christian Era	Recalibrated*	Cultural Affiliation
	Sosok-ni (*Misul Charyo,* no. 11 [1966] pp. 1–16; Kim 1969:6)	2340±120 2230±280	390±120 BC 280±280 BC	420±120 BC 250–380±280 BC	Polished adze
KAERI-80	Taegong-ni, Hwasun, South Chŏlla	2560±120	610±120 BC	750±120 BC	Fine decorated bronze mirror, bronze objects in burial, wood from coffin, 2 m below surface
N-236	Yangsan shell mound, Tabang-ni, Ryangsan-ŭp, South Kyŏng-sang (charcoal), layer I, site S-1 (Kim 1969:8; Yamasaki, Hamada, and Fujiyama, 1967: 307)	1750±120	AD 200±120	AD 260±120	
N-237	Yangsan shell mound, charcoal, layer 2, site S-6	1520±120	AD 430±120	AD 530–510±120	
N-238	Yangsan shell mound, charcoal from bottom of layer III, site S-6	1750±120	AD 200±120	AD 260±120	
N-239	Yangsan shell mound, charcoal from layer III, site N-2, 125 cm below surface	1840±110	AD 110±110	AD 170±110	
N-240	P'ungnam-ni Earth Fortress, Kwangjang-dong, Seoul (Yama-saki, Hamada, and Fujiyama 1967:307)	1720±110	AD 230±110	AD 290±110	Ancient dwelling site in fortress of early Three Kingdoms period (Paekche), floor of site overlain by layer with pot sherds
M-303	Kap'yŏng, Machang-ni (*Science,* vol. 127, pp. 1104–1105)	1700±250	AD 250±250	AD 320–290±250	Iron slag found in association
	Indong, Hwangsam-dong, tomb 1, Ch'ilgok-kun, North Kyŏng-sang	1710±180 1750±270	AD 240±180 AD 200±270	AD 320–290±180 AD 260±270	
	Indong, Hwangsam-dong, tomb 2 (Kim 1969:11,12), Ch'ilgok-kun, North Kyŏngsang	1420±160	AD 530±160	AD 600±160	
M-1491	Yŏngjong Island, Puch'ŏn-gun, Kyŏnggi (*Radiocarbon* 10(1)(1968): 111); dolmen site	720±100 880±110	AD 1230±100 AD 1070±110	AD 1250±100 AD 1120–1090±100	Northern-type dolmen excavated by Inchon City Museum; deposit is mixed with Koryŏ ceramics and also Comb Pattern Pottery. Date seems to be Koryŏ or else sample contaminated after collection
KAERI-74	Wangjin-ri, Ch'ŏngnam-myŏn, Ch'ŏngyang-gun, South Ch'ungch'ŏng; no. 1 wood from black soil layer, bottom of kiln 4 (02-021:194)	1330±70	AD 620±70	AD 670±70	Paekche kiln sites
M-1181	Ungch'ŏn shell mound, Ch'angwŏn-gun, Sŏngnae-ri, South Kyŏngsang (Crane and Griffin 1963:250)	1910±150	AD 40±150	AD 130–110±150	Kimhae period

TABLE I *(continued)*
Radiocarbon Dates from Korea

Number	Site and Provenience	Date BP	Date Christian Era	Recalibrated*	Cultural Affiliation
	Koryŏng, Koa-dong Pyŏkhwa (Kim 1969:12)	1780±130	AD 170±130	AD 250–220±130	Three Kingdoms period
N-351; N-352	Hwang'o-ri 1; Hwang'o-ri 2: wooden portion of saddle from tomb 34, Kyŏngju City (Yamasaki, Hamada, and Fujiyama 1968:342)	1630±110; 1580±115	AD 320±130; AD 370±110	AD 400±110; AD 440±110	Expected date 5th to 6th century AD
KAERI-75	Wangjin-ri no. 2, charcoal from blackish soil layer, bottom of kiln 4 (02-021:194)	1660±170	AD 290±70	AD 390–370±70	Kiln used to supply ceramics for the Paekche capital of Puyo; KAERI-75 is thought by excavators to be too early
KAERI-75	Wangjin-ri no. 3, charcoal from first step fireplace, kiln 4 (02-021:194)	1400±70	AD 550±70	AD 620±70	
KAERI-77	Tomb of King Muryŏng, ruler of Paekche, AD 501–523; Ungjin-dong, Kongju-ŭp, South Chungch'ŏng (02-021:194)	1470±70	AD 480±70	AD 570±70	
KAERI-98	Tomb 155; Kyŏngju no. 730713; charcoal (02-021:197)	1630±70	AD 320±70	AD 400±70	Sample part of wooden coffin from layer yielding gold crown and other grave goods
KAERI-97	Cist coffin, charcoal from Tunma-ri, Namha-myŏn, Kŏch'ang-gun, South Kyŏngsang (02-021:197)	720±100	AD 1230±100	AD 1250±100	Date thought to be accurate

REFERENCES CITED

This section contains references other than the English-language materials contained in the bibliography.

CH'OE, Mong-yong. "Kankoku dōka ni tsuite—toku ni keishiki bunrui o chūshin to shite." *Chōsen kōkogaku nempō* 2(1971):21–41.

———. "Chŏnnam sajŏn chŏkyumul chimyŏng p'yo." *Honam munhwa yŏn'gu* 6(1974):97–202.

CHŎN, Yŏng-nae. "Puan chibang kodae wigwak yujŏk kwa kŭ yumul." *Chŏnbuk yujŏk chosa pogo* 4(May 1975).

HAN, Byŏng-sam. "The Shido Shellmounds." *National Report of Antiquities Investigation* 8(1970). English translation by Alexander Townsend.

Han'guk Chungang Kungnip Pangmulgwan. *Paekche Muryŏng wang nŭng yumul t'ŭkpyŏlchŏn.* Seoul: 1971.

ICHIKAWA, K., I. FUJITA, and M. SHIMAZU. *The Geology of the Japanese Island.* Tokyo: Tsukiji Shokan, 1970.

KIM, Sin-gyu. "Waga kuni no genshi iseki ni mirareru honyu dōbutsuso (2)." *Chōsen gakujutsu tsūhō* 9(2)(1974): 44–63.

KIM, Wŏn-yong. *Sinch'ang-ni onggwan myoji.* Archaeological and Anthropological Papers of Seoul National University, vol. 1. Seoul: 1964.

———. "Pungnam-ni t'osongnae p'ohamch'ŭng chosa pogo." *Sŏul Taehakkyo kogo illyuhak ch'onggan.* Archaeological and Anthropological Papers of Seoul National University, vol. 3. Seoul: 1967.

———. "Han'guk kogohak esŏŭi pangsasŏng t'anso nyŏndae." *Kogohak* (Archaeology)2(June 1969). Seoul: Han'guk Kogohakhoe.

LEDYARD, G. "The Thalassocracy of Wa: The Political

Projection of Late Yayoi Culture." Unpublished manuscript. 1976.

National Museum of Korea. *Treasures from the Tomb of King Munyong* [Muryŏng] *of the Paekche Dynasty.* In Korean. Pp. 501–523. Seoul: 1971.

NISHITANI, Tadashi (ed.). *Chōsen kōkogaku nempō.* Vol. 2. In Japanese. Tokyo: Azuma Shuppan, 1975.

REFERENCES FOR ISOLATED RADIOCARBON
DATES

CRANE, H. R. and James B. GRIFFIN. University of Michigan Radiocarbon Dates VIII. *Radiocarbon* 5(1963):228–254.

_____. University of Michigan Radiocarbon Dates XII. *Radiocarbon* 10(1968):61–114.

YAMASAKI, Fumio, Tatsuji HAMADA, and Chikako FUJIYAMA. Riken Natural Radiocarbon Measurements III. *Radiocarbon* 9(1967):301–308.

_____. Riken Natural Radiocarbon Measurements IV. *Radiocarbon* 10(1968):333–343.

NOTE

Thanks are offered to the Canada Council, to the University of British Columbia Research Committee, and to the Joint Council on Korean Studies of the Social Science Research Council and the American Council of Learned Societies for their support in this research.

BIBLIOGRAPHY

02-001. CHARD, Chester S. "Neolithic Archaeology in North Korea." *Asian Perspectives* 4(1961):151–155. Contains a summary of the Chit'am-ni site (romanized as Ditap-li, near Sariwŏn) translated into English from the Russian. Problems with the romanization from Korean to English through Russian make correlation of sites and geographical names difficult. The interesting point is made that the black pottery of North Korea has direct analogies with later wares of the Soviet Union, which are said to be associated with the first appearance of iron (p. 153).

02-002. _____. *Northeast Asia in Prehistory.* Madison: University of Wisconsin Press, 1974. While this book does not aim at providing a definitive statement of Korean prehistory, it is indispensable for background to the entire area of Northeast Asia, particularly Japan and Siberia. The Japanese material, necessarily selective, gives one of the very best introductions in English. Chard suggests that Korea may have acted as a barrier between China and Japan in the prehistoric period.

02-003. CHASE, David. "A Limited Archaeological Survey of the Han River Valley in Central Korea." *Asian Perspectives* 4(1961):141–149. Reports the survey of seventeen sites found in 1960 in the Han River valley between Seoul and a point about 20 miles east of the city. The ceramics of three sites—Soksil, Misa-ri, and Toksŏ-ri—are described in some detail, and a series of types is worked out.

02-004. GARDINER, K. J. H. *The Early History of Korea: The Historical Development of the Peninsula up to the Introduction of Buddhism in the Fourth Century A.D.* Honolulu: University of Hawaii Press, 1969. Provides important background for the archaeology of the historical periods and reviews the Japanese excavations, particularly in the Taedong area. Appendix I contains a detailed discussion of the Tung Shou tomb found in 1949 at Anak, north of Sinch'ŏn. After presenting various interpretations, the author concludes that the tomb was built for Tung Shou, the last governor of Lolang before its fall to the Koguryŏ.

02-005. HAN, Pyŏng-sam. "Neolithic Culture of Korea." *Korea Journal* 14(4)(April 1974):12–17. The author proposes two temporal divisions of the Comb Pattern Pottery period—an early (nonagricultural) and a late (incipient agricultural) time division. It is suggested that the Pre-Comb Pattern Pottery period, which may be indicated by the bottom layers of the Unggi and Tongsam-dong sites, needs further research before it can be securely established. The article relies on some outdated concepts which can cause confusion, such as the term *Kammkeramik* for Comb Pattern Pottery. The dating given for Yang-shao is far too late, and that of Isakovo is given as firm whereas it is in fact very shaky.

02-006. HENTHORN, William E. "Recent Archaeological Activity in North Korea: (1) The Cave of Misong-ni." *Asian Perspectives* 9(1966):73–78. Translation with detailed comments of reports by Kim Yong-gan appearing in the journal *Munhwa yusan* 1(1961):45–57 and 2(1961): 23–32. Two cultural strata were excavated: the lower is a "Neolithic" layer earlier than 2000 BC; the upper layer has been dated to the first millennium BC. There is a brief mention of faunal remains.

02-007. HEWES, Gordon. "Archaeology of Korea: A Selected Bibliography." *Research Monographs on Korea,* series F, no. 1, 1947. This pioneering bibliography gives a great many of the early Japanese sources.

02-008. KIM, Chewon and Moo-Byong YOUN. *Studies of*

Dolmens in Korea. Report of the Research of Antiquities of the National Museum of Korea. Vol. 6. Seoul: National Museum of Korea, 1967. The 32-page English summary plus captions to more than 150 plates of the Korean work published under the title of *Han'guk chisŏngmyo yŏn'gu* make this publication of use to the English reader. Detailed information on each site is presented only in Korean, however. Dolmens are divided into a number of types and their associated artifacts are discussed. It is suggested that the table-form northern dolmen is earlier than the southern form, which consists of very large boulders and smaller rocks. The northern forms could be as early as the eighth century BC; the last dolmen forms are thought to have disappeared from the southern part of the peninsula by about 200 BC.

02-009. KIM, Chong-gi. "Dwelling Sites of the Geometric Period, Korea." *Asian Perspectives* 18(2)(1975). Translation from Japanese of a chapter of Kim Jeong-hak, *Kankoku no kōkogaku* (1972), dealing specifically with house remains, distribution of artifacts within houses, and changes in architectural style.

02-010. KIM, Jeong-hak. *The Prehistory of Korea.* Translated by Richard J. Pearson and Kazue Pearson. Honolulu: University Press of Hawaii, 1979. Professor Kim's book, published originally in Japanese (*Kankoku no kōkogaku,* Kawaide Shobō, Tokyo), is the most comprehensive, illustrated summary of Korean archaeology up to the late 1960s. The book includes work done in the North and South as well as earlier studies by the Japanese. The translated portion extends from the Paleolithic to the beginning of the Three Kingdoms. In conjunction with *The Traditional Culture and Society of Korea: Prehistory,* edited by Richard J. Pearson (see 02-024), it will provide a definitive coverage of Korean prehistoric research up to about 1970.

02-011. KIM, Jung-bae. "Bronze Age Culture in Korea." *Korea Journal* 14(4)(April 1974):18–31. A reduced version of the paper presented at the Conference on the Traditional Society and Culture of Korea, 1971, in Honolulu. The paper gives a rather thorough summary of the remains known to date. The repeated statements that Japanese Yayoi culture is borrowed wholesale from Korea are erroneous; a good deal of internal development from Jōmon into Yayoi can be documented. Further, the identification of the bronze culture with Ko Chosŏn is accomplished with virtually no documentation.

02-012. KIM, Wŏn-yong. "Dolmens in Korea." *Journal of Social Sciences and Humanities* 16(June 1962):1–11. A useful, brief, illustrated discussion of dolmens with particular emphasis on the author's own research and Japanese materials. The time period proposed for the southern dol-

mens, extending into the first centuries AD, seems to be too late in the light of recent discoveries outlined in *The Prehistory of Korea* by Kim Jeong-hak (02-010) and *Studies of Dolmens in Korea* by Kim Chewon and Youn Moobyong (02-008).

02-013. _____. "Some Aspects of Comb Pattern Pottery of Prehistoric Korea." *Arctic Anthropology* 1(1962):42–50. This brief summary has been superseded by Kim's later articles. Briefly outlines regional design variants, chronology, and origins. Mentions direct connections across Eurasia linking Korean pottery with the Eastern Baltic and other obsolete theories suggesting that Comb Pattern Pottery is the predecessor of Early Yayoi ceramics. The bibliography of early Japanese sources is useful for historical perspective.

02-014. _____. "New Lights on Korean Archaeology." *Asian Perspectives* 10(1967):39–55. A useful overview from Paleolithic times to the Iron Age, with current news of sites such as Yangsan and Yongjin-ni. Many photographs are included.

02-015. _____ (ed.). *Archaeology in Korea: An Annual Review of Korean Archaeology.* Vol. 1. Seoul: Department of Archaeology and Anthropology, Seoul National University, 1973. Contains a profusely illustrated résumé of the year's major excavations (including Silla tombs 98, 110, 155) and a list of field activities, museum activities and exhibitions, and publications. This annual publication fills a great need in Korean archaeology. Both English and Korean sections are provided.

02-016. KIM, Yong-jin. "Annotated Bibliography of North Korean Publications in Archaeology." *Asian Perspectives* 19(1973):29–32. Brief bibliography (1957–1966) of publications in several North Korean series and journals.

02-017. KNEZ, Eugene and Chang-su SWANSON. *A Bibliography of Korean Anthropology.* Seoul: National Assembly Library, 1968. Bibliography, to 1965, on ethnology, social anthropology, material culture, linguistics, and physical anthropology. Some 262 items in Korean and Japanese are included in archaeology and material culture. Some materials published in Pyongyang are also cited.

02-018. LEE, Sung-nyong (ed.). *Korean Studies Today.* Seoul: Institute of Asian Studies, Seoul National University, 1970. Contains a brief résumé of archaeology, focusing on contributions of Korean scholars in the fifties and sixties, with some reference, usually negative, to earlier Japanese work. Useful for pointing the reader to important work done by the Koreans in classification and interpretation. Contains no mention of North Korean work except for the site of Kul'po.

02-019. McCUNE, E. *The Arts of Korea: An Illustrated His-*

tory. Rutland, Vt.: Tuttle, 1962. A detailed account of the art and archaeology of Korea. Pages 1–156 contain a well-documented exposition of archaeological materials from earliest times to the end of Silla. Although the section on prehistory is now completely out of date, the portion on the Lolang colony is particularly useful, since Lolang is often played down in recent works as something external to the pattern of Korean development. The large number of illustrations and the discussions of the Three Kingdoms can also serve as a good introduction for students.

02-020. NELSON, Sarah Milledge. "Chulmun Period Villages on the Han River in Korea: Subsistence and Settlement." PhD dissertation, University of Michigan, 1973. 190 pp. Abstracted in *DAI* 35(July 1974):353-A; UM 74-15,811. Six possible settlement and subsistence patterns are proposed for testing on site in the Middle Han River valley near Seoul—seasonal use for hunting and gathering; settled hunting and gathering; seasonal use of sites for fishing; settled fishing; seasonal planting at sites with return for harvesting; and settled planting. It is suggested that the sites, spaced at about 2-kilometer intervals and in part contemporary (for example, Misa-ri, Amsa-ri, Tong-mak), were supported by broad-spectrum utilization of available food resources through collecting but also by planting crops for winter storage. Possible plant domesticates in the Comb Pattern Pottery period are turnip, Chinese cabbage, millet, grain sorghum, hemp, and soybeans. A portion of this research has appeared as "The Subsistence Base of Middle Han Sites of the Chulmun Period," *Asian Perspectives* 18(1)(1975).

02-021. PAK, Chan-kirl and Kyung-rin YANG. "KAERI Radiocarbon Measurements III." *Radiocarbon* 16(2)(1974): 192–197. Contains dates from the Korean sites of Wangjin-ni, the Paekche tomb of Muryŏng, Taegong-ni, Yanggun-ni, Sangjap'o-ri, Tunma-ri, and Silla tomb 155.

02-022. PEARSON, Richard J. "Archaeology in Korea." *Antiquity* 46(183)(1972):227–230. Gives a summary outline of the archaeology papers presented at the Conference on the Traditional Culture and Society of Korea held at the University of Hawaii in 1971.

02-023. _____. "Further Bibliography of North Korean Archaeology from North Korean Sources." *Asian Perspectives* 14(1973):33–34. Provides contents from some Pyongyang publications (1962–1967).

02-024. _____ (ed.). *The Traditional Culture and Society of Korea: Prehistory.* Occasional Papers of the Center for Korean Studies, no. 3. Honolulu: University of Hawaii, 1975. Contains three summary papers: the Paleolithic by Sohn Pow-key, the "Neolithic" by Kim Wŏn-yong, and the Bronze Period by Kim Jung-bae. Comments and com-

parative notes are provided by Chang Kwang-chih, Serizawa Chōsuke, Sato Tatsuo, and Okazaki Takashi. An introduction by Richard Pearson provides a summary of Korean prehistory and a sketch of Korean people-land relationships. Charts and maps give locations of sites and illustrate some categories of artifacts. The articles are fully documented with references in East Asian and European languages.

02-025. _____. "Prehistoric Subsistence and Economy in Korea—An Initial Sketch." *Asian Perspectives* 17(2) (1974):93–101. An attempt to bring together what is known of Korean prehistoric human ecology and to suggest directions in which future research might move. Vegetation is briefly reviewed, and there are discussions of house remains, faunal materials, and what can be determined of general subsistence patterns.

02-026. PEARSON, Richard J. and H. J. IM. "Preliminary Archaeological Research on Cheju Island and Its Implications for Korean Prehistory." *Proceedings of the VIIIth International Congress of Anthropological and Ethnological Sciences III.* Tokyo: Science Council of Japan, 1968. Report of a brief archaeological survey of Cheju Island undertaken in July 1967. Covers a number of sites, particularly dolmens. This work has been largely superseded by the discovery of both Paleolithic and later groups of sites in the past few years.

02-027. SAMPLE, Lillie Laetitia. "Culture History and Chronology of South Korea's Neolithic." PhD dissertation, Univeristy of Wisconsin, 1967. 414 pp. Abstracted in *DAI* 28(February 1968):3142-B; UM 12,156. Provides a summary review of Japanese and early Korean contributions to the study of Comb Pattern or Geometric Pottery as well as a detailed report of the excavations at Tongsamdong, Pusan. Two aspects are particularly worthy of note. The first is the detailed analysis of the ceramics, with stratigraphic control, which is almost always lacking in studies dealing with this time period. The second is the analysis of faunal materials. One might question the adequacy of the sample in each case; however, compared to what has been done previously the work represents a major step forward. Radiocarbon dates are presented for Tongsam-dong. The reader is directed to the discussion of Tongsam-dong in Pearson (see 02-024:112–125) and the forthcoming publications of the National Museum of Korea following its excavation project of the same site.

02-028. _____. "Tongsamdong: A Contribution to Korean Neolithic Culture History." *Arctic Anthropology* 11(2) (1974). Publication, with some revision and updating, of Sample's dissertation (see 02-027).

02-029. SAMPLE, Lillie Laetitia and A. MOHR. "Progress

Report on Archaeological Research in the Republic of Korea." *Arctic Anthropology* 2(1964):99–140. Gives preliminary results of survey in Kangwŏn province, the Kŭm River drainage, and the south coast. About one hundred sites were located in the summer and fall of 1962. Surface finds from the Kŭm River area give the first indications of Paleolithic occupation and it is suggested that the lowest layers of the Tongsam-dong site in Pusan may be preceramic.

02-030. SOHN, Pow-key. "Palaeolithic Cultures of Korea." *Korea Journal* 14(4)(April 1974):4–12. Brief paper which summarizes the finds from Sŏkchang-ni by layer, also mentioning Sangwŏn Cave, near Pyongyang, which has yielded faunal remains, Billemot Cave (Pillemok) on Cheju Island, Chŏnmal Cave in Chech'ŏn, and petroglyphs from Ch'ŏnjŏn-ni, Onyang-myŏn, and Ulchu-gun.

02-031. _____. *The Upper Palaeolithic Habitation Sokchang-ni, Korea: A Summary Report.* Yonsei University Museum, English Series, no. 1. Seoul: 1973. Description of the Upper Paleolithic occupation at Locality 1, Sŏkchang-ni, near Kongju. The local environment is briefly described according to fossil pollen distribution, and the function and technology of the tools are mentioned. Some postulated examples of Paleolithic art are discussed and the distribution of artifacts within a habitation is given.

02-032. SOHN, Pow-key, Chol-choon KIM, and Yi-sup HONG. *The History of Korea.* Seoul: Korean National Commission for UNESCO, 1970. A brief but effective summary (pp. 3–78) covering nearly all cultures from the Paleolithic to the rise of Silla, Koguryŏ, and Paekche. Much of the outline seems to be developed from historical sources rather than from excavation. Of particular interest is the account of the traditional ethnic groups in Korea in the latter part of the first millennium BC. This article might be used as an initial introduction to the reader totally unfamiliar with Korean prehistory. The statements concerning the immigrant groups who left China at the fall of the Shang are yet to be substantiated by archaeology. A bibliography of Korean sources is provided, as well as illustrations; the text, however, is not footnoted. Part 2, which is a historical outline of Koguryŏ, Paekche, and Silla, is followed by a section on Parhae (Pohai) and the decline of Silla. No archaeological materials are used in these sections; however, they are of great use as background for recent excavation.

02-033. TOWNSEND, Alexander. "Cultural Evolution of the Neolithic Period of West Central Korea." PhD dissertation in Anthropology, University of Hawaii, 1975. Presents a review of information on sites of the "Neolithic" period, with emphasis on the Han River drainage, in addition to a series of hypotheses on the chronological and adaptive relationships of sites in this area. One of the more significant of these is that later sites of the Comb Pattern Pottery period were located in areas marginal for incipient agriculture—the seacoast and offshore islands and the interior highlands (p. 202). Thus at the end of the Comb Pattern Pottery period, broad-spectrum hunting and gathering occurred in marginal areas while the middle-range plains were being used by cultivators. This hypothesis appears to be supported by evidence from sites such as Karang-ni and Yŏksam-dong, although Sarah Nelson postulates agriculture at an earlier date further upstream on the Han River. This dissertation contains useful summaries and illustrations.

02-034. YANG, Kyung-rin. "Atomic Energy Research Institute of Korea: Radiocarbon Measurement I." *Radiocarbon* 12(2)(1970):350–352. The first publication of archaeological dates of the Radiocarbon Dating Laboratory, Atomic Energy Research Institute, Seoul. Sites dated include Tongnae, Yangsan, Sŏkchang-ni, and Tongmang-ni.

02-035. _____. "Atomic Energy Research Institute of Korea: Radiocarbon Measurements II." *Radiocarbon* 14(1972):273–279. Presents further radiocarbon dates for Sŏkchang-ni and Tongsam-dong in addition to determinations for Shido, Kosŏng, Songp'a-dong, and Ch'ungsŏng.

CHAPTER 3
History

Yŏng-ho Ch'oe

with contributions by *Hugh Kang* and
*Michael E. Macmillan, Young Ick Lew,
Seong Rae Park, Li Ogg*

I. GENERAL
by Yŏng-ho Ch'oe

INTRODUCTION

KOREA has a long and varied history of historical writing. The oldest historical accounts of Korea, however, are found in Chinese historical sources. Ever since the tradition of compiling an official history was established in China by Ssu-ma Ch'ien (145–86 BC), the official dynastic histories of China included some references to Korea in varying degrees. Up until the period covered in the two Korean historical sources, *Samguk sagi* and *Samguk yusa*, compiled in the twelfth and thirteenth centuries respectively, the accounts given in these Chinese histories are the only written reference to Korea we now have except for a few inscriptions that have survived. Hence Chinese histories, such as *Shih-chi, Han-shu,* and *San-kuo-chih,* are invaluable sources in understanding ancient Korean history.[1]

HISTORICAL WRITING DURING THE THREE KINGDOMS PERIOD

Koguryŏ, first of the three kingdoms, began to emerge by the beginning of the first century as a centralized state in the area covering part of present southern Manchuria and North Korea, and it was then followed by the rise of two other kingdoms, Paekche in southwestern Korea and Silla in southeastern Korea, in the third and fourth centuries respectively. In time, all three kingdoms maintained close contacts with China and adopted many aspects of her civilization. Among the more important ideas borrowed from China by these Korean kingdoms were the Chinese writing system and historical writing.

Although none of the Korean historical writing dating back to the Three Kingdoms period has survived, we know from various other references that each of the three kingdoms did have some sort of historical record keeping. Koguryŏ was the first kingdom known to have compiled its own historical records. According to *Samguk sagi,* Koguryŏ kept in its early period a historical record called *Yugi* [Records of memorabilia], amounting to as many as 100 chapters *(kwŏn),* and in AD 600 an academy scholar named Yi Mun-jin compiled a new history called *Sinjip* [New collection] in five chapters, based on earlier historical records.[2] Unfortunately, however, this is about all the reference we have with regard to the Koguryŏ historical writings, and neither *Yugi* nor *Sinjip* has survived. Thus we know nothing about the nature and contents of these earliest known Korean historical works.

The introduction of historical writing into Paekche is believed to have come much later than in Koguryŏ. According to *Samguk sagi,* Paekche had no writing system until the rule of King Kŭnch'ogo (reigned AD 346–375), when a scholar named Kohŭng first recorded *Sŏgi* [Chronicle].[3] Although the term *Sŏgi* may mean simply "written records," most scholars nowadays tend to interpret it to be a historical record. Unfortunately, *Sŏgi*, too, was lost long ago and we have at present no way of knowing its contents or nature. Nevertheless, we can get some ideas on the nature of historical writings developed in Paekche from Japanese historical sources because a great deal of Paekche histories were transmitted to Japan and have survived there. *Nihon shoki* [Chronicle of Japan], the oldest history book in Japan (compiled in AD 720), cites a number of Korean sources, among which the most notable are *Kudara ki (Paekche ki* in Korean*), Kudara hongi (Paekche pon'gi), and Kudara shinsen (Paekche sinch'an)*. These Paekche historical records are believed to have been compiled either by scholars in Paekche or by Paekche expatriates who sought refuge in Japan after the demise of their kingdom in the seventh century. Many modern Japanese scholars agree that these Paekche history books exerted a profound influence upon the compilation of *Nihon shoki* as they provided its historical concept, organizational structure, and chronology as well as historical data.[4]

The first reference to historical writing in Silla dates back to AD 545, about which *Samguk sagi* gives the following account:

> The first grade official Isabu memorialized: "a nation's history records good and evil acts of kings and subjects so as to praise and censure them for tens of thousand generations. If history is not compiled, how will the posterity know?" The king thereupon agreed wholeheartedly and ordered the fifth grade official Kŏch'ilbu and others to assemble scholars widely and had them compile [a history].[5]

Unfortunately, the historical work compiled by Kŏch'-ilbu and his colleagues is not extant, but at least some parts of it may have survived long enough to have been incorporated into *Samguk sagi* in the twelfth century. What is interesting in the reference quoted above, however, is the underlying objective of the compilation of the first known Silla history, which follows very much a Confucian concept of history and indicates a strong Chinese influence on the historiography of Silla.

After Korea achieved the first political and territorial unification in the seventh century under the aegis of

Silla with the alliance of T'ang China, Silla's contact with China went apace in all areas. Especially noteworthy was the cultural and scholarly interchange between the two countries. It is believed that the tradition of historical writing started in Silla by Kŏch'ilbu in the sixth century was not only carried on but further developed during the Unified Silla period. Once again, no historical work dating back to this period has survived, but there are a number of references to historical works compiled after the Silla unification. Perhaps most noteworthy among them are several works authored by Kim Tae-mun—*Kyerim chapchŏn* [Miscellaneous stories of Korea], *Kosŭng chŏn* [Biographies of eminent monks], *Hwarang segi* [History of *hwarang*], and *Hansan ki* [Gazetteer of Hansan]. A Seoul National University historian, Ko Pyŏng-ik, making a particular note of the authorship of several different works by one man, Kim Tae-mun (fl. 704), recently suggested that the writing at this time may have been addressed not merely to posterity but also to contemporary readers as there may have been a substantial literate audience.[6]

HISTORICAL WRITING DURING THE KORYŎ PERIOD

The importance of history was recognized very early in the Koryŏ dynasty. *Koryŏ sa* [History of Koryŏ] records that the History Office known as Sagwan—later changed to Ch'unch'ugwan—was organized from the beginning of the dynasty,[7] but modern scholars believe that the actual establishment of the History Office may not have taken place until the reign of King Sŏngjong (reigned 981–997).[8] The rather elaborate structure and staffing of the office as well as other evidence indicate that a careful and systematic effort was instituted to keep the daily administrative record known as *Sijonggi* and preserve this and other historical records for posterity. The practice of compiling and safekeeping of the Veritable Records *(sillok)* in Korea also began during the Koryŏ dynasty, although it is not clear when it started or whose reigns the *sillok* covered. The Veritable Records were still available in the fifteenth century and became one of the main sources for the compilation of the official Koryŏ history, *Koryŏ sa*.

The most important historiographical work of the Koryŏ period, however, is *Samguk sagi* [Historical record of the Three Kingdoms], which was completed in 1146 and is the oldest extant history book in Korea. Compiled by Kim Pu-sik (1075–1151) at the command of King Injong (reigned 1122–1146), *Samguk sagi* is an official history in the tradition of the standard dynastic histories in China. Following the Chinese *chi-chüan* (annal-biography) format, it consisted of four parts— *pon'gi* (*pen-chi* in Chinese or "annals"), *yŏnp'yo* (*nien-piao* in Chinese or "tables"), *chi* (*chih* in Chinese or "treatises"), and *yŏlchŏn* (*lieh-chuan* in Chinese or "biographies"). Covering the history of Korea from the beginning of the Three Kingdoms through the fall of Unified Silla in 938, this is in fact the only historical work that treats Korea's ancient period systematically and comprehensively.

In compiling *Samguk sagi,* Kim Pu-sik was assisted by ten other scholar-officials to carry out an extensive research collecting whatever materials were available at the time. Altogether some 123 different titles of historical sources are cited in *Samguk sagi,* according to Suematsu Yasukazu's study; of these 69 are Korean and the rest are Chinese works.[9] A title which later historians call *Ku samguk sa* [Old Three Kingdoms history] had apparently been in existence for some time before the compilation of *Samguk sagi,* and Kim Pu-sik is believed to have relied heavily on it. Moreover, among the many Chinese works he consulted, Ssu-ma Kuang's *Tzu-chih t'ung-chien* [Comprehensive mirror for aid in government] was an important source for Kim Pu-sik that often filled the gaps not covered in Korean materials.

One basic principle that had guided the compilation of the *sagi,* according to Kim Pu-sik, was to bring out "the good and wicked acts of the rulers, the loyalty and evil doings of the subjects, the safety and crises of the nation, and the peaceful and rebellious acts of the people" so that these would provide lessons to posterity.[10] This "praise and blame" concept of history suited the Confucian Kim Pu-sik, who injected frequently his own moralistic historical judgment by adding his personal comment on many historical issues.

Because of its historical importance, *Samguk sagi* has been in the center of controversy for a long time. Some Neo-Confucian scholars of the Yi dynasty accused Kim Pu-sik of including stories of a "wild and nonsensical nature" such as mythical and supernatural tales found

in the origins of the Three Kingdoms.[11] The bitterest attack against the *sagi,* however, came in 1925 when Sin Ch'ae-ho published an article called "Chosŏn yŏksa sang ilch'ŏnnyŏn nae cheil taesagŏn," which may be translated as "the greatest incident in the past one thousand years of Korean history." In this article, Sin Ch'ae-ho claimed that Kim Pu-sik was the leader in suppressing Korea's nativistic tradition and independent spirit in favor of the Chinese civilization and Confucian culture when he defeated the rebellion led by Monk Myoch'ŏng in 1135 and further accused Kim Pu-sik of fabricating and distorting Korea's ancient history to suit his Confucian world view in *Samguk sagi.*

Such a Manichaean interpretation of history did provide a convenient answer to many frustrated and disgruntled intellectuals of the early twentieth century who had helplessly witnessed the demise of their country as an independent nation. Thereafter *Samguk sagi* and its compiler Kim Pu-sik have become a favorite target of criticism by a number of modern historians—largely on the ground that Kim Pu-sik reflected the China-centered Confucian world view in the *sagi.* This controversy is still being debated among scholars in South Korea. For example, Kim Ch'ŏl-chun of Seoul National University has recently argued eloquently that Kim Pu-sik, because of his Confucian outlook, high political position, and aristocratic background, tended to have a low opinion of Korea's nativistic tradition and that he compiled *Samguk sagi* in contravention to the then existing *Ku samguk sa* for the purpose of either obliterating the indigenous historical sources still extant at his time or obviating their value.[12] Recently, however, a new trend is afoot among scholars to give Kim Pu-sik and *Samguk sagi* credit. Ko Pyŏng-ik denies that Kim Pu-sik was subservient to China in his approach to the history of the Three Kingdoms and concludes that there is no evidence that he fabricated or distorted the ancient history, although he may have eliminated or abridged certain myths and legends.[13]

Some 140 years after the completion of *Samguk sagi,* another history of the Three Kingdoms called *Samguk yusa* [Memorabilia of the Three Kingdoms] was compiled by a Buddhist monk named Iryŏn (1206–1289). Because both books cover the history of the same Three Kingdoms, they have inevitably been compared and contrasted with each other. Unlike the *sagi,* the *yusa* is a work of an individual scholar achieved at his own initiative without government support or sanction. While Kim Pu-sik was a Confucian scholar-official whose entire career was spent in public service, Iryŏn was a Buddhist monk who devoted his life to the work of his religious belief. These personal differences of the two authors certainly affected the nature of the two historical works.

Essentially, *Samguk yusa* is a collection of tales and stories of the Three Kingdoms, not strictly a history. It followed no particular format originally until Ch'oe Nam-sŏn in 1926 reclassified the contents into nine different headings. These headings can in turn be divided simply into two large groups as Yi Ki-baek suggests— namely the supernatural stories of historical incidences and the Buddhist accounts of various nature.[14] In marked contrast to Kim Pu-sik's rational narration of *Samguk sagi, Samguk yusa* abounds with stories of wonder and miracle that defy any rational imagination. Nevertheless, these tales and stories take us back to the world of folk belief, superstition, legend, and myth in ancient Korea, and herein lies the book's historical value.

Largely because of this folkish characteristic, nationalistic-minded Korean scholars in the twentieth century have placed a great value on *Samguk yusa* as a historical source, and some have gone even to the extent of attaching greater importance to it than to the *sagi.* To them, the *sagi* is a China-centered work while the *yusa* represents nativistic tradition. Furthermore, the *yusa* includes the legend of Tan'gun, the mythical founder of ancient Korea, at the beginning of the work, which further enhances the nationalistic value of the book in the eyes of many modern Koreans. Be that as it may, the true value of the *yusa* lies in the fact that it contains histories that are not found in the *sagi* and vice versa. Thus the two works complement each other and neither is dispensable in understanding the history of the Three Kingdoms.

HISTORICAL WRITING DURING THE YI DYNASTY

As can be expected in a Confucian state, Yi Korea placed a great emphasis on the importance of history.

Indeed, very few states in the world can claim to be more conscious of history than was the Yi dynasty, and this consciousness is well reflected in the prodigious amount of historical writings it has left. The historical works of the Yi dynasty can be divided largely into two categories: official histories and unofficial histories. The official histories are works that received state sponsorship for their compilation; the unofficial histories are the work of private scholars without official auspices.

The first important official history of the Yi dynasty is *Koryŏ sa* [History of Koryŏ], compiled within the Chinese tradition of dynastic histories. *Koryŏ sa* follows the *kijŏn* (or *chi-chüan* in Chinese) format and is divided into four parts—*sega* (royal families) in 46 chapters, *chi* (monographs) in 39 chapters, *yŏnp'yo* (tables) in 2 chapters, and *yŏlchŏn* (biographies) in 50 chapters, along with 2 additional chapters of contents, altogether consisting of 139 chapters. Based on a number of primary and secondary sources such as *sillok* and *Kŭmgyŏng nok* [Records of golden mirror] among others, *Koryŏ sa* is by far the most important source in understanding the history of Koryŏ. The basic principle that guided the compiling of *Koryŏ sa* was the Confucian notion of history as an instrument of moral lessons for posterity, and certain Confucian prejudices were inevitably reflected in the editorial tone of the work. As Kim Ch'ŏl-chun points out, for example, although the Koryŏ civilization cannot be properly understood without its Buddhistic element, *Koryŏ sa* has no monograph or special section devoted to Buddhism.[15]

In addition to historical considerations, there was a distinctive political motive in the compilation of *Koryŏ sa* and that was to justify the inauguration of the new Chosŏn dynasty replacing Koryŏ. In spite of such political undertones, *Koryŏ sa* is an impressive work of scholarship based meticulously on the primary and secondary source materials. Now that most of the primary sources of Koryŏ have been lost, *Koryŏ sa* is an indispensable work for understanding the medieval period of Korea.

In addition to *Koryŏ sa,* the Yi dynasty also compiled another Koryŏ history called *Koryŏsa chŏryo* [Abridged essence of Koryŏ history]. Completed in 1452, one year after the completion of *Koryŏ sa, Koryŏsa chŏryo* is not a summary or condensation of *Koryŏ sa* and was in fact compiled independently of *Koryŏ sa;* hence it contains much valuable information not found in that work. It follows the annalistic format known as *p'yŏnnyŏn* (*pien-nien* in Chinese).

Several other histories were also compiled under the auspices of the state in the early years of the Yi dynasty; among these, *Tongguk t'onggam* [Complete mirror of the Eastern Country] is particularly important from the point of historiography. Based largely on *Samguk sagi, Samguk yusa,* and various Chinese sources, the *t'onggam* is the only officially sanctioned history that covers the entire Korean history from Tan'gun through the fall of the Koryŏ dynasty and was perhaps the most widely read Korean history text during the Yi dynasty. Compiled under the editorial leadership of Sŏ Kŏ-jŏng (1420–1488), the *t'onggam,* as the title suggests, was originally intended as a Korean version of Ssu-ma Kuang's *Tzu-chih t'ung-chien* and reflects strongly the Neo-Confucian world view of history. As a general history of Korea, however, the *t'onggam* has often been criticized for its many errors and omissions.

While the Yi dynasty spent considerable intellectual effort in compiling various histories, it also used a prodigious amount of energy in preserving historical records. There were several different offices involved in keeping and safeguarding records. The Ch'unch'ugwan (Bureau of State Records), under the charge of the three high state councillors, functioned as the state archive keeping all the administrative records of government. The actual duties of the historians, who kept a daily record of the official activities around the throne, however, were entrusted to eight diarists of the seventh, eighth, and ninth ranks in the Office of Royal Decrees (Yemungwan). These diarists, especially those of the lowly ninth rank, were usually known as *hallim* and carried the highest prestige for the young bureaucrats in the Yi dynasty government. Their selection and appointment followed stringent procedures: those participating in the selection were required to make a special oath that they would do their utmost to choose the best-qualified men.

The *hallim* were normally selected from the recent graduates of the higher civil service examination so that they were relatively free from vested interest or personal prejudice. It was hoped that their youth and idealism would "keep their brush straight" without fear in recording daily activities around the throne. Moreover, these historians accompanied the king constantly, and it became an established practice for rulers not to transact official business without the presence of a historian. This ubiquitous presence of a historian—and the concomitant fear of their deeds and speeches being recorded for posterity—often put the Yi dynasty rulers in a defensive situation, and thus, as Pow-Key Sohn ably argues, history became an effective instrument in checking the growth of the monarchical authority and power during the Yi dynasty.[16]

After the death of each king, the veritable records *(sillok)* of his reign were compiled by an ad hoc committee which included the highest officials as well as the ablest scholars. The *sillok* is based on the various primary sources of the foremost importance such as the historians' diaries, the administrative records known as *sijŏnggi,* and other government records including *Sŭngjŏngwŏn ilgi* and is one of the most important sources of information. To ensure the safekeeping of the *sillok,* four copies were printed and each was kept in a different locality. During the Hideyoshi invasion, all but one copy were lost, and the successful effort to save the last remaining set of the *sillok* against the hazard of war was almost heroic and indicated the degree of historical consciousness of the Yi dynasty. Following the end of the Japanese invasion, one of the first major acts of the Yi government was to reprint three additional sets of the *sillok.*[17] Thanks to these efforts, the complete sets of the Yi dynasty *sillok* have been preserved and the recent facsimile reprints by the National History Compilation Committee in Seoul and also by Gakushūin University in Tokyo have made it readily available to scholars.

In addition to the *sillok,* three more Yi dynasty documents of prime historical importance have been made available to the general public in recent years: *Sŭngjŏngwŏn ilgi* [Daily records of the Royal Secretariat], *Pibyŏnsa tŭngnok* [Records of the Border Defense Command], and *Ilsŏngnok* [Records of daily reflection]. Sŭngjŏngwŏn or the Office of the Royal Secretariat handled the transmission of all the documents to and from the throne, and the royal secretaries attended all audiences before the king including the important royal lectures. All the activities of the Royal Secretariat were recorded daily, and these records were in turn bound normally in one volume (sometimes more than one when there were greater activities) at the end of each month as *Sŭngjŏngwŏn ilgi*. Although the earlier records were lost, those covering the period from 1623 to 1910 have been preserved together in 3245 volumes and these vast documents are now being published by the National History Compilation Committee in Seoul after retranscribing the original grass writing into the standard characters with punctuation. So far, the portions covering the periods from 1623 to 1805 and from 1864 to 1910 have been published.[18]

First organized in the early sixteenth century as a consultative body on national security affairs, Pibyŏnsa or the Border Defense Command had developed after the Hideyoshi invasion into the highest policymaking organ of the Yi government, superseding in fact the authority of the Council of State (Uijŏngbu) until it was abolished in 1865 by the Taewŏn'gun. *Pibyŏnsa tŭngnok* is the official record of the transactions of this command, and its historical value as a primary source thus can easily be recognized. All the surviving documents dating from 1617 to 1892 have been published by the National History Compilation Committee in twenty-eight volumes.[19]

Ilsŏngnok [Records of daily reflection] was first started by King Chŏngjo (reigned 1776–1800) in 1760 when he began to keep a diary for his personal reflection as the crown prince, and after he ascended the throne, he ordered the secretaries of the newly organized Kyujanggak (Royal Library) to continue keeping daily records of all activities surrounding the throne. In addition to being a valuable primary source, *Ilsŏngnok* is convenient for its users because all the entries are recorded under classified headings. *Ilsŏngnok* was bound into one volume at the end of each month and some 2329 such volumes covering events until 1910 have survived and are now being published in a facsimile production by the Seoul National University. So far the portions covering the reign of King Kojong (reigned 1863–1907) and the first few years of King Ch'ŏljong's reign (reigned 1849–1863) have been published.[20]

All three records—*Sŭngjŏngwŏn ilgi, Pibyŏnsa tŭngnok,* and *Ilsŏngnok*—contain firsthand information on the major activities of the central government of the Yi dynasty and include, among other texts, memorials presented to the throne, edicts and decrees issued from the throne, verbatim reports of formal audiences held by the kings, transcripts of royal lectures, censorate reports, and reports from local government and other agencies. They are primary historical sources of foremost importance for the period they deal with.

In the meantime, there developed during the latter half of the Yi dynasty a new trend of historical scholarship of compiling histories by individual scholars without government sanction or support. The rise of this private historical scholarship coincided with the emergence of the new intellectual movement in the seventeenth and eighteenth centuries that came to be known later as the *sirhak* or the pragmatic learning school. Of many individual works, three—*Tongsa kangmok* by An Chŏngbok, *Haedong yŏksa* by Han Ch'i-yun, and *Yŏllyŏsil kisul* by Yi Kŭng-ik—deserve some attention here.

Not satisfied with *Tongguk t'onggam* and other history books on Korea, An Chŏng-bok (1712–1791) compiled his own *Tongsa kangmok* [Abridged view of Korean history], the first serious and systematic history of Korea by a private scholar covering the period from Kija (Chi-tzu in Chinese) through the fall of Koryŏ. As the title of the book suggests, An Chŏng-bok used Chu Hsi's *Tzu-chih t'ung-chien kang-mu* as a model and followed the basic principle as well as the format of the *kang-mu.* Thus An Chŏng-bok's foremost concern throughout the *kangmok* was the rectification of names, placing great emphasis on the idea of legitimacy *(chŏngt'ong).* Of particular interest in the book, however, is the section on addenda *(pu)* at the end. It is here that the author explains his conclusion on various issues and problems in Korean history, such as Tan'gun, Kijun, and geographical boundaries of various states, after discussing the merits and demerits of various references—including Chinese—related to the topics. From these discussions, one can get an idea as to how sophisticated, careful, and independent-minded a historian An Chŏng-bok was.[21]

Haedong yŏksa [Encyclopedic history of Korea] by Han Ch'i-yun (1765–1814) is an encyclopedic history of Korea, apparently modeled after the popular Chinese history with the similar title *I-shih* (*yŏksa* in Korean) by Ma Su of early Ch'ing. In this work Han Ch'i-yun has extracted relevant materials on various topics from a vast number of sources and put them together in a systematic manner. His sources were predominantly foreign materials including, as he lists at the beginning of the book, some 523 different Chinese as well as 22 Japanese sources, and he compared and collated them against Korean materials with his own comments. The section on treatises is of special value: there the author treats many diverse subjects such as institutions, music, economy, social customs, dialects, housing, flora, animals, fishes, and insects in an encyclopedic way, and the information found in it is still very useful.

The third private history of great importance is *Yŏllyŏsil kisul* [Narration from the Yŏllyŏ chamber] by Yi Kŭng-ik (1736–1806). Unlike other histories so far mentioned, *Yŏllyŏsil kisul* is a history of the Yi dynasty from its beginning to the end of King Sukchong's reign (1674–1720) and follows the narrative format known as *kisa ponmal* (*chi-shih pen-mo* in Chinese) from beginning to end. The whole *Yŏllyŏsil kisul* can be divided largely into two parts. The first part covers the history of each monarchical rule separately; the major events that took place during the reign are fully narrated, topic by topic, and then biographies of important officials as well as scholars during the reign are provided. The second part consists of *pyŏlchip* or addenda; a large number of special topics, such as various government institutions and their practices, diplomatic relations with China and other neighboring countries, land and tax system, household registry, marriage customs, penal system, astronomy and natural phenomena, and so on are explained.

The narrative method Yi Kŭng-ik used in the compilation of the *kisul* is also somewhat unique. Throughout the book, the author refrains from expressing his personal view and does not add his own words. Instead, he puts together various references either in verbatim quotations or in extracts from different sources in order to preserve the intent of the original. Yi Kŭng-ik feared that personal bias associated with factional affiliation might intrude into the historical writing; to prevent such a lapse, he tried to be as objective as possible by letting "fact speak for itself" as it were. Thus *Yŏllyŏsil kisul* is basically a collection of quoted or extracted statements on various historical subjects and topics arranged under topical headings. Drawn from more than four hundred different sources, the *kisul* is a meticulously researched

work and remains one of the most useful histories of the Yi dynasty. (Minjok Munhwa Ch'ujinhoe in Seoul has recently published a new twelve-volume edition in modern Korean translation together with the original Sino-Korean text and index.)

CONTRIBUTIONS OF MODERN JAPANESE SCHOLARS

The centuries-old Confucian tradition of historiography in Korea finally gave way to the modern scientific approach to history around the turn of the twentieth century. The first to apply the modern historical methodology of the West in studying Korean history were Japanese scholars, who virtually dominated the historical scholarship on Korea during the first half of this century. Although Japanese scholars have made important contributions to the better understanding of Korean history, many of them have been guilty of distorting that history. Space does not permit us to go into a detailed discussion of the modern Japanese historiography on Korea;[22] however, a few salient points regarding Japanese scholarship need to be mentioned.

Critics of Japanese historical scholarship usually cite three main characteristics. The first is the assertion that both the Japanese and the Korean people shared a common ancestral origin—the thesis known in Japan as *Nissen dōsoron*. Tracing its intellectual genesis back to the "National Learning" (*kokugaku*) of the Tokugawa period, this thesis was first expounded by three prominent scholars of Tokyo Imperial University in their influential history textbook called *Kokushi gan* [A survey of Japanese history], published in 1890. In this book, the Tokyo University professors characterized the historical relationship between Japan and Korea from the ancient through the modern periods largely in terms of Japan's subjugation and control of Korea.[23] This view soon became accepted widely in Japan, and many scholars thereafter built up their studies based on this assertion. It is not difficult to see that this *Nissen dōsoron* provided a convenient academic justification for Japan's political annexation of Korea and also for her attempt to eradicate Korea's cultural heritage.

The second characteristic of the pre-1945 Japanese historical studies on Korea is the notion that Korea was historically backward. This view was first expounded by

Fukuda Tokuzō, himself not a historian but an economist who had studied in Germany. Based on his brief visit to Korea in 1902, Fukuda wrote an article called "Kankoku no keizai soshiki to keizai tan'i" [Korea's economic structure and economic unit] in which he claimed that since Korea had not yet gone through a feudalistic stage, the country at the turn of the twentieth century was situated historically only at the stage equivalent to the Fujiwara period in Japan. This notion of Korea's historical backwardness subsequently received various "confirmations" by such well-known Japanese scholars as Kuromasa Iwao, Kawai Hirotami, Moritani Katsumi, Inaba Iwakichi, and Shikata Hiroshi, among others.[24]

The third feature is the treatment of Korean history as part of the so-called *Mansen shi* (Manchuria-Korea history). This seemingly innocuous approach, probably started after the turn of the century, led in the end to a rather disastrous conclusion in the interpretation of the nature of Korean civilization and society. Made academically respectable by Inaba Iwakichi in the 1920s and 1930s, those who followed the *Mansen shi* approach took the position that Korea had historically as well as geographically been inseparably connected with the Asian continent, especially with Manchuria, and that Korea had historically been dominated by alien influence in politics and economy as well as in all aspects of her civilization. Thus, they concluded, Korea had historically lacked the spirit of independence and originality. This notion was further developed by scholars like Mishina Shōei into the so-called thesis of "heteronomous determination" *(taritsusei)*—namely, Korea traditionally lacked an internal dynamic of her own and hence her history had largely been shaped by external influence.[25]

In the meantime, the Japanese Government-General of Korea organized the Society for the Compilation of Korean History (Chōsenshi henshūkai), whose main contribution to historiography was the publication of some twenty different titles of major historical sources. In addition, this society compiled and published *Chōsen shi* [History of Korea] in thirty-six volumes, which is essentially a collection of extracts drawn from a number of historical sources—Korean, Japanese, and Chinese—in chronological order from antiquity to 1894. Until the recent publication of many important primary sources,

this *Chōsen shi* had been used more or less as a historical source of primary nature and thus it had a considerable influence upon the studies of Korean history. *Chōsen shi,* however, was criticized by one eminent South Korean historian on the grounds that the biases and prejudices prevalent during the Japanese rule over Korea weighed greatly in the compilation of this massive work and that studies based on this title as a source would naturally tend to distort the picture.[26] Be that as it may, *Chōsen shi* is still very useful for students of Korean history as it can at least be used as a convenient guide to primary sources.

In spite of such historiographical problems, Japanese scholarship did lay the basic groundwork for modern historical studies on Korea and has made many important contributions to that discipline.

MODERN NATIONALIST HISTORIANS OF KOREA

While Japanese scholars began to dominate the studies of Korean history in the early decades of the twentieth century, there emerged a small number of Korean intellectuals, now identified with the school of "nationalist history" *(minjok sahak),* who explored Korean history from a different perspective. The major figures of this school include Sin Ch'ae-ho (1880–1936), Mun Il-p'yŏng (1888–1939), Ch'oe Nam-sŏn (1880–1957), An Chae-hong (1891–1965), and Chŏng In-bo (1892–?). These Korean scholars received, unlike their Japanese contemporaries, no formal training in modern historical craft and engaged in historical scholarship largely because of their desperate nationalistic concern.[27]

The historical outlook of these nationalist historians appears to have been shaped largely by two factors. One was the disintegration of Korea's traditional order leading ultimately to the loss of her political identity as an independent nation. As they had witnessed this process helplessly in their youth, they developed little attachment to Korea's old order, which they regarded as bankrupt. The other factor was the onslaught of Japanese scholarship in belittling and distorting Korean history. These Korean intellectuals were thus caught in a dilemma: on the one hand they were forced to admit the moral bankruptcy of the traditional order of their country; on the other they were obliged to defend their country against the pejorative treatment of Japanese scholars. Thus constricted, the Korean nationalist historians were obliged to discover a new identity and purpose, not only for themselves but also for their people, which would replace the tattered image of their country's immediate past history while at the same time challenging the new myth being created by the Japanese.

The nationalist historians turned their attention mostly to ancient history for two main reasons. One was that the image of ancient Korea suffered most from mutilation by Japanese historiography; the other was their anxious desire to discover the genuine indigenous tradition unaffected by any foreign influence, especially by that of China, in the ancient period. Thus we have Chŏng In-bo's agonizing search for Korea's soul or spirit *(ŏl)* in his *Chosŏnsa yŏn'gu* [Study of Korean history] and An Chae-hong's new synthesis integrating both Tan'gun and Kija within the framework of ancient Korean society as a prelude to the rise of the Three Kingdoms in his *Chosŏn sanggosa kam* [Mirror of Korea's ancient history].

Of all the nationalist historians, it is Sin Ch'ae-ho and Ch'oe Nam-sŏn who stand out. Sin Ch'ae-ho is best known for his blistering attack against Kim Pu-sik, as we have seen earlier in the discussion of *Samguk sagi.* In addition, he also is known for his rather idiosyncratic view of history, which he articulated in *Chosŏnsa yŏn'gu ch'o* [A draft study of Korean history]. Apparently influenced by Herbert Spencer and Karl Marx, Sin Ch'ae-ho regarded history as an endless struggle between the forces of what he termed "we" *(a)* and "non-we" *(pi-a)*—one country against another, proletariats against capitalists, and so on—in which an antagonistic alignment was determined by the relationship between the subjective "ego" and those who were opposed to it. Such a view of history made him one of the most militantly nationalistic Korean historians. His outlook bordered on xenophobia, and his intense nationalism plunged him into the whirlwind of the nationalistic struggle against Japan in China and Manchuria until he finally joined the Asian Anarchists' League. He was later arrested by the Japanese and died in 1936 while serving a ten-year prison term at Port Arthur.[28]

Ch'oe Nam-sŏn was perhaps the best known and most influential of all the Korean historians before 1945. Among his voluminous writings on many diverse subjects, his studies of Tan'gun are probably most im-

portant historiographically. Determined to repudiate the Japanese contention regarding the origin of the Korean people, Ch'oe Nam-sŏn reinterpreted the Tan'gun legend not as a historical figure who founded a nation but as a religious chief of sun-worshipping people in a primitive society. Based on his extensive comparative study of folk beliefs and religious practices of the Altaic peoples, Ch'oe Nam-sŏn went even so far as to claim that ancient Korea had at one time been a center of the civilization (which he called the *purham* civilization) that had extended far in northeast Asia—a contention obviously aimed at challenging the origin of civilization advanced in Japan's founding myth as well as disputing China's claim to being the source of Asian civilization. In spite of his long and close association with Korea's nationalist movement against Japan, Ch'oe Nam-sŏn finally succumbed to Japanese pressure and became a collaborator with the Japanese authorities in the last years of their rule. Largely because of this, he still remains discredited in the eyes of many Koreans, and his scholarship has drawn little serious attention in spite of the important role he once played as a leading intellectual as well as historian.[29]

From the academic standpoint, these claims by Sin Ch'ae-ho and Ch'oe Nam-sŏn had obviously little chance of withstanding the rigorous test of objective historical criticism. It is, however, important for us to keep in mind the peculiar environment in which they lived and the particular purposes they wanted to serve in writing their historical works. If their nationalist image of Korean history was extreme, they lived in a time of extremes. Desperate to regain self-respect and self-identification not only for themselves but also for their compatriots as well, these nationalist historians were unable to luxuriate in the calm and unbiased examination of history which we now generally value. For them, the study of Korean history was also a weapon to serve the higher goal of regaining their country's freedom and independence from Japanese rule.

MODERN KOREAN HISTORIOGRAPHY

As we move into the 1930s, we begin to see the emergence of a new breed of Korean scholars who received formal training in modern scientific historical methodology. They received their higher education either in universities in Japan or at the Keijō Imperial University in Seoul and in general followed the Rankean tradition of historical craft that had dominated modern Japanese historiography. Having initially published their works individually in Japanese journals, these Korean scholars got together in 1934 to organize Chindan Hakhoe (Chindan Academic Society) and began to publish a scholarly journal known as *Chindan hakpo*. It can be said that, with the publication of this journal, historiography in Korea finally entered the modern age. As the journal published many serious scholarly articles based on objective scientific research, Korean historians were able to challenge for the first time at least certain aspects of the prejudicial Japanese historiography on Korea, and their scholarly works could weather the strictest scrutiny of historical criticism.

Yi Pyŏng-do, Yi Sang-baek, Kim Sang-gi, and Kim Sŏk-hyŏng were among the representative scholars of this new academic society and continued to carry on their significant contributions to Korean historiography even after Korea's liberation from Japan in 1945. Two of those just mentioned—Yi Pyŏng-do and Kim Sŏk-hyŏng—have become the doyen of historians in South and North Korea respectively. In fact, following the end of Japanese colonial rule, the task of rebuilding historical scholarship in Korea and training a new generation of Korean historians fell upon the shoulders of these scholars under extremely adverse circumstances, and in this task they have been greatly successful. The study of Korean history is now largely dominated by those who received historical training from them, and this fact may very well be the single biggest tribute one can bestow upon these pioneers.

The 1930s also witnessed the publication of two books which are of major historical importance. Authored by Paek Nam-un in Japanese, they are *Chōsen shakai keizaishi* [Social and economic history of Korea] and *Chōsen hōken shakai keizaishi* [Feudalistic social and economic history of Korea], published in 1933 and 1937 respectively in Tokyo. In these two works, Paek Nam-un for the first time attempted to apply systematically the Marxian principle in the interpretation of Korean history. Repudiating the notion that Korean history had followed a unique path, Paek Nam-un took the position that the "entire course of Korea's historical development . . . has followed virtually the same pat-

tern of progression as those of other peoples in accordance with the unilinear historical principle of world history."[30] He then applied the schematic stages of Marxian history to Korea—classifying the period before the Three Kingdoms as the primitive communal society, the Three Kingdoms period as the slave society, and the period after the Silla unification through the Yi dynasty as "centralized feudal" society.

As part of his ambitious project to render his Marxian analysis on the entire Korean history, Paek Nam-un was able to complete only the first two volumes. The first volume, *Chōsen shakai keizaishi,* covers the communal and slave societies from antiquity to the unification of Silla; the second, *Chōsen hōken shakai keizaishi,* deals with a part of the feudal period from the Silla unification through the end of Koryŏ.

In addition to being the first serious Marxian history of Korea, these two works by Paek Nam-un had an important impact upon challenging the theory of backwardness of Korean history popularized by the Japanese scholars, whose claim was based largely on the notion that feudalism had been absent in Korean history. Not only did Paek Nam-un "prove" the existence of "the feudal period" in Korean history but also, by asserting the course of Korean history to be in parallel with world history, he tried to repudiate totally the idea of Korea's historical stagnation.

STUDIES OF KOREAN HISTORY AFTER 1945

Since 1945, when Korea was finally freed from the Japanese yoke, the study of Korean history has become the domain of Korean scholars as it should. The territorial and ideological divisions had an inhibiting influence upon the research efforts of Korean scholars at an early stage. But once the political situation became stabilized after the Korean War, a large number of important studies began to be published in both North and South Korea. In spite of the ideological polarity that separates North and South, there is not much difference in the basic approach to the traditional history of Korea among their historians. There are, in fact, many common elements in the historiography of divided Korea.

When one reads the representative historical studies of both North and South Korea, one is immediately struck by their intense nationalistic tone. Considering the bitter frustration that Korean nationalism had suffered at the hands of Japanese colonial rule, this tone is perhaps understandable—after all, history is often looked upon as a source of pride and inspiration for nationalistic causes. What is more interesting, however, is that the tone of nationalism exhibited in North Korean historical works is far more militant than that displayed in the South. In fact, the unrestrained outburst of nationalism in North Korean history gives a distinct impression that historiography in the North may be following nationalistic lines rather than Marxist. One ramification of such nationalism is the tendency to emphasize in both North and South Korean history what they call the "superiority" *(usu-sŏng)* and "advanced progress" *(sŏnjin-sŏng)* of Korea's historical development.

The other striking similarity in the historiography of North and South Korea is the acceptance of the notion that history progresses through certain preclassified stages—namely, communal, slave, feudal, and capitalistic societies—essentially, a Marxian concept. That North Korea, being openly committed to Marxian ideology, should embrace such a historical concept is not surprising. But it is ironic indeed that many, though by no means all, historians in the militantly anticommunist South Korea should accept such a view—although they naturally disavow any connection with Marx.

Once the notion of historical stages is accepted, then the question of periodization becomes extremely important. Not surprisingly, historians in both North and South Korea have devoted a great amount of time and effort to attempting to classify traditional Korean history into various historical stages. Only in recent times, after many years of heated scholarly debate, has the official history of North Korea apparently been settled on this question of periodization. The ancient Ko Chosŏn, Puyŏ, and Chin-guk, according to North Korean history, were slave societies which in turn gave way to feudal society with the emergence of the Three Kingdoms in the first century BC. Feudalism, according to the North Korean historians, had prevailed in Korea during most of historical times until the nineteenth century, when what is called "the capitalistic relations" in Korea gathered enough historical momentum for the bourgeois class to launch its first attempt at its own class revolution, albeit unsuccessful, under the leadership of Kim Ok-kyun in 1884. The overriding concern of North Korean historians in this periodization attempt, apparently, is to "prove" the superiority of Korean civilization by pushing the beginning of each historical stage as far back as possible chronologically.

In South Korea, where pluralism prevails, historians maintain relatively divergent views on the question of periodization and the debate is still going on. As to when the slave society came to an end and the feudal period began, South Korean views range from as early as the beginning of the Three Kingdoms period to as late as the beginning of the Yi dynasty in the late fourteenth century. While they agree that the modern period began some time in the middle to late nineteenth century, they more or less accept the recent thesis that the economic growth Yi Korea had achieved in the eighteenth century showed signs of "incipient capitalism," a view quite similar to that of North Korea.

While there are basic similarities in the historiography of North and South Korea, North Korean official history makes two claims that deviate strikingly from the traditional interpretation. One is a startling new proposal on the question of Nangnang (Lolang in Chinese). Until North Korea's recent challenge, it had been universally accepted that Nangnang (Lolang) was a commandery established by China in the northwestern region of Korea after Han Wu-ti militarily defeated Wiman Chosŏn in 108 BC. This commandery, it was said, flourished until AD 313 and produced a brilliant civilization which came to be known through the excavations of a large number of tombs in and around the present city of Pyongyang in the early part of the twentieth century.

North Korea now insists there were two Nangnangs—one a Chinese commandery and the other an independent Korean state. The Chinese commandery Nangnang (Lolang) discussed in various Chinese historical sources was actually located in the Liao River region in present-day southern Manchuria, not in the Korean peninsula, according to North Korean history. This Chinese commandery is to be distinguished from another Nangnang of a Korean state which flourished for five centuries from the second century BC until the third century AD with its capital located in the present city of Pyongyang.

All the archaeological artifacts that have been discovered from hundreds of tombs in that city in the twentieth century actually belong to this Nangnang of Korean origin. In other words, the brilliant Nangnang civilization that flowered at one time around Pyongyang was a product of a native Korean state, not a Chinese colony as has hitherto been believed. The historical "distortion" of Nangnang, according to North Korean history, was first started in the sixth century by chauvinistic Chinese historians and was further perpetrated by imperialistic Japanese historians in our times. According to the official North Korean history, the "true picture" has come to light only very recently through the systematic studies of both archaeological and historical evidence by North Korean scholars.

The other interpretation that differs from the traditional view deals with the question of Korea's first territorial and political unification. The traditional view has been that Korea emerged historically as a homogeneous unitary state after Silla's unification of the Three Kingdoms in the mid-seventh century. North Korea now takes the position that the Silla unification brought political unity only within the Korean peninsula and that a large part of the former Koguryŏ territory and population came under the rule of Parhae (Pohai in Chinese), which became the legitimate successor to Koguryŏ. Thus the first political unification of Korea did not come until the early part of Koryŏ, to whom both Silla and Parhae surrendered in the tenth century. The basic reason for such an interpretation seems to lie in their attempt to incorporate the hitherto neglected history of Parhae as an integral part of Korean history—an idea that has begun to receive wide support among South Korean historians as well.

Except for a small number of South Korean scholars' works carried in English translation in *Korea Journal* (Korean National Commission for UNESCO in Seoul) and *Journal of Social Sciences and Humanities* (Bulletin of the Korean Research Center in Seoul), few works by Korean historians are available in English or in any other Western language.

Studies of Korean history in the United States as well as in other parts of the West were long hampered by lack of interest among scholars and by the woefully meager resources and facilities made available for research. Only in very recent years has this situation begun to be changed, and signs of growing interest in Korean history can now be detected. In spite of such a disadvantageous situation, a small number of dedicated Korean specialists in the United States have produced some very important works. Of these, covering the traditional period before 1876, the following four works may be singled out as having made major contributions to the study of Korean history.

For the Koryŏ period, H. W. Kang's "The First Succession Struggle of Koryŏ in 945: A Reinterpretation" deals with perhaps a turning point in Korean history, one which has hitherto completely escaped the attention of other scholars—namely, the confrontation between the aristocratic-oriented socioeconomic order of Silla on the one hand and, on the other, the new force of upstarts which gained strength during the Silla-Koryŏ dynastic transition and which was diametrically opposed to the long-entrenched Silla aristocracy. The outcome of this confrontation, according to the author, had a profound impact on the fundamental character of Korea's subsequent politico-socio-economic order, which at least partly explains the rigid characteristics of Koryŏ and Yi society.

The remaining three works deal with the Yi dynasty. Pow-Key Sohn's unpublished dissertation, "Social History of the Early Yi Dynasty: 1392–1592" (University of California, Berkeley, 1963), analyzes the roles and functions of the ideology and major offices in the central government to assess the power relationship between the monarch on the one hand and the *yangban* bureaucracy on the other by applying the Weber-Parsonian theory. Although one can take issue with many points the author raises, this pioneering study provides important groundwork in understanding the power structure and the working of the Yi dynasty government. Regrettably, this provocative study has not yet drawn much scholarly attention.

In examining the political conflict of the early Yi dynasty, Edward W. Wagner traces in his recently published book, *The Literati Purges,* the growth of power on the part of the censorial organs, which had a profound impact on the distribution of power within the central government. Not only does this study provide a fresh new interpretation of the literati purges *(sahwa)* of early Yi Korea but it also explains how the Yi government's pattern of decision-making came into being.

The end of the traditional period is usually marked with the end of the Taewŏn'gun's rule in the 1870s, which is the subject of James B. Palais' study in his *Politics and Policy in Traditional Korea*. In examining and evaluating the Taewŏn'gun's policies, Palais points out the basic limitations and weaknesses of the late Yi political, social, and economic order in the face of the impending challenge that was to come from Japan and the West. This book is analytical and interpretive history at its best and sets a new standard for the study of Korean history in the United States.

The period from 1876, when traditional Korea first opened her door to the outside world, to 1910, when Korea lost her independence, has received more attention than any other period in Korean history as far as English works are concerned. The primary sources for the study of this period are no longer limited to Korean materials; the source materials in Western languages as well as in Japanese and Chinese are important and available in relative abundance, as Professor Young Ick Lew shows in a later section of this chapter. As for the study of the period, the aspect of international relations has received overwhelming attention while domestic issues have drawn little interest among scholars—as though internal problems did not exist or did not matter. During the nineteenth century, stresses came from both within and without, and Korea's traditional order began to be torn apart from pressures external and internal. But, unfortunately, we know very little about even what sort of domestic problems Korea faced.

Undoubtedly, the central issue of the last half of the nineteenth century was the idea of enlightenment. There has so far been no adequate study in English on this subject. In fact, the only good study available in any language is the two-volume Korean work by Yi Kwang-rin, *Han'guk kaehwasa yŏn'gu* [A study of the history of enlightenment in Korea] and *Kaehwadang yŏn'gu* [A study of the party of enlightenment]. Recently, however, as a counterpoint to the enlightenment movement, an interesting new thesis has been put forth by Ch'oe Ch'ang-gyu, a young political scientist at Seoul National University, with regard to the conservative Confucianists' reaction against the challenges thrust forward by the Westerners. The ultimate issue the orthodox Confucianists saw with regard to the coming of the West, according to Ch'oe Ch'ang-gyu, was the question of national survival. Only preservation of the traditional order would assure Korea's political entity. Thus the dilemma that confronted those who were genuinely concerned with Korea's identity at the time was, writes Ch'oe Ch'ang-gyu, "national interest vs. antinational interest," not "reaction vs. progress," and the Confucianists' cry of *wijŏng ch'ŏksa* in their categorical rejection of the West was motivated by this nationalistic concern. Such a view fits well with the rising neotraditionalist mood of nationalism in present-day South Korea. One big problem with this thesis, however, is the underlying assumption that the Confucianists alone had a monopoly of nationalism and the followers of progressive causes had no interest in preserving Korea's national identity or promoting Korea's interest. Nevertheless, Ch'oe Ch'ang-gyu's study does throw new light on why and how Korea had in the past (and still has) a problem with the concept of "modernization."

Transcending such a nationalistic emotion, Young Ick Lew of the University of Houston has made a series of studies focusing on the *Kabo* ("1894") reform movement bringing about a significant revision of the historical interpretation of this important reform, especially with regard to the role played by Korean reformers. The widely held view before Lew's study had been that the 1894 reform was sponsored and carried out largely by Japanese officials who employed Korean officials as their front men. Lew's careful research repudiates such a view and instead establishes that it was the Korean reformers, like Pak Yŏng-hyo, who actually drew up and pushed through most of the reform programs enacted during 1894–1895.

The 35-year period of Japanese rule from 1910 to 1945 still evokes emotionally charged reactions from many Koreans. Yet, in spite of the chronological proximity and relative abundance of the related source materials, this period has surprisingly drawn little scholarly attention. And those studies that have appeared in Korea and Japan have largely been hampered by either a nationalistic or an ideological preoccupation. Most of the South Korean works tend to emphasize two aspects —namely, the harsh exploitative nature of the Japanese colonial rule and the painstaking search for hitherto un-known resistance activities of Korean nationalists against Japan. Japanese scholarship on the same period has not moved much beyond the Marxian conceptual framework of the evils of capitalism and imperialism. North Korean historiography, on the other hand, dem-onstrates a classic example of history toeing the party line. Studies of the period are all but taken up by de-tailed depictions and glorifications of the nationalistic activities of Kim Il Sung (and his immediate family members), at least some parts of which are obviously fictitious.

In the meantime, scholars in the West are in an en-viable position to make important contributions to the studies of Korea under Japanese rule if they can take ad-vantage of the academic climate that transcends the nar-row nationalistic and ideological outlook. Interestingly, studies of this period have attracted greater interest among political scientists in the United States than among historians. Some of these political scientists have published major works, among them *The Politics of Korean Nationalism* by Chong-sik Lee, which remains a standard reference for the subject it covers, and *The Korean Communist Movement, 1918–1948* by Dae-sook Suh and *Communism in Korea* (Part 1: The Movement) by Robert A. Scalapino and Chong-sik Lee, both of which treat the subject comprehensively. As for the eco-nomic aspect of Japanese rule in Korea, *Modern Korea* by Andrew J. Grajdanzev, published in 1944, is very critical of Japanese policies in Korea and still stands out as the most authoritative and comprehensive, if contro-versial, study.

NOTES

This essay is based largely on various secondary sources. Although there is really no systematic historiographical study encompassing the whole of Korean history, there are a number of useful studies dealing with specific aspects of historiography, many of which are cited in the text. *Kuksa taesajŏn* [Encyclopedia of Korean history] (Seoul: Chi-mungak, 1968), edited by Yi Hong-jik, gives an outline summary of the historiography. *Han'guk ŭi yŏksa insik* [Perceptions of Korean history] (Seoul: Ch'angjak kwa pip'yŏngsa, 1976), edited by Yi U-sŏng and Kang Man-gil in two volumes, contains the most useful articles on various **aspects of Korean historiography.** *Uri yŏksa rŭl ŏttŏk'e*

polkŏsinga [How to view our history] (Seoul: Samsŏng munhwa chaedan, 1976) is a verbatim report of dialogues on a broad aspect of Korean historiography conducted by several leading historians of South Korea.

1. The *Wei shu* account and other references to Korea ap-pearing in the Chinese dynastic histories from *Shih chi* on through the T'ang period are conveniently reprinted in vol-ume 3 of the first series of *Chōsen shi,* compiled by Chō-senshi henshūkai.
2. *Samguk sagi,* 20, 2a.
3. Ibid., 24, 9a.
4. See Inoue Hideo, "Chōsen no shiseki ni yotte *Nihon shoki* wa kōsei sareta" [*Nihon shoki* was structured on the basis of Korean historical records], in *Seminā Nihon to Chōsen no rekishi,* edited by Inoue Hideo et al. (Tokyo: 1972), pp. 11–101; Tsuda Sōkichi, "Kudara ni kansuru *Nihon shoki* no kisai" [Records relating to Paekche in *Nihon shoki*], in his *Kojiki oyobi Nihon Shoki no kenkyū* (Tokyo: 1923); and Kinoshita Keiji, "*Nihon shoki* ni mieru Kudara shiryō no shiryōteki kachi ni tsuite" [On the histor-ical value of Paekche historical sources appearing in *Nihon shoki*], *Chōsen gakuhō,* 21/22 (1961).
5. *Samguk sagi,* 4, 6b.
6. Yi Ki-baek et al., *Uri yŏksa rŭl ŏttŏk'e polkŏsinga* [How to view our history] (Seoul: Samsŏng munhwa chae-dan, 1961), p. 24.
7. *Koryŏ sa,* 76, 26a–27b.
8. Kim Sang-gi, *Koryŏ sidaesa* [History of the Koryŏ pe-riod] (Seoul:1961), pp. 853–854.
9. Suematsu Yasukazu, "*Sankoku shiki* no keiseki kankei kiji" [Bibliographic references recorded in *Samguk sagi*], in his *Seikyū shisō,* Vol. 2 (Tokyo: 1960), pp. 29–45.
10. See the dedication of *Samguk sagi* found in *Tong-mun-sŏn* [Selections from the literary writings from Korea] (Seoul: Kyonghŭi ch'ulp'ansa, 1966), Vol. 2, pp. 585–586.
11. Ko Pyŏng-ik, "*Samguk sagi* e issŏ sŏ ŭi yŏksa sosul" [Historical narration in *Samguk sagi*], in Yi U-sŏng and Kang Man-gil (eds.), *Han'guk ŭi yŏksa insik,* Vol. 1, pp. 51–55.
12. Kim Ch'ŏl-chun, "Koryŏ chunggi ŭi munhwa ŭisik kwa sahak ŭi sŏngkyŏk" [Cultural consciousness and histo-riographical characteristics in the mid-Koryŏ period], in *Han'guk ŭi yŏksa insik,* Vol. 1, pp. 64–110.
13. Ko Pyŏng-ik, pp. 31–47. See also John C. Jamieson, "The *Samguk sagi* and the Unification Wars," PhD disserta-tion, University of California, Berkeley, 1969.
14. Yi Ki-baek, "*Samguk yusa* ŭi sahaksa chŏk ŭiŭi" [His-toriographical significance of *Samguk yusa*], in *Han'guk ŭi yŏksa insik,* vol. 1, p. 119.

15. Kim Ch'ŏl-chun, *"Koryŏ sa,"* in *Han'guk ŭi kojŏn paeksŏn* (*Sin Tong'a* monthly special supplement, January 1969), p. 94.

16. See Pow-key Sohn, "Social History of Early Yi Dynasty, 1392–1592," PhD dissertation, University of California, Berkeley, 1963, chap. 3.

17. See also George M. McCune, "The Yi Dynasty Annals of Korea," *Transactions of the Korea Branch of the Royal Asiatic Society* 25 (1939); Suk-ho Shin, "Yijo Sillok," *Journal of Social Sciences and Humanities* 12 (May 1960); and Suematsu Yasukazu, "Richō Jitsuroku Kōryaku" [A summary study of the veritable records of the Yi dynasty], in his *Seikyu shisō*, vol. 2, pp. 267–360.

18. See Suk-ho Shin, "Sŭngjŏngwŏn Ilgi," *Journal of Social Sciences and Humanities* 15 (December 1961); and James B. Palais, "Records and Record-keeping in Nineteenth Century Korea," *Journal of Asian Studies* 30 (1971).

19. See Suk-ho Shin, "Bibyonsa Dungnok," *Journal of Social Sciences and Humanities* 17 (December 1962); and James B. Palais, "Records and Record-keeping."

20. See Chŏn Hae-jong, *"Ilsŏngnok haeje"* [An explanatory note to *Ilsŏngnok*], in *Ilsŏngnok, Kojong p'yŏn,* vol. 44 (Seoul: Seoul Taehakkyo Kojŏn kanhaenghoe, 1967); and James B. Palais, "Records and Record-keeping."

21. For An Chŏng-bok, see Hwang Wŏn-gu, "Sirhakp'a ŭi sahak iron" [Historical theory of the Sirhak school], in *Han'guk ŭi yŏksa insik,* vol. 2, pp. 384–385; and Yi U-sŏng, *"Tongsa kangmok,"* in *Han'guk ŭi kojŏn paeksŏn.* For the North Korean view, see Kim Sa-ŏk, "An Chŏng-bok ŭi yŏksagwan kwa kŭŭi choguk yŏksa p'yŏnsa e taehayŏ" [On An Chong-bok's historical view and his compilation of the fatherland's history], *Yŏksa kwahak* 5 (1965).

22. For a stimulating discussion, see H. W. Kang, "Images of Korean History," in Andrew C. Nahm (ed.), *Traditional Korea—Theory and Practice* (Kalamazoo: Center for Korean Studies, Western Michigan University, 1974).

23. Hatada Takashi, *Sinpojiumu Nihon to Chōsen* [Symposium on Japan and Korea] (Tokyo: 1969), pp. 1–16.

24. Ibid.

25. Ibid. See also Kim Yong-sŏp, "Ilbon Han'guk e issŏsŏ ŭi Han'guksa sŏsul" [Narrations of Korean history in Japan and Korea], *Yŏksa hakpo* 31(August 1966):133–134.

26. Kim Yong-sŏp, pp. 134–135.

27. See H. W. Kang, "Images of Korean History"; Kim Yong-sŏp, "Ilbon Han'guk . . . "; Kim Yong-sŏp, "Uri nara kŭndae yŏksahak ŭi sŏngnip" [The establishment of modern historiography in our country], in *Han'guk ŭi yŏksa insik,* vol. 2, pp. 421–449; and Kim Yong-sŏp, "Uri nara kŭndae yŏksahak ŭi paldal" [Development of modern historiography in our country], op. cit., pp. 474–499.

28. An Pyŏng-jik, "Tanje Sin Ch'ae-ho ŭi minjok chuŭi [Nationalism of Sin Ch'ae-ho], in *Han'guk ŭi yŏksa insik,* vol. 2, pp. 450–472; and Yi Ki-baek, "Minjok sahak ŭi munje" [Problems in the nationalist historiography], in his *Minjok kwa yŏksa* (Seoul: 1971).

29. Ibid.

30. Paek Nam-un, *Chōsen shakai keizaishi* (Tokyo: 1933), p. 9.

BIBLIOGRAPHY

GENERAL HISTORICAL SURVEYS

03-001. BOSCARO, Andriana. "Storia della Corea." In B. Brocchieri and A. Boscaro (eds.), *Storia del Giappone e della Corea.* Milan: Marzorati, 1973.

03-002. Center for East Asian Cultural Studies (comp.). *A Short History of Korea.* Tokyo: Center for East Asian Cultural Studies, 1963. Distributed by East-West Center Press, Honolulu. This is a slightly modified English translation of a book originally written by a Japanese scholar and published by the Japanese Government-General of Korea in 1937 in commemoration of the twenty-fifth anniversary of Japanese rule of Korea. As such, the book, even in its English version, strongly reflects the "official" view of the Japanese Government-General toward Korea and is full of distortions and misrepresentations intended to belittle Korean history in spite of the claim made at the beginning that "some passages in the original that were heavily Japan-centered have been omitted and corrections have been made." When published, it was severely criticized by many historians in the United States and in South Korea. "Japanese Studies in Korean History" in Appendix 1, however, gives a useful short account of how the study of Korean history progressed in Japan from the late nineteenth century.

03-003. CHOY, Bong-youn. *Korea: A History.* Rutland, Vt.: Tuttle, 1971. A political history of Korea from the Three Kingdoms period until the early 1960s based almost entirely on secondary sources. The first five chapters, covering traditional Korea before 1910, contain many errors and are almost totally devoid of scholarly value. The bulk of the book, however, covers the modern period, treating in considerable detail such topics as the Japanese domination, the anti-Japanese struggle, political development in post–World War II Korea, Syngman Rhee's rule, the Korean War, the student revolution of 1960, the military coup of 1961, South Korea's economy, Soviet control of North Korea, and North Korea's economy. Although the treatment of the modern period is much more useful than that of the traditional period, the book still suffers from superficiality, unevenness, and unreliability. Inconsistency in the use of romanization throughout the book further detracts from its scholarly value.

03-004. ECKARDT, André. *Korea—Geschichte und Kultur.* Baden-Baden: Blower, 1960. Emphasizes the history of Korean culture.

03-005. FAIRBANK, John K., Edwin O. REISCHAUER, Albert M. CRAIG. *East Asia: Tradition and Transformation.* Boston: Houghton Mifflin, 1973. In this authoritative survey of East Asian civilization, two chapters are devoted to traditional Korea: chap. 11 covers "Early Korea: The Emergence of a Chinese Type of State," and chap. 12 treats "Yi Dynasty Korea: A Model Confucian Society." In addition, modern history is covered in chap. 20 under the section heading "Korea's Response to the Outside World" and in chap. 27 under the headings "Japanese Colonialism in Taiwan and Korea" and "Korea Since World War II." Korean history is briefly surveyed in this book, largely within the purview of East Asian history. Traditional Korea is treated as a variant of Chinese cultural patterns, and the latest scholarly findings are not well reflected.

03-006. GALE, James S. *The History of the Korean People.* Seoul: Christian Literature Society, 1927. See Richard Rutt (03-016).

03-007. GRIFFIS, William Elliot. *Corea: The Hermit Nation.* 9th ed., revised and enlarged. New York: Scribner's, 1911. Reprinted New York: AMS Press, 1971. First published in 1882, this book went through nine different editions with revision and enlargement until 1911 and was by far the most widely read book on Korea in English prior to World War II. The author, who lived in Japan, used mostly Japanese sources, supplemented by some Western works then available to him, and the book hence reflects strongly the "imperial" view of Meiji Japan with all her biases toward Korea.

03-008. HAN, Woo-keun. *The History of Korea.* Translated by Kyung-shik Lee and edited by Grafton K. Mintz. Honolulu: University Press of Hawaii, 1971. A detailed survey of Korean history from prehistory to about 1960. Written originally in the Korean language by one of the leading historians in South Korea, this book has been competently translated and edited to make it easier for English readers to follow. The book is divided into seven parts with thirty-four chapters. Part 1 covers the primitive and tribal societies. Parts 2 and 3 deal with the Three Kingdoms and Unified Silla respectively under the heading

of the Ancient Period. Part 4 deals with the Medieval Period covering the entire Koryŏ dynasty. Part 5, under the heading of the Modern Period I (which should have been translated as the Early Modern Period), covers the Yi dynasty up to the coming of Japan and the Western powers in the mid-nineteenth century. Part 6 discusses Korea during the nineteenth century when she was challenged by Japan and the Western powers. Part 7 covers what the author calls the Contemporary Period, in which Korea's unsuccessful resistance to Japanese annexation, Japanese rule, and Korea after the liberation are discussed. Practically every important aspect of Korean history, including politics, society, economy, religion, literature, and art, is competently treated. The book, however, is mostly descriptive and lacks interpretive discussion, and the treatment of the twentieth century is not adequate. Nevertheless, this is the most comprehensive and probably the best general history of Korea so far available in English.

03-009. HATADA, Takashi. *A History of Korea.* Translated and edited by Warren W. Smith, Jr., and Benjamin H. Hazard. Santa Barbara: ABC Clio, 1969. This is the English translation of perhaps the best and the most widely read Korean history book in Japan, written by a prominent Japanese historian whom many Korean historians regard as a judicious specialist on Korea. This is essentially a concise survey of political, social, and economic history from prehistory to the outbreak of the Korean War in 1950, reflecting strongly the author's concept of history largely as a function of economic and social forces. Some aspects of the book, however, such as the socioeconomic condition of the seventeenth and eighteenth centuries, are outdated. The translators' preface gives a succinct but informative review on the status of Korean historiography in the West, in Korea, and in Japan. The glossary at the end prepared by the translators is also very useful.

03-010. HENTHORN, William E. *A History of Korea.* New York: Free Press, 1971. A concise and yet comprehensive history of Korea from antiquity to the nineteenth century. In addition to political history, the author attempts to provide a balanced account of society, foreign relations, religion, literature, and various aspects of the arts. In three appendixes, the author also offers short but interesting discussions of the Korean language, Korea's foundation myth, and his view of Korean history in general.

03-011. HULBERT, Homer B. *The History of Korea.* Seoul: Methodist Publishing House, 1905. 2 vols. See Clarence Norwood Weems (03-018).

03-012. JOE, Wanne J. *Traditional Korea: A Cultural His-*

tory. Seoul: Chung'ang University Press, 1972. A detailed survey of Korean history from prehistoric times to the rule of the Taewŏn'gun in the mid-nineteenth century by a Korean scholar. The work is based largely on secondary source materials written in the Korean language. The author makes a valiant attempt to maintain a balance between a political-social and a cultural history, devoting considerable space to discussing intellectual and religious development and the literary and artistic tradition in which the treatment of Buddhism and arts is particularly useful.

03-013. LI, Ogg. *Histoire de la Corée.* Paris: Presses Universitaires de France, 1969. A survey of Korean history. Instead of adopting a format in which the narration would be relatively longer for the more recent period, the author allocated the same number of pages to each period (ancient, medieval, early modern, and modern). Unfortunately, this format and the restriction of the total length (128 pp.) make detailed narration impossible. The bibliography at the back of the book lists European-language articles related to Korean history.

03-014. LONGFORD, Joseph H. *The Story of Korea.* New York: Scribner's, 1911. A survey of Korean history from ancient times to the Japanese annexation in 1910 based primarily on the secondary Western sources available at the time of writing, such as Dallet's *Histoire de l'Église de Corée* and Hulbert's *History of Korea.* Although this book gained some popularity when first published, it no longer has any scholarly value except perhaps for historiographical use in understanding the degree of Western knowledge of Korea at the beginning of the twentieth century.

03-015. ROSS, John. *History of Corea, Ancient and Modern: With Description of Manners and Customs, Language and Geography.* London: Elliot Stock, 1891. First published in 1880, this was the first book on Korean history to appear in English. Written by a Scottish missionary who spent seven years in Manchuria and based almost entirely on old Chinese historical sources, the book is in reality a history of various ethnic groups that rose and fell in Korea and Manchuria—groups such as Chaohsien (Old Chosŏn), Hsienbi (Hsien-pei), Yen, Gaogowli (Koguryŏ), Sinlo (Silla), Kitan (Khitan), and Nujun (Jurchen). Since the territorial boundary of old Korea extended to much of present-day Manchuria, the author treats the history of these ethnic groups in Manchuria as part of Korean history. The history of Korea proper is brought down to 1876 largely as it pertains to Korea's relationship to China. The description in the last three chapters of Korea's social cus-

toms, religion, and government as of the mid-nineteenth century is interesting. Other than its historiographical value as the first Korean history in English, the book is hopelessly outdated.

03-016. RUTT, Richard. *James Scarth Gale and His History of the Korean People.* Seoul: Royal Asiatic Society, Korea Branch, 1972. Originally published serially in a missionary journal in Korea in the 1920s, *The History of the Korean People* by James S. Gale is largely a cultural and literary history from antiquity to Korea's loss of independence in 1910. Relying on the traditional Korean interpretation of history, Gale recounts interesting anecdotes, folklore, and customs. Of particular use is Gale's elegant translation of many Korean poems and examples of prose originally written in the classical *hanmun.* In the new edition published in 1972, Richard Rutt appends a detailed and authoritative biography of Gale, notes identifying Gale's original sources, and an annotated bibliography in addition to romanizing Korean names and words according to the McCune-Reischauer system.

03-017. SOHN, Pow-key, Chol-choon KIM, Yi-sup HONG. *The History of Korea.* Seoul: Korean National Commission for UNESCO, 1970. A concise and yet comprehensive history from prehistory to 1961 by three prominent scholars in South Korea. Like many history books on Korea, the theme of this book centers on the political development of the country interspersed with brief accounts on such topics as social structure, arts, and intellectual trends where appropriate. Part 1, dealing with prehistoric Korea, gives a good summation of the latest archaeological discoveries in Korea so far available in English. Parts 2 and 3 provide a good account of the history of the Three Kingdoms and the Koryŏ dynasty respectively, successfully incorporating an amazingly large amount of factual information on the period. Part 4 gives an interesting account of Yi (Chosŏn) dynasty state and society. The last three parts, dealing with Korea during the last half of the nineteenth century, the Japanese encroachment against Korea, and South Korea after regaining independence, are, however, the weakest sections of the book and should be used with caution—especially by those who are not familiar with the peculiar nationalistic sentiment prevalent in South Korea. Although the book as a whole lacks unity and suffers from uneven English editorial work, it is nevertheless an informative general history of Korea.

03-018. WEEMS, Clarence Norwood (ed.). *Hulbert's History of Korea.* 2 vols. New York: Hillary House, 1962. *The History of Korea* by Homer B. Hulbert first appeared serially in the *Korean Review* (1901-1905) and then was published in two volumes by the Methodist Publishing House in Seoul in 1905. For several decades thereafter, it remained the most detailed account of Korean history in English and was used as a standard history of Korea in the West. Based largely on traditional Korean historical sources, the book traces the development of Korean history—mainly political—chronologically in an "annalistic" style from antiquity to 1904 and follows the old storytelling fashion. Although the book is by now completely outdated, it still contains much useful factual information, especially on the last few decades of the Yi dynasty, during which the author was in a position to observe political developments in Korea personally. Moreover, this book has an important historiographical value for it was one of the most influential sources of Korean history in English. In reissuing this book, the original edition has been reproduced in facsimile and the editor has added a very helpful introduction in which he discusses Hulbert's sources, corrects errors, and supplements weak parts with additional information. The editor also provides in the new edition a valuable biographical sketch of thc author, who went on to become an important personage in the modern history of Korea.

POLITICS AND SOCIETY

03-019. HENDERSON, Gregory. *Korea: The Politics of the Vortex.* Cambridge, Mass.: Harvard University Press, 1968. A provocative analysis and interpretation of Korean politics in modern times by an American scholar drawn from his personal observations while serving as a US Foreign Service officer in South Korea and based on his penetrating study of a wide range of literature related to Korea and the social sciences. Although the bulk of the book deals with political developments in South Korea after 1945, the author develops his thesis on Korea's political culture by drawing generalizations largely from his understanding of the political pattern that existed in traditional Korea. The author's thesis is that Korea had traditionally been a highly homogeneous and centralized society in which centripetal force always swept as a great vortex. He traces such a vortex pattern of politics in Korean history, especially during the Yi dynasty, by examining such aspects as the decision-making process within the government, the recruitment system, factional strife, and the social and class structure, among others, and analyzes how Korea's sociopolitical culture was affected by Japanese rule. The author's observations of Korea's traditional history are often stimulating but sometimes misleading. Nevertheless, this is an extremely important, albeit contro-

versial, work of value in understanding the politics of both modern and traditional Korea.

03-020. KANG, Chinch'ol. "Traditional Land Tenure Relations in Korean Society: Ownership and Management." In Hugh H. W. Kang (ed.), *The Traditional Culture and Society of Korea: Thought and Institutions.* Honolulu: Center for Korean Studies, University of Hawaii, 1975. A broad study of land tenure relations from the Three Kingdoms period through the Yi dynasty with special emphasis on the question of land control. The author follows the recently popular revisionist view that the nature of the land system in traditional Korea was private ownership rather than public ownership. Should be used with the thoughtful commentary by Hugh H. W. Kang in the epilogue.

03-021. KANG, Hugh H. W. (ed.). *The Traditional Culture and Society of Korea: Thought and Institutions.* Occasional Papers of the Center for Korean Studies, no. 5. Honolulu: Center for Korean Studies, University of Hawaii, 1975. Contains three papers selected from those presented to the International Conference on Traditional Korean Culture and Society held at University of Hawaii in 1971: Lee Kibaik, "Korea—The Military Tradition" (see 03-025); Kang Chinch'ol, "Traditional Land Tenure Relations in Korean Society: Ownership and Management" (see 03-020); and Lee Woosung, "Korean Intellectual Tradition and the *Sirhak* School of Thought" (see 03-228). In the epilogue, Hugh H. W. Kang makes very useful critical commentaries on all three papers.

03-022. KIM, Bong-gi. *Brief History of the Korean Press.* Seoul: Korean Information Service, 1965. 114 pp. Gives a short outline history of newspaper publishing in Korea from the publication of *Hansǒng sunbo* in 1883 until the end of the Japanese rule in 1945.

03-023. KIM, Dong-uk. "On the Dual System of Korean Dress and Clothing." *Journal of Social Sciences and Humanities* 18(June 1963):58–71. Gives a short outline history of costumes Koreans wore from the time of the Three Kingdoms through the Yi dynasty with special emphasis on the influence received from China. The author believes that while dress worn on official occasions was affected greatly by Chinese influence, daily costume used at home underwent little change.

03-024. LEDYARD, Gari. "Chinese Institutions on Korean Soil." *Phi Theta Papers* 7(May 1962):1–10. A short essay reflecting on the author's belief that "we cannot accept Korea as a microcosm of China" in spite of the long continuous Chinese influence upon Korea.

03-025. LEE, Kibaik. "Korea—The Military Tradition." In Hugh H. W. Kang (ed.), *The Traditional Culture and So-*

ciety of Korea: Thought and Institutions. Honolulu: Center for Korean Studies, University of Hawaii, 1975. The author traces in broad outline the historical development of military institutions in traditional Korea from ancient tribal society through the Yi dynasty with special emphasis on the nature of the service performed by military organizations and the social base of soldiers recruited for duty.

03-026. LOH, Keie-hyun. "Territorial Division of Korea—A Historical Survey." *Korean Affairs* 3(1)(April 1964):103–119. After examining various proposals for territorial division of Korea made during the Hideyoshi invasion and around the turn of the twentieth century, the author analyzes Korea's division along the 38th parallel in 1945 and along the cease-fire line in 1953.

03-027. WAGNER, Edward W. "Modernization Process in Korea: Some Historical Considerations." *Koreana Quarterly* 5(3)(Autumn 1963):30–36. An interesting essay reflecting on how certain salient features of Korean history, such as weakness of monarchical power, factionalism, and a tradition of dissent, could play negative or positive roles in the process of modernization.

RELIGION AND EDUCATION

03-028. CLARK, Charles Allen. *Religions of Old Korea.* New York: Revell, 1932. Reprinted Seoul: 1961. A comprehensive study of Korean traditional religions—Buddhism, Confucianism, Ch'ŏndogyo, shamanism, and other Asian religious sects—by a Protestant missionary in Korea who taught theology in the Presbyterian Theological Seminary in Seoul. This work is based on Western sources and is considerably out of date, but it remains one of the most comprehensive accounts of Korean religion and philosophy in English.

03-029. PALMER, Spencer J. *Korea and Christianity: The Problem of Identification with Tradition.* Seoul: Royal Asiatic Society, Korea Branch, 1967. Protestant Christianity has achieved remarkable success in Korea, compared to other countries in Asia. This is a study of how certain characteristics of Korean tradition were conducive to the growth of Christianity in contrast to the situation in China. The book is divided into two parts; the first "explores the question of contact between Christianity and the traditions of China and Korea," and the second "deals with the particular set of circumstances and conditions among which both Koreans and Chinese engaged the modern world." The author finds the weakness of the pre-Christian religions—the long decay of Buddhism, the position of Confucianism, which never gripped the masses, and the prevalent practice of shamanism—as the main rea-

son for the success of Christianity in Korea. Once Christianity gained a foothold, however, the author contends that the growth and decline in church membership are correlated to international developments surrounding Korea, especially her relations with Japan.

03-030. YANG, Key P. and Gregory HENDERSON. "An Outline History of Korean Confucianism. Part 1: The Early Period and Yi Factionalism." *Journal of Asian Studies* 18(1)(November 1958):81–101. This article traces the development of Confucianism in Korea from the Lolang period (108 BC–AD 313) through the end of the Yi dynasty. After briefly describing the status of Confucian teachings during various historical periods, the authors discuss in some detail the transmission of the Neo-Confucianism of the Chu Hsi school in late Koryŏ, its acceptance as the state creed under the Yi dynasty, and its relationship with factionalism in Yi Korea. Based largely on secondary Korean and Japanese sources, this article follows more or less the traditional interpretation of Confucian history in Korea.

03-031. _____. "An Outline History of Korean Confucianism. Part 2: The Schools of Yi Confucianism." *Journal of Asian Studies* 18(2)(February 1959):259–276. This article classifies Confucianism of the Yi dynasty into various schools, such as *sŏngni, yehak,* and *sirhak,* and explains their basic doctrines. Some may question the classifications and even disagree with the explanations given for the different doctrines. It also gives a useful description of the various institutions that promoted Confucian teachings under the Yi dynasty.

FOREIGN RELATIONS

03-032. CHUN, Hae-jong. "China and Korea—An Introduction to the Sino-Korean Relations." *Journal of Social Sciences and Humanities* 29(December 1968):1–15. A historical overview of Korea's traditional relationship with China reflecting upon the nature of the intercourse—tributary, cultural, and so forth—with various Chinese and non-Chinese dynasties that rose and fell in China.

03-033. _____. "A Historical Survey of the Sino-Korean Tributary Relationship." *Journal of Social Sciences and Humanities* 25(December 1966):1–31. A systematic survey of the history of Korea's tributary relationship to China from the Three Kingdoms period through the Yi dynasty. After classifying various aspects of the Sino-Korean relationship, the author traces the historical origin and development of the tributary relations. A scholarly work.

03-034. EIKEMEIER, Dieter. "Koreanisch–chinesische Beziehungen." In *China Handbuch.* Düsseldorf: Bertelsmann Universitätsverlag, 1974. On Sino-Korean relations throughout history.

03-035. HSU, Shuhsi. *China and Her Political Entity: A Study of China's Foreign Relations with Reference to Korea, Manchuria and Mongolia.* New York: Oxford University Press, 1926. This book is primarily a study of the rising diplomatic tension between China and Japan over Korea and Manchuria from the mid-nineteenth century until 1915. After a useful short review of the historical background of Sino-Korean relations from antiquity through the Ch'ing dynasty based primarily on the official Chinese dynastic histories, the author traces the diplomatic problems China encountered in Korea and Manchuria from Japan and other powers from 1868 to 1915. Though outdated somewhat, the book still has some merits.

03-036. KOH, Byung-ik. "The Attitude of Koreans toward Japan." In Marshall R. Pihl (ed.), *Listening to Korea: A Korean Anthology.* New York: Praeger, 1973. A stimulating essay reflecting on how the Korean people came to develop a less than friendly attitude toward Japan in modern times. This is an English translation of an article written for a popular monthly magazine in 1965 by a distinguished Korean historian.

03-037. KUNO, Yoshi S. *Japanese Expansion on the Asiatic Continent: A Study in the History of Japan with Special Reference to Her International Relations with China, Korea, and Russia.* 2 vols. Berkeley: University of California Press, 1937–1940. This important work consists of monographic text and appendixes of translated documents selected from Japanese, Chinese, and Korean sources. Volume 1 begins with the ancient period and ends with the Hideyoshi invasion in the late sixteenth century; Volume 2 covers the entire Tokugawa period. The coverage of Korea is rather extensive in Volume 1. Published before World War II, some parts of the author's discussion and selected documents inevitably reflect the now outdated "imperial" Japanese scholarship, especially in dealing with Japan's early contact with Korea, but the author's approach as a whole is judicious and the work is still very valuable.

03-038. NELSON, M. Frederick. *Korea and the Old Orders in Eastern Asia.* Baton Rouge: Louisiana State University, 1945. Reprinted New York: Russel and Russel, 1967. A pioneering and thorough study of Korea's relationship with foreign countries, both under the traditional Confucian world order and under the Western international system before the Japanese annexation of Korea. The author expounds on the Confucian world order, in which Korea's relationship with China stood as "the most perfect example." Although much of the factual information embod-

ied in the book is outdated and romanization of Korean names and terms follows the rarely used Gale system, this is still an extremely important work, not only on Korea's foreign relations but also in understanding the traditional international system that prevailed in East Asia for many centuries.

03-039. SANTANGELO, Paolo. "Sulla natura dei rapporti fra Cina e Corea." *Annali dell'Istituto Universitario Orientale* (Naples), 34 (1974). On Sino-Korean relations.

03-040. WALKER, Hugh D. "Traditional Sino-Korean Diplomatic Relations: A Realistic Historical Appraisal." *Monumenta Serica* 24(1955):155–169. Attempts to characterize traditional Sino-Korean relations by comparing the patterns of dynastic cycle in China and Korea. Concludes that Korea had pursued a realistic policy toward China to safeguard her independence prior to the Yi dynasty and that only after the coming of the Confucianized state of Yi did Korea accept the concept of a Confucian "family of nations."

03-041. _____. "Korea and the Chinese Imperium." *Orient/ West* 9(2)(1964):90–98, 115–117. The bulk of this article is devoted to a narrative account of the rise and fall of Chinese and Korean dynasties from the Ch'in dynasty of China until modern times to illustrate the proposition that the dynastic cycles of Chinese history were an important influence on Korea, but that the concept of dynastic cycle is not in itself applicable to Korean history.

KOREANS ABROAD

03-042. GARDNER, Arthur L. *The Koreans in Hawaii: An Annotated Bibliography.* Hawaii Series, no. 2. Honolulu: Social Science Research Institute, University of Hawaii, 1970. Comprehensive bibliography with excellent annotations listing all the publications related to the Koreans in Hawaii, available documents and records of various Korean community organizations, and private manuscripts and memoirs. Indispensable for studying Koreans in Hawaii.

03-043. HOCHINS, Lee and Chang-su HOCHINS. "The Korean Experience in America, 1903–1924." *Pacific Historical Review* 43(1974):548–575. A detailed scholarly study of the experience of the Korean immigrants in the United States and Hawaii with emphasis on the political history and the patterns of the immigration process from 1904 to 1924.

03-044. KIM, Bernice B. H. "The Koreans in Hawaii." Master's thesis (Sociology), University of Hawaii, 1937. 209 pp. "Based on fieldwork undertaken between 1932 and 1936, this thesis is still the only serious study in English of

Hawaii's Korean community. At that time the author personally interviewed a large and representative cross-section of the Korean population. The main purpose of the study was to examine the adjustment of the Korean immigrants to the American social and economic environments and the effects of the adjustment on individual and group.'' From Arthur Gardner's *The Koreans in Hawaii* (03-042).

03-045. KIM, Hyung-chan. "History and Role of the Church in the Korean American Community." *Korea Journal* 14(8)(August 1974):26–37. A good survey of the growth of the Christian churches organized by the Korean immigrants in the United States (mostly in Hawaii and California) from 1903 to the present. Since church-related activities inevitably involved politics within the Korean communities, this article is also useful in understanding certain political and social aspects of the Korean immigrants in the United States.

03-046. _____. "Korean Community Organizations in America: Their Characteristics and Problems." *Korea Journal* 15(11)(November 1975):29–42. Gives a good account of the activities of major Korean community organizations in America such as Kungminhoe (Korean National Association), Hŭngsadan (Corps for the Advancement of Individuals), and Tongjihoe (Comrade Society).

03-047. KIM, Hyung-chan and Wayne PATTERSON. *The Koreans in America, 1882–1974: A Chronology and Fact Book*. Ethnic Chronology Series, no. 16. Dobbs Ferry, N.Y.: Oceana Publications, 1974. A brief chronology of events involving the Koreans in the United States from 1882 to 1974. Though it contains much useful factual information, the book suffers from unevenness in coverage and many inconsistencies such as in romanization. The book also includes sixteen selected documents and journal articles related to Korean immigration to the United States and Korean life in America.

03-048. KIM, Warren Y. *Koreans in America*. Seoul: Po Chin Chai Printing Co., 1971. A short history of the political, religious, educational, and cultural activities of Korean immigrants in America before 1948. Based on primary sources and the author's personal experiences with many organizational activities, this book contains valuable information.

03-049. KOH, Seung-Jae. "A Study of Korean Immigrants to Hawaii." *Journal of Social Sciences and Humanities* 38(June 1973):19–33. A survey study of Korean emigration to Hawaii and of emigrant life there before 1940.

03-050. LYU, Kingsley K. "Korean Nationalist Activities in Hawaii and the Continental United States, 1900–1945."

Amerasia Journal 4(1977):1–2. Gives an extremely valuable account of the nationalist activities of Koreans living in the United States, particularly in Hawaii, based on the author's firsthand observations and interviews of important individuals. Contains much useful information.

03-051. SHIN, Linda. "Koreans in America, 1903–1945." *Amerasia Journal* 1(3)(November 1971):32–39. Also in Amy Tachiki et al. (eds.), *Roots: An Asian American Reader* (Los Angeles: Continental Graphics, 1971). A brief account of the history of Korean immigration to the United States and the immigrants' political and other organizational activities before 1945.

03-052. STEPHAN, John J. "The Korean Minority in the Soviet Union." *Mizan* 13(1971):138–150. An excellent study of the Korean minority in the Soviet Union. Traces the main lines of development of Koreans in Russia since 1860 and gives an account of the economic and social conditions of Soviet Koreans today.

03-053. YUN, Yŏ-jun. "Early History of Korean Emigration to America." *Korea Journal* 14(6)(June 1974):21–26 and 14(7)(July 1974):40–45. A study of the first Korean emigration to Hawaii and Mexico from 1902 to 1905. The author examines the motivation and social background of the emigrants, the means by which they were recruited, the plight of emigrants in Mexico, and the reaction within Korea.

HISTORIOGRAPHY

03-054. CH'OE, Yŏng-ho. "History in North Korea: Its Role and Characteristics." *Journal of East and West Studies* 5(1)(April 1976). Studies how history is perceived and utilized in North Korea and analyzes the main characteristics of North Korean historiography.

03-055. CHUN, Hae-jong. "Dynastic Changes in China and Korea—A Comparative Study of Factors Causing the Changes." *Korea Journal* 11(4)(April 1974):32–36. An interesting comparison of similarities and dissimilarities in the rise and fall of the main dynasties in Chinese and Korean history by an eminent Korean historian of East Asia.

03-056. KANG, Hugh H. W. "Images of Korean History." In Andrew C. Nahm (ed.), *Traditional Korea—Theory and Practice*. Kalamazoo: Center for Korean Studies, Western Michigan University, 1974. A critical study of the major writings of important Japanese historians on Korea before 1945 who gave distorted images of Korean history in modern times. The representative writings of a few Korean nationalistic historians are also examined briefly as a counterpoint. This article is an important and authoritative study of modern Korean historiography.

03-057. KAWASHIMA, Fujiya. "Historiographic Development in South Korea: State and Society from the Mid-Koryo to the Mid-Yi Dynasties." *Korean Studies* (Honolulu), 2 (1978):29–56. A detailed and comprehensive review of the historical works published in South Korea since the mid-1950s.

03-058. Korean National Committee of Historical Sciences. *Historical Studies in Korea: Recent Trends and Bibliography (1945–1973).* Seoul: 1975. A report submitted to the XIVth International Congress of Historical Sciences held at San Francisco in August 1975, this is essentially a comprehensive list of historical studies (books, monographs, and articles) published in Korea from 1945 to 1973. Almost all the works are written in Korean, and each entry lists the author, date of publication, title of the work and its English translation, and title of the journal where the

work appears. The romanization follows the system devised by the Ministry of Education in Seoul. Divided into three parts covering Korean, Asian, and Western history; Korean history takes up the bulk of the book. Each part has an English introduction explaining the trend of research among historians in Korea.

03-059. TEWKSBURY, Donald G. (comp.). *Source Materials on Korean Politics and Ideologies.* Vol. 2: *Source Books on Far Eastern Political Ideologies.* New York: Institute of Pacific Relations, 1950. Mimeographed. Contains basic documents that in large measure shaped the history of modern Korea since 1871—such as diplomatic agreements, key official statements, memorials, proclamations, and constitutions. The book is divided into three parts: Part 1, From Isolation to Annexation by Japan; Part 2, From Annexation by Japan to World War II; and Part 3, From World War II to the Korean Crisis of 1950. The title of the book is misleading.

II. ANCIENT CHOSŎN, THREE KINGDOMS, AND KORYŎ

*by Hugh H. W. Kang
and Michael E. Macmillan*

INTRODUCTION

WESTERN INTEREST in the study of Korean history before the Chosŏn dynasty is a fairly recent phenomenon, having grown out of a boom in interest in Korea during the Korean conflict of 1950–1953. Research on this period therefore remains limited to a small number of scholars, mostly products of this postwar interest, who have been pioneering the field in the West for more than two decades. The titles annotated in this section are mainly works of these historians, supplemented by a few Korean and Japanese scholars' studies published in English. The number of entries is necessarily small but includes studies that broke new ground in the field.

The early history of Korea, while sharing problems common to the ancient history of most areas—scarcity of primary sources, inadequate or uneven secondary sources, and so forth—also poses unique historiographical problems. To begin with, the surviving written

records dealing with Korea before the Three Kingdoms are mostly of Chinese and not Korean authorship. The absence of Korean records necessitates dependence on Chinese accounts, which, tendentious and fragmentary in most cases, invariably reduce Ancient Korean (Ko Chosŏn) to but an appendage of China and her great civilization. Korean history, according to these accounts, began under the civilizing influence of a Chinese culture-bearer, the loyal Shang dissident statesman Chitzu (Kija in Korean), who settled in Korea and reputedly taught the native inhabitants the essentials of civilized life. From this alleged dawn of civilization to the fall of the Chinese colony of Lolang in AD 313, the principal figures on the Korean historical stage are said to have been men of Chinese, not Korean, origin. In such circumstances, the events of early Korea cannot escape being treated as marginal happenings on the periphery of Greater China; in fact, they are often relegated in these accounts to be incidental to Chinese history.

The Korean tradition of Confucian historiography compounds this problem through its ready acquiescence in the Chinese view of ancient Korea. Historical writing in premodern Korea developed as an integral part of the extensive cultural borrowing from China. Koreans learned the art of writing history from the Chinese and produced works patterned after the Chinese model.

While the adoption of this model helped Koreans develop a strong tradition of historical writing, it also resulted in acceptance of the early Chinese account of Korea together with its Confucian biases. Ancient Korean legends explaining the mythical foundations of early Korean kingdoms were often looked upon by later Korean Confucian historians as lacking credibility, particularly when compared to what they believed to be authentic Chinese historical accounts. The result was frequent abandonment or adulteration of old indigenous records, banishing the native development of early times into historical obscurity. It is thus no historical accident that the Tan'gun legend, describing the mythical but independent foundation of Korean civilization, was preserved only through a thirteenth-century historical work by a Buddhist monk, Iryŏn, nor that the Koryŏ Confucian statesman-historian Kim Pu-sik (1075–1151) was derided by later Neo-Confucian critics for his inclusion, even in a much abridged version, of the mythical foundation stories in the official history of the Three Kingdoms. In fact, Confucian historiography had such a strong grip on the intellectual world of traditional Korea that acquiescence to the early Chinese account of Korea was seldom challenged until modern times.

Modern iconoclastic scrutiny of Confucian historiography was made possible by the introduction of Western methods of historical inquiry, first applied to Korean history by Japanese academic historians around the turn of the century. Through relentless textual criticism of traditional Chinese and Korean sources on early Korea, these historians rejected both the Tan'gun and Chi-tzu stories as historical fabrications, leaving Wei-Man Ch'ao-hsien (in Korean, Wiman Chosŏn, 195–109 BC) to be the first authentic kingdom in the Korean peninsula. Japanese excavations of historical sites in Korea turned up nothing to contradict this assertion. Moreover, numerous artifacts unearthed in tombs in the vicinity of Pyongyang were determined to be those of high-ranking Chinese colonial officials of Lolang (109 BC–AD 313) and helped to confirm the view that the transplantation of advanced Chinese culture to the peninsula had been decisive in the rise of Korean civilization. Thus the Chinese beginnings of Korean history, while being stripped of Confucian approbation, were given new validity through the Japanese studies.

If the Japanese academic historians succeeded in discrediting Confucian historiography in Korea, their own studies of early Korea unfortunately were not altogether untainted by the politics of the Japanese colonization of Korea. Their effort to authenticate the historicity of ancient Japanese control of Mimana (Imna in Korean) in southeastern Korea evinced, perhaps more than anything else, the prepossession of many Japanese studies on early Korea to provide historical justification for modern Japanese imperialistic expansion. In marked contrast to their stringent textual criticism of old Korean and Chinese sources, few Japanese historians demonstrated readiness to apply similar scrutiny to early Japanese sources, though admittedly of dubious historical reliability, when they used the latter to document Japan's ancient control of Mimana. Although a passage in the inscription on the stele commemorating King Kwanggaet'o (391–412) of Koguryŏ was believed to offer evidence of Japanese control, numerous Japanese expeditions turned up little material evidence to corroborate it. Yet the existence in Korea of a headquarters of the ancient Japanese Yamato state exercising political control over the lower Naktong River basin, as asserted by the *Nihon shoki,* was accepted as an indisputable historical fact until its validity was challenged by revisionist historians in the 1970s.

Aside from the ancient Chinese and Japanese colonizations of the Korean peninsula, pioneer Japanese scholars showed their greatest research interest in the Three Kingdoms. Generally displaying a prepossession similar to that seen in studies on early Korea, Japanese academics dismissed the foundation legends of the Three Kingdoms as myths and directed their research toward the historically reliable period in the history of the kingdoms, stressing the outside influences they believed to be the principal stimuli for organized political life in the peninsula. Many of these pioneering studies, however, were merely factual verifications of the political and military history of the period undertaken not necessarily as groundwork for a broader historical inquiry but for the sake of factual verification.

Their stress on factual verification, though a natural consequence of having discredited Confucian historiography, was also a result of having characterized Korean culture as borrowed. The importance attached to external relations was therefore not so much for analysis of cultural interactions between the native people and outsiders as it was for mechanical confirmation of contacts between the two. The assumption underlying this approach was that Korea was historically devoid of any strong indigenous initiative to create an original native culture or to develop independent political power. Rather, the decisive influence always came from outside; imitation of the neighboring civilization was substituted for creation of a uniquely Korean culture. Consequently, little attention was paid to acculturation as a creative process of historical growth in Korean society —or, more specifically in this case, to enrichment of Korean culture through importation and absorption of a rich and sophisticated civilization from China. Even when Japanese academics did take up the internal developments of the Korean kingdoms, they tended to treat them more as a historically dormant and static phenomenon than as a dynamic and functionally creative process of history. Accordingly, little was done to investigate the positive accomplishments in Korean history, be they examples of exceptional political leadership or of creative artistic achievements or of brilliant intellectual and spiritual growth.

Modern Korean academic historians, few in number and mostly trained in Japanese universities, appeared first in the 1920s and 1930s. In their historical inquiries they focused their attention mainly on the ancient history to rediscover the indigenous civilization and, at the same time, refute what they considered to be the adulterated interpretations of Japanese scholars. This mere handful of pioneers, working in the adverse circumstances created by Japanese colonial policy, could do little to achieve their objectives, however. Their publications were limited in number and overshadowed by the numerically superior Japanese works. Indeed, the Japanese works, including newer studies made by a growing number of young scholars, continued to hold a monolithic grip on historical research of Korea and even produced a few studies of outstanding quality, some of which were now probing the histories of Unified Silla (668–935) and Koryŏ (918–1392). A few of these studies, branching out into socioeconomic and institutional history, attempted to examine the dynamics of Korean historical development through an analysis of the socioeco-

nomic and political forces at work. Promising though these studies were, the urgent demands of the war years interrupted scholarly endeavors, leaving the burden of producing a new comprehensive history of Korea to the historians of liberated Korea and postwar Japan.

Liberated Korea, though ideologically divided, assumed the principal responsibility for the monumental task of reexamining her history. In addition to training new historians and making available scarce source materials to facilitate a rapid growth of Korean historical studies, her task included wrestling with the difficult problem of undoing the wrongs done to Korean history by traditional Confucian historians and prewar Japanese historians. New studies by postwar Japanese revisionist historians, who have gradually been regaining the ground lost after Japan's withdrawal from Korea, have also been important in providing necessary reexamination of selected topics. A general survey of these studies published in Korea and Japan since 1945 is far beyond the scope of this brief introduction. It is sufficient here to say that the outpouring of studies on pre-Chosŏn history since the mid-1950s has definitely registered an unprecedented advance in Korean historical scholarship. Noteworthy among the achievements of these postwar studies are the works of North Korean historians on early Koguryŏ, Parhae (Po-hai in Chinese), and early Korea-Japan relations, as well as on periodization based on the Marxian scheme of historical development. For Western academics, however, studies by South Korean and postwar Japanese historians have been invaluable in broadening our knowledge, particularly on socioeconomic, political, and military institutions of Silla and Koryŏ.

Taking advantage of these works, Western historians too have been steadily increasing their contributions, assuming their share of the painstaking toil necessary for the growth of scholarship in the field. Although their studies have been directed mainly toward the period after the fourteenth century, they have published several important studies on earlier periods as well.

Not a few Western studies of Korea before the Chosŏn dynasty have dealt with early history, perhaps reflecting the interest in this period shown by pioneering Korean and Japanese scholars in the past. Observable in these studies are problems of fact and interpretation arising from the legacy of historiographical inadequacy and bias mentioned earlier. Studies of ancient Korea and its relations with adjacent countries (for example, the works of K. H. J. Gardiner, James K. Ash, Boleslaw Szczesniak, and Gari Ledyard) demonstrate the difficulties stemming from the paucity of source materials, particularly when compounded by the cultural idiosyncrasies of the countries involved. Although the studies of Shiratori Kurakichi, Ikeuchi Hiroshi, and Suematsu Yasukazu represent perhaps the high point of prewar Japanese scholarship, even these works embody typical shortcomings of their times, in particular a tendency to stress Korea's historical dependence on outside forces, be they Chinese or Japanese. On the other hand, studies by Kim Chŏng-bae, Ch'ŏn Kwan-u, and Yi Pyŏng-do typify the new Korean effort to refute this stress by focusing on the uniqueness and independent nature of ancient Korean historical development. Similarly, in the area of institutional history, the works of Yi Ki-baek and Kang Chin-ch'ŏl emphasize facts that support the independent development thesis postulated primarily by the postwar Korean historians.

Through the works just mentioned and others (for example, those by Michael C. Rogers and Chŏn Hae-jong), Korea's place in East Asian history has been probed with increasing zeal. Yet Korea's part in expanding the Chinese world order, as in, for example, her role in extending Sino-Buddhistic civilization to Japan, has not received similar scrutiny. From the emergence of the ancient Korean kingdoms through the fall of Silla, the dominant influence on Korean life was unquestionably derived from Sino-Buddhism, but virtually no study has appeared in the West on this vital influence. Peter H. Lee's studies stand alone in lifting the veil obscuring this important aspect of Korean history. The deep marks left by Buddhism on the institutions and thought of Korea from the Three Kingdoms through Koryŏ are too often simply lumped together with the general borrowings from China with little attention to Buddhism itself as a unique source of influence.

The widening cultural traffic between Unified Silla and T'ang China afforded Korean erudites opportunities to become immersed in Confucian secular learning, setting in motion a trend toward the secularization of intellectual life, including political ideology. One result was the increased importance of Confucian scholar-officials in government and society. Epoch-making though this was, no comprehensive study has yet been made of the process of this crucial intellectual transformation. Only a few of the political and socioeconomic institutions of Silla, as well as her unification and eventual demise, have attracted interest; examples are the inquiries by John C. Jamieson, Chong Sun Kim, Richard Rutt, and Ellen S. Unruh, which shed light on the forces that generated the energy and ferment leading to the rise and fall of Silla and the subsequent founding of Koryŏ, which eventually reunified the Later Three Kingdoms. The vitality of Koreans at the height of Silla's growth apparently spilled over into the coastal communities of central China, and Korean activities in these communities have been interestingly recaptured by Edwin O. Reischauer in his study of the Japanese monk Ennin's travel to T'ang China.

Large-scale borrowing of Chinese institutions, actively promoted with much success in the first and last centuries of Koryŏ, has yet to capture the fascination of historians in the West. My own study of the introduction of the Chinese civil service examination opens only a crack in the formidable subject of cultural borrowing and acculturation in traditional Korea. A unique blend of elements from the indigenous and borrowed cultures evidently resulted from this massive cultural transplantation. The delineation of pre-Koryŏ institutions, including the sociopolitical order, unquestionably necessary before one can apprehend this intricate process of cultural borrowing, still awaits scholarly probing. Even in Korea and Japan, only a few embryonic studies on this topic have begun to appear in recent years.

The fusion of the two cultures, while enriching life in Korea, also produced certain contradictory forces in society. Elements of this contradiction that ultimately found expression in an open clash between civil aristocratic interests and their military counterparts have received attention in the West only in Edward J. Shultz's study, although the same subject attracted some attention in Korea and Japan earlier. In the domestic developments along indigenous lines during the military rule of the Ch'oe house and in the record of Koryŏ's thirty-year resistance to the invading Mongols, one wonders whether one may not find a clue to Korea's ability to sustain political and cultural identity despite the magnetism of and borrowing from a highly developed foreign culture. Works by William E. Henthorn and Gari Ledyard on the Mongol-Koryŏ relationship, interesting though they are, only touch upon the aspects of the relationship between the victorious overlord and the humbled but tenacious vassal. Perhaps equally significant from the standpoint of broader Korean developments are the intellectual fermentation and socioeconomic changes that occurred following the renewed contact with China under the Mongols. But here again no Western studies exist yet. It may be a proper conclusion to this short introductory essay to say that this and many other subjects of equal, if not greater, importance quietly beckon the student of history in both East and West who would take up this young, fascinating field—not in spite of, but rather because of, the challenge it presents.

BIBLIOGRAPHY

POLITICS AND SOCIETY
Ancient and Three Kingdoms Periods

03-060. ANSELMO, Valerio. "Una ricerca sul nome Kudara." In *Gururajamanjarica: Studii in onore di Giuseppe Tucci.* Naples: Istituto Universitario Orientale, 1974. An article on historical and linguistic research into the etymology of the name Kudara (Paekche).

03-061. BAELZ, E. "Dolmen und alte Königsgräber in Korea." *Zeitschrift für Ethnologie* 42 (1910). Research on dolmens and ancient royal tombs.

03-062. DE ROSNY, Léon. *Les Coréens, aperçu ethnologique et historique.* Paris: Maisonneuve, 1886. The author states (p. 37): "There is a reason to believe that the present Korean nation, far from being constituted of one pure race, is the result of a mixture of the most diverse ethnic elements." Thus he concludes that, viewed historically, the Korean race is a mixture of various northeast Asian races such as the Chinese, Tungus, and others.

03-063. GARDINER, K. H. J. *The Early History of Korea: The Historical Development of the Peninsula up to the Introduction of Buddhism in the Fourth Century AD.* Honolulu: University of Hawaii Press, 1969. 78 pp. This brief outline history is aimed, according to the author, "at presenting Sinologists and Japanologists with essential information and the bibliography necessary to pursue further studies." A synthesis of a large number of modern studies, it is a lucid introduction to early Korean history, primarily from the vantage point of the interactions of the peninsular peoples and their neighbors, particularly China. It exhibits a ready acceptance of Japanese interpretations, notably in the matter of Japanese control of a portion of southern Korea, that have come under attack recently by Korean historians and does so without much acknowledgment of the existence of alternative interpretations. In separate chapters, Gardiner treats the historical background up to the Han Chinese conquest in 108 BC, the development of the Chinese colonies in Korea from 108 BC to the end of the third century, the history of Koguryŏ to AD 245, and the conditions that gave rise to strong native kingdoms and other important developments of the fourth century. Suggestions for further reading at the end of each chapter provide a good guide to specialized studies on various topics, mostly in Japanese and Chinese. In addition, there are in the appendixes an interesting discussion of the interpretation of the Tung Shou tomb and a survey of the principal primary sources for the history of early Korea.

03-064. _____. "The Beginnings of Korean History." *Journal of the Oriental Society of Australia* 4(1)(June 1960): 77–90. The author summarizes in briefest fashion the information available in early Chinese sources on the origins of the political entities on the Korean peninsula and compares this with the accounts found in later Korean sources such as the *Samguk sagi*. In particular, he disputes three of the stories of legendary origins that found their way into some early Western writings: the Tan'gun myth, the story of a Kija dynasty lasting from the eleventh until the third century BC, and the account of a kingdom of Mahan ruled by the descendants of the Kija dynasty. Gardiner discounts the *Samguk sagi* dates for the establishment of Silla (57 BC), Koguryŏ (37 BC), and Paekche (18 BC) and concludes that Korean history as a subject in its own right properly begins with the events of the fourth century AD.

03-065. _____. "Some Problems Concerning the Founding of Paekche." *Archiv Orientalni* 37(4)(1969):562–588. Relying on Chinese sources and the research of Japanese scholars, Gardiner theorizes that Paekche was established by members of the ruling family of Puyŏ, who were pushed southward from Manchuria by Mu-jung Hui in 286 and subsequently, under pressure from an expanding Koguryŏ in the third century, pushed further south into the Mahan area where, with superior weapons and social solidarity, they carved out a kingdom, absorbing Chinese from the Chinese colonies in Korea and Koreans from the Han tribes.

03-066. HAGUENAUER, Charles. "À propos de nouvelles recherches concernant le Liao-tong, la Corée et le Japon (Shikoku) antique." *Journal asiatique* (July–September 1936). Describes archaeological excavations in Manchuria, Liaotung, Korea, and Japan and attempts to define the relationships among these regions.

03-067. _____. "Encore la question des Gores." *Journal asiatique* (January–March 1935). This and the following entry attempt to trace the etymology of the names Korea, Corée, and Corea to "Koryǒ."

03-068. _____. "Les Gores." *Bulletin de la Maison franco-japonaise* (Tokyo), 3(3)(1930). See the preceding entry.

03-068. _____. "Les récentes fouilles japonaises en Corée," *T'oung Pao* 23 (1924). Based on the 1924 excavations by Hamada, a Japanese, as reported in *Shūkan Asahi* (20 July 1924).

03-070. HENDERSON, Gregory. "Korea through the Fall of the Lolang Colony." *Koreana Quarterly* 1(1)(1959): 147–168. This article deals in summary fashion with the history of the Korean peninsula from prehistoric times to AD 313. It recounts the legends of Tan'gun and Kija, outlines archaeological findings, discusses the introduction of metal culture, surveys the rise and fall of the Han Chinese colonies, and concludes with brief accounts of the development of Koguryǒ and the Han tribes.

03-071. ILYON. *Samguk Yusa: Legends and History of the Three Kingdoms of Ancient Korea.* Translated by Tae-Hung Ha and Grafton K. Mintz. Seoul: Yonsei University Press, 1972. 456 pp. This is the first published translation into English of the *Samguk yusa* [Memorabilia of the Three Kingdoms], compiled in the thirteenth century by the Buddhist monk Iryǒn. While adequate as an introduction to the work, this edition contains too many errors, inaccuracies, confusions, and other deficiencies to satisfy the requirements of the specialist. A definitive translation of this important source for the early history of Korea remains to be published.

03-072. KIM, Chewǒn. "Han Dynasty Mythology and the Korean Legend of Tan Gun." *Archives of the Chinese Art Society in America* 3(1948–1949):43–48. Kim compares the Tan'gun legend of Korea's founding, as given in the *Samguk yusa,* with the scenes depicted on two of the Wu Liang Tz'u stone slabs of Han dynasty China and concludes that the scenes probably represent a Chinese prototype of the Tan'gun legend.

03-073. KIM, Chǒng-bae. "Racial Composition and Cultural Complex in Ancient Korea." *Korea Journal* 12(9)(September 1972):4–17. In this article, Kim uses the findings of modern archaeological studies to bolster a reinterpretation of the Ancient Chosǒn period stressing indigenous development and connections with North Asia and deemphasizing the influence of Chinese culture. He relates the legend of Tan'gun to the Neolithic inhabitants of Korea, whom he identifies as one of the "ancient Asian races" pushed out of the Siberian region. He holds that Neolithic society, characterized by adherence to a bear cult, continued until the twelfth century BC and was then assimilated by immigrants of Altaic stock, makers of undecorated earthenware, whom he identifies as the Yemaek. Kim disclaims any archaeological evidence for the existence of a Kija Chosǒn dominated by Chinese and argues against any profound Chinese influence in the period known as Wiman Chosǒn. Rather, he maintains that in the period referred to as Kija Chosǒn the Yemaek developed a bronze culture and later, perhaps as early as the seventh century BC, an iron culture, retaining its power in the peninsula even after the coming of Wiman.

03-074. _____. "Characteristics of Mahan in Ancient Korean Society." *Korea Journal* 14(6)(June 1974):4–10. Kim here applies anthropological theories of society to the information on Mahan contained in early Chinese sources to argue against defining Mahan as a tribal state. He maintains instead that prior to the Three Kingdoms period Mahan had reached the stage of development of a "semi-state," vaguely defined as being more advanced than a tribal society but short of having become a genuine state.

03-075. LEE, Ki-baik. "The Crime of Jealousy in Puyǒ." *Journal of Social Sciences and Humanities* 18(June 1963):72–78. The author maintains that jealousy was a harshly punished offense for women not only in Puyǒ but in Koguryǒ and other Korean kingdoms as well and that this treatment probably arose from the need to maintain order in a family system based on polygamy.

03-076. LI, Ogg. "À propos des Ye et Mäk." *Annuaire de l'École Pratique des Hautes Études—IVe section* 106 (1973–1974):777–779. One section of the synopsis of Li's lectures on the racial makeup of the Koguryǒ people.

03-077. _____. "Aspects economiques dans l'histoire de la Corée à l'époque des trois royaumes." *Annuaire de l'École Pratique des Hautes Études—IVe section* 103 (1970–1971) and 104(1971–1972). On the land system of the Three Kingdoms period and the question of land cultivation by *haho* and slaves.

03-078. _____. "Aspects sociaux dans l'histoire de la Corée à l'époque des trois royaumes." *Annuaire de l'École Pratique des Hautes Études—IVe section* 105(1972–1973).

Analysis of materials on the question of marriage practices during the Three Kingdoms period.

03-079. SHIRATORI, Kurakichi. "The Legend of the King Tung-ming, the Founder of Fu-yü-kuo." *Memoirs of the Research Department of the Tōyō Bunko* 10(1938):1–41. This is a detailed study of the legends claiming Tong-myŏng (Tung-ming) as founder of both Puyŏ (Fu-yü) and Koguryŏ. Shiratori argues that only one claim can be correct and attempts through philological and geographical evidence to demonstrate that the legend properly applies to the founding of Puyŏ. He holds that Koguryŏ, having come to dominate the Puyŏ people, appropriated the legend in order to give the impression that its rulers had descended from the same royal family as those of Puyŏ. This, he argues, was intended to help pacify Puyŏ and provide a basis for Puyŏ aid against Paekche.

03-080. WATSON, Burton (trans.). *Records of the Grand Historian of China.* 2 vols. New York: Columbia University Press, 1961. A translation of the *Shih chi* by Ssu-ma Ch'ien. The account of Ch'ao-hsien (Chosŏn), describing the flight of Wei Man (Wiman) to Korea and the Han campaigns against his descendants in 108–109 BC, is found in vol. 2, pp. 258–263.

Silla

03-081. ITO, Akio. "Zür Chronologie der frühsillazeitlichen Gräber in Südkorea." PhD dissertation, Munich, 1971. A chronology of early Silla tombs.

03-082. JAMIESON, John Charles. "The *Samguk sagi* and the Unification Wars." PhD dissertation, University of California, Berkeley, 1969. 351 pp. Abstracted *DAI* 30(November 1969):1984-A; UM 69-18,938. Jamieson attempts to illuminate Silla's rise to dominance in Korea in the latter half of the seventh century through an examination of the materials related to the peninsular wars of this period contained in the *Samguk sagi*. The major portion of this study is an annotated translation of this material, including the Silla annals for 660–681 and the biographies of eleven major figures (notably omitting Kim Yu-sin on the grounds that this important biography had already appeared in a German translation). A two-part introduction consists of a discussion of the composition, nature, and usefulness of the *Samguk sagi* and an essay analyzing the information in the translated material. Two appendixes provide the names and order of positions in the Silla seventeen-rank bureaucracy and modern equivalents of place-names in the text.

03-083. KIM, Chong-Sun. "The Emergence of Multi-Centered Despotism in the Silla Kingdom: A Study of the Origin of Factional Struggles in Korea." PhD dissertation, University of Washington, 1965. 585 pp. Abstracted in *DAI* 27(August 1966):427–428-A; UM 65-15,391. Regarding the Silla period as a formative era in which the essential characteristics of traditional Korean civilization, including a proclivity for factional strife, took shape, Kim elaborates in this study the fundamental social and economic institutions of Silla, including the *kolp'um* system, the *hwarang,* slavery, and, particularly, the landholding system. He casts Sillan history in the framework of a "multicentered despotism" characterized by conflict among the aristocracy, the bureaucracy, and kings bent on autocracy. Much of the conflict, according to Kim, arose out of tension between state ownership of land and the desire for private ownership and led to fragmentation of power within the centralized government. Kim concludes with a theory of dynastic cycles in Korean history in which these economic conflicts lead to the fall of Silla and the successive rise and fall of Koryŏ and Chosŏn and eventually to the rise of the twentieth-century Japanese colonial regime.

03-084. _____. "The Kolp'um System: Basis for Sillan Social Stratification." *Journal of Korean Studies* 1(2) (January–June 1971):43–69. The author first discusses the origin and meaning of the word *kolp'um* and then describes the hierarchical structure of the *kolp'um* system and the restrictions it imposed on various social and economic activities. The article concludes with a critical examination of several hypotheses proposed to explain the demise of the *sŏnggol,* the highest stratum of the *kolp'um* order, the disappearance of which Kim believes undermined the stability of Sillan society. An appendix gives the *kolp'um* regulations governing clothing, housing, carts, and riding equipment.

03-085. _____. "Sources of Cohesion and Fragmentation in the Silla Kingdom." *Journal of Korean Studies* 1(1)(July–December 1969):41–72. This essay on the institutional bases of Sillan society emphasizes the relationship of various institutions to the emergence of factional struggles during the Silla period. Kim discusses the part played by the *hwabaek* council, the *kolp'um* rank system, and the *hwarang* (here interpreted as an educational system for training aristocratic leaders) in the early strength and later decline of Silla. He also discusses the role of the taxation system, shamanism, and the landholding system. In treating the land system, which he interprets as a form of state ownership, he gives particular attention to disputing interpretations that find in the Silla period the beginnings of a feudalistic society.

03-086. _____. "Slavery in Silla and Its Sociological and Economic Implications." In Andrew C. Nahm (ed.), *Traditional Korea—Theory and Practice*. Kalamazoo: Center for Korean Studies, Western Michigan University, 1974. The author challenges the view held by some historians that Sillan society was based on a slave economy and contends that such views are based on dubious interpretations of the documentary evidence. He argues instead that Silla was an agricultural economy heavily dependent on peasant labor and in which slaves played only a minor economic role. He maintains that the military aristocracy lacked the capacity to conduct the kind of supervisory administration associated with large slave holdings and, since landholdings were fragmented, had nothing to gain from a large-scale slave system.

03-087. RUTT, Richard. "The Flower Boys of Silla." *Transactions of the Korea Branch of the Royal Asiatic Society* 37(October 1961):1–66. This is the most extensive treatment of the Sillan *hwarang* organization available in English. Rutt summarizes the accounts of the *hwarang* contained in the two principal sources, the *Samguk sagi* and *Samguk yusa*, and provides brief biographies of the persons identified in these sources as *hwarang*. His discussion also covers the development of the *hwarang* after Silla, the connection between *hwarang* and Buddhism, homosexuality among *hwarang*, and the organization of the *hwarang*. This institution has been variously interpreted as a shamanistic organization, an educational movement, and, more popularly, as a military cult for the training of Sillan leaders. Rutt specifically disputes the latter interpretation, attributing it to a desire to view the institution in terms of modern patriotism. Rather, he interprets the *hwarang* as a band of adolescents of high moral purpose, essentially religious, but at least quasi-military. The military aspects, he maintains, were a transitory phenomenon that stemmed from the nature and needs of the society in which the *hwarang* flourished.

03-088. UNRUH, Ellen S. "Reflections of the Fall of Silla." *Korea Journal* 15(5)(May 1975):54–62. Largely an examination of the principal Korean sources for the history of Silla, particularly the *Samguk yusa*, this article maintains that imposition of Chinese concepts in the writing of history obscured the existence of indigenous cultural traditions that were important factors in the fall of Silla. Unruh cites several indications that Sillan centralized control and cultural unification of the peninsula were incomplete: persistence of tribal-aristocratic practices alongside new bureaucratic governmental structures; use of local Paekche and Koguryŏ families in the lower ranks of the bureaucracy; language differences; differences in shamanistic practices; and concentration of rebel bases in the former Paekche and Koguryŏ areas during the insurrections at the fall of the dynasty. She concludes that consciousness of ancient cultural traditions and desire to restore them were major forces binding the antidynastic elements.

03-089. YI, Pyong-do. "On the Primitive Assembly and Namdang (South Hall) Systems in Ancient Korea." *Journal of Social Sciences and Humanities* 12(May 1960):1–10. Yi traces in cursory fashion the evolution of what he regards as a primitive form of democratic organization in Silla, beginning with clan and village councils and developing into tribal councils, tribal federations, and eventually into the *hwabaek* council of Unified Silla. He maintains that the change in the title of Silla's rulers from *nisagŭm* to *maripkan* in the latter half of the fourth century reflects a change from a tribal-controlled society to a centralized state.

Koryŏ

03-090. HAZARD, Benjamin H. "The Creation of the Korean Navy During the Koryŏ Period." *Transactions of the Korea Branch of the Royal Asiatic Society* 48(1973):10–28. Hazard surveys the naval activity during the Koryŏ period that formed the base for the extensive development of Korean naval power under the Yi dynasty. Particular attention is given to the restraints imposed on Koryŏ by the Mongols, the stimulus given to ship construction by the Japanese pirate *(wakō)* raids after the mid-fourteenth century, and the key role of the development of shipborne firearms in enabling Koreans to seize the initiative in naval warfare from the *wakō* in the 1380s.

03-091. KANG, Hi Woong. "The Development of the Korean Ruling Class from Late Silla to Early Koryŏ." PhD dissertation, University of Washington, 1964. 357 pp. Abstracted in *DAI* 28(July 1967):166-A; UM 65-5432. This study attempts to show that a basic continuity was maintained in the social composition and power configuration of the ruling class despite the dynastic change from Silla to Koryŏ. The writer analyzes the stratified social system of Silla under the *kolp'um* system and examines in detail the major political developments and currents of thought in the period of dynastic change and the formative period of the Koryŏ government before the military coup d'état of 1170. Kang maintains that Koryŏ policies were based on preserving the essence of the Sillan social order and eventually permitted a resurgence of the Silla aristocratic families in the government of Koryŏ. Despite the adoption of names and forms patterned after medieval Chinese political institutions, governmental practices continued to reflect the Sillan social order and political traditions in which birth was the basis of power and merit and education were of secondary importance.

03-092. _____. "Institutional Borrowing: The Case of the Chinese Civil Service Examination System in Early Koryŏ." *Journal of Asian Studies* 34(November 1974): 109–125. The first part of this article examines the role of the Chinese adviser Shuang Chi in the establishment of a Chinese-style civil examination system *(kwagŏ)* by King Kwangjong in 958 as part of his effort to consolidate monarchical power. The second part of the study focuses on the bases for the successful implementation of the system, among them the prior Chinese experience of Shuang Chi in government centralization, the modest objectives of the system, the preservation of traditional channels of official recruitment, and the compromises made with the indigenous order.

03-093. _____. "The First Succession Struggle of Koryŏ in 945: A Reinterpretation." *Journal of Asian Studies* 36(3) (May 1977):411–428. This article maintains that traditional interpretations of the AD 945 succession struggle, emphasizing legitimacy and individual ambitions, have overlooked important aspects of the dispute. The writer asserts that the true significance of the struggle lay in its nature as a contest between two principal groups with incompatible socioeconomic and regional interests within the Koryŏ ruling class, the strength of one group being based on its descent from the former Silla aristocracy and the strength of the other deriving from its success in maritime trade. The eventual triumph of the Silla aristocratic group, it is argued, foreclosed an opportunity for broadening the bases of power in early Koryŏ and contributed to continuity in the social order.

03-094. MIN, Pyŏng-ha. "An Hyang—Introducer of Chu Hsi's Neo-Confucianism." *Korea Journal* 14(1)(January 1974):36–40. The bulk of this article is devoted to a general account of political conditions and government-sponsored educational enterprises in the thirteenth century. It deals only with the career of An Hyang, who is said to have been the first to bring the works of Chu Hsi to Korea from China.

03-095. SHULTZ, Edward J. "Institutional Developments in Korea under the Ch'oe House: 1196–1258." PhD dissertation, University of Hawaii, 1976. 389 pp. Shultz attempts a comprehensive reassessment of the period of military dominance that followed the coup d'état of 1170, which traditional historians have presented in terms of military usurpation of authority, power struggles, and rampant disorder. Through analysis of the institutions of the Koryŏ

dynastic government of the de facto rulers of the Ch'oe house, he attempts to illuminate accomplishments as well as disruptions, institutional innovations, and changes in the social and economic structure during this period. In addition to examining the organization and personnel of the dual structure created by imposition of Ch'oe house organs on the existing dynastic agencies, the writer treats in detail the fiscal structure and land system, Ch'oe house relations with the peasant and *ch'ŏnmin* classes, and the contradictions growing out of the dual structure—contradictions which ultimately contributed in large measure to the collapse of Ch'oe rule.

Others

03-096. HENTHORN, William E. "Some Notes on Parhae." *Transactions of the Korea Branch of the Royal Asiatic Society* 37(1961):65–81. This article provides a brief narrative account of the founding of Parhae in western Manchuria at the end of the seventh century, of Parhae's relations with China, and of the final disintegration of Parhae in the early tenth century. Appendixes contain a comparison of two Chinese accounts of the founding of Parhae, a list of rulers, and a chart showing the organizational structure of the government.

RELIGION AND EDUCATION

03-097. CHUN, Shin-Yong (ed.). *Buddhist Culture in Korea.* Korean Culture Series, no. 3. Seoul: International Cultural Foundation, 1974. 289 pp. Three of the essays in this bilingual volume deal with aspects of Buddhism in traditional Korea: "The Thought and Life of Wonhyo" by Hong Jung-shik; "Buddhist Sculpture in the Silla Period" by Hwang Soo-yong; and "Publication of Buddhist Scriptures in the Koryŏ Period" by Ahn Kai-hyon. A fourth essay, by Encho Tamura, deals with the influence of Sillan Buddhism on Japan in the sixth, seventh, and early eighth centuries.

03-098. EIKEMEIER, Dieter. "Rechtswirkungen von heiligen Stangen, Pfleilergottheiten und Steinhaufengottheiten in Korea." *Oriens Extremus* (Hamburg), 21(2)(1974). On the *sin'gan, sinju,* and *nusŏktan.* This supplements Haguenauer's study of the *sodo* (see 03-101).

03-099. HAGUENAUER, Charles. "Le *Ki-Kouei* de Yi-tsing et le Kye-rim de l'histoire." In *Kariyo kyōju kanreki kinen Shigaku ronsho.* Kyoto: 1928. On the role of the rooster in ancient Korean religion, particularly in the Silla period.

03-100. _____. "Note sur l'existence d'un culte du coq á Silla." *Bulletin de la Maison franco-japonaise* (1931). Supplements the preceding entry.

03-101. _____. "Lieux d'asile au Japon et en Corée." *Jour-*

nal asiatique (July–September 1934). Research on the *sodo* mentioned in the section on the Han tribes in the chapter on Eastern Barbarians in the *San-kuo chih.*

03-102. HENTZE, Carl. "Schamanenkronen zur Han-Zeit in Korea." *Ostasiatische Zeitschrift* (Berlin), 10(5)(1935). Discusses the ancient religion of Korea as seen in the gold crowns which have been discovered in the original Silla region and compares it with the indigenous folk religions of northeast Asia.

03-103. KIM, Doo Hun. "The Rise of Neo-Confucianism against Buddhism in Late Koryŏ." *Journal of Social Sciences and Humanities* 12(May 1960):11–29. This article describes the campaigns of late-Koryŏ Confucian scholars against Buddhism and discusses both the ideological and the economic bases of their opposition. Particular attention is given to Chŏng To-jŏn's criticism of Buddhism.

03-104. LEE, Ki-baik. "Wŏn'gwang and His Thought." *Korea Journal* 14(6)(June 1974):34–40. A brief biographical sketch of the Sillan monk Wŏn'gwang (553–636) with some interesting observations on his motivation, his relationship to the Sillan government, and the interplay of shamanism and Buddhism.

03-105. LEE, Peter H. *Lives of Eminent Korean Monks: The Haedong Kosŭng Chŏn.* Harvard-Yenching Institute Studies, no. 25. Cambridge, Mass.: Harvard University Press, 1969. 116 pp. An annotated translation of the two extant chapters of the *Haedong kosŭng chŏn,* compiled in 1215, an important source of information about the development of Buddhism in Korea from its introduction until the seventh century. The extant portion of the work deals with early propagators of Buddhism. The first chapter contains biographies of three monks of Koguryŏ, two of Silla, and three of foreign origin; the second chapter deals with Silla monks who traveled to China and India. An introduction by the translator places the work in its historical context and comments on its purpose and value.

03-106. _____. "The Life of the Korean Poet-Priest Kyunyŏ." *Asiatische Studien* 9(1957–1958):42–72. This article consists of an English translation of the *Kyunyŏ chŏn,* a brief account of the life and achievements of the Great Priest Kyunyŏ (917–973), whose writings are regarded as typifying the indigenous culture of Silla, and a short introductory commentary on the origins and publication of the work and its importance in the study of both Korean literature and the development of Buddhism in Korea.

03-107. _____. "Fa-tsang and Ŭisang." *Journal of the American Oriental Society* 82(1)(January–March 1962): 56–62. This short article consists of a translation of passages in the *Samguk yusa* concerning the Silla Buddhist

monk Ŭisang, a disciple of the Hwaŏm (Hua-yen) school who studied in China in the 660s, together with a translation of a well-known letter addressed to Ŭisang by the Chinese monk Fa-tsang in 692.

03-108. LI, Ogg. "À propos de Tangun." *Annuaire de l'École Pratique des Hautes Études—V^e section* (Paris), 78(1970–1971). A study on the chapter on "Tan'gun Chosŏn" in vol. 1 of the *Samguk yusa* as it relates to religious history.

03-109. _____. "Djumong et Tangun." *Annuaire de l'École Pratique des Hautes Études—V^e section* (Paris), 79(1971–1972). On the significance of the Chumong myth in terms of religious history; includes a comparison to the Tan'gun myth.

03-110. _____. "À propos de Čumong." *International Journal of Korean Studies* (Seoul), 1(1973). Compares the Chumong myth with northeast Asian shamanism and explores the significance of this myth in ancient Korean religion. (There are so many typographical errors in this article that it is hardly usable.) This article was published in Korean translation as "Chumong yŏn'gu" in *Han'guksa yŏn'gu* 7(February 1972).

03-111. _____. "Pak Hyŏkkŏse." *Annuaire de l'École Pratique des Hautes Études—V^e section* (Paris), 80(1971–1972) and 81(1972–1973). Research on the myth of Pak Hyŏkkŏse. The same topic is treated in somewhat more detail by the same author in "Pulgunae wang sinhwa" in *Yi Sŏn-gŭn Paksa kohŭi kinyŏm nonmunjip: Han'gukhak nonch'ong* (Seoul: 1974).

03-112. _____. "Karak Kukki." *Annuaire de l'École Pratique des Hautes Études—V^e section* (Paris), 80(1971–1972) and 81(1972–1973). A study of the history of the Karak nation in vol. 2 of the *Samguk yusa* from the viewpoint of religious history. This article was expanded and published in Korean under the title "Suro wang sinhwa" in *Ch'oe Ho-jin paksa hwagap kinyŏm nonch'ong* (Seoul: 1974), vol. 1.

03-113. _____. "T'alhaewang." *Annuaire de l'École Pratique des Hautes Études—V^e section* (Paris), 82(1973–1974). On the significance to religious history of the myth of King T'arhae.

03-114. PAIK, Nak Choon. "Tripitaka Koreana." *Transactions of the Korea Branch of the Royal Asiatic Society* 32(1951): 62–78. A survey of the introduction of Buddhist literature to Korea from China and of the printing of Korean editions of the standard Buddhist works during the Koryŏ period.

03-115. RHI, Ki-yŏng. "Wŏnhyo and His Thought." *Korea Journal* 11(1)(January 1971):4–9. A brief sketch of the life and career of the Buddhist monk Wŏnhyo (617–686) is followed by a list of his extant writings and an examination of some of the major themes in these writings, particularly his concept of enlightenment and his views of morality.

03-116. VOS, Frits. "Kim Yusin, Persönlichkeit und Mythos." *Oriens Extremus* (Hamburg), 1(1954) and 2 (1955). On religious characteristics seen in the biography of Kim Yu-sin of Silla.

03-117. ZABOROWSKI, Hans-Jurgen. "Der Gelehrte und Staatman Mogŭn Yi Saek." PhD dissertation, Frankfurt, 1971. On the life of Yi Saek (1328–1396), scholar and statesman.

FOREIGN RELATIONS
Korean-Chinese Relations

03-118. IKEUCHI, Hiroshi. "A Study of Lo-lang and Tai-fang, Ancient Chinese Prefectures in Korean Peninsula." *Memoirs of the Research Department of the Tōyō Bunko* 5(1930):79–95. The first part of this article describes the seizure of Liaotung and the Lolang commandery by Kung-sun Tu and Kung-sun K'ang during the declining years of the Han dynasty and the subsequent partition of Lolang to form the separate prefecture of Tai-fang in order, according to Ikeuchi, to improve administrative control and to safeguard Lolang against incursions by the Han tribes of southern Korea. The remainder of the article recounts the Wei dynasty takeover of the Kung-sun peninsular holdings and attempts to elucidate the passages of the *Wei chih* describing the investiture of Han tribal chiefs with titles and seals, the transfer of certain tribal communities from the jurisdiction of Tai-fang to that of Lolang, and the suppression of an ensuing revolt by the Han tribes in 246.

03-119. REISCHAUER, Edwin O. *Ennin's Travels in T'ang China.* New York: Ronald Press, 1955. 341 pp. An interesting picture of the activities of Koreans in ninth-century T'ang China is contained in chap. 8 of this account of the travels of the Japanese Buddhist monk Ennin (793–864), based on his diary. Ennin's observations suggest that Koreans from Silla dominated the East Asian maritime trade during the period of his travels (838–847). Reischauer has added, from other sources, a good summary of the career of Chang Po-go, a Korean who migrated to China, became wealthy, and returned to Korea, where his control of commercial activities led to involvement in politics and, ultimately, to his assassination.

03-120. ROGERS, Michael C. "Sung-Koryŏ Relations: Some Inhibiting Factors." *Oriens* 2(1958):194–202. This article describes the exchange of official envoys between Koryŏ and the Sung court from 1069, when the decline of the Khitan Liao dynasty enabled Koryŏ to resume its former contacts with China, until 1127, when pressure from the

rising Jurchen forced another severance of relations. Rogers focuses on the opposition of certain Sung statesmen to continuation of relations with Koryŏ, illustrating their opposition with excerpts from the memorials of Su Shih, who criticized the size of government expenditures and the private hardships entailed in the trade-tribute system, complained that the Koreans would give vital security information to the Khitan, and expressed the belief that the system was being maintained only for the benefit of Sung traders who sought profit from overseas ventures.

Korean-Japanese Relations

03-121. ANSELMO, Valerio. "Fonti coreani sul Giappone protostorico." In *Il Giappone.* Rome: 1970. Korean-Japanese relations during the fourth and fifth centuries AD.

03-122. ASH, James K. "Korea in the Making of the Early Japanese State: Preliminary Survey to 815 AD." *Journal of Social Sciences and Humanities* 35(December 1971): 31–48. Ash gives a critical assessment of the character of Japanese studies on early Korean-Japanese relations. He then presents a concise summary of recent research that points to extensive cultural influence of peninsular peoples on Japan up to the ninth century and to the possible identity of the founders of the Yamato state as invaders of Manchu-Korean stock.

03-123. CH'ŎN, Kwan-u. "A New Interpretation of the Problems of Mimana." *Korea Journal* 14(2)(February 1974):9–23 and14(4)(April 1974):31–44. This two-part article attempts to refute the view of many Japanese scholars that Japanese from the Yamato state governed a portion of southern Korea known as Mimana from the middle of the fourth century until the latter part of the sixth century. In the first part, Ch'ŏn questions whether the capability existed for Japanese to send an expedition to the peninsula or to control a large portion of it. He contrasts the Korean and Japanese sources on the subject, attempts to define the location of Mimana, and examines such evidence as the inscription on the stele commemorating King Kwang-gaet'o and the Paekche sword preserved in the Ishikami temple in Japan. The second part of the article is a detailed examination of the account of Mimana in the *Nihon shoki,* the major source for the Japanese interpretation. Ch'ŏn concludes that a Japanese expedition, perhaps from northern Kyushu rather than the Yamato region, did operate on the peninsula for six years (399–404) before being destroyed by Koguryŏ, but that no Japanese government of Mimana ever existed. He hypothesizes that the *Nihon shoki* account is an adaptation of Paekche accounts of its relations with Kaya to describe supposed Japanese relations with Mimana and that this was the result of deliberate misrepresentation by Paekche scholars who participated in the writing of the Japanese work.

03-124. COURANT, Maurice. "La Corée jusqu'au IXe siècle." *T'oung Pao* 1(9)(1898). On Korean-Japanese relations before the ninth century and Korean influence on the formation of Japanese culture.

03-125. HAZARD, Benjamin Harrison, Jr. "Japanese Marauding in Medieval Korea: The Wakō Impact on Late Koryŏ." PhD dissertation, University of California, Berkeley, 1967. 379 pp. Abstracted in *DAI* 28(January 1968):2617-18-A; UM 68076. This study deals primarily with the Japanese pirate *(wakō)* activity in Korea during its peak period: from the first major raid in 1350 until the overthrow of Koryŏ in 1392. In addition to a chronological narrative of the *wakō* raids of this period, Hazard discusses the nature of traditional Korean-Japanese relations and the earlier *wakō* raids. He examines the conditions that gave rise to piratical activities, the identity and motives of the *wakō*, the influence of the Mongols and conditions in China on Korea's attempts to cope with the pirates, and the impact of the raids on the economy of Koryŏ and the fate of the ruling dynasty.

03-126. _____. "The Formative Years of the Wakō, 1223-68." *Monumenta Nipponica* 22(3/4)(1967):260-277. This article centers on the conditions that gave rise to the Japanese pirate raids on the southern coast of Korea in the early thirteenth century and analyzes the effects of the raids on Koryŏ relations with Japan.

03-127. SEOH, M. S. "A Brief Documentary Survey of Japanese Pirate Activities in Korea in the 13th–15th Centuries." *Journal of Korean Studies* 1(1)(July–December 1969):23–39. Though lacking in focus, this article, drawn from the writer's MA thesis, provides a modest amount of information on sources available for the study of Japanese pirate raids in Korea, the frequency of the raids, and some of the causes of the piracy.

03-128. SUEMATSU, Yasukazu. "Japan's Relations with the Asian Continent and the Korean Peninsula (Before 950 AD)." *Cahiers d'Histoire Mondiale* 4(3)(1958):671–687. In this largely narrative account of Japanese relations with the continent from earliest contacts with the Han Chinese colonies in Korea until the T'ang era, Suematsu gives a concise statement of the view widely accepted among Japanese scholars regarding the existence of a Japanese-governed state of Mimana in southern Korea. Japanese domination, if not organized government, in this area is said to have begun around 366 and to have lasted until 562, with a strong Japanese influence being maintained in the peninsula even thereafter. The latter part of the article

stresses Japanese efforts to import Chinese culture, first through Paekche and Silla and then directly from Sui and T'ang.

03-129. SZCZESNIAK, Boleslaw. "The Sumu-Sanu Myth." *Monumenta Nipponica* 10(1/2)(April 1954):107–126. Szczesniak compares the foundation myth of the ruling dynasty of Japan as recorded in the *Kojiki* and *Nihon shoki* with the foundation myth of Koguryŏ as recorded on the stele commemorating King Kwanggaet'o and in earlier Chinese sources. He adduces common features in the myths to support the proposition that the Japanese myth was derived from the earliest Korean myth of Chu-mong.

03-130. THAYER, Nathaniel B. "The Suppression of Japanese Piracy Along the Korean Coast in the Second Half of the Fourteenth Century." *Researches in the Social Sciences of Japan* 2(1959):1–8. This is a summary of a longer, unpublished research paper examining the basis of Korean success in suppressing Japanese piracy in the latter part of the Koryŏ period and the early years of the Yi dynasty. This summary treats concisely the reasons for the growth of piracy in the fourteenth century, Korean diplomatic exchanges with the Ashikaga authorities in Kyōto and Kyushu, domestic policies initiated to prevent piracy after the beginning of the Yi dynasty, and Korean negotiations with the powerful Japanese families controlling the Shimonoseki Straits and Tsushima.

03-131. TSCHÖ, Hyŏnbä. "Beziehungen zwischen Japan und Korea in alter Zeit." In *Koreanica*. Baden-Baden: August Lutzeyer, 1960. A clarification of the Korean origins of Japanese civilization, mostly from the linguistic and historical viewpoints.

Korean-Mongol Relations

03-132. HENTHORN, W[illiam] E. *Korea: The Mongol Invasions*. Leiden: Brill, 1963. 252 pp. Part 1 of this study, constituting about four-fifths of the book, is a chronological narrative account of the Mongol invasions of Korea from 1218 until the final submission of Koryŏ with the collapse of the revolt of the Three Patrols (Sambyŏlch'o) in 1270–1273. Part 2 provides an analysis of the demands made by the Mongols on Koryŏ, including the sending of hostages, payment of tribute, submission of population registers, provisioning of the Mongol army, various levies and gifts, ship construction, and establishment of post stations and resident commissioners. In an appendix, the author discusses the origins, composition, and function of various Koryŏ military units.

03-133. LEDYARD, Gari. "Two Mongol Documents from the Koryŏ Sa." *Journal of the American Oriental Society* 83(2)(April–June 1963):225–239. Texts and English translations, with commentary, of two Mongol documents presented to Koryŏ authorities in 1231–1232 and preserved in the *Koryŏ sa.* The documents (an edict and a letter) are interesting examples of the demands made upon Korea by the invading Mongols.

Others

03-134. ANSELMO, Valerio. "Alcune inedattezze a proposito delle invasioni dei Rebelli rossi in Corea (1359, 1361)." *Annali dell' Istituto Universitario Orientale* (Naples), 32(1972). A study of the Red Turbans invasions in the fourteenth century.

03-135. KOH, Byong-ik. "Korea's Contacts with 'The Western Regions' in Pre-Modern Times." *Sahoe kwahak* 2(1958):55–73. Koh surveys contacts between Korea and the countries of southwest and west Asia from the fourth century to the end of the Koryŏ period, when such contacts were cut off by the adoption of a pro-Ming, anti-Mongol policy. Most attention is given to the travels of monks who went as far as India in search of scriptures after the introduction of Buddhism to Korea in the late fourth century, to the activities of Arab merchants who visited the peninsula during the Koryŏ period, and to the role of Muslims in Korea during the period of Mongol domination.

03-136. ROGERS, Michael C. "The Regularization of Koryŏ-Chin Relations (1116–1131)." *Central Asiatic Journal* 6(1)(1961)51–84. An account of the diplomatic relations between Koryŏ and the Jurchen at the time of the founding of the Chin dynasty, which claimed the vassalage of Koryŏ by virtue of conquest of the Khitan Liao state. Much of the account centers on the Jurchen demand for a sworn oath of allegiance and Korean resistance to that demand. In addition, the article recapitulates Koryŏ relations with Liao and examines the effect of the Jurchen on Koryŏ relations with the Sung court of China. Also of interest is Rogers' characterization of the contending factions in the debate over Koryŏ policy toward Chin: one faction is portrayed as conservative, Confucianistic, and realistic in international relations; the other is depicted as nativistic, imperialistic, and visionary.

03-137. _____. "Koryŏ's Military Dictatorship and Its Relations with Chin." *T'oung Pao* 47(1/2)(1959):43–62. This study, based on a comparison of accounts in the *Koryŏ sa* and the *Chin shih,* centers on the representations and misrepresentations made by Koryŏ in order to secure investiture by the emperor of Chin of Kings Myŏngjong (reigned 1171–1197), Sinjong (reigned 1198–1204), and Kangjong (reigned 1212–1213), whose accessions to the throne were dictated by the military officials who dominated the Koryŏ government during the years following the coup d'état of 1170.

HISTORIOGRAPHY

03-138. CHAVANNES, Edouard. "Les monuments de l'Ancien royaume coréenne Kao-kiu-li." *T'oung Pao* 2(9) (1908). Translation and explanation of the inscription on the monument of King Kwanggaet'o (375–431).

03-139. GARDINER, K. H. J. "The Hou-Han-shu as Source for the Early Expansion of Koguryŏ." *Monumenta Serica* 28(1969): 148–187. After a close comparison of sources, Gardiner concludes that the *Hou-Han shu* contains much valuable information not otherwise available on political developments in northern Korea and Manchuria during the first and second centuries AD, particularly regarding the expansion of Koguryŏ, although the *San-kuo chih* must be considered the basic source for information about the tribal structure of this region. Substantial portions of the article consist of direct comparisons of passages from the annals and the chapter on the Eastern Barbarians of the *Hou-Han shu* and from the section on the Eastern Barbarians in the *Wei shu* of the *San-kuo chih.*

03-140. _____. "The Samguk-sagi and Its Sources." *Papers on Far Eastern History* 2(September 1970):1–42. Gardiner first discusses the salient characteristics of the *Samguk sagi,* including Kim Pu-sik's adaptation of the structure of the Chinese dynastic histories; the paucity of his sources as indicated by the frequent repetition of material; his selective reliance on Chinese histories (sometimes altering or ignoring their accounts, sometimes adopting them *in toto*); his imposition of a Confucian tone on ancient Korean records; and his emphasis on legitimate succession. Gardiner then discusses the sources used by Kim Pu-sik in compiling the histories of the Three Kingdoms, with particular attention to identifying the earlier works that may have survived as major elements in the *Samguk sagi.*

03-141. JAMIESON, John C. "Collapse of the T'ang Silla Alliance—Chinese and Korean Accounts Compared." In Frederic Wakeman, Jr. (ed.), *"Nothing Concealed": Essays in Honor of Liu Yü-yün.* Occasional Series, no. 4. Taipei: Chinese Materials and Research Aids Service Center, 1970. The writer shows in this article that the *Samguk sagi,* while generally disappointing as an independent source for the study of Korean-Chinese relations, contributes significantly to an understanding of the events of the 670s when Silla, having defeated Paekche and Koguryŏ in alliance with T'ang China, then maneuvered to expel the Chinese from the peninsula. A comparison of the information in the Silla annals of the *Samguk sagi* with the accounts of the activities of the six T'ang military officials known to have participated in the peninsular campaigns recorded in the *Chiu T'ang shu, Hsin T'ang shu,* and *Tzu-chih t'ung-chien* suggests deliberate efforts to gloss over the T'ang defeat and testifies, Jamieson argues, to the independent historiographical attitude of the compiler of the *Samguk sagi.*

03-142. LI, Ogg. "Sources historiques pour l'histoire de Koguryŏ." Doctoral dissertation, University of Paris, 1968. Mimeographed. Contains a translation of the section on Koguryŏ in the *Samguk sagi,* as well as comparative examination of this account and the accounts in Chinese and Japanese historical documents. Supplemented by abundant annotation.

03-143. ROGERS, Michael C. "The Thanatochronology of Some Kings of Silla." *Monumenta Serica* 19(1960):335–348. This article analyzes Kim Pu-sik's use of Chinese sources on Silla-T'ang relations in the compilation of the *Samguk sagi* and attempts to judge which account is the more reliable in those cases in which Kim diverges from the Chinese chronology. Study of the dates of death of the nine kings of Silla from 702 to 826 indicates that Silla sometimes kept the T'ang court ill-informed about successions; Kim apparently could not accept the possibility of deliberate subterfuge in Silla's relations with the Chinese and hence adjusted the dates of certain investitures and embassies. In a number of cases, Rogers attempts to refute the conclusions of Suematsu Yasukazu in his *Shiragi-shi no shomondai.*

03-144. _____. "Some Kings of Koryŏ as Registered in Chinese Works." *Journal of the American Oriental Society* 81(4)(September–December 1961):415–422. Rogers here examines the omission from Chinese sources of the third

king of Koryŏ (Chŏngjong; reigned 945–949), probably as a result of Korean subterfuge stemming from the succession struggle after the death of the founder of the dynasty. Rogers also investigates the substitution of the name of the omitted king for that of the eleventh ruler (Hŏnjong; reigned 1094–1095) and the appearance of a fictitious ruler said to have reigned in the early eleventh century.

03-145. _____. "Sukchong of Koryŏ: His Accession and His Relations with Liao." *T'oung Pao* 47(1/2)(1959):30–42. A comparative analysis of the *Koryŏ sa* and *Liao shih* accounts of the accession of King Sukchong (reigned 1095–1105), who succeeded to the throne under suspect conditions following the brief reign of his juvenile nephew. Reveals considerable subterfuge and fabrication of documents on the part of Koryŏ officials and illustrates the need for caution in using the Koryŏ dynastic annals as a source for the study of international relations.

03-146. SAISON, Camille. *Les origines de la Corée.* Peking: Typographie du Pe-t'ang, 1895. The title of this book indicates that it treats the origins of the Korean people, but actually it is a translation, with brief annotation, of the first chapter of the *Tongguk t'onggam,* by Sŏ Kŏ-jŏng (1420–1488) et al. Entitled "Oe Ki," the chapter covers Tan'gun Chosŏn, Kija Chosŏn, Wiman Chosŏn, the Sagun (the Four Commanderies), Ibu, and Samhan.

03-147. SZCZESNIAK, Boleslaw. "The Kōtaiō Monument." *Monumenta Nipponica* 7(1/2)(1951):242–268. In the first half of this article, the author describes the stele erected to commemorate the Koguryŏ king Kwanggaet'o in 414, the inscription on the monument, and the various reproductions made of the inscription. The latter half of the article consists of the text of the inscription in Chinese characters and English translation based on three different rubbings and a number of published readings.

III. THE YI (CHOSŎN) DYNASTY BEFORE 1876

by Yŏng-ho Ch'oe

INTRODUCTION

THE YI DYNASTY (also known as the Chosŏn dynasty for its official designation) was one of the longest continuous regimes in the annals of humankind, lasting 518 years from 1392 to 1910. Chronologically, it was during this dynasty that the world witnessed the rise of the Western nations to a position of dominance throughout the world. As an aftermath of this dramatic change, Korea was compelled to move from what is now known as the traditional to the modern era during the last several decades of the Yi dynasty—a transition that resulted in the loss of its political entity as an independent state.

Historiographically, the last dynasty of Korea received unusually harsh treatment until very recently. Indeed, few regimes in world history have been more reviled by posterity. Perhaps two factors may explain this treatment. First, the study of Korean history in modern times before 1945 was largely dominated by Japanese scholars, many of whom consciously or unconsciously distorted Korean history by presenting Korean society as backward and dormant in order to justify Japanese rule. Second, the trauma the Korean people experienced in losing independence for the first time in their long history was so shocking that it led many Korean intellectuals to look for a scapegoat upon whom they could heap all the blame. For them, the Yi dynasty represented an era of domination by the alien ideology of Confucianism and corrosive decline in independent spirit.

Since Korea's liberation from Japan in 1945, however, historians in both North and South Korea, inspired by a new nationalistic ethos, have assumed the ambitious task of rediscovering their historical legacies and have published a number of important studies offering significant new interpretations of Yi dynasty history. Although one may fault the intemperate nationalistic exuberance that often overflows in Korean scholarship, these new studies in general mark a substantial advancement in historical studies in both North and South Korea.

Historical scholarship in South Korea in recent years has been particularly facilitated by the publication and reprinting of a large number of important historical source materials and works. Especially significant are the publications—brought out under the auspices of Kuksa P'yŏnch'an Wiwŏnhoe (The National History Compilation Committee) in Seoul—of source materials of prime historical importance. These publications include *Chosŏn wangjo sillok* [The veritable records of the Yi dynasty], *Pibyŏnsa tŭngnok* [The records of the Border Defense Command], *Sŭngjŏngwŏn ilgi* [The daily records of the Royal Secretariat], and the writings and works of private individuals. Easy availability of these primary sources, combined with more sophisticated and careful scholarship, has elevated historical studies in Korea to new heights. Unfortunately, most of these works are not available in English. Only a limited number of them appear in English translations in two journals: the *Journal of Social Sciences and Humanities,* published by the Korean Research Center as its bulletin, and *Korea Journal,* published monthly by the

Korean National Commission for UNESCO, both in Seoul. Fujiya Kawashima has made a useful survey of the historical studies in South Korea published in a recent issue of *Korean Studies* under the title "Historiographic Development in South Korea: State and Society from the Mid-Koryŏ to the Mid-Yi Dynasty." On North Korea's historiography, Yŏng-ho Ch'oe's study explains how history is perceived and used in North Korea.

Founded by Neo-Confucian scholar-officials, the Yi dynasty accepted from its inception the teachings of Chu Hsi as its official ideology, and the zealous scholar-officials attempted in good faith to realize the ideal world envisioned by the Confucian sages throughout the dynasty. In spite of the importance of the Neo-Confucian ideology, there have been very few studies on the subject. There are, however, three studies worth mentioning here. Pow-Key Sohn, in one of his dissertation chapters, discusses how China-centered ideology competed against Korea-centered ideology during the first two hundred years of the dynasty. Martina Deuchler posits in her short essay the interesting hypothesis that, in constructing the ideological foundation of Neo-Confucianism for the Yi dynasty, Neo-Confucianists applied and elaborated the concept of "proper ritual behavior" *(ye)* during the dynastic transition. Chŏng To-jŏn, on the other hand, was one of the main architects and the chief ideologist in the founding of the dynasty, and Korean scholar Han Yŏng-u recently made a comprehensive study of the thought of Chŏng To-jŏn; a part of this study appears in an English version in *Korea Journal.*

In the middle of the sixteenth century, Korea produced a host of Neo-Confucian studies and developed a metaphysical system based largely on Chu Hsi-ist themes. Yi Hwang (T'oegye) was undoubtedly most influential in defining the Korean orthodoxy of Chu Hsi philosophy through the voluminous commentaries and interpretations for which he was widely respected by Confucian scholars not only in Korea but also in Tokugawa Japan. Contrary to the criticism often lodged against him by modern scholars, Yi Hwang was not an obsequious follower of Chu Hsi who accepted the latter's teachings uncritically. He was a man of independent mind, who, as Abe Yoshio points out, even took issue with Chu Hsi on some points. Yi Hwang, however, represented an extreme conservative wing of Neo-Confucianism subscribing to a rigid interpretation of the Chu Hsi doctrine. (Largely because of Yi's condemnation, the teachings of Wang Yang-ming were branded as heresy and attracted only a small number of followers in Korea.) Yi I (Yulguk), on the other hand, was a practical thinker. Devoting most of his career to government service, Yi I advocated a number of reforms, mostly aimed at alleviating the burdens of the peasants. Unlike many of his contemporaries, Yi I believed in revising those laws that had become obsolete or served no useful purpose. Sŏ Kyŏng-dŏk (Hwadam) enjoyed a far less illustrious career than the other two, having spent most of his life in humble circumstances. Many modern scholars, however, regard him to have been a greater seminal mind than Yi Hwang or Yi I. Sŏ's metaphysical system was built upon the notion of the absolute primacy of ch'i (ether; ki in Korean).

One intellectual issue that preoccupied the mind of most Yi dynasty scholars was the debate over li (principle; i in Korean) and ch'i. Interestingly, each of the three scholars just mentioned maintained his own unique position on this issue. While Sŏ Kyŏng-dŏk believed in the supremacy of ch'i, Yi Hwang supported the primacy of li over all other elements. Yi I, on the other hand, adhered to the notion that li and ch'i are inseparable and that neither can function without the other. Scholars in Yi Korea in general followed one of these three positions and consumed much of their energy and time debating this issue. For a long time, an outline study by Key P. Yang and Gregory Henderson was the sole English work on the philosophical and metaphysical aspect of Yi Neo-Confucianism. Recently, however, Munsang Seoh has published a very perceptive study on the metaphysical issue of li and ch'i as debated by Yi Hwang and Yi I and their respective followers, delineating at the same time factional ties that arose from the disputes. Moreover, in his recent University of Hawaii dissertation, "Portents and Politics in Early Yi Korea, 1392–1519," Seong Rae Park has made a provocative study of how the Neo-Confucianists used extraordinary natural phenomena—which they called portents—to establish their own orthodox system of Neo-Confucianism in the early part of the Yi dynasty.

As is well known, the basic governmental institutions of the Yi dynasty were largely borrowed from China; but they were modified to suit the needs and climate of Korea. Although a comprehensive treatment in English of the organization and working of the Yi government is still lacking, Edward Wagner provides a succinct summary of the duties and functions of the major offices in the central government in his book *The Literati Purges*. In exercising the royal authority, the Yi rulers in general, unlike the Chinese emperors, enjoyed no prerogatives of absolute rule. As Pow-Key Sohn points out in his important dissertation, "Social History of the Early Yi Dynasty," powerful ideological and institutional checks were placed upon the monarchs, and it was extremely difficult, if not impossible for the Yi rulers to exercise their authority arbitrarily. If Yi Korea produced no despotic rulers like Hung-wu or Yung-lo of Ming China, she also permitted no single minister or official like Chang Chu-chen or Wei Chung-hsien of Ming to gain preponderant political power. As Edward Wagner's studies indicate, the censorate institutions under the Yi dynasty played an extremely important role in providing checks and balances in the allocation of power and authority within the government. The process of decision-making is also a subject that has received little attention among scholars and, hence, very little is known. From Ching Young Choe's study, "Kim Yuk and the Taedongbŏp Reform," however, one gets some idea of the tortuous way a decision was reached on a major reform program within the Korean court.

Being a Confucian state, the Yi dynasty placed utmost emphasis on rule by men of virtue and merit and immediately instituted the civil service examination system as the main channel of recruiting officials for government services. The officials so selected were then subject to periodic evaluation of their public performance, which in turn provided the basis for promotion within the bureaucratic ranks. Yŏng-ho Ch'oe's studies focus upon the civil service examination and its effect on the social structure of early Yi.

Toward the end of the fifteenth century, however, a serious split within the bureaucratic ranks began to surface and eventually led to the bloody literati purges and the factional strife that bedeviled the politics and government of Yi Korea. Historians in Korea and Japan explain the literati purges largely in terms of a conflict between the old aristocrats *(hun'gu)* and a new breed of scholar-officials *(sarim)* involving different ideological outlooks and economic interests. Edward Wagner's studies inject a new element in the interpretation of the literati purges. The purges, according to Wagner, involved a fundamental constitutional issue arising from sustained conflict between the monarchical and executive authority on the one hand and the censorial organs that demanded a greater voice in the council of government on the other. Wagner traces the growth of power on the part of the censorial organs during these purges. On the obviously important question of the factional strife, however, studies thus far have not progressed much beyond mere anecdotal recountings of events centering on the personality differences of the individuals involved.

Of all the historical periods of Korea, the historian's view of the late Yi dynasty period after the Hideyoshi and the Manchu invasions of the late sixteenth and early seventeenth centuries has perhaps undergone the most substantial revision in recent years. It was long believed that Yi Korea was never able to recover politically, socially, and economically from the devastation suffered from the two foreign invasions and that she remained stagnant and sterile until the coming of Japan and the Western powers in the last half of the nineteenth century. A number of recent studies in both South and North Korea have exploded this view. These studies show that considerable economic activity and growth took place during the period, and scholars in both North and South Korea claim, reaching a similar conclusion independently, that the rise of "incipient capitalism" (within the Marxian historical stages) can be traced to as early as the seventeenth or eighteenth century. Although certain emotional partiality is evident in some of these studies, the evidence presented seems sufficient to revise our earlier notion of the economic doldrums and backwardness of late Yi Korea. In the United States, in the meantime, Susan Shin has studied the question of land tenure and the agrarian economy in the seventeenth and eighteenth centuries from a more detached perspective. She finds the socioeconomic problems engendered by the economic changes far more complex than have hitherto been believed and concludes: "Economic advances undoubtedly occurred, but official inertia and traditional corruption often prevented these advances from making their full impact."

The discovery of a group of scholars of the seventeenth and eighteenth centuries now identified as the school of practical learning *(sirhak)* has been a source of great pride for Korean historians, and a large number of works—some of which have been translated into English—have appeared in Korea studying their life, thought, and wide-ranging reform programs. Against the background of the rigid Neo-Confucian orthodoxy, the *sirhak* scholars' scientific and pragmatic approach and their genuine concern for the welfare of the ordinary people and biting criticism of the prevalent socioeconomic inequities and the *yangban* establishment are understandably very appealing to the present generation of Korean scholars who are anxious to find a source of inspiration for their nationalism. In their enthusiasm for the *sirhak,* more and more scholars are now discovering the seeds of Korean "modernism" in the *sirhak* ideas, long before the coming of Japan and the West. Although it is true that many iconoclastic aspects of *sirhak* thought are surprisingly modern, it is important to keep in mind that the *sirhak* scholars of the seventeenth and eighteenth centuries were essentially Confucianists who envisioned restoration of what they believed to be the proper Confucian order that had gone astray.

While the new interpretation of the economy and the intellectual trend of late Yi has been brought about almost entirely through the work of Korean historians, scholars in the United States have made some important contributions to the studies of the social stratification in the last half of the dynasty. The pioneering studies on this question were made by a Japanese scholar, Shikata Hiroshi, in the 1930s with his analyses of the household registers *(hojŏk)* of the city of Taegu in four different periods from 1690 to 1858, during which time Shikata found a tremendous upward social mobility. In the 1960s, Kim Yong-sŏp published a series of articles studying the land registers of several districts in the eighteenth and early nineteenth centuries, establishing correlation between landownership and social mobility. While John Somerville's study of social mobility in the district of Ulsan in the eighteenth century generally confirms the conclusions of Shikata and Kim Yong-sŏp, studies of the late seventeenth century by Susan Shin and Edward Wagner of Kŭmhwa and the Northern District of Seoul, respectively, show a strong downward social mobility. Although the conclusions reached by Shikata, Kim, and Somerville, on the one hand, and by Wagner and Shin, on the other, seem at variance on the surface, they are not necessarily inconsistent when closely examined. The compositions of status classification as of the late seventeenth century in all three studies by Shikata, Wagner, and Shin are not much different from each other; and, according to Shikata, Kim, and Somerville, the trend of upward mobility took place in the eighteenth and nineteenth centuries—the period which Wagner and Shin did not cover. Whatever the trend of social change may have been, it is important to keep in mind that the increase in the proportion of the *yangban* population did not necessarily entail a corresponding rise in opportunities for power and privilege for those with newly acquired *yangban* status.

As we move into the nineteenth century, the socioeconomic changes had been so extensive that the traditional order was no longer able to contain the ferment that had been brewing for some time. To compound the situation, the royal family was simply biologically unable to sire an heir who could live long enough to reach maturity. For more than sixty years after the death of King Chŏngjo in 1800, the throne was occupied by boy kings in succession, and twice during that period the heir had to be adopted into the royal family from an obscure line. Such a situation created a power vacuum at the apex of the government, permitting the consort families to wield undue influence. Signs of the disintegration of the traditional order were evident in many sectors, and the central government was unable to cope with the situation effectively. The series of rebellions that Korea witnessed during the period were at once a reflection and a cause of such crisis. The challenge of the Western powers against the century-old East Asian world order came just at this junction.

Such an unsettling climate certainly was conducive to the rise of new religions. Catholicism was first introduced into Korea by a group of intellectuals by way of China during the seventeenth century. Fascinated at first by the new science and technology the Jesuit missionaries had brought into China, a small number of Korean scholars began to embrace the Catholic belief and in time it spread to a substantial number of people of all ranks in late Yi Korea. Korean historians cite political, social, economic, and psychological factors to explain this phenomenon. Charles Dallet's two-volume work, *Histoire de l'église de Corée,* published in 1874, remains not only a classic study but also a valuable source for further studies. Chai-sik Chung gives a masterful analysis of the intellectual arguments against the Catholic teaching made by the representative Neo-Confucian scholars in Korea.

Of the many native religions and beliefs that rose in this period, the Tonghak was by far the most important. It was as a reaction to the spread of Catholicism that the Tonghak teaching was first expounded and proselytized by its founder, Ch'oe Che-u, and it quickly spread among the peasants and other underprivileged people. Its egalitarian concept of *in nae ch'ŏn* (''Man is God'') and the promise of a paradise in this world were particularly appealing to the downtrodden and the discontented. The subsequent growth of the Tonghak into a formidable political and nationalistic force is well known. Benjamin B. Weems gives a concise general history of the Tonghak up to 1950 in his *Reform, Rebellion and the Heavenly Way.* The eclectic nature of Ch'oe Che-u's doctrine is analyzed by Key Ray Chong, while various theological aspects are studied by Yong Choon Kim. The interpretation of the role that Tonghak played as a political and social force in the 1890s has undergone significant revision since 1945. The earlier view of the Tonghak movement as a reactionary and xenophobic force has generally been rejected, and scholars in both North and South Korea now treat it as a patriotic and progressive revolutionary force. Chong-sik Lee, in his classic study of modern Korean nationalism, places the Tonghak movement of the 1890s within the purview of modern nationalism.

The ascension to the throne by twelve-year-old King Kojong in 1864 provided the opportunity for his father, Taewŏn'gun, to seize power and rule the country with an iron hand for the next twelve years. Rarely, if ever, had Korea witnessed such a concentration of power in the hands of one man. Exercising his authority as de facto regent, the Taewŏn'gun instituted many far-reaching reforms. The nature and objectives of the Taewŏn'gun's reform program are still very controversial and being debated among scholars in Korea as well as the United States. The Taewŏn'gun himself is depicted in varying characterizations ranging from a reactionary xenophobe to an early modernizer. Two recent works published in the United States make important contributions to the understanding of the Taewŏn'gun's rule. In *Rule of the Taewŏn'gun*, Ching Young Choe characterizes him as an intellectual heir to the *sirhak* reformers of the seventeenth and eighteenth centuries, who attempted to restore the sagging dynastic fortune to the state of former vigor that he believed had existed at the beginning of the dynasty. James B. Palais' study of the Taewŏn'gun's rule, *Politics and Polity in Traditional Korea,* is one of the most important works on Korea to have come out in many years and elevates American scholarship on Korean history to a new height. The Taewŏn'gun, according to Palais, was basically a pragmatic reformer who wanted to create a virile monarchy and strong central government and sought to preserve the traditional order, but his pragmatic and vigorous approach often came in conflict with the vested interests of the privileged *yangban* and the orthodox Confucian literati. The implications of Palais' study go much beyond the confines of the evaluation of the Taewŏn'gun's rule. His theory of equilibrium and stability as applied to the traditional Yi political order is refreshing and goes far to explain why and how the traditional order was unable to cope with the extraordinary situation Korea came to confront in the nineteenth century.

Korea's diplomatic relations with China during the Yi dynasty were governed largely by the concept known as *sadae* (respect for the senior state). The term *sadae,* however, has become to the nationalistic-minded Koreans in the twentieth century a pejorative word synonymous with servile and obsequious in dealing with a foreign country. This is a rather unfortunate distortion of Korea's traditional relationship with China that has been caused largely by applying the yardstick of the modern Western concept of international relations to the traditional world order in East Asia before the arrival of the Western powers. If we are to gain a proper understanding of Korea's controversial relations with China, it is vitally important that we take several hitherto unexamined factors into consideration—the cultural milieu within which the two countries interacted, the configuration of power between the two, and the common military interests shared by both China and Korea against the threat of the so-called northern barbarians.

The Chinese World Order edited by John K. Fairbank contains several articles explaining the Chinese perception of the Asian world order. Frederick Nelson in his *Korea and the Old Orders in Eastern Asia* gives the most perceptive explanation and analysis so far of the theoretical basis on which Korea's traditional relations with China operated. Yŏng-ho Ch'oe's study on the other hand examines the tension and problem created in the traditional Sino-Korean relations when challenged by France and the United States in 1866 and 1871, respectively, applying largely Nelson's theoretical framework and partly expanding on it. Several studies by Hae-Jong Chun illustrate the actual operation of Korea's diplomatic relationship with Ch'ing, including a detailed account of expenditures involved.

BIBLIOGRAPHY

POLITICS AND SOCIETY
Politics

03-148. BACON, Wilbur D. (trans.). "Records of Reprimands and Admonitions (Chingbirok)." *Transactions of the Korea Branch of the Royal Asiatic Society* 47(1972): 7-24. A translation of a portion of the introductory part of *Chingbirok,* an important Korean account of the Hideyoshi invasion of 1592 by Yu Sŏng-yong (1542-1607), who was one of the key officials during the war.

03-149. CHOE, Ching Young. "Kim Yuk (1580-1658) and the Taedongbŏp Reform." *Journal of Asian Studies* 23(November 1963):21-35. This is a study of Kim Yuk's role in the introduction of Taedongbŏp, an important land tax reform, in the seventeenth century. In addition to explaining the nature of the tribute tax system, it gives a good picture of how a decision was made on a major issue at the highest level of the Yi dynasty government by carefully examining the process of enactment of the Taedongbŏp.

03-150. CH'OE Ch'ang-gyu. "Remonstration System from Politico-Cultural Viewpoint." *Korea Journal* 14(2)(February 1974):30-33. A short essay on the system of remonstrance that discusses its role and characteristics during the Yi dynasty.

03-151. CH'OE, Sŭng-hi. "Interrelations of the Monarch and

the Remonstrants in the Early Yi Dynasty.'' *Korea Journal* 15(5)(May 1975):4–11. An interesting study of one aspect of the censorial system in the early Yi dynasty: remonstrance. Treating the system of remonstrance largely as a function of freedom of speech, this article recounts the main incidents involving remonstrance under the first nine rulers of the Yi dynasty and briefly examines the tension they created in the relationship between the monarchs and the censorial officials.

03-152. CH'OE, Yŏng-ho. ''The Civil Examinations and the Social Structure in Early Yi Dynasty Korea: 1392–1600.'' PhD dissertation, University of Chicago, 1971. 251 pp. In studying how the civil examinations might have affected the social structure of early Yi dynasty Korea, the author examines the structure of government and the recruitment system, the organization and processes of civil examinations, the educational system as it related to the examinations, and the social groups that were allowed in the civil examinations.

03-153. CHOI, Suk. ''The Factional Struggle in the Yi Dynasty of Korea, 1575–1725.'' *Koreana Quarterly* 8(1)(Spring 1965):60–91 and 8(2)(Summer 1965):70–96. Gives a relatively detailed factual account of the factional struggle of the period based mostly on secondary sources.

03-154. DALLET, Charles. *Traditional Korea.* Behavior Science Translations. New Haven: Human Relations Area Files, 1954. The English translation of the introduction to a two-volume work, *Histoire de l'Église de Corée,* published in 1874 and based on letters and reports received from French missionaries working in Korea. This is an important work containing valuable information on many aspects of eighteenth- and nineteenth-century Korea: government and politics, the tax system, language, class structure, social life, religious beliefs. Dallet's description of Korea catches her just when the traditional order began to disintegrate, and a biased view of Western missionaries is pronounced throughout the book.

03-155. HAHM, Pyong-Choon. ''A Historical Study of Discriminatory Legislation against the Descendants of Concubines during the Yi Dynasty.'' *Transactions of the Korea Branch of the Royal Asiatic Society* 42(1966). (See 03-174.)

03-156. HAN, Yŏng-u. ''Chŏng To-Jŏn: His Political Reform Thought.'' *Korea Journal* 14(7)(July 1974):45–51 and 14(8)(August 1974):56–61. Chŏng To-jŏn (1337–1398) was one of the main architects in founding the Yi dynasty and acted as chief ideologist and brain trust for the dynastic founder, Yi Sŏng-gye. This is the first English work that studies the political thought of Chŏng To-jŏn. After examining the social conditions leading to the dynastic change and Chŏng's family background, the author analyzes his views on people-centered government (*min-bon,* translated here as ''democracy'') and revolution, benevolent politics and virtuous government, literati, educational opportunity, centralization of government authority, and remonstrance.

03-157. HULBERT, Homer B. ''National Examination in Korea.'' *Transactions of the Korea Branch of the Royal Asiatic Society* 14(1923):9–32. A chronological account of state-sponsored examinations (nature, types, curriculum) to recruit government officials from the Three Kingdoms period through the Yi dynasty based largely on *Chŭngbo munhŏn pigo* and other Korean sources. Contains some erroneous information and not always reliable.

03-158. KAWASHIMA, Fujiya. ''Clan Structure and Political Power in Yi Dynasty Korea—A Case Study of the Munhwa Yu Clan.'' PhD dissertation, Harvard University, 1972. 316 pp. The author examines ''the clan structure by tracing the development of the Munhwa Yu clan and exploring the extent to which the clan maintained political power in traditional Korea'' and argues that ''traditional Korea placed a high value on lineage in the determination of social status and that, for this reason, in studying the *yangban* the individual or his nuclear family cannot be treated apart from'' the clan. By carefully analyzing more than 25,000 members listed in the 1803 edition of the Munhwa Yu genealogy, Kawashima studies, with forty-five different tables and fourteen illustrations, the origins and developments of Korean clans in general as well as the Munhwa Yu clan. He also investigates the relationships between the clan and the *munkwa* lineage, official status and lineage background, clan residence and geopolitics, and mate selection and officialdom.

03-159. KIM, Tschong Dae. ''Die Genremalerei der Yi-zeit als reflecktiertes Bild des Sozialwandels im 18 Jahrhundert.'' *Ostasienwissenschaftliche Beiträge zur Sprache, Literatur, Geschichte, Geistesgeschichte, Wirtschaft, Politik und Geographie.* Vol. 2. Wiesbaden: Veröffentlichungen des Ostasieninstituts der Ruhr-Universität Bochum, 1974. On social changes and customs during the eighteenth century.

03-160. KIM, Yŏng-mo. ''The Social Background and Mobility of State Ministers of the Yi Dynasty.'' *Korean Affairs* 3(2)(July 1964):238–260. A study of the social background of those who served in the three highest posts in the Yi dynasty government, Ŭijŏngbu (The State Council), by a Korean sociologist. Using 352 sample officials selected from the entire Yi period, the author makes a quantitative analysis of their social origin, status background, clan affiliation, and marriage ties in order to determine the extent of social mobility.

03-161. King Seijong Memorial Society. *King Seijong the Great: A Biography of Korea's Most Famous King.* Seoul: 1970. An old-fashioned eulogistic account of the remarkable achievements attained during the reign of King Sejong (reigned 1418–1450) in many fields—the promotion of scholarship, the invention of the Korean alphabet known as *han'gŭl,* the inventory of music, various scientific and technological inventions, reforms in the government and tax system, and securing the northern border of Korea.

03-162. LEE, Kwang-rin. "Census-taking under the Yi Dynasty." *Transactions of the Korea Branch of the Royal Asiatic Society* 35(1959):33–50. A brief study largely of the rules and regulations governing the census-taking system, the *Hop'ae* (Identity Tag) system, and the *Ogat'ong* (Five Households) system to control population registration during the Yi dynasty.

03-163. LEE, Peter H. *Songs of Flying Dragons: A Critical Reading.* Cambridge, Mass.: Harvard University Press, 1975. Prepared as a eulogy cycle of poems to celebrate the founding of the Yi dynasty, the *Songs of Flying Dragons (Yongbi ŏch'ŏn ka)* are important historical, philological, and literary documents. Historically, they are a "manifesto of the policies of the new state and a mirror for future monarchs," in addition to being a valuable historical source for the founding of the Yi dynasty. In this book, the author provides a magnificent historical and literary interpretation and commentary to the *Songs* as well as a superb English translation.

03-164. _____. "The Life and Poetry of Yun Sŏn-do, the Greatest Poet in the *Sijo* Form." *Monumenta Serica* 22(1963): 79–120. One can get a good glimpse of the political situation in seventeenth-century Korea rent by factional struggle from the careful account of the turbulent political career of the great poet Yun Sŏn-do (1587–1671) given in the first ten pages of this article devoted to the study of poetry.

03-165. MESKILL, John. *Ch'oe Pu's Diary: A Record of Drifting across the Sea.* Tucson: University of Arizona Press, 1965. This is a translation of *P'yohae-rok,* a record of drifting across the sea, by Ch'oe Pu (1454–1504). On his way back from the island of Cheju to observe the mourning of his father's death, Ch'oe Pu, a Confucian scholar and middle-rank government official, was inadvertently driven to China by adverse weather. Upon his return to Korea, he recorded meticulously his experiences and observations of the entire journey across the sea and central and northern China. In addition to the detailed description of China, Ch'oe Pu entered his conversations with Chinese officials, in which he explained Korean institutions and social customs. A glimpse into Sino-Korean relationships is also revealing. Of particular interest, however, are the beliefs and deportment of a Korean Neo-Confucianist as depicted illuminatingly throughout Ch'oe Pu's own record. The translator gives a very useful introduction, discussing the characteristics and significance of the book, and also provides helpful footnotes that enhance one's understanding of the main text.

03-166. PALAIS, James B. "Stability in Yi Dynasty Korea: Equilibrium Systems and Marginal Adjustment." *Occasional Papers on Korea* 3(June 1975):1–18. Edited by James B. Palais and Margery D. Lang. This short essay attempts a provocative new interpretation of Yi dynasty history, rejecting the conventional characterizations of Yi history as overly harsh. Holding the view that "one of the main accomplishments of traditional Koreans was the creation of a state, polity, and society that was so self-sufficient and stable that it could continue to hold together for five hundred years, despite all the maladies that beset it," the author discusses very persuasively two concepts—patterns of equilibrium tension and reform as marginal adjustment—as basic to an understanding of the stability and longevity of the Yi dynasty. This important essay also alludes to possible new directions for future study, not only of Yi but also of modern Korean history.

03-167. SCHERZER, M. F. "Tchao-sien-tche." *Journal asiatique* (1886). A translation of the *Chosŏn chi.*

03-168. SOHN, Pow-key. "Social History of the Early Yi Dynasty, 1392–1592: With Emphasis on the Functional Aspects of Governmental Structure." PhD dissertation, University of California, Berkeley, 1963. 523 pp. Abstracted in *DAI* 24(June 1964):5368; UM 64-5307. This is a major study of the Yi dynasty ideology and institutions—the decision-making, the historians, the censorate—that examines in detail the functioning of these institutions, especially the power relationships between the monarchy and the *yangban* bureaucracy. The author's main thesis is that the Confucian ideology and institutions borrowed from China were utilized by the *yangban* officials in the early Yi dynasty to curtail the power and authority of the Korean kings. This is an extremely important and provocative study of the Yi dynasty government. A part of chap. 1 (The Monarch and Ideology) is reproduced in "Power Versus Status: The Role of Ideology During the Early Yi Dynasty," *Tongbang hakchi* 10(1969):209–253. A part of chap. 3 (The Monarchy and the Historians) appears in

"The Concept of History and Korean Yangban," *International Journal of Korean Studies* 1(1973):93–115. (See 03-268.)

03-169. SONG, June-ho. "The Government Examination Rosters of the Yi Dynasty." In Spencer J. Palmer (ed.), *Studies in Asian Genealogy*. Provo, Utah: Brigham Young University Press, 1972. After giving an outline of the examination system of the Yi dynasty, the author explores the nature and purpose of publishing various kinds of examination rosters and their value as research material. Nine tables given at the end on such themes as the frequency of the examination and the number of graduates, the major clan representation, and the postexamination careers of *saengwŏn* and *chinsa* are very useful.

03-170. WAGNER, Edward Willett. *The Literati Purges: Political Conflict in Early Yi Korea*. Cambridge, Mass.: East Asian Research Center, Harvard University, 1974. This book is a detailed study, based on *sillok* (veritable records) and other primary sources, of the first three of the four major literati purges that broke out from 1489 to 1545. Treating the purges as an early manifestation of the factional strife that characterized the politics of the Yi dynasty after the mid-sixteenth century, the author introduces a fresh interpretation by focusing on the growth of power on the part of the censorate. He contends that the purges came about as a result of sustained conflict between the censoring organs and the more highly constituted authority of the government and the palace. The author concludes that although the censoring bodies suffered a temporary setback at each of the purges, they in effect gained greater stature and power in the end and eventually became an instrument of a single power group who gained office, serving their parochial interests and abdicating their original role as arbiter. The author then posits an interesting hypothesis that the factional strife in Yi Korea may have served a certain functional purpose in resolving political conflict. This is an extremely important study of the politics and institutions of the early Yi dynasty. Appendix A gives lists of government offices and posts in the Yi government in both Korean and English which can be used as a standard reference.

03-171. _____. "The Recommendation Examination of 1519: Its Place in Early Yi Dynasty History." *Chōsen gakuhō* 15(1969):1–80. This is a study of the literati purge that took place in 1519, in which the recommendation examination became the focal point of contention. After examining the historical background, the author analyzes various factors that contributed to the outbreak of the 1519 purge. The author's thesis, as embodied in greater

scope in his recent book, *The Literati Purges: Political Conflict in Early Yi Korea,* is that the purge was essentially the result of conflict between the censorial organs and the more highly constituted governmental authority. This is an important study not only of the politics but also of the censorial institutions and some aspects of the examination system in early Yi Korea.

03-172. WŎN, Yu-han. "On the Monetary Theory of Yu Hyŏng-wŏn (Pan'gye)." *Journal of Social Sciences and Humanities* 33(December 1970):1–12. Studies of Yu Hyŏng-wŏn's idea in advocating the use and circulation of currency as a medium of exchange.

03-173. _____. "Socio-Economic Thought of Kim Yuk." *Korea Journal* 15(1)(January 1975):44–54. The adoption and implementation of the *Taedongbŏp* (the law of great equity), which imposed a uniform tax on land and commuted all other sundry tribute tax, and the circulation of currency in the mid-seventeenth century were the main stimulants of the economic growth of the last half of the Yi dynasty. The man chiefly responsible for the adoption of these two reform measures was Kim Yuk (1580–1658). This article is a simple account of the historical background on how Kim Yuk pushed the two measures through to final implementation.

Law

03-174. HAHM, Pyong-Choon. *The Korean Political Tradition and Law: Essays in Korean Law and Legal History.* Seoul: Royal Asiatic Society, Korea Branch, 1967. This is a collection of essays dealing with the law and legal history of Korea by an eminent legal scholar. Of the nine essays in this collection, the first three deal with historical issues. The first essay, "The Korean Political Tradition and Law," is a lengthy study of the relationship between the political tradition and law in traditional Korea. After explaining the peculiar aspects of the Korean adoption and adaptation of Confucian ideologies, the author discusses how Korea came to value the rule of ethic rather than the rule of law. Throughout the essay, the author makes many interesting, even provocative, observations on the Korean political tradition from the standpoint of a modern legal historian. The second essay, "The Rule of Royal Succession During the Yi Dynasty," is a general discussion of the ways in which royal successions were carried out throughout the Yi dynasty. As there existed no expressly formulated rules on royal succession, the author delineates the customary rules that obtained during the dynasty. One peculiar aspect of Yi Korea was the sustained social discrimination against the descendants of concubines, who were by statute barred from participating in all civil examinations. The third essay, "An Historical Study of Discriminatory Legislation against the Descendants of Concubines in Korea, 1415–1894 AD," examines the circumstances leading to the enactment of the discriminatory statute, discusses problems it created, and traces various attempts to do away with the discretionary restriction until it was finally abrogated in 1894.

03-175. SHAW, William. "Traditional Korean Law: A New Look." *Korea Journal* 13(9)(September 1973):40–53. A thought-provoking essay reflecting on several aspects of law under the Yi dynasty. After repudiating the notion that there was no written, established, and consistently applied body of law in traditional Korea, the author argues that law and Confucian moral conceptions might have worked together rather than becoming a source of tension. He also explains how law sometimes acts as "a leveling influence" in spite of its manifested class biases, describes how the king was restrained in the legislative process, and finally discusses popular attitudes toward the law.

Economy

03-176. CHUNG, Young-iob. "Kye: A Traditional Economic Institution in Korea." In Andrew C. Nahm (ed.), *Traditional Korea—Theory and Practice*. Kalamazoo: Center for Korean Studies, Western Michigan University, 1974. An economist's study of *kye,* a unique Korean institution that has played multiple roles in both traditional and modern society. The author examines the nature and historical background of *kye* and evaluates its economic contribution in modern times.

03-177. KANG, Man-kil. "A Study of the Punwŏn." *Transactions of the Korea Branch of the Royal Asiatic Society* 44(1968): 71–127. *Punwŏn* was the government ceramic factory located in Kwangju, outside Seoul, during the Yi dynasty. This detailed study of the ceramic factory examines its location, facilities, management, financing, disposition of the products, and the living and working conditions of the artisans. A useful study not only for some aspects of ceramic production of the period but also for the state of handicraft industry during the latter half of the Yi dynasty.

03-178. KIM, Byung-ha. "Cloth Money in the Early Yi Dynasty Era." *Journal of Social Sciences and Humanities* 32(June 1970):9–24. A study of the use of cloth as a medium of exchange in the early Yi period from 1364, when cotton seeds were introduced into Korea. Also discussed are cloth as a trade item coveted by Japanese and the Yi government's unsuccessful attempts to promote the

use of metallic and paper currencies during the same period.

03-179. _____. "The Question of Silver–Ginseng in the Latter Period of the Yi Dynasty." *Journal of Social Sciences and Humanities* 37(December 1972):1–18. A study of Korean export of ginseng to Tokugawa Japan in exchange for silver during the seventeenth and eighteenth centuries.

03-180. KIM, Yŏng-ho. "The Manual Industries Prior to Korea's Opening." *Journal of Social Sciences and Humanities* 39(June 1974):1–36. A study of various developments within handicraft industries in the eighteenth and nineteenth centuries: the author finds many signs of a capitalistic economy before Korea was open to the outside world. Poorly translated into English from the Korean original.

03-181. PARK, Byong-ho. "The Legal Nature of Land Ownership in the Yi Dynasty" *Korea Journal* 15(10)(October 1975):4–10. Whether the nature of landownership in the Yi dynasty was public or private has been a main concern for many economic historians in recent years. A legal historian examines in this article the legal provisions and other practices that protected the rights of private ownership of land to underscore the view that the Yi dynasty land system was essentially that of private ownership. Gives no footnotes.

03-182. PARK, Won-Son. "The Merchant System Peculiar to Korea." *Journal of Social Sciences and Humanities* 25(June 1967):100–113. This article is useful in understanding mercantile practices in traditional Korea as it explains many terms used by merchants: *sangmae, chwamae, haengsang, kaekchu,* and others.

03-183. SHIN, Susan Sandler. "The *Kye:* A study of Social Change in Korean Villages." In *Papers on Japan.* Vol. 4. Cambridge, Mass.: Harvard University, 1967. Mimeographed. After examining the origin of *kye* and its development into an economic and administrative association in rural villages as a self-governing mutual-aid organization during the Yi dynasty, the author analyzes its decline under the colonial rule of Japan, brought about by far-reaching economic changes and political restrictions imposed by the colonial government. Useful for understanding rural society in traditional Korea and its economic and social changes during Japanese rule.

03-184. _____. "Land Tenure and the Agrarian Economy in Yi Dynasty Korea: 1600–1800." PhD dissertation, Harvard University, 1973. 176 pp. After examining the land reform instituted at the beginning of the Yi dynasty, the author concludes that it paved the way for the rise of the "latifundia-minifundia" type of private ownership of land and large-scale tenancy. The author then analyzes the distribution of landownership by social class and the nature of land tenure in three southern districts (Hwasun, Yonggung, and Namhae) based on the land registers *(yang'an)* of 1720 and evaluates several factors that contributed to the increase in agricultural productivity in late Yi dynasty, such as agricultural technology, rice transplanting and double cropping, and the introduction of currency and growth of market. A careful study of the agrarian economy and land tenure in Yi Korea.

03-185. WŎN, Yu-han. "An Observation on Monetary Policy of Taewongun in Power." *Journal of Social Sciences and Humanities* 39(June 1974):43–62. A study of the monetary policy of the Taewŏn'gun that focuses on the issuance of the new high-denomination coin known as *tang-baekchŏn.*

03-186. _____. "A Survey of Monetary Policy in the Later Period of the Yi Dynasty—With the Proposed Casting of Large Coins as the Central Topic." *Journal of Social Sciences and Humanities* 34(June 1971):119–148. Discusses the monetary policy of the Yi government in the seventeenth through nineteenth centuries and explores the debates surrounding the issuance of coins in higher denominations.

The Taewŏn'gun

03-187. CHOE, Ching Young. *The Rule of the Taewŏn'gun, 1864–1873: Restoration in Yi Korea.* Cambridge, Mass.: East Asian Research Center, Harvard University, 1972. One of the most colorful and dynamic personalities in modern Korean history is the Taewŏn'gun, who ruled the country as de facto regent for his son, King Kojong, from 1864 to 1873. This book is a study of the Taewŏn'gun's regency and especially his attempts to meet the diverse threats to Korean society and the dynasty both from within and without. After briefly examining the social and economic conditions before 1860, the reformist thought of the *sirhak* scholars, and social unrest on the eve of the Taewŏn'gun's rise to power, the author discusses various reform measures introduced by the Taewŏn'gun—the economic reconstruction programs, the reorganization of the government, the reform of officialdom, the consolidation of the Royal House, and the drastic cultural policies that undermined the power base of the parasitic Confucian scholars. The strict isolationist foreign policy of the Taewŏn'gun that brought about the French and American expeditions of 1866 and 1871 respectively and the strained diplomatic relations with the newly born Meiji Japan are also discussed in detail. The book concludes with an exam-

ination of the circumstances and forces that led to the downfall of the Taewŏn'gun in 1873. The author's thesis is that the Taewŏn'gun was a follower of the *sirhak* tradition and that his reform measures were essentially aimed at restoring Yi Korea to what he believed to be the dynamic state at the beginning of the dynasty (and hence the book's subtitle).

03-188. KIM, Sŏng-jong. "Letters of Taewŏn-gun." *Korea Journal* 13(12)(December 1973):31–33. A number of private letters and writings of the Taewŏn'gun have been uncovered in recent years, and this article contains an English translation of five private letters the Taewŏn'gun wrote to his wife and son during and after this abduction to China in 1882. The originals of these five letters can be found in *Munhak sasang* 14(November 1973).

03-189. PALAIS, James B. *Politics and Policy in Traditional Korea.* Harvard East Asian series, no. 82. Cambridge, Mass.: Harvard University Press, 1975. A major study of various aspects of the Taewŏn'gun's rule and its ramifications from 1864 to 1876 with three objectives: "to reexamine previous interpretations of the nature and aims of the reform effort of the 1860s; to identify the major obstacles to reform in terms of some of the salient characteristics of the traditional order; and to emphasize the intimate relationship between socioeconomic interest, ideology, and politics on the eve of the modern era in Korea." An extremely important book for understanding the political, social, and economic order of premodern and modern Korea.

Society

03-190. CHANG, Dae Hong. "A Study of the Korean Cultural Minority: The Paekchŏng." In Andrew C. Nahm (ed.), *Traditional Korea—Theory and Practice.* Kalamazoo: Center for Korean Studies, Western Michigan University, 1974. A study of *Paekchŏng,* an outcast social group in traditional Korea, by a sociologist. Based largely on secondary sources.

03-191. CH'OE, Yŏng-ho. "Commoners in Early Yi Dynasty Civil Examinations: An Aspect of Korean Social Structure, 1392–1600." *Journal of Asian Studies* 33(August 1974):611–631. In order to determine whether or not the civil examinations were open only to men born to *yangban* status and closed to all commoners, the author examines qualifications to take part in the civil examinations—such as legal stipulations, the educational system, lineage, and sample individual cases. He concludes that the channel of mobility for qualified commoners to rise above their social status was not totally closed during the early period of the

Yi dynasty. The author also hypothesizes that the pursuance of Confucian scholarship may have been more important than birth into a *yangban* family in determining *yangban* status.

03-192. HA, Hyon-kang. "Preference for Male Issue in Korean History." *Korea Journal* 15(6)(June 1975): 44–53. Traces the historical background of the preference for male issue in Korean families.

03-193. KAWASHIMA, Fujiya. "Lineage Elite and Bureaucracy in Early to Mid-Yi Dynasty Korea." *Occasional Papers on Korea* 5(March 1977). Edited by James B. Palais and Margery D. Lang. Studies the success of the Munhwa Yu clan in the civil bureaucracy and the problems the clan faced in the Yi dynasty. An exploratory study of a potentially very important subject.

03-194. KOH, Hesung Chun. "Reflections on Social Patterns in the Yi Kinship System: An Analysis of Yi Criminal Laws." In Andrew C. Nahm (ed.), *Traditional Korea— Theory and Practice.* Kalamazoo: Center for Korean Studies, Western Michigan University, 1974. Examines "Korean tradition as reflected in the family and kinship system through an examination of the laws and regulations" of the Yi dynasty. The author concludes that the Yi social pattern is characterized by "the primacy of the integrative system-maintenance values over the goal attainment or adaptive values."

03-195. PASSIN, Herbert. "The Paekchong of Korea: A Brief Social History." *Monumenta Nipponica* 12(1956–1957):195–240. An informative study, based primarily on secondary Japanese works, of the nature and development of the outcast social group *Paekchŏng* by a well-known anthropologist.

03-196. PETERSON, Mark. "Adoption in Korean Genealogies; Continuation of Lineage." *Korea Journal* 14(1) (January 1974):28–35. An interesting study of the adoption system in Yi dynasty Korea based on the Tŏksu family genealogy. Useful in understanding some aspects of Yi dynasty kinship and social behavior.

03-197. SHIN, Susan. "The Social Structure of Kŭmhwa County in the Late Seventeenth Century." *Occasional Papers on Korea* 1(April 1974):9–35. Edited by James B. Palais. A study of the social structure of Kŭmhwa county based on analysis of the census register of 1672. After a brief observation on the nature of census registers in Yi Korea and on the status change following the Japanese invasion, the author discusses the social structure of Kŭmhwa county with useful explanation of various civil and military titles assigned to each individual. She concludes that the general trend in social mobility over five

generations as recorded in the Kŭmhwa register was overwhelmingly downward. The glossary at the end of the article giving English equivalents of Yi dynasty titles and occupations that appear in the register is also very useful.

03-198. _____. "Some Aspects of Landlord-Tenant Relations in Yi Dynasty Korea." *Occasional Papers on Korea* 3(June 1975):49–88. Edited by James B. Palais and Margery D. Lang. The first part of this paper characterizes landlord-cultivator relationships at the beginning of the Yi dynasty and then points out certain changes in the agrarian labor supply. The second part deals "in more detail with aspects of landlord-tenant relationship in the eighteenth and nineteenth centuries" and attempts to "show that in the course of the dynasty unfree laborers such as slaves and bond servants were largely replaced by commoner tenants whose relationship to the landowners was more contractual than personal." This is a very carefully researched study. Yi dynasty measurements such as *kyŏl, malkari, majigi, sŏk,* and *mal* given in the appendix are also very useful.

03-199. SOMERVILLE, John Nottingham. "Success and Failure in Eighteenth Century Ulsan—A Study in Social Mobility." PhD dissertation, Harvard University, 1974. 197 pp. A detailed study of the demography and social structure of the county of Ulsan based largely on genealogies *(chokpo)* and the household registers *(hojŏk)* of 1729, 1753, 1765, and 1804 to enhance "our understanding of the diversity of life at the county level, the dynamics of a changing society, and the importance of the rural aristocracy *(hyangban)* to dynastic welfare."

03-200. *Upper-Class Culture in Yi-dynasty Korea.* Korean Culture Series, no. 2. Seoul: International Cultural Foundation, 1973. Prepared in Korea to introduce the *yangban* culture of traditional Korea to Western readers, this small book contains several short essays, all but one of which are written by Korean scholars and translated into English. In the introduction, Lee Kwang-rin gives an overview of the *yangban*. Richard Rutt renders an English translation with an introduction of *Yangban chŏn* or the *Tale of a Yangban,* a novella by Pak Chi-wŏn (1737–1805) which criticized through biting satire *yangban* who failed in the ideals of their class. Lee Wu-song explains the introduction of Neo-Confucianism into Korea and the rise of the scholar-official class in late Koryŏ and early Yi Korea. Kim Tong-Wook's essay explains the organization of the Confucian college at the Sŏnggyun'gwan and the life and activities of scholars enrolled in that institution. The last article, by Lee Dong-Ju, provides a brief sketch of the life of Kim Chŏng-hŭi (1786–1856), the great master of brush, both in calligraphy and in painting, and discusses his influence upon literati painting in late Yi Korea.

03-201. WAGNER, Edward W. "The Korean *Chokpo* as a Historical Source." In Spencer J. Palmer (ed.), *Studies in Asian Genealogy*. Provo, Utah: Brigham Young University Press, 1972. The author attempts "to introduce the Korean *chokpo* (genealogy) as a record of lineage structures produced historically in Korea and as a generic class of documentation of immense potential use for the historian of Korean culture and society."

03-202. _____. "The Ladder of Success in Yi Dynasty Korea." *Occasional Papers on Korea* 1(April 1974):1–8. Edited by James B. Palais. This is a preliminary observation on a large research project dealing with aspects of social mobility achieved through the civil examination process during the Yi dynasty. After a brief explanation of source materials used, the author comments on some of his findings including statistics on overall success of certain clans in the civil examinations and the geographical background of the graduates.

03-203. _____. "Social Stratification in Seventeenth-Century Korea: Some Observations from a 1663 Census Register." *Occasional Papers on Korea* 1(April 1974):36–54. Edited by James B. Palais. A study of social stratification in seventeenth-century Korea based on the census register for the northern suburb of Seoul in 1663. After explaining the nature of the document, the author analyzes the social demography of Seoul's northern section, classifying inhabitants into three social classes—*Yangban,* commoners, and slaves. In the conclusion, the author observes that *yangban* status as conceived by Korean society in 1663 may have been more complex than hitherto believed, that there was substantial and increasing downward social mobility, and that the percentage of slave households and population was surprisingly high.

RELIGION AND EDUCATION
Confucianism and Catholicism

03-204. AN, Pyŏng-ju. "Yi I (Yulgok) and His Thought. *Korea Journal* 11(4)(April 1971):13–19. A brief account of the life and thought of Yi I (Yulgok) (1536–1584), an important scholar-official in the sixteenth century.

03-205. CHOE, Andreas. "L'érection du premier vicariat apostolique et les origines du catholicisme en Corée (1592–1837)." *Nouvelle Revue de Science Missionnaire* (Fribourg), (1961). This doctoral dissertation presented at the University of Bonn concerns the establishment of the Catholic church in Korea.

03-206. CHONG, Chong-bok. "The Life and Thought of Sŏ

Kyŏng-dŏk" *Korea Journal* 14(5)(May 1974):63–66. A short discussion on the basic thought of Sŏ Kyŏng-dŏk (Hwadam), a Confucian philosopher in the early Yi dynasty who maintained the monist view of the primacy of *ch'i* (*ki* in Korean).

03-207. CHUNG, Chai Sik. "Christianity as a Heterodoxy: An Aspect of General Cultural Orientation in Traditional Korea." In Yung-hwan Jo (ed.), *Korea's Response to the West*. Kalamazoo: Korea Research and Publications, 1971. Mimeographed. One of the most scholarly studies of the Korean Confucianists' rejection of Christianity. Treating the Korean response to Christianity within the broader context of traditional Korean attitudes toward alien systems of thought, the author analyzes how and why Confucian scholar-officials, such as An Chŏng-bok and Yi Hang-no, branded Christianity as heterodoxy, fundamentally inimical to their world view and social order, and urged its outright rejection by those who wished to uphold the orthodoxy of Confucianism.

03-208. DEUCHLER, Martina. "Neo-Confucianism in Early Yi Korea: Some Reflections on the Role of *Ye*." Korea Journal 15(5)(May 1975):12–18. A stimulating essay on how the Neo-Confucianists of early Yi Korea applied and elaborated the concept of *ye* (proper ritual behavior; *li* in Chinese) in laying the foundation for the Confucian state of Yi during the dynastic transition.

03-209. KIM, Hyong-hio. "A Comparative Study of Yulgok and Merleau-Ponty." *Korea Journal* 15(8) (August 1975):32–37. In this short paper, the author examines Yi I's (Yulgok) metaphysics and its organic relation to the thought of twentieth-century French philosopher Merleau-Ponty to determine "how Merleau-Ponty would have evaluated Yulgok's theory of psychology in the light of his phenomenology with the aid of Gestalt-psychologie." In making comparison, the author gives succinct explanation of Yulgok's concept of *T'aegŭk* (the great ultimate) as the basis of both the negative and the positive and his theory of *i* (principle; *li* in Chinese) and *ki* (material force; *ch'i* in Chinese) as inseparable.

03-210. MINN, Young-gyu. "A Tychonic Theory Developed in the 17th Century Korea—Kim Sŏk-mun's *Yŏkhak tohae,* 6 vols., etc." *Korea Journal* 13(6)(June 1973):8–11. A commentary on *Yŏkhak tohae* [Illustrated explanation of changes] by Kim Sŏk-mun (1658–1735).

03-211. SEOH, Munsang. "The Ultimate Concern of Yi Korean Confucians: An Analysis of the *i–ki* Debates." *Occasional Papers on Korea* 5(March 1977). Edited by James B. Palais and Margery D. Lang. A very perceptive scholarly study of the *i (li)–ki (ch'i)* debate, one of the fundamental philosophical issues that preoccupied the minds of the Yi Korean Neo-Confucianists. After a concise summation of Chu Hsi's metaphysical system, the author makes a penetrating analysis of the views held by Yi Hwang (T'oegye) and Yi I (Yulgok) on *i* (principle) and *ki* (material force) and subsequent debates among followers of the two scholars, pointing out not only metaphysical issues but also political (factional) connections involved in the controversy. Also included is a good discussion on some key *sirhak* scholars' positions on the debate and their intellectual affinities, which in turn influenced their concepts of reform.

03-212. YOUN, Laurent E. *Le Confucianisme en Corée.* Paris: P. Guéthner, 1939. Divided into five chapters which treat religion before the introduction of Confucianism, the development of Neo-Confucianism, the confrontation of Confucianism and Buddhism, and the triumph of Confucianism and its consequences. Serves as an introduction to the subject.

Education

03-213. CHOO, Young Ha. *The Education in the Yi Dynasty.* Seoul: Soodo Women's Teachers College, 1961. A general survey of the educational system during the Yi dynasty. One must exercise caution in using this book for it contains a number of errors.

03-214. KIM, Chong-guk. "Some Notes on the Songgyun'gwan." *Transactions of the Korea Branch of the Royal Asiatic Society* 38(1961):69–91. A brief description of various functions of the Sŏnggyun'gwan (Confucian Academy) and the life and customs of students enrolled in this Confucian institution during the Yi dynasty.

03-215. SMITH, Warren William, Jr. "The Rise of the *Sŏwŏn:* Literary Academies in Sixteenth Century Korea." PhD dissertation, University of California, Berkeley, 1971. 250 pp. In this study of the very important Yi institution of private academies, the author is primarily concerned with the causes for the rise of the *sŏwŏn* in the sixteenth century and with the characteristics of the early *sŏwŏn.* Subjects dealt with include the Chinese *shu-yüan* and its Korean models, the advent of the Yi dynasty and the encouragement of Confucianism, the "history and literati" purges and their results, and the establishment and chartering of the early *sŏwŏn* in perspective.

The *Sirhak* School

03-216. CHŎN, Hae-jong. "Kim Chŏng-hŭi—Master Calligrapher and Epigraphist." *Korea Journal* 13(4)(April 1973):49–56. In addition to being perhaps the greatest master of calligraphic art in Korean history, Kim Chŏng-hŭi was a renowned scholar in the early nineteenth century, especially in the field of epigraphy. This is a general account of Kim Chŏng-hŭi's life and work, including how he came under the strong intellectual influence of the "Han Learning" of Ch'ing China.

03-217. CH'ŎN, Kwan-u. "Hong Tae-yong (1731–1783)." *Korea Journal* 12(11)(November 1972):34–39. A general account of the life and thought of Hong Tae-yong, a noted *sirhak* scholar in the eighteenth century who was the first Korean to have proposed the theory of earth rotation.

03-218. EIKEMEIER, Dieter. *Elements im politschen Denken des Yon'am Pak Chiwon (1737–1805).* Leiden: Brill, 1970. The most significant European work on this period. Focuses attention on Sino-Korean cultural interchange and gives a detailed discussion of the life of Pak Chi-wŏn, *sirhak* concepts and the *sirhak* school, and the relationship between the thought of Pak Chi-wŏn and Chinese thought. The description of Yi dynasty socioeconomic conditions needs further study.

03-219. HAN, Yong-u. "Chŏng Yak-yong: The Man and His Thought." *Korea Journal* 11(8)(August 1971):24–35. A short but informative account of the life and thought of Chŏng Yag-yong (1762–1836), including his views on human nature, government, and economy.

03-220. HENDERSON, Gregory. "Chŏng Ta-san: A Study of Korea's Intellectual History." *Journal of Asian Studies* 16(May 1957):377–386. This is a short but useful study of the life and thought of Chŏng Yag-yong (1762–1836), better known by his pen name Tasan, a great scholar-official of late Yi Korea. In examining the career and works of Tasan, the author traces the early impact of Western thought among Korean intellectuals in the eighteenth century and the difficulties Tasan encountered with factional politics in the late Yi dynasty.

03-221. HONG, I-sŏp. "Yi Chung-hwan's Geographical Thought in *T'aengniji.*" *Korea Journal* 14(3)(March 1974):40–44. An informative essay on the circumstances surrounding the compilation of *T'aengniji* by Yi Chunghwan and his political and social ideals incorporated in this important geographical book.

03-222. HWANG, Wŏn-gu. "An Chŏng-bok: New Discovery of Korean History." *Korea Journal* 13(1)(January 1973): 43–49. A brief biographical sketch of An Chŏng-bok, a noted *sirhak* scholar known for his historical work *Tongsa kangmok.*

03-223. KALTON, Michael C. "An Introduction to Sirhak." *Korea Journal* 15(5)(May 1975):29–46. A good English overview of *sirhak,* an important intellectual movement in late Yi Korea. Based largely on secondary works written in Korean, this study examines how the modern studies of *sirhak* came about, presents a summary description of *sirhak,* traces the Chinese and Western as well as the indigenous Korean influences upon *sirhak,* and assesses its significance in Korea's intellectual history.

03-224. KANG, Man-gil. "Sirhak Thought and Its Reflection in Policies." *Korea Journal* 14(5)(May 1974):4–13. An informative discussion of the reform ideas of the *sirhak* scholars in the areas of land reform, military service, and slavery, with emphasis on the extent to which their ideas influenced government policy.

03-225. KIM, Yong-dǒk. "The Life and Thought of Pak Che-ga." *Korea Journal* 12(7)(July 1972):40–43. A brief account of the life and ideas of Pak Che-ga (1750–?), a *sirhak* scholar noted for his iconoclastic views. Offers a glimpse of his ideas on agriculture, wealth, foreign trade, and military defense.

03-226. KIM, Yong-sǒp. "Two Sirhak Scholars, Agricultural Reform Theories." *Korea Journal* 14(10)(October 1974): 13–26. A study of agrarian reform programs proposed by Chǒng Yag-yong and Sǒ Yu-gǒ, the two foremost agricultural specialists in the late eighteenth and early nineteenth centuries, who were largely concerned with an increase in productivity and more equitable distribution and efficient use of land. Approaching the agrarian questions from two distinct perspectives, the two men differed in their reform programs, and those programs also underwent substantial changes at different stages in their careers. Although translated into awkward English, this article is an important and useful one, not only on the question of agriculture but also on the changing attitudes among Korean intellectuals toward economic development of the period.

03-227. KO, Byung-ik. "Chung Yak-yong's View of Progress —As Expressed in his *Kiye-Ron* (Essays on Arts and Technique)." *Journal of Social Sciences and Humanities* 23(1965):29–36. An interesting short essay discussing the idea of progress found in the writings of Chǒng Yag-yong, explaining its nature, limitation, and intellectual basis. This English translation of an article appearing elsewhere in Korean does not match the standard of the original.

03-228. LEE, Woosung. "Korean Intellectual Tradition and the *Sirhak* School of Thought." In Hugh H. W. Kang (ed.), *The Traditional Culture and Society of Korea: Thought and Institutions.* Honolulu: Center for Korean Studies, University of Hawaii, 1975. A study largely of the socioeconomic factors that contributed to the rise of *sirhak* thought from 1700 to 1850, which the author divides into three groups: the school of "governing for

maximum utility," the school of "utility and social welfare," and the school of "search for the truth in empirical evidence."

03-229. PAK, No-ch'un. "Pak Chi-wǒn, Satirist of the Aristocratic Society." *Korea Journal* 13(3)(March 1973):48–54. After giving a brief biographical sketch of Pak Chi-wǒn (1737–1805), a *sirhak* scholar known particularly for his biting satires of idle literati, the author provides a short summary of two of Pak's stories, *Yangban chǒn* and *Hǒsaeng chǒn.*

03-230. PARK, Chong-hong. "Empiricism of Ch'oe Han-gi." *Korea Journal* 15(6)(June 1975):54–69. Only in recent years have the voluminous writings of Ch'oe Han-gi (1803–1879) begun to attract the attention of Korean scholars, and as his works began to be studied, it became quite clear that he was a man of extraordinary intellect and a profoundly seminal thinker. The author of this article, a well-known Korean philosopher who introduced the thought of Ch'oe Han-gi for the first time in the 1960s, discusses his empiricism which, rejecting any a priori knowledge not based on experience, formed the basis of all his ideas. The author cites extensively from Ch'oe's writings.

03-231. SONG, Chu-yǒng. "Practical Learning of Yi Ik." *Korea Journal* 12(8)(August 1972):38–45. A general account of the social criticism of Yi Ik, an important *sirhak* scholar in the eighteenth century.

03-232. _____. "Yu Hyǒng-wǒn." *Korea Journal* 12(7)(July 1972):33–39. Discusses mostly the economic ideas of Yu Hyǒng-wǒn, an important reform-minded scholar in the seventeenth century, based on his work *Pan'gye surok.*

The Tonghak Movement

03-233. CHONG, Key Ray. "Ch'oe Che-u's Tonghak Doctrine: Its Sources and Meanings, 1860–1864." *Journal of Korean Studies* 1(2)(1971):71–84. Explains the eclectic nature of the original doctrine of Tonghak expounded by Ch'oe Che-u as having borrowed ideas from Christianity, Confucianism, Buddhism, Taoism, shamanism, and other traditional beliefs. The author also contends that the primary concern of the Tonghak founder was spiritual reform of individuals, rather than the social or political issues of the period.

03-234. _____. "The Religious Meaning of Ch'oe Che-u's Tonghak Doctrine, 1860–1864." In Robert J. Miller (ed.), *Religious Ferment in Asia.* Lawrence: University Press of Kansas, 1974. See preceding entry.

03-235. CHUNG, Chai Sik. "Religion and Cultural Identity —The Case of Eastern Learning." In *International Year-*

book for the Sociology of Religion. Vol. 5. Köln and Opladen: Westdeutscher Verlag, 1969. Analyzes the Tonghak from a comparative perspective as a "nativistic" movement in which the search for personal and cultural identity has particular relevance.

03-236. KIM, Young Choon. "The Concept of Man in Ch'ŏndogyo." PhD dissertation, Temple University, 1969. 280 pp. The dissertation includes the historical background of Ch'ŏndogyo (Religion of Heavenly Way), originally called Tonghak (Eastern Learning), which was founded by Ch'oe Suun (Che-u) in 1860. It includes the chapters on humanity's origin, nature, conduct, and destiny. The syncretistic aspects of Ch'ŏndogyo, the idea of unity of mortal and God, the humanistic ethics and eschatology, and the impact of Ch'ŏndogyo thought on Korean society, especially through the Tonghak Revolution, are discussed.

03-237. _____. "The Ch'ŏndogyo Concept of the Origin of Man." *Philosophy East and West* 22(4)(October 1972): 373–384. Discusses the philosophical concept of Ch'ŏndogyo regarding the origin of humankind by explaining how Ch'ŏndogyo affirms a natural human development which basically differs from the Christian concept of creation but is akin to that of Taoism and other Oriental philosophies. Also comments on how the Ch'ŏndogyo concept of "evolution from the totality" is different from "scientific evolution."

03-238. _____. "The Essentials of Ch'ondogyo Ethics." *Journal of Social Sciences and Humanities* 38(June 1973):85–100. Deals with the basic ideas of Ch'ŏndogyo, such as the concept of good and evil, the changing nature of ethics, unity with virtue, the treatment of human as God, and respect for material matters—all of which became the ethical basis of the Ch'ŏndogyo religion.

03-239. _____. "The Ch'ondogyo Concept of the Nature of Man." *International Philosophical Quarterly* 13(1973): 209–228. Discusses the basic Ch'ŏndogyo concepts of *in nae ch'ŏn* (Man is God), the relationship between soul and body, and good and evil in human nature.

03-240. WEEMS, Benjamin B. *Reform, Rebellion and the Heavenly Way.* Tucson: University of Arizona, 1964. A comprehensive study of the development of Ch'ŏndogyo from its inception as Tonghak to about 1950. After providing a short explanation of basic doctrines of the religion, the author examines the evolution of Ch'ŏndogyo in three stages: the first stage (1860–1905), when it stimulated and led a reform movement directed against the social, economic, and political abuses of the times that culminated with the great rebellion of 1894; the second period (1905–1945), when it became a major anti-Japanese

nationalist force leading the nonviolent independence uprising of 1919 and eventually suffered Japanese persecution; and the third period (1945–1950), when it was caught up in the problems spawned by the ideological as well as territorial division of the country.

FOREIGN RELATIONS
Korean-Chinese Relations

03-241. CH'OE, Yŏng-ho. "Sino-Korean Relations, 1866–1876: A Study of Korea's Tributary Relationship to China." *Asea yŏn'gu* 9(1)(March 1966):131–184. After explaining how Korea's tributary relations with China functioned in the traditional East Asian world order, the author examines how this relationship came to be challenged by France and the United States, who, not understanding the East Asian world order, tried unsuccessfully to open Korea in 1866 and 1871, respectively, and how Japan adroitly exploited her knowledge of both Western and Asian world orders and successfully induced Korea to sign the first modern treaty in 1876.

03-242. CHUN, Hae-jong. "Sino-Korean Tributary Relations in the Ch'ing Period." In John K. Fairbank (ed.), *The Chinese World Order.* Cambridge, Mass.: Harvard University Press, 1968. This authoritative study of Korea's tributary relations with Ch'ing China examines in detail various aspects of Korean embassies to China—their missions, appointment and composition of embassies, the route they took, ceremonies and activities in Peking, and frequency of embassies. Of particular value is the careful analysis of economic aspects of the tributary relations, including the gifts and goods exchanged, travel expenses, and a general outline of trade between the two countries.

03-243. FAIRBANK, John K. and Ssü-yu TENG. "On the Ch'ing Tributary System." *Harvard Journal of Asiatic Studies* 6(1941):135–246. Reprinted in *Ch'ing Administration: Three Studies* (Cambridge, Mass.: Harvard University Press, 1961). A comprehensive study of the tributary system of Ch'ing China, in which Korea was an important participant. Based chiefly on the various editions of *Ta-Ming hui-tien,* this study provides an extensive English translation and analysis of China's diplomatic relations with other countries.

03-244. GOODRICH, L. Carrington. "Korean Interference with Chinese Historical Records." *Journal of the North China Branch of the Royal Asiatic Society* 48(1937): 27–34. A factual account of how the Ming and Ch'ing courts in China responded in complying with the requests of Yi Korea to rectify the erroneous information on the family backgrounds of two Yi dynasty rulers—T'aejo (reigned 1392–1398) and Injo (reigned 1623–1649)—that had entered into some Chinese history books. The study is based mostly on Chinese sources.

03-245. _____. "Sino-Korean Relations at the End of the XIVth Century." *Transactions of the Korea Branch of the Royal Asiatic Society* 30(1940):33–46. A study of the diplomatic difficulties Korea encountered with the Ming founder, T'ai-tsu, during the transition from the Koryŏ to the Yi dynasty. The trouble arose when the Chinese emperor found many Korean actions toward China insulting, including the use of improper phraseology in Korea's diplomatic documents. For this discourtesy, Korea was threatened, her trade with China was interrupted, and her officials visiting China on mission were detained or sent into exile.

03-246. LEDYARD, Gari. "Korean Travelers in China over Four Hundred Years, 1488–1887." *Occasional Papers on Korea* 2(March 1974):1–42. Edited by James B. Palais. This is an introduction to the *Yŏnhaengnok sŏnjip,* a collection of diaries written by Yi dynasty Koreans during their trips to Peking, published in Seoul in two volumes in 1960 and 1962. In pointing out the importance of the book as a valuable source for the study not only of Sino-Korean diplomatic relations but also of Chinese history during Ming and Ch'ing times, the author makes thoughtful and interesting comments on several topics selected from the book—including the route the Korean missions took to visit Peking, the nature of the diaries collected in the book, diplomacy and ceremony in Peking, life in China as observed and recorded by Koreans, the activities of members of Korean embassies in Peking, and one rather unusual encounter in 1712 with a Chinese who claimed to be a descendant of the Ming royal family. This is more than a simple introduction to a book; it provides a fascinating glimpse into little-known but important aspects of Korean travelers in China.

03-247. ROCKHILL, William Woodville. *China's Intercourse with Korea from the XVth Century to 1895.* London: Luzac, 1905. This pioneering study of Korea's traditional relationship wtih China during the Yi dynasty examines Korea's status vis-à-vis Ming and Ch'ing China (based mostly on Chinese sources). Also gives the author's own observations on Korea's law and customs as he learned of them during his residence in Seoul as the United States chargé d'affaires in 1886–1887.

03-248. WALKER, Hugh Dyson. "The Yi-Ming Rapprochement: Sino-Korean Foreign Relations, 1392–1592." PhD dissertation, University of California, Los Angeles, 1971. 355 pp. Abstracted in *DAI* 32(6)(December 1971):3189-90-A; UM 72-1511. "The three main areas considered are: (1) ancient ideas and traditions of China and Korea which influenced their respective sense of national identity, and, conversely, affected their attitudes toward other peoples; (2) a survey of the actual nature of relations between the two countries prior to 1392, based upon Chinese imperial expansion and contraction, through an analysis of the effect of Chinese 'dynastic cycles' upon Korean political development; (3) background and nature of the extended *rapprochement* between Yi Korea and Ming China."

Korean-Japanese Relations

03-249. CODECASA, Maria Silvia. "A Korean's Drift to the Ryukyus in the 15th Century." *Korea Journal* 15(9)(September 1975):42–49. In 1477, a Korean officer named Kim Pi-i and eight of his men, sailing from Cheju Island bound for Mokp'o, met a typhoon and drifted until they reached the Ryūkyū Islands, where they were rescued. After Kim Pi-i returned to Korea in 1479 via Kyushu and Tsushima, Japan, he wrote a report describing his ordeal and his observations of social customs in Okinawa and western Japan. The article is an English summary of the Korean translation from the *hanmun* original that appeared in *Cheju sinmun* in August 1970.

03-250. HAGUENAUER, Charles. "Relations du Royaume des Ryukyu avec les pays des mers du Sud et la Corée." *Bulletin de la Maison franco-japonaise* (Tokyo), 3(1–2) (1931). On relations between Ryūkyū and Korea during the Yi dynasty period.

03-251. JHO, Sung-do. *Yi Sun-shin (Yi Sun-sin): A National Hero of Korea.* Chinhae, Korea: Choongmoo-kong Society, 1970. An old-fashioned biography of the great Korean naval hero of the Hideyoshi invasion. The bulk of the book is devoted to recounting various naval battles Yi Sun-sin won against the Japanese. Based largely on primary sources, the work includes Yi's own records, though without footnotes or bibliography. Following the praise-and-blame style of biographical writing, this book depicts Yi Sun-sin as one who did no wrong.

03-252. KIM, Ha-tai. "The Transmission of Neo-Confucianism to Japan by Kang Hang, a Prisoner of War." In *Yongjae Paek Nak-chun paksa hwan'gap kinyŏm kukhak nonch'ong.* Seoul: 1955. Also reproduced in *Transactions of the Korea Branch of the Royal Asiatic Society* 37(April 1961):83–103. An interesting study of how the Neo-Confucianism of Chu Hsi as expounded by Yi Hwang (T'oegye) was transmitted to Japan by Kang Hang, a Korean scholar-official who was taken to Japan as a prisoner of war during the Hideyoshi invasion.

03-253. MCCUNE, George M. "The Exchange of Envoys between Korea and Japan During the Tokugawa Period." *Far Eastern Quarterly* 5(May 1946):308–325. A study of the diplomatic exchange of envoys between the Korean government under the Yi dynasty and the Tokugawa shogunate of Japan from the early seventeenth to the mid-nineteenth century. Issues discussed include the resumption of diplomatic intercourse after the Hideyoshi invasion, the formalities and practices of the exchange of envoys, and the role Tsushima played in the diplomatic schemes between Korea and Japan. A scholarly and pioneering study of the diplomatic relationship between the two countries.

03-254. _____. "The Japanese Trading Post at Pusan." *Korean Review* (Seattle), 1(June 1948):11–15. A short but reliable study of the Japanese trading post permitted at the port of Pusan by the Yi government during the Tokugawa period.

03-255. SANSOM, George. *A History of Japan, 1334–1615.* Stanford: Stanford University Press, 1961. Chapter 22 (The Invasion of Korea) gives a good account of Japanese military activities in Korea during the Hideyoshi invasion.

03-256. STELCHEN, M. "Expédition du Taiko Hideyoshi en Corée (1592–1599)." In *Les daimyo chrétiens, ou un siècle de l'histoire politique et religieuse du Japon (1549–1650).* Tokyo: 1904. On the invasion of Korea by Toyotomi Hideyoshi.

03-257. TOBY, Ronald T. "Korean-Japanese Diplomacy in 1711: Sukchong's Court and the Shogun's Title." *Chōsen gakuhō* 74(January 1975):256–231. A study of the diplomatic relationship between Yi dynasty Korea and Tokugawa Japan focusing on a "crisis" that arose in 1711 when the Tokugawa government, under the prodding of Arai Hakuseki, demanded that Korea, in addressing official communications to the Tokugawa government, refer to the shogun as "King of Japan" instead of "Great Prince of Japan." The author examines the motivations behind Arai's move and describes a series of discussions that took place within the Korean government in determining its response. This is an interesting and useful study not only of the Korean-Japanese relationship but also of the decision-making procedures within the Yi dynasty government.

Korea and the West

03-258. HALL, Captain Basil. *Voyage to Corea and the Island of Loo-choo.* 2nd ed. London: John Murray, 1820. In 1816 two British ships, *Alceste* and *Lyra,* which had carried Lord Amherst and his embassy to China, made the return trip by way of the western coast of the Korean peninsula, surveying the navigability of the region. This narrative of that journey describes the events and the people they encountered on Korea's offshore islands from

Hwanghae to Ch'ungch'ŏng provinces. Of the three chapters, only chap. 1 deals with Korea.

03-259. HAMEL, Hendrik. *An Account of the Shipwreck of a Dutch Vessel on the Coast of the Isle of Quelpaert, Together with the Description of the Kingdom of Corea.* When, in July 1653, the Dutch ship *Sparrow Hawk* sailed from a base in Taiwan headed toward Nagasaki in Japan, it was damaged in high seas by a storm and inadvertently reached Korea. For the next thirteen years, the Dutch crew was forced to live in Korea among all ranks of life until some of them finally escaped to Japan. Hendrik Hamel, the secretary of these Dutch sailors, wrote an account of their adventures and experiences in Korea that became the first book on Korea to be published in Europe. Hamel's narrative consists of two parts—one is an account of the experiences of the castaways; the other is a description of Korea and its people, including geography, political divisions, coasts, boundaries, fisheries, climate, products, the monarchy, military administrations, state council, revenues, justice, religion, houses, marriages, education, parents and children, mourning, funerals, the disposition of the Koreans, tobacco, trade, weights and measures, writing, printing, and the manner of the king's going abroad. In general, according to Gari Ledyard, Hamel's "Account seems remarkably objective." This is a valuable description of Korea in the mid-seventeenth century as seen by a foreigner. Originally written in Dutch, Hamel's *Account* has appeared in several English versions, none of which is a complete translation. The most authoritative English edition, by John Churchill, first published in 1704, is reprinted in Gari Ledyard, *The Dutch Come to Korea* (Seoul: Royal Asiatic Society, Korea Branch, 1971).

03-260. KOH, Byong-ik. "On Negro Slaves Who Drifted to the Korean Shore in the Year 1801. In *Second Biennial Conference Proceedings.* Taipei: International Association of Historians of Asia, 1962. Relying on contemporary descriptions found in private and official records, the author makes a careful analysis of the circumstances leading to the landing of five Negroes on Cheju Island in 1801—the first black men known to have reached Korea —and of their national origin.

03-261. LEDYARD, Gari. *The Dutch Come to Korea.* Seoul: Royal Asiatic Society, Korea Branch, 1971. Using Hamel's *Narrative* as well as Korean and Japanese sources, the author narrates the adventures and experiences of the Dutch sailors, including their shipwreck on Cheju Island, their encounter with another Dutchman who had adopted a Korean name (Pak Yŏng), their life in Seoul and in Chŏl-la province, their final escape to Japan, and the subsequent diplomatic negotiations between Korea and Japan on the release of the remaining Dutch crew in Korea. In a chapter entitled "Afterthoughts," the author gives an interesting discussion of the early Korean contacts with the West—largely intellectual and religious—through the Jesuits in China. In the two appendixes, the author gives "Bibliographic Notes on Hendrik Hamel's *Narrative* and Its Early Printed Editions" and "Text of the Interrogation Given Hamel by the Japanese Authorities in Nagasaki." In addition, the text of Churchill's English edition of Hamel's *Narrative* is reprinted at the end. This book is also useful in understanding the political and social condition of mid-seventeenth-century Korea.

03-262. ORANGE, Marc. "L'attitude de réserve observée par la France à l'égard de la Corée entre l'expédition de l'Amiral Roze et la traité franco-coréen de 1886." In *Yi Sŏn-gŭn paksa kohŭi kinyŏm nonmunjip: Han'gukhak nonch'ong.* Seoul: 1974. Discusses the indifferent political stance reflected in French polity on Korea from the time of the French invasion of Korea in 1866 to the Franco-Korean Friendship Treaty of 1886.

HISTORIOGRAPHY

03-263. McCUNE, George M. "The Yi Dynasty Annals of Korea." *Transactions of the Korea Branch of the Royal Asiatic Society* 29(1939):57–82. A good account of how the annals (*sillok;* usually translated now as "veritable records") of the Yi dynasty were compiled and preserved for posterity. Also useful for understanding the historiography of Yi Korea.

03-264. PALAIS, James B. "Records and Record-keeping in Nineteenth-Century Korea." *Journal of Asian Studies* 30(1971):583–591. An informative discussion of how such important historical sources as the *Veritable Records (Sillok),* the *Records for Daily Reflection (Ilsŏngnok),* the *Records of the Border Defense Command (Pibyŏnsa tŭngnok),* and the *Daily Records of the Royal Secretariat (Sŭngjŏngwŏn ilgi)* are kept; also examines their value and weaknesses as historical sources.

03-265. SHIN, Suk-ho. "Bibyonsa Dungnok (Pibyŏnsa Tungnok)." *Journal of Social Sciences and Humanities*

17(December 1962):67–77. Gives a brief outline of the evolution of the office of *Pibyŏnsa* (Border Defense Command) and the disposition of *Pibyŏnsa tŭngnok* [Records of the Border Defense Command], which is one of the main primary sources of Yi dynasty history.

03-266. _____. "Sungjong-won Ilgi [Diary of the Sŭngjŏngwŏn]." *Journal of Social Sciences and Humanities* 15(December 1961):104–111. A useful account of how *Sŭngjŏngwŏn ilgi* [Records of the Royal Secretariat], one of the most important primary sources of the Yi dynasty, was compiled and preserved.

03-267. _____. "Yijo sillok [Annals of the Yi Dynasty]." *Journal of Social Sciences and Humanities* 12(May 1960): 37–43. A succinct account of how the *sillok* (veritable records) of the Yi dynasty was compiled and preserved.

03-268. SOHN, Pow-key. "The Concept of History and Korean Yangban." *International Journal of Korean Studies* (Seoul), 1(1973):91–113. This major comprehensive study of the official historiography under the Yi dynasty centers on the author's thesis that the *yangban* officials used the authority of historical writing as an instrument to gain the upper hand over the monarch. It examines, among other things, how history was perceived under the Yi dynasty, how various offices related to historical compilations were organized, how the official histories were compiled, how the historians were selected, and why the potential power of historians was so formidable. It also makes a number of useful comparisons with Chinese historiography. This is an authoritative and important study not only of the historiography but also of the government under the Yi dynasty.

03-269. SUEMATSU, Yasukazu. "Introduction to the Ri [Yi] Dynasty Annals." *Memoirs of the Research Department of the Tōyō Bunko* 17(1958):97–166. After briefly reviewing the history of the compilation of veritable records (*sillok*) in China and Koryŏ, the author gives a detailed description of the compilation of *sillok* and its preservation during the Yi dynasty and examines the circumstances surrounding the *sillok* compilation for each monarchical reign.

IV. THE LATE YI (CHOSŎN) DYNASTY: 1876–1910

by Young Ick Lew

INTRODUCTION

In 1876 Yi dynastic Korea, through the Japanese- imposed Treaty of Kanghwa, ceased to be a hermit kingdom. With the wall of seclusion breached, the Korean peninsula was soon engulfed by a tide of Japanese, and then Western, imperialist aggression. Ch'ing China, Korea's traditional suzerain, attempted to stem this tide by dispatching garrison forces and governmental advisers to Korea after the *Imo* ("1882") Mutiny in mid-1882. China accelerated this process by appointing a resident in Korea in the wake of the abortive pro-Japanese coup d'état, called the *Kapsin* ("1884") Coup, in late 1884. China's decade-long attempt to maintain Korea as a virtual protectorate thereafter, however, came to an ignominious end in 1894 with the outbreak of the Sino-Japanese War (1894–1895). Japan's stunning victory in this war helped extricate Korea from the age-old bond to the Chinese tribute system—only to make her a pawn in the nascent Russo-Japanese rivalry over Korea. Korea remained "independent" under a quasi Russo-Japanese condominium from 1896 to 1904.

Unsupported by any major paternalistic power like China, the Korean "Empire"—so-called from 1897—quickly degenerated into an incompetent autocracy. Japan intruded into Korea once more in 1904 by starting the historic Russo-Japanese War (1904–1905). Simultaneously Japan embarked upon a program to secure Korea as her protectorate and, as a victor in the war, crowned this effort by annexing Korea as part of the Japanese empire in 1910. The convulsive history of the 34-year period from 1876 to 1910 was essentially one of steady demise of the ancient, Sino-centric Korean kingdom under the mounting pressure of modern imperialism led by expansive Meiji Japan.

The history of Korea from 1876 to 1910 is also a history of incipient modernization or westernization. The Yi Korean leadership launched a rather vigorous "enlightenment" campaign in the early 1880s in emulation of Meiji Japanese and Ch'ing Chinese modernization movements. This effort came to a premature end in 1884 due to Chinese containment of Korean nationalism. No major progress was achieved in Korean modernization between 1885 and 1894. A pro-Japanese reform movement, known as the *Kabo-Ulmi* ("1894–1895") Reforms, erupted after the outbreak of the Tonghak Rebellion and the Sino-Japanese War in 1894. This Japanese-oriented reform movement, however, quickly subsided due to the sudden eclipse of Japanese political influence in Korea following the Triple Intervention (May 1895). Another reform movement led by the American-inspired Independence Club took over this unfinished task from 1896 to 1899. The benighted Yi dynastic leaders antagonized and suppressed this movement, however, an action which resulted in their own demise. By the time the Japanese invaded the country in 1904, the Korean body politic sadly lacked the sinews of modern "wealth and power" to withstand this aggressive neighbor. The last-minute efforts to salvage national independence among the Korean people between 1904 and 1910 proved to be unavailing in the face of a determined Japanese drive for annexation. The Yi dynasty and its people paid dearly for their failure to achieve timely modernization in the nineteenth century. Along with the kaleidoscopic power politics which the imperialist nations played in Korea, this aspect of Korea's stultifying internal transformation remains an intriguing subject for historians.

Unlike the history of the previous era, Korean history of this period was shaped more by external stimuli than by internal dynamism. Therefore foreign historical sources, particularly Chinese, Japanese, and American, constitute basic materials which rival domestic sources in the study of this period. English-language materials bequeathed by a small but educated community of contemporary American and British diplomats, advisers, missionaries, and travelers in Korea provide very valuable information regarding Korean external and internal conditions rarely found in other national archival sources. The very fact that the United States and Great Britain maintained a relatively detached diplomatic posture vis-à-vis Korea while China, Japan, and Russia developed a serious power rivalry enhanced the objectivity of their citizens' observations regarding Korea. The primary sources cited in the following bibliography represent a part of this valuable body of historical material hitherto made available to historians.

The tradition of secondary writing in English on Korean history of this period dates back to 1906, when Homer Hulbert published his *Passing of Korea*. If modern historical scholarship failed to develop in Korea in the subsequent years, it was undoubtedly due to the disintegration of the Korean kingdom in 1910. Nevertheless, a few high-quality monographs and articles relevant to nineteenth-century Korea did begin to appear from the 1920s with the heightened interest of the American people in East Asia. They included, in chronological order: Tyler Dennett, *Americans in East Asia: A Critical Study of the Policy of the United States with Reference to China, Japan, and Korea in the Nineteenth Century* (New York: 1922); L. George Paik, *The History of Protestant Missions in Korea, 1832–1910* (Pyongyang: 1927); Harold J. Noble, "The United States and Sino-Korean Relations, 1885–1887," *Pacific Historical Review* 2(3) (1933); T. F. Tsiang, "Sino-Japanese Diplomatic Relations, 1870–1894," *Chinese Social and Political Science Review* 17 (1933–1934); T. C. Lin, "Li Hung-chang: His Korea Policies, 1870–1885," ibid., 19 (1935); Fred H. Harrington, *God, Mammon, and the Japanese: Dr. Horace N. Allen and Korean-American Relations, 1884–1905* (Madison, Wisc.: 1944); and M. Frederick Nelson, *Korea and the Old Orders in Eastern Asia* (Baton Rouge: 1945). Except for the works of Paik, Tsiang, and Lin, these studies were based on Western-language sources, but the authors' application of modern analytic methods set their works apart from the more descriptive traditional writings. Along with the two-volume work of a Japanese historian, Tabohashi Kiyoshi, entitled *Kindai Nissen kankei no kenkyū* [Modern Japanese-Korean relations] (Keijō: 1944), these works—particularly Harrington's—contributed to setting a new standard of historical scholarship on modern Korean history.

Active research and writing on late nineteenth- century Korean history commenced after 1945 with the restoration of Korean independence. The availability of Korean and Japanese archival sources and the outbreak of the Korean War in the early 1950s stimulated the growth of a multiarchival historical scholarship relevant to Korea. The first major works included: Hilary Conroy, *The Japanese Seizure of Korea, 1868–1910: A Study of Realism and Idealism in International Relations* (Philadelphia: 1960) and C. I. Eugene Kim/Han-Kyo Kim, *Korea and the Politics of Imperialism* (Berkeley: 1967). The former used major Japanese primary and secondary sources, whereas the latter put to use Korean and Chinese materials, in addition to Japanese, in surveying the entire range of Korean-Japanese relations in the late nineteenth century. Together, these two books established a convenient frame of reference for students who approach modern Korean history with topical interest. They remain prerequisite readings for those who embark on serious research on modern Korea, just as Sun Keun Lee's weightier volumes in Korean—*Han'guksa: ch'oegŭnse p'yŏn* [Korean history: modern era] (Seoul: 1961) and *Han'guksa: hyŏndae p'yŏn* [Korean history: contemporary era] (Seoul:1963) —are for native Korean scholars.

After these two books came out, a number of studies based on theme or incident emanated from American and Korean scholars in the United States. As a result, by the 1970s dozens of monographs and dissertations in English have illuminated selective features or turning points of modern Korean history. Identifying some representative works here by historical sequence will help clarify the current frontier of our knowledge in late nineteenth-century Korean history.

For the eventful years from 1876 to 1884, two monographs have recently appeared: Martina Deuchler, *Confucian Gentlemen and Barbarian Envoys: The Opening of Korea, 1875–1885* (Seattle: 1977) and Harold F. Cook, *Korea's 1884 Incident: Its Background and Kim Ok-kyun's Elusive Dream* (Seoul: 1972). The former admirably covers the traumatic Korean encounter with Japan and the West from the time of the Kanghwa Treaty to the Li-Itō Convention of Tientsin (1885). The latter deals in depth with the all-important *Kapsin* Coup. Together with numerous additional monographs published in Korean on the pre-1885 period—including Kwang-rin Lee's *Han'guk kaehwasa yŏn'gu* [Studies on the Korean enlightenment movement] (Seoul: 1969) and *Kaehwadang yŏn'gu* [Studies on the Progressive Party] (Seoul: 1973)—these two volumes help clarify the early history of the period under discussion.

No major monographic study has yet been published in English covering the Chinese-dominated decade of 1885–1894. However, at least three PhD dissertations have been completed since the mid-1950s dealing with various aspects of this period: Robert Edwin Reordan, "The Role of George Clayton Foulk in the United States–Korean Relations, 1884–1887" (Fordham, 1955); Dalchoong Kim, "Korea's Quest for Reform and Diplomacy in the 1880's: With Special Reference to Chinese Intervention and Control" (Fletcher, 1972); and Bonnie B. Oh, "The Background of Chinese Policy Formation in the Sino-Japanese War of 1894–1895" (Chicago, 1974). Among these studies, Kim's work emphasizes the frustrating reform attempts of Korean leaders under the dominant Min clan during Yüan Shih-k'ai's residency (1885–1894) and helps complement Lin Ming-te's more narrowly focused monograph in Chinese on Yüan's role in Korea, *Yüan Shih-k'ai yü Ch'ao-hsien* (Taipei, 1970). Despite the high quality of these works, the history of this particular decade remains rather opaque. More active research in the future dealing with the Min clan oligarchy, Yüan's relationship with the Korean leadership, or the Tonghak agitations during 1892–1894 may help bring the picture of this era into clearer focus.

For the dramatic years of the Japanese ascendancy and the Tonghak Rebellion (1894–1896), Young I. Lew and, to a lesser degree, Bonnie B. Oh have utilized mainly Korean, Japanese, and American sources and analyzed Korean reform efforts. Lew's dissertation, "The Kabo Reform Movement: Korean-Japanese Reform Efforts in Korea, 1894" (Harvard, 1973), and related articles concentrate upon the Japanese-oriented Korean reform movements in 1894 and 1895 and their relevance to the conservative Tonghak Rebellion. When future research illuminates such incidents as Queen Min's assassination (October 1895) and the Korean royal flight to the Russian legation (February 1896), we will gain a clearer picture of Korean-Japanese relations during these tumultuous years. In order to complete the picture of Korean history of this period, however, we still need a solid study exploring Russo-Korean relations with focus perhaps on the role of Karl Waeber, the Russian minister to Korea from the mid-1880s to 1895.

Like the decade of Chinese domination prior to 1894, the history of 1895–1904, characterized by Russo-Japanese rivalry over the Korean "Empire," remains in an embryonic stage of development. Seung Kwon Synn's PhD dissertation, "The Russo-Japanese Struggle for Control of Korea, 1894–1904" (Harvard, 1967), helps supplement our knowledge on the period imparted by such previous works as Harrington's previously mentioned book and Andrew Malozemoff's *Russian Far Eastern Policy, 1881–1904: With Special Emphasis on the Causes of the Russo-Japanese War* (Berkeley, 1958). A recently completed PhD dissertation centering on the Independence Club by Vipan Chandra, entitled "Nationalism and Popular Participation in Government in Late 19th Century Korea: The Contribution of the Independence Club (1896–1898)" (Harvard, 1977), along with a comparable study in Korean by Yong-ha Shin, *Tongnip hyŏphoe yŏn'gu* [A study on the Independence Club] (Seoul, 1976), significantly raises our level of understanding regarding Korean domestic politics during this time. Future studies centering on Korean-Russian relations, Korean-Japanese relations, and the decadent Yi court will produce a more balanced perspective on this period.

The history of Korean-Japanese relations between 1904 and 1910 was covered by Conroy's and Kim and Kim's aforementioned works, as well as by numerous articles. Furthermore, Chon Dong's PhD dissertation, "Japanese Annexation of Korea: A Study of Korean-Japanese Relations to 1910" (Colorado, 1955), is devoted to Korean-Japanese relations of this period. In spite of these works, more research is needed in this period dealing with such neglected subjects as the Korean Patriotic Enlightenment movement and the Righteous Army movement. A solid study on Japanese policy toward Korea, with focus on the role of Japanese Resident-General Itō Hirobumi, may yield new insight into an old problem.

The works I have cited generally fall into the category of political-diplomatic history. A few studies pursuing different lines of disciplinary interest have emerged in recent years. For example: Benjamin B. Weems, *Reform, Rebellion and the Heavenly Way* (Tucson, 1964); Carlos Kenneth Quinones, "The Prerequisite for Power in Late Yi Korea, 1864–1894" (PhD dissertation, Harvard, 1975); and Wayne Patterson, "The Korean Frontier in America: Immigration to Hawaii, 1896–1910" (PhD dissertation, Pennsylvania, 1977). As pioneer studies in intellectual-political history, social-political history, and diplomatic-social history, respectively, they have opened up new possibilities for more diversified historical studies. Needless to say, a similarly creative approach is possible and indeed necessary in the future in such neglected fields as cultural history and, above all, economic history. A monograph on the history of modern Korean education based on American missionary documents seems to be feasible. Moreover, a history of early modern Korean finance could be written on the basis of customs records and the private papers of MacLeavy Brown, a Briton who served as chief commissioner of Korean Customs (1893–1913).

The following bibliography also presents a select list of monographs, articles, and unpublished dissertations relevant to Korean history from 1876 to 1910. I have exercised discretion in selecting, annotating, and organizing the entries from among more than five hundred titles. In providing annotations for unpublished PhD dissertations, however, I relied on the authors' own synopses if available. I thank Professors Vipan Chandra, Key Ray Chong, Chai-sik Chung, K. H. Kim, Yong Choon Kim, John E. Merrill, Bonnie B. Oh, Wayne Patterson, and C. Kenneth Quinones for their cooperation in furnishing me with synopses of their works. When such information was unavailable, I made my own annotation or relied on Frank J. Shulman, *Japan and Korea: An Annotated Bibliography of Doctoral Dissertations in Western Languages, 1877–1969* (London: 1970). I would like to extend my special appreciation to Dr. Yŏng-ho Ch'oe of the University of Hawaii at Manoa and Professor Donald M. Bishop at the United States Air Force Academy for their unstinted help in obtaining rare materials. They also provided me with draft annotations for some important entries—I used Professor Bishop's annotations for entries 03-271, 276, 280, and 285, with little modification, for example. Any error of commission or omission remains subject to future revision.

BIBLIOGRAPHY

PRIMARY SOURCES
Archival Sources

03-270. Great Britain. Foreign Office. *British and Foreign State Papers,* 1812–1964. Published from 1841 in series.

Presently compiled and edited in the Library and Records Department of the Foreign and Commonwealth Office and published through Her Majesty's Stationery Office. Volumes 73 (1881–1882) through 103 (1909–1910) give major international agreements Korea concluded under the title of Corea. Volume 78 (1886–1887) includes the "Correspondence between Great Britain, China, and Corea, respecting the Occupation of Port Hamilton by Great Britain,1885–87" (pp. 143–169). Otherwise this source book contains little information on Korea.

03-271. _____. Public Record Office. London. The extensive holdings of the British National Archives in the Public Record Office are yet to be fully exploited for their materials on Korean history. There are several major series of records relating to late Yi dynasty Korea. Series FO 17 (Foreign Office: General Correspondence: China) includes dispatches from the consul general at Seoul (1890–1905). Series FO 371 (Foreign Office: General Correspondence: Political) consists of letters received at the Foreign Office from British diplomatic and consular representatives abroad, from individuals writing from the country concerned, from foreign diplomatic representatives in London, and from institutions, individuals, and British government agencies. (Correspondence in this series relating to Korea may be searched by using a card index located at the Public Record Office.) Series FO 523 (Foreign Office: Embassy and Consular Archives: Korea) covers the period 1891–1902 and 1909. Series FO 228 (Foreign Office: Embassy and Consular Archives: China) includes material on Korea to 1901. Series FO 262 (Foreign Office: Embassy and Consular Archives: Japan) covers the period from 1904. Series ADM 125 (Admiralty: Station Records: China) contains a certain amount of material on Korea.

The records held in the British National Archives are extensively described in: *Public Record Office List(s) and Index(es),* 55 nos. (London: Her Majesty's Stationery Office, 1892–1936; reprint ed., New York: Kraus Reprints, 1963–1966); *Supplementary Series,* 15 nos. to date (London: Her Majesty's Stationery Office, 1892–; reprint ed., New York: Kraus Reprints, 1964–). References to the materials on Korea cited above are found in: ADM 125: *PRO L&I, Supplementary,* no. 6, v. 2; FO 17: *PRO L&I, Supplementary,* no. 13, v. 2; FO 228: *PRO L&I, Supplementary,* no. 13, v. 6; FO 262: *PRO L&I, Supplementary,* no. 13, v. 7; and FO 523: *PRO L&I, Supplementary,* no. 13, v. 7. Records of the Foreign Office are generally described in *The Records of the Foreign Office, 1782–1939,* Handbook no. 13 (London: Her Majesty's Stationery Office, 1969).

03-272. _____. *Parliamentary Papers, 1803–1903.* Also known as the Blue Books. Consists of papers presented to the British Parliament at the request of the British crown, the parliament, or the cabinet. Remains the key diplomatic source of the British government relative to late Yi dynasty Korea. Korean issues are covered in the sections dealing with China, Japan, and Russia. For details of this source, see Harold W. V. Temperley and Lilian M. Penson (eds.), *A Century of Diplomatic Blue Books, 1814–1914* (New York: Barnes and Noble, 1938).

03-273. Koryŏ taehakkyo. Asea munje yŏn'guso (Korea University Asiatic Research Center) (comp.). *Ku-Han'guk oegyo munsŏ* [Diplomatic papers relating to late Yi dynasty Korea]. 22 vols. Seoul: Koryŏ taehakkyo ch'ulp'anbu (Korea University Press), 1965–1973. Volumes 10 (1882–1894), 11 (1894–1900), and 12 (1900–1906) of this collection are designated as *Mi-an* [United States documents]; vols. 13 (1882–1898) and 14 (1898–1905) are *Yŏng-an* [British documents]. They consist of correspondence from the American and British diplomatic and consular representatives in Seoul to the Korean foreign office. Entries are partly in English and partly in literary Chinese. Useful as a supplement to the US and British archival sources.

03-274. *Krasnyi Archiv* [Red Archives]. 106 vols. A collection of historical documents pertaining to Tsarist Russia compiled by the Soviet government (1922–1941). A portion of this important Russian archival source dealing with Korea directly and indirectly is available in English translation: "First Steps of Russian Imperialism in Far East, 1888–1903" (from *Krasnyi Archiv,* vol. 52, pp. 54–124), appears in *Chinese Social and Political Science Review* 18(2) (1934):236–281; "Russian Documents Relating to Sino-Japanese War, 1894–1895" (from *Krasnyi Archiv,* vol. 50–51, pp. 3–63) appears in *Chinese Social and Political Science Review* 17(1935–1936):125–139; and "On the Eve of the Russo-Japanese War" (from *Krasnyi Archiv,* vol. 2 (63), pp. 7–54) appears in *Chinese Social and Political Science Review* 17(1934–1935):572–594 and 19(1935–1936):125–139.

03-275. *Korean-American Relations: Documents Pertaining to the Far Eastern Diplomacy of the United States.* 2 vols. Vol. 1: *The Initial Period, 1883–1886.* Edited by George McCune and John A. Harrison. Vol. 2: *The Period of Growing Influence, 1887–1895.* Edited by Spencer J. Palmer. Berkeley: University of California Press, 1951–1963. Select diplomatic documents—generally dispatches from the American minister in Seoul and instructions from the secretary of state—drawn from the original papers in the National Archives. (See 03-277.) Edited under strict guidelines and grouped topically. Each volume contains an introduction by the editors and appen-

dixes. Indispensable for the study of Korean-American relations from 1883 to 1895.

03-276. United States. Department of State. *Papers Relating to the Foreign Relations of the United States.* Washington: Government Printing Office, 1865–. Contains diplomatic correspondence between the US State Department and the diplomatic and consular representatives in Korea. Standard published record of the United States' foreign relations. Thirty-six of the volumes between 1866 and 1910 deal with late Yi dynasty Korea. Unfortunately, however, the State Department editors often deleted sensitive portions of dispatches before publication. Texts which appear in these volumes should not be accepted as authoritative until compared to the National Archives microfilms. (See 03-277.)

03-277. _____. National Archives. Washington. Several series of records preserved in the National Archives relate to Korea between 1876 and 1910. The most important record groups and subseries are listed below; several have been microfilmed.

Record Group 59 (General Records of the Department of State): "Despatches from United States Ministers to Korea, 1883–1905" contains many important documents not included in published works mentioned above (see entries 03-275 and 03-276); available on microfilm, 22 rolls, National Archives Microcopy 134. "Diplomatic Instructions from the Department of State—Korea, 1883–1905" is an important series defining the official American foreign policy toward Korea; roll 109 of National Archives Microcopy 61. "Notes to Foreign Legations and Consuls—Korea" is a portion of roll 68, Microcopy 38. "Notes from Foreign Legations—Korea, 1883–1906" is on one roll, Microcopy 166. "Consular Despatches—Seoul, 1886–1906" contains much material concerning Korean commerce and economics and American business interests in Korea; two rolls, Microcopy 167.

Record Group 84 (Naval Records Collection of the Office of Naval Records and Library): "Letters Received by the Secretary of the Navy from Commanding Officers of Squadrons"; subseries "The Asiatic Squadron Letters." The dispatches from the admiral commanding the Asiatic Squadron to the secretary of the navy. Dispatches from 1876 to 1885 comprise rolls 262–271 of National Archives Microcopy 89.

Private Papers

03-278. *The Allen Papers.* Deposited at the Manuscript Division, New York Public Library. Consists of the private diary, letters, press copy books, official documents, contemporary newspapers, and a collection of books on Korea of Dr. Horace N. Allen (1858–1932). Allen was active in Korea first as a pioneer missionary doctor (1884–1887) and then as a diplomat (1890–1905). One of the most important private primary sources for the study of late nineteenth-century Korean history.

03-279. *The Foulk Papers.* Deposited at the Manuscript Division, New York Public Library. Consists of a part of the papers belonging to George C. Foulk (1856–1893), who was attached to the first Korean mission to the United States in 1883 and then active in Korea as the naval attaché and chargé d'affaires in the US Legation in Seoul (1883–1887). Essential source for the understanding of Korean internal, as well as external, politics.

03-280. _____. A second collection of Foulk papers is preserved in the Library of Congress, Manuscript Division, by the Naval Historical Foundation. Foulk's private letters to his family included in this collection are a rich supplement to his official dispatches. (See entries 03-275, 276, 277, and 279.)

03-281. *The Griffis Papers.* Deposited in the Rutgers University Library. Consists of pamphlets, newspaper clippings, and other materials collected by William Elliot Griffis (1843–1928), the author of *Corea: The Hermit Nation.* For additional information, see Ardath W. Burks and Jerome Cooperman, "The William Elliot Griffis Collection," *Journal of Asian Studies* 28(November 1960): 61–69.

03-282. *The Merrill Papers.* Deposited in the Houghton Library, Harvard University. Consists of the letter-books and other miscellaneous records of Henry F. Merrill (1853–1935), the American chief commissioner of the Korean Customs from 1885 to 1899. Merrill's letters in this collection are addressed mainly to Robert Hart.

03-283. *The Rockhill Papers.* Deposited in the Houghton Library, Harvard University. The papers of William W. Rockhill (1854–1914), the United States chargé d'affaires in Seoul from December 1866 to April 1887. This collection includes Rockhill's correspondence with Dr. Horace N. Allen from 1891 to 1905 and with George C. Foulk from 1887 to 1888.

03-284. *The Shufeldt Papers.* Preserved in the Library of Congress. These papers consist of the diary, personal memoranda and letters of Commodore Robert W. Shufeldt (1822–1895), who was instrumental in concluding the Korean-American Treaty of 1882.

03-285. *The Straight Papers.* Preserved in the John M. Olin Library, Cornell University. Willard Dickerman Straight went to Korea in 1904 as a correspondent covering the Russo-Japanese War. In the summer of 1905 he became private secretary to American Minister to Korea Edward Morgan. The papers contain much material—generally in the form of drafts for news articles—on the crumbling strength of Korea in its domestic and international affairs. Straight's correspondence from the Associated Press indicates a news service policy to avoid comment on Japanese high-handedness in Korean affairs. The collection has been microfilmed, and a guide has been published by the library.

03-286. YUN, Ch'i-ho. *Yun Ch'i-ho Ilgi* [Yun Ch'i-ho diary]. 6 vols. Seoul: Kuksa p'yŏnch'an wiwŏnhoe (National History Compilation Committee), 1973–. Yun Ch'i-ho (1865–1946), one of the most distinguished Christian leaders in modern Korea, was active in the reform movement of the late Yi dynasty during the 1890s. He kept his diary in English from 7 December 1889 to 3 July 1906. This diary reveals the mind of a Korean reformist thinker very well. An indispensable source for the study of Korean political and intellectual history of the late nineteenth century.

Official Government Publications

03-287. China. Inspectorate General of Customs. *Returns of Trade and Trade Reports.* Published by order of the Inspector General of Customs, Shanghai, 1883–1920. 38 vols. under slightly varying titles. The portions for the period 1885–1893 contain appendixes dealing with trade conditions of Korea, including statistical reports on the import and export at Inch'ŏn, Pusan, and Wŏnsan. A very important source for the study of Korean economic development.

03-288. Japan. Residency General of Korea (comp.). *Annual Report of Reforms and Progress in Korea* (1907–1923). Seoul: HIJM's Residency General, 1908–1923. Official publication of the Japanese protectorate regime in Korea to justify Japanese administration of Korea. Although politically biased, the first three issues of *Annual Report* provide useful information on Korean political and economic conditions on the eve of Japanese annexation of Korea in 1910.

03-289. _____. Bureau of Customs. *Report on the Foreign Trade of Korea and Abstract of Statistics* (1907); *Reports of the Foreign Trade and Shipping* (1908); *Report on the Foreign Trade* (1909). Title varies. Continuation of the Chinese serial reports mentioned in entry 03-287.

Contemporary Periodicals

03-290. *The Independent.* The Korean-English bilingual newspaper known in Korea as *Tongnip sinmun* was founded by Dr. Sŏ Chae-p'il (Philip Jaisohn) in April 1896. As the organ of the Independence Club (Tongnip hyŏphoe), this newspaper contains ideas and issues concerning Korean politics of the late 1890s. It was edited by Yun Ch'i-ho and Henry G. Appenzeller (1858–1902) from 1898 to 1899. One of the most important sources for the study of the Korean political and intellectual history of the late Yi dynasty period. Available partly in photoduplicate editions (Seoul: Segye Ilbosa, 1959).

03-291. *Japan Weekly Mail*. Yokohama: 2 January 1886–12 February 1916. Available in microfilm (21 reels). Contains articles on Korea although Japan was the primary interest of this newspaper. Edited after 1880 by Frank Brinkley, R.A., the Yokohama correspondent for *The Times* (London). Since Brinkley accepted a subsidy from the Japanese government after 1900, the post-1900 issues should be read with care.

03-292. *Korea Review*. Seoul: Methodist Publishing House, 1901–1906. Monthly journal edited by Homer B. Hulbert (1863–1949). Similar to *Korean Repository* in organization of contents. Carried scholarly articles on Korean life and history. To be distinguished from *Korea Review* of the Korean Information Bureau (Philadelphia, 1919–1922) and *Korean Review* of the Korean-American Cultural Association (Seattle, 1948–1949).

03-293. *Korean Mission Field*. Seoul: General Council of Evangelical Missions in Korea, 1896–1941. Monthly publication. The standard missionary journal published by the evangelical missions in Korea. Contains good articles on Korean life and history.

03-294. *Korean Repository*. Seoul: Trilingual Press, 1892; 1895–1898. Monthly journal edited first by Franklin Ohlinger (1892) and then by Henry G. Appenzeller and George H. Jones. Carried news features and articles of general interest on Korea, penned mainly by Western residents in Korea. Constitutes a literary treasure and an invaluable historical source for the period covered. Available in photoduplicate edition by the Paragon Book Reprint Corp. in 5 vols.

International Agreements

03-295. Carnegie Endowment for International Peace. *Korea: Treaties and Agreements*. Washington: 1921. Contains copies of twenty-two treaties and proclamations by Korea, China, Japan, Russia, and Great Britain from 1882 to 1910. A highly selective collection.

03-296. China. Imperial Maritime Customs. *Treaties, Regulations, etc., between Corea and Other Powers, 1876–1889.*

Shanghai: Statistical Department of the Inspectorate General of Customs, 1891. 386 pp. Contains, in Chinese and English, all the major international treaties and agreements that Korea entered into from 1876 to 1889.

03-297. CHUNG, Henry (comp.). *Treaties and Conventions between Corea and Other Powers*. New York: H. S. Nichols, 1919. Contains forty-one treaties and agreements with reference to Korea by Austro-Hungary, Belgium, China, Denmark, France, Germany, Great Britain, Italy, Japan, and the United States from 1876 to 1910. Arranged chronologically by nation, this source book provides most of the important treaties and agreements which the Yi dynasty Korean government concluded with foreign powers as a sovereign nation. This collection was motivated by the compiler's desire to buttress Korean independence vis-à-vis Japanese colonial rule in 1919.

03-298. ROCKHILL, William W. (ed.). *Treaties and Conventions with or Concerning China and Korea, 1894–1904, together with Various State Papers and Documents Affecting Foreign Interests*. Washington: Government Printing Office, 1904. Part 2 of this collection is devoted to Korea, covering the international treaties, arrangements, and protocols Korea entered into with foreign powers (for example, Japan and Russia from 1894 to 1904) and the contracts, concessions for railways and mining, and regulations concerning other concessions that the Korean government signed with foreign powers from 1895 to 1899. Ten important documents are listed in chronological order. The addendum, an alphabetical index of Korean treaties and agreements, is useful.

Memoirs, Travel Accounts, and Contemporary Treatises

03-299. ALLEN, Horace N. *Korea: Fact and Fancy*. Seoul: Methodist Publishing House, 1904. 285 pp. The first two chapters of this book deal with the author's impression of the Korean people, the government, and the sights of the capital city which he observed in the early 1880s as a pioneer medical missionary. "A Chronological Index" (pp. 139–271) provides a detailed chronology of the major internal and external events of Korea from antiquity to 1904 with emphasis on the late nineteenth century. Five additional appendixes contain very useful data for students of diplomatic history.

03-300. _____. *Things Korean: A Collection of Sketches and Anecdotes, Missionary and Diplomatic*. New York: Revell, 1908. 256 pp. Casual memoirs of Horace N. Allen as a missionary-diplomat in Korea from 1884 to 1905. Contains the author's reminiscences of the 1884 coup d'état, the Korean mission to the United States in 1887, and the episodes behind the concession of the Unsan gold mines in 1895.

03-301. BISHOP, Isabella L. Bird. *Korea and Her Neighbours: A Narrative of Travel with an Account of the Recent Vicissitudes and Present Condition.* 2 vols. London: John Murray, 1897. Reprinted Seoul: Yonsei University Press, 1970. As the first woman to be honored as a fellow of the Royal Geographical Society, the author of this travel account made intermittent trips through Korea in 1894 and 1895. Based on her personal contact with Korean leaders, including the royal couple and the populace, this travel account provides an intimate and incisive description of internal conditions at a crucial historical turning point. A very important source for the study of the late Yi dynasty Korea.

03-302. CARLES, William R. *Life in Corea.* London: Macmillan, 1888. 317 pp. This is an eyewitness account by a British vice-consul in Korea of the country's internal conditions in the early 1880s. The author's main interest lies in Korea's trade and industrial potential, but he gives an illustrated account of the Korean life-style.

03-303. CURZON, George Nathaniel. *Problems of the Far East: Japan–Korea–China.* London: Longmans, Green, 1894. 411 pp. A reliable account of the Korean internal and external conditions prior to the outbreak of the Sino-Japanese War (1894–1895) by a renowned British scholar-statesman, Lord Curzon, who visited Korea in 1892. More than one-third of this book (chaps. 4 to 7) is devoted to the analysis of the Korean situation. One of the most reliable eyewitness accounts of the Korean domestic situation; includes thirty-six illustrations of Korean scenes and leaders.

03-304. DENNY, Owen N. *China and Korea.* Shanghai: Kelly and Walsh, 1888. 47 pp. A caustic denunciation of Yüan Shih-k'ai's high-handed policies in Korea by an American adviser to the Korean king between 1886 and 1890. Judge Denny defends the cause of Korean independence mainly on modern juristic grounds. This pamphlet is reprinted in the *Congressional Record,* 50th Cong. 1st sess., 8138–8140.

03-305. FRAZER, Everett. *Korea and Her Relations to China, Japan and the United States.* Orange, N.J.: Chronicle Book and Job Printing Office, 1884. 52 pp. In this short but interesting pamphlet, the author, a prominent New England merchant who had business interests in China and Japan, recounts his relationship with such diplomats or semidiplomats as Shufeldt, Foote, and Foulk and reveals his experiences in conducting the first Korean

mission to the United States in 1883 on a tour of observation in New England. Frazer (1835–1901) later served as Korean honorary consul in New York for eleven years after 1884. An important source shedding light on the interrelationship between American business and diplomacy in Korea in the early 1880s.

03-306. GALE, James S. *Korean Sketches.* Nashville: Publishing House of the M.E. Church South, 1898. 271 pp. An outline of the Korean situation as observed by a leading Presbyterian missionary who entered Korea in 1888. Particularly good for understanding the Korean Protestant missionary movement and the domestic political conditions following the Sino-Japanese War of 1894–1895. Although copyrighted in 1898, the book actually covers the author's experience up to 1903.

03-307. GIFFORD, Daniel L. *Every-day Life in Korea: A Collection of Studies and Stories.* New York: Revell, 1898. 231 pp. A well-organized description of the growth of Protestant churches, modern schools, and various other modern institutions in Korea by a missionary who entered Korea in 1890. An accurate and systematic description of Korea in the 1890s.

03-308. GILMORE, George W. *Korea from Its Capital: With a Chapter on Missions.* Philadelphia: Presbyterian Board of Publication and Sabbath-School Work, 1892. 32 pp. The author was an American teacher of the Royal College (Yugyŏng kongwŏn) from 1886 to 1889. He provides an overall impression of the Korean situation—government, language, religion, foreign relations, missionary work—from a rather critical standpoint.

03-309. LADD, George Trumbull. *In Korea with Marquis Ito.* New York: Scribner's, 1908. 477 pp. An overtly pro-Japanese account of Japanese-dominated Korea in the wake of the Russo-Japanese War by a prominent professor of Yale University who visited Korea in 1906 at Japanese invitation. The book consists of two parts: "A Narrative of Personal Experiences" and "A Critical and Historical Inquiry."

03-310. LENSEN, George Alexander (ed.). *Korea and Manchuria between Russia and Japan, 1895–1904: The Observations of Sir Ernest Satow.* Tallahassee: Diplomatic Press, 1966. 296 pp. A lifelong orientalist and an intimate friend of Japanese statesmen, Sir Ernest Satow was HM Minister to both Japan (1895–1900) and China (1900–1906). The excerpts from Satow's personal diaries printed in this book are a valuable source for understanding the thoughts of the Japanese policymakers toward Korea during the decade which preceded the Russo-Japanese War.

03-311. LOWELL, Percival. *Choson: The Land of the Morning Calm—A Sketch of Korea*. Boston: Ticknor and Co., 1888. 412 pp. Percival Lowell (1855–1916) served as "Secretary and Counsellor" to the Korean special mission to the United States in 1883. This book is based on his personal experience in Seoul as a royal guest during the winter of 1883–1884. Covers a wide range of subjects including Korean geography, government, popular mores, and religion. A rather superficial account of Korea.

03-312. MOOSE, J. Robert. *Village Life in Korea*. Nashville: Publishing House of the M.E. Church, 1911. 242 pp. An intimate account of the "heathen" way of life as observed by an American medical missionary after 1899. It deals with various aspects of Korean life, both in the countryside and in the capital city, in an easy style of writing. Although intended to be an introductory survey of Korean native culture for prospective missionaries, this book is actually a sort of anthropolitical survey of Korean society at the turn of the century.

03-313. OPPERT, Ernest. *A Forbidden Land: Voyages to Corea*. London: Sampson Low, Marston, Searle and Rivington, 1880. After outlining Korean geography, government, history, social customs, and language, Oppert dwells on his two voyages along the Korean coast and provides his own story regarding the infamous and abortive adventure to dig up the tomb of the father of the (Hungson) Taewon'gun in 1868.

03-314. SANDS, William F. *Undiplomatic Memories: The Far East, 1896–1904*. New York: McGraw-Hill, 1930. 238 pp. Sands (1874–1946) was secretary of the American legation in Seoul (1898–1900) and "Advisor to the Korean Emperor" (1900–1904). In this memoir, he provides a very intimate and vivid picture of Korean court life, the rebellion of Cheju Island in 1901, the concession rivalry among the great powers in Korea, and other important features of Korean domestic and foreign politics in which he was personally involved. A major source for the study of the Korean politics prior to Japanese absorption of Korea.

03-315. UNDERWOOD, Lillias Horton. *Fifteen Years among the Top-knots, or, Life in Korea*. Rev. ed. New York: American Tract Society, 1908. 354 pp. (1st ed., 1904). An intimate account of Korean life by the wife of the Rev. H. G. Underwood, a woman medical missionary who arrived in Korea in 1888. Aside from the details of the evangelical activities in which the Underwoods took the lead, the author recounts how the American Protestant missionaries were involved in Korean domestic politics. Accounts dealing with the missionaries' relationship with the court, the Independence Club, and the Righteous Army movement are particularly useful.

03-316. WILKINSON, William H. *The Corean Government: Constitutional Changes, July 1894 to October 1895, with an Appendix on Subsequent Enactments to 30th June 1896*. Shanghai: Statistical Department of the Inspectorate General of Customs, 1897. A study based on Korean sources of the late nineteenth-century Korean political and social institutions, focusing on the drastic institutional changes between 1894 and 1896. The author arrived in Seoul as the acting consul general of Great Britain in 1889 and remained in Korea during the *Kabo* reform movement of 1894–1896. This book provides much useful information; of special value is an English translation of Korean institutional terms. Although it lacks a proper historical perspective, this work remains an invaluable manual for the study of the late Yi dynasty institutional history.

GENERAL

03-317. BOURDARET, Émile. *En Corée*. Paris: Plon, 1904. A firsthand account of folkways, religion, historical landmarks, social conditions, and government of the time.

03-318. HULBERT, Homer B. *The Passing of Korea*. New York: Doubleday Page, 1906. Reprinted Seoul: Yonsei University Press, 1969. 473 pp. A general discussion of Korean history, culture, and society up to the Russo-Japanese War, with emphasis on Japan's wartime encroachments into Korea. Also provides an excellent firsthand account of such domestic incidents as the assassination of Queen Min (1895) and the activities of the Independence Club.

03-319. JANSEN, Marius B. *Japan and China: From War to Peace, 1894–1972*. Chicago: Rand McNally, 1975. 547 pp. This up-to-date textbook on modern East Asian history contains an excellent summary of Korean history from 1866 to 1910.

03-320. KIM, C. I. Eugene and Han-Kyo KIM. *Korea and the Politics of Imperialism, 1876–1910*. Berkeley and Los Angeles: University of California Press, 1967. 260 pp. A well-balanced, objective, and lucid account of Korean political development from 1876 to 1910 in the context of international power rivalry impinging on the Korean peninsula. This volume, based on multiarchival research, will remain a standard work on late Yi dynasty Korean political history for a long time.

03-321. McGRANE, George A. *Korea's Tragic Hours: The Closing Years of the Yi Dynasty*. Edited by Harold F. Cook and Alan M. MacDougall. Seoul: Taewon Publishing Co., 1973. 85 pp. This posthumous booklet, based on the author's lectures delivered to newly arrived foreigners in Seoul, provides a brief overview of Korean history from 1882 to 1910. The discussion on the early phase of modern Korean history is generally outdated, but the treatment of Korean resistance against the Japanese from 1905 to 1910 is good.

03-322. McKENZIE, Frederick Arthur. *Tragedy of Korea.* London: Hodder and Stoughton, 1908. Reprinted Seoul: Yonsei University Press, 1969. McKenzie (1869–1931), a Canadian journalist representing the *Daily Mail* of London from 1900 to 1910 and the author of *Korea's Flight for Freedom* (1920), treats the process of the Japanese penetration into Korea and the Korean reaction to it from 1876 to 1907. This volume contains an eyewitness account of the Korean Righteous Army *(Uibyŏng)* active in 1907. In appendixes the author lists the findings of the Japanese Minister Miura's trial in the Hiroshima court in conjunction with the assassination of Queen Min, a series of international treaties relevant to Korea from 1876 to 1907, and the petition of the Korean residents in Hawaii to President Roosevelt.

03-323. PALAIS, James B. "Political Participation in Traditional Korea, 1876–1910." *The Journal of Korean Studies* (Seattle) 1(1979):73–121. In this provocative essay dealing with the origins of mass participatory democracy and nationalism in modern Korea, the author examines the salient features of the enlightenment movement of the 1880s, the *Kabo* ("1894") Reforms of 1894–1896, the activities of the Independence Club (1896–1898), the Tonghak-inspired peasant movement, and a variety of political and educational movements which cropped up between 1904 and 1910—including those of the Progressive Society *(Chinbohoe),* the Unity and Progress Society *(Ilchinhoe),* The Great Korean Association *(Taehan hyŏphoe),* the Northwest Academic Association *(Sŏbuk hakhoe),* and the Righteous Army *(Ŭibyŏng).* The author concludes that "the record of participatory activity and organization for the period from 1896–1910 was impressive," but their sustained growth was impeded by "the continued presence of domestic and foreign governmental authorities overtly hostile to the growth of political participation." This essay is recommended highly not only for its analytical insights but also for an up-to-date selective bibliography contained in its footnotes.

03-324. YI, Kyu-tae. *Modern Transformation of Korea.* Translated by Sung Tong-mahn et al. Seoul: Sejong Publishing Co., 1970. 327 pp. An English version of the author's contributions in Korean to a daily newspaper in Seoul under the title of "One Hundred Views of Korean Enlightenment" *(Kaehwa paekkyŏng).* Deals in a journalistic style with myriad aspects of Korean life in transformation from 1876 to 1919.

POLITICS AND SOCIETY

03-325. CHANDRA, Vipan. "Nationalism and Popular Participation in Government in Late 19th Century Korea: The Contribution of the Independence Club (1896–98)." PhD dissertation, Harvard University, 1977. 298 pp. "The dissertation discusses at length the political ideology and the political activities of the Independence Club, a mass pressure group of late 19th-Century Korea. Two specific questions form the focus of the author's inquiry: One, what was the aim of its movement, and two, what were its accomplishments and shortcomings. The Club's pronounced aim was to protect Korean sovereignty from foreign encroachments and to see Korea transformed into a prosperous and strong political entity. It considered popular participation in government important to the achievement of this aim. The thesis goes on to examine the club's activities in pursuit of its aim and finds that while achieving much success in spreading a new nationalistic consciousness in Korea, its leaders failed in displaying solidarity, dedication and self-sacrifice in moments of crisis. This, together with the fact that the Club was not a revolutionary body, but a gradualist-reformist group working within the traditional political structure of Korea, in the judgment of the author, constituted the major shortcoming of the Club's movement which ultimately led to its quick and easy suppression by the government."

03-326. _____. "An Outline Study of the Ilchin-hoe (Advancement Society) of Korea." *Occasional Papers on Korea* 2(March 1974):43–72. Edited by James B. Palais. A study of the pro-Japanese Korean association organized by Yi Yong-gu (1868–1912) and Song Pyŏng-jun (1858–1925) on the eve of Japanese annexation of Korea in 1910. Analyzes the ideology and activities of the society in connection with the Pan-Asiatic movement in Asia at large. Based on Japanese and Korean primary sources.

03-327. _____. "The Independence Club and Korea's First Proposal for a National Legislative Assembly." *Occasional Papers on Korea* 4(September 1975):19–35. This article discusses the reasons behind the Independence Club's call for a Korean national assembly and examines at length the various features of the proposed body. The proposal showed that its authors had a fair, though incomplete, understanding of the Western parliamentary model and that the club's stress on keeping the assembly initially under the direction of the nation's elite perhaps was inspired by the Japanese example. An expanded and revised version of this article forms part of the author's PhD dissertation (03-325).

03-328. CHUN, Hae-jong. "The Origin and Development of the Tongni Amun and Its Significance in Modernization." In *Proceedings of Conference on Modernization of East Asia.* Seoul: Korea University Press, 1969. An important study dealing with the genesis of Korea's first foreign office, T'ongni Kimu Amun, in 1881–1882. Very useful for the study of institutional modernization in late Yi dynasty Korea.

03-329. COOK, Harold Francis. *Korea's 1884 Incident: Its Background and Kim Ok-kyun's Elusive Dream.* Royal Asiatic Society Korea Branch Monograph Series, no. 4. Seoul: Taewon Publishing Co., 1972. 264 pp. As a distillation of the author's PhD dissertation (Harvard University, 1969), this volume presents the thesis that the 1884 coup d'état was worked out mainly by Korean reformist officials clustered around Kim Ok-kyun, with little decisive influence from the Japanese. A detailed study based on Japanese and Korean primary sources. This volume, however, lacks footnotes.

03-330. DEUCHLER, Martina. *Confucian Gentlemen and Barbarian Envoys: The Opening of Korea, 1875–1885.* Published for the Korea Branch of the Royal Asiatic Society. Seattle: University of Washington Press, 1977. 310 pp. This is a well-informed and carefully documented study on the initial phase of "Confucian" Korea's opening to the "barbarian" Japan and West. Deuchler opens this book by examining domestic and international conditions leading to the momentous Kanghwa Treaty in 1876. She then delves into the questions of how Korean leaders reacted to the challenge of modern civilization, how new treaty ports were established, and how Korea came to conclude treaties with the United States and other Western powers in the early 1880s. She also discusses the development of China's aggressive policy toward Korea after mid-1882, which culminated with the Li-Itō Convention at Tientsin in 1885. In analyzing Korean domestic development, Deuchler credits the youthful King Kojong—characterized as "sophisticated" and "pragmatic"—for breaking the Korean-Japanese diplomatic stalemate prior to 1876 and for launching the self-strengthening movement in 1880. Korean modernization during 1875–1885 was retarded, according to Deuchler, because of the strong influence of Neo-Confucian conservative ideology, the

overcentralization of the Korean government, the slow development of capitalist economy, the smallness of the territory, the interference of foreign powers in Korean internal affairs, and the defeat of the progressive "Enlightenment Party" *(Kaehwadang)* by the more conservative Min clan party in the power struggle of 1884. The changing condition of Korea's early open ports, Korean diplomatic and cultural missions to Japan and China, the growth of Korea's early modern institutions (T'ongni Kimu Amun, for example, and the Maritime Customs Service), and the roles played by such foreign advisers as Paul G. von Möllendorff are described succinctly in this volume. This multifaceted study based on Korean, Chinese, Japanese, and Western sources will long remain a valuable guide for students interested in Korea's early response to the West.

03-331. HAHM, Pyong-Choon. "Korea's Initial Encounter with the Western Law: 1866–1910 A.D." *Korea Observer* 1(2)(January 1969):80–93. The author analyzes Korea's first exposure to Western law in three stages: (1) the opening of Korea, (2) the *Kabo* Reforms and their aftermath, and (3) the Japanese protectorate and annexation. He concludes that "every step of the 'reform' and 'modernization' was accompanied by a progressive loss of national independence."

03-332. KIM, Yong-sŏp. "Absentee Landlord System during the 19–20th Century in Korea—Aggravations in the Landlord and Agromanagerial Means in Chaeryŏng, Tōtaku Farmlands." *Journal of Social Sciences and Humanities* 37(December 1972):27–63. This is an important study of how a vast amount of land owned by the Korean Royal Household of the Yi dynasty eventually came to be possessed by the Oriental Development Company (Tōtaku) of Japan. By delving into the case of the Yi dynasty Royal Household land located in Chaeryŏng, Hwanghae province, as a typical example, the author examines the changes in land tenure system prior to 1894, the incorporation of all of the Royal Household lands into the post and garrison lands *(yŏktunt'o)* during the Japanese Residency-Generalcy (1906–1910), the establishment of the Oriental Development Company and its subsequent absorption of these lands, and the land tenure disputes raised by Korean tenants in the post-1910 period.

03-333. LEE, Hyon-jong. "On Political, Journalistic, and Social Organizations in the Days of the Taehan Empire." *Journal of Social Sciences and Humanities* 28(June 1968):31–41 and 29(December 1968):100–117. A comprehensive survey of various organizations, political and social, in the last years of the Yi dynasty.

03-334. LEE, Kwang-rin. "On the Publication of *The Independent* by Suh Jae-pil (Philip Jaisohn)." *Journal of Social Sciences and Humanities* 43(June 1976):1–43. In this fascinating and well-documented article, Professor Lee describes how *The Independent (Tongnip sinmun)*—Korea's first Korean-English newspaper—came into being in April 1896, how it was closed down in December 1899, and how its editorship changed hands from Sǒ Chae-p'il to Yun Ch'i-ho and, then, to H. Emberly. The author reveals the personal motives of Sǒ Chae-p'il and his early helpers, including Yun Ch'i-ho and Yu Kil-chun, in launching the newspaper and explores the reasons for its suppression by the Yi government in 1898. As a study utilizing the diary of Yun Ch'i-ho and the Japanese-Korean newspaper *Kanjō Shimpō (Hansǒng sinbo),* it sheds much light on the inner workings of Korean politics during the turbulent years of 1895–1899.

03-335. LEW, Young Ick. "The Kabo Reform Movement: Korean and Japanese Reform Efforts in Korea, 1894." PhD dissertation, Harvard University, 1972. 660 pp. An in-depth analysis of the ideas and behavior of the Korean and Japanese leaders related to the historic reform movement starting in 1894. Particular emphasis is placed on the motivations and roles of the Korean royal coterie, reformer-officials of the Deliberative Council *(Kun'guk kimuch'ǒ),* the Tonghak rebels, and the Japanese representatives in Seoul. Based on Korean and Japanese primary source materials.

03-336. _____. "The Reform Efforts and Ideas of Pak Yǒng-hyo, 1894–1895." *Korean Studies* 1(December 1977). This article deals with the role of Pak Yǒng-hyo in the reform movement of 1894–1895 under the aegis of the Japanese Minister Inoue Kaoru. The author argues that Pak espoused an ambitious reform program of his own, independent of the Japanese plan, and that he attempted to implement radical reforms against Japanese wishes.

03-337. NAHM, Andrew Changwoo. "Kim Ok-kyun and the Korean Progressive Movement, 1882–1884." PhD dissertation, Stanford University, 1961. 406 pp. Abstracted in *DA* 22(November 1961):1603-04; UM 61-4149. "Focuses upon the goals of the Progressive Party, the forces which nurtured the growth of progressive ideas and the nationalist movement in Korea, and China's policy for reasserting its overlordship in Korea." Also studies the support extended by the United States and Japan to the progressives.

03-338. _____. "Reaction and Response to the Opening of Korea, 1876–1884." In Robert K. Sakai (ed.), *Studies on Asia 1965.* Lincoln: University of Nebraska Press, 1965. Deals with the initial reaction of the antiforeign groups to the opening of Korea. The emphasis is on their ideological and political rationale and the clash between the conservative party and the reformist party culminating with the coup of December 1884.

03-339. QUINONES, Carlos Kenneth. "The Prerequisites for Power in Late Yi Korea: 1864–1894." PhD dissertation, Harvard University, 1975. 259 pp. A study of Yi Korea's governmental leadership between 1864 and 1894 with a view to ascertaining factors that enabled an individual in late Yi Korea to acquire a position of political influence. The author uses quantitative methods to analyze the examination, clan, and geographic backgrounds of some 375 individuals who held high offices and concludes that "there were three crucial prerequisites for achieving a position of political and bureaucratic influence between 1864 and 1894. Listed in the order of their importance, these were: success in an examination, especially the *munkwa;* being from the area surrounding Seoul; and membership in a family of established socio-political importance." A solid study based on extensive genealogical and examination records.

03-340. _____. "The Impact of the Kabo Reforms upon Political Role Allocation in Late Yi Korea, 1884–1902." *Occasional Papers on Korea* 4(September 1975):1–18. In this carefully researched article based on traditional lineage records, examination rosters, and other bibliographic sources, the author attempts to ascertain whether any major change was introduced into the Yi Korean policy of recruitment by the *Kabo* Reforms of 1894–1896. By noting that little change appeared in the percentage of traditional examination passers among the ruling elite of 1884–1894 and that of 1896–1902, the author concludes that the effect of the *Kabo* Reforms was slight and "success in the traditional examination continued to be a fundamental prerequisite for entrance into the ruling elite after 1896."

03-341. WEEMS, Clarence Norwood, Jr. "The Korean Reform and Independence Movement, 1881–1889." PhD dissertation, Columbia University, 1954. 557 pp. Abstracted in *DA* 14(October 1954):1704-05; UM 8859. Analyzes the failure of the nineteenth-century Korean reform movement in terms of the failure of the reformist Tonghak Society and the independence movement to combine forces.

03-342. WǑN, Yu-han. "A Study on the Introduction of German Coinage Technique to Korea." *Korea Journal* 14(11) (November 1974):4–11. Deals with the Korean government's attempt at monetary reform in the 1880s by the introduction of modern minting techniques from Germany.

03-343. WOO, Philip Myungsup. "The Historical Development of Korean Tariff and Customs Administration, 1875–1958.'' PhD dissertation, New York University, 1963. 292 pp. Abstracted in *DA* 27(June 1967):4321-A; UM 64-1792. The author concludes that "the tariff process pursued by the Korean government is a linear one"—that is, its formulation, enactment, and execution "are administered by the customs service without implicit consent of the interested public.'' Contents: The Royal Korean Maritime Customs: Initial Period (1876–1883); The Royal Korean Maritime Customs: European Era (1883–1905); The Japanese Era, I: The Korean Customs in the Period of a Vanished Kingdom (1910–1945); The Japanese Tariff System; Customs; Administration, Postwar Period; Tariff Making Power; Legal Framework of the Customs Institution; Summary; Conclusion.

RELIGION AND EDUCATION

03-344. AN, Pyong-uk. "Tosan: The Man and His Thought." *Korea Journal* 11(6)(June 1971):33–42. Tosan is the pen name of An Ch'ang-ho (1878–1938).

03-345. ASH, James Kenneth. "The Tonghak Rebellion: Problems and Interpretations." *Journal of Social Sciences and Humanities (Bulletin of the Korean Research Center)* 32(March 1970):89–106. A provocative survey of some interpretative problems regarding the Tonghak movement from the 1860s to 1910, with emphasis on the Tonghak "rebellion" of 1894. The author refutes the conspiracy theories that the Japanese assisted the Tonghak uprising, that the Taewŏn'gun and Chŏn Pong-jun collaborated, and that the Chinese instigated the rebellion.

03-346. CHUNG, Chai Sik. "Protestantism and the Formation of Modern Korea, 1884–1894." PhD dissertation, Boston University, 1964. 322 pp. Abstracted in *DA* 26(July 1965):328; UM 64-11,603. "The involvement of Protestantism in the inceptive process of the formation of modern Korea is studied as a case of culture contact with the West and subsequent social change. Attention is focused on the nature and process of the contact and the extent and direction of mutual accommodation during the inceptive stage. The role of the religious factor in the evolution of Korean society is seen to be crucial."

03-347. CLARK, Charles Allen. *Religions of Old Korea.* New York: Revell, 1932. Reprinted in Seoul, 1961. A comprehensive study of Korean traditional religions—Buddhism, Confucianism, Ch'ŏndogyo, shamanism, and other Asiatic religious sects—by a Protestant missionary in Korea who taught theology in the Presbyterian Theological Seminary in Seoul. This work is based on Western sources and is out of date, but it remains one of the most

comprehensive accounts of Korean religion and philosophy in English.

03-348. DALLET, Charles *Histoire de l'Église de Corée.* Paris: V. Palme, 1874. 2 vols. Reprinted by the Royal Asiatic Society, Korea Branch, Seoul, 1975. The classic study on the history of the Catholic church as well as on the sociopolitical conditions of the period. Based on letters and reports received from French missionaries, this famous work is still very useful.

03-349. HA, Hyon-gang. "The Life and Thought of Sin Ch'ae-ho." *Korea Journal* 12(9)(September 1972):49–92. A brief survey of the life and ideas of Sin Ch'ae-ho (1880–1936), an important Korean nationalist historian at the turn of the century.

03-350. JO, Yung-hwan (ed.). *Korea's Response to the West.* Kalamazoo: Korea Research and Publications, 1971. Mimeographed. A collection of ten papers, of uneven quality, dealing with various aspects of Korean attempts to cope with the challenge of the West. This edition comprises the following: Hugh D. Walker, "The Weight of Tradition: Preliminary Observations on Korea's Intellectual Responses"; Young-ho Kim, "The Acceptance of Western Technology in Early Modern Korea"; Hong-ryol Ryu, "The Acceptance of Western Culture in Korea"; W. J. Kang, "Early Korean Contact with Christianity and Korean Response: An Historical Introduction"; Chai Sik Chung, "Christianity as a Heterodoxy: An Aspect of General Cultural Orientation in Traditional Korea" (03-207); Spencer J. Palmer, "Western Religion and Korean Culture"; Soo-bock Choi, "Korea's Response to America and France in the Decade of the Taewongun, 1864–1873"; Andrew C. Nahm, "Reaction and Response to the Opening of Korea, 1876–1884" (03-338); Clarence N. Weems, "Reformist Thought of the Independence Program (1896–1898)" (03-361); Daniel S. Juhn, "Korean Industrial Entrepreneurship, 1924–1940."

03-351. KANG, Thomas Hosuck. "Confucian Behavior Toward the Modernization of Korea, 1864–1910." *Korea Journal* 13(7)(July 1973):4–15. Using the author's "model of mathematical function," this paper "attempts to analyze the pattern of Confucian behavior in Korea . . . and the factors involved in the response of Korean Confucian society to the challenge of modernity from 1864 to 1910."

03-352. KIM, Hyung-chan. "Yu Kil-chun: A Korean Crusader for Reform." *Korea Journal* 12(12)(December 1972): 36–42. This brief article gives a biographical sketch of a Korean "enlightenment" thinker, Yu Kil-chun (1856–1914), and summarizes the thoughts on enlightenment, government, and education which appear in his *Sŏyu kyŏnmun* [Observations on a tour of the West].

03-353. KIM, Young-Ho. "Yu Kil-chun's Idea of Enlightenment." *Journal of Social Sciences and Humanities* 33 (December 1970):37–60. The author details the ideas of enlightenment available in Yu Kil-chun's *Sŏyu kyŏnmun* after providing personal and intellectual data on its author as backdrops.

03-354. LEE, Kwang-rin. "'I-yen' and the Ideas of Enlightenment in Korea." *Journal of Social Sciences and Humanities* 31(December 1969):1–9. An authority on the Korean enlightenment movement of the late nineteenth century examines how a book written by a Chinese reform thinker, Cheng Kuan-ying (1841–1920), was introduced into Korea and subsequently influenced the reform-minded Korean intellectuals. A major study in Korean intellectual history of the nineteenth century.

03-355. _____. "Royal College: The Earliest Modern Government School in Korea." *Journal of Social Sciences and Humanities* 21(December 1964):26–42. This is an informative study on the first government-sponsored modern educational institution in Korea—the *Yugyŏng kongwŏn* (Royal College), founded in 1886. The author details the background leading to its creation, the recruitment of foreign instructors, the organization of its curricula, the social background and behavior pattern of its students, and the reasons for its eventual failure in making any significant contribution to Korean modernization.

03-356. _____. "Western Korea and Protestantism in the Enlightenment Period: A Case Study in the Reception of Protestantism." *Journal of Social Sciences and Humanities* 41(June 1975):1–16. A provocative sociointellectual study relating the high receptivity of Protestantism in the northwestern provinces in Korea to the prevalence of non-*yangban* middle class, including merchants, in that region. The author also finds an affinity between Protestant ethics and the relatively active political, social, educational, and economic movements among the northwesterners in modern times.

03-357. LEW, Young Ick. "An Analysis of Reform Documents of the Kabo Reform Movement, 1894." *Journal of Social Sciences and Humanities* 40(December 1974): 29–85. An analysis of the reform documents adopted by the reform-promoting Deliberative Council *(Kun'guk kimuch'ŏ),* from July to October 1894, with a view to refuting the conventional thesis that the *Kabo* ("1894") reform movement was a heteronomous movement wholly dictated by the Japanese against Korean wishes.

03-358. PAIK, Lak-Geoon George. *The History of Protestant Missions in Korea, 1832–1910.* Pyongyang: Union Christian College Press, 1927. Reprinted Seoul: Yonsei University Press, 1970. 470 pp. A monumental study of the Protestant missionary movement in Korea from its inception in 1832 to the time of Korean incorporation into the Japanese empire in 1910, based on a solid research into a vast amount of primary sources in English. The author covers practically all important aspects of missionary activities in Korea, including evangelical, medical, and educational undertakings, which had a profound impact on Korean modernization in the late nineteenth century. A work of high scholarship, it has withstood the test of time and remains the standard work on the subject. The author improved on the contents of this book in the 1970 edition by adding minor modifications in the text of the first two chapters, standardizing romanization of proper nouns, and updating footnotes and bibliography. The 1970 version contains a brief biographical sketch of the author by Samuel H. Moffett.

03-359. SIN, Yong-ha. "Social Philosophy of Tongnip Hyŏphoe." *Korea Journal* 14(3)(March 1974):21–30. A short discussion of the basic ideas of the Tongnip Hyŏphoe (Independence Club), including the concepts of independence, civil liberties, and reform. The author has written a book in Korean on the club.

03-360. SOHN, Pow-Key. "The Opening of Korea: A Conflict of Traditions." *Transactions of the Korea Branch of the Royal Asiatic Society* 36(April 1960):101–128. This is a study on how a Confucian-oriented Korean official, Kim Ki-su, heading the first diplomatic mission to Japan in 1876, reacted to the "new civilization" of Meiji Japan. Based on an analysis of Kim's diary.

03-361. WEEMS, Clarence N. "Reformist Thought of the Independence Program (1896–1898)." In Yung-hwan Jo (ed.), *Korea's Response to the West.* (See 03-350.) The most comprehensive treatment in English of the political, social, and other reform programs advocated by the Independence Club.

FOREIGN RELATIONS
Multinational Relations

03-362. DE LAGUÉRIE, Villetard. *La Corée et la Guerre russo-japonaise.* Paris: Delagrave, 1909. A general description of Korea, her government and economy, and the economic and political developments following 1898. Also explains the Russo-Japanese agreement on the Korean problem and the commencement of hostilities between Russia and Japan.

03-363. DONG, Chon. "Korea and the Russo-Japanese

War.'' *Koreana Quarterly* 1(2)(Winter 1959):22–72. A detailed study of the Russo-Japanese rivalry over Korea from 1895 to the termination of the Russo-Japanese War of 1904–1905.

03-364. GORRINI, G. ''La Corea e la guerra fra la Cina e il Giappone.'' *Nuova Antologia* (Rome), 52(1894). Inquiry into the causes of the Sino-Japanese War.

03-365. HONG, Soon-ho. ''La question coréenne face au conflit sino-japonaise de 1894–1895.'' PhD dissertation, University of Paris, 1969. Discusses the connection between the Sino-Japanese War and the Korean problem.

03-366. KIM, Chang-hoon. ''Les relations internationales de la Corée de la seconde moitié du XIXe siècle à la perte de son indépendance (1910).'' PhD dissertation, University of Paris, 1959. Discusses Korean foreign policy in the last half of the nineteenth century and the early twentieth century and explores the international situation affecting Korea during that period.

03-367. KIM, K. H. ''The Last Phase of the East Asian World Order: The Sino-Japanese Rivalry and the Opening of Korea, 1870–1882.'' PhD dissertation, University of California, Davis, 1975. ''In the mid-nineteenth century the traditional world order in East Asia and Chinese supremacy in that order faced two major challenges which were ultimately to cause the demise of that order: Western expansion and the rise of Meiji Japan. Because of Korea's pivotal geographical position in East Asia and its position as the keystone of the Chinese tribute system, its opening was a process that represented both the last phase of the traditional world order and the rising Sino-Japanese rivalry for hegemony in East Asia.''

03-368. KOH, Byong-ik. ''The Role of the Westerners Employed by the Korean Government in the Late Yi Dynasty.'' In *International Conference on the Problems of Modernization in Asia*. Seoul: 1965. In this knowledgeable article, a German-trained Korean historian explores the political background leading to Yi Korean employment of European and American advisers from 1882 to 1910 and evaluates their contribution to Korea's early modernization. The author's emphasis is on Paul G. Möllendorff, Henry F. Merrill, O. N. Denny, Charles W. LeGendre, and McLeavy Brown, who worked for the Korean customs service, foreign office, and finance department. The author concludes that their contribution to Korean modernization was ''far from outstanding'' for a number of historical reasons, including a lack of commitment to the goal of modernization among the Korean employers. This short article serves as a useful introduction to the subject.

03-369. LEE, Bae-yong. ''Competitive Mining Survey by Foreign Powers in Korea—With Emphasis on the 1880s.'' *Journal of Social Sciences and Humanities* 36(June 1972): 12–41. An interesting study on the competitive attempts of Japan, Great Britain, Germany, and the United States to obtain mining concessions from the Korean government in the 1880s and Korea's reaction to them.

03-370. OH, Bonnie Bongwan. ''The Background of Chinese Policy Formation in the Sino-Japanese War of 1894–1895.'' PhD dissertation, University of Chicago, 1974. 508 pp. ''A study of the background of the Sino-Japanese War with emphasis on the reasons for China's inability to avoid the war, which few Chinese, even including the so-called war party, desired. This study includes a fairly thorough survey of Korean-Chinese-Japanese relations, the events in early 1894, and the interplay of the Powers in East Asia in the late nineteenth century. Based on Chinese, Korean and Japanese documents and materials, as well as English, French, and Russian sources.''

03-371. TSIANG, T. F. ''Sino-Japanese Diplomatic Relations, 1870–1894.'' *Chinese Social and Political Science Review* 17(1933–1934):1–106. A masterly survey of the development of Sino-Japanese diplomacy regarding Formosa, the Liu-ch'iu (Ryūkyū) Islands, and Korea from 1870 to 1894 from the Chinese point of view. Special emphasis is given to Chinese policies toward Korea surrounding the stormy years of 1882 and 1884. The author's treatment of Sino-Japanese-Korean relations of the post-1885 period is superficial, but it remains one of the best on the subject in English.

Korean-American Relations

03-372. ARNOLD, Dean Alexander. ''American Economic Enterprises in Korea, 1895–1939.'' PhD dissertation, University of Chicago, 1954. 515 pp. Contents: Korea in 1895; American Concession Hunting, 1895–1897; International Rivalries and American Financial Promotion, 1897–1898; The Greater Concession, 1899–1900; From McKinley's Re-Election to the Russo-Japanese War, November 1900–February 1904; The Russo-Japanese War and American Enterprises in Korea, 1904–1905; The Kapsan Concession, 1900–1915; The Suan Concession, 1905–1924; The Oriental Consolidated Mining Company, 1905–1939.

03-373. BISHOP, Donald M. ''Sustaining Korean Independence: American Military Mission to Korea, 1882– 1887.'' MA thesis, Ohio State University, 1974. 143 pp. Studies on the roles of Ensign George C. Foulk, the Asiatic Squadron, and the American military instructors, including Gen. William McEntyre Dye (1831–1899), in Korean domestic development from 1882 to 1897. The author brings into relief many unknown or neglected aspects of Korean-American relations in the late nineteenth century by tapping the vast amount of American primary sources and utilizing the limited number of Korean secondary sources. He writes with unusual insight and empathy with regard to the subjects under consideration.

03-374. CHAY, Jongsuk. "The Taft-Katsura Memorandum Reconsidered." *Pacific Historical Review* 37(1968):321–326. Reviews the legal aspects of the Taft-Katsura memorandum and refutes thc claim of Raymond A. Esthus that it was a mere exchange of views (see 03-383). The author concludes that "the conversation was highly significant to President Roosevelt," who "knew well that his approval of the Japanese position in Korea and Japanese policy toward the Philippines was involved in the conversation. Although not an international agreement in words, the conversation amounted to an informal and tacit understanding between the two countries."

03-375. _____. "The United States and the Closing Door in Korea: American-Korean Relations, 1894–1905." PhD dissertation, University of Michigan, 1965. 192 pp. Abstracted in *DA* 27(August 1966):435-A; UM 66-6581. "The objective of this study is to examine America's policy toward Korea during the period of 1894–1905 and to evaluate it on the bases of her interest in Korea and the situation in the Far East." Contents: The Bases of American Policy toward Korea; Offer of Good Offices for Korea: The Policy of Strict Neutrality; Theodore Roosevelt and Korea; (1) The Policy of Indifference, (2) The Policy of Reality.

03-376. CHOE, Choon. "Korean-American Negotiations Regarding Copyright of 'Independent' Newspaper." *Journal of Social Sciences and Humanities* 30(June 1969):1–23. A detailed study of the circumstances leading to the final closing of the newspaper *Tongnip sinmun (The Independent)*.

03-377. CHOI, Dong Hoon. "The United States Policy toward the Japanese Protectorate and Annexation in Korea, 1904–1910." PhD dissertation, Fletcher School of Law and Diplomacy, 1965. 228 pp. Contents: Korea and the Outside World: From the Treaty of Kanghwa (1876) to the Japanese Annexation of Korea (1910); Korean-American Relations: From the Treaty of Shimonoseki to the Russo-Japanese War; United States Policy toward the Japanese Absorption from the Protectorate Agreement to the Hague Affair; United States Policy toward the Japanese Annexation of Korea.

03-378. DENNETT, Tyler. *American in Eastern Asia: A Critical Study of the Policy of the United States with Reference to China, Japan and Korea in the Nineteenth Century.* New York: Macmillan, 1922. Reprinted New York: Barnes and Noble, 1963. A comprehensive and authoritative study of the origin and development of American policy in East Asia in the nineteenth century with a substantial coverage on Korea. Dennett was the first scholar to exploit systematically the diplomatic records of the Department of State. The resulting book is still remarkable for its analysis and depth of scholarship despite its exclusive reliance on American records.

03-379. _____. "American Choices in the Far East in 1882." *American Historical Review* 30(1924):84–108. In this article, the author examines the text of the official dispatch and enclosures submitted to the secretary of state by John Russel Young, the United States minister to China, concerning the domestic as well as the international situation following the political disturbance within Korea in July 1882—an affair which resulted in the forcible removal of the Taewŏn'gun from Korea by China. The documents under scrutiny are not included in the published State Department records.

03-380. _____. "Early American Policy in Korea, 1883–87: The Services of Lieutenant George C. Foulk." *Political Science Quarterly* 38(1923):82–103. A systematic study, based on the Foulk papers and other Western primary sources, of the diplomatic services rendered by George C. Foulk as a United States representative in Korea. The author is very critical of the State Department's contemporary indifference toward Korea.

03-381. _____. "President Roosevelt's Secret Pact with Japan." *Current History* 21(1924):15–21. In this article, the distinguished American diplomatic historian reveals what he calls "the most remarkable 'executive agreement' in the history of the foreign relations of the United States" concluded by the Japanese and the American governments after a conversation between Katsura Tarō and William Howard Taft in July 1905. With that pact, Japan promised to renounce any aggressive design on the Philippine Islands in return for American acquiescence in Japan's subjugation of Korea.

03-382. DORWART, Jeffery M. "The Independent Minister: John M. B. Sill and the Struggle against Japanese Expansion in Korea, 1894–1897." *Pacific Historical Review* 44(1975):485–502. Traces the activities of John M. B. Sill as the United States minister to Korea from 1894 to 1897. Recognizing irreconcilable Japanese-American differences in East Asia, Sill tried to persuade his own government to alter her policy toward Japan and attempted to resist Japanese expansion in Korea, all in vain.

03-383. ESTHUS, Raymond A. "The Taft-Katsura Agreement—Reality or Myth?" *Journal of Modern History* 31(1959):46–51. The author rebuts Tyler Dennett's characterization (see 03-378) of the Taft-Katsura conversation and the subsequent exchange of memoranda in July 1905 as a "secret pact" or "agreement." Esthus contends that no agreement was reached or intended, nor was there a quid pro quo involved between Japan and the United States: the conversation was merely "an honest exchange of views" on the general situation in East Asia, in which the Korean question was only one of the topics discussed.

03-384. GRAVES, Louis. "Willard Straight at the Legation in Korea." *Asia* 20(1920):1079–1086. Reprinted in 1922 in a book entitled *Willard Straight in the Orient*. Straight, a well-known American diplomat and businessman, was secretary to Minister Edward Morgan in Korea in 1905.

03-385. HARRINGTON, Fred Harvey. *God, Mammon, and the Japanese: Dr. Horace N. Allen and Korean-American Relations, 1884–1905*. Madison: University of Wisconsin Press, 1944. One of the most enduring and valuable studies of Korean-American relations from 1884 to 1905. Horace N. Allen (1858–1932) came to Korea in 1884 as the first American Protestant medical missionary and served as American minister to Korea from 1897 to 1905. This monographic study of his variegated career in the general context of Korean-American relations focuses on his contribution to Korea as a missionary ("God"), as a proponent of American business enterprises in Korea ("Mammon"), and as a diplomat ("the Japanese"). The work is based on extensive use of the Allen Papers.

03-386. HONG, Soon C. "The Active Diplomatic Role Taken by American Minister Foote During the Post-Kapsin Coup Period: December 4, 1884–January 9, 1895." *Journal of Korean Studies* 1(2)(1971):85–95. A study of the intermediary role played by Lucius H. Foote, American minister to Korea, during the negotiations between Korea and Japan which followed the abortive coup of 1884.

03-387. KIM, Won-mo. "American 'Good Offices' in Korea, 1882–1905." *Journal of Social Sciences and Humanities* 41(June 1975):93–139. A critical review of the failure of the United States government to carry out its responsibility, under the good offices clause included in the Korean-American Treaty of 1882, to mediate on Korea's behalf during a series of international crises such as the Kŏmundo (Port Hamilton) Incident (1885) and the Sino-Japanese War (1894–1895). The author emphasizes Theodore Roosevelt's pro-Japanese policy prior to Japan's takeover of Korea in 1905.

03-388. LEE, Yur-bok. *Diplomatic Relations between the United States and Korea, 1866–1887*. New York: Humanities Press, 1970. 211 pp. This thorough treatment of American diplomacy in Korea, based on American sources, emphasizes the roles of the first American minister, Lucius H. Foote, and chargé d'affaires, George C. Foulk.

03-389. _____. "American Policy toward Korea during the Sino-Japanese War of 1894–1895." *Journal of Social Sciences and Humanities* 43(June 1976):81–97. In this well-documented article, the author examines why the United States government under the Cleveland administration opted for a passive policy of minimum involvement or strict neutrality vis-à-vis Korea before and during the Sino-Japanese War, in spite of repeated Korean requests for American good offices and British overtures for joint intervention. This study is based on United States archival sources relevant mainly to Secretary of State Walter Q. Gresham.

03-390. MERRILL, John Espy. "American Official Reactions to the Domestic Policies of Japan in Korea, 1905–1910." PhD dissertation, Stanford University, 1954. 388 pp. Abstracted in *DA* 14(October 1954):1689; UM 9510. "The purpose of this dissertation is to describe the reactions of American officials, in particular, to the Japanese policies relating to domestic administration in Korea under the Japanese protectorate. First, the foreign attitudes toward the various steps preparatory to the establishment of the protectorate are discussed. Second, the first two years of the protectorate are dealt with and the foreign reaction to that government's establishment down to and including the failure of Prince Itō's advisory efforts at reform is detailed. Third, the period in which the old emperor of Korea was forced to abdicate and Korean riots and attempted Japanese reforms played an alternating tattoo on the senses of foreigners in Korea is delineated. Finally, the work concludes with the foreign reaction, generally acquiescence, to the outstanding events of the last year of the protectorate and to the events surrounding the annexation itself."

03-391. NAHM, Andrew C. (ed.). *The United States and Korea*. Kalamazoo: Center for Korean Studies, Western Michigan University, forthcoming. This conference volume contains the papers presented to the Sixth Conference on Korea at the Center for Korean Studies, Western Michigan University, in November 1976. Among the articles included are: Donald M. Bishop, "Policy and Personality in Early Korean-American Relations: The Case of George Clayton Foulk"; Young I. Lew, "American Advisers in Korea, 1885–1894: The Case of Failure"; Andrew C. Nahm, "Durham White Stevens and the Japanese"; Bonnie B. Oh, "John M. B. Sill, American Minister to Korea,

1894–1897''; and Wayne Patterson, ''Horace N. Allen and Korean Immigration to Hawaii.''

03-392. NOBLE, Harold Joyce. ''Korea and Her Relations with the United States before 1895.'' PhD dissertation, University of California, 1931. 2 vols. 598 pp. This dissertation represents a pioneer study on the variegated aspects of early Korean-American relations from 1850 to 1895. The Korean-born American author highlights the United States–Korean treaty of 1882, the achievements of George C. Foulk in Korea during 1884–1887, United States policy toward Korea during the period of Chinese domination (1885–1894), and the roles played by American advisers and missionaries in Korea prior to 1895. Regarding American policy toward Korea prior to 1895, the author concludes: ''American policy in regard to Korea was largely a passive one, that of neutrality, that of avoiding favoring either China, Japan or Korea in peninsular or Far Eastern politics. . . . But under no circumstances would the government of the United States intervene to protect Korea or to establish an independence which the government of Korea was unable to secure for itself.'' This work is based on English-language sources, including the archival documents of the American legation in Seoul and the private papers of Foulk. Some of the author's findings in this dissertation have been extracted as articles.

03-393. _____. ''The Korean Mission to the United States in 1883—The First Embassy Sent by Korea to an Occidental Nation.'' *Transactions of the Korea Branch of the Royal Asiatic Society* 18(1929):1–21. A factual account of the activities of the first Korean mission, headed by Min Yŏng-ik, to the United States in 1883.

03-394. _____. ''The United States and Sino-Korean Relations, 1885–1887.'' *Pacific Historical Review* 2(3)(September 1933):292–304. A general but sympathetic study of the diplomatic role played by George C. Foulk as an American representative in Seoul from 1885 to 1887. Foulk operated under very difficult circumstances, having been placed in opposition to Yüan Shih-k'ai, the Chinese resident in Seoul.

03-395. PALMER, Spencer J. ''American Gold Mining in Korea's Unsan District.'' *Pacific Historical Review* 31 (1962):379–391. A survey of the history of gold mining at Unsan by an American firm from 1895 to the 1940s, with emphasis on the techniques, operations, and development of mining in Korea.

03-396. PATTERSON, Wayne. ''The Korean Frontier in America: Immigration to Hawaii, 1896–1910.'' PhD dissertation, University of Pennsylvania, 1977. 741 pp. ''The seven thousand Korean immigrants who arrived in Hawaii between 1902 and 1905 represented the culmination of ef-

forts by the Hawaiian Sugar Planters' Association in Honolulu and U.S. Minister to Korea, Horace N. Allen, in Seoul. The Planters wanted to offset the Japanese labor monopoly and Allen wanted to promote American economic interests to force the State Department into an activist policy toward Korea. In the process, Allen and the Planters knowingly conspired to break American immigration laws and confuse the Korean governmental officials but the opposition from the Japanese government was to prove the most powerful. In 1905 the Japanese were able to halt this movement when it became clear that the continued exodus of Koreans to Hawaii was partly responsible for anti-Japanese sentiment in the mainland United States.''

03-397. PAULLIN, Charles Oscar. *Diplomatic Negotiations of American Naval Officers, 1778–1883*. Baltimore: Johns Hopkins Press, 1912. Chapter 10 of this book (''The Opening of Korea, 1855–1883'') deals with the efforts of Commodore Robert Shufeldt to open Korea, including his negotiations with Li Hung-chang in 1882. Based primarily on Navy Department documents, this study first appeared in *Political Science Quarterly* 25(1910):470–499.

03-398. POLLARD, Robert T. ''American Relations with Korea, 1882–1895.'' *Chinese Social and Political Science Review* 16(October 1932):425–471. Though written in the 1930s, this remains a useful study of American-Korean relations from 1882 to 1895. In examining major American involvement in Korea during the given period, the author takes the position that the first treaty signed by the two countries in 1882 marked ''an important step in the rivalry of China and Japan over Korea.''

03-399. REORDAN, Robert Edwin. ''The Role of George Clayton Foulk in United States–Korean Relations, 1884–1887.'' PhD dissertation, Fordham University, 1955. 306 pp. This is a well-researched and cogently argued study on the role of George C. Foulk as naval attaché and then chargé d'affaires of the American legation in Seoul from 1884 to 1887 with emphasis on the circumstances leading to his abrupt recall in June 1887. The author sheds much light on Foulk's background prior to his appointment to the Korean post and United States–Korean relations before 1884. The author is sympathetic toward Foulk's inveterate concern over Korean independence and reform but he is critical of United States policy toward Korea. Reordan contends: ''The history of early relations between the United States and Korea is one of hesitating and indecisive American retreat from a responsibility assumed too lightly, culminating in abject capitulation to Chinese demands that the American representative who was the conspicuous advocate of Korean independence be recalled.''

This dissertation is based on extensive use of the archival documents of the State and Navy Departments and the personal papers of Foulk and Horace N. Allen.

03-400. WALTER, Gary D. "The Korean Special Mission to the United States of America in 1883." *Journal of Korean Studies* (Seattle), 1(1)(1969):89–142. This informative study of the first Korean mission to the United States in 1883 emphasizes the itinerary and activities of the mission members and the impact of their visit. Appendixes 3 ("Correspondence of the Special Mission") and 4 ("Newspaper Accounts of the Special Mission") are useful. Generally supersedes the work of Harold J. Noble on the same topic (03-392).

Korean-Chinese Relations

03-401. CHIEN, Frederick Foo. *The Opening of Korea: A Study of Chinese Diplomacy, 1876–1885.* Hamden, Conn.: Shoestring Press, 1967. 364 pp. A work stemming from the author's PhD dissertation at Yale and based on Chinese sources. There are many minor mistakes regarding details of Korean history—particularly the pronunciation of Korean proper nouns. Nonetheless, this work is useful for its inclusion of many unknown Chinese documents in English translation as well as for the author's fresh insights into problems related to Sino-Korean relations during the given period.

03-402. DUSTIN, Frederick H. "Li Hung-chang and His Policies in Korea." *Chung'ang taehakkyo nonmunjip* 4(1959):153–164. Examines the motivation behind Li Hung-chang's policies toward Korea from 1882 to 1894.

03-403. KIM, Dalchoong. "Korea's Quest for Reform and Diplomacy in the 1880s: With Special Reference to Chinese Intervention and Control." PhD dissertation, Fletcher School of Law and Diplomacy, 1972. 589 pp. In this dissertation, the author advances the bold thesis that the Mins in power in the early 1880s were realistic and could have responded progressively to the challenges of the modern world, had not their attempts at modernization been thwarted by the increased control imposed by China's resident in Korea from 1885 to 1894, Yüan Shih-k'ai. The author characterizes this Chinese policy of control over Korea during the 1880s as a manifestation of modern, security-oriented imperialism, rather than an extension of the unique Sino-Korean tributary relations. Based on Chinese, Japanese, and Korean primary sources.

03-404. LIN, T. C. "Li Hung-chang: His Korean Policies, 1870–1885." *Chinese Social and Political Science Review* 19(1935):202–233. An important study of the evolution of Li Hung-chang's policy toward Korea from 1870 to 1885. Based on Chinese sources.

03-405. TREAT, Payson J. "China and Korea, 1885–1894." *Political Science Quarterly* 49(1933):506–543. An indictment of Chinese policy toward Korea from 1885 to 1894. Based on American diplomatic sources.

03-406. WRIGHT, Mary C. "The Adaptability of Ch'ing Diplomacy: The Case of Korea." *Journal of Asian Studies* 17(May 1958):363–381. An excellent case study of the late Ch'ing diplomacy toward Korea which supports the thesis that China's response to Japanese and Western challenges in Korea through the 1870s and 1880s was very resilient. Based on Chinese sources.

03-407. YIM, Dong Jae. "The Abduction of the Taewŏn'gun, 1882." *Papers on China* (East Asian Research Center, Harvard University), 21(February 1968):99–130. A careful study of the dramatic decision-making process in China regarding the abduction of the Taewŏn'gun in the wake of the *Imo* ("1882") Mutiny. Based on Chinese and Korean primary sources.

Korean-Japanese Relations

03-408. CHOI, Woonsang. *The Fall of the Hermit Kingdom.* Dobbs Ferry, N.Y.: Oceana Publications, 1967. 179 pp. A study of Japanese foreign policy toward Korea, and the Korean response to it, from 1870 to 1910. The emphasis is on the question of how Japan's initial pursuit of economic interests in Korea led to her political domination of the country. Heavily reliant on Korean and Japanese secondary sources.

03-409. CONROY, Hilary. *The Japanese Seizure of Korea, 1868–1910: A Study of Realism and Idealism in International Relations.* Philadelphia: University of Pennsylvania Press, 1960. 544 pp. This is an interpretive history of Japanese-Korean relations from the Meiji Restoration (1868) to the Japanese annexation of Korea (1910). Conroy identifies three political groups in Japan who helped form and execute Meiji Japanese policy toward Korea: (1) the realistic Meiji oligarchs including Ōkubo Toshimichi and Itō Hirobumi; (2) the idealistic liberals, including the members of the Liberal Party and the followers of Fukuzawa Yukichi; and (3) the "reactionary" idealists, including the members of the Kokuryūkai (such as Uchida Ryōhei). These groups, according to Conroy, affected the outcome of Japanese-Korean interaction in 1873, 1876, 1882, 1884, 1894–1895, and 1905–1910 to varying degrees. It was, however, the position of the realistically minded oligarchs that ultimately guided the course of Japanese relations with Korea. The main thesis of this book is that the oligarchic leadership consistently followed a "safe and sane" policy based on "enlightened self-interest"—including Japan's security considerations and concern for the welfare of the Korean people—in formulating its Korea policy. Conroy disputes the widely accepted hypothesis that "Japan always had her eye on Korea." That is to say, he attempts to prove that Japan did not plot to seize Korea by pointing out, for example, that "improvisation rather than calculation underlay the moves of Japanese policy makers" in the case of the Sino-Japanese War of 1894. Moreover, Conroy argues that Itō Hirobumi originally intended to promote "a mild, benevolent, and helpful" government for the poverty-stricken Korean people when he assumed the post of resident-general in 1906 but was compelled to change his policy because of the "betrayal" of the Korean emperor in 1907. The Japanese decision to annex Korea in 1910, according to this book, was a function of two causes: Itō's change of mind in 1907 and pressure for an early merger of Japan and Korea drummed up by the "reactionary" Japanese idealists and the pro-Japanese Korean Ilchinhoe between 1907 and 1910. The author parenthetically refutes a Marxian theory that Japanese annexation of Korea was motivated by capitalist economic interest by pointing out the absence of such an interest. Conroy's work is noteworthy for its provocative thesis, which rejects conventional views on Korean-Japanese relations. It also helps to set a new standard of research on the subject by utilizing massive data in Japanese as well as in Western languages. Nationalistic Korean historians nevertheless have vehemently criticized the author's thesis as a purposeful condonation or justification of Japanese imperialism based on selective use of pertinent documents. For all these reasons, this book has to be scrutinized by anyone who wants to study Japanese-Korean relations in the late nineteenth century.

03-410. DAUGNY, J. "L'annexion de la Corée." *La Nouvelle Revue* (Paris), (1910). An article on the Japanese annexation of Korea.

03-411. DE LAGUÉRIE, Villetard. *La Corée indépendante, russe ou japonaise.* Paris: Hachette, 1898. Investigates the infiltrations of Japanese power in Korea, Japan's policy on Korea, and the state of Korean politics after the Sino-Japanese War.

03-412. DONG, Chon. "Can Aggression Be Justified and Imperialism Rationalized by 'Realism'?: A Review of Hilary Conroy's *The Japanese Seizure of Korea, 1868–1910.*" *Journal of Social Science and Humanities* 14(1961): 69–105. A caustic criticism of Hilary Conroy's book (03-409) with emphasis on the Japanese policy toward Korea between 1905 and 1910. Defends the pro-Korean scholarly tradition of Homer B. Hulbert, F. A. McKenzie, and Andrew J. Grajdanzev.

03-413. _____. "Japanese Annexation of Korea: A Study of

Korean-Japanese Relations to 1910." PhD dissertation, University of Colorado, 1955. 391 pp. Abstracted in *DA* 17(September 1957):1992; UM 16,932. Contents: Pt. 1: From the Earliest Contacts through the Era of Hideyoshi's Invasion; Pt. 2: The Sino-Russo-Japanese Contest over Korea (1876–1905); Pt. 3: The Final Stage of Annexation. For a critical examination of this dissertation, see Hilary Conroy, *The Japanese Seizure of Korea, 1868–1910,* pp. 369–381 (entry 03-409).

03-414. KIM, C. I. Eugene. "Problem in Japan's Control of the Press in Korea, 1906–1910." *Pacific Historical Review* 21(November 1962):393–402. The coauthor of *Korea and the Politics of Imperialism, 1876–1910* (see 03-320 above) examines the case of Japanese persecution of Ernest T. Bethell (1872–1909) who, as editor of *Korea Daily News* from 1905 to 1909, printed articles denouncing Japanese policy toward Korea.

03-415. KIM, Ui-hwan. "Japanese in Pusan (Fusan) after Opening of Port." *Journal of Social Sciences and Humanities* 40(December 1974):87–102. A very critical study of the process of Japanese economic encroachment at the port city of Pusan from 1876 to 1910 centering on the often illicit and deceptive practices of Japanese merchants under the protection of the Japanese government.

03-416. LEE, Sun-keun. "Historical Recollection of Korean-Japanese Relations: Japan's Policy of Aggression and Problems of Modern Age." *Journal of Social Sciences and Humanities* 19(December 1963): 1–28. A sweeping generalization of modern Korean-Japanese relations (1876–1910) based on the thesis that Japanese aggression against Korea hampered Korean modernization. The author is a representative nationalist historian in Korea and this article is from his books in Korean: *Han'guk sa: ch'oekŭnse p'yŏn* (Seoul: Ŭryu munhwasa, 1961) and *Han'guk sa: hyŏndaep'yŏn* (Seoul: Ŭryu munhwasa, 1963).

03-417. LEE, Young Bum. "The Annexation of Korea—Japanese Policy: 1905–1910." *Koreana Quarterly* 7(3) (1965): 50–82. An examination of the policies pursued by Yamagata Aritomo, Kokuryūkai (Black Dragon Society), and Itō Hirobumi toward Korea from 1905 to 1910. The author concludes that "whether or not Itō was in favor of the annexation of Korea is really not the question. His activities during the period of his Residency-General clearly indicate his policy of a gradual approach to annexation."

03-418. LEW, Young I. "Minister Inoue Kaoru's Mission to Korea, 1894–1895: An Abortive Japanese Attempt to Control Korea During the Sino-Japanese War." *The Journal of Korean Studies* 2 (forthcoming). This article, based on Korean, Japanese, and American archival sources, reveals the abortive attempt of the Japanese leaders to "Egyptianize" Korea during and after the Sino-Japanese War by means of large-scale loans and grants to the bankrupt Yi Korean royal court and government. Minister Inoue Kaoru's failure to achieve this end is related to the collapse of the Japanese-sponsored reform movement in early 1895 and Minister Miura's attempt on Queen Min's life in October 1895.

03-419. _____. "Korean-Japanese Relations, 1876–1910." In *Encyclopaedia of Japan*. Tokyo: Kōdansha International, forthcoming. In this short introductory article, the author provides a bird's-eye view of the panoramic history of Korean-Japanese relations in the late nineteenth century. This article contains a useful bibliography of representative secondary sources in Korean, Japanese, Chinese, and English.

03-420. NAHM, Andrew C. (ed.). *Korea under Japanese Colonial Rule*. Kalamazoo: Center for Korean Studies, Western Michigan University, 1973. 290 pp. In the introduction (pp. 17–38) of this book on the Japanese colonial rule of Korea from 1910 to 1945, the editor provides an informative overview of the process of Japanese penetration, domination, and eventual annexation of Korea from 1876 to 1910.

03-421. OH, Bonnie Bongwan. "The Kabo Kaengjang of 1894 in Korea and the Policy of Mutsu Munemitsu." *Journal of Social Sciences and Humanities* 44(December 1976):85–103. In this article dealing with the process of Japanese policy formulation leading to the proposal for reform on the eve of the Sino-Japanese War, the author probes into the motives of Japanese policymakers, including Foreign Minister Mutsu Munemitsu, in pressuring reforms on Korea. Also discusses the contents of the reform proposals.

03-422. PARK, Seong-Rae. "Fukuzawa Yukichi on Korea." *Journal of Social Sciences and Humanities* 45(June 1977): 33–48. This article analyzes the writings of Meiji Japan's foremost publicist, Fukuzawa Yukichi (1835–1901), with emphasis on his editorial essays in *Jiji shimpō* from 1882 to 1901. The author characterizes Fukuzawa as a nationalist and pragmatic realist who advocated Japanese domination of Korea under the euphemism of supporting Korean "independence" or spreading the "benefits of civilization" to the Korean people. This article also touches on Fukuzawa's frustrating personal relationship with Korean reformers in the 1880s and 1890s.

03-423. SUNOO, Hag-won. "A Study of the Development of the Technique of Japanese Imperialism in Korea, 1904–1910." *Korean Review* 1(1)(1948):27–51. A pioneer study in English on the process of Japanese annexation of Korea from 1904 to 1910. The emphasis is on the roles of Itō Hirobumi and Hayashi Gonsuke in obtaining a series of treaties leading to the annexation and on the collaboration of "corrupt" Korean officialdom. The author also dwells at length on the economic motivation behind Japanese imperialism in Korea and the Korean nationalist resistance against Japanese encroachment.

Korea's Relations with Britain, France, Italy, and Russia

03-424. HAMILTON, A. W. "Origins of British Interest in Korea in the Nineteenth Century." *Korea Journal* 14(5) (May 1974):25–33. Also appears in *Asea Yŏn'gu* 17(2) (July 1974):275–286. Traces Great Britain's strategic, evangelistic, and commercial interests in Korea and evaluates her knowledge of Korean internal affairs in the nineteenth century.

03-425. KIM, Yung Chung. "Great Britain and Korea, 1883–1887." PhD dissertation, Indiana University, 1965. 247 pp. Abstracted in *DA* 26(November 1965):2712; UM 65-10,856. "Examines British policy toward Korea from the beginning of treaty relations to the withdrawal of the British squadron from Port Hamilton." Contents: Great Britain and the Opening of Korea; The Background: The Treaty Relations; Sino-Japanese Intervention; Anglo-Russian Crisis, 1885; Port Hamilton; Great Britain and Chinese Supremacy.

03-426. LI, Kitak. "Un aspect de la politique russe en Extrême Orient—la Russie et la Corée (1860–1904)." PhD dissertation, University of Paris, 1969. Discusses Russia's Far Eastern policy with emphasis on Russo-Korean relations. Uses almost all materials available on both the Korean and the Russian sides.

03-427. MALOZEMOFF, Andrew. *Russian Far Eastern Policy, 1881–1904: With Special Emphasis on the Causes of the Russo-Japanese War*. Berkeley: University of California Press, 1958. 358 pp. In this general study of Russian policy in Asia, Korean affairs receive serious attention. This is one of the few works on Russian diplomacy in East Asia with a thorough grounding in Russian sources. The sections dealing with Korea, however, are based on secondary sources.

03-428. ORANGE, Marc. "La politique de la France en Corée a l'époque de son annexion par le Japon." In *Ch'oe Ho-jin paksa hwagap kinyŏm nonch'ong*. Vol. 1. Seoul: 1974. Investigation of the reasons why France made no objection to the Japanese annexation of Korea.

03-429. SANTANGELO, Paolo. "Relazione fra i regni di Corea e d'Italia." *Annali dell'Istituto Universitario*

Orientale (Naples), 31(1971). Discusses the 1894 Korean-Italian Friendship, Trade, and Navigational Treaty.

03-430. SYNN, Seung Kwon. "The Russo-Japanese Struggle for Control of Korea, 1894–1904." PhD dissertation, Harvard University, 1967. 479 pp. "The purpose . . . is to present a comprehensive analysis of the policies of Russia and Japan toward Korea from 1894 to 1904." Contents: Sino-Japanese Rivalry over Korea, 1873–1893; The Outbreak of the Sino-Japanese War; Japan's Attempt to Seize Korea, 1894–1895; Russian Policy toward Korea, 1894–1895; The Murder of Queen Min; Russo-Japanese Rivalry over Korea, 1896–1898; The Rise of Japanese Influence, 1898–1900; On the Eve of the Russo-Japanese War.

BIOGRAPHICAL STUDIES

03-431. CLARK, Donald N. "Yun Ch'i-ho (1864–1945): Portrait of a Korean Intellectual in an Era of Transition." *Occasional Papers on Korea* 4(September 1975):36–76. Edited by James B. Palais and Margery D. Lang. This is a balanced biography of Korea's leading educator, diplomat, and journalist in the late Yi dynasty and Japanese colonial period: Yun Ch'i-ho. The author treats Yun's entire career with emphasis on his activities prior to 1910. This biography is based on Korean, Japanese, and American sources, except for Yun's all-important diary.

03-432. COOK, Harold. "Pak Yŏng-hyo: Background and Early Years." *Journal of Social Sciences and Humanities* (Bulletin of the Korean Research Center), 31(December 1969):11–24. A reliable account of Prince Pak Yŏng-hyo's (1861–1939) background up to the bloody coup of 1884—an event in which he played a role second in importance only to that of Kim Ok-kyun. Based on Korean and Japanese primary sources.

03-433. GOMPERTZ, G. St. G. M. "Archbishop Mutel: A Biographical Sketch." *Transactions of the Korea Branch of the Royal Asiatic Society* 27(1937):56–132. A sympathetic account of the life of Archbishop Mutel, a Catholic missionary in Korea from 1880 to 1933, based on Mutel's own narratives and diaries. The author recounts Mutel's experiences during the political turmoil of 1882 and 1894 and his conferment of baptism on the Taewŏn'gun's wife in 1896.

03-434. GRIFFIS, William E. *A Modern Pioneer in Korea: The Life of Henry G. Appenzeller.* New York: Revell, 1912. A rather superficial biography of the first American Methodist missionary in Korea. Arriving in 1885, Appenzeller founded the Paejae Boys School and was active

in the translation of the Bible into Korean until his sudden death in 1902.

03-435. JAISOHN, Muriel. "Philip Jaisohn, B.S., M.D. (1869–1951)." *Medical Annals of the District of Columbia* 21(1952):350–353. An obituary of Sŏ Chae-p'il (Philip Jaisohn) by his daughter giving a brief review of his life. Account of Sŏ's activities in the United States is useful.

03-436. KATZ, Herman M. *KMAG's Heritage: The Story of Brigadier General William McEntire Dye.* [Seoul ?]: Headquarters, Eighth United States Army, n.d. 44 pp. This is a short biographical account of General Dye's life and his contribution to the Korean military training program from 1888 to 1895 as the precursor of the Korean Military Advisory Group (KMAG), US Army. Based largely on secondary English sources.

03-437. LIEM, Channing. *America's Finest Gift to Korea: The Life of Philip Jaisohn.* New York: William-Frederick Press, 1952. 89 pp. A sympathetic biography of Sŏ Chae-p'il (Philip Jaisohn), who was active as one of the junior reformers in the coup of 1884 and then as the leader of the Independence Club movement from 1896 to 1898. Because the author of this biography was a close associate of Sŏ, this work is not wholly objective; useful nevertheless.

03-438. OLIVER, Robert T. *Syngman Rhee: The Man Behind the Myth.* New York: Dodd Mead, 1954. 380 pp. The first part (pp. 1–92) of this "official" biography of Yi Sŭng-man (1875–1965) is devoted to Yi's childhood, his early career as a member of the Independence Club, and his life in the United States as a diplomatist and student from 1905 to 1910. This biography is based on Yi's private papers.

03-439. RUTT, Richard. "A Biography of James Scarth Gale." In *James Scarth Gale and His History of the Korean People.* Published for the Korea Branch of the Royal Asiatic Society. Seoul: Taewon Publishing Co., 1972. 396 pp. The first part of Rutt's book (pp. 1–88) is a biography of Gale (1863–1937), a Canadian-born American Presbyterian missionary in Korea from 1888 to 1927. In a masterly and critical style, the author deals with Gale's multifarious activities as missionary, pastor, educator, translator, and lexicographer.

03-440. WEEMS, Clarence N. "Profile of Homer Belazell Hulbert." In Clarence N. Weems (ed.), *Hulbert's History of Korea.* Vol. 1. New York: Hilary House, 1962. A short biographical sketch of the career of Homer B. Hulbert (1863–1949) in Korea as a teacher, missionary, magazine editor, and, finally, personal envoy of the Korean emperor to the United States from 1886 to 1907.

V. THE JAPANESE COLONIAL PERIOD

by Yŏng-ho Ch'oe

INTRODUCTION

ANNEXED BY JAPAN in 1910, Korea came under Japanese colonial rule in the following thirty-five years until 1945 when Japan was defeated in World War II. Although thirty-five years is merely a speck in a broad perspective of historical time, the period of Japanese rule is of great historical significance for modern Korean history. For one thing, the Japanese rule from 1910 to 1945 was an unprecedented experience for Korea in her long history. Never before since the formation of the Three Kingdoms had she lost her independent political integrity and been subject to direct control by an alien power.

Moreover, the imposition of Japanese colonial rule came at a crucial juncture in history when Korea was at the threshold of transformation into the modern age. Hence whatever modernization Korea experienced during the first half of the twentieth century was carried out largely at the hands of Japan to suit her objectives. To be sure, there were a number of movements and activities waged by enlightened Korean leaders to awaken the Korean public to the urgent need for modernization, but their worthy causes were either preempted by the Japanese, thus losing their Korean character, or rendered ineffective because of Japanese suppression. Thus the nature of Korean society in its transformation from traditional to modern was shaped largely by the Japanese.

If one views modernization in terms of westernization, the modern ideas and institutions that had been introduced into Korea during the Japanese rule were not direct importations in their original forms from the Western world but truncated versions that had gone through the grinding mills of Japan. This at least partly explains the preponderant presence of Japanese vestiges in many aspects of present Korean society in spite of the nationalistic attempts to eliminate them after 1945.

Nevertheless, it would be wrong to say that tradition died in Korea with the coming of Japanese rule. On the contrary, one effect of that rule was that the contest between tradition and modernism which usually takes place in non-Western countries with the coming of Western influence became blurred in the case of Korea. For the Koreans in their anger and resentment against Japan tended to identify her with modernity and the destruction of Korea's own tradition. Hence modernity is regarded by many Koreans as something to be resisted rather than welcomed. As a consequence, rigorous intellectual debate has never really addressed the question of tradition versus modernity, largely because of the intrusion of Japanese control in Korea.

As for the historical studies of this period, there are some important English works in addition to the books mentioned in the introduction to this chapter. The Center for Korean Studies at Western Michigan University has put out two books, *Korea under Japanese Colonial Rule* and *Korea's Response to Japan,* that are collections of scholarly articles on various aspects of the Japanese colonial period. In "Japan's Experiment in Korea," David Brudnoy renders a critical assessment of the Japanese rule as a whole and points out its ideological basis and weaknesses. In "The Japanese Colonial Administration in Korea," in *Korea under Japanese Colonial Rule* edited by Andrew C. Nahm, Han-Kyo Kim gives not only a perceptive overview but also future research suggestions. In *Korea: The Politics of the Vortex,* Gregory Henderson provides a very lucid and original interpretation of the Japanese colonial period in which he discusses how his characterization of Korea's "mass society" became affected by the Japanese rule within the framework of his vortex theory.

The economic aspect of Japanese rule is understandably very controversial. Those who are critical of that rule tend to minimize the impact of Japanese economic policy while the official Japanese position and those who favored Japan are inclined to emphasize the positive aspects. Nevertheless, even the critics of Japan in general recognize significant economic growth during Japanese rule; their question is whether or not the Koreans really benefited from the growth. James I. Nakamura has made a comparative study of Japanese agrarian policies in Korea and Taiwan in "Incentive, Productivity Gaps, and Agricultural Growth Rates in

Prewar Japan, Taiwan, and Korea,'' in *Japan in Crisis,* edited by Bernard Silberman and H. D. Harootunian. Nakamura concludes that, from the economic standpoint, Korean agriculture benefited greatly from the Japanese policies because of a greater increase in productivity. On the other hand, in *Growth and Structural Changes in the Korea Economy, 1910–1940,* Sang-Chul Suh has produced one of the most comprehensive and scholarly studies of the Korean economy under Japanese rule. He documents quantitatively and qualitatively a substantial growth in productivity in all sectors of the Korean economy during the period. He finds, however, that such a growth had taken place largely at the expense of creating dual structure: the great majority of Koreans, he contends, actually suffered a decline in their living standards.

Many areas await further study. For one thing, preoccupied mostly with Japanese colonialism and Korean nationalism, scholars in the past have approached the period largely within the framework of what Japan did in Korea and how the Koreans reacted. Important though these issues are, there were other changes that transcend the context of colonialism and nationalism, such as the traditional value and structure of family, clan, community relations, and social stratification.

In the realm of intellect, some South Korean scholars have examined the historiographies of certain individual historians (which Western scholars may find useful for further studies), but that is about all there is. Certainly we can gain greater insight into the period by having perceptive studies on such influential individuals as Yun Ch'i-ho, An Ch'ang-ho, Yi Sang-jae, Cho Man-sik, Kim Sŏng-su, Yŏ Un-hyŏng, Yi Kwang-su, and Ch'oe Nam-sŏn.

BIBLIOGRAPHY

POLITICS AND SOCIETY
Colonial Rule and Institutions

03-441. BORTON, Hugh. "Korea: Internal Political Structure." US Department of State. *Bulletin* 21(1944): 578–583. Gives a good description and discussion of the organization, administration, and policies of the Government-General of Korea under Japan, including education, health, and sanitation. Also gives a brief discussion of the nature and possible ramifications of the new change enacted in 1942 with regard to the administration of the Japanese empire.

03-442. BROWN, Arthur Judson. *The Korean Conspiracy Case.* Northfield, Mass.: Northfield Press, 1912. 27 pp. A carefully prepared paper representing the position of several American missionary organizations connected with Korea toward the so-called Korean conspiracy case of 1912, which it condemns. Various other factors, including the relationship between the Japanese government in Korea on the one hand and the American missionaries and the Korean Christians on the other are also examined.

03-443. _____. *The Mastery of the Far East: The Story of Korea's Transformation and Japan's Rise to Supremacy in the Orient.* New York: Scribner's, 1919. An authoritative study of Korea and Japan from the late nineteenth century until the eve of the March First movement in 1919 with special emphasis on (1) how Japan gained control of Korea, which the author regards as "the strategic point in the mastery of the Far East," (2) evaluating the Japanese rule over Korea in its early stage, and (3) reviewing the nature and objectives of the Christian missions in Korea and Japan. The author's coverage of the missionaries' activities in Korea is particularly useful.

03-444. BRUDNOY, David. "Japan's Experiment in Korea." *Monumenta Nipponica* 25(1970):156–195. A critical evaluation of Japanese rule in Korea with emphasis on the ideological aspect that underlay the Japanese policy. A comprehensive and scholarly treatment.

03-445. BUTLER, Sir Paul. "A Korean Survey." *International Affairs* 5(12)(December 1919):21–34. A critical survey of Korea-Japan relations in modern times with an assessment of Japanese colonial rule in Korea. The author had served for a long time as a British consular general in Asia.

03-446. CHANG, Yunshik. "Colonization as Planned Changes: The Korean Case." *Modern Asian Studies* 5(1971):161–186. A study of the economic and social changes that took place in Korea under Japanese rule. The first part discusses "reorganization of the traditional economy by changes in institutional control over it, and the second part describes the growth of the economy" and its impact on demographic trend.

03-447. CHEN, Edward I-te. "Japan: Oppressor or Modernizer?: A Comparison of the Effects of Colonial Control in Korea and Formosa." In Andrew C. Nahm (ed.), *Korea under Japanese Colonial Rule.* Kalamazoo: Center for Korean Studies, Western Michigan University, 1973. In this short essay, the author delineates certain similar and contrasting factors in the Japanese colonial administration toward Korea and Formosa.

03-448. _____. "Japanese Colonialism in Korea and Formosa: A Comparison of the Systems of Political Control." *Harvard Journal of Asiatic Studies* 30(1970): 126–158. An informative study comparing the systems of political control used by Japan in Korea and Formosa centering on three major areas: "(1) the governor-general—his appointment, the scope of his power, and his relationship with Tokyo; (2) the composition and functions of various local governments; and (3) the degree of participation permitted the natives in so-called local 'autonomy.' "

03-449. _____. "Japanese Colonialism in Korea and Formosa: A Comparison of Its Effects upon the Development of Nationalism." PhD dissertation, University of Pennsylvania, 1968. 376 pp. Abstracted in *DA* (January 1969): 2317-A; UM 69–76. A comparison of the ways in which Koreans and Formosans responded to Japanese rule—the nature of their resistance movements, the techniques they employed, and the repression they invited.

03-450. CHUNG, Henry. *The Case of Korea: A Collection of Evidence on the Japanese Domination of Korea, and on the Development of the Korean Independence Movement.* New York: Revell, 1921. A powerful indictment of the Japanese encroachment and domination of Korea from the late nineteenth century through the March First movement in 1919. Marshals concrete evidence of Japanese atrocities in Korea.

03-451. CHUNG, Joong-Gun. "Japanese Colonial Administration in Korea, 1905–1919." PhD dissertation, Claremont Graduate School, 1971. 214 pp. Abstracted in *DAI* 32(4)(October 1971):2150-A; UM 71-21,661. An analysis of Japanese administrative machinery, laws, and principles in Korea.

03-452. DONG, Wonmo. "Assimilation and Social Mobilization in Korea." In Andrew C. Nahm (ed.), *Korea under Japanese Colonial Rule.* Kalamazoo: Center for Korean Studies, Western Michigan University, 1973. A scholarly analysis of the goals, instruments, and socioeconomic and cultural effects of the assimilation policy pursued by the Japanese government in Korea with an attempt to determine quantitatively the degree of social mobilization and political integration the Japanese policy had brought about.

03-453. _____. "Japanese Colonial Policy and Practice in

Korea, 1905–1945: A Study of Assimilation." PhD dissertation, Georgetown University, 1965. 542 pp. Abstracted in *DAI* 26(December 1965):3466-67; UM 65-12,510. A study of the failure of Japanese assimilation policy in Korea which overemphasized language but resulted in the inhibition of assimilation. The study includes useful statistical computations.

03-454. GRAJDANZEV, A[ndrew J.]. "Korea: Example of 'De-Colonization.' " *Amerasia* 4(1941):513–517. "Examines statistically the main features of industrialization . . . and comes to the conclusion that there is no basis for the claim that Korea is emerging from a colonial status to a place of equality in the Japanese empire."

03-455. _____. "Korea in the Postwar World." *Foreign Affairs* 22(1944):479–483. Provides a thoughtful discussion, along with the author's own suggestions, on the economic, political, and international problems Korea would likely encounter after the war.

03-456. _____. *Modern Korea.* New York: Institute of Pacific Relations, 1944. The most comprehensive and scholarly study so far available in English on Korea under Japan. It examines and evaluates virtually every aspect of Japanese rule in Korea. Of particular interest and value are the author's ingenious analyses of various economic aspects of colonial rule.

03-457. _____. *Korea Looks Ahead.* IPR Pamphlet 15. New York: American Council, Institute of Pacific Relations, 1944. A compact and yet remarkably good assessment of many aspects of Korea—people, agriculture and industry, Japanese rule, prospects after the war—on the eve of Japan's military defeat in World War II. Points out problems Korea might encounter once freed from Japan.

03-458. HAYDEN, Ralston. "Japan's New Policy in Korea and Formosa." *Foreign Affairs* 2(1924):479–487. A very sympathetic account of Japanese rule in Formosa and Korea (the latter, particularly, under Governor-General Saitō Makoto). Also gives a brief discussion of Korean nationalists abroad.

03-459. HENDERSON, Gregory. "Japan's Chosen: Immigrants, Ruthlessness and Development Shock." In Andrew C. Nahm (ed.), *Korea under Japanese Colonial Rule.* Kalamazoo: Center for Korean Studies, Western Michigan University, 1973. An essay reflecting the author's hypothesis that certain shocks Koreans suffered during the Japanese intrusion might have given impetus to Korea's economic development.

03-460. _____. *Korea: The Politics of the Vortex.* Cambridge, Mass.: Harvard University Press, 1968. A major study of politics in modern Korea in which the authoritarianism and centralist orientation of Korean political culture is analyzed historically. The Japanese colonial period is treated within the context of the author's theory of politics of the vortex.

03-461. IRELAND, Alleyne. *The New Korea.* New York: E. P. Dutton, 1929. Reprinted Seoul: 1975. A detailed account of "the aims, the methods, and results of Japanese administration in Korea." Concludes that "Korea is today infinitely better governed than it ever was under its own native rulers."

03-462. Japan. Government-General of Chosen. *Annual Report on Administration of Chosen.* Keijō (Seoul): 1907–1937. Title varies: *Annual Report of Reforms and Progress in Korea* (1908–1910); *Annual Report of Reforms and Progress in Chosen* (1911–1922); *Annual Report on Administration of Chosen* (1923–1937). Official reports of the Government-General on history, organization, finance and economy, education, religion, social work, communication, and other topics. Contains statistical tables and photographs.

03-463. _____. _____. *Thriving Chosen: A Survey of Twenty-five Years' Administration.* Keijō (Seoul): 1935. An official publication of the Japanese Government-General in Korea showing the progress made during the 25-year period of Japanese rule. Includes many photographs.

03-464. Japan Chronicle. *The Korean Conspiracy Trial.* Kōbe, Japan: 1913. Full report on the proceedings in appeal of the conspiracy trial of 1911–1913, known as the 105 Men incident. A valuable source.

03-465. KIM, C. I. Eugene and Doretha E. MORTIMORE (eds.). *Korea's Response to Japan: The Colonial Period.* Kalamazoo: Center for Korean Studies, Western Michigan University, 1975. Proceedings of the Conference on Korea. Papers deal with various reactions of the Korean people against Japanese colonialism.

03-466. KIM, Han-Kyo. "The Japanese Colonial Administration in Korea: An Overview." In Andrew C. Nahm (ed.), *Korea under Japanese Colonial Rule.* Kalamazoo: Center for Korean Studies, Western Michigan University, 1973. A good overview of Japanese rule in Korea that points out salient features of its administration and suggests further research possibilities.

03-467. LI, Ogg. "Les Japonais et la langue coréenne, aperçu historique sur l'oppression des Coréens par l'autorité japonaise." *Revue de la Deuxième Guerre Mondial* (Paris), (January–March 1973). On Japanese colonial policy in Korea, especially the policy to eradicate Korean language and culture.

03-468. LUCY, L. W. Wilson. "The Reality in Korea." *The Century* 99(February 1920):536–548. A report on the situation in Korea after the March First movement. Points out several reasons why Japan failed and aroused antagonism in Korea in spite of certain beneficial policies.

03-469. McCUNE, G[eorge M.]. "Korea: A Study in Japanese Imperialism." *World Affairs Interpreter* 11 (1940): 77–85. A critical review of Japanese rule in Korea.

03-470. MOSCOWITZ, Karl. "The Creation of the Oriental Development Company: Japanese Illusions Meet Korean Reality." *Occasional Papers on Korea* 2(March 1974):73–121. Edited by James B. Palais. A useful study of the reasons for creating Tōyō takushoku kabushiki kaisha (Oriental Development Company) and why some of the company's original objectives were altered.

03-471. NAHM, Andrew C. (ed.). *Korea under Japanese Colonial Rule: Studies of the Policy and Techniques of Japanese Colonialism.* Kalamazoo: Center for Korean Studies, Western Michigan University, 1973. Collection of papers presented at the conference held at Western Michigan University in November 1970. The book is divided into five parts: (1) the functions and mechanics of control, (2) economic policy and change, (3) education and social change under the colonial situation, (4) Korean response and reactions, and (5) Japanese colonial rule: an evaluation.

03-472. NOBLE, Harold J. "Korea under Japanese Rule." *Current History* 33(1930):78–81. A short essay discussing the difficult economic condition of Korea under Japan.

03-473. OLIVER, Robert T. *Korea: Forgotten Nation.* Washington: Public Affairs Press, 1944. This booklet gives a brief account of Korean nationalist activities abroad and repressive conditions within Korea under Japanese rule.

03-474. REW, Joung Yole. "A Study of the Government-General of Korea: With an Emphasis on the Period between 1919–1931." PhD dissertation, American University, 1962. 312 pp. Abstracted in *DAI* 23(March 1963): 3460-61; UM 62-4526. A study of the administrative and political structure of the Japanese Government-General in Korea following the March First movement. The study includes a discussion of internal Japanese politics with regard to Korea at the time.

03-475. RHEE, Syngman. *Japan Inside Out: The Challenge of Today.* New York: Revell, 1941. Written to warn the United States against Japan's aggressive designs prior to Pearl Harbor, this book makes an eloquent and powerful indictment of Japan that reveals the militaristic side of the

Japanese empire. Syngman Rhee also makes an effective appeal for Korea's independence and records some of his personal experiences.

03-476. SAITO, Makoto. "A Message from the Imperial Japanese Government to the American People—Home Rule in Korea?" *The Independent* (31 January 1920):167–169. The new governor-general of Korea explains his position and the reform policies and intentions of the Japanese government in Korea. Obviously aimed at placating American public sentiment toward Korea aroused in the wake of the March First movement.

03-477. STEVENSON, Frederick Boyd. "The Truth about Korea." *World Outlook* 5(12)(December 1919):21–34. A critical report on Japanese rule in Korea with many good photographs.

03-478. WHITE, Oswald. "Japanese Administration of Korea and Manchuria." *Royal Central Asian Journal* 33(1943):19–36. The first half of the paper is devoted to discussing why Japanese rule in Korea was resented by Koreans in spite of many reforms instituted by Japan. The author at one time served as a British counselor in Korea.

03-479. YANAIHARA, Tadao. "Problems of Japanese Administration in Korea." *Pacific Affairs* 11(1938):198–207. A Japanese scholar examines Japan's assimilation policy of paternalistic protection in Korea by analyzing financial expenditure, industrial promotion, and educational expansion in Korea. He concludes that Japanese policy will only lead to oppressive bureaucratic control and that Japan's colonial rule over Korea is a national burden on Japan both financially and militarily.

03-480. YOO, Jong Hae. "The System of Korean Local Government." In Andrew C. Nahm (ed.), *Korea under Japanese Colonial Rule*. Kalamazoo: Center for Korean Studies, Western Michigan University, 1973. Traces the system of local government in Korea under Japan from 1910 to about 1930 and analyzes the role of local government within the context of the overall control mechanism instituted by the Japanese Government-General.

Korean Nationalism

03-481. AMIRAULT, Jacques. "La résistance coréenne de 1907 à 1919 et la formation d'un gouvernement provisoire de la Republique de Corée." *Revue de Corée* 7(3)(Autumn 1975). Discusses the Korean resistance movement from 1907 to 1919 and the establishment of the Provisional Government of Korea.

03-482. *First Korean Congress*. Philadelphia: 1919. 82 pp. Proceedings of the first Korean Congress held on 14–16 April 1919 in Philadelphia in support of Korea's independence. Among the participants were Philip Jaisohn and Syngman Rhee.

03-483. FITCH, Geraldine T. "Korea's Hope of Freedom." *Amerasia* 5(1942):494–498. A brief sympathetic review of Korea's struggle to regain freedom from Japan.

03-484. KENDALL, Carlton Waldo. *The Truth about Korea*. San Francisco: Korean National Association, 1919. 104 pp. A pamphlet giving a short account of Japanese oppression and the March First movement in Korea. Includes official statements: "Aims and Aspirations of the New Korean Republic" by the first Korean Congress held in Philadelphia, "Provisional Constitution" of the Provisional Government in Shanghai, and "the Claim of the Korean People and Nation" presented to the Peace Conference at Paris.

03-485. *Korea and the Pacific War: Condensed Reference*. Los Angeles: United Korean Committee in America, Planning and Research Board, 1943. 76 pp. A very interesting document originally prepared for the US Office of Strategic Services at its invitation by an anonymous Korean "as a partial plan for more effective participation by the Korean people" in the Pacific war and "as a guide to an understanding of Korea's present and post-war problems, her economic status and the capacity of her people to carry on an enlightened and stable self-government." Includes a brief survey of Koreans in the United States who could be mobilized into the proposed Korean Army to be used for and after the war. Certain sensitive matters are deleted in the pamphlet.

03-486. Korean Commission to America and Europe. *Korea Must Be Free*. [New York: 1930.] 32 pp. A pamphlet indicting the wrongs committed by Japan in Korea and appealing for Korea's freedom.

03-487. *Korean Liberty Conference*. Los Angeles: United Korean Committee in America, 1942. 103 pp. The proceedings of the United Korean Committee conference held at Washington, D.C., on 27 February–1 March 1942, which adopted several resolutions in support of Korea's independence. The participants include Syngman Rhee, Philip Jaisohn, and Homer B. Hulbert. In app. 1, Hulbert gives a brief account of the secret mission entrusted him by King Kojong in 1905 to appeal directly to President Roosevelt for Korean causes.

03-488. LEE, Chong-sik. "The Korean Nationalist Movement, 1905–1945." PhD dissertation, University of California, Berkeley, 1961. 836 pp. Although this dissertation became the basis of the author's *Politics of Korean Na-*

tionalism, it still contains much valuable information not included in the published book.

03-489. _____. *The Politics of Korean Nationalism.* Berkeley: University of California Press, 1965. A comprehensive and authoritative study of Korean nationalism and the nationalist movement from the Tonghak uprising in 1894 to 1945. The author traces, analyzes, and assesses with an extraordinary perspicacity the major nationalist activities, including the Tonghak, the Independence Club, the Righteous Armies, the March First movement, the Provisional Government in exile, the nationalists abroad, and the Sin'-ganhoe and other movements within Korea. This book will remain a standard reference on the subject for a long time to come.

03-490. LEE, Hi-seung. "Recollections of the Korean Language Society Incident." In Marshall R. Pihl (ed.), *Listening to Korea: A Korean Anthology.* New York: Praeger, 1973. A personal account of the author's own experiences in the Korean Language Society incident in the 1940s, in which a number of prominent Korean linguists were arrested and tortured by the Japanese police.

03-491. LEE, Ki-Baek. "Historical View of Nationalism in Korea under Japanese Occupation." *Journal of Social Sciences and Humanities* 27(Winter 1967):1–18. A summary review of how nationalism affected the thinking of five prominent Korean intellectuals during Japanese rule. They are Sin Ch'ae-ho, Ch'oe Nam-sŏn, Chŏng In-bo, Mun Il-p'yŏng (all historians), and Yi Kwang-su, a novelist.

03-492. McKENZIE, F. A. *Korea's Fight for Freedom.* New York: Revell, 1920. Reprinted Seoul: Yonsei University Press, 1969. An impassioned account of Japanese encroachment and abuses in Korea and Korea's struggle against Japan from the late nineteenth century through the March First movement in 1919. The book may be divided into two parts: the first part, covering the period up to 1908, is an extract with revision from the author's earlier book, *The Tragedy of Korea;* the second part covers the Korean conspiracy case (105 Men incident) and the March First movement.

03-493. MESLER, David P. "Korean Literature of Resistance: A Case of Chong Pi-sok." In Andrew C. Nahm (ed.), *Korea under Japanese Colonial Rule.* Kalamazoo: Center for Korean Studies, Western Michigan University, 1973. After a short introduction to a few representative works of the resistance literature, the author analyzes the symbolic significance of Chŏng Pi-sŏk's novel, *The Village Shrine (Sadang).*

03-494. ROBINSON, Michael E. "Ch'oe Hyon-bae and Korean Nationalism: Language, Culture, and National Development." *Occasional Papers on Korea* 3(June 1975):19–33. Edited by James B. Palais and Margery D. Lang. A thoughtful analysis and evaluation of the nationalistic ideas and activities of Ch'oe Hyŏn-bae, who dedicated his life to rediscovering Korea's own language and culture.

03-495. SUH, Dae-sook. "The Korean Revolutionary Movement: A Brief Evaluation of Ideology and Leadership." In Andrew C. Nahm (ed.), *Korea under Japanese Colonial Rule.* Kalamazoo: Center for Korean Studies, Western Michigan University, 1973. A brief essay evaluating the role played by ideology and leadership in the Korean revolutionary movement during the Japanese period.

The March First Movement

03-496. AMIRAULT, Jacques. "La délégation coréenne à la Conférence de la Paix de Paris (1919–1920) et les *lobbies* pro-coréens en Occident." *Hanbul Munhwa* (Seoul), 1(1974). On the March First movement: covers the activities of the Provisional Government delegation at the Paris Peace Conference and the actions of the pro-Korean European lobbies.

03-497. BALDWIN, Frank Prentiss, Jr. "The March First Movement: Korean Challenge and Japanese Response." PhD dissertation, Columbia University, 1969. 343 pp. Abstracted in *DAI* 33(1)(July 1972):244-A; UM 72–20, 026. An objective and authoritative study of the March First movement of 1919. The author carefully traces and analyzes the movement—its inception, the Wilsonian idealism and its impact, preparation by various groups, execution, nature of demonstrations, Japanese reprisals, impact upon Korean nationalists abroad, attempts to appeal to the Paris Peace Conference, the Japanese response, and the evaluation of the Saitō administration.

03-498. _____. "Missionaries and the March First Movement: Can Moral Men be Neutral?" In Andrew C. Nahm (ed.), *Korea under Japanese Colonial Rule.* Kalamazoo: Center for Korean Studies, Western Michigan University, 1973. A scholarly study of how the Christian missionaries were torn between remaining neutral politically in the confrontation between the Japanese authorities and the Korean nationalists on the one hand and, on the other, following the moral dictates of their conscience provoked by the atrocities committed by the Japanese during the March First movement.

03-499. Federal Council of the Churches of Christ in

America. Commission on Relations with the Orient. *The Korean Situation: Authentic Accounts of Recent Events by Eye Witnesses.* New York: 1920. 125 pp. Collection of reports, personal letters, and signed affidavits of eyewitnesses on the March First movement. A valuable source.

03-500. Japan Chronicle. *The Independence Movement in Korea: A Record of Some Events of the Spring of 1919.* Kōbe, Japan: 1919. Reprint of news and comments on the March First movement carried in the *Japan Chronicle* from 4 March till 20 June 1919. A valuable contemporary account.

03-501. KO, Seung Kyun. "The March First Movement: A Study of the Rise of Korean Nationalism under the Japanese Colonialism." *Koreana Quarterly* 14(1/2)(Spring/Summer 1972):14–33. Examines the March First movement of 1919 within the conceptual framework of nationalism and investigates the reasons for Japan's failure to integrate the Korean people into the Japanese polity.

03-502. LEE, Ki-baek. "The March First Movement." In Marshall R. Pihl (ed.), *Listening to Korea: A Korean Anthology.* New York: Praeger, 1973. A short essay by a prominent South Korean historian reflecting on the historical significance of the March First movement.

03-503. McCUNE, Shannon. *The Mansei Movement, March 1, 1919.* Colloquium Paper no. 5. Honolulu: Center for Korean Studies, University of Hawaii, 1976. 39 pp. An interesting personal reflection on the March First movement from three different aspects: as a child participant, as the son of a well-known American missionary, and as a geographer.

03-504. SCHOFIELD, Frank W. "What Happened on Sam Il Day March 1, 1919." In In-hah Jung (ed.), *The Feel of Korea: A Symposium of American Comment.* Seoul: Hollym Corporation, 1966. A Canadian missionary who played a key role in the March First movement recollects what happened and what he did on that memorable day.

Communism

03-505. BAIK, Bong. *Kim Il Sung: Biography.* Tokyo: Miraisha, 1969–1970. 3 vols. Translation of *Minjok ŭi t'aeyang Kim Il-sŏng changgun.* A semiofficial biography of the North Korean leader giving a detailed and panegyric account of his activities and achievements from his birth in 1912 until 1967.

03-506. KIM, G. F. "The Formation of the Korean Proletariat," *Soviet Sociology* 4(4)(Spring 1966):12–23. Translation of a Russian article. The author, a Russian scholar of Korean ancestry, attempts to show, mostly with secondary sources, that the formation of the industrial working class

took place in Korea during World War I, not before as claimed by some North Korean scholars.

03-507. KIM, Il Sung. *The Just Fatherland Liberation War of the Korean People for Freedom and Independence.* Pyongyang: Ministry of Culture and Propaganda, 1955. In this North Korean official publication, Kim Il Sung is lauded as the most important revolutionary for Korean independence.

03-508. LEE, Chong-sik. "Korean Communists and Yenan." *China Quarterly* 9(January–March 1962):182–192. A study of Korean communist groups in Yenan and their relationship with the Chinese Communist Party.

03-509. _____. "Witch Hunt among the Guerrillas: The Min-Sheng-T'uan Incident." *China Quarterly* 26(April–June 1966):107–117. A detailed study of the Min-sheng-t'uan (Minsaengdan) incident of the 1930s, in which a number of veteran Korean communists were executed by Chinese communists under false charges in Manchuria.

03-510. PAIGE, Glenn D. "Korea and the Comintern, 1919–35." *Journal of Social Sciences and Humanities* 13(December 1960):1–25. One of the earliest English studies of the Korean communist movement and its relations with the Comintern from 1919 to 1935.

03-511. SCALAPINO, Robert A. and Chong-sik LEE. *Communism in Korea.* 2 vols. Berkeley: University of California Press, 1972. The most comprehensive study so far available in English tracing the development of communism in Korea from its inception to the present and analyzing the contemporary North Korean communist system. The first volume of this award-winning work deals with the history of the communist movement; the period before 1945 is covered in the first three chapters.

03-512. _____. "The Origins of the Korean Communist Movement." *Journal of Asian Studies* 20(1)(November 1960): 9–31; 20(2)(February 1961):149–167. A detailed study of the earliest stage of the Korean communist movement tracing the activities of the Korean communists in Siberia, China, and Manchuria from 1918 until the establishment of the first Korean Communist Party within Korea in 1925. The study also offers a perceptive analysis of various problems the movement encountered during the period.

03-513. SUH, Dae-sook. *Documents of Korean Communism, 1918–1948.* Princeton: Princeton University Press, 1970. Sixty-six documents related to the Korean communist movement are divided into six parts with the author's commentary at the beginning of each part. The documents selected in the book are not otherwise readily available. Written originally in Korean, Japanese, Chinese, and Russian, they formed the basis of the author's earlier work, *The Korean Communist Movement.*

03-514. _____. *The Korean Communist Movement, 1918–1948.* Princeton: Princeton University Press, 1967. A pioneering study of the Korean communist movement since its inception in 1918 until the rise of Kim Il Sung in 1948. Relying on exhaustive research of primary and secondary sources, the author meticulously traces and analyzes the movement's origins, its early relations with Russia and the Comintern, its penetration into Korea, its activities within Korea, its problems with factions, and its relations with Korean nationalism. Perhaps most significant, however, is the objective and authoritative uncovering of Kim Il Sung's past before his rise to power.

03-515. WALES, Nym and San KIM. *Song of Ariran: A Korean Communist in the Chinese Revolution.* New York: John Day, 1941. Rev. ed. San Francisco: Ramparts Press, 1972. A fascinating account of the life and activities of a Korean nationalist (pseudonym Kim San) who joined the Chinese communists in Yenan.

03-516. WASHBURN, John N. "Soviet Russia and the Korean Communist Party." *Pacific Affairs* 23(1950): 59–64. A brief outline history of the Korean Communist Party and its relations with the Soviet Union. Based primarily on Soviet materials available in the United States at the time of writing.

03-517. YOO, Se Hee. "The Communist Movement and the Peasants: The Case of Korea." In John Wilson Lewis (ed.), *Peasant Rebellion and Communist Revolution in Asia.* Stanford: Stanford University Press, 1974. Examines "the relationship between the peasantry and the Communist movement in Korea in the 1920's and 1930's, and particularly the relationship between the peasantry's economic grievances and its susceptibility to Communism."

03-518. _____. "The Korean Communist Movement and the Peasantry under Japanese Rule." PhD dissertation, Columbia University, 1974. 353 pp. A study of the relationship between the Korean communist movement and the Korean farmers during the Japanese period.

Economy

03-519. BUNCE, Arthur C. "The Future of Korea." *Far Eastern Survey* 13(8)(April 1944):67–70 and 13(10)(May 1944):85–88. In pt. 1, the author discusses "the political problems of organizing a democratic state, the broad question of the type of economy that might be developed, and the need for far-sighted planning for independence by Korean leaders" after Korea is freed from Japan. In pt. 2, the author points out problems and suggests possible courses of actions on land tenure, industry, finance, trade, and employment in postwar Korea. A farsighted article.

03-520. CHEN, Ta. "The Labor Situation in Korea." *Monthly Labor Review* 31(1930):1070–1080. A Chinese scholar examines economic and social conditions of factory workers and miners, the agrarian situation, labor movement and unrest, and labor's outlook in Korea as of 1930.

03-521. CHEVALIER, Henri. "Des réformes et des progrès réalisés Corée par le gouvernement général japonais." *Bulletin de la Maison franco-japonaise* (Tokyo), 30(1913) and 31–32(1914). A representative work on political and economic changes during the period of Government-General rule.

03-522. CHŎNG, To-Yong. "Korea's Foreign Trade under Japanese Rule." *Journal of Social Sciences and Humanities* 27(December 1967):19–44. An economist analyzes the structure of Korea's foreign trade under Japanese rule from 1910 through 1939 and concludes that it "contributed to the advancement of capitalism . . . and to the imperialistic advancement of Japan" while hampering economic development in Korea.

03-523. CHUNG, Young-iob. "Japanese Investment in Korea, 1904–1945." In Andrew C. Nahm (ed.), *Korea under Japanese Colonial Rule.* Kalamazoo: Center for Korean Studies, Western Michigan University, 1973. A summary report on Japanese investment and its impact in Korea from 1904 to 1945. The author points out that while Japanese investment made positive contributions to the growth of the Korean economy, there were a number of areas where Korea received less favorable results.

03-524. JUHN, Daniel Sungil. "The Development of Korean Entrepreneurship." In Andrew C. Nahm (ed.), *Korea under Japanese Colonial Rule.* Kalamazoo: Center for Korean Studies, Western Michigan University, 1973. Examines the economic policies of the Government-General and some cultural factors that affected the development of entrepreneurship in Korea during Japanese rule.

03-525. _____. "Entrepreneurship in an Underdeveloped Economy: The Case of Korea, 1890–1940." DB dissertation, George Washington University, 1965. 225 pp. Abstracted in *DAI* 27(October 1966):863-64-A; UM 65-14,632. Historical study of the growth of indigenous Korean entrepreneurship during the Japanese colonial administration.

03-526. KANG, Chul Won. "An Analysis of Japanese Policy and Economic Change in Korea." In Andrew C. Nahm (ed.), *Korea under Japanese Colonial Rule.* Kalamazoo: Center for Korean Studies, Western Michigan University, 1973. After examining overall quantitative and qualitative changes in the Korean economy under Japanese colonial rule, the author concludes that the Korean economy did grow in terms of output but failed to generate genuine economic development.

03-527. KIM, Kwan Suk. "An Analysis of Economic Change in Korea." In Andrew C. Nahm (ed.), *Korea under Japanese Colonial Rule.* Kalamazoo: Center for Korean Studies, Western Michigan University, 1973. Analyzes the economic changes brought about by Japan from 1910 to 1945 and evaluates their impact on the living conditions of Koreans.

03-528. KOH, Sung-Jae. "Contrasting Characteristics of Industrial Entrepreneurship in Japan, India and Korea." *Journal of Social Sciences and Humanities* 29(December 1968):16–51. A provocative study analyzing socioeconomic factors that affected the development of industrial entrepreneurship in modern Japan, India, and Korea.

03-529. _____. "The Development of the Modern Banking System in Korea." *Koreana Quarterly* 1(2)(1959):82–92. A factual survey of the development of the modern banking system in Korea from the late nineteenth century to the 1920s.

03-530. _____. "The Role of the Bank of Chosen (Korea) and the Japanese Expansion in Manchuria and China." *Journal of Social Sciences and Humanities* 32(June 1970): 25–36. An interesting study of how the Japanese government "used the Bank of Chōsen as a financial instrument for accomplishment of the Japanese imperialistic expansion into Manchuria and China" from 1904 until about 1932.

03-531. KWON, Ik Whan. "Japanese Agricultural Policy on Korea:1910–1945." *Koreana Quarterly* 7(3)(Autumn 1965):96–112. A critical study of Japanese agricultural policy in Korea with special attention to land reform and rice export policies. Repudiates the claim that Japanese policy contributed to the growth of Korea's economy.

03-532. _____. "Japanese Industrialization in Korea, 1930–1945: Idealism or Realism?" *Koreana Quarterly* 8(2)(Summer 1966):80–95. After examining the background of the Japanese decision to industrialize Korea after 1930, the author analyzes Japan's policies of industrialization in Korea and concludes that "the Japanese government frankly and deliberately imposed an unbalanced economic structure on Korea in order to fulfill Japan's military adventure over the Asiatic Continent."

03-533. LEE, Hoon K. *Land Utilization and Rural Economy in Korea.* Chicago: University of Chicago Press, 1936. Reprinted New York: Greenwood Press, 1969. A comprehensive and detailed study of Korean agriculture and rural economy as of 1930. Contents: general conditions, characteristics of Korean agriculture, land use, landownership and tenancy, the utilization of forest, urban, and mineral land, capital investments other than in land, farm labor, rural credit, marketing and prices of farm products, farm income and expenses, the standard of living, and agricultural colonization. A very important work.

03-534. NAKAMURA, James I. "Incentives, Productivity Gaps, and Agricultural Growth Rates in Prewar Japan, Taiwan and Korea." In Bernard S. Silberman and H. D. Harootunian (eds.), *Japan in Crisis: Essays on Taisho Democracy.* Princeton: Princeton University Press, 1974. An authoritative comparative analysis of agricultural growth in Korea and Taiwan under Japanese rule. Using the increase in land productivity as the basis for agricultural growth, the author delineates several factors that contributed to the development of traditional agriculture in Korea and Taiwan—which he calls "a success without precedent in the world."

03-535. SCHUMPETER, S. B. (ed.). *The industrialization of Japan and Manchukuo, 1930–1940: Population, Raw Materials and Industry.* New York: Macmillan, 1940. In this important study of Japanese industry before World War II, certain aspects of the Korean economy, particularly agriculture, mineral resources, and trade and industry, are examined within the context of the overall industrialization of Japan.

03-536. SHIN, Yong-ha. "Land Tenure System in Korea, 1910–1945." *Social Science Journal* (Korean National Commission for UNESCO), 1(1973):65–84. A scholarly analysis of the land tenure system under Japanese rule; discusses the nature of land tenure, changes in land tenancy and rural stratification, and rent.

03-537. SUH, Sang Chul. *Growth and Structural Changes in the Korean Economy, 1910–1940.* Cambridge, Mass.: Council on East Asian Studies, Harvard University, 1978. An important and authoritative study by an economist of the Korean economy during the Japanese rule. It attempts to measure the rates of economic growth by estimating production in agriculture, forestry, fishery, mining, and manufacturing; examines structural changes by analyzing the composition of commodity production and labor force by industries. Extensive quantitative findings are often supplemented by qualitative materials to give historical perspective.

Society

03-538. BERGMAN, Stan. *In Korean Wilds and Villages.* Translated by Frederic Whyte. London: Travel Book Club, 1938. The author, a Swede, made an expedition in northern Korea in 1935 to study the life and distribution of birds. This is an account of his experience and observation depicting Korea's flora and fauna and social customs. Particularly useful for understanding Korea's nature and wildlife. Contains many helpful photographs.

03-539. BRUNNER, Edmund de S. *Rural Korea.* New York: International Missionary Council, 1942. A good description of colonial realities of rural Korea under Japan. Based on firsthand observation and highly critical of Japanese exploitation.

03-540. CLIPPINGER, Morgan E. "The Development of Modernized Elites under Japanese Occupation." *Asiatic Research Bulletin* 6(6)(September 1963):1–11. A perceptive analysis of the emergence of new elites in Korea during the Japanese occupation. Describes the extent to which Korea was able to produce modernized elites in various fields and suggests several factors which hindered the growth of a modernized Korean elite.

03-541. DRAKE, H. B. *Korea of the Japanese.* London: John Lane, 1930. An account of the author's impression of life and social conditions in Korea in the 1920s based on his experience of living there as an English instructor. Unabashedly favoring imperialism as the white man's burden, the author is convinced that the Japanese were doing in Korea what the English were doing in India.

03-542. KIM, Yong-mo. "Social Background and Mobility of the Landlords under the Japanese Imperialism in Korea." *Journal of Social Sciences and Humanities* 34(June 1971): 87–109. An analysis of the social background and mobility of Korean landlords under Japanese rule. Based on interviews with some 233 sample individuals throughout South Korea.

03-543. WAGNER, Ellasue. *Korea: The Old and the New.* New York: Revell, 1931. An impressionistic sketch of Korean life in the midst of transition from the old to the new as observed by a Western missionary.

Koreans in Japan

03-544. MITCHELL, Richard H. *The Korean Minority in Japan.* Berkeley: University of California Press, 1967. Traces the development of the Korean minority in Japan and analyzes the controversies that arose between Korean immigrants and the Japanese from 1919 to 1963. Also discusses the role of Korean students in Japan in the March First movement, the communist and nationalist movements among Koreans in Japan, problems of assimilation, and the ideological split and intensification of political activity after World War II.

03-545. WAGNER, Edward W. *The Korean Minority in Japan, 1904–1950.* New York: Institute of Pacific Relations, 1951. Mimeographed. A judicious study of the mi-

gration of Koreans to Japan in the years between 1904 and 1950. Traces the history of migration and problems of the Korean minority in Japan. Chapters 2 and 3 cover the period before 1945.

RELIGION AND EDUCATION
Religion

03-546. CLARK, Allen D. *History of the Korean Church.* Seoul: Christian Literature Society, 1961. A survey history of the activities of Christian missionaries and the growth of the church in Korea until the 1950s.

03-547. KANG, Wi Jo. "Japanese Government and Religions in Korea." PhD dissertation, University of Chicago, 1967. A study of Japanese policies toward various religions in Korea under Japanese colonial rule.

03-548. _____. "Japanese Rule and Korean Confucianism." In Andrew C. Nahm (ed.), *Korea under Japanese Colonial Rule.* Kalamazoo: Center for Korean Studies, Western Michigan University, 1973. A short survey of the policies of the Japanese Government-General toward the Korean Confucianists in the early stage of colonial rule. Focuses largely on educational institutions.

03-549. SHEARER, Roy E. *Wildfire: Church Growth in Korea.* Grand Rapids, Mich.: Eerdmans, 1966. A scholarly study of the growth of the Protestant churches in Korea from 1832 to 1964 based on extensive use of primary sources. Includes many statistical tables and figures.

Education

03-550. ABE, Hiroshi. "Higher Learning in Korea under Japanese Rule: Keijo Imperial University and the 'People's University' Campaign." *Developing Economies* 9(2)(June 1971):174–196. Examines critically the policies of the Japanese Government-General in Korea regarding higher education and traces the circumstances leading to the establishment of Keijo Imperial University and the unsuccessful campaign among Koreans to organize a People's University *(Millip taehak)* in the 1920s.

03-551. FISHER, James Earnest. *Democracy and Mission Education in Korea.* New York: Columbia University Press, 1928. Reprinted Seoul: Yonsei University Press, 1970. Examines some of the aims and activities of the mission education in Korea "in the light of a democratic philosophy of education" and points out problems such an education entails, especially the tension between Japanese authorities and Korean nationalists. A scholarly and authoritative work.

03-552. KIM, C. I. Eugene. "Education in Korea under the Japanese Colonial Rule." In Andrew C. Nahm (ed.), *Korea under Japanese Colonial Rule.* Kalamazoo: Center for Korean Studies, Western Michigan University, 1973. A brief survey of Japanese educational policies in Korea under Japanese rule.

03-553. KIM, Helen Kiteuk. *Rural Education for the Regeneration of Korea.* New York: Columbia University Press, 1931. A study of the development of modern education, particularly vocational, in Korea's rural areas during the Japanese colonial period.

03-554. TOBY, Ronald. "Education in Korea under the Japanese: Attitudes and Manifestation." *Occasional Papers on Korea* 1(April 1974):55–64. Edited by James B. Palais. A brief essay reflecting on the attitudes and manifestations of the Japanese colonial educational system in Korea.

03-555. UNDERWOOD, Horace Horton. *Modern Education in Korea.* New York: International Press, 1926. An account of the development of modern education in Korea from the late nineteenth century until 1923 with special emphasis on missionary education by an American missionary who played an important role in the mission education there. Contains many useful statistical tables and figures as well as photographs. A valuable source.

03-556. YIM, Han-yong. "Development of Higher Education in Korea during the Japanese Occupation (1910–1945)." EdD dissertation, Teachers' College, Columbia University, 1952. A critical analysis of the totalitarian Japanese colonial educational system in Korea.

INTERNATIONAL RELATIONS

03-557. CHO, Soon Sung. *Korea in World Politics, 1940–1950.* Berkeley: University of California Press, 1967. The author traces and examines the development of the Korean question from the Cairo Declaration of 1943 to the eve of the Korean War in 1950 with special emphasis on the role of the United States in Korea. For the period before 1945, the first two chapters present a good discussion of American policy toward Korea at Cairo, Teheran, Yalta, and Potsdam and the division of Korea at the 38th parallel.

03-558. DENNETT, Tyler. "In Due Course." *Far Eastern Survey* 14(January 1945):1–4. A distinguished diplomatic historian reflects on the future status of Korea after being freed from Japan in the light of the Dumbarton proposals prepared for the forthcoming United Nations organization.

03-559. KIM, Kyu-sik. "The Asiatic Revolutionary Movement and Imperialism." *Communist Review* 3(3)(July 1922):137–147. Reprinted in Dae-sook Suh, *Documents of Korean Communism, 1918–1948.* (Princeton: Princeton University Press, 1970). A well-known leader of the Korean independence movement discusses the political sit-

uation in the Far East. The author is extremely critical of both Japanese imperialism and American indifference and concludes that "the Korean question is the crucial point in the Far Eastern situation."

03-560. LEE, Won-sul. "American Preparedness on the Korean Question in 1945: A Study on the Question of Power and Morality in American Foreign Policy." *Journal of Social Sciences and Humanities* 22(June 1965): 53–68. A critical analysis of American wartime policy toward Korea. Concludes that miscalculation of national interests, not naivete, on the part of America's wartime leaders virtually led North Korea to fall under Russian control.

BIOGRAPHIES

03-561. KANG, Younghill. *The Grass Roof.* New York: Scribner's, 1931. A literate autobiographical description of a Korean boy growing up in the early part of the twentieth century who is caught between tradition and modernism and between Korean nationalistic sentiment and Japanese encroachment. Offers considerable insight into individual, family, and community relations.

03-562. KIM, Richard E. *Lost Names: Scenes from a Korean Boyhood.* New York: Praeger, 1970. A brilliant autobiographical novel depicting the life of a Korean boy growing up under Japanese colonial rule. One can get an intimate feeling of how a Korean family responded to harsh Japanese rule.

03-563. LI, Mirok. *The Yalu Flows: A Korean Childhood.* Translated by H. A. Hammelmann. East Lansing: Michigan State University Press, 1956. Originally written in German, this autobiography poignantly recounts the author's early life during the first two decades of the twentieth century—growing up in an old traditional family environment while tradition was fast vanishing, the coming of the Japanese, his quest for "the new learning," and his participation in the March First movement as a young student in Seoul.

03-564. NEW, Ilhan. *When I Was a Boy in Korea.* Boston: Lothrop, Lee and Shepard Co., 1928. Born in 1894 in Pyongyang, the author was educated in the United States and became a successful businessman in Korea. He gives a good account of social customs in the Korea of his boyhood but explains very little about his own life or experience.

03-565. OLIVER, Robert T. *Syngman Rhee: The Man Behind the Myth.* New York: Dodd, Mead, 1954. An authoritative biography of Syngman Rhee by one of his close associates who had access to the subject's personal records and documents. Rhee's activities abroad during the Japanese period are covered in chaps. 6 through 11.

03-566. PAHK, Induk. *September Monkey*. New York: Harper, 1954. An autobiography of a Korean woman who was born into a tradition-bound family around the turn of the century and became one of the first "modernized" women in Korea through her Christian education. In spite of the missionary tone of the book, it gives a good account of the life of a Korean woman.

03-567. YI, Pangja. *The World Is One: Princess Yi Pangja's Autobiography*. Seoul: Taewon Publishing Co., 1973. Yi Pangja, born of a noble Japanese family (née Princess Masako), was married largely through a political arrangement to Prince Ŭn, who, as last heir to the throne of the Yi dynasty, was forced to spend most his life from early boyhood in Japan. In this autobiography, the author gives a moving account of her life with the Korean prince from her engagement to him in 1917 till the prince's return to Korea in 1963 as an invalid. She also ably depicts the sentiment and reactions of her family toward many turbulent events that took place during the period.

03-568. YIM, Louise. *My Forty Year Fight for Korea*. Seoul: International Culture Research Center, Chungang University, 1951. A close associate of Syngman Rhee, Louise Yim (Im Yŏng-sin) is a well-known educator and a women's leader in South Korea. This personal account of her life from her birth in rural Korea until the outbreak of the Korean War in 1950 depicts her struggle for education, for Korea's independence, and for the school she founded. Events narrated in the memoir are not always reliable, however.

VI. THE HISTORY OF SCIENCE
by Seong Rae Park

INTRODUCTION

ALTHOUGH KOREA has made a number of significant contributions to the world of science, studies of the history of science have unfortunately been neglected for a long time. Only in recent years have we begun to see serious efforts by Korean scholars to rediscover the scientific achievements of traditional Korea.

In modern times Korea's development of science and technology first drew the attention of a few Japanese scholars in the early twentieth century. Wada Yuji, for example, wrote a series of articles in Japanese on Korea's astronomy and meteorology which attracted attention in the Western world. Western scholars, mostly missionaries who were stationed in Korea, sustained the interest by publishing useful studies on various aspects of science and technology in *Transactions of the Korea Branch of the Royal Asiatic Society*—Bowman wrote on "The History of Korean Medicine" (1915), Underwood on "Korean Boats and Ships" (1934), Boots on "Korean Weapons and Armor" (1934), and Rufus on "Astronomy in Korea" (1936).

The first serious study of the general development of science in Korea was not made until 1944 when Hong I-

sŏp published his pioneering work *Chosŏn kwahaksa* [History of science in Korea], which was originally published in Japanese under the title *Chōsen kagakushi*. Although this book deals with many aspects of science and technology in traditional Korea, it is strictly speaking a cultural history since topics of scientific import are treated within a broader context of the development of civilization at different periods in Korean history. Thus it is the work of a general historian, not of a scientist working on the history of science.

In 1966, more than twenty years after the first publication of Hong I-sŏp's work, Chŏn Sang-un (Sangwoon Jeon) published a new title called *Han'guk kwahak kisulsa* [History of science and technology in Korea]. In this book we have, for the first time, a comprehensive study of science and technology in traditional Korea by a scholar trained in the field of science. The same author published an English version, titled *Science and Technology in Korea*, which competently reviews various aspects of the technical accomplishments of traditional Korea.

Although these works by Hong I-sŏp and Chŏn Sang-un are major scholarly achievements, they are essentially encyclopedic collections of various data on scientific relics and cannot in a strict sense be regarded as works of "history of science and technology"—if, to borrow Nathan Sivin's definition, "by that we mean a reconstruction of the interplay of forces which accounts for

Korea's own balance between constancy and change or between fluctuating social circumstances and the unfolding inner potentialities of ideas and techniques."[1] The history of science in Korea is yet to be written, for there is still much basic research to be done on many aspects of science and technology. Nevertheless, these pioneering works have made very useful beginnings.

Ideally, the historian of science should have adequate training in both science and historical craft as well. In Korea today, however, we have two groups of scholars with different backgrounds working in this field. The first group comprises the professional historians, such as Yi Yong-bŏm, Yi Kwang-rin, Hŏ Sŏn-do, and Kang Man-gil, whose primary interests lie in general history. Although they do not have much training in science and technology, these professional historians have contributed greatly by pointing out areas in which notable scientific achievements have been made. The second group comprises the scientist-historians, who are scientists by profession but amateurs in historical craft. Their interest in the history of science is a relatively recent phenomenon but already they are beginning to make significant contributions to our knowledge of science and technology in traditional Korea.

Studies of the history of science in traditional Korea have made great strides in the last two decades. During this period, professional historians as well as scientist-historians have conducted basic research on "the world's first discoveries"—the astronomical observatory, the rain gauge, movable type, the warship covered with iron spikes, and the first Asian to propose the idea of earth rotation. Especially noteworthy is the emergence in recent years of a small number of scientist-historians who are able to attack technical problems that professional historians have been obliged to ignore. In the not too distant future, we may perhaps witness more systematic and comprehensive studies of the history of science in traditional Korea. In the meantime, notable studies have been made in certain areas: astronomy and meteorology by Chŏn Sang-un (Sang-woon Jeon), Yi Yong-bŏm, Pak Sŏng-nae (Seong Rae Park), and Tamura Sennosuke; mathematics by Kim Yong-un; firearms by Hŏ Sŏn-do; printing by Kim Tu-jong, Kim Wŏn-yong, and Son Po-gi (Pow-key Sohn); geography by Yi Ch'an and Shannon McCune; geomancy by Yi

Pyŏng-do; technicians by Kang Man-gil; shipbuilding by Kim Chae-gŭn; modern technology by Kim Yong-ho and Im Ch'ae-wŏn; biology by Yi Tok-pong; agriculture by Yi Ch'un-nyŏng; irrigation by Yi Kwang-rin; and medicine by Kim Tu-jong and Miki Sakae.[2]

Korean scholars engaged in the study of science and technology in traditional Korea are handicapped by an almost total lack of institutional support. There is not a single college or university in South Korea today that offers any organized curriculum to teach the history of science. It is hardly surprising, then, that there are only about half a dozen scholars who are full-time historians of science (not including the professional or scientist-historians). That only a handful of scholars can devote their time to the study of science and technology in traditional Korea is deplorable. Nevertheless, an organization called the History of Science Society of Korea was formed about ten years ago for those engaged in the study of science history in Korea, and its activities are slowly gaining the attention of other scholars.

In 1977, three important new books in Korean were published. One is Kim Chae-gŭn's study on the history of shipbuilding in Yi Korea, the second is Kim Yong-un's study of the history of mathematics in Korea, and the third is the revised edition of Chŏn Sang-un's earlier work on science and technology. These pioneering works have made significant contributions to our understanding of the subjects. It is also important to note the suggestion made by Kim Yong-un in his study of mathematics in traditional Korea. During the Yi dynasty, mathematicians and astronomers, as well as other scientists and technicians, were usually included in the separate class of people known as *chungin* or "middle people," and Kim suggests that further studies on the social backgrounds of scientists would throw new light on hitherto unknown aspects of the social history of Korea. Clearly, greater consideration should be given to the role of science in Korean history.

Science as a mode of understanding nature has exerted a powerful influence on human thinking. Keeping this in mind, I have tried to demonstrate how the changing views of nature in early Yi Korea influenced Confucian political views of the period.[3] Confucianism in Korea was above all a political ideology, but it also had a holistic tendency to subsume all human understanding of nature within its political framework. In this sense the political ideas of Confucianism cannot be properly understood, not to mention appreciated, without an adequate grasp of the Confucian view of nature—an important reason for the intellectual historian to keep an eye on the history of science.

As we can see from the Western historiography of science, especially the "internalist-externalist" controversy over the place of science in history, science is an intellectual effort of individuals as much as a product of society. Maybe we are already at the threshold of a new stage in this study, for Korean historians of science are gradually moving into the historians' province with the materials traditionally taken to be too "scientific" and "technical" if not "esoteric." Both general historians and historians of science should benefit from this new development.

NOTES

1. Sang-woon Jeon, *Science and Technology in Korea: Traditional Instruments and Techniques* (Cambridge, Mass.: MIT Press, 1974), p. xiv.

2. For the full citation of their works, see bibliography in Sang-woon Jeon, *Science and Technology in Korea,* and Hong I-sŏp, "Han'guk ŭi kwahak [Science in Korea]," in Seoul taehakkyo, Tonga munhwa yŏn'guso, *Han'gukhak* (Seoul: Hyonamsa, 1972), pp. 537–559.

3. Seong Rae Park, "Portents and Politics in Early Yi Korea, 1392–1519." PhD dissertation, University of Hawaii, 1977.

BIBLIOGRAPHY

GENERAL

03-569. HONG, I-sup. "Western Science in Yi Korea." *Korea Journal* 4(11)(November 1964):4–7. A short survey of the sciences and technology Korean scholars acquired from the Jesuit missionaries in China and of their impact on scholarship—*sirhak* in particular—in the latter half of the Yi dynasty.

03-570. JEON, Sang-woon. *Science and Technology in Korea: Traditional Instruments and Techniques.* MIT East Asian Science Series, no. 4. Cambridge, Mass.: MIT Press, 1974. The first serious systematic study of science and technology in traditional Korea in any Western lan-

guage. The author discusses the development of Korean science, especially scientific instruments, which he describes in great detail in chapters on astronomy, meteorology, physics and physical technology, chemistry and chemical technology, and geography and cartography. The author points out Korea's unique contributions to the history of science and technology as well as her role as a bridge between Japanese and Chinese science and civilization. Very informative and useful.

03-571. _____. "Understanding of Science in History of Korea with Emphasis on Scientists in Early 15th Century." *Japanese Studies in the History of Science* 6(1967): 124–137. A bibliographic review of achievements in the study of the history of science in Korea, with a brief survey of scientific works in King Sejong's reign in the first half of the fifteenth century.

03-572. King Seijong Memorial Society. *King Seijong [Sejong] the Great: A Biography of Korea's Most Famous King.* Seoul: King Seijong Memorial Society, 1970. A biography of King Sejong (reigned 1418–1450) in an old-fashioned eulogistic style. The achievements in science and technology during his reign are explained in chap. 7 (publication of books, many of them on science and technology), chap. 9 (science and invention), and chap. 10 (movable bronze type printing).

MATHEMATICS, PHYSICS, AND ASTRONOMY

03-573. CH'ŎN, Kwan-u. "Hong Tae-yong (1731–1783)." *Korea Journal* 12(11)(November 1972):34–39. A general account of the life and thought of Hong Tae-yong, a noted *sirhak* scholar who is known as the first Korean to have proposed the theory of the earth's rotation.

03-574. CHŎN, Sang-un. "Astronomy and Meteorology in Korea." *Korea Journal* 13(12)(December 1973):13–18. A brief survey of the development of astronomy and meteorology in traditional Korea from the Three Kingdoms period through the Yi dynasty.

03-575. _____. "Chang Yŏng-sil: The Galileo of the Yi Dynasty." *Korea Journal* 14(2)(February 1974):44–48. Born as a slave, Chang Yŏng-sil rose to become a noted inventor and chief engineer in early Yi dynasty Korea. This is a general account of the works in which he is believed to have had a hand during the reign of King Sejong (reigned 1418–1450).

03-576. _____. "Ch'ŏmsŏngdae and Astronomical Observation." *Korea Journal* 12(2)(February 1972):20–25. In recent years, scholars have challenged the old view that Ch'ŏmsŏngdae, which still stands in the old capital of Silla, was constructed as a dome-type observatory. Here the author posits the theory that it may have been used as a gnomon to measure the shadow from outside (rather than inside) the tower. Also suggested is the possible use of the tower as the standard of definite directions.

03-577. KIM, Yong-woon. "Introduction to Korean Mathematical History." *Korea Journal* 13(7)(July 1973):16–23; 13(8)(August 1973):27–32; and 13(9)(September 1973): 35–39. A survey of mathematics in traditional Korea from the Three Kingdoms period on. It examines the major textbooks of mathematics, various calculating devices, the theory of equations, surveying, and "magic squares"—all with sample problems and solutions. This valuable study is the first on the subject.

03-578. _____. "Structure of Ch'ŏmsŏngdae in the Light of the Choupei Suanchin." *Korea Journal* 14(9)(September 1974):4–11. A mathematician examines the structural aspects of Ch'ŏmsŏngdae based on the old Chinese book on astronomy and mathematics and posits a new thesis that the tower was built not for astronomical observation but for symbolic demonstration of Silla's scientific prowess.

03-579. _____. "T'aegŭk Pattern of a Stone at Kamŭn-sa Temple." *Korea Journal* 15(1)(January 1975):4–10. Arguing that the zigzag design on a foundation stone discovered in the old site of Kamŭn-sa is related to the quadrature of the circle, the author discusses the probable mathematical system developed in Silla times and its relationship with metaphysical thought.

03-580. _____. "Origins of Time-keeping Mechanisms: Similarities in China and Korea." *Korea Journal* 15(8)(August 1975):4–11. The author examines a fragment of a stone sundial of Silla, now being preserved in a museum in Kyŏngju, along with other timekeeping mechanisms developed in traditional China and Korea and compares the origins of timekeeping in the two countries.

03-581. NEEDHAM, Joseph. *Science and Civilization in China.* Vol. 3: *Mathematics and the Sciences of the Heaven and the Earth.* London: Cambridge University Press, 1959. In every volume of this great work, Needham tries to incorporate as much information on Korean science as possible into his discussion of Chinese science. This volume has discussions on the Korean sundial, armillary sphere, cosmography, observatory, comets observed, rain gauge, map, and star chart. At the end of this volume is an addendum on Korea (pp. 682–683) emphasizing the importance of the study of history of Korean sciences for better understanding of Far Eastern civilizations.

03-582. _____. "A Korean Astronomical Screen of the Mid-Eighteenth Century from the Royal Palace of the Yi Dynasty." *Physics* 8(2)(1966):137–162. A description is given of a folding screen now in the Whipple History of Science Museum at Cambridge. It contains the traditional Korean planisphere of 1395 together with two Jesuit planispheres dated ca. 1357. Inscriptions on the screen are translated. The origin of the screen is traced back to the friendship between two Koreans, An Kuk-pin and Pyŏn Chung-hwa, and two Jesuits in China, Ignatius Koegler and Andrea Pereira, in 1741.

03-583. RUFUS, W. Carol. "Astronomy in Korea." *Transactions of the Korea Branch of the Royal Asiatic Society* 26(1939):1–48. The best chronological survey of Korean astronomy. Covers Lolang remains, the records of eclipses and comets in the Three Kingdoms and Koryŏ periods, the cosmologies of Yi scholars, the inventions during the reign of King Sejong, and the Jesuit astronomy introduced to Korea.

03-584. _____. "The Celestial Planisphere of King Yi Tai-jo." *Transactions of the Korea Branch of the Royal Asiatic Society* 4(3)(1913):23–72. A detailed discussion of the *Ch'ŏnsang yŏlch'a punya chido,* a constellation chart prepared on a stone slab by Kwŏn Kŭn and others at the beginning of the Yi dynasty. Well illustrated. Author gives English translations of the original explanations inscribed on the stone (still preserved in Seoul).

03-585. _____. "A Korean Star Map." *Isis* 35(1944):316–326. Good supplement to the preceding entry by the same author. All terms in the chart are translated into English.

03-586. _____. "The Observatory of Silla." *Popular Astronomy* 25(1917):490–496. Author believes Ch'ŏmsŏngdae was used in Silla times as an open-dome type of observatory for nighttime astronomical observations.

03-587. RUFUS, W. Carol and Won-chul LEE. "Marking Time in Korea." *Popular Astronomy* 44(1936):252–257. A brief survey of calendars, sundials, and clepsydras in Korean history.

03-588. SUDZUKI, Osamu. "A Concave Mirror of Koryo Dynasty and Its Earlier Phases." *Chōsen gakuhō* 14 (1959):625–644. With additional twenty-one photos. A comparative study of old mirrors discovered in Korea and those of neighboring civilizations from the archaeological standpoint. Little to do with optics or metallurgy.

03-589. WADA, Yuji. "A Korean Rain Gauge of the 15th Century." *Quarterly Journal* (Royal Meterological Society of London), 37(1911):83. The first short announcement to the West that Koreans had, for the first time in the world, invented a rain gauge in the reign of King Sejong (reigned 1418–1450) to measure the rainfall nationwide for agricultural purposes.

MEDICINE AND BIOLOGY

03-590. AVISON, O. R. "Disease in Korea." *Korean Repository* 4(1897):90–94 and 207–211. Though impressionistic, this is a valuable source on the health problems of the Koreans at the end of the nineteenth century. Based on three years' experience at the Government Hospital in Seoul, the author comments on widespread diseases such as syphilis, skin disease, eye disease, parasites, fever-related diseases, smallpox, tuberculosis, and indigestion. Also offers short comments on "not too many" cases of leprosy and bad teeth.

03-591. BOWMAN, Newton H. "The History of Korean Medicine." *Transactions of the Korea Branch of the Royal Asiatic Society* 6(1915):1–34. Largely translations from the medical texts used by Korean herbalists at the turn of this century. The translation is often inaccurate and confusing. Also included are discussions of basic techniques of Korean doctors in herbs and acupuncture, along with anatomical charts.

03-592. BUSTEED, J. B. "The Korean Doctor and His Methods." *Korean Repository* 2(1895):188–193. A brief survey of traditional therapy of fracture, fever, chronic dyspepsia, and eczema; also explains the use of acupuncture and moxa.

03-593. KIM, Du-chong. "Middle Eastern and Western Influence on Development of Korean Medicine." *Korea Journal* 2(12)(December 1962):5–7. Traces Arabic influence during the Koryŏ period, such as the introduction to alcohol distillation, and examines Adam Schall's translation of Western medicine and other medical books introduced into Yi Korea by *sirhak* scholars.

03-594. KIM, Kwang-il. "Shamanist Healing Ceremonies in Korea." *Korea Journal* 13(4)(April 1973):41–47. A neuropsychiatrist evaluates "the manner of shamanist performances in the treatment of patients in terms of their mechanism and psychodynamism, and their cultural connotation regarding personality in Korea."

03-595. LANDIS, Eli Barr. "The Korean Pharmacopae." *Korean Repository* 5(1898):448–464. An introduction to the most celebrated text of Korean traditional medicine: *Tong'ŭi pogam* (1613) by Hŏ Chun. Includes a partial translation from the text on "Remedies from the Invertebrates."

03-596. NO, Chong-u. "Chinese Medicine in Korea." *Korea*

Journal 11(2)(February 1971):24–29 and 11(3)(March 1971):15–18. Argues that Oriental medicine, though it originated in China, experienced a unique development in Korea, which he calls *Tong ŭihak* (Eastern medicine or Korean medicine). Proposing five periods in the development of Korean medicine, the author finds the uniqueness of "Eastern medicine" manifest in *"sasang"* medicine of Yi Che-ma and the acupuncture and moxabustion techniques developed by Sa-am.

03-597. _____. "Hŏ Chun: Medical Sage of Korea." *Korea Journal* 14(4)(April 1974):53–56. Biography of the author of the best-known text of Korean medicine, *Tong'ŭi pogam* (1613). Hŏ Chun (1546–1615) was born the son of a concubine in the famous family that produced Hŏ Kyun, author of *Hong Kil-tong chŏn,* and became a famous doctor and compiler of many medical books.

GEOGRAPHY AND GEOMANCY

03-598. CHŎNG, Hyŏng-u. "Kim Chŏng-ho's Map of Korea." *Korea Journal* 13(11)(November 1973):37–42. Short account of the life of Kim Chŏng-ho, a nineteenth-century cartographer, and a commentary on his *Taedong yŏjido.*

03-599. HULBERT, Homer B. "An Ancient Gazetteer of Korea." *Korean Repository* 4(1897):407–416. Guide to the best-known gazette of Korea in the Yi period: *Tongguk yŏji sŭngnam.* A portion of the book, on the city of Kyŏngju, is translated as a sample.

03-600. _____. "An Ancient Map of the World." *Bulletin of the American Geographical Society* 36(1904):600–605. Translation and identification of 155 terms used in an old map of the world found in Korea. No effort is made to identify the map itself.

03-601. _____. "The Geomancer." *Korean Repository* 3(1896):387–391. Explains half a dozen basic ideas behind the traditional geomancy practiced in Korea. Concepts are from the Yi period's standard geomancy text, *Ch'ŏn'gi taeyo.*

03-602. KIM, Young Il and Norman J. W. THROWER. "Dong-kook-yu-ji-do [Tongguk yŏjido]: A Recently Discovered Manuscript of a Map of Korea." *Imago Mundi* 21 (1967):30–49. Description of *Tongguk yŏjido,* a well-known map of Korea made by Chŏng Sang-gi in the eighteenth century. Some technical innovations used in making the map are also noted. Has detailed photos of all the provinces of Korea from the map.

03-603. LANDIS, E. B. "Geomancy in Korea." *Korean Repository* 5(1898):41–46. Thirteen basic rules in the practice of Korean geomancy, fifteen points of Tosŏn's teaching in geomancy, and fifteen points of Muhak's teaching in geomancy are translated into English.

03-604. LEE, Chan. "Old Maps of Korea." *Korea Journal* 12(4)(April 1972):4–14. Good survey of the history of cartography during the Yi dynasty. Examines four old maps to demonstrate the technical level reached by each map.

03-605. NAKAMURA, Hiroshi. "Old Chinese World Maps Preserved by the Koreans." *Imago Mundi* 4(1947):3–22. Author classifies all the known old maps of Korea in the Yi period into twelve groups, each with different features. He believes that all the maps are slavishly copied from Chinese prototypes (hence the title).

03-606. _____. "Old Chinese World Maps Preserved by the Koreans." *Chōsen gakuhō* 39/40(1966):1–73. Additional information in Japanese (pp. 1–10) and in English (pp. 10–12) concerning the preceding article; addenda and corrigenda to the preceding article (pp. 13–15); French original writing (pp. 15–61) from which the English version was translated; and an additional report on the placenames in Japanese (pp. 61–73).

03-607. ROH, Do-yang. "History of Korean Geography." *Korea Journal* 13(12)(December 1973):19–30. A useful introduction to the development of geography in traditional Korea.

TECHNOLOGY

03-608. BOOTS, John L. "Korean Weapons and Armor." *Transactions of the Korea Branch of the Royal Asiatic Society* 23(2)(1934):1–42. Discusses features of the weapons and armor in traditional Korea, including archery, swords, spears, firearms, armor, shields, and castles. Brief yet well illustrated and informative.

03-609. CHŎN, Sang-un. "Korean Printing with Movable Metal Types." *Korea Journal* 11(4)(April 1971):4–10. Good survey of the development of movable metal type printing in Korea. After tracing the world's first use of such printing as early as 1234, the author explains various improvements made in the printing technique during the Yi dynasty.

03-610. CH'ŎN, Hye-bong. "Pulcho Chikchi Simch'e Yojŏl." *Korea Journal* 13(4)(April 1973):10–16. After the first public display in Paris in 1972, it was determined by Korean specialists on book printing that this old Buddhist text published in 1377 was the world's oldest extant book printed by metallic type. The author examines the developments leading to the invention of metallic type and the printing of this Buddhist text.

03-611. HULBERT, Homer B. "A Korean Mint." *The Korea Review* (Seoul), 5(3)(March 1905):87–97. Good description with illustrations of how coins were made in traditional Korea.

03-612. MILLS, Edwin W. "Gold Mining in Korea." *Transactions of the Korea Branch of the Royal Asiatic Society* 7(1916):5–39. Tools and methods of gold mining in traditional Korea are explained with ample illustrations. The author comments that "tools look primitive but Koreans have attained great skill."

03-613. NEEDHAM, Joseph. *Science and Civilization in China.* Vol. 4, pt. 2: *Mechanical Engineering.* London: Cambridge University Press, 1965. Korean technology as manifested in the folding fan (p. 150), irrigation (pp. 348–349), and clockwork (pp. 516–522) is discussed. Needham reiterates here that "the Koreans were probably more interested in science and mechanical technology than any other people on the periphery of the medieval Chinese culture area."

03-614. _____. *Science and Civilization in China.* Vol. 4, pt. 3: *Civil Engineering and Nautics.* London: Cambridge University Press, 1971. The author discusses Chang Po-go's adventures in the Yellow Sea toward the end of the Silla period (pp. 453–454) and the technical innovations in Admiral Yi Sun-sin's "turtle ship" (pp. 683–685). Also noted is a Korean world map prepared by Yi Hoe and Kwŏn Kŭn in early Yi Korea that reflected the knowledge of world geography held by the peoples of East Asia (p. 499).

03-615. SOHN, Pow-key. *Early Korean Typography.* Seoul: Korean Library Science Research Institute, 1971. Written in Korean and in English. Sohn's essay "Early Korean Printing" (pp. 31–48) is an excellent survey of the field, giving attention to the political, social, and cultural milieu for the development of printing in traditional Korea. The rest of the book is devoted to a Korean version of the English essay (with slight difference in content), forty-four specimen pages from different type sets with bilingual explanations, and an index prepared both in Korean and English.

03-616. _____. "Early Korean Printing." In Hans Widmann (ed.), *Der Gegenwärtige Stand der Gutenberg-forschung.* Vol. 1. Stuttgart: A. Hiersemann, 1972. Reprint of the essay described in the preceding entry.

03-617. _____. "Early Korean Printing." *Journal of the American Oriental Society* 79(1959):99–103. Earlier version of the same essay.

03-618. UNDERWOOD, H. H. "Korean Boats and Ships." *Transactions of the Korea Branch of the Royal Asiatic Society* 23(1934):1–99. Excellent survey on all aspects of traditional navigation techniques. Includes types of ships, techniques of shipbuilding, rites and customs related to navigation, history of shipbuilding, and Admiral Yi Sunsin's naval campaign. Well illustrated, with bibliography and glossary.

03-619. VIESSMAN, Warren. "Ondol—Radiant Heat in Korea." *Transactions of the Korea Branch of the Royal Asiatic Society* 31(1948–1949):9–22. Mechanical engineer's assessment of the structure and thermal efficiency of the traditional heating device in Korea. Not a historical study.

03-620. WŎN, Yu-han. "A Study on the Introduction of German Coinage Techniques to Korea." *Korea Journal* 14(2)(November 1974):4–11. Explains the Korean government's efforts and eventual failure to introduce Western coinage techniques in 1880s. Traditional minting techniques, largely drawn from Hulbert's article (03-611), are briefly explained.

03-621. YI, Ch'un-yŏng. "A Historical Survey of Agricultural Techniques in Korea." *Korea Journal* 14(1)(January): 21–27. An outline of the development of agricultural techniques in traditional Korea.

CHAPTER 4
Philosophy and Religion

Kah-Kyung Cho

INTRODUCTION

THE PRIMITIVE RELIGIONS of Korea belong to the animistic and shamanistic traditions prevalent in Northeast Asia. Objects in nature are believed to be literally animated and alive, having souls which enter into relationships with the souls of living and dead humans. The happiness and well-being of the people are thus influenced by the spirits of mountains and rivers, trees and rocks, and deceased persons. To exorcize the evil spirits, the shaman, acting as a medium, invokes gods of good fortune and performs colorful rites for believers. Foreign visitors to modern Korea may witness the noisy ceremonies with gongs, dances, and incantations that fill the night life of many villages. However, it is not unusual for believers to invite the shaman to their urban abodes for what may be called semireligious and semisuperstitious services.

One major reason why shamanism continued to exercise such a strong influence on Koreans until only recently can be seen in the ascendancy of Confucianism to the position of a state religion during the Yi dynasty (1392–1910). The Yi dynasty rejected Buddhism, which had enjoyed the patronage of ruling kings in the previous Koryŏ dynasty (918–1392) and which had become corrupt toward the end of the Koryŏ period. The basically sober, pragmatic ethics of Confucianism, however, deprived the common populace of their opportunity to believe in supernatural powers. Besides, at the center of

Confucianism was a study of classical Chinese literature, and only the members of the upper class who were naturally bent on becoming government officials were able to afford the energy and time necessary for its study. Humble Koreans, the perpetual underdogs in a strictly status-oriented society, took recourse to shamanistic practices in order to vent their supercharged emotions.

Though it is certain that magic rites and religious aberrations will gradually disappear with the advance of modern education, shamanism has been a significant factor in Korean religious life, since it functions as a barometer of social instability and spiritual restlessness. Geomancy, fortune-telling, and numerous semireligious fads arose in Korea in the past whenever there was a national crisis. Given that Koreans have had to reckon with prolonged crises most of the time, it must be recognized that there has been a persistent demand for such religious outlets throughout that country's history. The success of Christianity in modern Korea clearly reinforces this point. When Roy E. Shearer says that "shamanism, or animism, had actually prepared the nation to receive Christianity,"[1] we can understand his statement in light of the underlying cause of the rise of the shamanistic form of religion. The appeal of the supernatural increases in proportion to one's disillusionment with reality. Thus, in Shearer's words, Korea had for centuries been "plowed by Shamanistic efforts to communicate with higher beings, and when the seeds of

Christianity were placed in this rich, plowed soil, they flourished and produced the fruit of Christian disciples."[2]

The widespread influence of shamanism can also be traced in the pattern of interaction that existed among Korea's major religious elements. Though some rivalry between Buddhism and Confucianism—or, for that matter, between Confucianism and Taoism—was inevitable, Korea was by and large a syncretic climate in which those traditional religions flourished until the arrival of Christianity. Indeed, not only did Confucianism, Buddhism, and Taoism coexist in Oriental societies, but it was not uncommon for the same individual to embrace these beliefs alternatively at different stages of life. It was even possible for some people to embrace them all at once. This spirit of reconciliation was already manifest in China. When Buddhism crossed the border from India, its otherworldly outlook found a sympathetic philosophy in Taoism. That the doctrinal substance of Buddhism had to undergo a certain modification through the agency of Taoism was not really disturbing because the idea of possessing the absolute truth to the exclusion of all other views was after all alien to the Chinese mind. Thus, in Korea, even the austere Confucian ethics would align with shamanism to the point of holding the spirits of the deceased in awe. On the negative side of the balance, however, this eclecticism resulted in superficial assimilation, so that, for example, a modern, educated, Christian leader of Korea can sometimes still be an authoritarian Confucianist and repressive patriarch at heart.

But while coexistence of traditional religions has been characteristic of all nations in East Asia, certain contrasting patterns emerge in various countries. China, the land which produced Confucianism and Taoism, understandably showed greater flexibility of spirit. Furthermore, regional differences were bound to arise, even in the application of the same system, due to the vast expanse of its territory. The island nation of Japan, on the other hand, was able to maintain some measure of autonomy, if for no other reason than the existence of the Korean buffer zone through which she enjoyed a somewhat discriminating access to Chinese culture. Korea's geographical proximity to China, finally, must account for the overwhelming Chinese influence on her (especi-

ally in the case of Confucianism). Unlike Buddhism, which, as a religion in the proper sense of the word, was primarily concerned with spiritual welfare, Confucianism was more broadly applied to Korean life. It dictated the form of government and bureaucracy, prescribed the examination system for public servants, and inculcated the moral behavior of all men and women according to a strictly hierarchical social order.

It has been said that Koreans have "out-Chinesed the Chinese" in their enthusiastic assimilation of Confucian culture. Though not intended as a compliment, this appraisal of the situation plainly indicates that Koreans have not blindly imitated or passively tolerated the significant product of China's ancient civilization. As a matter of fact, Koreans have taken the moral philosophy of Confucius so much to heart that they have earned the nickname of "the courteous people of the East." More important, Confucianism has sparked in many Koreans an insatiable zeal for learning which has produced both positive and negative results. On the positive side, it has nurtured the popular ideal of a "cultured man," an accomplished person of learning who is well versed in the literature of ancient sages and the history of past dynasties. Though the immediate incentive for mastering the classics was provided by the traditional state examination which was a passport to a prestigious career in the government, the Confucian philosophy tended to encourage education for Korean children at all cost. Learning, even in the opinion of the humblest farmers, has become an unquestioned goal of life and an end in itself.

A host of schools, public and private, flourished during the Yi dynasty, and out of the higher institutions of Confucian learning emerged a group of eminent scholars whose fame reached China and Japan. One of the most outstanding Neo-Confucian scholars was Yi Hwang (1501–1570). His books, including *On Reflection* and *Essence of Neo-Confucianism,* were published in Japan. Yamazaki Ansai, a noted Neo-Confucian scholar of Japan, praised Yi for his profound mastery of the spirit of Confucianism, and his classics were edited in ten volumes of excerpts by another Japanese, Suguri Gyokusui. The well-known edict of Emperor Meiji on Japanese education was drafted by Motoda Tōya, who admitted that he was a follower of Yi

Hwang's teachings. Much later, in 1926, Peking's Shang Te Women's College was reported to be selling reprints of Yi Hwang's "Ten Diagrams of Royal Learning" for the purpose of raising funds. Neo-Confucian pundits of comparable stature to Yi were not few. Their effort widened the horizon of Confucian philosophy and demonstrated the "theoretical" acumen of Korean scholars—hence "Koreanizing" the originally Chinese philosophy.

On the negative side, however, their hair-splitting arguments on cosmological issues and mind versus matter dualism deteriorated in partisan rivalry and factionalism. Because the abstract controversy could not be settled by clear-cut empirical proof, the best scholarship was eventually wasted in a wrangle over personal trivialities, such as whether one had membership in the Eastern or Western or the Northern or Southern factions. Dissatisfied with this state of Confucianism and with the distressing social order of the day, some scholars saw a need for reform. Although the reforms were to be a return to the old teaching of Confucius and Mencius, they were in effect programs of social and public welfare with emphasis on the application of Western scientific technology. The movement was called *sirhak,* or "practical learning." Noted representatives were Pak Chi-wŏn (1737–1805) and Chŏng Yag-yong (1762–1836). Their progressive programs included reform plans for the economic, educational, and legal systems and for agriculture and land redistribution. But an instrumental element of this outwardly Confucian movement was a forbidden religion of the West, Catholicism, which acted as the transmitter of scientific and technical knowledge. Pak Chi-wŏn first came in contact with Catholicism during his trip to China. The *sirhak* school could not long survive—partly because of its leaders' association with the "heresy" of Western religion, but mostly because the majority of the policymakers of the state were conservatives. Nevertheless, the movement is a significant chapter in the history of Korean Confucianism. It signifies an attempt to reconcile The Master's teaching with the knowledge of the modern West, even though it involved the risk of coming into close contact with the wholly alien religion of Catholicism.

Confucianism, which came to Korea during the Three Kingdoms era (AD 313–668), was soon to be followed by Buddhism, the second major religion to mold Korean thought. The principal characteristics of Korean Buddhism, as compared with Indian or Chinese Buddhism, consist of its historical role as the powerful medium of the nation's spiritual unity. Since Buddhism was primarily known for its otherworldly orientation, this may sound unusual. Besides, the Chinese Buddhism that sponsored the Korean version was highly sectarian. Here again, however, the unique pattern of practical adaptation occurred. Officially, the teaching of Gautama first found patronage in Korea's royal household. The first recorded introduction of Buddhism to Korea was in the second year of King Sosurim (AD 372) of the Koguryŏ dynasty. The height of its dissemination was reached during the Silla dynasty, when kings and queens had their heads shaved, changed their names in Buddhist fashion, and became monks and nuns. During the time of peace, the rulers built imposing pagodas and temples to elevate national prestige as well as to express their gratitude for Buddha's blessings. When a calamity of one sort or another befell the kingdom, it was customary for the reigning dynasty to offer prayers and sacrifices to repel the misfortune. Thus the ruler's patronage of Buddhism had the practical purpose of laying the spiritual foundation of the state. In other words, Buddhism became fundamentally a faith that was oriented more to earthly happiness than to life hereafter.

This "Koreanization" of Buddhism was possible, as indicated above, because of the deep-rooted shamanistic tradition in the Korean peninsula. While Confucianism ignored the superstitions of the peasants and had little in common with shamanistic practices except for ancestor worship, the Buddhist belief in the supernatural being conformed more readily to the shamanistic mentality. Buddhism in Korea had become, in effect, an instrument of securing good fortune and a happy life both now and in the hereafter. In this general orientation, there was no difference between the upper class and the masses. Just as a king would offer prayers and sacrifices in the hope of averting a national crisis, a foreign invasion from the north, or a widespread famine, so a lay family would pray in Buddha's name to be cured of a disease or to be blessed with a long-awaited baby son.

The common beliefs of Korean Buddhists and those practicing shamanistic rites were based on the presence of a heavenly being or supernatural powers. But neither shamanism nor Buddhism portrayed the afterlife in any detail. True, stories of the reincarnation of heroes occur repeatedly in Buddhist literature, and the theory of the transmigration of the soul is accepted at face value, as are other doctrinal matters. Nevertheless it is safe to say that Korean people for the most part were simply contented with applying the power of Buddha to life of this world. The telos of Nirvana, the quietistic negation of life that constitutes the ultimate message of Buddhism, remained too esoteric for most Koreans. Instead, Buddhism had to serve their more urgent needs. For instance, there has been a perpetual exigency for Korea's ancient kingdoms to entreat Buddha's heavenly power for protection against their enemies. The splendid temples, pagodas, statues, and other ornaments were not works of art wrought by leisurely hands for aesthetic pleasures. They were the diverse forms of entreaties for the peace and security of a nation under stress. The mammoth project of carving the wooden printing blocks known as Tripitaka Koreana—the most complete collection of Buddhist literature known in the world, capable of printing 160,000 pages, and twice duplicated by King Kojong of the Koryŏ dynasty—was carried out under the impending pressure of Mongolian invasion. It was a spiritual bulwark to fend off the evil, just as the armies on the battlefield were the physical force employed for the same purpose.

But in spite of the pomp and expenditure for spiritual welfare, Korea's Buddhist art did not become lost in the otherworld. Compared with Indian Buddhism, which was propagandistic and noted for its mythological exuberance, the artistic representations of Korean Buddhism have been relatively free of bold fantasy. Having absorbed the more naturalistic tendency of Chinese interpreters, Koreans have cultivated an aesthetic sensibility which is akin to the Taoist notion of rustic simplicity. (Symbol of such simplicity is the "uncarved block" repeatedly alluded to in *Tao te ching* XV, XIX, XXVIII, and XXXII.) This sensibility becomes especially apparent in the typical sculpture of Buddha by Korean artists. Instead of the usual celestial grandeur, some critics find archaic simplicity and childlike warmth of expression evincing a sort of melancholic humor.

Speaking of the influence of Taoism, it is mostly in the area of art and literature that the world-retreating philosophy of Lao Tzu had its greater appeal. As in China, Taoism in Korea stood in the shadow of both Confucianism and Buddhism, which were alternately assuming the role of state religion or official philosophy. Even during the Yi dynasty, however, when Confucians controlled the state's bureaucracy, the study of Lao Tzu and Chuang Tzu remained despite a public policy of discouragement. Noted Confucian scholars considered it the ultimate refinement to be versed in Taoist philosophy, and some even sought to propagate the virtue of Taoism as a political and moral philosophy by challenging the monopoly of the Confucian orthodoxy. Pak Se-dang (1629–1703), who interpreted Lao Tzu's *Tao te ching* as a moral and political corrective to create a rule of virtue among kings and subjects, belongs to a group of stalwart Taoists in the eighteenth-century Yi dynasty.

Although Buddhism, Confucianism, and Taoism had reached Korea centuries earlier, it was not until the seventeenth century that Christianity arrived on the scene. After some Korean scholars visiting Peking had been converted to Catholicism there, missionaries from Europe, especially France, began arriving in Korea. The Church of Rome was established in Korea in the late eighteenth century, and despite the severe persecutions by the government, the number of Korean Catholics grew rapidly. The last persecution of Catholic believers and priests in 1866 caused an international uproar and resulted in the eventual adoption of an open-door policy toward the West and the cessation of anti-Christian activity by the Korean government.

In 1885, two American Protestant missionaries—Horace G. Underwood, a Presbyterian, and H. G. Appenzeller, a Methodist—landed in Inch'ŏn to start what was to become the most successful missionary drive in the Orient. Other missionaries of various denominations soon followed. Some allied themselves with Koreans to reform the government and strengthen the nation against Japan's pressure for colonization; others gained influence at court with their knowledge of advanced medicine and technology. Through subsequent stages of upheaval—the annexation of Korea by Japan in 1910, the March First movement of 1919, the liberation of Korea at the end of World War II in 1945, the North Korean invasion of 1950—Christianity emerged with renewed vigor after initial setbacks. The reason for this extraordinary growth of Christianity has already been pointed out. Along with the shamanistic heritage which prepared Korean soil for organized religion, the fact that Korea's past history on the whole was a record of successive spiritual trials should be kept in mind.

Students interested in the dynamics of Christianity's growth in Korea would not be at a loss to find reports, articles, and books written by Western missionaries. Indeed, the history of the churches belongs to the best-researched and documented chapter in the history of Korean religions. While most of the literature has been provided by Western missionaries, it may be noted that more and more Koreans trained in the theological seminaries at home and abroad are contributing to the study of Korea's church history. Beyond that, there are also movements among Christian leaders and theology professors to "autochthonize" Korean Christianity. This naturalization movement signals the maturity of Christianity in Korea and finds its intellectual underpinnings in the comparative studies of Christianity and the traditional religions of Korea. The Korea Theological Seminary was founded to answer the call for the naturalization of Christian theology, and its graduates, some of them trained further in overseas seminaries, are active in evangelism, teaching, and research. Studies on "Christianity and Korean Thought" by Yun Song-bŏm (Methodist Seminary of Seoul) and "Korean Religions and Christianity" by Yu Tong-sik, to name but two, are typical products of this trend. Nineteenth-century antagonism has given way to better understanding between Christianity and Korean religions.

Buddhism and Confucianism, which came to Korea from China, found a fertile soil for growth in the peninsula and enjoyed the privilege of being declared national religions for centuries. Though no such special status is accorded Christianity in present-day Korea, where politics and religion have become separated, Christianity has grown into the largest and most active organized religion in the nation. Total membership in the Roman Catholic Church and the Protestant churches (the Presbyterian ranking foremost) amounts to nearly 4 million and is still increasing so rapidly that accurate statistics are not readily available. More important, Christianity is undergoing the process of "Koreanizing" just as Confucianism and Buddhism underwent a similar process of assimilation in earlier ages.

But the remarkable success of Christianity in Korea cannot completely overshadow the tendency among religious conservatives to rally around the banner of traditional Eastern thought. In 1861, Ch'oe Che-u, a scholar from the southern part of Korea, founded a religious reform movement, first called Tonghak (Eastern Learning) and later, especially since 1894, Ch'ŏndogyo (Religion of the Heavenly Way). As the original title suggests, the movement arose in opposition to "Western Learning," or Christianity, and promised to furnish the Korean people with a new Oriental faith and ideal. In Tonghak were combined various elements of traditional religions: heaven worship, Confucianism, Buddhism, and shamanism. But central to it is a unique credo that Man is equal to Heaven. The latter appellation of Ch'ŏndogyo or Heavenly Way is derived from this belief. According to this theory, there should be no distinction in class or occupation. The ruler does not have a born privilege over the ruled, since he himself is selected from among the ruled.

Ch'ŏndogyo thus marked a stage in the development of philosophical ideas in Korea: for the first time the concept of human dignity and equality was openly registered. But what gives Ch'ŏndogyo its peculiar religious status is not so much the "democratic" philosophy around which some political forces can be rallied (as in rebellious movements against the corrupt Yi court and the Japanese rulers) as the emphasis on the feeling of reverence and sincerity toward others. Humanity should be revered and served as one would revere and serve Heaven. This message is combined with an equally strong premium placed on learning and diligence. Today Ch'ŏndogyo followers number nearly half a million and represent a significant force of organized religion in Korea.

Finally, a brief account of the influence of modern Western philosophy must be given. During the three decades prior to the end of World War II, about a dozen pioneers who studied in Japanese universities or visited Europe and America had already brought home the prevailing Western philosophical ideas—the philosophy of science and positivism in general; the pragmatism of James and Dewey in particular. The major figures of nineteenth-century German philosophy from Kant to Hegel, as well as the twentieth-century Neo-Kantians, Dilthey and Simmel, Eucken and Bergson, phenomenology and existentialism, were also introduced. Since many universities were founded after 1945, the study of

Western philosophy has become a major area of interest for Korean students, some of whom have received further education in Europe and the United States. In fact, the number of graduate students specializing in European philosophy is much greater than the number of those who pursue the study of traditional Confucian or Buddhist philosophies.

Major universities in Korea have journals of philosophy in which articles on current Western philosophy are published (often complete with English excerpts). The Korean Philosophical Association has its own journal. Nevertheless, an overall view of the acculturation of Western philosophy in Korea, by either Korean or foreign writers, is not available at present. Several such surveys are currently being made in the Korean language, however, and a bibliography including all the Korean-language studies in Western philosophy, as well as some theses and articles by Korean students published in Western languages, is being planned by the Korean Academy of Sciences. One of the immediate tasks facing Korean philosophers today is to assess the impact of Western philosophies on the sociocultural development of modern Korea. It is a task worthy of serious attention if Western philosophy is to secure its place as a moral and intellectual guide in the complex stream of life in Korea.

NOTES

1. Roy E. Shearer, *Wildfire: Church Growth in Korea* (Grand Rapids, Mich.: Eerdmans, 1966), p. 30.
2. Ibid., pp. 30–31.

BIBLIOGRAPHY

GENERAL WORKS

04-001. CHANG, Pyŏng Gil. "Religious Landscape of Korea." *Koreana Quarterly* 6(3)(Autumn 1964):90–96. A brief sketch of the faith in heaven in Korea's religious tradition. Three features are pointed out: (1) heaven realizes its will on earth; (2) heaven, from the beginning, exists only for earth; (3) heaven and earth are amalgamated into one.

04-002. CHUNG, David Tae-wi. "Religious Syncretism in Korean Society." PhD dissertation, Yale, 1959. 306 pp. Abstracted in *DAI* 30(February 1970); UM 70-1750. A historical case study of the religious aspects of Korean soci-

ety's cultural contacts with the outside world (including the West).

04-003. CLARK, Charles Allen. *Religions of Old Korea.* New York: Revell, 1932. The most comprehensive study of Korean religions. Contains lectures (delivered at the Princeton Theological Seminary in 1921) on Buddhism, Confucianism, Ch'ŏngdogyo, shamanism, and other Asiatic sects and on the early phase of Christianity in Korea. Describes their history, doctrines, literature, and arts in Korea. Written by a missionary who, except for some information given him by Korean associates, relied upon Western sources and sometimes accepted accounts of Korean history which have been proved erroneous.

04-004. DALLET, Charles. *Traditional Korea.* New Haven: Human Relations Area Files, 1954. A translation of an ethnographic introduction to the author's *Histoire de l'Église de Corée* written at the end of the nineteenth century. The work is important since it is still the only attempt at a complete ethnography of traditional Korea written in a Western language. Contains a section on religious practices and beliefs.

04-005. GRAF, Olaf. "Ein Abriss der Religionsgeschichte Koreas." In *Cristus und Religionen der Erde: Handbuch der Religionsgeschichte.* Vienna: Verlag Herder, 1951. The most recent survey of Korean religious development in German by an authority on Japanese and Chinese religion and philosophy.

04-006. GUNDERT, Wilhelm. *Japanische Religionsgeschichte: Die Religionen der Japaner und Koreaner in geschichtlichem Abriss dargestellt.* Tokyo: Japanisch-Deutsches Kulturinstitut, 1935. Although mostly concerned with Japan, this volume surveys traditional Korean religion and philosophy and is in many ways superior to Graf's work (04-005).

04-007. Hakwon-sa. *Korea, Its Land, People and Culture of All Ages.* 2nd ed. Seoul: Hakwon-sa Publishing Co., 1963. Chapter on "Thoughts and Religion" contains: (1) General Remarks on Korean Thought, (2) Confucianism in Korea, (3) Korean Buddhism, (4) Christianity in Korea, (5) The Tonghak Movement, (6) Taejonggyo, (7) Shamanism and Aberrations, and (8) Modern Korean Thought. There is an informative chapter on shamanism in the section on "Manners and Customs." Articles in this collection give a fairly rounded picture of all aspects of Korean philosophy and religion on a popular rather than a scholarly basis.

04-008. HULBERT, Homer B. *The History of Korea.* 2 vols. Seoul: Methodist Publishing House, 1905. Although published over half a century ago and primarily a political history, this work still contains much valuable information concerning religious and philosophic development in Korea up to 1904.

04-009. KENYON, Albert. *Valiant Dust: Graphic Stories from the Life of Herbert A. Lord.* London: Salvationist Publishing and Supplies, 1966. 96 pp.

04-010. KOH, Hesung C. "Religion, Social Structure, and Economic Development in Yi Dynasty Korea." PhD dissertation, Boston University, 1959. 267 pp. Abstracted in *DA* 20(November 1959):188–189; UM 59-3459.

04-011. OSGOOD, Cornelius. *The Koreans and Their Culture.* New York: Ronald Press, 1951. A general work on Korea unusual in content and arrangement. Part 1 is an ethnographic village study and thus contains material on religious practice and beliefs. Part 2 is a description of the culture and values of the aristocracy and also deals with religion and philosophy.

04-012. PALMER, Spencer J. "The New Religions of Korea." *Transactions of the Korea Branch of the Royal Asiatic Society* 43(1967):1–10.

04-013. RUTT, Richard. "Some Problems in the Study of Korean Religion." *Korean Affairs* (Seoul), (1962): 256–260.

04-014. SHIN, Myŏng-sŏp. "The Religious Implications of the 'Sacred Calendar' of Korea." *Korea Journal* 10(7)(July 1970):16–20.

04-015. SOK, Do-Ryun. "Non-Western Religion." *Korea Journal* 7(2)(February 1967):11–15.

04-016. VINACKE, Harold M. *The History of the Far Eastern Asia.* New York: Crofts, 1941.

04-017. YE, Yun Ho. *A New Cult in Postwar Korea.* Princeton: Princeton Theological Seminary, 1959. Mimeographed.

PRIMITIVE AND NATIVE RELIGIONS

04-018. ALLEN, H. N. "Some Korean Customs: The Mootang." *Korean Repository* (Seoul), 3(1896):163–165.

04-019. AN, Ho-sang. "Dae-Jong-Gyo: Religion of God-Human Being." *Korea Journal* 2(5)(May 1963):9–13.

04-020. CANANOWICZ, I. M. "Paraphernalia of a Korean Sorceress in United States National Museum." *Proceedings* (United States National Museum), 51(1917):591–597.

04-021. GALE, J. S. "Korean Beliefs." *Folklore* (London), 11(1900):325.

04-022. GIFFORD, D. L. "Ancestral Worship as Practiced in Korea." *Korean Repository* (Seoul), 1(1892):169–172.

04-023. HULBERT, Homer B. "The Geomancer." *Korean Repository* (Seoul), 3(1896):381–391.

04-024. JONES, Rev. G. H. "The Spirit Worship of the Koreans." *Transactions of the Korea Branch of the Royal Asiatic Society* (Seoul), 2(1901):37–85.

04-025. LAMBUTH, David Kelly. "Korean Devils and Christian Missionaries." *Independent* (New York), 63(1907): 287–288.

04-026. LANDIS, E. B. "Geomancy in Korea." *Korean Repository* (Seoul), 5(1898):41–46.

04-027. _____. "Korean Geomancy." *China Review* (Hong Kong), 23(1898–1899):37–45.

04-028. _____. "Notes on the Exorcism of Spirits in Korea." *Journal of the Buddhist Text and Research Society* 3(3) (1895):1–8; *China Review* (Hong Kong), 12(1894–1895): 399–404.

04-029. LEE, Kang-O. "Jingsan-gyo: Its History, Doctrines, and Ritual Practices." *Transactions of the Korea Branch of the Royal Asiatic Society* 43(1967):28–103.

04-030. PAI, Paul. *Les Croyances populaire en Corée.* Lyon: 1956. 139 pp. Text in French.

04-031. REISCHAUER, Edwin. "On the Cult of the Grain-Spirit in the Religious Administration of Ancient Korea." *Harvard Journal of Asiatic Studies* 2(1937):39–43. Reischauer's abstract of a lengthy article in the Japanese periodical *Shirin* by the Japanese scholar Mishina. Mishina discusses Korea's ancient myths of a grain spirit in the light of comparative ethnological studies in Europe.

04-032. _____. "Groves and the Religious Administration in Ancient Korea and Japan." *Harvard Journal of Asiatic Studies* 2(1939):43–44. Reischauer's abstract of Mishina's article in the Japanese periodical *Shigaku zasshi* on the groves that were the sites of worship as well as of government in ancient Korea and Japan.

04-033. _____. "The Origin and the Development of the Hoa-ra in Silla." *Harvard Journal of Asiatic Studies* 2(1937):45–47. Reischauer's abstract of Mishina's article in the Japanese periodical *Shigaku zasshi* concerning the function of Hoa-ra (Hwarang) in Korea's ancient society.

CONFUCIANISM

04-034. AHN, In-sik. *Ri Yul-Kok, His Life and Works.* Seoul: Far Eastern Research Center, Sung-Kyun-Kwan University, 1958. 19 pp.

04-035. CHOI, Min-hong. "Der Einfluss der konfuzianischen Ethik in Korea." Unpublished dissertation, University of Munich, 1961.

04-036. CHUNG, David. "The Problem of Analogy between Christianity and Confucianism." *Koreana Quarterly* (Seoul), 1(2)(1959):115–130.

04-037. HAFNER, Ambrosius. "Der Konfuzianismus in koreanischen Volk." *Benediktinische Monatschrift* 34(1958): 99–110.

04-038. HENDERSON, Gregory. "Chŏng Ta-san: A Study in Korea's Intellectual History." *Journal of Asian Studies*

16(3)(1957):377–386. The career and thought of a Korean scholar-official whose life spanned the eighteenth and nineteenth centuries (1762–1836). His thinking reflects the philosophic factionalism of the period and the impact of Western thought.

04-039. HETT, G. V. "Some Ceremonies at Seoul." *Geographical Magazine* 3(1936):179–184.

04-040. HONG, I-sop. "Political Philosophy of Korean Confucianism." *Korea Journal* 3(9)(September 1963):12–16.

04-041. KIM, Doo-hun. "The Rise of Neo-Confucianism against Buddhism in Late Koryo." *Bulletin of the Korean Research Center* 12(May 1960):11–19.

04-042. KIM, Ha-Tai. "The Transmission of Neo-Confucianism to Japan by Kang Hang, a Prisoner of War." *Transactions of the Korea Branch of the Royal Asiatic Society* 37(1961):83–103.

04-043. KO, Byung-ik. "Chung Yak-yong's View of Progress —As Expressed in His Kiye-Ron (Essay on Arts and Techniques)." *Bulletin of the Korean Research Center* 23(December 1965):29–36.

04-044. LEE, Sang-eun. "On the Criticism of Confucianism in Korea." *Korea Journal* 7(9)(September 1967):4–18.

04-045. OLIVER, Egbert S. "Korea and China: The Confucian Pattern." *Korean Studies* 6(February 1957):3–5.

04-046. OLIVER, Robert T. "Confucian Rhetorical Tradition in Korea During the Yi Dynasty (1392–1910)." *Quarterly Journal of Speech* 45(1959):363–373. A discussion of the basic differences between Confucian and Aristotelian logic as reflected in the major schools of Confucianism of the Yi period.

04-047. PARK, Chong-Hong. "Historical Review of Korean Confucianism." *Korea Journal* 3(September 1963):5–11.

04-048. YANG, Key P. and Gregory HENDERSON. "An Outline History of Korean Confucianism: I and II." *Journal of Asian Studies* 17(1)(1958):81–101 and 18(2)(1959): 259–276. Part 1 gives a summary of the development and growth of Confucian thought to the end of the nineteenth century. The emphasis is on the Yi period (1392–1910). Part 2 goes into greater detail on the nature and great variety of Confucian schools in the Yi period. It emphasizes the factionalism of these schools and the effects of this factionalism.

04-049. YI, Myonggu and William A. DOUGLAS. "Korean Confucian Today," *Pacific Affairs* 40(Spring/Summer 1967):43–59. This article is devoted to the study of the structures of Confucian institutions which survived the collapse of the Yi dynasty. The study is based on six field trips to local Confucian institutions and detailed questionnaires sent to the 228 local chapters of the Confucian Association.

04-050. YOUN, Eul-sou (Abbé Laurent). *Le Confucianisme en Corée*. Paris: 1939. Studies from a historical and political-social viewpoint on the manner in which Confucianism became the basis of the ideology and political actions as well as social actions of the Korean people.

04-051. YUN, Sŏng-sun. "The Influences of Confucianism and Christianity upon Korean Education." PhD dissertation, American University, 1932. 240 pp.

BUDDHISM
General Bibliography

04-052. *Bibliographie Bhouddique*. Paris: Geuthner, 1928–. This bibliography appears irregularly but contains complete listings of all works written on Buddhism. The last issues (vols. 24–27) appeared in 1958 and cover the years 1950 to 1954.

04-053. HANAYAMA, Shinsho. *Bibliography on Buddhism*. Edited by the Commemorative Committee for Professor Shinsho Hanayama's Sixty-first Birthday. Tokyo: Hokuseidō, 1961. Provides a complete bibliography up to 1928 and contains a number of listings on Korea.

04-054. MARCH, Arthur C. *A Buddhist Bibliography*. London: Buddhist Lodge, 1935. Contains a few entries on Korea and many on China and Japan.

Books and Articles

04-055. AHN, Kye-Hyŏn. "Buddha Images in Korean Tradition." *Korea Journal* 10(3)(March 1970):7–14.

04-056. *Buddhism and Its Culture in Korea*. Seoul: Dongguk University Press, 1964. 46 pp.

04-057. CHO, Myung-ki. "Prominent Buddhist Leaders and Their Doctrines." *Korea Journal* 4(5)(May 1964):15–21.

04-058. DUMOULIN, Heinrich. "Buddhismus in heutigen Korea." *Saeculum* 20(1969):281–290.

04-059. ECKARDT, Andreas. "Verehrung Buddhas in Korea." *Geist des Ostens* 2(34/37)(April 1914/April 1915): 146–158.

04-060. EIDMANN, P. K. "An Introduction to the History of Buddhism in Korea." *Maha bodhi* 68(1960):114–122, 186–192.

04-061. GORDON, E. A. "Some Recent Discoveries in Korean Temples . . ." *Transactions of the Korea Branch of the Royal Asiatic Society* 5(1914):1–39.

04-062. HEYMAN, Alan C. "Historical Document in Sound: Korean Buddhist Ceremony Recorded in Its Entirety." *Korea Journal* 8(July 1968):36–38.

04-063. KAKHUN (comp.). *Lives of Eminent Korean Monks: The Haedong kosŭng chŏn*. Translated with an introduction by Peter H. Lee. Harvard-Yenching Institute Studies, no. 25. Cambridge, Mass.: Harvard University Press, 1969. 116 pp.

04-064. KIM, Tong-hwa. "The Buddhist Thought in the Paekche Period." *Journal of Asiatic Studies* (Seoul), 5(1)(1962):83–85.

04-065. _____. "The Buddhist Thought in the Silla Period." *Journal of Asiatic Studies* (Seoul), 5(2)(1962):59–62.

04-066. KWON, Sang-no. "History of Korean Buddhism." *Korea Journal* 4(5)(May 1964):8–14.

04-067. LANDIS, E. B. "Buddhist Chants and Processions." *Korean Repository* (Seoul), 2(1895):123–126.

04-068. LEDYARD, Gari. "Cultural and Political Aspects of Traditional Korean Buddhism." *Asia* 10(Winter 1963): 46–61.

04-069. LEE, Peter H. "The Life of the Korean Poet-Priest Kyunyŏ." *Asiatische Studien* 9(1958):42–72.

04-070. LONG, Charles Chaillé. "Art and the Monastery in Corea." *Cosmopolitan* (New York), 10(1890):73–80.

04-071. MOORE, S. F. "Present Day Buddhism in Korea." *Missionary Review of the World* (New York, London), 30(1907):647–651.

04-072. OHLINGER, F. "Buddhism in Korean History and Language." *Korean Repository* 1(1892):101–108.

04-073. PARK, Chong-hong. "Buddhist Influence on Korean Thought." *Korea Journal* 4(5) (May 1964):4–7.

04-074. RHI, Ki-yŏng. "Won Hyo's Moral Concepts—according to his Po-sal ke-bon-ji-bom-yo-ki (Notes on the Good Observance of the Boddhisattva Sila Manual)." *Korea Observer* 1(2) (January 1969):103–115.

04-075. SEO, Kyung Bo. "A Study of Korean Zen Buddhism Approached through the Chodangjip." PhD dissertation, Temple University, 1969. 429 pp. Abstracted in *DAI* 30 (December 1969):2611-A; UM 69-16, 815. Contents: Pt. 1: The History of Legend of Zen in India and China, According to the Chodangjip; pt. 2: The Nine Zen Schools of Silla; pt. 3: The Teachings of Master Sunji; pt. 4: The Developments in Korean Zen in the Koryŏ and Yi Dynasty.

04-076. SOK, Do-ryun. "Modern Son Buddhism in Korea." *Korea Journal* 5(1)(January 1965):26–30; 5(2)(February 1965):27–32; 5(4)(April 1965):17–22.

04-077. _____. "Buddhist Images of Popular Worship." *Korea Journal* 10(7)(July 1970).

04-078. "Son Buddhism in Korea." *Korea Journal* 4(1) (January 1963):34–40; 4(3)(March 1964):41–47; 4(4)(April 1964):32–37; 4(5)(May 1964):31–36; 4(6)(June 1964):28–31.

04-079. STARR, Frederick. *Korean Buddhism.* Boston: Marshall Jones Co., 1918. Contains three lectures— "History," "Condition," "Art." Supports the argument that Buddhism is still an influential religion in contemporary Korea. Although neither a profound nor a detailed work, it is based on personal observation and contains suggestions for further study. It is also one of the very few Western studies of Korean Buddhism.

04-080. _____. "Korean Buddhism." *Journal of Race Development* 9(1918):71–84.

04-081. TROLLOPE, Mark Napier. "Introduction to the Study of Buddhism in Corea." *Transactions of the Korea Branch of the Royal Asiatic Society* 8(1917):1–41. A brief but informative history of Buddhism in Korea and a summary of its creeds. Contains suggestions for future researchers.

04-082. TSUKAMOTO, Zenryu. "Buddhism in China and Korea." In Kenneth W. Morgan (ed.), *The Path of the Buddha: Buddhism Interpreted by Buddhists.* New York: Ronald Press, 1956. Devoted almost entirely to developments in China but indicates the sects of Buddhism and their historical movement into Korea.

TONGHAK (EASTERN LEARNING) AND CH'ŎNDOGYO (RELIGION OF THE HEAVENLY WAY)

04-083. CHOI, Dong-hi. "Tonghak Movement and Chundogyo." *Korea Journal* 3(5)(May 1963):14–19.

04-084. HULBERT, Homer B. "The Religion of the Heavenly Way." *Korea Review* 6(11)(November 1906):418–424; 6(12)(December 1906):460–465.

04-085. KANG, Wi Jo. "Belief and Political Behavior in Ch'ondogyo." *Review of Religious Research* 19(Fall 1968):38–43.

04-086. KIM, Yong Choon. "The Concept of Man in Ch'ŏndogyo." PhD dissertation, Temple University, 1969. 280 pp. A study of Ch'ŏndogyo, a modern mass religion in Korea whose adherents number over half a million. The major portion of the work deals with the origin and nature of man, ethics, and eschatology.

04-087. LANDIS, E. B. "The Tonghaks and Their Doctrine." *Journal of the North China Branch of the Royal Asiatic Society* 21(1903):123–129.

04-088. WEEMS, Benjamin. "Ch'ondogyo Enters Its Second Century." *Transactions of the Korea Branch of the Royal Asiatic Society* 43(1967):157–166.

04-089. _____. *Reform, Rebellion and The Heavenly Way.* Tucson: University of Arizona Press, 1964. A study of Ch'ŏndogyo or the Religion of the Heavenly Way from its beginning in the late Yi dynasty to the period 1945–1950. Contains illustrations, glossary, bibliography, and index.

PHILOSOPHY

04-090. BAEK, Se Myung. "The Origins of Korean Thought." *Koreana Quarterly* 4(1)(Autumn 1962): 151–159. A brief survey of the ancient myth (the story of Tan'gun) and native Korean thought, Confucian and Buddhist influences, Hwarang-do, modern Western learning, the Tonghak school, and recent philosophic ideas.

04-091. CHO, Ji-hoon. "Tradition of Korean Thought." *Koreana Quarterly* 1(2)(1960):72–84.

04-092. CH'OE, Dong-hul. "Object of Faith in Eastern Language." *Korea Journal* 5(12)(December 1965):4–8.

04-093. CHOI, Kwang-sok. "Philosophy in North Korea." *Koreana Quarterly* 8(2)(Summer 1966):60–69. Analyzes the North Korean ideological claim for autonomy in achieving the communist revolution in the North as distinct from the Russian revolution and examines North Korea's claim for national identity and self-revival, especially after the Korean War.

04-094. JI, Myung Kwan. "Thinking and Religion of Korean People." *Koreana Quarterly* 6(2)(Summer 1964):82–87. Special focus placed on the influence of the state authority and politics on Korean religions.

04-095. KIM, Tae-Kil. "Pragmatism and Modernization of Korea." *Koreana Quarterly* 8(4)/9(1)(Winter 1966/Spring 1967):56–68. Influence of pragmatism on the process of modernization in Korea is traced by the author in the following areas: (1) rise of interest in social reality as the major theme of philosophy; (2) pluralistic empiricism and relativistic theory of values; (3) peaceful reform instead of radical change through violence; (4) respect for science.

04-096. LEE, Hang Nyung. "Korean Thought and Its Natural Features." *Koreana Quarterly* 6(2)(Winter 1962): 117–121. Briefly examines the correlation between physical and geological features of Korea and the type of life that is reflected in Korean culture as distinct from that of the West.

04-097. OTT, Alfons. "Die Elementenlehre im chinesisch-koreanischen Denken." In *Koreanica,* a collection of essays in honor of Andrć Eckardt. Baden-Baden: 1960.

04-098. PARK, Chong-hong. "Ch'oe Han'gi's Experimentalism." *Journal of Asiatic Studies* (Seoul), 8(4)(December 1965):35–41. Ch'oe Han-gi is seen as a pioneer of Korea's empiricist-experimentalist approach to philosophy. Text in Korean, résumé in English.

04-099. _____. "Postwar Currents of Thought and New Ethics." *Korea Journal* 4(12)(December 1964):4–8.

04-100. _____. "Tasks for Korean Studies: Thought and Philosophy." *Asiatic Research Bulletin* 8(7)(October 1965):1–8.

CHRISTIANITY
General Bibliographies

04-101. ELROD, Jefferson McRee. *An Index to English Language Periodical Literature Published in Korea, 1890–1940.* Seoul: Yonsei University, 1960. (Distributed in the United States by J. McRee Elrod, Peabody Library School, George Peabody College, Nashville, Tennessee.) While not a bibliography, this index is useful because it is a guide to a number of missionary journals such as *The Korea Mission Field* (1904–1940), *The Korea Field* (1901–1904), and *The Korea Methodist* (1904–1905). This index also includes the important *Transactions of the Korea Branch of the Royal Asiatic Society.* Articles on Korea's old religions and philosophies appeared in these journals. The index is also available on microfilm.

General Reports

04-102. "Annual personal, station and mission reports written to the Board of Foreign Missions of the Presbyterian Church in the USA from its missionaries in Korea." Microfilm. New York: United Presbyterian Library, 1884–1911.

04-103. "Annual personal and station reports written to the Board of Foreign Missions of the Presbyterian Church in the USA and the United Presbyterian Church in the USA." New York: Files of the Commission on Ecumenical Mission and Relations of the United Presbyterian Church in the USA, 1912–1962.

04-104. "Fifth Annual Meeting of the Federal Council of Protestant Evangelical Missions in Korea." Seoul: YMCA Press, 1916.

04-105. "General Council of Protestant Evangelical Missions in Korea, First Annual Meeting." Seoul: 1905.

04-106. "General Council of Protestant Evangelical Missions in Korea, Second Annual Meeting." Seoul: 1906.

04-107. "General Council of Protestant Evangelical Missions in Korea, Seventh Annual Meeting." Seoul: 1911.

04-108. Korea Mission of the Presbyterian Church USA. "Annual Meeting Reports" of 1909, 1913, 1914, 1916, 1918, 1949–1953, 1954–1956.

04-109. "Korea Section of Annual Reports of the Board of Foreign Missions of the Presbyterian Church USA and the Commissions on Ecumenical Mission and Relations of the United Presbyterian Church in the USA." New York: United Presbyterian Library, 1885–1962.

04-110. "Statistics from the Printed Minutes of the General

Assembly of the Presbyterian Church in Korea.'' Photographed from General Assembly files. Seoul: 1913–1942.

04-111. ''Statistics from the Printed Minutes of the Presbyterian Church in Korea.'' Photographed from General Assembly files. Seoul: 1908–1912.

General Books and Articles

04-112. AHN, Yong Choon. *The Seed Must Die.* London: Inter-Varsity Fellowship, 1965. 94 pp.

04-113. AWE, Chulho. *Decision at Dawn: The Underground Christian Witness in Red Korea.* New York: Harper & Row, 1965.

04-114. BATEMAN, Doris. *We Went to Korea.* London: Society for the Propagation of the Gospel in Foreign Parts, 1956.

04-115. BEGUIN, O. ''Korean Suspense.'' *Bulletin of United Bible Society* 41(1960):12–15.

04-116. BISHOP, Isabella Bird. *Korea and Her Neighbors.* New York: Revell, 1897.

04-117. BLAIR, Herbert E. *Stewardship in Korea.* Seoul: Christian Literature Society of Korea, 1938.

04-118. BUTTERFIELD, Kenyon L. *The Rural Mission of the Church in Eastern Asia.* New York: International Missionary Council, 1931.

04-119. CAMPBELL, Arch. *The Christ of the Korean Heart.* London: Christian Literature Crusade, 1957. (1955 ed. by Falco Publications, Columbus, Ohio.)

04-120. CLARK, Allen D. *History of the Korean Church.* Seoul: Christian Literature Society of Korea, 1961.

04-121. _____. *A Study of Religion and the State in the Japanese Empire with Particular Reference to the Shrine Problem in Korea.* Thesis, Princeton Theological Seminary, 1939.

04-122. CLARK, Charles A. *First Fruits in Korea.* New York: Revell, 1921.

04-123. _____. *The Korean Church and the Nevius Methods.* New York: Revell, 1930.

04-124. _____. *The National Presbyterian Church of Korea as a Test of the Validity of the Nevius Principles of Missionary Method.* Chicago: 1929. A study of the missionary methods suggested by Dr. John L. Nevius in 1886 and implemented by Presbyterian missionaries to Korea in 1890 and thereafter.

04-125. EDDY, Sherwood. *I Have Seen God Do It.* New York: Harper, 1940.

04-126. Federal Council of Missions in Korea. *The Korea Missions Yearbook.* Seoul: Christian Literature Society of Korea, 1928, 1932.

04-127. FENWICK, Malcolm C. *The Church of Christ in Corea.* New York: Hodder & Stoughton, 1911.

04-128. FULTON, C. Darby. *Star in the East.* Richmond, Va.: Presbyterian Committee of Publication, 1938.

04-129. GALE, James Scarth. *Korea in Transition.* Copyrighted by the Young People's Missionary Movement of the United States and Canada. New York: Educational Department Board of Foreign Missions of the Presbyterian Church in the USA, 1909. A general introduction to Korea. Contains chapters on the beliefs of Korean people, pioneering methods of Western missionaries, and statistics of Protestant missions in Korea as an appendix.

04-130. GEHMAN, Richard. *Let My Heart Be Broken.* New York: McGraw-Hill, 1960.

04-131. GOFORTH, Jonathan. *When the Spirit's Fire Swept Korea.* Grand Rapids, Mich.: Zondervan, 1942.

04-132. GRAFFSHAGEN, Stephan. *Treffpunkt Korea: Ein Spiel von Gottes und der Menschen Gerechtigkeit.* Kassel: Barenreither, 1957. 44 pp.

04-133. HAN, Ki-shik. ''The Christian Impact and the Indigenous Response in the 18th and 19th Century Korea.'' *Koreana Quarterly* 10(1)(Spring 1968):1–25. A sociopsychological analysis of a ''miracle'': that many Koreans became Christians without planned efforts by Western missionaries and withstanding social disapproval and political persecution.

04-134. JI, Won-yong. ''Christian Church and Sects in Korea.'' *Korea Journal* 5(9)(September 1965):4–11.

04-135. _____. ''The Role of Missionary Today.'' *Korea Journal* 7(1)(January 1967):20–23.

04-136. KANG, Won Yong. ''The Korean Church in the World Community.'' *Koreana Quarterly* 3(2)(Summer 1961):113–125.

04-137. _____. ''A Study on the Family System of Korea: The Christian Approach to Its Changing Situation.'' New York: Union Theological Seminary, 1956.

04-138. KAY, Il Seung. ''Christianity in Korea.'' Thesis, Union Theological Seminary, 1950.

04-139. KIM, Chung-Choon. ''The Confessing Church in Korea.'' *Southeast Asia Journal for Theology* 8(1)(July/October 1966):183–196.

04-140. KIM, Eui Whan. ''The Korean Church under Japanese Occupation with Special Reference to the Resistance Movement within Presbyterianism.'' PhD dissertation, Temple University, 1966. 253 pp. Abstracted in *DA* 27(October 1966):1103-04-A; UM 66-9214.

04-141. KIM, Hyung Tae. ''Relationships between Personal Characteristics of Korean Students in Pennsylvania and Their Attitude toward the Christian Churches in America.'' PhD dissertation, University of Pittsburgh, 1966. 172 pp. Abstracted in *DA* 27(8)(February 1967):2415-A; UM 66-13,486.

04-142. KIM, Yang Sun. *History of the Korean Church in the Ten Years Since Liberation.* Translated by Allen Clark. Mimeographed. Seoul: 1962.

04-143. KIM, Yun Kuk. ''The Korean Church Yesterday and Today.'' *Korean Affairs* 1(1962):81–105. A résumé of the history of the Korean church and its interpretation in the present situation.

04-144. KO, Hyun Bong. *A Historical Study of the Characteristics of the Christian Church in Korea.* Dallas: Dallas Theological Seminary, 1965. 523 pp.

04-145. *The Korean Situation.* New York: Commission on Relations with the Orient of the Federal Council of the Churches of Christ in America, 1919.

04-146. LATOURETTE, Kenneth S. *Advance Through Storm: AD 1914 and After, with Concluding Generalizations.* Vol. 8 of *A History of the Expansion of Christianity.* New York: Harper, 1945. Korea is included in the chapter ''The Japanese Empire,'' and the book contains a description of the developments up to World War II.

04-147. _____. *The Great Century: In Northern Africa and Asia, AD 1800–AD 1914.* Vol. 6 of *A History of the Expansion of Christianity.* New York: Harper, 1944. There is a chapter devoted to Korea alone that gives an excellent summary of Christian activities both Catholic and Protestant in the period of great missionary activity.

04-148. LEE, Reverend Gabriel Gab-Soo. ''Sociology of Conversion: Sociological Implications of Religious Conversion to Christianity in Korea.'' Dissertation, Fordham University, 1961. 308 pp. Abstracted in *DA* 22(October 1961):1290-91; UM 61-1572.

04-149. McKEE, Thomas. ''Korean Mission Parish.'' *Mission Bulletin* 10(September 1958):647–650.

04-150. MILLER, Frederick S. *The Gospel in Korea.* New York: Revell, 1939.

04-151. MOFFETT, Samuel Hugh. *The Christians of Korea.* New York: Friendship Press, 1962.

04-152. MOOSE, J. Robert. *Village Life in Korea.* Nashville: Publishing House of the Methodist Episcopal Church, 1911.

04-153. MOTT, John R. ''The Rural Mission of the Church in Eastern Asia.'' *Cooperation for the Christian Advance in Rural Korea* 4(13–15)(1931).

04-154. *National Christian Council of Korea: New Forms of Christian Service and Participation in Korea.* Report of the consultation held 13–16 April 1962 at Onyang, Korea. n.p. Committee on Inter-Church Aid and on Church and Society of the East Asia Christian Conference, 1962. 58 pp.

04-155. NOBLE, Mattie Wilcox. *Victorious Lives of Early Christians in Korea.* Seoul: Christian Literature Society of Korea, 1927.

04-156. NORTH, Eric M. *The Kingdom and the Nations.* West Medford, Mass.: Central Committee on the United Study of Foreign Missions, 1921.

04-157. O'BRIEN, B. Thomas. ''Missionary Successes in Korea.'' *Mission Bulletin* 10(June 1958):535–540.

04-158. PALMER, S. J. ''Korea and Christianity: Equivocal Success in Post-Independence Times.'' *Journal of Korean Affairs* 3(1)(April 1973):3–20. Examines three major sources of Christian growth in postindependence times: (1) shamanism provides vital underpinnings for Christian growth; (2) Christianity appeals to Koreans through its sponsorship of Korean independence and nationalism; (3) Christianity provides inspiration for leadership in Korea's modernization efforts.

04-159. PARK, Bong Bae. ''The Encounter of Christianity with Traditional Culture and Ethics in Korea: An Essay in Christian Self-Understanding.'' PhD dissertation. Vanderbilt University, 1970. 317 pp. Abstracted in *DAI* 31(10)(April 1971):5512-A; UM 71-10,459.

04-160. PERRY, Jean. *Twenty Years a Korea Missionary.* London: S. W. Partridge, 1911.

04-161. PYUN, Y. T. *My Attitude Towards Ancestor Worship.* Seoul: Christian Literature Society, 1926.

04-162. RUTT, Richard. ''Concerning the New Translation of the Korean Bible.'' *Bible Translator* 15(April 1964):80–83.

04-163. _____. *Korean Works and Days: Notes from the Diary of a Country Priest.* Rutland, Vt.: Tuttle, 1964.

04-164. SHEARER, Roy E. *Wildfire: Church Growth in Korea.* Grand Rapids, Mich.: Eerdmans, 1966. A case study of missionary activity in Korea by the Presbyterian and other major denominations, with consideration given to the religious, social, political, and geographical realities affecting church growth.

04-165. _____. ''The Evangelistic Missionary's Role in Church Growth in Korea.'' *International Review of Missions* 54(October 1965):462–470.

04-166. SHELDON, Robert Lewis. *Daybreak in Korea.* Nashville: Southern Publishing Association, 1965.

04-167. UNDERWOOD, Horace G. *Tragedy and Faith in Korea.* New York: Friendship Press, 1951.

04-168. VAN BUSKIRK, James Dale. *Korea, Land of the Dawn.* New York: Missionary Education Movement of the United States and Canada, 1931.

04-169. WANGERIN, Theodora S. *God Sent Me to Korea.* Washington: Review and Herald Publishing Association, 1968.

04-170. WASSON, Alfred W. *Church Growth in Korea.* New York: International Missionary Council, 1934.

04-171. _____. *Factors in the Growth of the Church in Korea.* Chicago: 1931.

Catholicism

04-172. BYON, Douglas. "Faith's Rising Tide in Korea." *Catholic Digest* 20(October 1956):39–44.

04-173. CH'OE, Sŏk-U. "Catholic Church and Modernization in Korea." *Korea Journal* 7(1)(January 1967):4–9.

04-174. DALLET, Charles. *Histoire de L'Église de Corée.* Paris: Librairie Victor Palmé, 1874. 2 vols. The first systematic account of Catholicism in Korea. The long introduction to vol. 1 describes Korean history, institutions, language, morality, and customs (see 04-004); the rest of the work is a detailed account of the Roman Catholic Church in Korea from its introduction in 1784 to the persecution of 1866.

04-175. DESTOMBES, Paul. *Au pays du matin calme, les martyrs de 1866.* Paris: Apostolat des éditions, 1968. 240 pp.

04-176. HAFNER, Ambrosius. *Längs der Roten Strasse.* St. Ottilien: EOS Verlag, [1967]. 169 pp.

04-177. HERLIHY, Francis. *Now Welcome Summer.* Melbourne: Hawthorne Press, 1946. Recounts the experiences of the author, a former Catholic missionary in Korea, during the period of Japanese rule. Gives considerable information on Japanese policy toward Christianity and activities of the Catholic church.

04-178. HEUKEN, Adolf. *Auf allen Wegen: Das absenteuerliche Leben des ersten koreanischen Priesters Andres Kim-tai-ken.* Donauworth: Auer Cassianeum, 1957. 84 pp.

04-179. KIM, Ch'ang-Mun (ed.). *Catholic Korea, Yesterday and Today.* Compiled and edited by Joseph Chang-mun Kim and John Jae-sun Chung. Seoul: Catholic Korea Publishing Co., 1964. 964 pp.

04-180. LATOURETTE, Kenneth S. *Three Centuries of Advance: AD 1500–AD 1800.* Vol. 3 of *A History of the Expansion of Christianity.* New York and London: Harper, 1939. The chapter on the "Chinese Empire" contains a brief outline history of the development of Catholicism in Korea.

04-181. MAXWELL, Murray. "Catholic Significance in Korea." *Koreana Quarterly* 1(2)(1960):105–119.

04-182. MUTEL, Gustave. *Documents relatifs aux martyrs de Corée de 1839 et 1846.* Hong Kong: Société des missions Etrangeres de Paris, 1924. Contains translations of the sections of the *Sŭngjŏng-wŏn Ilgi, Hŏnjong Sillok,* and other Korean official documents which contain accounts of the persecutions of Christians in Korea in 1839 and 1846.

04-183. YOON, Matheous. "Catholicism in Korea." *Koreana Quarterly* 4(1)(Autumn 1962):124–133.

Protestantism

04-184. BLAIR, William Newton. *Gold in Korea.* New York: Central Distributing Department of the Presbyterian Church in the USA, 1946.

04-185. BROWN, Arthur Judson. *Report on a Second Visit to China, Japan and Korea.* New York: Board of Foreign Missions of the Presbyterian Church in the USA, 1909.

04-186. _____. *The Korean Conspiracy Case.* New York: Board of Foreign Missions of the Presbyterian Church, USA, 1912. Attempts to establish the political neutrality of Christian churches, especially American missionaries, in Korea. Refutes Japanese charges against them regarding an alleged conspiracy on the life of Governor-General Terauchi in 1911.

04-187. _____. *The Mastery of the Far East.* New York: Scribner's, 1919. A general account of the power struggle between China, Japan, and Russia over Korea is supplemented by an evaluation of the place and influence of Christian missions. Christianity is seen as one of the most potent of the enlightening and reconstructive forces operating in the Far East.

04-188. BROWN, George Thompson. "A History of the Korean Mission Presbyterian Church United States, 1892–1962." Thesis, Union Theological Seminary, 1963. 762 pp.

04-189. _____. *Mission to Korea.* Nashville: Board of World Missions, Presbyterian Church US, 1962.

04-190. CHO, Timothy Hyo-Hoon. "A History of the Korea Baptist Convention: 1889–1969." PhD dissertation, Southern Baptist Theological Seminary, 1970. 290 pp. Abstracted in *DAI* 31(12)(June 1971):6698-A; UM 71-12,426.

04-191. CHUN, Sung-chun. "Schism and Unity in the Protestant Churches of Korea." Dissertation, Yale University, 1955. 214 pp. Historical study of the unifying factors and the various schisms.

04-192. CLARK, Charles Allen. *Digest of the Presbyterian Church of Chosen.* Seoul: Presbyterian Publication Fund, Christian Literature Society, 1934.

04-193. COOPER, S. Kate. *Evangelism in Korea.* Nashville: Board of Missions, Methodist Episcopal Church South, 1930.

04-194. CORFE, C. J. *The Anglican Church in Korea*. London: Rivingtons, 1906. 139 pp.

04-195. CUMMINGS, Malcolm Stanley. *A Manual of Personal Evangelism for Korean Communities*. Greenville, S.C.: Bob Jones, 1967. 241 pp. Contents: Personal Evangelism; Its Scriptural Basis; Requirements for Success; Its Basic Method; The Approach; Opportunities; Suggestions for Tract Distribution; Dealing with the Unconcerned and Procrastinators; Dealing with Those Who Offer Sincere Excuses; Dealing with Those Who Believe in Heathen Religions; Dealing with Those Who Believe in False Cults; Summary, Conclusion, and Recommendations.

04-196. HAN, Sun Nam. "History of Methodism in Korea, 1931–1965." PhD dissertation, Temple University, 1970. 309 pp. Abstracted in *DAI* 31(12)(June 1971):6701-A; UM 71-10,573.

04-197. HOOPER, James Leon. *Mission Study*. Extracts from the material of the Board of Foreign Missions of the Presbyterian Church in the USA. New York: 1949.

04-198. HWANG, Sŏng-Mo. "Protestantism and Korea." *Korea Journal* 7(2)(February 1967):4–10.

04-199. JONES, George Heber and Arthur NOBEL. *The Korean Revival*. New York: Board of Foreign Missions of the Methodist Episcopal Church, 1910.

04-200. *Jubilee Papers*. Fiftieth Anniversary Celebration of the Korea Mission of the Presbyterian Church in the USA. Seoul: 1934.

04-201. KIM, Changyup Daniel. "Seventy-eight Years of the Protestant Church in Korea." PhD dissertation, Dallas Theological Seminary, 1963. 330 pp.

04-202. *Korea Handbook of Missions*. Federal Council of Korea and the Interchurch World Movement of North America, 1920.

04-203. *Korea Mission Field*. Seoul: Evangelical Missions of Korea, 1905–1941.

04-204. Korea Mission of the Presbyterian Church, USA. *Presentation of Difficulties Which Have Arisen*. A petition, statement, and correspondence by the missionaries and Board of Foreign Missions of the Presbyterian Church USA. Printed for private use, 1918.

04-205. Korea Mission of the Presbyterian Church, USA. *Quarto Centennial Papers Read before Annual Meeting*. Pyongyang: 1909.

04-206. *Korea*. Philadelphia: Women's Foreign Missionary Society of the Presbyterian Church USA, 1897.

04-207. *Letters of the Presbyterian Church in the USA Korea Missionaries Written to the Board of Foreign Missions Staff*. Microfilm. New York: United Presbyterian Library, 1884–1911.

04-208. LIEROP, Peter Van. "The Development of Schools under the Korea Mission of the Presbyterian Church in the USA, 1919–1950." PhD dissertation, University of Pittsburgh, 1955. 276 pp. Abstracted in *DA* 16(January 1956):170; UM 15,109.

04-209. NEVIUS, John L. *Planting and Development of Missionary Churches*. From articles printed in 1885. Philadelphia: Presbyterian and Reformed, 1958.

04-210. NISBET, Anabel Major. *Day In and Day Out in Korea*. Richmond: Presbyterian Committee on Publication, 1919.

04-211. PAIK, L. George. *The History of Protestant Missions in Korea (1832–1910)*. Pyongyang: Union Christian College Press, 1929. The definitive history of Protestant missions in Korea by a Korean scholar trained in Western historical methods. Paik uses a few Oriental sources, but his bibliography in Western languages is exhaustive. The introduction furnishes a succinct and useful account of Korea and its religions.

04-212. PALMER, Spencer J. "Protestant Christianity in China and Korea: The Problem of Identification with Tradition." PhD dissertation, University of California, Berkeley, 1964. 199 pp. Abstracted in *DA* 25(January 1965):4111-12; UM 64-13,073.

04-213. PARK, Pong Nang. "Karl Barth's Doctrine of Inspiration on the Holy Scriptures with Special Reference to the Evangelical Churches in Korea." PhD dissertation, Harvard University, 1959. 319 pp.

04-214. RHODES, Harry A. *History of the Korea Mission, Presbyterian Church USA: 1884–1934*. Vol. 1. Seoul: Chosen Mission of the Presbyterian Church USA, 1934.

04-215. ⸺. *History of the Korea Mission, Presbyterian Church USA*. Vol. 2: 1935–1950. Vol. 3: 1950–1954. New York: United Presbyterian Library, 1954. Mimeographed.

04-216. RO, Bong Rin. "Division and Reunion in the Presbyterian Church in Korea, 1959–1968." PhD dissertation, St. Louis Seminary, 1968.

04-217. RYANG, J. S. *Southern Methodism in Korea: Thirtieth Anniversary*. Seoul: Board of Missions of Methodist Episcopal Church South, 1927.

04-218. SAUER, Charles A. *Within the Gate*. Seoul: Korea Methodist News Service, 1934.

04-219. STOKES, Charles Davis. "History of Methodist Missions in Korea, 1885-1930." PhD dissertation, Yale University, 1947. 421 pp. Abstracted in *DA* 25(December 1964):3721; UM 64-11,999.

04-220. WHELAN, J. B. "The Anglican Church in Korea." *International Review of Missions* 49(1960):157–166.

CHAPTER 5
Language and Linguistics

Chin-W. Kim

with contribution by
Seok Choong Song

INTRODUCTION

THE KOREAN LANGUAGE

THE KOREAN LANGUAGE is spoken primarily by people living in the Korean peninsula. The population of North Korea is approximately 15 million and that of South Korea 34 million. Outside Korea proper, there are sizable numbers of residents who speak Korean: in China including Manchuria (1.5 million), in Japan (600,000), in the United States (400,000), and in the Soviet Union (400,000).

Korean is generally regarded to belong to the Altaic language family, which includes Turkic, Mongolian, and Tungusic as major branches. Although the similarities between Korean and these languages are not so striking as to quiet all skeptics, Korean nonetheless displays many Altaic features.

Before turning to the salient features of Modern Korean, I wish to touch upon the history of the Korean language. Scholars differ in their demarcation of Korean into periods. (See 05-066 for a proposal available in English.) Here I will follow the scheme advanced by Ki-Moon Lee:

Old Korean: prehistory to tenth century
Middle Korean: eleventh century to sixteenth century
Modern Korean: seventeenth century to present

Lee's demarcation is based on the changing features of the language itself, not on historical events external to it. Yet the invention of *han'gŭl* (the Korean script) by King Sejong in the fifteenth century must be regarded as the greatest achievement and the single most important event in the history of the Korean language. Up to that point, the Chinese characters were borrowed in an attempt to record Korean (the so-called *idu*). Since Korean and Chinese belong to two different language families and are quite different both syntactically and phonologically, the *idu* system must have been awkward at best. The scanty extant material is frequently subject therefore to ambiguous interpretation.

The earliest period for which there are materials available in relative abundance is the latter half of the fifteenth century. Korean-language materials before the introduction of the script are meager, and even such prominent features of Middle Korean (MK) as vowel harmony and tones cannot be traced to Old Korean (OK) with continuity and confidence.

From the barren land of Old Korean, one suddenly comes upon an oasis in the fifteenth century. Textual sources of Middle Korean are redeemingly abundant. A brief exploration reveals certain characteristics of Middle Korean. There is, for example, the consonant system:

p	*t*	*k*	*ch*	*s*	*h*
p'	*t'*	*k'*	*ch'*		
pp	*tt*	*kk*		*ss*	*hh*
β				*z*	*ĥ*
m	*n*	*ŋ*			
	l				

Note that Middle Korean developed tense obstruents (including *hh* = *[x]*?, but not *cc*). Note also that Middle Korean had voiced fricatives: *β, z,* and *ɦ*. Restricted distribution and light functional load were responsible for the gradual disuse and final disappearance of some of these consonants: *β, z, ɦ, hh.*

The vowel system underwent the following changes:

Old Korean			Middle Korean			Modern Korean			
i	*u*	*o*	*i*	*ŭ*	*u*	*i*	*ü*	*ŭ*	*u*
ə	*ɔ*		*ŏ*	*o*		*e*	*ö*	*ŏ*	*o*
ʌ	*a*		*a*	*ɒ*		*æ*	*a*		

(with arrows: Old Korean → Middle Korean → Modern Korean)

With subsequent monophthongization of many diphthongs at the end of the eighteenth century, Modern Korean has now a maximum of ten vowels. But simplification occurred in the loss of "low" *a* (*ɒ*) and in the loss of vowel harmony in the eighteenth century. The loss of "low" *a* is generally credited as responsible for the destruction of symmetry in the vowel system on which a smooth operation of vowel harmony depended.

As for suprasegmentals, it is known that Middle Korean had tones. The exact number of tones (tonemes), whether they were true tones or pitch accents, their correlation with vowel length, and the cause of their sudden disappearance have been the subject of much discussion among Korean scholars. (For a recent treatise in English by a Westerner, see Rosén 1974; 05-254.)

I now wish to survey some characteristic features of Modern Korean regarding phonology, lexicon, syntax, and semantics. In the sound pattern, Korean is characterized by the three series of obstruent consonants (tense, lax, and aspirated), which is unusual in the sense that all of them are voiceless. This characteristic has been a major source of difficulty for foreigners trying to learn Korean as well as for scholars trying to analyze the exact phonetic nature of these obstruent consonants.

In the lexicon, one is immediately struck by the great proportion of Chinese loanwords in the Korean vocabulary. In *K'ŭn sajŏn* [Great dictionary] edited by Han'gŭl Hakhoe (Korean Language Society), 54 percent of its entries are of Chinese origin. This situation is by no means unique to Korean. About half the English lexicon is said to be of Romance origin; most of these words entered English during the three centuries following the Norman conquest. But there is a great difference between the two cases. In the case of English and French, both belong to the same language family, and the marriage of the two met with little difficulty and produced no mutation. In the case of Korean and Chinese, however, the matrimony involved two languages belonging to two entirely different stocks. This union created a situation of two strange bedfellows, and to this day consummation has not been achieved.

A dual system of Korean and Sino-Korean words pervades almost the entire structure of Korean, from the two sets of numerals and common words to noun phrase construction. Consider, for example, the following doublets:

Korean	Sino-Korean	
mok-sŭm	*saeng-myŏng*	life
mul-kyŏl	*p'a-do*	waves
saram	*in-gan*	man

Rules that govern the proper usage of these and other parallel words are too complex to mention. Sometimes there is complete interchangeability—for example, Korean *ŏrini* and Sino-Korean *adong* (child)—but sometimes one member of the doublet is designated as the honorific and no interchange is allowed. With Korean *nŭlgŭni* and Sino-Korean *noin* (an old man), for example, the latter is honorific, so that honorification of the former is normally unacceptable (that is, **nŭlgŭni-kkesŏ* [*kkesŏ* = honorific subject marker]). In telling time, the hour is told with Korean numbers but the minute with Sino-Korean numbers—for example, *tu-si osip-pun* (2:50).

Recently there has been much debate about the *han-tcha p'yeji* (disuse of Chinese characters) movement. In discussing this matter, it must be understood from the outset that neither Chinese characters nor Chinese loanwords are the Chinese language. A strange bedfellow he may be, but he has now become part of the family. Both pronunciation and usage have long been Koreanized. Thus cries of unpatriotism or toadyism by purists are groundless. On the other hand, opponents of *han'gŭl chŏnyong* (exclusive use of the Korean alphabet) misunderstand much of the proponents' intentions. To begin with, the proponents have never argued that all Chinese loanwords must be replaced by the equivalent of pure Korean words. Examples like Korean *pŏngae-ttalttari* (electric rattler; for Sino-Korean *chŏnhwa*, telephone) and Korean *olm-sari* (for Sino-Korean *tongmul*, animal) were not made by the proponents of *han'gŭl* but were concocted by opponents as preposterous examples in analogy with some less wild suggestions made by the proponents—for example, *nal-t'ŭl* (for Sino-Korean *pihaenggi*, airplane) and *ne-mokkol* (for Sino-Korean *sa kak-hyŏng*, a rectangle). And the proponents' suggestions must be understood in the proper historical perspective. It was the *han'gŭl* scholars who suffered jailing and torture during the Japanese occupation because of their determined movement against the colonial policy to abolish Korean (see Song 1975; 05-036). It is understandable, then, that when the end of the war came, these *han'gŭl* scholars wanted to restore the status of the Korean language and actually did so with some success. Many Japanese loanwords were replaced by equivalent Korean words—for example, *tŏp-pap* (for *domburi*, omelet) and *sae-ch'igi* (for *yokodori*, cutting in).

In syntax, Korean is characterized by an extremely richly developed set of derivative and conjugational affixes. These affixes agglutinate one after another. They indicate different styles of speech, express every conceivable mood and aspect, and function as honorific markers, case markers, connectives, postpositions, and sentence-type markers. In the following phrases, several sentential connectives combine with the verb *ha-* (to do): *ha-go* (do and); *ha-myŏ* (while doing); *ha-ni* (as (I) do); *ha-myŏn* (if I do); *ha-ja* (as soon as I do); *ha-nikka* (as I finished doing); *ha-doe* (though I do).

A liberal use of such affixes (connectives) naturally makes sentences quite lengthy, while honorific and sentence-type markers make possible an unusual number of elliptical sentences in Korean. For instance, nouns (subject as well as object nouns) are frequently deleted in Korean even in nonimperative sentences. Yet there is almost no difficulty in determining the subject or object of the sentence. Given a particular set of honorific markers, a sentence-type marker, and so forth, the subject and object of the sentence can be easily determined by computing, on the basis of affixes, the relationship they hold with respect to the speaker and the hearer.

A semantic characteristic of Korean is the ability to express minute nuances with a richly developed system of phonetic symbolism. Observe for instance the following expressions, all describing the flow of water: *chol-jol, chul-jul, chŏl-jŏl, chwal-jwal, cil-jil, cal-jal; churuk-churuk, ch'ullŏng-ch'ullŏng, chilgŭm-jilgŭm, ch'alssak-ch'alssak; ppŏl-ppŏl, ttok-ttok, ttuk-ttuk.* These expressions describe different motions of water—from the drizzling of a cat to the pouring of rain, from the murmur of a gentle brook to the breaking of ocean waves, from the dripping of sweat to a gushing flood.

The net effect of all these features—a complex phonetic system, a dual lexicon, an intricate honorific system, different styles of speech, an indefinite concatenation of clauses, a rich set of tense, mood, and aspect—is to make Korean a difficult language to learn, at least as a second language. In fact, the complexity is such that it will inevitably generate its opposite—already there are signs of a tendency toward simplification. In phonology, for example, we see a leveling of final consonants. More increasingly, we hear: *tag-i, tag-ŭl* (chicken) instead of *talgi, talgŭl; puŏg-i, puŏg-e* (kitchen) instead of *puŏk'i, puŏk'e;* and so forth. All dental and palatal obstruents tend to be neutralized to *s* before an affixal vowel—for example, *kkoch'i→kkosi* (flower), *pat'e→pase* (field), and so forth. In syntax also, the trend is toward simplification. A complex agglutination of affixes to denote many different styles and levels of speech will be gradually simplified. Indefinite concatenation of sentences is rapidly going out of style, perhaps due to the influence of heavy punctuation and laconism in sentences of Western languages.

Along with simplification of the language, some sort of stabilization or unification should occur. With the tremendous mobility and the mass media of communication in modern society, the dialectical differences will gradually disappear and a uniform and standard language will emerge.

ORIGINS OF THE KOREAN LANGUAGE

How did the Korean language come to be spoken in the Korean peninsula? When did the first speakers of Korean come to the peninsula? Were there already inhabitants there? If so, what language did these people speak? And if there was an aboriginal language, what role did it play in the making of the Korean language? These are fascinating questions, but we do not have sufficient data about the ancient past to permit a reasonable reconstruction.

What seems to be quite certain is that there was no homogeneous people of which Koreans are direct descendants. Nor was there a homogeneous language on the Korean peninsula from time immemorial. But the problem of whence Koreans came is as many-sided as a quadrangle: some theorize that they came from the north; others propose the south; others suggest the east; still others argue for the west. It should be mentioned here that there is a scale in the degree of plausibility—it is, in decreasing order, north, south, west, and east.

The East theory proposes that the Korean people and language originated from the east: namely, Japan and its neighboring islands. Holders of this view attempt to relate Korean to Japanese (or Ainu) by claiming that Old Korean was the peninsular dialect of Old Japanese. That is, they regard Korean as an early variety of Japanese found on the Korean peninsula. This view is largely colonialistic and merits little further mention. If anything, Old Japanese was the insular dialect of Korean.

Actually, there is some indication that the language of Koguryŏ, the nation that occupied southern Manchuria and the northern half of the Korean peninsula from the first century BC to the seventh century AD, and Old Japanese were more closely related to each other than has been hitherto thought. Ki-Moon Lee has recently uncovered a significant number of lexical correspondences. For example:

Koguryŏ	Old Japanese	
osagum	*wusagi*	rabbit
mit	*mil*	three
utsu	*itu*	five
nanin	*nana*	seven
poksa	*fuka*	deep

Murals and other art objects found in royal tombs near Kyoto have also been linked to those of Koguryŏ. The full significance of these findings must await further definitive studies.

The West theory has two unrelated versions. One is held primarily by German scholars (Eckardt, Koppelmann; 05-238, 261) who attempt to relate Korean to Indo-European. Eckardt, for example, gives archaeological and ethnic as well as linguistic correlations between the two. Among some 150 lexical correspondences he offers are:

Korean	Indo-European
iss (be)	Gk. *esti;* L. *est, esse;* G. *ist*
kiph (deep)	Skt. *kup* (to sing); G. *tief* (deep)
korŭ (choose)	G. *küren* (choose)
kul (cave, hole)	Skt. *guh* (hide); Gk. *koilos* (hollow); Toch. *kukul* (hole)
nŭngari (snake)	Lith. *unguris* (eel); L. *anguilla* (eel)
pulŭ (full)	L. *plenus* (full); G. *voll* (full)

These examples, though ingenious and impressive, are nonetheless mere coincidences that have no bearing whatsoever on the genesis of language.

The other version of the West theory was proposed by Homer B. Hulbert, who attempted to argue that Korean is related to the Dravidian languages of India by observing that Korean and Dravidian share quite remarkable syntactic similarities—for example, both have the word order Subject-Object-Verb (while it is typically S-V-O in Indo-European languages); both have postpositions instead of prepositions; both have neither relative pronouns nor an explicit gender system; both have modifier clauses always in front of the modified; both have two forms of *be,* one copulative, the other existential. Today these correspondences would be called typological similarities, and it is an accepted view that two or more totally unrelated languages may nevertheless share typological similarities. Three quarters of a century ago, however, linguistics was still in its infancy. One can imagine how striking and suggestive the typological similarities between Korean and Dravidian must have looked to Hulbert, especially when Indo-European languages, about the only well-established language family then, shared a different typology.

There is still a grain of possibility that Hulbert was conceivably right. Speakers of Dravidian languages in use today in the southern part of the Indian subcontinent and Sri Lanka (Ceylon) migrated to the present areas when pushed by the invading Aryans who now occupy northern India. The Dravidian homeland was probably farther to the north, near Central Asia, the supposed *Urheimat* of Altaic languages. Since the increasingly popular North theory, to be discussed below, claims that Korean is an Altaic language, it is theoretically conceivable that Korean and Dravidian were once neighbors. However, one can hardly hope to see a family tree germinating out of this grain.

It is therefore safe to state that both the East and the West theories are now of only passing historical interest, and that their defense on both flanks lost ground to assaults from the front and rear.

The ancient road leading to Northeast Asia from the south has been largely explored by a Japanese scholar named Susumu Ohno, who holds the view that the Malayo-Polynesian people whose homes stretch from Madagascar to Hawaii, came to Japan and settled there, laying the foundation of the Japanese language. It must be pointed out from the outset that (1) Korean is relevant to Ohno's theory only to the extent that Korean and Japanese are closely related, and (2) Ohno himself does not deny the Northern Altaic elements in Japanese and Korean. He claims only that, at least for Japanese, the migration of the northern Altaic people to Japan was small in number, and therefore that, although they became the upper echelon in the Japanese society after their arrival, the Altaic elements did not influence the native language greatly, but were quickly absorbed by it.

There are both linguistic and anthro-archaeological findings that suggest that more than a passing glance at the South theory is warranted. Rice cultivation, tatooing, a matrilineal system of family, myths about royal births, and other recent discoveries in paleolithic or pre-ceramic cultures indicate the existence of shared life among Koreans, Japanese, and their southern neighbors. Linguistically, a good number of names of various parts of the human body show a semisystematic correspondence which is not found elsewhere. For example:

Japanese	Korean	
para	*pae*	belly
cici (titi)	*chyŏch*	breast
kuti	*aguri*	mouth
kösi	*hŏri*	waist

Ohno cites one item, *puka* 'lungs', as having cognates in such diverse languages as Korean *puxua (puhwa), puka* in Maori of New Zealand, *bagga* in Mentawai of Suma-tra, *poka* in New Guinea, *baga* in the Visayan of the Philippines, and so forth.

Names of the body parts form a subset of core vocabulary, and as such, they are thought to be resistant to substitution from borrowing. If this is the case, how is one to explain the similarity of body-part names among these languages? Furthermore, on a less tangible side, there are other features in Korean and Japanese that are shared by none of the other Altaic languages, but are shared to some extent by some Polynesian languages. These include a phonological structure of open syllables, the honorific system, tones, and the semantics of numerals. Old Korean, like modern Japanese and Polynesian languages but unlike many Altaic languages, was open-syllabic. The honorific system, so unique in Japanese and Korean among Altaic languages, is reported to exist also in Ponapean, Thai, and Javanese. It is believed that *tas-* or *tasŏs* 'five' in Korean originated from a verb stem *tat-* 'to close', and that *yŏl* 'ten' was derived from the verb stem *yŏl-* 'to open'. If one imagines counting from one to ten using one hand, it is easily seen why closing of the fist means a count of five and opening the fist, ten. Again, this kind of numerical semantics is not found in Altaic languages. It is also significant to note that a sizable number of lexical items have no cognates in other Altaic languages than Japanese and Korean. For example:

Japanese	Korean	
sima	*syŏm*	island
pata	*pat'*	field
wata	*pata*	ocean
mu	*mom*	body
nata	*nat*	sickle
yörö 'ten thousand'	*yŏrŏ*	many

In discussing the early history of man in Northeast Asia, one must keep in mind that during the glacial age there was a land bridge in the Yellow Sea connecting the Korean peninsula to that of Shantung. Likewise, the Korean Strait and the Taiwan Strait linked the islands to the continent by land. Even without these land bridges, the Philippine Islands, Taiwan, and the Ryukyu Islands form stepping stones for the northward passage, and it is easily conceivable that they served as a migrational channel for early men. (There is a parallel channel to the east formed by a chain of islands—the Palaus, Marianas, and Bonins.) It is not surprising, then, that one finds southern elements in Korean. The problem is that the amount is so scanty that it is overshadowed by the somewhat overwhelming presence of northern elements.

The North theory is generally known as the Altaic theory. It stipulates that Korean belongs to a language family called Altaic, which has three major branches—Turkic, Mongolian, and Tungusic—and whose domain encompasses the entire breadth of the Asian continent from the Black Sea to the Pacific.

For much of the linguistic evidence relating Korean to the Altaic family we are indebted to the Finnish linguist and diplomat Gustaf J. Ramstedt (1873–1950). He was a scholar with boundless energy whose field trips took him as far south as Afghanistan and as far east as Lake Baikal in Siberia. In 1919, at the end of World War I, he was appointed by the Finnish government as consul to Japan and China, and lived in Tokyo for eleven years. It was during this period that he came in contact with some Koreans living in Japan. From them he learned enough Korean to make a major contribution to both Korean and Altaic linguistics. There were a few minor stars in the field, to be sure (e.g. E. D. Polivanov, 05-242), but it was chiefly Ramstedt (see 05-104, 243) who took Korean out of a linguistic orphanage and put it into the Altaic family.

A few examples of lexical correspondences will show rather unmistakably a genetic affinity among them (Ma., Manchu; Mo., Mongolian; MMo., Middle Mongolian; Mgu., Monguor):

K. *pom* 'spring', Ma. *fon* 'season', Mo. *on* 'year', MMo. *hon* 'year', Mgu. *fän* 'spring'

K. *pul* 'to blow', Ma. *fulgije,* Lamut *hu-,* Mo. *ulije-,* MMo. *hulie-* 'to blow'

K. *pil* 'to pray', Ma. *firu* 'to pray', Evenki *hiruge-* 'to pray', Mo. *iruüge* 'prayer', MMo. *hirüer-* 'to pray'

K. *pus* 'to pour', Ma. *fusu-* 'to sprinkle', Ulcha *pisuri-,* Mo. *ösür-,* Mgu. *fudzuru-,* Goldi *pis-* 'to pour'

These examples illustrate one of the most revealing and systematic phonological correspondences in various Altaic languages for proto-Altaic initial *p*. The correspondences with Korean *P* are:

Tungusic: P (Goldi, Ulcha); *f* (Manchu); *x* (Udehe); *h* (Lamut, Evenki); *Ø* (Salon)
Mongolian: *h* (Middle Mongolian); *f* (Monguor); *x* (Dagur); *Ø* (elsewhere)
Turkic: *h* (Southwest and Eastwest dialects); *Ø* (Old Turkish and elsewhere)

Today the Altaic theory of Korean is generally, if often uncritically, accepted. Its proponents include Nicholas Poppe, Samuel Martin (05-264, 265), Sung-nyŏng Lee, Roy A. Miller (05-266, 267), and Ki-Moon Lee (05-241). Needless to say, there are still a few skeptics. Among them are Denis Sinor, G. Clauson, and Bo-gyŏm Kim (05-240).

One must bear in mind, however, that even with generous application of imagination, the number of lexical items having a systematic sound-meaning correspondence does not exceed two hundred. Granted that the influx of Chinese loanwords drove much of the native vocabulary into oblivion, granted that separation of Korean from its ancestral language happened such a long time ago that much of its true form has now been obscured, yet two hundred is still too small a number to constitute fibers of a firm genetic band. To be sure, there are features other than lexical correspondence that are said to show the common properties in Korean and other Altaic languages. But in general these are more or less negative properties—that is, features that are commonly absent. Thus, compared to Indo-European languages, all Altaic languages are noticeably void of grammatical number, gender, articles, overt copula, inflexion, voice, relative pronouns, and conjunctives. There are a few positive features, such as vowel harmony and the process of agglutination, that are commonly present in most Altaic languages. But, unfortunately, these are mostly typological features. That is, vowel harmony and the process of agglutination are found among non-Altaic languages as well.

The most reasonable position is that Korean is a language created from the grafting of two different stocks. Situated at the periphery of the Asian continent, both Korea and Japan were the ends of the road of migration. The two migratory paths, one northerly and the other southerly, must have collided in the Korean peninsula and the Japanese islands. That a language born of this collision possesses the genes of both sides is by no means an unnatural view. Of course, the degree of influence of either side could be different. Personally, I believe that in Japan the Altaic element played the role of superstratum, while in Korea the southern influence was much weaker than the northern and became only a substratum to the language of northerners.

A small but interesting piece of information that has a bearing on this issue is recorded in *Chou shu* (AD 636). There it is written that "in Paekche the ruling class call their king *ŏraha,* while the common people call him *kŏngilchi.*" Fragmentary as the information may be, it shows symbolically the difference that must have existed between the northern language and the southern language during the pre–Three Kingdom period in Korea, for we know that the ruling class of Paekche came from Puyŏ, a northern nation, while people of Paekche were of the Mahan tribe of Three Han nations in southern Korea and in all probability spoke its vernacular, a southern tongue. We also know that the Saro tribe near Kyŏngju, who also spoke a Han language, annexed the neighboring Kaya nation in the sixth century and then unified the peninsula in the following century. This is the nation of Silla. The Silla language gradually spread the entire length of the peninsula, and Modern Korean is a direct descendant of this Unified Silla tongue. What was it like? What was its ethnic and linguistic relation to the northern tribes of Puyŏ and Koguryŏ? What was their exact relationship to Old Japanese? Today, these questions remain among the most important ones in the history of the Korean language and people.

KOREAN LINGUISTICS IN THE WEST

Much linguistic research, especially studies of the so-called Middle Korean period, has of course been done by native scholars, who by and large have concentrated their efforts on identifying Middle Korean and tracing its subsequent development into Modern Korean. For a review of Korean linguistics in South Korea, see Ki-Moon Lee (05-029, 031) and Lukoff (05-033); for North Korea, see Chin-W. Kim (05-026). Japanese scholars have also made a significant contribution, notably Ogura and Koono. But most of their works are in Japanese, and no single review of the Japanese contribution is available in English.

Studies on the Korean language by Westerners were begun around the turn of the century by American and French missionaries in Korea. They were mostly concerned with two problems: romanizing the Korean script and learning and teaching Korean as a foreign language. Most of their contributions appeared as short articles in *Korean Repository* and *The Korea Review,* both published in Seoul. Their works, however, were primarily pedagogical despite the publication of several grammar books along with manuals, dictionaries, and phrase books, and they now have only a historical interest. The amateurism of their studies is reflected in the fact that one ventured to suggest that Korean and English were genetically related!

It was the Finnish scholar G. J. Ramstedt who, with his meticulous studies on Korean etymology (05-104) and by comparing Korean with various Altaic languages, firmly laid the foundation stone of Korean as an Altaic language. One may argue with N. Poppe's statement that Ramstedt's *Korean Grammar* (05-156) has been unsurpassed; one may also contend that Ramstedt's evidence of Korean-Altaic affinity would not be admissible in an "Indo-European" court; but his monument stands tall and alone in the entire continent of Eurasia.

It must be mentioned here, however, that a Russian linguist, E. D. Polivanov, observed as early as 1916 the existence of vowel harmony in Korean and subsequently suggested the affinity of Korean to the Altaic language family (Polivanov 1927; 05-242). It is noteworthy that this suggestion precedes Ramstedt. (Ramstedt was apparently not aware of Polivanov's works.)

Because a part of the northern frontier of Korea abuts upon Siberia, and because the Soviet Union has been traditionally interested in Altaic linguistics (certainly more than the United States has been), there is a sizable body of studies on Korean by Russian scholars (see Kontsevich 1967; 05-028). The most recurring names are those of Kontsevich, Mazur, Nikolski, and Kholodovich; their works, however, appear exclusively in Russian.

In Prague, Alena Skaličková has made some experimental studies in Korean phonetics (05-058, 061). In Germany, P. A. Eckardt, H. F. T. Junker, and Bruno Lewin have been very active in Korean-language studies

—Eckardt in grammar and genealogy, Junker in phonology, Lewin in morphology. Recently, contributions in Korean linguistics have also been coming from Sweden (05-066, 254) and from Italy (Istituto Universitario Orientale, Naples). These European works have remained relatively unknown to outsiders because of the languages in which they were written. The situation should be corrected by way of reviews and English synopses.

In the latter half of this century, the United States has been the major scene of Korean linguistic research in the West. At the University of Washington, great names like Nicholas Poppe, Roy A. Miller, and Fred Lukoff have provided a backbone in comparative-historical Korean linguistics.

On the East Coast at Yale University, Samuel E. Martin has made his works—in Korean phonology (05-093, 094); in historical-comparative Korean (05-264); and a Korean-English dictionary (05-322)—a testimony of his scholarship. He is now engaged in a monumental work called *Korean Reference Grammar,* which, I am certain, will supersede Ramstedt's *Grammar.* We owe much to Professor Martin. Without him, the field of Korean linguistics would be bleak indeed.

At the moment, Korean programs exist in one form or another in the following universities: California at Berkeley, Columbia, Harvard, Hawaii, Illinois, Washington (Seattle), Western Michigan (Kalamazoo), Yale; and at the US Foreign Service in Washington and the US Army Language School in Monterey, California. The University of Hawaii has the largest student enrollment in Korean, and the recent establishment of the Center for Korean Studies on its campus should provide moral support to students and scholars of the Korean language not only in Hawaii but throughout the United States.

In 1967, three doctoral dissertations on Korean syntax were written by young Korean scholars at three major American universities: Seok Choong Song (05-215, Indiana), Soon-Ham Park Kim (05-173, Michigan), and Maeng Sung Lee (05-191, Pennsylvania). The demarcation in the following bibliography of grammars into pre-1967 and post-1967 is due as much to this epochal event as to the fact that they were the first significant studies done by anyone on Korean syntax within the framework of the "generative-transformational" theory of language. Since 1967, steady and solid progress has been made in the scholarship of Korean linguistics. Nearly two dozen doctoral dissertations both in phonology and syntax have appeared, some subsequently making their way to publication, and more and more articles on Korean linguistics both by native and by foreign scholars are appearing in international journals.

Scholarly meetings have been no less evident. There have been four panels in Korean linguistics in the annual meetings of the Association for Asian Studies (1969 in Boston, 1973 in Chicago, 1975 in San Francisco, 1977 in New York), and ASPAC (Asian Studies in Pacific Coasts) has a Korean language/linguistics section in its annual conferences. An international symposium on Korean linguistics was held in August 1977 at the University of Hawaii in conjunction with the Linguistic Institute of the Linguistic Society of America. The International Circle of Korean Linguistics was formed in 1975 to promote and coordinate Korean linguistic studies throughout the world. Indeed, Korean linguistics has put on new wings.

BIBLIOGRAPHY

In the following bibliography, unpublished papers have been excluded except for doctoral dissertations and papers definitely scheduled to appear soon in print. Book reviews are not listed separately but are given following the annotation of the books they review. Translations have been treated similarly. The classification scheme is my own, and the order of subfields has no inherent significance. Major sections are preceded by a brief note of overview.

No annotation should be regarded as a normative description, let alone prescription. Nor should the present bibliography be taken as exhaustive. I have summarily excluded all items that appeared before the turn of the century and some that were published during the first half of the century. In reviewing the works in Russian, I was greatly helped by Kanno Hiroomi's translation into Korean of L. R. Kontsevich, "Koreiskii yazyk [The Korean language]," in *Sovetskoe yazykoznaniye za 50 let* [50 years of Soviet linguistics], Moscow, 1967, pp.

298–311. The translation with Kanno's excellent and detailed footnotes following the text appears in *Asea yŏn'gu* [Asiatic research bulletin], 14(2)(1971):187–216.

A special acknowledgment is due to Professor Seok C. Song of Michigan State University for writing annotations to the works in syntax and semantics, especially the contemporary ones.

BIBLIOGRAPHIES AND ANTHOLOGIES

A quite extensive, classified, and fairly up-to-date bibliography in Korean language and linguistics is found in Rosén (05-007). In Ogura (05-004) the bibliography compiled by Kōno Rokurō includes works written in non-Western languages.

Two anthologies are of particular interest: *Koreiskii yazyk* [The Korean language] (Moscow: 1961) and A. A. Kholodovich (ed.), *Voprosy koreiskogo i kitaiskogo yazykoznaniya* [Studies in Korean and Chinese linguistics] (Moscow: 1958). They embody Korean linguistic studies in Soviet Russia during the 1950s.

A collection of papers presented at the Korean linguistics panel in the annual meeting of the Association for Asian Studies in 1973 in Chicago appeared, together with comments made by official panel members, in *Language Research (Ŏhak yŏn'gu),* (1973). Those presented at the 1975 AAS meeting in San Francisco appeared in *Language Research* 11(1)(1975). Proceedings of the 1975 meeting of Asian Studies on Pacific Coasts in Honolulu appeared as a monograph from the Center for Korean Studies at the University of Hawaii (05-012). These publications represent the current state of Korean linguistics in North America, especially in the United States.

Bibliographies

05-001. *Bibliography of Korean Studies.* Seoul: Asea Munje Yŏn'guso (Asiatic Research Center), Korea University, 1961. A bibliographic guide to Korean publications on Korean studies appearing from 1954 to 1958. Korean language and linguistics are discussed on pp. 155–229.

05-002. California, University of. Institute of East Asiatic Studies. *Korean Studies Guide.* Edited by Richard Marcus; compiled by B. H. Hazard, Jr., J. Hoyt, H. T. Kim, and W. W. Smith. Berkeley and Los Angeles: University of California Press, 1954. 220 pp. See reviews by Seung-bog Cho in *Ural-Altaische Jahrbücher* 26(1954):247–250; by D. L. Olmsted in *Far Eastern Quarterly* 14(1954/1955):127–128; by W. E. Skillend in *Bulletin of School of Oriental and African Studies* 17(1955):405–406; by F. Vos in *T'oung Pao* (Leiden), 43(1955):408–431; and by E. Wagner in *Far Eastern Quarterly* 14(1954/1955):225–260.

05-003. KONTSEVICH, L. R. "Bibliograficheskii ukazatel' rabot po koreiskomu yazykoznaniyu [Bibliographic material on Korean linguistics]." In *Voprosy grammatiki i istorii vostochynkh hazykov* [Grammar and historical studies of Oriental languages]. Moscow and Leningrad: Akademija Nauk, 1958.

05-004. OGURA, Shimpei. *Chosengogaku shi* [History of Korean linguistic studies]. Tokyo: Tōkō-shoin, 1964. There is an expanded and classified bibliography (in all languages) by Kōno Rokurō at the end.

05-005. PETROVA, O. P. "Sobranie koreiskikh pis'mennykh pamjatnikov Instituta Vostokovediniya AN SSSR [Korean collection of the Institute of Oriental Studies of the Soviet Academy of Sciences]." In *Uchenye zapiski.* Vol. 9. Moscow: Instituta Vostokovediniya, AN SSSR, 1954. See review by G. D. Paige, "The Korean Collection of the Division of Oriental Manuscripts, Institute of Oriental Studies, Academy of Sciences of the USSR," *Harvard Journal of Asiatic Studies* 19(1956):409–411.

05-006. _____. *Opisanie pis'mennykh pamyatnikov koreiskoi kul'tury* [Annotated material in Korean culture]. Vol. 1, Moscow and Leningrad, 1956; vol. 2, Moscow, 1963. For language, see vol. 2, chap. 11.

05-007. ROSÉN, Staffan (ed.). *A Bibliography of Korean Studies.* Stockholm: Institute of Oriental Languages, Stockholm University, [1970?]. Mimeographed. Bibliographic data of most works on Korea and Korean studies, excluding those on the Korean War, written in Western languages from about 1800 to 1969. For language and linguistics, see pp. 38–82.

Anthologies and Festschrifts

05-008. JUNKER, H. F. J. (ed.). *Koreanische Studien.* Abhandlungen der deutschen Akademie der Wissenschaften zu Berlin, no. 5. Berlin: 1955. 127 pp. See reviews by L. R. Koncevic in *Kratkie soobscenija Instituta Vostokovediniya* (Akademiya Nauk), 24(1958):110–117 and by W. E. Skillend in *Bulletin of School of Oriental and African Studies* 22(1959):195–196.

05-009. KHOLODOVICH, A. A. (ed.). *Voprosy koreiskogo i kitaiskogo yazykoznaniya* [Studies in Korean and Chinese linguistics]. Uchenye zapiski, LGU (Leningrad University research bulletin), no. 236, Serija vostokovednykh nauk (Oriental study series), part 6. Leningrad and Moscow: 1958.

05-010. *Koreiskii yazyk* [The Korean language]. Moscow: Akademiya Nauk, SSSR, Institut Naradov Azii (Institute of Asian Peoples, USSR Academy of Sciences), 1961. 237 pp. A summary of the state of Korean linguistics in Soviet Russia by 1960.

05-011. RIEKEL, A. (ed.). *Koreanica: Festschrift Dr. André Eckardt zum 75 Geburtstag*. Baden-Baden: 1960.

05-012. SOHN, Ho-min (ed.). *The Korean Language: Its Structure and Social Projection*. Honolulu: Center for Korean Studies, University of Hawaii, 1975. Contains nine papers presented at the Annual Conference of Asian Studies on Pacific Coasts held at the University of Hawaii, 19–21 June 1975. Topics range from comparative and historical to syntactic and semantic studies and include questions of romanization and nonverbal communication.

GENERAL STUDIES

As yet there is no adequate, up-to-date, and comprehensive description of the Korean language in English à la R. A. Miller's *The Japanese Language* (1967). Kim (05-022) may be the best popular introduction to the language. For a general survey of the current state of Korean linguistics, see Lee (05-031). For a sweeping review of linguistic activities in post-war South Korea, see Lukoff (05-033). For surveys of Korean linguistics in North Korea and in Soviet Russia, see Kim (05-026) and Kontsevich (05-028). Strangely, and unfortunately, there is no survey, except a brief account in Suh (05-037), of Korean linguistics in the United States despite the strong interest and activity there, particularly in recent years.

General Descriptions

05-013. HAGUENAUER, Charles. "Le coréen." In *Les Langues du Monde*. Rev. ed. Paris: Société linguistique de Paris, 1952.

05-014. HSIANG, P. S. "What Is the Korean Language?" *Modern Language Journal* 34(1950):441–443.

05-015. KIM, Hyong-kyu. "The Korean Language." *Korean Report* (Seoul), 2(4)(1962):21–24.

05-016. KIM, Yungyŏng. "Zum Aufbau der koreanischen Sprache." In *Koreanica: Festschrift Dr. André Eckardt zum 75 Geburtstag*. Baden-Baden: 1960.

05-017. RAMSTEDT, G. J. "Remarks on the Korean Language." *Mémoires de la Société Finno-Ougrienne* 58(1928):441–453. This short introduction to the language surveys vowels, consonants, and verbal conjugation. Although the survey is brief, insightful observations are made here and there. For example, via internal reconstruction Ramstedt speculates that there must have been a historical vowel shift since clusters like *ps*—as in the old spelling of *psu-* (to use) and *ptal* (daughter)—must have derived from a suppression of a short reduced vowel between the two consonants (compare Goldi *putula*, girl) and that a final consonant *g* must be posited for *namu* (tree) because of such forms as *namge* (dial.) and *namaksin* (wooden shoes).

05-018. SUH, Cheong-soo. "Some Characteristics of Korean Language." In Cheong-soo Suh and Chun-kun Pak (eds.), *Aspects of Korean Culture*. Seoul: Soodo Women's Teachers College Press, 1974.

05-019. VOS, Frits. "Korean Language and Culture." In J. K. Yamagiwa and P. V. Hyer (eds.), *Papers of the CIC Far Eastern Language Institute*. Ann Arbor: University of Michigan, 1963.

History of the Korean Language

05-020. HUH, Woong. "Development of Korean Language." *Korea Journal* 3(7)(1963):4–7.

05-021. KASSA, T. "A Brief Historical Review of the Korean Language." *Korea Review* (Washington), 1(1948):53–58.

05-022. KIM, Chin-W. "The Making of the Korean Language." *University of Hawaii Working Papers in Linguistics* 6(2)(1974):69–92. Also in *Korea Journal* 14(8)(1974): 4–17. Kim reviews several hypotheses of the origin of Korean and surveys salient features of Modern Korean.

05-023. LEE, Ki-Moon. "Formation of the Korean Language." *Korea Journal* 11(12)(1971):4–9.

05-024. VOS, Frits. "History of the Korean Language." In J. K. Yamagiwa and P. V. Hyer (eds.), *Papers of the CIC Far Eastern Language Institute*. Ann Arbor: University of Michigan, 1963.

History of Korean Linguistics

05-025. CHOI, Den Khu [Ch'oe Chŏn(g)-hu]. "Iz istorii yazykoznaniya v koree [A history of linguistics in Korea]." *Voprosy yazykoznaniya* [Linguistic studies], 4(1954):116–124.

05-026. KIM, Chin-W. "Linguistics and Language Policies in North Korea." In *The Proceedings of the Conference on North Korea*. Honolulu: Center for Korean Studies, University of Hawaii (forthcoming).

05-027. KIM, Min-su. "Korean Language Studies." *Asea yŏn'gu* (Seoul), 5(1)(1962):1–6.

05-028. KONTSEVICH, L. R. "Koreiskii yazyk [The Korean language]." In *Sovijetskoe yazykoznaniye za 50 let* [50 years of Soviet linguistics]. Moscow: 1967. Surveys the history of linguistics in Soviet Russia from 1917 to 1967. For a translation with notes into Korean, see Kanno Hiroomi in *Asea yŏn'gu* (Seoul), 14(2)(1971):187–216.

05-029. LEE, Ki-Moon. "Korean Studies in Seoul 1945–1959." *Ural-Altaische Jahrbücher* 32(1960):126–129.

05-030. _____. "Korean Linguistics: Retrospect and Prospect." *Koreana Quarterly* 5(1)(1963):119–134. Lee believes that Korean scholars can make an important contribution through studies of Manchu and Mongolian materials.

05-031. _____. "Linguistics." In Sung-nyŏng Lee (ed.), *Korean Studies Today*. Seoul: Tong'a munhwasa, 1970. Lee surveys Korean studies done up to 1968, primarily by native scholars, although those by Japanese and Western scholars are also included. A good survey and bibliography at the end.

05-032. LEE, Sung-nyŏng. "A Note on Korean Language Study." *Korean Affairs* 1(3)(1962):248–255. Lee urges that foreign scholars of Altaic studies make greater use of Korean materials.

05-033. LUKOFF, F. "Linguistics in the Republic of Korea." In T. Sebeok (ed.), *Current Trends in Linguistics*. Vol. 2. The Hague: Mouton, 1967. A sweeping review of postwar linguistics in South Korea.

05-034. MAZUR, Yu. N. "Koreiskaya Narodno-demokraticheskaya respublika [Korean People's Democratic Republic]." Seriya "yazykoznanie za rebezom" (Linguistics Abroad series), *Voprosy yazykoznaniya* [Linguistic studies], 3(1952):119–122.

05-035. PASKOV, B. K. "Koreiskii yazyk v sovetskom yazykoznanii [Korean language in Soviet linguistics]." In *Koreiskii yazyk* (Moscow: Akademiya Nauk, 1961). See 05-010.

05-036. SONG, Seok-Choong. "Grammarians or Patriots: Struggle for the Linguistic Heritage." *Korea Journal* 15(7)(1975):29–44. Describes the struggle of Korean scholars to preserve, promote, and reform the language during the period of Japanese colonial rule.

05-037. SUH, Doo-Soo. "Korean Studies in the U.S." *Koreana Quarterly* 4(1)(1962):119–123.

05-038. VOS, Frits. "Historical Survey of Korean Language Studies." In J. K. Yamagiwa and P. V. Hyer (eds.), *Papers of the CIC Far Eastern Language Institute*. Ann Arbor: University of Michigan, 1963.

THE SOUND SYSTEM

Korean presents a complex sound system and has been the subject of intensive study by both native and foreign scholars. The three series of Korean obstruents, for example, have been a constant puzzle to many general phoneticians as well as Korean linguists. For discussions on this topic, see Han and Weitzman (05-042), Hirose et al. (05-045), Kagaya (05-047, 048), Kim (05-050, 051), and Rachkov (05-057). The most extensive overall treatment of Korean phonetics using the instruments in experimental phonetics available in the 1950s was done by a Czech phonetician, Alena Skaličková (05-059, 060).

In Korean phonology, which is no less complicated than Korean phonetics, Samuel E. Martin has laid a structural foundation with his "phonemics" (05-093) and "morphophonemics" (05-094). Studies in Korean phonology within the framework of transformational-generative linguistics have been explored in a series of articles by Chin-W. Kim (05-072, 078). His view (05-073) on the system of Korean vowels is controversial (see B.-G. Lee, 05-088, for a critical review). Kim-Renaud's dissertation (05-083) represents the most current and extensive treatment of Korean consonantal phonology.

Phonetics

05-039. ABBERTON, Evelyn. "Some Laryngoscopic Data for Korean Stops." *Journal of International Phonetic Association* 2(1972):67–78.

05-040. ABRAMSON, Arthur S. and Leigh LISKER. "Voice Timing in Korean Stops." In *Proceedings of the Seventh International Congress of Phonetic Sciences*. The Hague: Mouton, 1972. The authors try to categorize three series of stops in one dimensional scale: voicing lag after the oral release.

05-041. HAN, Mieko S. *Studies in the Phonology of Asian Languages*. Vol. 1: *Acoustic Phonetics of Korean* (UCLA, 1964). Vol. 2: *Duration of Korean Vowels* (Acoustic Phonetics Research Laboratory, USC, 1964). Vol. 3 (with R. S. Weitzman): *Acoustic Characteristics of Korean Stop Consonants* (USC, 1965). Vol. 7 (with S. B. Ross): *Korean Affricates* (USC, 1968). Exclusively spectrographic examinations of Korean sounds. Measurements of formants, duration, transitions, and other purely phonetic details.

05-042. HAN, M. S. and R. S. WEITZMAN. "Acoustic Features of Korean /P,T,K/, /p,t,k/ and /ph, th, kh/." *Phonetica* 22(1970):112–128.

05-043. HAN, Young-hie. "The Duration of the Intervocalic Obstruents in Korean." *Ŏnŏ* (Linguistic journal of Korea), 1(1)(1976):1–21.

05-044. HARDCASTLE, W. J. "Some Observations on the Tense-Lax Distinction in Initial Stops in Korean." *Journal of Phonetics* 1(1973):263–272.

05-045. HIROSE, H., C. Y. LEE, and T. USHIJIMA. "Laryngeal Control in Korean Stop Production." *Journal of Phonetics* 2(1974):145–152. An electromyographic study of Korean stops.

05-046. HOANG, Hee Young. "Internal Structure of Absolute Phonemes and Formant Chart Analysis of Vowels." *Han'guk ŏnŏmunhak* (Seoul), 5(1968):112–126. Formant charts of ten Korean vowels spoken by two female and two male speakers of Korean.

05-047. KAGAYA, R. "Laryngeal Gestures in Korean Stop Consonants." *Annual Bulletin* 5(1971):15–23. Research Institute of Logopedics and Phoniatrics, University of Tokyo. Using a technique of fiberscope photography, the author finds that the degree of aspiration is proportional to the degree of glottal opening at the time of oral release.

05-048. _____. "A Fiberscopic and Acoustic Study of the Korean Stops, Affricates and Fricatives." *Journal of Phonetics* 2(1974): 161–180. An expanded version of the preceding entry.

05-049. KIM, Byoung Wook. "Physiological Production Mechanisms of Korean Stop Consonants and Word Level Suprasegmentals." PhD dissertation, University of Wisconsin at Madison, 1971. 139 pp. Abstracted in *DAI* 32(6)(December 1971):3690-B.

05-050. KIM, Chin-W. "On the Autonomy of the Tensity Feature in Stop Classification: With Special Reference to Korean Stops." *Word* 21(1965):339–359. With experimental data on three series of stops, Kim demonstrates that voicing and tensity are two independent phonetic phonological features.

05-051. _____. "A Cineradiographic Study of Korean Stops." *Quarterly Progress Report* 86(1967):259–272. Research Laboratory of Electronics, MIT. Three measurements are reported: the glottal height, the glottal width, and the width of the pharyngeal cavity. A portion of this paper was published as "A Theory of Aspiration," *Phonetica* 21(1970):107–116. There Kim argues that aspiration can be defined as a function of the glottal opening at the time of release of the oral closure of a stop and demonstrates the explanatory elegance of the theory.

05-052. KIM, Kong-On. "Temporal Structure of Spoken Korean: An Acoustic Phonetic Study." PhD dissertation, University of Southern California, 1974. 235 pp. Abstracted in *DAI* 34(10)(April 1974):6618-A.

05-053. _____. "The Nature of Temporal Relationship between Adjacent Segments in Spoken Korean." *Phonetica* 31(1975):259–273. Kim finds that the duration of a consonant has a systematic relationship with the duration of the adjacent vowel and argues that segments, rather than syllables, are the units of time programming in speech production.

05-054. LEE, Hey-Sook. "Acoustical Transitional Cues for Korean Semivowels." In *Ehwa University 80th Anniversary Thesis Collection, Humanities.* Seoul: 1966. A spectrographic study of semivowels /w/ and /y/. Measurements of the rate, direction, and duration of transitions.

05-055. LEE, Jae-Ho. "A Unified Phonetic Study of Korean Stop Consonants." *Language Research (Ŏhak yŏn'gu),* 2(1)(1966):1–17.

05-056. LEE, Ik-Mo. "A Study of Laryngeal Source Variables: Their Employment as Distinctive Cues for the Plosive Consonants of English, Hindi, and Korean, and Their Inherent Distinguishability as Measured in a Nonlinguistic Perception Test." PhD dissertation, Georgetown University, 1971. 293 pp. Abstracted in *DAI* 32(10)(April 1972):5765-A.

05-057. RACHKOV, G. E. "Shumnye smychnye soglasnye v sovremennom koreiskom yazke [Voiceless obstruent consonants in modern Korean]." In *Voprosy koreiskogo i kitaiskogo yazykoznaniya.* Leningrad and Moscow: 1958. A kymographic examination of Korean stops.

05-058. SKALIČKOVÁ, A. "Vocalický systém korejštiny [Vocalic system of Korean]." *Universitas Carolina, Philologica* (Prague), 1(1)(1955):67–73.

05-059. _____. "The Korean Vowels." *Archiv Orientalni* (Prague), 23(1955):29–51. See review by H. F. J. Junker in *Zeitschrift für Phonetik und allgemeine Sprachwissenschaft* 9(1956):285–287.

05-060. _____. *The Korean Consonants.* (Rozpravy Československé akademie věd, Ročnik 70, Sešit 3.) Prague: 1960. The preceding two papers (05-058, 059) present the most extensive overall treatment of Korean phonetics with the instruments available in the 1950s. The author differentiates three series of stops in terms of "linkage" with a preceding vowel: close link (tense series), basic link (basic series), and loose link (aspirated series).

05-061. _____. "Some Problems of General Phonetics (Demonstrated on the System of Korean Consonants)." *Acta Universitatis Carolinae, Philologica* (Prague), 1(1959):29–39. A discussion of aspiration in Korean stops in terms of a general phonetic theory.

05-062. SKALOZUB, L. G. "Soglasnye fonemy koreiskogo yazyka [Consonant phonemes of Korean]." *Naukovi zapiski kievskogo derzhavnogo univ.* (Kiev University Journal), 16(7)(1957). Uses kymograph, oscillograph, artificial palate, and x-ray pictures to investigate physiology of consonants.

05-063. SOHN, Han. "A Cineradiographic Study of Selected Korean Utterances and Its Implications." PhD dissertation, University of Illinois at Urbana-Champaign, 1976. 99 pp.

05-064. TCHEU, Soc-Kiou. "Mémoires sur les occlusives coréennes." *Tongbanghakchi* (Seoul), 5(1961):297–324.

05-065. VASIL'EV, I. V. "K voprosu o kolichestve glansnogo v sovremennom koreiskom yazyke [On vowel quantity in present-day Korean]." *Archiv Orientalni* (Prague), 28(1966):368–398.

Phonology

05-066. CHO, S. B. *A Phonological Study of Korean.* Acta Universitatis Upsaliensis. Studia Uralica et Altaica Upsaliensia, no. 2. Uppsala: Almqvist & Wiksells, 1967. Cho discusses all aspects of Korean phonology, including history, graphemics, and suprasegmentals. See reviews by Soc-Kiou Tcheu in *Bulletin de la Société de Linguistique de Paris* 63(1968):339–341; by Pentti Aalto in *Finnisch-ugrische Forschungen* (Helsinki), 37(1969):173–176; and by A. Rygaloff in *Linguistique* 2(1969):158–159.

05-067. COOK, Eung-Do. "Double Consonant Base Verbs in Korean." *Language Research (Ŏhak yŏn'gu)* (Seoul), 9(2)(1973):264–273. Posits *-lt* and *-wp* as underlying the so-called *t*-irregular and *p*-irregular verbs. See comment by Chin-W. Kim in the same issue, pp. 292–294.

05-068. HA, Chong-on. "Generative Approach to Korean Phonology." In *30th Anniversary Thesis Collection.* Seoul: Hanyang University, 1969.

05-069. JUNKER, H. F. J. "Über Phoneme im Koreanischen." *Wissenschaftliche Zeitschrift der Humboldt-Universität zu Berlin, Gesellschafts- und Sprachwissenschaftliche Reihe* 3(1)(1953–1954):25–31.

05-070. _____. "Zur System der koreanischen Laute." In *Koreanische Studien.* Berlin: 1955. (See 05-008.)

05-071. _____. "Das koreanische Lautwesen." In *Koreanische Studien.* Berlin: 1955. (See 05-008.)

05-072. KIM, Chin-W. "Some Phonological Rules in Korean." *Ŏmun yŏn'gu* [Studies in language and literature] (Taejon), 5(1967):153–177. Presents distinctive feature classification of phonemes, obligatory rules, optional rules, special rules, and sample derivations.

05-073. _____. "The Vowel System of Korean." *Language* 44(1968):516–527. Kim examines four alternative analyses of the vowel system: (1) traditional phonemics, (2) distinctive feature analysis, (3) generative phonology, and (4) componential analysis. See note by G. L. Trager in *Language* 44(1968):918 and a critique by Lee (05-088).

05-074. _____. "Boundary Phenomena in Korean." *Papers in Linguistics* 2(1970):1–26. A systematic examination of the *"sai sios"* phenomenon and related topics in the framework of generative phonology. For follow-ups, see C. B. Kim (05-079) and Lee (05-089).

05-075. _____. "Regularity of the So-called Irregular Verbs in Korean." In C. W. Kisseberth (ed.), *Studies in Generative Phonology.* Edmonton, Alberta, Canada: Linguistic Research Inc., 1972. A Korean version appeared in *Han'guk ŏnŏmunhak* [Korean language and literature], 8/9(1971):1–11. Kim argues that the conjugation of the so-called irregular predicates can be regarded as phonologically regular by positing different basic (underlying) shapes for the stems—for example, *tŏw-* instead of *tŏp-*. This is the first time a regular solution has been proposed, but for further discussion see Kim-Renaud (05-082), Keedong Lee (05-092), and Sohn (05-095).

05-076. _____. "Gravity in Korean Phonology." *Language Research (Ŏhak yŏn'gu)* (Seoul), 9(2)(1973):274–281. A Japanese version appeared in *Han* (Tokyo), 1(10)(1972):88–97. Kim observes that the peripheral consonants *(p, m, k)* behave as a group differently from the central consonants *(t, n, ch, s)* and that, in general, there is a tendency for articulation to move toward the peripheral region in the vocal tract.

05-077. _____. "Rule Ordering in Korean Phonology." *Ŏnŏ* (Linguistic journal of Korea), 1(1)(1976):60–83. Also appeared in *Korean Studies* (Honolulu), 1(1977):1–20.

05-078. _____. "Vowel Length in Korean." *Studies in Linguistic Sciences* 7(2)(1977):184–190.

05-079. KIM, Choong-Bae. "Tensification Revisited." *Language Research (Ŏhak yŏn'gu),* 10(2)(1974):129–142. Extension and reexamination of Kim (05-074) and Lee (05-089).

05-080. KIM, Kong-On and M. SHIBATANI. "Syllabification Phenomena in Korean." *Language Research (Ŏhak yŏn'gu)* 12(1)(1976):91–98.

05-081. KIM, Soo-Gon. "Palatalization in Korean." PhD dissertation, University of Texas at Austin, 1976. 201 pp. Also published by Tower Press (Seoul: 1976).

05-082. KIM-RENAUD, Young-Key. "Irregular Verbs in Korean Revisited." *Language Research (Ŏhak yŏn'gu),* 9(2)(1973):206–225. Kim-Renaud argues that the alternation of *p~w, t~r, s~Ø*, and so forth is an intervocalic "weakening process" conditioned by the length of a vowel preceding the final stem consonants.

05-083. _____. "Korean Consonantal Phonology." PhD dissertation, University of Hawaii, 1974. 314 pp. Abstracted in *DAI* 36(2)(August 1975):869-70-A. A fresh treatment of some aspects of the Korean consonantal system in the framework of generative phonology. Particularly interesting is Kim-Renaud's treatment of the alternation of the stem-final consonants of "irregular" verbs as the process of intervocalic weakening (see preceding entry).

05-084. _____. "On *h*-deletion in Korean." *Kugŏhak* (Journal of Korean linguistics), 3(1975):45–64.

05-085. _____. "Semantic Features in Phonology: Evidence from Vowel Harmony in Korean." In *Papers from the 12th Meeting of the Chicago Linguistic Society.* Chicago: Chicago Linguistic Society, 1976.

05-086. _____. "Syllable Boundary Phenomena in Korean." *Korean Studies* (Honolulu), 1(1977):243–273.

05-087. KONTSEVICH, L. R. "Priroda fonematicheskoi dlitel'nosti glasnykh-monoftongov koreiskogo yazyka [Nature of phonemic length of Korean monophthongal vowels]." In *Koreiskii yazyk* [The Korean language].

Moscow: Akademiya Nauk, 1961. Author argues that vowel length is phonemic in Korean.

05-088. LEE, Byung-Gun. "Underlying Segments in Korean Phonology." PhD dissertation, Indiana University, 1973. 176 pp. Lee attempts to determine the underlying segments in Modern Korean with an ancillary examination of vowel and consonant evolution since the fifteenth century.

05-089. LEE, Chungmin. "Boundary Phenomena in Korean Revisited." *Papers in Linguistics* 5(3)(1972):454–474. A review, extension, and reexamination of C.-W. Kim (05-074).

05-090. LEE, Hye-Sook. "Lexical-feature Redundancy Rules of Korean." *Language Research (Ŏhak yŏn'gu)* 4(1) (1968):92–108.

05-091. LEE, Ik-Hwan. "Korean Vowel System: Abstract Solution?" *Texas Linguistic Forum* 4(1976):57–70.

05-092. LEE, Keedong. "On the So-called *s*-irregular and *t*-irregular Verbs in Korean." *Working Papers in Linguistics* (University of Hawaii), 5(6)(1973):129–138. Lee argues that *t∼r, s∼∅* alternation in the so-called irregular verbs is phonologically conditioned by the length of the stem vowel.

05-093. MARTIN, Samuel E. "Korean Phonemics." *Language* 27(1951):519–533. Reprinted in M. Joos (ed.), *Readings in Linguistics.* Washington: American Council of Learned Societies, 1958. Shows that the same body of phonetic facts of Korean can be analyzed in three different ways according to three different theoretical frameworks: in terms of (1) articulatory components, (2) auditory qualities, and (3) distinctive oppositions. The most exhaustive analysis of Korean phonemes in the tradition of structural linguistics.

05-094. _____. *Korean Morphophonemics.* Baltimore: Linguistic Society of America, 1954. 64 pp. An extensive treatise on phonological alternations in Modern Korean from segments to intonation. A classic and the best in the tradition of structural linguistics. See reviews by D. L. Olmstedt in *Far Eastern Quarterly* 15(1)(1955):134–136 and by C. F. Hockett in *Language* 32(1956):184–189.

05-095. SOHN, Han. "On the Regularization of the Irregular Verbs in Korean." *Language Research (Ŏhak yŏn'gu)* 13(1) (1977):49–59.

05-096. TCHEU, Soc-Kiou. "La neutralisation et le consonantisme coréen." *La Linguistique* 2(1967):85–97.

05-097. TRAGER, G. L. "Korean Syllabics." *Studies in Linguistics* 13(1958):73–77. An *ad libitum* extension of Martin's (05-093) "componential" analysis of phonemes. See comment in C.-W. Kim (05-074; n. 3, p. 22).

05-098. UMEDA, H. "The Phonemic System of Modern Korean." *Gengo Kenkyū* (Journal of Linguistic Society of Japan), 32(1957):60–82. Sets up two phonemes for two different pronunciations of *o,* one short and low [ʌ] and the other high and long [ŭ:] or [ə:] as in *ŏp-ta* (to carry on the back) versus *ŏps-ta* (there isn't).

05-099. ZINDER, L. R. "Glasnye koreiskogo yazyka: sostov fonem koreiskogo yazyka [Korean vowels: phonemic construction of Korean]." *Sovetskoe vostokovedenie* [Soviet oriental studies], 3(1958):91–103. From the official English summary: "The author observes that the definition of vowel phonemes in the Korean language depends upon the phonemic interpretation of the palatal and labial consonants as well as the sonants *j* and *w*. Inasmuch as all these consonants do not occur as independent phonetic units, they do not represent separate phonemes. Combinations of the type of *ja, wa,* etc. are monophonemic units. It follows that the Korean language has 8 simple vowel phonemes (i, e, ɛ, a, ɔ, o, u, ɯ), 12 diphthongoids (i$_e$, i$_\epsilon$, i$_a$, i$_\supset$, i$_o$, i$_u$, u$_i$, u$_e$, u$_\epsilon$, u$_a$, u$_\supset$, u$_o$[? CWK]) and one diphthong (ɯ)." Descriptions of simple vowels as pronounced in Seoul are given on the basis of experimental data (spectrograms, roentgenograms, kymograms, and photographs).

LEXICAL STRUCTURES

The best studies in Korean etymology are those of Ramstedt (05-104, 105). See also Rahder (05-103) and Martin (05-113). The study on word formation in Korean has been quite ignored both in Korea and in the United States. The most substantial contribution to this field has come from Russia: see the works by Mazur, Nikolskii, Pak, and Vasil'ev. Particularly interesting are the studies of mimetic words (phonetic symbolism) by G. A. Pak (05-121, 122); see also Kim (05-111) and Martin (05-113). Morphology plays a great role in Russian linguistics, and its influence on Korean linguistics is reflected in the works of Russian and North Korean linguists.

Etymology

05-100. ANSELMO, Valerio. "A proposito di *qum (sabbia, terra) nel coreano antico [On *qum (sand, earth) in Old Korean]." *Annali, Istituto Universitario Orientale* (Naples), 32(1972):535–539.

05-101. HAGUENAUER, Charles. "De la survivance possible de particules enclitiques -et et -ka en coréen." In *Paek Nak-chun Festschrift.* Seoul: Sasanggye-sa, 1955.

05-102. _____. "À propos de coréen *nä* 'riviere' et *mö* 'montagne.' " In *Lee Pyŏng-do Festschrift.* Seoul: Ilcho-gak, 1956.

05-103. RAHDER, Johannes. "Etymological vocabulary of

Chinese, Japanese, Korean and Ainu." Pt. 1: Monograph 16, *Monumenta Nipponica* (Tokyo: Sophia University, 1956). Pt. 2: *Asea yŏn'gu* [Asiatic research bulletin], 2(1)(1959):317–406. Pt. 3: *Asea yŏn'gu* 2(2)(1959): 307–371. See review in *Anthropos* 54(1047) (1959).

05-104. RAMSTEDT, G. J. *Studies in Korean Etymology.* Mémoires de la Société Finno-Ougrienne, no. 95. 2 vols. Helsinki: Suomalais-ugrilainen Seura, 1949–1953. Despite a few far-fetched interpretations, Ramstedt's investigations into Korean etymology are perceptive. This monograph, more than anything else, established the affinity of Korean to other Altaic languages. See reviews by N. Poppe in *Harvard Journal of Asiatic Studies* 13(1949): 568–581; by A. Sauvageot in *Bulletin de la Société de linguistique de Paris* 46(133)(1950):226–228; by J. Rahder in *Monumenta Nipponica* 8(1952); by P. Aalto in *Ural-Altaische Jahrbücher* 24(3/4)(1952):122–126; by A. Raun in *Word* 8(1952):190–191; by R. Austerlitz in *Word* 11(1955):190; and by F. Vos in *Lingua* 6(1956/1957):108–109.

05-105. RAMSTEDT, G. J. and P. AALTO. "Additional Korean Etymologies." *Journal de la Société Finno-Ougrienne* 57(3)(1953):1–23. Posthumous addenda to the preceding work by Ramstedt's student and colleague.

Morphology and Word Formation

05-106. BECKER, Anne-Katrein. "Das mehrdeutige Monem *i* in der modernen koreanischen Sprache." *Zeitschrift für Phonetik* 22(1969):533–540.

05-107. FABRE, André. *Les mots expressifs en coréen moderne.* Paris: Université de Paris, 1971. 175 pp.

05-108. JUNKER, H. F. J. "Zu den koreanischen Zahlwörtern." *Mitteilungen des Instituts für Orientforschung der deutschen Akademie der Wissenschaften zu Berlin* (Berlin), 1(2)(1953):298–312.

05-109. KIM, Bo-gyŏm. "Das koreanische Zahlsystem." In *Koreanica: Festschrift Dr. André Eckardt zum 75 Geburtstag.* Baden-Baden: 1960.

05-110. KIM, Han-Kon. "Korean Kinship Terminology: A Semantic Analysis." *Language Research* 3(1)(1967): 70–81.

05-111. KIM, Kong-On. "Sound Symbolism in Korean." *Journal of Linguistics* 13(1)(1977):67–75.

05-112. LEWIN, Bruno. *Morphologie des koreanischen Verbs.* Wiesbaden: Otto Harrassowitz, 1970. 256 pp. See review by W. E. Skillend in *Bulletin of School of Oriental and African Studies* 34(1971):640.

05-113. MARTIN, Samuel E. "Phonetic Symbolism in Korean." In *American Studies in Altaic Linguistics.* Uralic and Altaic Series, vol. 3. Bloomington: Indiana

University Press, 1962. A structural analysis of mimetic words (phonomimes and phainomimes) in Korean. Martin describes alternations in initial consonants *(podong, ppodong, p'odong)*, in vowels *(kkal, kkil, kkol)*, and in syllable-final consonants—for example, *-l* (smooth or liquid) *(kkol, pudul, sol-sol); -ng* (round or hollow) *(ping, ssing, kkwang); -k* (abrupt, tight) *(ppak, ssuk, ssaktok)*.

05-114. MAZUR, Yu. N. "Struktura slova v koreiskom yazyke [Lexical structure of the Korean language]." In *Koreiskii yazyk.* Moscow: Akademiya Nauk, 1961. Mazur proposes strict classification of different processes of word construction in Korean: (1) phonemic-morphological, as in *kŏch'il-da kkach'ilhada;* (2) lexico-syntactic, as in *pojalkŏt-ŏpta;* (3) morphologico-syntactic, as in *ponttŭgi, ŏkchiro;* (4) morphological.

05-115. _____. *Sklonenie v koreiskom yazyke* [Declension in Korean]. Moscow: 1962. Mazur classifies cases in Korean into (1) nominative, *-ka, -i;* (2) genitive, *-ŭy;* (3) accusative, *-ŭl, -rŭl;* (4) dative, *-e, -ege;* (5) ablative, *-esŏ;* (6) instrumental, *-ro, -ŭro;* (7) comitative, *-wa, -kwa;* (8) vocative, *-a, -ya.* The author uses the term *case analogs* for such forms as *-kkeso, -hant'e, -rossŏ, -hago.*

05-116. NIKOLSKII, L. B. "O 'nepolnoznachnykh imenakh sushchestivetel 'nykh' v koreiskom yazyke [On the "dependent noun" in Korean]." In *Voprosy koreiskogo i kitaiskogo yazykoznaniya.* Leningrad and Moscow: 1958. (See 05-009.) The author classifies "dependent" nouns into three types: (1) those that decline, such as *-kŏs, -i;* (2) those that conjugate, such as *-tŭs sip'ta, -man hada;* (3) invariants, such as *ppun, ch'ŏk, mank'ŭm.*

05-117. _____. *Sluzhbenye slova v koreiskom yazyke* [Complementary words in Korean]. Moscow: Institut Narodov Azii, AN SSSR, 1962. 180 pp. "Complementary" words belong to the third category of the following classification of words: (1) independent: independent nouns and verbs; (2) dependent: as in *-kŏs, -i;* (3) nonindependent (complementary): numerals, postpositions, conjunctives, auxiliary verbs. See review by V. N. Dmitrieva in *Narodyi Azii i Afriki* [Asian and African peoples], 4(1964):226–228.

05-118. _____. "Ob upotreblenii koreiskikhpadezhnykh okonchanii [On the use of case endings in Korean]." *Kratkie soobshcheniya Instituta Narodov Azii,* AN SSSR [Research bulletin of Institute of Asian Nations, Soviet Academy of Sciences], 72(1963):151–155.

05-119. _____. "O leksiko-grammaticheskoi prirode koreiskoi obstojatel'stvennoi formy na *'ke* [On the lexico-grammatical characteristics of the Korean aspect morpheme *-ke*]." *Kratkie soobshcheniya Instituta Narodov Azii,* AN SSSR, 72(1963):156–159.

05-120. OOE, Takao. "On the indicative endings in modern

Korean." *Gengo Kenkyū (Journal of the Linguistic Society of Japan)*, 34(1958):1–40.

05-121. PAK, G. A. "Morfologicheskie osobennosti izobrazitel'nykh slov v koreiskom yazyke [Morphological characteristics of mimetic words in Korean]." In *Voprosy koreiskogo i kitaiskogo yazykoznaniya*. Leningrad and Moscow: 1958. (See 05-009.) Pak illustrates morphological processes in constructing mimetic words in Korean.

05-122. _____. "Slovoobrazovanie na baze izobrazitel'nykh slov [Word construction based on phonetic symbolism]." In *Koreiskii yazyk*. Moscow: Akademiya Nauk, 1961. (See 05-010.) Pak notes the following types of derivation from onomatopoeic words: (1) into adverbs, as in *kyaus-i;* (2) into verbs, as in *hundulgŏri-da, kalp'ang chilp'ang-hada;* (3) into adjectives, as in *panjirŭrŭ-hada, ulgutpulgut-hada;* (4) into nouns, as in *ttungttung-po, ttalkkak-chil.*

05-123. PAK, N. S. "Priimennaya morfema 'ne' i ee znachenie [Nominal suffix "ne" and its meaning]." In *Voprosy koreiskogo i kitaiskogo yazykoznaniya*. Leningrad and Moscow: 1958. (See 05-009.) Pak says that *ne* is neither a dative nor a plural affix but a morpheme denoting a group whose members are of the same kind.

05-124. RAMSTEDT, G. J. "The nominal postpositions in Korean." *Mémoires de la Société Finno-Ougrienne* 67(1933):459–464. Ramstedt lists twenty-eight nominal positions (such as *an, ap', wi,* and *kyŏt*), gives possible cognates in other Altaic languages, and speculates on their grammatical functions.

05-125. _____. "Koreanische *kes* 'Ding, Stück.' " *Journal de la Société Finno-Ougrienne* 48(1937):4–10.

05-126. _____. "Two words of Korean-Japanese." *Journal de la Société Finno-Ougrienne* 55(1951):25–30.

05-127. REE, J. J. "A Semantic Analysis of *(ŭ)ni* and *(e)se.*" *Language Research* 11(1)(1975):69–76. An interesting attempt to elucidate the subtle distinction between near-synonymous conjunctions *(ŭ)ni* and *(ĕ)sĕ* on the basis of their different syntactic and semantic behavior. A useful guide to a language teacher.

05-128. SIBATA, Takesi. "Korean Sibling Terms and Their Structure." In R. Jakobson and S. Kawamoto (eds.), *Studies in General and Oriental Linguistics* (Hattori Festschrift). Tokyo: TEC Co., 1969.

05-129. VASIL'EV, A. G. "Infinity na -*ki* v sovremennom koreiskom yazyke [Infinitival affix -*ki* in Modern Korean]." *Filologiya i istoriya stran vostoka* [Oriental philology and history], 12(1961):163–188. Uchenye zapiski LGU (Leningrad University research bulletin) no. 294, Seriya vostokevedcheskikh nauk (Oriental Study Series). The author gives the verbal paradigm of -*ki* (according to tense, aspect, and modality) and analyzes the use of -*ki* in

different cases: (1) nominative, as in -*ki(ga) cohta;* (2) accusative, as in -*ki (rŭl) coha hada;* (3) dative, as in -*ki(e) him ssŭda;* (4) instrumental, as in -*ki(ro) irŭm nada;* (5) comparative, as in -*ki poda coh -ta.*

05-130. _____. "Substantivirovannyj infinitiv na -*m* v koreiskom yazyke [Nominalizing infinitival affix -*m* in Korean]." *Filologiya stran Vostoka* [Oriental philology], 286(1963):12–31. Vasil'ev distinguishes between "lexicalized" -*m (nŭkkim, midŭm, kŭrim, chim, kippŭm)* and "nominalized" -*m (cŏlmŭm, coyongham).*

Loanwords

05-131. COLHOUN, E. R. and T. W. KIM. "English Loanwords in Korean—Lexical and Phonological Problems." *Ŭngyong-ŏnŏhak* [Applied linguistics], 8(2)(1976):237–250.

05-132. KHEGAI, M. A. "O morfologii russkikh zaimstvovanii v koreiskom yazyke [On morphology of Russian loanwords in Korean]." *Narody Azii i Afriki* [Asian and African peoples], 5(1965):151–154. The author says that there are about five hundred Russian loanwords currently used in Korean.

05-133. LEE, Ki-Moon. "Mongolian Loan-Words in Middle Korean." *Ural-Altaische Jahrbücher* 34(1964):188–197.

05-134. PAI, Yang-Seo. "English Loan-Words in Korean." PhD dissertation, University of Texas, 1967. 199 pp.

GRAMMARS (SYNTAX AND SEMANTICS)

The year 1967 is a landmark in the history of Korean grammatical studies, for in that year three doctoral dissertations on Korean syntax written by young Korean scholars in the United States (Song, 05-215; Kim, 05-173; Lee, 05-191) appeared simultaneously. Up to that point, all studies in Korean grammar were either pedagogical or descriptive. Lukoff (05-148), Ramstedt (05-156), Sunoo (05-158), and Kholodovich (05-144) are most representative of the pre-1967 period. Then the three dissertations, written within the framework of the "generative-transformational" theory of language, heralded a new trend in Korean syntax. This is the sole reason for dividing this section into pre-1967 and post-1967. It is more than a mere chronological demarcation.

The generative-transformational study of Korean syntax and semantics has made steady and remarkable progress since 1967. In the decade or so since then, there have appeared nearly one hundred scholarly articles and fifteen dissertations on syntax and semantics alone. Prominent and recurrent themes are negation, relativization, complementation, causativization, sentence types, case marking, and the speech act.

The controversy on negation, touched off by Song's (05-215, 216) separate underlying structure hypothesis for two types of negative sentences, still continues. Articles by Lee (05-182) and Oh (05-194) are representative of the single underlying structure hypothesis that challenges Song's original proposal. Song (05-218) offers the response; Cho (05-164) and I. Yang (05-228) present logical extensions and elaborations, but they fail to relate semantics to syntax.

Relativization was first dealt with by M. Lee (05-191) and was taken up by Ree (05-202), Oh (05-195), I. Yang (05-233), and finally by D. Yang (05-227). M. Lee views relativization as an extraction transformation while others derive relative clauses either by embedding or conjunctions. All have made some contributions to the topic. The most novel treatment is found in Oh's conjunctions theory. The most interesting is D. Yang's universalist view, which if substantiated will constitute a significant contribution to general theory of language.

Song (05-215), H. Lee (05-181), I. Yang (05-233, 235, 236), Park (05-197), and Shibatani (05-204, 205) have all discussed causativization. Yang and Shibatani's exchanges on lexical versus periphrastic/phrasal causatives have been stimulating. Patterson (05-200) exquisitely combines the best of two approaches to her advantage.

S.-H. Kim (05-173) and Song (05-215) first discussed sentence types, but an advanced treatment of the subject is found in H. Lee's (05-182) performative and Chang's (05-160, 161) discourse approaches. I. Yang (05-232) is also interesting in this respect. Chang's contribution, especially his study of modality, is noteworthy. The study of the speech act is first incorporated in H. Lee (05-182) and then in Chang (05-160), but C. Lee (05-178) should be singled out for his perceptive analysis.

Korean linguistics has made progress in leaps and bounds since 1967 and seems to have come of age in the past few years. At long last, Korean syntacticians and semanticists are making headway in the international community of linguists. The breadth of topics, the height of quality, and the depth of insight they have demonstrated are now of international standards.

Pre-1967

05-135. CHANG, Suk-Jin. "Some Remarks on Korean and Nominalizations." *Language Research* 2(1)(1966):18–31.

05-136. DMITRIEVA, V. N. "Ob obrazovanii i upotreblenii zalogov v koreistom yazyke [On the formation and use of voice in Korean]." In *Koreiskii yazyk*. Moscow: Akademiya Nauk, 1961. (See 05-010.) The author sets up four voices in Korean: (1) active (basic); (2) causative; (3) middle voice; and (4) passive.

05-137. ECKARDT, A. *Studien in die koreanische Sprache.* Heidelberg: Julius Groos Verlag, 1960.

05-138. _____. *Grammatik der koreanischen Sprache (Studienausgabe).* Heidelberg: Julius Groos Verlag, 1962. 244 pp.

05-139. _____. *Studien zur koreanischen Sprache (Studienausgabe).* Heidelberg: Julius Groos Verlag, 1965. 226 pp.

05-140. FIGULLA, H. H. "Prolegomena zu einer Grammatik der koreanischen Sprache." *Mitteilungen des Seminars für orientalische Sprachen* (Berlin), 38(1)(1963): 101–121.

05-141. GUSEVA, E. K. *Sistema vidov v sovremennom koreiskom yazyke* [Aspectual system in Modern Korean]. Moscow: Izd. vostochnoj literatury, 1961. 119 pp. See review by A. Fabre in *Bulletin de la Société de Linguistique de Paris* 58(1963):326–327.

05-142. _____. "Zametki o sposobakh vyrazheniya vidovykh znachenii v sovremennom koreiskom yazyke [A treatise on the method of expression of aspectual meanings in Modern Korean]." In *Koreiskii yazyk*. Moscow: Akademiya Nauk, 1961. (See 05-010.) The author sets up three aspects in Korean verbs: (1) continuative, as in *-ko, iss-ta, -a ka-da;* (2) terminative, as in *-a pŏrida, -ko malda;* (3) repetitive, as in *-kon hada, -a ssah-ta.* A Korean version is found in *Chosŏn ŏmun* 4(1959):62–71.

05-143. JUNKER, H. F. J. "Grundfragen des koreanischen Satzbaues." *Wissenschaftliche Zeitschrift der Humboldt-Universität* (Berlin), 7(1957/1958):329–350.

05-144. KHOLODOVICH, A. A. *Grammatika Koreiskogo yazyka* [A Korean grammar]. Pt. 1: Morphology. Moscow: 1939. The first scientific grammar of Korean in Russian. A detailed description of verb morphology, which is categorized into five modalities: person, tense, aspect, mood, and voice. The author points out the syntactic equivalence of verbs and adjectives but argues that there are enough morphological differences to warrant their designation as separate parts of speech.

05-145. _____. *Ocherk grammatiki koreiskogo yazyka* [An outline of a grammar of Korean]. Moscow: 1954. 320 pp. Discussions on word formation (divided into eleven types), verb categories, and sentence types. See reviews by Ju. N. Mazur in *Voprosy yazykoznaniya* 2(1957):139–143; by A. Eckardt in *Literatur-Zeitung für Kritik der internationalen Wissenschaft* 77(2)(1956):91–95; and by Kanno Hiroomi in *Gengogaku* (Tokyo), 6(1965):45–55.

05-146. _____. "O predel'nikh i nepredel'nykh glagolakh (po dannym koreiskogo i yaponskogo yazykov) [On limited and unlimited verbs (according to Korean and Japanese data)]." In *Filologiya stran vostoka* [Oriental philology]. Leningrad: Leningrad University, 1963. The author classifies verbs according to co-occurrence restrictions.

05-147. LEE, Hong-Bae. "A Transformational Outline of Korean." *Language Research (Ŏhak yŏn'gu)* (Seoul), 2(3)(1966). Originally an MA thesis, Brown University, 1966. See review by Eung-Do Cook in *Language Research* 3(2)(1967):139–156.

05-148. LUKOFF, Fred. "A Grammar of Korean." PhD dissertation, University of Pennsylvania, 1954. 265 pp.

05-149. MALKOV, F. V. "Leksiko-grammaticheskie osobennosti kachestvennykh prilagatel'nykh v sovremennom koreiskom yazyke (Sposoby vyrazheniya intensivosti kachestva) [Lexico-grammatical characteristics of character adjectives in Modern Korean (expression of intensity of character)]." In *Voprosy filologii* [Philological studies]. Moscow: Institut Mezhdunarodnykh Otnoshenii, 1957.

05-150. _____. "Skhodstvo i razlichie predikativnykh prilagatel'nykh i glagolov v koreiskom yazyke [Similarities and differences of predicative adjectives and verbs in Korean]." In Yu. N. Mazur, *Koreiskii yazyk* [The Korean language]. Moscow: Izd. vost. lit., 1960.

05-151. MAZUR, Yu. N. *Koreiskii yazyk* [The Korean language]. Moscow: Izd. vost. lit., 1960. 118 pp.

05-152. PIHL, M. R., Jr. *A Study on Non-conclusives in Modern Korean.* Seoul: T'ongmun-kwan, 1965.

05-153. RACHKOV, G. E. "Vremena deeprichastii pervov i vtoroi grupp v sovremennom koreiskkom yazyke [Tense of group 1 and group 2 verbs in Modern Korean]." In *Voprosy koreiskogo i kitaiskogo yazykoznaniya.* Leningrad and Moscow: 1958. (See 05-009.) Rachkov divides verbal connectives into five groups according to co-occurrence restrictions with tense affixes; he discusses the first two groups.

05-154. _____. "Predel'nye glagoly v koreiskom yazyke [Limited verbs in Korean]." *Filologiya stran Vostoka* [Oriental philology], 16(1962):32–45. Uchenye Zapiski, LGU (Leningrad University rescarch bulletin). Intransitive verbs express "state" with *-a iss-ta,* while transitive verbs denote "state" with *-ko iss-ta* (not progressive). But some verbs cannot co-occur with these connectives—hence the following four classes of verbs: (1) intransitive limited (cannot take *-a iss-ta*), as in *nol-da, *nora iss-ta;* (2) intransitive unlimited, as in *nam-ta, nam-a iss-ta;* (3) transitive limited (cannot take *-ko iss-ta*), as in *tŭt-ta, *tŭk-ko iss-ta;* (4) transitive unlimited, as in *kaji-da, kaji-go iss-ta.*

05-155. _____. "Dva tipa razdelitel'nykh deeprichastii v koreiskom yazyke [Two types of disjunctive adverbial verbs in Korean]." *Vestnik LGU* (Leningrad University bulletin), 4(20)(1963):128–131. Rachkov examines the following two types of constructions: (1) X-*kŏna* Z (as in *ka-kŏna, sa-kŏna);* (2) X-*kŏna* Y-*kŏna* Z (as in *o-kŏna ka-kŏna, sa-kŏna p'al-kŏna).*

05-156. RAMSTEDT, G. J. *A Korean Grammar.* Helsinki: 1939. 232 pp. This classic work is the first serious grammatical study of Korean by a professional linguist of the West. Although it is morphology-oriented grammar with only four pages devoted to syntax (versus 130 pages for morphology), Ramstedt's grammar is replete with insightful observations and perceptive remarks. Particularly detailed are descriptions of verbal endings. The book is not only of historical interest but will remain informative and instructive. N. Poppe remarks in his *Introduction to Altaic Linguistics* (Wiesbaden: 1965) that Ramstedt's grammar is "still unsurpassed." See reviews by A. Eckardt in *Deutsche Literaturzeitung für Kritik der internationalen Wissenschaft* (Berlin), 70(1949):484–490; by W. A. Unkorig in *Sinica* 15(1941):152–159; and by H. H. Figulla in *Deutsche Literatur-Zeitung* 70(1949): 484–490. There is a Russian translation by B. K. Pastov: *Grammatika koreiskogo yazyka* (Moscow: 1951).

05-157. ROGERS, M. C. *Outline of Korean Grammar.* Berkeley: University of California Press, 1953.

05-158. SUNOO, Hag-Won (Harold). *A Korean Grammar.* Prague: Státní pedagogické nakladaterlství, 1952. Also published by Korean-American Cultural Association, Seattle Branch, 1952. 189 pp. The only Korean grammar written in English by a native grammarian. A typical structural description of Modern Korean consisting mainly of classification of grammatical elements and their arrangements. Half the book is devoted to verb and adjective conjugations (including auxiliary verbs and predicate adjectives) and the copula. Abundant examples illustrating usage will be helpful to students learning Korean. As a linguistic description, it is of little theoretical interest.

Post-1967

05-159. ABASOLO, Rafael (OFM). "Basic Semantic Structures of Korean." PhD dissertation, Georgetown University, 1974. 401 pp. Abstracted in *DAI* 35(7)(January 1975):4471-A.

05-160. CHANG, Suk-Jin. "Some Remarks on 'Mixed Modality' and Sentence Types." *English Language and Literature* (Seoul), 44(1972):95–110.

05-161. _____. *A Generative Study of Discourse: Pragmatic Aspects of Korean with Reference to English.* Seoul: Language Research Institute, Seoul National University, 1973. 149 pp. Originally PhD dissertation, University of Illinois at Urbana-Champaign, 1972; abstracted in *DAI* 33(10)

(April 1973):5702-A. This is a pioneering work that broadens the domain of the linguistic description of Korean beyond sentence grammar. Chang discusses the interesting questions of deixis (person, time, place, and so on) and direct and indirect discourse, which he claims are not transformationally relatable. The chapter on discourse levels and honorification contains illuminating analysis of complex problems peculiar to Korean. Chang also treats presupposition-bearing elements like *man, to, majŏ*. The final chapter deals with modality and sentence types in a most perceptive manner. The treatment of the suspective morpheme *chi* is especially interesting. Although highly exploratory, this is an imaginative treatment of various aspects of Korean syntax and semantics. It will undoubtedly become a landmark in the syntactic description of Korean. Good bibliography.

05-162. _____. "A Generative Study of Discourse in Korean: On Connecting Sentences." *Language Research* (Seoul), 9(2)(1973):226–238. An innovative and insightful treatment of the conjunction phenomenon within the discourse frame that Chang is advocating (see his dissertation; 05-161). This article is especially valuable in providing perceptive semantic analysis of *ko* and other sentence connectives.

05-163. CHANG, Sun. "Korean Reflexive Pronoun *caki* and Its Referent NP's Point of View." *Language Research* (Seoul), 13(1)(1977):35–48.

05-164. CHO, Choon-Hak. "The Scope of Negation in Korean." In Ho-min Sohn (ed.), *The Korean Language*. Honolulu: Center for Korean Studies, University of Hawaii, 1975. Also in *Working Papers in Linguistics* 8(4)(1976):121–132 (Department of Linguistics, University of Hawaii). An interesting discussion of preverbal and postverbal negation in Korean and their relation to quantifiers, delimiters, presupposition-bearing elements, and sentence conjunction.

05-165. CHWAE, Seung-Pyung. "Korean Verb Inflection: A Tagmemic Study of the Verb *ka-*." *Language Research* (Seoul), 5(1)(1969):73–103. A tagmemic analysis of the verb inflection in Korean. Inflectional endings consist of mood, aspects, tense, and voice. The voice includes active, passive, causative, and negative. Descriptive, data-oriented, and useful for language learners.

05-166. COOK, Eung-Do. "Embedding Transformations in Korean Syntax." PhD dissertation, University of Alberta, 1968. An interesting and lucid treatment of embedding processes in Korean.

05-167. _____. "Korean Verbal Affixes: A Generative View." *Canadian Journal of Linguistics* 16(2)(1971):81–

91. The first serious attempt to relate sentence final verbal endings to those of an embedded sentence.

05-168. HAN, Young-Hie. "Some Aspects of Passivization in Korean." *Ŭngyong-ŏnŏhak* [Applied linguistics], 8(2)(1976):223–235.

05-169. KIM, Han-Kon. "A Semantic Analysis of the Topic Particles in Korean and Japanese." *Language Research* (Seoul), 3(2)(1967):106–117.

05-170. KIM, Jong Yule. "Base Structure and Transformational Derivations of Complex Sentences in Korean." PhD dissertation, Columbia University, 1974. 229 pp. Abstracted in *DAI* 35(2)(August 1974):1080-A. A classic study of Korean complementation à la Rosenbaum supervised by Rosenbaum himself. The introduction contains a vigorous review of the previous literature. Grammatical Model (chap. 2) is a concise introduction to transformational grammar. Base structure rules and their justification constitute chaps. 4 and 5; five types of complement sentences are given in chap. 4. Kim's complement phrase embedding deserves further study. His treatment of *ha* as a modal is original and interesting but its justification still inconclusive. Although his analysis of Korean data may be questioned, Kim's thorough mastery of Rosenbaum's theory of complementation and its application to Korean gives this work a unique status among similar studies.

05-171. KIM, Nam-Kil. "Studies in the Syntax of Korean Complementation." PhD dissertation, University of Washington, 1974. 154 pp. Abstracted in *DAI* 35(9)(March 1975):6121-A. A lucid, original, and perceptive treatment of Korean complementation. It contains chapters on factive and nonfactive, question, exclamatory, and quotative complementations. Kim's arguments are well motivated syntactically as well as semantically.

05-172. _____. "The Double Past in Korean." *Foundations of Language* 12(1975):529–536. A breakthrough in the treatment of the double past in Korean. A persuasive argument is presented for treating the second element of the *ŏss-ŏss* sequence as the "experiential-contrastive" aspect rather than a tense.

05-173. KIM, Soon-Ham Park. *A Transformational Analysis of Negation in Korean.* Seoul: Paekhap Ch'ulp'an-sa, 1967. Originally a PhD dissertation, University of Michigan, 1967. 167 pp. Abstracted in *DA* 28(7)(January 1968): 2666-A. The first major study of negation in Korean within the framework of generative-transformational grammar. The author's distinction between sentence and constituent negation is valid.

05-174. _____. "On the Prefixal Negatives in Korean." *Language Research* (Seoul), 5(1)(1969):1–17. A slightly revised version of a portion of Kim's dissertation. The first systematic account of a constituent negation in contrast with a sentence negation. The distinction between the constituent and sentence negation in terms of the scope of application is well motivated. Sample lexicon and derivations are provided.

05-175. KIM, Tae Han. "Ross's Coordinate Structure Constraint in Korean." *Ŏmunhak* (Seoul), 33(1975):145–146.

05-176. KIM, Wha-Chun. "The Theory of Anaphora in Korean Syntax." PhD dissertation, MIT, 1976.

05-177. LEE, Chungmin. "Presupposition of Existence of Theme for Verbs of Change (in Korean and English)." *Foundations of Language* 9(4)(1973):384–388. An extract from Lee's dissertation (05-178). In this highly condensed and technical paper, Lee presents an interesting and convincing argument for the existence of underlying inchoative for every occurrence of causative.

05-178. _____. *Abstract Syntax and Korean with Reference to English.* Seoul: Pan Korea (Pŏmhan) Book Corporation, 1974. Originally a PhD dissertation, Indiana University, 1973. 196 pp. Abstracted in *DAI* 34(8)(February 1974):5146-47-A. This monograph contains an abstract, highly sophisticated, and technical exposition of a variety of topics of current interest. Lee critically reexamines illocution, modality, and implicature along the line of pragmatics. He presents a revealing analysis of the Korean honorific system, reflexivization, causative, passive, and inchoative. His strong claim that both lexical and periphrastic causatives can be derived from the identical abstract structure remains an open question. (See Patterson, 05-200). Lee's analysis of the irregular passive is perceptive and revealing. Up-to-date bibliography.

05-179. _____. "The Korean Modality in the Speech Act." *Working Papers in Linguistics* 2(1975). University of Michigan.

05-180. _____. "Cases for Psychological Verbs in Korean." *Ŏnŏ* (Linguistic journal of Korea), 1(1)(1976):256–296.

05-181. LEE, Hong-Bae. *A Study of Foreign Syntax.* Seoul: Pan Korea (Pŏmhan) Book Corporation, 1970. 229 pp. Originally a PhD dissertation, Brown University, 1970. Abstracted in *DAI* 31(2)(June 1971):6581-A. Contains chapters on performatives, complementation, negation, and causation flanked by introduction and concluding remarks. Lee's theoretical orientation is generative-transformational, and he specifically introduces Ross's performance hypothesis to the study of Korean syntax for the first time. The most interesting description is the section dealing with sentence endings and speech levels and the honorific system. The description of complementation

is essentially correct, but his treatment of complementizers is problematic. The chapter on negation is revealing but inconclusive (see 05-182). Lee's discussion of the causative is limited to lexical causative and formalization of generative rules. See the review (in Korean) by Suh Cheong-soo in *Language Research* (Seoul), 8(1)(1972):147–166.

05-182. _____. "On Negation in Korean." *Language Research* (Seoul), 6(2)(1970):33–59. A chapter from Lee's PhD dissertation (05-181). It contains a critical review of previous literature and his new proposal to treat negation as object NP complementation.

05-183. _____. "The Category of Mood in Korean Transformational Grammar." *Language Research* (Seoul), 7(1) (1971):53–78. Lee discusses constraints on the occurrences of mood morphemes (sentence endings) and problems of base-generated category of mood in embedded sentences.

05-184. _____. "Problems in the Description of Korean Negation." *Language Research* (Seoul), 8(2)(1972):60–75.

05-185. _____. "Notes on Pronouns, Reflexives, and Pronominalization." *Language Research* (Seoul), 12(2) (1976):253–263.

05-186. LEE, Hong-Bae and E. R. MAXWELL. "Performatives in Korean." In *Papers from 6th Meeting of Chicago Linguistic Society.* Chicago: Chicago Linguistic Society, 1970.

05-187. LEE, Hyun Bok. "A Study of Korean Syntax." PhD dissertation, School of Oriental and African Studies, University of London, 1969. 344 pp.

05-188. LEE, Keedong. "Lexical Causatives in Korean." *Language Research* (Seoul), 11(1)(1975):17–24.

05-189. _____. "Arguments against Lexicalization: With Reference to Deadjectival Causatives in Korean." *Ŏnŏ* (Linguistic journal of Korea), 1(1)(1976):237–255.

05-190. _____. "Auxiliary Verbs and Evaluative Viewpoints." *Ŏnŏ* (Linguistic journal of Korea), 1(2)(1976): 47–69.

05-191. LEE, Maeng Sung. "Nominalization in Korean." PhD dissertation, University of Pennsylvania, 1967. Published as supplement to *Language Research* (Seoul), 4(1) (1968). The first systematic study of nominalization in Korean. It deals with pseudo-cleft sentence formation, a type of topicalization, and adverbialization as well. Lee provides a detailed list of verbs classified according to their operands and identifies four types of complementizers (nominalizers)—*kŏs, m, ki,* and *chi*—and six types of nominalized constructions based on their formal characteristics.

05-192. NAM, Ki Shim. "An Analysis of True Contractions and Quasi-Contractions of Quotative Verb Forms in

Korean.'' *Kyemyŏng Nonch'ong* 4(1967):129–151. Taegu: Kyemyŏng University. Contains many interesting examples and useful information on contracted forms involving the quotative marker *ko*.

05-193. OH, Choon-Kyu. ''Spurious Counterexamples to the Complex NP Constraint Including a 'Variably Crazy Rule' in Korean Syntax.'' *Working Papers in Linguistics* 2(9)(1970):105–124. Department of Linguistics, University of Hawaii. An interesting account of Korean counterexamples to Ross's complex NP constraint. Oh discusses the relatedness between relativization and topicalization in processes in Korean.

05-194. _____. ''On the Negation of Korean.'' *Language Research* (Seoul), 7(2)(1971):45–66. An article with cogent arguments to present a new hypothesis on Korean negation. Oh discusses three possible approaches to the question: (1) separate underlying structures for two types of negation (05-215, 216); (2) the neg-transportation approach (05-181, 182); (3) his own neg-incorporation theory.

05-195. _____. ''Aspects of Korean Syntax: Quantification, Relativization, Topicalization, and Negation.'' *Working Papers in Linguistics* 3(6) (1971). Department of Linguistics, University of Hawaii. Originally a PhD dissertation, University of Hawaii, 1971. The first wholesale application of the generative semantic approach to analysis of Korean. Oh's treatment of quantification is interesting, but the syntactic support for his argument is weak. Oh claims that both restrictive and unrestrictive relative clauses are derived from underlying conjunctions. Oh's analysis of topicalization is innovative and sheds new light on the age-old problem of choice between *nŭn* and *i/ka*. His hypothesis on negation is most interesting and better than those of his predecessors but not without weaknesses of its own. See Eung-Do Cook, ''Notes on Oh's Analysis of Korean,'' *Working Papers in Linguistics* 3(8)(1971): 55–63 (Department of Linguistics, University of Hawaii); and Oh's ''Comments on Cook's Note,'' ibid., pp. 65–75.

05-196. _____. ''Topicalization in Korean: NIN vs. KA (Comparable to Japanese WA vs. GA).'' *Papers in Linguistics* 5(4)(1972):624–659.

05-197. PARK, Byung-Soo. *Complement Structures in Korean: A Syntactic Study of the Verb ''ha.''* Seoul: Kwangmunsa, 1974. Originally a PhD dissertation, University of Pittsburgh, 1972. 166 pp. This is a comprehensive treatment of the verb *ha* as a higher predicate requiring various sentential complements. Also included in the discussion are subject and object NP complementation

associated with incomplete nouns like *tŭs, kŏs, moyang, ch'ŏk* plus *ha*. Park speculates on the relation between direct and indirect discourse and concludes that indirect discourse is an instance of VP complementation. Finally, he touches upon the question of sentence endings (declarative, interrogative, and so on) and argues against a performative approach.

05-198. _____. ''On the Multiple Subject Construction in Korean.'' *Linguistics* 100(1973):63–76. An ambitious attempt to challenge the theoretical adequacy of the phrase structure rules of Chomsky and the case frames of Fillmore on the ground that their frameworks do not readily accommodate ''multiple subject'' construction in Korean. Park's confusion of the deep and surface case relationship, however, casts doubt on the validity of his new proposal.

05-199. _____. ''The Korean Verb *ha* and Verb Complementation.'' *Language Research* (Seoul), 10(1)(1974):46–82. A slightly revised and abridged version of chap. 2 of Park's dissertation (05-197).

05-200. PATTERSON, Betty Soon-Ju. ''A Study of Korean Causatives.'' *Working Papers in Linguistics* 6(4)(1974): 1–52. Department of Linguistics, University of Hawaii. Contains a critical review of previous studies of both a theoretical and descriptive nature. A perceptive treatment of the subject that differentiates two types of causative on syntactic and semantic grounds. The real contribution of Patterson's thesis is her analysis of case markers and their roles in causative construction. A good up-to-date bibliography.

05-201. REE, (Joe) Jung-no. ''Does Korean Have Relative Clauses?'' *Papers in Linguistics* 3(1)(1970):147–160.

05-202. _____. *Topics in Korean Syntax with Notes to Japanese.* Seoul: Yonsei University Press, 1974. 117 pp. A revised publication of Ree's doctoral dissertation: ''Some Aspects of Korean Syntax,'' Indiana University, 1969; abstracted in *DAI* 30(3)(September 1969):1160-A. An abstract discussion of syntax and semantics of two markers in Korean: subject and topic markers. After in-depth study of surface distribution of these markers both in simple and complex sentences, Ree speculates on their generative sources. His analysis of ''double subject'' is perceptive and well motivated. Ree also examines various aspects of relativization.

05-203. _____. ''Demonstratives and Number in Korean.'' In Ho-min Sohn (ed.), *The Korean Language.* Honolulu: Center for Korean Studies, University of Hawaii, 1975. Deals with the deictic uses of Korean demonstratives and the form *ku* with regard to anaphoric reference. It also touches upon the relationship between the demonstratives and plural marking.

05-204. SHIBATANI, M. "Lexical versus Periphrastic Causatives in Korean." *Journal of Linguistics* 9(1973): 281–298. The author argues against Yang's claim (05-233) that both lexical (suffixal) and periphrastic (phrasal) causatives are synonymous. He critically examines the claims of generative semanticists and counters their position by presenting contradictory evidence from Korean.

05-205. _____. "On the Nature of Synonymy in Causative Expressions." *Language Research* (Seoul), 11(2)(1975): 267–274.

05-206. _____. "Relational Grammar and Korean Syntax." *Language Research* (Seoul), 12(2)(1976):241–251.

05-207. SOHN, Ho-min. "Coherence in Korean 'Auxiliary' Verb Construction." *Language Research* (Seoul), 9(2)(1973):239–251. Sohn demonstrates that a similarity exists between auxiliary and main verbs which take a sentential complement. He enumerates at the same time many important differences between the auxiliary and main verbs on syntactic as well as semantic grounds.

05-208. _____. "A Re-examination of 'Auxiliary' Verb Constructions in Korean." *Working Papers in Linguistics* 5(3)(1973):63–88. Department of Linguistics, University of Hawaii. An expanded version of the preceding entry. Sohn adds some important justifications for treating the auxiliary as a "pure" complement verb.

05-209. _____. "Modals and Speaker-Hearer Perspective in Korean." *Papers in Linguistics* 7(1974):493–520. A lucid and perceptive analysis of Korean modals associated with the speaker and the hearer within the framework of generative semantics. Sohn's original contribution lies in his semantic analysis of the retrospective -*ti*/-*tŏ*.

05-210. _____. "Case Incorporation in English Verbs with Reference to Korean Structure." *Working Papers in Linguistics* 6(4)(1974):53–72. Department of Linguistics, University of Hawaii. Sohn compares semantic structures of English and Korean verbs in terms of case incorporation with the framework of case grammar. An illuminating discussion of double (or multiple) subject construction in Korean is touched upon with great insight. His exploratory discussion of English and Korean verbs sheds new light on surface differences between the two languages and points to their deeper similarity.

05-211. _____. "Case Incorporation in English Verbs with Reference to Korean Structure." *English Language and Literature* (Seoul), 46(1974):431–455.

05-212. _____. "Retrospect in Korean." *Language Research* (Seoul), 11(1)(1975):87–103. An original analysis of semantic components of the syntactic verbal affix -*tŏ* as consisting of "reporter" (speaker/hearer), "past" (tense), and "perceive" (abstract predicate). Sohn elucidates many puzzling features associated with "retrospective" such as first person subject constraint, the relation between tense of events (of embedded sentence), and that of -*tŏ* (of an observer) as well as its semantic contents. One of the finest generative semantic studies on Korean. The best formal characterization of "retrospective" in Korean.

05-213. _____. "Semantics of Compound Verbs in Korean." *Ŏnŏ* (Linguistic journal of Korea), 1(1)(1976):142–150.

05-214. _____. "Goal and Source in Korean Locatives with Reference to Japanese." *Eoneohag* (Journal of Linguistic Society of Korea), 2(1977):73–98.

05-215. SONG, Seok Choong. "Some Transformational Rules in Korean." PhD dissertation, Indiana University, 1967. 254 pp. Abstracted in *DA* 28(9)(March 1968): 3660-A. One of the earliest PhD dissertations on Korean by a native speaker. Generative-transformational in approach, it covers fairly comprehensive topics such as negation, passive and causativization, and quantity phrase. Song's new hypothesis on negation has touched off a controversy that continues today.

05-216. _____. "A Note on Negation in Korean." *Linguistics* 76(1971):59–76. A slightly revised version of a portion of the chapter on negation in Song's dissertation (05-215). Song argues on syntactic grounds that two types of allegedly synonymous negative sentences in Korean have different deep structures. The crux of his argument hinges upon the identification of *chi* as a negative counterpart of the nominalizer *ki*.

05-217. _____. "On the Disappearing 'Nominative Marker' in Korean." *Papers in Linguistics* 5(3)(1972):434–453.

05-218. _____. "Some Negative Remarks on Negation in Korean." *Language Research* (Seoul), 9(2)(1973): 252–263. Song provides semantic grounds for differentiating two types of negative sentences in Korean.

05-219. _____. "Rare Plural Marking and Ubiquitous Plural Marker in Korean." In *Papers from the 11th Regional Meeting*. Chicago: Chicago Linguistic Society, 1975. Also published in *Language Research* (Seoul), 11(1)(1975): 77–86. Deals with two disparate aspects of plural marking in Korean. First, Song challenges the traditional descriptions that plural marking is optional and presents evidence for a case of obligatory plural marking. Second, he discusses a ubiquitous plural marker, which invariably signals plurality of a subject noun although it actually occurs in various positions in a sentence.

05-220. _____. "A Suspicious Analysis of the Suspective Morpheme and Its Homonyms." *Language Research* (Seoul), 11(1)(1975):1–8. A critical examination of the Korean form *chi*, which Song considers a homophonous realization of four distinct morphemes on syntactic grounds.

05-221. _____. "On an Abbreviation Phenomenon in Korean." *Ŏnŏ* (Linguistic journal of Korea), 1(2)(1976): 70–88.

05-222. SUK, Kyoung-Jing. "The Syntax of Sentence Enders [in Korean]." *Language Research* (Seoul), 12(1)(1976): 99–119.

05-223. TAGASHIRA, Yoshiko. "Relative Clauses in Korean." In *The Chicago WHICH Hunt.* Chicago: Chicago Linguistic Society, 1972.

05-224. YANG, Dong-Whee. "'Double Subject' Verbs in Korean." *Working Papers in Linguistics* 10(1971):231–244. Ohio State University. Yang makes an attempt to account for the "double subject" construction within the framework of Fillmore's case grammar. "Double subject" verbs are classified into four categories in accordance with combinations of cases they occur with.

05-225. _____. "'Island Constraints' and Pro-deletion Phenomena in Korean." *Language Research* (Seoul), 9(2)(1973):144–160. An interesting and plausible account of Korean counterexamples that apparently violate Ross's "island constraints."

05-226. _____. "Inner and Outer Locatives in Korean." *Language Research* (Seoul), 9(1)(1973):27–45. Yang tries to show that Korean *e* "locative," *e* "directional," *esŏ* "locative," and *esŏ* "source" are a single element *E* on an abstract level of analysis.

05-227. _____. "Topicalization and Relativization in Korean." PhD dissertation, Indiana University, 1973. 220 pp. Abstracted in *DAI* 34(3)(September 1973):1270-A. Yang discusses three topics of current interest: pronominalization, topicalization, and relativization. He claims that topical sentence and relative clause structures have similar underlying structures and that both are subject to the same constraints. He also argues against a straight deletion and advocates conjunction of pro-formation and pro-deletion instead. Lastly, he speculates on a universal theory of relativization.

05-228. _____. "Korean Negation Revisited." *Ŏnŏ* (Linguistic journal of Korea), 1(1)(1976):183–217.

05-229. _____. "On Complementizers in Korean." *Ŏnŏ* (Linguistic journal of Korea), 1(2)(1976):18–46.

05-230. _____. "Pragmantax of Modality in Korean." *Ŏnŏ* (Linguistic journal of Korea), 2(2)(1977):85–96.

05-231. _____. "Instrumental Causation [in Korean]." *Language Research* (Seoul), 13(1)(1977):87–90.

05-232. YANG, In-Seok. "Double Modality in Korean." *Language Research* (Seoul), 7(1)(1971):23–36. Yang presents a clear and plausible analysis of double modality in "filtered quotative" (*nŭn-ta-n-ta, nŭn-ta-p-ni-ta,* and so forth) through Ross's performative approach.

05-233. _____. *A Korean Syntax: Case Markers, Delimiters, Complementation, and Relativization.* Seoul: Paekhapsa, 1972. Originally a PhD dissertation, University of Hawaii, 1972. Also published as *Working Papers in Linguistics* 4(6) (1972), Department of Linguistics, University of Hawaii. The first major treatment of many interesting aspects of Korean syntax and semantics within the framework of Fillmore's case grammar. Fillmore's treatment of causatives is still controversial. Yang's analysis of the verb *swipta* is perceptive. Moreover, his distinction between verbs of self-judgment *(choh, silh, kippu, ch'up)* and their transitivized construction with *-ha* in terms of role structure of the subject is insightful.

05-234. _____. "Semantics of Delimiters in Korean." *Language Research* (Seoul), 9(2)(1973):84–121. An illuminating discussion of the sociopsychosemantics of Korean delimiters *(nŭn, ya, to, na, lato).* Yang elucidates elusive semantic contents of these forms in terms of presuppositions, assertions, and implication.

05-235. _____. "Two Causative Forms in Korean." *Language Research* (Seoul), 10(1)(1974):83–117. A defense of Yang's earlier view that lexical and periphrastic causatives are synonymous against Shibatani's challenge (see 05-204). He offers five syntactic arguments to demonstrate his synonymy hypothesis against the nonsynonymy hypothesis of his opponent.

05-236. _____. "Semantics of Korean Causation." *Foundations in Language* 14(1)(1976):55–87.

05-237. _____. "Progressive and Perfective Aspects in Korean." *Ŏnŏ* (Linguistic journal of Korea), 2(1)(1977): 25–40.

HISTORICAL AND COMPARATIVE STUDIES

Genealogy was one of the first questions raised by Westerners when they (primarily missionaries) discovered Korean in the nineteenth century. Suggestions, some incidental and semischolarly, linked Korean to such diverse groups as Uralic, Altaic, Indo-European, Dravidian, Malayo-Polynesian, Japanese, and Ainu. German scholars (Eckardt, 05-238; Koppelmann, 05-261) had Korean belonging to "Indo-germanisch," while Japanese scholars (Hattori, 05-259; Kanazawa, 05-239) related Korean to Japanese. Hulbert (05-260) was the lone force behind the Korean-Dravidian hypothesis. Today most scholars follow Polivanov (05-242) and Ramstedt (05-243) in granting a filial relationship between Korean and Altaic on the one hand and in recognizing a fraternal affinity with Japanese on the other—an affinity which has found firmer ground in recent years (see Ki-Moon Lee, 05-241; Martin, 05-264, 265; Miller, 05-266, 267).

Naturally, historical studies of Korean have been most extensively done in Korea by native scholars, and the number of items cited here does not reflect the amount of knowledge gained on the history of Korean. It must be mentioned, however, that even in Korea most historical studies have dealt with the post–Middle Korean period. Scarcity of documents makes it difficult and often impossible to go beyond the fifteenth century.

GENEALOGY

05-238. ECKARDT, A. *Koreanisch und Indogermanisch: Untersuchungen über die Zugehörigkeit des koreanischen zur indogermanischen Sprachfamilie.* Heidelberg: Julius Groos Verlag, 1966. 240 pp.

05-239. KANAZAWA, Shōsaburō. *The Common Origin of the Japanese and Korean Languages.* 2nd ed. Tokyo: 1910. This work laid the foundation for the comparative study of Korean and Japanese. Comparison of words and grammatical forms constitute the main study. The author's etymologies, however, are nothing more than probable candidates and have not been established on systematic sound-meaning correspondence relations.

05-240. KIM, Bo-gyŏm. "Gehört die koreanische Sprache zur altaischen Sprachfamilie?" *Hanguk Munhwa Yŏn'guwŏn Nonch'ong* (Seoul), 2(1)(1960):115–175. Ehwa Women's University. Also published in *Koreana Quarterly* 5(4) (1963):97–126 and 6(1)(1964):97–128. Kim doubts that Korean belongs to the Altaic language family.

05-241. LEE, Ki-Moon. "A Genetic View on Japanese." *Chōsen Gahukō* 27(1963):94–105. Lee demonstrates that the extant vocabulary of the Koguryŏ language shows great similarities with that of Old Japanese; he argues that this finding bridges the gap of the great divergency between Altaic on the one hand and Korean and Japanese on the other.

05-242. POLIVANOV, E. D. "K voprosu o rodstvennykh otnosheniyakh koreiskogo i 'altaiskikh' yazykov [On the problem of a genetic relationship between Korean and "Altaic" languages]." *Izvestiya Akademii Nauk* (Moscow), series 6, 21(15–17)(1927):1195–1204.

05-243. RAMSTEDT, G. J. "Über die Stellung des Koreanischen." *Journal de la Société Finno-Ougrienne* 55(1951):47–58.

05-244. RUDNEV, A. "Über die Zugehörigkeit des Koreanischen zur altaischen Sprachgruppe." *Finnisch-ugrische Forschungen* 27(1941):55–60.

05-245. TSCHE, Djon Chu [Ch'oe Chŏng-hu]. "Einige Fragen zur Entstehung und Entwicklung der koreanischen Sprache." *Wissenschaftliche Zeitschrift der Humboldt-Universität* (Berlin), 10(1961):217–229.

Historical Studies

05-246. ANSELMO, Valerio. "Armonica consonantica nel coreano antico." *Annali, Istituto Universitario Orientale* (Naples), 33(1973):61–76.

05-247. CHEUN, Sang-Buom. *Phonological Aspects of Late Middle Korean.* Seoul: Pan-Korean (Pŏmhan) Book Corporation, 1975. Originally a PhD dissertation, Indiana University, 1975. 227 pp. Deals in depth with vowel harmony, hiatus as shown in endings, and consonant clusters in Late Middle Korean.

05-248. LEE, Ki-Moon. "On the Breaking of *i in Korean." *Asea yŏn'gu* [Asiatic research bulletin], 2(2)(1959): 131–137. Seoul: Korea University.

05-249. LEE, Sang Oak. "Conspiracy in Korean Phonology Revisited: As Applied to Historical Data." *Studies in Linguistic Sciences* 7(2)(1977):1–23. University of Illinois at Urbana-Champaign.

05-250. MÁRTONFI, F. "On Some Problems of a Generative Phonology of Middle Sino-Korean." *Acta Orientalia Acad. Sci. Hung.* (Budapest), 26(1972):299–307.

05-251. MOON, Yang-Soo. "A Phonological History of Korean." PhD dissertation, University of Texas at Austin, 1974. 193 pp. Abstracted in *DAI* 35(1)(July 1974):433-A. Moon treats the development of Korean phonology from the fifteenth century to the present. He postulates *ɒ* (the so-called *arae a*) as an unround mid-back vowel and speculates that *ɒ* disappeared because it alone lacked the *long* counterpart. In consonants, Moon sets up /b, d, z, g/ as phonemes to explain the verb morphophonemics (the so-called *pyŏnch'ŭk yong'ŏn*). Moon suspects that tones in Middle Korean were redundant, the length being the primary distinctive feature.

05-252. RAMSEY, S. Robert. "Middle Korean *W-, z,* and *t/l-* Verb Stems." *Language Research* (Seoul), 11(1) (1975):59–67. Argues that *W, z,* and *t/l* developed from the lenition of *p, s, t* respectively and that these verb stems should be reconstructed with a stem-final vowel.

05-253. _____. "Accent and Morphology in Korean Dialects: A Descriptive and Historical Study.'' PhD dissertation, Yale University, 1975. 308 pp. From a comparative study of Middle Korean and modern Hamgyŏng and Kyŏngsang dialects, Ramsey supports the hypothesis that certain consonants in the central dialect arose through lenition and that there are systematic correspondences in the pitch patterns of the three. Particular attention is given to verb morphology, and insightful solutions are proposed for many accentual and segmental irregularities.

05-254. ROSÉN, Staffan. *A Study on Tones and Tonemarks in Middle Korean.* Stockholm: Institute of Oriental Languages, Stockholm University, 1974. 147 pp. The Middle Korean tone system is divided into four subtypes:

    I. Tone system of pure Korean reference
        Ia. Standardized (represented by early *chŏng'ŭm* documents)
        Ib. Nonstandardized (represented by later Middle Korean documents)
    II. Tone system of Sino-Korean reference
        IIa. Standardized (represented by *Tongguk-chŏng'ŭm*)
        IIb. Nonstandardized (represented by *Hunmong-chahoe*)

Rosén suggests a long preexistence of tone in Korean and examines traces of tonality in the Silla language. He also compares the Middle Korean tone system with that of the contemporary Kyŏngsang-do dialect and argues that the Middle Korean tone system may be reduced to two tonemes: high *(ko-sŏng)* and low *(p'yŏng-sŏng),* the rising tone *(sang-sŏng)* being the juxtaposition of the two in the sequence low-high.

05-255. SONG, Seok Choong. ''Synchronic Alternation and Diachronic Change.'' In Adam Makkai and Valerie B. Makkai (eds.), *The Second Lacus Forum.* Columbia, S.C.: Hornbeam Press, 1975. Song speculates that two coexisting morphemes *ki* and *ti* in Middle Korean merged into a single morpheme when their distribution became complementary. The palatalization process converts *ti* to *chi* to produce the alternation of *ki* and *chi* in Modern Korean. This work constitutes a historical backdrop supportive of his hypothesis on negation in Korean (05-215, 216, 218).

05-256. TOH, Soo-Hee. ''Glide *y* in Korean Historical Phonology.'' *Studies in Linguistic Sciences* 7(2)(1977):178–183. University of Illinois at Urbana-Champaign.

Comparative Studies

05-257. ASTON, W. G. ''A Comparative Study of the Japanese and Korean Languages.'' *Journal of Royal Asiatic Society of Great Britain and Ireland* (London), new series, 11(3)(August 1879):317–364. This article, the first to suggest the genetic relationship of Korean and Japanese, later motivated Japanese scholars (like Kanazawa; 05-239) to undertake the comparative study of Korean and Japanese.

05-258. ECKARDT, André. ''Altkorea und die Tocharer.'' *Sinologica* 9(1967):96–107. Archaeological, historical, cultural, and linguistic relations between the two tongues.

05-259. HATTORI, Sh. ''The Relationship of Japanese to the Ryukyu, Korean, and Altaic Languages.'' *Transactions of Asiatic Society of Japan,* series 3, 1(1948):101–133.

05-260. HULBERT, H. B. *A Comparative Grammar of the Korean Language and the Dravidian Dialects of India.* Seoul: 1905. Largely on the basis of typological similarities, Hulbert argues that Korean and Dravidian are genetically related. Hulbert's examples of lexical similarities are accidental and spurious.

05-261. KOPPELMANN, D. H. *Die Eurasische Sprachfamilie: Indogermanische, Koreanisch und Verwandtes.* Heidelberg: 1933. See reviews by Charles Haguenauer in *Journal Asiatique* 228(1936):346 and by Ogura Shimpei in *Gengo Kenkyū* 1(1939).

05-262. KWON, Hyogmyon. ''Das koreanische Verbum vergleichen mit dem altaischen und japonischen Verbum.'' Dissertation, University of Munich, 1962. 144 pp.

05-263. LEE, Ki-Moon. ''A Comparative Study of Manchu and Korean.'' *Ural-Altaische Jahrbücher* 30(1958):104–120.

05-264. MARTIN, Samuel E. ''Lexical Evidence Relating Korean to Japanese.'' *Language* 42(1966):185–251. A meticulous study surpassing Kanazawa (05-239) and Ramstedt (05-104) in many respects. The article also includes some pertinent remarks on Middle Korean phonology (pp. 193–194).

05-265. _____. ''Grammatical Evidence Relating Korean to Japanese.'' In *Proceedings of the 8th Congress of Anthropological and Ethnological Sciences.* Tokyo and Kyoto: 1968. Martin compares Korean *-m, -n,* and *-l* to Ryukyuan *-m, -n,* and *-r,* assuming that these represent proto-Japanese verb endings. Martin suggests that Korean genitive *-uy* and nominative *-i* may have a common origin.

05-266. MILLER, Roy A. ''Old Japanese Phonology and the Korean-Japanese Relationship.'' *Language* 43(1967):278–302.

05-267. _____. *Japanese and the Other Altaic Languages.* Chicago: University of Chicago Press, 1971. There are relevant chapters and sections on Korean. See review by J. J. Chew in *Language* 45(1969):203–205.

05-268. SOHN, John Young. ''A Study of Grammatical Cases of Korean, Japanese and Other Major Altaic Languages.'' PhD dissertation, Indiana University, 1973. 432 pp. Abstracted in *DAI* 34(7)(January 1974):4235-36-A. The first systematic and most comprehensive study of grammatical cases in Korean and Japanese with a chapter on a comparative survey of the Altaic cases. The model of description is Fillmore's case grammar. Sohn discusses divergent (more forms for a single function) and converging (a single reflex for more than one function) relations and explores topics of current interest (topicalization, causative, passive, psych-movement) in depth.

05-269. VOS, Frits. *Volken van Een Stam? Engine Beschouwingen over de problemen van een Koreans-Japanse Taalen Kultuur- verwantschap* [People of one stock? An investigation into the problem of Korean-Japanese linguistic and cultural relationship]. The Hague: Mouton, 1950.

DIALECTOLOGY AND SOCIOLINGUISTICS

Most studies in Korean dialects are fragmentary, and as yet there is no full-scale dialect atlas. For a general survey, see Ogura (05-272).

The Korean War, mass communication, and a mobile society have been obliterating dialect boundaries, but six major dialect areas are still recognized: central (Seoul and Kyŏnggi), northwest (P'yŏng'an), northeast (Hamgyŏng), southwest (Chŏlla), southeast (Kyŏngsang), and Cheju. One may also cite Ch'ungch'ŏng, Kangwŏn, and Hwanghae provinces as distinct dialect areas, although these are often regarded as belonging to the central dialect. The most striking of them all is the Cheju dialect, due to its long geographical separation from the mainland. Because of the belief that this conservative dialect holds a key to identification of several sounds that have been either lost or drastically changed in the mainland dialects, it has attracted the most attention in Korea.

Standardization of Korean, though only a recent process, has been quite successful despite minor problems and variations that still exist (see Martin, 05-277). A major problem will arise, however, if and when the unification of North and South is achieved. The long separation with independent language policies has already given rise to considerable discrepancies between the two "political" dialects. For discussion and examples, see Kim (05-026).

Sociolinguistics is still in its infancy in Korea. Only recently have serious studies been made (Choi, 05-279; Hwang, 05-281).

Dialectology

05-270. LEE, Pyong-geun. *Phonological and Morphological Studies in a Kyŏnggi Subdialect.* Seoul: T'ongmun'gwan, 1970.

05-271. MAZUR, Yu. N. "Zametki po koreiskoi dialektolo-

gii [A treatise on Korean dialectology]." In *Koreiskii yazyk.* Moscow: Akademiya Nauk, 1961. (See 05-010.)

05-272. OGURA, Shimpei. *The Outline of the Korean Dialects.* Memoirs of the Research Department of Tōyō Bunko, no. 12. Tokyo: 1940. Summary in English of the results of Ogura's investigations for more than a decade into Korean dialects. The only study of its kind available in English.

05-273. PAIK, Keum-ju. "Tonal Characteristics of Kyŏngsang Dialect." *Sogang Review* (Seoul), 1(1973):18–27. Paik examines whether the tones in Kyŏngsang dialect are true tones like Chinese tones or merely pitch accents like accents in Japanese. A tentative conclusion: the latter.

05-274. UMEDA, Hiroyuki. "On the Phonemes of Cheju Dialect of Korean." *Nagoya University Thesis Collection* 22(1960):17–46.

Language Standardization

05-275. ANDERSON, P. S. "Korean Language Reform." *Modern Language Journal* 32(1948):508–511.

05-276. KIM, Min-su. "The Modernization of the Korean Language." *Asea yŏn'gu* 6(2)(1963):1–4. Seoul: Asiatic Research Institute, Korea University.

05-277. MARTIN, Samuel E. "Korean Standardization: Problems, Observations, and Suggestions." *Ural-Altaische Jahrbücher* 40(1968):85–114. Martin makes many pertinent observations about the variant forms and their standardization in Korea. Discussions include not only variant Korean spellings but also different proposals of romanization from McCune-Reischauer to the Yale system. Some suggestions: that the infinitives of bases ending in *e, eŏ, wi,* and *we* be written in unshortened forms like *pe-ŏ-sŏ* instead of *pe-sŏ;* that full, not contracted, forms of the copula and *ha-* be written, like *an-ha-go* instead of *an-k'o* and *sae-i-da* instead of *sae-da.* Martin contends that there is overdifferentiation in such contrasts as *ŭm-ŭro* (with) versus *ŭ-mŭro* (because of) and *ŭ-mae* (thereupon) versus *ŭ-me* (on——ing), but he wants to keep distinct the three endings: *ŭmyŏn, -ŭmyŏ-n(ŭn),* and *-ŭmyŏn-ŭn.*

05-278. NIKOLSKII, L. B. "Iz istorii stanovleniya nacional'nogo literaturnogo yazyka v koree [On the history of the formation of the standard national language in Korea]." *Problemy vostokovedeniya* [Oriental problems], 6(1960):59–69.

Sociolinguistics

05-279. CHOI, Young-soon Park. "Honorification and Levels of Deference in Korean: A Developmental Sociolinguistic Study in Communicative Competence." PhD dissertation, University of Illinois at Urbana-Champaign, 1977.

05-280. DREDGE, Paul. "Social Rules of Speech in Korean: The Views of a Comic Strip Character." *Korea Journal* 16(1)(1976):1–14.

05-281. HWANG, Juck-ryoon. *Role of Sociolinguistics in Foreign Language Education with Reference to Korean and English Terms of Address and Levels of Deference.* Seoul: Tower Press, 1976. Originally a PhD dissertation, University of Texas at Austin, 1975. See review (in Korean:) by Kyoung-jing Suk in *Ŏnŏ* (Linguistic journal of Korea), 2(1)(1977):171–182.

05-282. JO, Mi-Jeung. "The Retrospective Suffix and Speech Levels of Narration in Korean." *Ŭngyong ŏnŏhak* [Applied linguistics], 8(1976):57–79.

05-283. KIM-RENAUD, Young-Key. "Variation in Korean Negation." *Language Research* (Seoul), 10(2)(1974):1–21. Report of an experiment on the acceptability of two types of negative sentences with variables such as stative/nonstative predicate, monosyllabic/polysyllabic, pure Korean/Sino-Korean vocabulary.

05-284. MARTIN, S. E. "Speech Levels in Japan and Korea." In Dell Hymes (ed.), *Language in Culture and Society.* New York: Harper & Row, 1964.

05-285. SONG, Yo-In. *Translation: Theory and Practice.* Seoul: Dongguk University Press, 1975. The multifaceted cross-lingual process of equivalence-matching is analyzed semantically, syntactically, stylistically, and culturally, as well as from the standpoint of discourse analysis. Song draws illustrative data primarily from Korean and English.

05-286. _____. "Some Implications of *Weltanschauung* in Translation Theory with Special Reference to English and Korean." *Ŏnŏ* (Linguistic journal of Korea), 1(1)(1976): 89–120.

WRITING SYSTEMS

The elegance, simplicity, and ingenuity of *han'gŭl* have been admired by all. One linguist, in fact, has called it "the world's best alphabet" (Vos; 05-320:31). Worthy of mention are a series of articles by F. Z. Kim (05-293, 296) on the history of the Korean alphabet and by Ledyard (05-300) arguing that the shapes of several original *han'gŭl* letters were imitations of the *hPhags-pa* (or square) script of Middle Mongolian. See Cho (05-288), however, for an interesting counterargument using x-ray technique. The best and most compact overall history of the Korean writing system is the English synopsis at the end of Lee's book (05-304).

Romanization of Korean is in a quite congested, if not confused, state. Currently, there are four major competing systems in use with little prospect of unification in sight: (1) the Yale system (used by Korean linguists in North America); (2) the McCune-Reischauer system (used by most social scientists in the United States); (3) the South Korean system; and (4) the North Korean system. See the chart and discussions in Martin (05-277) and in Martin, Chang, and Lee (05-322). This is no place to discuss the relative merits of different systems except to say that my personal preference is the Yale system. There is no standard Koreanization of roman scripts. For a suggestion, see Daniel Jones' letter to the late Hyon-bai Choe, published in translation by Chin-W. Kim in *Han'gŭl* 124(1959): 7–24.

The life of Chinese characters in Korea is a long and strange one. For a discussion of their status in Korean and the rationale behind the movement to abolish the use of *hantcha* in Korea, see Kim (05-022).

The Korean Alphabet *(han'gŭl)*

05-287. CHANG, Duk-sun. "Hangul—A Historical Review." *Korea Journal* 1(4)(1961):6–8.

05-288. CHO, Sek Yen K. *Verification of the Relationship between the Graphic Shapes and Articulatory-Acoustic Correlates in the Korean Consonants of 1446 (Using Cineradiographic Technique).* Seoul: Tower Press, 1977. 153 pp. Originally a PhD dissertation, State University of New York at Buffalo, 1977. Using cineradiographic data from a male Korean speaker, Cho attempts to support the hypothesis that, in designing the original consonant graphemes of *han'gŭl*, the inventors ensured that each graphic stroke was made to reflect an associated articulatory-acoustic feature.

05-289. ECKARDT, André. "Zum Ursprung der koreanischen Buchstabenschrift." *Zeitschrift für Phonetik* 17(1964/1965):505–513.

05-290. HOPE, E. R. "Letter Shapes in Korean Onmun and Mongol hPhags-pa Alphabets." *Oriens* (Leiden), 10(1) (1959):150–156.

05-291. JUNKER, H. F. J. "Die Umschrift des Koreanischen." *Mitteilungen des Instituts für Orientforschung der deutschen Akademie der Wissenschaften zu Berlin* (Berlin), 2(1)(1954):144–164.

05-292. KHOLODOVICH, A. A. "O proetke reformy koreiskoi ortografii 1949. [On the spelling reform in Korean orthography of 1949]." In *Voprosy koreiskogo i kitaiskogo yazykoznaniya.* Leningrad and Moscow: 1958. (See 05-009.) A criticism of North Korea's ill-fated spelling reform in 1949 in which two obsolete fifteenth-century symbols were revived and four new symbols were created to regularize verb morphology.

05-293. KIM, F. Z. "Printsipy postroeniya koreiskikh grafem [The constructive principles of Korean graphemes]." *Voprosy Yazykoznaniya* (Moscow), 4(1960):85–96. Kim argues that *han'gŭl* letters were shaped after the articulatory configurations assumed in pronouncing the respective letters.

05-294. _____. "Vozniknovenie i ischeznovenie nekotorykh zvukov v koreiskom yazyke [Development and decline of some Korean sounds]." In *Koreiskii yazyk*. Moscow: Akademiya Nauk, 1961. (See 05-010.)

05-295. _____. "Sozdanie koreiskogo zvutovogo pis'ma khunmin chonym [Invention of the Korean alphabet *Hunmin chŏng'ŭm*]." In *Voprosy filologi sbornik statei*. Moscow: 1957.

05-296. _____. "Iz istorii razvitiya koreiskogo alfavitnogo pis'ma khunmin chonym [A history of the development of the Korean alphabet *Hunmin chŏng'ŭm*]." In *Koreiskii yazyk*. Moscow: Akademiya Nauk, 1961. (See 05-010.)

05-297. KIM, Yun-kyung. "Written Language of Korean." *Koreana Quarterly* (Seoul), 1(1)(1959):121–129.

05-298. _____. "Chu Si-kyong and Modernization of Hangul." *Korea Journal* (Seoul), 1(4)(1961):9–10.

05-299. KONTSEVICH, L. R. "Pervyj pamyatnik koreiskoi pis'mennosti (Opyt sostavleniya kriticheskogo teksta perevoda) [The first writings in Korean scripts (a textual criticism)]." *Narody Azii i Afriki* [Asian and African peoples] (Moscow), 4(1965):160–173. Russian translation of *Hunmin chŏng'ŭm* with critical notes, especially on the difference between the *han'gŭl* version *(ŏnhaebon)* and the Chinese version *(hanmunbon)*.

05-300. LEDYARD, Gari Keith. "The Korean Language Reform of 1446: The Origin, Background, and Early History of the Korean Alphabet." PhD dissertation, University of California, Berkeley, 1966. 427 pp. Abstracted in *DA* 27(October 1966):1031-32-A. Extensive bibliography; excellent translations of important historical material. Ledyard argues that the shapes of the half-dozen original letters of *han'gŭl* were imitations of the *hPhags-pa* script of Middle Mongolian.

05-301. LEE, Hi-seung. "The Position of the Hun-Min-Jong-Um in the History of Writing Systems." *Koreana Quarterly* 4(2)(1962):103–109.

05-302. LEE, Jeong-Ho. "A Philosophical Study of the Korean Alphabet." *Chungnam University Thesis Collection* 11(1972).

05-303. _____. *Explanation and Translation of Hunmin-*

chŏng'ŭm. Seoul: Korean Library Science Research Institute, 1973.

05-304. LEE, Ki-Moon. "A Historical Study of the Korean Writing Systems." English synopsis of Lee's *Kugŏ p'yogipŏb ŭi yŏksajŏk yŏn'gu*. Seoul: Han'guk yŏn'guwŏn, 1963.

05-305. LEE, Sang-beck. *The Origin of the Korean Alphabet Hangul According to New Historical Evidence*. Publications series A, no. 2. Seoul: National Museum, 1957.

05-306. LEE, Sung-nyŏng. "Hangul in Comparative Linguistics." *Korea Journal* 1(4)(1961):4–6.

05-307. PULTR, A. and V. Pucek. "Z historie koreského písma [On the history of the Korean script]." *Nový Orient* (Prague), 24(1969):202–208.

05-308. WHANG, Won-Koo. "King Sejong—Versatile Monarch Gives the Nation Own Alphabet." *Korea Journal* 1(4)(1961):11–12.

Romanization

05-309. AHN, Ho-Sam. "The Romanization of the Korean Language." *English Language and Literature* (Seoul), 4(1967): 295–305.

05-310. ANSELMO, Valerio. *La Traslitterazione del Coreano*. Naples: Istituto Universitario Orientale, Seminario di Yamatologica, 1973. 124 pp.

05-311. HAGUENAUER, C. "Système de transcription de l'alphabet Coréen." *Journal Asiatique* 222(1933):145–162.

05-312. KONTSEVICH, L. R. "Pravila peredachi koreiskikh imen, nazavanii i terminov [Rules for transcribing Korean names, titles, and terminology]." In *Pravila izdaniya serii pamyatniki pis'mennosti vostoka*. Moscow: 1966.

05-313. MCCUNE, G. M. and E. O. REISCHAUER. "Romanization of the Korean Language." *Transactions of the Korea Branch of the Royal Asiatic Society* 29(1939):1–55. An abbreviated version was later reprinted in the *Transactions* 38(1961):121–128.

05-314. ZŎNG, In-Sŏb. "The Unified System for the Romanization of Korean." *Chōsen Gahukō* 6(1954):1–28 and 171–198. Also in *Chung-Ang University Thesis Collection* (Seoul), 5(1961):1–16.

Chinese Characters *(hantcha and idu)*

05-315. ALLOCCO, Vincent Anello. "Phonetic Orthographic Method of Organizing Chinese Characters Used in the Republic of Korea: An Alternative to Rote Memorization." PhD dissertation, US International University, 1972. 185 pp. Abstracted in *DAI* 33(3)(September 1972): 1035-A.

05-316. KIM, Hyŏng-kyu. "Chinese Characters and Korean Language." *Korea Journal* 3(7)(1963):11–13.

05-317. MÁRTONFI, F. "On Sino-Korean Finals." *Acta Orientalia Academiae Scientiarum Hungaricae* (Budapest), 25(1972):83–99.

05-318. TCHEU, Soc-Kiou. "Correspondences phonologiques du sino-coréen à l'ancien chinois." *Langues et Techniques* 1(1972):237–256.

05-319. VOS, Frits. "Korean Writing: The Hyang'ga." In J. K. Yamagiwa and P. V. Hyer (eds.), *Papers of the CIC Far Eastern Language Institute.* Ann Arbor: University of Michigan, 1963.

05-320. _____. "Korean Writing: Idu and Hanglu." In J. K. Yamagiwa and P. V. Hyer (eds.), *Papers of the CIC Far Eastern Language Institute.* Ann Arbor: University of Michigan, 1963.

05-321. YU, Chang-Kyun. "The Systems and Characteristics of Modern Sino-Korean Pronunciations." In R. Jakobson and S. Kawamoto (eds.), *Studies in General and Oriental Linguistics.* Tokyo: TEC Corporation, 1969.

DICTIONARIES

The character of a Korean-English dictionary depends on whether it is compiled for use by Koreans or by English speakers. Not only will the choice of lexical entries be different (no pronunciation guide is necessary for Koreans, for example) but the explanations will tend to be paraphrases for English speakers but equivalent words for Koreans. The best Korean-English dictionary is that prepared by Martin, Lee, and Chang (05-322). There is no English-Korean counterpart.

A standard Korean-Russian dictionary is Kholodovich (05-324), and a standard Russian-Korean dictionary is Usatov, Mazur, and Mozdykov (05-328). It is mentioned in Kontsevich (05-028) that a Korean-Russian dictionary (of about 150,000 entries) has been compiled jointly by the Institute of Asian Peoples of the Soviet Academy of Sciences and Ŏnŏ yŏn'guso (Institute of Linguistic Research) of the Academy of Sciences, Democratic People's Republic of Korea. But no word of publication has yet been received.

Dictionaries of Korean and other Western languages are surprisingly few in number. This section omits recent dictionaries published in Korea for the sake of aiding Koreans learning a foreign language.

Korean and English

05-322. MARTIN, S. E., Y. H. LEE, and S.-U. CHANG. *A Korean-English Dictionary.* New Haven: Yale University Press, 1967. Also Seoul: Minjungsŏqwan, 1968. The best, most comprehensive, and most linguistically oriented dictionary of its kind available today. The introductory section includes a complete description of the Yale romanization system and a set of pronunciation rules by which actual pronunciation forms can be derived from the morphophonemic forms used in lexical entries. Particles, endings, and other bound morphemes are listed individually.

05-323. UNDERWOOD, Joan V. *Concise English-Korean Dictionary.* Rutland, Vt.: Tuttle, 1954. 320 pp. "The 8000 most useful English words and phrases with Korean equivalents in both Roman and Korean letters." See reviews by S. McCune in *Far Eastern Quarterly* 14(2)(1954):128–129; by R. B. Jones in *Journal of American Oriental Society* 74(1954):282; and by F. Vos in *Lingua* 5(1955):306–307.

Korean and Russian

05-324. KHOLODOVICH, A. A. *Koreisko-russkii slovar'* [Korean-Russian dictionary]. Moscow: 1st ed. 1951; 2nd ed. 1958; 3rd ed. 1959. 896 pp. 60,000 entries. Order of entries: *han'gŭl,* Chinese characters if applicable, pronunciation in Russian script, translation. No parts of speech. No vowel length distinction. Some examples in sentences. *Han'gŭl* orthography is according to North Korea's 1954 "New Orthography." See review by L. B. Nikolskii in *Narody Azii i Afriki* 2(1961):214–216.

05-325. KIM, Gi Yun [Gi-yun Kim], Zhen Tser KIM [Yongch'ŏl Kim], and L. N. KARSHINOV. *Russko-koreiskii i koreisko-russkii vneshnetorgovyi slovar'* [Russian-Korean and Korean-Russian commercial dictionary]. Moscow: 1961.

05-326. MAZUR, Yu. N., V. M. MOZDYKOV, and D. M. USATOV. *Kratkii russko-koreiskii slovar'* [A short Russian-Korean dictionary]. Moscow: 1st ed. 1958; 2nd ed. 1959; rev. ed. 1964. 614 pp. 25,000 entries.

05-327. NIKOLSKII, L. B. *Koreisko-russki voennyi slovar'* [Korean-Russian military dictionary]. Moscow: 1966.

05-328. USATOV, D. M., Yu. N. MAZUR, and V. M. MOZDYKOV. *Russko-koreiskii slovar'* [Russian-Korean dictionary]. Moscow: 1951; 3rd ed. 1954. Appendix by Yu. N. Mazur: "Kratkii ocaerk grammatiki sovremennogo koreiskogo yazyka [A short outline of a grammar of Modern Korean]."

Others

05-329. ECKARDT, A. *Wörterbuch: Chinesisch-Koreanisch-Deutsch (Studienausgabe).* Heidelberg: Veröffentlichung des Ostasiatischen, Seminars der Universität München, 1966. See review by Karl-Heinz Reck in *Mitteilungen des Instituts für Orientforschung* Berlin), 13(1967):307–310.

05-330. _____. *Wörterbuch der deutsch-koreanischen Sprache*. Heidelberg: Julius Groos Verlag, 1969. 208 pp.

05-331. PULTR, A. *Příruční slovník česko-korejský* [A Czech-Korean dictionary]. Prague: 1954. 253 pp.

05-332. UMEDA, Hiroyuki. *A Classified Dictionary of Modern Korean, with Korean, English, and Japanese Indexes*. Tokyo Institute for the Study of Languages and Cultures of Asia and Africa. Tokyo: Tokyo Gaikokugo Daigaku, 1971. 224 pp.

PEDAGOGICAL MATERIALS

While there is a host of materials and textbooks for teaching Korean to foreigners (primarily to English speakers), an authoritative text has yet to emerge. It appears that—from the University of Hawaii to the Foreign Service Institute in Washington—every institution offering Korean instructions compiles and uses its own text. Hence the multitude of textbooks, of which the following are worthy of mention: Lukoff (05-344), Horne and Yun (05-341), Park (05-349), Martin and Lee (05-346), and Wagner and Kim (05-356).

Korean, because of its inherent complexity, is one of the most difficult tongues to learn as a second language. To alleviate the problem somewhat through a different teaching method, Lee (05-343) has developed an audiovisual text.

With many Korean students coming to the United States to study TESL, there should be many contrastive studies between Korean and English, but most of them apparently remain as unpublished MA theses. Whang et al. (05-364) have prepared the only extensive report.

Learners and Readers

05-333. ALLEN, Clark. *A Korean Grammar for the Language Students*. Seoul: Christian Society of Korea, 1965.

05-334. CHANG, Choo-Un. *An Intermediate Korean Reader*. New Haven: Institute of Far Eastern Languages, Yale University Press, 1960.

05-335. CHANG, Sung-Un. *Korean Newspaper Readings: An Introductory Text*. New Haven: Yale University Press, 1960.

05-336. CHANG, Sung-Un and S. E. MARTIN. *Readings in Contemporary Korean*. 2nd ed. Institute of Far Eastern Languages. New Haven: Yale University Press, 1968.

05-337. CHANG, Sung-Un and Robert P. MILLER. *Imme-* *diate Korean*. Mirror Series, K 10. New Haven: Institute of Far Eastern Languages, Yale University Press, 1959. 472 pp.

05-338. CHOY, Bong-Y. *Korean Reader: A Textbook for Beginners*. Syllabus Series, no. 287. Berkeley and Los Angeles: University of California Press, 1943.

05-339. ECKARDT, A. *Koreanische Konversations-Grammatik*. Heidelberg: Julius Groos Verlag, 1923. There is a Russian translation of this book by A. A. Kholodovich: *Grammatika razgovornogo koreiskogo yazyka* (Moscow: 1951).

05-340. _____. *Übungsbuch der koreanische Sprache*. Heidelberg: Julius Groos Verlag, 1964. 200 pp.

05-341. HORNE, Elianor C. and Sang Soon YUN. *Introduction to Spoken Korean*. 2 vols. New Haven: Institute of Far Eastern Languages, Yale University Press, 1950–1951. 311 pp.

05-342. LEE, Chang-Hei. *Practical Korean Grammar*. Seattle: University of Washington Press, 1955. 225 pp. See review by M. C. Rogers in *Far Eastern Quarterly* 15(1955/1956):431–432.

05-343. LEE, Maeng-Sung. *Korean by the Audio-Visual Method*. Philadelphia: Center for Curriculum Development, 1971.

05-344. LUKOFF, F. *Spoken Korean*. 2 vols. New York: Holt, 1945–1947.

05-345. MARTIN, S. E. *Korean in a Hurry*. Rev. ed. Rutland, Vt.: Tuttle, 1960. See review by M. C. Rogers in *Far Eastern Quarterly* 15(1956):430–431.

05-346. MARTIN, S. E. and Y.-S. C. LEE. *Beginning Korean*. New Haven: Yale University Press, 1969.

05-347. OLMSTEDT, D. L. *Korean Folklore Reader*. Indiana University Publications in Uralic and Altaic series, vol. 16, 1963. 97 pp. Texts with presyntactic analysis. See review by W. E. Skillend in *BSOAS* 28(1965):426.

05-348. PAI, Edward W. *Conversational Korean*. Washington: Korean Affairs Institute, 1944.

05-349. PARK, Bong-Nam. *Korean Basic Course*. 2 vols. Washington: Foreign Service Institute, 1968–1969.

05-350. PARK, Chang-Hai. *An Intensive Course in Korean*. Vol. 1. Seoul: Yonsei University Press, 1961. 736 pp.

05-351. PULTR, A. *Lehrbuch der koreanischer Sprache*. Berlin: 1958; Niemeyer: 1960. Translation of *Učebnice korejštiny* [Korean handbook]. Ceskoslovenské Akademie Věd. Sekce jazyka a literatury. Jazykovědné priručku a učebnice, Sv. 1. Prague: 1954. 280 pp. See reviews by C. Haguenauer in *T'oung Pao* 46(1958):448–452; by A. Eckardt in *Deutsche Literaturzeitung für Kritik der internationalen Wissenschaft* (Berlin), 80(1959):974–977; by

M. C. Rogers in *Journal of American Oriental Society* 79(1959):161–162; by I. V. Vasil'ev in *Archiv Orientální* (Prague), 28(1960):508–510; and by W. E. Skillend in *Orientalistische Literaturzeitung* (Berlin), 56(1961):94–96.

05-352. SUH, Doo Soo. *Korean Literary Reader*. Seoul: Dong-A Publishing Co., 1965. 908 pp. See review by W. E. Skillend in *Asia Major* 14(1968):258–260.

05-353. US Army Language School (ed.). *Readings from Spoken Korean*. Monterey, Calif.: 1953.

05-354. _____. *Comprehensive Course in Korean*. Monterey, Calif.: 1955.

05-355. _____. *Korean: Reading and Conversation*. Monterey, Calif.: 1956.

05-356. WAGNER, Edward W. and Chongsoon KIM. *Elementary Written Korean*. 3 vols. Pt. 1: Sino-Korean Text. Pt. 2: Han'gul Text (Cambridge, Mass.: Harvard-Yenching Institute, 1963). Pt. 3: Grammar, Vocabulary, and Notes (Cambridge, Mass.: Sin Fac Minor, 1971).

05-357. YOUNG, John et al. *Learn Korean*. 4 vols. College Park: University of Maryland Press, 1965.

Contrastive Studies

05-358. BECKER, Anne-Katrein. *Untersuchung der Funktionen der Kasuskonstruktionen im Koreanischen und* *deren Konfrontation mit dem Deutschen*. Berlin: Humboldt-Universität, 1970. 77 pp.

05-359. _____. "Betrachtungen zur Konfrontation des Nominativs, Deutsch-Koreanisch." *Zeitschrift für Phonetik* 23(1970):461–474.

05-360. KIM, Sun Jai. "Contrastive Study of Complex Verb Constructions between English and Korean." *Working Papers in Linguistics* 3(4)(1971):25–33. Department of Linguistics, University of Hawaii.

05-361. PAE, Yang-seo. "English Sounds Perceived by Korean Speakers." *Language Research* (Seoul), 3(1)(1967):118–124.

05-362. SONG, Yo-In. "The Consonant Systems of English and Korean." *Dongguk Journal* (Seoul), 3(1) (1968).

05-363. SUH, Cho-soon. "A Contrastive Analysis of Stop Consonants in English and Korean for the Teaching of English to Koreans." *Ŏmunhak* (Seoul), 31(1974):91–110.

05-364. WHANG, Chan-Ho, Han-Kon KIM, Choon-Hak CHO, and Ke-Soon LEE. *The Grammatical Structures of Korean and English: A Contrastive Analysis*. Seoul: Language Research Institute, Seoul National University, 1969. 132 pp.

CHAPTER 6
Literature and Folklore

Peter H. Lee

INTRODUCTION

IN PREPARING this survey of Korean literature and folklore in translation for use in general education, I am again reminded of the paucity of translations that are at once accurate and readable. Loose definitions of terms and concepts, poor English or at times nonlanguage, egregious proofing, rehashing of prior views or readings without a new clarification or synthesis—these are the principal faults of some publications, mostly those printed in Korea. I doubt that even the interested but uninformed reader will be happy with such material; indeed, I feel myself morally bound to omit them or offer warnings to the reader. What follows is therefore a critical selection.

POETRY

Although earlier attempts were made to introduce Korean poetry in English—by some Westerners in Korea and Koreans in Korea and elsewhere—a systematic translation of the national poetic tradition began only in the fifties. In 1954 the *Hudson Review* published a group of Old Korean poems in translation: *saenaennorae* (or *hyangga*) written between the seventh and tenth centuries. Subsequently Old Korean poetry was the subject of investigation in *Studies in the Saenaennorae: Old Korean Poetry* (06-022). The book opens with a historical survey of the subject, followed by a comparison of Japanese and Korean readings of the twenty-five extant poems. Chapter 3 provides the romanized texts, glosses, and literal and literary translations along with a critical analysis of the poems. The development of historical and comparative philology in recent decades notwithstanding, the substance of the poems remains the same. The background of Middle Korean poems *(changga* or *pyŏlgok),* which flourished from the eleventh to fourteenth centuries, was the subject of an article (1958) that was later incorporated in chap. 2 of *Korean Literature: Topics and Themes* (06-003).

Toward the end of the fourteenth century a new verse form—the *akchang* (eulogy)—emerged. The culmination of literary activities in the subsequent century was the compilation in 1445–1447 of *Songs of Flying Dragons,* a great eulogy cycle in 125 cantos composed by a committee of literary men to celebrate the founding of the Yi dynasty in 1392. The first part of *Songs of Flying Dragons: A Critical Reading* (06-023) studies the cycle's multiple motives and complex structure and offers a sustained analysis of 248 poems with appropriate parallels drawn from Western literature. An introductory chapter provides a short account of the Korean events to which the poems refer; then follows an analysis of the form and structure of the work. Two chapters on "The Confucian Soldier" and "The Confucian Statesman" set the themes of the *Songs* into the framework of Confucian politico-moral thought and explore the Confucian view of man and his conduct in the world. The subject of the fifth chapter is traditional *topoi* and symbolism as well as folklore and myth based on the macrocosmic-microcosmic correspondence employed in the creation of hero and the atmosphere of the work. The last chapter, through an analysis of the symbolism of the "sacred" tree, explores from yet another angle the East Asian view of man and history. The second part consists of annotated translations of the 248 poems, followed by chronology, bibliographic notes, and extensive bibliography.

Perhaps the most popular and enduring Korean poetic form is the *sijo,* which consists of three lines, each divided into four phrase groups. The form has hitherto attracted most translators, as evinced by a number of collections in English—*The Bamboo Grove* (06-028) comprises some 250 classic and modern examples, especially 22 *sasŏl sijo,* an expanded form of the regular *sijo,* which became popular in the eighteenth century. *Kasa,* on the other hand, is a more leisurely discursive verse, like the Chinese *fu* or rhymeprose, characterized by verbal and grammatical parallelism, the absence of stanzaic division, and a tendency toward description and exposition. Examples of *kasa* poetry are included in *Poems from Korea* (06-020). Of the five native poetic genres, *sijo* is the only form which is alive, and many modern poets have written individual *sijo* and *sijo* cycles. *An Anthology of Korean Sijo* is a collection of modern *sijo* poems by some seventy poets (06-029).

Twentieth-century Korean poetry encompasses the widest range of matter and manner. A poetry produced to satisfy the wishes and needs of "hungry generations" shows how Korean poets responded to the common problems of modern life and how they attempted to solve them. Several anthologies of modern Korean poetry exist—notably *Poems from Modern Korea,* compiled by the Korean Poets Association (06-016), in which 42 poets are represented; *Modern Korean Poetry* by the Korean PEN (06-018), which includes 64 poets (pt. 2 lists 31 *sijo* poems); and Won Ko's *Contemporary Korean Poetry* (06-015), comprising 181 poems by 141 poets. The problem with these anthologies is the one-poem-to-one-poet format: it attempts to make a meal out of hors d'oeuvres. There are also translations of se-

lected works of individual poets, Han Yong-un (1879–1944), Kim Sowŏl (1903–1934), Cho Pyŏng-hwa (born 1921), Pak Tu-jin (born 1916), and Kim Chi-ha (born 1941).

To date, the only anthology of Korean poetry devoted to the country's whole poetic tradition is *Anthology of Korean Poetry* (06-019), the revised edition of which was published under the title *Poems from Korea: A Historical Anthology* (06-020), which takes into account the latest Korean scholarship. It contains 292 poems spanning fourteen centuries—from the Old Korean "Song of Mattung" (ca. 600) to the poetry of Cho Pyŏng-hwa. Two major traditional poets, Chŏng Ch'ŏl (1537–1594) and Yun Sŏn-do (1587–1671), are generously represented. Another historical anthology in German, *Kranich am Meer* (06-021), ends with the eighteenth century.

FOLKLORE

Although the novel in the modern sense began in the seventeenth century in Korea, its ancestors—legends, anecdotal narratives, and tales—are as old as human history itself. There is a rich collection of folktales in the form of myths, fables, fairy tales, novellas, hero tales, sagas, etiological stories, and jests. The oldest surviving examples of such tales, foundation myths of ancient Korean kingdoms and unusual Buddhistic and shamanistic stories, are preserved in earlier collections. In later times, folktales and songs were collected by The Establishment to gauge the mood of the people and their response to the government. From the middle of the thirteenth century, story collecting became a vogue, and collectors not only gleaned the stories but also added a personal touch to make them more entertaining or didactic. It is a commonplace that there is a correlation between the study of folklore and the rise of nationalism, and recent activities in Korea, both North and South, may reflect the reawakening of national consciousness and solidarity. A study of Korean popular traditions—together with traditional ceremonies and festivals, popular beliefs and folk expressions, social structure and regional variations—helps one to trace the oral origins of vernacular stories, dramas, and songs as well as folk motifs in traditional verse and prose.

Adapting Korean folktales seems to have been a favorite pastime among Western residents in Korea: Allen's *Korean Tales* (06-032), Griffis' *The Unmannerly Tiger and Other Korean Tales* (06-035), Metzger's *Tales Told in Korea* (06-038), Carpenter's *Tales of a Korean Grandmother* (06-033). Collections by Koreans include *The Story Bag* (06-037), *Folk Tales from Korea* (06-039), and recently *The Folk Treasury of Korea* (06-034).

Earlier collections, compiled for story content rather than for folkloristic study, are dated and out of print. Later collections do not always inform the reader from whom the stories were collected—sex, age, and profession of the storyteller—or what method of recording—dictation, memory, or reconstruction—was used. They also suffer from loose terminology and simplification of genres, as in *Folk Tales from Korea* and *The Folk Treasury of Korea*. In the former, myth is defined as "those tales which describe the creations of the world and natural beings"; the latter designates "Myth I" (foundation myths of earlier Korean states) and "Myth II" (descriptions of rituals and genealogy of local deities recited or changed by the shaman). The former also includes legends, fairy tales, fables, and old novels; the latter, legends and folktales. Mere etiological tales, such as why the ant has a slender waist, why the bedbug is flat, or why the louse has a spot on his back (*Folk Tales from Korea,* nos. 16 and 20), are not myths. Moreover, "The Sun and the Moon" (no. 3), "The Seven Stars of the North" (no. 5), and "The Jewel of the Fox's Tongue" (no. 9) are *Märchen,* not myths. The "Nine-tailed Fox" (no. 22) is not a myth but a fable, since an actual maxim is attached at the end of the story, distinguishing it from other animal tales. Of course, there are borderline cases, such as "The Mud-snail Fairy" (no. 13), which is a *Sage* in the southwest of Korea but has a happy ending when told in the area of Seoul. Whether myth is understood as a symbolic description of natural phenomena, wish fulfillments for a society, a repository of allegorical instruction, a rationalization of fundamental social needs, a by-product of living faith in need of miracles, or a system of word symbols, the systematic elucidation of Korean myths has just begun.

Foundation myths and dynastic origin stories, mostly written down in Chinese by official historians, are not "unrecorded mentifacts," but they may contain "floating intercultural narrative elements"—that is, motifs like the "exposed child" motif in the birth story of King Tongmyŏng, founder of Koguryŏ). The extent of the expurgation of the more primitive aspects in these tales is difficult to assess, but older material may remain embedded in them. Mythological and folkloristic archetypes and symbols may be found in traditional narrative, especially in the portrayal of heroes. But research at its current state has not yet been able to determine the origins of these stories, their evolution, diffusion, and displacement, and their importance in the literature and intellectual history of Korea.

Heroes from all parts of the world have common features. The common biographical patterns of heroic lives have been seen in terms of traditional narrative formula, human psychology, myth and ritual, or monomyth. Heroes in Korean history and literature also tend to conform to a type or types. Such motifs as miraculous conception, physiognomy (large ears, dragon forehead, long hands), magical animals (especially prophetic, helpful, or speaking ones), dream vision, prophecy by gnomic charts and oracles, and portents and strange eruptions—divine instruments of fear and warning, encouragement and solace—adorn the lives of heroes, from great historical personages to folk heroes. Just as there is a great deal of folklore in Western epics and a great many folkloristic motifs and mythical themes in tales of epic heroes, so the portrayal of Korean heroes involves a set of motifs and patterns drawn from myth and folklore.

The frequency of the word *life* or *record* in the titles of Yi dynasty stories seems to attest a close relation between biography (and history) and fiction. Lives of kings, great men, and eminent monks were popular in Korean culture, and life writing, conceived as a patchwork for exemplary deeds, offered little characterization. In spite of such artistic defects, they performed an important function in the development of fiction proper. A close analysis of verbal texture and normative structure, as well as the traditional and conventional values that underpin the stories, will help answer some of the basic questions concerning the nature, subject, and theme of Yi dynasty stories.

For students of Korean literature perhaps the most interesting possibilities of investigation are offered by children's stories and folktales turned into written literature: "The Pumpkin Seeds" (*The Story Bag,* no. 23),

"Two Sisters, Rose and Lotus" (*Folk Tales from Korea,* no. 97), "Korean Cinderella, K'ongjwi and P'atchwi" (*The Folk Treasury;* also in Metzger, Griffis, and Carpenter), and "Shim Ch'ŏng" (in Allen, Carpenter, and Metzger). These furnish valuable data for a study of the interaction between oral and written literature.

As yet there is no complete classification of Korean folktales according to type and motif. So far only *The Folk Treasury of Korea* provides in its introduction some types and motifs to a number of folktales (pp. 15–20). Many types and motifs in East Asian folktales are not incorporated in Aarne-Thompson's *The Types of the Folktale* (Helsinki: 1961) and Thompson's *Motif-Index of Folk Literature* (Copenhagen and Bloomington: 1955–1958), but those motifs which apply to Korean tales should be identified. A listing of such elementary constituents would provide a convenient reference for tracing themes and the migration of folktales.

FICTION

The most popular Korean works of fiction from among five hundred known stories are the *Nine Cloud Dream* and *Spring Fragrance.* Written in the seventeenth century, the *Nine Cloud Dream* (or *A Dream of Nine Clouds*) is a Buddhist romance on the familiar theme that the fame and glory of human existence are but a dream. The "nine" of the title refers to the nine main characters, who transmigrate from the life of Buddhist devotees to the dream of worldly life; "cloud" is a common symbol of the transience of life. Archetypal patterns of withdrawal-transformation-return, the elements of quest, inward associations with dream, blurred barriers between reality and fantasy, episodic plot, high stylization (including interspersed poems in the narrative)—all seem to point to the story's nature. The first translation by Gale (London: 1922) is faulty, but a more reliable version is provided by Richard Rutt in *Virtuous Women: Three Masterpieces of Traditional Korean Fiction* (06-057).

Written by an anonymous hand, *Spring Fragrance* is the story of a romance between the son of an upper-class family and the daughter of a socially despised *kisaeng* or female entertainer. They marry secretly, but the hero is soon ordered to accompany his father to the capital. The new governor of the town, enraptured by the beauty of Spring Fragrance, wishes to make her his concubine. But she refuses and is imprisoned. In the meantime, the boy passes the civil service examination and returns to town as the Secret Royal Inspector in the guise of a beggar. He punishes the evil one and delivers his faithful wife. The story contains brilliant characters: beautiful and virtuous Spring Fragrance, her devoted and shrewd mother, the passionate and upright hero, and his cunning but loyal servant are masterly inventions. The people delight to see in *Spring Fragrance* a paragon of chastity and a model of the virtuous wife; others read the book for its protest against the privileged class and defense of human rights. The story has been told countless times in prose and verse, as opera, drama, and film, and in the town associated with her name there is a shrine dedicated to her memory. Earlier translations or adaptations suffer from one defect or another, but a quite readable version is included in *Virtuous Women* (06-057).

Twentieth-century Korean fiction has matured in a most turbulent setting: Japanese occupation (1910–1945), collapse of the independence movement (1919), World War II, the liberation (1945), the Korean War (1950–1953), and revolutions (1960, 1961). Few people have experienced so many political and spiritual crises in a span of fifty years. But what is important is that these crises were occasions for the emergence of a new generation with a new voice. Each time, new writers subjected the ruling literary fashions to a fresh valuation. Each time, they succceded in reshaping the literary medium adequate to contain the quality of new values and new visions. Indeed, these cultural and moral crises not only fostered the experimental movements but effected the modernization of language and the liberalization of techniques.

Examples from this bountiful harvest of new fiction have appeared in journals, notably *Korea Journal* (the first issue appeared in September 1961), a monthly publication of the Korean National Commission for UNESCO (06-051). Some found their way into international collections like *Asian Literature: Short Stories and Plays* (06-040), compiled by the Asian Writers' Translation Bureau, where Korea is represented by six stories; five stories are included in the miscellany *Listening to Korea* (06-055). To date, the most comprehensive collection of twentieth-century Korean stories is *Flowers of Fire* (06-052), which comprises twenty-one stories by seventeen writers—from "Fire" (1925) to "The River" (1968). Earlier decades are somewhat meagerly covered, but the postliberation years, especially those after the Korean War, are generously represented. The collection gives an adequate notion of the diversity of modern Korean stories. Mention should be made of another collection in German, *Die Bunten Schuhe* (06-056), which contains nineteen stories by fifteen writers. Selections are not always based upon literary importance, and the translator's German at times fails to do justice to the originals.

Modern Korean writers continue to write some of their best works in the short story form, but the novel, as a protean form of literature, has also flourished and is read widely, often serialized in the daily newspapers for a diversified audience. Such advocates of the V Narod (To the People) movement as Yi Kwang-su's *Soil* (1932–1933) and Shim Hun's *The Evergreen* (1935) and such sociological novels as Yŏm Sang-sŏp's *Three Generations* (1931) and Ch'ae Man-sik's *Muddy Stream* (1938) were first serialized. In recent decades, the historical, sociological, and psychological novels have come into vogue, some panoramic, some dramatic, some sentimental best-sellers. Hwang Sun-wŏn's *Descendants of Cain* (1954) deals with a struggle between landowner and tenant in the North after 1945; An Su-gil's *North Kando* (1959–1967) concerns the struggles of Korean settlers in Chientao in southern Manchuria. Hwang has produced other prize-winning novels: *Trees Standing on the Slope* (1960) delves into the spiritual crises of a soldier and *The Sun and the Moon* (1964) explores the alienation and solitude of a young architect, a descendant of the despised butcher class, as a symbol of alienated modern man. One of the foremost writers of the *roman-fleuve,* a long epic fiction around one or more families' progress or decline, is Pak Kyŏng-ni (born 1927), whose *T'oji* (*Land,* 1969-) has been acclaimed for its commanding style and narrative techniques. These works skillfully explore complex contemporary realities and universal human concerns and deserve to be better known to the West.

The twentieth century has produced a number of Koreans who write in Western languages. Li Mirok (1899–1950), a medical doctor in Bavaria, wrote *The Yalu Flows* originally in German (Munich: 1946); later it was translated into English (06-053). Younghill Kang

(1903–1972), Yong Ik Kim (born 1920), and Richard E. Kim (born 1932) have written their representative works in English. Kang's *The Grass Roof* (06-043) and Richard Kim's *Lost Names* (06-046), together with *The Yalu Flows,* represent three definitions or metaphors of self, more or less in the form of autobiography. Kang and Li deal with the traumatic years before and after the Japanese seizure of Korea in 1910; Richard Kim concerns himself with the last fifteen years of the occupation. All deal with the disintegration of traditional systems and values, conflicts between the old and the new, ourselves and others, and within one's own self, and the awakening of nationalism and the discovery of individual identity.

"Life in such country districts as mine," says the narrator in *The Grass Roof,* "was a long unbroken dream lasting thousands of years, in which the same experiences, the same thoughts, the same life came unceasingly, like the consistently reappearing flowers of spring, whose forms and attributes were the same, although the individuals were changing." Into this Arcadia intrudes cataclysmic change, which is depicted as a raging flood, unbound and mutinous, portending death and disaster. But Kang is not writing a historical novel; he is happy in portraying such characters as his prodigal-son uncle, crazy-poet uncle, aunts, and grandmother. Grandmother is matriarch of a family comprising her three sons and their wives and their in-laws, one of whom is a newly rich widow with no respect for the scholar-poet family. Grandmother's job is to maintain order and degree in the teeth of poverty and frustration. Consider her tragic, lonely figure in the following passage (p. 85):

Now in her land of religious Utopia beside the lotus pool in the garden, my grandmother could forget her domestic trouble, and all the agonizing pains and tears that simple human life brings from day to day.

Yet she believed thoroughly in the domestic life, even as she mounted into the world of Buddha. She believed in raising children, and in getting her children and grandchildren married. It seemed to her that the only progress possible was through the domesticity of life. But somehow she could not bear this time to see the night go and the dawn break.

"Don't come—I don't want you!" she thought as a wan streak came. "I don't want to be seen. The sun shames me."

And it seemed like a man's hand upon her soul, calling it back. Night, the time of her woman's supremacy, was ebbing. She could no longer rest with perfect understanding upon the dark. But she raised her eyes to the pine tree outlined against the rosied sky.

"O let my heart be inspired by that tall pine tree!"

Lost Names by Richard Kim refers to one of the measures initiated by the Japanese in February 1940, when Koreans were ordered to adopt Japanese names. Kim's father, a Protestant pastor in Pyongyang, was, like most Korean Christians at the time, involved in some form of independence movement and was under Japanese surveillance. Kim, who was then no more than ten, does not fully realize the enormity of the humiliation suffered by his elders when they gathered around ancestors' graves to repent their sins and announce to the spirits the inevitability of their deed. But the boy ("I" in the narrative) cries out: "Stop! Please stop! . . . What is the matter with you all, you grown-ups! All this whining, wailing, chanting, bowing to the graves, sorrowful silence, meaningless looks, burning tears. . . ." The story ends with Korea's liberation. When his father tells him, "The liberation is a gift . . . and not something that we have fought for and won. . . . And perhaps that's why most of us, grown-ups, are confused and bewildered and feel at a loss," the boy assures him, "We will be all right, Father. We are going to be different from your generation, stronger and more confident. I mean, sir, my generation is beginning with our liberation and freedom, which your generation didn't have. That ought to make all the difference."

Kim's first novel, *The Martyred* (06-047), is again set in Pyongyang, now occupied by the advancing UN forces during the Korean War. The narrator is Captain Lee, a South Korean political intelligence officer whose job is to investigate the circumstances of the execution of twelve Christian ministers by the retreating North Korean army. Adopting the role of inquisitor, the captain sets out to discover why fourteen were arrested and only twelve killed. One of the survivors has become insane. The other, Mr. Shin, the real hero and martyr, knows how the ministers died—"like dogs, whimpering, whining, wailing, begging for mercy, denouncing their God for abandoning them." Shin survived, as a captured North Korean major reveals, not because of his

collaboration but on account of his bravery. Although Shin confesses to his congregation that he was the betrayer, what he conceals from them is that he can no longer believe in an unjust God. Despite these terrifying doubts that torment him, when the Chinese communists intervene and the UN forces are compelled to withdraw, Shin chooses to remain with his flock: "I must make them believe God cares for them and I care for them." Will Captain Lee be able to reconcile the conflicting voices, "one from within history, the other from far beyond history, each promising [the people] salvation and justice, each asking them to pledge themselves to its promise"? It is a moving story well told. Kim has seldom written better since.

In *The Diving Gourd* (06-048), as in all Yong Ik Kim's stories, such as *Love in Winter* (06-049), there are admirable scenes that evince his firsthand knowledge of the regions and their people. As the subtitle suggests, it is a novel of farmers, fisherfolk, and the Korean earth. Bosun, a diving woman, lives with her son Bau on the southeastern coast and supports her family by her catches from the sea. She realizes that "a woman and diving do not go together," but her zeal for independence and freedom drives her to the sea, which she calls her nunnery. Bau falls in love with Songha, the daughter of a cattle farmer who sneers at his mother's trade. As the boy and the girl get intimate, Bosun's loneliness becomes unbearable. When her son returns after a night with Songha on the beach, Bosun's bitter anger erupts. "She snatched Bau's kite from the wall and smashed it with her hands and threw it at him. With mouth open and eyes wide open, Bau stared at this crumpled kite. He kicked open the swinging door and dashed from the room. Bosun heard her *dyun bak* crash in the yard. Has he thrown my diving gourd on the steps? No, he wouldn't—he couldn't—that supported catches and my tired body on the surface of the water." Such scenes and symbols point to the story's larger metaphorical patterns. In Yong Ik Kim we see that traditional subjects and modern techniques are inseparable.

DRAMA

Korean drama had its origin in the agricultural festivals of primitive times, when dances were performed to the rhythmic accompaniment of chorus or drums and other musical instruments. During such festivals, celebrants are believed to have worn masks—hunting, totemic, demon, or masks of mountain gods. Remnants of such mask dances, especially tiger and lion dances, have been preserved. The earliest record of the performance of "a hundred shows" by mimes, acrobats, jugglers, singers, and dancers occurs in AD 32. The most famous dances in Silla were sword, Ch'ŏyong (exorcism), and Buddhist dances.

The mask and puppet plays are of folk origin and closely associated with the popular religions: shamanism and Buddhism. The most famous mask play is the *sandae,* which probably originated toward the end of the fourteenth century and was developed in the fifteenth. Performed by masked actors following a script which presented a story with spoken lines and intermittent dances and songs, a version of the *sandae* performed in Yangju, near Seoul, has eight acts with prologue and epilogue. As in all such plays, the function of *sandae* was didactic and satirical, pouring scorn upon the nobility as well as on apostate monks. In addition to official occasions, it was performed in open air in the village square, adjacent to a sloping hillside, on New Year's day, the eighth day of the fourth month, the fifth day of the fifth month, or the fifteenth day of the eighth month in the lunar calendar. The seven-act *pongsan* mask-dance play, performed in Hwanghae province, is characterized by lively dances (incorporating also a lion dance) and allusive dialogue. Consisting generally of five (or seven) acts, the *Ogwangdae* play of South Kyŏngsang province is rich in local color and performed usually on the fifteenth day of the first month. Both plays contain bitter attacks on the bureaucracy, Buddhist clergy, and shamans and on current fashions of thought and behavior.

The representative puppet play is the *Kkoktukaksi* (or *Pak Ch'ŏmji* or *Hong Tongji*). "*Pak*" in *Pak Ch'ŏmji* refers to the gourd dipper (masks were made of dried gourds), the surname Pak and *pak* (gourd) being homonyms in Korean; *Kkoktu* is believed to have been derived from the Mongol word for mask. The length of the performance, seven to eleven acts, depends on the circumstances and the interpretation of the narrator. The play's major concerns are a satire on the rapacious nobility and apostate clergy, exposure of the poverty of the masses, ridicule of double moral standards, and es-

pousal of Buddhism as a means of ensuring future happiness. The text of the play achieves a fair degree of thematic unity and tone.

In another form of entertainment popular in the late Yi dynasty—the *p'ansori*—the singers, like the minstrels in medieval Europe, recreated, dramatized, and sang known tales and narratives with gestures and the accompaniment of instruments. It flourished in the eighteenth and nineteenth centuries, chiefly in the southeast. Many popular novels, such as *Spring Fragrance* and *Sim Ch'ŏng,* were outgrowths of the *p'ansori,* demonstrating their origin in their style, especially their incorporation of popular folk songs. The *p'ansori* version of *Spring Fragrance,* for example, represents a comic variant of stylization, parody, and satire complementing and enhancing each other. The purpose of burlesque is to ridicule a whole range of traditional poetic style prevalent among the literati class by means of a comically distorted imitation. The interaction of story writing and *p'ansori* (story singing) is a fascinating topic of study—the narrative skill of singers of tales, the use of formulas and songs, and the function of singers as oral poets. The *p'ansori* version of *Sim Ch'ŏng* was the subject of a thesis at Harvard University (1974).

The so-called new drama began in November 1908 with the performance of Yi In-jik's *The Silver World* at the Wŏn'gaksa amphitheater. Like most new writings in the beginning of this century, the play's intent was didactic: a political and social means of persuasion and enlightenment. Following decades saw the rise and fall of small theater groups, their repertory consisting mainly of adaptations from Japanese "new" plays. The T'owŏrhoe, organized in 1923 by a group of Korean students studying in Tokyo, consciously attempted to launch the modern drama movement. Their maturity was inhibited, however, by inadequate translations and adaptations from the originals, haphazard selection of repertory, and, finally, compromise with commercialism. Only the formation in 1931 of the Theatrical Arts Research Society by members of a Western literature research society brought vitality to the Korean stage. Through their experimental theater, they staged contemporary Western plays, and the creative theater program encouraged writing of original plays (such as Yu Ch'i-jin's *Clay Hut* in 1933). As amateurs they strove to preserve the integrity of the theater arts and, until their dissolution by the Japanese authorities in 1938, contributed to the growth of modern Korean drama.

The paucity of first-rate playwrights and actors, the dearth of plays which satisfy dramatic possibilities, and the general living standards of the audience have been cited as chief causes for the relative inactivity in the field in the twentieth century. Unlike China and Japan, Korea had no tradition of drama to speak of, except for court pageants for the nobility and folk plays for the peasantry. Domestic plays and historical pieces continue to be written and staged, but the future of the dramatic arts in contemporary Korea is uncertain. Except for a few individual plays, there is no comprehensive anthology of modern Korean plays in a Western language.

BIBLIOGRAPHY

GENERAL

06-001. CHŎNG, Pyŏng-uk. "Korean Literature." In *The New Encyclopedia Britannica.* 1974.

06-002. KIM, Kay H. "Korean Literature." In *Encyclopedia of World Literature in 20th Century.* 1969.

06-003. LEE, Peter H. *Korean Literature: Topic and Themes.* Tucson: University of Arizona Press, 1965. 141 pp. See reviews in *Korea Journal* 6(1)(1969):25; *Archiv Orientalni* (Warsaw), 39(1971):254–255; *Monumenta Serica* 28(1969):480–482.

06-004. SKILLEND, W. E. "Korean Literature." In *A Guide to Eastern Literatures.* New York: Praeger, 1971.

06-005. UNDERWOOD, Horace H. "Korean Literature in English: A Critical Bibliography." *Transactions of the Korea Branch of the Royal Asiatic Society* 51(1976): 65–115. To be used with caution.

POETRY

06-006. Asian Writers' Translation Bureau (ed.). *Asian Literature: Poetry, Short Stories and Essays.* Seoul: 1975. Includes poems by Cho Pyŏng-hwa (three), Kim Su-yŏng (two), Ku Sang (one), Pak Tu-jin (two), Shin Kyŏng-nim (two), Shin Suk-chŏng (one), and Yun Tong-ju (two).

06-007. CHO, Byung-hwa. *Fourteen Poems by Cho Byung-hwa.* Translated by Kevin O'Rourke and Norman Thorpe. Seoul: Kyung-hee University, 1973. 33 pp. In Korean and English. Somewhat wordy renderings with Cho's biographical data and publications at the end.

06-008. HAN, Young-un. *Meditations of the Lover.* Translated by Younghill Kang and Frances Keely. Seoul: Yonsei

University Press, 1970. 219 pp. See review in *Korea Journal* 11(9)(1971):44–45. Free and faulty translations; to be used with caution.

06-009. KIM, Chi-ha. *Cry of the People and Other Poems.* Hayama, Japan: Autumn Press, 1974. 112 pp. See review in *Books Abroad* 50(4)(1976):957. Introduction by Nicola Geiger and excerpts from conversation with Kim precede somewhat wooden and literal translations of twelve poems followed by notes and excerpts from Kim's statement before the military tribunal.

06-010. KIM, Jaihiun. *The Immortal Voice: An Anthology of Modern Korean Poetry.* Seoul: Inmun Publishing Co., 1974. 293 pp. Free and faulty translations. For example, in Yi Yuksa's poem, "Twilight" (p. 80), "The stars spangling in the December constellation" should read "Glittering stars in the Twelve Houses." "Twelve" refers not to "December" but to twelve "lunar mansions, equatorial divisions, or segments of the celestial sphere bounded by hour-circles"—see Joseph Needham, *Science and Civilisation in China,* vol. 3 (Cambridge: Cambridge University Press, 1959), p. 231 passim and table 24.

06-011. KIM, Jong Gil. "T. S. Eliot's Influence on Modern Korean Poetry." *Literature East and West* 13(3–4)(1969): 359–376. T. S. Eliot's influence on such poets as Kim Ki-rim (born 1909), Song Uk (born 1925), and Min Chae-sik (born 1932).

06-012. KIM, Sowŏl. *Selected Poems of Kim So-wol.* Translated by Dong Sung Kim. Seoul: Sung Moon Gak, 1959. 105 pp.

06-013. ———. *Lost Love: 99 Poems by Sowol Kim.* Translated by Jaihiun Kim. Seoul: Pan-Korea Book Corporation, 1975. 100 pp. In Korean and English. See review in *Korea Journal* 15(8)(1975):52–53. A revised version of Kim's earlier *Azaleas: Poems by Sowol Kim* (Han'guk University of Foreign Studies Press, 1973).

06-014. KIM, U-chang. "Sorrow and Stillness: A View of Modern Korean Poetry." *Literature East and West* 13(1–2)(1969):141–166. An intelligent discussion of what the author calls "the tradition of partial transcendence." Poets confront misery and suffering not with defiance but with lamentation and resignation which, in the author's view, constitute "the last expression of the native Korean ethos" in modern Korean poetry written before 1950.

06-015. KO, Won (comp. and trans.). *Contemporary Korean Poetry.* Iowa City: University of Iowa Press, 1970. 211 pp. See review in *Korea Journal* 11(2)(1971):38–39. From Chu Yo-han's "A Spring Dream Passes" to Ma Chong-gi's "A Mental Hospital Ward." The book has an introduction and index of authors.

06-016. Korean Poets Association (ed.). *Poems from Modern*

Korea. Seoul: 1961. 89 pp. A revised and expanded version of *Korean Verses* (1961), omitting classical poems and seven modern poets and adding some thirty new selections.

06-017. _____. (ed.). *Korean Verses.* Seoul: Munwon Publishing Co., 1961. 128 pp. The original texts are appended.

06-018. Korean PEN (ed.). *Modern Korean Poetry.* Seoul: 1970. 258 pp. Reprints a number of poems included in *Poems from Modern Korea* but gives a generous sampling of modern *sijo.*

06-019. LEE, Peter H. (comp. and trans.). *Anthology of Korean Poetry from the Earliest Era to the Present.* New York: John Day, 1964. 196 pp. See reviews in *Hudson Review* 18(1965):300; *New York Times Book Review* (24 May 1964):4; *Journal of Asian Studies* 24(1964):167–168; and *Korea Journal* 4(6)(1964):19–21.

06-020. _____. (comp. and trans.). *Poems from Korea: A Historical Anthology.* Honolulu: University Press of Hawaii, 1974. 196 pp. See reviews in *Journal of Asian Studies* 34(1974):207–210; *Books Abroad* 48(4)(1974):845. Ch'oe Nam-sŏn drafted the "Declaration of Independence" but did not sign it (p. 161).

06-021. _____. *Kranich am Meer: Koreanische Gedichte.* Munich: Carl Hanser, 1959. 130 pp. See reviews in *Books Abroad* 35(1961):61 and *Journal of Asian Studies* 20(1960):385. The first representative anthology of classic Korean poetry in German. Comprises *hyangga* (seventeen), *changga* (nine), *sijo* (eighty-five), and *kasa* (six), followed by an epilogue, chronology, index with notes on the poets, and bibliography.

06-022. _____. *Studies in the Saenaennorae: Old Korean Poetry.* Rome: Istituto Italiano per il Medio ed Estremo Oriente, 1959. 212 pp. See reviews in *Journal of Asian Studies* 20(1960):113; *Journal of American Oriental Society* 81(1961):74–76; *Comparative Literature* 12(1960):376–377; and *T'oung Pao* 48(1960):282–287.

06-023. _____. *Songs of Flying Dragons: A Critical Reading.* Cambridge, Mass.: Harvard University Press, 1975. 314 pp. See reviews in *Journal of Asian Studies* 35(1976):337–339; *Korea Journal* 16(4)(1976):64–68; *Journal of the American Oriental Society* 98(1978):186–187; and *Korean Studies* 1(1977):275–278.

06-024. *Literature East and West* 14(3)(1970). The Korean literature issue is a small anthology of verse and prose in translation. Divided into "poetry and early prose" (three pieces), *sijo* (twenty), *sijo* cycle (one), and *kasa* (two); prose ("The Tale of Hong Kil-tong"), modern poems (nine), modern *sijo* (three), and modern prose (three).

06-025. McCANN, David R. "The Structure of the Korean *Sijo.*" *Harvard Journal of Asiatic Studies* 36(1976):114–

134. Studies syntactic and prosodic structure, musical setting, and syllabic distribution in the *sijo* and concludes that Korean is "accentual, not syllabic."

06-026. _____. "Weighing the Balance: Form and Content in the Korean *Kasa.*" In *Korean Studies Forum.* Vol. 1 Seoul and Pittsburgh: 1976–1977. A study of *kasa* poems by Chŏng Ch'ŏl (1536–1593) and Pak Il-lo (1561–1642).

06-027. PAK, Tu-jin. *Sea of Tomorrow: Forty Poems of Pak Tu-jin.* Translated by Edward W. Poitras. Seoul: Il Cho Kak, 1971. In English and Korean. 104 pp. Literal, not always readable, translations.

06-028. RUTT, Richard. *The Bamboo Grove: An Introduction to Sijo.* Berkeley: University of California Press, 1971. 177 pp. See reviews in *Journal of Asian Studies* 31(1972):427–428; *Journal of American Oriental Society* 92(1972):588–589; *Harvard Journal of Asiatic Studies* 33(1973):272–277; and *Literature East and West* 15(1971):319–323. The book has an introduction, texts and sources, index of authors, and index of first lines. Errors in translations have been pointed out in the reviews; Rutt is at his best in *sasŏl sijo* (nos. 223–244). Poems are grouped according to themes—history, politics, drinking, morality, loyalty, love, solitude, music, mortality, nature, retirement, and rustic life. Such thematic classifications are arbitrary, for many poems can be entered in more than one category: poems on nature, for example, also deal with retirement, rustic life, solitude, and wine.

06-029. _____. *An Anthology of Korean Sijo.* Taejon: Ch'ongja Sijo Society, 1970. In English and Korean. 194 pp. Ten classic *sijo* poems are followed by a generous sampling of modern *sijo* in bilingual form. Translations are free and at times faulty.

06-030. _____. "Kim Sakkat, Vagabond Poet." *Transactions of the Korea Branch of the Royal Asiatic Society* 41(1964): 59–87. Translations of some humorous and satiric poems by Kim Ip (1807–1863), also known as Kim Sakkat.

06-031. _____. "Traditional Korean Poetry Criticism." *Transactions of the Korea Branch of the Royal Asiatic Society* 47(1972):105–143. Fifty pieces of poetic criticism or talks on poetry *(sihwa)* written in Chinese by Koryŏ and Yi scholars are divided into four sections: technique, poetry and experience, criticism, and poetry and life. This pioneering translation is marred by a number of errors.

FOLKLORE

06-032. ALLEN, Horace Newton. *Korean Tales.* New York and London: Putnam, 1889. 193 pp.

06-033. CARPENTER, Frances. *Tales of a Korean Grandmother.* Garden City: Doubleday, 1947. 287 pp.

06-034. CHANG, Tok-Sun (comp.). *The Folk Treasury of Korea: Sources in Myth, Legend and Folktale.* Translated by Tae-sung Kim. Seoul: Society for Korean Oral Literature, 1970. 298 pp.

06-035. GRIFFIS, William Elliot. *The Unmannerly Tiger and Other Korean Tales.* New York: Crowell, 1911. 155 pp.

06-036. IM, Pang and Yuk YI. *Korean Folk Tales: Imps, Ghosts and Fairies.* Translated by James S. Gale. Tokyo: Tuttle, 1963. 233 pp. Fifty-three tales by Im Pang (1640–1724) and Yi Yuk (1438–1498) written in Chinese, some of which are portraits and anecdotes. This is a reprint of the 1913 edition—hence the large number of errors in dates, romanization, and translation of technical terms.

06-037. KIM, So-un. *The Story Bag.* Rutland, Vt.: Tuttle, 1957. A collection of thirty folktales gathered by Kim and translated freely into English. Contains such stories as "The Man Who Planted Onions" (should read "garlic"); "The Tiger and the Rabbit" (also in Griffis); "The Deer and the Woodcutter" (also in Metzger and Zong); "The Magic Gem" (also in Allen, Griffis, Metzger, and Zong); "The Pumpkin Seed" (the story of Hŭngbu); and "The Bridegroom's Shopping" (also in Metzger as "The Magical Moon").

06-038. METZGER, Berta. *Tales Told in Korea.* New York: Frederick A. Stokes, 1932. 247 pp.

06-039. ZONG, In-sob. *Folk Tales from Korea.* London: Routledge & Kegan Paul, 1952. 257 pp. See review in *Comparative Literature* 7(1955):162–164.

FICTION

06-040. Asian Writers' Translation Bureau (ed.). *Asian Literature: Short Stories and Plays.* Seoul: 1973. 311 pp. See review in *Korea Journal* 13(11)(1973):64–65. Includes six modern stories; translations uneven.

06-041. _____. (ed.). *Poetry, Short Stories and Essays.* Seoul: 1975. Includes five stories; translations uneven.

06-042. HONG, Myoung-hee (trans.). *Korean Short Stories.* Seoul: Il Ji Sa (Ilchisa), 1975. 227 pp. See review by Kevin O'Rourke in *Korea Journal* 15(10)(1975):61–62. An anthology of eight modern Korean stories, such as "At the Time When the Buckwheat Blooms," "The Third Human Type," and "Picture of a Sorceress" (also in *Flowers of Fire*). The reviewer says the style of Hong is "jerky and over-punctuated."

06-043. KANG, Younghill. *The Grass Roof.* Chicago: Follett, 1966. 377 pp.

06-044. KIM, Chong-un (trans.). *Postwar Korean Short Stories.* Seoul: Seoul National University Press, 1974. 353 pp. See review in *Journal of Asian Studies* 35(1975):

155–157. In the compiler's words, his anthology contains "examples of 'war realism' along with 'social realism' . . . 'stories of atmosphere,' whose main strength is the general drift of the narrative rather than the plot . . . 'stories of ideas,' in which intellectual themes are tapped and developed as their plot unfolds, and even some stories that can be pigeon-holed as black humor." The book has an introduction and notes on the writers.

06-045. KIM, Richard E. *The Innocent.* New York: Ballantine, 1969. 403 pp.

06-046. _____. *Lost Names: Scenes from a Korean Boyhood.* New York: Praeger, 1970. 195 pp.

06-047. _____. *The Martyred.* New York: G. Braziller, 1964. 316 pp.

06-048. KIM, Yong Ik. *The Diving Gourd.* New York: Knopf, 1962. 244 pp.

06-049. _____. *Love in Winter.* Garden City: Doubleday, 1969. 206 pp.

06-050. *Korea Journal* 11(9)(1971). See index (from September 1961 to August 1971) on pp. 55–79 and subsequently annual index.

06-051. Korean National Commission for UNESCO (ed.). *Synopses of Korean Novels: Reader's Guide to Korean Literature.* Seoul: 1972. 100 pp. Divided into two parts: pt. 1 lists forty-one classical tales; pt. 2 lists forty modern novels and stories. Each entry gives the author's name, the date of publication, if known, and a synopsis with occasional comments on the writer and the work. No attempt is made, however, to classify works by narrative type—tales of the marvelous, the romance, the picaresque, historical tale—or by form—short story, novel, diary, and so forth. Errors in dates and romanization abound.

06-052. LEE, Peter H. (ed.). *Flowers of Fire: Twentieth Century Korean Stories.* Honolulu: University Press of Hawaii, 1974. 486 pp. See reviews in *Journal of Asian Studies* 35(1975):121–128; *Korea Journal* 15(3)(1975):58–60; *Books Abroad* 49(3)(1975):609–610; and *Bulletin of the School of Oriental and African Studies* 39(1976):721.

06-053. LI, Mirok. *The Yalu Flows: A Korean Childhood.* East Lansing: Michigan State University Press, 1956. 149 pp. Contains a large number of errors in romanization and translation of technical terms.

06-054. O'ROURKE, Kevin. *Ten Korean Short Stories.* Seoul: Yonsei University Press, 1973. 274 pp. See review in *Korea Journal* 13(7)(1973):67–69. "Potatoes" and "Cranes" are also included in *Flowers of Fire*.

06-055. PIHL, Marshall R. (ed.). *Listening to Korea: A Korean Anthology.* New York: Praeger, 1973. 249 pp. See review in *Journal of Asian Studies* 33(1974):495–496. The anthology is divided into six parts: (1) Koreans and Japanese; (2) The Press in Korea; (3) Liberation, the War, and After; (4) From the City and the Country; (5) Youth and Age; and (6) Two Critics View Their Society.

06-056. RHIE, Tschang-boum (trans.). *Die Bunten Schuhe und andere koreanische Erzählungen.* Herenalb: Horst Erdmann, 1966. 384 pp.

06-057. RUTT, Richard and Chong-un KIM (trans.). *Virtuous Women: Three Masterpieces of Traditional Korean Fiction.* Seoul: Korean National Commission for UNESCO, 1974. 333 pp. See reviews in *Korea Journal* 14(7)(1975):53–54 and *Journal of Asian Studies* 35(3) (1976):511–513. Readable but not always accurate translation, especially in classical allusions and technical terms, of three classic Korean narrative works: *Kuun mong; Inhyŏn wanghu chŏn,* an anonymous story of court intrigue involving two queens of King Sukchong; and *Ch'unhyang ka,* which should have been rendered in verse.

06-058. SKILLEND, W. E. *Kodae Sosŏl: A Survey of Traditional Korean Style Popular Novels.* London: School of Oriental and African Studies, University of London, 1968. 268 pp. See review in *Journal of American Oriental Society* 17(1972):159–161. The compilation lists, in Korean alphabetical order, 531 titles of Korean traditional-style popular stories and novels. A typical entry contains information on different editions (listed in order of date, the dated manuscripts preceding the undated), different titles, and, occasionally, the available summary in, or translations into, Western languages. The purpose of the catalog, in the compiler's words, is to "serve as a basic point of reference for westerners who wish to investigate the subject in general, any aspect of the subject, or any particular story or work of literature" and to "make known to westerners where they may find texts of these stories." The book contains a fair number of errors in logographs, romanization, and translation of titles.

06-059. _____. "The Texts of the First New Novel in Korean." *Asia Major* 14(1968):21–62. A textual analysis of the 1906, 1907, 1940, and 1957 editions of Yi In-jik's *Tears of Blood.*

06-060. UNDERWOOD, Horace H. and Norman THORPE. "Modern Korean Fiction in English: A List." *Korea Journal* 15(9)(1975):53–68.

DRAMA

06-061. HENTHORN, William E. "The Early Days of Western Inspired Drama in Korea." *Yearbook of Comparative and General Literature* 15(1966):204–213.

06-062. YI, Tu-hyŏn. *Han'guk shingŭksa yŏn'gu* [History of modern Korean drama]. Seoul: Seoul National University Press, 1966. English synopsis on pp. 321–331. This useful study is divided into five periods: 1902–1910; 1911–1920; 1921–1930; 1931–1939; and 1940–1945. Chronology and index; illustrated.

06-063. *Korean Mask-Dance Drama.* Seoul: Ministry of Culture and Information, 1969. English synopsis on pp. 433–456. The book is divided into five chapters: (1) outline of primitive masks; (2) names of Korean masks; (3) development of the Korean mask play; (4) transmission of Korean masks and the mask play; and (5) ethnography of the Korean mask and puppet play. Illustrated.

PHD DISSERTATIONS

06-064. BOUCHEZ, Daniel. "Les peregrinations de Dame Xie dans le Sud: étude sur un roman coréen." Université de Paris, 1975. 251 pp.

06-065. CHANG, Chung-oung. "Étude sur le Hong Kil-tong Côn: traduction annotée avec introduction." Université de Paris, 1972. 174 pp.

06-066. CHO, Oh Kon. "Chi-Jin Yoo: A Patriotic Playwright of Korea." Michigan State University, 1972. 352 pp. Abstracted in *DAI* 33(9)(March 1973):5334-A; UM 73-5344.

06-067. HAN, Ponghum. "Schillers 'Räuber' und Ho Gyuns 'Hong Kil-tong': Vergleichende Untersuchung zur Literatur zweier Kulturkreise." Freien Universität, Berlin, 1962.

06-068. HOYT, James. "Korean Literature: The Rise of the Vernacular, 1443–1592." University of California, Berkeley, 1962.

06-069. McCANN, David R. "The Prosodic Structure of Pre-Modern Korean Verse." Harvard University, 1976. 167 pp.

06-070. ORANGE, Marc. "Monographie de Dame Pak: roman coréen du XVIIIe siècle. Texte présenté, traduit et annoté." Université de Paris, 1970. 146 pp.

06-071. PIHL, Marshall R. "The Tale of Sim Ch'ŏng: A Korean Oral Narrative." Harvard University, 1974. 391 pp.

06-072. SOLBERG, Sammy Edward. "The Nim-ui Chimmuk (Your Silence) of Han Yong-un: A Korean Poet." University of Washington, Seattle, 1971. 232 pp. Abstracted in *DAI* 32(3)(September 1971):1531-A; UM 71-24,085.

06-073. SUNG, Ok Ryen. "L'univers pédagogique des contes coréens." Université de Paris, 1970. 278 pp.

CHAPTER 7
Art, Music, and Drama

Lena Kim Lee

with contributions by
Bang-song Song
Du-Hyun Lee

INTRODUCTION

STUDIES IN KOREAN ART have long been delayed not only in the West but in Korea as well. The Japanese were the first to start collecting and studying Korean art in the early years of the twentieth century, and most of the preliminary works were written in Japanese. Buddhist sculpture and architecture have received special attention from Japanese scholars, perhaps because they are closely related to the beginnings of Japanese art. In the West, Korean ceramics have drawn the notice of scholars and collectors alike. Painting, on the other hand, is the least explored field of all.

A gradual recognition of the importance and the uniqueness of Korean art is developing, however, and many students in Oriental art are now turning their attention to Korean art. It is still an open field with many untouched materials and unsolved problems of importance. Those with the background in Oriental art or culture are very much needed in this field to explore what is specifically "Korean" in Korean art—as compared to Chinese or Japanese art—and to place it in the proper context of the development of East Asian art.

ART/*Lena Kim Lee*
AESTHETIC CHARACTERISTICS

The artistic creations of a nation reflect the cultural and intellectual traditions of its people. As part of the larger entity of East Asian culture over which China exerted influence, Korean art was greatly inspired, though not overwhelmed, by Chinese art forms, philosophical and aesthetic concepts, motifs, and techniques. A major factor in the formation of early Korean art was the introduction of Buddhism and the artistic activities that accompanied the propagation of the new faith. While Buddhism flourished for several centuries in Korea and had a profound impact on Korean culture, the nature-oriented philosophy of Taoism also found its way from China to Korea and is reflected in certain motifs in Korean art. Although Neo-Confucian thought and ethics were introduced later, they gradually gained prominence and, by the beginning of the Yi dynasty, they predominated, at least in the thought and artistic output of the upper-class circles.

The Neo-Confucian domination lasted almost four hundred years, but it did not nullify the earlier influences of Buddhism and Taoism on Korean art forms. These alien elements were superimposed upon the deeply rooted naturalistic and shamanistic beliefs of native Korean culture. Notwithstanding the important influence of Buddhist, Taoist, and Confucian elements, the overwhelming majority of Korean art retains an integrity of its own that can be attributed only to an indigenous gift for beauty. Thus, while Korean art shares much of the same cultural background as that of China and Japan, it has developed a distinctive style that can be distinguished from those of neighboring countries.

The art forms of Korea are an expression of her people's needs, tastes, and perceptions of beauty.

In the field of ceramics, for instance, one can easily find Chinese prototypes—in form or in technical process—for Korean wares, but there are slight differences in shape, color, and decorative design that are distinctively Korean. If Chinese ceramics can be described as austere, regular in shape, and perfect in technique, Korean ware may be typified as irregular but naturally spontaneous in shape and rough and inferior in technical skill. Chinese wares have a variety of colored glazes and are often decorated with detailed overall designs, but most Korean wares are plain or subdued in color. Pigments are sparsely used to draw simple designs on the side of a porcelain vessel: there is never a desire to fill the entire surface. The design of Korean wares is carefree, often exhibiting a certain degree of naiveté. As a whole, while Chinese wares are impersonal and balanced in form and ornamentation, the unpretentious Korean wares are intimate and personal in expression. In contrast to both, Japanese wares are deliberately irregular in shape, and their coloring is either artificially rustic or extremely decorative and varied in design. Often Japanese wares are highly sophisticated but lacking in naturalness.

The preceding remarks may be simple generalizations but they nonetheless illustrate the basic differences that initially distinguish the ceramic arts of the three countries. One can always cite the admiration showered upon Korean wares by the famous Japanese aesthete Yanagi Sōetsu, who praised the natural beauty and the unsophisticated charm of Korean ware so much loved by Japanese tea masters. He comments:

> One who has the chance of visiting a Korean pottery may notice that the wheel used for throwing pots is never exactly true. Sometimes it is so crudely set up that it is not even horizontal. The asymmetrical nature of Korean pots comes partially from the uneven movement of the surface of the wheels. But we must understand that Koreans do not make such wheels because they like unevenness and dislike evenness, but they just make their wheel in that happy-go-lucky way. The unevenness is but a natural outcome of the untrammelled state of their minds. They never concern themselves with either this or that but just make wheels. They live just as circumstances permit without any sense of artificiality. Of course if the wheel slopes too much, they may correct it to some extent, but that will not mean precision even then. They hardly trouble about accuracy or inaccuracy. They live in a world where accuracy and inaccuracy are met, yet differentiated. This state of mind is the very foundation from which the beauty of the Korean pots flows.[1]

Yanagi's observations are particularly applicable to Yi dynasty *punch'ŏng* or white wares, for they are simpler in form and more naive in design than the refined and elaborate Koryŏ celadons. Yet when the Koryŏ wares are compared with Chinese celadons, one can only be impressed by the subtle coloring of the blue-green glaze and by the subdued decoration typified by such quiet and charming scenes as ducks in a pond by willow trees or cranes amidst clouds. The subdued coloring, the simple and intimate design, and the combination of elegance and asymmetric charm differentiate Korean wares from those of other countries. Certainly these differences reflect the taste, environment, and artistic traditions of the Korean people.

It also seems to be true that the preceding characteristics apply to most other art forms of the three countries. Buddhist sculptures, for instance, are religious images of Indian origin, and since their prototypes may be found in India or along the pilgrimage road to Central Asia and China, a line of formal and stylistic development can be established. It is clear that when Buddhism reached Korea, local characteristics undeniably influenced the creation of sculpture. This is apparent in the carving technique, the facial expressions, and the choice of types and forms. Often the technical skill lacks detailed refinement and does not match the perfection found in Chinese or sometimes in Japanese images. However, Korean images declare an interest in simple form, plasticity, and overall harmony. There is also an undeniable inviting human warmth in posture and facial expression which is absent from the dignified faces of Chinese images and serene expressions of Japanese figures.

Such differences are equally apparent in architecture. Chinese palaces are massive in scale and monumental in appearance. Although Korean palaces, being smaller replicas of Chinese models, retain much of the weightiness of their Chinese prototypes, they exhibit a grace attributable in part to a judicious use of gently curving lines in the design of the roofs. Koreans tend to shun extremes: for example, perfectly straight or exaggerated curved lines are both avoided. While larger public buildings and palaces possess a remote charm, Korean architecture's most distinctive personality is expressed in the private quarters of royal residences. Here, in the residential buildings, the tendency of Korean architecture to merge man-made structures with their natural surroundings is most apparent. The respect for the needs of the individual which one finds in a myriad of details in the Korean home is also visible in temple architecture and shrines throughout the country. Korean architecture invites; it does not overwhelm.

On the whole, Korean art is closer in feeling to Chinese art than to Japanese art. For instance, the stylistic changes and the philosophical content of Korean paintings follow closely the changing patterns found in Chinese paintings. The general nature of Buddhist art in Korea including its rise and decline is also similar to that of China. Korea's artistic posture is more complex than it might appear, however. Not only did Korea facilitate the flow of East Asian civilization from China to Japan, but her own artistic movements and contributions also influenced Japanese art. Sometimes Korea influenced Japan; other times they shared common styles. In yet other instances native Korean influences were dominant, allowing Korea to develop her own distinct art forms.

Certainly, from a purely academic point of view, a knowledge of Korean art is of great scholarly worth, particularly for those who are interested in the transmission of art forms from one country to another. But ultimately Korean art is of greatest value when considered in its own right. Its charm, grace, and human warmth make it a personal expression of the human creative endeavor. Seldom monumental and never coldly remote, it fits into people's lives; it does not overwhelm the beholder. In sum, Korea's art invites the viewer to participate in the aesthetic experience.

A Brief Outline
Three Kingdoms Period: Koguryŏ; Paekche; Silla

Though the artistic record of the prehistoric peoples who inhabited the Korean peninsula is still incomplete, even a cursory glance at the pots and stone implements

that have been unearthed reveals the nascent forms of the characteristics that typify Korean art. To date, however, art historians have paid little attention to these often sophisticated remains. In the absence of solid research findings on the prehistoric period, we too begin our discussion of Korean art with the Three Kingdoms period, the first period where a written record supplements the visual one.

Koguryŏ (?37 BC–AD 668), the northernmost kingdom on the Korean peninsula (which also occupied much of southern Manchuria), was the first to be exposed to Chinese culture, and it established its own austere cultural pattern in Northeast Asia. The first significant contact between Koguryŏ and China occurred when a Han Chinese colony was established in Nangnang (Lolang) (108 BC–AD 313) in the present-day Pyongyang area. This appears to have contributed considerably to the formation of early Koguryŏ art, which in turn was transmitted to Paekche (?18 BC–AD 660). Situated in the southwestern part of the peninsula, Paekche also received southern Chinese influences, especially during the Liang dynasty (502–557), via sea routes. Silla (?57 BC–AD 668), located in the southeastern part of the peninsula, was by contrast rather slow in receiving outside influences, and its art forms retained much of their native character.

The major artistic productions of the Three Kingdoms period can be divided into two groups. The first includes the works fashioned for luxurious burials including the construction of tombs and the creation of murals, ceramics, metal ornaments, and jewelry. The second group consists of works inspired by Buddhism which, according to written record, was officially introduced into Koguryŏ in 372, to Paekche in 384, and to Silla in 527, although actual propagation of the faith had presumably begun earlier. Temples, pagodas, and Buddhist images or reliquaries attest to the rapid assimilation of the new faith.

Architecture. The tomb constructions of Koguryŏ are of two types: mounded tombs and stone-chambered tombs. Many of the latter are decorated with murals. The motifs of these paintings include both the exterior wooden pillars and interior scenes of Koguryŏ dwellings, thus giving us an idea of early Koguryŏ architectural forms. Some of these painted tombs have lantern ceilings which indicate a cultural connection with the Near East, where similar tombs are found. No original

Koguryŏ Buddhist architecture remains except for a few temple foundations. One in Ch'ŏng'am-ni, near Pyongyang, shows a temple plan with one octagonal wooden pagoda surrounded by three main halls, the same plan as the earliest known type of temple plan in Japan (the Asuka-dera near Kyoto).

Among the extant tombs of Paekche, those in the Kongju area (the capital in 475–538) were constructed with bricks and were modeled after the tombs of the Liang dynasty in China. The most representative tomb among them is that of King Muryŏng (reigned 501–523) and his queen, which yielded, among other objects, several gold ornaments, painted wooden headrests, and an inscribed, dated stone tablet. No original temple buildings of Paekche remain. However, some foundation stones of temple and palace sites do suggest the general nature of Paekche architecture. A temple plan in Kunsu-ri, Puyŏ (the capital in 538–660), for instance, also reveals one pagoda and three main halls, a system similar to those in Ch'ŏng'am-ni of Koguryŏ and Asuka-dera in Japan. Another temple site at Tongnam-ni, also in Puyŏ, shows a more highly developed type of plan in which one pagoda and one main hall are arranged on a north-south axis. As for the pagodas of Paekche, two examples remain. One, the Mirŭk-sa pagoda in Iksan, was constructed of granite in the early seventh century and modeled after the shape of wooden structures. Later pagodas became smaller and simpler. Representative of this later type is the one now standing on the temple site of Chŏngnim-sa in Puyŏ.

Silla tombs were huge mounds covered with earth. The wooden coffin and burial objects were placed underneath the mound, so no architectural form was constructed. No Silla temples are extant; only foundation stones remain. Recent excavation of the temple site of Hwangnyŏng monastery (finished in 584; pagoda in 645) revealed one pagoda, one main hall, two subsidiary halls on either side of the main hall, and a lecture hall on a north-south axis. Today a Silla pagoda in Punhwang-sa dating from 634 remains. It is constructed of stone, but it imitates Chinese brick pagodas. Another example of Silla stone architecture is the Ch'ŏmsŏngdae, thought to be an astronomical observatory, which is built of rectangular stones with openings on top and on one side.

Painting. The paintings decorating the walls of the stone-chambered tombs of Koguryŏ are representative of the pictorial arts of the Three Kingdoms period. Painted tombs are scattered throughout the Tung-kou area near the Korean-Manchurian border and in the Pyongyang area. They may be grouped into three periods: the early period, the second period, and the final period.

In the early Koguryŏ period—the fifth century—portraits of the deceased master and his wife are included. Black, brownish red, deep yellow, green, and blue are used. The pictures resemble those of the late Han tombs in the Honan and Liaotung areas in their frontally seated postures and in their use of wiry outlines.

In the second Koguryŏ period—the early sixth century—slight changes occur in the depiction of the deceased. A view of the deceased engaging in some important event such as hunting or entertaining during his lifetime replaces the solemn frontal view. Primitive representations of landscapes appear; mountain ridges are depicted by thick and thin wavy lines and trees are suggested by simple fernlike shapes. Distance is suggested by overlapping and by the placement of images in different planes. However, no adequate naturalistic principles of proportion and scale are applied.

In the third and final Koguryŏ period—the late sixth and early seventh centuries—portraiture of the deceased disappears from the main walls of the burial chamber, giving way to a depiction of the spiritual deities of four quarters of the universe. There is great movement and dynamism in the use of fluid lines and varying intensities of color.

In Paekche, too, some tombs were decorated with paintings. One Songsan-ni tomb in Kongju has the four direction deities on brick surfaces. Another one in Nŭngsan-ni, Puyŏ, shows a painting of lotus-shaped flowers and clouds on the ceiling and four deities on the plain-surfaced stone walls. The workmanship of these Paekche wall paintings resembles that of the last period of Koguryŏ wall paintings.

No painted tomb comparable to those in Koguryŏ or Paekche has been discovered in Silla. However, an important specimen of Silla pictorial art can be seen in a pair of flying horselike animals, birds, and floral decorations painted on the quilted bark of white birch. These examples were discovered in the Ch'ŏnma Ch'ong (Flying Horse tomb) in Kyŏngju and probably date from the sixth century.

Sculpture. A small gilt bronze Buddha discovered in the Seoul area is considered to be a fifth-century work. Its close affinity to Chinese images of the same period suggests, however, that the image's place of origin might be China. Most of the extant early images from the Three Kingdoms date from the sixth century.

A gilt bronze standing Buddha inscribed with cyclical year *chi-wei* of Koguryŏ is thought to date from 539 and is the earliest datable piece among Korean Buddhist statues. It shows influence of the early sixth-century Northern Wei style in its elongated face, in its flared garment folds, and in the workmanship of the flaming decoration of the mandorla. Terra-cotta images found at the temple site near Pyongyang are also important for the study of the types and styles of early Koguryŏ Buddhist art.

The gilt bronze Bodhisattva and a soapstone seated Buddha discovered at the Kunsu-ri temple site are thought to be early examples of Paekche sculpture. These pieces show slight differences in workmanship from those of Koguryŏ. The modeling is rounder and softer; facial expressions are characterized by warm smiles; and drapery fold lines are relaxed and harmonize with the body structure. These differences are attributable both to the influence of the southern Chinese Liang dynasty and to the particular artistic perception of Paekche artisans. Another important group of sculptures includes the rock-cut Buddha triad at Sŏsan, dating from around AD 600. Carved in relief on outdoor natural rock, it is a modified version of the cave temples that were in fashion in India, Central Asia, and China. Here again an inviting human warmth characterizes the images. Among the Paekche images of a slightly later date (probably mid-seventh century) are two gilt bronze Bodhisattva images found at the Kyuam-ni temple site. These two images reflect the stylistic influence of Sui sculpture in their slightly bent postures and in the arrangement of their scarves and jewels.

Many early Silla sculptures are carved in stone, most of it from the Kyŏngju area. Although some pieces may date from the sixth century, the earliest pieces which can be dated with certainty are the four pairs of Dvarapalas from the entrances of Punhwang-sa pagoda, which probably dates from 634. They show a stylistic affinity to Sui and early T'ang sculpture. The Buddha triad at Pae-ri, and those from Samhwaryŏng of Namsan, all in Kyŏngju, date from the mid-seventh century and reflect the sculptural interest in massiveness. The heads tend to be large in proportion to the bodies and the facial expressions tend to be solemn.

Among the Buddhist sculptures of the Three Kingdoms, one particular type, the meditating Bodhisattva, becomes popular in the late sixth to early seventh centuries. This development coincides with the popularity of the same type in China. A little later the type is also found in Japan. Belief in Maitreya was in vogue in China at this time, and this particular type of Bodhisattva is generally identified as a Maitreya Bodhisattva, the Buddha-to-be. Nearly twenty sculptures of meditating Bodhisattvas are known. Most are of gilt bronze though several stone statues have also been found. Among them, two large gilt bronze images can be singled out as masterworks of bronze casting of the Three Kingdoms. The modeling of the round faces, the clearly articulated facial features, the well-proportioned bodies, the naturalistic drapery—all suggest the excellent workmanship at the turn of the seventh century. Similar images were also made in Japan at the same time, and some of them are thought to have been brought from Korea or to have been made by Korean artisans who emigrated from the peninsula.

Ceramics. No significant pottery is known from Koguryŏ except for some roof tiles. Roof tiles from Paekche which have been preserved exemplify a different style of workmanship in line and modeling from those of Koguryŏ. Many floor tiles discovered at the temple site of Kyuam-ni, Puyŏ, show relief representations of stylized landscapes, birds, and demon figures typified by a sense of movement and freedom in design.

Of the pottery of the Three Kingdoms, Silla pottery is most representative. The high-fired nonporous gray stoneware, often covered by accidental ash glaze on top, is uniquely Korean in shape and style. Although the earliest Silla pottery may have been inspired by early Han ware technique, the rectangular and triangular openings in the bases and the miniature figurines and incised animal drawings on the tops or sides of Silla wares are characteristically Korean. The Sue pottery of the Tumulus period in Japan is the Japanese version of this Silla pottery.

Applied Arts. Metalwork is representative of this genre in the Three Kingdoms. From Koguryŏ only a few gilt bronze ornaments from crowns are known, but they exhibit fine openwork technique and fluent lines as decoration. From Paekche, the gold objects found in the tomb of King Muryŏng (reigned 501–523) who was buried in 525 and his queen who was buried in 529 are representative. The items include an openwork gold headdress, earrings, necklaces, bracelets, and belts. Another important item found in Naju is a gilt bronze crown formed of an inner cap covered by an outer part in the form of a diadem with upright tree-shaped ornaments which are similar to the more stylized tree-shaped uprights of Silla crowns.

The best preserved metalwork comes from the intact Silla mounded tombs. A large number of crowns, earrings, belts, necklaces, and other ornaments in gold, silver, jade, and glass have been unearthed and they show fine and sophisticated craftsmanship. Certain ornamental elements, such as the tree-shaped upright motif, suggest cultural ties with the nomadic tribes of Northwest Asia. Among the burial items quite a number of glass objects were found. Many experts believe that they were imported from Near Eastern countries, probably via China, but some may also have been manufactured locally.

Unified Silla Period

The Unified Silla period (668–935) was the golden age of Korean art and was predominantly Buddhist in nature. Buddhism enjoyed renewed prosperity and became an important source of inspiration for every artistic aspect of the period. Numerous temples and pagodas were built, large bronze images were cast, and in pottery, burial urns were produced in large numbers. Many Silla monks and scholars traveled to T'ang China and some ventured even further west into Central Asia and India. China conducted an active trade with the Arabs, and the T'ang capital Ch'ang-an became the cosmopolitan center of East Asian culture. All these activities provided Silla art with a strong international flavor. One can detect many common motifs and stylistic affinities among the artworks of T'ang China, Silla Korea, and Nara and Tempyō Japan.

Architecture. Temples were planned with two pagodas and one hall. The foundations of Sach'ŏnwang-sa, completed in 679, show a plan which included two wooden pagodas and a main hall on a north-south axis.

At the temple site of Kamŭn-sa, finished in 682, two three-story stone pagodas still stand. It seems to have been about this time that stone became the most popular material for pagodas as well as for Buddhist images. Pulguk-sa, at the foot of Mount T'oham, is still extant and is certainly the best known of the Silla temples. The major construction effort began in 751. The temple plan is divided into two complexes. The gates of both complexes are approached by a pair of staircases constructed with elaborate arches beneath. Two stone pagodas stand inside the main gate: one is a typically well-balanced three-story pagoda named Sŏkka-t'ap (Pagoda of Śākyamuni); the other is an unusually elaborate pagoda called Tabo-t'ap (Pagoda of Prabhūtaratna). Behind these pagodas lie the Main Hall and the Lecture Hall, which are arranged on a north-south axis; these buildings are connected by roofed corridors. The other complex, which is on a lower level, is dominated by the Central Hall of the Western Paradise. The extant wooden structure dates from the seventeenth century (Yi dynasty). As a special annex to this temple, an artificially constructed cave temple, Sŏkkuram, appears at the top of the same mountain. Constructed with stone panels, the main hall is a circular structure with a domed ceiling. It is a unique structure which imitates the natural cave temples of India and China.

Burial tombs of the Unified Silla period are stone-chambered constructions covered with earthen mounds. The bases of these tombs are surrounded by stone panels and have relief representations of the twelve animals of the zodiac, which are uniquely Korean. Some representative tombs are those of General Kim Yu-sin (595–673), King Sŏngdŏk (702–737), and King Wŏnsŏng (785–798). In the case of the last-named tomb, known as Kwaenŭng, stone figures of military and civilian officers and animals are lined up on either side of an approaching road.

Painting. Historic records mention the names of several painters—Solgŏ is said to have painted the temple wall of Hwangnyong-sa and many other Buddhist deities—but no Buddhist painting or painted tomb of Unified Silla has yet been found.

Sculpture. Many fine sculptures, mostly Buddhist, date from the Unified Silla period. The late seventh century was the formative period during which sculptors well versed in the Old Silla style absorbed artistic elements from the fallen kingdoms of Paekche and Koguryŏ and added fresh ideas from early T'ang art. Granite became the favorite material and natural rocks were carved with relief images; Namsan, a mountain south of Kyŏngju city, became the active center of Buddhist art and worship. While several stelae from the Yŏn'gi area represent the workmanship of Paekche artisans still active in the area, the Kunwi Amitābha triad near Taegu shows new stylistic interests in the modeling of the massive but well-proportioned bodies. A gentle sway in the stance of the attendant Bodhisattva indicates the late Sui and early T'ang influence. The workmanship of the four guardian kings of the Kamŭn-sa reliquary also reveals the rising influence of the early T'ang sculptural art around 682. From the beginning of the eighth century the assimilation of the T'ang sculptural idiom was successfully achieved, as can be seen in the seated Buddha from the Hwangbok-sa reliquary which bears the inscribed date 706.

The first half of the eighth century can be characterized as the period of the international style, during which the arts of thc Unified Silla shared many formal and stylistic characteristics with those of T'ang China and Nara and Tempyō Japan. Some of the characteristic features include the easy and relaxed stances, naturally balanced body proportions, full, round faces, and a treatment of the garment folds which harmonizes with the modeling of the body. Statues from Kamsan-sa of 719 show a developed form of T'ang style with a slight modification by the local Silla element of stiffness. Dating from the mid-eighth century, images in the Sŏkkuram cave mark the high point of Silla sculpture. Imposing in size and majestic in posture, the refined modeling of the main Buddha and his clinging garments reflect the inner strength of the spiritual quality of the Buddha. The high degree of carving skill is also apparent in the graceful linear treatment of the attendants' figures which are carved in relief on stone panels and arranged in a circle around the Buddha. When compared with full T'ang T'ien-lung-shan sculptures from China, these Silla images do not possess the feminine quality and the sensuous modeling of the body seen in the Chinese examples.

In the late eighth century a gradual decline in the sculptural style began. The garment folds became mannered, and the facial expressions lost their vigor and in-

ner spiritual power. Bronze images degenerated both in artistic quality and in casting technique. The Buddha of Medicine and Healing (Bhaisajyaguru) of Paengnyul-sa and the Amitābha and Mahāvairocana statues from Pulguk-sa perhaps represent the last fine examples of large bronze images from late eighth-century Silla.

From the mid-ninth century, the two Mahāvairocana statues in Porim-sa and Top'ian-sa indicate the presence of esoteric Buddhism in late Silla and the increasing use of iron for large images. The stylized garment folds, shrunken bodies with small heads, and sloping shoulder lines point to a stylistic aspect of late Silla sculptural art.

Ceramics. High-fired stone wares of Old Silla type continued to be produced during the Unified Silla period, but yellowish or brownish lead glazes were often applied. Many old shapes disappeared but new types, especially urns, were made in abundance. Decorative designs such as floral and geometric shapes were stamped on the surface. Some rare specimens made in imitation of T'ang three-colored wares have been found, but they were not as successful in color tone as the models.

Applied Arts. Bronze bells may be the most representative examples in this field. While the Sangwŏn-sa bell with a known date of 725 and with relief decoration of goddesses *(apsaras)* playing music is the earliest dated piece, the Pongdŏk-sa bell, now in the Kyŏngju Museum, was finished in 771 and is the largest surviving bell from the Unified Silla period. The relief images of kneeling apsaras holding incense burners and the floral bands on the surface again mark the accomplished workmanship of bronze casters.

Also important among the applied arts are the Buddhist reliquaries most commonly found in stone pagodas. These form elaborately shaped miniature shrines which hold little glass *śarīra* containers. Many are datable from historical records of the temple or from inscriptions on the reliquary. Those from Kamŭn-sa pagoda (AD 682), from Hwangbok-sa pagoda (706), and from Pulguk-sa pagoda (ca. 751) are especially famous.

Koryŏ Dynasty

The court of the Koryŏ dynasty (918–1392) avidly patronized Buddhism. Koryŏ Buddhism, in contrast to the Buddhism of earlier periods, was strongly Ch'an, or

Zen, in practice. Thus little attention was given to the production of Buddhist images. Although a decline in workmanship was apparent in Buddhist sculpture, the addition of local elements often made Koryŏ sculpture more distinctively Korean. Buddhist painting, on the other hand, seems to have gained popularity, and a great many paintings are extant, mostly in Japanese collections. Koryŏ developed strong cultural ties with the Sung court (960–1279) but maintained friendly relations with Liao (916–1125) and Chin (1115–1234) on its northern border. Mongol influence predominated from the late thirteenth century through the end of the Koryŏ dynasty. In Buddhism, Lamaist elements were introduced to the Koryŏ court from the Yüan court in China and are reflected in the forms of Buddhist figures, reliquaries, and pagodas.

The ceramic art of Koryŏ, especially the celadon, is greatly admired for its clear blue-green glaze, elaborate shapes, and refined designs, which certainly reflect the needs and sophisticated taste of the aristocratic nobility and the powerful Buddhist community of Koryŏ society.

Architecture. Some of the oldest extant wooden constructions in Korea date from the Koryŏ period. In the wooden architecture of Korea two systems of bracketing are known. The earlier system is called the *chusimp'o* style, or column-head bracket style. The earliest example of this style is the Kŭngnak-chŏn (Hall of Western Paradise) in Pongjŏng-sa, which dates from the mid-Koryŏ period. The Muryangsu-jŏn (Hall of Eternal Life) and Chosa-dang (Hall of Patriarchs) of Pusŏk-sa are also built in the *chusimp'o* style and reflect the architectural trends of the mid-Koryŏ period, even though both buildings bear the inscribed date of the restorations in the 1370s. The other system is a more complicated, intercolumnar bracket system called the *tap'o* style, which was introduced in late Koryŏ and became popular during the Yi period. The Ŭngjin-jŏn of Sŏgwang-sa in North Korea is a representative *tap'o*-style building of the fourteenth century. The earlier *chusimp'o* style may be described as simple, static, and elegant with straight linear expression; the *tap'o* style is more elaborate and dynamic with curving lines of baroque expression.

Some of the early Koryŏ stone pagodas, such as the one in Kaesim-sa constructed in 1010, continued the tradition of Silla pagodas; new types of pagodas were also constructed, however. The towering octagonal pagoda of Wŏlchŏng-sa exhibits influence from Liao-Sung China, while multiphased pagodas, such as the Kyŏngch'ŏn-sa of 1348, now in Kyŏngbok Palace, show Yüan dynasty (Mongol) influence—particularly since the surface of the pagoda is carved with relief images of Buddhist deities.

Numerous memorial pagodas of Ch'an monks, called *pudo,* were made to enshrine their *śarīra* and many are datable from the inscriptions or accompanying memorial stelae.

Sculpture. Despite the decline in sculptural art during this period, several large bronze and iron images exist. Some follow the Silla sculptural style, others show Sung-Liao influence, and yet others are typically Koryŏ with friendly faces and plump bodies. Few of them are dated, however. The large iron Buddha from Kwangju, now in the National Museum, is usually placed in the tenth century and is quite similar to the Sŏkkuram Buddha. Only the sharply raised eyes and nose and the angularity in the garment folds mark the difference. The Buddha of Pusŏk-sa, made with layers of clay and hemp cloth, is the earliest extant example of this technique among Korean sculptures. The image follows the Sŏkkuram Buddha type, but the modeling of the body and the treatment of the garment folds lack the typical Silla vitality. As a late fourteenth-century image, an ornate gilt bronze Avalokiteśvara from Hoeyang is a fine example which reflects the influence of the Lamaist Buddhism of the Yüan court.

Another important area of Koryŏ sculptural art is the theatrical shaman mask carved in wood, especially the famous masks from Hahoe and Pongsan which are thought to date from mid-Koryŏ. Made of wood with lacquered surfaces, the grotesque looking masks are typified by a few simple facial planes, deep-set eyes, and enlarged noses. The asymmetrically shaped face is employed to show dynamically changing expressions of the character under the play of changing light and shade.

Painting. Many Buddhist paintings from the Koryŏ period exist today, but most of them are in Japan and a few in America. Representative examples are the portrait of Priest Hsianghsiang in Tōdai-ji, which dates from 1185, and the painting of the Avalokiteśvara in Senso-ji inscribed by the artist Hyehŏ. In addition, a small black lacquer screen painted on both sides with Buddhist images in gold by Noyŏng in 1307 is in the National Museum in Seoul. The depiction of the Buddha's garment folds in this screen is characterized by thin wiry lines, a treatment probably of Central Asian origin.

Few ink paintings from Koryŏ remain. The paintings of "Three Friends of Winter" signed by Haeae (now in Myōman-ji) and a summer landscape with an inscription by the Japanese monk Zekkai Chūshin(1336–1405) in Shōkoku-ji, both in Japan, are rare examples from Koryŏ. Recently a seemingly genuine Koryŏ work called "Winter Hunting Scene" was uncovered; it was painted and signed by a high official named Yi Che-hyŏn (1287–1367) who was acquainted with the literati circle of Chao Meng-fu in the Yüan court. King Kongmin (reigned 1352–1374) is also thought to have been an accomplished artist, and a painting of a hunting scene attributed to him shows a very detailed depiction of horses.

As to temple wall paintings, a depiction of flowers and flying angels once decorated the Sudŏk-sa wall. The painting dates from 1307 but has been destroyed. Perhaps the best-known temple paintings are the depictions of the Four Guardians (Lokapalas) and Brahamā and Indra on the wall of Chosa-dang of Pusŏk-sa dating from 1377. Among tomb paintings, an interesting depiction of a flying deva was found in a tomb in Kŏch'ang but the draftsmanship is not very accomplished.

Ceramics. Among Koryŏ ceramics, celadon wares may be cited as the supreme achievement. They are outstanding for their distinctive beauty of form, somber decoration, and deep greenish-blue glaze. The celadon glaze first appeared in the tenth century and the earliest dated jar is from 993. By the late eleventh and early twelfth centuries, Koryŏ was producing very fine plain celadon wares, some of which are decorated with incised, engraved, or molded designs. Sometime during the second quarter of the twelfth century inlaid celadons began to be made. In this form the incised areas were filled with white and black clays before glazing. This inlay technique, inspired by either inlaid nacre lacquer ware or metal inlay, is a unique invention of Koryŏ potters. Copper red underglaze began to be applied to the celadon wares of the late twelfth or thirteenth centuries, much earlier than the Yüan underglaze red-painted

wares. In the late Koryŏ period, from the late thirteenth and fourteenth centuries, celadon glazes became yellowish from the oxidizing kiln atmosphere and designs became coarse and loose. Among late Koryŏ celadon wares some are painted with iron brown underglaze and show free and fluent lines that reflect the spontaneous artistic touch of Koryŏ potters.

Applied Arts. Bronze bells were made in abundance, but they became smaller in size and inferior in craftsmanship to Silla bells. Some fine dated pieces include the Ch'ŏnhŭng-sa bell (dated 1010) and the Sangp'umni bell of Yŏju (dated 1058). Other bronze items include incense burners in the shape of mounted cups with gracefully curving silhouettes. Most of them are decorated with silver inlay on the body representing *siddham* characters to symbolize a particular Buddha image. The famous *kundikā* (water sprinkler) in the National Museum is also of bronze with silver inlay: it shows a beautiful scene of ducks swimming in a pond surrounded by willow trees, fishing figures, and flying geese, a design typical in inlaid celadon wares too.

Yi Dynasty

The Yi dynasty (1392–1910) was a Neo-Confucian oriented society where court ceremonies, ancestor worship, and Confucian education were highly emphasized. The art forms, architectural design, and ceramics and paintings reflect the needs, thoughts, and aesthetic taste of such a society. Moreover, in much of the art produced in the Yi dynasty, the indigenous artistic sense of the craftsman comes to the fore. And in many respects the Yi craftsman was far more immune to foreign influences than his Koryŏ predecessor. Painting may be the least successful field in this respect, yet one can always detect a "Koreanness" upon careful observation and comparison.

This dynasty saw the decline of Buddhism, and few sculptures of artistic importance remain. Private devotion to the faith continued, however, and many Buddhist paintings, some patronized by royal families, remain today. These paintings, particularly those of the late Yi dynasty, are a fascinating amalgamation of Buddhist, Confucian, and shamanistic elements and many include genre scenes.

Furthermore, at the end of the dynasty, particularly

from the last decade of the nineteenth century when Korea was opened to European countries and the United States, the impact of Western culture began to be felt in various fields of Korean art.

Architecture. Most of the temple buildings, royal palaces, and ancestral shrines date from the Yi dynasty. Many were destroyed, however, during the Hideyoshi invasion in 1592–1598. The column-head bracketing of the *chusimp'o* style continued in early Yi buildings, but the dominant type was the intercolumnar bracket or *tap'o* style. Some early examples of Yi architecture are the South Gate in Seoul built in 1398, the Kŭngnak-chŏn (Western Paradise Hall) of Muwi-sa built in 1476, and the Tosan sŏwŏn (the Confucian academy) in An-dong built in 1574. Major palace buildings in Seoul were also constructed in the early Yi period, but most of the remaining ones are reconstructions done after the seventeenth century. The Kyŏngbok and Ch'angdŏk Palaces are representative buildings and were modeled after Chinese Ming and Ch'ing palaces; Korean examples are smaller in scale and have an intimate, quiet atmosphere. Visiting these palaces, once the center of power and politics, one can freely imagine scenes of court life, official ceremonies, the intrigues and political struggles of the old dynasty.

Western influence is clearly revealed in the two stone buildings in the Tŏksu Palace, which was designed by a British architect in neoclassical style and completed in 1909. Glass was used for windows and European-style furniture was installed.

Sculpture. There are very few known religious sculptures of importance from the period. A set of gilt bronze images found in the pagoda of Sujong-sa and dated 1628 show distinctive stylistic features such as squat proportions of the body, a lack of vitality, and emotionless expressions. Among secular sculptures are the stone statues of civil and military officers or animals standing in line in front of the royal tombs. Though possessing an appeal of their own, they are columnar and frontal in posture with oversized heads and lack naturalistic modeling.

Painting. Yi dynasty paintings may be divided into three periods: the early, the middle, and the late.

In the early period (fifteenth to mid-sixteenth centuries), the major portion of early Yi paintings follow the landscape tradition established by Kuo Hsi of the Northern Sung dynasty and his followers. An Kyŏn, active around the mid-fifteenth century, is the representative court painter of the Kuo Hsi school. His famous work of *A Dream Visit to the Peach Blossom Spring* is now in the Tenri University Library. Yang P'aeng-son (1488–1545) may be singled out as the main follower of An Kyŏn in the early half of the sixteenth century. Painters such as Kang Hŭi-an (1419–1464) were aware of the Ma-Hsia tradition of the Southern Sung as well as the Ming court style and Che school manner. Yi Sang-jwa, a contemporary of Yang P'aeng-son in the early sixteenth century, also favored the Ma-Hsia tradition as one can see in his famous painting *Moon Viewing under a Pine Tree.*

In the middle period (mid-sixteenth and seventeenth centuries), there was a gradual decline of the Kuo Hsi tradition and the growing dominance of the Che school. Yi Ching (1581–?) painted landscapes in the stylized Kuo Hsi manner; Ham Yun-dŏk (active in the mid-sixteenth century) and Yi Kyŏng-yun (1545–?) worked in the Che school manner; Yi Chŏng (1578–1607) worked in the Che school manner and in the broken ink style. Kim Myŏng-guk, active in the first half of the seventeenth century, is a representative figure who, working in the radical Che school manner, carried this style to the extreme in developing his own personal brushwork. He also painted Buddhist and Taoist figures and his paintings were popular in Ch'an circles in Japan during his two visits there in 1636 and 1643. His extant painting of Bodhidharma is famous.

In the late period (eighteenth and nineteenth centuries), paintings of the literati in the prevailing styles of the late Ming and Ch'ing periods were dominant. Chŏng Sŏn (1679–1759), an academy painter, started working in both the Che school and literati manners, but later he developed his distinctive personal styles in theme and brushwork. He is acclaimed as a pioneer in freely depicting native subject matter, especially scenic spots and native dress. Painters like Sim Sa-jŏng (1707–1769), an academician, worked in the Chinese literati manner practiced by the late Ming painters whereas scholar painters such as Kang Se-hwang (1713–1793) and Kim Chŏng-hŭi (1786–1857) provided much of the theoretical background for literati circles. Kim

Hong-do (1745–ca. 1818), also a professional painter, is recognized for his Buddhist and Taoist figures and for his genre paintings, which exhibit his distinctively powerful brushwork. His landscapes are also representative of the late phase of Yi paintings. Sin Yun-bok, another genre painter of the late eighteenth century, should also be mentioned. His work depicts love scenes and entertainment scenes of court life and scholars. The rise in the standard of living of the lower classes seems to have encouraged artistic interest in the commoners' activities and the vivid expression of their emotions and humor. Chang Sǔng-ǒp (1843–1897) may be one of the last representative figures of Yi dynasty painting while An Chung-sik (1861–1919) and Cho Sǒk-chin (1853–1923) carried this traditional Korean painting style into the modern period. It is also to be noted that late Yi painters, whether amateur or professional, worked mostly in the literati manner and, except for folk paintings, that style completely dominated the output of paintings in the last years of the dynasty.

Another area where Korean painters showed particular skill is in portraiture. The many paintings that remain are very linear and detailed and capture the essence of the subject but are suggestive rather than photographic.

Ceramics. Ceramic art of the Yi dynasty is an important genre that contributes to our understanding of the aesthetics of the Yi people. In the early Yi dynasty, Koryǒ inlaid celadon types continued to be produced, but the most representative type was *punch'ǒng* ware, known as *mishima* in Japanese. The ware is characterized by the use of white slip to decorate a coarse grayish-blue body. Various decorative techniques were applied in *punch'ǒng* including incised, inlaid, carved, and stamped patterns. Sometimes the plain surface was coated with white slip either by dipping the vessel into the slip or by brushing the slip over the surface. *Punch'ǒng* employed a technique derived from Koryǒ inlaid celadons, but these vessels were mass produced. These *punch'ǒng* wares were highly praised by Japanese potters and tea masters since the sixteenth century for their rustic simplicity and spontaneous and naturally irregular shape. The Hideyoshi invasion of 1592 put an end to the *punch'ǒng* production in Korea; instead, the cap-

tured Korean potters developed a new ceramic tradition in Japan.

Plain white porcelain was also produced from the early years of the Yi dynasty; these pieces were highly valued, especially for Confucian ceremonies and ancestor worship. Even decorated white wares with blue, iron-brown, and copper-red underglaze retained the basic nature of white porcelain through sparing use of decorative pigments. Colored ceramic wares as one finds in Chinese examples were not produced in Korea; nor was enamel applied for overglaze decorations. Designs were thus very simple and restrained with an original touch. These Korean decorated wares show a marked contrast to the overall surface design of Chinese blue-and-white wares, a difference certainly resulting from the different tastes and preferences of the Yi people.

Folk Art. Many charming works which belong to the folk art category have been handed down from the late Yi period. Most of them date from the eighteenth and nineteenth centuries. Popular motifs in paintings include symbols of longevity, good luck, exorcism, success in civil service examinations, and natural symbols of eternity which are strongly shamanistic in nature. The painters employ simple forms but reveal the common people's unpretentious charm and humorous naiveté. These folk art paintings also reveal the complex mixture of Confucian, Buddhist, and Taoist elements, mingled together with shamanistic and animistic ones that form the philosophical and cultural background of the daily life and customs of Korean people today.

The Modern Period

From the early years of the twentieth century, styles of Korean art began to change under Japanese and European influence. While painters like An Chung-sik (1861–1919) and Cho Sǒk-chin (1853–1911) continued to work in the late Yi dynasty style, which was developed from the Yüan, Ming, and Ch'ing literati style, many went to Japan to learn a new approach to Oriental as well as Western oil painting. Yi Sang-bǒm (1897–1972), Pyǒn Kwan-sik (1899–1976), Hǒ Paek-nyǒn (1891–1977), No Su-hyǒn (born 1899), Pae Ryǒm (1911–1968), and Kim Ki-ch'ang (born 1913) were some of the representative painters who further developed this traditional painting style with a personal and modern touch. Many contemporary artists try to use the traditional painting medium (paper, Chinese ink, and brush), Korean themes, and native color scheme to create works of Western-inspired expression. Recently Kim Ki-ch'ang, for instance, has been known for painting Korean folk themes, while Yi Ŭng-no, active now in Paris, has developed calligraphic forms near abstraction.

Western oil painting began to appear in the early twenties of this century when Ko Hŭi-dong (1886–1965) went to Japan in 1909 as one of the earliest students to study the new style. Painters like To Sang-bong (1902–1977) and Kim In-sŭng (born 1911) belong to one group who paint in very realistic representation; Yi Chung-sŏp (1916–1956), who died young in Japan, worked in a Fauvist style, and Kim Hwan-gi (1913–1974) and Nam Kwan (born 1911) represent the group who work in abstract form. Although this Western mode of abstraction is a dominant trend among contemporary artists, many still work in an impressionistic style.

Ceramic art in modern Korea is now experiencing a revival. Many have tried to combine the old techniques and old forms of Koryŏ and Yi wares but mostly end up imitating them rather than creating new forms to suit modern taste. Some contemporary artists treat ceramic ware as an art object of distorted or sculptural form after the Western mode of expression.

In Korean art today we have traditional style as well as very avant-garde abstract forms. While many artists are trying to create a synthesis of the new and old, only a few have succeeded in translating individuality and originality into works of philosophical substance.

MUSIC/*Bang-song Song*

Two distinct musical cultures exist in Korea today: Western music and traditional music. The latter—*kugak* (the national music) or *Han'guk ŭmak* (Korean music) —is scarcely known and inadequately appreciated in the West. This section focuses on the traditional music of Korea, which occupies a significant position in the musical culture of East Asia.

Although Korea shares much of the same musical background with China and Japan, she has developed and maintained her own musical tradition that is uniquely Korean. During the Three Kingdoms and Unified Silla periods, Korea came under the strong influence of the fully matured Chinese culture as a steady stream of Chinese music and musical instruments reached Korea. The flow of musical culture was not unidirectional, however, and historical records indicate the presence of Korean orchestras in the T'ang and Sui courts of China as well as in the Nara court of Japan. Subsequently, a dichotomy between *tangak* (music from China) and *hyangak* (native music) came to be recognized. Certain elements in Korea's musical traditions are in marked contrast to those of her neighbors: for example, the triple rhythm in Korean music is easily distinguishable from the duple rhythm in the music of China or Japan. Korean music also has a unique mensural notation system that was designed to indicate the duration of a note. The study of Korea's traditional music is, therefore, a culturally enriching experience which opens a new vista in our understanding of East Asian musical culture.

According to the conventional classification scheme, three main categories of music traditions are recognized: court music, folk music, and religious music. The court music consists of various types of music which can be subdivided according to their ceremonial uses: ritual music (Confucian temple music), banquet music (*hyangak* and *tangak),* and military music *(ch'wit'a).* Folk music's wide variety of musical genres are subdivided into two classes: instrumental music (*chŏngak, sanjo, nongak,* and others) and vocal music (*kagok, sijo, kasa, p'ansori, minyo,* and others). Religious music and dance are part of Buddhist and shamanistic traditions.

COURT MUSIC
Ritual Music

Confucian Temple Music. The tradition of Confucian ritual music is the most unique and ancient heritage alive in East Asia. An authentic performance of Confucian rites can still be observed at the Confucian temple *(munmyo)* located on the present-day campus of Sŏnggyun'gwan University in Seoul. The Confucian ritual music is performed twice a year in the second and eighth months of the lunar calendar. The first Confucian ritual music and instruments came from China to the Koryŏ court in 1116 during the reign of Emperor Hui-tsung of the Sung dynasty. Centuries later, during the reign of King Sejong (1418–1450) of the Yi dynasty, Pak Yŏn restored the original Chou dynasty form using as one of the main documentary sources *Ta-ch'eng yüeh-p'u* (*Taesŏng akpo* in Korean) by Lin Yü of the Yüan dynasty. The original texts and notations by Pak appeared in the Sejong Annals (137:25a–27b).

Confucian ritual music is performed antiphonally by two orchestras: the terrace orchestra *(tŭngga)*, situated on the terrace of the main temple, and the ground orchestra *(hŏn'ga)* in the courtyard. (For a musical example see side I, bands 1 and 2, in *Korean Court Music* by Lyrichord; hereafter roman numerals refer to the side and arabic numerals signify the bands of a phonograph record.) Theoretically, these orchestras must include instruments that represent all of the eight materials: metal, stone, silk, bamboo, gourd, clay, leather, and wood. Thus the instrumentation includes such rare instruments as a set of bronze bell chimes *(p'yŏnjong)*, a set of stone chimes *(p'yŏn'gyŏng)*, a tiger scraper *(ŏ)*, a wooden box *(ch'uk)*, and a baked clay jar *(pu)*. Since ritual dance is an integral part of Confucian ceremony, two dances are performed at the temple: one is the "civil dance" *(munmu)*; the other is the "military dance" *(mumu)*. Sixty-four dancers are now used at the Confucian ceremony.

Ancestral Temple Music. The royal ancestral temple music is performed once a year in May at the royal ancestral temple *(chongmyo)* located in the heart of downtown Seoul. Chinese *ya-yüeh* (*aak* in Korean; *gagaku* in Japanese) had originally been used at the royal ancestral temple before 1464, when it was replaced by Korean music such as the *Pot'aep'yŏng* and *Chŏngdaeŏp*. Since the royal ancestral ceremony follows the general pattern of Confucian rites, the musical performance is also very similar to the Confucian ritual music. The music, therefore, is performed by two orchestras and accompanied by ritual dances. (See II:12 in *Folk and Classical Music of Korea* by Folkways.) Its instrumentation, however, differs slightly: besides stone and bell chimes, the orchestras include such instruments as a large transverse flute *(taegŭm)*, a Chinese oboe *(tang p'iri)*, and a set of tuned iron slabs *(panghyang)*.

Banquet Music and Military Music

Hyangak. The majority of pieces of court repertory belong to the category of banquet music, which includes *hyangak* (Korean music) and *tangak* (Chinese music). The *Sujech'ŏn*, commonly known as *Chŏngŭp*, is the best-known piece in the *hyangak* repertoire. (See I:4 in *Korean Court Music* by Lyrichord; and I:1 in *UNESCO Collection* by Philips.) The piece is believed to be the oldest of all court orchestral pieces. The main melodic line is carried by cylindrical oboes *(p'iri)* and large transverse flutes *(taegŭm)*. The scale is based on the pentatonic: C, E flat, F, G, and B flat. The overall impression of the piece is very majestic.

Tangak. The term *tangak* literally means the music of T'ang China. In the broadest sense of the word, however, it also includes the music from the Sung dynasty. The *Nagyangch'un* (*Lo-yang-ch'un* in Chinese) and the *Pohŏja* (*Pu-hsü-tzu*) are in the existing *tangak* repertoire. (For *Nagyangch'un* see I:3 in *Korean Court Music* by Lyrichord.) When they were introduced to the Koryŏ court, the two pieces were the *tz'ŭ* music of Sung, which was the Chinese irregular verse form with an instrumental accompaniment. Later the texts were excluded and the *tz'ŭ* melodies were no longer vocal music accompanied by an orchestra. Thus the contemporary music is purely instrumental. The orchestra consists not only of Chinese instruments such as stone chimes, bell chimes, Chinese transverse flute *(tangjŏk)*, and Chinese oboe *(tang p'iri)* but also includes a Korean instrument: a large transverse flute *(taegŭm)*.

Military Music. The royal military music was mainly performed by two bands: a louder band at the head of the royal procession and a softer band to follow the king's carriage. The front band was called *tae ch'wit'a* or *muryŏngjigok* (see I:3 in the *UNESCO Collection* by Philips); the rear band was called *ch'wit'a* or *manp'a chŏng sikchigok* (II:4 in *Korean Court Music* by Lyrichord). The front band consisted of brass trumpets *(nabal)*, conch shell trumpets *(nagak)*, conical oboes *(taep'yŏngso)*, cymbals *(chabara)*, gongs *(ching)*, and drums *(changgo and yonggo)*. The instrumentation of the rear band consisted of cylindrical oboes *(p'iri)*,

Chinese transverse flutes *(tangjŏk),* two-stringed fiddles *(haegŭm),* hourglass drums *(changgo),* and barrel drum *(chwago).*

FOLK MUSIC
Instrumental Music

Chŏngak. The term *chŏngak* literally means "right (or correct) music," and its tradition includes both instrumental and vocal music, which were cultivated mainly by the upper-class literati of Yi society. The *Yŏngsan hoesang* is the main repertoire of instrumental *chŏngak* tradition and the most representative chamber ensemble of Korea. The title is derived from a Buddhist chant with the short text "Yŏngsan hoesang pulbosal," which literally means "Buddha and Bodhisattvas meet at the Spirit Vulture Peak." The Buddhist music with the texts notated in the fifteenth-century manuscript *Taeak hubo* was a vocal work accompanied by an orchestra. The contemporary piece, however, is a purely instrumental suite consisting of nine movements. Because a complete performance of the suite takes approximately forty-five minutes, only segments are usually performed: the first and the second movements, for example, or the third and the fourth, and so on. (See I:4 in *UNESCO Collection* by Philips.) At the present time there are three versions of *Yŏngsan hoesang* classified according to their instrumentation: "String Ensemble," commonly known as the *chul p'ungnyu* (string music); "Wind Ensemble," known as the *tae p'ungnyu* (bamboo music); and "Wind and String Ensemble." The first version—the mainstay of the chamber ensemble repertoire—is called *Kŏmun'go hoesang* or *Chunggwangjigok.*

Sanjo. The word *sanjo* literally means "scattered melodies," and it refers to virtuoso solo instrumental music that is the core of folk instrumental music. The solo music developed in the southwestern part of Korea, chiefly Chŏlla province, during the second half of the nineteenth century. The historical development of *sanjo* was greatly influenced by two other musical traditions: the vocal *p'ansori* and the shamanistic dance music, *sinawi.* It was Kim Ch'ang-jo (1867–1919) who organized the overall form of the genre as played today and played first on his *kayagŭm.* (See I:3 in *P'ansori* by Nonesuch Records; and side I in *Music from Korea* by East-West Center.) When Kim Ch'ang-jo's *kayagŭm sanjo* had become well known, *sanjo* was first played on *kŏmun'go* by Paek Nak-chun (1884–1934) at the opening of this century. (See I:1 in *Korean Social and Folk Music* by Lyrichord; and II:2 in *P'ansori.*) Since then, other instrumentalists found *sanjo* to be a perfect vehicle for their musical idioms and they established various *sanjo* traditions: *taegŭm sanjo* by Pak Chong-gi, *haegŭm sanjo* by Chi Yong-gu, *p'iri sanjo* by Ch'oe Ŭng-nae, *ajaeng sanjo, hojŏk sanjo,* and so on. (See I:2 and 3 in *Korean Social and Folk Music*; and II:1 in *P'ansori.*)

A *sanjo* is performed by a solo instrument accompanied by the hourglass drum, *changgo.* The musical characteristics of *sanjo* include subtle melodic progressions and a fantastic variation of rhythmic patterns. *Sanjo* is made up of several movements in different rhythmic cycles *(changdan).* The fundamental movements of a *sanjo* are the slow *chinyangjo,* the moderate *chungmori,* and the fast *chajinmori.* The movements of the *sanjo* proper are played without interruption: the first movement begins in a slow tempo and gradually accelerates toward the next movement. In the course of a performance the *sanjo* player displays an immense variety of rhythmic patterns and melodic progressions. A complete *sanjo* performance lasts for over thirty minutes, but a long one may take as much as an hour. Today one may hear many short versions of *sanjo* performance lasting five to ten minutes, but these are simplified arrangements.

Nongak. The word *nongak* means "farmers' music" and represents an important musical genre that has been developed mainly by peasants in the agricultural society of Korea. The farmers' music is performed typically in an open area of the village. The organization of *nongak* varies according to locality and performing groups, and today there are a great number of regional styles. However, they share at least the following features.

A full program includes not only a variety of music but also other entertainment such as dance, acrobatics, and singing. The entertainment begins with a group of dance and formation, followed by individual performances. The *nongak* band consists of small gongs *(kkwaenggwari),* large gongs *(ching),* hourglass drums, barrel drums *(puk),* and several hand drums *(sogo).* The small gong player called *sangsoe* functions as the leader among the players, and he provides various rhythmic patterns *(soe karak)*. The most important melodic instrument, *nallari* or *hojŏk*, is added to the band (II:3 in *Korea: Vocal and Instrumental Music* by Folkways).

Vocal Music

There are three genres of classical vocal songs: long lyric songs *(kagok)*, short lyric songs *(sijo)*, and narrative songs *(kasa)*. They belong to the vocal *chŏngak* tradition which was developed chiefly by the educated singers of the literati class during the late Yi period. The vocal genres have been cultivated in close relationship with Korean poetic genres. The term *sijo*, for example, was originally the musical term for the short lyric songs consisting of three sections *(chang)*, but it also came to designate a short poetic genre in this century. *Kasa* likewise designates both musical and poetic genres. The musical characteristics of the vocal songs are marked by their subtle dynamics and melismatic progressions.

Kagok. The long lyric song is the best vocal genre of the *chŏngak* tradition. No other vocal genre can compare with *kagok* in beauty of form, standardization of accompanying instrumentation, and range of expressiveness. The refinement of vocal techniques and richness of repertoire have been well established in the course of its development. A *kagok* singer would be accompanied by an instrumental ensemble which must include at least the five basic instruments: a *kŏmun'go*, a soft oboe *(se p'iri)*, a *taegŭm*, a *haegŭm*, and a *changgo*. The formal structure of *kagok* consists of five sections *(chang)* with an instrumental interlude *(chungyŏŭm)* and an instrumental postlude or prelude *(taeyŏŭm)*. *Kagok* repertoire is divided into two groups based on the form of the text. The first group consists of *ch'osudaeyŏp, isudaeyŏp,* and *samsudaeyŏp,* the verse form of which is the basic poem of *sijo*. The second group consists of *nong, nak,* and *p'yŏn,* the verse form of which differs from the basic *sijo* form.

The two groups are also distinguishable by their different *changdan*: the first group is based on the sixteen beats of *changdan*; the second is based on the ten beats of *changdan*. Two modal systems are found in *kagok* repertory: *u* mode *(ujo)* and *kyemyŏn* mode *(kyemyŏnjo)*. Today there are forty-one songs in the *kagok*

repertoire, and the entire repertoire has been given the collective name *Mannyŏn changhwanjigok* or "Song of Ten-Thousand-Year Joy." (See II:11 in *Folk and Classical Music* by Folkways; and II:6 in *UNESCO Collection* by Philips.)

Sijo. The short lyric song *sijo* is more widely popular than *kagok*, particularly among the older generations. Its formal structure is divided into three *chang* or sections: each is sung to an entire line of *sijo* text. A *changgo* is the standard accompaniment, but a *se p'iri, taegŭm,* and *haegŭm* may be added for more elaborate performances. *P'yŏng sijo* is the basic melody, and it has a number of variants such as *chirŭm sijo* and *sasŏl sijo*. The musical beauty of *sijo* singing is attained by delicate gradation of intensity, dynamics, falsetto, and vibrato (II:3 in *Korean Court Music* by Lyrichord).

Kasa. The narrative song *kasa* has relatively long texts. It is musically less well organized than either *kagok* or *sijo* because it lacks both a strict structural framework and a uniform singing style. Its singing style is said to hold a midway position between the song styles of common people and those of the aristocracy. A *taegŭm* and *changgo* are the most common instrumental accompaniments, but a *se p'iri* and *haegŭm* may be added. The aesthetic value of *kasa* lies not in the melodies but in its use of falsetto, dynamics, vibrato, and quiet singing style. The *Ch'unmyŏn'gok* or "Spring Sleep" is the best-known piece of *kasa* repertoire.

P'ansori. This vocal genre is the most unique musical-dramatic tradition of Korea. The term *p'ansori* is derived from *p'an* (gathering place) and *sori* (singing). Like *sanjo* its tradition has developed, since the eighteenth century, in the southwestern part of Korea, mainly in Chŏlla province, by professional folk musicians. In the nineteenth century when *p'ansori* reached the zenith of its popularity, Sin Chae-hyo (1812–1884) revised, polished, and rewrote six *p'ansori* texts: *Ch'unhyangga* or the Song of Ch'unhyang; *Simch'ŏngga* or the Song of Sim-ch'ŏng; *Hŭngbuga* or the Song of Hŭngbu; *Sugungga* or the Song of the Underwater Palace; *Chŏkpyŏkka* or the Song of the Red Cliff; and *Pyŏn'gangsoe t'aryŏng* or the Song of Pyŏn'gangsoe. Of the six texts the last piece is no longer performed but the other five are still heard today. At the beginning of this century *p'ansori* was threatened by the advent of *ch'anggŭk* (sung drama), a new version of *p'ansori* which imitates certain aspects of Western operatic style.

A *p'ansori* performance is presented by two musicians: a solo singer and a *puk* player. When performing a long dramatic song, the *p'ansori* singer employs singing *(sori),* speech *(aniri),* and dramatic actions *(pallim),* whereas the drummer keeps basic rhythmic cycles, sometimes giving the singer calls of encouragement *(ch'uimsae)* at phrase endings: *choch'i!* (nice!), *kŭrŏch'i!* (perfect!), and the like. The song is built on fixed rhythmic cycles *(changdan)* and on a large number of modes or melody types *(cho). Changdan* and *cho* change according to the mood of the text. Speech includes both half-singing, half-talking passages similar to ariosos in Western opera, and normal conversational recitative. While singing and speaking, the soloist often indicates dramatic actions with gesture and by using the fan and handkerchief as props. The audience is captured by the abundant expressiveness of *p'ansori* performance found in the great variety of dramatic expressions, rhythmic patterns, and subtle melodic progressions. (See I:1 and II:4 in *P'ansori* by Nonesuch Records; and II:1 in *Korea* by Folkways.)

Folk Song. The Korean concept of folk song is quite different from that of its Western counterpart. The Korean definition would include not only the simple work song of the peasant but also the polished song of the professional singer. *Minyo* or folk song belongs to the first category whereas *chapka* (miscellaneous song) belongs to the second. *Chapka* is divided into two types based on the singing style: the standing song *(ipch'ang)* and the sitting song *(chwach'ang).* There are a large number of songs in the *chapka* category which reflect different regional styles: *sŏdo chapka* or *chapka* of the western province, *kyŏnggi chapka* or *chapka* of the central province, and so on. These refined songs are performed by the professional singers of entertainment troupes.

The majority of folk songs *(minyo)* are farmers' songs which reflect the life-style of the traditional agrarian society. Most folk songs are in the form of call and response—the leader sings an improvised solo tune, and the chorus answers with a repeated refrain. Although the scale of the Korean folk song varies according to locality, pentatonic and tetratonic are the most common scale systems. Korean folk song is characterized by its rhythmic structure. The rhythm of most Korean folk songs is triple meter; duple meter is the outstanding feature of Japanese and Chinese folk songs. The triplet is very common in the Korean folk song, while dotted rhythm is characteristic of Chinese and Japanese folk songs. (See II:2 and 3 in *Korean Social and Folk Music* by Lyrichord; and II:7 and 8 in *UNESCO Collection* by Philips.)

RELIGIOUS MUSIC
Buddhist Music

Korean Buddhism is marked by its variety of ritual music and dance. Since the introduction of Buddhism into Korea, the ritual music and dance have played a vital role in intensifying the religious experiences of Buddhist rites. Early Buddhist music of Korea reveals Chinese influence, but Korean Buddhist music has developed a unique style that is different from those of China and Japan. The acceptance of Buddhism as a national religion during the Koryŏ period stimulated the development of Buddhist ritual performing arts. In spite of the official rejection of Buddhism in the Yi period, the tradition of Buddhist music has survived to the present time.

Buddhist ritual performing arts include chant, ritual dance, and outdoor band music. Of these, ritual chant occupies the most important place in a Buddhist rite. There are two types of Buddhist chant in Korea: *pŏmp'ae* and *yŏmbul. Yŏmbul,* literally "praying to Buddha," which has a simple singing style, is used in recitations and is sung by all Buddhist monks. *Pŏmp'ae* is more complex in its singing style and is sung by trained monks. The term *pŏmp'ae* corresponds to the Chinese *fan-bai* and the Japanese *bombai* and is derived from the Sanskrit *Brahma (fan)* and the root *bhan (bai),* meaning "sacred chanting." The Korean *pŏmp'ae* encompasses two styles of singing: *chissori* and *hossori.* The latter, meaning "simple chant," is used for short ceremonies and makes up the great majority of the repertoire. Its texts are quatrains of Chinese verses in lines of five or seven syllables. The *chissori,* more "elaborated chant," has the most extraordinary melismas, employs a wide range of tone, and makes use of falsetto singing. The *chissori* singing is not confined to any limitation of time: it can be prolonged or abridged according to the requirements of a given performance. (See I:1 and II:1–4 in *Musique bouddhique de Corée* by Disques Vogue.)

Ritual dance, an integral part of the Buddhist ceremony, is performed in conjunction with Buddhist chant. Three kinds of ritual dance have survived: Butterfly Dance *(nabich'um)*, Cymbal Dance *(parach'um)*, and Drum Dance *(pŏpkoch'um)*. These dances are given during the *Yŏngsanjae,* the greatest ceremony for a dead person.

Shamanistic Music

Shamanism is an indigenous religious tradition that has had a pervasive impact on the mind of Korean people. Since shamanistic music is the oldest of all religious music in Korea, it has exerted a strong influence on the development of other folk music traditions in the course of Korea's long history. In a contemporary shaman's rite called *kut,* a shaman (usually a female, *mudang*) sings, dances, intones magic spells, and performs the other acts necessary for the ceremony. The most important shamanistic music is performed when instrumentalists accompany the female shaman's ritual dance. The shamanistic dance music is known as *sinawi. Sinawi* music is improvised by instrumentalists and may be prolonged according to the length of the shaman's dance performance. The main melodic instruments of the *sinawi* ensemble are *p'iri, taegŭm,* and *haegŭm.* The *sinawi* ensemble also includes such percussive instruments as *changgo* or *puk,* a large gong *(ching)* or cymbals *(para),* and small gong *(kkwaenggwari),* all of which provide a variety of rhythmic patterns.

The melodic progressions and rhythmic cycles used in *sinawi* music are typical of southern provinces, chiefly Chŏlla province. The basic musical elements of *sinawi* music are identical with those found in *p'ansori* and *sanjo. Kyemyŏnjo,* the most common melodic type, for example, is an important melodic feature not only in *sinawi* music but also in *sanjo* and *p'ansori.* When *sinawi* players perform solo versions without a shamanistic ceremony, they seek more organized melodies and rhythmic beauty, displaying virtuoso instrumental techniques. This sort of solo *sinawi* music is believed to have been a prototype of early *sanjo* music. When observing contemporary performances of shamanistic music, one may recognize the real essence of musical characteristics in Korean folk music tradition—a tradition that has been transmitted by rote from generation to generation.

DRAMA AND DANCE/*Du-Hyun Lee*
A BRIEF OUTLINE

The remote origin of the drama in Korea lies in the ancient religious rituals. According to historical documents, Korean tribes had heaven-worship festivals once or twice a year in which they played music and danced. It is believed that a form of unconscious drama developed from these festivals.

It was in the Three Kingdoms period, however, that the drama as an art form began to develop; external stimuli, such as Buddhism, and the music of the dance from China and Central Asia were contributing factors. In the Koryŏ dynasty, plays such as *sandae chapkŭk* and *narye* were extensively used in governmental ceremonies and in entertaining royal familiies and the nobility. The drama of the Koryŏ dynasty seems to have been influenced by Chinese court music and dances.

It was in the latter part of the Yi dynasty that the Korean theatrical arts began to be used for the entertainment of common people. The mask-dance drama, the puppet play, and *p'ansori* (a form of opera) were popular in the Yi dynasty. Beginning with the twentieth century, Western drama was introduced to Korea through Japan.

REPRESENTATIVE PLAYS
The Ancient Period

In some historical documents, such as the *Biography of Eastern Barbarians, San-kuo chih, Wei chih,* and other fragmentary Chinese historical notes, we find references to the cultural condition of the various tribes inhabiting the Korean peninsula around the third century AD. According to these documents, each tribe had some kind of heaven-worship festival once or twice a year. In conjunction with these celebrations, members of each tribe performed a variety of singing-dancing plays. Typical of these festivals were the *Yŏnggo* of Puyŏ, *Tongmaeng* of Koguryŏ, *Much'ŏn* of Ye, *Kye yok* of Karak, and the spring and autumn farm festivals of Mahan. It is believed that Korean drama developed from these festivals.

Three Kingdoms and Unified Silla

In the period of the Three Kingdoms (Koguryŏ, Paekche, and Silla), Koguryŏ (37 BC–AD 688) developed its *angmu* (music and dance) under the influence of the Central Asian music and dance which also influenced the court music and dance programs of Sui and T'ang China. Of the twenty pieces of Koguryŏ music, twelve were for the performance of mask dances. Available records also show the existence of the puppet show in Koguryŏ, which seems to have been succeeded by the folk puppet show of the present day: *norŭm*.

Paekche (18 BC–AD 660) also developed a mixed form of dance, music, and drama called *kiak* (Japanese *gigaku*). *Kiak* originated in Central Asia and was brought to Paekche through China. *Kiak* was then taken to Japan by Mimaji in AD 612; it had a great influence on the development of the dramatic arts in both Korea and Japan.

The Unified Silla period (AD 668–935) also developed various forms of plays. Among these, *kŏmmu, muae mu, ch'ŏyong mu,* and *ogi* are best known today. *Kŏmmu* (sword dance), also called *hwangch'ang mu*, has been handed down to the present. *Muae mu* was transmitted to the Yi dynasty as a court dance. *Ch'ŏyong mu* was performed throughout the Koryŏ and Yi dynasties; it was a mask-dance play and the players wore *ch'ŏyong* masks. The *ogi*, a synthetic form of play, was composed of *kumhwan, wŏlchon, taemyŏn, soktok,* and *sanye*: the *kumhwan* was an acrobatic play in which several gilt balls were tossed in the air; the *wŏlchon* was a form of mask-dance play of farcical comedy; the *taemyŏn* was comparable to the Chinese *tai-mien* and the Japanese *ranryō-ō; soktok* was a group dance; *sanye* was a lion dance.

Koryŏ Dynasty

The Koryŏ dynasty (918–1392) inherited the *P'algwan hoe,* a Buddhist festival held under royal sponsorship, from the Silla period, and it was held every year in midwinter until the middle of the thirteenth century. *Yŏndŭng hoe* (Lantern Festival), another festival of Buddhist origin, was also held every year on the fifth of

January in the lunar calendar. Both in *P'algwan hoe* and *Yŏndŭng hoe,* the "one hundred shows" were performed by mimes, acrobats, jugglers, singers, and dancers according to tradition. The substance of the "one hundred shows" was most likely the precursor of the *sandae chapkŭk* that was composed by Yi Saek at the end of the Koryŏ period. The *sandae chapkŭk* consisted of a variety of performances including songs, music, dances (among them *ch'ŏyong mu*), and acrobatic feats such as stilt-walking, which delighted the spectators largely through sensual excitement. It is recorded that the *sandae chapkŭk* was performed not only at the time of *Yŏndŭng hoe* and *P'algwan hoe* but also on the occasions of the travel of kings, various festivals, and the welcoming of victorious generals.

There was also another form of play in the Koryŏ dynasty. Called *narye,* it was originally a religious ceremony to expel epidemic devils, but gradually it changed into a spectacle to delight the spectators—that is, a dramatic performance. According to the records of the twelfth century, this development gave rise to professional actors who performed *uhi* (actors' plays) or *chaphi* (various plays) along with the *narye.*

Yi Dynasty

Because its national ideology was anti-Buddhist, the Yi dynasty (1392–1910) did not inherit the *Yŏndŭng hoe* and *P'algwan hoe* festivals from the Buddhist dynasty of Koryŏ. It did retain the *sandae chapkŭk* and *narye,* however, and expanded the various dramatic sections of the plays while deemphasizing ritual exorcism. These plays were used extensively for entertaining Chinese emissaries whenever they visited Korea, as well as on such occasions as the winter *narye* rituals, the king's return to the palace from religious ceremonies, royal visits to Confucian shrines, welcoming of provincial governors, and the like. An official, called *Narye togam* or *Sandae togam,* took charge of *sandae* and *narye* plays. In the latter part of the Yi dynasty, however, these plays ceased to be performed altogether at official ceremonies and became folk drama. They then developed regional and other varieties: the *sandae* play of the *Kyŏnggi* region; the *pongsan t'alch'um* of Hwanghae province; *ogwangdae* and *yaryu* of the southern province; and the puppet show. These are mostly mask-dance dramas which have mime and action accompanying the dialogue and song.

In the latter part of the Yi dynasty, there also was a particular genre of drama called *p'ansori*—a form of dramatic song in the mode of a solo performance. It was established by such pioneers as Ha Han-dam and Ch'oe Sŏn-dal during the seventeenth and eighteenth centuries. By the middle of the eighteenth century, this form of drama came to embrace a repertory of twelve popular stories. Following the founding of the Wŏngaksa Theater in 1908 by Yi In-jik, Kim Ch'ang-hwan endeavored to develop a new format for *p'ansori* by separating casts and unit divisions. The new *p'ansori* was performed by the Chosun Vocal Music Association and then transformed into the *ch'anggŭk,* an "opera-type" performance.

The Modern Period

The first page of the history of modern Korean drama was written by Yi In-jik on 26 July 1908 with the opening of the Wŏngaksa Theater. A dramatic version of Yi's novel *The Silver World* was produced on the Wŏngaksa stage later in the same year, thus marking the beginning of modern dramatic performance. Soon thereafter, the *sinp'a* or "new style plays" started when, in the winter of 1911, the Hyŏksindan (Revolutionary Drama Group) led by Im Song-gu performed *The Robber with a Six-Barreled Gun.* The *sinp'a* drama was popular and many small groups of *sinp'a* drama made brief appearances.

In the early 1920s, the *sinp'a* drama was replaced by modern drama in a real sense. The T'owŏrhoe Dramatic Group, organized by a group of college students in 1923, presented Pak Sŭng-hui's original play *Kilsik,* Anton Chekhov's *The Bear,* G. B. Shaw's *How He Lied to Her Husband,* and Eugene Pillot's *The Famine.* The T'owŏrhoe thus played a pioneer's role in introducing the new dramatic movement of the 1930s.

In July 1931, Kŭkyesul yŏn'guhoe (Society for Research in Dramatic Art) was organized to promote the study of dramatic arts and the new dramatic movement. It sponsored a summer seminar on dramatic arts in August 1931 and organized the Experimental Theater in November of the same year. The Experimental Theater presented a number of plays including the first original

Korean play: *The Clay Hut,* written by Yu Ch'i-jin. In the eight years of its existence, the Experimental Theater made lasting contributions to the establishment and enhancement of the standards of *sin'gŭk* (New Drama), an important milestone in the history of Korean dramatic art.

During the period of the Sino-Japanese conflict and World War II, repressive Japanese controls forced Koreans to undertake reactionary dramatic activities. The result was a dark age for drama. With the liberation from Japan on 15 August 1945, however, the Korean dramatic world resumed its normal activities only to be abruptly interrupted by the Korean War. After the war, the "little theater" movement of young dramatists and players newly graduated from college began reviving the dying art of drama. In 1962, Yu Ch'i-jin founded the Drama Center and the Central National Theater was revived (both located in Seoul). This infused a new vitality into the hard-pressed dramatic world. The completion of a 1812-seat national theater in 1974 marked another turning point in the long history of Korean drama.

NOTE

1. Yanagi Sōetsu, "The Mystery of Beauty: A Tribute to the Korean Craftsman," *Far Eastern Ceramic Bulletin* 9(3/4)(September/December 1957):8–9.

BIBLIOGRAPHY

ART/*Lena Kim Lee*
General Works
Books

07-001. BARINKA, J. *The Art of Ancient Korea.* Translated from German by Iris Urwin. London: Peter Nevill Ltd., 1962. The book deals with painting, sculpture, applied arts, and ceramics. The illustrations are mostly from the collections in North Korea, which are very weak in late period pieces. The author tries to cover the historical, philosophical, and social background of Korean art but fails to give coherent coverage of art objects themselves. The text includes some erroneous spellings for Korean names and wrong information in dating and personal history.

07-002. ECKARDT, P. Andreas. *A History of Korean Art.* Translated from German by J. M. Kindersley. London and Leipzig: E. Goldston, 1929. This is the earliest book on the general history of Korean art written in a Western language. The text deals with sculpture, painting, ceramics, and various minor arts like bronze articles, silver and gold works, lacquer, wood carving, embroidery, and folk arts. The book is marred by a superficial approach and is somewhat out of date now, but it still retains some value since it illustrates many rare old materials *in situ*.

07-003. *Encyclopedia Brittanica*. 15th ed. Vol. 19: Visual Art, East Asian II, Visual Arts of Korea. Prepared by Won-yong Kim, this is a very concise and well-written outline of Korean art from the ancient period to the modern.

07-004. FONTEIN, Von Jan and Rose HEMPEL (eds.). *Propyläen Kunst Geschichte*. Vol. 17: *China, Korea, Japan*. Berlin: Propyläen Verlag, 1968. Two sections are devoted to Korean art: one (pp. 75–85) is by Jan Fontein, "Die Kunst der Koreaner"; the other (pp. 225–235) is the list of important sites, art objects, and artists arranged by Jan Fontein and Chewon Kim, "Koreanische Kunst: Architectur, Kunst-handwerk, Plastick, Malerei."

07-005. KIM, Chewon, Alexander GRISWOLD, and Peter H. POTT. *Burma, Korea, Tibet*. Art of the World Series. London: Methuen, 1964. The section on Korea (pp. 63–149) is one of the earliest authoritative works on Korean art to appear in the West. It is a very general and readable survey which includes ceramics, sculptures, paintings, and metal works.

07-006. KIM, Chewon and Won-yong KIM. *Treasures of Korean Art: 2000 Years of Ceramics, Sculpture, and Jeweled Arts*. New York: Abrams, 1966. (Published in Great Britain as *The Arts of Korea: Ceramics, Sculpture, Gold, Bronze and Lacquer*. London: Thames & Hudson, 1966.) A highly recommended book to general readers as well as to serious students. It has an authoritative text and excellent illustrations with beautiful color plates. The chapter on Buddhist sculpture shows an attempt to place Korean sculpture in chronological order with stylistic comparisons with Chinese and Japanese materials. Painting, an important field in Korean art, is not included in the discussion, however.

07-007. KIM, Chewon and Lena Kim LEE. *Arts of Korea*. Tokyo: Kodansha International, 1974. So far the most recent and scholarly approach to Korean art. Includes a general introduction to Korean history and a very thorough analysis of Buddhist sculpture and painting in comparison with related Chinese and Japanese materials. The discussion of applied arts covers ceramics and tomb furnishings. Highly recommended for general readers as well as for serious students who specialize in Asian or Korean art.

07-008. Korea, Republic of. Ministry of Culture and Infor-

mation. Bureau of Cultural Property (comp.). *The Arts of Ancient Korea*. Seoul: Kwang Myong Publishing Co., 1975. This book covers painting, sculpture, Buddhist art, folk art, ancient tomb furnishings, ceramics, and stone and wooden architecture. The text is rather fragmentary and very general, but the illustrations cover a variety of Korean arts in color plates.

07-009. _____. National Academy of Fine Arts. *Survey of Korean Arts: Fine Arts I*. Seoul: 1972. This book is divided into sections prepared by different writers: pt. 1, Painting by Yŏng-gi Kim; pt. 2, Sculpture by Su-yŏng Hwang; pt. 3, Calligraphy by Ch'ung-hyŏn Kim; pt. 4, Architecture by Chŏng-gi Kim.

07-010. _____. *Survey of Korean Arts: Fine Arts II*. Seoul: 1972. The second volume deals with the arts of modern Korea. Pt. 1, Oriental Painting in Korea since 1910 by No-soo Park; pt. 2, Contemporary Korean Sculpture by Kyung-seong Kim; pt. 3, Modern Painting in Korea by Kyeong-seong Yi; pt. 4, Contemporary Craft by Kyeong-seong Yi; pt. 5, Contemporary Korean Architecture by In-guk Chong.

07-011. McCUNE, Evelyn. *The Arts of Korea: An Illustrated History*. Rutland, Vt.: Tuttle, 1962. As the title indicates, this work illustrates art objects rather than discussing the history of Korean art. It is, however, about the only book in English dealing with Korean archaeology, architecture, sculpture, painting, ceramics, and minor arts. Illustrations are lavish but the text contains a disturbing number of errors and some mistakes in romanizing Korean proper names.

07-012. SWANN, Peter. *Art in China, Korea and Japan*. 3rd ed. New York: Praeger, 1965. This is the only book dealing with Korean art that compares it systematically with Chinese and Japanese arts. Although the discussion on Korean art is very brief, it points out the common stylistic aspects that Korean art shared with neighboring countries and also the differences in technique and expressive idiom that characterize Korean art. A very good introduction to Korean art in the context of Asian art.

Catalogs

07-013. Art Council of Great Britain. *An Exhibition of National Art Treasures of Korea*. London: 1961. The exhibition was held in the Victoria and Albert Museum and the catalog was prepared by G. St. G. M. Gompertz. Many of the illustrations are the same as those used in *Masterpieces of Korean Art* (see 07-017).

07-014. ELISSEEFF, Vadime (ed.). *Trésors d'art Coréen*. Paris: Musée Cernuschi, 1961–1962. The same objects as shown in London (see 07-013) but rearranged and with additional illustrations. The exhibition was also shown at The Hague, Frankfurt, and Vienna.

07-015. National Museum of Korea. *Guide Book: National Museum of Korea.* 2nd rev. ed. Seoul: 1968.

07-016. _____. *Kyŏngju and Kyŏngju Museum.* Seoul: 1966. Both 07-015 and 07-016 are catalogs of the representative selection of the National Museum collection. (The National Museum merged with the Tŏksu Palace Museum in 1972.)

07-017. PAINE, Robert Treat, Jr. (ed.). *Masterpieces of Korean Art.* Boston: 1957. A catalog of exhibitions held in eight major museums in the United States during 1957 and 1958. It includes a fine selection of Korean art comprising sculpture, painting and ceramics, and minor arts. The text has a short introductory note and each item is supplied with a detailed explanation.

Architecture
Book

07-018. ADAMS, Edward B. *Palaces of Seoul.* Seoul: Taewon Publishing Company, 1972. A very useful book on Korean architecture of the Yi dynasty as well as a guidebook on ancient remains in Seoul. Important palaces, gardens, and ancestral shrines are presented with plan drawings, photos, and maps. Also illustrated are the actual ceremonial scenes of the Confucian rite of ancestral worship.

Articles

07-019. BACON, Wilbur. "Tombs of the Yi Dynasty Kings and Queens." *Transactions of the Korea Branch of the Royal Asiatic Society* 33(1957):1–40. A very interesting article about the forty royal tombs. Describes their shapes and the arrangement of the civil and military officers and animals in stone sculpture aligned on either side of the approaching road.

07-020. CHAPIN, Helen B. "Puyŏ, One of Korea's Ancient Capitals." *Transactions of the Korea Branch of the Royal Asiatic Society* 32(1951):51–61.

07-021. _____. "Kyŏngju, Ancient Capital of Silla." *Transactions of the Korea Branch of the Royal Asiatic Society* 33(1957): 55–72. The same article first appeared in *Asian Horizons* (1948):36–45. A short introductory article to give a general idea about the ruins of the Buddhist architecture, tombs, and Buddhist images in Kyŏngju, once the flourishing capital city of Silla.

07-022. _____. "A Little Known Temple in South Korea and Its Treasures." *Artibus Asiae* 11(3)(1948):189–195. A brief introduction to the temple known as Chongnyang-sa from the Great Silla epoch. The author discusses its monument as well as its sculptural program.

07-023. _____. "Palaces in Seoul." *Transactions of the Korea Branch of the Royal Asiatic Society* 32(1951):3–50. Introduction to the palaces in Seoul including Kyŏngbok, Ch'angdŏk, Ch'anggyŏng, and Tŏksu. Gives maps and names of each palace building and discusses the symbolism in the decorative designs on the walls and building details.

07-024. CHONG, In-kook. "Two Styles of Korean Wooden Architecture." *Korea Journal* 15(2)(February 1975):4–15. A study of Korean wooden architecture of the Koryŏ and Yi dynasties divided into two bracketing styles. The earlier style is called *chusimp'o* (or columnar bracket style); the latter is called *tap'o* (or intercolumnar bracket style). Names of representative buildings of each style are mentioned and their characteristics are discussed.

07-025. LEE, Kyu. "Aspects of Korean Architecture." *Apollo* 88(August 1968):94–103. A brief survey of remaining Korean architecture from the Three Kingdoms to the Yi dynasty.

07-026. VIESSMAN, Warren. "Ondol—Radiant Heat in Korea." *Transactions of the Korea Branch of the Royal Asiatic Society* 31(1948–1949):9–22. The author, a mechanical engineer, observes the old Korean heating system and finds a similar principle in the West. He states that the structure of the *ondol* shows the technical ingenuity of the Koreans in developing a combined heating and cooking system. It is economical in operation since it is easily constructed and uses native materials.

Sculpture
Catalog

07-027. SOPER, Alexander. *Chinese, Korean and Japanese Bronzes.* Series Orientale Roma, no. 35. Rome: IsMEO, 1966. A catalog of the Aurity collection donated to IsMEO and preserved in the Museo Nazionale d'Art Orientale in Rome. Ten pieces of Korean bronze statues are included. Although the Korean pieces are not of a high quality, the explanatory notes for each object are very helpful for grouping and dating Silla bronze Buddhist statues.

Articles

07-028. BERTHIER, François. "A propos une statuette de Bodhisattva en méditation conservée au Musée Guimé." *Arts Asiatique* 32(1976):140–161.

07-029. COHN, William. "Zur Deutung der Sculpturen des

Sok-kul-am [Sŏkkuram]." *Ostasiatische Zeitschrift* 9(1922):306–309.

07-030. HWANG, Su-yŏng. "On the Stone Triad from Namsan, Kyŏngju." *Transactions of the Korea Branch of the Royal Asiatic Society* 44(1968):139–150. A study of probably a Maitreya Triad from Samhwaryŏng, in the mountain Namsan, located south of the ancient capital Kyŏngju. It is thought to date from about 644.

07-031. KIM, Chewon. "The Stone Pagoda of Koo-Hwang-li [Kuhwang-ni] in South Korea." *Artibus Asiae* 13(1/2) (1950):25–38. About the findings from the *śarīra* container with inscribed cover which describes the construction of the pagoda at the site of Hwangbok-sa in 692 and the placement of the *śarīra* and other objects in 706. Two fine statues of Buddha images were found inside.

07-032. KIM, Won-yong. "An Early Chinese Gilt-bronze Seated Buddha from Seoul." *Artibus Asiae* 23(1)(1961): 67–71. An interesting study of a fifth-century Buddha image, found in a suburb of Seoul, that closely resembles the early fifth-century seated Buddha statues from China. Dr. Kim places the piece as Chinese in origin. If it is a Korean piece, it is perhaps the oldest remaining type dating from the fifth century.

07-033. SECKEL, Dietrich. "Some Characteristics of Korean Art." *Oriental Art* 23(1)(Spring 1977):52–61. A study on the Koreanization of Korean art and changing patterns and designs through history.

07-034. TOMITA, Kojiro. "A Korean Statue of the Healing Buddha Eighth Century." *Bulletin of the Museum of Fine Arts* (Boston), 31(185)(1933):38. A short introductory note on a gilt bronze image of Medicine Buddha in the Museum of Fine Arts in Boston. It discusses the nature of Medicine Buddha and his twelve vows to save suffering beings. This eighth-century work reflects the stylistic elements of T'ang China and Nara Japan.

07-035. WATSON, William. "The Earliest Buddhist Images of Korea." *Transactions of the Oriental Ceramic Society* (London), 31(1957–1959):83–94. Perhaps the earliest article written on Korean Buddhist sculpture in a Western language. Names of dynasties are written after Japanese pronunciation and new findings have since been added.

Unpublished Dissertation

07-036. LEE, Lena Kim. "Korean Buddhist Sculpture of the Unified Silla Dynasty (A.D. 668–935)." PhD dissertation, Harvard University, 1972. 362 pp. Abstracted in *DAI* 32(8)(February 1972):4197-98-A; UM 72-3,092. A first attempt in English to establish a stylistic and typological development of the Unified Silla Buddhist sculptures, com-

paring them with related Chinese and Japanese examples. First the historical background of Silla Buddhism is discussed on such subjects as the Buddhist sects, active monks, and external contacts with Indian, Chinese, and Japanese Buddhist communities. Then comes a brief analysis of materials and techniques used in Silla sculptures. The next section deals with major sculptural groups dated (or datable) either by inscription or historical sources; their stylistic and iconographic importance is then discussed. The last section is devoted to the stylistic analysis of extant Silla Buddhist sculptures based on datable Silla pieces and on comparison with other major Asian examples.

Painting
Books

07-037. JANATA, Alfred. *Korean Painting*. Translated by Margaret Shenfield. Movements in World Art Series. New York: Crown, 1964. (First published by Verlag Brüder Rosenbaum, Vienna, in 1963 as *Koreanische Malerei*.) A catalog type of book with a very brief introductory note and twenty-four color plates each supplied with explanations of the pictures and the biographies of the painters and their styles.

07-038. KIM, Yong-joon. *Dan Won: Kim Hong Do*. Pyongyang: Foreign Languages Publishing House, 1956. Mostly a biography of the painter Kim Hong-do (active in the latter half of the eighteenth century). Also discusses other professional and literary painters of the time and the influence of Western culture which came through China.

07-039. Korean National Commission for UNESCO. *Modern Korean Painting*. Seoul: 1971. A brief outline of the development of Korean painting in the modern period (early twentieth century onward). Selected works by twenty artists are illustrated in color.

07-040. YU, Joon-young. *Chŏng Sŏn (1676–1759), ein koreanischer Landschaftsmaler aus der Yi-Dynastie*. Cologne: Universität zu Köln, 1976. This is a doctoral dissertation in paperback bound for the University of Cologne. It discusses a famous painter, Chŏng Sŏn, active in the early half of the eighteenth century, in the following order: I. Introduction; II. Korea in the Seventeenth and Eighteenth Centuries; III. Biography of Chŏng Sŏn; IV. Chŏng Sŏn's Works; V. Conclusion; VI. Catalogue and Illustrations; VII. Appendix; VIII. Plates.

Articles

07-041. AHN, Hwi-Joon. "Two Korean Landscape Paintings of the First Half of the 16th Century." *Korea Journal*

15(2)(February 1975):31–41. A brief yet very analytical study of two works of the first half of the sixteenth century: one by Yang P'aeng-son and the other an eightfold screen (by an anonymous painter) brought to Japan in 1539. His comparison with the fifteenth-century Korean painter An Kyŏn and related works indicates the lineage of the Kuo-Hsi tradition in early Yi dynasty painting which remained in vogue until the middle of the sixteenth century.

07-042. COX, Susan. "An Unusual Album by a Korean Painter Kang Se-hwang." *Oriental Art* 19(2)(Summer 1973):157–168. A discussion of an album painting by the eighteenth-century scholar-painter Kang Se-hwang. The text seems to be based on comments made by Korean experts rather than original analytical study of the album itself.

07-043. DAVIDSON, J. Le Roy. "An Unpublished Korean Album." *Bulletin of New York Public Library* 39(1935): 595–604. A study of a rare album painting depicting eight horses with poems which is in the collection of the New York Public Library. The text consists mostly of descriptions of the paintings and translations of the poems, but it indicates a highly scholarly approach. The writer suggests that the work might date from the late seventeenth to early eighteenth century, but the painting style closely resembles the brushwork of Tanwŏn, Kim Hong-do (1745–ca. 1818).

07-044. GAZZARD, Barry. "Korean Buddhist Painting." *Oriental Art* 15(4)(Winter 1969): 263–268. A short article on Korean Buddhist paintings seen as a pictorial version of Buddhist teaching. The text is mostly on the nature of Korean Buddhist painting and some specific Korean characteristics. No particular attention is given to stylistic or iconographic analysis of each painting.

07-045. LEE, Lena Kim. "Chŏng Sŏn: A Korean Landscape Painter." *Apollo* 88(August 1968):84–93. A short article about a pioneering Korean landscape painter active in the early half of the eighteenth century. Clearly demonstrates the painter's achievement in establishing an original style which distinguishes his from other Chinese-style works.

07-046. LOEHR, Max. "An Eleventh-Century Korean Copy of the Pi-tsang-ch'uan." In *Chinese Landscape Woodcuts*. Cambridge, Mass.: The Belknap Press, Harvard University Press, 1968. An introduction to an eleventh-century Korean woodblock-printed landscape painting which decorates the frontispiece of sūtras now in Nanzenji temple in Kyoto, Japan. Korean examples are discussed for comparative study of earlier tenth-century Chinese Sung works of the same type.

07-047. PAK, Young-Sook. "Ksitigarbha as Supreme Lord of the Underworld." *Oriental Art* 23(1)(Spring 1977):96–104.

07-048. UMEHARA, Sueji. "The Newly Discovered Tombs with Wall Paintings of Kao-Ku-li [Koguryŏ] Dynasty." *Archives of the Chinese Art Society of America* 6(1952): 5–17. Discusses the wall paintings of Chinp'ai-ri tomb near Pyongyang. The writer seems to believe that the Koguryŏ wall paintings were done by Chinese. Names are also written according to Chinese pronunciation.

Unpublished Dissertation

07-049. AHN, Hwi-Joon. "Korean Landscape Painting in the Early Yi Period: The Kuo Hsi Tradition." PhD dissertation, Harvard University, 1974. 347 pp. Available at the Harvard University Archives, Widener Library, call no. HU90.10502.10. The first attempt in a Western language to analyze the early phase of Yi dynasty painting, especially the paintings after the Li Ch'eng and Kuo Hsi tradition. The thorough and in-depth research on the subject is indispensable for the serious student of Korean painting.

Ceramics
Books

07-050. GOMPERTZ, G. St. G. M. *Korean Celadon and Other Wares of the Koryŏ Period*. London: Faber & Faber, 1963. Impressive scholarship and faultless prose, the hallmarks of Gompertz' work, are particularly evident in this book. Of special interest to the scholar is his detailed study of the relationship between Yüeh ware and Koryŏ celadon as well as the treatment of the lesser-known Koryŏ work, particularly the black ware. The illustrations are admirably matched to the textual material, though the color plates are not as good as one might wish. An excellent book that should appeal to both the specialist and the general student of Korean culture.

07-051. _____. *Korean Pottery and Porcelain of the Yi Period*. London: Faber & Faber, 1968. (American edition published by Praeger, New York, 1968.) A comprehensive, scholarly, but above all interesting study of the various ceramic wares of the Yi period. The historical background, technical information, and aesthetic evaluation are well balanced, thus giving this book a wider appeal than others of its kind. Of particular interest to the student of Korean ceramics is the chapter on "black-glazed and other wares." The illustrations are good—though too few are in color—and a relatively broad spectrum of Yi dynasty wares is illustrated.

07-052. _____. *Celadon Wares*. London: Faber & Faber, 1968. A charming little book. Though Gompertz deals with the celadon production of China, Japan, Korea, and Thailand, his stated preference for Korean celadon is very obvious. His description of the appeal of celadon in his general introduction is perhaps one of the best attempts to translate a visual reaction into the verbal medium. The chapter on Korea is, in the context of the book, quite well done though limited. The photographs effectively illustrate the points made in the text—particularly on the comparison between Korean and Chinese celadons.

07-053. HONEY, William Bowyer. *Corean Pottery*. London: Faber & Faber, 1947. (American edition published by Van Nostrand, New York, 1948.) This book should be recognized for what it is: a pioneering work introducing Korean ceramics to the West. Though scholarship in the field has advanced rapidly in the last decade, Honey's artistic observations remain valid—though, it should be pointed out, not all his historical data. Indeed, scholars such as Gompertz often refer to his work. Of particular interest are Honey's comments on the form and shape of Korean ceramics, for it is here, more than anywhere else, that Honey communicates his appreciation of the Korean ceramic genius.

07-054. _____. *The Ceramic Art of China and Other Countries of the Far East*. London: Faber & Faber, 1945. An outstanding work containing a brief survey of Silla, Koryŏ, and Yi period pottery (pp. 167–176).

07-055. _____. *The Art of the Potter: A Book for the Collector and Connoisseur*. London: Faber & Faber, 1964.

07-056. KIM, Chewon and G. St. G. M. GOMPERTZ. *The Ceramic Art of Korea*. London: Faber & Faber, 1961. (American edition published by Yoselloff, New York, 1961.) Illustrations in color and monochrome are supplemented by descriptions and a short historical introduction. The first authoritative account of Yi period wares to appear in the West. Color plates are not as good as those in later publications. The same work has been distributed by the Republic of Korea, Ministry of Foreign Affairs, under the title *Korean Art*, vol. 2: *Ceramics* (Seoul: 1961).

07-057. KIM, Won-yong. *Studies on Silla Pottery*. Publication of the National Museum of Korea, series A, vol. 4. Seoul: Eul-yoo Publishing Co., 1960. This work is based on Kim's dissertation under the same title (New York University, 1959). A highly informative and systematic study that centers on the problem of the origin and dating of Silla stonewares. Should be read by anyone with more than a casual interest in Korean ceramics. The quality of the illustrations could be improved, but they are admirably matched to the text.

07-058. YANAGI, Sōetsu. *The Unknown Craftsman: A Jap-*

anese Insight into Beauty. Foreword by Hamada Shōji; adapted by Bernard Leach. Tokyo: Kodansha International, 1972. This book deals primarily with Japanese ceramic wares, but the author often mentions the natural beauty and spontaneous charm of Korean wares, which had great influence on the development of Japanese tea bowls.

Catalogs

07-059. GRIFFING, Robert P., Jr. *The Art of the Korean Potter: Silla, Koryŏ, Yi*. New York: Asia Society, 1968. This catalog of an exhibition confined to Korean pottery in the United States contains excellent photographs and a highly readable text. The text itself, though cursory, provides a good survey of Korean ceramic history for the general reader. Owing to the special nature of the exhibition, a full range of ceramic arts was not included in the display; nonetheless, as indicated by the catalog, it was an interesting and visually exciting exhibition.

07-060. HENDERSON, Gregory (ed.). *The Columbia University Exhibition of Ceramics and Bronzes of Korea*. New York: Columbia University Press, 1965. A potentially useful catalog of pieces from the Sackler collection that is severely marred by the absence of photographs. This flaw is especially unfortunate as the coverage is fairly extensive and, judging from the text, representative (though by no means exhaustive). The individual description of the Koryŏ celadons, for example, is particularly well done, but again the lack of illustrations reduces the usefulness of this catalog for those with limited knowledge of Korean ceramics and bronzes. The text itself, written by Henderson, provides a good general introduction to Korean ceramics.

07-061. _____. *Korean Ceramics: An Art's Variety*. From the collection of Mr. and Mrs. Gregory Henderson. Exhibition Catalog at Divisions of Art Gallery, Ohio State University, 9 February–9 March 1969. A marvelous catalog, both in terms of the text and photographs. The text is at once subjective and informative, and the collection itself clearly illustrates the collector's love and knowledge of Korean pottery. In sum: a collector's collection.

07-062. HOBSON, R. L. *The Catalogue of the George Eumorfopoulos Collection of Chinese, Corean and Persian Pottery and Porcelain*. 3 vols. London: E. Benn, 1925–1926.

07-063. MEDLEY, Margaret (comp.). *Korean and Chinese Ceramics from the 10th to the 14th Century*. Catalog of a loan exhibition sponsored jointly by the Fitzwilliam Museum and the Percival David Foundation of Chinese Art, 24 February–28 March 1976, at the Fitzwilliam

Museum, Cambridge, England. A very good catalog demonstrating the interrelationship between Sung wares and Koryŏ celadon wares.

07-064. Museum of Far Eastern Antiquities, Stockholm. *Koreansk Keramik—Korean Ceramics.* Stockholm: 1966.

07-065. Museum of Fine Arts of Boston. *The Charles B. Hoyt Collection Memorial Exhibition.* Boston: 1952.

07-066. RACKHAM, Bernard. *Catalogue of the Le Blond Collection of Corean Pottery.* London: Victoria and Albert Museum, 1918.

Articles

07-067. GOMPERTZ, G. St. G. M. "Seventeen Centuries of Korean Pottery." *Apollo* 88(August 1968):104–113.

07-068. _____. "Hsü Ching's Visit to Korea in 1123." *Transactions of the Oriental Ceramic Society* 33(1960–1962):1–21.

07-069. _____. "The Appeal of Korean Celadon." *Oriental Art* 23(1)(Spring 1977):62–67.

07-070. _____. "A Royal Pavilion Roofed with Celadon Tiles." *Oriental Art* 3 (n.s.) (3)(1957):104–106.

07-071. _____. "Gilded Wares of Sung Koryŏ." *Burlington Magazine* 98(September–November 1956):300–308, 400–402.

07-072. _____. "Koryŏ Inlaid Celadon Wares." *Transactions of the Oriental Ceramic Society* 28 (1953–1954).

07-073. _____. "Koryŏ Ware and Ying-ch'ing." *Burlington Magazine* 95(June 1953):188–193.

07-074. _____. "The Koryŏ White Porcelains." *Transactions of the Oriental Ceramic Society* 27(1951–1953):21–22.

07-075. _____. "The 'Kingfisher Celadon' of Koryŏ." *Artibus Asiae* 16(1953):5–24.

07-076. _____. "Black Koryŏ Wares." *Oriental Art* 3(2)(1950):61–67.

07-077. _____. "A Trip through Southern Korea." *Transactions of the Oriental Ceramic Society* 36(1964/1965, 1965/1966):1–36.

07-078. GRIFFING, Robert P., Jr. "Some Koryŏ Celadons in the Collection of the Honolulu Academy of Arts." *Oriental Art* 23(1)(Spring 1977):68–79. An introductory note to nine Korean celadon wares in the Honolulu Academy of Arts.

07-079. HENDERSON, Gregory. "Dated Late Koryŏ Celadons: New Finds and New Theory." *Far Eastern Ceramic Bulletin* 11(2)(December 1959):1–8.

07-080. _____. "Korean Ceramics: Problems and Sources of Information." *Far Eastern Ceramic Bulletin* 10(1/2)(March/June 1958):5–28.

07-081. _____. "Pottery Production in the Earliest Years of the Yi Period." *Transactions of the Korea Branch of the Royal Asiatic Society* 39(December 1962):5–22.

07-082. HOBSON, R. L. "Corean Pottery: I. The Silla Period; II. The Koryŏ Period." *Burlington Magazine* 56(324)(1930):154–164, 186–193.

07-083. HONEY, William Bowyer. "Corean Wares of the Koryŏ Period." *Transactions of the Oriental Ceramic Society* 22(1946/1947):9–18.

07-084. _____. "Corean Wares of the Yi Dynasty." *Transactions of the Oriental Ceramic Society* 20(1944/1945):11–24.

07-085. KIM, Chewon. "Random Notes on Literary References to Koryŏ Ceramics." *Far Eastern Ceramic Bulletin* 9(3/4)(September/December 1957):30–34.

07-086. LEE, George J. "On the Relationship of Early Korai [Koryŏ] Celadon to the Chinese Wares of Yueh." *Far Eastern Ceramic Bulletin* 1(3)(November 1948):20–25. An excellent brief study with reference to Japanese sources.

07-087. _____. "Two Korean Ceramic Ewers." *Museum Bulletin of the Brooklyn Institute of Arts and Sciences* 20(Summer 1959):1–6.

07-088. MEDLEY, Margaret. "Korea, China and Liao in Koryŏ Ceramics." *Oriental Arts* 23(1)(Spring 1977):80–86.

07-089. STERN, Harold Philip. "A Contemporary Korean Kiln." *Far Eastern Ceramic Bulletin* 10(1/2)(March/June 1958):1–4.

07-090. WARNER, Lorraine d'O. "Korean Grave Pottery of the Korai [Koryŏ] Dynasty." *Bulletin of the Cleveland Museum of Art* 6(3)(April 1919):46.

07-091. _____. "Korai [Koryŏ] Celadon in America." *Eastern Art: An Annual* 2(September/December 1930):37–121. For many years this article has been the most comprehensive study of Koryŏ celadon published in the West. Now somewhat out of date, it remains a valuable and stimulating introduction to the subject.

07-092. YANAGI, Sōetsu. "A Note on the Pottery Kilns of the Korai [Koryŏ] Dynasty." *Eastern Art: An Annual* 2(September/December 1930):122–125.

07-093. _____. "The Mystery of Beauty: A Tribute to the Korean Craftsman." *Far Eastern Ceramic Bulletin* 9(3/4)(September/December 1957):6–11. A well-known Japanese aesthete praises the shape, color, and design of Korean wares and notes the spontaneous and natural attitudes of the potters who produced them.

Applied Arts

07-094. CABLE, E. M. "Old Korean Bells." *Transactions of the Korea Branch of the Royal Asiatic Society* 16(1925):1–45.

07-095. FIGGESS, John. "Mother of Pearl Inlaid Lacquer of the Koryŏ Dynasty." *Oriental Art* 23(1)(Spring 1977): 87-95.

07-096. FONTEIN, Jan. "Masterpieces of Lacquer and Metalwork." *Apollo* 88(August 1968):114-119.

07-097. _____. "Notes on Korean Lacquer." *Bulletin of Vereeniging von Vrieden der Asiatische Kunst* 6(1956): 88-93.

07-098. GRAY, Basil. "The Inlaid Metalwork of Korea." *British Museum Quarterly* 20(1956):92-95.

07-099. KIM, Chewon. "Die Steinpagoden des Kamun-sa und des Pulguk-sa in Korea und ihre Schätze." *Propyläen Kunstgeschichte China, Korea, Japan.* Berlin: Propyläen Verlag, 1968. A study of gilt bronze Buddhist reliquaries of fine workmanship found in stone pagodas of Kamŭn-sa (datable from 682) and Pulguk-sa (around 751). The items include Buddhist images, glass objects, and woodblock-printed sūtras.

07-100. _____. "Treasures from the Songyim-sa [Songnim-sa] Temple in South Korea." *Artibus Asiae* 22(1/2)(1959): 95-112. A study of a gilt bronze Buddhist reliquary from which a glass bottle and a cup were discovered. The glass cup, probably a work of the eighth century, resembles closely the famous Shōsōin glass cup probably of Sassanian origin.

07-101. _____. "Two Old Silla Tombs." *Artibus Asiae* 10(3)(1947):169-192. A preliminary report on Ho'uch'ong, which yielded a covered bronze bowl with inscriptions of Koguryŏ King Kwanggaet'o (dated 415), and also on Ŭnyŏng-ch'ong, which yielded a lacquered mask among other excavated items. (See also 07-031.)

07-102. TOMITA, Kōjiro. "Korean Silver-work of the Koryo Period." *Bulletin of the Museum of Fine Arts* (Boston), 39(231)(1941):2-7. Study of a silver plaque and a Buddhist reliquary in the Museum of Fine Arts, Boston. The plaque depicts a dragon with pearl-shaped balls in repoussé and is dated to the late eleventh or early twelfth century. Another item discussed is a small Lamaist stupa-shaped reliquary which contains five smaller pagodas inscribed with names, of which two are identified as monks active in the fourteenth century in Korea. Very little discussion is given to the art objects themselves.

07-103. _____. "A Han Lacquer Dish and a Koryŏ Silver Ware from Korea." *Bulletin of the Museum of Fine Arts* (Boston), 33(199)(1935):64-69.

Folk Art
Books

07-104. Korea, Republic of. National Academy of Fine Arts. *Survey of Korean Arts: Folk Arts.* Seoul: 1974. Chapter 5 is divided into two sections: folk painting by Za-yong Zo and folk craftsmanship by Yong-hae Ye.

07-105. ZO, Zayong (ed.). *The Humor of Korean Tiger.* Seoul: Emille Museum, 1970. A charming series of varying aspects of Korean folk art has been published by the Emille Museum with Zo as chief editor. He has almost single-handedly brought Korean folk art to the attention of the general public and his love of that genre infuses his books. Zo's highly intimate and subjective style is in some ways quite amateurish yet very interesting, particularly for general readers.

07-106. _____. *The Spirit of Korean Tiger.* Seoul: Emille Museum, 1970.

07-107. _____. *Folkism.* 2 vols. Seoul: Emille Museum, 1971-1972.

07-108. _____. *Diamond Mountains.* 2 vols. Seoul: Emille Museum, 1975.

07-109. _____. *The Life of Buddha in Korean Paintings.* Seoul: Emille Museum, 1975. A joint project of the Emille Museum and the Korea Branch of the Royal Asiatic Society. The depiction of the eight great events during the life of Śākyamuni in temple paintings and woodblock prints.

07-110. _____. *Introduction to Korean Folk Painting.* Seoul: Emille Museum, 1977.

Articles

07-111. PAI, Man-sill. "Patterns of Furniture Design during the Yi Dynasty." *Transactions of the Korea Branch of the Royal Asiatic Society* 44(1968):129-138.

07-112. STARR, Frederick. "Corean Coin Charms and Amulets: A Supplement." *Transactions of the Korea Branch of the Royal Asiatic Society* 8(1917):42-79.

Catalogs

07-113. KIM, Man-Hee (ed.). *The Collection of Korean Folklore Pictures [Han'guk minsok togam].* Seoul: Asian and Pacific Culture Association, 1973.

07-114. _____. *Folklore Pictures [Torok].* Seoul: Research Institute of Folklore Painting, 1974.

07-115. _____. *Korean Folklore Pictures [Minsok torok].* Vols. 3 and 4. Seoul: Research Institute of Folklore Painting, 1975. These catalogs contain interesting drawings of ornamental designs in Korean houses, costumes, and various handicrafts, household furnishings, folkdance masks, musical instruments, and almost everything related to traditional Korean life. The captions for each object are written both in Korean and English. Unfortunately the contents are not systematically arranged and hence it is difficult to locate specific items.

MUSIC /*Bang-song Song*
Books

07-116. CHANG, Sa-hun. *Han'guk akki taegwan* [Korean musical instruments]. Seoul: Korean Musicological Society, 1969. 315 pp. A comprehensive study of Korean musical instruments with an English summary divided into four parts: Classification of Korean Musical Instruments; Wind Instruments, String Instruments, and Percussion; Orchestrations in the Old Music; and The Court Musicians. Illustrated by 8 color and 140 black/white pictures.

07-117. _____. *Glossary of Korean Music.* Seoul: Korean Musicological Society, 1972. 118 pp. Reprint of Chang's first publication in 1961 by Radio Management Bureau, Republic of Korea. The work consists of three parts: Musical Instruments; Court Music; and Folk Music. It was compiled as a reference for those who work in the broadcasting field.

07-118. _____. *Han'guk chŏnt'ong ŭmak yŏn'gu* [Studies in Korean traditional music]. Seoul: Po Chin Chai Printing Co., 1975. 461 pp. A collection of fifteen essays with an English summary. Contents: Part 1: Development of Traditional Music Including "A Study of *Pohŏja* (II)," "Performance Practice of *Kŏmun'go,*" "Historical Changes in *Kŏmun'go* Tuning," "On the Historical Development of the *Yŏgan-pŏp* Ornament," and "Past and Present Forms of the *Taegŭm* and *Chunggŭm*." Part 2: Characteristics of Traditional Music ("Appoggiatura Techniques in *Kŏmun'go* Performance" and "An Attempt to Define the Characteristics of Korean Music"). Part 3: Traditional Vocal Music ("*Ŏllong* and *Ŏlp'yŏn,*" "Musical Characteristics of *Kasa,*" and "On the Actual Beat in *Sijo* Singing"). Part 4: Musical Sources ("Korean Traditional Notations," "An Explanation of Symbols," "Yang's *Kŏmun'go* Book," "Fifteenth-Century Court Music," and "A Transcription of *Changgo* Rhythmic Patterns").

07-119. ECKARDT, Andreas. *Koreanische Musik.* Tokyo: Deutsche Gesellschaft für Natur und Völkerkunde Ostasiens, 1930. 63 pp. Contains a short history and description of Korean music with an analysis of Korean songs and melodies. Transcriptions and photographs of the various Korean instruments are included.

07-120. _____. *Musik, Lied, Tanz in Korea.* Bonn: H. Bouvier and Co. Verlag, 1968. 168 pp. The work is divided into five chapters: Einführung; Musikinstrumente; Tanz und Lied; Lieder zum Tanz; and Musikbeispiele. Forty-three photographs and a bibliography are appended.

07-121. KAUFMANN, Walter. *Musical Notations of the Orient.* Bloomington: Indiana University Press, 1967. 498 pp. Includes such notational systems as *yulchabo* (Chinese *lü-lü* notation), *kongch'ŏkpo* (Chinese *kung-ch'e* notation), *chŏngganbo* (Korean mensural notation), *oŭm yakpo* (Korean five-tone notations), *yukpo* (Korean solmization notation), *kuŭm* (Korean syllable notation), and *yŏnŭmp'yo* (Korean neumatic notation).

07-122. KEH, Chung-sik. *Die koreanische Musik.* Strassburg: Heitz & Co., 1935. 77 pp. Originally a doctoral dissertation submitted to the University of Strassburg in 1934. Contains a historical survey of Korean culture and discusses the philosophy of Korean music, the essence of Korean music, the form and method of playing instruments. Includes transcriptions of seventeen phonograph records.

07-123. Korean Musicological Society. *Yi Hye-gu paksa songsu kinyŏm ŭmakhak nonch'ong* [Essays in ethnomusicology: a birthday offering for Lee Hye-ku]. Seoul: Seoul National University Press, 1969. 433 pp. An essay collection on Korean music and ethnomusicology. The work is roughly divided into two parts: the first contains ten articles in Korean by Korean scholars; the second includes eleven essays in foreign languages by Oriental and Western scholars.

07-124. LEE, Hye-ku. *Han'guk ŭmak sŏsŏl* [Topics in Korean music]. Seoul: Seoul National University Press, 1975. 510 pp. A revised edition of Lee's publications of 1967. A collection of nineteen articles with an English summary. The entire text of "Musical Paintings in a Fourth-Century Korean Tomb" is translated by Robert C. Provine, Jr.; it was published in *Korea Journal* 14(3)(March 1974):4–14.

07-125. _____. *Han'guk ŭmak nonch'ong* [Essays on Korean music]. Seoul: Sŏmundang, 1975. 426 pp. A collection of fifteen essays with an English summary. It contains such essays as "A Short History of Korean Music," "Les charactéristiques de la musique coréenne," "The Preface to the *Aakpo* in the Annals of King Sejong," "Music in the Confucian Shrines of Korea with Comparison to the Current Situation in China," "Chronology of Pak Yŏn's Pitch Pipes," and "The Kwansŭp Togam." English translations by Robert C. Provine, Jr.

07-126. PROVINE, Robert C., Jr. *Drum Rhythm in Korean Farmers' Music.* Seoul: Sinjin munhwasa, 1975. 53 pp. An intensive study of hourglass drum *(changgo)* playing under the guidance of Kim Pyŏng-sŏp during the period of his field research (1973–1975). The work is divided into two parts: "Survey of Drum Rhythm in Korean Farmers' Music" and "Transcriptions of 305 *Changgo* Rhythmic Patterns" (241 in app. 1 and 64 in app. 2).

07-127. ROCKWELL, Coralie. *Kagok: A Traditional Korean Vocal Form.* Providence: Asian Music Publications,

Brown University, 1972. 302 pp. Originally a master's thesis submitted to UCLA in 1969. Contents: History and Introduction to *Kagok;* Instruments in the *Kagok* Ensemble; Male and Female Vocal Technique and Ornamentation; The *"Jo"* of *Kagok;* The Relationship of Mode and Text in the *Kagok* Form; Melodic Titles in Modal Variation: *P'yŏngjo* and *Kemyŏnjo.* Appendix contains musical transcriptions of *kagok.*

07-128. SONG, Bang-song. *An Annotated Bibliography of Korean Music.* Providence: Asian Music Publications, Brown University, 1971. 250 pp. The work is divided into two parts: pt. 1 deals with 792 entries in the Korean language; pt. 2 deals with 477 entries in foreign languages including English, Japanese, French, and German. Addenda contain fifty entries in Korean and Japanese. Included are indexes of names, subjects, and publications.

07-129. _____. *The Korean-Canadian Folk Song: An Ethnomusicological Study.* Ottawa: Canadian Centre for Folk Culture Studies, National Museum of Man, 1974. 222 pp. An analytical study of the Korean-Canadian community, their folk songs, and their music as recorded in Metropolitan Toronto in 1973. Part 1 contains an introduction to the Korean people and their cultural traditions, a survey of the Korean immigrants and their music in Canada, and an analysis of twenty-one folk songs. Part 2 contains transcriptions of twenty-one folk songs and nine pieces of instrumental folk music. A glossary-index is appended.

Articles

07-130. COURANT, Maurice. "La musique en Corée." In Albert Lavignac (ed.), *Encyclopédie de la musique et dictionnaire.* Vol. 1. Paris: Charles Delagrave, 1913–1931. A brief survey of Korean music including descriptions of musical instruments, a short history, and the influence of China on musical form and dances in Korea.

07-131. DEUCHLER, Martina and Hye-ku LEE. "Koreanische Musik." In Frederich Blume (ed.), *Die Musik in Geschichte und Gegenwart.* Supplement. Kassel and Basel: Bärenreiter Verlag, forthcoming.

07-132. HAHN, Man-young. "Religious Origins of Korean Music." *Korea Journal* 15(7)(July 1975):17–21. An attempt to view traditional Korean music *(p'ansori, kagok, sanjo, nongak, sijo)* from the standpoint of religious origins such as shamanism, Buddhism, Confucianism, and Christianity.

07-133. LEE, Byong-won. "A Short History of *Pŏmp'ae*: Korean Buddhist Ritual Chant." *Journal of Korean Studies* (Seattle), 1(2)(1971):109–121. Historical survey of Korean Buddhist chant covering the Three Kingdoms period to the Yi period. Discusses "Genealogy of *Pŏmp'ae* between 15th and 18th Century" and "Genealogy of *Pŏmp'ae* Musicians after 1900."

07-134. _____. "Korean Music and Dance." In *Grove's Dictionary of Music and Musicians.* 6th ed. London: Macmillan, forthcoming.

07-135. LEE, Hye-ku. "The *Yukcha-paegi.*" *Asian Music* (New York), 2(2)(1971):18–30. A critical examination of Keh Chung-sik's transcription and analysis of the *Yukcha paegi* in his *Koreanische Musik* (Strassburg: 1935) (07-122).

07-136. _____. "Musical Painting in a Fourth-Century Korean Tomb." *Korea Journal* 14(3)(March 1974):4–14. An intensive study of musical paintings uncovered in an archaeological excavation at Anak, Hwanghae province. This is an English translation of Lee's previous essay published in *Chindan hakpo* (Seoul: 1962) and reprinted in *Han'guk ŭmak sŏsŏl* (Seoul: 1967). The translation was done by Robert C. Provine, Jr. A translator's preface is added.

07-137. LEE, Kang-Sook. "Providing Korean Rhythmic Experiences in the Classroom." *Korea Journal* 15(12)(December 1975):25–30. The author discusses his experiences teaching Korean *changgo* rhythms in American classrooms. Originally a chapter in his doctoral dissertation: "The Development and Trial of Korean-based Musical Activity for the Classroom" (University of Michigan, 1975).

07-138. PROVINE, Robert C., Jr. "The Treatise on Ceremonial Music (1430) in the Annals of the Korean King Sejong." *Ethnomusicology* (Ann Arbor), 18(1)(January 1974):1–29. An intensive study of a Korean musical source containing sections on "Historical Background," "Background and Purpose of the *Treatise on Ceremonial Music,*" "Neo-Confucian Task and Its Source Materials," "Four Korean Versions," "Analysis of the Lin Yü Melodies," and "Antecedents and Descendants."

07-139. _____. "Sejong and the Preservation of Chinese Ritual Melodies." *Korea Journal* 14(2)(February 1974): 24–39. Examines some aspects of an important musical document—the *Treatise on Ceremonial Music (Aakpo),* prepared in 1430 by order of King Sejong.

07-140. _____. "Brief Introduction to Traditional Korean Folk Music." *Korea Journal* 15(1)(January 1975):29–31. An attempt to define the Korean concept of folk music, which usually includes not only the polished songs of professional singers but also highly developed art forms like *p'ansori* and *sanjo* performed by professional troupes of entertainers.

07-141. ROCKWELL, Coralie. "The Traditional Music of Korea." *Korea Frontier* 10(October 1971):10–13. A brief introduction to Korean music including history, categories of music (court music and noncourt music), vocal music, and folk music.

07-142. _____. "Trends and Developments in Korean Traditional Music Today." *Korea Journal* 15(3)(March 1974): 15–20. A general observation of recent trends in Korean music during the period of the author's field research in Seoul (1973–1974). Includes court music, Confucian ritual music, and *kayagŭm sanjo.*

07-143. SONG, Bang-song. "The Korean *Pip'a* and Its Notation." *Ethnomusicology* (Ann Arbor), 17(3)(September 1973):460–493. A comprehensive study covering two topics: one is a historical investigation of the migration of lute-family instruments from Central Asia through China; the other is a deciphering of a sixteenth-century tablature of Korean *pip'a.* Appended are the original notation of *pip'a,* its transcription in Western notation, and a glossary.

07-144. _____. "Korean *Kwangdae* Musicians and Their Musical Tradition." *Korea Journal* 14(9)(September 1974):12–18. Presents a comprehensive summary of current knowledge on *kwangdae* musicians and suggests a possible direction for future research. The paper tries to answer two questions: How did *kwangdae* musicians come to establish their professionalism in the traditional society of Korea? And how have they contributed to Korea's musical history?

07-145. _____. "*Kagok,* a Traditional Korean Vocal Form." *Ethnomusicology* (Ann Arbor), 18(2)(May 1974):315–321. A critical review of *Kagok, a Traditional Korean Vocal Form* (Providence: Asian Music Publications, 1972) by Coralie Rockwell (07-127).

07-146. _____. "*P'ansori:* Korea's Epic Vocal Art and Instrumental Music." *Yearbook of the International Folk Music Council* 6(1974):166–168; and *Asian Music* 5(2) (1974): 66–71. Review of a record: *P'ansori: Korea's Epic Vocal Art and Instrumental Music* (see 07-178).

07-147. _____. "Supplement to *An Annotated Bibliography of Korean Music (I–V),*" *Korea Journal* 14(12)(December 1974–April 1975):59–72; 15(1):59–72; 15(2):58–68; 15(3): 64–70; and 15(4):69–76. Contains 643 items—books, reviews, essays, and articles in Korean and foreign languages—which have been published since the first edition of *An Annotated Bibliography of Korean Music* in 1971 (07-128). Alphabetically arranged with annotations.

07-148. _____. "The Etymology of the Korean Six-Stringed Zither, *Kŏmun'go:* A Critical Review." *Korea Journal* 15(10)(October 1975):18–23. A critical review of theories on the etymology of the Korean *kŏmun'go* advocated by literary scholars and musicologists. Originally a chapter in

the author's doctoral dissertation: "*Kŏmun'go Sanjo:* An Analytical Study of a Style of Korean Folk Instrumental Music" (Wesleyan University, 1975).

07-149. _____. "The Selection of Korean Classical Music." *Ethnomusicology* (Ann Arbor), 19(3)(September 1975): 508–510. A record review of three discs: *Han'guk ŭmak sŏnjip* (Seoul: National Classical Music Institute, 1972), manufactured by Chigu Record Co.

07-150. _____. "Korean Music." *Asian Music* 7(1)(1975): 84–85. A record review of an LP disc: *Korean Music: UNESCO Collection Musical Sources* (see 07-179).

07-151. _____. "Sijo ŭmak non [A treatise on *sijo* music]." *Ethnomusicology* (Ann Arbor), 20(1)(January 1976): 140–141. A book review of *Sijo ŭmak non* (Seoul: Seoul National University Press, 1973) by Chang Sa-hun.

07-152. _____. "Korean Music in Canada." In Helmut Kallman (ed.), *Encyclopedia of Music in Canada.* Ottawa: National Library of Canada, forthcoming.

07-153. SONG, Kyŏng-nin. "Korean Music." *Arts of Asia* (Hong Kong), 2(5)(September/October 1972):52–57. A general introduction to Korean traditional music including twelve pictures of performance.

07-154. SUR, Donald. "Korea." In W. Apel (ed.), *Harvard Dictionary of Music.* 2nd ed. Cambridge, Mass.: Harvard University Press, 1969. A comprehensive introduction to Korean music covering history, kinds of music, notations, theory, and musical instruments. Includes a selected bibliography.

Unpublished Dissertations

07-155. ANDERSON, Sara May. "Korean Folk Songs." Master's thesis, Eastman School of Music, University of Rochester, 1940. 103 pp. Contains two parts: "Cultural Value of Folksongs in Public School Music" and "Cultural Value of Korean Folksong" (including historical background, the Korean philosophy of music, the nature of Korean folk songs, and analysis of twelve songs). Appended is transcription of twelve songs with piano accompaniment.

07-156. BREZETTE, Majel C. "The Music of China, Korea and Japan in Relationship to the Rest of the World." Master's thesis, Wayne State University, 1951.

07-157. CHI, Chul Young. "The Influence of Chinese Music on Korean Music." EdD dissertation, University of Northern Colorado, 1975. 171 pp.

07-158. KEH, Chung-sik. "Die koreanische Musik." PhD dissertation, University of Strassburg, 1934. For an annotation of the work see 07-122.

07-159. KIM, Chin-gyun. "Musikethnologische Studien über

das koreanische Volklied.'' PhD dissertation, Universität Wien, 1964. 228 pp. General remarks on the study of folk song and examination of the characteristics of Korean folk song (for example, *Arirang*) with twenty-nine musical examples. The dissertation manuscript is available at the Universität Wien library (call number D12,911).

07-160. KIM, Soon-ae. "Traditional Musical Instruments and Folksongs of Korea." Master's thesis, Eastman School of Music, University of Rochester, 1956. 95 pp. Consists of three chapters: I. Survey of Korean Music (including historical background, scales, accompaniment, and notations); II. Korean Musical Instruments; and III. Analysis of 12 Korean Folksongs. Included are diagrams, photographs, tables, and a bibliography.

07-161. LEE, Byong-won. "*Hossori* and *Chissori* of *Pŏmp'ae*: An Analysis of Two Major Styles of Korean Buddhist Ritual Chant." Master's thesis, University of Washington, 1971. 111 pp. Contents: I. A Short History of Buddhist Rituals and *Pŏmp'ae*; II. Forms in Buddhist Music; III. Structure of *Hossori Pŏmp'ae*; IV. Structure of *Chissori Pŏmp'ae*; V. Analysis of *Ch'ohalryang*; VI. Analysis of *Porye*; and Conclusion.

07-162. _____. "An Analytical Study of Sacred Buddhist Chant of Korea." PhD dissertation, University of Washington, 1974. 206 pp. Available from University Microfilm: UM 74-28,666. Contents: I. Background and Purpose of the Study; II. History of Buddhist Ritual Performing Arts; III. Introduction to Buddhist Rites, Ritual Music, and Dance; IV. Theoretical Structure of *Hossori Pŏmp'ae*; V. Analysis of Three *Hossori Pŏmp'ae*; VI. Theoretical Structure of *Chissori Pŏmp'ae*; VII. Analysis of Two *Chissori Pŏmp'ae*; and VIII. Conclusion.

07-163. LEE, Kang-sook. "The Development and Trial of Korean-Based Musical Activities for the Classroom." PhD dissertation, University of Michigan, 1975. 277 pp. Available from University Microfilm: UM 75-20,390. Contents: I. Introduction; II. Korean Music Culture; III. Orientation; IV. Musical Notation; V. Teaching Korean Musical Concepts through the Elements: Rhythm, Melody, and Form; VI. A Summation of Musical Elements; VII. Summary, Recommendations and Implications; Appendix A: Korean Modes.

07-164. PARK, Chong Gil. "Ornamentation in Korean Court Music." Master's thesis, University of Washington, 1970. 107 pp. An analytical study of ornamentation based primarily on the contemporary performance practices of court musicians in the National Classical Music Institute.

07-165. ROCKWELL, Coralie. "A Study of *Kagok*, a Traditional Korean Vocal Form, and an Analysis of Thirty-four Songs of the Repertoire." Master's thesis, University of

California, Los Angeles, 1969. For an annotation of Rockwell's work see 07-127.

07-166. SMITH, Lenore K. "The Korean *Sanjo-Taegŭm* and Its Music." Master's thesis, Wesleyan University, 1970. 71 pp. An analytical study of *taegŭm sanjo* based on the Han Pŏm-su school. Discusses such topics as historical survey, construction, structure, relationship between *taegŭm* and Chinese *ti*, tuning method, and notation. A transcription in graphic notation is appended.

07-167. SONG, Bang-song. "*Kŏmun'go Sanjo*: An Analytical Study of a Style of Korean Folk Instrumental Music." PhD dissertation, Wesleyan University, 1975. 464 pp. Available from University Microfilm: UM 75-23, 004. Part 1: History and Theory: I. A Short History of *Kŏmun'go*; II. The Instrument and Its Etymology; III. Physical Description; IV. Historical Source of *Kŏmun'go* Music; V. Forms of *Kŏmun'go* Notation; and VI. Standard Pitch and Tuning. Part 2: Music and Musicians: VII. Socio-Historical Background of *Kwangdae* Musicians; VIII. Relationships of *Sanjo* to Other Performing Arts; and IX. An Historical Survey of *Sanjo*. Part 3: Analysis and Discussion: X. Tonal Structure; XI. Rhythmic Structure; XII. Other Features; XIII. Improvisation in *Kŏmun'go Sanjo*; and XIV. Summary and Conclusion. Part 4: Transcriptions include *Kŏmun'go Sanjo* of Sin K'we-dong and *Kŏmun'go Sanjo* of Paek Nak-chun. Appended are a glossary, source readings in *kŏmun'go* literature, transcriptions of Korean zither tablature, and field research data.

07-168. SUH, In-jung. "Traditional Korean Stringed Instruments." Master's thesis, Indiana University, 1972. Contents: I. Introduction; II. Bowed Instruments: *Ajaeng* and *Haegŭm*; III. Plucked Instruments: *Kŏmun'go, Kayago, Taejaeng, Kŭm, Sŭl, Hyang-pip'a, Tang-pip'a, Wŏlgŭm, Konghu (Su-konghu, Wa-konghu, Tae-konghu, So-konghu)*; IV. Struck Instrument: *Yanggŭm*; and V. Conclusion.

07-169. TIANEN, Walter. "Melodic Movement in *Yŏngsan Hoesang*." Master's thesis, University of Washington, 1971. 125 pp. Contents: I. Brief Survey of Korean Court Music; II. The *Kŏmun'go, Tanso*, and *Changgo*; III. The *Kŏmun'go* Melody (Melodic Analysis); and IV. The *Tanso* Melody (Notation and Ornamentation).

Selected Discography

This discography is based primarily on records manufactured in the United States and still available in American stores. All the records are LP 33 1/3 rpm discs. Side and band numbers are abbreviated in roman and arabic numerals: II:1, for example, indicates side II and band 1.

07-170. Disques Vogue. *Musique bouddhique de Corée*. One disc, Collection Musée de l'Homme, LVLX-253, 1968. Recorded and noted by John Levy. I:1 *Koryŏngsan*. II:1. *Samgŭi-ŭirye;* 2. *Panya simgyŏng;* 3. *Hwach'ŏng;* 4. *Ch'ŏnsubara.*

07-171. East-West Center. *Music from Korea*. Vol. 1: *The Kayakeum*. One disc, East-West Recording Stereo, EWS-1001, 1965. Performed by Byongki Hwang and noted by Barbara B. Smith. I:1. *Kayagŭm Sanjo*. II:1. The Fall composed by B. Hwang; 2. The Pomegranate House composed by B. Hwang; 3. The Forest composed by B. Hwang.

07-172. Folkways Records and Service Corp. *Folk and Classical Music of Korea*. One disc, Ethnic Folkways Library, FE 4424, 1951. Noted by Park Kyung Ho. I:1. *Ch'angbu t'aryŏng;* 2. *Tan'ga;* 3. *Chŏkpyŏkka;* 4. *Yukchabaegi;* 5. *Norae Karak;* 6. *Chajin nongbuga*. II:7. *Chŏngak (Kyemyŏn);* 8. *Chŏngak (Ujo);* 9. *Changch'unbullojigok;* 10. *Manp'asik;* 11. *Kagok: Ŏllak;* 12. *Chongmyoak: Yŏngsin.*

07-173. _____. *Music of the World's People*. Vol. 4. Two discs, Ethnic Folkways Library, FE-4507, 1958. Edited by Henry Cowell. IV:67. Classical Song from Harold Courland Collection.

07-174. _____. *Music of the Orient in Hawaii: Japan, China, Korea, and Philippines*. One disc, Folkways Records, FW-8745, 1963. Recorded by Jacob Feurring. II:2. Drum solo played on nine *puk* by Pai Bok Soon; 3. *Kayagŭm* solo *"Chajinmori"* by Sung Keum Sun; 4. *Chukchang manghye* accompanied by *kayagŭm*, Sung Keum Sun; 5. *Kutkŏri t'aryŏng* by Sung Keum Sun.

07-175. _____. *Korea: Vocal and Instrumental Music*. One disc, Ethnic Folkways Library, FE-4325, 1965. Noted by Paul M. Ochojski. I:1. *Aak;* 2. *Arirang;* 3. *Toraji t'aryŏng;* 4. *Tan'ga*. II:1. *Ch'anggukcho;* 2. *T'aryŏng;* 3. *Nongak;* 4. *Kayagŭm Sanjo.*

07-176. Lyrichord Discs. *Korean Social and Folk Music*. One disc, Lyrichord, LLST-7211, 1970. Noted and recorded by John Levy. I:1. *Kŏmun'go sanjo* by Sin K'we-dong; 2. *Ajaeng sanjo* by Han Il-sŏp; 3. *Hojŏk sanjo* by Han Il-sŏp; 4. *Sae t'aryŏng* with *kŏmun'go* accompaniment by Sin K'we-dong. II:1. *P'ansori, Ch'unhyangga* by Pak Ch'o-wŏl; 2. Four northwestern folk songs *(Kin ari, Chajin ari, Susimga,* and *Chajin nanbongga)* sung by Yi Ch'ang-bae; 3. Four Central Province folk songs *(Norae karak, Arirang, Ibyŏlga,* and *Chŏngsŏn arirang)* by Yi Ch'ang-bae.

07-177. _____. *Korean Court Music*. One disc, Lyrichord Stereo, LL-7206, 1969. Performed by the National Classical Music Institute and recorded by John Levy. I:1. *Ŭnganjiak* (Confucian); 2. *Sŏnganjiak* (Confucian); 3. *Nagyanch'un;* 4. *Sujech'ŏn;* 5. *Kŏmun'go tasŭrŭm* with *taegŭm*. II:1. *Kagok* sung by Hong Wŏn-gi; 2. *Kagok* sung by Hong Wŏn-gi; 3. *Sijo* sung by Chi Hwa-ja; 4. *Ch'wit'a;* 5. Stone chimes *(p'yŏn'gyŏng)* and bronze bells *(p'yŏnjong).*

07-178. Nonesuch Records. *P'ansori: Korea's Epic Vocal Art and Instrumental Music*. One disc, Explorer Series, H-72049 (stereo), 1972. Noted by Jonathan Cott and David Lewiston. I:1. Scene from *Hŭngbuga* sung by Kim So-hŭi; 2. *P'yŏngjo hoesang (p'iri* solo) by Chi Yŏng-hui; 3. *Kayagŭm sanjo* by Sŏng Kŭm-yŏn. II:1. *Haegŭm sinawi* by Chi Yŏng-hŭi; 2. *Kŏmun'go sanjo* by Kim Yun-dŏk; 3. *Ch'angbu t'aryŏng (p'iri* solo) by Chi Yŏng-hŭi; 4. Scene from *Simch'ŏngga* by Kim So-hŭi.

07-179. Philips. *UNESCO Collection Musical Sources: Korean Music*. One disc, Art Music from the Far East, VIII-1. Philips, 5686-011, 1973. Noted by Alain Daniélou. I:1. *Sujech'ŏn;* 2. *Manp'a chŏngsikchigok;* 3. *Tae ch'wit'a;* 4. *Samhyŏn yŏngsan*. II:5. *Ch'ŏngsŏng chajinhanip;* 6. *Mannyŏn changhwanjigok;* 7. The Waterfall of Pak Yŏn; 8. *Chŏngsŏn arirang;* 9. *Kayagŭm sanjo* by Sŏng Kŭm-yŏn.

Korean Music and Dance on Film

The following films on Korean dance and music are part of the Ethnic Music and Dance Series, which has been produced under the direction of Professor Robert Garfias by the University of Washington Press in Seattle. The films are intended to be used as a documentary record of authentic performances of traditional music. The films can be purchased from the University of Washington Press, Attn: Mr. Ott Haytt, 1416 N.E. 41st Street, Seattle, WA 98105.

07-180. *Five Korean Court Dances*. 33 minutes, color, $370 (rental $16). The performances include a solo Nightingale Dance and four group dances: a Flower Dance, a Drum Dance, a Ball Game Dance, and five men in a masked dance.

07-181. *Buddhist Dances of Korea*. 18 minutes, color, $200 (rental $9.50). The performances include the Butterfly Dance, the Cymbal Dance, and a Monk's Dance. Also shown is a performance by the instrumental ensemble of the old royal processional music.

07-182. *Korean Court Music*. 15 minutes, color, $170 (rental $8.25). The musicians of the National Classical Music Institute perform several different examples of court music, both the ceremonial and the entertainment music. A chamber ensemble also performs two selections from the court entertainment music repertoire.

07-183. *Yangju Sandae Nori: Masked Drama of Korea.* 33 minutes, color, $370 (rental $16). The masked drama has evolved into a folk drama consisting of a number of short acts using stock characters: the nobleman, the shaman, the policeman, the errant monk, the wife of the nobleman, and the seductive female shaman or courtesan.

07-184. *Pongsan T'al Ch'um: Northern Korean Masked Drama.* 32 minutes, color, $360 (rental $15). *T'al ch'um* is another form of traditional masked drama. This one has its origin in the region around Pongsan in North Korea.

07-185. *Korean Vocal Music.* 14 minutes, color, $160 (rental $7). The first example is a lyrical form *(tan'ga)* accompanying a *kayagŭm.* The second is an excerpt from the *p'ansori* repertory sung by Kim So-hŭi.

07-186. *Korean Folk Dances.* 25 minutes, color, $280 (rental $12.75). Contains Rope Dance *(chult'agi)* and Farmer's Dance *(nongak).* The latter usually takes place during the harvest season.

07-187. *Salp'uri: Korean Improvisational Dance.* 25 minutes, black/white, $110 (rental $6). The film includes two separate performances which are executed with a high degree of spontaneous spirit.

07-188. *Sanjo: Korean Improvisational Music.* 21 minutes, black/white, $110 (rental $11.50). This film includes three performances of *sanjo*—two on the traditional instrument for this music *(kayagŭm)* and a third on a seven-stringed bowed zither *(ajaeng).*

07-189. *Three Dances from Chŏlla-do, Korea.* 23 minutes, color, $260 (rental $12.75). Presents three different types of dance from the southwestern province of Korea: Buddhist monk's dance, a solo improvisational dance *(salp'-uri),* and a popular group dance *(kanggang sulle).*

DRAMA AND DANCE/*Du-Hyun Lee*
Books

07-190. CHO, Won-Kyung. *Dances of Korea.* New York: Norman J. Seaman, 1962.

07-191. CHOE, Sang-su. *A Study of the Korean Puppet Play.* Korean Folklore Studies Series, no. 4. Seoul: Korea Books Publishing Company, 1961. A comprehensive survey of the Korean puppet play including themes, content, costumes, and props. Contains pictures of puppets and scenes from puppet plays.

07-192. _____. *A Study of the Mask Play of Ha-hoe.* Korean Folklore Studies Series, no. 2. Seoul: Korea Books Publishing Company, 1959. A survey of *Hahoe* masks and mask-dance drama including themes, content, masks, costumes, and props. Contains pictures of masks and props.

07-193. CHONG, Pyong-hi. *Danses masquées et jeux de marionnettes en Corée.* Paris: Publications Orientalistes de France, 1975. The first introductory book in French on the Korean mask-dance and puppet show. The book is based on Chae-Ch'ŏl Kim's *A History of Korean Drama* and Tu-Hyŏn Yi's *Korean Mask-dance Drama* (both in Korean).

07-194. FREEDLEY, George and John A. REEVES. *A History of the Theatre.* New York: Crown, 1968. Chapter 14 devotes one and a half pages (pp. 195–196) to the old theater in Korea. Chapter 27, written by John Kardoss, presents a helpful outline of Korean drama.

07-195. GASSNER, John and Edward QUINN (eds.). *The Reader's Encyclopedia of World Drama.* New York: Crowell, 1969. Offers a brief and comprehensive survey of Korean theater arts written by John Kardoss (pp. 509–516). It deals with not only the history but also the contemporary theater and explains the contents of mask-dance drama, stage, types of masks, music, and so on.

07-196. HEYMAN, Alan. *Dances of the Three Thousand League Land.* Seoul: Myongji College, 1966. A brief description of Korean court dance, religious dance, folk dance, and mask dance.

07-197. KARDOSS, John. *An Outline History of Korean Drama.* Greenvale, N.Y.: Long Island University Press, 1966. A brief history of Korean drama from the Silla dynasty until the 1960s. Contains mask dances, *narye* and *sandae* plays of the Yi dynasty, puppet plays, *p'ansori,* and others. This is a good introductory book for students interested in Korean drama.

07-198. Korea, Republic of. National Acadamy of Arts. *Survey of Korean Arts: Folk Arts.* Seoul: 1974. Chapter 2, Folk Drama, has four entries: (1) Mask-Dance Drama by Du-Hyun Lee; (2) Puppet Play by Sang-su Choe; (3) *P'ansori* by Han-yŏng Kang; (4) Folk Plays by Sang-su Choe. Chapter 7, devoted to Namsa-dang, is by U-sŏng Sim.

07-199. Korean National Commission for UNESCO. *Traditional Performing Arts of Korea.* Seoul: 1975. Divided into the following sections: Introduction and Folk Songs by Man-yong Han; Farmers' Band Music by Sa-hun Chang; Mask-Dance Drama by Du-Hyun Lee; and Folk Plays by Tong-gwon Im. Superb color illustrations.

07-200. LEE, Peter H. *Korean Literature: Topics and Themes.* Tucson: University of Arizona Press, 1965. Chapter 9 deals briefly with Korean drama, including traditional mask-dance drama, puppet play, *p'ansori,* and modern drama.

07-201. SOBEL, Bernard (ed.). *The New Theatre Handbook*

and Digest of Plays. New York: Crown, 1959. Contains a cursory introductory article on Korean theater (pp. 214–217). Also contains unconfirmed and largely incorrect data.

07-202. SUH, Doo-Soo. *Korean Literary Reader with a Short History of Korean Literature.* Seoul: Dong-A Publishing Co., 1965. Chapter 3 presents a brief history of Korean drama describing *sandae nori* (mask drama), *kkotu kaksi norŭm* (puppet play), *p'ansori* and *ch'anggŭk* (singing play), and *sin'gŭk* (modern play).

07-203. ZONG, In-sob. *Plays from Korea.* Seoul: Chung-ang University Press, 1968. Contains English versions of twelve Korean plays and a brief history of Korean drama.

07-204. _____. *An Introduction to Korean Literature.* Seoul: Hyangnimsa Publishing Co., 1970. Chapter 9 offers a good introduction to Korean drama. Discusses the development, characteristics, contents, themes, costumes, and other aspects of the mask plays, puppet plays, old plays, *sinp'a* plays, and *sin'gŭk.*

Articles

07-205. CHOE, Sang Su. "The Contents and Significance of the Korean Puppet Play." *Koreana Quarterly* 5(1)(Spring 1963):109–118.

07-206. _____. "Mask Dance Charmers Spirit Ridicules Yangban Class." *Korea Journal* 3(1)(January 1963): 11–13. A brief introduction to Korean mask-dance drama including types and themes with an analysis of *Hahoe* mask-dance drama.

07-207. CHUNG, Won-Si. "Das koreanische Theater." In *Fernöstliches Theater.* Stuttgart: Alfred Kröner Verlag, 1966. A history of ancient Korean theater arts, especially mask-dance drama, from an intercultural viewpoint dealing with Korean, Japan, and China.

07-208. LEE, Du-Hyun. "History of Korean Drama." *Korea Journal* 4(6)(June 1964):4–7. A brief description of the modern history of Korean drama from 1902 until 1945 divided into five subperiods. A careful analysis of the development of modern Korean theater.

07-209. _____. "Korean Masks and Mask Dance Plays." *Transactions of the Korea Branch of the Royal Asiatic Society* 42(1966):49–67. A brief introduction to Korean masks and mask-dance drama. Contains pictures of typical masks and scenes from mask-dance plays.

07-210. _____. "Korean Masks and Mask Dance Dramas." *Korea Journal* 8(3)(1968):4–10. A comprehensive survey of Korean masks and mask-dance drama including discussion of types, themes, content, and costumes.

07-211. _____. "Korean Folk Play." In *Folk Culture in Korea.* Seoul: International Cultural Foundation, 1974. A detailed explanation of the origin, development, features, and themes of several varieties of drama such as *Hahoe* mask-dance drama, *sandae* mask-dance drama, Yangju mask-dance drama, Pongsan mask-dance drama, T'ong yŏng and Kosŏng mask-dance drama, Pukch'ŏng lion play, and puppet play. Contains two pictures of masks and eight pictures of scenes from mask-dance plays.

07-212. _____. "Dramatic Arts." In Sung-nyong Lee (ed.), *Korean Studies Today.* Seoul: Institute of Asian Studies, Seoul National University, 1970. Chapter 8 describes the development of Korean dramatic arts from the ancient period to 1970. The author divides the history of Korean drama into classical and modern periods and further divides the modern period into six subperiods: 1902 to 1910; 1911 to 1920; 1921 to 1930; 1931 to 1939; 1940 to 1945; and the postwar period, 1945 to 1970.

07-213. YOH, Suk-kee. "Traditional Korean Plays and Humor: With Special Reference to *Sandae* Mask Play." *Korea Journal* 10(5)(May 1970):19–22. The author discusses traditional Korean plays and the humor hidden in those plays with emphasis on the Yangju *sandae* mask-dance play.

07-214. _____. "Korean Mask Plays." *Drama Review* 15(3) (Spring 1971):143–152. The author explains a typical Korean mask-dance drama—Yangju *Pyŏl sandae*—and the characters, masks, and themes of the play. Also presented are the dialogues of the play and pictures of the masks and the scenes. Highly recommended reading.

Unpublished Dissertations

07-215. CHO, Oh-Kon. "Chi-jin Yoo: A Patriotic Playwright of Korea." PhD dissertation, Michigan State University, 1972. 352 pp. Abstracted in *DAI* 33(9)(March 1973):5334-35-A; UM 73-5344. The purpose of this study is to analyze seven plays of Ch'i-Jin Yoo which represent the best of his historical, anti-Japanese, and anticommunist plays.

07-216. CHOE, Suk-hee. "Yangju Byol Sandae Nori: A Translation and Critical Introduction." MA thesis, University of Kansas, 1974. An English translation of Yangju *Sandae nori,* a typical Korean mask-dance drama. Presents a short history of Korean mask-dance drama and explains the technical terms of dance action and mime.

07-217. KIM, Ho-soon. "The Development of Modern Korean Theatre in South Korea." PhD dissertation, University of Kansas, 1974. 180 pp. Abstracted in *DAI* 36(2)(August 1975):605-A; UM 75-17, 624. This study traces the development of modern Korean theater from 1945 until 1970. Worthwhile reading.

CHAPTER 8
Education

Don Adams

INTRODUCTION

THE STUDY of Korean education may be roughly divided into five periods. The overwhelming influence of Chinese educational ideas and institutions characterized the first period, which ended in the late nineteenth century. The second period, beginning in the 1880s, witnessed the entrance of Christian missionaries and the introduction of Western concepts of schooling. The third period covers the years of Japanese rule (1910–1945) when Japanese language and educational institutions were introduced into Korea in an attempt to eliminate national identity. In the fourth period, the emergence of two Koreas after 1945 led to the development of two distinct patterns of education—one strongly influenced by the United States and Western educational philosophies, the other drawing extensively from communist educational models. In the current and fifth period, a new sense of nationalism permeates educational systems within the ideological frameworks of anticommunism in the South and communism in the North.

HISTORICAL SURVEY
THE PERIOD OF CHINESE INFLUENCE

There is no major published history of Korean education in English which treats the subject in detail before the nineteenth century, although most descriptions of contemporary Korean education published in Korea do present brief historical introductions. Moreover, a number of master's theses and doctoral dissertations prepared in American universities by young Korean scholars offer general historical descriptions. From such sources some insights may be gleaned regarding the pervasive influence of Chinese ideology vis-à-vis education.

Prior to the latter part of the nineteenth century there was no well-articulated general system of education in Korea. Formal education was essentially a private affair and available only to a small proportion of the population. A type of basic education for some children was provided in the *sŏdang,* which could be found in many Korean villages from the eleventh century onward. The *sŏdang* offered training in the pronunciation of Chinese characters, in calligraphy, and in the meaning of selected passages from Chinese and Korean classical literature. A number of advanced private schools were created from time to time by Confucian scholars. At the close of the fourteenth century the highest state institution was renamed Sung Kyun Kwan (Sŏng-gyun'gwan). This institution, like the few state schools of lesser stature, gathered "gifted youths of the Chinese classics so that they might acquaint themselves with Confucian moralism and philosophy as a guide for politics and economy."[1] Until 1882, however, when a royal decree opened the state-operated schools to common citizens, the "gifted youth" were largely limited to applicants from the *yangban,* or upper class.

A major element of advanced Korean education prior to the twentieth century was the system of examinations designed to select public servants for the nation. These examinations, modeled after those created in China to select government officials, played an important role in the history of the Korean nation. In principle, the evaluation of a candidate's understanding of Chinese classics, histories, and literature represented a process for unprejudiced selection of wise and just leaders. In practice, a strong nobility blunted the potential of the examinations by seeking to perpetuate ascriptively derived privileges. Moreover, the reinforcement given by the examinations to a curriculum limited by the Confucian classics severely constrained innovation. The elimination of the public service examination in 1894 heralded an opportunity for change in Korean education.

INITIAL WESTERN CONTACTS

The educational goals and activities of the Western missionary societies are reasonably well documented. One of the basic references describing missionary work in education is Horace Underwood's study published in 1926 (08-038). It provides information on educational institutions developed by the Protestant missionaries during the latter part of the nineteenth century and the early twentieth century under Japanese annexation. Christian schooling, because of its radically different curriculum, its tie to Western religion, and its attention to instruction of girls, was suspected by many Koreans. Moreover, the avoidance of Chinese language and literature made such schooling inferior in the eyes of many of the upper class. The early missionary work in education was modest in scope. Often it consisted of the irregular instruction of a few orphan children in the home of a missionary. Yet by the turn of the twentieth century the demand for new kinds of learning was becoming increasingly evident. Christian schooling at all levels rapidly grew in popularity and competed with other private institutions created to introduce Western learning.

JAPANESE RULE

The initial Japanese policy after annexation of Korea in 1910 was to maintain a dual system of education: one set of schools for Japanese children and another set for Korean children. The basic argument for the continued segregation was simply that a "different standard of living did not permit amalgamation."[2] This and subse-

quent annual reports provided descriptions of the status of Korean education during the colonial period. An imperial ordinance in 1911 established a structure of schooling for Koreans which included a four-year common school followed by either a four-year higher common school or any of a variety of industrial schools. During the early years of the annexation only one institution was available to Koreans who were graduates of the higher common school.

The educational objectives of the Japanese have been tersely described by a Korean scholar: "Denationalization, Vocationalization, Deliberalization, and Discrimination."[3] Denationalization meant forcing the Korean people to substitute loyalty to the Japanese emperor for that formerly given to their own rulers. Vocationalization implied concentration on those skills necessary to prepare Koreans to be low-level tradesmen. Deliberalization referred to a curriculum for Koreans which ignored both the liberal subjects and the advanced technical courses. Discrimination suggested that Japanese students were offered better and more advanced educational opportunities than Koreans.

These accusations are, of course, similar to those which have been leveled at colonial education throughout the world. Japanese policy was to integrate Korea into its empire and make Koreans productive and loyal workers. In this process Korean language, literature, and culture were deemphasized in order to teach the Japanese heritage. Moreover, since leadership would largely be restricted to Japanese, advanced liberal or professional education was considered irrelevant for Koreans.

A new educational ordinance in 1922 was designed to provide an integrated system of schooling which enrolled both Koreans and Japanese. The ordinance further encouraged limited attention to Korean history and geography. With the opening of a university in Seoul (Keijō Imperial University), higher education became available to Koreans. Educational opportunity for Koreans was thus, in principle, extended and the curriculum was made more responsive to Korean culture. As World War II approached, however, the process of assimilation was hastened. Koreans and Japanese attended the same schools and studied the same curriculum. The study of the Korean language was completely discontinued and students outside of school as well as inside were rigidly forbidden to speak the native tongue. The needs of a wartime economy were particularly felt in the secondary schools and colleges which, in addition to sending military volunteers, were instructed to emphasize vocational and technical subjects.

THE POSTWAR PERIOD

With the creation of two Koreas after World War II, educational policies became strongly influenced by the two powers which for all practical purposes controlled North and South Korea: the Soviet Union and the United States.

In South Korea, under the US Military Government in Korea (USMGIK), Americans served in many leadership roles in education and directed or advised on policies affecting educational development. Although frequently there was much confusion regarding educational responsibility, a centralized administrative structure extending from the national level to the provincial level emerged. A new organizational ladder was implemented along the 6-3-3-4 pattern (6 years in elementary education, and so on) typical in the United States. Compulsory education was limited to common primary school, which was followed by selective 3-3 secondary schools. The basic degree program of colleges and universities was four years in length. The Educational Law of 1949 and its amendment in 1951 established the 6-3-3-4 ladder as the national system of education in the Republic of Korea.

In North Korea, the new communist government initiated a number of changes designed to bring education into line with ideological and economic goals. In 1946 the Provisional People's Committee created an organizational structure consisting of a four-year people's school, a three-year junior middle school, and a three-year senior middle school. Moreover, technical secondary schools and a large number of specialized training institutes were built to support an ambitious program of industrialization. Kim Il Sung University was erected as the capstone of the system.

CONTEMPORARY SYSTEMS

North and South Korea achieved increasing independence from the counsels of the USA and the USSR and,

as the two Korean political entities solidified, two distinct patterns of education evolved. In the Republic of Korea this pattern was distinguished by its anticommunist orientation, the rapid extension of formal schooling to the young, and the move toward a common ladder of public education. In the Democratic People's Republic of Korea, education took on the three characteristics which have become so familiar in communist countries: the explicit and self-conscious ideological characteristics, the orientation toward vocational, technical, and applied knowledge, and the extension of educational programs into major places of work such as the factory and farm. Within these guidelines, however, North Korean education developed a national distinctiveness.

EDUCATION IN THE SOUTH

In terms of administration, all schools in South Korea are under the control of the central government. The Ministry of Education as the central administrative body exercises wide supervision over such areas as curriculum and textbook standards, teacher qualifications, tuition fees, certain fiscal allocations, and the entrance examination system. Colleges and universities are included in the jurisdiction of the Ministry of Education; however, they have relatively more freedom than the elementary and secondary schools.

Since the early 1950s some decentralization has been evolving in the management and control of education. Local authorities in the form of city, county, and provincial boards of education have been formed. These appointed boards select the superintendent of schools who, as executive officer of the board and acting on authority delegated by the ministry, has a wide range of discretionary power.

The curriculum offerings, time allocation for subject matter, and teaching materials are subject to regulatory standards under educational law or guided by ministry policy. In addition to the general curriculum offerings found in most countries, special courses on anticommunism and morals are also included in all elementary and secondary schools. In the middle schools (grades 7 to 9), vocational subjects occupy a minimum of 15 percent of the total curriculum time. Foreign languages are required in all secondary schools (grades 7 to 12); English, the first foreign language, is introduced in the seventh grade. In vocational high schools vocational subjects occupy over 50 percent of the curriculum. Graduation from degree-granting colleges and universities requires a minimum of 160 credit hours of which 31 percent are typically general education, 51 percent specialized courses, and 18 percent electives.

The growth in enrollment since national independence has been remarkable. By 1974 over 98 percent of the children aged six to twelve were enrolled in elementary schools. The middle-school entrance examination was abolished in 1969, and 1980 was the target date set to extend compulsory education through grade nine. High schools, covering grades ten through twelve, were enrolling 67 percent of the middle-school graduates by 1974. Girls comprised about 40 percent of the total secondary school population.

Approximately 250 institutions make up the system of higher education. Included in this number are 69 universities and degree-granting colleges; the remainder are mainly two-year junior colleges. Institutions of higher education are typically coeducational and, with the exception of junior teachers colleges, the great majority are privately controlled and supported. The usual range of curriculum offerings may be found in the arts, sciences, and professional schools. Teacher education for elementary teachers is provided in special two-year colleges, while four-year colleges of education exist for the preparation of secondary school teachers. Approximately 26 percent of the student population in colleges and universities is female.

CHANGING GOALS IN THE SOUTH

The Educational Law promulgated in 1949 states that education is guided by the ideal of *hong'ik in'gan* (benefits for all mankind). This general principle presumably has deep roots in Korean history and thus provides continuity as a central aspiration. Article II of the law declares some of its broad social aims: "cultivation of an indomitable spirit," "development of a patriotic spirit," "preservation and enhancement of national culture," "development of an aesthetic appreciation," and "cultivation of thrift and faithfulness to one's work in order to become an able producer and a wise consumer."

Such aspirations must be implemented, of course, by explicit policies and plans. In the Republic of Korea policy guidelines emanating from the Ministry of Education and the comprehensive Long-Range Educational Plan are the best guideposts to the educational future. The picture which emerges from scrutiny of these sources suggests that the coming years will see a concentration of effort in certain areas: improvement of curriculum, teaching methods, and educational management; research to relate education to the demands of the economy; sustained efforts to teach anticommunism and national loyalty; reduction of the educational advantages of children from privileged families; expansion of community-centered education, adult education, and nonformal education; and increased research and development vis-à-vis educational policies.

Certain problems are visible on the horizon. For one thing, the capacity of the educational system cannot keep up indefinitely with the widespread demand for schooling. For another, the economic system cannot absorb greater and greater numbers of the highly educated indefinitely. In the minds of many, probably most, Korea's high educational attainment must be accompanied by a correspondingly high social and economic status. In the last two decades a fluid social structure and a rapidly expanding economy have allowed a high level of opportunity for educated youth. That level may be difficult to maintain.

EDUCATION IN THE NORTH

The administration of all major educational efforts and institutions in North Korea is highly centralized in national ministries. The Communist Party maintains a deep involvement in education, however, and assumes much of the responsibility for the creation of major policies and the enunciation of priorities.

The structure and content of education in North Korea have undergone—and continue to undergo—a number of changes in keeping with technical, cultural, and ideological goals. There have been adjustments in the length of primary and secondary education. There has been experimentation with a number of patterns of vocational and technical training. There have been a variety of innovations with part-time adult literacy. New specialized schools in foreign languages and the arts have been developed; preschool institutions and programs have been extended. Although many combinations have been attempted, the evolving structure of formal education appears to be a ten-year compulsory system. (With a year of preprimary schooling, this becomes an eleven-year system.) However, all indications are that North Korean leaders will continue to respond pragmatically and create new institutional arrangements as the need arises.

Often the structure and content of education have been revised to increase the number and quality of skilled manpower. To meet the need for new cadres required by national economic plans, a variety of short-term and long-term institutes and training programs have been introduced. Institutions comprising the main educational ladder have also been forced to adjust. In 1956 the prestigious but "bourgeois" academic middle school was terminated. In its place the technical school and technical high school became the only path open to all youth seeking advanced education. During the early 1960s, the emphasis on "factory colleges" represented a further attempt at promoting the unity of education and labor. Each of these colleges offered preparation, both theoretical and practical, for a single industry like fishing or construction.

In 1966 the senior middle school was in effect reintroduced under the new name of "high school." This date perhaps marks the beginning of a new period of synthesis in North Korean education. The vocational, technical, and applied content of education remains important, it is true. Moreover, adult education continues to represent a prominent part of the educational scene. Yet the introduction of the high school would seem to suggest a recognition of the significance of a basic academic curriculum.

CHANGING GOALS IN THE NORTH

By controlling the learning environment of the young in particular, the North Korean leaders are attempting to alter the national identity and create a new communist society. Teaching and learning should not only result in acquisition of scientific knowledge *(kyoyuk)* but also in communist indoctrination or cultivation *(kyoyang)*. The goals that should guide all educational and social institutions in North Korea have been repeatedly identified by Kim Il Sung:

To indoctrinate in the superiority of socialism and communism over capitalism.

To indoctrinate in the truth that things new are destined to conquer things old.

To eliminate individualism and egoism and to indoctrinate in collectivism and love for organization.

To indoctrinate in socialist patriotism and proletarian internationalism.

To indoctrinate love for socialist labor.

To indoctrinate in incessant revolutionary ideology.

In spite of the rhetoric which gives an international flavor to *kyoyuk* and *kyoyang,* these processes are ultimately defined in the national context. In 1955 Kim Il Sung identified the concept of *chuch'e* as a central guide to a communist society in Korea. *Chuch'e,* typically translated as national identity or national individuality, reflects the intent of North Korean leadership to avoid mere imitation of communist institutions found elsewhere and to promote pride in Korea's heritage. North Korean leaders have argued that the long subjection of the Korean people to another nation left a servile mentality which needed to be erased. While a "Korea for Koreans" or a "Made in Korea" movement can be seen in both South and North, it is pushed with more consistent vigor in the latter.

In summary, then, for the last two decades educational policy in the North has reflected three main objectives: the ideological reorientation of the total population; the integration of all instruction; and the renewal of nationalistic culture. North Korean sources frequently report dramatic progress in the achievement of all three objectives. Frustration or doubt concerning either the direction or magnitude of the tasks undertaken is seldom voiced. Moreover, the absence of independent social research, the secrecy with respect to statistical data, and the penchant for substituting slogans for achievements cloud any careful assessment of progress.

FUTURE PROSPECTS

Looking to the future, there appear to be certain common directions in education in both North and South Korea. The great demand for education is likely to require continued expansion of the formal school system or the creation of new nonformal alternatives. Moreover, with the demands for literacy and vocational skills being rapidly met, the next few years should offer the opportunity to turn to qualitative improvements in instruction at all levels. In North Korea the basic principle of wedding theory and practice will probably continue to guide the organization of learning. Efforts in this direction are present in South Korea but are more explicit in the North.

The attention to political, historical, and moral instruction will probably remain unabated in both nations. The ideological differences between North and South Korea, both presumed and real, will continue to be emphasized by all educational institutions so long as leaders of both nations view such distinctions as essential to the achievement of national policies.

NOTES

1. *University of Sung Kyun Kwan Bulletin* (Seoul), (1955):1.
2. Japan, Government-General of Chōsen, *Annual Report of Reform and Progress in Chōsen [Korea], 1910–1911* (Keijō [Seoul]: 1911), p. 1.
3. Han Young Rim, "Development of Higher Education in Korea during the Japanese Occupation (1910–1945)," PhD dissertation (Teachers College, Columbia University, 1952).

BIBLIOGRAPHY

This bibliography lists materials in English; most of them appeared during the last twenty years. There is some overlapping among the various parts of this bibliography, and disagreement is possible over the choice of heading for a particular entry. Entries are arranged by heading and then alphabetized within each group by author.

BIBLIOGRAPHIES, SOURCE MATERIALS, AND PERIODICALS
Bibliographies

08-001. FRASER, Steward E., Hyong-Chan KIM, and Sun-Ho KIM. *North Korean Education and Society: A Select and Partially Annotated Bibliography Pertaining to the Democratic People's Republic of Korea.* London: Institute of Education, University of London, 1972. 149 pp.

08-002. KANG, Kil-Su. *A Short Bibliography in the English Language Material on Korea and Its Education.* Pittsburgh: IDEP, University of Pittsburgh, 1968. 16 pp.

08-003. United Nations. Asian Institute for Economic Development and Planning. *Education in Asia: A Bibliography.* Bangkok: 1969. 34 pp.

08-004. UNESCO. Regional Office for Education in Asia. *Economic and Educational Planning in Asia: A Selected List of Books and Periodical Articles.* Bangkok: 1969.

Source Materials: Yearbooks, Statistics, and Annual Surveys
A general yearbook from South Korea, *Korea Annual* (see 01-129), contains a section on education and provides relevant statistical data. JPRS translations of excerpts from the North Korean yearbook, *Chosŏn chung'ang yŏn'gam* [Korean central yearbook], include general information and statistical data on North Korean education (see 01-118). Listed here are more specialized publications.

08-005. Korea, Republic of. Ministry of Education. *Education in Korea.* Annual publication since 1960. Contents typically include: the geographic, historical, and cultural backdrop to education; the history of education; the legal basis of education; administration and finance; and a description of each level and type of schooling.

08-006. _____. _____. *Survey of Education in Korea.* Annual publication, 1963–1974. These statistical reports provide basic data on South Korean education including number of schools, classes, students, and teachers, school facilities, employment of graduates, and educational expenditures for all school levels ranging from kindergarten to college and university.

08-007. UNESCO. "Republic of Korea." *International Yearbook of Education.* Geneva: International Bureau of Education, UNESCO, 1963–. These publications offer brief outlines of the organization, administration, curriculum and method, professional personnel, auxiliary services, and qualitative development of the school system.

08-008. _____. *World Survey of Education.* Paris: UNESCO, 1955–. The first volume (1955) presents general educational information for 196 states and territories and is designed to contribute to the comparative study of education. The next three volumes deal respectively with primary (1958), secondary (1961), and higher education (1966) in national systems.

08-009. _____. Regional Office for Education in Asia. *Bulletin of the UNESCO Regional Office for Education in Asia.* Bangkok. Published twice annually from 1966 to 1972. From 1973, an annual publication.

Periodicals

08-010. *Comparative Education Review.* Official journal of the Comparative and International Education Society. Los Angeles, California.

08-011. *Education.* Quarterly journal which publishes investigations and theoretical papers dealing with innovations in learning, teaching, and education. Chula Vista, California.

08-012. *Peabody Journal of Education*. A quarterly journal primarily concerned with teacher education. Published by George Peabody College for Teachers. Nashville, Tennessee.

08-013. *Phi Delta Kappan*. A comprehensive monthly journal of education. Bloomington, Indiana.

GENERAL AND HISTORICAL

08-014. ADAMS, Don. "Problems of Reconstruction in Korean Education." *Comparative Education Review* 3(3) (February 1960):27–32.

08-015. _____. "Cultural Pitfalls of a Foreign Educational Adviser." *Peabody Journal of Education* 36(6)(May 1959): 338–344. Using Korea as a case in point, Adams describes some of the cultural pitfalls facing an American working in that country. Differences are noted between Western and Korean values vis-à-vis time orientation, man-nature orientation, and power and status orientation.

08-016. ADAMS, Don and Chong Chol KIM. "South Korea." In *Encyclopedia of Education*. Vol. 5. New York: Macmillan, 1971.

08-017. BENBEN, John. "Korea and Education." *Education* 76(10)(June 1956):618–622. A brief historical description of Korean education during the following four phases: Pre-Japanese Occupation, Japanese Occupation (1910–1945), Liberation (1945–1949), Korean War (1950–).

08-018. BOWEN, Genevieve. "Ninety Days in the Orient." *Pennsylvania School Journal* 96(1)(September 1947): 14–15. A brief account by an educational consultant urging American assistance for Korean education.

08-019. CHŎNG, T'ae-Si. "Twenty Years of Korean Education through Statistics." *Korea Journal* 8(8)(August 1968):4–13. This article surveys the twenty-year growth of Korean education from 1945 to 1967 through various statistics. No qualitative inferences are drawn from data.

08-020. _____. "Yesterday of Korean Education." *Korea Journal* 3(4)(April 1963):16–19. Historical description of Korean education. Begins with the influence of Confucianism, Buddhist, and indigenous Korean elements and proceeds to modern education and the anti-Japanese movement.

08-021. _____. "Korean Education: Yesterday and Tomorrow." *Koreana Quarterly* 12(3)(Autumn 1970):66–76. A review of twenty-five years of education and a look at the targets expressed in the Long-Range Educational Development Plan of Korea (1972–1986).

08-022. FOGG, Helen. "Three Significant Years of Korean Education (1952–1955)." *Korea Survey* 5(June/July 1956):5–7. A report on educational projects sponsored by the Unitarian Service Committee.

08-023. FRASER, Mowart G. "Educational Progress in Korea." *Institute of International Education Bulletin* 31(June 1956):13–16. As chief of the Education Division, American-Korean Foundation, Fraser describes school conditions, including crowded classrooms and the shortage of facilities and equipment. He concludes that economic and educational aid from the United States must be maintained for some years to come.

08-024. FRASER, Stewart. "North Korea." In *Encyclopedia of Education*. Vol. 5. New York: Macmillan, 1971. A descriptive review of North Korean culture and education.

08-025. HAHN, Ki-Un. "Study of the Democratization of Education in Korea Based on the History of Education Thought." *Korea Observer* 1(3/4)(April/July 1969):11–31. Traces the course of democratization of education in Korea viewed in three historical stages: (1) democratic tradition of Korean education (before 1876); (2) attempts to democratize Korean education (1876–1945); (3) democratic evolution of Korean education (after 1945).

08-026. HALL, Budd L. "Adult Education in the People's Republic of Korea." *Convergence* 7(4)(1974):70–74. The task of systematically reducing illiteracy by means of formal and nonformal educational institutions is traced from the mid-1940s. Describes the opportunities for technical and cultural education for the new literates.

08-027. KIM, Yong-Shik. "Korean Education in Historical Perspective." *Korea Journal* 10(10)(October 1970):20–24. A history of Korea and its education beginning from the "Hermit Kingdom" era to 1970. The 1960s are identified as the beginning of an era of "heightened motivation and achievement" in Korean life and education. Significant changes in education in recent years include: the abolition of entrance examinations for middle schools, the promulgation of the National Education Charter of 1968, and the creation of the National Council for Long-Range Comprehensive Educational Planning in 1968.

08-028. *Korea: Its Land, People and Culture of All Ages*. Seoul: Hakwon-Sa, 1963. The chapter on education presents an encyclopedic survey of Korean education by three contributors: In-Ky Yi, Han-Yong Rim, and Yang-Su Chong.

08-029. *Korea: Past and Present*. Seoul: Kwang Myong Publishing Co., 1972. The chapter on education (pp. 229–250) offers a brief description of educational activities in each level of schools. Contributed by Sik-Young Chung.

08-030. Korean National Commission for UNESCO. *Review of Educational Studies in Korea*. Vol. 1. Seoul: Korean National Commission for UNESCO, 1972. 129 pp. This publication presents abstracts for research papers submitted to the Korean National Commission for UNESCO. It represents a major source of empirical studies of Korean education.

08-031. _____. *UNESCO Korean Survey.* Seoul: Dong-A Publishing Co., 1960. This survey is regarded as an encyclopedia of Korean education, science, and culture. The main chapter on education attempts to give a comprehensive review of modern education as it exists in Korea at the present time, tracing its development from 1945.

08-032. NORTH, Richard. *Educator's Guide to Korea.* Seoul: Civil Affairs Division, US Army, 1948. 18 pp. An introduction to the culture and society of South Korea. A sketch of the educational system is included.

08-033. OH, Chae-Kyong. "Education." In *Handbook of Korea.* New York: Pageant Press, 1958. A brief survey of the organization of education.

08-034. PAIK, Hyon-Ki. "The Present Status of Modern Education." *Korea Journal* 3(4)(April 1963):4–15. The author discusses the present status of the Korean educational system after giving a brief history of the system.

08-035. PARK, Dong-Wa. "Historical Background of Yi Dynasty Chu Hsiism (Meta-physical Rationalism) and Its Influence on Education." *Korea Observer* 1(3/4)(April/ July 1969):32–41. Park considers the rise of Neo-Confucianism in Korea during the Yi dynasty set against its historical background. Discusses its influence on educational thinking and more generally on the formation of national characteristics.

08-036. PARSONS, Howard L. "A Transformation in Education." *Korea Focus* 1(2)(Spring 1972):31–34. Parsons describes the educational system of North Korea, focusing on its expansion since 1965.

08-037. RHEE, Yu-Sang. "Korean Education, 1956–1965." *Bulletin of the Korean Research Center* 31(December 1969):25–45. A survey of the dimensions of a decade of rapid educational growth and the many attendant problems.

08-038. UNDERWOOD, Horace Horton. *Modern Education in Korea.* New York: International Press, 1926. 336 pp. This book represents one of the earliest and most thorough accounts of the educational institutions created by the various Christian missions in Korea. The author traces the founding and growth of what have become some of the best-known secondary schools and universities in contemporary Korea. The early educational changes initiated by the Japanese are identified and the tenuous position of mission schools under the Japanese occupation is elaborated. Includes a brief account of the March First movement of 1919 and the response of the Japanese authorities.

08-039. UNESCO. "Education in the Republic of Korea." *Bulletin of the UNESCO Regional Office for Education in Asia* 6(2)(1972):99–106. A summary of the characteristics of the educational system followed by identification of emerging problems.

08-040. _____. "Republic of Korea." *World Survey of Education: Handbook of Educational Organization and Statistics.* Paris: UNESCO, 1955. A survey of the legal basis, administration, and finance of education followed by a review of teacher education.

08-041. WERTH, Richard. "Educational Development under the South Korean Interim Government." *School and Society* 69(20 April 1949):305–309. A brief survey of conditions and problems during the period when educational policies were strongly influenced by Americans.

08-042. WOOD, C. W. "Post-Liberation Problems in Korean Education." *Phi Delta Kappan* (December 1957):115 –118. Special Issue on the Problems on Education in Asia. The author analyzes the problems of postliberation Korean education under five headings: organization and administration; financial support; teacher education; curriculum; and physical facilities.

08-043. YANG, Key P. and Chang-Boh CHEE. "North Korean Educational System: 1945 to Present." *China Quarterly* 14(April/June 1963):125–140. The present educational system of North Korea is seen as supporting a redefinition of its cultural heritage and paving the path for communism. The authors identify three primary objectives: (1) the socialistic reorientation of the younger generation and the adult population; (2) the revival of nationalistic patriotism; and (3) integration of theory and practice. The authors review three stages: the pre–Korean War period (1945–1950) characterized by a strong Russian influence; the Korean War period characterized by patriotism and nationalistic fervor; and the post–Korean War period (1953–) characterized by a wedding of theory and practice and by the concept of dignity of labor. The authors are optimistic about North Korea's plans and development.

08-044. YU, Hyung-Jin. "Educational Developments in the Republic of Korea: 1957–1967." *Bulletin of UNESCO Regional Office of Education in Asia* 2(1)(September 1967):37–43. A general description.

PRIMARY, SECONDARY, AND HIGHER EDUCATION (INCLUDING TEACHER EDUCATION)

08-045. ADAMS, Don. "Teacher Education in Modern Korea." *School and Society* 80(2173)(23 April 1960):207– 209. This article deals with the problems of teaching and teacher education created by the sudden expansion of schools in Korea between 1945 and 1959, the uncertain direction of Korean society, and the changing image and role of the teacher.

08-046. _____. *Higher Educational Reforms in the Republic of Korea*. Contract 05-64-58 with the Office of Education, US Department of Health, Education, and Welfare. Washington: Government Printing Office, 1965. 63 pp. This study presents a historical survey but focuses on the changes of organizational structure and instructional program in the field of higher education of the Republic of Korea since the fall of the First Republic in the spring of 1960.

08-047. BARTZ, Carl F., Jr. "Higher Learning in the Third Republic." In A. C. Nahm (ed.), *Studies in the Developmental Aspects of Korea*. Proceedings of the Conference on Korea held at Western Michigan University, 1969. Focuses on academic freedom and university autonomy. The author reviews the historical foundations of these two concepts in Korean higher education, examines their constitutional and legal bases, and interprets their current status. He concludes that academic freedom is established to a considerable degree but university autonomy will not be realized in the near future.

08-048. CHOE, W. P. "The Largest Women's University in the World." *Korean Survey* 8(8)(October 1959):6–7. Choe sketches the history of Ewha Women's University in Seoul.

08-049. CHŎNG, T'ae-Si. "Problems Facing the Enhancement of the Status of Teachers in Korea." *Korea Journal* 6(7)(July 1966):13–17. Deals with the present status of teachers in Korea. The author discusses the academic background of teachers, teacher qualifications, teacher training institutes, teaching careers, teachers' families, class size, and salary. Suggests steps for improvement of teachers' status.

08-050. EDMAN, Marion L. *Primary Teachers of Korea Look at Themselves*. Seoul: CERI, 1962. 123 pp. This study, conducted in cooperation with the Central Education Research Institute, is an attempt "to find out who the Korean teachers are, what they do, how they are regarded in general, and how adequate their salary is. Beyond this it tries to find out the opinion and judgement of primary teachers concerning a number of important matters relating to education in Korea." Interviews with education officials and questionnaires filled out by teachers were used as data sources. The author's findings suggest that the primary teacher is still most often a man, who is, in general, indifferent to in-service training for upgrading himself. The average Korean teacher would like to see more decentralization of authority in the schools. There are more

women among younger teachers; they are less conservative; and they show a slight disposition to want more democratic procedures in the classroom. There seems to have been no clear pattern showing urban teachers to be more liberal than their rural counterparts. In general, primary school teachers do not exert great effort to improve their status (which they regard as low) and they seem to be unaware of the limitations of their training or experience.

08-051. EVERSULL, Frank L. "Some Observations for Higher Education in Korea." *School and Society* 65(1674) (25 January 1947):51–53. The author was chief of colleges and teachers colleges under the American military government. He offers a brief description of Korea's history of higher education, the creation of Seoul National University, the quantity and quality of equipment and plant at Seoul National University, and the typical methods of instruction.

08-052. HONG, Woong-Sun. "Liberal Education in Korean Universities." *Korea Observer* 1(3/4)(April/July 1969): 49–66.

08-053. HWANG, Chul-Su. "Primary Education in Revolution?" *Korea Journal* 9(7)(July 1969):18–20. Hwang discusses the abrogation of the middle-school entrance examination, enforced in 1969 through the assignment of all applicants by lottery. The entrance examination had been a major barrier to significant changes in elementary education.

08-054. KEH, Young-He. "Communization of Education in North Korea: Technical Education for Economic Development." In Andrew C. Nahm (ed.), *Studies in the Developmental Aspects of Korea*. Proceedings of the Conference on Korea held at Western Michigan University, 1969. A general descriptive review of educational developments in North Korea and their relation to economic needs. Keh points out that the ideal "socialist man" under Marxist-Leninist doctrine is one who possesses at least one technical skill. Data are provided on the number of schools and students, the growth in number of technicians and specialists, and the ratios of supply and demand of technicians by major industry.

08-055. KIM, Chong-Chol. "Higher Education in the Republic of Korea." *Bulletin of the UNESCO Regional Office of Education in Asia* 7(1)(September 1972):89–99. The author gives a brief history of the significant changes in higher education in Korea followed by a description of the existing system of higher education. There are four tables at the end of the article describing enrollment at the third level (1967–1971); number of teaching staff (1967–1971); number of institutions (1967–1971); and number of graduates by field of study (1967–1971).

08-056. KIM, T'ae-Gil. "Korea and the Mission of Universities." *Korea Journal* 9(2)(February 1969):16–21. The author questions the functions of the Korean university, its students, and its professors. He recommends that the university should abandon the ivory tower and join in the struggle for a true democracy.

08-057. Korean Federation of Education Associations. "Organizations for Teaching Profession." *Korea Journal* 3(4)(April 1963):20–23. The article describes various teachers' organizations that began to emerge around 1945, most of which did not survive the Korean War because of their left-wing orientation. One of the surviving organizations is the Korean Federation of Education Associations, which was founded in November 1947. It is designed to promote the economic, social, academic, and professional status of teachers by strengthening the teaching profession rather than by "adopting union methods." The article outlines the objectives of the KFEA, its organizational structure, and its activities.

08-058. KWON, O-Sik. "Eleven-Year Compulsory Education Introduced in Tosan County." *Korea Today* 6(213) (1974):41–42. Kwon describes educational growth in Tosan County, North Korea.

08-059. LI, Kang-Jong. "Samhung Middle School—Trainer of Children into a New Communist Type of Man." *Korea Today* 6(213)(1974):33–34. Li delineates the daily school life of pupils in Chŏllima Samhŭng Middle School located in Mangyŏngdae district, Pyongyang, North Korea.

08-060. PERLO, Ellen. "Happy Children: Asia's Future Is in Their Hands." *Korea Focus* 1(2)(Spring 1972):37–38. After visiting the children's palace, kindergartens, and nurseries in factories and on farms, Perlo describes the child care system of North Korea. Some statistics on child care facilities are included.

08-061. STODDARD, George D. "Problems of Higher Education in Korea." *School and Society* 88(23 April 1960): 210–211. This article is the result of a one-man mission to Korea to study US financial commitments in higher education. Stoddard reports on the acute shortage of books, journals, and laboratory apparatus and comments on the comparatively fewer educational opportunities for Korean women.

08-062. UNDERWOOD, Horace G. "International Symposium on Innovation in Higher Education." *Korea Journal* 12(11)(November 1972):17–21. Report on a symposium held at Yonsei University, Seoul, in October 1972.

08-063. UNESCO. "Democratic People's Republic of Korea." *World Survey of Education.* Vol. 4: *Higher Education.* Paris: UNESCO, 1966. A survey of higher education in North Korea.

08-064. _____. "North Korea." *World Survey of Education.* Vol. 3: *Secondary Education.* Paris: UNESCO, 1961. A survey of secondary education beginning with a brief description of the educational system in North Korea followed by an account of the development of secondary education. Describes the types of secondry education: secondary schools, technical schools, higher technical schools, schools for workers, specialized educational establishments, teacher training schools, out-of-class activities.

08-065. _____. "People's Democratic Republic of Korea." *World Survey of Education.* Vol. 2: *Primary Education.* Paris: UNESCO, 1958. A report on primary education in North Korea.

08-066. _____. "Republic of Korea." *World Survey of Education.* Vol. 2: *Primary Education.* Paris: UNESCO, 1958. A survey of primary school education beginning with a brief historical summary of education (1910–1955). There is a summary of school statistics (1950–1954) at different levels: preprimary, primary, secondary, higher, special, adult.

08-067. _____. "Republic of Korea." *World Survey of Education.* Vol. 3: *Secondary Education.* Paris: UNESCO, 1961. A survey of secondary school education beginning with a brief description of the whole educational system. Statistics for the years 1953–1957 are given for the different levels: preprimary, primary, secondary, higher, and special.

08-068. _____. "Republic of Korea." *World Survey of Education.* Vol. 4: *Higher Education.* Paris: UNESCO, 1966. A survey of higher education beginning with a brief description of the whole educational system. Some statistics for all levels: preprimary, primary, secondary, higher, and special education.

08-069. US Operations Mission to Korea. *Report on Survey of National Higher Education in the Republic of Korea.* Seoul: USOM/Korea, 1960. 80 pp.

ADMINISTRATION, POLICY, AND PLANNING

08-070. CHEE, Chang-Boh. "North Korea: Manpower Training Reflected in Social and Cultural Movements." *Asia* 7(Spring 1967):78–98. Examines how North Korea has made progress through effective planning, control, and mobilization of economic resources and manpower. Chee regards "education" as the most effective means of manpower training in North Korea.

08-071. CHŎNG, Bŏm-Mo. "Problems Facing Education Planning." *Korea Journal* 6(7)(July 1966):4–8. The author suggests that the tasks facing Korean education must be deduced from the movements for national identity, modernization, and democratization. The article stresses the need for long-range educational planning which is closely integrated with the country's total development.

08-072. KAUH, Kwang-Man. "A Critical Analysis of Korean Education." *Phi Delta Kappan* (December 1957):112–114. Special issue on the problems of education in Asia. A brief summary of the origin of school education in Korea is followed by an analysis of the present status of Korean education.

08-073. KIM, Chong-Chŏl. "Long-Range Educational Planning in Korea." *Korea Journal* 2(10)(October 1971):5–11. Between 1969 and 1972 South Korea evolved a comprehensive long-range educational plan. This fifteen-year plan, beginning in 1972, consisted of three consecutive five-year plans. Kim outlines the scope of the plan and the major directions the plan suggests. He leaves for others to argue whether or not the results will be worth the effort.

08-074. KIM, Dae-Kwan. "Social Trends in Korea in the 1970's and Educational Policies." *Koreana Quarterly* 12(1/2)(Spring/Summer 1970):25–30. After discussing the scope and intensity of social changes in the coming decade in Korea, the author suggests the following policy approaches: (1) a new value system to combine foreign influence and traditional culture; (2) an educational policy to prevent polarization and stratification of society; (3) an educational policy to encourage individual ingenuity; (4) policies designed to narrow the gap between classroom reality and social reality.

08-075. LEE, Kyu-Hwan. *The Equalization Policy of Middle Schools in the Republic of Korea.* Seoul: Ewha Women's University, 1972. Mimeographed. Since 1968, the entrance examination for middle schools has been discontinued and assignment of middle school places has been made by lottery. Lee assesses the early effects of the new policy.

08-076. MORGAN, Robert and C. B. CHADWICK. *System Analysis for Education Change: The Republic of Korea.* Contract AID/ea-120. Tallahassee: Florida State University, 1971. 325 pp. The authors use a broad "systems approach" to examine the operation of the Korean educational system in its economic and social context. A number of recommendations are offered in terms of subsystem priorities—primary and middle schooling should be emphasized, for example, and curriculum and teaching methods should be improved. Considerable attention is given to ways of improving administration and instruction.

08-077. PAIK, Hyun-Ki. "Nonformal Education in Korea: Program and Prospects." In C. S. Brembeck and T. J. Thomson (eds.), *New Strategies for Education Development.* East Lansing: IIS, Michigan State University,

1973. A discussion of some contemporary educational trends and problems of nonformal education in Korea.

08-078. _____. "Role of University in National Development." *Koreana Quarterly* 10(3)(Autumn 1968):244–252. After interpreting the role of the university in the economic, political, and social development of a nation, the author indicates the problems confronting higher educational institutions in Korea.

08-079. _____. "Problems Facing Revision of School System." *Korea Journal* 4(12)(December 1964):16–20. Paik weighs the merits and demerits of the proposed revision from the present 6-3-3-4 school system to a 6-5-5 system.

08-080. PAIK, L. George. "The Future of University Education." *Koreana Quarterly* 10(3)(Autumn 1968):239–243. Paik discusses the university's role in nation-building.

08-081. PARK, Tai-Sun. "The Role of University Education for National Development." *Korea Observer* 1(3/4) (April/July 1969):3–10. A discussion of the relationships between the university and national development. Park stresses such areas as: university control, curricula and teaching, student guidance, and faculty research and activities.

08-082. UNESCO. *An Asian Model of Educational Development: Perspective for 1965–1980.* Paris: UNESCO, 1966. 126 pp. This model was prepared by five UNESCO consultants for the implementation of the Karachi plan for free and compulsory education of a minimum seven years' duration. The Republic of Korea is one of the eighteen countries included.

08-083. _____. "Democratic People's Republic of Korea." *World Survey of Education.* Vol. 5: *Educational Policy, Legislation and Administration.* Paris: UNESCO, 1971. Surveys the broad national aims of education, government policies, organizational structure, finance, educational planning, and research.

08-084. _____. "Republic of Korea." *World Survey of Education.* Vol. 5: *Educational Policy, Legislation and Administration.* Paris: UNESCO, 1971. Describes the broad national aims of education, government policies, organizational structure, administrative structure, and responsibilities of the Ministry of Education. Statistics are given for 1961 to 1965 on educational expenditure. Statistics for different school levels—preprimary, primary, secondary, higher, vocational—are also given.

08-085. UNESCO. Regional Advisory Team for Educational Planning in Asia. *Long-Term Projections for Education in the Republic of Korea.* Bangkok: UNESCO, Regional Office for Education in Asia, 1965. 97 pp. The advisory team examines the problems of educational planning in the context of the socioeconomic environment.

08-086. UNESCO/UNKRA. Educational Planning Mission to Korea. *Rebuilding Education in the Republic of Korea.* Paris: UNESCO, 1956. 221 pp. This is the report of a joint UNESCO/UNKRA educational mission. After spending approximately three months in Korea, the mission transmitted a survey of educational conditions along with recommendations for action.

08-087. US Operations Mission to Korea. "Ministry of Education." *Organizations and Functions of the Government of the Republic of Korea.* Seoul: Public Service, USOM/KOREA, 1966.

SCHOOLING AND SOCIETY

08-088. CHOE, Chae-Sŏk. "Family Relations and Education in Korea." *Korea Journal* 13(3)(March 1973):43–47. An examination of the influence of family relations on the formation of personality and social behavior patterns. Choe argues that in school (as a study of textbooks shows) too much space is given to family ethics, while too little space is allotted to social ethics and public morality.

08-089. CHŎNG, Bŏm-Mo. "Impact of American Culture on Korea through Educational Exchanges." *Koreana Quarterly* 9(4)(Winter 1967): 74–87. The author focuses on the relationship between acculturation and educational exchanges between Korea and the United States and examines the cultural impact of such exchanges on Korea. Using an empirical survey of Korean students who went abroad, he describes the impact the returning students have had on Korea from an economic, social, and cultural point of view. He concludes that notwithstanding all the conflicts, self-contradictions of personality, and individual differences, Korean–American cultural exchanges do work and will continue to have an impact on political, economic, and cultural change in Korea.

08-090. KAUH, Kwang-Man. "Problems Concerning Student Participation in Korean Society." *Korea Journal* 8(7)(July 1968):29–34. The author examines the questions being raised by students in secondary schools and universities regarding their role in school and society. He briefly traces Korean student movements from 1919 to the 1960 student revolution. The author argues that students are an inevitable pressure group in most contemporary nations, including Korea. The task of the educator, he suggests, is to guide the students to participate responsibly.

08-091. _____. "Problems Concerning Student Participation in Korean Society." *Koreana Quarterly* 10(Autumn 1968): 253–262. The author discusses student activism in Korea and other parts of the world. He describes the Korean student movements and concludes that students cannot be unconditionally suppressed.

08-092. KIM, Hyung-Chan. "Ideology and Indoctrination in the Development of North Korean Education." *Asian Survey* 9(11)(November 1969):831–841. Kim examines four educational reforms in North Korea during the last twenty years: the reforms of 1946, 1953, 1959, and 1966.

08-093. _____. "Patterns of Political Socialization in North Korean School." *Peabody Journal of Education* 50(4)(July 1973):265–275. Political socialization is seen as having two main functions in North Korean schools: as a means of "eliminating the old ideology" and as a means for developing a new communist morality. Two major processes are employed in socializing the young into communism: *kyoyuk* (education) and *kyoyang* (indoctrination). *Kyoyuk* implies the total educational process including the acquisition of a wide variety of information, skills, and knowledge. *Kyoyang* refers to a process of imparting the explicit values, information, and knowledge necessary to develop an acceptable personality.

08-094. KO, Hwang-Kyong. "Korean Women and Education." *Korea Journal* 4(2)(February 1964):10–13. An examination of the special problems facing the education of women in South Korea and future prospects.

08-095. LEE, Hwa-Soo. "A Study of Political Socialization Process: Family, Political Efficacy and Legitimacy: The Case of Secondary School Students in Korea." *Koreana Quarterly* 10(2)(Summer 1968):156–197. This empirical study of political socialization focuses on eighth- and eleventh-grade students in four private schools. The independent variables were defined as: political orientation of the family, socioeconomic status, sex, grade, parents' religion, father's and mother's education, urban-rural background. Two dependent variables were selected: political efficacy and political legitimacy. Lee concludes that the political system's legitimacy is a sufficient but not a necessary condition for political efficacy (the belief that one can effectively participate in politics and influence political decisions).

08-096. LEE, Yung Dug. *Educational Innovations in the Republic of Korea.* Geneva: International Bureau of Education, 1974. 50 pp. The author reviews recent innovations in curriculum, structure of the educational system, school selection procedures, instructional techniques, and educational management.

08-097. OH, Byung-Hun. "University Students and Politics in Korea." *Koreana Quarterly* 9(4)(Winter 1967):1–40. Analyzes the political activities of Korean students—first by following the history of student movements, then by depicting current campus life, and lastly by explaining the political aspects of student activities. Oh recommends that students be given more genuine freedom without ulterior political motives.

08-098. PAIK, Hyon-Ki. "Population Increase and Educational Problems." *Korea Journal* 4(8)(August 1964): 14–17. Paik discusses the far-flung effects of the population boom on education and argues that quality must keep pace with quantitative growth.

09-099. _____. "The Social Structure of Korea and Its Implications for Korean Education." *Korea Journal* 8(3) (March 1968):11–15. Paik ventures certain generalizations about the Korean people, including rural and urban distinctions. He argues that social class distinctions persist, as do Confucian influences in family life. He sees education gradually "welding together the old and new values."

08-100. YOO, Hyong-Jin. "The Charter of National Education." *Korea Journal* 9(8)(August 1969):4–7. The author describes the Charter of National Education—announced in December 1968 as "the supreme guideline for the nation's life"—and expresses hope that it will provide Korean education with a sense of direction. Yoo expands on the basic ideas underlying the charter: an emphasis upon national identity and a balance between the needs and obligations of the individual and the state.

CONTENT AND METHODS

08-101. KANG, Hui-Su. "Utilization of Mass Media for Education." *Korea Journal* 8(1)(January 1968):10–12. A summary of the use of the mass media in "radio school" and "film school" is followed by a description of how such facilities are used in formal schooling. The author gives a statistical account of the growth of mass media in Korean education and discusses the factors which have inhibited this growth in formal schools and in social education. He suggests in conclusion how the mass media can contribute substantially to Korean education.

08-102. KANG, Kil-Soo. "Recent Efforts to Improve the Quality of Education." *Korea Journal* 10(11)(November 1970): 10–12. Kang describes three educational projects to improve the quality of school learning: the Mastery Learning Project launched by the Korean Institute for Research in the Behavioral Sciences; the Education Development Project run by Yonsei University; and the educational projects supervised by the Central Education Research Institute.

08-103. KIM, Ho-Gwon. "Master Learning in the Korean Middle Schools." *Bulletin of the UNESCO Regional Of-fice for Education in Asia* 6(1)(1971):50–60. Kim reports results of the Mastery Learning Project, which derived its basic theory from Bloom's strategy for mastery learning and Carrol's model of school learning. Although the project is still in an experimental stage, the interim results are encouraging.

08-104. KIM, Hyung-Chan. "Teaching Social Studies in North Korean Schools under Communism." *Social Education* 34(5)(May 1970):528–533. Describes the social studies programs in North Korean schools and estimates the degree of their success.

08-105. _____. "The Teaching of Social Studies in North Korean Schools." *Social Studies* 62(3)(March 1971): 120–124. This article focuses on certain characteristics of social studies teaching and curriculum in primary and secondary schools of North Korea. The author points out that it is difficult to determine whether social studies instruction has succeeded in changing behavior in the approved direction. He also stresses the consistent concern for patriotism, collectivism, and revolutionary ideology.

08-106. LEE, Yong-Kul. "The Curriculum: Current Status and Prospects." *Korea Journal* 10(10)(October 1970):25–30. This article explains the inadequacies of the national curriculum implemented in 1955 and details the process of preparation and approval of new textbooks. During the late 1960s the Ministry of Education initiated a comprehensive revision of curriculum. The long-term educational plan (1972–1976) gives top priority to curriculum, and the author identifies the general guidelines for future curriculum changes.

08-107. NOBLE, G. A. "Science Education in Korea." *Science* 107(9 January 1948):31–32. A consultant in biology for the American Military Government in Korea offers an impression of science education at the time.

08-108. OH, Ki-Hyong. "Innovation in Korean Education: Reorganization of Structure of Education." *Koreana Quarterly* 13(4)(Winter 1971):53–68. Oh, director of the Education Development Project, Yonsei University, explains the integrated teaching-learning model.

08-109. PAIK, Hyon-Ki. "Development of Educational Research and Its Status in Korea." *Korea Journal* 7(7)(July 1967):9–14. The author gives a brief account of the development of educational research at the primary and secondary school levels and the activities and organization of the Central Education Research Institute. He also discusses control of the forty-five educational research institutes and their major functions.

08-110. YOO, Tai-Yong. "Audio-Visual Education in Korea." *Korea Observer* 1(3/4)(April/July 1969):42–48.

After describing the development of audiovisual education in Korea during the last twenty years, Yoo discusses the agencies responsible for such education.

DOCTORAL DISSERTATIONS

08-111. ADAMS, Donald Kendrick. "Education in Korea 1945–1955. PhD dissertation, University of Connecticut, 1955. 328 pp. Abstracted in *DA* 16(9)(September 1956): 1630; UM 18,314. A descriptive analysis of the educational goals, organizational structure, and administrative and teaching practices in South Korea. The major educational developments are discussed in the context of the changing Korean society.

08-112. AUH, Paul (Ch'ŏn-Sŏk). "Education as an Instrument of National Assimilation." PhD dissertation, Teachers College, Columbia University, 1931. 246 pp.

08-113. BANG, Hung-Kyu. "Japan's Colonial Educational Policy in Korea." PhD dissertation, University of Arizona, 1972. 241 pp. Abstracted in *DAI* 33(7)(January 1973): 3,522-A; UM 72-31,848. Historical treatment of the first two and a half decades of education under Japanese administration. Attention is given particularly to Japanese educational policies believed to be discriminatory against Koreans.

08-114. BARNES, Elaine Milam. "The Schools of Taegu, Kyongsang Pukto Province, Korea in 1954–55: An Investigation into the Interaction between Culture and Education." EdD dissertation, University of Maryland, 1960. 310 pp. Abstracted in *DA* 22(December 1961):1873; UM 61-5391. A description of the response of a city school system to national goals and policies requiring the fostering of democratic concepts and practices in primary schools.

08-115. CHEY, Soon-Ju. "A Suggested Commercial Curriculum for the Chosen Christian College of Korea." PhD dissertation, New York University, 1930. 271 pp. Presents a brief historical survey of general education. Examines the development of commercial education in Korea; the general trend of economic conditions; defects in the economic system and the educational means for correcting them. Evaluates the curriculum of Chosen Christian College and proposes a commercial curriculum.

08-116. CHO, Seung-Hak. "A Study of the Korean Elementary School Curriculum." PhD dissertation, University of Wisconsin, 1937. 200 pp. Describes the extent to which psychological principles have been used to guide instruction in elementary education and curriculum development.

08-117. CHOE, Byung-Sook. "The Impact of the Government Policy on the Development of Education in the First Republic of Korea, 1948–1960." PhD dissertation, Uni-

versity of Pittsburgh, 1971. 292 pp. Abstracted in *DAI* 32(9)(March 1972):4998-A; UM 72-7,884. A general descriptive study of the major developments in Korean education during the period 1948–1960 with particular attention to political influences.

08-118. CHOE, Sae-Hyun. "Family and Social Relationships as Factors Related to Academic Achievement of Korean Secondary School Students." PhD dissertation, Fordham University, 1971. 111 pp. Abstracted in *DAI* 32(2)(August 1971):781-A; UM 71-20,197.

08-119. CHOI, Sung-Pyo. "The Problems of Reconstructing Korean Education in Historical Perspectives." PhD dissertation, University of Illinois, 1960. 350 pp. Abstracted in *DA* 21(March 1961):2575-76; UM 61-103. In this historical survey of South Korea and its educational heritage, the author views the main obstacles to improved education as the nation's low economic development and the Korean people's lack of experience in democracy. American educational advisers are criticized for their perpetuation of class-oriented educational policies.

08-120. CHOY, Young-Ho. "Reorganization of Private Education in Korea: With Special Emphasis on the Rural Secondary Phase." PhD dissertation, University of Indiana, 1930. 139 pp. A descriptive study which includes: historical background of Korean education; private education in Korea; mission education in Korea; government education in Korea; educational needs of Korea; suggested reorganization.

08-121. CHUNG, Sae-Gyu. "The Political Socialization of Selected Elementary and Middle School Students in the Republic of Korea: Political Knowledge, Political Trust and Political Efficacy." PhD dissertation, Florida State University, 1973. 105 pp. Abstracted in *DAI* 34(4)(October 1973):1473-74-A; UM 73-24,288. Describes the current political orientation of Korean elementary and middle school students; explains how political orientation changes from grade to grade; and assesses the influence of factors outside and inside school.

08-122. CHUNG, Young-Hwan. "The Study of Some Aspects of Educational Administration with Implications for the Korean Public School System." PhD dissertation, University of Oklahoma, 1965. 163 pp. Abstracted in *DA* 26(September 1965):1445; UM 65-9,743. Draws from modern management principles and techniques in educational administration to formulate proposals for improving Korean education.

08-123. DODGE, Herbert Wesley. "A History of the U.S. Assistance to Korean Education: 1953–1966." EdD dissertation, George Washington University, 1971. 326 pp. Abstracted in *DAI* 32(6)(December 1971):3067-A; UM

72-456. During the academic year 1952–1953 the investigator was a member of the Unitarian Service Committee's first American Education Mission to Korea. The purpose of this study was to recommend improvements in the system of teacher education for elementary school personnel in the Republic of Korea. A nationwide survey was made to determine typical conditions and practices in Korean schools. A questionnaire, an interview schedule, and an observation schedule were used to collect data.

08-124. FISHER, James Earnest. "Democracy and Mission Education in Korea." PhD dissertation, Teachers College, Columbia University, 1928. 187 pp. Contents include: a general survey of the situation and an outline of the problem; modern conceptions of democracy in education; basic assumptions and experimental results; a criticism of the aims of mission education in Korea from a democratic standpoint; the relation of mission education to political and economic problems of the Korean people; the relation of mission education to indigenous Korean culture; problems in individual and social adjustment between missionary and native educational workers; the growing conflict between intellectual liberalism and religious authoritarianism in Korea.

08-125. HARRIS, Sue Ann. "The Present Status of Vocational Education in Selected High Schools of South Korea." EdD dissertation, University of California, Los Angeles, 1970. 250 pp. Abstracted in *DAI* 31(4)(October 1970):1702-A; UM 70-19,852. The proper balance between vocational and academic secondary education has been a subject for debate in South Korea for many years. By means of documents and a questionnaire, the author assesses the current status, problems, and potential of vocational high schools.

08-126. KIM, Helen Kiteuk. "Rural Education for the Regeneration of Korea." PhD dissertation, Teachers College, Columbia University, 1931. 124 pp. Contents include: general conditions in rural Korea and the educational problems; how the present educational system meets the educational needs of rural people (elementary, secondary, and agricultural schools; facilities for adult rural education); contributions of other agencies toward the education of rural people; what other countries (Denmark and Russia) are doing under similar circumstances; reasonable objectives for rural education in Korea.

08-127. KIM, Hyun-Chul. "History of Education in Korea." PhD dissertation, American University, 1931. 291 pp. Contents include: beginning of educational effort; development of education during the Three Kingdoms period, the Koryŏ dynasty, and the Yi dynasty; system and methods of education; transition to modern education.

08-128. KIM, Hyung-Chan. "A Study of North Korean Education under Communism Since 1945." EdD dissertation, George Peabody College for Teachers, 1969. 1162 pp. Abstracted in *DAI* 30(11)(May 1970):4685-A; UM 70-7615. Historical study of the development of North Korean education. Volume 1 (711 pp.) includes a detailed description of the educational system; vol. 2 (409 pp.) presents translations of key educational documents. The study is both thematic and chronological. Volume 2 includes a detailed and annotated bibliography of over five hundred references concerning education in North Korea; it incorporates a variety of English, German, Chinese, Japanese, and Korean sources.

08-129. KIM, Jin-Eun. "An Analysis of the National Planning Process for Educational Development in the Republic of Korea." PhD dissertation, University of Wisconsin, 1973. 274 pp. Abstracted in *DAI* 34(12)(June 1974):7490-91-A; UM 74-9,003. This study asks three questions: What was the political-administrative environment of national educational planning? What was the national planning activity for educational development? What was the educational change in relation to the planning goals? Assesses the changes in educational planning—from merely responding to social demand in the 1950s to attempting to fulfill the economic needs and academic goals of the 1970s.

08-130. KIM, Myung-Han. "The Educational Policy-Making Process in the Republic of Korea: A Systems Analysis." EdD dissertation, North Texas State University, 1974. 201 pp. Abstracted in *DAI* 35(7)(January 1975):4079-80-A; UM 75-887. Examines the relationship between politics and education; applies a systems analysis to the process of educational policymaking; and examines the problems in the educational policymaking process. Policymaking is viewed as an input-conversion-output process. Within this systems scheme, the author examines the forces influencing educational policy and offers an evaluation of the limitations on the existing process of decision-making.

08-131. KIM, Ran-Soo. "Perceived Need for Academic Reform in Higher Education: With Some Reference to Korean Colleges and Universities." PhD dissertation, George Peabody College for Teachers, 1972. 169 pp. Abstracted in *DAI* 33(7)(January 1973):3323-A; UM 72-34,206. An empirical study of how certain American and Korean educators regard academic reforms in higher education. Points out the problems perceived as peculiar to Korean higher education by Korean educators and summarizes the perceptions by category of respondent.

08-132. KIM, Shin-Bok. "A Systemic Sub-Optimization Model for Educational Planning: With Application to

Korea.'' PhD dissertation, University of Pittsburgh, 1973. 193 pp. Abstracted in *DAI* 35(3)(September 1974):1385-86-A; UM 74-15,554. This study attempts to develop an integrated approach to educational planning and to provide policy guidelines for the Korean educational system. The study proceeds along three major lines. The projection of educational trends with emphasis on student flow suggests the future educational structure and offers some clues on possible constraints. The manpower forecast predicts the demand from the viewpoint of structural adaptation of education to economic growth. The estimates of supply and demand are also analyzed.

08-133. KIM, Sun Ho. ''Education in North Korea: Technical, Manpower and Ideological Development.'' PhD dissertation, George Peabody College for Teachers, 1971. 579 pp. Abstracted in *DAI* 32(4)(October 1971):1751-A; UM 71-26,212. This study is concerned with North Korea's attempts to improve the quantity and quality of education for technicians and engineers. The author examines the history of technical and higher education in North Korea, the methods of manpower training in secondary schools and colleges, and the ideological aspects of technical education.

08-134. KIM, Sung-Il. ''A Study of Certain Aspects of Educational Administration and Their Historical Roots in the Republic of Korea.'' PhD dissertation, Syracuse University, 1961. 656 pp. Abstracted in *DA* 22(June 1962): 4240; UM 62-1106. A detailed description of the organization and administration of South Korean education. Extensive historical material is also included.

08-135. KIM, Tuk-Yul (Andrew). ''The Problem of Growing Disunity in the Presbyterian Church in Korea and a Suggested Approach for the Christian Education of Young Koreans.'' PhD dissertation, Hartford Seminary Foundation, 1961. 259 pp. Abstracted in *DA* 23(July 1962): 332-33; UM 62-145. The contents include: the general background of the problem; some factors operating in the growing disunity in the Presbyterian Church in Korea; a critical restatement of the problem and related factors with implications for Christian education; an approach to the Christian education of young people.

08-136. KIM, Uk-Hwan. ''An Examination of the Interplay of Culture and Education in Korea: A Comparative Study.'' PhD dissertation, Claremont Graduate School, 1972. 275 pp. Abstracted in *DAI* 33(5)(November 1972): 2075-A; UM 72-3,059. Explores the culture's characteristics and examines its effect on the educational system. Suggests intervention in the educational program of Korean schools within a cultural context. If Korea is to utilize the dynamic characteristics of democratic thinking, she must recognize the presence of undemocratic cultural forces. The study is conducted as a cross-cultural comparison in the anthropological sense. Kim argues that if educational reform is to succeed in Korea, its teachers must be cognizant of cultural influences that are working against them.

08-137. KIM, Young-Shik. ''Education of Elementary School Teachers and Administrators in the Republic of Korea.'' PhD dissertation, George Peabody College for Teachers, 1968. 333 pp. Abstracted in *DA* 29(November 1968): 1465-A; UM 68-16,344. Contents include: historical background of teacher education from the late 1890s through the 1950s; preservice education of elementary teachers from the late 1950s through 1964; the in-service education of elementary schoolteachers and administrators from the late 1950s through 1964.

08-138. KWAK, Soo-Il. ''Applying the Systems Approach to an Educational System of the Republic of Korea.'' PhD dissertation, University of Washington, 1974. 194 pp. Abstracted in *DAI* 35(8)(February 1975):4789-90-A; UM 75-4006. Through a ''systems approach'' the author examines the characteristics of Korean education with particular focus on the preparation of skilled manpower and the relation of system output to employment. A systems model for the management of Korean education is also elaborated.

08-139. LEE, Sung-Hwa. ''The Social and Political Factors Affecting Korean Education, 1885–1950.'' PhD dissertation, University of Pittsburgh, 1958. 235 pp. Abstracted in *DA* 19(December 1958):1284-85; UM 58-5619. Contents include: introduction of modern education, 1885–1910; Japanese national education, 1910–1945; educational reform since liberation, 1945–1950.

08-140. MIN, Leo Yoon-Gee. ''Mathematical Programming Model of Educational Planning with Quantitative and Qualitative Sub-Objectives: A Case of Korea.'' PhD dissertation, Stanford University, 1971. 317 pp. Abstracted in *DAI* 32(3)(September 1971):1195-A; UM 71-19,729. A macroplanning approach to the determination of educational needs. A linear programming model was constructed, and optimal solutions were obtained for individual and social objectives. Particular contributions of this study include the attempt to distinguish between wants and needs and the employment of ''qualitative'' as well as quantitative social objectives.

08-141. NAM, Byung-Hun. ''Educational Reorganization in South Korea under the United States Army Military Government, 1945–1948.'' PhD dissertation, University of

Pittsburgh, 1962. 275 pp. Abstracted in *DA* 23(December 1962):1996-97; UM 62-6677. A descriptive analysis of the educational reorganization activities of the US Army Military Government in South Korea from September 1945 to August 1948. The conclusions of the study are presented under the following headings: administrative reorganization; reorganization of schools; reorganization of higher education.

08-142. PAIK, Hyun-Ki. "Designing County Cooperative Services for the Improvement of the School and Community in the Rural Areas of Korea with Special Attention to Audio-Visual Service." PhD dissertation, Teachers College, Columbia University, 1956. 246 pp.

08-143. PARK, Bong-Mok. "An Analysis of the Ideas of John Dewey and Reinhold Niebuhr on Social Justice and the Implications of These Ideas for Korean Education." PhD dissertation, New York University, 1968. 262 pp. Abstracted in *DA* 30(August 1969):624-A; UM 69-11,767. This study analyzes and compares the theories of Niebuhr and Dewey on social justice. The author then uses the ideas of these philosophers in defining a number of reforms in Korean education.

08-144. PARK, Hun. "The Relationships between the Principal's Rating of Teacher Effectiveness and Certain Selected Teacher Variables in Korea." PhD dissertation, University of Southern California, 1972. 126 pp. Abstracted in *DAI* 32(12)(June 1972):6722-A; UM 72-17,498. The purposes of this study are (1) to identify the relationships between teacher effectiveness as rated by school principals and certain teacher characteristics; (2) to determine the significance of these relationships; and (3) to present recommendations for improving the administration of the nation's teaching personnel.

08-145. PARK, Thomas Choonbai. "Proposal for Improvement of Korean Schools through Development of a Co-curricular Program." EdD dissertation, University of Florida, 1961. 195 pp. Abstracted in *DA* 24(November 1963):1945; UM 63-7495. Contents include: the cocurricular program in the United States; a survey of the literature; a brief description of Korean education with emphasis on the curricular program; basis for a cocurricular program; a recommended curricular program for Korean elementary and secondary schools.

08-146. PARK, Young-Youl. "Education in South Korea: Schools in Transition." EdD dissertation, University of California, Los Angeles, 1967. 232 pp. Abstracted in *DA* 28(August 1967):548-49-A; UM 67-7,386. Contents include: education prior to 1945; postwar trends in Korean education; the implications of educational reform.

08-147. RIM, Han-Young. "Development of Higher Education in Korea during the Japanese Occupation." PhD dissertation, Teachers College, Columbia University, 1952. 246 pp.

08-148. ROE, Chungil Han. "The True Function of Education in Social Adjustment: A Comparative Estimate and Criticism of the Educational Teachings of Confucius and the Philosophy of John Dewey with a View to Evolving a Project for a System of National Education Which Will Meet the Needs of Korea." PhD dissertation, University of Nebraska, 1927. 60 pp.

08-149. SESSION, Eldred Steed. "An Analysis of the Contribution of the Educational Establishment to the Emergence of Korean National Identity: A Case Study of the Role of Education in Formulating a National Ethic in a Developing Country." PhD dissertation, Catholic University of America, 1969. 209 pp. Abstracted in *DAI* 30(6)(December 1969):2269-A; UM 69-19,693. Includes a historical treatment of moral education and relationships between students and government authorities. The author assesses democratic schooling as a force in promoting national identity.

08-150. SITLER, Lydia Arlene. "An Investigation of the Need for Increased Support and Improvement of Indigenous Graduate Education in Korea." PhD dissertation, University of Indiana, 1968. 350 pp. Abstracted in *DA* 29(10)(April 1969):3450-A; UM 69-6,774. Examines the causes and effects of the migration of Korean students and faculties to the United States for study or employment. An argument is made for strengthening Korean higher education.

08-151. SONG, Byung-Soon. "Comparative Study of Ideological Influences on Educational Theory and Practice in North and South Korea." PhD dissertation, Wayne State University, 1974. 181 pp. Abstracted in *DAI* 35(7)(January 1975):4277-78-A; UM 74-29,866. An examination of the major religious and political influences on education as Korean society evolved from a primitive homogeneous culture to a relatively high level of industrialization.

08-152. UNDERWOOD, Horace Horton. "Outline History of Modern Education in Korea." PhD dissertation, New York University, 1926. 393 pp. See annotation of related publication *Modern Education in Korea* (08-038).

08-153. WHANG, Hichul Henry. "The Tasks of Public Education as Perceived by the Public of Korea." PhD dissertation, University of Wisconsin, 1972. 149 pp. Abstracted in *DAI* 33(1)(July 1972):130-A; UM 72-13,116. Using the concepts of philosophy, the author identifies the tasks of Korean public education, determines the priority of these tasks, explains how various elements of the Korean public perceive the tasks of education, and compares American and Korean perceptions.

08-154. WILSON, Elizabeth Cecil. "The Problem of Value in Technical Assistance in Education: The Case of Korea 1945–1955." EdD dissertation, University of Maryland, 1959. 349 pp. Abstracted in *DA* 20(April 1960):4006; UM 60-1286. An experienced technical adviser examines the values which dominate Korean education and those held by American advisers.

08-155. YOO, Hyung-Jin. "An Intellectual History of Korea from Ancient Times to the Impact of the West with Special Emphasis upon Education." PhD dissertation, Harvard University, 1958. 292 pp. One of the most complete surveys in English of the intellectual and historical background to the introduction of Western institutions. Korea's cultural dependence on China is explored in detail.

08-156. YOO, Stanley-Sung Soon. "The Influences of Confucianism and Christianity upon Korean Education." PhD dissertation, American University, 1932. 240 pp. Presents a brief survey of Korean education and discusses the influence of Confucian education from its dominance over Buddhism until 1885, the early influence of Christianity upon Confucian education (1886–1895), and the Christian influence upon secondary and higher education (1896–1931).

08-157. YOO, Young-Dae. "Suggestions for the Improvement of Korean Educational Law in Terms of the Democratic Principles." PhD dissertation, George Peabody College for Teachers, 1960. 257 pp. Abstracted in *DA* 21(September 1960):533-34; UM 60-2190. The author establishes the following principles of educational organization and administration: universal free education, sharing of responsibility among central and local educational governments, continuous growth of the teaching profession, and individual self-realization, among others.

08-158. YOU, In-Jong. "The Impact of the American Protestant Missions on Korean Education from 1885–1932." PhD dissertation, University of North Carolina, 1967. 324 pp. Abstracted in *DA* 28(February 1968):2999-A; UM 68-2,254. Contents include: the social and educational background before the coming of the American Protestant missionary; the establishment of American Protestant missions and their early educational activities (1885–1896); the establishment of mission schools (1897–1910); the development of the secondary mission schools (1911–1932); the development of mission colleges as union institutions (1911–1932).

08-159. YUM, Ki-Sup. "The Development of a Korean Group Intelligence Test." EdD dissertation, Boston University, 1964. 240 pp. Abstracted in *DA* 26(April 1966):5887; UM 65-5,532. An attempt to develop a valid and reliable group test for evaluating the intelligence of Korean children between the ages of nine and twelve. After reviewing thirty standardized test scales and the concept of intelligence, the author selects the following item types: verbal synonyms; classification by similarities; analogies; word classification; picture classification; number sequences.

CHAPTER 9

Geography and Natural Environment

Shannon McCune

INTRODUCTION

GEOGRAPHY AND NATURAL ENVIRONMENT

THE GEOGRAPHICAL CHARACTERISTICS, the limitations of the natural environment, and the strategic peninsular location of Korea have been significant influences throughout the country's history. In fact, geography and history have always been closely related in the minds and writings of Korean scholars. Though Korean geographers are not strong in numbers, they are actively publishing worthwhile materials on Korean geography and the natural environment.

The peninsular location and character of Korea in the heart of the Far East have been discussed by many geographers since the days of the German Friedrich Ratzel a hundred years ago. In times of tension and aggression, the Korean peninsula has been invaded and conquered by outside forces. In times of peace, the peninsula has provided shelter for the Korean people. In 1945 the hitherto unified peninsula was divided. Two political areas were soon formed—the Republic of Korea in the south and the Democratic People's Republic of Korea in the north. These countries have been divided since 1953 by a highly fortified demilitarized zone.

THE TWO KOREAS

The two Koreas of the present day—North and South—have considerable contrasts in geography and natural environment. North Korea is larger in area (47,000 square miles) but smaller in population (an estimated 17 million people in 1978); whereas South Korea has an area of 38,000 square miles and an estimated 36 million people in 1978. North Korea has cold winters with average January temperatures of 17.5°F in Pyongyang and −6°F in Chunggangjin at the northern bend of the Yalu River. In contrast South Korea has relatively mild winters with average January temperatures of 24°F in Seoul and 32°F in Pusan. All of Korea has hot, humid summers with average July and August temperatures in the 70s and 80s. Summer temperatures are not so high, however, in the mountain areas of North Korea and along the deep Sea of Japan. Urbanization has increased in both North and South Korea: Pyongyang has an estimated population of over 1 million; Seoul has an estimated population of over 7 million and Pusan, over 2 million.

Half the population in both areas are engaged in the primary occupations of farming, fishing, and forestry. North Korea has more mineral and hydroelectric power resources than South Korea; South Korea has more arable land, some of which may be double-cropped.

Because of their strategic location, the two Koreas have been studied by a number of geographers. North and South Korea are discussed with varying emphasis in general books on Asian geography and in world political geographies. The most recent general works on Korea written by Western scholars have been those of the late Hermann Lautensach, Shannon McCune, Patricia B. Bartz, and Eckart Dege, whose writings are listed in the bibliography.

Geographers in the Republic of Korea have been very

active. They have written a great number of articles, monographs, and books; many of the journals and monographs, published by universities, are limited in circulation. There are numerous Korean-language textbooks for use in geography classes at all levels. (No attempt is made here to list them.) They usually follow a rather standardized format with discussions of the physical and cultural elements in the geography of Korea. In 1975 the Korean Geographical Society, the professional organization of geographers in South Korea, held a symposium reviewing the progress of research. A 182-page mimeographed summary of papers on various aspects of research was printed and discussed. These papers include extensive bibliographies on the topics of geomorphology, climatology, urban and settlement geography, economic geography, geographic education, and applied geography.

Geographers have been active in North Korea also. A brief *Outline of Korean Geography* was published in English in Pyongyang in 1957. The writings of two Russian geographers, V. T. Zaichikov and V. V. Martynov, give emphasis to North Korea; both have been translated into English and are available in mimeographed form. V. A. Dement'ev prepared a summary of geographical sciences in North Korea in 1958, but much advancement has taken place in the last twenty years.

Comparative studies of the changing geography of North and South Korea need to be made; such studies should be useful in considering the future of the divided peninsula. Both areas have been undergoing economic and political development, and their geography has accordingly changed greatly.

THE KOREAN PENINSULA AND ITS SURROUNDING SEAS

The 600-mile-long Korean peninsula, stretching from latitudes 43° to 33° north, has a broad base along its northern frontier with Manchuria. The land narrows to a waist between Pyongyang and Wŏnsan and then widens again to a fairly uniform width of some 160 miles to the south. On the west and south there are many islands and peninsulas. The relatively shallow Yellow Sea on the west contrasts with the deep Sea of Japan to the east. (In Korean this body of water is termed the Eastern Sea.) Out in the Sea of Japan off south-central Korea is small, volcanic Ullŭng (or Dagelet) Island and even smaller Tokto. Tokto (Takeshima in Japanese) has been claimed by Japan but is in the possession of the Republic of Korea. There are a number of studies by Japanese and Korean geographers of these uninhabited islands, called the Liancourt Rocks by early British surveyors. The southern shore of the Korean peninsula is a ria coastal zone with many islands and peninsulas along the crenulated coastline. It is warmed by offshoots of the Kuroshio (Black Current). The Korea Strait separates the Korean peninsula from Tsushima and Japan, some 120 miles distant. To the southwest, offshore some 60 miles, lies large, volcanic Cheju, or Quelpart Island as it was called on early European maps. It is elliptically shaped and slopes upward to the crest of Hallasan with an elevation of 6400 feet. The German geographer Hermann Lautensach wrote an interesting article in 1935 comparing the geography of Quelpart and Dagelet islands. More recently there have been many geographic studies of contemporary Cheju Island stressing its distinctive differences with peninsular Korea.

Only in recent years has much oceanographic research been carried on in the seas around the Korean peninsula. The ocean currents in the Sea of Japan and along the southern coast have a moderating effect on the climate. In the areas where the warm and cool currents meet are important fishing grounds. The nature of these currents, in particular the cool Liman Current which flows south along the shores of northeastern Korea, needs further research and description. The high tides of the Yellow Sea severely handicap the use of ports and estuaries along the west coast of Korea. Much research effort is being expended on the potential oil resources which are believed to be under the continental shelf to the south and west of Korea. The seaward political jurisdictions of South Korea and North Korea are matters of international dispute about which much has been written.

EARLY KOREAN DESCRIPTIONS

Korean scholars have long been writing of the geography of their land. Following the classical Chinese form of scholarship in which history and geography are closely related, early Korean accounts were in the nature of gazetteers and descriptions of places of interest rather than systematic and regional geographies. One of the most noteworthy of these is the *Tongguk yǒji sǔngnam* [Korean gazetteer], which was prepared in the early days of the Yi dynasty by a group of scholars, started by Yang Sǒng-ji in 1455 and completed by No Sa-sin in 1481. It was revised in later years: 1486, 1499, and 1531. These early geographical works stress the nature of the land and the relations of the villages and towns to county seats and of the counties to the eight provinces into which Korea was divided for many centuries.

Interesting descriptions of the eight provinces are found in Yi Chung-hwan's *T'aengniji* (sometimes entitled *P'aryǒkchi*: Guide to the Eight Provinces). This work was written while the scholar was banished from the Korean court and was completed shortly before his death in 1752. Many of the provinces and counties are described in gazetteers compiled by Korean scholars who were serving as governors or magistrates of these political units. The chapter on geography in an official Korean encyclopedia—the *Tongguk munhǒn pigo*, with editions of 1770, 1807, and 1908—summarizes the geographical materials from many of these descriptive works.

Though some of the works of early Korean scholars on the geography of Korea have been reprinted, few have been translated into English or analyzed with the care they deserve. In a chapter in his *Science and Technology in Korea*, Sang-woon Jeon discusses works on geography and cartography of Korea up to modern times; this study includes reproductions of Korean maps and, usefully, gives the Chinese titles of the various works.

Closely related to the study of geography, particularly before Confucian doctrine was firmly established, was the practice of geomancy in Korea. Though it was not officially recognized during the later years of the Yi dynasty, geomancy played, and still plays, a large role in the siting of Korean graves and houses. An excellent study of Korean geomancy was completed recently as a PhD dissertation at the University of California by a Korean scholar, Hong-key Yoon.

EARLY WESTERN DESCRIPTIONS

Early Western visitors to Korea found it difficult to penetrate the isolation of the Hermit Nation. In some cases Western exploration parties were able to go along the coasts or along the northern frontier. One of the first French Catholic missionaries, though unsuccessful in his attempts to enter Korea, described the land with its mountains and hills along the Yalu River—"like a sea tossed in a heavy gale." The account of a Dutch ship's clerk, Hendrik Hamel, shipwrecked in 1653, was published in European travel literature along with translations of the accounts of Chinese and Japanese travelers. Basil Hall and John M'Leod on a British expedition sailed along the west coast of Korea in 1816 and wrote of their inhospitable reception.

After Korea was opened to the outside world in 1876, a number of Western travelers wrote descriptions based on their excursions in Korea. William R. Carles, a British vice-consul in 1884–1885, wrote *Life in Corea* based on his experiences. A redoubtable English lady traveler, Isabella Bird Bishop, was in Korea a decade later and wrote *Korea and Her Neighbours*. Other travelers—Arnold Henry Savage Landor, Alfred E. Cavendish, Percival Lowell—wrote accounts of their travels and impressions for the benefit of armchair travelers in the United States and Europe. The writings of American, English, and French missionaries often included brief geographical descriptions. A three-volume description of Korea was published by the Ministry of Finance in St. Petersburg in Russian in 1900. It brought together most of the information available in Western languages on Korea at the turn of the century.

Some of the best descriptions of premodern Korea in Western languages have been written by expatriate Koreans who, thinking back to their childhood in Korean villages, wrote eloquently of their early life. Two such books are Younghill Kang's *The Grass Roof* and Mirok Li's *The Yalu Flows*. Though these books, as well as the travel accounts of Western writers, are not strictly geographical studies, they do provide the reader with a feel for traditional Korean life and ways, something much needed by all students of Korea.

In modern times many Westerners have visited Korea. In their writings one finds interesting and colorful descriptions of Korea. Articles in travel and popular magazines like the *National Geographic* have often been accompanied by picturesque photographs. Not so complimentary are the descriptions of Korea written by

Westerners during the Korean War, when the writers were impressed by the tragedies of conflict rather than the beauty of the landscape.

Numerous guidebooks designed for tourists have been published in English. These often are well illustrated and include maps and geographical descriptions. A guide to the national parks of Korea was published by the Ministry of Construction. Allen D. Clark and his son, Donald N. Clark, wrote an excellent guide to Seoul; Dorothy H. Middleton and her husband, William D. Middleton, wrote of Korean journeys which would take a tourist out of Seoul. There are many studies of Korean villages which provide details on local geography such as Pak Ki-hyŏk's study of three villages undergoing change and Vincent S. R. Brandt's study of a farming and fishing village.

GEOLOGY AND PHYSIOGRAPHY

Though there were earlier geological studies by Westerners searching for gold deposits, major research on the geology of Korea was conducted by the Japanese during their period of control (1910–1945). Koto Bunjirō carried out some pioneering research. A well-known Japanese geologist, Kobayashi Teiichi, did much field research and, many years later in 1953, summarized the work of Japanese geologists in a useful monograph—*The Geology of South Korea*—which really covers all of Korea in its Far Eastern geological setting.

The Geologic Survey of Korea, established by the Japanese, was expanded as a research and publication center by the Republic of Korea. The survey, together with various state agencies for mineral exploration and development, has published a number of geological studies of different areas and of the hydrogeology of certain river basins of Korea. Many of these publications have English abstracts or are in bilingual form and are listed in geological bibliographies. Of particular importance are the bilingual reports on the geology of individual topographic sheets or quadrangles at a scale of 1:50,000.

The Geologic Survey—which is now called the Geological and Mineral Institute of Korea—has been carrying on collaborative research with the Institute of Geological Sciences of London. A. J. Reedman, a British geologist, has collaborated with Sangho Um, a Korean geologist, in writing a brief and excellent *Geology of Korea*. The individual chapters cover the geological periods and conclude with detailed bibliographies. Useful maps and tables are included and the monograph has an appendix that lists with a locational map all of the 175 quadrangles for which geological surveys had been completed by 1975 in South Korea. Of special interest is a short discussion of the plate tectonics and Mesozoic orogeny of Korea, a topic on which research is just starting.

Geologically, Korea is an old portion of the earth's crust. The general trend of the gneisses, schists, and granites which make up the basic complex is from northeast to southwest. In the northern interior of the peninsula the high Kaema Plateau is dissected by the headwaters of the Yalu and Tumen rivers so that, though called a plateau structurally, it is a land of mountains. Mount Paektu, the highest of these at 9000 feet, is an extinct volcano with a crater lake. The crest has light-colored pumice rocks which make it appear white in the summer; in the fall, winter, and spring it is capped by snow. A rift structure that extends northeast from Seoul to Wŏnsan on the Sea of Japan is often used by writers to separate the Korean peninsula into to macrogeomorphological areas. South of this rift the T'aebaek Range parallels the east coast and forms the major drainage divide of southern Korea. Southwest from its central area branches the Sobaek Range, which culminates in the Chiri massif in southwestern Korea. Cheju and Ullŭng islands have been formed by relatively recent volcanism. During the Pleistocene glacial ages, changes in sea level joined Korea and China across the Yellow Sea. Though there was some mountain glaciation, the major effect of the glacial periods was the development of a series of three or four levels of erosion in the mountain areas and along the major river valleys of Korea. Within the complex geological structure are significant mineral deposits of particular concern to those engaged in geological research in Korea. A voluminous survey of the mineral resources of South Korea and their geology was prepared by David Gallagher and others of the US Geological Survey; an account of those in North Korea is in V. V. Martynov's economic-geographic study of Korea.

Since river valleys have been the habitat of most of

the Korean people through historic times, the Koreans link the ever-present mountains and the rivers closely. The major rivers flow to the west and south with the exception of the Tumen River, which forms the northeastern boundary of Korea. The Yalu River is the northwestern boundary. The Taedong flows past Pyongyang. The two major branches of the Han River join before it flows past Seoul. The Kŭm and Yŏngsan rivers in southwestern Korea are bordered by intensively cultivated plains. A large area of southeastern Korea is drained by the winding Naktong River. Taegu is on one of its tributaries; Pusan is in a sheltered bay near the mouth of the Naktong on the Korea Strait. The many tributaries of these major rivers and other smaller rivers have been described in early Korean geographical writings and are currently described in an excellent series of *Hydrogeological Maps of Korea* published by the Geological and Mineral Institute of Korea. The latter have lengthy English abstracts.

Because of the monsoonal climate the rivers of Korea fluctuate greatly in their flows between winter, late spring, and early summer. There is a constant problem of flooding if they are too constricted by man-made structures. Development of dams along them for hydroelectric power and irrigation has been based on detailed hydrological studies, including work in recent years in South Korea by United Nations experts. The Naktong, the Han, and rivers in southwestern Korea have been the subject of special studies with many reports. Many of these studies are relatively inaccessible to research workers, however, since they were prepared for Korean, United Nations, and United States agencies and never distributed. Some of them are listed in the useful bibliographies in Patricia M. Bartz's *South Korea*.

The terrain of Korea with its diversity depends upon the underlying geological structure and the faulting and uplift of this structure. The plate tectonics of the Korean peninsula in the Far East is the subject of interesting current geological research. There is a difference between the old and the young granites and their susceptibility to erosion. The alluvial terraces and depositions in the floodplains also give variation to the physical base of the land. These matters have been studied by many scholars. Some of the research has been very detailed—for example, a study of the size and shape of the pebbles

in alluvial deposits. General and regional studies of the physiography of Korea have also been written, some of them useful for military strategists and tactical army commanders. Attention should also be devoted, however, to the curtailment of serious erosion in the upland areas and the flooding of the plains.

CLIMATE

The climate of Korea, basic to agriculture and forestry, has been studied by a number of scholars. Centuries ago the Koreans developed rain gauges. Monthly rainfall data for Seoul go back to 1770, and data for numbers of rainy days per month go back to 1626. Under the Japanese a number of modern weather observatories were established in the major regions of Korea. These have been continued in both North and South. Although the current data from North Korea are not easily obtainable, summaries of climatic data from the official weather stations and from the information collected at schools and county offices in South Korea are prepared in various reports and are readily available. Annual reports and summary volumes are published by the Korean Central Meteorological Observatory in Seoul. A useful bibliography of Korean-language materials in geographical and meteorological journals is presented at the end of the chapter on climatology in the *30 Years Anniversary Symposium* published by the Korean Geographical Society in 1975.

The diversity of the humid continental climate of Korea is of particular interest. Though all of Korea, except the high mountain areas and the coastal zone along the deep Sea of Japan in northern Korea, has relatively warm moist summers, there is great regional variation in winter temperatures. Bitterly cold winters are experienced in the northern interior with five months having average monthly temperatures below freezing; by way of contrast, the southern coast and Cheju and Ullŭng islands have average temperatures in January slightly above freezing. There is also a regional contrast between the small climatic influence of the Yellow Sea and the pronounced maritime effect of the Sea of Japan. Research on the climatic regions in Korea has been carried out by a number of climatologists and geographers.

The climatic variations in Korea greatly affect agricultural and land use patterns and practices. Floods caused by heavy or unseasonal rainfall can cause great hardship. Any delay in the spring and summer rains may result in drought conditions with serious economic effects. Typhoons in late summer and early fall may damage the ripening rice. In terms of a modern scientific approach, the study of these climatic and flood hazards is just beginning.

NATURAL VEGETATION

The natural vegetation of Korea reflects the climatic and edaphic conditions with variations from north to south, from coastal areas to interior locations, and from lower elevations to mountainous areas. On Cheju and Ullŭng islands and along the southern coast of the Korean peninsula influenced by the maritime position and southern latitude, there is subtropical deciduous vegetation with some evergreen species, even subtropical fruits and flowers. Bamboo flourishes. The greater part of Korea has deciduous mixed forests of oaks, maples, birches, and, especially at higher elevations, pines. Azaleas, rhododendrons, and other flowering shrubs add color to the hillsides. The fall colors of these mixed forests interspersed with green pines are spectacular. Naturally, local differences in this forest cover occur. Some areas have been cut over repeatedly so that only scrub oaks and grass vegetation have been able to maintain a hold on the bare, eroded hill slopes, particularly where the granite rocks have weathered. There are very few stands of virgin forest. The tall pines in protected stands around Buddhist temples deep in the hills give an indication of what the natural vegetation could be, if only proper reforestation and control were maintained. In the higher mountains in the south and throughout the northern interior of the Korean peninsula, the predominantly pine and mixed forests are replaced by northern boreal forests with spruce, fir, and larch as dominant species. It is in these areas that commercial forestry was carried on by the Japanese. Both North and South Korea now have government forests for timber production.

Great efforts have been expended recently in North and South for the rehabilitation of forest resources. Though under the Japanese some reforestation programs were carried out, in the latter days of Japanese control, especially during World War II, these controls

were slackened and wood-hungry Koreans cut over many of the forested areas, particularly near the cities and towns; moreover the Japanese cut much timber for an unsuccessful wooden-shipbuilding program. New regulations and major reforestation programs were started in South Korea with American and United Nations assistance, particularly after the Korean War. Rigid controls have been instituted in North Korea and vast areas are reported to have been reforested. Though fire-field agriculture—the practice of burning a plot of forest and scrub land, planting crops of millet and barley for two or three years, and then abandoning the fields—has largely been stopped in South Korea, it is still practiced as it has been for centuries in the mountain lands of North Korea. Most of the economic exploitation of the forests is done in North Korea, but South Korea has an estimated 68 percent of its land area that could be used for forests. In South Korea substitution of other fuels for cooking and heating in the cities has decreased the demand for firewood and brush, though these are still gathered, often illicitly, and used in rural areas.

Japanese botanists were active in research on Korea's natural vegetation and published some excellent taxonomic studies. After a hiatus in such research from 1945 to 1953, Korean botanists are now continuing the research. The forestry services in both North and South Korea have been doing much to further reforestation along scientific lines. Research on insect infestation and control is of paramount concern; more damage is done by insects than by illicit cutting. Various tree planting programs have been quite successful. The clothing of the eroded hills with young trees, particularly pines, the planting of poplars and other fast-growing species along roads and stream banks, and the development of recreational parks have all met with remarkable success in South Korea.

NATURAL RESOURCES

Korea is not a land rich in natural resources. When the Japanese took complete control of Korea in 1910, they instituted projects to exploit the natural resources of their new colony. They conducted soil surveys, topographical and cadastral mapping programs, and geological surveys in order to inventory the available agricultural and mineral resources. In the post-1945 period, with Russian assistance in North Korea and with American, British, and United Nations assistance in South Korea, new intensive surveys of mineral resources have taken place. Moreover, engineering studies of water supplies for hydroelectric power, for irrigation water, and for drinking and industrial water have been carried out in North and South Korea. The potentialities for offshore oil deposits in the Yellow Sea and Korea Strait have also been studied recently. The economic development of such oil resources would have a tremendous impact on the Far East, which has few large petroleum fields.

Forest and soil constitute the basic natural resources of Korea. The soil classification systems in use are usually based on the geological structure of the land. Because most of the soils are lacking in important elements for good crop production, heavy fertilization and treatment of the soil are necessary for high yields. In both North and South Korea great efforts have been made to produce chemical fertilizers and to assure their distribution and effective use. Though barnyard manure has been used with care on the fields for centuries, today chemical fertilizers are increasingly substituted. Numerous studies have been made on the improvement of Korean agriculture through better soil use and treatment. The United Nations Korean Reconstruction Agency, for example, with the assistance of the Food and Agricultural Organization, published a voluminous report in 1954. In South Korea active experimental stations with well-qualified agronomists publish many reports and monographs in Korean.

WATER RESOURCES

Since rice is such a desired and high-yielding crop in Korea, irrigation water control has been of great importance for centuries. In modern times many dams and irrigation systems have been built. The Japanese were particularly active in such enterprises during their days of control, seeking to make southern and western Korea a major rice-producing area for the growing cities of Japan. In the post–World War II period, irrigation has been considerably expanded in North and South Korea by means of modern hydraulic engineering techniques. Cost-benefit studies have shown that many small proj-

ects may be more advantageous to Korea than a few large-scale ones. But large projects have prestige and political value. These projects, though often announced with fanfare, are not always completed.

The hydroelectric power resources of North Korea were initially developed by the Japanese. A series of dams was constructed on the headwaters of the Yalu, water being diverted from the reservoirs through tunnels down the eastern slopes of the mountains to provide hydroelectric power to new chemical and steel industries built in cities along the northeast coast. The Japanese also constructed dams on other streams and other tributaries of the Yalu. In the late 1930s they completed the Sup'ung Dam across the Yalu itself. At the time it was the largest hydroelectric power project in the Far East with 640,000 kilowatts installed capacity, equally divided between Korea and Manchuria. The threat to the Sup'ung Dam and its power resources by the advances of the United Nations forces during the Korean War was reportedly one reason why the Chinese Communists entered the war. Other dams have been built on the Yalu and its tributaries since the Korean War by the North Korean regime with the assistance of the Soviet Union, East European nations, and Communist China. Still other projects have been planned. In South Korea dams have been built on the headwaters of the Han River for multipurpose use, including hydroelectric power. Plans have been made for more such dams in South Korea.

MINERAL RESOURCES

The geological occurrence and character of the mineral resources of Korea have been studied intensively by Japanese and, later, by Russian and American mining geologists and engineers. Well-trained Koreans are now doing much of this research in both North and South Korea. The literature on the mineral resources of Korea is rather scattered or is found in government reports of limited circulation. A few general accounts have been published, but often these deal more with potentials than with actual production. Though under the Japanese the mineral resources in the north were more developed than those in the south, much exploration and development have taken place in South Korea in recent decades. The glowing reports of vast mineral resource development in North Korea often give production as a percentage increase over some previous year on which data are not available.

Because of the geological character of the Korean peninsula there are many and scattered mineral resources. The list is long, but few minerals are found in large enough deposits to be economically significant. One of the most important is the anthracite coal deposits in the Yŏngwŏl area of southeastern Korea. Even larger anthracite coal deposits are found near Pyongyang in North Korea. Lignite or brown coal is mined near the northern bend of the Tumen River in northeastern Korea. This coal has low caloric value, but the reserves are very large. Iron ore deposits south of Pyongyang were developed by the Japanese early in their days of control. Later they mined low-content iron ores in northeastern Korea and installed concentrating plants to enrich these ores, which have large reserves. These mines, though damaged during the Korean War, have been rehabilitated and reportedly expanded. Low-grade iron ore deposits, notably the field at Hongch'ŏn near Yŏngwŏl in South Korea, have been developed for domestic production and export to Japan.

The mineral resources in Korea, other than coal and iron ore, are mined by numerous enterprises. Output depends in large part upon world prices for gold, tungsten, copper, lead, zinc, graphite, and bismuth. Often these metals are mined from complex ores containing more than one of these metals and separated in the refining process. The reserves are large, but in small scattered deposits of complex ores, making economic development difficult.

HUMAN GEOGRAPHY

The close ties of the Korean people to their land have been part of their heritage. With modernization, however, many of these ties are being modified, particularly in the agricultural geography of Korea. The geographical patterns of Korea's agricultural land use have been studied by many Japanese and Korean scholars; some of the latter, such as Hoon K. Lee and Chung Myun Lee, were trained in America. These patterns reflect the physical features that set the framework for the varied land use. One-fifth of Korea may be cultivated. The intensity with which the land is used depends greatly upon the length of the growing season. In the southern part of

Korea a crop of barley may follow a crop of rice; the cold winters of central and northern Korea make this double cropping impossible.

The changing land use of South Korea has been studied by many Korean geographers and agricultural economists. Of particular value has been the land-use mapping program based largely upon the availability of air photographs. Almost all of Korea south of the Demilitarized Zone has now been mapped; the colored maps of land use at a scale of 1:25,000 are restricted in circulation, but collections may be consulted at universities and government agencies. Detailed land-use studies have been made of certain areas—for example, Cho Tong-gyu of Kyung Hee University has studied the shifting cultivation of a highland region near Kangnŭng in Kangwŏn province. The opening of the Seoul-Kangnŭng Express Highway in 1976 through this area is causing tremendous changes. Eckart Dege of Kiel University has been making land-use studies of South Korea with emphasis upon eight selected villages; the final results of his studies will be valuable.

Along the coasts some farmers carry on fishing as a part-time activity; in addition there are major fishing ports. Korean fishing vessels go out into the Sea of Japan, the Korean Strait, and the Yellow Sea, sometimes fishing in quite distant waters. Few studies have been done on the geography of these fishing activities, though it seems an important field for research. Government reports of various kinds have been published on the fishing industries of North and South Korea.

The population growth and distribution reflect differences in land use and the rapid urbanization which has taken place throughout Korea. The city of Seoul, for example—nothing but rubble at the end of the Korean War—has a population estimated at over 7 million. Though not at such a rapid pace, other cities in both North and South Korea have been growing. The geographical aspects of urbanization and the relationships of the cities to transportation facilities in South Korea have been studied by both Korean and American geographers, such as Forrest R. Pitts and Hong Kyung-hi. Migration patterns in Korea have been studied by another geographer, Han-soon Lee. There are many census reports and sociological studies of the Korean population.

The industrial complexes which have developed recently in both North and South Korea are of particular geographical interest, though not much comparative material has been published on these developments. A preliminary comparative study by Byung-ho Park is a start in this field. Rigid economic planning has been carried on under the communist regime of North Korea. Cities with extensive housing blocks for the workers have been built near factories and mines. In South Korea various five-year and sectoral economic development plans have been based on economic data collected in an increasingly sophisticated manner. In some of these plans greater attention might have been given to geographical factors; for example, there is a disturbing concentration of industry in the militarily vulnerable and presently overcrowded Seoul area. The overall economic progress of South Korea has been impressive and many studies of the "economic miracle" have been published. Few of these studies, however, are geographically based. Thorough geographical research on the changing economic patterns of South Korea, using some of the quantitative techniques and theories now available, would have significance.

The political and military geography of Korea has, of necessity, been a major concern in recent years. Much has been written on these subjects, but some of it has been fairly superficial. More detailed and objective research is needed on the divided land of Korea and its internal and international political geography. A Korean geographer, Im Tŏk-sun, has published textbooks in Korean on political geography and a number of articles on critical areas such as the Demilitarized Zone and Tokto.

CARTOGRAPHY

Korea is now a well-mapped land with many series of detailed topographical maps and thematic maps of various kinds and at various scales. Early Korean scholars appreciated maps and used them in their manuscripts and published works. European cartographers, as they attempted to map Korea, went through an interesting progression before the shape of the Korean peninsula became established in a map published in 1735 and copied from a Korean map. The Japanese in the early part of their period of control, 1910 to 1945,

prepared an important series of topographic sheets at a scale of 1:50,000 in over seven hundred sheets. These were widely used by American and Korean mapping agencies as the basis for other series. At present, data obtained from satellites are being used for updating the maps of Korea.

EARLY KOREAN MAPS

Early Korean mapmakers drew maps of the cities, counties, and provinces of Korea, as well as all of the Korean peninsula. These maps were included in historical works and descriptive accounts; they were often made or copied by administrative officials such as county magistrates to aid them in their duties. Most of the early Korean maps were drawn in the Chinese fashion: scale, if used at all, was based upon travel time from place to place; standardized forms for mountains and rivers were used; circles or boxes enclosed the names of cities and towns; color was used on the manuscript maps and sometimes added to the woodblock-printed maps. Usually the maps were adjusted to the size of the paper sheets and were thus distorted in shape and direction. Korean, Japanese, and Western scholars have devoted considerable research to this early Korean cartography. Korean maps, including copies of world maps obtained in Peking and reproduced in Korea, are often cited and illustrated in general works on the history of cartography. Yi Pyŏng-do, the eminent Korean historian, has written on early Korean maps, as have other Korean scholars, such as Yi Ch'an (Ch'an Lee), Kim Yang-sŏn, Chŏn Sang-un, U Nak-ki, Hyung Kie-joo, and Hong I-sŏp. Geographers in North Korea—most recently Mok Yong-man—have also been interested in the history of the cartography of Korea. Copies of early Korean maps are to be found in various libraries and in private collections. A list of the holdings in the major university and government libraries of South Korea is included as an appendix in Yi Ch'an's (Ch'an Lee's) monumental and valuable *Old Korean Maps* (1977).

Though often the early Korean maps were designed or used for scrolls and screens, atlases in woodblock or manuscript have intrigued many scholars, perhaps receiving more attention than they merit. The atlases usually include maps of the world, China, Japan, and the Ryūkyū Islands (Liu-ch'iu Kingdom), as well as maps of the Korean peninsula and the provinces of Korea. The map which has aroused the most interest is the world map drawn in a circular form—the *Ch'ŏnha to*—which has been reproduced in many forms. Nakamura Hiroshi, a Japanese cartophile, wrote a lengthy article on this map for *Imago Mundi.*

One of the most noteworthy early maps of Korea is that of Kim Chŏng-ho, published in woodblock form in 1861. As U Nak-ki has noted in a useful study, this map has a precursor, the *Ch'ŏnggu to,* drawn in manuscript by Kim Chŏng-ho in 1834. Both maps may have been based in part on the *Tongguk yŏjido,* a map drawn by Chŏng Sang-gi (1678–1752). Kim Chŏng-ho's map, printed by woodblocks in 1861 and reprinted in 1864, is made up of twenty-one sheets which when joined together make a map of Korea at a scale of roughly 1:160,000, or less than 3 miles to the inch. This map was reprinted in 1936 with an index prepared by the Japanese scholar Y. Suematsu; this version has since been reprinted a number of times.

EUROPEAN MAPS

As concern grew among nations in Europe for expansion in colonies, trade relations, and missionary activities in the Far East, Korea became a place of special interest. Efforts to map Korea correctly increased. A number of scholars, such as August Pawlowski as early as 1904, have written articles and notes based on European map collections at their disposal. Korean scholars have recently become interested in these maps, but the definitive work remains to be written. The evolution of Korea—from a place-name on the shores of China, to the shape of a circular island, to the shape of an elongated island, and finally to a peninsular shape—is fascinating to trace.

The turning point for European cartography of Korea came with the publication of J. B. Du Halde's *Description . . . de la Chine* in 1735 and d'Anville's *Nouvel Atlas de la Chine . . .* in 1735. The map of Korea in these publications was drawn from a map prepared by Father Regis, a Jesuit scholar-missionary, and his associates in the so-called Kang-hsi Atlas of China. Prepared for the Ch'ing emperor Kang-hsi, the atlas was presented to him in 1718. Father Regis, a most redoutable traveler and map surveyor, went along the northern frontier of Korea in 1709 and 1710. He used his geodetic

observations to orient a map of Korea which had been obtained in the royal court in Seoul by a Tartar lord and made available to Father Regis in Peking. The resulting map shows a relatively correct shape of the Korean peninsula; it was widely copied in European publications and atlases after 1737.

In modern times, many European exploratory expeditions went along the coast of Korea mapping (and naming) islands and shore lands. With the opening of Korea after 1876, numerous maps of Korea were published in Europe—especially during the Sino-Japanese (1894–1895) and Russo-Japanese (1904–1905) wars. Many of these were copies of Japanese maps. These European maps have a weird collection of place-names: some are derived from the names given by European explorers; others are taken from Chinese, Korean, or Japanese transcriptions, variously romanized.

MODERN JAPANESE MAPS

The Japanese early in their period of control (1910–1945) conducted cadastral surveys to ascertain ownership of fields, house lots, and forest lands. They also prepared in 1914–1918 a set of 722 topographic maps of Korea at a scale of 1:50,000. Each sheet covered an area of 15 minutes of longitude by 10 minutes of latitude. These maps were based on ground surveys and included contours and spot heights; they also had symbols for land use and cultural features. In some of the uninhabited and mountainous areas shading rather than contours was used. This series of maps is still useful as a resource for study of the changes which have taken place in the last half century. The Japanese prepared other series of maps at scales of 1:200,000 in sixty-five sheets and at 1:25,000 and 1:10,000 for cities. Maps of the thirteen provinces into which Korea was by then divided were published at a scale of 1:500,000. Many thematic maps, such as geological surveys and types of forests, were also published by Japanese government agencies. Numerous maps were made for tourists, including pictorial maps with changing scales for the major tourist areas such as the Diamond Mountains, Seoul, Kyŏngju, and Pyongyang.

AMERICAN MAPS

During World War II the US Army Map Service reprinted the Japanese 1:50,000 sheets with purple overlay for place-names. For strategic planning purposes up-to-date maps at a scale of 1:250,000 in forty-four sheets to cover Korea were published in 1944. Later—particularly during and after the Korean War—the Army Map Service published series at scales of 1:25,000; 1:50,000; 1:100,000; and 1:250,000. These were based partially on the old Japanese land survey but were brought up to date by the use of air photography. The Army Map Service published some photo maps at scales of 1:12,000 and 1:25,000. They also published for military usage during the Korean War many tactical maps and bilingual maps in Korean and English.

After the outbreak of the Korean War a number of American map companies published maps of Korea at scales of 1:1,000,000 or smaller scales. Recently the US Central Intelligence Agency has published useful desk maps of North and South Korea at scales of 1:1,220,000 with thematic map inserts. These are very useful for students and may be purchased from the Government Printing Office.

MODERN KOREAN MAPS

Both the Democratic People's Republic of Korea in the north and the Republic of Korea in the south have published maps of Korea at various scales. These are usually in Korean, though some published by the Republic of Korea are bilingual in English and Korean. Since the North Korean regime has divided the traditional provinces, their maps are of interest to show the new boundaries. The new South Korean map series have the same grid as the Japanese series and are updated by recent air photography. The 1:50,000 maps may be readily purchased, and city maps at scales of 1:5000 and 1:2500 are also available. The Republic of Korea has published various thematic maps—for example, on soils, geology, and forest cover. An excellent and useful series of colored land-use maps at a scale of 1:25,000 is being published for South Korea but may be obtained only for official use. Transportation and railroad maps have been published for both North and South Korea. For school use wall maps and atlases, among them some useful historical maps, have been published; these are usually only in Korean. Fortunately maps are a universal language. They represent valuable source materials for students interested in gaining knowledge of Korea and its geography and natural environment.

BIBLIOGRAPHY

GEOGRAPHY AND NATURAL ENVIRONMENT

Bibliographies, Journals, and Accounts of Geographical Studies
Bibliographies

09-001. COURANT, Maurice. *Bibliographie Coréenne.* Publications de L'École des Langues Orientales Vivantes, nos. 18–20. Paris: 1894–1897. *Supplement,* 1901. This bibliography includes brief accounts of many old Korean geographical descriptions, maps, and atlases.

09-002. FANG, Chaoying. *The Asami Library: A Descriptive Catalogue.* Edited by Elizabeth Huff. Berkeley: University of California Press, 1969. 424 pp. This annotated catalog has a chapter, "Geography" (pp. 168–180), that includes illuminating comments on a number of old Korean geographical works and maps. References to such works are to be found in other chapters also. The Asami collection is one of the best collections of old Korean materials in the United States.

09-003. GOMPERTZ, G. St. G. M. "Bibliography of Western Literature on Korea from the Earliest Times until 1950." *Transactions of the Korea Branch of the Royal Asiatic Society* 40 (1963). This bibliography is based in part on Horace H. Underwood's *Bibliography* (1931). It is a very good source for the travel literature on Korea by Western writers, including over 750 references to such travel accounts.

09-004. JONES, Helen Dudenbostel and Robin L. WINKLER (comps.). *Korea: An Annotated Bibliography of Publications in Western Languages.* Washington: Reference Department, Library of Congress, 1950. 155 pp. Mimeographed. This bibliography is of value for the large number of geographical works cited and annotated.

09-005. LAUTENSACH, Hermann. "Korea (1926–36) mit Nachträgen aus älterer Zeit." *Geographische Jahrbuch* 53(1938): 255–274. Lautensach, the German geographer who did fieldwork in Korea in 1933 and subsequently wrote many books and articles on Korea, prepared this useful bibliography on Korean geography, including materials from Japanese sources at a time when Korea was not well studied. A bibliography of recent materials to supplement his bibliography is being prepared by Eckart Dege of the University of Kiel.

09-006. MARCUS, Richard (ed.). *Korean Studies Guide.* Compiled for the Institute of East Asiatic Studies, University of California, by B. H. Hazard, Jr., James Hoyt, H. T. Kim, and W. W. Smith. Berkeley: University of California Press, 1954. 220 pp. This bibliographic study guide includes primary and secondary sources, monographs, and studies in Western languages, Korean, Japanese, and Chinese. The compilers, graduate students in Korean history, were assisted by specialist consultants. The chapter on "Geography" (pp. 29–37) annotates a number of significant early Korean geographical works.

Journals and Accounts of Geographical Studies

09-007. *Applied Geography*. Korean Institute of Geographical Research. 1975 onward. This new journal publishes articles dealing with geographical methodologies applied to contemporary problems.

09-008. *Chiri hak* [Geography]. Korean Geographical Society, Department of Geography, College of Education, Seoul National University. 1963 onward. This geographical journal has articles in Korean with English abstracts.

09-009. DEMENT'EV, V. A. "Geograficheskaiâ nauka v Koreĭskoĭ Narodno Demokraticheskoĭ Republike [Geographical sciences in the Korean People's Democratic Republic]." *Isvestiiâ Vsesoiûznogo Geogrfisheskogo Obshchestva* [Bulletin of the All-Union Geographical Society] 90(3)(May/June 1958):288–293. In Russian. A brief discussion of the work of Korean and other geographers in North Korea. Considerable expansion in the discipline of geography has taken place since this summary was written. A number of Korean geographers have received advanced training in the Soviet Union.

09-010. *Geography—Education*. Department of Geography, Graduate School of Education, Seoul National University. 1973 onward. This semiannual publication includes geographical articles with English abstracts as well as notes of materials of interest to teachers. Volume 5 (1975) includes a list of Master's theses and doctoral dissertations completed in American universities from 1939 to 1975 which dealt with Korea or were submitted by Korean students in the discipline of geography.

09-011. *Journal of Regional Development*. Institute of Land Development, Kyung Hee University, Seoul. 1971 onward. A number of articles in this journal are written by geographers.

09-012. *Korea, Its Land, People and Culture of All Ages*. 2nd ed. Seoul: Hakwon-sa, 1963. 739 pp. The first edition of this encyclopedic work was published in March 1960. Includes discussions on geographical studies.

09-013. Korean Geographical Society. *30 Years Anniversary Symposium*. Edited by Ch'an Lee. Seoul: 1975. 182 pp. Mimeographed. This summary of the development of research in the field of geography during the thirty-year existence of the Korean Geographical Society, the leading professional organization for geographers in Korea, is composed of an introduction on the growth of geography by Ch'an Lee and then papers on various aspects of geography; each of these has an extensive bibliography. This document was used for a lively discussion at the annual fall meeting of the society on 30 November 1975. It is expected that a revised edition of this symposium will be published by the society.

09-014. Korean National Commission for UNESCO (comp.). *UNESCO Korean Survey*. Seoul: Dong-A Publishing Co., 1960. 936 pp. This encyclopedic work includes a brief section (pp. 1–2) on the natural conditions of Korea, a colored map of Korea (p. 66) at the scale of 1:2,500,000, and a section on geography in the chapter on humanistic studies.

09-015. *Naksan chiri* [Geography of Naksan]. Department of Geography, College of Liberal Arts and Sciences, Seoul National University. 1970 onward. This geographical journal has articles in Korean with English abstracts.

Studies on Old Korean Geographical Works

09-016. HONG, I-sŏp. "Yi Chung-hwan's Geographical Thought in T'aengniji." *Korea Journal* 14(3)(March 1974):40–44. This is an interesting article on the life and work of Yi Chung-hwan, who completed the *T'aengniji* (or *P'aryŏkchi*) in 1752.

09-017. HULBERT, Homer B. "An Ancient Gazetteer of Korea." *Korean Repository* 4(1897):407–416. Homer B. Hulbert, an American who wrote widely on Korea in the last years of the Yi dynasty, wrote this note on the *Sinjŭng tongguk yŏji sŭngnam* [Revised Korean gazetteer] to bring this monumental work to the attention of Western readers.

09-018. JEON, Sang-woon. *Science and Technology in Korea: Traditional Instruments and Techniques*. MIT East Asian Science Series. Cambridge, Mass.: MIT Press, 1974. 383 pp. Professor Jeon has written a book in Korean on the history of science and technology in Korea (1966) and a number of articles on different aspects of science. In chap. 5 of this work he discusses advances in geography and cartography, particularly during the Yi dynasty.

09-019. NEEDHAM, Joseph and W. LING. *Science and Civilization in China*. Vol. 3: *Mathematics and Sciences of the Heaven and the Earth*. London: Cambridge University Press, 1959. The famous English historian of science in China discusses the geographic and cartographic contributions of old Korean scholars.

09-020. RHO, Do Yang. "A Study of Pal-yuk-ji [Livable places]." *Chiri hak* [Geography] 1(July 1963):91–96. English abstract: pp. 91–92. This note outlines the contents of a famous Korean work by Yi Chung-hwan: the *T'aengniji* (sometimes entitled the *P'aryŏkchi*).

09-021. WOO, Nak-ki. "Geographer Kim Chong-ho's Three Achievements." *Journal of Social Sciences and Humanities* (Korean Research Center), 38(June 1973): 69–83. Woo Nak-ki, director of the Korean Geographic Research Institute, discusses the life and work of Kim Chŏng-ho.

09-022. YI, Pyŏng-do. "The Impact of the Western World on Korea in the 19th Century." *Cahiers d'Histoire Mondiale* 5(1960):957–975. In this article, the eminent Korean historian summarizes the exchanges of geographical knowledge which took place.

09-023. YOON, Hong-key. *Geomantic Relationships between Culture and Nature in Korea.* Asian Folklore and Social Life Monographs, Vol. 89. Taipei: Orient Cultural Service, 1976. 279 pp. Yoon's doctoral dissertation at the University of California has been published in this form. The result of field research and training in geomancy in Korea, it is an interesting study of the subject. The author also draws on some of the classics in geomancy and a study by a Japanese scholar, Professor Murayama Chijun, published in 1931.

General Geographical Studies

09-024. BARTZ, Patricia M. *South Korea.* Oxford: Clarendon Press, 1972. 203 pp. Bartz, a geographer trained in Australia and at the University of California, has written a very useful and well-illustrated geography of the southern part of Korea. She follows a traditional approach with chapters on the various elements in the geography of South Korea. The last half of the book is a descriptive geography—first of Seoul and Pusan, then of four regions—based on the political provinces. In addition to its value as a geography, the book is a useful guidebook for a visitor or a Western resident of Korea, for the major cities and places of interest in each region are described.

09-025. DEGE, Eckart. *Korea: Führer zu einer landeskundlichen Exkursion.* Kiel: University of Kiel, 1977. 181 pp. Mimeographed. Dege has done fieldwork in Korea and served as a visiting professor at Kyung Hee University. This book was developed for the use of a group of German geography teachers who visited Korea in the spring of 1977. It does not pretend to be an exhaustive geographical study but gives useful background on certain features and places. Dege is publishing a number of other useful geographical studies including a chapter on Korea in a general book on the Far East edited by Peter Schöller.

09-026. KOLB, Albert. *East Asia: China, Japan, Korea, Vietnam; Geography of a Cultural Region.* Translated by C. A. Sym. London: Methuen, 1971. 591 pp. This book in German (under the title *Ostasien*) was first published in Heidelberg in 1963. The text and statistics were brought up to date for this English-language edition. The numerous colored maps have added to the cost of this book, written by a German geographer who has done fieldwork in the Far East. Chapter 6, "Korea: A Bridgehead," is a useful summary of the geography of Korea. It concludes with regional descriptions of North and South Korea and some comparisons between the two areas.

09-027. LAUTENSACH, Hermann. *Korea: Eine Landeskunde auf Grund eigner Reisen und der Literatur.* Leipzig: K. F. Koehler, 1945. 542 pp. Hermann Lautensach, a highly competent German geographer, wrote two books and some forty articles on the geography of Korea. He traveled extensively throughout Korea from March to November 1933. Returning to Germany with his field notes, pictures, list of plants, virtually complete sets of maps, and "hundreds of Japanese books and brochures," Lautensach started writing on aspects of his research. Some of the most significant articles are listed in a note by Shannon McCune, "Geographic Publications of Hermann Lautensach on Korea," *Far Eastern Quarterly* 5(3)(May 1946): 330–332. After his preliminary work, Lautensach wrote his definitive geography of Korea. This was completed in November 1942, but because of World War II the book was not published until 1945.

09-028. _____. *Korea: Land, Volk, Schicksal.* Stuttgart: K. F. Koehler, 1950. 135 pp. Since his major book on the geography of Korea was relatively inaccessible in 1950, Hermann Lautensach wrote a short book on Korea for the general reader. He brought some of the material up to date and emphasized the varied political and economic developments which had taken place in North and South Korea after 1945.

09-029. MARTYNOV, V. V. *Koreya: Economichasko-Geograficheskaya Kharakteristika KNDR i Yuzhnoy Korei* [Korea: An economic-geographic study of the Korean People's Democratic Republic and South Korea]. Moscow: MYSL Publishing House, 1970. 216 pp. A complete translation of Martynov's book has been published by the Joint Publications Research Service under the English-language title and the number JPRS 52032 (278 pp., mimeographed, 1970). Martynov received his Economic Sciences degree from the Moscow Economic Statistics Institute in 1963 with a 193-page dissertation: "An Economic and Statistical Examination of the Fuel and Power Resources of the Korean People's Democratic Republic.'' He evidently expanded that study for this book; almost all of the bibliography on North Korea consists of works dated prior to 1963.

09-030. McCUNE, Shannon. *Korea, Land of Broken Calm.* Princeton: Van Nostrand, 1966. 221 pp. This book is in the Asian Library series sponsored by the Asia Society of New York, but it has more geographical content than other books in the series.

09-031. _____. *Korea's Heritage: A Regional and Social Geography.* Rutland, Vt.: Tuttle, 1956. 250 pp. Shannon McCune, the son of American missionaries in Korea, spent part of his boyhood in Sŏnch'ŏn and some of his high school years in Pyongyang in northern Korea. He did his fieldwork for his doctoral dissertation in Korea in 1938–1939: ''The Climatic Regions of Tyosen (Korea) and Their Economy'' discusses the various elements in the geography of Korea and then describes the two divisions —North and South—and the ten geographical regions into which McCune divides Korea. Some of the geographical regions are further subdivided. The book has appendixes on mineral and hydroelectric power resources and on industrial patterns. There is a rather lengthy appendix annotating bibliographic references and notes. The pictures grouped in the text and the notes on the pictures given in an appendix supplement the book considerably.

09-032. *Outline of Korean Geography.* Pyongyang: Foreign Languages Publishing House, 1957. 119 pp. This small book includes quite a bit of propaganda but offers a brief account of Korean geography with some useful information on North Korea. The geographies of Korea written by geographers in North Korea are in Korean or in Russian; very little is written or even abstracted in English, though the Joint Publications Research Service of the US Department of Commerce has translated some of these articles into English.

09-033. ZAICHIKOV, V. T. *Geography of Korea.* Translated by Albert Parry with an introduction by Shannon McCune. New York: Institute of Pacific Relations, 1952. 142 pp. Mimeographed. This is a translation of the first edition of Zaichikov's *Koreia,* which was published in Moscow in 1947. An expanded second edition of Zaichikov's book was published in Moscow in 1951. Zaichikov's study is a rather dull compendium of geographical information. After a discussion of the various geographic elements, he describes the six regions into which he has divided Korea. Some of the regions he divides into subareas. He has been more careful in his regional description of North Korea than in that of South Korea.

Descriptions and Travel Accounts

09-034. BERGMAN, Stan. *In Korean Wilds and Villages.* Translated from *I Morganstillhetens Land* by Frederick Whyte. London: I. Gifford, 1938. 232 pp. This account of a Swedish naturalist's travels in Korea in 1935–1936 is of particular interest for the descriptions of the interior of northern Korea.

09-035. BISHOP, Isabella Bird. *Korea and Her Neighbors.* New York: Revell, 1898. 480 pp. Bishop, a British traveler, was in Korea from 1894–1897. Her impressions make interesting reading, though she was quite critical of some aspects of Korean society. Her views of the political situation are colored by the weakness of the Korean court at this time and the emerging power of Japan. This book was published in London in two volumes and was widely read at the time.

09-036. CARLES, William R. *Life in Corea.* New York: Macmillan, 1888. 217 pp. Carles was British vice-consul in Korea in 1884–1885 and traveled rather extensively in that country.

09-037. CAVENDISH, Alfred E. and Henry E. GOOLD-ADAMS. *Korea and the Sacred White Mountain.* London: G. Philip, 1894. 224 pp. The travels of two British army captains in Korea including their ascent of Mount Paektu on the North Korean boundary.

09-038. HALL, Basil. *Account of Voyage of Discovery to the West Coast of Corea and the Great Loo-choo Island.* London: John Murray, 1818. 222 pp. Hall's account of the inhospitable reception of a British surveying expedition in 1816 along the islands of southwestern Korea was published in a number of editions and translated into the major European languages; a pirated edition was published in Philadelphia. This is reported to have been the first book on Korea published in the United States. The Royal Asiatic Society, Korea Branch, has recently reprinted Hall's book with an introduction by Shannon McCune.

09-039. HETT, G. V. ''A Korean Journey.'' *Geographical Magazine* 3(2)(August 1935):274–292. This is a short but interesting account. A similar account was offered in Hett's ''In Korea, 1935,'' *Journal of the Royal Central Asian Society* 23(2)(April 1936):236–250.

09-040. KANG, Younghill. *The Grass Roof.* New York: Scribner's, 1931. 367 pp. A nostalgic and beautifully written account of a boyhood in Korea. Younghill Kang also wrote other books on Korea and translated Korean poetry.

09-041. KIM, H. Edward. ''Rare Look at North Korea.'' *National Geographic* 146(2)(August 1974):252–277. *National Geographic* was able to get a Korean-born photographer-writer into North Korea. His account, though noncontroversial and noncritical, is colorful.

09-042. LANDOR, Arnold Henry Savage. *Corea: Or Chosen, the Land of the Morning Calm.* London: Heinemann, 1895. 304 pp. Landor, a British traveler, visited Korea in 1890–1891 and wrote of his impressions.

09-043. LEDYARD, Gari. *The Dutch Come to Korea.* Seoul: Korea Branch of the Royal Asiatic Society and Taewon Publishing Company, 1971. 231 pp. This account of the life of the first Westerners in Korea (1653–1666) includes the account of the shipwreck of a Dutch vessel and the description of the Kingdom of Corea written by Hendrik Hamel in 1668.

09-044. LI, Mirok. *The Yalu Flows: A Korean Childhood.* Translated by H. A. Hammelmann. East Lansing: Michigan State University Press, 1956. 185 pp. This well-written account of his early years in Korea was written by a Korean who became an expatriate in Germany after 1919.

09-045. LOWELL, Percival. *Chosön, the Land of Morning Calm: A Sketch of Korea.* Boston: Tickner, 1885. 412 pp. Lowell was in Korea in 1884 and wrote of his impressions and travels.

09-046. M'LEOD, John. *Narrative of a Voyage in His Majesty's Late Ship Alceste, to the Yellow Sea along the Coast of Corea, and through its Numerous Hitherto Undiscovered Islands, to the Island of Lew Chew. . . .* London: John Murray, 1817. 288 pp. This account of the British expedition, like its companion volume by Basil Hall, has had several reprintings. A reprint with an introduction by Shannon McCune was published by Tuttle in 1963.

09-047. PAIK, L. George. "The Korean Record on Captain Basil Hall's Voyage of Discovery to the West Coast of Korea." *Transactions of the Korea Branch of the Royal Asiatic Society* 24(1935):15–19. The official Korean reaction to the British visit of 1816 was assembled and translated by an eminent Korean historian and educator.

09-048. SOCHUREK, Howard. "South Korea, Success Story in Asia." *National Geographic* 135(3)(March 1969):301–345. *National Geographic* has published articles on South Korea every few years; this one is written in glowing terms and with striking photographs.

09-049. WHITE, Peter T. "South Korea: What Next." *National Geographic* 148(3)(September 1975):394–427. Photographs by H. Edward Kim.

Government Publications

09-050. Canada. Department of Mines and Technical Surveys. *Korea: A Geographical Appreciation.* Foreign Geography Information Series, no. 4. Ottawa: 1951. 84 pp.

This brief study based on the available literature and including maps was edited by Gordon D. Taylor. It is a useful summary of Korean geography by a group of Canadian geographers.

09-051. SHINN, Rinn-Sup et al. *Area Handbook for North Korea.* Prepared by Foreign Area Studies, American University. DA Pamphlet 550-81. Washington: Government Printing Office, 1969. 481 pp. This handbook follows the rather rigid outline of the series. Chapter 2, "Physical Environment," is a brief description with a number of maps. The bibliography is useful, particularly for the listing of the articles and books translated by the Joint Publications Research Service of the Department of Commerce.

09-052. United States. Department of Army. *Area Handbook for South Korea.* Prepared by Foreign Area Studies, American University. DA Pamphlet 550-41. Washington: Government Printing Office, 1975. 413 pp. This handbook is a revision from a previous Area Handbook which covered all of Korea. Chapter 3, "Physical Environment and Population," is a summary of the geography of South Korea.

09-053. _____. Department of State. *Background Notes: North Korea.* Publication 8396, August 1973. 5 pp. Students find these Background Notes with their brief comments and bibliographies very useful. Especially helpful is the single-page map which may be reproduced easily and then colored to illustrate students' papers.

09-054. _____. _____. *Background Notes: South Korea.* Publication 7782, December 1975. 6 pp. These Background Notes are revised periodically. The summarized data, brief discussion, and selected bibliography are very useful for students, as is the single-page map.

09-055. _____. _____. Office of the Geographer. *China-Korea Boundary.* International Boundary Study no. 17, 1962. 4 pp. This study of the 880-mile boundary includes a discussion and map of the Mount Paektu area, which at the time this study was made was in dispute between China and the Democratic People's Republic of Korea. China has since acknowledged the validity of the Korean claims.

09-056. _____. _____. _____. *Korea "Military Demarcation Line."* International Boundary Study no. 22, 1963. 3 pp. This study has a clear map of the 148.5-mile-long "demarcation line" and the zones of 2 kilometers on each side of the line.

09-057. _____. _____. _____. *Korea–U.S.S.R. Boundary.* International Boundary Study no. 59, 1965. 4 pp. This study includes a colored map of the boundary that extends along the Tumen River for 10.4 miles. The principle of following the "thalweg," or main channel, is observed, so that the boundary is close to the Soviet Union's bank of the river. There is no explicit treaty on this boundary, which has effectively blocked Chinese access to the Sea of Japan.

Recent Guidebooks and Descriptive Studies

09-058. BRANDT, Vincent S. R. *A Korean Village between Farm and Sea.* Cambridge, Mass.: Harvard University Press, 1971. 252 pp. This study by an American anthropologist of a village on the Yellow Sea has much valuable geographical material.

09-059. CLARK, Allen D. and Donald N. CLARK. *Seoul, Past and Present: A Guide to Yi T'aejo's Capital.* Seoul: Korea Branch of the Royal Asiatic Society and Hollym Corporation, 1969. 242 pp. This is a perceptive guide by a father and son who know Seoul very well. There are a number of other guides written for tourists by Republic of Korea agencies. Some excellent guides have been written by Edward B. Adams, another American who knows Seoul and Korea well.

09-060. MIDDLETON, Dorothy H. and William D. MIDDLETON. *Some Korean Journeys.* Seoul: Korea Branch of the Royal Asiatic Society, 1975. 312 pp. The Middletons traveled extensively in the early 1970s and took some excellent pictures which effectively illustrate this interesting guide to areas away from Seoul in South Korea.

09-061. *National Parks of Korea.* Seoul: Ministry of Construction, Republic of Korea, 1975. 134 pp. This is a sumptuously illustrated guide to the nine national parks of South Korea; a foldout map accompanies each description.

09-062. PAK, Ki-Hyuk and Sidney D. GAMBLE. *The Changing Korean Village.* Seoul: Korea Branch of the Royal Asiatic Society and Shin-hung Press, 1975. 222 pp. This study of three villages was written by Pak and dedicated to Gamble, who inspired his research. The original field survey was done in 1961–1962; since then many changes have taken place in rural Korea.

Geology and Physiography

09-063. Japan. Government General of Chōsen. Geological Survey of Chōsen. *Bibliography on the Geology of Tyosen.* Prepared under the direction of Iwao Tateiwa, 1933. This bibliography contains 547 references and indicates how much geological research had been done by Japanese and other geologists prior to 1933. In recent years several Japanese geologists have been able to carry on fieldwork in South Korea; their publications may be found in Japanese geological journals.

09-064. KOBAYASHI, Teiichi. "A Sketch of Korean Geology." *American Journal of Sciences* 26(156)(December 1933):585–606. A good, brief summary of the geological structure of Korea by a well-known Japanese geologist.

09-065. ———. "Geology of South Korea: With Special Reference to the Limestone Plateau of Kogendo (Kangwŏn-do)." *Journal of the Faculty of Science* (University of Tokyo), 8(4)(1953):145–293. One of Japan's eminent geologists who had done research in Korea before World War II summarizes his findings and those of others in this study. Though the title seems to limit the study, it is in fact a geology of all Korea. The bibliography is especially valuable for its citation of Japanese publications.

09-066. Korea, Republic of. *Geological Survey of Korea: Hydrogeologic Maps of Korea: Anseong River Basin.* Vol. 1. Seoul: 1961. 48 pp. This is the first in a series of reports on the hydrology and geology of selected river basins in South Korea. Includes a ten-page English abstract and a foldout map.

09-067. ———. *Geological Survey of Korea: An Outline of the Geology of Korea.* Seoul: 1956. 29 pp. A brief summary of the geology of Korea. The Geological Survey of Korea has been publishing many reports and studies, often bilingually, on areas of geological significance and mineral resources.

09-068. KOTO, Bunjiro. "An Orographic Sketch of Korea." *Journal of the College of Sciences, Tokyo Imperial University* 19(1)(1903–1904):1–61. Koto was one of the first Japanese geologists to work in Korea. In this sketch he stresses the significance of the rift (which he called not too correctly a "graben") from Seoul to Wŏnsan which divides Korea into two geomorphic provinces.

09-069. ———. "Journeys through Korea." *Journal of the College of Sciences, Tokyo Imperial University* 26(2) (1909):1–207. Professor Koto traveled extensively, particularly in South Korea; his field notes and descriptions make interesting reading.

09-070. PARK, No-Sik. "Physiographic Provinces of Korea." *Chiri hak* [Geography], 6(May 1971):1–23. Park, an established geographer, made a study, based in part on topographic maps, of the physiographic regions of Korea. He stresses the significance of the division of Korea into two large provinces by the Seoul–Wonsan rift. He further divides Korea into 5 macroregions, 53 mesoregions, and 299 microunits. These are shown on a map and listed.

09-071. REEDMAN, Anthony John and Sangho UM. *The Geology of Korea.* Seoul: Geological and Mineral Institute of Korea, 1975. 139 pp. This excellent "account of the geological development of the Republic of Korea," as it is subtitled, is a product of the cooperative research of the

Korean Geological and Mineral Institute and the British Institute of Geological Sciences. It has many clear maps, cross sections, charts, and photographs. Each chapter concludes with a lengthy bibliography on the geological period which has been discussed. An appendix lists the geological quadrangles which have been mapped and discussed in bilingual reports. There is also a very helpful table of Japanese and Korean romanizations of stratigraphic names in Korea.

09-072. TATEIWA, Iwao. "Outline of the Geology of Korea." *International Geological Review* 2(12)(1960): 1053–1070. This is a brief review by a Japanese geologist who served as head of the Geological Survey of Chōsen for a number of years prior to 1945.

09-073. USSR. Geological Institute. *Geologiya Korei.* Prepared under the direction of B. A. Masaitis. Moscow: 1964. 263 pp. This Russian-language survey of the geology of Korea has a bibliography emphasizing Russian and North Korean sources.

09-074. YOSHIKAWA, Tarao. "Analysis of Late Mature and Old Mountains in Central Korea: An Approach to Quantitative Research on Physiographic Development of Mountains." *Japanese Journal of Geology and Geography* 37(1)(1956):67–78. The author is an eminent geomorphologist who has done fieldwork in Korea.

Mineral Resources

09-075. GALLAGHER, David, Montes R. KLEPPER, William D. OVERSTREET, and Raymond C. SAMPLE. *Mineral Resources of Korea.* 4 vols. Washington: US Geological Survey, 1962. 2239 pp. Mimeographed. This monumental compilation of data was prepared by the US Geological Survey assisted by geologists of the Korean Geological Survey and the Korean Institute of Mining Technology. Incorporated in the bibliography are annotations on Japanese publications prepared by Takeo Watanabe of Tokyo University shortly after 1945.

09-076. GALLAGHER, David. *Mineral Resources of the Republic of Korea.* Open File, Series 1184. Washington: US Geological Survey, 1968. 74 pp. This is a condensation and updating of various reports plus a very useful bibliography that includes United States and Korean government reports and studies.

09-077. KAWASAKI, S. "Geology and Mineral Resources of Korea." *Geology and Mineral Resources of the Japanese Empire* (Tokyo), (1926):109–126. This is an old study but still of some value.

09-078. *Mineral Resources of Southern Korea.* Natural Resources, no. 84. Tokyo: Supreme Commander Allied Powers, Natural Resources Section, 1947. This report,

written early in the period of the American occupation of Korea, is based largely on Japanese sources and lists the mineral resources alphabetically.

09-079. OGURA, Tautoma. *Geology and Mineral Resources of the Far East.* 3 vols. Tokyo: University of Tokyo Press, 1967–1971. This work includes a summary of Korean geology and mineral resources and a useful bibliography.

River and River Basin Studies

09-080. KANG, Dae Hyeon. "Flood Plain Settlements on the Han River." *Chiri hak* [Geography], 2(May 1966):14–26. This study by a Korean geographer includes an English summary (pp. 14–15).

09-081. LEE, Moon-chong. "Flood and Flood Adjustments to the Han River." *Chiri hak* [Geography], 7(May 1972): 24–39. Through a questionnaire the author found that the majority of the inhabitants in an area subject to flooding by the Han River in 1925, 1936, and 1965 "showed an environmental deterministic attitude" toward floods.

09-082. MEER, K. Van der. "Aspects of Reclamation of Tidal Flats in Korea." *Geografish Tijdschrift* 4(3)(June 1970):220–227. This study by a Dutch scholar on the Mokpo-Yŏngam area of southwestern Korea stresses that small reclamation projects would have greater economic impact and viability than large-scale projects.

09-083. PARDE, Maurice. "Les acrues phénomènales du Han en Corée." *Annales de Géographie* 420(March/April 1968):194–202. This study of the severe flooding of the Han River points out the real dangers of erosion in the Han's headwaters and flooding in the lower stretches, a phenomenon characteristic of the rivers in Korea.

09-084. United States. Bureau of Reclamation. *Han River Basin: Reconnaissance Report; Water Resources Study.* 4 vols. Washington: 1971. This study was prepared by the Bureau of Reclamation in cooperation with the US Geological Survey, the Republic of Korea Ministry of Construction, the Korea Water Resources Development Corporation, and the US Agency for International Development. This report is characteristic of many other studies —for example, of the Naktong River basin.

Weather and Climate

09-085. ARAKAWA, H. "On the Secular Variation of Annual Totals of Rainfall at Seoul from 1790 to 1944." *Archiv für Meteorologie, Geophysik und Bioklimatologie,* series B, 7(2)(1956):205–211. A Japanese climatologist studies the data on rainfall at Seoul compiled from the old records by Y. Wada in 1917. Wada's original work, published by the Central Meteorological Observatory at Inch'ŏn, has been reprinted recently by the Korean Meteorological Service in Seoul.

09-086. HUH, Woo Kung. "A Study of Climate Classification of Korea, after the Koppen System and Its Modified System." *Naksan chiri* 1(December 1970):20–26. Summarizes the patterns which may be developed according to the Koppen climatic system; the English summary is on p. 26.

09-087. KIM, Soon Tae. "Secular Precipitation Variations in Seoul, 1770–1968." *Naksan chiri* 1(December 1970):27–36. This article in Korean, with an English abstract (pp. 33–34), compares rainfall data with sunspot activity but discovers no relationship.

09-088. LEE, Byong-Sul. "A Synoptic Study of the Early Summer and Autumn Rainy Season in Korea and in East Asia." *Geographical Reports of Tokyo Metropolitan University* 9(1974):79–96. This study in English has a useful bibliography including Japanese and Korean-language references.

09-089. _____. "Weather Climatology of Changma (Early Summer Rainy Season) and Kaul Changma (Early Autumn Rainy Season) in Korea in Relation to Two Rainy Seasons in East Asia." *Geographical Review of Japan* 48(7)(1975):459–484. The maps of distributions of the polar fronts of distinctive years are especially interesting. Japanese article with an English abstract.

09-090. McCUNE, Shannon. "Climatic Regions of Korea and Their Economy." *Geographical Review* 21(1)(1941): 95–99. A summary of McCune's doctoral dissertation at Clark University. This dissertation, completed in 1939, was rearranged and published as a series in *Research Monographs on Korea*.

09-091. OKADA, Takematsu. "Winter Temperatures in Korea and Manchuria." *Proceedings of the Imperial Academy* (Tokyo), 8(1932):116–118. Okada, long the distinguished director of the Japanese Weather Observatories and an excellent scholar, made this brief study of the validity of an old Korean weather proverb: "Three cold days follow four warm days." He attributed this cycle of weather in the winter months to the passage of extratropical cyclonic storms.

09-092. United States. Weather Bureau. *An Annotated Bibliography on Climatic Maps of Korea.* Compiled by Allen Wallace, Jr., and Darthula M. Carraway. Washington: 1962. 20 pp. Mimeographed. A useful bibliography.

Natural Vegetation and Forestry

09-093. GOOD, Sister Alice Maria. "An Annotated Bibliography of the Flora of Korea." *Transactions of the Kentucky Academy of Science* 17(1)(February 1956):1–32.

This excellent bibliography, unfortunately rather obscurely published, is a real contribution to Korean studies, for information on the natural vegetation of Korea is widely scattered. It is a condensation of an MS dissertation at Catholic University. The bibliographer has examined all the pertinent bibliographies in Western languages. She did not list titles in Japanese or Korean, except those that had English abstracts or Latin names for species. She lists some fifty publications by Takeoshin Nakai, a Japanese botanist who spent his life working on the scientific aspects of Korean flora.

09-094. Korea, Republic of. Office of Forestry. *Forestry in Korea.* Seoul: 1968. 120 pp. This bilingual report on the forest resources of Korea and their use is well illustrated. Especially interesting are the comments on insect pests, which are of serious concern. There are many other reports on forestry in South Korea, including some prepared for United States and United Nations agencies.

Land Use and Agricultural Regions

09-095. BARTZ, Fritz. "Die Seefisherei Koreas." *Zeitschrift für Erdkunde* 8(11/12)(June 1940):296–303. This article, written before World War II, is one of the few studies in a Western language on the geography of fishing activities in Korea.

09-096. CHEN, Cheng-siang. *Agricultural Geography of Korea.* Research Report 31. Hong Kong: Geographical Research Center, University of Hong Kong, 1970. 90 pp. Largely a compendium of previous studies, but it is useful for its maps and bibliography.

09-097. CHO, Dong Kyu. "A Geographical Study on the Shifting Cultivation of High, Cool Lands in Taikwanryong Area." *Theses Collection, Kyung Hee University* 6(1970):143–226. A study of the upland area near Kangnŭng in Kangwŏn province.

09-098. _____. "Slash-Burn Cultivation in Korea." *Chiri hak* [Geography], 2(May 1966):57–65. A useful, though brief, study. Includes an abstract in English.

09-099. DEGE, Eckart. "Socio-Economic Research as a Tool for Regional Planning—Based on Examples from Korean Agricultural Regions." *Journal of Regional Development* (Kyung Hee University), 6(December 1975):53–69. A preliminary report on Dege's research on eight villages in different agricultural regions of Korea.

09-100. _____. "Stand und Entwicklung der Agrarstruktur Südkoreas." *Geographisches Taschenbuch* (1975–1976): 106–127. A general survey of the status and development of agriculture in South Korea with an excellent colored map of agricultural distribution.

09-101. Korea, Republic of. Office of Fisheries. *Fisheries in*

Korea. Seoul: 1966. 257 pp. A useful summary of official data in English on Korean fishing activities.

09-102. LAUTENSACH, Hermann. "Zur Geographie der künstlichen Bewässerung in Korea." *Petermanns Geographische Mitteilungen* 86(9)(September 1940):289–303. This study on irrigation in Korea was based in part on fieldwork in Korea in 1933; it is of value for the data it gives on the development of irrigation by the Japanese. An English translation by Shannon McCune is available in the Library of the American Geographical Society in New York.

09-103. _____. "Über den Brandrodungsfeldbau in Korea mit Bemerkungen zur Urlandschaftsforschung." *Petermanns Geographische Mitteilungen* 87(2)(February 1941): 41–54. This geographical study of the "fire-field" agriculture of Korea is based in part on Lautensach's field research in 1933.

09-104. LEE, Chung Myun. "A Study of Agricultural Regions in South Korea." *Chiri hak* [Geography], 2(May 1966):1–13. This brief study by a Korean geographer was followed by a more comprehensive work.

09-105. _____. "A Study of Agricultural Regions in South Korea." *Geographica Polonica* 19(1970):147–170. Lee has developed a very useful regional analysis of Korean agricultural land use. His report on land use prepared in Korean for the Ministry of Education in 1966 was 450 pages in length. This summary contains a large number of maps of South Korea which classify in various ways the data on the 1520 statistical units he used in his study. Patricia M. Bartz used a number of these maps in her *South Korea.*

09-106. LEE, Hoon K. *Land Utilization and Rural Economy in Korea.* Chicago: University of Chicago Press, 1936. 302 pp. Lee was a professor of agriculture and economics at the Union Christian College in Pyongyang at the time he wrote this book. He had written an earlier study on Korean migrants in Manchuria, published in Korean by the Union Christian College Press; an abstract was published in "Korean Migrants in Manchuria," *Geographical Review* 22(2)(April 1932):196–204. Lee's book was a noteworthy contribution for its time. He critically assessed the agricultural data being collected by the Japanese authorities and showed some of the weaknesses in those data.

09-107. McCUNE, Shannon. "Utilization of Upland Areas in Korea." In *The Development of the Upland Areas in the Far East.* Vol. 2. New York: Institute of Pacific Relations, International Secretariat, 1951. This study has some general materials on the physical basis of the upland areas and "fire-field" agriculture in Korea.

09-108. PITTS, Forrest R. *Mechanization of Agriculture in the Republic of Korea.* (n.p.); 1960. 28 pp. Mimeographed. In this report Pitts makes a suggestion for the greater use of mechanization, especially of powered rototillers.

09-109. *Rehabilitation and Development of Agriculture, Forestry and Fisheries in South Korea.* New York: Columbia University Press, 1954. 428 pp. This report was prepared for the United Nations Korean Reconstruction Agency by a mission selected by the Food and Agriculture Organization. A considerable amount of data is collected and summarized here.

09-110. SUH, Chan-ki. "A Study on the Spatial Model of Korean Agriculture: The Spatial Variation of Farming Intensity and Its Regression Analysis." *Chiri hak* [Geography], 9(1974):1–18. This is a quantitative geographical study with a one-page English abstract and English-titled maps.

Population

09-111. LEE, Han Soon. *A Study on Korean Internal Migration in the 1960's.* Seoul: Kyonghee University, 1973. 180 pp. During the period covered by this study the population of Seoul and certain other urban areas was increasing at a rapid rate while the rural areas were losing population. The bilingual maps and charts in this study, along with the lengthy English abstracts, make it useful for Western students.

09-112. TREWARTHA, Glenn T. and Wilbur ZELINSKY. "Population Distribution and Change in Korea, 1925–1949." *Geographical Review* 45(1)(January 1955):1–26. This analysis by two American geographers includes a number of useful maps and stresses the geographical shifts in population in Korea.

Economic Development, Manufacturing, and Urbanization

09-113. HONG, Kyung-hi. "Function of Central Places in the Area Surrounding Taegu City." *Oriental Culture Research* 2(1975):127–183. Includes an English abstract and English-titled maps and charts. Hong has applied central-place theory to the area around Taegu in a very interesting paper. The sophistication of her modern research techniques is characteristic of the work of contemporary Korean geographers.

09-114. _____. *An Industrial Analysis of Taegu City.* Taegu: Kyongbuk National University, 1969. 180 pp. English abstract (pp. 172–180). This study of the industries of Taegu was the result of Hong's research.

09-115. _____. "Urbanization in South Korea, 1960–1970."

Research Review of Kyungpook National University
17(1973):87–110. This is the third in a series of Hong's papers on urbanization in Korea. It has an English abstract and English-titled maps and charts. She has effectively used interregional telegram interchanges to depict tributary areas.

09-116. HYUNG, Kie Ju. "The General Pattern of Manufacturing Accumulation in Korea." *Chiri hak* [Geography], 2(May 1966):27–34. English abstract (p. 27). This brief geographical study of a Korean geographer notes the concentration of manufacturing around Seoul and in certain other areas of Korea.

09-117. _____. "A Study on the Localization Processes of Manufacturing Industries in Korea, 1910–1945—Methodology and Colonial Industrialization." *Chiri hak* [Geography], 12(December 1975):27–52. Hyung has been making an interesting study of the development of manufacturing and its geographical distribution in Korea.

09-118. LEE, Young-Ho. "Economic Development and Environmental Quality: An Analysis of Korean Attitudes." *Korea Journal* 12(6)(June 1972):21–29. Brief study of an increasingly important aspect of Korean life.

09-119. PARK, Byung Ho. "Natural Resources and Industrial Location in South and North Korea." In C. I. Eugene Kim (ed.), *Korean Unification: Problems and Prospects.* Kalamazoo: Korea Research and Publications, 1973. A brief, general survey of the subject with comparisons between North and South Korea. Other articles in this issue are also of interest, though without much geographical analysis.

09-120. PARK, Young-Han. "The Economic Structure of Korean Cities." *Naksan chiri* 1(December 1970):11–19. English abstract (pp. 17–18). A rather general study of the geographical characteristics of major cities of Korea.

09-121. PITTS, Forrest R. "A Factorial Ecology of Taegu City." In Mangap Lee and Herbert R. Barringer (eds.), *A City in Transition: Urbanization in Taegu, Korea.* Seoul: Hollym Corporation, 1971. An interesting study using new quantitative mapping techniques by an American geographer who has done much fieldwork in Korea.

09-122. RENAUD, Bertrand M. "Regional Policy and Industrial Location in South Korea." *Asian Survey* 14(5) (May 1974):456–477. Much of the new industrialization in South Korea has been financed by government loans and grants, some from foreign funding sources, so that decisions on industrialization locations are often made on the basis of politics.

09-123. STINE, James H. "Temporal Aspects of Tertiary Production Elements in Korea." In Forrest R. Pitts (ed.),

Urban Systems and Economic Development. Eugene: University of Oregon, 1962. This is essentially a theoretical study, but an interesting one, by an American geographer who has done fieldwork in Korea.

09-124. SURET-CANALE, Jean. "Le Development economique de la Republic Populaire Democratique de Corée." *Annales de Géographie* 81(443)(January–February 1972): 48–65. This article by a French geographer who traveled all over North Korea (except for the extreme north) in October 1969 includes data from North Korean sources for 1970. The maps and pictures are interesting. The English abstract is very short and carelessly translated.

Political Geography

09-125. FISHER, Charles A. "The Role of Korea in the Far East." *Geographical Journal* 120(3)(September 1954): 282–298. This is a short but excellent analysis by a British political geographer who has written considerably on the Far East. He gives emphasis to the period of Japanese political control (1910–1945).

09-126. IM, Duck-Soon. "A Political Geographical Study of Dok-Do Island." *Bulletin of Busan Teachers College* 8(1)(1972):45–54. This article has a brief English abstract. Tokto, or Takeshima in Japanese, is claimed by both Korea and Japan. It is now in the possession of the Republic of Korea: a small detachment of the ROK Coast Guard is perched on these rocks in the Sea of Japan.

09-127. _____. "A Study of the Armistice Line in Korea." *Chiri hak* [Geography], 7(1972):1–11. Im has written a number of articles and a textbook on political geography (in Korean) for use in Korean universities. This article has a brief English abstract and an interesting map showing the pressure on the Demilitarized Zone and the eccentric location of Seoul.

09-128. PARK, Choon-Ho. *Continental Shelf Issues in the Yellow Sea and the East China Sea.* Occasional Papers, no. 15, Law of the Sea Institute. Kingston: University of Rhode Island, 1972. 65 pp., 12 maps. Mimeographed. The footnotes for this interesting study provide a good bibliography of the problems associated with the territorial seas and the exploration for offshore oil resources under the continental shelf of the Far East. The same scholar has written *Fisheries Issues in the Yellow Sea and the East China Sea,* Occasional Papers, no. 18, 1973. Since these papers Park has written a number of other articles and monographs from the standpoint of an international lawyer on the various claims to the continental shelf areas of the Far East.

THE MAPS OF KOREA
Early Maps and Atlases

09-129. CORDIER, Henri. "Description d'un Atlas Sino-coréen manuscrit du British Museum." In *Recueil de Voyages et de Documents pour Servir a l'histoire de la Géographie, depuis le XIIIe jusqu'à fin de XVIe Siècle.* Paris: Section Cartographique, 1896. 13 maps. The diligence and expense taken to produce the parts of this old Korean manuscript atlas are rather amazing in light of the plenitude of such atlases.

09-130. *The History of Mapping in Korea.* Seoul: National Construction Research Institute, 1972. 24 pp.; 17 illustrations; one-page English abstract. This booklet notes both old and modern Korean mapping.

09-131. HYUNG, Kie Joo. "Materials on Old Maps of Korea." *Chiri hak* [Geography], 1(July 1963):97–101.

09-132. LEE, Ch'an. *Korean Old World Maps—Ch'onha-do and Hanilnangni-Yokdae-Kukdo-Chido.* Seoul: Graduate School of Education, Seoul National University, 1971. 40 pp. This monograph discusses two old Korean maps.

09-133. _____. *Old Maps of Korea.* Seoul: Korean Library Science Research Institute, 1977. 249 pp. This is a monumental quarto-size volume with many reproductions of Korean maps; one section presents full-color reproductions. Some maps fold out; all have brief descriptions in Korean. In an appendix Lee lists the major old maps in the main university and government libraries in Korea. The English-language summary (pp. 221–230) is very useful, as is the bibliography of major writings on old maps in Korean, Japanese, and English. This is a beautifully published and valuable book, well representative of modern Korean scholarship.

09-134. _____. "Old Maps of Korea: Historical Sketch." *Korea Journal* 12(4)(April 1972):4–14. In this English-language article Lee summarizes some of his work on the history of Korean cartography. The article concludes with a useful bibliography.

09-135. MCCUNE, Shannon. "Maps of Korea." *Far Eastern Quarterly* 5(3)(May 1946):325–329. A brief summary of the maps of Korea available at the end of World War II.

09-136. _____. "Old Korean World Maps." *Korean Review* 2(1)(September 1949):14–17. This note includes a review of Hiroshi Nakamura's article in *Imago Mundi* and a brief bibliography of articles on old Korean atlases.

09-137. _____. "Some Korean Maps." *Transactions of the Korea Branch of the Royal Asiatic Society* 50(1975): 70–102. A general survey of both modern and old Korean cartography that includes numerous footnote references.

09-138. _____. "Geographical Observations on Korea: Those of Father Regis in 1735." *Journal of Social Sciences and Humanities* (Seoul), 44(December 1976):1–19. Includes reproductions of Father Regis' maps as well as some background on this Jesuit missionary-geographer and his summary of the geography of Korea.

09-139. MOK, Yung-man. *Chido iyagi* [Story of maps]. Pyongyang: Kunjung munhwa chulp'ansa, 1965. 352 pp. This book on the old maps of Korea includes some reproductions and a commentary on the history of cartography. It is entirely in Korean and rather poorly printed, but it indicates the interest in the subject in North Korea.

09-140. NAKAMURA, Hiroshi. "Old Chinese World Maps Preserved by the Koreans." *Imago Mundi* 4(1947):3–22. This scholarly article by the eminent Japanese cartophile was written in 1934, but publication was delayed until 1948. It is a thorough study of an old Korean world map, the *Ch'ŏnhado,* in the hand atlases which Korean scholars had developed. Because of errors in translation as well as inadequacies in the original illustrations, Nakamura gave the original French-language article and its illustrations in an article with the same title in *Chōsen gakuho* (Journal of koreanology) (Tenri, Japan), 39–40(39/40)(April 1966): 1–73. In this article he also adds a section on the toponyms in the *Ch'ŏnhado,* many of which were drawn from mythical place-names on maps used by Taoist followers.

09-141. PAWLOSKI, Auguste. "Historique de la Connaissance de la Corée, d'après la Cartographie." *Bulletin de la Société de Géographie de Rochfort* 26(1904):216–225. An account of a scholar browsing through the European maps of Korea.

09-142. THROWER, Norman J. W. and Young Il KIM. *"Dong-kook-yu-ji-do:* A Recently Discovered Manuscript of a Map of Korea." *Imago Mundi* 21(1967):30–49. Using a manuscript map (probably copied in 1889) of the *Tong-guk yŏjido* of Chŏng Sang-gi of 1786, this interesting article reproduces each of the eight provincial maps in black and white and discusses early Korean cartography.

Gazetteers

09-143. Korea, Republic of. Ministry of Education. *Korean Gazetteer.* Seoul: 1972. 59 pp. This handy gazetteer gives the official Republic of Korea romanization of all major place-names in Korea. It includes lists in the Korean alphabet, in Chinese characters, in the Ministry of Education romanization, and in the McCune-Reischauer romanization for administrative units and noted spots for tourists. It also lists these place-names by the number of strokes in the Chinese characters and in English alphabetical order for the Ministry of Education romanization. A map of Korea in which the romanized place-names are given is indexed with the lists.

09-144. United States. Army Map Service. *Gazetteer to Maps of Korea.* 3 vols. Washington: 1950. This gazetteer lists all the names found on the common map series of Korea prepared by the Army Map Service. Vol. 1 has names south of 37° latitude; vol. 2 has names between 37° and 40° latitude; vol. 3 has names north of 40° latitude.

09-145. _____. _____. *Place Name Index for Korea (Chōsen).* Washington: 1943. 63 pp. This handy book includes a description of the McCune-Reischauer romanization system and a gazetteer in Korean, Japanese, and English (romanizations of Korean and Japanese).

Map Series

09-146. Chungang chido munhwasa. *Sinp'yŏn taehan minguk chŏndo* [New edition of the map of Korea]. Seoul: 1973. These are eight colored maps at the scale of 1:500,000. Relief is shown by contours and spot heights; roads, railroads, and cities are classified. In Korean.

09-147. _____. *Taehan minguk chŏndo* [Map of the Republic of Korea]. Seoul: 1974. This colored map at a scale of 1:1,000,000 has relief shown by gradient tints and spot heights. Depths are shown by gradient tints. Place-names are in Korean and English.

09-148. Han'gong chido kongŏpsa [Han Kong Map Reproduction Company]. *Korea (Southern).* Edited by Kim Min-Su. Seoul: 1972. This colored map at a scale of 1:500,000 has relief shown by shading and spot heights. It shows distances and air, road, and sea routes. It includes a location map and six insets. In Korean.

09-149. Japan. Government-General of Chōsen. *Chōsen 1:200,000 zu* [Korea 1:200,000 maps]. Seoul: 1921. These four-color maps of Korea with Japanese place-names give complete coverage of Korea in sixty-five sheets. Relief is shown by contours and spot heights; roads and railroads are classified; political boundaries of provinces and districts are shown along with city areas.

09-150. _____. Rikugun. Sambō Hombu. *Chōsen 1:50,000 Chikeizu* [Topographic maps 1:50,000 of Korea]. Tokyo: 1917-1937. These topographic maps at a scale of 1:50,000 show the relief by contours in light gray or brown or in brown shading; water bodies are in blue; roads are in red or black. Place-names, railroads, and provincial and district boundaries are in black and other cultural features

such as land use are rendered in black symbols. There were 722 of these sheets issued; there were some unissued sheets of strategic areas. During World War II these maps were reprinted in black with a purple overlay for romanized place-names by the US Army Map Service.

09-151. United States. Army Map Service. Far East. *Korea, 1:50,000.* AMS Series L 751. Washington: 1956. These maps were based on the grid of the Japanese Land Survey and issued on quadrangles 10 minutes of latitude by 15 minutes of longitude. Data were updated by air photography and, where feasible, by ground checking. These maps were also issued in bilingual Korean and English editions.

09-152. _____. _____. *Korea Photo Maps, 1:12,000.* AMS 1052. Washington: 1952. Aerial photography with place-names, geographic coordinates, and military grid overprinted. These maps are difficult to obtain and not all of Korea is covered.

09-153. _____. _____. *Korea, 1:100,000.* AMS Series L 651. Washington: 1958. The relief is shown in contours and spot heights; roads and railroads are classified. This is a very useful map series that is also available in a bilingual (Korean and English) edition: AMS Series L 653.

09-154. _____. _____. *Korea, 1:250,000.* AMS Series L 551 and L 552. Washington: 1950. These are issued in quadrangles 1° of latitude by 1½ to 2° of longitude. Korea is covered in forty-one sheets. The relief is indicated variously by contours, shading, and spot heights. Internal boundaries, five classes of roads, and four classes of railroads are shown. Bilingual (English and Korean) editions are also available.

Thematic Maps

09-155. Korea, Republic of. Central Meteorological Office. *Han'guk kihudo* [Climatic atlas of Korea]. Seoul: 1962. 299 pp. The scale of the colored maps is 1:5,000,000. Diagrams and tables are included.

09-156. _____. Office of Rural Development. Institute of Plant Environment. Korea Soil Survey. *Reconnaissance Soil Map of Korea.* 9 vols. Seoul: 1971. The maps in these volumes are overprinted on the topographic maps at a scale of 1:50,000. Each of the nine volumes covers a province. The city areas of Seoul and Pusan are included in the Kyŏnggi and Kyŏngsang Namdo volumes respectively. These soil maps are mainly in Korean but have some English.

CHAPTER 10
People, Family, and Society

Vincent Brandt
and Yun Shik Chang

INTRODUCTION

ALTHOUGH SOCIOLOGISTS and social/cultural anthropologists have been active in South Korea during the
past twenty-five years or so, one does not find many
published materials in Western languages of any length
that deal explicitly and rigorously with such topics as social organization, the family, social change, interpersonal relations, group behavior, institutional structure,
stratification, and social mobility. Apart from missionary and travelers' accounts from earlier periods, only
two attempts by foreigners to write a systematic, comprehensive, book-length interpretation of Korean society and behavior come to mind. One is by an anthropologist (Osgood, 10-007) who includes a brief village
study, a cultural history, and an account of political
events in the immediate post–World War II period; he
also offers free-swinging generalizations and psychological explanations of behavioral data (much of which
appear to have been gleaned from traditional Western
sources on Korea). The other work, by a missionary
doctor (Crane, 10-001), is a brief, popularly written,
somewhat patronizing, but nevertheless highly informative and provocative account of traditional values,
attitudes, and customs. Journal articles, short monographs, research papers, and academic theses are, of
course, much more numerous, and some are of extremely high quality, although frequently hard to obtain.
There is also a large body of unpublished conference

papers which, while inevitably uneven, probably comprises in its entirety the most authoritative and extensive
material in English on modern Korean society.

Until fairly recently much of the description and analysis by foreigners, while generally sympathetic to Korea
and Koreans, has embodied highly personal, and to a
considerable extent ethnocentric, accounts that have
concentrated on the exotic—what is or seemed to be
uniquely Korean in sharp and startling contrast to Western ways of thinking and behaving. And as a result, a
considerable literature (perhaps mythology is a better
term) exists that emphasizes such purported traits as the
Koreans' emotional volatility, undisciplined energy, inability to sustain productive effort for long periods,
cantankerous resistance to authority, heroic ambition,
cheerfulness in the face of disaster, pride, uncontrol-
lable rage, and obsession with family and hierarchy.
The extent to which these characteristics were more or
less prevalent in Korea than elsewhere is in any case
problematic. But where such behavior has been observed, it was probably as much a reflection of the
special (and usually extremely frustrating) cross-cultural
and historical context within which Koreans have encountered foreigners during the last hundred years or so
as it was representative of deep-rooted Korean cultural
themes. In emphasizing the superficial, the exceptional,
and the sensational, such accounts have probably expressed Western prejudices to a greater degree than they
have provided real insights into the fundamental rela-

tionships and cognitive orientations that exist among Koreans.

The astonishment of Americans and Europeans at Korea's economic "miracle" and the abrupt change in descriptions of national character that has taken place during the last ten or fifteen years are a measure of the extent to which this kind of "research" has been misleading. More recently the work of foreign sociologists and anthropologists has been less impressionistic and a good deal more solidly based on objective research. The dazzling generalization that tells us in one flash of understanding why Koreans behave the way they do is fortunately giving way to sober, disciplined research, as we realize how endlessly complex are the motives and situations that shape everyday behavior.

The work of foreigners is now overshadowed, however, both in quantity and in importance, by that of Korean social scientists. Good translations are increasingly available, and in the case of Koreans who have been trained abroad, research reports are often written in English. In general, a distinction can be made between two kinds of sociological writing. On the one hand there are rigorous efforts to apply Western (usually American) sociological theories and methods directly to Korea with little modification; on the other there are attempts at broad social interpretation based on the understandings that Koreans have had about their own traditions (particularly the Confucian heritage) and about contemporary processes of change. Sometimes the fine-grained research appears overly restricted in scope with abject submission to American academic jargon and findings that may seem trivial in their lack of relationship to other social phenomena; but this is perhaps a problem of the discipline rather than of research in Korea. Yet many of the efforts to explain the workings of Korean society in broad, fundamental terms have, until quite recently, been both simplistic and redundant, resting on a common body of conventional wisdom concerning the supposed effects of Confucian values and related behavior patterns on social change and modernization. A whole generation of Korean intellectuals has railed against the pernicious influence of ideological and social tradition in politics, family life, education, and economic behavior, but sometimes the clarity of analysis has been blurred by the ambivalent treatment of beliefs and customs to which there remains a strong emotional attachment. Moreover, many of the fundamental assumptions concerning development and its relation to Confucian values are increasingly open to question. In any case the intensification of national pride and self-confidence accompanying rapid economic development has encouraged Korean scholars to take a more positive attitude toward their cultural heritage in recent years.

TRADITIONAL PATTERNS

The social organization of villages in Korea before the Japanese annexation in 1910, and to a considerable extent until quite recently as well, has shared many features with traditional agricultural societies in other parts of the world. Community solidarity was based primarily on face-to-face interaction, and the hamlet or cluster of houses is still the basic residence unit. Before the onset of sustained urban growth and industrialization, the village was almost self-sufficient, politically as well as economically. Village communities were small, and most residents were born into families that had lived in the same place for generations.

The hamlet was characterized by its spatial isolation from other hamlets and by its settlement pattern in which the dense cluster of dwellings was surrounded by farm land. In everyday life the inhabitants of a community interacted with each other much more frequently than with outsiders, and their hamlet was almost a world in itself identified for residents by the term *we* in contrast to the *they* of the outside world.

No household within the hamlet was likely to specialize in activities other than farming. The largely obligatory cooperation among inhabitants extended widely into all spheres of life—labor exchange; sharing the expense and effort on various ceremonial occasions such as births, marriages, and deaths; and the performance of tutelary deity rites in the village shrine for the welfare of the community and for protection from calamities such as famine, drought, and infectious disease, over which residents had no control.

Mutual help within the rural community, while also comprising spontaneous acts of personal sympathy, usually reflected a strong sense of obligation and necessity. Such collective assistance ranked high in the hierarchy of values. The term *neighbor* had a special connotation since neighbors were mutually obligated to each other in everyday life, and an act that placed one in debt to others should always be reciprocated.

In the hamlet, where people interacted only with others whom they knew well over a long period of time, the forms of interaction were limited in number. Since these relations recurred frequently, the appropriate behavior in each case was well known. Most people had a clear idea—and within the same hamlet an almost identical idea—of how they should treat one another in most situations. This fairly elaborate and universally accepted code of conduct gained such force that its legitimacy was considered above question.

The entire village acted as an agency of social control. Severe violations of expected behavior within the hamlet were liable to various forms of sanction. The most notable was a withdrawal of cooperative aid by neighbors—an act which could make life economically very difficult for those who failed to observe the established rules. The "deviant" and his family were often socially ostracized by their neighbors—an act which could result in great emotional stress. The villager who was an object of gossip or had not been invited to a wedding in the same hamlet would feel extremely insecure. Outside his own hamlet, the individual could not easily find help or a basis for his own identity. There is a sense in which the solidarity of the hamlet was forced upon its individual members and households, since it is unbearable to live so physically and socially close to people and yet be completely alienated from them.

There was a good deal of give in the system, however. There was considerable tolerance for idiosyncratic behavior, provided it did not challenge the community's basic ideals too directly or too frequently. While everyone knew the code of proper behavior, considerable individual variation was accepted in practice. In most cases social control was exercised in a subtle and restrained way in order to maintain at least a minimally acceptable degree of conformity to the rules without the need for strong sanctions.

Social relations in small rural hamlets were highly particularistic. Individuals developed their conceptions of self and their role in the community as a result of intimate daily ties with specific individuals. Personal loyalties based on reciprocity, friendship, mutual indebtedness, or kinship generally took precedence over a sense of obligation to abstract principles or a territorial entity.

Historians and sociologists have only recently begun to interact in the social structure and personal relationships that characterized rural communities in traditional Korea. So far only a handful of articles and monographs have been published.

POPULATION

The population of Korea is believed to be going through the latter stage of what is commonly called the demographic transition. Mortality has been declining for some time, and there is solid evidence of a sustained decline in fertility with a resulting diminution of the overall growth rate. This discussion focuses on these population dynamics by reviewing Korean demographic trends over the past half century.

Population trends during the Yi dynasty period (1392–1910) appear to have been almost stable although there may have been a low level of population growth. Estimates from household registration data indicate that the annual growth rate ranged between zero and 5 per thousand total population.[1] Judging from fertility measures of more recent times and the social conditions that prevailed during the dynastic period, it seems safe to assume that the crude birth rate was in the range of 40 to 45 births per thousand. A variety of factors would account for the high level of traditional fertility. Women married early, and marriage was universal since it was a necessary condition for becoming an adult member of society.[2] Marital unions were seldom broken by divorce or separation.[3] The existence of concubinage and severe sanctions against remarriage of widows made divorce almost impossible. Positive value was placed on abundant reproduction, and attempts to control fertility within marriage were hardly ever condoned. This high fertility norm was presumably a reflection of the Confucian emphasis on family succession, which in turn led to the strong preference for sons that is still found in Korea. The contribution of this preference to a high fertility rate must have been strengthened by the prevailing high mortality, especially among infants and children. In the face of high infant mortality, having a large number of children was the best way to make sure that enough sons survived to adult age to succeed to the family leadership, provide for parents in their old age, and carry out the appropriate rituals after their death.

The death rate is assumed to have been equally high, although limited evidence suggests that mortality might have been slightly lower than fertility. The life expectancy at birth could not have been greater than thirty years. One can think of many reasons for the high mortality. The economy was predominantly self-sufficient, agricultural, and based on primitive techniques. What nature provided in terms of climate (drought and flooding) was, to a large extent, what people endured. The climate was uncontrolled and made farm yields precarious and highly variable from year to year. Malnutrition must have been ever-present and famine a continuous hazard.[4] At this stage of Korean history health conditions were extremely poor. Care of disease was left to herb doctors and other traditional healers. Folk medicine exerted little control over infectious and epidemic diseases and preventive medicine was nonexistent.

The traditional stability of Korean population growth began to break down during the first decade of the Japanese regime. This period marked the onset of the mortality decline that continued throughout the colonial period. This reduction in mortality may be ascribed partly to the increased regularity of food supplies resulting from increasing agricultural productivity and the reorganization of market exchange and distribution, together with technological development—especially in the field of communication and transportation. More directly, however, the mortality decline was due to advances in medicine, especially in public health, which were an integral part of the colonial regime in Korea. In 1910, the crude death rate was in the range of 32 to 37 deaths per thousand. Somewhat more accurate estimates derived from the census age data indicate that the same rate was approximately 29 deaths per thousand in the first intercensal period (1925–1930), 26 per thousand in 1930–1935, and 23 per thousand in 1935–1940. These figures lead us to believe that the crude death rate was about 20 deaths per thousand in 1945. In other words, the total reduction in the crude death rate over the three and a half decades of the colonial period was 12 to 17 points, or almost 40 percent. Life expectancy at birth

for both sexes for the intercensal periods shows an increase of about 6 years: from 37 in 1925–1930 to 43 in 1935–1940.

While mortality continued to decline, the fertility rate remained relatively stable. Birth rates estimated from census age distribution data are about 45 births per thousand total population throughout the census period (1925–1944) with only a slight fluctuation on the order of two points.[5] The number of children ever born to an average woman at the end of the childbearing span is slightly above six.[6] Although the age at the first marriage increased somewhat for both sexes during the Japanese regime, it was mostly accounted for by a reduction of women marrying in their teens. The custom of early marriage remained basically unchanged. In 1940, the average man married at age twenty-one, the average woman at seventeen; the great majority of women were married by twenty-five years of age.

The immediate result of the declining death rates and the unchanging birth rates was rapid population growth. The natural growth rate per annum indicates a steady increase: 1.7 percent in 1925–1930; 1.9 percent in 1930–1935, 2.2 percent in 1935–1940, and 2.0 percent in 1940–1944.[7] The magnitude of the population growth is perhaps more readily comprehended if one looks at the increase in the actual size of the population. In 1910, at the time of annexation, the population of Korea was estimated to be 17.5 million.[8] In 1944, one year prior to liberation, the population had increased to 25.2 million —7 million people had been added to the same territory. Increasing population pressure was, however, considerably reduced by emigration. There is a sense in which the growth of population outpaced that of the economy during the Japanese period, and a good proportion of the increment sought exodus, either in Japan or in Manchuria, for better economic opportunities. Estimation of the net loss of Koreans over the twenty-year census period (1925–1944) indicates that Korea lost about 120,000 during 1925–1930, 210,000 during 1930–1935, 1 million during 1935–1940, and 400,000 during 1940–1944. In other words, some 28 percent of the net increase of the population of Korea during the same period moved out of the country.

The population trends of the post liberation period (confined to South Korea only) stood in marked contrast to those of the colonial period. The mortality rate continued to decline, except for the war years when there was a temporary sharp rise as a result of war casualties. Within a quarter of a century, the death rate was reduced from 23 deaths per thousand total population in 1945 to 13 deaths in 1970—a decline of 10 points or 43.5 percent. On the other hand, life expectancy gained four years for both sexes during the fifteen-year period from 1955 to 1970. It went from 47 years to 51 years for men and from 52.5 years to 56.5 years for women.

The mortality decline and improved health conditions continued even during the hard years following liberation. Perhaps the fastest modernization in Korea took place in the fields of public health and medical care, even though a considerable number of Koreans are still living in towns and villages without resident doctors. Several new public health and medical facilities were introduced after the Pacific war, and chemicals such as DDT and antibiotics were made widely available through foreign aid. Campaigns to prevent serious epidemics and tuberculosis became major national programs, reaching even the most remote areas.

There were also significant changes in fertility during this period. The first decade of the republic, 1945 to 1955, experienced a slight decline in the birth rate. Estimates from the 1940 and the 1960 censuses indicate that the birth rate was in the neighborhood of 40 births per thousand total population—five points lower than that of the colonial period. This reduction must have been an outcome of the hardships the country suffered, politically as well as economically. The next five-year period, 1955 to 1960, was characterized by a resumption of the traditional high level of fertility. There was a brief baby boom. The birth rate estimated from the 1960 census was 45 births per thousand. A turning point came shortly, however, and a steady and rapid fertility decline was witnessed throughout the 1960s. The crude birth rate was reduced from 45 births per thousand in the 1955–1960 period to 42 births in the 1960–1966 period and then to 32 births in the 1966–1970 period—a total reduction of thirteen points or over 25 percent in a 25-year period. During the same period, the total fertility rate decreased from 6.3 to 4.6 children.

This remarkable reduction in fertility was due mainly to two reasons: (1) the continually decreasing proportion of married women in the age group fifteen to forty-nine caused mainly by increases of the age at marriage and (2) deliberate fertility control within marriage. The decline of early marriages which started during the Japanese period continued after liberation. By 1970, the custom of early marriage had virtually disappeared. The average woman in 1970 married at the age of twenty-four—a gain on the order of six years over that in 1945. The overwhelming majority of women in the youngest age group of the childbearing period (fifteen to nineteen) remain single. Even among women aged twenty to twenty-four, less than half are married.[9] In the 1960s deliberate fertility control spread widely among married women as contraceptive devices became easily available. Induced abortion is believed to have been practiced widely since the 1950s, even though it was illegal. Contraceptive practice began to spread spontaneously, first among urban women and later among rural women on an individual basis. It was then further reinforced when the government adopted a ten-year family planning program in 1962 as an integral part of the successive five-year economic plans. The Korean experience in family planning is commonly described as a success.

The combined effects of these changing vital rates are summarized in the changing growth rate. The natural growth rate was estimated to be 1.5 percent in 1945–1955. It reached the highest level in 1955–1960: 3 percent per annum. With the onset of the fertility reduction, the growth rate decreased to 2.6 percent in 1960–1966 and further to 1.9 percent in 1966–1970. In terms of absolute size of the total population, however, growth in the postliberation period has indeed been formidable. In 1945, the total number of people residing in South Korea alone was estimated to be about 16 million. In the following thirty-year period, this figure more than doubled, reaching 34 million in 1975.

Internal migration after 1945 did very little to lessen the burden of rapid population growth. The end of the colonial administration brought the repatriation of some 1.8 million Koreans mainly from Japan and Manchuria. In the process of territorial division a large stream of refugees from the North (on the order of 1 million) was added to the population of the South. The Korean War caused high casualties, but their effect on population growth in the South was largely offset by the influx of a vast number of refugees from the North. Except for the early periods population exchange was never of any significant scale, and no outlet of emigration was available for the population pressure which built up during the postliberation period. The net annual loss of population by emigration for the period from 1957 to 1965 ranged from a few hundred to a few thousand, totaling only 28,000. This figure increased substantially from 1966 to 1969, averaging 13,000 a year. The early 1970s witnessed an emigration boom: a large number, averaging 25,000, emigrated every year. Altogether 180,000 Koreans migrated overseas in sixteen years (1957–1973). This accounts for slightly less than 2 percent of the total population increase during the same period.

VALUES

A concern with moral principles is deeply rooted in the Korean tradition. The Confucian ideal of the superior individual who chooses to act virtuously on the basis of an abstract ethical code is a fundamental part of the East Asian world view. Most Koreans, therefore, seem to take for granted the conventional sociological notion that normal behavior is motivated by shared values rather than by deterministic factors of an ecological or economic nature or by an individual's rational assessment of alternative courses of action. Similarly the failure to act properly is almost invariably attributed to an inadequate education in morality. The concern with ethics combined with the belief that social harmony depends on value consensus is perhaps responsible for the great emphasis placed on attitude and value surveys by Korean scholars. Moreover, since the first modern educators and students of Korean culture and behavior were foreign missionaries, the native ideological orientation has been strongly reinforced by intellectual influences from the West.

In any case, value surveys seem to be the preferred method used by Korean social scientists in their efforts to account for contemporary behavior, although the likelihood that Koreans will reveal their innermost convictions to graduate students armed with questionnaires is certainly no greater than in other societies.

Whatever degree of value consensus may have existed among the aristocratic elite or in peasant villages in the past, today many fundamental ideas about right and wrong seem to be in a state of disorganized transition. For the foreign student it is perhaps worthwhile here to point out that moral values have been more closely linked to social relations in Korea than in the West. The ethical emphasis is on social obligation and propriety rather than on the struggles of an individual conscience to achieve personal salvation by means of direct transactions with the supernatural. The contrasting perspective of Christians, who comprise perhaps a tenth of the South Korean population, adds to the complexity of the contemporary situation.

The themes of value change, contrast, and contradiction appear in the work of many scholars. Pyong Choon Hahm (10-026) has emphasized the persistence of traditional ideals in the modern period, while other scholars such as Young Ho Lee (10-039, 040, 041), Sung Chick Hong (10-028, 029), and Kyong Dong Kim (10-049) have documented the changes they regard as particularly significant. Dae Hwan Kim (10-151), Man Gap Lee (10-099), Hy Sop Lim (10-042), and Yun Shik Chang (10-126) have focused specifically on value conflict.

There seem to be three main dimensions within which the contradictions between traditional and modern or Western ideas of what is right and valuable are particularly acute: (1) legitimate hierarchical authority as opposed to egalitarian participation in decision-making; (2) subordination of individual interests to collective goals and welfare as opposed to notions about the sanctity of individual rights and aspirations; (3) the primacy of spiritual and moral concerns in contrast to what is seen as the modern obsession with material goods. Some of these oppositions have been discussed in relation to social institutions by Kyung-won Kim (10-018), Yong-bok Ko (10-019), and Youngil Lim (10-020). Their resolution turns out to be difficult—not only between generations and among different sectors of society, but also in the thought of single individuals, most of whom have internalized parts of two quite different traditions. The problem raised by this ideological disarray and its relationship to individual behavior and the functioning of institutions provides an enormous and still largely unexplored field for sociological research.

FAMILY AND KINSHIP

Historically, kinship organization, ideology, ritual, and associated behavior have represented crucial, perhaps dominant, themes in Korean culture, particularly among the elite. Fundamental ideas about morality and the proper ordering of human relationships are closely associated with kinship values that are derived mainly from the Confucian concept of filial piety. The pervasive, highly elaborated system of lineages and branch lineages has provided the basic structural principle on which most groups in traditional society were organized. Kinship loyalties and obligations have generally taken precedence over other claims and commitments, both ideally and in terms of actual behavior.

As part of the modernization process profound changes have been taking place in the kinship system, particularly in the rapidly growing urban areas, and there has been considerable erosion of the dominance of family concerns. Nevertheless, ideals of family cohesion and solidarity retain their influence and the individual's emotional dependence on close kin is still very great.

Both Koreans and foreigners have been fascinated by the intricacy and intensity of kinship organization and behavior, and the number of studies in this area is substantial. Fortunately for the student, the Human Relations Area Files (HRAF) under the direction of Hesung Koh has compiled a comprehensive bibliography of materials on Korean kinship to be published in the near future.

Most eminent Korean sociologists and anthropologists have conducted research on some aspect or other of family and lineage organization, and a representative sample of their work has been translated into English. In particular, articles and books by Man Gap Lee, Kwang Gyu Lee, Hae Young Lee, Hyo Chai Lee, Taek Kyoo Kim, Jae Sok Choe, and Hyong Cho are outstanding. Although most of this research has been conducted through opinion surveys and interviews, Choe has emphasized historical description and comparative analysis while Cho has based her work with urban, middle-class families on participant observation. Research by Korean scholars has generally focused on the changes in values and behavior that have accompanied economic development. The theoretical issues that seem to fascinate non-Korean anthropologists specializing in kinship studies have been largely bypassed—perhaps because the traditional Korean conceptualization in both structural and moral terms has had such prestige that it has been accepted without question.

It has been suggested by some foreign scholars that Korean social scientists do not pay enough attention to dysfunctional aspects of contemporary kinship behavior because they themselves have so thoroughly internalized prevailing kinship values. In other words, Korean researchers may have a tendency to shy away from close scrutiny of domestic conflict, frustration, and instability because the family is inextricably associated for them at both the cognitive and emotional levels with ideas of harmony and solidarity. Thus it might be said that a kind of unconscious conspiracy exists—both among informants and their questioners—that is directed at preserving intact the traditional image of family loyalty and cohesion, despite the disorganizing effects of rapid industrialization and urbanization. In opposition to this view, the Korean might maintain that foreigners are distracted by superficial evidence of strain and tension without understanding the profound and continuing meaning that family and kinship has for the individual.

Whether such criticism is justified in the case of scholarly family studies or not, it certainly should not be applied to the writers of scenarios for movie, television, and radio dramas, who focus mainly on just this theme —the prevalence of tension and conflict in modern family life. In any case there is a good deal of ambivalence associated with the issue. The chief causes of family disorganization—the desire of the young for greater freedom from parental authority, the desire of wives for greater equality—are almost universally regarded in abstract terms as favorable aspects of progressive development. On the other hand, considerable concern has been expressed by social critics regarding the decline in family cohesion and morality that has accompanied the erosion of patriarchal authority.

Foreigners (mainly Americans) who write about Korean kinship tend either to emphasize structural aspects of the system (such as terminology and lineage organization) or to describe the social functions of kin groups within the context of a holistic, rural community study (Biernatzki, 10-067; Brandt, 10-077; Dredge, 10-178; Goldberg, 10-179; McBrian, 10-111; Janelli, 10-070; Osgood, 10-007). Although constantly confronted with the profound importance of kinship ties in everyday life, outsiders have found it extremely difficult to comprehend the situational and emotional complexity of such relationships. Possibly a younger generation of

Korean scholars who have spent many years abroad in an entirely different social context will be able to combine rigorous objectivity with the sensitivity to nuance that seems to be required.

Network theory, although ideally suited to the analysis of Korean social phenomena, has not been utilized to any significant extent for kinship studies. Organized lineage groups larger than the family have declined sharply in functional importance with modernization, but individual kinship ties beyond the immediate household and the values associated with them continue to influence behavior. As a result of greater geographic and social mobility the kinship networks of Koreans tend to be increasingly widespread, and they are used constantly and systematically in order to pursue personal goals. Claims are asserted, requests made, and obligations fulfilled (or evaded) as part of a continuing process that shapes many of the individual's most important decisions, as well as helping to determine their outcome. Further study of such systems of social linkage and communication would cast light on the general articulation that exists among different sectors in Korean society.

RURAL SOCIETY

Among the various studies of rural Korea a useful distinction can perhaps be made between two types: (1) those that attempt to interpret as a more or less integrated whole the actual situation in a particular village community and (2) those that are concerned primarily with defining social problems and promoting rural development. Usually the title of the work indicates whether the author is concerned mainly with social organization, interpersonal relationships, and beliefs or whether he or she has concentrated on practical problems associated with efforts to achieve specific economic and social goals. Both kinds of research must confront the realities of rapid social change, however, and there is inevitably a good deal of overlap in this area. But in general terms anthropologists have tended to produce community studies of a static and isolated nature (Biernatzki, 10-067; Brandt, 10-077; McBrian, 10-111; Janelli, 10-070; Knez, 10-110; Osgood, 10-007), while rural sociologists, political scientists, and economists have emphasized the linkages between village society and larger social units (Aqua, 10-075; Hong and Lee,

10-094; Keim, 10-096; B. C. Lee, 10-098; Moon, 10-101; Park, 10-103; Wang, 10-105). A few Korean scholars have combined both perspectives (S.-B. Han, 10-093; M. G. Lee, 10-082; Pak and Lee, 10-086), and Goldberg's forthcoming dissertation (10-179) will emphasize the relationship of one community to the central state apparatus.

Although many studies of shamanism, geomancy, ancestor worship, and folklore have been carried out within the context of village communities, only a handful of scholars have explored the implications of such beliefs and practices for rural social organization (Biernatzki, 10-067; Brandt, 10-077; Choi, 10-024; Dix, 10-177; Guillemoz, 10-180; Janelli, 10-033; T. G. Kim, 10-038; Knez, 10-110; Yun, 10-183).

As in other developing countries with a single primate city, the gap between a traditional, subsistence-oriented, agricultural way of life and a rapidly modernizing and expanding urban society has been very great. Most farmers in Korea not only have had lower incomes and material living standards than city dwellers, but also their access to educational opportunities, medical treatment, and cultural resources has been severely limited. They are now acutely aware of these disadvantages, and young people in particular are determined to participate in the benefits of modernization.

Until quite recently the authorities in Seoul have paid little attention to rural development, though large investments have been made to develop industry and improve urban amenities. By the end of the 1960s, however, the imbalance had become so extreme that the government was confronted with acute problems in at least three sectors of society: (1) extremely large and chaotic rural-urban migration had added greatly to administrative burdens in the cities and to the potential for social unrest; (2) the rural economy remained stagnant, and increases in agricultural productivity, particularly of grains, were insufficient to satisfy greater consumption and a rapidly growing population; and (3) an erosion of political support for the government in rural areas showed up dramatically in the presidential election of 1971.

The Park regime responded in the winter of 1971–1972 by launching the New Community Movement (NCM)—a highly organized, centrally directed effort to mobilize farmers on a national scale. From the start the movement has had political overtones. Its stated purpose was to upgrade the quality of village life by promoting cooperation, self-help, and the transformation of conservative rural attitudes. Although actual government investments in NCM projects were initially quite small as a proportion of total budget expenditures, the administrative and propaganda effort at both local and national levels has been intense. President Park has backed the NCM with the full weight and prestige of his office, and from 1972 to 1975 its momentum was not only sustained but even intensified. Every village in the country has to a greater or lesser extent felt the economic, political, and cultural pressures.

Because of the strong presidential backing and the identification of the movement with patriotism and nation-building, it has been difficult for the social scientist to carry out objective studies of its effects. Along with agricultural extension agents, county officials, and newspaper editors, academicians have also been mobilized as part of the effort. As a result most accounts stress its achievements in glowing terms. But even if the transformation of the countryside to date has been less revolutionary and less pervasive than government spokesmen habitually claim, a good deal has been accomplished, particularly in the area of stimulating the farmer's desire for further technological and social improvement. In any case, it is probably impossible to study the changing rural society of Korea during the 1970s without a thorough understanding of the goals, methods of operation, accomplishments, and shortcomings of the New Community Movement.

Except for official government publications (10-118) there are still few accounts of the NCM in English. A good deal of basic economic information is provided in Sung Hwan Ban's recent essay (10-076). The articles by N. B. Han (10-091) and I. C. Kim (10-097) generally duplicate the official point of view, while those of J. W. Cheong (10-090) and M. G. Lee (10-082) discuss the movement within the broad context of overall rural development. Further studies are now in progress; in particular, an evaluative and comparative report under UNESCO auspices by V. Brandt and M. G. Lee will soon be available.

A number of predominantly economic influences are helping transform rural society, and their total effect may be considerably greater in the long run than that of the social engineering being attempted by the administrators of the NCM.[10] Most important perhaps is the growing commercialization of agriculture, at least for those farmers with appropriate land and access to markets. Increased purchasing power and rapidly rising consumption standards in the cities have created a greater demand for agricultural products—and both the technical knowledge and the capital necessary to fill that demand now exist.

The introduction of advanced agricultural technology has been going on for many years in Korea under both public and private auspices, although the limited size of the extension service budget has been criticized by those who favor more balanced development. Since 1971, however, the success achieved by the Office of Rural Development with various strains of "miracle rice" has been particularly notable (10-116). Increased yields combined with high government subsidies have provided a secure economic base for efficient farmers and those with good paddy land. Thus, at the same time as the NCM has been promoting cooperation and community-oriented self-help, the opportunities for individuals to adopt innovative agricultural practices and increase their cash profits have also expanded. Although the rural-urban gap remains, real improvements in village incomes and living standards during the 1970s have significantly modified the grinding poverty and lack of opportunity that prevailed in most villages only a few years ago.

URBANIZATION

Urbanization may be viewed as a form of population redistribution in which the increasing population, largely agricultural, responds to the development of new opportunities in the cities—especially industrial employment. The growth of large-scale manufacturing industries in Korea which began in the late 1930s, although limited in scope and diversity, created economic opportunities outside of traditional agriculture and thus attracted the rural surplus population. In 1919 there were thirteen *pu* (incorporated cities) with 20,000 or more inhabitants, accounting for 3.5 percent of the total population. The number of *pu* increased to twenty with a total population of 2.8 million by 1945, thus constituting 11.6 percent of the total population. At the end of the Japanese period Korea remained predominantly rural.

The proportion and the absolute number of the urban population continued to grow after 1945 as the city played a prominent role in the process of population redistribution. In 1944, there were eleven *pu* with 1.6 million people, or 12.2 percent of the total population of the southern half of the country. By 1949, the urban population had increased to 3.5 million, more than doubling over the five-year period. Urban residents accounted for 17 percent of the total population. This rapid urban growth in the early stage of the republic was largely attributable to the influx of overseas repatriates and refugees from North Korea, most of whom found settlement in the cities. Natural increase contributed little.

The next stage of urbanization, 1949 to 1955, was marked by the Korean War, which contributed a great deal to the regional population movement. The *si* (city) population increased to 5.3 million in 1955, accommodating roughly one-fourth of the entire population. The annual growth rate of the city population was 4 percent during the same period, which can be contrasted with the rate of growth of the national population: 0.8 percent. The net increment of the city population, 1.1 million, constituted 68.7 percent of the total population growth. This was a remarkable increase, especially in view of the fact that the war hit the cities hardest, destroying their economic bases almost completely. The most characteristic feature of the rapid urbanization in this period is that it took place not through the development of urban industry but through an urgent need to accommodate homeless refugees created by the internal hostilities.

The turbulent years of the Korean War were followed by a period of stability and growth. The proportion of the total population residing in *si* (cities of 50,000 or more) increased from 24.5 percent in 1955 to 48 percent in 1975. If, however, we consider places with a population of 20,000 or more (a more widely used criterion), then in 1975 just under 60 percent of the population was living in urban places.[11] In absolute terms the urban population more than doubled over the fifteen-year period from 1960 to 1975, increasing to 20.5 million. The population explosion in the cities in each intercensal period constitutes a growing proportion of population increases in the nation as a whole: 49.2 percent in 1955–1960, 66.8 percent in 1960–1966, and 138 percent in 1966–1970. In other words, in net assessment, recent population increase has been largely accommodated by the cities. It should also be noted that, in the most recent intercensal period, the role of internal migration in urbanization became much greater than that of natural increase. This implies that the rural sector lost more inhabitants than it gained through natural increase. During the same period, the absolute size of the rural population decreased by about 4 percent. Korea has become an urban nation.[12]

As indicated above, a city consists of a large aggregate of people concentrated in an identifiable spatial boundary where the main means of livelihood is nonagricultural industry. The factors that permit such a large population concentration require a way of life markedly different from that of rural areas. The early generation of urban sociologists concluded that the new patterns of urban living lead to similar life-styles in cities all over the world. More recent evidence indicates that city life, though everywhere different from farm life, is by no means the same from culture to culture. Traditional patterns respond in varying ways to new city settings.

Unlike the small village where one interacts mostly with those known intimately for a long period of time, the urbanite constantly associates with strangers or those known only in specialized and limited roles. The urbanite is also dependent upon more people than the rural resident for the satisfaction of essentials. As a result, city dwellers tend to be associated with a greater number of organized groups but are less dependent upon particular persons. Moreover, in the city dependence upon others is often confined to highly fractionalized aspects of both ego's and alter's activity. Therefore, urban contacts inevitably become a good deal more impersonal, mechanical, and contractual than those in traditional sectors; contacts serve merely as a means to an end.

The social order envisaged by members of the urban community is public by nature. In Korea, however, the traditional orientation toward personalized human relations has survived rather well in the city. While urbanization has proceeded, personalism as a value has never been seriously challenged. The Korean urbanite tends to establish a network of close personal relationships. One also observes deliberate efforts by urbanites to widen their personal network of relations, perhaps in appreciation of its economic utility. To know people well is to have them obligated to you personally and to be obligated in return. The greater the number of persons you are personally acquainted with, the greater is your power and influence, the prestige accorded you, and your potential economic advantage. In one respect, the traditional legacy of personalism appears to have been strengthened in the city. The urbanite is free to disengage at will from primary relations, but such disengagement implies a violation of the ethic of mutual support. As long as personalism prevails in the city, the urban Korean is neither free from personal ties nor completely alienated from the community. Consequently, while the rules governing the relationship patterns characterized by personalism are elaborate and well agreed upon by the parties involved, those governing relations between strangers in the city are notably lacking. The urban Korean who is skillful in dealing with personal acquaintances is often completely at a loss upon encountering a person he has never met—because there are no rules to regulate how strangers interact in the impersonal context. In fact, the personalism that is still widespread in the value system of city people stands in the way of establishing a system of rules governing the interaction of individuals unacquainted with each other, whether in a community or in a formal organization.

At the present stage of urban development, the Korean city is far from being a moral entity with an integrated normative system regulating citizens' lives. This lack of integration allows an array of normative variations. In such a state of moral ambiguity, individual variation from the system is gradually gaining its own legitimacy, and the urban Korean, regardless of individual volition, is, to some extent, forced to be independent. Thus individualism is slowly rising in the city since the urbanite is frequently thrown into situations where the traditional culture fails to provide an adequate definition of appropriate behavior. It will be some time,

however, before individualism is fully institutionalized as part of the social structure—if indeed it ever is.

CLASS AND SUBCULTURE

Given the turbulent change and social mobility in certain sectors of Korean society during the last thirty years, it is hardly surprising that there is no clear-cut definition of contemporary class structure. The land reform of 1950, the massive disruption during the Korean War, the subsequent rise of new industrial, commercial, military, and professional elites—all have greatly modified traditional class parameters. On the other hand studies by Kyong Dong Kim, Kyu Taik Kim, Dong Suh Park, and Eugene Kim, among others, have shown that a disproportionate share of today's leaders in business and public administration are the sons of those who were landowners during the Japanese occupation, most of whom in turn came from formerly aristocratic lineages of the late Yi dynasty period. Thus there is a significant component of upper class continuity.

Efforts to analyze social stratification in recent years have generally been based on interpretations of income and occupation data derived either from census statistics or other surveys. The only systematic treatment in English is by Barringer (10-121, 138), who concludes that "class structure is beginning to approximate that of Western industrialized countries, the principal difference being in a larger lower class in Korea" (10-121:16). While recognizing that sampling biases and other methodological problems "probably produce a middle-class bias" in his work, Barringer nevertheless insists that the middle class is growing. The proportion of poor in "the total population is growing smaller rapidly," he argues, and the avenues for upward mobility are adequate to handle the influx of villagers into the cities (10-121: 31, 33).

Other sociologists, however, whose work has appeared only in Korean or as unpublished papers in English, maintain that substantial barriers to upward mobility do exist, and there is considerable speculation concerning the development of an increasingly rigid segregation of classes. According to this view, the high cost of a university education and the difficulty of finding a good job without educational qualifications or personal connections sharply limit the opportunities available to the poor. Thus the benefits of increasing national productivity and wealth do not really filter down to those engaged in manual labor and menial service occupations—particularly when there are more migrants each year to the cities than new opportunities for work. On the other hand, a recent paper by Renaud on the distribution of income shows that a considerably greater degree of economic equality exists in Korea than in most other developing countries. At present, the available statistical data do not permit a satisfactory resolution of these issues, but there are a number of studies of the urban poor in progress that should help to establish both the size of the lower-class population and the long-term trends in earning power and mobility.

While income and life-style are the usual criteria for determining class membership, other ranking systems based on status and power rather than wealth are also important in Korea. The difference between the salary of a pipe fitter and a university professor has narrowed significantly in recent years, for example, but the status of the intellectual remains high. In spite of the great wealth and power acquired by military officers since 1961, the prestige of a military career remains low while high bureaucratic office retains a special aura that is reinforced by the enormous influence officials can exert on commerce and industry. A vice-minister, for example, is treated by everyone with the respect and deference that a company president obtains only from his own subordinates. There is a great deal of popular and scholarly criticism of the contradiction between material rewards in Korean society and what are regarded as the most valuable social functions. As Barringer points out, little attention has been given to the way individuals categorize themselves in terms of class, although value surveys by occupation do in fact bear somewhat on this subject. At any rate it is probably safe to say that the traditional predilection for ranking classes of people on the basis of assumed moral worth is still in operation today.

Although both Korean and foreign observers continually point out that Korea has a remarkably homogeneous cultural tradition without significant ethnic or linguistic contrasts, urban society has recently become much more complex, with greater subcultural differentiation. A considerable amount of research has been carried out through surveys in an effort to discern patterns of individual and group behavior as well as the personal values and attitudes of administrators, professionals, student activists, workers, and intellectuals (D. S. Park, 10-164; S. J. Kim, 10-154; S. C. Hong, 10-149; W. K. Yoon, 10-171; S. C. Cho, 10-147; B. H. Oh, 10-163; K. H. O, 10-162). In addition, a few sociological studies deal specifically with such groups as women, lawyers, entrepreneurs, and juvenile delinquents.

There has been little work done so far on the relations between subcultures, but the lack of integration in Korean society is a frequent theme of social criticism, in which the alleged actual obsession with materialistic goals and power among leaders is usually contrasted with an idealized conception of cooperation and community. See the articles by Y. B. Koh (10-155) and D.-H. Kim (10-151) for representative samples.

One of the sharpest subcultural distinctions in Korea today is that between Christian congregations and the rest of society. While all kinds of variations exist in the degree of segregation, there are many instances, both in rural and urban environments, where Christians live in cohesive communities, partly isolated in terms of social interaction and ideology from the rest of Korean society. The situation is even more exaggerated with some of the "new religions" that have developed since 1945, often as exotic offshoots of Protestantism. There is an extensive literature on the Christian church in Korea, although not much attention has been paid to the separatist aspect in sociological terms. In any case Christians of the same denomination tend to live near one another, intermarry, and if possible work in a firm run by members of the same sect. A book on the new religions edited by Palmer (10-046)—particularly his introduction —marks a good beginning to the study of this fascinating social and ideological phenomenon, but a great deal more remains to be done. A study now in progress (10-176) promises to provide a fresh anthropological perspective.

SOCIAL CHANGE

Change is probably the single most persistent theme underlying sociological investigation in Korea during the past thirty years or so and possibly during the colonial period as well. Most Koreans have been conditioned to think of themselves as changing human beings in a rapidly changing world, and consequently the dynamic, diachronic perspective is rarely absent in contemporary research. One result is that findings are usually tentative. Moreover, there have not been many attempts to set down a definitive model of a situation that is perceived as temporary and transitional. Foreigners have until quite recently usually been conditioned to think of Korea as an unsatisfactory place that requires changing, and large numbers of them have done their best to speed up the process.

To a considerable extent the strong drive for industrialization has involved self-conscious westernization, and it has seemed natural and even desirable that social institutions, attitudes, and patterns of behavior should evolve in the direction of American models. In recent years, however, there has been more uncertainty regarding the preferred direction of change. Both the inevitability and the desirability of imitating the United States are increasingly questioned. Developing nationalism —based to a considerable extent on pride in Korea's economic accomplishments combined with some understanding of the extent of social problems in America— tends to encourage confidence in uniquely Korean responses to pressures for change. Although some foreign observers have pointed to close parallels between the process of development in Japan and Korea, Korean scholars have not devoted much attention to this theme. Comparisons with Japan, however well meant, are not accepted with much enthusiasm in Korea.

With regard to specific research there have been numerous surveys of attitudes and values within particular sectors of society that have attempted to measure cognitive predispositions for change. Sung Chick Hong, Young Ho Lee, Kyong Dong Kim, and Hy Sop Lim, among others, have made valuable contributions in this area. Although less attention has been devoted to studying changes in actual behavior, the work of Hae Yong Lee and Hyo Chai Lee on marriage institutions and that of In Keun Wang and Seung Gyu Moon on the adoption of agricultural innovations have dealt with practices as well as ideas. Moreover, changing behavior as well as attitudes associated with family planning and abortion have received a good deal of attention, largely because of the availability of ample research funds. Economists —and to some extent anthropologists as well—are in-

creasingly studying shifts in patterns of saving, consumption, and investment.

Another field where changing patterns of interpersonal behavior are under scrutiny is that of management, both in the bureaucracy and in private business. Nam Won Suh, Dong Suh Park, Suck Hong Oh, and Suk Choon Cho have provided detailed descriptions of some of the problems involved in reconciling traditional and modern practices and relationships within institutional contexts.

NOTES

1. Tai Hwan Kwon, Hae Young Lee, Yun Shik Chang, and Eui Young Yu, *The Population of Korea* (Seoul: Population and Development Studies Center, 1975), pp. 1–3.
2. According to the *Kyŏngguk taejŏn,* the standard Yi dynasty code of laws, boys were admitted to marriage at the age of fifteen and girls at the age of fourteen. Exceptions to this general rule were made when parents were very old (and therefore not likely to live until the children became of marriageable age).
3. However, marriage was frequently broken by death of one party, as the mortality rate was rather high. Mortality differentials in favor of women, together with the younger age of women at marriage, produced a large number of widows.
4. Irene B. Taeuber, "Japan and Korea: Population Growth," in Harold F. Williamson and John A. Buttrick (eds.), *Economic Development* (New York: Prentice-Hall, 1954), p. 455.
5. For the precensus period (1910–1925) we can assume that the birth rate was slightly lower than that of the census period since a mortality reduction in an early transition period was generally followed by a slight increase in fertility. A reasonable estimate of the crude birth rate for this period is 42 births per thousand total population. See Tai Hwan Kwon and others, *The Population of Korea,* p. 11.
6. Ibid., p. 11.
7. These estimates were derived from the census figures on total population with the immigrant figures adjusted back. That the natural growth rate was increasing indicates both the scope of population growth during the period under consideration and the greater potential for population growth in the future. The population of Korea was to accelerate much faster than during the colonial period as mortality decline continued.
8. The official estimate of the size of total population for 1910 was 14 million—which, considering the same figures for the later census years, was clearly an underestimate. See Tai

Hwan Kwon, "Population Change and Its Components," doctoral dissertation, Australian National University, 1972, chap. 1.

9. It should, however, be noted that the increasing age at marriage for women was not accompanied by a decline in the trend of universal marriage. Also intact were the traditional attitudes toward marital union in terms of its permanency as evidenced in an almost negligible divorce rate.

10. Actually the concept of the New Community Movement has been expanded recently to embrace practically everything of a positive nature that takes place in rural areas, whether planned and promoted by the authorities or not.

11. If we include in the city population those *ŭp* (townships) which were not promoted to *si* (city) status although they contained more than 50,000 residents, the urban sector would account for more than half the total population.

12. The rapidity with which urbanization is taking place in Korea is not merely ascribable to the net gain of population in the urban area. It is also due to spatial expansion of the urban area itself in the form of boundary change or promotion to urban status of towns with population growing beyond the 50,000 limit.

BIBLIOGRAPHY

GENERAL
Books and Monographs

10-001. CRANE, Paul. *Korean Patterns*. Seoul: Hollym, 1967. This account of traditional values, attitudes, customs, and personality has been widely read by foreigners trying to understand why Koreans act the way they do. The author spent more than twenty years in Korea as a missionary doctor.

10-002. DALLET, Charles. *Traditional Korea*. New Haven: HRAF, 1954. A nineteenth-century French missionary account of Korean manners, customs, morals, and attitudes. While often highly critical, Dallet provides a useful contrast to the conventional Confucian self-picture.

10-003. International Cultural Foundation (ed.). *Folk Culture in Korea*. Seoul: International Cultural Foundation, 1974. A collection of translated essays by Korean scholars on oral literature, popular dance drama, mythology, and shamanism.

10-004. _____. *Korean Society*. Seoul: International Cultural Foundation, 1977. Seven articles on family and genealogy, social strata and the traditional elites, village conventions, and the urban man.

10-005. *Korea: Its People and Culture*. Seoul: Hakwon Sa, 1970. A compendium of short essays by Korean specialists on every subject, this large volume contains sections of possible interest to the sociologist or anthropologist on people and language, social problems, thought and religions, social sciences, and manners and customs.

10-006. LEE, Ou Young. *In This Earth and in the Wind: This Is Korea*. Seoul: Hollym, 1967. A selection of short pithy essays that often illuminate aspects of Korean beliefs and attitudes that are not dealt with elsewhere.

10-007. OSGOOD, Cornelius. *The Koreans and Their Culture*. New York: Ronald Press, 1951. Contains a village ethnography (postliberation period), a historical summary (based on Hulbert), and a psychological interpretation of Korean character and personality.

10-008. PARK, Chong Kee. *Social Security in Korea: An Approach to Socio-Economic Development*. Seoul: Korea Development Institute, 1975. This pioneering work by an economist concludes that income security and economic development are not mutually exclusive goals. There is a detailed description with numerous statistical tables of demographic, labor force, and income factors in South Korea, followed by a critique of the National Welfare Pension System.

10-009. PIHL, Marshall. *Listening to Korea*. New York: Praeger, 1973. Good translations of well-chosen recent stories and essays by some of the best-known contemporary writers. Many of the works deal with sociological themes.

10-010. RUTT, Richard. *Korean Works and Days*. Rutland, Vt.: Tuttle, 1964. Written in diary form with a degree of bucolic lyricism, this account of rural customs and beliefs throughout the year is illuminated by the author's intimate knowledge of one community.

10-011. STANLEY, John W. *The Foreign Businessman in Korea*. Seoul: Kyumoon, 1972. A nonacademic but often penetrating discussion of Korean attitudes and behavior, particularly in the commercial and industrial sector.

10-012. YI, Kyu-tae. *Modern Transformation of Korea*. Seoul: Sejong, 1970. A fascinating collection of odds and ends of social history from the early modern period until after the Japanese takeover of Korea.

10-013. ZONG, In-sob. *Modern Short Stories from Korea*. Seoul: Munho Sa, 1958. The stories take place in the Japanese or immediate postliberation period and generally emphasize tragic themes or the seamy side of life. They provide revealing accounts of social interaction under difficult circumstances.

Articles

10-014. ADAMS, Don. "The Monkey and the Fish: Cultural Pitfalls of an Educational Advisor." In A. Dundes (ed.),

Every Man His Way: Readings in Cultural Anthropology. Englewood Cliffs, N.J.: Prentice-Hall, 1968. Discusses the contrasts between American and Korean concepts of education in terms of time perspectives, man-nature orientation, and power-status orientation. Educational practices are also related to societal behavior and efforts to promote planned change.

10-015. CUMINGS, Bruce. "Is Korea a Mass Society?" *Occasional Papers on Korea* 1(April 1974), 65–80. A thoughtful article that directly challenges Henderson's "vortex" theory as well as his assertion that Kornhauser's mass society model can be applied to traditional Korea.

10-016. KANG, Shin-Pyo. "Toward a New Understanding of the Culture of the East Asians: Chinese, Korean and Japanese." *Journal of East and West Studies* 3(1)(April 1974): 27–57. Following a discussion of the adequacy of anthropological theory for describing cultures, the author stresses the persistence of a distinctive "unconscious structure" in every Asian society despite strong Western influences.

10-017. KIM, Ki-hong. "Cross Cultural Differences between Americans and Koreans in Nonverbal Behavior." In *The Korean Language: Its Structure and Social Projection.* Honolulu: Center for Korean Studies, University of Hawaii, 1975. A useful summary from a Korean perspective of most of the cross-cultural differences that have been emphasized by foreign observers. The differences are grouped into the following categories: expressions of thoughts; interpersonal relationships; manners and courtesy in social life; privacy; gifts; and gestures.

10-018. KIM, Kyung-won. "Social Discontinuities and Korean Politics." *Journal of Asiatic Studies* (Seoul), 15(2) (June 1972):153–163. Discusses the "discontinuities" between rural and urban society, between generations, and between classes in relation to Korean modernization processes in general and the current political system in particular.

10-019. KO, Yŏng-Bok. "An Anatomy of Modern Korean Society." *Korea Journal* 12(3)(March 1972):18–24. A highly critical discussion of the lack of integration and humanistic values in Korean society despite recent changes in ideology, material living standards, education, and institutional structure.

10-020. LIM, Youngil. "Social and Economic Costs of Industrialization in Korea." *Korea Journal* 13(10)(October 1973):18–28. An economist discusses the major problems associated with development: income distribution, foreign debts, inflation, resource allocation, and urbanization. He concludes that more emphasis should be placed on investment in agriculture.

10-021. ROCKHILL, W. W. "Notes on Some of the Laws, Customs, and Superstitions of Korea." *American Anthropologist* 4(1891):177–187. Often perceptive comments on a great variety of matters from love of strong drink to the peculiarities of the penal code by a former American consul in Seoul.

Unpublished Dissertation

10-022. SHIM, Sang P'il. "Société Coréene Contemporaire: Analyse Economique et Sociale." Doctoral dissertation, Université de Paris, 1968.

VALUES, ATTITUDES, PSYCHOLOGY, AND FOLK RELIGION
Books, Monographs, and Articles

10-023. CHANG, Suk C. and Swang Iel KIM. "Psychiatry in South Korea." *American Journal of Psychiatry* 130(6) (June 1973):667–669. After a description of traditional mechanisms in Korea for dealing with anxiety and mental illness, the question is posed whether Western psychiatric methods are suitable in the Korean context. There is also a description of psychiatric facilities and the incidence of mental disorders.

10-024. CHOI, Hong-gi. "Rural-Urban Differences in Attitudes and Behavior." *Korea Journal* 12(2)(February 1972):4–13. A survey designed to measure differences in the modernity of attitudes of rural and urban residents. Includes a discussion of the causes of the observed differences.

10-025. GUILLEMOZ, Alexandre. "The Religious Spirit of the Korean People." *Korea Journal* 13(5)(May 1973): 12–18. An anthropological assessment of the religious significance to Koreans of shamanism.

10-026. HAHM, Pyong-Choon. *Religion and Law in Korea.* Kroeber Anthropological Society Papers, no. 41. Berkeley, Calif.: Kroeber Anthropological Society, 1969. An anthropological approach to a discussion of how law, morality, and religion exercise restraints on behavior. The emphasis is on traditional Korea.

10-027. HAN, Wan Sang. "Perception of Limited Opportunity and Self Ability and Deviation among Urban Adolescents: A Test of the Anomie Hypothesis." *Journal of East and West Studies* 2(1973):3–13. An effort to test Merton's anomie hypothesis to the effect that frustrated goals and expectations due to inadequate opportunity lead to delinquent behavior. The author finds significant contrasts with the West.

10-028. HONG, Sung Chick. *The Intellectual and Modernization: A Study of Korean Attitudes.* Seoul: Korea University, 1967. Reports the results of an extensive survey carried out in 1966 of the attitudes of professors and journalists regarding modernization and change, economic development, political development, and the role of intellectuals.

10-029. _____. "Perceived Intergenerational Value Gaps: Korea and Hong Kong." *Journal of East and West Studies* 3(1)(1973):101–121.

10-030. _____. "Values of College Students." *Journal of Asiatic Studies* (1963).

10-031. _____. "Values of Korean Farmers, Businessmen, and Professors." In *Report: International Conference on the Problem of Modernization in Asia.* Seoul: Asiatic Research Center, Korea University, 1965. These surveys of "values" (actually opinions) have a common theme in their attempts to gauge changing attitudes toward religion, the role of women, family and kinship, occupational roles, and political institutions as an indication of degree of modernization.

10-032. HWANG, Eung-yun. "A Study of Value Orientations of Korean University Students." *Journal of Social Sciences and Humanities* (Seoul), 41(June 1975):17–78. Korean Research Center. Values were measured for 860 students throughout Korea in six categories of orientation: social, political, economic, family, moral, and religious. There is an extended discussion of the theoretical background for relating psychological and attitudinal testing to behavior as well as a review of previous value surveys done in Korea. An ambitious study somewhat marred by the inadequacy of the English.

10-033. JANELLI, Roger. "Anthropology, Folklore, and Korean Ancestor Worship." *Korea Journal* 15(6)(June 1975):34–53. A summary of findings concerning ancestor worship in a village studied by a folklorist using anthropological methods. There is also material concerning status differences and accompanying behavior between the generations of the living.

10-034. KIM, Kwang-il. "Shamanist Healing Ceremonies in Korea." *Korea Journal* 13(4)(April 1973):41–47. An effort by a psychiatrist to evaluate the effectiveness of shamanistic ritual in treating mental illness. The ritual is analyzed in psychological terms.

10-035. _____. "Culture and Mental Illness in Korea." *Korea Journal* 14(2)(February 1974):4–8. A psychiatrist discusses how cultural factors determine what is abnormal, how people react to the behavior of psychotics, and the most frequent symptoms.

10-036. KIM, Kyong Dong. *Industrialization and Industrialism: A Comparative Perspective on Values of Korean Workers and Managers.* ILCORK Working Paper 1. Honolulu: University of Hawaii, 1971. This study challenges the idea that in industrializing countries changes in

values and attitudes follow the pattern set by the advanced Western countries as part of their modernizing process. A comparative survey of industrial attitudes in Korea, Japan, and the United States supports the hypothesis.

10-037. KIM, Se-jin. "Attitudinal Orientations of Korean Workers." *Korea Journal* 12(9)(September 1972):18–30. A large-scale survey of political attitudes among factory workers with regard to their union leaders, management, and the government. An effort is made to isolate problem areas.

10-038. KIM, T'ae-gon. "Components of Korean Shamanism." *Korea Journal* 12(12)(December 1972):17–25. A general description of Korean shamanism as a variant of a worldwide phenomenon. There is a case study of one *mudang* (sorceress), a list of gods worshipped in Korean shamanism, and a discussion of shamanistic chants and myths.

10-039. LEE, Young Ho. "Economic Growth vs. Political Development." *Korea Journal* 12(5)(May 1972):5–11.

10-040. _____. "The Korean People's Distributive Consciousness: An Analysis of Attitude." *Korea Journal* 12(9)(September 1972):31–39.

10-041. _____. "Modernization and Tradition: Korean Attitudes." *Korea Journal* 12(10)(October 1972):12–17. These three articles (10-039, 040, 041) report the result of a large-scale 1971 survey of the attitudes of ordinary Koreans compared with those of national assemblymen.

10-042. LIM, Hy Sop. "Continuity and Change of Development Values in Korea." *Journal of the Korean Sociological Association* 8(1973):81–89. Viewing development values as the hopes and aspirations of a people at any given historical period, the author traces the shifts in Korea from 1850 to 1973. The issue of managing tensions between such development values as democratization and economic growth is discussed.

10-043. _____. "A Study on Legal Values in Korea." *Seoul Law Journal* 15(1)(1974):56–81. There is a discussion of the relation of law to morality, state, and society framed entirely in terms of Western theory, followed by a report of a 1972 survey of Korean legal attitudes classified into cognitive, emotional, and behavioral aspects.

10-044. MIN, Pyung Kun. "Cultural Influence in Mental Disorders among Koreans." *Modern Medicine* 4(5)(1966). Also in *Korea Journal* 10(9)(October 1970).

10-045. MOOS, Felix. "Some Aspects of Park Chang No Gyo: A Korean Revitalization Movement." *Anthropological Quarterly* 37(July 1964):110–120. A sympathetic (in social-psychological terms) view of a popular "new religion" that has helped fill the psychological "vacuum" accompanying rapid social change and the erosion of traditional values. Statistics on membership may have more to do with the religion's claims than with reality.

10-046. PALMER, Spencer J. (ed.). "The New Religions of Korea." *Transactions of the Korea Branch of the Royal Asiatic Society* 43(1967). A collection of articles by Korean and American observers on some of the "new religions" that were active in the early 1960s. The introduction is particularly useful.

10-047. RUTT, Richard. "Some Problems in the Study of Korean Religion." *Korean Affairs* 1(3)(1962):256–260. This article points out the lack of modern interpretive studies of the history of religion in Korea in spite of the fact that a great deal has been written about Confucianism, Buddhism, and Christianity. Moreover, there is criticism of the lack of systematic studies of shamanism and the syncretic religions that have recently become widespread.

Unpublished Dissertations

10-048. BARRINGER, Herbert R. "The Aesthetic Theoretical Continuum: Primary and Secondary Values in Korea and the United States." PhD dissertation, Northwestern University, 1964. 286 pp. Abstracted in *DA* 25(January 1965):4289; UM 64-12,250. A summary statement of this thesis can be found in Barringer's article in C. I. E. Kim (ed.), *Aspects of Social Change in Korea* (Kalamazoo: Korea Research and Publications, 1969).

10-049. KIM, Kyong Dong. "Industrialization and Industrialism: Comparative Perspective on Values of Korean Workers and Managers." PhD dissertation, Cornell University, 1972. 224 pp. Abstracted in *DAI* 33(3)(September 1972):1239-40-A; UM 72-23672. For a summary of this dissertation, see 10-036.

FAMILY AND KINSHIP
Books and Monographs

10-050. CHANG, Dae Hong. "The Historical Development of the Korean Socio-Family System Since 1392: A Legalistic Interpretation." *Journal of East Asiatic Studies* 11(September 1967):1–124.

10-051. HILL, R. (ed.). *Families in East and West: Socialization Process and Kinship Ties.* The Hague: Mouton, 1970. This volume contains two articles on Korean kinship: Jae Suk Choi's "Comparative Study on the Traditional Families in Korea, Japan, and China" and Man Gap Lee's "Consanguinous Group and Its Function in the Korean Community."

10-052. KIM, Taek Kyoo. *The Cultural Structure of a Consanguinous Village.* Taegu: Ch'ong Ku University, 1964. A landmark study of a conservative *yangban* community with extensive treatment of the economic and political aspects of lineage organization.

10-053. *Korea Journal* 3(10)(October 1963). The entire issue is devoted to "Family Life in Korea."

10-054. YI, Hyo-jae. *Industrialization and the Family in Korea.* ILCORK working paper. Honolulu: University of Hawaii, 1971.

Articles

10-055. CHO, Hyoung. "The Kin Network of the Urban Middle Class Family in Korea." *Korea Journal* 15(6)(June 1975):22–33. Describes change, continuity, and the tensions characteristic of middle-class families in an industrializing society.

10-056. CHOE, Jae-Sok. "Étude Comparative sur la Famille Traditionelle en Corée, au Japon, et au Chine." *Revue de Corée* 7(2)(1975):29–36.

10-057. _____. "Family Relations and Education in Korea." *Korea Journal* 13(3)(March 1973):43–47. A highly critical view, using Western standards for comparison, of the traditional family system and the ethic of filial piety.

10-058. KIM, Jae-Un. "Psychological Structure of the Korean Family." *Bulletin of Korean Research Center* 40(December 1974):1–77. A "syndrome analysis" of parental behavior based on a Korean "Fels scale" of thirty variables. Results are of possible interest to psychologists.

10-059. LEE, Hae Young. "Modernization of the Family Structure in an Urban Setting." In *Report: International Conference on the Problems of Modernization in Asia.* Seoul: Asiatic Research Center, 1965. This report of a 1965 survey of 233 married women presents their attitudes regarding mate selection, happiness in married life, communications with their husbands, divorce, number of children, and dependency in old age.

10-060. LEE, Hyo-Chai. "The Changing Family in Korea." *Bulletin of Korea Research Center* 29(December 1968):87–99. An effort to assess the changes in family life, site, and composition resulting from the Korean War, industrialization, and American influence. Comparisons are made between rural and urban families and among different classes.

10-061. _____. "Changing Korean Family and the Old." *Korea Journal* 13(6)(June 1973):20–25. Examines the problem of providing financial and psychological support for the aged within the context of the changing family institutions of contemporary Korea. Frequent comparisons are made with American institutions.

10-062. _____. "Patterns of Change Observed in the Korean Marriage Institution." *Bulletin of Korean Research Center* 26(June 1967):34–55. Following a description of traditional and current marriage customs, there is a discussion of changes in mate selection, engagement practices, and wedding ceremonies.

10-063. LEE, Kwang Kyu. "The Korean Family in Changing Society." *East Asian Cultural Studies* (Tokyo University), 2(14)(1972):28–43.

10-064. LEE, Kwang Kyu and Youngsook HARVEY. "Teknonymy and Geononymy in Korean Kinship Terminology." *Ethnology* 12(1)(1973):31–45. In addition to a discussion of the frequent use by Koreans of teknonymy and geononymy (the use of place-names in terms of address) this article contains a highly condensed summary of Korean kinship terminology.

10-065. PETERSON, Mark. "Adoption in Korean Genealogies: Continuation of Lineage." *Korea Journal* 14(1) (January 1974):28–35. The record of adoptions over a 240-year period in Yi dynasty *yangban* lineage is examined through study of a written genealogy. Discusses changing customs and compares actual practice with the official law codes dealing with adoption.

10-066. YI, Hyo-Jae. "Les Relations Familiales en Corée." *Revue de Corée* 7(2)(1975):18–28.

Unpublished Dissertations

10-067. BIERNATZKI, William E. "Varieties of Korean Lineage Structure." PhD dissertation, St. Louis University, 1967. 635 pp. Abstracted in *DAI* 28(February 1968): 3141-B; UM 68-1251.

10-068. CHAI, Alice Y. "Kinship and Mate Selection in Korea." PhD dissertation, Ohio State University, 1962. 164 pp. Abstracted in *DAI* 23(August 1962):392; UM 62-3577.

10-069. CHANG, Dae Hong. "The Historical Development of the Korean Socio-Family System Since 1392: A Legislative Interpretation." PhD dissertation, Michigan State University, 1962. 312 pp. Abstracted in *DAI* 23(April 1963):4011; UM 63-1716.

10-070. JANELLI, Roger. "The Significance of Peasant Lineages: A Korean Example." MS thesis, University of Pennsylvania, 1974.

10-071. KAWASHIMA, Fujiya. "Clan Structure and Political Power in Yi Dynasty Korea." PhD dissertation, Harvard University, 1972. 316 pp.

10-072. LASSITER, D. "Changing Patterns of the Korean Family System." MA thesis, Harvard University, 1970.

10-073. PARK, Hyoung Cho. "The Urban Middle Class Family in Korea." PhD dissertation, Harvard University, 1973. 345 pp. A revealing account of many aspects of middle and upper middle class life in Seoul by a sociologist.

10-074. ROH, Chang Shub. "A Comparative Study of Korean and Japanese Family Life." PhD dissertation, Louisiana State University and Agricultural and Mechanical College, 1959. 310 pp. Abstracted in *DAI* 19(June 1959): 3408; UM 59-1546.

RURAL SOCIETY AND AGRICULTURAL DEVELOPMENT
Books and Monographs

10-075. AQUA, Ronald. *Local Institutions and Rural Development in South Korea.* Ithaca: Cornell University, Rural Development Committee, 1974. One of the few detailed descriptions in English of local government. This perceptive work by a political scientist also provides an account based on personal interviews of farmers' reactions to the New Community Movement in its initial stages.

10-076. BAN, Sung Hwan. *The New Community Movement in Korea.* Interim Report KDI. Seoul: 1975. A useful paper that provides complete statistical summaries of work accomplished under the New Community Movement through 1974. The account emphasizes accomplishments, echoing government rhetoric, while problems are largely ignored.

10-077. BRANDT, Vincent S. R. *A Korean Village: Between Farm and Sea.* Cambridge, Mass.: Harvard University Press, 1971. An anthropological community study in which the emphasis is on the settlement of disputes and the maintenance of village solidarity despite divisive structural factors. There are also discussions of kinship and village economics.

10-078. CHOI, Jae-sok. *Han'guk nongch'on sahoe yŏn'gu* [A study of rural Korean society]. Seoul: 1975. The results of a rural survey conducted by a Korean sociologist. There are also analytical sections on kinship and social structure. Summary in English.

10-079. HAN, Sang-Bok. *Korean Fisherman.* Seoul: Seoul National University Press, 1977. An ethnographic study of three fishing villages concerning their socioeconomic organizations, the direction and the rate of their development, and the factors involved in the change. Special emphasis is placed on the problem of cooperation among fishermen for ecological adaptation.

10-080. KIM, Taek-Kyoo. *The Cultural Structure of a Consanguinous Village.* Taegu: Ch'ong Ku University Press, 1964. 52 pp. This study and Item 10-082 are valuable pioneering studies that are well worth deciphering despite the poor quality of the English résumés. The author provides a detailed discussion of landownership, kinship relations, ideology, status, and leadership in the context of a single clan village.

10-081. *Korean Agricultural Sector Analysis and Recommended Development Strategies.* East Lansing: Korean Agricultural Study Team, Michigan State University, 1972. Although now out of date, this work contains a great deal of useful information as well as projections for the future.

10-082. LEE, Man Gap. *The Social Structure of a Korean Village and Its Change.* Seoul: University Press, 1973. The emphasis is on variations in lineage composition, leadership, village solidarity, and economic initiative in six different communities. A follow-up ten years later provides valuable perspectives on rural social and economic change. Summary in English.

10-083. MILLS, John (ed.). *Ethno-Sociological Reports of Four Korean Villages.* Seoul: USOM, 1960. Although the research and compilation were done by amateurs, and there is very little organization or theoretical integration, this work contains a good deal of interesting material on village customs, organizations, leadership, and economic life.

10-084. MOOSE, J. R. *Village Life in Korea.* Nashville: 1911. A Methodist missionary's sympathetic account of rural life around 1900.

10-085. *National Agricultural Cooperative Federation: An Appraisal.* East Lansing: Agricultural Economics Research Institute, Michigan State University, 1972. A detailed description and critique of the agricultural cooperative system with recommendations for reform based on American experience. The report is still useful, although now somewhat outdated because of changes in the NACF introduced in recent years.

10-086. PAK, Ki Hyuk and Seung Yun LEE. *Three Clan Villages in Korea.* Seoul: Yonsei University, 1963. Contains much valuable information on variations in lineage composition, village organization, leadership, and adaptation to change in Korean villages.

10-087. UPHOFF, N. T. and M. J. ESMAN. *Local Organization for Rural Development: Analysis of Asian Experience.* Ithaca: Cornell University, 1974. Compares the effectiveness of rural development efforts in eighteen Asian countries. Concludes that the relative success of Korea is due to its highly developed and adequately linked local governmental organizations.

10-088. YOON, Jong-Joo. *A Study on Rural Population.* Seoul: Seoul Women's College, 1974. Based on a 1971 survey, this study of an entire subcounty *(myŏn),* while primarily demographic in orientation, contains much information on kinship, living conditions, education, and values. There is also an extensive treatment of fertility and family planning, as well as of out-migration.

Articles

10-089. BRUNNER, E. de S. "Rural Korea." *International Missionary Council VI* (New York), (1928):84–172. A study of rural society, economy, and religion during the Japanese period. An effort is also made to describe the national character.

10-090. CHEONG, Ji Woong. "The Sae Maul Movement as I See It." *Community Development* (Seoul), (1973):401–411. One of the few articles on the New Community Movement that includes a critical discussion of problems encountered in addition to the usual praise of accomplishments.

10-091. HAN, Nae Bok. "The New Community Movement." *Korea Journal* 12(7)(July 1972):4–6. A succinct account of the backward state of the agricultural sector relative to industrial development, which by 1971 had reached the point where the government initiated a massive program to increase grain production and rural income.

10-092. _____. "Third Five Year Plan and the Green Revolution." *Korea Journal* 12(2)(February 1972):4–17. A discussion of the introduction of a new "miracle" rice variety in 1971 and the policy of maintaining higher rice prices. Obstacles to the achievement of planning goals are listed.

10-093. HAN, Sang-Bok. "Micro-Development of Farming and Fishing Villages: Theory and Policy." In *Development and Change.* Seoul: Seoul National University, 1973. This paper discusses basic problems of rural development in general theoretical terms and then emphasizes the importance in the case of Korea of promoting greater integration of villages with national economic, political, sociological, and cultural institutions.

10-094. HONG, Sung-Chick and Bok-Soo LEE. "The Expressway and the Process of Change in Rural Villages." *Social Science Journal* (Seoul), (1973):85–113. This survey of six villages bordering the new (1970) Seoul–Pusan expressway investigates associated changes in attitudes, farming practices, migration patterns, land prices, industrialization, and community development brought about by proximity to the highway.

10-095. KANG, Chinch'ol. "Traditional Land Tenure Relations in Korean Society: Ownership and Management." In H. Kang (ed.), *The Traditional Culture of Korea: Thought and Institutions.* Occasional Paper no. 5. Honolulu:

Center for Korean Studies, University of Hawaii, 1975. This study deals with the legal and administrative aspect of landownership throughout Korean history, particularly with regard to the distribution of land by the state and the increase of large private buildings among the aristocracy. Much of the discussion of peasant conditions is relegated to footnotes.

10-096. KEIM, Willard D. "The Attitudes of Korean Peasants." *Journal of East and West Studies* (Seoul), 3(1) (1974):65–100. A psychologically oriented survey that introduces provocative variables and reports survey results.

10-097. KIM, Il-Chul. "Community Development in Korea." *Final Report: International Seminar of the Cooperative Study of Community Development.* Seoul: Korean National Commission for UNESCO, 1973. A brief discussion of the goals, policy organization, and achievements of the New Community Movement, with some mention of the problems of leadership and participation.

10-098. LEE, Byung-Choon. "Agricultural Development and Rural Guidance Work." *Korea Journal* 13(4)(April 1972): 40–44. A brief but useful account of community development efforts prior to the launching of the New Community Movement in 1971. The stress is on the importance of education as a means of promoting rural development.

10-099. LEE, Man Gap. "Rural People and Their Modernization." In *Aspects of Social Change in Korea.* Kalamazoo: Korea Research and Publications, 1968. A penetrating discussion of the effects of social, political, economic, and ideological change on Korean farmers since 1945 and the relationship between such changes and agricultural development.

10-100. _____. "Socio-Cultural Aspects of the Community Development Movement in Korea." *Korea Journal* 13(1) (January 1973):25–33. A discussion of rural problems in terms of both traditional attitudes and contemporary change processes.

10-101. MOON, Seung Gyu. "Local Participation in Rural Development Planning in Korea: Its Functions and Disfunctions." *Korea Journal of Sociology* 4(1968). An account of community development efforts from 1958 to 1965 that examines the problem of why local participation has been low and failures frequent. The focus is on government policy, management, voluntary organizations, values, and social structure.

10-102. OH, Young-Kyun. "Agrarian Reform and Economic Development: A Case Study of Korean Agriculture." *Koreana Quarterly* 9(2)(1967):91–137. Emphasizes the economic disadvantages of the land reform, which created many small nonviable landholdings. Concludes that 20 percent of the farm population must leave the land. A

policy of selective taxation is recommended as a means of achieving this goal.

10-103. PARK, Sang-Yol. "The Social Structure of a Korean Village under the Control of Consanguinity." *Bulletin of Korea Research Center* 27(December 1967):70–98. This study of political power, economic and social status, and marriage patterns in a "clan village" (Hahoe tong) unfortunately replicates a more extensive work on the same community (by Taek Kyoo Kim) without adding much that is new.

10-104. SHIN, Susan S. "Some Aspects of Landlord–Tenant Relations in Yi Dynasty Korea." *Occasional Papers on Korea* 3(1975):49–77. Discusses the extent of tenancy, types of tenure, settlement of disputes, and the nature of social relationships among landlords and tenants. Also describes changes at the end of the Yi dynasty and the beginning of the Japanese period.

10-105. WANG, In Keun. "Relationship of Agricultural Adoption with Selected Variables in Korean Villages." *Seoul National University Faculty Papers* 1(B)(1971):130–158. An extensive survey which correlates agricultural innovation with a variety of individual social, economic, and psychological characteristics. The general implication is that innovative developmental activity only takes place where individual motivation is high.

Unpublished Dissertations

10-106. CHO, J. H. "Post 1945 Land Reforms and Their Consequences in South Korea." PhD dissertation, Indiana University, 1964. 215 pp. Abstracted in *DAI* 26(August 1965):740-41; UM 64-12,012.

10-107. HA, Joseph Man Kyung. "Politics of Korean Peasantry: A Study of Land Reforms and Collectivization with Reference to Sino Soviet Experiences." PhD dissertation, Columbia University, 1971. 498 pp. Abstracted in *DAI* 34(April 1974):6714-15-A; UM 74-8182.

10-108. HAN, Chungnim. "Social Organization of Upper Han Hamlet in Korea." PhD dissertation, University of Michigan, 1949. 238 pp. Abstracted in *Microfilm Abstracts* 9(2)(1949):180–181; UM 1245.

10-109. HAN, Sang Bok. "Socio Economic Organization and Change in Korean Fishing Villages: A Comparative Study of Three Fishing Communities." PhD dissertation, Michigan State University, 1972. 246 pp. Abstracted in *DAI* 34(November 1973):1845-B; UM 73-12,724.

10-110. KNEZ, Eugene I. "Sam Jong Dong: A South Korean Village." PhD dissertation, Syracuse University, 1959. 283 pp. Abstracted in *DAI* 20(February 1960):3016-17; UM 59-6308.

10-111. MCBRIAN, Charles D. "Kinship and Community in

a Korean Village.'' PhD dissertation, Harvard University, 1974. 160 pp. Available at the Harvard University Archives, Widener Library.

10-112. PAK, Ki Hyok. "Economic Analysis of Land Reform in the Republic of Korea with Special Reference to an Agricultural Economic Survey 1954–55." PhD dissertation, University of Illinois, 1959. 214 pp. Abstracted in *DAI* 16(November 1956):1977; UM 18,183.

10-113. SHIN, Susan. "Korean Village Associations: A Study of Social Change under Colonial Rule." MA thesis, Harvard University, 1966.

10-114. SWISHER, Ralph B. "Passing the Threshold to Modernity in Rural South Korea: The Convergence of Elite Communications, Popular Frame of Reference, and Institutional Capacity." PhD dissertation, University of Pittsburgh, 1972. 340 pp. Abstracted in *DAI* 33(May 1973): 6466-A; UM 73-12,359.

Documents

10-115. *Agricultural Cooperatives in Korea.* Seoul: National Agricultural Cooperative Federation, 1974. A description with simple statistical tables (designed to accentuate the positive) of activities undertaken by the National Agricultural Cooperative Federation.

10-116. *The Effectiveness of the Tongil Rice Diffusion in Korea.* Seoul: Office of Rural Development, Republic of Korea, 1975. A detailed description of the successful introduction of a new high-yield rice variety during the period 1971–1974.

10-117. *Rural Development Program in Korea.* Seoul: Office of Rural Development, Republic of Korea, 1975. A glowing description of the organization and operation of ORD's research stations and extension activities.

10-118. *SAEMAUL.* Seoul: Office of the President, Republic of Korea, 1974. A lavishly illustrated account of New Community Movement successes.

URBANIZATION AND MIGRATION
Books and Monographs

10-119. KWON, Tai Hwan. *Demography of Korea.* Seoul: Seoul National University, 1977. The author presents a comprehensive picture of population movements and changes in the southern half of Korea during the period from 1925 to 1966 through detailed analysis of patterns and trends in mortality, fertility, and migration.

10-120. LEE, Hyo-jae et al. "Life in Urban Korea." *Transactions of the Korea Branch of the Royal Asiatic Society* 46 (1971). A general survey of various aspects and modes of middle-class life in Seoul as exemplified in three wards. The study was "designed to help meet the needs of the urban planner." The emphasis here is overwhelmingly on the "typical": conflict, disorganization, and complexity are played down.

10-121. LEE, Man Gap and Herbert BARRINGER (eds.). *A City in Transition: Urbanization in Taegu, Korea.* Seoul: Hollym, 1971. A comprehensive study by a team of experts of Korea's third largest city with chapters on history, government, economics, social structure, migration, education, and religion.

10-122. MOON, Seung Gyu. *Outmigration from Families of Orientation in Two Rural Communities: A Case Study in Korea.* Seoul: Seoul National University, Population and Development Studies Center, 1972. Part of a general study of population changes and migration patterns in North Chŏlla province since 1945. This report concentrates on the migration of young people, asking such questions as when, where, why, how, and which children. Also discusses factors accounting for the chosen destinations.

10-123. *Report: International Conference on Urban Problems and Regional Development.* Seoul: Yonsei University, 1970. Includes articles on urbanization in Korea as well as other parts of the developing world. Both migration and the social consequences of urban growth are dealt with.

10-124. RO, Chung Hyun. *Population and the Asian Environment.* Paper presented at Michigan University, 1971. Despite the title this paper is concerned primarily with rural-urban migration and the situation of the urban poor in Korea. The general economic context is described with policy recommendations for administrative planners.

Articles

10-125. BRANDT, Vincent. "Mass Migration and Urbanization in Contemporary Korea." *Asia* 20(1970/1972):31–47. Discusses the rural-urban imbalance in contemporary Korea and suggests that an incipient form of the culture of poverty may be developing among the urban poor in Seoul due to social and economic discrimination and physical segregation.

10-126. CHANG, Yun-shik. "The Urban Korean as Individual." *Korea Observer* 3(3)(April 1971):3–15. Starting with an account of traditional social organization in Korea, this article provides a perceptive account of the shift in personal values, attitudes, and behavior that accompanies modernization and urbanization.

10-127. KIM, Chong Lim and Seong-tong PAI. *Urban Migration, Acquisition of Modernity, and Political Change.* Occasional Paper no. 5, Comparative Legislative Research Center. Iowa City: University of Iowa, 1975. An examination of the political implications of rapid urbanization in terms of modernization, political involvement, and stability.

10-128. KIM, Sungwoo. "Internal Labor Migration and Economic Development: A Case Study of Korea." *Asian Forum* 4(4)(1972):39–51. From an economic perspective, rural-urban migration is described as highly advantageous for both rural and urban sectors. Recommends that the costs of migration should be borne by government and the urban population.

10-129. LEE, Man Gap. "The Facts behind Seoul's Exploding Population" and "Pushing or Pulling?" In *Report: International Conference on Urban Problems and Regional Development*. Seoul: Yonsei University, 1970. These papers describe the dimensions of rural-urban migration until 1968 together with informed discussion of both the motives and the social consequences of large-scale population movement in Korea.

10-130. RO, Chung Hyun. "Housing Problems in Urban Korea." *Koreana Quarterly* 11(2)(1969):51–62. A critical view of government planning and policy measures designed to cope with severe housing shortages.

10-131. SLOBODA, John. "Urbanization, Migration and Socio-Economic Development: Contemporary Patterns in Korea." *Korea Journal* 14(11)(October 1974):27–36 and 14(12)(November 1974):20–32. Part 1 discusses various theories relating migration and urbanization to economic development. Part 2 presents a detailed account supported by statistics of migration patterns in Korea from 1910 to 1970.

10-132. WILKINSON, T. O. "The Pattern of Korean Urban Growth." *Rural Sociology* 19(March 1954):32–35.

Unpublished Dissertations

10-133. KENNEDY, Gerald F. "The Korean Fiscal Kye (Rotating Credit Organization): An Urban Accommodation in a Modernizing Society." PhD dissertation, University of Hawaii, 1973. 207 pp.

10-134. KIM, Seyeul. "The Economic and Social Determination of Rural-Urban Migration in Korea: A Case Study of North Cholla Province." PhD dissertation, University of Hawaii, 1974. 167 pp.

Documents

10-135. OTAM-METRA International. *Urban Development*. Seoul: 1971. This report by international urbanization experts describes the present status of urban development in terms of housing, medical facilities, education, tourism, and recreation. The main emphasis is on attempting to predict future trends and make policy recommendations.

10-136. *A Survey of the Housing Market in Urban Korea*. Seoul: USOM, 1972.

10-137. *A Survey on Slum Population in Seoul*. Seoul: Institute of Urban Studies, Yonsei University, 1971. A detailed statistical report of the most extensive survey yet undertaken of migrant squatter areas in Seoul. Presents information on social background, education, migration patterns, occupation, living standards, health, housing, and attitudes on political, economic, and cultural matters.

SOCIAL CHANGE, CLASS, AND SUBCULTURES
Books and Monographs

10-138. BARRINGER, Herbert. *Social Stratification and Industrialization in Korea*. ILCORK Working Paper 11. Seoul: 1971. Summarizes much of the available data on class and mobility. Concludes optimistically that there is a rapidly growing middle class and enough upward mobility to integrate most migrants successfully into urban society.

10-139. CH'OI, Jin Ho and Tai Hwan KWON (eds.). *Development and Change*. Seoul: Population and Development Studies Center, Seoul National University, 1973. This collection of papers from a 1973 conference in Seoul is mainly oriented toward theoretical and conceptual aspects of development.

10-140. KIHL, Young Whan. *Local Elites, Power Structure and the Legislative Process in Korea*. Occasional Paper no. 8, Comparative Legislative Research Center. Iowa City: University of Iowa, 1975. Provides background information on the political role of local provincial leaders and reports the results of a survey investigating their attitudes regarding democracy and the political process in Korea.

10-141. KIM, Chong Ik Eugene (ed.). *Aspects of Social Change in Korea*. Kalamazoo: Korean Research and Publications, 1969. A somewhat uneven collection of articles from the middle and latter 1960s by both Korean and American scholars on a wide variety of topics.

10-142. NAHM, Andrew (ed.). *Korea under Japanese Political Rule*. Kalamazoo: Center for Korean Studies, Western Michigan University, 1973. This is an outstanding collection of longer papers, each of which makes a substantial contribution to an understanding of social, economic, or political processes during the period of Japanese occupation. Throughout the book the focus is on modernization and development.

10-143. _____. (ed.). *Studies in the Developmental Aspects of Korea*. Kalamazoo: Center for Korean Studies, Western Michigan University, 1969. A collection of symposium papers that deal with contemporary (late 1960s) developmental changes in both North and South Korea.

10-144. *Report of a Seminar for the Improvement of Women's Status.* Seoul: Korean National Commission for UNESCO, 1975. This report contains articles by prominent Korean sociologists on such topics as educational opportunities for women, their social consciousness, and current changes in their roles.

10-145. *Upper Class Culture in Yi Dynasty Korea.* Seoul: International Cultural Foundation, 1973. Translations of articles by Koreans on the work and life-style of scholarly notables. This collection stresses both the high idealism and the exaggerated formality of the strict, Neo-Confucian life-style.

Articles

10-146. BARRINGER, H. R. "The Increasing Social Scale and Changing Social Character in Korea." In Dennis McElrath and Scott Grear (eds.), *The New Urbanization.* Evanston, Ill.: Northwestern University Press, 1968. An extension and refinement on the basis of further fieldwork of the research reported on in Barringer's doctoral dissertation (see 10-048).

10-147. CHO, Suk Choon. "The Korean Bureaucracy: Authority and Policy Formation Process." *Korean Journal of Administration* 8(1)(1970):153–164. After discussing the heterogeneous composition of the bureaucracy in terms of age, class, education, and experience, this article analyzes characteristics shared by bureaucrats under the headings of hierarchical human relations, specialization, and personalism. The implications of these properties for innovative policy formation are discussed.

10-148. HAHM, Pyong-Choon. "Korea and Asia: Crisis, Continuity and Change." In *Asian Perspectives.* Provo: Brigham Young University, 1975. A brief but perceptive comment on the way Koreans (or at least large numbers of Koreans) see themselves and their relationship with other nations.

10-149. HONG, Sung-chick and Kil-myong RO. "Measurement of Industrial Workers' Job Satisfaction." *Journal of Asiatic Studies* 16(2)(1973):391–398. A survey of attitudes in two factories with regard to income, job security, work supervision, welfare, union activity, and overall job satisfaction.

10-150. HWANG, Tong-gon. "Social Change and Education in Rural Communities." *Korea Journal* 13(8)(August 1973):1–12. A description of two villages where factories were built and the resulting adjustment of farmers. Attitudes toward money, cash dealings, and patterns of work are examined. The role of education in preparing villagers for such changes is stressed.

10-151. KIM, Dae-Hwan. "Industrialization and Social Change." *Korea Journal* 12(3)(March 1972):25–30. A discussion of problems of integration resulting from what is described as an overemphasis on material progress in formulating national goals.

10-152. _____. "Social Trends in the 1970's and Education Policies." *Koreana Quarterly* 12(1/2)(1970). The problems of social integration and youth that are associated with rapid economic development and structural change. A critical view of the government's accomplishments.

10-153. KIM, Kyong Dong. "Social Change in South Korea." *Journal of Korean Affairs* 4(4)(1975):3–15. A comprehensive summary description of recent economic progress and social problems. Agricultural-industrial imbalance, unequal income distribution, balance of payments, rural-urban migration, stratification, and mobility—all are examined from a critical perspective. The paper asks: Has real development taken place?

10-154. KIM, Se-jin. "Attitudinal Orientations of Korean Workers." *Korea Journal* 12(9)(September 1972):18–30. A highly condensed report of the results of a "massive" 1972 survey of the backgrounds and opinions of workers, union leaders, and management. The focus is mainly on political issues, job satisfaction, and ideas about the appropriate roles for unions and management.

10-155. KOH, Young Bok. "A Review of Post-War Social Change in Korea." *Asian Pacific Quarterly* 3(2)(1971):9–33. Rapid urbanization, changes in occupational structure, improvement of educational levels, and the organization of voluntary organizations are discussed in the context of economic development. Changes in human relations, the cultural system, and institutions are also mentioned.

10-156. LEE, Hong-Koo. "Political Culture and Political Development in Korea: An Aspect of the Political Behavior of Low-Income Groups in Seoul." *Korea Journal* 18(1) (January 1978):16–29. Analysis of survey data shows that low-income urban dwellers have low levels of civic consciousness and political involvement but high political perception.

10-157. LEE, Sang-Beck. "Social Stratification and Mobility in Three Cities of Korea." *East Asian Cultural Studies* 4(1/4)(March 1965):127–132. Seoul, Taegu, and Chŏnju were surveyed with regard to such categories as occupation, education, and self-identification of class. Comparisons were made of mobility within and across generations.

10-158. LEE, Young Ho. "Modernization and Tradition: Korean Attitudes." *Korea Journal* 12(10)(October 1972):

12–17. Reports the results of an attitude survey indicating that there is a contradiction between the conscious rejection of traditional practices and values on the one hand and unconscious, internalized beliefs and patterns of behavior on the other.

10-159. LIM, Hy-sop. "A Study on Legal Values in Korea: An Analysis of Attitude toward Law." *Social Science Journal* (Seoul), (1974):59–89. Presents the findings of a large-scale, carefully conducted survey examining legal attitudes in Korea from a moral, political, and sociological standpoint. The results have been analyzed in an effort to determine the frequency of various types of legal behavior.

10-160. LOVELL, John P., Hui Sok MUN, and Young Ho LEE. "Professional Orientation and Policy Perspectives of Military Professionals in the Republic of Korea." *Midwest Journal of Political Science* 13(3)(August 1969):415–438. An investigation of the extent to which military professionals and college students agree with the government's position on controversial issues. Findings are correlated with age, regional background, and religion.

10-161. NAM, Won-suh. *The Traditional Pattern of Korean Industrial Management.* ILCORK Working Paper 14. Honolulu: University of Hawaii, 1971. This paper describes the social background, age, education, and experience of the managerial class, most of whom have achieved success since 1960. There is an extensive discussion of typical authority relationships within the firm as well as of general organizational structure. Problems resulting from the effort to combine traditional and modern management practices are spelled out.

10-162. O, Kap Hwan. "Special and Economic Status of Korean Writers." *Korea Journal* 9(4)(1969):13–15. A condensed summary of the findings of a survey conducted among thirteen writers in 1969. Social background, income, class, status, and daily life-style were investigated.

10-163. OH, Byung Hun. "University Students and Politics in Korea." *Koreana Quarterly* 9(4)(1967):1–40. This wide-ranging article first describes the history of student movements in Korea and then examines the involvement of students in politics.

10-164. PARK, Dong Suh. "Korean Higher Civil Servants: Their Background and Morale." In B. C. Koh (ed.), *Aspects of Administrative Development.* Kalamazoo: Korea Research and Publications, 1967.

10-165. _____. "Study of Qualifications of Korean Administrative Executives." *Koreana Quarterly* 11(2)(1969):19–37. These two studies by a political scientist are basically sociological in orientation. In addition to social back-

ground, age, education, salaries, recruitment, and promotion policies, there is a discussion of social status and satisfactions of bureaucrats.

10-166. SHIN, Susan. "The Social Structure of Kumhwa County in the Late Seventeenth Century." In *Occasional Papers on Korea,* 1(April 1974):9–35. An analysis, based on detailed examination of a census register, of class hierarchy, personal status, and socioeconomic mobility in one local district.

10-167. WAGNER, Edward W. "Social Stratification in Seventeenth Century Korea: Some Observations from 1663 Seoul Census Register." In *Occasional Papers on Korea,* 1(April 1974):36–54. A detailed examination of status and wealth among a suburban Seoul population. Challenges many commonly held ideas about stratification and mobility in Yi dynasty Korea.

10-168. WHANG, In Joung. "Elite Change and Program Change in the Korean Government 1955–1967." *Journal of Public Administration* 7(1)(1969):235–264. A description of the shift in high administrative personnel that took place after the military coup in 1961. The author correlates this shift with the subsequent rapid economic development.

10-169. WON, George, Jang-Hyun LEE, and In Hwan OH. "Korean Lawyers: Self Evaluation and Occupational Satisfaction." *Korea Journal* 14(11)(November 1974):33–39.

10-170. _____. "The Korean Lawyer: A Study of Career Style." *Social Science Journal* (Seoul), (1974):81–89. These two articles (10-169, 170), which present the results of several surveys of lawyers in Seoul and other cities, deal with social background, mobility, career development patterns, and work satisfaction.

10-171. YOON, Woo-kon. "Korean Bureaucrat's Behavior: An Analysis of Personality and Its Effect." *Korea Journal* 14(7)(July 1974):22–35. A survey of 273 high-ranking and low-ranking bureaucrats was used in an effort to discover: (1) the bureaucratic behavior that causes administrative problems; (2) the reasons for such behavior; and (3) the administrative implications of such behavior.

Unpublished Dissertations

10-172. KIM, Quee-Young. "Social Structure and Student Revolt: A Quantitative Analysis of the Korean Case." PhD dissertation, Harvard University, 1975.

10-173. RYU, Jai Poong. "From 'Chosen' to 'Daehan': Social Change in Twentieth Century Korea." PhD dissertation, University of Minnesota, 1972. 354 pp. Abstracted in *DAI* 33(November 1972):2531-A; UM 72-27,802.

10-174. SOMERVILLE, John N. "Success and Failure in

18th Century Ulsan: A Study in Social Mobility.'' PhD dissertation, Harvard University, 1974.

Document

10-175. Asiatic Research Center. *Report: International Conference on the Problems of Modernization in Asia.* Seoul: Korea University, 1965.

RESEARCH IN PROGRESS

A number of exceptionally well-qualified PhD candidates in anthropology and sociology are now (1977) doing dissertation research in Korea. Since it seems likely that their work, when completed, will add significantly to the existing materials, a brief description follows.

Dissertations in Progress

10-176. COZIN, Mark L. "Sociological Aspects of New Religious Sects in South Korea." PhD dissertation, London School of Economics. Voluntary religious groups in post–Yi dynasty Korea are described from an anthropological perspective, both in terms of their internal social organization, ideology, and scope as well as in relation to recent Korean historical developments and social structure.

10-177. DIX, Griffin. "Confucian Social Values and World View in Contemporary Korean Rural Society." PhD dissertation, University of California at San Diego. The functions of Confucian ethics—in particular filial piety—are examined in relation to local political and economic behavior using case histories obtained from anthropological fieldwork.

10-178. DREDGE, Paul. "Speech Variation and Social Structure in a Korean Village." PhD dissertation, Harvard University.

10-179. GOLDBERG, Charles N. "Rural Korea in Transition: A Century of Social and Economic Change." PhD dissertation, Columbia University. Based on a year and a half of residence in a Korean village and an extensive analysis of local archives, this anthropological study deals with the relationships among kinship organization, class structure, and land tenure as these institutions have changed in response to external pressures over the past century. The research has been designed to provide a model of Korean rural society as well as to help refine the concept of peasant societies in general.

10-180. GUILLEMOZ, Alexandre. "Shamanism in an East Coast Village and in Seoul." Doctoral dissertation, École Normale et Superieur, Université de Paris.

10-181. HONG, Suhn-Kyoung. "Rural-Urban Migration and Squatter Settlements in Seoul." PhD dissertation, Harvard University. This study examines the causes of migration from villages to Seoul during the period 1962–1972 and interprets the experience of migrant squatters both in terms of their adaptation to urban socioeconomic structures and with reference to their own beliefs and attitudes.

10-182. SLOBODA, John. "Migration, Mobility and Socioeconomic Development in Korea." PhD dissertation, Harvard University. Two streams of analysis, one essentially structural and the other behavioral, are utilized to explore the role of urbanization and growth centers in the overall development/modernization process.

Postdoctoral Research

10-183. YUN, Soon Young. "A Comparative Study of the Role of Women in Korean Society with Particular Reference to Shamanistic Practitioners on Cheju Do." Seoul: Ehwa Women's University.

CHAPTER 11
The Economic System

Joseph Sang-hoon Chung

INTRODUCTION

SIGNIFICANCE OF THE ECONOMIC SYSTEM

FOLLOWING THE SURRENDER of Japan in August 1945, two opposing political systems came to be established in Korea. This, in turn, led to the adoption of two entirely divergent and competing economic systems. Thus in the Republic of Korea (South Korea) an economic system evolved that was based more or less on market economy while in the Democratic People's Republic of Korea (North Korea) a Soviet-type economic system developed consistent with its communist ideology and political system.

Since the division, and particularly after the Korean War, economic contacts between the two have been suspended. Each attempted to rebuild and attain economic viability in isolation from the other half that had long complemented its economy. The wide disparity between the economic systems and developmental patterns of South and North Korea, each based on its own political and ideological premises, offers an unusual opportunity for a comparative study.

An economic system represents a set of institutional arrangements and organizational interactions by which a society determines the production, distribution, and use of goods and services. By this system the society decides (1) what to produce (determination of the kind and quantity of goods and services from all possible choices); (2) how to produce it (determination of techniques of production, institutions, and the patterns of resource allocation); (3) how to share the national output and income among the people (choice regarding distribution of income); and (4) how to divide the national output between current and future use (determining the right mix of today's consumption and tomorrow's economic growth). These are the economic questions (functions) that every society must answer (perform). How these functions are performed varies from one economic system to another.

In this essay the economic systems of South and North Korea are analyzed and compared. Three major bases are used in comparing the two systems: (1) the nature and characteristics of the system and the mechanics of its operation; (2) factors influencing the system and determining its character and evolution; and (3) actual performance of the system with respect to its goals.

Broadly, the major forces that shape economic systems may be grouped into three categories. These must be borne in mind when the two economic systems of Korea are compared. They are the level of economic development, social and political-cultural forces, and the environment. Economic development alters the size and structure of the economy, and these transformations in turn influence the economic system.

Many aspects of society and culture determine the economic system. They involve religion, custom, tradition, values, and beliefs. Ideology is a major, often the dominant, influence. Thus communist nations typically adopt an economic system consistent with communist ideology. An economic ideology affects both the ends and the means, the institutions and instruments of the economic system, and the way the resources are allocated and utilized.

The physical environment of a society affects the economic system through its size (territory and population), climate, topography, natural resources, and geopolitics. These factors help determine not only the level of economic development but also the economic relations with neighbors and others in the world. These relations in turn affect the economic system.

THE KOREAN ECONOMY IN 1945

Substantial economic development and modernization did take place during the Japanese occupation (1910–1945) in all areas of the Korean economy. The Japanese had developed considerable heavy industry, particularly in the metal and chemical industries, hydroelectric power, and mining in the northern half of Korea. The southern half produced most of the rice and a majority of textiles. The mining methods introduced by the Japanese were modern. The hydroelectric power and chemical plants, both in terms of their scale and technology, were second to none in Asia. The same applied to such social overhead capital as railroad and communication networks.

There were serious defects in the industrial structures and their location, however. The Korean economy, geared primarily to benefit the Japanese, was made dependent on Japan for final processing of products: heavy industry was limited to the production of mainly raw materials, semifinished goods, and war supplies, which were then shipped to Japan proper for final processing and consumption. The dependence was particularly pronounced in regard to machine tools, for Japan did not allow Korea to develop an industry. In a classic colonial pattern, Korea acted as a supplier of important raw materials, semifinished products, and rice while providing a market for Japanese manufactured goods. Most industrial centers were strategically located on the eastern or western coastal areas near ports so as to connect them efficiently with Japan proper. The railroad networks, well developed by Asian standards, ran mainly along the north-south axis and facilitated Japan's access to the Asian mainland.

Very few Koreans were allowed to participate in government and industry as officials, managers, engineers, owners, or skilled personnel. As a result, Koreans did not benefit from the development experience, and neither did they acquire basic skills essential for modernization. The Japanese came to own and control almost all the key industrial and financial enterprises and to occupy all high civil service offices. Even in agriculture much land was transferred to Japanese ownership. Discrimination against Koreans in education compounded these problems.

The Japanese left behind an agrarian structure—land tenure system, size of landholdings and farm operation, pattern of land use and farm income—that needed much reform. One revealing indicator of the state of landownership and farm management toward the end of the Japanese occupation (1943) showed that about 50 percent of all farm households in Korea were tenants. Moreover, farms were fragmented and small in size and extreme inequality characterized the landownership.

The sudden withdrawal of the Japanese and the subsequent division of the country into North and South Korea created chaos in the economy. Severance of the "agricultural" South from the "industrial" North compounded the difficulties resulting from Japanese departure—all at once the traditional market for Korean products and the sources for food and raw materials were cut off. The South was cut off from its primary source of electricity and fertilizers and various minerals in the North, for example, while the latter lost its traditional source of food and light industrial goods. Links between industry and agriculture, between heavy industry and light industry, and between raw materials and finished products were disrupted. Furthermore, the industrial plants that Korea inherited from the Japanese were not in good operational condition due to matériel shortages, mismanagement in allocation, loss of managerial and technical personnel to the war effort, and unavailability of fuel. Furthermore, there were unconfirmed reports from North Korean sources that the fleeing Japanese had, in the face of the advancing Soviet Army, resorted to considerable destruction and sabotage in the north. Repatriation of trained Japanese personnel who used to occupy all key managerial and technical positions created a severe shortage of skilled manpower and managerial know-how.

THE SOUTH KOREAN ECONOMY

The South Korean economy is a mixed economy. While the basic tenets of private enterprise and the market economy are practiced, the government plays a crucial role in economic decision-making and resource allocation. The magnitude of the government's role in South Korea's economy is roughly comparable to that of Japan and other Western European countries such as West Germany and France, although it is perhaps more evident in South Korea than in these advanced nations. These countries share a basic adherence to the private enterprise system with strong governmental participation. Some scholars characterize these countries as "mixed economies of the Middle Way" in which the mixture between private and public sectors may vary. Countries like the United States and Canada, on the one hand, and the centrally planned economies, on the other, occupy opposing ends in the spectrum of private–government mixture.

The enormous exercise of government influence in the South Korean economy occurs in several important ways. First, since 1962 the South Korean government has introduced economic planning on a formal basis starting from the First Five-Year Plan. While South Korea's "indicative" plan does not directly compel the enterprises to adhere strictly to the specific and general targets set forth as does the Soviet type of "imperative plan," it does attempt to exert broad indirect pressure through the market mechanism. Private enterprises are asked to conform to the basic objectives of the plan, and the government resorts to fiscal, monetary, and other policies to achieve the planned goals. Since the end of the Korean War, South Korea had made a series of attempts to introduce planning. An American team produced in 1954 the first long-range economic plans—popularly known as the Nathan Report (see 11-080)—at the behest of a United Nations agency, but they were largely sidetracked due mainly to the lack of requisite political leadership. It was only in the 1960s that favorable political conditions for planning came to prevail. Following the First Five-Year Plan, two subsequent eco-

nomic plans—the Second Five-Year Plan (1967–1971) and the Third Five-Year Plan (1972–1976)—were implemented. It is the general conclusion among students of the South Korean economy that these plans have significantly influenced the private sector and the course and rate of economic development.

Second, the government budget (central and local), whose expenditures amount to a large proportion of national output (30 to 40 percent of the GNP in the 1960s and early 1970s), places the government in a position to exert a direct and significant influence upon the economy through the public sector.

Third, a major instrument of government influence is government enterprise. Such an enterprise is usually found in public utilities or in strongly monopolistic industries like railroads, electricity, the telephone system, and cigarettes. Moreover, the government is also a stockholder in more than thirty "government-invested corporations," most of which also have private stockholders.

Fourth, the government directly owns or controls nearly all the financial institutions including the Bank of Korea. Thus it can directly determine the interest rates and other quantitative and qualitative lending policies.

Fifth, the government exerts direct and powerful control over the foreign sector through its monopoly of foreign exchange, preferential tariffs and interest rates, and direct or indirect subsidies.

Sixth, the government exerts influence on the pattern of resource allocation and the course of economic development by means of certain other fiscal and monetary policies. In an effort to utilize domestic savings for capital formation, the South Korean government has instituted since 1961 various tax reforms. Until then foreign economic aid had served as the basis for reconstruction, stabilization, and growth. The reforms included: modernization and strengthening of tax machinery; increase in indirect taxes such as on liquor, oil, business license fees, and the sales tax; rational coordination and adjustment among various central, provincial, and local tax collection agencies; a punitive surtax on speculative real estate transactions to divert the financial resources from speculative to productive investment. The new tax policy was highly effective. Consumption was curtailed and domestic savings were substantially increased. Furthermore, enterprises in key industries were granted special tax exemptions or special depreciation allowances. Special treatment was extended to export firms via reduced tax rates. Imports of raw materials destined for the production of exportable goods were exempt from customs duties. A special tax concession was also made to encourage the inflow of foreign capital.

Monetary and financial reforms introduced during the 1960s also played an important role in achieving the goals of economic plans. These reforms included transfer of ownership of important private banks to the government, government assumption of partial ownership of financial institutions through stock holdings, raising of the official ceiling on nominal interest rates on time and savings deposits to a more realistic level, and introduction of a government guarantee of foreign loans. Through these measures the government has attempted to mobilize domestic resources and to attract foreign capital.

In sum, the South Korean system deviates from the model of a pure free enterprise economy. In this mixed system the government exerts a major influence on the course of the economy through planning, direct and indirect government ownership and control of enterprises and financial institutions, control of foreign exchange, and monetary and fiscal policies. Nevertheless, reliance on the market, private initiative, and pecuniary incentives remain the basic tenets of the system. The government's influence is used to change the parameters of the market and provide incentives in order to achieve the desired economic and social-political-cultural goals.

ECONOMIC DEVELOPMENT OF SOUTH KOREA

The political events of 1945 severely limited the potential of the South Korean economy and altered, for good, its course of development and pattern of domestic and external trade. The departure of Japanese management and technical know-how created a shortage of trained manpower; cutting off the electricity from the North made it necessary for the South to develop its own power sources nearly from scratch; traditional trade with North Korea and Japan was ruptured.

By the spring of 1950, however, there had been a gradual improvement in the economy with substantial foreign aid from the United States. Various institutional reforms such as land reform and the creation of a new central bank had been introduced. The economy seemed on its way to recovery from the effects of the division. However, all the gain was wiped out when the Korean War broke out in the summer of 1950. Nearly all the industrial facilities and urban centers (except the Pusan area) were either destroyed or heavily damaged during the war. The overall physical destruction was estimated to be $2 billion, roughly equal to the value of one year's GNP at that time. The war also brought hyperinflation; prices increased eighteen times between 1950 and 1953.

Postwar development can be conveniently divided into three distinctive periods: the reconstruction period of 1953-1958, a period of stagnation and political unrest during 1959-1962, and a period of rapid growth since 1963. In the first period a large-scale infusion of foreign aid made it possible for the economy to rebuild the war-damaged productive facilities. This period was also characterized by moderate growth which was, however, marred by imbalance and instability. At the same time, a high rate of inflation, averaging 30.1 percent per annum, continued to plague the economy. The second period saw the rate of inflation reduced to an annual average of 10.4 percent, but the pace of economic development slowed down somewhat from 5.5 percent per annum during the first period to 3.6 percent. The growth of national output in per capita terms declined to nearly zero. Dwindling foreign aid and import levels acted as a brake on production and investment. Economic stagnation was accompanied by political unrest. The Rhee government was overthrown in April 1960, but its successor, the Chang government, was in turn overthrown by a military coup in May 1961 marking the beginning of the present government of Chung Hee Park.

The rapid growth of recent years had its beginning in 1963, one year after the introduction of the First Five-Year Plan. The economy has since achieved a high rate of growth in output, income, and employment. At the same time, there have been rapid structural changes in the form of rising ratios of investment, saving, exports and imports, and industrial output. The GNP (in 1970 constant prices) grew from 1328.31 billion *wŏn* in 1963 to 4767.90 billion *wŏn* in 1976, registering an annual average growth rate of 10.3 percent for the thirteen years between 1964 and 1976. The GNP in 1976 was 12,143.36 billion *wŏn* (in current prices) or $25.1 billion. The per capita GNP rose from a mere $98 in 1963 to $713 in 1976 (assuming an estimated population of 35.2 million). Rapid industrialization has brought with it a significant shift in the structure of the economy. The share of the primary products (agriculture, forestry, fisheries) rose from 40.3 percent in 1954 to 42.2 percent in 1963 but declined sharply to 24.8 percent by 1976. In contrast, the share contributed by mining and manufacturing increased from 12.4 percent in 1954 to 16.6 percent in 1963 and finally to 31.0 percent in 1976.

The most dramatic indicator of South Korean growth has been a spectacular expansion in exports from a mere $39.6 million in 1953 to $86.8 million in 1963—and to $7715.3 million in 1976. The value of exports in 1976 was 194.8 and 88.9 times that of 1953 and 1963, respectively. In terms of annual average growth, exports grew at a rate of 41.2 percent during the thirteen years between 1964 and 1976. Such a record reflects not only quantitative advances but also impressive improvement in the quality of South Korean export products and their acceptance in international markets. Rapid growth increased the need for imports of necessary resources and, as a result, imports increased from $345.4 million in 1953 to $560.3 million in 1963—and to $8773.6 million in 1976, showing an annual growth rate of 26.3 percent during 1964–1976. Although South Korea has been plagued by chronic balance of trade deficits, the faster growth in exports than imports points to a gradual and steady reversal in the unfavorable balance. In 1973 South Korea became the twenty-fourth largest exporter in the world as compared to the ninety-fourth place she occupied in 1961. As a share of GNP, the value of exports rose from 2 percent in 1961 to 31 percent in 1976.

Rapid growth in international trade has been accompanied by a drastic change in the commodity composition of trade which, on the one hand, reflects the extent of economic development and import substitution and, on the other hand, played a major role in the development process. In exports the relative importance of primary products decreased while the share of manufactured goods increased to occupy more than 80 percent by the mid-1970s. In imports the most significant structural change has been the steady increase in capital goods, machinery, and transportation equipment.

Along with the high rate of growth, the South Korean government's vigorous stabilization measures have been successful in bringing the chronically high rate of inflation down to an average level of less than 10 percent (9.8 percent in wholesale price index and 9.4 percent in consumer price index) during the three years between 1971 and 1973.

In recent years South Korean growth has slowed down somewhat. Drastic changes in the international economic situation have confronted South Korea with difficult problems related to worldwide inflation and shortages of essential raw materials (particularly since the oil crisis of late 1973). These problems have exerted an adverse influence on production, exports, employment, balance of payments, and prices. Slackened exports due to the worldwide recession coupled with sluggish domestic demand for consumption and investment brought about a sharp reduction in the rate of economic growth during 1974–1975. Compared to the unprecedented 16.0 percent real growth attained in 1973, the rate of GNP growth declined to 8.7 and 8.3 percent, respectively, for the two years. Moreover, export growth slowed down from an astonishing increase of 98.6 percent in 1973 to 38.3 and 13.9 percent, respectively, in 1974 and 1975. Imports, in contrast, grew at a rate of 61.6 percent in 1974, although the following year saw a sharp reduction in the rate with 6.2 percent. The balance of international payment position worsened and the severe inflationary pressure returned. The annual rate of increase in the wholesale (consumer) price index rose from 6.9 percent (3.2 percent) in 1973 to 42.3 (24.3) and 26.4 percent (25.3 percent), respectively, in 1974 and 1975.

From all indications the South Korean economy has recovered from the temporary setback of 1974–1975. In 1976 the real GNP grew at 15.5 percent. Exports grew by 51.8 percent in 1976 as compared to 20.6 percent in imports. The rate of inflation slowed down considerably with the wholesale price index increasing 12.1 percent in 1976 and the consumer price index increasing by 15.3 percent. Responsible for the fast recovery were such factors as gradual improvement in international economic conditions—particularly the recovery of the United States and Japan, South Korea's principal trade partners—and South Korea's vigorous export promotion efforts, strong domestic stabilization measures, and continued energetic development programs through economic planning.

THE NORTH KOREAN ECONOMY

North Korea ranks as one of the world's most highly centralized and planned economies, even by communist standards. Complete "socialization" of the economy was accomplished by 1958 when private ownership of productive means, land, and commercial enterprises was replaced by state and cooperative (collective) ownership and control. Private garden plots and peasant markets remain, however, as minor exceptions.

Like other Soviet-type or "command" economies, North Korea's economy is run by means of commands from a central planning body. All economic decisions concerning the selection of output, output targets, allocation of inputs, prices, distribution of national income, investment, and economic growth are implemented through the "imperative" economic plan from the center, "blueprinted" by the State Planning Commission. In contrast to the "indicative" planning of South Korea, imperative planning is associated with the dominance of the economy by the state (public sector), which assumes direction by ownership, control, and regulation of all fields of economic activity.

After two one-year plans for 1947 and 1948 respectively, North Korea has instituted six distinct economic plans. Each of these plans expressed the broad and specific economic objectives to be achieved and the means and strategies necessary for their achievement:

One-Year Plan (1947): Peaceful Construction Period
One-Year Plan (1948): Peaceful Construction Period
Two-Year Plan (1949–1950): Peaceful Construction Period
Three-Year Plan (1954–1956): Postwar Reconstruction Period
Five-Year Plan (1957–1961): A de facto Four-Year Plan (terminated in 1960)
Seven-Year Plan (1961–1967): A de facto Ten-Year Plan (extended to 1970)
Six-Year Plan (1971–1976)
Second Seven-Year Plan (1978–1984)

North Korea wasted no time in implementing state and cooperative ownership of production, an organizational objective of the communist economic policy. Key industrial enterprises came first under the control of the People's Committee under the tutelage of the Soviet occupation force, even before the formal nationalization decree of 10 October 1946 by the Provisional People's Committee. State ownership and control of other industrial enterprises progressed until 1958 when "socialization" of industry and all other sectors of the economy was completed. The last remnants of private ownership and control of industrial enterprises had been eliminated from the North Korean scene altogether. As a result, industrial firms are today either state-owned or in the form of cooperatives, the former contributing a lion's share of the total (gross) industrial output (more than 90 percent in the 1960s).

Since 1945 there has been an equally drastic change in North Korea's land tenure system and in the organization and management of agricultural production. Private farming, which ironically had been given a boost through the land reform in 1946, declined rapidly after the Korean War. With the completion of collectivization in 1958, private farming as a type of agricultural organization and as a way of life totally disappeared from North Korea. Today basic farm production units are either state farms or collective farms. Unlike industry the collective arrangement is the predominant form of ownership and production in agriculture (contributing more than 80 percent of the total farm output and using more than 90 percent of the total cultivated land in the 1960s). The one negligible exception to state and collective ownership in agriculture is the ownership of small "garden plots" and fruit trees as well as the raising of poultry, pigs, bees, and the like, permitted both for consumption at home and sale at the peasant market. The rule allows 50 p'yŏng (or roughly 0.04 acre) as the maximum for the private plots.

State and cooperative ownership and control extend to foreign trade as well as to all other sectors of the economy such as banking, transportation, and communication. In commerce nearly all goods are distributed through either state-operated or cooperative stores. A small amount of retail transaction (less than 1 percent) is carried on at peasant markets where surplus farm products are sold at free-market prices through the interaction of supply and demand. Often the goods offered in these markets are of better quality than those provided by state stores. The North Korean leadership, however, is doctrinally opposed to the peasant markets, which are considered remnants of capitalism. The peasant markets seem to be a stop-gap device to provide consumers with much needed relief in daily necessities and to lessen black market activities.

Slowdowns in economic growth in the Soviet Union and Eastern European communist countries in the late 1950s and early 1960s started a chain of drastic institutional reforms which resulted in significant liberalization and decentralization in central planning. These reforms, aimed primarily at avoiding the declining efficiency of a central command-type economic system, have as their basic thrust a shift of emphasis from administrative and bureaucratic control to economic and pecuniary incentives. Elements of liberalization in central planning and decentralization in control were thereby introduced. In the context of these developments elsewhere, an appraisal of the nature and extent of reforms in North Korea's economic system patterned after the Soviet Union takes on special significance—particularly in the wake of North Korea's greatly reduced pace of economic growth since the 1960s. North Korea's unique record in this regard reveals much about the stage of its economic development and its sociopolitical environment.

While there have been scattered cases of economic "liberalization," these have been more than offset by countermovements that have brought the North Korean economic system closer to centralization. Greater reliance on nonmaterial incentive systems and the further strengthening of central planning are two most revealing testimonies of the trends. Political and ideological indoctrination, mass movements, and exhortations have been intensified recently as a means to motivate workers and managers. Nonpecuniary incentive systems such as the Taean industrial management system, the *chuch'e* ideology, the Ch'ŏllima movement, the Ch'ŏngsan-ni spirit, and mass-production campaigns like "Pyongyang Speed," "Kangsŏn Speed," "Carrying One More Load," and "Let's-fulfill-the-plan-as-a-present-for-Marshal Kim Il Sung's birthday," as well as translating national economic goals into so many "heights to scale," permeate every aspect of life in North Korea. More significant in its impact was the decision of the

leadership to tighten and strengthen central planning further through what the regime calls the "unified" and "detailed" planning system. This system was introduced, in the words of Kim Il Sung, "to further tighten the democratic centralist discipline in overall economic management and to develop our economy in a more planned and balanced way."

All in all, at a time when central planning is being significantly altered and the market mechanism is being increasingly enlisted, at least at the microlevel, in the Soviet Union and Eastern Europe, there is no evidence in North Korea of a general and consistent economy-wide trend toward reforms aimed at decentralizing the central planning. Except for minor innovations which tend to be stop-gap devices, the North Korean system has not diverged fundamentally from the Stalinistic command system which characterized the Soviet economy from the introduction of the first five-year plan in 1928 until about a dozen years after Stalin's death in 1953.

ECONOMIC DEVELOPMENT OF NORTH KOREA

Like South Korea, the North Korean economy has grown at a rapid rate since 1945 as measured by total and per capita national income. High growth has been accompanied by a fundamental shift in the structure of the economy and society.

Technically, national income in North Korea is different from the familiar GNP concept in noncommunist nations. Following the Marxian tradition, North Korea's concept of national output includes the value of income (output) generated only in the production of material goods and "productive services," and for this reason services not directly related to production and distribution are excluded. As a result, most personal and government services—passenger transportation, public health, private housing, and the like—are not included in national income calculations. In this sense, North Korea's national income corresponds to net material product rather than to gross national product, net national product, or national income at factor cost. This makes the conversion of North Korean national income into GNP very tricky and hazardous unless all relevant information is available for the purpose. Such information has been extremely scarce. Moreover, there is the problem of conversion into common currency. Official exchange rates used by North Korea for international trade (mostly bilateral) hardly reflect the market value of the North Korean *wŏn* in dollars.

Using official data, the North Korean national income in 1973 is estimated to have been 11.4 billion *wŏn* with a per capita income of 710 *wŏn*. At the official exchange rate of 2.5 *wŏn* per dollar, corresponding figures amounted to $4.6 billion and $284, respectively. Using a more realistic rate of 1.66 (or 1.2 as estimated by some) *wŏn* per dollar reflecting the purchasing power of North Korean *wŏn,* these statistics run to $6.9 ($9.5) billion and $428 ($592), respectively. Estimates by a US government agency show that the GNP of North Korea in 1974 and 1975 was, respectively $8.4 billion and $9.0 billion. The 1975 per capita GNP was estimated to be $545. Another US government agency estimates North Korean GNP and per capita GNP for 1976 at $10 billion and $590, respectively, in 1975 US dollars.

In terms of the rate of growth, the national income of North Korea in 1973 was 20.9 times that of 1946, 14.5 times that of 1953, and 3.1 times that of 1960. Translated into an annual average rate, national income grew at 12 percent during the twenty-seven years between 1947 and 1973 and 14 percent during the post–Korean War period (1954–1973). The corresponding growth rate of per capita income was 10 percent and 11 percent. While overall growth has been rapid, the rate of growth slowed down during the 1960s. National income growth declined from phenomenal rates of 30.0 percent and 21.0 percent, respectively, during the Three-Year Plan (1954–1956) and Five-Year Plan (1957–1960) to 7.5 percent (as compared to the planned rate of 15.2 percent) during 1961–1970. Per capita growth rates for the respective periods were 26.0, 16.6, and 5.5 percent. Slow growth in the first half of the 1960s compelled North Korea to extend the Seven-Year Plan for three additional years to 1970. Judging from a 14 percent national income growth reported during the three years between 1971 and 1973, North Korea appears to have recovered somewhat from the slow growth of the 1960s. The growth rate of 1971–1973 surpassed the 10.3 percent growth rate planned for the Six-Year Plan. According to the official announcement, North Korean national income at the end of August 1975 was 1.7 times that of

1970 as compared to the planned figure of 1.8 times to be achieved by the end of 1976—the equivalent of slightly more than an 11 percent rate of annual growth between 1 January 1971 and 31 August 1975.

Concomitant with a rapid growth in the total magnitude of national output there has been a dramatic and revealing change in the relative share of output, indicating the transformation of the economy from agricultural to industrial. Whereas in 1946 industrial and agricultural outputs were 16.8 percent and 63.5 percent, respectively, of the total national output, the relative position has reversed fundamentally so that around 1970 a rough estimate for industrial and agricultural outputs were 60 and 20 percent, respectively. This means that industrial output was recently three times the agricultural output.

Growth and changes in the structure and ownership pattern of the economy have brought with them changes in the labor force. Individual private farmers who once made up more than 70 percent of the labor force have been transformed into or replaced by collective farmers. Private artisans, merchants, and entrepreneurs have joined state or cooperative enterprises. Rapid urbanization has been another consequence of industrialization. Around 1970 the North Korean population was estimated to be distributed equally between rural and urban centers as compared to 1953 when 82.3 percent of the population lived in rural areas. The total population in 1976 was estimated to be roughly 17 million (at midyear) and had been growing at an annual rate of 3.0 percent during 1961–1976, showing a slightly declining trend relative to 3.3 and 3.6 percent, respectively, during the Three-Year and Five-Year Plans.

North Korea has made remarkable progress in industrialization. Her industrial output (gross industrial product) in 1973 was 528 percent of 1960 and about 110 times that of 1946. In the post–Korean War period (1954–1973) the annual rate of growth in industry was 22.6 percent. The trend has continued into the 1970s. According to the official North Korean pronouncement, the total industrial output in 1973 showed an increase of 60 percent over 1970, indicating an annual average growth rate of 17 percent during the first three years (1971–1973) of the Six-Year Plan. This is higher than the 14 percent rate of growth planned for the current economic plan. A high rate of 19 percent in industrial growth for 1973 and an annual average rate of 17 percent during 1971-1973 suggest that the North Korean economy has recovered from the slow growth it experienced at the inception of the Six-Year Plan. The latest official report indicates that the gross industrial product at the end of August 1975 was 2.2 times that of 1970 (as compared to 2.3 times planned by the end of 1976)—an annual growth rate of 18.4 percent.

Though the pace of industrialization during the Six-Year Plan, up to 1973, has fared better than the 12.8 percent rate of growth during the Seven-Year Plan, it is a far cry from an annual growth rate of 41.8 and 36.6 percent claimed, respectively, for the Three and Five-Year Plan periods. A complex of factors contributed to the differential growth during these periods—the nature of the North Korean command economic system, completion of reconstruction from the damages of the Korean War, bottlenecks in strategic resources, a heavy defense burden, cutbacks in foreign aid, planning errors, statistical overestimation of actual output, and the like.

Among economic factors, severe shortages in fuel and extractive industries and labor were said to be the main causes for the slowdown in the 1960s. Since the end of the 1960s an all-out national campaign to relieve these bottlenecks has been waged. North Korea brought three major responses to these pressing economic problems: first, assignment of top priority to developing the fuel, power, and extractive industries; second, a nationwide movement for technical improvements; and third, more efficient labor administration and deployment as a means to alleviate labor shortage and increase productivity.

Although progress has been made, agriculture has been lagging behind industry since the beginning of the regime in spite of a substantial and steady increase in mechanization, chemical fertilizers, irrigation, land use rate, and farm labor. The law of diminishing returns owing to the inevitably fixed supply of arable land undoubtedly offers one explanation for the poor performance. As is the case with the Soviet failure in agriculture, the lack of incentives on the part of collectivized peasants and the coercive nature of the farm organization and operation must also have played their part.

Also responsible for the agroindustry's development gap is a deliberate official investment allocation policy which favors industry, particularly heavy industry.

North Korea's total grain production increased from 1.9 million metric tons in 1946 to 3.9 million tons in 1960 and 7 million tons in 1970. The rate of growth in grain production fluctuated from 4.8 percent during the twenty-eight years between 1947 and 1974 to 5.4 percent between 1954 and 1974 and to 4.5 percent between 1961 and 1974. The greatest improvement in grain production occurred in 1974: an unprecedented 30 percent increase was claimed. Apart from the unpredictable nature of weather conditions affecting yearly harvests, it appears that intensified indoctrination and mass movements as well as recent innovations in farm policies have paid off.

These innovations include continued introduction of intensive methods of farming through multiple cropping, relatively extensive mechanization, and "industrialization" of agriculture. Following the more recently implemented policy of industrializing agriculture, particularly the livestock sector, modern "swine factories," mechanized and automated "dairy factories," and "chicken factories" have begun to be constructed throughout the country on a large scale. Large-scale canals and river projects to increase the reservoir and distribution capacity for irrigating paddy fields, increased electrification, and farm labor reorganization are other means used by the authorities.

North Korea's claim that it has become entirely self-sufficient in food is not true if one defines the term in the narrow sense that North Korea produces by itself all the food that it consumes. Economically, however, there is no reason why any nation should strive toward this goal as long as the nation has industrial and other products to pay for the importation of food. This importation makes sense, in fact, if one considers North Korea's lack of good fertile land. Thus in one sense North Korea does seem to have achieved self-sufficiency in food. Whether it has to give up industrial products or even rice is not the issue.

Although the total value of foreign trade has been expanding at a rapid rate, in absolute terms it amounted to only $1830 million in 1975 (exports, $755 million; imports, $1075 million). In 1976 both imports and exports declined substantially (exports, $555 million; imports, $825 million). (The decline in imports must be due to North Korea's poor credit rating.) Between 1970 and 1976 North Korean exports grew at 9.9 percent per annum.

North Korea has been a substantial net importer of cereals (mostly wheat) paid for partially by exports of rice, its main cereal export item. Interestingly, the neighboring People's Republic of China also resorted to imports in order to alleviate domestic food shortages while at the same time exporting rice to pay for wheat and barley.

Although North Korea trades with more than sixty nations in every part of the globe, communist nations headed by the Soviet Union and the People's Republic of China have been its major trade partners ever since the beginning of the Pyongyang regime. Since 1963, however, there has been a slow but steady expansion in North Korean trade with the noncommunist world, especially Japan and Western Europe.

In the mid-1970s the North Korean economy appeared to be facing serious and persistent difficulties with no easy solutions. The severity and the character of the problem can be gleaned from several recent developments. North Korea claimed that by the end of August 1975 the Six-Year Plan targets were fulfilled—one year and four months ahead of schedule. According to official statistics this is true for the total industrial output and a majority of industrial products. Individual products whose output fulfilled the plan targets include electricity, coal, chemical fertilizers, machine tools, tractors, textiles, marine products, and grains. Of the several important industrial products (pig iron, steel, cement) whose output did not reach the plan level by August 1975, the target output of steel and cement was fulfilled by the end of the final year (1976) of the Six-Year Plan by producing 4 million and 8 million tons, respectively. The fact that no mention was made of the total agricultural output as well as national income in the official announcements leads one to suspect that these targets were not met by the end of 1976.

In spite of the official claim for fulfilling the Six-Year Plan by August 1975, North Korea designated 1976 and 1977 as buffer years before a new economic plan was to be initiated. This is reminiscent of the Five-Year Plan

during which the final year was also officially named the buffer year. Designating 1977 as an additional buffer year rather than starting the next economic plan immediately is not only unprecedented but puzzling. Some observers conjecture from this that the North Korean economy is in such a serious state of disarray that the leadership has been unable to set feasible targets. It was as late as December 1977, two and a half years after completing the Six-Year Plan, that North Korea unveiled its Second Seven-Year Plan (1978–1984).

General targets for the new plan are lower than those of the Six-Year Plan and fewer details have been made public than for previous plans. Some of the major targets include raising national income by 90 percent (an annual rate of 9.6 percent) and industrial output by 120 percent (12.1 percent per annum). Output targets for major products are: electricity, 56 to 60 billion kwh; coal, 70 to 80 million tons; steel, 7.4 to 8.0 million tons; chemical fertilizers, 5 million tons; textiles, 800 million meters; marine products, 3.5 million tons.

North Korea attracted worldwide attention in 1976 by stopping payment of its international debts and requesting postponement of payment until later days. These were debts owed to Japan and various Western European countries. This apparently marks the first instance in which a communist nation has not been able to meet its debt obligation in dealing with private Western firms. This turn of events dramatized North Korea's severe balance of payments problem and depletion of its foreign exchange holdings. Several factors appear to have contributed to the debt problem.

First, in an all-out effort to complete the Six-Year Plan successfully, North Korea adopted, since entering the 1970s, a new trade policy of relying on Japan and Western Europe for advanced capital goods and technology. However, North Korea began to import Western machinery and plants with little regard for its foreign exchange earning capacity. Second, North Korea's expectation of expanded exports to the West was dealt a severe blow by the worldwide energy crisis, inflation, and recession. These factors also substantially raised the cost of its imports. Third, North Korea, anticipating a price rise in iron ores and zinc (which constitute more than half its exports), accumulated sizable inventories. When the anticipated price increase did not materialize,

North Korea incurred a heavy loss. Fourth, North Korea's allocation of priority to defense-related industries in recent years has diverted resources away from nondefense sectors, thus slowing down recovery and expansion in exports and other industrial projects.

It is estimated that North Korea's foreign debt increased from $1.7 billion in 1974 to $2.1 billion by 1975. If one considers that the total North Korean exports amounted to only $555 million in 1976, it is not difficult to see how far North Korea's debt payment capacity lags behind the debt and how serious is the country's foreign debt problem.

EVALUATION OF THE TWO ECONOMIES

The two competing economic systems that have evolved in the Korean peninsula appear to have been shaped largely by political-ideological factors and to a lesser extent by the stage of economic development. While South Korea's economy has adopted the modified market economy with strong governmental participation, North Korea remains one of the world's most centralized, socialized, and planned economies. In contrast to South Korea's reliance on pecuniary incentive systems, North Korea has become a mobilization economy attempting to raise production through heavy dependence on nonmaterial motivations.

The government plays an important role in both economies in terms of state ownership and control of enterprises, economic planning, and the state budget. But there is a fundamental qualitative difference. The government's policies and actions in South Korea are geared to affect the forces of the market within the basic framework of free enterprise. The North Korean leadership has rigidly adhered to the Stalinistic command system and has shown no inclination to introduce relaxation in central planning and control, as has been the case in Eastern Europe. Thus North Korea's experience runs counter to the pattern of a high correlation between the incidence of economic slowdowns and the timing of the reforms in Eastern Europe and the Soviet Union. The reasons appear to be partly economic and partly noneconomic. Students of comparative economic systems conjecture a positive correlation, other things being equal, between the stage of economic development and the vigor of instituted reforms as observed among the

countries of Eastern Europe and the Soviet Union. In this sense the lack of reforms in North Korea may simply be attributable to her early stage of development. More importantly and credibly, however, political considerations must have figured large in the North Korean response to liberalization movements in the communist countries of Europe and to their own economic slowdown. An economy-wide liberalization would not be consistent with the existing ideological, political, and power structure. Nor would it be compatible with the personality cult of the present ruler. Any regime which possesses the degree of doctrinal rigidity that North Korea manifests would fear that relaxation might open a Pandora's box and cause a loss of political control. The North Korean leadership may have decided that continuation of the centralized economic decision-making is a sure avenue to centralized political control (for military, ideological, and cultural reasons)—and, perhaps, the only road for the perpetuation of the regime.

The North is better endowed in natural resources than the South, although Korea as a whole ranks low among the nations of the world in this regard. South Korea has an advantage in human resources with roughly twice the population of the North. Owing to the continued confrontation between the two, both economies have been constrained by defense expenditures. North Korea's defense burden has been much higher with an estimated allocation of 15 to 20 percent of its GNP each year during the past decade. In comparison the South has expended an average of less than 5 percent during the same period. Moreover, its smaller population makes the alternative cost of maintaining a huge army even higher for North Korea relative to the South.

Both are committed to rapid economic growth through industrialization and have enjoyed a high rate of growth undergoing fundamental structural changes. In so doing both have progressed from predominantly agricultural to semiindustrial economies. This demonstrates that rapid growth is possible under divergent political-economic systems with different developmental strategies and with different results in human costs and distribution of benefits.

North Korea has emphasized heavy industry while South Korea has developed light industry for domestic and foreign markets with increasing attention given to heavy industry in the 1970s. South Korea has depended heavily on exports and foreign investment and technology while North Korea has extolled the virtue of self-reliance and self-sufficiency. In recent years North Korea has reversed its policy of autarky to some extent by resorting to importation of Western capital and technology. Ironically the new strategy has resulted in an accumulation of foreign debts beyond its capacity to earn foreign exchange. The international debt problem along with prolonged drought were among the major reasons for North Korea's inability to introduce the Second Seven-Year Plan in 1977. With an almost $10 billion debt at the end of 1976, South Korea's foreign debt is much larger. Because of the size and rapid growth in exports, however, South Korea is in a stronger financial position to repay its debt; the debt service ratio has declined from the level of 20 percent of its exports in the early 1970s to 11 percent in 1976.

A high-quality labor force has offset the limited supply of land and other natural resources of both Koreas. The labor force has been characterized by industriousness, adaptability, near total literacy, and a highly developed educational system relative to the stage of economic development. North Korea has been geared to technical education through a theory-practice concept in which the theories of the classroom are translated into active participation in productive activities. Apart from quality, the size of the labor force favors South Korea, which enjoys a large pool of unemployed and underemployed workers and low wages. Both Koreas have manifested a strong desire for achieving growth and modernization. They also enjoy a temperate climate.

Political stability, considered one of the preconditions of economic growth, and strong leadership by the central government have been essential components of Korean growth in both South and North. In the North Kim Il Sung has been an absolute ruler since the beginning under the monolithic Communist Party. North Korea has been generally free from the factionalism, revolutions, corruption, ineptitude, inflation, and unemployment that have demoralized and undermined many a developing nation. Such stability has probably exerted a favorable influence on economic growth. On the other side of the ledger, political stability achieved

under such conditions must have worked to dampen individual initiative and freedom. The beginning of South Korea's rapid growth coincided with the military revolution and the assumption of power by Park Chung Hee. It took the discipline of a military government to introduce aggressive economic planning which imposed austerity. Such stability also made the climate attractive to foreign investment.

Since the mid-1960s South Korea's growth has outpaced North Korea's. In the mid-1970s the South's GNP reached a level more than twice that of the North —enough to compensate for the South's larger population. As a result, North Korea, for the first time, slipped behind the South in per capita national income, an area where the North had kept an edge since the division of Korea. Several factors are responsible for the faster South Korean growth: its greater, better-educated, and better-trained manpower, especially in terms of economic planning, managerial skills, and technical and scientific expertise; its efficient use of Western capital and technology; its success in expanding foreign markets and foreign exchange generating capacity required for capital investment; and its ability to formulate disciplined and pragmatic economic planning.

To be sure, such international factors as a worldwide boom lasting up to the end of 1973 and windfalls from Vietnam War procurements have helped to expand foreign demand for South Korean products. The influence of Vietnam procurements on South Korea's development has been often exaggerated, however. South Korea received far less benefit from the Vietnam War than did Japan from the Korean War. Sales to Vietnam accounted for only 10 to 20 percent of current account receipts from 1966 through 1971. Moreover, South Korea's spectacular growth in exports and in national income continued after having suffered reverses caused by the oil crisis and worldwide inflation and recession of the mid-1970s. Factors other than these temporary phenomena are behind the rapid growth.

The remarkable rate of South Korea's growth has not been without serious problems which are expected to continue to challenge the economy in the immediate future. Severe inflation has been a fixed element in South Korea, although the rate was brought down to a more or less manageable level in the late 1960s and early

1970s. Many factors will continue to exert pressure on prices: maintenance of a large army; developmental financing by government budget; bank lending to finance investment; reduced supply of goods for domestic markets in order to increase exports; pressure from foreign exchange inflows arising from expanded exports and remittances from abroad; and worsening worldwide shortages (and higher prices) of raw materials, particularly oil. The last factor, along with the accompanying international recession, caused a sudden rise in prices that has persisted since the end of 1973, thus reversing a successful attempt to control inflation. Heavy dependence on exports and foreign capital for growth—and on the United States and Japan as principal trade partners—makes the South Korean economy extremely susceptible to external developments and introduces elements of high risk and instability. The same applies to high import contents of South Korea's exports and its chronically adverse international balance of payments.

Industrialization, accompanied by urbanization and growing output-per-worker differentials between industries, has widened inequality in the distribution of the benefits of growth in South Korea. Heavy concentration of export production in the Seoul–Inch'ŏn and Pusan areas for obvious locational advantages was one major cause of the widening income disparities among regions. Government labor and agricultural policies also have discriminated against the peasants and industrial workers. Pricing policies have been used by government to keep the cost of food and other wage goods low in the industrial sector. Restriction of labor union activities by government and its failure to enforce labor laws have helped employers to hold down wages while extracting long hours of work. Moreover, an increasing share of the growing output has been skimmed off for investment in further growth. The need to correct this growing imbalance was stressed in the Third Five-Year Plan. This is also the strategy behind the introduction of the New Community Movement *(Saemaŭl undong)* in 1972, which is intended to improve rural life.

In North Korea, dogmatic adherence to the Stalinistic model of a command economy will remain a stumbling block in the years to come as the nation attempts to transform itself into a truly industrial state. In the *extensive* stage of development, such a system probably

proved advantageous. At the beginning, the economy is relatively small. As the economy grows, the mathematical and physical complexity of planning and choice-making multiplies, making the slapdash nature of the centralized decision-making process progressively more inefficient and wasteful. The command economy is exceedingly well adapted for marshaling idle resources and manpower in the formative and reconstruction period when augmentation of efficiency is relatively unimportant in achieving growth. Sooner or later, however, as development progresses, opportunities for *extensive* growth—growth attained by expansion in the utilization of natural resources and unemployed or underemployed labor—diminish. As bottlenecks begin to proliferate, the economy has to shift from extensive to *intensive* exploitation of resources. At this stage the economy will experience diminishing returns and increasing inefficiencies. Further growth must come largely from raising productivity through the use of more advanced technology and greater efficiency. Nonmaterial incentive systems may work in the short run, but sooner or later promises of the future and fruits of the labor must be delivered to the workers. Agriculture appears to have suffered directly from the rigid North Korean system. Relaxation in central planning and liberalization in central control—along with greater reliance on pecuniary incentives and greater participation in international trade geared more for economic gains—might be one answer for continued future growth.

KOREAN ECONOMY STUDIES IN THE US

The study of the Korean economy in the United States is still in its infancy as measured by the number of specialists in the field, quantity of research and publications, and the sophistication of the methodologies employed. In fact, it has become somewhat of a stepchild in the Korean studies field (which itself suffers from underdevelopment). Furthermore, study of the Korean economy trails far behind the studies of the Chinese (People's Republic of China) and Japanese economies. The North Korean economy has received less attention than that of South Korea. In other words, the study of the Korean economy is yet underdeveloped both in absolute and in relative terms.

There are several reasons for the underdevelopment.

First of all there is the problem of language: Korean is required for handling primary sources, yet very few Americans have even a reading knowledge of Korean. This explains why the majority of Korean economy specialists are Korean-Americans. The language problem in economics, on the other hand, is not as acute as in disciplines such as political science, history, and anthropology. Many important economic data, particularly from South Korean government agencies, appear with English subtitles (for example, *Economic Statistics Yearbook* by the Bank of Korea). This is not generally true of North Korean publications.

Second, the scarcity of published economic data certainly inhibits study of the North Korean economy. The problem has worsened since the 1960s when North Korea stopped publishing economic statistics altogether, except for fragmentary information often clouded in indexes.

Third, very few economists become area specialists. Many Korean-Americans have written dissertations on the South Korean economy only to test more or less universal economic principles. Seldom have they become Korean specialists.

Fourth, the government, the general public, and scholars in the United States show far less interest in the Korean economy than in those of Japan and China. Undoubtedly the United States attaches greater strategic importance to Korea's neighbors in political, military, and economic affairs. This has adversely affected the availability of research funds for the study of the Korean economy, which, in turn, has inhibited study of the Korean economy.

Mathematical and econometric analyses have begun to be applied to the study of the South Korean economy in recent years. In the case of North Korea, however, lack of data has prevented the use of sophisticated quantitative tools. Indeed, the availability and reliability of economic statistics remain the thorniest problem faced by students of the North Korean economy. To begin with, economic data are extremely hard to come by due to the secretive nature of the North Korean regime. Further, the few statistics made available are more often than not fragmentary and misleading. Reliability of the little information that has been made available, therefore, poses a serious problem. Scrutiny of published speeches by political leaders in search of statistical information, often by reading between the lines, has become an unavoidable but all-important exercise for students of the North Korean economy as it has been for students of other communist economies.

It is strongly recommended that beginning students of the Korean economy read major works published in the United States. This task is made easier by the fact that there are only a handful of Korean economy specialists. For the South Korean economy the list should include Brown (11-196), Cole and Lyman (11-200), Hasan (11-202), Kuznets (11-212), Lim (11-217, 218, 219), and Renaud (11-139, 221). Recommended reading for the North Korean economy includes Brun and Hersh (11-227), Chung (11-039, 060, 087, 170, 230), Kuark (11-117, 145), J. K. Lee (11-172, 173), and P. S. Lee (11-146, 235, 236, 237).

Korean economy studies have just begun, and many challenging questions need answers. A few of the promising topics of research include: causes of growth, lessons to be learned from Korean experiences for other developing countries, the role of human capital in development, effects of rapid development (such as income disparity between regions and occupations), the role of foreign capital and technology in development, the role of monetary and fiscal policies in development, the role of foreign trade in development, and the long-run effects of heavy foreign dependence for trade, capital, and technology.

Korea offers a rare test case for evaluating the relative merits of capitalism and socialism. Competing economic systems with divergent strategies that produced a differential pace and pattern of economic development offer a unique opportunity for students of comparative systems and economic development to investigate all aspects of the relationship between the political-economic system and economic performance. But meaningful comparative study will require more data on North Korea than have so far been available. Perhaps the most urgent task is to reconstruct detailed and continuous national income accounts since 1945 if and when enough North Korean data become available. It is possible, however, even at present, to undertake a limited comparative study with available data and it should be encouraged.

BIBLIOGRAPHY

YEARBOOKS AND ANNUAL REPORTS
South Korea

11-001. Bank of Korea. *Economic Progress in Korea.* Seoul: annual. Reviews economic performance and change.

11-002. _____. *Economic Statistics Yearbook.* Seoul: annual. A most useful, comprehensive, continuous series of statistical information on the South Korean economy.

11-003. Hapdong News Agency. *Korea Annual.* Seoul: Hapdong News Agency, annual.

11-004. Korea, Republic of. Economic Planning Board. *Annual Report on the Economically Active Population.* Seoul.

11-005. _____. _____. *Annual Report on the Current Industrial Production Survey.* Seoul.

11-006. _____. _____. *Annual Report on the Family Income and Expenditure Survey.* Seoul.

11-007. _____. _____. *Korea Statistical Yearbook.* Seoul: annual.

11-008. _____. Ministry of Agriculture and Forestry. *Yearbook of Agriculture and Forestry Statistics.* Seoul: annual.

11-009. _____. Ministry of Health and Social Affairs. Office of Labor Affairs. *Yearbook of Labor Statistics.* Seoul: annual.

11-010. National Agricultural Cooperative Federation. *Agricultural Yearbook.* Seoul: annual.

11-011. United Nations. *Demographic Yearbook.* New York. Contains demographic information on South Korea.

11-012. _____. *Yearbook of National Accounts Statistics.* New York. Contains national income accounts of South Korea.

North Korea

11-013. United States. Department of Commerce. Office of Technical Service. Joint Publications Research Service. Excerpts from the annual issue of *Chosŏn chungang yŏn'gam* [Korean central yearbook] for the years 1958 through 1972. The most important source of North Korean economic statistics. For the JPSR serial numbers and publication dates see 15-017.

DOCUMENTS AND GENERAL REFERENCE WORKS
All Korea

11-014. United States. Department of Commerce. Office of Technical Services. Joint Publications Research Service.

Korea: An Economic-Geographic Study of the Korean People's Democratic Republic and South Korea. JPRS, no. 52032. Translation of the Russian work by V. V. Martynov, published by Moscow's MYSL Publishing House, 1970.

South Korea

11-015. Bank of Korea. *Quarterly Economic Review.* Seoul: published quarterly. Review of general trends of the South Korean economy during the previous quarter, particularly in the area of supply of credit and money and interest rates.

11-016. Korea, Republic of. Economic Planning Board. *Economic Survey.* Seoul: 1965–1971.

11-017. _____. _____. *Economic Survey of the 1971 Korean Economy.* Seoul: 1972. *Economic Survey of the 1972 Korean Economy.* Seoul: 1973.

11-018. LEE, Hyo Koo. "An Econometric Model of Korea: 1959–1970." PhD dissertation, Northwestern University, 1973. 201 pp. Abstracted in *DAI* 34(9)(March 1974): 5420-A; UM 74-7772.

11-019. SONG, Yoon Keun. "A Quantitative Model for the Korean Economy." PhD dissertation, University of Illinois at Urbana-Champaign, 1969. 218 pp. Abstracted in *DAI* 30(7)(January 1970):2685-A; UM 70-987.

11-020. REEVE, W. D. *The Republic of Korea: A Political and Economic Study.* London: Oxford University Press, 1961.

North Korea

11-021. *Democratic People's Republic of Korea.* Pyongyang: Foreign Languages Publishing House, 1958. A general introduction to North Korea including the economy.

11-022. *Documents and Materials of the Third Congress of the Workers' Party of Korea.* Pyongyang: Foreign Languages Publishing House, 1961.

11-023. *Documents of the Fourth Congress of the Workers' Party of Korea.* Pyongyang: Foreign Languages Publishing House, 1961.

11-024. *Documents of the National Congress of Agricultural Cooperatives.* Pyongyang: Foreign Languages Publishing House, 1959.

11-025. *Facts about Korea.* Pyongyang: Foreign Languages Publishing House, 1961. General survey of Korea including the economy.

11-026. KIM, Il Sung. *Report on Work of Central Committee to 5th Congress Worker's Party of Korea.* London: Africa-Magazine, 1971.

11-027. _____. "Report to the Fifth Congress of the Worker's Party of Korea on the Work of the Central Committee." In Kim Il Sung, *Selected Works*. Vol. 5. Pyongyang: Foreign Languages Publishing House, 1972.

11-028. _____. *Selected Works*. 5 vols. Pyongyang: Foreign Languages Publishing House, 1965–1972.

11-029. RYU, Hun. *Study of North Korea*. Seoul: Research Institute of Internal and External Affairs, 1966. Chapter 6 is devoted to a survey of the North Korean economy.

11-030. SCALAPINO, Robert A. and Chong-sik LEE. *Communism in Korea*. 2 vols. Berkeley: University of California Press, 1972. The most comprehensive and thorough book on the subject. Volume 2 contains two chapters related to economics: one on industry and the other on agriculture.

11-031. SHINN, Rinn-Sup et al. *Area Handbook for North Korea*. DA Pamphlet 550-91. Washington: Government Printing Office, 1976. Prepared by Foreign Area Studies of the American University. Contains an economic section made up of four chapters and bibliography on the North Korean economy. An updated version of the 1969 edition.

11-032. United States. Department of Commerce. Office of Technical Services. Joint Publication Research Service. *Translations on North Korea*. Washington: 1966–. Translations from all the major North Korean newspapers and journals. Results of amalgamating two previous translation series: *Political Translations on North Korea* (later *Translations of Political and Sociological Information on North Korea*) and *Economic Report on North Korea*.

11-033. _____. Department of State. *North Korea: A Case Study in the Technique of Takeover*. Department of State Publication no. 7118. Washington: Government Printing Office, 1961. Report based on interrogations of former North Korean government and party personnel and others plus captured North Korean and Russian documents. Includes survey of the North Korean economy before the Korean War.

11-034. YANG, Key P. "The North Korean Regime: 1945–1955." MA thesis, American University, 1958.

STATISTICS
South Korea

11-035. Bank of Korea. *Monthly Economic Statistics*. Seoul. Most useful, comprehensive, and continuous series of economic statistics covering principal economic indicators, money and banking, public finance, prices, foreign exchange, foreign trade, national income accounts, and balance of payments.

11-036. Korea, Republic of. Economic Planning Board. *Major Statistics in Charts, 1972*. Seoul: 1972.

11-037. _____. _____. *Major Statistics in Charts, 1973*. Seoul: 1973.

11-038. _____. _____. *Statistical Handbook of Korea, 1973*. Seoul: 1973.

North Korea

11-039. CHUNG, Joseph Sang-hoon. "Availability and Reliability in North Korean Statistics." *Asian Forum* (July/September 1973):117–126. Assesses the reliability and availability of North Korean economic statistics by checking internal consistency, input-output relationship, and pattern of data publication by the North Korean authorities. Concludes that, by and large, North Korean data are usable if handled with extreme care and investigated critically.

11-040. Korea, Democratic People's Republic of. State Planning Commission. Central Statistics Bureau. *Statistical Returns of National Economy of the DPRK (1946–1960)*. Pyongyang: Foreign Languages Publishing House, 1961. Collection of economic statistics covering population, index of national income, state budget, index of wages, industrial and agricultural output, transportation and communication, commerce and foreign trade.

PRE-1945 KOREAN ECONOMY

11-041. CHOI, Ho-Chin. *The Economic History of Korea, from the Earliest Times to 1945*. Seoul: Freedom Library, 1971. Pre-1945 economic history of Korea by one of the foremost Korean economic historians.

11-042. _____. "The Process of Industrial Modernization in Korea: The Latter Part of the Chosen Dynasty through 1960's." *Journal of Social Sciences and Humanities* (June 1967):1–33. Contains industrial history of Korea during the latter period of the Yi dynasty.

11-043. _____. "The Strengthening of the Economic Domination by Japanese Colonialism (1932–1945)." *Korea Observer* (Seoul), 2(4)(July 1970):49–79. Analysis of how "the workers and peasants of Korea were reduced from poor to complete bankruptcy" during the Japanese occupation period.

11-044. CHOI, Ho-Chin and To-Yong CHŎNG. "Korea's Foreign Trade under Japanese Rule." *Journal of Social Sciences and Humanities* 27(December 1967):19–44. Discusses Korea's foreign trade in 1910–1939.

11-045. CHUNG, Young-iob. "Japanese Investment in Korea, 1904–1945." In Andrew C. Nahm (ed.), *Korea under Japanese Colonial Rule.* Kalamazoo: Center for Korean Studies, Western Michigan University, 1973. Based on the author's larger study of the economic development of Korea. Analysis of Japanese investment in Korea from 1904 to 1945 and evaluation of its impact on Korea's early stage of modernization.

11-046. DALLET, Charles. *Traditional Korea.* Behavior Science Translations. New Haven: Human Relations Area Files, 1954. Originally published as the "Introduction" in his *Histoire de L'Église de Corée.* Paris: Victor Palmé, 1874. Based on letters of French missionaries to the author. Contains descriptions of general economic conditions during the third quarter of the nineteenth century.

11-047. GRAJDANZEV, Andrew J. *Modern Korea.* New York: Institute of Pacific Relations, 1944. A very useful source for descriptions of economic conditions and statistics during the Japanese occupation.

11-048. Japan. Government-General of Chōsen. *Annual Report on Administration of Chōsen.* Keijō (Seoul): 1907–1937. English-language publication with varying titles. Contains official statistics and narrative texts on aspects of the Korean economy under Japanese rule.

11-049. JUHN, Daniel Sungil. "The Development of Korean Entrepreneurship." In Andrew C. Nahm (ed.), *Korea under Japanese Colonial Rule.* Kalamazoo: Center for Korean Studies, Western Michigan University, 1973. Traces the development of Korean entrepreneurship during the Yi dynasty and Japanese occupation; emphasis is on the latter period. Included are such topics as commerce and industry in the last years of the Yi dynasty, economic policies of the Government-General, and entrepreneurship by types of activity.

11-050. KANG, Chul Won. "An Analysis of Japanese Policy and Economic Change in Korea." In Andrew C. Nahm (ed.), *Korea under Japanese Colonial Rule.* Kalamazoo: Center for Korean Studies, Western Michigan University, 1973. Shows that output did grow during the Japanese colonial period but failed to generate genuine economic development.

11-051. KIM, Kwan Suk. "An Analysis of Economic Change in Korea." In Andrew C. Nahm (ed.), *Korea under Japanese Colonial Rule.* Kalamazoo: Center for Korean Studies, Western Michigan University, 1973. Analyzes the pace and direction of economic changes in Korea during the Japanese occupation and explores the economic implications of Japanese colonial policies.

11-052. KOH, Sung-Jae. "The Role of the Bank of Chosen (Korea) and the Japanese Expansion in Manchuria and China." *Journal of Social Sciences and Humanities*

32(June 1970):25–36. A critical assessment by an economic historian.

11-053. LEE, Hoon K. *Land Utilization and Rural Economy in Korea.* Shanghai and Hong Kong: Kelly and Walsh Ltd., 1936.

11-054. MCCUNE, George M. *Korea Today.* Cambridge, Mass.: Harvard University Press, 1950. Contains considerable discussion and statistical tables on the Korean economy under Japanese rule in chap. 2 and elsewhere.

11-055. MOSCOWITZ, Karl. "The Creation of the Oriental Development Company: Japanese Illusions Meet Korean Reality." *Occasional Papers on Korea* 2(March 1974):73–121. Edited by James B. Palais. An interesting study of the huge agrobusiness corporation that was originally created to carry out large-scale Korean agriculture.

11-056. SHIN, Susan S. "Some Aspects of Landlord–Tenant Relations in Yi Dynasty Korea." *Occasional Papers on Korea* 3(June 1975):49–84. Edited by James B. Palais and Margery D. Lang. Refutes the popular conception of Yi dynasty society as being feudal and argues that, for more than two centuries until 1945, "land tenure in Korea had assumed the latifundia-minifundia pattern."

11-057. SUH, Sang-Chul. "Growth and Structural Changes in the Korean Economy Since 1910." PhD dissertation, Harvard University, 1966. 313 pp.

THE ECONOMIC SYSTEM

11-058. BREIDENSTEIN, Gerhard. "Capitalism in South Korea." *Internationales Asienforum* (Munich), 3(April 1972):212–234. Overall interpretation of the economic, social, and political situation in contemporary South Korea.

11-059. _____. "Economic Comparison of North and South Korea." *Internationales Asienforum* (Munich), 5(1974): 209–222. Comparative study of the economic performance of North and South Korea.

11-060. CHUNG, Joseph Sang-hoon. "North Korea's Economic System and Development: Recent Trends and Their Implications on Unification." *Journal of Asiatic Studies* 13(4)(December 1970):261–277. Also reprinted in *Proceedings of International Conference on the Problems of Korean Unification* (Seoul: Asiatic Research Center, Korea University, 1971). Summary of North Korea's economic system and development. Review of recent trends in the economic system and development "with a view to emphasizing those factors that might either hinder or facilitate any attempt at integrating the two systems (South and North Korea)."

11-061. _____. "North Korea's Economic System and the

New Constitution.'' *Journal of Korean Affairs* 3(1)(April 1973):28–34. Overall characteristics of the North Korean economic system based on North Korea's new constitution proclaimed in December 1972. The new constitution is a significant economic document; one chapter of its seventeen articles is devoted completely to the economy.

11-062. HAN, Sung-joo. "South Korea: The Political Economy of Dependency.'' *Asian Survey* 14(1)(January 1974): 43–51.

11-063. KIM, Il Sung. "On Some Theoretical Problems of the Socialist Economy.'' In Kim Il Sung, *Selected Works.* Vol. 5. Pyongyang: Foreign Languages Publishing House, 1972. Exposition of North Korea's official position on various issues including the economic system and strategies of economic development.

ECONOMIC PLANNING
South Korea

11-064. ADELMAN, Irma. "A Non-Linear Dynamic, Micro-Economic Model of Korea: Factors Affecting the Distribution of Income in the Short Run.'' Discussion Paper no. 36, presented at Woodrow Wilson School of Public and International Affairs. Obtained from US Department of State, Office of External Research, Foreign Affairs Research Paper FAR 16951.

11-065. _____ (ed.). *Practical Approaches to Development Planning: Korea's Second Five-Year Plan.* Baltimore: Johns Hopkins, 1969. Description of "a planning experience of highly technical caliber and considerable real success: the formulation of the second five-year Development Plan (1967–1971) of the Republic of Korea.'' It is composed of three parts ("Economic Perspective,'' "Planning Models,'' and "Plan Implementation'') with eleven articles by American and Korean economists. It is the outgrowth of a conference held in St. Charles, Illinois, in June 1968 under the sponsorship of the Ford Foundation-supported Council for Intersocietal Studies of Northwestern University. Contains a bibliography divided into "General Literature on Planning,'' "Literature on Korea,'' and "Korean Statistics.''

11-066. CHO, Sun. "Korean Economy and the Third Five-Year Plan.'' *Korea Journal* 12(3)(March 1972):14–17.

11-067. CHOO, Hakchung John. "An Industrial Analysis of Development Planning and Performance: A Case Study of the Korean First Five-Year Plan, 1962–1966.'' PhD dissertation, Clark University, 1970. Abstracted in *DAI* 31(7) (January 1971):3148-A; UM 71-13.

11-068. KICKMAN, Bert G. *The Korean War and United States Economic Activity, 1950–1952.* New York: National Bureau of Economic Research, 1953.

11-069. KIM, Hyon-cho. "Population and the Third Five-Year Plan.'' *Korea Journal* 12(3)(March 1972):8–13.

11-070. Korea, Republic of. Economic Planning Board. *Overall Resources Budget for 1974: The Third Year of the Third Five-Year Economic Development Plan.* Seoul: 1974.

11-071. _____. *A Summary of the First Five-Year Economic Plan, 1962–66.* Seoul: 1962.

11-072. _____. *A Summary of the Second Five-Year Economic Plan, 1967–71.* Seoul: 1966.

11-073. _____. *A Summary of the Third Five-Year Economic Plan, 1972–76.* Seoul: 1971.

11-074. _____. *The Third Five-Year Economic Development Plan, 1972–1976.* Seoul: 1971.

11-075. _____. Ministry of Public Information. *The Road toward Economic Self-sufficiency and Prosperity.* Seoul: 1966. Discusses the accomplishments of the First Five-Year Plan and lays out strategies for the Second Five-Year Plan.

11-076. LEE, Kie Wook. "Efficiency of Resource Allocation in Traditional Agriculture: A Case Study of South Korea.'' PhD dissertation, Vanderbilt University, 1968. Abstracted in *DA* 29(January 1969):2011-A; UM 68-17,980.

11-077. LEWIS, J. P. *Reconstruction and Development in South Korea.* Planning Pamphlet 94. Washington: National Planning Association, 1955. After reviewing previous recovery programs, the author offers "a workable reconstruction pattern'' and "needed supporting policies.''

11-078. NAM, Duck Woo. "Korea's Experience with Economic Planning.'' In Sang-eun Lee (ed.), *Report of International Conference on the Problems of Modernization in Asia.* Seoul: Asiatic Research Center, Korea University, 1966.

11-079. NORTON, R. D. "Planning with Facts: The Case of Korea.'' *American Economic Review Papers and Proceedings* 60(2)(May 1970):59–64.

11-080. United Nations. *An Economic Program for Korean Reconstruction.* New York: United Nations Korean Reconstruction Agency, 1954. A report prepared by Robert R. Nathan Associates under a contract from the UN Korean Reconstruction Agency. Represents the first major economic planning document for South Korea.

11-081. _____. *Rehabilitation and Development of Agriculture, Forestry, and Fisheries in South Korea.* New York: Columbia University Press, 1954. A report prepared for the UN Korean Reconstruction Agency by a mission selected by the Food and Agriculture Organization.

11-082. WESTPHAL, Larry Edward. "A Dynamic Multi-Sectoral Programming Model Featuring Economies of Scale: Planning Investment in Petrochemicals and Steel in Korea." PhD dissertation, Harvard University, 1969. 341 pp.

11-083. WESTPHAL, Larry E. and Irma ADELMAN. *Reflections on the Political Economy of Planning: The Case of Korea.* ILCORK Working Paper 3. Seoul: 1971.

11-084. WHANG, In-Joung. "Leadership and Organizational Development in the Economic Ministries of Korean Government." *Asian Survey* 11(10)(October 1971):992–1004.

11-085. WOLF, Charles, Jr. "Economic Planning in Korea." *Asian Survey* 2(10)(December 1962):22–28.

North Korea

11-086. CHUNG, Joseph Sang-hoon. "A Model of Post-Reconstruction Stagnation: North Korea's Seven Year Plan." *Asian Forum* 1(3)(October 1969):30–36. Analysis of the factors contributing to slowdown in economic growth during the Seven-year Plan coming after the completion of reconstructing a war-torn economy.

11-087. _____. "North Korea's Seven Year Plan (1961–70): Economic Performance and Reforms." *Asian Survey* 12(6)(June 1972):527–545. Assessment of North Korea's economic performance during the Seven-Year Plan and analysis and causes of slowdowns during the period. Includes an appraisal of economic reforms and their impact on economic development.

11-088. _____. "The Six Years Plan (1971–1976) of North Korea: Targets, Problems and Prospects." *Journal of Korean Affairs* 1(2)(July 1971):15–26. Analysis of the contents of the Six-Year Plan of North Korea. Compares them with those of previous plans and evaluates the strength, weaknesses, and potentials of the North Korean economy as disclosed by the comparative study. Also examines prospects for the economy during and at the end of the Six-Year Plan.

11-089. KIM, Joungwon Alexander. "The 'Peak of Socialism' in North Korea: The Five and Seven Year Plans." In Jan S. Prybyla, *Comparative Economic Systems.* New York: Appleton-Century-Crofts, 1969. Analysis of the outcome, problems, and effects of the Five Year Plan. Kim also touches on the Ch'ŏllima movement, North Korea's striving toward an independent economy, the outlook for agriculture, and the standard of living.

11-090. KIM, Il Sung. *All for the Post-war Rehabilitation and Development of the National Economy.* Pyongyang: Department of Cultural Relations with Foreign Countries, Ministry of Culture and Propaganda, 1954. Kim's policies for reconstructing the war-torn economy and call for an all-out effort on the part of the populace. Basic developmental policies are laid out for industry, transportation and communications, agriculture, forestry, cities, and education.

11-091. KUARK, J. Y. T. "Economic Planning in North Korea." Paper presented at the Conference on Korean Studies held on 6–7 April 1967 at Western Michigan University.

AGRICULTURE, COLLECTIVIZATION, AND PEASANTRY
All Korea

11-092. PAK, Ki Hyuk. "A Comparative Study of the Agrarian Systems of North and South Korea." In W. A. Douglas Jackson, *Agrarian Policies and Problems in Communist and Non-Communist Countries.* Seattle: University of Washington Press, 1971.

South Korea

11-093. BAN, Sung Hwan. "The Long-Run Productivity Growth in Korean Agricultural Development, 1910–1968." PhD dissertation, University of Minnesota, 1971. 243 pp. Abstracted in *DAI* 32(7)(January 1972):3518-A; UM 71-28,299.

11-094. CHANG, Oh-Hyun. *Land Reform in Korea: A Historical Review.* Madison: University of Wisconsin, 1973.

11-095. HAN, Hae-Bok. "Third Five-Year Plan and Green Revolution." *Korea Journal* 12(3)(March 1972):4–7.

11-096. KEIM, Willard D. "The South Korean Peasantry in the 1970s." *Asian Survey* 14(9)(September 1974):854–868.

11-097. KIM, Dong Hi. "Economics of Fertilizer Use in Production of Food Grains in Korea." PhD dissertation, University of Hawaii, 1971. 187 pp.

11-098. KIM, Hyoung Yul. "Development Administration: The Case of South Korea with Reference to the Agricultural Development Program, 1962–1973." PhD dissertation, University of Maryland, 1974. 358 pp. Abstracted in *DAI* 35(7)(January 1975):4666-A; UM 74-29,081.

11-099. KIM, Seyeul. "The Economic and Social Determinants of Rural-Urban Migration in Korea: A Case Study of North Cholla Province." PhD dissertation, University of Hawaii, 1974. 167 pp.

11-100. Korea Institute of Agricultural Economics. *A Study of Food Grains Policy in Korea.* Seoul: 1965.

11-101. Korea Land Economics Research Center. *A Study of Land Tenure System of Korea.* Seoul: 1966.

11-102. Korea University. College of Agriculture. International Agricultural Resource Research Institute. *A Study of the Regional Characteristics of Korean Agriculture.* Seoul: 1967.

11-103. Korean Agricultural Sector Study Team. *Korean Agricultural Sector Analysis and Recommended Strategies, 1971–1985.* East Lansing: Michigan State University Press, 1972.

11-104. MOON, Pal Yong. "An Analysis of Foodgrain Market in Korea." PhD dissertation, Oregon State University, 1973. 163 pp. Abstracted in *DAI* 33(9)(March 1973): 4637-A; UM 73-7841.

11-105. PAK, Ki Hyuck and Kee Chun HAN. *Analysis of Food Consumption in the Republic of Korea.* Seoul: Yonsei University Press, 1969. A report prepared for the Economic Research Service of the US Department of Agriculture under contract with Yonsei University. The study describes the findings of research on food consumption in South Korea during 1964–1967 and projected consumption for 1968 through 1971.

11-106. PARK, Young June. "Land Reform in South Korea." PhD dissertation, Temple University, 1974. 329 pp. Abstracted in *DAI* 35(6)(December 1974):3242-A; UM 74-28,383.

11-107. RHEE, Jae Han. "Inflation and Agricultural Development in Korea." PhD dissertation, Pennsylvania State University, 1971. 230 pp. Abstracted in *DAI* 33(1)(July 1972):47-A; UM 72-19,367.

11-108. United Nations. Food and Agricultural Organization. *Agricultural Survey and Demonstration in Selected Watersheds: Republic of Korea.* Report prepared for the Republic of Korea by the FAO acting for the UN Development Programme. Rome: UN Development Programme, 1969.

11-109. WIDEMAN, Bernard. "Political Economics of Factor Inputs in Korean Agriculture." *Korea Journal* 13(1) (January 1973):19–24.

North Korea

11-110. *Agricultural Cooperativization in D.P.R.K.* Pyongyang: Foreign Languages Publishing House, 1958.

11-111. *The Historical Experience of the Agrarian Reform in Our Country.* Pyongyang: Foreign Languages Publishing House, 1974.

11-112. KIM, Il Sung. "All Efforts to Attain the Goal of Eight Million Tons of Grains." *Pyongyang Times* 4(536) (25 January 1975). A speech made by Kim Il Sung at the National Congress on Agriculture.

11-113. _____. *Let Us Further Consolidate and Develop the Great Successes Achieved in the Building of a Socialist Countryside.* Pyongyang: Foreign Languages Publishing House, 1974.

11-114. _____. *On the Victory of Socialist Agricultural Collectivization and the Future Development of Agriculture in Our Country.* Pyongyang: Foreign Languages Publishing House, 1974.

11-115. _____. *The Results of the Agrarian Reform and Future Tasks.* Pyongyang: Foreign Languages Publishing House, 1974.

11-116. _____. *Theses on the Socialist Agricultural Question in Our Country.* Pyongyang: Foreign Languages Publishing House, 1964. A major official farm policy statement which has become a bible for agriculture.

11-117. KUARK, Yoon T. "North Korea's Agricultural Development during the Post-war Period." *China Quarterly* 14(April–June 1963):82–93. Discussion of North Korea's development in agriculture roughly between 1946 and 1959 in terms of farm investment, mechanization, production, the work incentive system, and land use. In addition, Kuark appraises the impact of the Flying Horse (Ch'ŏllima) movement on agriculture.

11-118. LEE, Chong-Sik. "Land Reform, Collectivization and the Peasants in North Korea." *China Quarterly* 14(April–June 1963):65–81. One of the early Western articles on the subject. The author describes the process, the political implications, and the peasants' reaction to land reform and collectivization.

11-119. MOAK, Samuel K. "Farm Management and Incentive Problems in North Korean Collective Farms." *Asian Profile* (Hong Kong), 1(3)(December 1973):440–456.

11-120. _____. "North Korea's Agricultural Policies in Collectivization." *Journal of Korean Affairs* 3(4)(January 1974):25–36. Review of farm problems and major farm policies of North Korea.

11-121. United States. Department of State. *Land Reform in North Korea.* DRF Information Paper no. 419. Washington: 1951.

11-122. _____. Bureau of Intelligence and Research. *The Role of Agriculture in North Korea's Development.* Research Memorandum RSB-105. Washington: 1962. An independent estimate of farm output based on internal consistency and crop yields and tested with observed food supply. Shows that the North Korean official agricultural output figures are exaggerated.

INDUSTRY
South Korea

11-123. BALASSA, Bela. "Industrial Policies in Taiwan and Korea." *Weltwirtschaftliches Archiv* 106(1)(1971):55–76.

11-124. BYUN, Hyung-yoon. "Industrial Structure in Korea: With Reference to Secondary Industry." *Seoul National University Economic Review* 1(December 1967):33–69.

11-125. CHA, Byung-kwon. "The Resource Allocation Pattern for Korea's Import Substitution Industries." *Korea Observer* (Seoul), 1(2)(January 1969):45–65.

11-126. CHUNG, Kae H. "Industrial Progress in South Korea." *Asian Survey* 14(5)(May 1974):439–455.

11-127. HAN, Kee Chun. *Estimates of Korean Capital and Inventory Coefficients in 1968.* Seoul: Yonsei University, 1970.

11-128. JEONG, Changyoung. "Production Functions in Korean Manufacturing: An Analysis of Trade Policy and Its Effect on Technological Change." PhD dissertation, University of Southern California, 1971. 135 pp. Abstracted in *DAI* 32(8)(February 1972):4196-A; UM 72-6068.

11-129. KIM, Kwan S. "Labour Force Structure in a Dual Society: A Case Study of South Korea." *International Labour Review* (Geneva), 101(1)(January 1970):35–48.

11-130. KIM, Young Chin and Jane K. KWON. *Capital Utilization in Korean Manufacturing, 1962–1971: Its Level, Trend and Structure.* Seoul: Korean Industrial Development Research Institute, 1973.

11-131. Korea Development Bank. *Industry in Korea, 1972.* Seoul: 1972.

11-132. Korea, Republic of. Development Research Institute. *Preliminary Review of Heavy and Chemical Industry Development Policy in Korea.* Seoul: 1973.

11-133. _____. Heavy and Chemical Industry Promotion Council. Planning Office. *Heavy and Chemical Industry Development Plan.* Seoul: 1973.

11-134. _____. *Heavy and Chemical Industry Development Policy of Korea.* Seoul: 1973.

11-135. Korean Development Association. *Effective Protective Rates of Korean Industries.* Seoul: Korean Development Association, 1967.

11-136. KUZNETS, Paul W. *Korea's Emerging Industrial Structure.* ILCORK Working Paper 6. Seoul: 1971.

11-137. Medium Industry Bank. *An Introduction to Small Industries in Korea.* Seoul: 1966.

11-138. RENAUD, Bertrand M. "Regional Economic Disparities and Economic Planning Policies Affecting Industrial Location in Korea." Paper presented by the Southeast Asia Development Advisory Group (SEADAG) on Korea, June 1970–December 1971. Obtained from US Department of State, Office of External Research, Foreign Affairs Research Paper FAR 19604-P.

11-139. _____. "Regional Policy and Industrial Location in South Korea." *Asian Survey* 14(5)(May 1974):456–477.

11-140. United States. Department of Interior. Bureau of Mines. *The Mineral Industry of the Republic of Korea:*

Reprint from the 1972 Bureau of Mines Minerals Yearbook. Washington: Government Printing Office, 1974.

North Korea

11-141. CHUNG, Joseph Sang-hoon. "The North Korean Industrial Enterprise: Size, Concentration and Managerial Functions." In Robert K. Sakai (ed.), *Studies on Asia, 1966.* Lincoln: University of Nebraska Press, 1966. Analyzes the process of eliminating private industry and introducing the cooperatization and nationalization of industry. Also discusses the managerial decision-making process as well as the size and concentration of industrial enterprises.

11-142. "Conversion into a Socialist Industrial State." *Link* (New Delhi), 16(6)(16 September 1973):41–42.

11-143. JUHN, Daniel Sungil. "The North Korean Managerial System at the Factory Level." *Journal of Korean Affairs* 2(1)(April 1972):16–21. Examination of the Taean managerial system at the factory level.

11-144. KLOTH, Edward W. "The Korean Path to Socialism: The Taean Industrial Management System." *Occasional Papers on Korea* 3(June 1976):34–48. Challenges previous views on the subject by showing that the Taean work system is an attempt to mold a Korean model of industrial management rather than an imitation of the Chinese or Russian systems.

11-145. KUARK Yoon T. "North Korea's Industrial Development during the Post-war Period." *China Quarterly* 14(April–June 1953):51–64. Review of the process of nationalization, industrial output, developments in selected industrial sectors, wage level, and foreign aid.

11-146. LEE, Pong S. "Overstatement of North Korean Industrial Growth, 1946–1963." *Journal of Korean Affairs* 1(2)(July 1971):3–14. Recalculation of the index of industrial growth between 1946 and 1963. Finds that the North Korean official index is overstated.

11-147. SCALAPINO, Robert A. and Chong-Sik LEE. "Industrialization and the Worker." In *Communism in Korea.* Pt. 2. Berkeley: University of California Press, 1972. A comprehensive treatment of development in industry and the workers.

11-148. United States. Department of Commerce. Office of Technical Services. Joint Publications Research Service. *North Korean Study of the Economy of Industrial Establishments.* JPRS nos. 1537-N, 1550-N, 1585-N, 1598-N, 1620-N. Washington: 1959. Translation of the Korean-language material of the same title. North Korean study on the various aspects of industrial enterprises. Covers such topics as "the system of computation and statistics," "fixed assets and production capacity," "current funds and supplies of equipment and materials," "original cost and price of industrial products and return," and "analysis of management activities."

11-149. United States. Department of Interior. Bureau of Mines. *The Mineral Industry of North Korea: Reprint from the 1972 Bureau of Mines Minerals Yearbook.* Washington: Government Printing Office, 1974.

FOREIGN TRADE AND ASSISTANCE
South Korea

11-150. HAN, Kee-chun. "An Analysis of the Relationship between U.S. Aid and Korea's Balance of Payments." *Korea Observer* (Seoul), 1(2)(January 1969):3–25.

11-151. KIM, Chan Jin. "Foreign Investment in Korea: Law and Administration." PhD dissertation, University of Washington, 1972. 329 pp. Abstracted in *DAI* 33(9)(March 1973):5209-10-A; UM 72-28,617.

11-152. KOH, Soo Kohn. "Commodity Composition of Exports of Manufactures from a Developing Country: The Case of Republic of Korea." PhD dissertation, New York University, 1973. 161 pp. Abstracted in *DAI* 34(8)(February 1974):4530-31-A; UM 74-1915.

11-153. Korea, Republic of. Economic Planning Board. *A Guide to Investment in Korea.* Seoul: 1972.

11-154. KRAZKIEWICZ, T. Mark. *Republic of Korea.* US Bureau of International Commerce. Washington: Government Printing Office, 1969.

11-155. LEE, Dae Sung. "International Trade in the Economic Development of the Korean Economy." PhD dissertation, University of Massachusetts, 1970. Abstracted in *DAI* 30(12)(June 1970):5124-25-A; UM 70-9857.

11-156. LEE, Hy Sang. "International Trade of South Korea." In Young C. Kim (ed.), *Foreign Policies of Korea.* Washington: Institute for Asian Studies, 1973. Study of foreign trade of South Korea "with an intent to delineate her position in the political economy of the world." Covers the decade between 1961 and 1971.

11-157. LIM, Youngil. "South Korea's Foreign Trade: Possible Impacts of Trade with North Korea." Paper presented at the 26th Annual Meeting of the Association for Asian Studies, Boston, 1–3 April 1974. Uses the Leontief input-output technique in discussing the potential commodities to be traded, the magnitude of trade, and the benefits to South Korea of a prospective South Korea–North Korea trade.

11-158. LYONS, Gene. *Military Policy and Economic Aid: The Korean Case, 1950–1953.* Columbus: Ohio State University Press, 1961. A detailed study of complex problems

of coordinating the economic aid activities of the UN Command in Korea and the UN Korean Reconstruction Agency (UNKRA) in 1950–1953. Lyons worked for UNKRA in 1951–1956. Appendixes include texts of relevant UN and US documents.

11-159. MOST, Amicus. *Expanding Exporters: A Case Study of the Korean Experience.* Washington: US Agency for International Development, 1969.

11-160. _____. *A Guide to Investment in Korea.* Seoul: 1974.

11-161. _____. *Korean Economy and Foreign Equity Investment.* Seoul: 1974.

11-162. PARK, Seong Ho. "Export Expansion and Import Substitution in the Economic Development of Korea, 1955–1965." PhD dissertation, American University, 1969. 165 pp. Abstracted in *DAI* 30(5)(November 1969):1700-A; UM 69-18,811.

11-163. REUBENS, Edwin P. "Commodity Trade, Export Taxes and Economic Development: The Korean Experience." *Political Science Quarterly* 71(March 1956):55–62.

11-164. United States. Comptroller General of the United States. *U.S. Assistance for the Economic Development of the Republic of Korea.* Series B-164264. Washington: US General Accounting Office, 1973.

11-165. United States. Department of Commerce. Bureau of International Commerce. Domestic and International Business Administration. *Foreign Trade Regulations in Korea.* Overseas Business Reports, OBR 73-66. Washington: Government Printing Office, 1973.

11-166. VOIVODAS, Constantin. "Exports, Foreign Capital Inflow, and South Korean Economic Growth." *Economic Development and Cultural Change* (April 1974):480–484.

11-167. WATANABE, Susumu. "Exports and Employment: The Case of the Republic of Korea." *International Labour Review* (Geneva), 106(6)(December 1972):495–526.

11-168. YANG, Yung Yong. "The Response of Korean Exports to Variations in the Effective Export Price." PhD dissertation, University of Oregon, 1974. 115 pp. Abstracted in *DAI* 35(8)(February 1975):4840-A; UM 75-3934.

11-169. YOON, Suk Bum. "A Macroeconomic Analysis of the Impact of Foreign Capital Investment in an Underdeveloped Economy: The Case of Korea." PhD dissertation, University of Pennsylvania, 1971. 254 pp. Abstracted in *DAI* 32(4)(October 1971):1718-A; UM 71-26,117.

North Korea

11-170. CHUNG, Joseph Sang-hoon. "North Korea's International Trade: Appriasal and Prospects." In Young C. Kim (ed.), *Foreign Policies of Korea.* Washington: 1973.

Analysis of the trade value, commodity composition, and direction of North Korean trade in the 1960s with emphasis on her economic relations with the major powers.

11-171. LEE, Chong-Sik. "Notes on North Korean Import and Export of Cereals." *Journal of Korean Affairs* 1(4)(January 1972):54–56. Analysis of North Korean trade statistics. The North was a sizable net food importer and, surprisingly, a rice exporter.

11-172. LEE, Joong-Koon. "North Korean Foreign Trade in Recent Years and the Prospects for North–South Korean Trade." *Journal of Korean Affairs* 4(3)(October 1974): 18–32. Analysis of the commodity composition of North Korean trade in recent years and a comparative commodity structure of trade between South and North Korea in order to determine the potential characteristics and scope of a South–North trade.

11-173. LEE, J. K. and Donald WELLINGTON. "North Korea's Trade with the West: 1956–68." *Journal of Korean Affairs* 1(1)(April 1971):25–33.

11-174. THOMAS, S. B. "The Chinese Communists' Economic and Cultural Agreement with North Korea." *Pacific Affairs* 27(March 1954):61–65.

11-175. United States. Department of Commerce. Office of Technical Services. Joint Publications Research Service. *Economic Progress and Development of Foreign Economic Relations of North Korea.* JPRS no. 878-D. Washington: 1959. Translation of the Russian work by Nikolai Ivanovich Samsonov.

FINANCE, MONEY, AND BANKING

11-176. AHN, Seung Chul. "A Monetary Analysis of the Korean Economy, 1954–1966, on the Basis of Demand and Supply Functions of Money." PhD dissertation, University of California, Berkeley, 1968. 88 pp. Abstracted in *DA* 29(March 1969):2847-A; UM 69-3555.

11-177. CAMPBELL, Colin D. "The Velocity of Money and the Rate of Inflation: Recent Experiences in South Korea and Brazil." In David Meiselman (ed.), *Varieties of Monetary Experience.* Chicago: University of Chicago Press, 1970.

11-178. CAMPBELL, Colin D. and Chang-Shick AHN. "Kyes and Mujins—Financial Intermediaries in South Korea." *Economic Development and Cultural Change* (October 1962):55–68.

11-179. CAMPBELL, Colin D. and Gordon TULLOCK. "Some Little-understood Aspects of Korea's Monetary and Fiscal Systems." *American Economic Review* 47(June 1957):336–349.

11-180. CHUNG, Joseph Sang-hoon. "Recent Trends in the North Korean State Budget: With Special Reference to 1971 and 1972." *Journal of Korean Affairs* 2(4)(January 1973):24–30.

11-181. First National City Bank. Seoul Branch. *Investment Guide to Korea.* Seoul: 1973.

11-182. GURLEY, John G., H. T. PATRICK, and E. S. SHAW. *The Financial Structure of Korea.* Reprint. Seoul: Bank of Korea, 1965.

11-183. JIN, Hyung Ki. "Stabilizing the Exchange Rates: Behavior of Floating Rates in a Developing Economy." PhD dissertation, University of Southern California, 1971. Abstracted in *DAI* 32(6)(December 1971):2849-A; UM 71-27,931. Focuses on South Korea.

11-184. KIM, In Kie. "The Sources of the Stock of Money in the Case of Korea, 1954–1969." PhD dissertation, University of Maryland, 1972. 202 pp. Abstracted in *DAI* 34(1)(July 1973):48-A; UM 73-19,039.

11-185. KIM, Jung-sae. *The Evolution of the Financial Structure for Industrialization.* ILCORK Working Paper 13. Seoul: 1971.

11-186. KIM, Seung Hee. "The Korean Balance of Payments and Economic Development." PhD dissertation, New York University, 1969. 246 pp. Abstracted in *DAI* 30(5)(November 1969):1720-A; UM 69-16,765.

11-187. KIM, Sung Tae. "Indicators of Liquidity and Debt Servicing Difficulties of Developing Countries: The Short and Long-Run Empirical Analyses." PhD dissertation, Catholic University of America, 1974. 224 pp. Abstracted in *DAI* 35(3)(September 1974):1341-A; UM 74-20,160.

11-188. Korea, Republic of. Ministry of Finance. *Outline of Banking System and Policy of Korea.* Seoul: 1966.

11-189. Korea, Republic of. Ministry of Finance. Office of National Tax Administration. *An Introduction to Korean Taxation.* Seoul: 1968.

11-190. KWACK, Yoon Chick et al. *Credit and Security in Korea: The Legal Problems of Development Finance.* Manila: Asian Development Bank, 1973.

11-191. LEE, Eric Youngkoo. "The Effects of Exchange-Rate Devaluation on the Dynamics of Inflation in Korea." PhD dissertation, Columbia University, 1973. 208 pp.

11-192. LEE, Seung Yun and Byong Kuk KIM. *Determinants of Money Supply and the Scope of Monetary Policy: 1954–1964.* Seoul: Research Institute for Economics and Business, Sogang College, 1968.

11-193. OH, Kwan Chi. "The Economics of Kye: An Informal Association of Individuals for Savings and Loans in Korea." PhD dissertation, Vanderbilt University, 1972. 116 pp. Abstracted in *DAI* 33(8)(February 1972):3924-A; UM 73-17,039.

11-194. PARK, Chin Keun. "The Role of the Exchange Rate in a Developing Economy: A Case Study of Korea." PhD dissertation, University of California at Los Angeles, 1972. 204 pp. Abstracted in *DAI* 33(1)(July 1972):55-A; UM 72-20,466.

ECONOMIC DEVELOPMENT
All Korea

11-195. CHUNG, Joseph Sang-hoon (ed.). *Patterns of Economic Development: Korea*. Kalamazoo: Korea Research and Publications, 1966. Contains four articles each on South and North Korea. A "Selected Bibliography of Materials on Korean Economy" was compiled primarily from Korean-language materials in the Library of Congress.

South Korea

11-196. BROWN, Gilbert T. *Korean Pricing Policies and Economic Development in the 1960's*. Baltimore: Johns Hopkins, 1973. Assesses the relationship between major shifts in economic policy and rapid economic growth in South Korea since 1963.

11-197. CHAPIN, Emerson. "Success Story in South Korea." *Foreign Affairs* 47(April 1969):560–574.

11-198. CHINN, Dennis Leslie. "Potential Effects of Income Redistribution on Economic Growth Constraints: Evidence from Taiwan and South Korea." PhD dissertation, University of California at Berkeley, 1974. 146 pp. Abstracted in *DAI* 34(11)(May 1974):6822-A; UM 74-11,887.

11-199. CHOI, Choong-shik. "A Study of the Structural Change in a Developing Country's Industrial Growth: The Case of Korea." PhD dissertation, Columbia University, 1973. 330 pp. Abstracted in *DAI* 34(7)(January 1974): 3643-A; UM 73-28,192.

11-200. COLE, David D. and Princeton N. LYMAN. *Korean Development: The Interplay of Politics and Economics*. Cambridge, Mass.: Harvard University Press, 1971. A joint work by political scientist Lyman and economist Cole covering political and economic progress and their interplay during the crucial period of transformation between 1963 and 1967. One of the few comprehensive books on the South Korean economy in English. Of eleven chapters, the following cover economic development: chap. 4, "Growing Economic Emphasis"; chap. 6, "The Dimensions of Economic Growth and Structural Change"; chap. 7, "The Causes of Economic Growth"; chap. 8, "The Patterns of Economic Policy"; chap. 9, "The Significance of Economic Planning"; and chap. 11,

"Lingering Constraints." Contains a six-page bibliography covering materials on South Korea.

11-201. HAHN, Youngki. "Foreign Resources and Economic Growth: An Alternative Model for Korea." PhD dissertation, University of California at Riverside, 1971. 166 pp. Abstracted in *DAI* 32(9)(March 1972):4791-92-A; UM 72-10,385.

11-202. HASAN Paryez. *Korea: Problems and Issues in a Rapidly Growing Economy*. Baltimore: Johns Hopkins, 1976. Published as one of the World Bank series of "country economic reports," the work concentrates on problems the South Korean economy has faced and is likely to face in sustaining a high rate of growth. Analyzes resource mobilization, resource allocation, and distribution of the benefits of growth. A 73-page statistical appendix provides ready reference for all aspects of the economy.

11-203. HONG, Sung-chick. "Intellectuals' Attitudes towards Economic Development in Korea." *Korea Observer* (Seoul), 1(2)(January 1969):26–44.

11-204. KANESA-THASAN, S. "Stabilizing an Economy: A Study of the Republic of Korea." *International Monetary Fund Staff Papers* 16(1)(March 1969):1–26.

11-205. KIM, Se Jin. "South Korea's Involvement in Vietnam and Its Economic and Political Impact." *Asian Survey* 10(6)(June 1970):319–333.

11-206. KIM, Seung-hee. "Economic Development of South Korea." In Se Jin Kim and Chang-Hyun Cho (eds.), *Government and Politics of Korea*. Silver Spring, Md.: Research Institute on Korean Affairs, 1972. Examines the role of government in the economic development of South Korea through capital formation during 1945–1970.

11-207. _____. *Foreign Capital for Economic Development: A Korean Case Study*. New York: Praeger, 1970.

11-208. _____. "Politics and Economic Development in Korea." Paper presented at Association for Asian Studies Annual Meeting, March 1972. Obtained from US Department of State, Office of External Research, Foreign Affairs Research Paper FAR 15768-P.

11-209. Korea, Republic of. Economic Planning Board. *The Korean Economy: Present and Future*. Seoul: 1973.

11-210. _____. *Major Economic Indicators of the Korean Economy, 1953–61*. Seoul: 1973.

11-211. _____. *Major Economic Indicators, 1962–1973*. Seoul: 1974.

11-212. KUZNETS, Paul W. *Economic Growth and Structure in the Republic of Korea*. New Haven: Yale University Press, 1977. The most up-to-date and authoritative work on the subject. Describes and analyzes economic development and structural change in South Korea since

1953 based primarily on quantitative information. Emphasizes factors responsible for accelerated growth. A must for students of the South Korean economy. Contains a twelve-page bibliography.

11-213. _____. "The Korean Take-Off." *Journal of Korean Affairs* 3(3)(October 1973):3–23. The evidence, causes, and consequences of the South Korean takeoff covering the period between 1953 and 1971.

11-214. LEE, Hyun-jae. "A Study of the Structural Change of Expenditures on Gross National Product in the Process of Economic Growth: With Special Reference to the Korean Economy." *Asian Economies* (Seoul), 6(September 1973):5–38.

11-215. LEE, Kyung-Sook Chang. "Korean Economic Policies and Economic Development, 1945–1960." PhD dissertation, New York University, 1971. 362 pp. Abstracted in *DAI* 32(8)(February 1972):4197-98-A; UM 72-3092.

11-216. LEE, Takyun John. "Potential Output and Sources of Economic Growth: Korea 1962–1968." PhD dissertation, State University of New York at Binghamton, 1971. 141 pp. Abstracted in *DAI* 32(3)(September 1971):1174-75-A; UM 71-22,698.

11-217. LIM, Youngil. "Foreign Influence on the Economic Change in Korea." *Journal of Asian Studies* 38(1)(November 1968):77–99. Exploration of the characteristics of the South Korean economy in historical context and appraisal of the foreign impact on the Korean economy since the beginning of Western influence.

11-218. _____. *Gains and Costs of Postwar Industrialization in South Korea.* Occasional Paper Series, no. 2. Honolulu: University of Hawaii, Center for Korean Studies, 1973.

11-219. _____. "Social and Economic Costs of Industrialization in Korea." *Korea Journal* 13(10)(October 1973):18–28.

11-220. LYMAN, Princeton N. "Economic Development in South Korea: Prospects and Problems." *Asian Survey* 6(7)(July 1966):381–388.

11-221. RENAUD, Bertrand M. "Conflicts between National Growth and Regional Income Equality in a Rapidly Growing Economy: The Case of Korea."*Economic Development and Cultural Change* 21(3)(April 1973):429–445.

11-222. RHEE, T. C. "South Korea's Economic Development and Its Socio-Political Impact." *Asian Survey* 13(7)(July 1973):677–690.

11-223. SHIN, Bong Ju. "Inflation and Economic Growth: An Empirical Study Based on the Korean Experience, 1948–1967." PhD dissertation, Ohio State University, 1969. 313 pp. Abstracted in *DAI* 30(10)(April 1970):4126-A; UM 70-6881.

11-224. SONG, Byung Nak. "A Theory of Regional Economic Growth: Growth Poles and Development Axes." PhD dissertation, University of Southern California, 1970. 275 pp. Abstracted in *DAI* 31(11)(May 1971):5651-A; UM 71-12,418. South Korea is used as a major case study.

11-225. WHANG, Byung-Joon. "Inflation and Economic Growth: A Dynamic Analysis of Deficit Finance." PhD dissertation, State University of New York at Binghamton, 1974. Abstracted in *DAI* 35(4)(October 1974):1857-58-A; UM 74-21,446. Uses South Korean data.

North Korea

11-226. BRUN, Ellen. "North Korea: A Case of Real Development." *Monthly Review* 22(2)(June 1970):25–37.

11-227. BRUN, Ellen and Jacques HERSH. *Socialist Korea: A Case Study in the Strategy of Economic Development.* New York: Monthly Review Press, 1976. A nontechnical treatise on North Korean economic development through roughly 1973 by specialists in international affairs with Marxian bias. Lacks critical analysis of North Korean official data and policies. Good source for North Korean views of economic policies and economic development.

11-228. CHUNG, Joseph Sang-hoon. "Economic Development of North Korea, 1945–1970." In Se-jin Kim and Chang-Hyun Cho, *Government and Politics of Korea.* Silver Spring, Md.: Research Institute on Korean Affairs, 1972. Survey of North Korea's development during the period 1945–1970 covering industry, agriculture, foreign trade, and the economic system.

11-229. _____. "A Model of Post-Reconstruction Stagnation: North Korea's Seven Year Plan." *Asian Forum* 1(3)(October 1969):30–35. Analyzes the nature and causes of economic slowdown since the beginning of the Seven-Year Plan in 1961.

11-230. _____. *The North Korean Economy: Structure and Development.* Hoover Institution Publications, no. 132. Stanford: Stanford University, Hoover Institution Press, 1974. The first comprehensive English-language study of the North Korean economy. It treats agricultural development (chap. 2), industrial development (chap. 3), foreign trade (chap. 4), and an overall evaluation of the economy (chap. 5). Contains two appendixes: one on economic plans and the other on the availability and reliability of North Korean statistics. The bibliography lists Korean, Japanese, and English-language sources on the North Korean economy.

11-231. JONES, P. H. M. "Economic Survey of North Korea." In *The Far East and Australasia.* London: Europa Publications, 1974.

11-232. KARSHINOV, L. N. *People's Democratic Republic of Korea: Russian Economic Study.* JPRS: 3822(1960). 81 pp.

11-233. KIM, Il Sung. *For Socialist Economic Construction in Our Country.* Pyongyang: Foreign Languages Publishing House, 1958.

11-234. KIM, Ilpyong J. "North Korea: Economic Development" *Problems of Communism* 22(1)(January–February 1973):44–54.

11-235. LEE, Pong S. "The Economy and Foreign Trade of North Korea." Paper presented at the Conference on Korea and the Major Powers, Washington, 1–3 May 1975. Developments in agriculture, industry, and foreign trade in the early 1970s.

11-236. _____. "An Estimate of North Korea's National Income." *Asian Survey* 12(6)(June 1972):518–526. Estimates North Korea's national income and the gross value of social product (GVSP) between 1946 and 1966. The author also discusses various aspects of the exchange rate between the US dollar and the North Korean *wŏn* with a view to deriving a purchasing power parity for comparing national income accounts.

11-237. _____. "North Korean Economy in the Seventies: A Survey." *Journal of Korean Affairs* 4(3)(October 1974): 3–17. Surveys a few aggregate series of the North Korean economy including national income and foreign trade in the early part of the 1970s.

11-238. ROBINSON, Joan. "Korean Miracle." *Monthly Review* (January 1965):545–548. A sympathetic article by the noted British economist after her tour of North Korea.

11-239. RUDOLPH, Philip. "North Korea and the Path to Socialism." *Pacific Affairs* 32(2)(June 1959):131–143.

11-240. _____. *North Korea's Political and Economic Structure.* New York: Institute of Pacific Affairs, 1959. One of the earliest English-language studies on North Korea. Part of the work appeared in the article the author wrote for the June 1959 issue of *Pacific Affairs.* The aim of the study is "to analyze how the Communist system has been applied to North Korea through an examination of the development of the major political and economic institutions in North Korea since 1945." Chapter 2, titled "Economics Institutions," treats industry, finance, trade, and agriculture using largely Russian-language sources.

11-241. WHITE, Gordon. "North Korean Chuch'e: The Political Economy of Independence." *Bulletin of Concerned Asian Scholars* (April–June 1975):44–50. Description of the origins and content of *chuch'e* and how this concept has shaped North Korea's economic policy. Challenges the view of "scholars in the United States, notably Chung,

Scalapino and Lee, [who] tend to present *chuch'e* as merely a defense-mechanism against the unreliability of the Soviet Union as an ally or aid-giver, or as a cynical tool used by Kim Il-song to discredit factions within the KWP."

LABOR

11-242. CHO, Yong Sam. *Disguised Unemployment in Underdeveloped Areas with Special Reference to South Korean Agriculture.* Berkeley: University of California Press, 1963. Examines various widely accepted theories of surplus labor and establishes "a more realistic and workable definition of surplus labor." With this new definition Cho proceeds to "develop a method for measuring true surplus labor, with rural [South] Korea as an example."

11-243. CHOE, Ehn-hyun. *Population Distribution and International Migration in Korea.* 1960 Census Monograph Series. Seoul: Bureau of Statistics, Economic Planning Board, 1966.

11-244. Chung-Ang University. Institute of Social Science. *Income Distribution and Consumption Structure in Korea.* Seoul: Chung-Ang University Press, 1966.

11-245. KIM, Han Keyn. "On the Role of Human Capital in Optimal Growth." PhD dissertation, Stanford University, 1972. Abstracted in *DAI* 32(10)(April 1972):5459-A; UM 72-11,585. Focuses on South Korea.

11-246. KIM, Hwang Joe. "An Analysis of the Interindustry Wage Structure of Mining and Manufacturing Industries in Korea." PhD dissertation, University of Massachusetts, 1973. 278 pp. Abstracted in *DAI* 34(10)(April 1974): 6207-A; UM 74-8563.

11-247. KIM, San-O. "Labour Force Structure in a Dual Economy: A Case Study of South Korea." *International Labour Review* (Geneva), 51(1)(January 1970):35–48.

11-248. KUZNETS, Paul W. "Labor Absorption in Korea Since 1963." Working Paper 16. Bloomington: Indiana University, International Development Center, 1972.

11-249. MCVOY, Edgar C. *Manpower Development and Utilization in Korea.* Washington: US Department of Labor, 1965.

11-250. MOON, Won-taik. "South Korean Labor and Labor Policies and Their Relationships to Developmental Administration." PhD dissertation, George Washington University, 1971. 262 pp. Abstracted in *DAI* 32(8)(February 1972):4699-A; UM 72-7606.

11-251. OGLE, George Ewing. "Labor Unions in Rapid Economic Development: Case of the Republic of Korea in the 1960s." PhD dissertation, University of Wisconsin at

Madison, 1973. 423 pp. Abstracted in *DAI* 34(10)(April 1974):6213-A; UM 74-3539.

11-252. SUH, Sang Mok. "The Determinants of Personal Income Distribution and Its Relationship to Aggregate Saving and Employment with an Application to the Korean Economy." PhD dissertation, Stanford University, 1974. 173 pp. Abstracted in *DAI* 35(5)(November 1974):2501-A; UM 74-20,240.

11-253. United States. Department of Labor. Bureau of Labor Statistics. *Directory of Labor Organizations in the Republic of Korea.* Washington: Government Printing Office, 1969.

11-254. _____. *Labor Law and Practice in the Republic of Korea.* BLS Series, no. 361. Washington: Government Printing Office, 1969.

11-255. WOO, Ki-do. "Labor Force, Wage Level and Economic Growth in Korea." *Asian Economies* (Seoul), 6(September 1972):12–51.

CHAPTER 12
Government and Politics

C. I. Eugene Kim

INTRODUCTION

THIS CHAPTER deals with the contemporary government and politics of both North and South Korea. Korea was liberated from Japanese colonial rule at the end of World War II. American troops occupied the area south of the 38th parallel, and Soviet troops occupied the region north of it. This division of the Korean peninsula resulted in the establishment of two separate governments in 1948—the Republic of Korea in the south and the Democratic People's Republic of Korea in the north. The period immediately preceding the establishment of the two Koreas is important for proper understanding of the dynamics and processes of contemporary Korean politics, as it bears directly on the two Koreas' initial state-building processes.

Government and politics are essentially about people —their values, aspirations, and interactions in the decision-making process. This chapter emphasizes a broad syncretic approach. It covers not only government structures and their operations but also the political dynamics and processes.

THE REPUBLIC OF KOREA
GENERAL

Since its establishment in 1948, the South Korean republic has experienced much political instability, punctuated by the Korean War (1950–1953) and its aftermath, frequent constitutional crises, student uprisings, and military coups d'état. Altogether, there have been four major constitutional changes and a succession of four "republics"; the last change, in 1972, resulted in the creation of South Korea's fourth republic. A reader who is interested in a one-volume work that describes and explains the whys and hows of these changes, however, may not easily find it. While there is no dearth of English-language literature on Korean government and politics, no single volume that would satisfy the needs of such a reader appears to be available. One must draw a composite picture from many different works that cover various topics and different periods.

Henderson's *Korea: The Politics of the Vortex* (12-012) may be the most comprehensive one-volume study of South Korean government and politics, but this book was published in 1968. Moreover, its basic thesis regarding the existence of a political vortex operating in a homogeneous, "mass" society is open to question. Recent general works that are useful include the books by Cole and Lyman *(Korean Development: The Interplay of Politics and Economics)* (12-006), J. Alexander Kim *(Divided Korea: The Politics of Development, 1945–1972)* (12-021), and Vreeland and others *(Area Handbook for South Korea)* (12-060). The books by Allen *(Korea's Syngman Rhee: An Unauthorized Portrait)* (12-121), John K. Oh *(Korea: Democracy on Trial)* (12-045), and Reeve *(The Republic of Korea: A Political and Economic Study)* (12-052) contain good treatments of the First Republic (1948–1960); and Sungjoo Han's

The Failure of Democracy in South Korea (12-009) is an excellent study of the failure of the Second Republic (1960–1961). The military coup of 1961 is well treated by Se-Jin Kim in his *Politics of Military Revolution in Korea* (12-024), and the political role of the military in South Korea is the topic of a series of analytical studies by John Lovell and C. I. Eugene Kim. Kyung Cho Chung's *Korea: The Third Republic* (12-004) has a good coverage of the Third Republic (1963–1972).

Since 1962, *Asian Survey* has annually carried an excellent summary article of South Korean events and developments, and these summaries together constitute a useful source of information. An article by Palais— " 'Democracy' in South Korea, 1948–72" (12-050)— successfully draws them together. Some useful collections of articles include Kim and Cho's *Korea: A Divided Nation* (12-025) and Wright's *Korean Politics in Transition* (12-063).

POLITICAL CULTURE, IDEOLOGY, AND POLITICAL SOCIALIZATION

Political culture refers to the attitudes and behavior that affect the way people perceive and act in the political system. Political culture provides a general framework in which the game of politics is played. People interact politically on the basis of perceptions molded by the general cultural framework in which they are born, brought up, and socialized. While they may be ideologically motivated in their behavior, such motivation may itself be a cultural expression.

In Korea, modernity is highly valued but the traditional norms of behavior still operate. Although democratic aspirations exist, traditional authoritarianism frequently governs interpersonal relationships and the decision-making process. When aspirations and realities are disparate, the resulting frustration may be manifested in popular distrust of government and politics. A significant segment of the population may become alienated from the political process. This feeling of alienation is shared particularly by students and intellectuals. With more education, people generally become more knowledgeable about government and politics. In South Korea, however, more knowledge has meant not increased political participation but increased political cynicism or a sense of apathy in the political process.

Political culture in South Korea is also characterized by diversity. Unlike North Korea, South Korea has no comprehensive ideology. The people are pragmatic and tend to go their independent ways. At the same time, the political process has long been highly centralized and bureaucratized, one of the legacies of the Confucian state of the recent past. The system of representation, a recent import from the West, is yet in its early phase of development. In this stage of transition, political integration of the leaders and the led is a difficult challenge.

Only a limited number of published works are available in this area. A good historical analysis of the centralistic, authoritarian political culture is presented by Henderson's *Korea: The Politics of the Vortex* (12-072) and Pyong-choon Hahm's *The Korean Political Tradition and Law: Essays in Korean Law and Legal History* (12-068). Some recent empirical works include Young-ho Lee's "The Political Culture of Modernizing Society: Political Attitudes and Democracy in Korea" (12-100), Sung-chick Hong's *The Intellectual and Modernization: A Study of Korean Attitudes* (12-073), Osgood's *The Koreans and Their Culture* (12-047), and Brandt's *A Korean Village between Farm and Sea* (12-065).

President Park's collected essays and speeches have appeared in several volumes that reveal both his own prescriptions for Korean modernization and the ideological emphasis in South Korea. Among works on political socialization, the most comprehensive and analytical is a doctoral dissertation by Sae-gyu Chung ("The Political Socialization of Selected Elementary and Middle School Students in the Republic of Korea") (12-067). *Source Materials on Korean Politics and Ideologies,* compiled by Tewksbury (12-056), and *Aspects of Social Change in Korea,* edited by C. I. Eugene Kim and Ch'angboh Chee (12-078), are two readily available reference sources.

POLITICAL LEADERS, LEADERSHIP STYLE, AND DECISION-MAKING

The study of political leaders is particularly important for gaining an understanding of progressive changes in developing countries because such leaders effect momentous changes often unfettered by institutional restraints and significant political input by the populace.

In developing countries such as Korea, we find the political input for decision-making limited and uninstitutionalized.

Studies show that the postliberation leaders in South Korea are generally those who are: (1) of middle and lower-middle social status, (2) primarily non-Confucian in their values, (3) predominantly Christian or have no religious affiliation, (4) educated in the Western tradition and familiar with the Western legal system, (5) of largely middle economic level, and (6) overwhelmingly westernized in attitudes and beliefs. Particularly since the 1961 military coup in South Korea, furthermore, South Korea's westernized elites have increasingly come to assume a technocratic orientation. They are task-oriented technicians and administrators engaged in problem-solving in increasingly specialized and compartmentalized sectors of modern society. The political leader, backed by the two most powerful political groups in the country—the military establishment and the civilian bureaucracy—has a vast array of de jure and de facto power and utilizes an extensive patronage system to reward and punish his followers.

Among works on South Korea's political leaders and their leadership styles, the books by Henderson (12-134) and J. Alexander Kim (12-147) are good historical accounts. Changes in the socioeconomic background of South Korean leaders over the years are statistically analyzed by Chan Kwon ("Social Backgrounds of the Emergent Political Leadership of Korea, 1948–60") (12-152) and by Hahn and Kim ("Korean Political Leaders (1952–62): Their Social Origins and Skills") (12-130).

For other general studies of the elites, the best recent collection of analytical works is Suh and Lee's *Political Leadership in Korea* (12-171). Complementing this volume are works by Young Whan Kihl ("Leadership and Opposition Role Perception among Party Elite") (12-136), Kim and Rocco ("Political Orientations of Military and Non-military Party Elites in South Korea") (12-139), Kim and Woo ("Social and Political Background of Korean National Assemblymen: The Seventh National Assembly") (12-142), and Mangap Lee ("Korean Village Politics and Leadership") (12-156).

"Political Elites and the Socio-Economic Development of South Korea, 1948–72" by Yong Sun Lee (12-157) and "Development Patterns, Leadership Styles and Popular Attitudes: Korea's Development Politics (1948–1972)" by Young-June You (12-176), both doctoral dissertations, apply a sophisticated quantitative analysis to show correlations between elite changes in South Korea and socioeconomic development.

Only a limited number of political biographies are available in English for South Korean leaders. Allen's *Korea's Syngman Rhee: An Unauthorized Portrait* (12-121) is a critical portrayal of Syngman Rhee and his First Republic of Korea, whereas Oliver's *Syngman Rhee: The Man Behind the Myth* (12-161) is a sympathetic account of Rhee. Sungjoo Han's *The Failure of Democracy in South Korea* (12-133) contains a good analysis of Chang Myŏn, prime minister of the short-lived Second Republic of Korea. For President Park of the Third and Fourth Republics of Korea, his many essays and speeches provide the best sources to the man and his leadership style. Chong-shin Kim's *Seven Years with Korea's Park Chung-hee* (12-143) is an insightful account of President Park.

POLITICAL PARTICIPATION, POLITICAL PARTIES, AND ELECTIONS

With the sole exception of the caretaker government headed by Hŏ Chŏng for a brief period in 1960, the reins of government in the Republic of Korea changed hands only through extraconstitutional means. This record is one that compounds the usual difficulties experienced by most new nations in creating the legitimacy and stability of governance. Peaceful transfer of power has been notably absent in South Korean politics.

Each succeeding regime has attempted to ensure political stability by means designed to reduce the power of opposition parties and groups. Denied a meaningful role in the political process and divided among themselves, the forces of political opposition have been weak and ineffectual. Under these circumstances, a series of interrelated phenomena, called the "opposition syndrome" by some, has been almost inevitable. The behavior of political opposition groups has often reflected a sense of alienation, a proclivity to oppose for the sake of opposition, a tendency to condemn any compromise and assume a dogmatic posture, and an emotional preference for violent means to effect political change.

Elections, though held often, have never resulted in a peaceful transfer of power. Nevertheless, voter participation has been moderately high. Interestingly, voter turnout is highest among the rural, uneducated populace. Rural voters are more susceptible to mobilization by the government and the ruling party than their urban, more politically sophisticated counterparts. It has also been shown that traditional ties of kinship and localism continue to exert a strong influence on voter behavior.

Generally, the process of political development in Korea has been uneven among various sectors of the society. The most highly developed political sector is that of the leaders; their political capabilities have increased to an extremely sophisticated degree. The most politically underdeveloped sectors are found among the rural voters. The leaders have used all available means to exploit the democratic processes in order to mobilize rural voters for maximum advantage.

A corollary to this type of elite–mass relationship is the low developmental level of various interest groups and political parties. While they do exist in impressive profusion, their primary role in political communication is focused on the downward, rather than upward, direction; in other words, they convey the decisions made at the center down to the masses more than they articulate and aggregate the interests of their own membership. Thus the political system provides for little input from the people; its emphasis is on output.

Political participation, political parties, and elections have been the focus of many empirical studies. Most of them, however, are article-length analyses and doctoral dissertations. A singular exception, perhaps, is Kwan Bong Kim's detailed study of the Democratic Republican Party of the Third Republic: *The Korea–Japan Treaty Crisis and the Instability of the Korean Political System* (12-220). Lee and Barringer's volume, *A City in Transition: Urbanization in Taegu, Korea,* is a significant study of various socioeconomic and political aspects of urbanization in Korea (12-234).

Some of the excellent article-length studies include: Hyo-won Cho, "An Analytical Study of Some Characteristics of Korean Political Parties" (12-181); Bae-ho Hahn, "The Parties and Politics in Two Koreas: A Pre-

liminary Comparative Analysis" (12-191); Ki-shik Han, "Development of Parties and Politics in Korea (12-192); Y. C. Han, "Political Parties and Political Development in South Korea" (12-197); Jewell and Kim, "Sources of Support for the Legislature in a Developing Nation: The Case of Korea" (12-201); Young Whan Kihl, "Urban Political Competition and the Allocation of National Resources: The Case Study of Korea" (12-206); C. I. Eugene Kim, "Significance of the 1963 Korean Elections" (12-209), "Patterns in the 1967 Korean Election" (12-208), and "The Meaning of the 1971 Korean Elections: A Pattern of Political Development" (12-207); Kim, Kihl, and Chung, "Voter Turnout and the Meaning of Elections in South Korea" (12-212); Kim and Koh, "Electoral Behavior and Social Development in South Korea: An Aggregate Data Analysis of Presidential Elections" (12-219); Kyu-taik Kim, "Statistical Analysis of the Elections in Korea" (12-222); Kim, Ham, and Yoon, "Korean Voting Behavior and Political Orientation" (12-224); Young-bok Ko, "Political Parties and Factionalism in Korea" (12-228); Chae-jin Lee, "Urban Political Competition in a Developing Nation: The Case of Korea" (12-229); and Joung-sik Lee, "Development of Party Politics in Korea" and "Voting Behavior in Korea" (12-232 and 12-233). Kim and Kihl's *Parties and Electoral Politics in Korea* (12-211) is a useful collection of some of these articles.

The following doctoral dissertations should be of special interest: Byong Man Ahn, "Congressional Elections in Korea, 1954–1971: An Analysis of Crucial and Normal Elections" (12-177); Ken Ahn, "Mobilization and Participation in Elections: A Study of Korean Voting Behavior" (12-179); Bae-ho Hahn, "Factions in Contemporary Korean Competitive Politics" (12-190); Chulsu Kim, "Parties and Factions in Korean Politics" (12-218); Loo, "A Comparative Study of Governmental Treatment of Interest Groups in South Korea and North Korea, 1954–1964" (12-237); Won-Taik Moon, "South Korean Labor and Labor Policies and Their Relationship to Developmental Administration" (12-241); Ky-moon Oum, "Urban Growth and Political Participation in Korea (1962–1973): A Comparative Analysis of 32 Cities" (12-248); Ogle, "Labor Unions in Rapid Economic Development: The Case of the Republic of Korea in the 1960's" (12-242); Han-shik Park, "Voting Participation and Socio-economic Status in the U.S. and Korea: A Comparative Study" (12-250); Sung-Chul Yang, "Revolution and Change: A Comparative Study of the April Student Revolution of 1960 and the May Military Coup d'Etat of 1961 in Korea" (12-257); and Suk Ryul Yu, "Role of Interest Groups in Emerging Nations: A Case of Korea" (12-261).

CONSTITUTIONAL DEVELOPMENT AND GOVERNMENTAL STRUCTURE

With the birth of the Republic of Korea, a Western-style constitution was drawn up and put into effect. This constitution lasted only for a short time in its original form, however. A series of amendments, followed by more basic constitutional changes, ensued.

Syngman Rhee was the first and only president of the First Republic under its presidential system of government. Massive student uprisings, protesting the March 1960 elections that had been rigged in order to keep the ruling Liberal Party in power, led to the overthrow of this autocratic government. The general populace supported the students' protest against a regime that had become increasingly discredited over the years. In the end, even the troops that had been mobilized to enforce martial law refused to fire on the demonstrators. Rhee was forced to resign and left for Hawaii.

Following Rhee's resignation, an interim civilian caretaker government headed by Hŏ Chŏng served until a new constitution was promulgated on 15 June 1960, and a new election was held in July. A cabinet system of government was created in the Second Republic under the premiership of Chang Myŏn (John M. Chang) of the Democratic Party.

Although the Second Republic was born in reaction to the autocratic rule of the First Republic, its leadership was uncertain about making democracy work in Korea and proved powerless against the multiple problems arising from the overthrow of the First Republic. The ruling Democratic Party, itself divided into two opposing factions, was unable to provide leadership and direction to the country. The Second Republic was overthrown by a military coup, led by Major General Park Chung Hee (Pak Chŏng-hŭi), on 16 May 1961. The military junta ruled the country for almost two and a half years before a new constitution came into force in December 1963; and Korea's Third Republic was created with General Park himself as president.

The Third Republic was a highly centralized administrative state, a development which reflected the junta's distrust of "politicians" and its own vision of a better Korea. Since the third constitution limited the president to two consecutive terms, an amendment was passed in 1969 by the National Assembly, which was controlled by the ruling Democratic Republican Party, to permit President Park's third term. President Park was then reelected in 1971. A year later, the government introduced sweeping constitutional changes which amounted to a coup in office. Thus was the Fourth Republic of Korea created.

Only a limited number of studies are available in the area of South Korean constitutional development and governmental structure. Governmental structure itself is adequately treated, however, by the *Korea Annual,* which, though largely descriptive, is based on up-to-date information. The system of local government is studied in detail by Chang-Hyun Cho in his doctoral dissertation ("The System of Local Government in South Korea as Affected by Patterns of Centralized Control") (12-263). Kim and Cho's *Korea: A Divided Nation* (12-280) and Wright's *Korean Politics in Transition* (12-063) also contain articles on the constitutional system of South Korea.

Some useful and critical analyses of the constitutional development include: C. I. Eugene Kim, "South Korean Constitutional Development: The Meaning of the Third Constitution" (12-272) and "Korea at the Crossroads: The Birth of the Fourth Republic" (12-273); Y. C. Han, "The 1969 Constitutional Revision and Party Politics in South Korea" (12-269); and Chi-Young Pak, "The Third Republic Constitution of Korea: An Analysis" (12-283). Kyu Sung Kim's doctoral dissertation, "The History of Constitutional Development in the Republic of Korea 1948–1972" (12-279) is the most comprehensive work thus far. Kyung Cho Chung's *Korea: The Third Republic* (12-004) has a good coverage of the constitutional structure of the Third Republic.

PUBLIC ADMINISTRATION, BUREAUCRACY, AND
GOVERNMENT PERFORMANCE

South Korea maintains a large civilian bureaucracy. Constitutionally, bureaucrats exist to serve the people, but Korea has traditionally been a bureaucrat-dominant system.

Bureaucratic positions are highly desired and they are filled competitively, very often by graduates of the country's prestigious universities. Many positions have also been filled in recent years by retired military officers. Public bureaucracy has too often been politically manipulated, however, and has failed to maintain political neutrality. It has too often been identified with the party in power. Under the supreme leader, it has proved an effective tool for carrying out his orders.

South Korea has recently experienced a remarkable rate of economic development. The government has proved itself capable not only of meeting challenges to its power but also of accomplishing rather ambitious goals for economic development. It has been willing to experiment, and its successive five-year plans and New Community Movement *(Saemaŭl undong)* have been effectual. South Korea today represents a most dynamic growth economy.

A large number of studies have been published on public administration, bureaucracy, and government performance in South Korea. An excellent analysis of the role performed by high civil servants in South Korea's development is Hahn-Been Lee's *Korea: Time, Change and Administration* (12-311). The same theme is also emphasized by In-joung Whang's "Elites and Economic Programs: A Study of Changing Leadership for Economic Development in Korea 1955–1967" (12-336) and Yong-Sun Lee's "Political Elites and Socio-Economic Development of South Korea, 1948–1972" (12-314)—both doctoral dissertations. Another excellent study which highlights Korean development is *Korean Development: The Interplay of Politics and Economics* by Cole and Lyman (12-295). More critical of the South Korean developmental pattern are doctoral dissertations by Bom Hu ("A Social Information System for National Development Planning of a Developing Country: Korea") (12-298) and Doh Chull Shin ("Socio-Economic Development and Democratization in the South: A Time-Series Analysis") (12-332) and an article by Wideman ("The Plight of the South Korean Peasant") (12-340).

Other useful studies on public administration and bureaucracy include: Dong-suh Bark, "Comparison of Administration under Different Ideologies" (12-287); Chung and Pae, "Orientation of the Korean Bureaucrats toward Democracy: A Study of Background and Institutional Characteristics" (12-294); and Lee and Bark, "Political Perception of Bureaucratic Elites in Korea" (12-309). In addition, B. C. Koh's *Aspects of Administrative Development in South Korea* (12-306) and Wright's *Korean Politics in Transition* (12-342) present a good collection of articles for ready use. Doctoral dissertations by Wanki Paik ("Modernization of Korean Bureaucracy") (12-324) and Woo-kon Yoon ("The Effect of Personality on Bureaucrats' Behavior in the Case of South Korea") (12-347) are useful additions to the field.

THE DEMOCRATIC PEOPLE'S REPUBLIC OF KOREA
GENERAL

The Democratic People's Republic of Korea (DPRK) was established in 1948 as a communist system based on the Soviet pattern. Kim Il Sung (Kim Il-sŏng), then in his early thirties, was placed at the helm of this regime. Earlier, Kim had led anti-Japanese guerrilla fighters active in the Manchurian-Korean border area. Later, in the early 1940s, he had moved to Siberia and from there was brought to Korea in 1945 together with the Soviet-Korean members of the Soviet occupation forces. Why was Kim selected and not somebody else, perhaps someone older, more mature, and established? By what process was he selected? These are questions that remain unanswered. Clear enough, however, is the fact that Kim's leadership forcefully molded the subsequent North Korean development.

At the outset, Kim was not without rivals. He had three communist groups to contend with: the domestic communist group, the so-called Yenan group from China, and the Soviet-Korean group. Kim found his initial power base, supported by the Soviet occupation authorities, among the Soviet-Korean group, but subsequent loyal followers were comrades of his earlier guerrilla days on the Manchurian-Korean border.

Kim's achievement of power early in the history of the DPRK insulated the regime from constitutional instability. As supreme leader, Kim has been able to monopolize political power. He has performed chief executive functions as premier (1948–1972) and as president (since 1972) under the new constitution; he has effectively headed the Workers' Party of Korea (Korean Communist Party) since its establishment in 1949; and he has been commander in chief of the armed forces. Even the tragic consequences of the misguided Korean War could not dislocate his power and supreme leadership position. Kim's monocratic position in the North Korean power hierarchy has not only made him an absolute leader but has also enabled him to elevate his family members to influential political positions. Under Kim, North Korea today is a highly mobilized state that remains militant in its determination to reunify the Korean peninsula under communist rule.

Works on North Korea are much more limited in number and scope than those on South Korea, since the closed nature of the North Korean political system denies easy access to outside researchers. North Korean studies have, however, produced a seminal work by Scalapino and Lee *(Communism in Korea)* (12-394). This two-volume work is thus far the most comprehensive, in-depth analysis of the North Korean system. Those interested in shorter but useful general treatments may consult the following books: J. Alexander Kim, *Divided Korea: The Politics of Development, 1945–1972* (12-367); Ilpyong J. Kim, *Communist Politics in North Korea* (12-366); Paige, *The Korean People's Democratic Republic* (12-385); and Vreeland and others, *Area Handbook for North Korea* (12-402). Students may also wish to compare the contrasting views on North Korea presented by Hun Ryu, *Study of North Korea* (12-391), and Brun and Hersh, *Socialist Korea: A Case Study in the Strategy of Economic Development* (12-350). Some useful articles are collected in Kim and Cho's *Korea: A Divided Nation* (12-370) and Scalapino's *North Korea Today* (12-393).

As on South Korea, *Asian Survey* has published an-

nual survey articles on North Korea since 1963. These excellent articles taken together provide a composite picture of recent North Korean events and developments. For a short introduction to North Korea, articles by Chong-Sik Lee ("Stalinism in the East: Communism in North Korea") (12-382) and Bae-ho Hahn ("Toward a Comparative Analysis of the South and North Korean Systems") (12-357) are also excellent.

POLITICAL CULTURE, IDEOLOGY, AND POLITICAL SOCIALIZATION

Words and examples of Kim Il Sung form the supreme guidelines for socialist action in North Korea. The population has been regimented in a military pattern and organized into production units. Agriculture and industry are collectivized; personal desires are subordinated to collective needs. Instead of more consumer goods, Kim has called for more austerity and patriotic demonstrations. The people have constantly been exhorted to produce more, purportedly in order to help their brethren in the South.

Out of the chaos following Korea's liberation, Kim has created a new political culture in the North. It is a totalitarian culture singularly guided by the personality cult of Kim himself. Since the establishment of the DPRK some thirty years ago, Kim has created a new Korean Communist personality, totalitarian and highly mobilized. All socializing agents—the family, schools, work places, communications media—have been mobilized for this purpose.

One major political theme in the North is *chuch'e*—meaning the independent solution of all revolutionary and nation-building problems in accordance with actual conditions in Korea. *Chuch'e* rejects dependency on both the USSR and the People's Republic of China, emphasizing North Korean political sovereignty and calling for a self-sufficient economy and self-defense. Since its first enunciation in December 1955, it has become increasingly an expression of the nationalistic sentiment of the North Korean people.

The importance of political culture, ideology, and political socialization in North Korea is reflected in a relatively large number of studies on these subjects. However, the collection of Kim Il Sung's speeches and writings edited by Yuk-sa Li, *Juche: The Speeches and Writings of Kim Il-sung* (12-422) is still the best one-volume reading on the *chuch'e* ideology. A five-volume set of Kim's selected works is also available. More analytical works include those by Scalapino and Lee, *Communism in Korea* (12-426); Ilpyong J. Kim, *Communist Politics in North Korea* (12-412); Cumings, "Kim's Korean Communism" (12-407); and B. C. Koh, "Chuch'esŏng in Korean Politics" (12-417) and "Ideology and Political Control in North Korea" (12-418). Useful articles and doctoral dissertations on eduction and political socialization include works by Hyung-chan Kim, "Ideology and Indoctrination in the Development of North Korean Education" (12-410); Sun Ho Kim, "Education in North Korea: Technical, Manpower and Ideological Development" (12-414); Young-horm Park, "The School System of North Korea" (12-424); and Yang and Chee, "The North Korean Educational System: 1945 to Present" (12-428).

POLITICAL LEADERS, LEADERSHIP STYLE, AND DECISION-MAKING

In North Korea, the cult of Kim Il Sung reigns unchallenged. In his mid-60's, he remains a dynamic figure with unchecked personal power. The decision-making process, in which only a limited circle of his loyal followers participates, is marked by the heavy imprint of his own personality and the *chuch'e* idea.

Chuch'e claims that the North Korean people, guided by the hero of Korea's anti-imperialist revolution, are more nationalistic than the South Koreans, who are still protected by the American "imperialist." It asserts that South Korea needs national liberation under the North Korean leadership. In this way, *chuch'e* is intended to replicate in Korea the successes of Chinese and Vietnamese national liberation. *Chuch'e,* however, disguises to some extent the foreign origin of the North Korean system and Kim's adaptation of the successful Chinese and Vietnamese formula of revolution for communization of the whole Korean peninsula.

The "mass line" approach is Kim's technique of mobilizing the masses. The masses must be educated to become dedicated members of the society and transformed into revolutionaries for a new communist Korea. This approach also strongly emphasizes closing the gap between leaders and the led. What is often called the *Ch'ŏngsan-ni* method states that "the higher organ helps the lower; the superior assists his inferiors and always goes down to work areas in order to get a good grasp of actual conditions." This method was enunciated in connection with the reorganization of management and administration of agricultural cooperatives. The Taean system, on the other hand, was implemented to encourage greater participation of industrial workers in management.

Voluminous North Korean publications are available on Kim Il Sung. These works, epitomized by Bong Baik's three-volume work *(Kim Il Sung: Biography)* (12-430), are unswerving in the adulation of their hero. More balanced assessments of Kim and his leadership style are found in: J. Alexander Kim, *Divided Korea: The Politics of Development, 1945–1972* (12-367); Ilpyong J. Kim, *Communist Politics in North Korea* (12-366); Scalapino and Lee, *Communism in Korea* (12-394); Koon Woo Nam, *The North Korean Communist Leadership, 1945–1965* (12-462); and Dae-Sook Suh, *The Korean Communist Movement, 1918–1948* (12-465). Other studies on leadership and decision-making in North Korea are limited in number, but some useful works include: Nam-shik Kim, "The Decision-Making Process in the Foreign Policy of North Korea" (12-444); Tae-ho Kim, "The Ruling System of the North Korean Regime" (12-446); B. C. Koh, *The Foreign Policy of North Korea* (12-450); articles by Chong-Sik Lee and Dae-Sook Suh in Suh and Lee (eds.), *Political Leadership in Korea* (12-467); and Ho-min Yang, "The Personality Cult of Kim Il-sŏng as a Strategy for National Unification" (12-470). Also highly recommended is an interesting participant account of North Korean negotiating behavior by Charles Turner Joy: *How Communists Negotiate* (12-433).

POLITICAL PARTICIPATION, POLITICAL PARTIES, AND ELECTIONS

In North Korea, the Workers' Party of Korea is the leading organ of power. Other major organizations include the military structure and civilian government bureaucracy. Kim Il Sung, as supreme leader, heads all three.

While elections are held in North Korea, no party opposed to the Workers' Party is tolerated. Organized on the principle of democratic centralism, the masses are encouraged to interact in decision-making at the primary level.

Research on North Korean political participation, political parties, and elections—subjects which carry different meanings in North and South Korea—suffers from the closed nature of the North Korean political system. No empirical studies have been possible. Among useful works, however, Bae-ho Hahn's "The Parties and the Politics in Two Koreas: A Preliminary Comparative Analysis" (12-191) should be read by anyone interested in this field. This and other useful articles are collected in Kim and Kihl's *Parties and Electoral Politics in Korea* (12-480). A good coverage of this area is also found in Scalapino and Lee, *Communism in Korea* (12-394); US Army Joint Publications Research Service, *On Party Leadership, Training, and Policy Implementation in North Korea* (12-495); Loo, "A Comparative Study of Governmental Treatment of Interest Groups in South Korea and North Korea, 1954–1964" (12-489); Ch'ang-sun Kim, "The North Korean Communist Party: Historical Analysis" (12-481); and Dae-Sook Suh, "Communist Party Leadership" in Suh and Lee's *Political Leadership in Korea* (12-467).

Constitutional Development and Government Structure

Kim Il Sung's undisputed leadership rapidly filled the postwar political vacuum in North Korea and provided for much more unity and stability than in the South.

Initially structured along the Soviet line, the North Korean constitutional system experienced little change until 1972, when wholesale revision was undertaken. The purpose of this revision was to institutionalize Kim's supreme leadership position. Whereas he had earlier been the premier of the North Korean state, Kim was made president in the 1972 constitution. Under Kim, North Korea remains a tightly regimented garrison state. Party and government are present in every aspect of people's lives.

Only a limited number of publications are available that deal exclusively with North Korean constitutional development and governmental structure. The following works, however, provide sufficiently useful cover-

age of the field: Scalapino and Lee, *Communism in Korea* (12-510); Chong-sik Lee, "The 1972 Constitution and Top Communist Leaders" (12-507); Tae-suh Kim, "North Korea's New Constitution and New Power Structure" (12-506); Bae-ho Hahn, "Toward a Comparative Analysis of the South and North Korean Political Systems" (12-501); Sung Yoon Cho, "The Judicial System of North Korea" (12-499); and Koo-chin Kang, "Comparison of the Legal System between North and South Korea" (12-502). Kim and Cho's *Korea: A Divided Nation* (12-504) also contains useful articles for ready use.

Public Administration, Bureaucracy, and Government Performance

Politically, the DPRK is a highly regimented state, and the masses are mobilized for social construction. Economically, no private enterprises are permitted, and the concept of private property is meaningless. Socially, equality is emphasized, and the mass-line approach purports to homogenize the entire population and eliminate class distinctions.

Recovering quickly from the ravages of the Korean War, North Korea has created one of the most industrialized states in Asia. But North Korea has displayed an uneven record of development. Its high industrial achievement has not contributed to the production of more consumer goods or to general liberalization of the regime. Recently, signs of weakness have also appeared in its developmental pattern, and its economy has been growing at a much slower pace than in earlier years.

Among the works on North Korea's achievements, *Socialist Korea: A Case Study in the Strategy of Economic Development* by Brun and Hersh (12-515) is the latest of those that are one-sidedly laudatory. For more balanced views, Scalapino and Lee, *Communism in Korea* (12-534), J. Alexander Kim, *Divided Korea: The Politics of Development, 1945–1972* (12-527), and Joseph S. Chung, *The North Korean Economy* (12-518), are excellent sources. For public administration and bureaucracy, some useful additions to sources listed are: Lee and Kim, "Control and Administrative Mechanisms in the North Korean Countryside" (12-530); and Dong-suh Bark, "Comparison of Administration under Different Ideologies" (12-513).

BIBLIOGRAPHY

THE REPUBLIC OF KOREA
General

12-001. CHAPIN, Emerson. "Success Story in South Korea." *Foreign Affairs* 47(3)(April 1969):560–574. A laudatory account of the progress and political stability South Korea has achieved under President Park's leadership.

12-002. CHO, Soon-Sung. "North and South Korea: Stepped-up Aggression and Search for New Security." *Asian Survey* 9(1)(January 1969):29–39. A survey of events and developments in 1968.

12-003. CHOI, Sung-il. "Typological Model of Political Development: Korea, A Preliminary Test." PhD dissertation, University of Kansas, 1971. 160 pp. Abstracted in *DAI* 32(4)(October 1971):2149-50-A; UM 71-27,133. Analysis of Korean political development in terms of three interdisciplinary variables—social and economic differentiation, cultural secularization, and system adaptability.

12-004. CHUNG, Kyung Cho. *Korea: The Third Republic.* New York: Macmillan, 1971. 269 pp. An account of the rise of the military in Korean politics—its achievements and problems.

12-005. _____. *New Korea: New Land of the Morning Calm.* New York: Macmillan, 1962. 274 pp. A journalistic treatment of the downfall of Syngman Rhee and the eventual rise of the military junta in Korea under General Park.

12-006. COLE, David C. and Princeton N. LYMAN. *Korean Development: The Interplay of Politics and Economics.* Cambridge, Mass.: Harvard University Press, 1971. 320 pp. A scholarly examination of political and economic development and their interplay in Korea from 1961 to 1971, which highlights the highly successful period of Korea's Third Republic under President Park.

12-007. HAHN, Bae-ho. "Toward a Comparative Analysis of the South and North Korean Political System." *Social Science Journal* (1973):7–21. A study of the emergence of two different systems in North and South Korea: their different ideologies and operative principles and politics.

12-008. Hapdong News Agency. *Korea Annual.* Seoul: annual. Descriptive but up-to-date information.

12-009. HAN, Sungjoo. *The Failure of Democracy in South Korea.* Berkeley: University of California Press, 1974. 240 pp. A detailed, scholarly account of the Second Republic of South Korea under Chang's premiership, which unsuccessfully tried for a liberal democracy.

12-010. _____. "South Korea: The Political Economy of Dependency." *Asian Survey* 15(1)(January 1974):43–51. A survey article of events and developments in South Korea in 1973. Highlights the theme of foreign and domestic linkage in South Korea's economic development.

12-011. _____. "South Korea in 1974: The Korean Democracy on Trial." *Asian Survey* 16(1)(January 1975): 35–42. A survey of events and developments in South Korea in 1974 emphasizing an increasingly authoritarian tendency of the incumbent Park regime.

12-012. HENDERSON, Gregory. *Korea: The Politics of the Vortex.* Cambridge, Mass.: Harvard University Press, 1968. 479 pp. A major political history of Korea. The authoritarian and centralistic culture is historically analyzed. The characterization of Korean politics as the politics of the vortex is controversial.

12-013. _____. "Korea." In Gregory Henderson, Richard Ned Lebow, and John G. Stoessinger (eds.), *Divided Nations in a Divided World.* New York: McKay, 1974. A succinct survey of the origin, evolution, and effects of Korea's territorial division.

12-014. JO, Yung-hwan. "Whither Two Koreas?" *Pacific Community* 5(4)(July 1974):565–578. Examines how the North–South dialogue toward peaceful reunification has influenced politics in North and South Korea.

12-015. KANG, Pyung-kun. "Recent Changes in Korean Politics." *Philippine Journal of Public Administration* 12(2) (April 1968):165–174. A review of Korean political developments particularly since 1961.

12-016. KEON, Michael. *Korean Phoenix: A Nation from the Ashes.* Englewood Cliffs, N.J.: Prentice-Hall, 1977. 234 pp. A personal, journalistic account of the achievements of President Park in providing political stability and promoting socioeconomic development in South Korea. The book is also a biography of Park.

12-017. KIHL, Young Whan. "Korea's Future: Seoul's Perspective." *Asian Survey* 17(11)(November 1977): 1064–1076. A survey article. Analyzes South Korea's perception of the stalemate on the Korean peninsula, its position on various international proposals on Korea, and its thinking on the critical factors affecting future North–South relations.

12-018. KIM, C. I. Eugene (ed.). *A Pattern of Political Development: Korea.* Kalamazoo: Korea Research and Publications, 1964. 200 pp. A collection of papers dealing with structural-functional aspects of Korean political development.

12-019. _____. "Korea in the Year of ULSA." *Asian Survey* 6(1)(January 1966):34–42. A survey of events and developments in Korea in 1965.

12-020. KIM, C. I. Eugene and Lawrence ZIRING. "Korea:

The Politics of a Divided Nation.'' In *An Introduction to Asian Politics*. Englewood Cliffs, N.J.: Prentice-Hall, 1977. A concise summary of Korean political dynamics and processes.

12-021. KIM, Joungwon Alexander. *Divided Korea: The Politics of Development, 1945–1972*. Cambridge, Mass.: East Asian Research Center, Harvard University, 1975. 471 pp. A scholarly work on developments in the two Koreas particularly in regard to the roles played by leaders and their uses of different political tools.

12-022. _____. ''Divided Korea, 1969: Consolidating for Transition.''*Asian Survey* 10(1)(January 1970):30–42. A survey of events and developments in Korea in 1969.

12-023. _____. ''The Republic of Korea: A Quest for New Directions.'' *Asian Survey* 11(1)(January 1971):92–103. A survey of events and developments in South Korea in 1970.

12-024. KIM, Se-Jin. *The Politics of Military Revolution in Korea*. Chapel Hill: University of North Carolina Press, 1971. 239 pp. A detailed account of the forces which led to the 1961 military coup in Korea and the subsequent military government.

12-025. KIM, Se-Jin and Chang-hyun CHO (eds.). *Korea: A Divided Nation*. Silver Spring, Md.: Research Institute on Korean Affairs, 1976. 330 pp. A revised edition of *Government and Politics of Korea* (1972). Includes some new papers.

12-026. KIM, Youngjeung. ''Korea—Ten Years after Liberation.'' *Foreign Affairs Report* (New Delhi), 4(June 1955): 6–18. A historical account of the oppressive rule of President Rhee of South Korea.

12-027. KOH, B. C. ''Two Koreas.'' *Current History* 58(April 1970):209–216. A discussion of politics and foreign policy in North and South Korea. The study shows that they pursue the same goals but their means are diametrically opposed.

12-028. Korea, Republic of. Bureau of Statistics, Economic Planning Board. *Korea Statistical Yearbook*. Seoul: Dong-A Publishing Co., annual. A useful research tool. Statistical information on various topics.

12-029. _____. Kukka Chaegŏn Ch'oego Hoeŭi [Supreme Council for National Reconstruction]. *The Military Revolution in Korea*. Seoul: Secretariat, SCNR, 1961. 235 pp. An official justification of the 1961 military coup in South Korea.

12-030. Korea University, Asiatic Research Center. *Report: International Conference on the Problems of Korean Unification*. Seoul: 1971. 1251 pp. Proceedings of the International Conference on the Problems of Korean Unification

held in Seoul in 1970 under the sponsorship of the Asiatic Research Center of Korea University. Most comprehensive coverage of various problems regarding Korean reunification. Includes papers on the North and South Korean political systems.

12-031. _____. *Report: International Conference on the Problems of Modernization in Asia*. Seoul: 1965. 821 pp. Proceedings of the International Conference on the Problems of Modernization in Asia held in Seoul in 1965 under the sponsorship of the Asiatic Research Center of Korea University. Comparative, international in coverage. A total of sixty-two papers were presented at the conference, many of them dealing directly with Korea.

12-032. Korean National Commission for UNESCO (comp.). *Korean Survey*. Seoul: Dong-A Publishing Co., 1960. 936 pp. A general survey of Korea including sections on government and politics.

12-033. LEE, Chae-Jin. ''South Korea: Political Competition and Government Adaptation.'' *Asian Survey* 12(1)(January 1972):38–45. A survey of events and developments in South Korea in 1971.

12-034. _____. ''South Korea: The Politics of Domestic Foreign Linkage.'' *Asian Survey* 13(1)(January 1973):94–101. A survey of events and developments in South Korea in 1972.

12-035. LEE, Chong-sik. ''Korea: In Search of Stability.'' *Asian Survey* 4(1)(January 1964):656–665. A survey of events and developments in Korea in 1963.

12-036. LEE, Joung-sik. ''The Prospects of Korean Politics in the 1970's: Problems of Political Development.'' *Koreana Quarterly* 12(1/2)(Spring/Summer 1970):1–17. A brief but perceptive summary of Korean politics in the 1960s and some predictions for the future.

12-037. LEE, Kyu-tae. *Modern Transformation of Korea*. Seoul: Sejong Publishing Co., 1970. 327 pp. An extensive study of cultural and social transformation of Korea during the last hundred years.

12-038. McCUNE, George M. *Korea Today*. Cambridge, Mass.: Harvard University Press, 1950. 327 pp. The first comprehensive study of North and South Korea since the 1945 liberation from Japanese imperialism. Particularly useful for the 1945–1948 period.

12-039. McCUNE, Shannon. *Korea: The Land of Broken Calm*. New York: Van Nostrand, 1961. 221 pp. A general introduction to the history and culture of the Korean people.

12-040. MEADE, E. Grant. *American Military Government in Korea*. New York: Columbia University Press, 1951. 281 pp. A detailed, critical study of American military government in Korea, particularly at the local and provincial levels.

12-041. MIN, Byong-tae. "Political Development in Korea: 1945-1965." *Korea Journal* 5(9)(September 1965):28–33. A historical account of political development in South Korea from 1945 to 1965.

12-042. MOON, Chang-joo. "Development of Politics and Political Science in Korea after World War II." *Koreana Quarterly* 10(Autumn 1968):282–302. A survey of South Korean political development since the liberation and the role played by political scientists in Korea.

12-043. MORLEY, James William. *Japan and Korea: America's Allies in the Pacific.* New York: Walker, 1965. 152 pp. A section on Korea includes useful statistical data.

12-044. NAHM, Andrew C. (ed.). *Studies in the Developmental Aspects of Korea.* Kalamazoo: School of Graduate Studies, Western Michigan University, 1969. 255 pp. Papers presented at a conference on Korea at Western Michigan University.

12-045. OH, John Kie-chiang. *Korea: Democracy on Trial.* Ithaca: Cornell University Press, 1968. 240 pp. A concise but scholarly treatment of South Korea's unsuccessful experimentation with Western democracy, particularly in the first and second republican periods and the military coup in 1961.

12-046. _____. "South Korea 1976: The Continuing Uncertainties." *Asian Survey* 17(1)(January 1977):71–80. A survey of developments in South Korea in 1976. Discusses domestic politics in South Korea and South–North relations.

12-047. OSGOOD, Cornelius. *The Koreans and Their Culture.* New York: Ronald Press, 1951. 387 pp. A pioneering anthropological work on a farming village on the island of Kanghwa. It also includes a political history of the peninsula through 1950.

12-048. PAIGE, Glenn D. "Some Implications for Political Science of the Comparative Politics of Korea." In Fred W. Riggs (ed.), *Frontiers of Developing Administration.* Durham: Duke University Press, 1970. North and South Korean development strategies present useful empirical cases for comparative study.

12-049. _____. "1966: Korea Creates the Future." *Asian Survey* 7(1)(January 1967):21–30. A survey article of events and developments in Korea in 1966.

12-050. PALAIS, James B. "'Democracy' in South Korea, 1948-72." In Frank Baldwin (ed.), *Without Parallel.* New York: Pantheon Books, 1973. A useful summary of political developments in South Korea from 1948 to 1972, highlighting South Korea's difficulties with its experiment in democracy.

12-051. RHEE, Yong Pil. "The Breakdown of Authority Structure in Korea in 1970: A Case Study of the Failure of Concerted Feedback." *Journal of East and West Studies* 4(1)(April 1975):3–44. A systematic study of the downfall of the Rhee regime of Korea's First Republic, which was unable to meet the critical overflow of demand-input stress during the 1960 political disturbance. A summary of the author's doctoral dissertation on the same topic at the University of Chicago (1974).

12-052. REEVE, W. D. *The Republic of Korea: A Political and Economic Study.* London: Oxford University Press, 1963. 197 pp. A detailed, useful study of the Rhee government of South Korea's First Republic, its administration, and its performance.

12-053. SAWYER, Robert. *Military Advisors in Korea: KMAG in Peace and War.* Washington: Office of the Chief of Military History, 1962. 216 pp. An important work on the role of American military advisers in the establishment of the ROK armed forces.

12-054. SCALAPINO, Robert A. "Which Route for Korea?" *Asian Survey* 2(9)(September 1962):1–13. A discussion of political problems and constitutional issues facing the military government in their quest for "Koreanized" democracy. The possibility of some form of joint military-civilian administration is noted for the future.

12-055. STEINBERG, David I. *Korea: Nexus of East Asia— An Inquiry into Contemporary Korea in Historical Perspective.* New York: American-Asian Educational Exchange, 1968. 71 pp. A brief historical survey of political and economic development of South and North Korea. Emphasis on Korea's geopolitical position.

12-056. TEWKSBURY, Donald G. (comp.). *Source Materials on Korean Politics and Ideologies.* New York: Institute of Pacific Relations, 1950. 190 pp. A useful collection of historical documents and other source materials, compiled and translated.

12-057. United Nations. *Report of the United Nations Commission for the Unification and Rehabilitation of Korea.* New York: United Nations, annual. A useful summary of major political developments in the Korean peninsula as reported each year by the commission until 1973, when it was dissolved.

12-058. United States. Army. South Korean Interim Government. *South Korean Interim Government Activities.* Seoul: August 1947–August 1948. An official record of activities of the US Command in Korea and the South Korean Interim Government. A useful day-to-day account.

12-059. _____. Congress. House of Representatives. Committee on Foreign Affairs. *Human Rights in South Korea:*

Implications for U.S. Policy. Washington: Government Printing Office, 1975. 293 pp. A collection of statements and documents provided by government officials, scholars, clergymen, and others who discussed the problems of human rights in South Korea before the Subcommittee on Asian and Pacific Affairs and on International Organizations and Movements.

12-060. VREELAND, Nena, Rinn-Sup SHINN, and others. *Area Handbook for South Korea.* 2nd ed. Washington: Government Printing Office, 1975. 394 pp. A comprehensive summary of the dominant social, political, economic, and military aspects of South Korea. The handbook includes an extensive bibliography in four parts: (1) social, (2) political, (3) economic, and (4) national security.

12-061. WAGNER, Edward W. "Failure in Korea." *Foreign Affairs* 40(October 1961):128–135. A critical observation of the 1961 military coup.

12-062. WEEMS, Clarence Norwood. *Korea: Dilemma of an Underdeveloped Country.* New York: Foreign Policy Association, World Affairs Center, 1960. 62 pp. A perceptive study of the problems faced by South Korea as a developing nation.

12-063. WRIGHT, Edward R. (ed.). *Korean Politics in Transition.* Seoul: Korea Branch of the Royal Asiatic Society, 1974. 399 pp. A useful collection of papers on South Korean politics, both historical and contemporary. Various topics are covered by specialists.

Political Culture, Ideology, and Political Socialization

12-064. AN, Rosario Lee. "Political Socialization of Korean Children in a Comparative Perspective: Comparison of Political Learning in Korea with Political Learning in the United States and Its Systematic Effects." PhD dissertation, Rutgers University–State University of New Jersey, 1975. 244 pp. Abstracted in *DAI* 36(2)(August 1975):1056-57-A. An empirical, comparative study of early childhood political socialization and its impact on adult political behavior in South Korea and the United States.

12-065. BRANDT, Vincent S. R. *A Korean Village between Farm and Sea.* Cambridge, Mass.: Harvard University Press, 1971. 252 pp. A scholarly anthropological and political work on a Korean village. Includes a detailed account of informal village decision-making process.

12-066. CHANG, Yun-shik. "Urban Korean as Individual." *Korea Observer* 3(3)(April 1971):3–15. Korea's new urban man is characterized as individualistic and egalitarian.

12-067. CHUNG, Sae-gyu. "The Political Socialization of Selected Elementary and Middle School Students in the Republic of Korea: Political Knowledge, Political Trust and Political Efficacy." PhD dissertation, Florida State University, 1973. 105 pp. Abstracted in *DAI* 34(4)(October 1973):1473-74-A; UM 73-23,283. A survey. Analysis of the various political and nonpolitical agencies in the development of the sense of political efficiency among elementary and middle school students in Korea.

12-068. HAHM, Pyong-Choon. *The Korean Political Tradition and Law: Essays in Korean Law and Legal History.* Seoul: Hollym Corporation, 1967. 249 pp. A historical and scholarly treatment of Korea's concept of law and authoritarian political tradition. See 03-174.

12-069. HAHN, Sung-joe. *The Korean Way to Democracy.* Seoul: Pŏmmun-sa Publishing Co., 1976. 382 pp. Identifies three forms of democracy—Western democracy or individualistic democracy; Eastern democracy or totalitarian democracy; and emerging nation's democracy or various forms of authoritarian democracy. Korean democracy is posited as neither Western nor Eastern, but suited to the existing conditions of Korea.

12-070. HAN, Wan-sang. "A Conceptual Clarification of 'Mass Society' for a Better Understanding of Mass Tendencies in Korean Society." *Korea Observer* 3(4)(July 1971):3–22. Analysis of the gradually emerging mass tendencies in Korea.

12-071. HAN, Yung Chul. "Traditionalism and the Struggle for Political Modernization in Contemporary Korea: With Special Reference to the Development of Political Parties." PhD dissertation, New York University, 1966. 277 pp. Abstracted in *DAI* 27(June 1967):4311-12-A; UM 67-6026. Analysis of the causes for the failure of political modernization and party institutionalization in South Korea.

12-072. HENDERSON, Gregory. *Korea: The Politics of the Vortex.* Cambridge, Mass.: Harvard University Press, 1968. 479 pp. A good, albeit controversial, discussion of Korean political culture. See 12-012.

12-073. HONG, Sung-chick. *The Intellectual and Modernization: A Study of Korean Attitudes.* Seoul: Korea University, 1967. 268 pp. A collection of surveys conducted by the author. Includes a discussion of intellectuals' attitudes toward democracy and individual freedom.

12-074. _____. "Political Diagnosis of Korean Society: A Survey of Military and Civilian Values." *Asian Survey* 8(5)(May 1967): 329–340. A survey. Shows value differences between the military and civilian sectors of society.

12-075. _____. "Values of Korean College Professors." *Koreana Quarterly* 7(4)/8(1)(Winter 1965/Spring 1966):62–73. A survey of Korean intellectuals.

12-076. HUNT, Walter E. "Attitudes of Korean Farmers, Businessmen and Professors toward Social Change." *Koreana Quarterly* 11(1)(Spring 1969):75–89. A survey.

Shows the respondents' mixed reactions toward modernization and social change.

12-077. JEWELL, Malcolm E. and Chong Lim KIM. "Sources of Support for the Legislature in a Developing Nation: The Case of Korea." *Comparative Political Studies* 8(4)(January 1976):461–489. A survey to discover the basis of individual support for the Korean legislature. The study finds greater legislative support among persons in the higher political strata as measured by knowledge, activity, and efficacy.

12-078. KIM, C. I. Eugene and Ch'angboh CHEE (eds.). *Aspects of Social Change in Korea*. Kalamazoo: Korea Research and Publications, 1969. 272 pp. A collection of articles on various aspects of social change in Korea since 1945. A broad area of change is covered.

12-079. KIM, C. I. Eugene and C. HUNT. "Education and Political Development: A Comparison of Korea and the Philippines." *Journal of Developing Areas* 2(3)(April 1968):407–420. A comparative study of different colonial experiences and patterns of development in Korea and the Philippines.

12-080. KIM, C. I. Eugene and Hyung-chin YOO. "Political Socialization in Korea: A Pilot Study." *Korean Political Science Review* 3(1969):259–269. Findings of a survey of public and middle school students. The sources of political alienation are explained.

12-081. KIM, Chin-man. "Korean Thought Patterns: How Koreans Think and Solve Problems." *Koreana Quarterly* 11(4)(Winter 1969–1970):67–82. An essay on the Korean people as "a peaceful, friendly, fun-loving people eager to make the best of things given to them."

12-082. KIM, Chong Lim and Gerhard LOWENBERG. "The Cultural Roots of a New Legislature: Public Perceptions of the Korean National Assembly." *Legislative Studies Quarterly* 1(3)(August 1976):371–387. A survey of public attitudes toward the National Assembly conducted in 1973. The study finds that public support for the National Assembly is high, particularly among citizens familiar with the assembly and with their own legislators and those in the modern sector of society.

12-083. KIM, Kyung-won. "Ideology and Political Development in South Korea." *Pacific Affairs* 38(4)(Summer 1965):164–176. A discussion of the South Korean ideology as a mixture of nationalism and anticommunism. The study shows no genuine ideological development in South Korea.

12-084. KIM, Pyung-ku. "The Image of Korean Intellectuals." *Korea Journal* 8(6)(June 1968):17–25. A survey of Korean intellectual movements from the early 1920s to the present. The survey also discusses the role of Korean intellectuals in Korea's reunification.

12-085. KIM, Se Jin. "Attitudinal Orientations of Korean Workers." *Korea Journal* 12(9)(September 1972):18–30. A survey on the attitudes of Korean workers toward management and the political system.

12-086. KIM, T'ae-gil. "The Changing Morals of Korean Students." *Korea Journal* 6(3)(March 1966):11–15. A survey of the changing morals of Korean students from their Confucian tradition to a more egalitarian and materialistic orientation.

12-087. _____. "What Korean Students Think Most Valuable." *Journal of Asiatic Studies* 9(1)(March 1966):57–63. A survey of the values and ideals held by Korean students.

12-088. KIM, Yoon H. "Provincialism in Korea." *Journal of Korean Affairs* 4(2)(July 1974):8–23. A survey of strong provincialism in Korea, which still exists.

12-089. KIM, Young-mo. "Consciousness Structure of Korean Farmers." *Korea Observer* 3(3)(April 1971):16–25. Analysis of young versus old value structures in relation to modernization. Discusses the continuing sources of the old value structure among the rural community.

12-090. KO, Yong-bok. "Leading Class and Leadership in Korean Nationalism." *Korea Journal* 6(12)(December 1966):25–30. A discussion of the emergence of a new nationalism in South Korea.

12-091. KOH, B. C. "Chuch'esŏng in Korean Politics." *Studies in Comparative Communism* 7(1/2)(Spring/Summer 1974):83–106. Analysis of the meaning of "independent orientation" in North and South Korean politics—their similarities and differences.

12-092. LEE, Chul-hyun. "Political Modernization with Special Reference to the Republic of Korea: Theoretical, Historical and Comparative Study." PhD dissertation, New York University, 1971. 347 pp. Abstracted in *DAI* 32(11) (May 1972):6509-10; UM 72-3091. A historical and comparative treatment of Korea's process of political modernization and an analysis of difficulties arising from Korea's centralistic, authoritarian tradition.

12-093. LEE, Hwa-soo. "A Study of Political Socialization Process: Family, Political Efficacy and Legitimacy: The Case of Secondary School Students in Korea." *Koreana Quarterly* 10(2)(Summer 1968):156–197.

12-094. _____. "An Analysis of the April Revolution in Korea." *Koreana Quarterly* 8(2)(Summer 1966):96–110. A survey of the motivating factors behind the 1960 student movement.

12-095. LEE, Hyo-chai. "The Korean's Understanding of Democracy." *Korean Affairs* 2(13)(1962):12–19. This survey notes the general awareness of the ideals of democracy.

12-096. LEE, Ick-whan. "Motivations of the Student Movement in Korea." *East-West Center Review* 2(3)(February 1966):20–33. This survey reveals the personal and social frustrations of students in Korea.

12-097. LEE, Joung-sik. "Some Characteristics of Korean Political Culture: A Study on Korean Political Leaders' Statements, 1948–60." *Koreana Quarterly* 8(3)(Autumn 1966):3–14. A content analysis.

12-098. LEE, Young-ho. "The Korean People's Political Orientations: Multivariate Analysis." *Koreana Quarterly* 13(1/2)(Spring/Summer 1971):11–30 and 13(3)(Autumn 1971):19–42. A survey of the relationship between popular orientations toward democracy and political involvement.

12-099. _____. "Modernization as a Goal Value in Korean Society." *Korea Journal* 12(4)(April 1972):15–25 and 12(5)(May 1972):5–11. A survey on the popular view of modernization. Modernization is often associated with industrialization.

12-100. _____. "The Political Culture of Modernizing Society: Political Attitudes and Democracy in Korea." PhD dissertation, Yale University, 1969. 291 pp. Abstracted in *DAI* 30(7)(January 1970):3519-20-A; UM 70-2760. A survey on the extent of the civic and democratic orientation of the Korean people.

12-101. LEWIS, David M. and Dae Hong CHANG. "Youth's Perception of the Prestige of Positions in Government and Military Service in Japan and Korea." *Asian Forum* 2(1)(January–March 1970):1–9. Findings of a comparative survey on prestige occupations.

12-102. LIM, Bang-hyun. "Koreanization of Democracy: A Target of October Reforms." *Koreana Quarterly* 14(4) (Winter 1972–1973):26–42. A discussion of the so-called October Reforms of 1972 and President Park's strategy of modernization.

12-103. LYMAN, Princeton N. "Students and Politics in Indonesia and Korea." *Pacific Affairs* 38(3/4)(Fall/Winter 1965–1966):282–293. A discussion of student movements and the educational system. The educational system tends to set apart the new generation of students as a distinct and restless group.

12-104. MIN, Suk-Hong. "Problems Incidental to Application of Western Ideology to Modernization of Korea." *Koreana Quarterly* 8(4)/9(1)(Winter 1966/Spring 1967):3–20. A discussion of the impact of rapid industrialization upon promotion of freedom and equality in a developing country such as Korea.

12-105. OH, Byung-hun. "University Students and Politics in Korea." *Koreana Quarterly* 9(4)(Winter 1967):1–40. A survey of higher educational institutions and students' political activism in Korea.

12-106. OH, John Kie-chiang. "Role of the United States in South Korea's Democratization." *Pacific Affairs* 43(2) (Summer 1969):164–177. A discussion of America's contribution to the establishment of a democratic republic in South Korea.

12-107. PARK, Chung Hee [PAK, Chŏng-hŭi]. "Korean Political Philosophy: Administrative Democracy." *Korean Affairs* 1(1962):111–121. The concept of administrative democracy in South Korea as explained by President Park himself.

12-108. _____. *Our Nation's Path: Ideology of Social Reconstruction by Park Chung Hee.* Seoul: Dong-A Publishing Co., 1962. 252 pp. One of the first essays by President Park in justification of the 1961 military coup and the plan for development instituted by the junta.

12-109. _____. *Selected Works of President Chung-hee Park.* 6 vols. Seoul: Chimoon-gak, 1969. A collection of essays and addresses by President Park.

12-110. _____. *To Build a Nation.* Washington: Acropolis Books, 1971. 216 pp. An essay by President Park revealing his prescription for Korean modernization.

12-111. PARK, N. Y. "Should We Impose Democracy on Korea?" *Current History* 41(December 1961):341–349. A discussion of the lack of training and experience with democratic process in Korea.

12-112. RHEE, Syngman. *Korea Flaming High: Excerpts from Statements by President Syngman Rhee, 1953–1955.* 2 vols. Seoul: Office of Public Information, Republic of Korea, 1956. A collection of speeches by President Rhee.

12-113. SHIN, Il-ch'ol. "Marxism and Korea." *Korea Journal* 7(1)(January 1967):10–19. A history of modern Korean political thought. Includes a discussion of the Shinganhoe in the 1920s.

12-114. SONG, Byung Soon. "Comparative Study of Ideological Influences on Educational Theory and Practice in North and South Korea." PhD dissertation, Wayne State University, 1974. 181 pp. Abstracted in *DAI* 35(7)(January 1975):4277-8-A; UM 74-29,866. A historical and analytical comparison of the ideology–education causal connection in the different systems of North and South Korea.

12-115. SPRINGER, John Frederick. "Role Integration among Development Administrators: A Cross-national Comparison." PhD dissertation, University of California at Davis, 1974. 305 pp. Abstracted in *DAI* 36(1)(July 1975):518-19-A. A survey to discover the extent of integration of new and "modern" roles in the lives of individuals. Certain personal characteristics and experiences of individual officials are said to condition their role perception. The Republic of Korea is compared with three Southeast Asian countries.

12-116. SWISHER, Ralph Blakeslee. "Passing the Threshold to Modernity in Rural South Korea: The Convergence of Elite Communication, Popular Frame of References, and Institutional Capacity." PhD dissertation, University of Pittsburgh, 1972. 340 pp. Abstracted in *DAI* 33(11)(May 1973):6466-A; UM 73-12,359. This survey shows among other things that "shared improvement and expectations associated with governmental effectiveness tend to increase perceptions of governmental legitimacy."

12-117. YANG, Sung Chul. "Political Ideology, Myth and Symbol in Korean Politics." *Asian Forum* 4(3)(July–September 1972):30–42. A quantitative analysis of political symbols used by Korean leaders, particularly Presidents Rhee and Park.

12-118. YI, Man-gap. "Socio-cultural Aspects of the Community Development Movement in Korea." *Korea Journal* 13(January 1973):25–33. Analysis of the traditional, rural group organizations and the developmental roles and problems of the Community Development Movement.

12-119. YI, Myonggu and W. A. DOUGLAS. "Korean Confucianism Today." *Pacific Affairs* 40(1/2)(Spring/Summer 1967):43–59. A discussion of the role of Confucianism in contemporary Korea. Analyzes the contrasting rates of change in urban and rural areas.

12-120. YOU, Young-June. "Development Patterns, Leadership Styles, and Popular Attitudes: Korea's Development Politics (1948–1972)." PhD dissertation, University of Hawaii, 1974. 214 pp. Abstracted in *DAI* 37(1)(July 1976):583-4-A; UM 75-21,620. Development as an alien concept. Needed for Korea is "a more 'human-populist' type of development and a more 'democratic but consistent' political leadership."

Political Leaders, Leadership Style, and Decision-making

12-121. ALLEN, R. C. *Korea's Syngman Rhee: An Unauthorized Portrait.* Rutland, Vt.: Tuttle, 1960. 259 pp. The authoritarianism of the First Republic of South Korea traced to the personal shortcomings of its president, Syngman Rhee.

12-122. BRIGGS, Walter. "The Military Revolution in Korea: Its Leaders and Achievements." *Koreana Quarterly* 5(2)(Summer 1963):17–34. A discussion of the military coup of 1961—the way it was brought about, its leaders, and its achievements.

12-123. CHAI, Jae Yung. "The Military and Modernization in Korea." PhD dissertation, Case Western Reserve, 1972. 214 pp. Abstracted in *DAI* 33(6)(December 1972):2985-86-A; UM 72-26,142. Analysis of the military as a modernizing force. Argues that the military in power in Korea is yet to develop a stable and viable political system.

12-124. CHANG, David W. "The Military and Nation-Building in Korea, Burma and Pakistan." *Asian Survey* 9(11)(November 1969):818–830. A comparative study of the political role of the military elite for nation-building and modernization.

12-125. CHOI, Sung-il. "The Social Dynamics of Elite Circulation: A Case Study of Korea, 1948–1967." *Journal of Korean Affairs* 4(1)(April 1974):9–21. A quantitative analysis of the relationship between social change and the transformation of legislative elite characteristics between 1948 and 1967.

12-126. CHOI, Yearn H. "Decision-Making in Korean Government: Between Student Uprising and Military Coup d'Etat." PhD dissertation, Indiana University, 1974. 206 pp. Abstracted in *DAI* 35(7)(January 1975): 4663-A; UM 75-1682. Analysis of the failure of the Chang government of Korea's Second Republic to survive.

12-127. DOUGLAS, William A. "South Korea's Search for Leadership." *Pacific Affairs* 27(1)(Spring 1964):20–36. An overview of political events in Korea since 1960. The study emphasizes a need for new party leadership.

12-128. GIBNEY, Frank. "Syngman Rhee: The Free Man's Burden." *Harper's* 208(February 1954):27–34. An observation of President Syngman Rhee as a despotic leader.

12-129. HAHN, Bae-ho. "Factions in Contemporary Korean Competitive Politics." PhD dissertation, Princeton University, 1971. 293 pp. Abstracted in *DAI* 32(3)(September 1971):1851-A; UM 71-23,360. Analyzes the nature of factional politics within the ruling and opposition parties in the Rhee and the Park era of South Korean politics. The study examines the importance of the supreme leader who dictates, arbitrates, or neutralizes factional struggles.

12-130. HAHN, Bae-ho and Kyu-taik KIM. "Korean Political Leaders (1952–62): Their Social Origins and Skills." *Asian Survey* 3(7)(July 1963):305–323. A quantitative analysis of the background data of Korean political leaders between 1952 and 1962. The study shows changes in their characteristics over the years.

12-131. HAN, Jong-il. "Decision-making Process in the Korean Legislature." *Korea Journal* 13(7)(July 1973): 29–43. Analysis of the legislature which has traditionally been subservient in its decision-making to the executive.

12-132. HAN, Ki-shik. "Political Leadership and Development in Postwar Korea: Continuity and Change between the Rhee and Park Regimes.'' PhD dissertation, University of California, 1972. Analysis of leadership change and political development from the First to the Third Republic of Korea.

12-133. HAN, Sungjoo. *The Failure of Democracy in South Korea.* Berkeley: University of California Press, 1974. See 12-009.

12-134. HENDERSON, Gregory. *Korea: The Politics of the Vortex.* Cambridge, Mass.: Harvard University Press, 1968. See 12-012.

12-135. KEON, Michael. *Korean Phoenix: A Nation from the Ashes.* Englewood Cliffs, N.J.: Prentice-Hall, 1977. See 12-016.

12-136. KIHL, Young Whan. ''Leadership and Opposition Role Perception among Party Elite.'' *Korea Journal* 13(9)(September 1973):4–23. The survey shows different opinions held by the sample respondents on the role of political opposition.

12-137. KIM, C. I. Eugene. ''The South Korean Military Coup of May, 1961: Its Causes and the Social Characteristics of Its Leaders.'' In Jacques Van-Doorn (ed.), *Armed Forces and Society.* The Hague: Mouton, 1968. Analysis of the causes of the 1961 military coup and the social background of participants and nonparticipant military leaders.

12-138. _____. ''Transition from Military Rule: The Case of South Korea.'' *Armed Forces and Society* 1(3)(May 1975): 302–316. A case study of the general problems of transition from military rule in developing areas. The study shows that the transition from military rule in South Korea did not mean liberalization of the political process.

12-139. KIM, C. I. Eugene and Kenneth ROCCO. ''Political Orientations of Military and Non-Military Party Elites in South Korea.'' *Journal of Korean Affairs* 4(1)(January 1975):16–26. Findings of a survey of party elites. The study shows that those with military and those with non-military backgrounds show no significant differences in their political orientation.

12-140. KIM, Chong-Lim and Byung-Kyu WOO. ''The Patterns of Recruitment and Political Representation in Korea.'' *Asian Profile* 2(1)(February 1974):31–44. A survey showing the relationship between the pattern of one's recruitment in the legislature in Korea and one's perception of a certain representation role.

12-141. _____. ''The Role of Legislative Elites in Democratic Change: An Analysis of Democratic Commitment among Korean National Legislators.'' *Comparative Political Studies* 6(3)(October 1973):349–379. A survey on the func-

tion performed by legislative elites for democratic change in Korea and in developing systems generally.

12-142. _____. ''Social and Political Background of Korean National Assemblymen: The Seventh National Assembly.'' *Asian Forum* 3(July/September 1971):123–137. A survey of members of the Seventh National Assembly elected in 1967. The Korean national assemblymen are a highly selected group sharing many social background characteristics.

12-143. KIM, Chong-shin. *Seven Years with Korea's Park Chung-hee.* Seoul: Hollym Corp., 1967. 306 pp. An intimate and valuable account of President Park before the 1961 military coup.

12-144. KIM, Jai-hyup. ''The Political Involvement of Military Elites: A Comparative Study of a 'Garrison State' in Japan during the 1930s and 1940s and Korea during the 1960s and 1970s.'' PhD dissertation, Indiana University, 1976. 334 pp. Abstracted in *DAI* 37(11)(May 1977):7288-9-A; UM 77-10,967. The Park regime, like the Japanese military regime in the 1930s and 1940s, is a garrison state that is totally geared for war. The author notes that ''as the regimes move toward a full garrison state, civilian and military domains tended to become fused in political decision-making.''

12-145. KIM, Jong-pil. ''The Ethos of October Reforms.'' *Koreana Quarterly* 14(4)(Winter 1972–1973):10–17. The meaning of the so-called October Reforms of 1972 as explained by the prime minister of South Korea at the time.

12-146. _____. ''Political Conception and Leadership in Korea.'' *Koreana Quarterly* 7(3)(Autumn 1965):1–10. An article written by one of the prime movers of the 1961 military coup.

12-147. KIM, Joungwon Alexander. *Divided Korea: The Politics of Development, 1945–1972.* Cambridge, Mass.: East Asian Research Center, Harvard University, 1975. See 12-021.

12-148. _____. ''Korean Kŭndaehwa: The Military as Modernizer.'' *Journal of Comparative Administration* 2(3)(November 1970):355–371. An evaluation of the extent of the modernization in Korea under the direction of the 1961 military coup leaders.

12-149. KIM, Kyu-taik. ''The Behavior Patterns of the Rulers and Ruled in Korean Politics.'' *Korean Affairs* 1(1962):319–326. A perceptive discussion of similarities and differences in the behavior pattern of the rulers and the ruled between Korea's ''traditional despotic society and modern society.''

12-150. KOH, Kwang Il. ''In Quest of National Unity and Power: Political Ideas and Practices of Syngman Rhee.''

PhD dissertation, Rutgers University, 1963. 283 pp. Abstracted in *DA* 24(September 1963):1231-A; UM 63-5888. Analysis of the political style of President Syngman Rhee and the causes of failure of Korea's presidential system under him.

12-151. KWON, Chan. "The Leadership of Syngman Rhee: The Charisma Factor as an Analytical Framework." *Koreana Quarterly* 13(1/2)(Spring 1971):31–48. Analysis of the charismatic quality of President Rhee's leadership and South Korea's political culture.

12-152. _____. "Social Backgrounds of the Emergent Political Leadership in Korea, 1948–60." *Koreana Quarterly* 12(1/2)(Summer/Spring 1970):41–63. A study of the social backgrounds of South Korean political leaders which show change from traditional to modern characteristics —more middle class and higher education.

12-153. LEE, Eun Ho. "The Role of the Military in Nation Building: A Comparative Study of South Vietnam and South Korea." PhD dissertation, Southern Illinois University, 1971. 325 pp. Abstracted in *DAI* 33(2)(August 1972): 997-A; UM 72-22,485. A comparative study of the political and developmental roles played by the military in South Korea and South Vietnam. Concludes that "there are significant limitations on the military's capacity as a political stabilizer."

12-154. LEE, Joung-sik. "Some Characteristics of Korean Political Culture: A Study on Political Leaders' Statements, 1948–60." *Koreana Quarterly* 8(3) (Autumn 1966): 3–14. A content analysis.

12-155. _____. "The Social Origin of Members of the Sixth Assembly." *Korean Affairs* 3(1) (April 1964):1–19. Analysis of social background data of members of the Sixth National Assembly elected in 1963.

12-156. LEE, Mangap. "Korean Village Politics and Leadership." *Korean Affairs* 1(1962):398–412. A pioneering survey of community power structure and leadership at the village level.

12-157. LEE, Yong Sun. "Political Elites and the Socio-Economic Development of South Korea, 1948–1972." PhD dissertation, Wayne State University, 1976. 328 pp. Abstracted in *DAI* 37(11)(May 1977):7289-A; UM 77-9420. A quantitative study of the political elites of South Korea and their performance in the socioeconomic development from 1948 to 1972. Several propositions are tested against the political economy of development model of Norman T. Uphoff and Warren E. Ilchman. The study shows among other things that "in an early stage of national building, leadership's reliance on administrative and police machinery tends to increase its effectiveness."

12-158. LOVELL, J. P., Hui Sok MUN, and Young Ho LEE. "Recruitment Patterns in the Republic of Korea Military Establishment." *Journal of Comparative Administration* 1(4)(February 1970):428–454. Importance of military elites in the Korean political process. Analyzes recruitment patterns in the Korean military academy.

12-159. _____. "Professional Orientations and Policy Perspectives of Military Professionals in the Republic of Korea." *Midwest Journal of Political Science* 13(3) (August 1969):415–438. A survey showing different generational political outlooks within the military profession.

12-160. OH, John Kie-chiang. "The Political Role of the Korean Military: The Making of the Third Republic." *Studies on Asia* 8(1967):72–86. A study of the institution-building process of the 1961 military coup leaders in the creation of Korea's Third Republic.

12-161. OLIVER, Robert T. *Syngman Rhee: The Man Behind the Myth.* New York: Dodd, Mead, 1954. 380 pp. President Syngman Rhee's biography by his close friend and confidant.

12-162. PAIK, Sang-ki. "A Study of Decision-Making Process in the Chung-wa-dae." *Koreana Quarterly* 11(2) (Summer 1969):38–50. A study of the institutionalization of decision-making within the Blue House of President Park.

12-163. PARK, Chung Hee [PAK, Chŏng-hŭi]. *To Build a Nation.* Washington: Acropolis Books, 1971. See 12-110.

12-164. _____. *Our Nation's Path: Ideology of Social Reconstruction by Park Chung Hee.* Seoul: Dong-A Publishing Co., 1962. See 12-108.

12-165. _____. "Korean Political Philosophy: Administrative Democracy." *Korean Affairs* 1(1962):111–121. See 12-107.

12-166. _____. *Selected Works of President Chung-hee Park.* 6 vols. Seoul: Chimoon-gak, 1969. See 12-109.

12-167. _____. "What Has Made the Military Revolution Successful." *Koreana Quarterly* 3(1)(Summer 1961):20–27. Analysis of the success of the coup by its prime mover.

12-168. PARK, C. J. "Influence of Small States upon the Superpowers: United States–South Korean Relations as a Case Study, 1950–53." *World Politics* 28(October 1975): 97–117. Includes a discussion of several efforts made by President Rhee of South Korea and techniques used to influence American decision-makers for help in the war (1950–1953).

12-169. RHEE, Syngman. *Korea Flaming High: Excerpts from Statements by President Syngman Rhee, 1953–1955.* 2 vols. Seoul: Office of Public Information, Republic of Korea, 1956. See 12-112.

12-170. SOHN, Jae-Souk. "Political Dominance and Political Failure: The Role of the Military in the Republic of

Korea.'' In Henry Bienen (ed.), *The Military Intervenes.* New York: Russell Sage Foundation, 1968. A critical review of the political role of the military in South Korea. The study points to the military's shortcomings in assuming political power.

12-171. SUH, Dae-Sook and Chae-Jin LEE (eds.). *Political Leadership in Korea.* Seattle: University of Washington Press, 1975. 256 pp. Contains studies on the traditional Yi dynasty political leadership, on more contemporary legislative, party, and bureaucratic establishment, and on the current political leaders in South Korea.

12-172. VINOCOUR, Seymour Murray. "Syngman Rhee: Spokesman for Korea (June 23, 1951–October 8, 1952): A Case Study in International Speaking." PhD dissertation, Pennsylvania State University, 1953. 462 pp. A study of Syngman Rhee's positions on major issues.

12-173. WHANG, In-joung. "Elites and Economic Programs: A Study of Changing Leadership for Economic Development in Korea, 1955–1967." PhD dissertation, University of Pittsburgh, 1968. 216 pp. Abstracted in *DAI* 30(February 1970). Finds a correlation between elite changes and economic development in Korea.

12-174. WOO, Byung-Kyu and Chong Lim KIM. "Intra-Elite Cleavages in the Korean National Assembly." *Asian Survey* 11(6)(June 1971):544–561. Findings of a survey research of national assemblymen. Differences between their role perceptions and behavior are found.

12-175. YIM, Yong Soon. "Politics of Korean Unification: A Comparative Study of Systematic Outputs in Two Different Political Systems." PhD dissertation, Rutgers University, 1974. 343 pp. Abstracted in *DAI* 35(6)(December 1974). Decision-making in North and South Korea in the 1954–1965 period regarding Korea's unification. The study finds that the closed political system of North Korea allows a lesser degree of penetration from foreign inputs into domestic politics.

12-176. YOU, Young-June. "Development Patterns, Leadership Styles and Popular Attitudes: Korea's Development Politics (1948–1972)." PhD dissertation, University of Hawaii, 1974. See 12-120.

Political Participation, Political Parties, and Elections

12-177. AHN, Byong Man. "Congressional Elections in Korea, 1954–1971: An Analysis of Crucial and Normal Elections." PhD dissertation, University of Florida, 1974. 180 pp. Abstracted in *DAI* 36(3)(September 1975):1766-A; UM 75-16,345. A study of congressional elections in terms of crucial–normal categories, interparty competition, and socioeconomic change.

12-178. AHN, Cook-chin. "Platforms of Major Political Parties." *Korean Frontier* 2(3)(March 1971):8–9. A comparison of the platforms of major political parties competing in the 1971 general elections.

12-179. AHN, Kenneth K. "Mobilization and Participation in Elections: A Study of Korean Voting Behavior." PhD dissertation, University of Georgia, 1975. 284 pp. Abstracted in *DAI* 36(12)(June 1976):8264-A. A statistical study of the relationship between socioeconomic conditions and voting participation. The study shows that poorly educated rural voters are most likely mobilized voters.

12-180. CALDWELL, John C. *The Korea Story.* Chicago: Regnery, 1952. 180 pp. A personal, critical account of the American occupation of South Korea. "It is a story of great opportunities not seized upon, of mistakes made and not corrected." Covers the first election in Korea in 1948.

12-181. CHO, Hyo-won. "An Analytical Study of Some Characteristics of Korean Political Parties." *Journal of Social Science* (Seoul), 2(March 1958):131–151. A comparative analysis of some of the common characteristics of political parties in Korea.

12-182. CHO, Soon Sung. "Korea: Election Year." *Asian Survey* 8(1)(January 1968):29–42. A survey of the events and developments in 1968. Covers the 1967 general elections in South Korea.

12-183. CHU, Shao-hsien. "Past and Present of the Political Parties in the Republic of Korea." *Issues and Studies* 1(10)(July 1965):20–30. A historical analysis of political parties—their roles and characteristics.

12-184. CHUNG, Chong-shik. "Political Parties and Funds in Korea." *Korean Affairs* 3(December 1964):286–295. A journalistic but incisive account of political funds and corruption in the Korean party political process.

12-185. CUMINGS, Bruce. "Korea: The Politics of Liberation, 1945–47." PhD dissertation, Columbia University, 1975. A detailed account of various group interactions in the initial state-building process under American occupation.

12-186. DOUGLAS, William A. "Korean Students and Politics." *Asian Survey* 3(12)(December 1973):584–595. Analysis of student politics in South Korea. Discusses factionalism, corruption, and careerism among student leaders.

12-187. EARL, David M. "Korea: The Meaning of the 2nd Republic." *Far Eastern Survey* 29(November 1960):169–175. A discussion of the causes of the 1960 student movement and the significance of the Second Republic's political experiment.

12-188. GARVER, R. A. "Communication Problems of Underdevelopment: Cheju-do, Korea, 1962." *Public Opinion Quarterly* 26(Winter 1962):613–625. A field study of the island province of Cheju and its underdevelopment of communications of all types.

12-189. GORDENKER, Leon. "The United Nations, the United States Occupation and the 1948 Election in Korea." *Political Science Quarterly* 73(3)(September 1958):426–450. Analysis of the circumstances of the American decision to establish the Republic of Korea in the South, thus contributing to the permanent division of the Korean peninsula. Includes a discussion of the first election in South Korea.

12-190. HAHN, Bae-ho. "Factions in Contemporary Korean Competitive Politics." PhD dissertation, Princeton University, 1971. 293 pp. Abstracted in *DAI* 32(3)(September 1971):1582-A; UM 72-23,360. Analysis of the nature of factional politics within the ruling and opposition parties during the Rhee and the Park era. The study discusses the importance of the supreme leader who dictates, arbitrates, or neutralizes factional struggles.

12-191. _____. "The Parties and Politics in Two Koreas: A Preliminary Comparative Analysis." *Journal of Asiatic Studies* 13(4)(December 1970):251–260. A model for a comparative study of the South and North Korean political systems. Includes a good discussion of different political practices in North and South Korea.

12-192. HAN, Ki-shik. "Development of Parties and Politics in Korea." *Korea Journal* 14(9)(September 1974):37–49. A discussion of party development in South Korea in the 1960s and 1970s. South Korea's party system is viewed as being competitive.

12-193. HAN, Tae-Soo. "The Results of National Referendum and the Future Prospects of Korean Politics." *Koreana Quarterly* 11(4)(1969–1970):12–20. Analysis of the results of a national referendum on the 1969 constitutional amendments.

12-194. _____. "Results of National Referendum and Its Significance." *Koreana Quarterly* 5(1)(Spring 1963):7–16. Analysis of the results of a national referendum on the third republican constitution held in 1962.

12-195. _____. "A Review of Political Party Activities in Korea (1945-1954)." *Korean Affairs* 1(1962):413–427. Discusses the various political parties that proliferated following the liberation and examines their activities.

12-196. HAN, Y. C. "The 1969 Constitutional Revision and Party Politics in South Korea." *Pacific Affairs* 44(2)(June 1971):242–258. A critical analysis of the 1969 constitutional revision—the circumstances which led to the revision and its passage.

12-197. _____. "Political Parties and Political Development in South Korea." *Pacific Affairs* 42(4)(Winter 1969–1970):444–464. A critical assessment of the ineffectiveness of political parties in South Korea in the performance of their functions.

12-198. HAN, Yung Chul. "Traditionalism and the Struggle for Political Modernization in Contemporary Korea: With Special Reference to the Development of Political Parties." PhD dissertation, New York University, 1966. 277 pp. Abstracted in *DAI* 27(June 1967):4311-12-A; UM 67-6026. Analysis of the causes for the failure of political modernization and party institutionalization in South Korea.

12-199. HENDERSON, Gregory. *Korea: The Politics of the Vortex.* Cambridge, Mass.: Harvard University Press, 1968. Chapters on functionalism, political parties, and the military. See 12-012.

12-200. HUANG, Sung-mo. "Whither the Revolution in Korea." *Korean Affairs* 2(1)(1963):44–59. A critical analysis of events in Korea during the Chang government of the Second Republic and the military coup in 1961.

12-201. JEWELL, Malcolm E. and Chong Lim KIM. "Sources of Support for the Legislature in a Developing Nation: The Case of Korea." *Comparative Political Studies* 7(4)(January 1976):461–489. See 12-077.

12-202. KANG, Han Mu. "The United States Military Government in Korea, 1945–1948: An Analysis and Evaluation of Its Policy." PhD dissertation, University of Cincinnati, 1970. Part 3 deals with the elections of 1948 and the establishment of the Republic of Korea. 301 pp. Abstracted in *DAI* 31(8)(February 1971):4242-A; UM 71-1527.

12-203. KEIM, Willard D. "The South Korean Peasantry in the 1970's." *Asian Survey* 14(9)(September 1974):854–868. Analysis of the deprived status of the South Korean peasantry and a critical review of the new community movement.

12-204. KIHL, Young-Whan. "Public Policy, Socioeconomic Development and Electoral Competition in Korean Cities: A Preliminary Analysis." *Koreana Quarterly* 15(1/2)(Spring/Summer 1973):3–25. A quantitative analysis of the impact of public policy on electoral competition in urban areas.

12-205. _____. "Research on Party Politics in Korea: An Analytical Scheme." *Korean Political Science Review* 6(June 1972):279–296. Presentation of an analytical scheme for the systematic study of party politics in Korea.

12-206. _____. "Urban Political Competition and the Allocation of National Resources: The Case Study of Korea." *Asian Survey* 13(4)(April 1973):366–379. A study of the politics of allocation of national resources by the ruling party. The findings show the importance of central planning.

12-207. KIM, C. I. Eugene. "The Meaning of the 1971 Korean Elections: A Pattern of Political Development." *Asian Survey* 12(3)(March 1972):213–224. A detailed analysis of the 1971 general elections in South Korea; notes the increasing sophistication of South Korean voters.

12-208. _____. "Patterns in the 1967 Korean Election." *Pacific Affairs* 41(1)(Spring 1968):60–70. Analysis of the uneven pattern of political development seen through the 1967 Korean general election.

12-209. _____. "Significance of the 1963 Korean Elections." *Asian Survey* 4(3)(March 1964):765–773. Analyzes the meaning of the 1963 elections in which General Park won his presidency by a much narrower margin than generally expected.

12-210. KIM, C. I. Eugene and Ke-soo KIM. "The April 1960 Korean Student Movement." *Western Political Quarterly* 17(1)(March 1964):83–92. A survey of participants in the movement. Students are viewed as the carriers of modernization in a repressive traditional society.

12-211. KIM, C. I. Eugene and Young Whan KIHL (eds.). *Parties and Electoral Politics in Korea.* Silver Spring, Md.: Research Institute on Korean Affairs, 1975. 195 pp. A collection of papers dealing with party development and electoral politics and political participation. North Korea is also covered.

12-212. KIM, C. I. Eugene, Young Whan KIHL, and Doock-kyu CHUNG. "Voter Turnout and the Meaning of Elections in South Korea." *Asian Survey* 13(11)(November 1973):1962–1974. Presents findings of a survey of the 1971 Korean elections and analyzes the meaning of the low turn-out rate in urban areas.

12-213. KIM, Chi-Sun. "The Changes in Labor Force Structure and Their Causes in Korea." *Koreana Quarterly* 14(1/2)(Spring/Summer 1972):34–41. Analysis of the changing composition of Korea's labor forces—its reasons and future impact.

12-214. KIM, Chong Lim and Gerhard LOWENBERG. "The Cultural Roots of a New Legislature: Public Perceptions of the Korean National Assembly." *Legislative Studies Quarterly* 1(3)(August 1976):371–387. See 12-082.

12-215. KIM, Chong Lim and Ji Hwan OH. "Perceptions of Professional Efficacy among Journalists in a Developing Country." *Journalism Quarterly* 51(1)(Spring 1974):73–78. Analysis of different perceptions of efficacy of journalists by type of assignments, professional commitment, and length of career in journalism.

12-216. KIM, Chong Lim and Byung-kyu WOO. "The Pat-terns of Recruitment and Political Representation in Korea." *Asian Profile* 2(1)(February 1974):31–44. See 12-141.

12-217. _____. "Political Representation in the Korean National Assembly." *Midwest Journal of Political Science* 16(4)(November 1972):626–651. A survey of Korean national assemblymen. Investigates their perceptions of their representation role.

12-218. KIM, Chulsu. "Parties and Factions in Korean Politics." PhD dissertation, University of Massachusetts, 1973. 352 pp. Abstracted in *DAI* 34(10)(April 1974):6716-A; UM 73-31,105. Analysis of Korean political parties and processes. Notes the importance of factions.

12-219. KIM, Jae-on and B. C. KOH. "Electoral Behavior and Social Development in South Korea: An Aggregate Data Analysis of Presidential Elections." *Journal of Politics* 34(3)(August 1972):825–859. A statistical analysis of the three presidential elections in Korea in 1963, 1967, and 1971. Particularly noted is the government mobilization of voters.

12-220. KIM, Kwan Bong. *The Korea–Japan Treaty Crisis and the Instability of the Korean Political System.* New York: Praeger, 1971. 350 pp. A detailed study of the early and formative years of South Korea's Third Republic. A good treatment of the formation of the Democratic-Republican Party of South Korea.

12-221. KIM, Kyong-dong. "Political Factors in the Formation of the Entrepreneurial Elite in South Korea." *Asian Survey* 16(5)(May 1976):465–477. Analyzes the interplay of politics and economy in South Korea's economic development and in the formation of its entrepreneurial elite. The pattern of South Korea's entrepreneurial behavior is also discussed.

12-222. KIM, Kyu-taik. "Statistical Analysis of the Elections in Korea." *Koreana Quarterly* 9(Summer 1967):60–84. A statistical analysis of several elections in South Korea. Some general trends are explained.

12-223. KIM, Myong-Whai. "The Presidential Election in Korea, 1963." *Korean Affairs* 2(1963):372–378. A statistical analysis of the 1963 presidential election marking the beginning of the presidency of General Park.

12-224. KIM, Myong-Whai, Eui-Yong HAM, and Hyoung-sup YOON. "Korean Voting Behavior and Political Orientation." *Korea Observer* 3(2)(January 1971):51–58. A survey on the meaning of elections and the extent of democratic practices in South Korea.

12-225. KIM, Se-Jin. "Attitudinal Orientations of Korean Workers." *Korea Journal* 12(9)(September 1972):18–30. See 12-085.

12-226. KIM, Song-Hui. "The Third Republic Moves Toward Stability—DRP." *Korean Affairs* 3(1)(April 1964): 52–62. Analyzes the ruling party of South Korea's Third Republic—its organization and activities.

12-227. KIM, Sung-sik. "Youth-Student Movement in Korea." *Korea Journal* 4(4)(April 1964):24–27. A discussion of various youth-student organizations and their activities.

12-228. KO, Young-bok. "Political Parties and Factionalism in Korea." *Koreana Quarterly* 9(2)(Summer 1967):18–37. Discusses the lack of institutionalization of Korean political parties and the prevalence of factional and personal politics.

12-229. LEE, Chae-Jin. "Urban Political Competition in a Developing Nation: The Case of Korea." *Comparative Political Studies* 4(1)(April 1971):107–116. A statistical analysis of the extent of urbanization and intensity of political competition.

12-230. _____. "Urban Electoral Participation in Korea." *Midwest Journal of Political Science* 16(2)(May 1972): 303–312. A statistical analysis of voting participation in South Korea's urban centers. The study shows a negative relationship between nonvoting and higher levels of education and affluence.

12-231. LEE, Jang-hyun. "Social Background and Career Development of the Korean Jurists." *Korea Journal* 14(6) (June 1974):11–20. A survey of Korean jurists.

12-232. LEE, Joung-sik. "Development of Party Politics in Korea." *Koreana Quarterly* 9(2)(Summer 1967):1–17. A useful summary of the origin and development of party politics in Korea since the liberation.

12-233. _____. "Voting Behavior in Korea." *Korean Affairs* 2(3–4)(1963). A useful review of Korean voting and attitudinal studies. The study shows the importance of personal rather than party preference in voting decisions.

12-234. LEE, Man-Gap and Herbert BARRINGER (eds.). *A City in Transition: Urbanization in Taegu, Korea: An IL-CORK/AID Research Report*. Seoul: Hollym Corp., 1971. An intensive work on Taegu's urbanization problems by a team of researchers. Covers various topics.

12-235. LEE, Taikwhi. "Urbanization and Its Political Implication." *Korean Affairs* 3(3)(December 1964):304–314. Analysis of political parties as possible channels for political participation by the rapidly urbanizing masses.

12-236. LIM, Sang-un. "An Analysis of Electoral Behavior in South Korea." PhD dissertation, Syracuse University, 1968. 328 pp. Abstracted in *DA* 29(December 1968): 1934-A; UM 68-13,844. A study of electoral dynamics and the development of party politics (1948–1960).

12-237. LOO, Robert Kalei Wah Kit. "A Comparative Study of Governmental Treatment of Interest Groups in South Korea and North Korea, 1954–1964." PhD dissertation, New York University, 1970. 391 pp. Abstracted in *DAI* 31(12)(June 1971):6681-82-A; UM 71-13,652. Analysis of differences in the treatment of various interest groups in North and South Korea.

12-238. MIN, Byong-Gi. "Political Parties and Diplomatic Policy." *Korea Journal* 7(6)(June 1967):31–38 and 8(12) (December 1968):5–11. Analysis of the foreign policy planks of major political parties.

12-239. MOBIUS, J. Mark. "Japan–Korea Normalization Process and Korean Anti-Americanism." *Asian Survey* 6(April 1966):241–248. Notes anti-Americanism in the 1965 student demonstration in opposition to Korea's normalization of relations with Japan.

12-240. _____. "The Korean Press and Public Opinion about Japan." *Journalism Quarterly* 42(Autumn 1965): 623–631. A survey of news reporting about Japan, particularly in relation to the Korea–Japan diplomatic normalization treaty.

12-241. MOON, Won-Taik. "South Korean Labor and Labor Policies and Their Relationship to Developmental Administration." PhD dissertation, George Washington University, 1971. 262 pp. Abstracted in *DAI* 32(8)(February 1972):4699-A; UM 72-7606. A comparative analysis of the labor policies and developmental administration of Presidents Syngman Rhee and Chung Hee Park. Shows among other things that "labor militancy is not a direct function of the level of industrial advancement of society."

12-242. OGLE, George Ewing. "Labor Unions in Rapid Economic Development: The Case of the Republic of Korea in the 1960's." PhD dissertation, University of Wisconsin at Madison, 1973. 423 pp. Abstracted in *DAI* 34(10)(April 1974):6213-A; UM 74-3539. Historical analysis of the development of labor unions in Korea and the meaning of "guided capitalism" in Korea in the 1960s.

12-243. OH, Byung-hun. "Party System in Korea." *Bulletin of the Korean Research Center* 21(December 1964):58–67. Analysis of the history and development of the Korean party system.

12-244. OH, In-hwan. "Korean Journalists: Their Perception of Roles." *Korea Journal* 15(3)(March 1975):4–12. A survey of working journalists employed by general Korean newspapers and news agencies. Surveys journalists' conceptions of four different roles (enlightenment role, watchdog role, political stabilizer role, and roles related to right and accountability).

12-245. _____. "The Korean Journalist—A Study of Dimensions of Role." PhD dissertation, University of Hawaii,

1974. 339 pp. Abstracted in *DAI* 35(9)(March 1975): 6250-A; UM 75-5038. A survey of the roles which Korean journalists perceive themselves playing.

12-246. OH, Jin Hwan. "Toward a Practical Approach to Journalism in Developing Countries: The Case Study of South Korea." PhD dissertation, University of Iowa, 1974. 158 pp. Abstracted in *DAI* 35(7)(January 1975): 4412-A; UM 75-1239. A study of journalism as a tool for national development.

12-247. OH, Jin Hwan and Young-geun KIM. "Mass Media Diffusion in the Process of Development in Korea." *Korea Journal* 14(12)(December 1974):23–31. Analysis of the diffusion of mass media, particularly newspapers, in Korea. Regional variations are noted. Newspaper circulation has been increasing faster in the country than in cities in South Korea.

12-248. OUM, Ky-moon. "Urban Growth and Political Participation in Korea (1962–1973): A Comparative Analysis of 32 Cities." PhD dissertation, University of Cincinnati, 1976. 263 pp. Abstracted in *DAI* 37(11)(May 1977):7292-3-A; UM 77-11,217. A quantitative study of the relationship between urbanization and support for government party, between the rate of participation and the rate of government party support, and between election results and institutional changes. The study shows that electoral participation differs according to the level of urban growth.

12-249. PAK, Kwon-sang. "Party Politics in Korea." *Korea Journal* 6(2)(February 1966):4–10. A critical survey of party politics in South Korea from its inception in 1945.

12-250. PARK, Han-shik. "Voting Participation and Socio-Economic Status in the U.S. and Korea: A Comparative Study." PhD dissertation, University of Minnesota, 1971. 156 pp. Abstracted in *DAI* 32(8)(February 1972):4686-A; UM 72-5617. Analyzes the difficulties with democratic institutions in Korea. Notes different meanings of political participation in the United States and Korea.

12-251. PARK, Hee-bum. "Political Parties and Economic Policies in Korea." *Koreana Quarterly* 9(2)(Summer 1967):38–59. Analysis of different economic development strategies offered by different parties.

12-252. PARK, Yong-ki. "Trade Unionism in Korea." *Free Labor World* 41(January 1963):11–15. A brief history and status of Korea on trade unionism.

12-253. SOHN, Yun-Mok. "Comparison of Policy Commitment by Government and Opposition Parties in the 1967 Presidential Election." *Koreana Quarterly* 9(2)(Summer 1967):138–151. An item-by-item comparison of party campaign platforms for the 1967 presidential election.

12-254. VALENCE, D. "Opposition in South Korea." *New Left Review* 77(January–February 1973):77–89. A discussion of the growing and increasingly effective domestic opposition, particularly by students and labor groups, at the time when President Park declared a "national state of emergency" in December 1971.

12-255. WIDEMAN, Bernie [Bernard F.]. "The Plight of the South Korean Peasant." In Frank Baldwin (ed.), *Without Parallel*. New York: Pantheon Books, 1973. A critical analysis of the South Korean development which has enriched people at the top at the sacrifice of those at the bottom: the peasants.

12-256. WOO, Byung-kyu. "The Disposal of Legislative Information in Korea." *Koreana Quarterly* 11(4)(Winter 1969–1970):21–30 and 12(1/2)(Spring/Summer 1970):64–74. A discussion of the legislative process and the working of various committees.

12-257. YANG, Sung-Chul. "Revolution and Change: A Comparative Study of the April Student Revolution of 1960 and the May Military Coup d'État of 1961 in Korea." PhD dissertation, University of Kentucky, 1970. 308 pp. Abstracted in *DAI* 31(10)(April 1971):5487-A; UM 71-8607. A comparative analysis of the causes of the 1960 and 1961 revolutions in South Korea and their impact on South Korea's political development.

12-258. YI, Gouzea. "Some Organizational Characteristics of the DRP of Korea." *Koreana Quarterly* 10(1)(September 1968):75–91. Analysis of the organization and development of the DRP as the government party.

12-259. YI, Hu-Rak. "Why is a Pan-national Party Necessary?" *Koreana Quarterly* 5(2)(Summer 1963): 11–16. An article by one of the leading figures of the Park regime calling for a single-party system for South Korea.

12-260. YOON, Chun-joo. "Urbanization and Political Participation in Korea." *Koreana Quarterly* 4(Autumn 1962): 62–89. A pioneering survey of urbanization and political participation in Korea. The findings show no necessary correlation.

12-261. YU, Suk Ryul. "Role of Interest Groups in Emerging Nations: A Case of Korea." PhD dissertation, University of Missouri, 1974. 540 pp. Abstracted in *DAI* 36(3)(September 1975):1784-5-A; UM 75-20,175. A documentary and empirical study of the nature, organization, and internal democracy of interest groups in South Korea. Emphasizes government control of interest group activities.

12-262. ZEON, Young-cheol. "The Politics of Land Reform in South Korea." PhD dissertation, University of Missouri, 1973. 335 pp. Abstracted in *DAI* 35(1)(July 1974): 549-50-A; UM 74-10,012. A survey of the political effect of land reform, particularly during the Rhee government of Korea's First Republic.

Constitutional Development and Government Structure

12-263. CHO, Chang-Hyun. "The System of Local Government in South Korea as Affected by Patterns of Centralized Control." PhD dissertation, George Washington University, 1968. 369 pp. Abstracted in *DA* 29(November 1968):1588-A; UM 68-14,590. A detailed study of the patterns of local government control in South Korea.

12-264. CHO, Suk Choon. "Administrative Decentralization in the Government of the Republic of Korea." PhD dissertation, University of Minnesota, 1965. 479 pp. Abstracted in *DA* 29(March 1966):5537-A; UM 65-15,247. Analysis of the centralist tradition in South Korea. The need in Korea for administrative decentralization is stressed. The thesis includes case studies.

12-265. CHOI, Sung-il. "The Electoral Reform, the New National Assembly, and Democracy in South Korea: A Functional Analysis." *Asian Survey* 13(12)(December 1973):1092-1101. Analysis of the electoral reform in 1972 and its manifest and latent functions.

12-266. HAN, Tae-Soo. "Results of National Referendum and Its Significance." *Koreana Quarterly* 5(1)(Spring 1963):7-16. See 12-194.

12-267. _____. "The Results of National Referendum and the Future Prospects of Korean Politics." *Koreana Quarterly* 2(4)(1969-1970):12-20.

12-268. HAN, Tai-yon. "Constitutional Development in Korea." *Koreana Quarterly* 5(1)(Spring 1963):45-55. A discussion of constitutional development from 1948 to 1963. The article also explains reasons for constitutional instability in South Korea.

12-269. HAN, Y. C. "The 1969 Constitutional Revision and Party Politics in South Korea." *Pacific Affairs* 44(2)(June 1971):242-258. See 12-196.

12-270. Hapdong News Agency. *Korea Annual*. Seoul: annual. Descriptive but up-to-date information.

12-271. KAL, Bong-Keun. "Characteristics of the New Constitution." *Koreana Quarterly* 14(4)(Winter 1972-1973):52-66. A summary and analysis of South Korea's fourth republican constitution of 1972.

12-272. KIM, C. I. Eugene. "South Korean Constitutional Development: The Meaning of the Third Constitution." *Papers of the Michigan Academy of Arts and Sciences* 49(1964):301-312. A comparative historical analysis of South Korea's three different constitutions between 1948 and 1963.

12-273. _____. "Korea at the Crossroads: The Birth of the Fourth Republic." *Pacific Affairs* 46(2)(Summer 1973):211-231. Analyzes the forces which brought about the creation of the Fourth Republic through a coup in office and discusses the meaning of the new constitution in terms of internal power politics.

12-274. _____. "The Military in the Politics of South Korea: Creating Political Order." In Jacques Van Doorn and Morris Janowitz (eds.), *On Military Intervention*. Rotterdam: Rotterdam University Press, 1971. A detailed account of the institution-building process associated with the creation of South Korea's Third Republic following the 1961 military coup.

12-275. KIM, Chae-Kwang. "Amendment to the Constitution Lacks Logical Foundation." *Koreana Quarterly* 11(3)(Autumn 1969):14-25. Written by a leader of the opposition New Democratic Party.

12-276. KIM, Jong-pil. "The Ethos of October Reforms." *Koreana Quarterly* 14(4)(Winter 1972-1973):10-17. See 12-145.

12-277. KIM, Ki-bom. "Revisions of the Korean Constitution." *Korea Journal* 14(7)(July 1974):4-13. Analysis of the new constitution of South Korea's Fourth Republic.

12-278. _____. "Certain Features of the Constitution." *Korean Affairs* 3(1)(April 1964):20-28. An explanation of some features of the 1963 constitution as revised from the original 1948 constitution of the Republic of Korea.

12-279. KIM, Kyu Sung. "The History of Constitutional Development in the Republic of Korea, 1948-1972." PhD dissertation, St. John's University, 1973. 221 pp. Abstracted in *DAI* 34(7)(January 1974):4124-A; UM 73-29,960. Analysis of the constitutional changes since 1948 and the meaning of South Korea's "democratic authoritarianism."

12-280. KIM, Se-Jin and Chang-Hyun CHO (eds.). *Korea: A Divided Nation*. Silver Spring, Md.: Research Institute on Korean Affairs, 1976. 330 pp. Includes articles on the constitutional system of South Korea. See 12-025.

12-281. Korea, Republic of. Oemubu (Ministry of Foreign Affairs). *The Military Revolution in Korea*. Seoul: 1961. An official justification of the 1961 coup.

12-282. _____. Supreme Council for National Reconstruction. *A Commentary on the Constitution of the Republic of Korea as Submitted to National Referendum*. Seoul: 1962. A useful document.

12-283. PAK, Chi-Young. "The Third Republic Constitution of Korea: An Analysis." *Western Political Quarterly* 21(1)(March 1968):110-122. Analysis of the third constitution—its similarities and differences compared with the first constitution.

12-284. RHI, Sang-Kyu. "The Structure of Government." *Korean Affairs* 3(1)(April 1964):29–43. Analysis of the third republican government and the meaning of the change from a parliamentary to a presidential system.

12-285. YU, Chin-o. "The Constitution of the Republic of Korea: Its Ideal and Reality." *Koreana Quarterly* 1(2) (1959):5–10. Analysis of the first constitution of the Republic of Korea by one of its chief architects.

Public Administration, Bureaucracy, and Government Performance

12-286. ADELMAN, Irma (ed.). *Practical Approaches to Development Planning: Korea's Second Five-Year Plan.* Baltimore: Johns Hopkins Press, 1969. 306 pp. A collection of papers dealing with successful economic planning efforts by foreign experts and South Korean planners.

12-287. BARK, Dong-suh [PAK, Tong-sŏ]. "Comparison of Administration under Different Ideologies." *Journal of Asiatic Studies* 13(4)(December 1970):279–292. A comparative study of administration in North and South Korea. The study emphasizes their similarities.

12-288. _____. "An Ecological Analysis of Korean Administration." *Koreana Quarterly* 9(4)(1967):55–73. A political and cultural interpretation of administration in South Korea.

12-289. _____. "Public Personnel Administration in Korea: A Mixed Heritage in Contemporary Practice." PhD dissertation, University of Minnesota, 1962. 469 pp. Abstracted in *DA* 23(April 1963):3959-60; UM 63-2306. A critical historical analysis of the system of public personnel administration in South Korea. Suggests reforms.

12-290. _____. "Study on Qualification of Korean Administrative Executives." *Koreana Quarterly* 11(2)(Summer 1969):19–37. A study of biographical backgrounds of high-ranking officials of the South Korean bureaucracy from 1948 to 1967.

12-291. CHA, Marn J. "Pollution Control Policy in Korea: An Assessment." *Koreana Quarterly* 14(3)(Autumn 1972): 33–59. Historical analysis of pollution politics. The public nuisance law, its effects, and enforcement problems.

12-292. CHO, Suk Choon. "Administrative Decentralization in the Government of the Republic of Korea." PhD dissertation, University of Minnesota, 1965. See 12-264.

12-293. CHU, Shao-hsien. "The Republic of Korea Actively Strengthening Its Defense Capabilities." *Asian Outlook* 3(June 1968):23–33. A review of the military capabilities

of South Korea, particularly in view of increasing North Korean provocation.

12-294. CHUNG, Joong-gun and Sung-moun PAE. "Orientation of the Korean Bureaucrats toward Democracy: A Study of Background and Institutional Characteristics." *Korea and World Affairs* 1(2)(Summer 1977):219–236. Findings of a survey conducted in the summer of 1975 on relationships between personal backgrounds and attitudes toward democratic cultural values. Younger, lower- ranking bureaucrats seem to show more democratic orientation.

12-295. COLE, David C. and Princeton N. LYMAN. *Korean Development: The Interplay of Politics and Economics.* Cambridge, Mass.: Harvard University Press, 1971. See 12-006.

12-296. HAN, Kiuk. "An Analysis of Government Administration of Communication Media in the Republic of Korea." PhD dissertation, New York University, 1967. 211 pp. Abstracted in *DA* 28(May 1968):4691-92-A; UM 68-6070. A survey of the ways government controls the mass communication media and the impact of such control.

12-297. Hapdong News Agency. *Korea Annual.* Seoul: annual. Useful statistical information. See 12-008.

12-298. HU, Bom. "A Social Information System for National Development Planning of a Developing Country: Korea." PhD dissertation, State University of New York at Buffalo, 1974. 242 pp. Abstracted in *DAI* 35(10)(April 1975):6794-95-A; UM 74-19,990. Critical analysis of the prevalent concepts and practices of national planning. Emphasizes the need for "a new knowledge of monitoring changes toward the fuller realization of what the future society should be in terms of the quality of human life."

12-299. JUN, Jong-sup. "Some Considerations of the Role of Bureaucracy: Effecting Modernization of Korea." *Koreana Quarterly* 10(January 1968):26–33. Analysis of the contributions made by the bureaucracy toward South Korea's modernization.

12-300. KANG, Pyung-kun. "Administrative Structure and Management in Regional Development: The Case of Korea." *Koreana Quarterly* 10(2)(Summer 1968):121–132. Critical analysis of the organization and management of regional development in South Korea.

12-301. _____. "The Role of Local Government in Community Development in Korea." PhD dissertation, University of Minnesota, 1966. 428 pp. Abstracted in *DA* 28(February 1968):3236-37-A; UM 68-1171. A survey of how the Korean people perceive the role of local government in community development. Also analyzes the structure and power allocation of local governments in South Korea.

12-302. KIHL, Young Whan. "Urban Political Competition and the Allocation of National Resources: The Case of Korea." *Asian Survey* 13(4)(April 1973):366–379. See 12-206.

12-303. KIM, Hyoung Yul. "Development Administration: The Case of South Korea with Reference to the Agricultural Development Program, 1961–1973." PhD dissertation, University of Maryland, 1974. 358 pp. Abstracted in *DAI* 35(7)(January 1975):4666-A; UM 74-29,081. Analysis of South Korea's agricultural development program—its planning, coordination, and execution. Concludes that "the effective accomplishment of program objectives depends upon the coordinated use of the administrative system and other action instruments."

12-304. KIM, Se-Jin. "South Korea's Involvement in Vietnam and Its Economic and Political Impact." *Asian Survey* 10(6)(June 1970):519–532. Concludes that South Korea's involvement in the Vietnam conflict was beneficial to President Park and his government.

12-305. KIM, Yung Sam. "The Government's Basic Orientation Vague—Minjung-dang." *Korean Affairs* 3(1)(April 1964): 63–72. Critical analysis of the government's developmental programs by one of the opposition party leaders.

12-306. KOH, B. C. (ed.). *Aspects of Administrative Development in South Korea.* Kalamazoo: Korea Research and Publications, 1967. 144 pp. A useful collection of papers on administrative development in South Korea.

12-307. Korea, Republic of. Bureau of Statistics, Economic Planning Board. *Korea Statistical Yearbook.* Seoul: Dong-A Publishing Co., annual. See 12-028.

12-308. Korea University. Asiatic Research Center. *Report: International Conference on the Problems of Modernization in Asia.* Seoul: 1965. Papers on public administration and bureaucracy. See 12-031.

12-309. LEE, Chae-Jin and Dong-Suh BARK. "Political Perception of Bureaucratic Elite in Korea." *Korea Journal* 13(10)(October 1973): 29–41. A survey on the extent of politicization of the South Korean bureaucracy and the political role that it plays.

12-310. LEE, Hahn-Been. "The Role of the Higher Civil Service under Rapid Social and Political Change." In Edward Weidner (ed.), *Development Administration in Asia.* Durham: Duke University Press, 1970. A discussion of the developmental role of the higher civil service in a country such as South Korea.

12-311. _____. *Korea: Time, Change and Administration.*

Honolulu: East-West Center Press, 1968. 240 pp. A major theoretical analysis of South Korea's administrative development and governmental performance.

12-312. LEE, Hahn Been and In-Joung WHANG. "Development of Senior Administrators: The Korean Experience." *Koreana Quarterly* 12(3)(Autumn 1971):1–19. A discussion of the ways Korea's senior bureaucrats have contributed to national development.

12-313. LEE, Won Sul. "The Embryo of Korean Bureaucracy in 1945." *Koreana Quarterly* 7(3)(Autumn 1965):32–49. A discussion of the Korean bureaucratic structure in 1945 as inherited from the Japanese colonial administration.

12-314. LEE, Yong Sun. "Political Elites and the Socio-Economic Development of South Korea, 1948–1972." PhD dissertation, Wayne State University, 1976. See 12-157.

12-315. LEE, Young-ho. "Economic Growth vs. Political Development: The Issue of Relative Emphasis in Modernization, Part II." *Korea Journal* 12(5)(May 1972):5–11. A discussion of the need for balanced growth of the economy and democratic political system.

12-316. LYMAN, Princeton N. "Economic Development in South Korea: Prospects and Problems." *Asian Survey* 6(July 1966):381–388. Discussion of the remarkable rate of growth of the South Korean economy and its future, particularly political and social, implications.

12-317. LYONS, Gene M. *Military Policy and Economic Aid: The Korean Case, 1950–1953.* Columbus: Ohio State University Press, 1961. 298 pp. An important work on the impact of America's foreign and military policies on the economic aid program for Korea during and after the Korean War. The study also deals with the background of social, political, and military events in Korea at the time.

12-318. MIN, Pyong-chon. "Non-Military Aspects of Korean National Defense." *Korea Observer* 3(1)(October 1970):3–23. A discussion of the integrated nature of economic, social, cultural, and political aspects of defense. Emphasizes a need for effective coordination of defense and economic growth.

12-319. MOON, Won-Taik. "South Korean Labor and Labor Policies and Their Relationship to Developmental Administration." PhD dissertation, George Washington University, 1971. See 12-241.

12-320. OH, Suck Hong. "A Separate Monitoring Agency in the Administration Control System: A Study of the Board of Audit and Inspection of the Government of the Republic of Korea." PhD dissertation, University of Pittsburgh, 1969. 350 pp. Abstracted in *DAI* 31(3)(September 1970):1357-A; UM 70-5286. A study of the working of a control system in Korea for the enforcement of administrative responsibility.

12-321. OH, Chung Hwan. "The Civil Service of the Republic of Korea." PhD dissertation, New York University, 1961. 352 pp. Abstracted in *DA* 27(December 1966):1901-02-A; UM 66-9730. Analysis of the South Korean civil service system—its origins and development.

12-322. PAE, Sung-moun. "Beyond Rationality and Self-Actualization: A Study of Korean Bureaucracy." *East Asian Review* 4(2)(Summer 1970):158–180. A survey of central and local government officials of various departments in South Korea. The study argues that scientific management and human relations management need not be incompatible and concludes that a combination of the two management approaches "represents the reality of South Korean bureaucracy."

12-323. PAIGE, Glenn and Doo Bum SHIN. "Aspiration and Obstacles in Korean Development Administration: An Application of Self-Anchoring Scaling." *Public Policy* 16(1967): 3–28. Introduction of self-anchoring scaling for the study of South Korea's development administration.

12-324. PAIK, Wanki. "Modernization of Korean Bureaucracy." PhD dissertation, Florida State University, 1972. 168 pp. Abstracted in *DAI* 33(11)(May 1973): 6437-A; UM 73-11,323. Analysis of the modernization process of South Korea's bureaucratic organizations and processes.

12-325. PARK, Moon Ok. "The Process of Korean Administrative Modernization." *Koreana Quarterly* 7(1)(Spring 1965): 111–125. A discussion of administrative and bureaucratic modernization in South Korea.

12-326. PARK, Nei Hei. "A Comparative Study of Managerial Job Attitudes in the U.S. and Korean Civil Services." PhD dissertation, American University, 1974. 131 pp. Abstracted in *DAI* 35(6)(December 1974):3223-23-A; UM 74-22,273. A comparative survey of different management organizations and differences in managerial job satisfaction.

12-327. REEVE, W. D. *The Republic of Korea: A Political and Economic Study*. London: Oxford University Press, 1963. See 12-052.

12-328. RHEE, Chongik. "Central Budget Administration and Its Structure in the Republic of Korea, 1961–1963." PhD dissertation, New York University, 1969. Abstracted in *DAI* 31(3)(September 1970):1357-A; UM 70-16,096. A study of the administrative structure and process of central budgeting.

12-329. RHEE, T. C. "South Korea's Economic Development and Its Socio-Political Impact." *Asian Survey* 13(July 1973):677–690. A critical evaluation of strengths and weaknesses of the Park regime, which has largely been instrumental in bringing about rapid economic development.

12-330. RHEE, Yong Pil. "The Breakdown of Authority Structure in Korea in 1960: A Case Study of the Failure of Concerted Feedback." *Journal of East and West Studies* 4(1)(April 1975):3–44. See 12-051.

12-331. RO, Chung-Hyun. "A Comparative Study of Manpower Administration in Developing Countries: With Special Reference to South and North Korea." PhD dissertation, New York University, 1962. 173 pp. Abstracted in *DA* 29(July 1968):313-14-A; UM 63-7197. A comparative study of the patterns of supply and use of trained manpower in North and South Korea.

12-332. SHIN, Doh Chull. "Socio-Economic Development and Democratization in South Korea: A Time-Series Analysis." PhD dissertation, University of Illinois at Urbana-Champaign, 1972. 196 pp. Abstracted in *DAI* 33(11)(May 1973):6422-A; UM 73-10,052. A statistical analysis of negative correlation of socioeconomic development and democratization in South Korea.

12-333. SHIN, Roy W. "The Politics of Foreign Aid: A Study of the Impact of United States Aid to Korea from 1945 to 1966." PhD dissertation, University of Minnesota, 1969. 313 pp. Abstracted in *DAI* 30(6)(December 1969): 2588-A; UM 69-20,094. A study of the contribution American aid has made to Korea's economic and political development.

12-334. SPRINGER, John Frederick. "Role Integration among Development Administrators: A Cross-National Comparison." PhD dissertation, University of California at Davis, 1974. See 12-115.

12-335. SWISHER, Ralph Blakeslee. "Passing the Threshold to Modernity in Rural South Korea: The Convergence of Elite Communications, Popular Frame of Reference, and Institutional Capacity." PhD dissertation, University of Pittsburgh, 1972. See 12-116.

12-336. WHANG, In-joung. "Elites and Economic Programs: A Study of Changing Leadership for Economic Development in Korea, 1955–1967." PhD dissertation, University of Pittsburgh, 1968. See 12-173.

12-337. _____. "Integration and Coordination of Population Policies in South Korea." *Asian Survey* 14(11)(November 1974):985–999. A discussion of the government's performance in the administration of population control policy.

12-338. _____. "Leadership and Organizational Development in the Economic Ministries of the Korean Government." *Asian Survey* 11(10)(October 1971):992–1004. An evaluation of organizational changes within the bureaucracy introduced by political leaders for better performance and more effective political control.

12-339. WIDEMAN, Bernard F. "The Political Economics of Factor Inputs in Korean Agriculture." *Korea Journal* 13(January 1973):19–24. Analyzes the government's "export first" policy and discusses the growing disparity between urban workers and farm laborers.

12-340. WIDEMAN, Bernie [Bernard F.]. "The Plight of the South Korean Peasant." In Frank Baldwin (ed.), *Without Parallel*. New York: Pantheon Books, 1973. See 12-255.

12-341. WOLF, Charles, Jr. "Economic Planning in Korea." *Asian Survey* 2(December 1962):22–28. A discussion of the history of economic planning in South Korea and the First Five-Year Plan instituted in 1962.

12-342. WRIGHT, Edward R. (ed.). *Korean Politics in Transition*. Seoul: Korea Branch of the Royal Asiatic Society, 1974. Includes papers on public administration and bureaucracy.

12-343. YIM, Yong Soon. "A Comparative Study of Systematic Outputs in Two Koreas: A Theoretical Framework." *Journal of Korean Affairs* 4(4)(January 1975):39–48. A research note for comparative study of the performance of the North and South Korean political systems. Introduces some research hypotheses.

12-344. YOO, Hoon. "Social Background of Higher Civil Servants in Korea." *Koreana Quarterly* 10(1)(1968):35–55. A quantitative analysis of the social background of higher civil servants in South Korea showing changes over the years.

12-345. YOO, Jong Hae. "National Planning for Development: The Case of Korea." PhD dissertation, University of Michigan, 1968. 240 pp. Abstracted in *DA* 30(July 1969):309-A; UM 69-12,279. A study of the substance and process of national planning for development since 1953 in Korea.

12-346. YOON, Woo-kon. "Korean Bureaucrats' Behavior: An Analysis of Personality and Its Effect." *Korea Journal* 14(7)(July 1974):22–29. Survey on the authoritarian personality of the Korean people and its effect on South Korean bureaucrats' behavior.

12-347. _____. "The Effect of Personality on Bureaucrats' Behavior in the Case of South Korea." PhD dissertation, New York University, 1972. 258 pp. Abstracted in *DAI* 33(7)(January 1973):3753-54-A; UM 72-31,146. Survey findings show that South Korean bureaucrats are highly authoritarian in their personality manifestations. Suggests that the more authoritarian they are, the more compulsive desire for power they manifest along with their personal inclinations.

12-348. YU, Hoon. "The Budgeting Process in Korea." PhD dissertation, University of Minnesota, 1974. 297 pp. Abstracted in *DA* 25(February 1965):4807; UM 65-1026. A study of the South Korean budget system and the way it works.

12-349. YU, Tal-Young. "The National Reconstruction Movement in Retrospect and Prospect." *Korean Affairs* 1(1962):291–299. Discusses the workings of the national reconstruction movement instituted by the military leaders soon after the 1961 coup.

THE DEMOCRATIC PEOPLE'S REPUBLIC OF KOREA
General

12-350. BRUN, Ellen and Jacques HERSH. *Socialist Korea: A Case Study in the Strategy of Economic Development*. New York: Monthly Review Press, 1976. 422 pp. Argues for the case of North Korean strategy for development as relevant to many countries that are trying to find their own roads of development. A laudatory account of North Korean development by European writers largely on the basis of personal observation.

12-351. BUCHER, Lloyd M. (with Mark Rascovich). *Bucher: My Story*. Garden City: Doubleday, 1970. 447 pp. A personal, revealing account of his experience in North Korea by the commander of the *Pueblo*, an American intelligence ship captured by North Korea.

12-352. CHO, Soon Sung. "Korea: Election Year." *Asian Survey* 8(1)(January 1968):29–42. Covers events and developments in North Korea in 1967.

12-353. _____. "North and South Korea: Stepped-up Aggression and Search for New Security." *Asian Survey* 9(1)(January 1969):29–39. See 12-002.

12-354. _____. "The Politics of North Korea's Unification Policies: 1950–65." *World Politics* 19(2)(January 1967): 218–241. A detailed discussion of factors affecting North Korean policies toward South Korea and its Korean reunification strategies and tactics.

12-355. CHUNG, Henry. *The Russian Came to Korea*. Seoul and Washington: Korean Pacific Press, 1947. 212 pp. Analysis of Russia's intentions in Korea in both historical and contemporary contexts. Warns against the Russian intention to stay in Korea.

12-356. HAHN, Bae-ho. "Some Methodological Aspects of North Korean Studies." *East Asian Review* 1(1)(Spring 1974):2–11. A discussion of difficulties plaguing North Korean studies and its future research needs.

12-357. _____. "Toward a Comparative Analysis of the South and North Korean Political Systems." *Social Science Journal* (1973):7–21. See 12-007.

12-358. Hoover Institution. Stanford Univeristy. *Yearbook on International Communist Affairs.* Stanford: Hoover Institution Press, annual. The section on North Korea includes discussions of leadership, organization, and other topics.

12-359. JANG, Woo Tai and others. "Socialist Korea: A Korean Marxist View." In Harry G. Shaffer (ed.), *The Communist World: Marxist and Non-Marxist View.* New York: Appleton-Century-Crofts, 1967. A collection of articles on various aspects of North Korean development. Articles appeared in *Korea Today* and *Democratic People's Republic of Korea,* periodicals in the English language published in North Korea.

12-360. JO, Yung-hwan. "Whither Two Koreas?" *Asian Survey* 6(1)(January 1966):34–42. Covers events and developments in North Korea in 1965. See 12-014.

12-361. KIM, C. I. Eugene. "Korea in the Year of ULSA." *Asian Survey* 6(1)(January 1966):34–42. Covers events and developments in North Korea in 1965.

12-362. _____ (ed.). *Korean Unification: Problems and Prospects.* Kalamazoo: Korea Research and Publications, 1973. Includes papers on North Korea.

12-363. KIM, C. I. Eugene and Lawrence ZIRING. "Korea: The Politics of a Divided Nation." In *An Introduction to Asian Politics.* Englewood Cliffs, N.J.: Prentice-Hall, 1977. See 12-020.

12-364. KIM, Chang-sun. *Fifteen-Year History of North Korea.* Washington: Joint Publications Research Service, 1963. 198 pp. Historical survey of North Korea, its changes, and its developments. Includes government and politics.

12-365. KIM, Il Sung. *Report at the Celebration Meeting of the 10th Anniversary of the Founding of the Democratic People's Republic of Korea.* Pyongyang: Foreign Languages Publishing House, 1958. 43 pp. A ten-year summary of the progress North Korea has made.

12-366. KIM, Ilpyong J. *Communist Politics in North Korea.* New York: Praeger, 1975. 121 pp. A study of systematic political changes in North Korea as they have been forcefully engineered by the Pyongyang regime.

12-367. KIM, Joungwon Alexander. *Divided Korea: The Politics of Development, 1945-1972.* Cambridge, Mass.: East Asian Research Center, Harvard University, 1975. Covers North Korea. See 12-021.

12-368. _____. "Divided Korea 1969: Consolidating for Transition." *Asian Survey* 10(1)(January 1970):30–42. Covers events and developments in North Korea in 1969. See 12-022.

12-369. _____. "Soviet Policy in North Korea." *World Politics* 22(2)(January 1970):237–254. Developments in North Korea since 1945, particularly regarding its relationship with the Soviet Union.

12-370. KIM, Se-Jin and Chang-Hyun CHO (eds.). *Korea: A Divided Nation.* Silver Spring, Md.: Research Institute on Korean Affairs, 1976. Includes papers on North Korea. See 12-025.

12-371. KIM, Young C. "North Korea in 1974." *Asian Survey* 15(1)(January 1975):43–52. A survey of events and developments in North Korea in 1974.

12-372. KIM, Uoong Tack. "Sino-Soviet Dispute and North Korea." PhD dissertation, University of Pennsylvania, 1967. 385 pp. Abstracted in *DA* 28(November 1967): 1879-A; UM 67-12,766. Analysis of North Korean political developments within the overall context of Sino-Soviet relations.

12-373. KOH, B. C. "North Korea and the Sino-Soviet Schism." *Western Political Quarterly* 22(December 1969): 940–962. Analysis of North Korean reactions to and exploitation of the Sino-Soviet schism.

12-374. _____. "North Korea: A Breakthrough in the Quest for Unity." *Asian Survey* 13(1)(January 1973):83–93. A survey of events and developments in North Korea in 1972.

12-375. _____. "North Korea 1976: Under Stress." *Asian Survey* 17(1)(January 1977):61–70. A survey of developments in North Korea in 1976. Covers the 1976 Panmunjŏm incident and changes in North Korea's power hierarchy.

12-376. Korea University. Asiatic Research Center. *Report: International Conference on the Problems of Korean Unification.* Seoul: 1971. Papers on North Korea. See 12-030.

12-377. LEE, Chong-Sik. "The Impact of the Sino-American Detente on Korea." In Gene T. Hsiao (ed.), *Sino-American Detente and Its Policy Implications.* New York: Praeger, 1974. Discusses North Korean reactions.

12-378. _____. "Korea: In Search of Stability." *Asian Survey* 4(1)(January 1964):656–665. Covers events and developments in North Korea in 1963.

12-379. _____. "Korea: Troubles in a Divided State." *Asian Survey* 5(1)(January 1965):25–32. Covers events and developments in North Korea in 1964.

12-380. _____. "New Paths for North Korea." *Problems of Communism* 26(March 1977):55–66. A survey of recent developments in North Korea. Highlights North Korea as being in a state of flux and some significant leadership changes.

12-381. _____. "Politics in North Korea: Pre-Korean War Stage." *China Quarterly* 14(April/June 1963):3–16. Analysis of the power structure of North Korea at the time of liberation and Kim Il Sung's eventual rise to power.

12-382. _____. "Stalinism in the East: Communism in North Korea." In Robert A. Scalapino (ed.), *The Communist Revolution in Asia*. Englewood Cliffs: Prentice-Hall, 1965. One of the first systematic studies on North Korean communism—Kim Il Sung's rise to power and his imposition of Stalinism in North Korea. Includes a discussion of government and politics.

12-383. NAHM, Andrew C. (ed.). *Studies in the Developmental Aspects of Korea*. Kalamazoo: School of Graduate Studies, Western Michigan University, 1969. Includes papers on North Korea. See 12-044.

12-384. NOBLE, Harold J. "North Korean Democracy: Russian Style." *New Leaders* 30(22)(31 May 1947):1–12. Analysis of the formative years of the North Korean regime under Russian influence and supervision.

12-385. PAIGE, Glenn. *The Korean People's Democratic Republic*. Stanford: Stanford University Press, 1966. 60 pp. A study of North Korean development, particularly her relationships with the other communist bloc nations. North Korea's increasingly independent posture is noted.

12-386. _____. "Korea." In Cyril E. Black and Thomas P. Thornton (eds.), *Communism and Revolution: The Strategic Use of Violence*. Princeton: Princeton University Press, 1964. Analyzes the meaning of political violence in the development of North Korean communism and the way political violence has been used as a means for national unification.

12-387. _____. "North Korea and the Emulation of Russian and Chinese Behavior." In A. Doak Barnett (ed.), *Communist Strategies in Asia*. New York: Praeger, 1963. A succinct summary of the North Korean system and its relationships with the USSR and the People's Republic of China.

12-388. PAIGE, Glenn and Dong Jun LEE. "The Post-war Politics of Communist Korea." *China Quarterly* 14 (April/June 1963):17–29. Analysis of the major political developments in North Korea during 1952–1953 as they were affected by internal and international politics.

12-389. RILEÝ, John W. and Wilbur SCHRAMM. *The Reds Take a City: The Communist Occupation of Seoul with Eyewitness Accounts*. New Brunswick: Rutgers University Press, 1951. 210 pp. A scholarly assessment of communist techniques in occupied areas during the Korean War. South Korean officials and citizens who remained under communist occupation were interviewed.

12-390. RUDOLPH, P. "North Korea and the Path to Socialism." *Pacific Affairs* 32(2)(June 1959):131–143. Historical account of North Korea's collectivization program and ideological transformation.

12-391. RYU, Hun. *Study of North Korea*. Seoul: Research Institute of International and External Affairs, 1963. 317 pp. A critical survey of North Korean government, politics, and rulership structure. Also covers economy, education, and culture.

12-392. SALISBURY, Harrison E. *To Peking and Beyond*. New York: Quadrangle Books, 1973. 308 pp. Contains a report of personal observation of North Korea.

12-393. SCALAPINO, Robert A. (ed.). *North Korea Today*. New York: Praeger, 1963. 141 pp. A collection of papers on North Korea which appeared originally in *China Quarterly* (April/June 1963). Covers various aspects of the North Korean political system.

12-394. SCALAPINO, Robert A. and Chong-Sik LEE. *Communism in Korea*. 2 vols. Berkeley: University of California Press, 1972. The most comprehensive work available in the English language on the communist movement in Korea and the communist North Korean regime. Contains a valuable annotated bibliography.

12-395. SCHRAMM, Wilbur, J. W. RILEY, Jr., and F. W. WILLIAMS. "Flight from Communism: A Report on Korean Refugees." *Public Opinion Quarterly* 15(Summer 1951):274–286. A report of interviews with refugees from North and South Korea during the Korean War. North Korean refugees show more anticommunist feelings than South Korean refugees.

12-396. SCHUMACHER, F. Carl, Jr., and George WILSON. *Bridge of No Return: The Ordeal of the USS Pueblo*. New York: Harcourt, Brace, Jovanovich, 1970. 242 pp. Account of a crew member of the intelligence ship captured by North Korea.

12-397. SIMMONS, R. "North Korea: Silver Anniversary." *Asian Survey* 11(1)(January 1971):104–110. A survey of events and developments in North Korea in 1970.

12-398. _____. "North Korea: Year of the Thaw." *Asian Survey* 12(1)(January 1972):25–31. A survey of events and developments in North Korea in 1971.

12-399. SUH, Dae-Sook. *The Korean Communist Movement, 1918–1948*. Princeton: Princeton University Press, 1967. 406 pp. A pioneering work in the English language of the Korean communist movement since its inception in 1918.

12-400. _____. *Documents of Korean Communism, 1918–1948*. Princeton: Princeton University Press, 1970. 570 pp. A collection of documents showing the development of the Korean communist movement leading to the establishment of the Democratic People's Republic of Korea. Translated and edited.

12-401. United States. Department of State. *North Korea: A Case Study in the Techniques of Takeover*. Washington:

Government Printing Office, 1961. 121 pp. Report of a State Department team sent to Korea in 1950.

12-402. VREELAND, Nena, Rinn-Sup SHINN, and others. *Area Handbook for North Korea. DA* Pamphlet 550-81. Washington: Government Printing Office, 1976. 481 pp. A useful exposition and analysis of the dominant social, political, and economic aspects of North Korea. The study includes many illustrative tables and a lengthy bibliography.

12-403. WHITE, D. G. "Democratic People's Republic of Korea through the Eyes of a Visiting Sinologist." *China Quarterly* 63(September 1975):515–522. Account of a personal visit to North Korea. Compares the North Korean and Chinese roads to socialism and notes the importance of *chuch'e*-ism in North Korea.

12-404. YUN, Ki-bong. *North Korea as I Knew It [Naega bon pungnyŏkttang].* Seoul: Buk-han Research Institute, 1974. 232 pp. Personal account of a life of regimentation in North Korea by a former North Korean espionage agent dispatched to South Korea. The author defected to South Korea. Some useful insights.

Political Culture, Ideology, and Political Socialization

12-405. AN, Thomas. "New Winds in Pyongyang?" *Military Review* 46(November 1966):75–81. A discussion of North Korean national interest and the rise of a new sense of nationalism and independence.

12-406. CHOI, Yung. "The Comparative Study on the Thought of Mao Tsetung and Chuch'e Thought." *East Asian Review* 2(1)(Spring 1975):2–23. The thought of Mao and *chuch'e* thought of Kim Il Sung as variations of the mass-line approach of mobilization.

12-407. CUMINGS, Bruce G. "Kim's Korean Communism." *Problems of Communism* 23(2)(March 1974):27–40. Analyzes the emergence of the Korean brand of communism in North Korea since 1945. A useful summary of its operative principles and realities.

12-408. HAHM, Pyong-Choon. "Ideology and Criminal Law in North Korea." *American Journal of Comparative Law* 17(1969):77–93. A study of the North Korean legal system, which has been molded after Stalinist law. Its operative principle is viewed as being primarily a political expression.

12-409. KIM, Gaab Chol. "Reflections on the Origin and Development of the Chuche Idea in North Korea: The Impact of Sino-Soviet Competition." *East Asian Review* 2(2) (Summer 1975):145–165. Historical account of the origin and development of the *chuch'e* idea in North Korea.

12-410. KIM, Hyung-Chan. "Ideology and Indoctrination in the Development of North Korean Education." *Asian Survey* 9(11)(November 1969):831–841. A discussion of major educational reforms in North Korea since 1945 and the importance of the "thoughts of Kim Il Sung" in ideological indoctrination.

12-411. KIM, Il Sung. *Selected Works.* 5 vols. Pyongyang: Foreign Languages Publishing House, 1971. A collection of various works by President Kim Il Sung.

12-412. KIM, Ilpyong J. *Communist Politics in North Korea.* New York: Praeger, 1975. Includes a discussion of North Korean ideology.

12-413. _____. "The Mobilization System in North Korean Politics." *Journal of Korean Affairs* 2(1)(April 1972):3–15. Analysis of the North Korean mobilization system—North Korea's stress on the ideological and cultural revolution to mold the consciousness of the people.

12-414. KIM, Sun Ho. "Education in North Korea: Technical, Manpower and Ideological Development." PhD dissertation, George Peabody College for Teachers, 1971. 579 pp. Abstracted in *DAI* 32(4)(October 1971):1751-A; UM 71-26,212. Analysis of North Korea's manpower training programs at the secondary and higher educational levels and their stress on the principles of unity between education and productive labor.

12-415. KIM, Young C. "North Korea's Reunification Policy: A Magnificent Obsession?" *Journal of Korean Affairs* 3(4)(January 1974):15–24. A personal account of talks with North Korean leaders.

12-416. KOH, B. C. *The Foreign Policy of North Korea.* New York: Praeger, 1969. 237 pp. References to the role ideology plays in North Korea's modernization.

12-417. _____. "Chuch'esŏng in Korean Politics." *Studies in Comparative Communism* 7(1/2)(Spring/Summer 1974):83–106. See 12-091.

12-418. _____. "Ideology and Political Control in North Korea." *Journal of Politics* 32(3)(August 1970):655–674. A full account of development of the thoughts of Kim Il Sung and their place in North Korean society.

12-419. _____. "North Korea and Its Quest for Autonomy." *Pacific Affairs* 38(3/4)(Fall/Winter 1965–1966):294–306. Discusses North Korea's vast economic improvement and its newfound policy of neutrality and nonalignment.

12-420. LEE, Chong-Sik. "North Korea between Dogmatism and Revisionism." *Journal of Korean Affairs* 1(1)(April 1971):14–24. A useful survey of changes in the North Korean system in its attempt to cope with dogmatism and revisionism in the international communist movement. Views the North Korean communists as ideologically orthodox and committed to war to attain their victory.

12-421. _____. "The 'Socialist Revolution' in the North Korean Countryside." *Asian Survey* 2(10)(October 1962): 9–22. Analysis of the agricultural cooperatives in North Korea.

12-422. LI, Yuk-sa (ed.). *JUCHE: The Speeches and Writings of Kim Il Sung.* New York: Grossman Publishers, 1972. 271 pp. Kim is lauded as a spokesman for pluralism and nationalism within the communist movement. His concept of *chuch'e* is regarded as a creative application of Marxism-Leninism to the historical and national characteristics of each country.

12-423. PAGE, Ben. "North Korea: Sitting on Its Own Chair." *Monthly Review* 20(January 1969):15–31. An assessment of the independent philosophical and ideological position of North Korea in relation to the USSR and China.

12-424. PARK, Young-horm. "The School System of North Korea." *East Asian Review* 4(1)(Spring 1977):43–67. Also examined are the North Korean educational policy and its basic objectives.

12-425. RUDOLPH, P. "North Korea and the Path to Socialism." *Pacific Affairs* 32(2)(June 1959):131–143. Notes the importance of ideology. See 12-390.

12-426. SCALAPINO, Robert A. and Chong-Sik LEE. *Communism in Korea.* 2 vols. Berkeley: University of California Press, 1972. Chapter 2 deals with ideology. See 12-394.

12-427. SONG, Byung Soon. "Comparative Study of Ideological Influences on Educational Theory and Practice in North and South Korea." PhD dissertation, Wayne State University, 1974. See 12-114.

12-428. YANG, K. P. and C. B. CHEE. "The North Korean Educational System: 1945 to Present." *China Quarterly* 14(April/June 1963):125–140. Historical study of the North Korean educational system and its development.

12-429. YIU, Myung Kun. "Sino-Soviet Rivalry in North Korea Since 1954." PhD dissertation, University of Maryland, 1969. 375 pp. Abstracted in *DAI* 31(3)(September 1970):1353-A; UM 70-14,953. A study of the evolution of Kim Il Sung's policy of *chuch'e* and the Sino-Soviet responses to it.

Political Leaders, Leadership Style, and Decision-making

12-430. BAIK, Bong. *Kim Il Sung: Biography.* 3 vols. Tokyo: Miraisha, 1969–1970. An official biography. Contains useful details on Kim's life and career.

12-431. CHUNG, Chin O. "The Central Government and Power Structure of North Korea." *Korean Affairs* 1(3) (October 1971):3–11. Analyzes the governmental structure of North Korea and the power alignment within it.

12-432. CHUNG, Kiwon. "The North Korean People's Army and the Party." *China Quarterly* 14(April/June 1963): 105–124. Analyzes the North Korean People's Army—its organization and the method of political control over it.

12-433. JOY, Charles Turner. *How Communists Negotiate.* Santa Monica, Calif.: Fidelis Publishers, 1970. 178 pp. An account by the chief UN negotiator at the Panmunjŏm truce talks.

12-434. KANG, Young Hoon. "North Korea's Mysterious Kim Il-Sŏng." *Communist Affairs* 2(March 1964):21–26. A study of Kim's background and his rise to power.

12-435. KIM, Byong-sik. *Modern Korea: The Socialist North, Revolutionary Perspectives in the South and Unification.* Translated by Takeshi Haga and edited by Victor Perlo. New York: International Publishers, 1970. 319 pp. A laudatory account of North Korea's socialist transformation and Kim Il Sung's strategies and tactics regarding unification.

12-436. KIM, Dong Su. "Future Revolutionaries." *Democratic People's Republic of Korea* 135(1967):8–11. An official report on the Mangyŏngdae Institute in North Korea where future leaders are trained.

12-437. KIM, Il Sung. *Answers to the Questions Raised by Foreign Journalists.* Pyongyang: Foreign Languages Publishing House, 1974. On national reunification and other topics.

12-438. _____. *For the Independent Peaceful Reunification of Korea.* Rev. ed. New York: Guardian Associates, 1976. 246 pp. A collection of speeches in the 1960–1976 period.

12-439. _____. *Selected Works.* 5 vols. Pyongyang: Foreign Languages Publishing House, 1971. A collection of various works by Kim Il Sung.

12-440. KIM, Ilpyong J. *Communist Politics in North Korea.* New York: Praeger, 1975. Includes a discussion of North Korean leadership techniques. See 12-366.

12-441. KIM, Joungwon Alexander. *Divided Korea: The Politics of Development, 1945–1972.* Cambridge, Mass.: East Asian Research Center, Harvard University, 1975. Includes a discussion of Kim Il Sung and his leadership. See 12-021.

12-442. _____. "North Korea's New Offensive." *Foreign Affairs* 48(1)(October 1969):166–179. Analysis of Kim Il Sung's drive for reunification at any cost.

12-443. _____. "Pyongyang's Search for Legitimacy." *Problems of Communism* 20(January/April 1971):37–44. A discussion of North Korea's need to establish and substantiate Kim Il Sung's claim to be the legitimate leader of the North as well as all Korea.

12-444. KIM, Nam-shik. "The Decision-Making Process in

the Foreign Policy of North Korea." *East Asian Review* 1(1)(Spring 1974):66–87. Importance of the Communist Party in North Korean foreign policy decision-making. The discussion includes an analysis of the North Korean foreign policy decision-making structure.

12-445. KIM, Roy U. T. "Sino–North Korean Relations." *Asian Survey* 8(8)(August 1968):708–722. North Korea's autonomy and independence vis-à-vis China as resulting from North Korea's development.

12-446. KIM, Tae-ho. "The Ruling System of North Korean Regime." *Korean Affairs* 2(2)(1963):174–186. Analysis of the North Korean leadership structure.

12-447. KIM, Tae-suh. "North Korea's New Constitution and New Power Structure." *East Asian Review* 4(1) (Spring 1977):23–43. Analysis of the new North Korean constitution adopted on 27 December 1972. The succession question in North Korea is also treated.

12-448. KIM, Young Jeh. "The Purpose of North Korea's Guerrilla Warfare and the Republic of South Korea." *Issues and Studies* 6(11)(August 1970):16–28.

12-449. KIM, Yu-nam. "External Inputs and North Korea's Confrontation Policy: A Case Study of Linkage Politics." PhD dissertation, North Texas State University, 1973. 333 pp. Abstracted in *DAI* 34(4)(October 1973):1999-2000-A; UM 73-23,738. Analysis of the North Korean confrontation policy from 1953 to 1970 as resulting from "fused linkage" between her international environment and internal need for economic development and political stability.

12-450. KOH, B. C. *The Foreign Policy of North Korea.* New York: Praeger, 1969. See 12-416.

12-451. _____. "Anatomy of a Revolution: Some Implications of the Fifth KWP Congress." *Journal of Korean Affairs* 1(3)(October 1971):22–36. Analysis of the Fifth Congress of the Korean Workers' Party of North Korea.

12-452. _____. "Ideology and Political Control in North Korea." *Journal of Politics* 32(3)(August 1970):655–674. See 12-418.

12-453. _____. "North Korea: Profile of a Garrison State." *Problems of Communism* 18(January 1969):18–27. Discusses the cult of Kim Il Sung and his political goals and analyzes North Korea as a militant state.

12-454. _____. "The *Pueblo* Incident in Perspective." *Asian Survey* 9(4)(April 1969):264–280. Analysis of North Korea's various tactical responses to the changing politico-economic situation in South Korea. Regards North Korea's foremost strategic objective as the communization of the South.

12-455. _____. "The Revolutionary Strategy of North Korea." *Pacific Community* 2(2)(January 1971):354–368. A discussion of the revolutionary strategy of North Korea to consummate its revolution in all parts of Korea. Includes an analysis of a report by Kim Il Sung to the Korean Workers' Party conference in October 1966.

12-456. Korea, Democratic People's Republic of. Party History Institute. *Brief History of the Revolutionary Activities of Comrade Kim Il Sung.* Pyongyang: Foreign Languages Publishing House, 1969. 295 pp. North Korea's official record of Kim's revolutionary activities and leadership style.

12-457. KIYOSAKI, Wayne S. *North Korea's Foreign Relations: The Politics of Accommodation, 1945–75.* New York: Praeger, 1976. 133 pp. Includes a discussion of leadership and the political ideology of Kim Il Sung. North Korea's accommodation to pressures from Moscow and Peking is viewed as positive accommodation, not merely passive acquiescence.

12-458. LEE, Chong-Sik. "Kim Il-sŏng of North Korea." *Asian Survey* 7(6)(June 1967):374–382. Analysis of the life of Kim Il Sung and his leadership style.

12-459. _____. "New Paths for North Korea." *Problems of Communism* 26(March 1977):55–66. Covers recent leadership changes.

12-460. LEE, Chong-Sik and K. W. OH. "Russian Faction in North Korea." *Asian Survey* 8(April 1968):270–288. Historical and biographical account of a dominant power group in North Korea.

12-461. LEE, Sang-min. "The Factual Sampling Analysis on the Personality Cult of Kim Il-sŏng." *East Asian Review* 4(3)(Autumn 1974):301–329. Extent of the personality cult of Kim Il Sung as revealed by published materials in North Korea.

12-462. NAM, Koon Woo. *The North Korean Communist Leadership, 1945–1965: A Study of Factionalism and Political Consolidation.* University: University of Alabama Press, 1974. 214 pp. A study of power struggle and President Kim Il Sung's rise to power and prominence in North Korea.

12-463. _____. "North Korean Non-Communist Leaders and Political Effects of the 'Democratic' Reforms." *Journal of Korean Affairs* 2(2)(October 1972):29–43. Discusses the fate of noncommunist leaders in North Korea and the way they have been purged.

12-464. SCALAPINO, Robert A. and Chong-Sik LEE. *Communism in Korea.* 2 vols. Berkeley: University of California Press, 1972. Chapter 9 covers leadership. See 12-394.

12-465. SUH, Dae-Sook. *The Korean Communist Movement, 1918–1948.* Princeton: Princeton University Press, 1967. See 12-399.

12-466. _____. "North Korea: Emergence of an Elite Group." In Richard Staar (ed.), *Aspects of Modern Communism*. Columbia: University of South Carolina Press, 1968. Analysis of the new, emergent leadership structure of North Korea.

12-467. SUH, Dae-Sook and Chae-Jin LEE (eds.). *Political Leadership in Korea*. Seattle: University of Washington Press, 1975. A section on North Korea. See 12-171.

12-468. SOHN, Jae-souk. "Factionalism and Party Control of the Military in Communist Korea." *Koreana Quarterly* 9(3)(1967):16–40. Analysis of North Korea's civil-military relations. Various factions in North Korea's power structure are discussed.

12-469. United States. Army. Joint Publications Research Service. *On Party Leadership, Training, and Policy Implementation in North Korea*. Washington: 1960. Collection and translation of the North Korean literature on the working of the Korean Workers' Party and its cadres.

12-470. YANG, Ho-min. "The Personality Cult of Kim Il-sŏng as a Strategy for National Unification." *Journal of Asiatic Studies* 13(4)(December 1970):317–332. A succinct account of the development of the personality cult of Kim Il Sung in North Korea.

12-471. YIM, Yong Soon. "Politics of Korean Unification: A Comparative Study of Systematic Outputs in Two Different Political Systems." PhD dissertation, Rutgers University, 1974. See 12-175.

12-472. YIU, Myung Kun. "Sino-Soviet Rivalry in North Korea Since 1954." PhD dissertation, University of Maryland, 1969. See 12-429.

12-473. YOO, Ki Hong. "A Study of North Korean Communism as Related to the Rise of Kim Il-sŏng." PhD dissertation, American University, 1969. 253 pp. Abstracted in *DAI* 31(3)(September 1970):1353-A; UM 70-15,456. A historical treatment of Kim's rise to power and his responses to changes in world politics, particularly within the international communist movement.

12-474. ZAGORIA, Donald S. and Young Kun KIM. "North Korea and the Major Powers." *Asian Survey* 15(12) (December 1975):1017–1035. Analysis of North Korea's foreign policy decision-making. Maintains that "North Korea is not likely to return to a full-scale policy of military confrontation against the South."

Political Participation, Political Parties, and Elections

12-475. CHO, Jaekwan. "A Comparative Analysis of the Communist Cadre System." PhD dissertation, University of California, Berkeley, 1972. 268 pp. Includes North Korea.

12-476. CHUNG, Kiwon. "The North Korean People's Army and the Party." *China Quarterly* 14(April/June 1963): 105–124. See 12-432.

12-477. ELLO, Paul Stephen. "The Commissar and the Peasant: A Comparative Analysis of Land Reform and Collectivization in North Korea and North Vietnam." PhD dissertation, University of Iowa, 1967. 564 pp. Abstracted in *DA* 28(July 1967):268-69-A. Analysis of land reform and collectivization in North Korea between 1945 and 1960 and the Russian influence on their origin and development.

12-478. HA, Joseph Man-kyung. "Politics of Korean Peasantry: A Study of Land Reforms and Collectivization with Reference to Sino-Soviet Experiences." PhD dissertation, Columbia University, 1971. 216 pp. Abstracted in *DAI* 31(7)(January 1971):3630-31-A; UM 71-1459. Analysis of the North Korean method of land use and land redistribution as a model for modernization and development.

12-479. HAHN, Bae-ho. "The Parties and the Politics in Two Koreas: A Preliminary Comparative Analysis." *Journal of Asiatic Studies* 13(4)(December 1970):25–61. See 12-191.

12-480. KIM, C. I. Eugene and Young Whan KIHL (eds.). *Parties and Electoral Politics in Korea*. Silver Spring, Md." Research Institute on Korean Affairs, 1975. Contains a section on North Korea. See 12-211.

12-481. KIM, Ch'ang-sun. "The North Korean Communist Party: Historical Analysis." *Korean Affairs* 2(2)(1963): 130–139. Analyzes the origin and development of the North Korean Communist Party.

12-482. KIM, Doo Yung. "Labor Legislation in North Korea." *Amerasia* 11(May 1947):156–160. Translation of an article which first appeared in the Japanese radical periodical *Zenei* [Vanguard] in January 1947. The Labor Law of 24 June 1946 is discussed.

12-483. KIM, Ilpyong J. *Communist Politics in North Korea*. New York: Praeger, 1975. Includes a discussion of mass mobilization techniques.

12-484. _____. "North Korea's Fourth Party Congress." *Pacific Affairs* 35(1)(Spring 1962):37–50. Meaning of the Fourth Party Congress following de-Stalinization—intensification of Kim's personality cult.

12-485. KOH, B. C. "Anatomy of a Revolution: Some Implications of the Fifth KWP Congress." *Journal of Korean Affairs* 1(3)(October 1971):22–36.

12-486. LEE, Chong-Sik. "Land Reform, Collectivization and the Peasants in North Korea." *China Quarterly* 14(April/June 1963):65–81. Analysis of land reform in North Korea—its origin and development and the actual condition of the peasants.

12-487. _____. "Politics in North Korea: Pre–Korean War Stage." *China Quarterly* 14(April/June 1963):3–16. See 12-381.

12-488. _____. "The 'Socialist Revolution' in the North Korean Countryside." *Asian Survey* 2(10)(October 1962): 9–22.

12-489. LOO, Robert Kalei Wah Kit. "A Comparative Study of Governmental Treatment of Interest Groups in South Korea and North Korea, 1954–1964." PhD dissertation, New York University, 1970. See 12-237.

12-490. NAM, Koon Woo. *The North Korean Communist Leadership, 1945–1965: A Study of Factionalism and Political Consolidation.* University: University of Alabama Press, 1974. See 12-462.

12-491. _____. "North Korean Non-Communist Leaders and Political Effects of the 'Democratic' Reforms." *Journal of Korean Affairs* 2(2)(October 1972):29–43. See 12-463.

12-492. SCALAPINO, Robert A. and Chong-Sik LEE. *Communism in Korea.* 2 vols. Berkeley: University of California Press, 1972. Includes chapters on intellectuals, workers, and peasants. See 12-394.

12-493. SCHRAMM, Wilbur, J. W. RILEY, Jr., and F. W. WILLIAMS. "Communication in the Sovietized State, as Demonstrated in Korea." *American Sociological Review* 16(December 1951):757–766. A study of the mechanisms of control instituted in South Korea by North Korea during the Korean War.

12-494. SOHN, Jae-souk. "Factionalism and Party Control of the Military in Communist Korea." *Koreana Quarterly* 9(3)(1967):16–40. See 12-468.

12-495. United States. Army. Joint Publications Research Service. *On Party Leadership, Training, and Policy Implementation in North Korea.* Washington: 1960. See 12-469.

12-496. WASHBURN, J. N. "Soviet Russia and the Korean Communist Party." *Pacific Affairs* 23(March 1950):59–65. Historical assessment of the North Korean position within the communist bloc and its relationship with the USSR.

12-497. YUN, Ki-bong. *North Korea as I Knew It [Naega bon pungnyŏkttang].* Seoul: Buk-han Research Institute, 1974. See 12-404.

Constitutional Development and Government Structure

12-498. CHO, Chang-Hyun. "The System of Local Government in North Korea: An Introduction." *Journal of Korean Affairs* 1(3)(October 1971):12–21. Analysis of the centralist structure of North Korea at the local level.

12-499. CHO, Sung Yoon. "The Judicial System of North Korea." *Asian Survey* 11(12)(December 1971):1167–1181. Analysis of the North Korean judicial system as modeled after the Stalinist system.

12-500. CHUNG, Chin O. "The Central Government and Power Structure of North Korea." *Korean Affairs* 1(3) (October 1971):3–11. See 12-431.

12-501. HAHN, Bae-ho. "Toward a Comparative Analysis of the South and North Korean Political Systems." *Social Science Journal* (1973):7–21. See 12-357.

12-502. KANG, Koo-chin. "Comparison of the Legal System between North and South Korea." *Seoul Law Journal* 12(2)(1971):5–23. A detailed study of the North Korean legal system.

12-503. KIM, Ilpyong J. "The Judicial and Administrative Structure in North Korea." *China Quarterly* 14(April/June 1963):94–104. A study of the North Korean institutional framework wherein the legal and administrative function with the party and politics held supreme.

12-504. KIM, Se-Jin and Chang-hyun CHO (eds.). *Korea: A Divided Nation.* Silver Spring, Md.: Research Institute on Korean Affairs, 1976. 331 pp. Includes papers on North Korea's constitutional and administrative structures. See 12-025.

12-505. KIM, Tae-ho. "The Ruling System of North Korean Regime." *Korean Affairs* 2(2)(1963):174–186. See 12-446.

12-506. KIM, Tae-suh. "North Korea's New Constitution and New Power Structure." *East Asian Review* 4(1) (Spring 1977):23–43. See 12-447.

12-507. LEE, Chong-Sik. "The 1972 Constitution and Top Communist Leaders." In Dae-Sook Suh and Chae-Jin Lee (eds.). *Political Leadership in Korea.* Seattle: University of Washington Press, 1976. A detailed analysis of the 1972 constitution of North Korea.

12-508. PAIGE, Glenn D. *The Korean People's Democratic Republic.* Stanford: Stanford University Press, 1966. Still useful as a referent point. See 12-385.

12-509. RUDOLPH, P. *North Korea's Political and Economic Structure.* New York: International Secretariat, Institute of Pacific Relations, 1959. 72 pp. A survey of the North Korean communist system. One of the first systematic studies on North Korea.

12-510. SCALAPINO, Robert A. and Chong-Sik LEE. *Communism in Korea.* 2 vols. Berkeley: University of California Press, 1972. Includes various documents. See 12-394.

12-511. WASHBURN, J. N. "Russia Looks at Northern Korea." *Pacific Affairs* 20(June 1947):152–160. Analysis of Soviet influence on the North Korean political organization as viewed by the Soviet press and radio while North Korea was occupied by the Soviet Union.

12-512. YANG, K. P. and C. B. CHEE. "The North Korean

Educational System: 1945 to Present." *China Quarterly* 14(April/June 1963):125–140. A study of the North Korean educational system and its development.

Public Administration, Bureaucracy, and Government Performance

12-513. BARK, Dong-suh. "Comparison of Administration under Different Ideologies." *Journal of Asiatic Studies* 13(4)(December 1970):279–292. See 12-287.

12-514. BRUN, Ellen. "North Korea: A Case of Real Development." *Monthly Review* 22(2)(June 1970):25–37. An uncritical report on the growth and development of socialism in a developing country such as North Korea.

12-515. BRUN, Ellen and Jacques HERSH. *Socialist Korea: A Case Study in the Strategy of Economic Development.* New York: Monthly Review Press, 1976. See 12-350.

12-516. BURCHETT, Wilfred G. *Again Korea.* New York: International Publishers, 1968. 188 pp. A report by a veteran Australian communist reporter of the progress North Korea has made.

12-517. CHUNG, Joseph S. "The North Korean Industrial Enterprise: Control, Concentration, and Managerial Functions." *Studies on Asia* 7(1966):165–185. Analyzes the totalitarian aspect of the North Korean communist system.

12-518. CHUNG, Joseph Sang-hoon. *The North Korean Economy: Structure and Development.* Stanford: Hoover Institution Press, 1974. 212 pp. The most comprehensive account of the North Korean economy—its structure, transformation, and growth since 1945.

12-519. ELLO, Paul Stephen. "The Commissar and the Peasant: A Comparative Analysis of Land Reform and Collectivization in North Korea and North Vietnam." PhD dissertation, University of Iowa, 1967. See 12-477.

12-520. JUHN, Daniel Sungil. "The North Korean Managerial System at the Factory Level." *Journal of Korean Affairs* 2(1)(April 1972):16–21. Analysis of the Taean system of collective leadership of engineers and party cadres.

12-521. KIM, Byong-sik. *Modern Korea: The Socialist North, Revolutionary Perspectives in the South and Unification.* Translated by Takeshi Haga and edited by Victor Perlo. New York: International Publishers, 1970. See 12-435.

12-522. KIM, Han-ju. *Great Victory in Agricultural Cooperatization in the DPRK.* Pyongyang: Foreign Languages Publishing House, 1959. 71 pp. Justifies and explains the development of agricultural cooperatives in North Korea.

12-523. KIM, Il Sung. *All for the Post-War Rehabilitation and Development of the National Economy.* Pyongyang: Ministry of Culture and Propaganda, 1954. 147 pp. A

policy statement delivered at the sixth plenum of the Central Committee of the Workers' Party of Korea, Pyongyang, 5 August 1953 and other documents.

12-524. _____. *The Present Situation and Tasks of Our Party.* Report delivered at the Conference of the Workers' Party of Korea in 1970. Tokyo: Central Standing Committee of the General Association of Korean Residents in Japan, 1970. 123 pp. A comprehensive and revealing document about the role and status of the Workers' Party of North Korea.

12-525. _____. *Theses on the Socialist Agricultural Question in Our Country.* Pyongyang: Foreign Languages Publishing House, 1964. 55 pp. A major statement on agriculture.

12-526. KIM, Ilpyong J. "The Judicial and Administrative Structure in North Korea." *China Quarterly* 14(April/June 1963):94–104. See 12-503.

12-527. KIM, Joungwon Alexander. *Divided Korea: The Politics of Development, 1945–1972.* Cambridge, Mass.: East Asian Research Center, Harvard University, 1975. Includes a discussion of North Korean development. See 12-021.

12-528. _____. "The Peak of Socialism in North Korea: First Five and Seven-year Plans." *Asian Survey* 5(5)(May 1965):255–268. Analyzes the development plans of North Korea for industrialization and socialistic economy and construction.

12-529. LEE, Chong-Sik. "Land Reform, Collectivization and the Peasants in North Korea." *China Quarterly* 14(April/June 1963):65–81. See 12-486.

12-530. LEE, Chong-Sik and Nam-sik KIM. "Control and Administrative Mechanisms in the North Korean Countryside." *Journal of Asian Studies* 29(2)(February 1970):309–326. Analyzes the system of control and administration at the local level in North Korea.

12-531. MOAK, Samuel K. "North Korea's Agricultural Policies in Collectivization." *Journal of Korean Affairs* 3(4)(January 1974):25–36. A study of collectivization of agriculture—its structure and practices and their rationale.

12-532. RO, Chung-Hyun. "A Comparative Study of Manpower Administration in Developing Countries: With Special Reference to South and North Korea." PhD dissertation, New York University, 1962. See 12-331.

12-533. ROBINSON, Joan. "Korean Miracle." *Monthly Review* 16(January 1965):541–549. A well-known leftist British economist's glowing account of North Korean economic development.

12-534. SCALAPINO, Robert A. and Chong-sik LEE. *Communism in Korea.* 2 vols. Berkeley: University of California Press, 1972. See 12-394.

12-535. SHABAD, T. "North Korea's Postwar Recovery." *Far Eastern Survey* 25(June 1956):81–91. Analyzes the development strategy of North Korea as a way of quick recovery from the war damages.

12-536. SUH, Dae-Sook and Chae-Jin LEE (eds.). *Political Leadership in Korea.* Seattle: University of Washington Press, 1975. Includes papers on the North Korean government structure and bureaucracy. See 12-171.

12-537. YIM, Yong Soon. "A Comparative Study of Systematic Outputs in the Two Koreas: A Theoretical Framework." *Journal of Korean Affairs* 4(4)(January 1975):39–48. Covers North Korea's system performance. See 12-343.

CHAPTER 13
The Legal System

Chin Kim

INTRODUCTION

WESTERN STUDIES on the Korean legal system have hitherto been neglected. The prevailing notion has been that no special effort is needed to study Korean law because it has traditionally been modeled after Chinese law and, moreover, modern Korean law derives from that of Japan. This notion conveys a narrow outlook which disregards indigenous Korean legal culture. It is true that Chinese legal institutions and Japanese law (essentially German and French in origin) have influenced the Korean legal system, but there are more valid questions to consider: To what extent, under what conditions, and with what effects do these foreign-imported systems function? These questions are difficult to answer and suggest a future area of research. Furthermore, during the three decades since 1945 there have been a series of significant legal developments that warrant a closer examination of the South and North Korean legal systems. In this guide, primary emphasis will be placed on the South Korean legal system, as the study of current practices in the North has not been possible to date.

HISTORY OF KOREAN LAW

According to *Samguk sagi* [Historical Record of the Three Kingdoms], written in 1145, the first promulgation of *yul* (code) by a Koguryŏ king could be dated in AD 373 and *yullyŏng* (code and substatutes) were en-acted by a Silla king in 520. An epigraph written in 924 during the Silla dynasty commemorates the promulgation of a code. Despite the existence of these historical records and the chronology of political events between the Silla and T'ang dynasties, we know little about the types of codes and substatutes that had been promulgated and enforced during the Silla period. In 1933, however, a partial answer to this enigma was offered by the discovery of the so-called civil governance document of Silla villages (presumably dated AD 755), which indicates the influence of T'ang administrative statutes on Silla households and tilled land.

Information regarding legal institutions and their functions during the Koryŏ dynasty is also sketchy. The *Hyŏngpŏp chi* [Treatise on penal law] of the *Koryŏ sa* [History of Koryŏ], written in 1453, simply lists the headings of seventy-one articles whose texts cannot be found elsewhere. However, a perusal of the Koryŏ code as presented in the *Koryŏ sa* reveals that the organization of the code and the classes of penalty with a grading scale were influenced by T'ang and Sung codes. On the other hand, the administration of codes could have been influenced by the Yüan code, since the Yüan dynasty actually controlled the Koryŏ dynasty for approximately ninety years.

T'aejo, the founder of the Yi dynasty, set an example by codifying the laws, and his successors continued the endeavor. T'aejo ordered that an office be established to collect, compile, and publish all laws and decrees from the time of the last king of the Koryŏ dynasty down to his own time. The culmination of this work, the *Kyŏngje yukchŏn* [Six codes of governance], is not extant today. In the annals of the law codifications throughout the Yi dynasty, the *Kyŏngguk taejŏn* [Great code of state governance] is an important work, as it became the basic guide to administration after 1470. It sanctioned the application of the *Ta-Ming lü* [Code of the Great Ming] as the common law consisting of six codes that corresponded to the six departmental divisions of the government: personnel *(i)*, revenue *(ho)*, rites *(ye)*, war *(pyŏng)*, punishment *(hyŏng)*, and works *(kong)*. The section on personnel covered appointment of officials, titles and ranks, and general structure of the government; the section on revenue dealt with the census, landholdings, and taxation; the section on rites treated such matters as official attire, foreign relations, the government service examination system, and education; the section on war covered military organization and administration; the section on punishment was largely concerned with trials of criminals, prison administration, and slave ownership and status; and the section on works dealt with such matters as civil engineering, maintenance of public buildings and ships, weights, scales, and artisans. Enactment of the Chinese-oriented *Kyŏngguk taejŏn* was followed by a series of new codes during the Yi dynasty—a revision and elaboration of each code based on its predecessors. The last of these, the *Taejŏn hoet'ong* [Comprehensive code of administration], was completed in 1866. Like the earlier codes, it, too, was influenced by the Chinese codes.

As a result of the *Kabo* Reforms of 1894, gazettes appeared announcing newly promulgated laws. Another significant legal development was the enactment of the *Hyŏngpŏp taejŏn* [Complete criminal code] in 1905, which was based on the traditional law and the Japanese Penal Code of 1882. *Hyŏngpŏp taejŏn* underwent two revisions and was incorporated into the 1910 *Hanguk pŏpchŏn* [Korean legal code] under the new title of *Hyŏngpŏp* [Penal law].

The Japanese annexation of Korea in 1910 introduced the civil law system. The Government-General of Korea functioned through the Japanese governor-general as an autonomous body. All decrees of the governor-general had to receive the approval of the Japanese emperor, however, and jurisdiction over finances and legislation on broad policies concerning Korea was in the hands of the Imperial Diet in Tokyo. The colonial government in Korea consisted of the secretariat and seven departments *(kyoku)*, one of which supervised the administration of justice. During this colonial period, at least five discernible bodies of law were in force: first, laws promulgated by the Japanese between 1905 and 1919; second, special statutes particularly directed to Korean affairs adopted by the Japanese Imperial Diet; third, applied Japanese codes and statutes *mutatis mutandis* by virtue of the governor-general's action; fourth, Korean customary law on family relations and inheritance based on the Korean Civil Decree of 1912; and fifth, other legal measures issued by the Government-General. The judiciary was built under a three-instance system—the district and the branch courts; the courts of review; and the Supreme Court. The Supreme Court, located in Seoul, consisted of a chief judge and nine judges. Attached to the courts of each instance were the prosecutor's offices. Prosecutors exercised wide authority by enjoying the same status as the judges in importance and rank.

The laws in force at the time of Korea's liberation in 1945 remained effective in the area south of the 38th parallel for three years until the establishment of the Republic of Korea in 1948. Among other legislative reforms, the Republic of Korea made laborious efforts to adopt new basic legal codes, which were enacted in the following sequence: criminal in 1953, criminal procedure in 1954, civil in 1958, civil procedure in 1960, and commercial in 1962. The constitution, the other basic code, was originally adopted in 1948 and has been amended several times since. The latest amendment of 1972 has substantially reduced the power of the judiciary. Meanwhile, the regime in North Korea has been developing a new legal order based on socialist legality.

SOURCES AND STRUCTURE OF LAW IN SOUTH KOREA

The emphasis on codified statutes is one of the principal features of the Korean legal system. A set of five legal codes (Civil Code, Criminal Code, Commercial Code, Code of Civil Procedure, and Code of Criminal Procedure), plus the constitution, are collectively known as the *yukpŏp*—literally, the six codes. The codes are the main principles of law supplemented by a host of laws. Laws enacted and promulgated by state authorities pursuant to the constitution are recognized as the primary source of law. Thus a variety of terms are used to designate South Korean laws, usually denoting the issuing authorities. Laws may be divided into three main classes: statutes passed by legislation; decrees issued by executive organs and rules and regulations by the local self-governments; and international agreements. What authority is given to customary law and to the doctrine of stare decisis? Customary law could be defined as the regular and general practice of law based on opinio necessitatis. The Civil Code prescribes that in the absence of a statute, customary law—and if the latter is lacking, sound reasoning (recta ratio)—is to serve as the basis for deciding civil cases. The Commercial Code also prescribes that "in commercial cases, commercial custom applies in the absence of provisions in the present code, and in the absence of commercial custom, the provisions of the Civil Code shall apply." This legal formula cannot be applied to criminal cases, however, due to the constitutional requirement of nulla poena sine lege. As far as the effect of doctrine of stare decisis is concerned, judicial precedent is not a primary source of law in South Korea, but a decisional rule admitted to be a binding authority only where there has developed a series of consistent decisions. Thus every court is theoretically free not to follow the judicial decisions of courts even when they are superior. In practice, however, a judge, in deciding a case, will closely examine relevant previous decisions. Furthermore, the lower courts can be expected to pay a great deal of attention and respect to judgments of higher courts—especially the higher court in their own district.

There are various ways in which South Korean law can be divided. One of the best-known systematic divisions is that of public and private law. Public law regulates the state and other public corporations and their relations either *inter se* or with the individual citizen. Public law comprises *inter alia* constitutional law, nationality law, administrative law, criminal law, and public international law. The entire law of procedure is also considered as public law because it deals with the relations between the citizens and courts in their capacity as organs of the state. Thus not only the law of crimi-

nal procedure, but also the law of civil procedure and the law of bankruptcy, are considered as part of public law. On the other hand, private law regulates mainly the relations between private individuals. Private law includes the so-called civil law (which includes the law of real and personal property, contracts, torts, domestic relations, and succession); commercial law; private international law; and copyright and patent law.

The law regulating legal relations is so extensive that it cannot be listed here in its entirety. The following paragraphs summarize the major sources of South Korean law.

Constitutional Law. Legal rules form a hierarchy at the top of which stand the rules of constitutional law. All laws and other public acts must derive their validity from the constitution, which is the ultimate basis of all law. The present constitution, approved by referendum in 1972, formally concentrates all effective power in the office of the presidency.

Administrative Law. Administrative law is a branch of law that controls or is intended to control the administrative agencies and their operations and remedies. There is no administrative code. The main statutes are the Government Organization Law, Local Autonomy Law, National Public Servants Law, Administrative Litigation Law, and laws related to land reform. Another important legislative measure of recent origin in the field of administrative law is the Foreign Capital Inducement Law, which is designed to induce and administer foreign equity investments, foreign loans, and foreign technology for the development of the economy. This statute and the tax laws are closely interrelated.

Labor Law. Labor law consists of those constitutional provisions, statutes, executive decrees, and administrative regulations that regulate labor relations. Basic statutes are the Labor Union Law, Labor Dispute Adjustment Law, Labor Standard Law, and Labor Committee Law.

Criminal Law. Criminal law is a body of legal rules which treats of crimes and their punishment. The main source of criminal law is the Penal Code. There are a number of ancillary laws which include the National Security Law and Juvenile Law.

The Law of Criminal Procedure. The law of criminal procedure prescribes procedural rules connected with the prosecution of a person charged or to be charged with the commission of a crime. The primary source of this field of law is the Code of Criminal Procedure, which sets out general rules, trial procedure at the first instance, appeals, special proceedings of trial, and execution of decision.

Public International Law. Public international law is the law of the world community which relates to states, international organizations, and private individuals. Sources of public international law are international customary law and international agreements. The present constitution sanctions that "treaties duly ratified and promulgated in accordance with this Constitution and the generally recognized rules of international law shall have the same effect as domestic laws of the Republic of Korea."

Civil Law. Civil law is known as a general private law which consists of the Civil Code of 1958 together with several ancillary laws. In its form, the Korean Civil Code follows the so-called pandect system. It is divided into five books. The first three books of the Korean Civil Code, dealing with general provisions, property rights, and obligations in general, resemble the German Civil Code, while the fourth and fifth books, covering family and successions, are based on Korean customs.

Commercial Law. Commercial law is the body of special rules of private law applicable only to those legal relations which arise from commercial intercourse. The most important source of commercial law is the Commercial Code, which consists of five books: General Part; Commercial Transactions; Commercial Companies; Insurances; and Maritime Commerce. The important ancillary laws are the Enforcement Law of the Commercial Code, the Law on Bills of Exchange and Promissory Notes, the Cheques Law, and the Corporate Reorganization Law.

The Law of Civil Procedure. The law of civil procedure is a branch of law which is concerned with civil actions to settle compulsorily disputes among private individuals. The main source of law regulating civil actions is the Code of Civil Procedure, which consists of seven chapters: General Rules; Procedure in First Instance; Appeal; Retrial; Summary Procedure; Public Summons Procedure; and Execution. Main ancillary laws are the Arbitration Law and the Law of Procedure on Noncontentious Matters.

Private International Law. The main source of private international law is Private Law Involving Foreign Elements, which is designed to "determine the applicable law to the matters involving foreign elements wherein aliens within the Republic of Korea, or the nationals of the Republic of Korea abroad, become parties." This law sets out the choice-of-law rules and is organized into three parts: general rules, rules concerning civil matters, and rules concerning commercial matters. The important ancillary laws are the National Law and the Code of Civil Procedure, which contains rules related to the jurisdiction, the recognition, and the enforcement of foreign judgment.

Laws Governing Industrial Property Rights and Copyright. Korean law protects the following four industrial property rights: patent, utility model, trademark, and design. These rights are recognized and protected only when they are registered upon application. The main source of protection of copyright is the Copyright Law, which is also based on the principle of registration. South Korea is not a signatory to any bilateral or multilateral international agreement related to copyright.

JUDICIAL ADMINISTRATION IN SOUTH KOREA

ORGANIZATION OF COURTS

South Korean courts are organized on the three-tier system. District courts, their branch courts, and family courts are courts of first instance. Appellate courts are intermediate, and the Supreme Court is the highest court of appeal. Ten district courts have civil law and criminal law divisions, except in Seoul, where a separate Seoul Civil District Court and a Seoul Criminal District Court have been created. The Seoul Family Court hears cases related to domestic relations. Three appellate courts are organized respectively into civil, criminal, and special divisions. A special division tries administrative cases. The Supreme Court is composed of a chief justice and fifteen associate justices given rule-making power to supervise judicial administration.

JUDICIAL PROCEEDINGS

The South Korean judge is not simply an arbiter between two sides but a "seeker of justice" who guides the trial, questions the witnesses, and develops facts in the interest of truth. Oral hearings are quite brief. On request, the judge may allow the parties to the action to ask supplementary questions. Judicial proceedings can roughly be divided into three kinds: civil and administrative actions; criminal actions; and action to test the constitutionality of a law.

The Code of Civil Procedure sets out a number of general principles related to civil and administrative actions. Among these principles are representation of both parties, oral presentation, bilateral hearing, immediacy, and free admissibility of evidence. In a Korean court, it is not the universal rule for witnesses to give evidence on oath. The evidence given by the party, whether as witness or by questioning in the court, is considered a secondary means of evidence. An administrative action is also carried out pursuant to the code of civil procedure. An appellate court exercises exclusive jurisdiction with authority over the place of residence where the defendant is situated. As a prerequisite to initiation of administrative litigation, a person deprived of his or her rights by an illegal or unjust action on the part of an administrative agency has to exhaust administrative remedies in accordance with the Administrative Litigation Law. The present constitution establishes the principle of judicial review of administrative acts.

In a criminal action, the judge has no function until a charge has been brought by the prosecutor, who has not only the right but the legal obligation to initiate and conduct an investigation into any complaint with a view to bringing a charge. The onus of proving the guilt of an accused person rests on the prosecutor. The prosecutor may request that a case be referred for summary judgment when a minor offense is involved. The accused may request a formal trial within seven days from receipt of notification of summary judgment, but if he fails to do so, or withdraws his request, the summary judgment becomes a final judgment. Cross-examination has never been prevalent before the Korean criminal courts. Questioning by the court is preferred, and although the judge may permit supplemental questions to be addressed directly by the prosecutor or defense counsel, questioning does not reach the intensity of the American system. The accused is asked whether he wishes to reply to the charges made against him. If he chooses to answer, he is not sworn. Similarly, relatives of the accused do not give testimony on oath. For the same reason, the evidence of a party in a civil action is generally deemed unacceptable. In a criminal case, the temptation of the accused to lie may be very great; hence he should not be forced to speak, nor should he swear to his testimony.

Action to test the constitutionality of a law has to pass the Constitution Committee, which was created by the 1972 constitution. This committee has the power to review and declare the unconstitutionality of a law at the request of the court.

JUDGES, PROSECUTORS, LAWYERS, AND AUXILIARY PERSONNEL

The graduates of the law faculty in South Korea enter diverse occupations; only a minor portion of them pursue professional legal careers. To become a member of the bar, one must pass the state judicial examination and then complete two years of a practical training course at the Institute of Judicial Training, which is now an organ of the Supreme Court. Upon completion of two years' apprenticeship, the new member of the bar may be invited to become a judge or a prosecutor, or he may engage in private practice.

Judges. In South Korea, becoming a judge is not a reward for long and successful practice as a member of the bar. It is only the beginning of a career in the civil service. Under the 1972 constitution, the tenure of the chief justice of the Supreme Court is six years, whereas all judges, including associate justices of the Supreme Court, have a limited tenure of ten years subject to reappointment.

Prosecutors. To become a prosecuting and public attorney is also considered entering a civil service career. Prosecutors engage in investigation and prosecution of crimes; they bring actions in the name of the public, they supervise the execution of penalty; and they also represent the public interest in civil cases. The highest-ranking prosecutor is the prosecutor-general, who is next in rank and authority to the minister of justice and is assigned to the Supreme Court. The prosecutor-general supervises all prosecutors throughout the country under the principle of so-called unity and indivisibility of the prosecution. Prosecutors are assigned to each court on all levels and perform their function independently of the court.

Lawyers. Lawyers are generally admitted to local bars. The local bar associations and the national bar association are not effective as a collegial body and not so influential as their counterparts in other countries on legal developments and reforms. The activity of the bar association generally tends to be limited to protecting the interests of its members. A typical Korean law office is conducted by a single lawyer or by two or three persons who share offices and practice. The name of a person who is either dead or no longer a partner is not used on the letterhead of partnership. Thus it is more correct to speak of "law offices" than of "law firms."

Notary Public, Patent Specialist, and Judicial Scrivener. Any member of the bar can be appointed as a notary public by the minister of justice, who supervises notaries public and assigns them to the district prosecutor's office. Notaries public prepare notarial deeds, which include the issuance of certificates of self-executing obligation and articles of incorporation. Any nonlawyer who meets special qualifications under the existing statute can become a patent specialist. Patent specialists represent their clients in the administrative agency and the court in any matter related to industrial property rights. Paraprofessionals play an important role in judicial administration. Judicial scriveners, for instance, draft legal documents, including court papers. Their training ranges from self-education to postgraduate university qualifications.

COURTS AND PROCURACY IN NORTH KOREA

Administration of justice under the 1948 constitution of North Korea, following the Russian model of 1936 and the post–World War II constitutions of other socialist countries, was the responsibility of two units. The courts, the first element, were comprised of the Supreme Court (elected by the highest legislative body) and lower courts at each level of state authority (elected by the corresponding legislative unit). The second element, the procuracy, was headed by a legislatively elected procurator-general, who then appointed procurators to each lower level. Both the Supreme Court and the procurator-general were accountable to the Supreme People's Assembly (SPA) which elected them, and each was responsible for supervising the work of its lower units. The lower-level courts, however, were also answerable to the legislative bodies which elected them, while the appointed procurators at the lower levels were free from local legislative supervision.

The scope of this section only allows for a broad outline of North Korea's justice system with special reference to courts and procuracy as it appears to exist under the 1972 constitution. Although it was reported in 1970 that revisions of the Criminal and Civil Codes plus the codes of criminal and civil procedure were under way in North Korea, they have not yet been announced. It is assumed that such older statutes as the Law Concerning the Organization of the Courts and the Code of Criminal Procedure, as amended in 1954, are still in force. However, an effort will be made to distinguish clearly between provisions of the 1972 constitution, those of the old one, and extraconstitutional sources. A special attempt will be made to point out apparent changes wrought by the new basic law.

COURTS

North Korea's courts, under the new basic law, are charged with three broad tasks: first, providing formal legal support for the existing socialist state, specifically including the protection of state and cooperative property and the guarding of citizens' constitutional rights in general; second, educating organizations and citizens as to their legal duties and arousing them to fulfill these requirements; and third, performing certain bureaucratic functions (like notarial work) commonly associated with the legal system.

These three main court functions, which were entirely lacking in the original constitution, are to be carried out by three-person courts composed of one judge and two people's assessors (except for special cases which may require three judges), who are to be independent and act "in strict accordance with the law." Cases are to be heard in public, with some exceptions, and defendants are guaranteed the right to a defense. While proceedings are to be conducted in Korean, foreigners may use their own languages. Basic judicial tasks were formulated shortly after the first constitution was promulgated, and their essential thrust is preserved in the new 1972 document. Also included in the current basic law is the article which deals with the election of special court members. In the earlier constitution it was merely stated that special courts would be provided for by law. Such legislation was adopted, and it is this law, alluded to in the 1948 constitution, which is now embedded in the present basic law.

General provisions for the judicial system under the 1972 constitution differ in a few respects from those mandated by the 1948 constitution. Most important, in the 1948 document, as is typical of socialist basic law, the highest body, called the Supreme Court, was elected by the Supreme People's Assembly as a whole and held a shorter term of office than did the latter body. Somewhat atypically, the Supreme Court was responsible to the SPA alone. The original constitution also had a recall provision for all elected judicial officers; that provision is missing from the current constitution. Additionally, the original article concerning people's assessors clearly indicated that they did not hear appeals, whereas the new article covering the subject implies that under some conditions they may.

"Justice is administered by the Central Court, the court of the province (or municipality directly under the central authority), the people's court, and the special court," according to the 1972 constitution. In addition to these four constitutionally designed courts, it is reported that separate arbitration courts exist for settling disputes "between state enterprises and/or other Socialist organizations." At the apex of the judicial administration is the Central Court, which "supervises the judicial work of all the courts." Its members are elected by the SPA's standing committee, but it is responsible to the president of the People's Republic and the Central People's Committee (the CPC), as well as to the body of the SPA. Members of the provincial court and people's court "are elected by the people's assembly at the corresponding level," while the Central Court appoints the president and judges of the special court. The people's assessors of each of the latter, however, are elected by those who are within its jurisdiction. The term of office for members of provincial courts is four years; their counterparts in the people's courts serve for only two years. It has been reported that professionalism, even among judges, is not fostered under the North Korean system, since the court's political judgment is of primary importance. While judges serve full time during their designated terms, people's assessors are supposed to serve only fourteen days per year; if a proceeding requires additional time, however, the assessors are to continue and hence avoid disruption of the judicial process. Wage earners are paid their regular earnings while they serve, and assessors who are not wage earners are given the same salary as a judge for his service period.

People's Courts. The people's court is North Korea's lowest-level general court and is the court of first instance for most criminal and civil cases. Its criminal jurisdiction covers the following crimes: those against state order, state, cooperative, and private property, and the person, plus those involving labor legislation, official duties, the economy, the administrative system, health and social safety, and a residual category of crimes not within the jurisdiction of any other court.

Provincial Courts. Provincial courts play a dual role in North Korea's judicial system. Under their original jurisdiction lie crimes of a serious nature such as those against state sovereignty, grave crimes against the person, and especially significant crimes against state and cooperative property and official duties, as well as civil actions involving North Korean nationals and aliens. As an appellate court, the court of the province hears appeals and protests from the decisions of the people's courts within its jurisdiction. Additionally, provincial courts have the discretionary power to hear, as a court of first instance, any case which arises within one of its subordinate people's courts and can transfer cases between these courts. These middle-level courts are divided into civil and criminal departments, but each one apparently fulfills both the original and appellate roles within its sphere of competency.

Special Court. Currently, the only special courts in existence are military courts which exercise jurisdiction over crimes committed by armed forces personnel and members of the Ministry of Social Safety's security organs, in addition to others, such as workers on military bases, as authorized by law. Special courts are supervised by a special chamber of the Central Court.

Central Court. North Korea's highest judicial body, now called the Central Court, is made up of three chambers—criminal, civil, and special. It acts as a dual-instance tribunal much like the provincial courts. The only duties specifically cited as being within its original jurisdiction, however, are criminal ones involving especially serious crimes against state sovereignty and official crimes committed by high-level elected representatives and judges. As a court of second instance, the Central Court has jurisdiction over appeals and protests from original decisions of the provincial and special courts. Like the provincial courts, the Central Court may choose to hear as a court of first instance any case within the jurisdiction of a lower court or to transfer the case to another court of equal authority.

A unique feature of the Central Court is its authority under the extraordinary appeal arrangement. For the most part, the North Korean court system, though a three-tiered one, is of the two-instance variety; that is, only one appeal is allowed from the original decision. There exists, however, an exception to this rule in the ability of the president of the Central Court and the procurator-general to demand a case for an extraordinary appeal to the Central Court "at any stage in the judicial proceeding from any judicial organ."

The essential import of the extraordinary appeal concept is that it provides one way for the Central Court to control at least the most obvious deviations of lower courts. Thus the president of the Central Court or the procurator may suspend the judgment entered in a case and bring it before the high court for review (even if an appeal has already been heard on the matter below). This device may also be used, however, to correct decisions made by one of the Central Court's chambers alone. The judgment of the latter cannot be immediately suspended, but the same officials responsible for extraordinary appeals of lower-court decisions can demand a plenary session of the Central Court where the judges of all three chambers, the president and vice-president of the Central Court, and the procurator-general decide the issue together.

The Central Court fulfills its responsibility of supervising the lower courts in two other ways besides the use of ordinary and extraordinary review: by issuing "guiding directives" and by publishing other materials (such as selected cases, decisions, and memoranda) which it is thought will be of assistance to the inferior tribunals. "Guiding directives" are summaries of cases actually heard by the court, and their holdings are binding precedents for all lower courts. The other materials are of a more instructive nature by way of general comment and analysis.

PROCURACY

The other major component of the North Korean legal system that is distinguished constitutionally is the procuracy. According to the 1972 constitution, "procuration affairs are conducted by the Central Procurator's Office." Procurator's offices on each of the other levels of state administration, including a special procurator's office, also exercise such functions. The Central Procurator's Office, headed by the president whom the SPA appoints for an apparently open term, is responsible for coordinating the work of all lower-level procurator's offices. While the Central Procurator's Office is responsible for its work to the SPA, the president of the People's Republic, and the CPC, the lower-level procurators are subordinated to their higher analogs alone. No representative body at their corresponding levels have constitutional authority over them in any way.

Like the courts, procurators' offices have three basic constitutional functions: the first is to supervise the observance of state laws by organizations and individuals; the second is to be sure that "decisions and directives of state organs" do not conflict with the official pronouncements of the SPA, its standing committee, the president of the People's Republic, the CPC, and the State Administration Council; the third, similar to the first duty mentioned in regard to the courts, is to protect the current political system, state and cooperative property, and the individual's constitutional rights—but, unlike the courts, through means of uncovering threatening activity and prosecuting its perpetrators.

These 1972 articles covering the procuracy elaborate on their analogs in the old constitution and add one especially noteworthy feature. Although the functions mandated to the office of the procurator in the old constitution were generally the same as those in the new one noted above, in the former no explicit mention was made of the procuratorial duty "to expose and institute penal proceedings." Undoubtedly this was thought to be implicit in the procuracy's responsibility to "ensure precise and honest observation and execution of the law.'' The fact that such a function was more specifically enunciated in the 1972 constitution, as it is in other Marxist constitutions, seems to call attention to its importance. The noteworthy addition to the new document's provisions concerning the procuracy is the final one indicating to whom the central procurator is to be responsible. In both the old and new constitutions, as in the socialist method, the procurators below the central authority are not subject to local agencies. In the original document, the procurator-general answered only to the SPA; in the new one, the Central Procurator's Office must also respond to supervision from the presidency and the CPC.

Nonconstitutional sources reveal in greater detail the type of activities which fall to the procuracy. For example, procurators are expected to represent citizens in complaints against government agencies and to look after the public interest in civil cases which might have a significant social impact. More important, though, as the ''watchdog of socialist legality'' the procuracy is to supervise inquiries into criminal activities and supervise or conduct pretrial investigations (in addition to prosecuting criminal cases) and see that trials are properly conducted. In cases concerning state sovereignty, however, the Code of Criminal Procedure apparently gives authority for all inquiry and pretrial preparation to state security agencies.

Perhaps the most critical extraconstitutional, yet official, function of the procuracy is its role in ''safeguarding a consistent application of the policy of the Worker's Party, . . . publicity for that policy, strengthening of the ideological system, and conscious implementation of Party policies.''

BIBLIOGRAPHY

INTRODUCTION

There is no work yet written in a Western language specifically designed to explain both the South and the North Korean legal systems. However, the following four publications are useful as an introduction to the South Korean legal system.

13-001. Korea, Republic of. Supreme Court. *Korean Legal System.* Seoul: 1964. 151 pp. A brief survey of the history of the Korean judicial system and an explanation of court organization and jurisdiction and Korean civil and criminal trials.

13-002. RYU, Paul Kichyon. ''Republic of Korea.'' In Viktor Knapp (ed.), *International Encyclopedia of Comparative Law: National Reports.* Vol. 1. R Series. Tübingen: J. C. B. Mohr, [1970?]. Provides a brief outline of the basic principles of the Korean legal system, including its constitutional system based on the 1962 constitution and sources of law, with particular emphasis on private and commercial law.

13-003. SHIN, Woong Shik. *Comparative Analysis of Korean and American Judicial System.* Chicago: American Judicature Society, 1974. 228 pp. Serves as an introduction to the South Korean legal system and judicial power, court organization, administration, and personnel.

13-004. World Peace Through Law Center. *Law and Judicial Systems of Nations: Korea.* Washington: 1968–. Looseleaf. Includes such basic information as the legal system, requirements to practice law, the organization of the bar, information on law schools and law students, and a descriptive analysis of court organization and function.

HISTORY OF KOREAN LAW

Writings on traditional Korean law are much desired, especially for the pre–Yi dynasty period. The following four works are helpful background readings.

13-005. HAHM, Pyong-Choon. *The Korean Political Tradition and Law: Essays in Korean Law and Legal History.* Seoul: Hollym Corporation, 1967. 249 pp. Discusses Korean political institutions and values and explores various historical and contemporary Korean problems related to the field of law. See 03-174.

13-006. HYUN, Soong-Jong. ''The Traditional Laws of Korea and the Modern Laws of the West.'' *Korea Journal* 15(10)(1975):11–17. Discusses the role of Confucian rules of propriety in Korean dispute settlement with reference to the reception of Western law.

13-007. KIM, Chin. *Korea.* No. E/12 of John Gilissen (ed.), *Bibliographical Introduction to Legal History and Ethnology.* Brussels: Université Libre de Bruxelles, 1970. 24 pp. A selective bibliographic guide to studies of Korean legal history and ethnology.

13-008. _____. ''Legal Privileges under the Early Yi Dynasty Criminal Codes, I and II.'' *Korea Journal* 15(4)(April

1975):34–44 and 15(5)(May 1975):19–28. Treats the history of traditional Korean penal codes.

Introduction of Yi dynasty legal history to the West is also unsatisfactory; at least ten items, however, are noteworthy.

13-009. CHANG, Dae Hong. "The Historical Development of the Korean Socio-Family System Since 1392—A Legalistic Interpretation." *Journal of East Asiatic Studies* 11(September 1967)(pt. 2):1–124. Discusses family law of Yi dynasty.

13-010. CHANG, Tŏk-sun. "Cérémonies de la majorité, du mariage, des funérailles, et des offrandes pour les morts." *Revue de Corée* 8(4)(1976):33–53. Discusses ceremonies related to the adulthood, marriage, and offerings for the deceased in traditional society that may be useful in the study of Yi dynasty law.

13-011. EIKEMEIER, Dieter. "Villages and Quarters as Instruments of Local Control in Yi Dynasty Korea." *T'oung Pao* 62(1–3)(1976):71–110. Discusses local government and law of Yi dynasty.

13-012. PAK, Pyŏng-Ho. "Caractéristique de la loi coréenne traditionnelle." *Revue de Corée* 8(4)(1976):3–21. Discusses traditional law with reference to family and property.

13-013. PARK, Byong Ho. "Characteristics of Traditional Korean Law." *Korea Journal* 16(7)(1976):4–16. Treats subjects of family and ownership within the context of traditional law and argues that such customs as adopting a son-in-law and equal inheritable shares of family property for sons and daughters are uniquely Korean.

13-014. _____. "The Legal Nature of Land Ownership in the Yi Dynasty." *Korea Journal* 15(10)(1975):4–10. Tries to characterize the proof of Yi dynasty landownership based on documentary evidence and explains various relevant legal terms.

13-015. _____. "Traditional Korean Society and Law." *Seoul Law Journal* 15(1)(1974):107–134. Probes traditional Yi dynasty law with reference to family, legal capacity, and property ownership.

13-016. _____. "Traditional Korean Society and Law." *Korean Journal of Comparative Law* 5(1977):1–26. Discusses traditional law related to family, legal capacity, and property ownership.

13-017. SHAW, William. "Traditional Korean Law: A New Look." *Korea Journal* 13(9)(1973):40–53. Outlines research possibilities on Yi dynasty law and hypothesizes on the roles of law in Yi society.

13-018. TJONG, Zong Uk. "Traditionelles und modernes Strafrecht in Korea." *Zeitschrift für die gesamte Strafrechtwissenschaft* 88(3)(1976):785–812. Discusses traditional criminal law.

For the period from the *Kabo* Reforms of 1894 until the Japanese annexation of Korea, three items are notable.

13-019. CRÉMAZY, Laurent. *Le Code Pénal de la Corée, Tai-Han Hyeng Pop.* Seoul: Seoul Press, Hodge & Co., 1904. 182 pp. Provides a French translation and analysis of the draft on *Hyŏngpŏp taejŏn* [The complete criminal code] in light of the Ch'ing dynasty and Vietnamese penal codes.

13-020. _____. *Texte Complémentaire de Code Pénal de la Corée.* Paris: Marchal et Billard, 1906. 28 pp. Supplements Crémazy's 1904 work by referring to the finalized text (680 articles) of the 1905 *Hyŏngpŏp taejŏn*.

13-021. WILKINSON, W. H. *The Corean Government: Constitutional Changes, July 1894 to October 1895.* Shanghai: Statistical Department of Inspectorate General of Customs, 1897. 192 pp. Discusses judicial administration before and after 1894 with specific references to the 1894 reform.

The subject of Japanese administration of justice from 1910 to 1945 also wants systematic research. Three publications are relevant to this subject.

13-022. GRAJDANZEV, Andrew J. *Modern Korea.* New York: Institute of Pacific Relations, 1944. Offers a brief description of the judicial system under Japanese colonial rule.

13-023. Japan. Government General of Chosen. *Annual Report on Administration of Chosen.* Keijo [Seoul]: 1907–. Contains a section on "Justice."

13-024. LYMAN, Albert. "Notes on Japanese Law: The Administration of Justice in Korea." *American Bar Association Journal* 35(4)(1949):303–305. Gives a brief introduction to the Korean legal system under the Japanese Government-General covering the period from 1910 through 1945.

A glimpse of the administration of justice under the US Military Government in an area south of the 38th parallel can be attained through the following book.

13-025. LYMAN, Albert (ed.). *Selected Legal Opinions: Opinions Rendered in the Role of Legal Adviser to the*

Military Government of Korea and Covering a Period from March 1946 to August 1948. 2 vols. Seoul: US Military Government, 1948. 511 pp. Compiles legal opinions given by the Opinion Bureau based on requests by various agencies of the military government.

SOURCES AND STRUCTURE OF LAW IN SOUTH KOREA

A systematic exposition of South Korean law based on logical and practical classification into public and private law has yet to be written in a Western language. Major sources of South Korean law in their English textual format appear in the following book.

13-026. Korean Legal Center. *Laws of the Republic of Korea.* Seoul: 1975. 1565 pp. Contains the English translation of 101 laws (including the basic six codes) of South Korea, effective January 1975.

Constitutional Law

For the study of the 1972 constitution, two works are useful.

13-027. FLANZ, Gisbert H. In Albert P. Blaustein and Gisbert H. Flanz (eds.), *Constitutions of the Countries of the World.* Vol. 6 (June 1974 Supplement). New York: Oceana Publications, 1974. Loose-leaf. Contains constitutional chronology, English text of the 1972 constitution, and annotated bibliography.

13-028. KIM, Ki-Bŏm. "Revisions of the Korean Constitution." *Korea Journal* 14(7)(July 1974):4–13 and 14(8) (August 1974):18–25. Discusses constitutional changes since 1948 and presents special features of the 1972 constitution.

The following seven items are relevant for a grasp of constitutional history.

13-029. DULL, Paul S. "South Korean Constitution." *Far Eastern Survey* 17(17)(September 1948):205–207. Gives a brief description of the South Korean constitution.

13-030. FLANZ, Gisbert H. "Korea and Vietnam—Two Constitutional Experiments." *St. John's Law Review* 42(1967–1968):18–37. Discusses the work of the Constitutional Deliberation Committee on the 1962 constitution.

13-031. HENDERSON, Gregory. *Korea: The Politics of the Vortex.* Cambridge, Mass.: Harvard University Press, 1968. Contains an appraisal of South Korea's constitutional development.

13-032. KIM, Youn-Soo. "Die Verfassung der Republik Korea—Geschichte und Kommentar." *Verfassung und Recht in Übersee* 6(1)(1971):31–40. Describes constitu-

tional history until the adoption of the 1962 constitution and analyzes that constitution.

13-033. PAK, C. Y. "Third Republic Constitution of Korea: An Analysis." *Western Political Quarterly* 21(March 1968):110–122. Analyzes the characteristics of the 1962 constitution.

13-034. REEVE, W. D. *The Republic of Korea: A Political and Economic History.* London: Oxford University Press, 1963. Includes a section entitled "Constitutional and Political Development, 1948–60."

13-035. YUN, Kun-Shik. "Die Verfassungsentwicklung der Republik Korea seit 1948." *Jahrbuch des Öffentlichen Rechts der Gegenwart* 12(1963):461–503. Provides a survey of constitutional history from the original constitution to the 1962 constitution including an English translation of the 1962 constitution.

Western-language translations of past constitutions can be located through the following five sources.

13-036. Asian-African Legal Consultative Committee. *Constitutions of Asian Countries.* Bombay: N. M. Tripathi Private Ltd., 1968. Gives the English text of the 1962 constitution.

13-037. Korea, Republic of. Central Election Management Committee. *Korean Constitution, Election and Political Party Law.* Seoul: 1964. Offers a compilation of the English text of the 1962 constitution and the legislative and executive measures related to election and political parties.

13-038. PEASLEE, Amos J. (ed.). *Constitutions of Nations.* Vol. 2. 2nd ed. The Hague: Martinus Nijhoff, 1956. Contains an English translation of the constitution of the Republic of Korea (12 July 1948).

13-039. _____. *Constitutions of Nations.* Vol. 2. 3rd rev. ed. The Hague: Martinus Nijhoff, 1966. Contains an English translation of the 1962 constitution.

13-040. PUGET, Henry (ed.). *Les Constitutions d'Asie et Australasie.* Paris: Les Editions de L'Epargne, 1965. Includes a French translation of the 1962 constitution.

Administrative Law

No comprehensive treatise on South Korean administrative law is yet available in a Western language. There have been extensive writings, however, on the Foreign Capital Inducement Law and related subjects. At least fourteen publications are worth noting.

13-041. CALHOUN, Alexander D. and others. "Foreign Investment in the Republic of Korea." *Hastings Law Journal* 20(1)(1968):245–271. Introduces to American lawyers the relevant points of Korean laws concerning business organization, foreign capital investment, and taxation.

13-042. CHUNG, Kuang-Hsung. "Investment Laws in the Republic of China and the Republic of Korea: A Comparative Study." *Journal of Law and Economic Development* 4(2)(1969):338–385. Appraises the economic and legal effects of the investment laws of South Korea and examines tax concessions and laws for the protection of foreign property.

13-043. DIAMOND, Walter H. (ed.). *Foreign Tax and Trade Briefs: Republic of Korea.* 2 vols. Loose-leaf. New York: Matthew Bender, [1974?]. Provides a general picture of taxation and trading laws with an updating loose-leaf service.

13-044. International Centre for Settlement of Investment Disputes. *Investment Laws of the World: South Korea.* Vol. 2. New York: Oceana Publications, 1974–. Loose-leaf. Presents the English text of the laws affecting investment with a compilation of constitutional, legislative, regulatory, and treaty materials.

13-045. KIM, Chan-Jin. "Foreign Investment in Korea: Law and Administration." PhD dissertation, University of Washington, 1972. Abstracted in *DAI* 33(9)(March 1973): 5209-10-A; UM 72-28,617. Discusses investment law and its administration.

13-046. _____. "Legal Aspects of Foreign Investment in Korea." *Korea Journal of Comparative Law* 1(1973): 2–60. Explains the legal environment of foreign investment in Korea.

13-047. KIM, Chin and Robert H. ROGIER. "International Trade and Investment Law in the Republic of Korea." *Journal of World Trade Law* 10(1976):462–477. Aims at providing American business people and lawyers with background and the principal sources of information on trade and investment law in the Republic of Korea.

13-048. KIM, Hong Han. "Foreign Investment Laws of Korea." In V. S. Cameron (ed.), *Private Investments and International Transactions in Asian and South Pacific Countries.* New York: Matthew Bender, 1974. Treats origin and features of foreign investment laws in South Korea.

13-049. KIM, Joungwon A. "South Korea: A Summary of the Existing Legal System and Future Trends in Respect to Foreign Trade and Investment." In Richard C. Allison (ed.), *Current Legal Aspects of Doing Business in the Far East.* Chicago: American Bar Association, 1972. Makes an inquiry into the legal climate for investment and trade in South Korea.

13-050. KIM, Young Moo. "Legal Forms of Doing Business in Korea." *Korea Journal of Comparative Law* 2(1974): 58–84. Explains the legal forms and procedures of doing business in Korea by aliens and related legal problems.

13-051. KOH, Kwang Lim. "Korea." In G. Wolfgang and R. Pugh (eds.), *Legal Aspects of Foreign Investment.* Boston: Little, Brown, 1958. Discusses the initial period of drafting a law for foreign investment.

13-052. Korean Traders Association. *Laws Relating to Foreign Trade.* Seoul: 1973. 380 pp. Includes the English text of the Trade Translation Law, Foreign Exchange Control Law, Foreign Capital Inducement Law, and related laws, as well as an English translation of the tariff table.

13-053. YOON, Ho Il. "Legal Aspects of Foreign Investment in the Republic of Korea." *International Lawyers* 10(4) (1976):729–754. Examines the laws and regulations of the Republic of Korea concerning direct foreign investment, licensing, loans, foreign exchange, business organization, and taxation.

13-054. _____. "Taxation of Foreign Investment and Trade: The Need for Harmonization." *Korean Journal of Comparative Law* 5(1977):48–68. Discusses briefly the impact of the present system of taxation of individual countries on the foreign investment and trade engaged in by multinational enterprises by referring to the tax laws of the Republic of Korea and the United States.

Land reform legislation, in spite of its importance, has received less attention.

13-055. CHOY, Bong-youn. *Korea: A History.* Rutland, Vt.: Tuttle, 1971. May serve as background reading; especially informative on the subject of land reform from traditional to modern Korea.

13-056. MITCHELL, Charles Clyde, Jr. *The New Korea Company Limited: Land Management and Tenancy Reform in Korea against a Background of U.S. Army Occupation, 1945–1948.* Cambridge, Mass.: Harvard University Press, 1949. Administration of the New Korea Company set up by the American occupation for the management of former Japanese properties in Korea.

13-057. ZEON, Young-cheol. "The Politics of Land Reform in South Korea." PhD dissertation, University of Missouri at Columbia, 1973. 335 pp. Abstracted in *DAI* 35(1)(July 1974):549-50-A; UM 74-10,012. A survey of the political effect of land reform—particularly during the Rhee government of Korea's First Republic.

The tax law is complicated and its changes are frequent. The following six publications are relevant.

13-058. Foreign Tax Law Association. *Foreign Tax Law Bi-Weekly Bulletin.* Ormond Beach, Fla.: 1950–. Often carries the latest developments on tax law revision of various countries, including South Korea.

13-059. _____. *Tax Laws of the World: Korea.* Loose-leaf. Ormond Beach, Fla., [1970?–]. Periodically updates Korean income tax law data in English translation.

13-060. Korea, Republic of. Office of National Tax Administration. *Major Tax Laws of the Republic of Korea.* Seoul: 1968. Translates tax laws into English.

13-061. LEE, Samuel Sang-ok. "The Effects of Inflation and Legal Remedies on Accounting in Korea Since 1945." PhD dissertation, Columbia University, 1964. 171 pp. Abstracted in *DA* 25(June 1965):7006; UM 65-5858. Studies two Korean laws (1958 and 1962) relating to price-level adjustment and their background.

13-062. LEE, Tai Ro. "Value Added Tax Act of 1976." *Korean Journal of Comparative Law* 5(1977):27–47. Outlines and examines the Value Added Tax Act of 1976.

13-063. YUN, Seung-Young. "Alien Income Tax in Korea." *Korean Journal of Comparative Law* 1(1973):61–100. Explains Korean income tax law as it relates to aliens.

Labor Law

No comprehensive treatise on labor law has been written in a Western language. However, the following publications may serve as background sources.

13-064. BLEECKER, Theodore. "Labor Legislation in the Republic of Korea." *Labor Development Abroad* 11(1) (1966):1–6. Summarizes labor legislation in Korea as of 1965.

13-065. KIM, Chi Sun. "The Changes in Labor Force Structure and Their Causes in Korea." *Koreana Quarterly* 14 (1/2) (Spring/Summer 1972):34–41. An analysis of the changing composition of Korea's labor forces—its reason and future impact.

13-066. _____. "Legal Control of Labor-Management Relations of Foreign Capital-Invested Enterprises in Korea." In V. S. Cameron (ed.), *Private Investments and International Transactions in Asian and South Pacific Countries.* New York: Matthew Bender, 1974. Discusses general law governing labor-management relations with reference to foreign capital-invested enterprises.

13-067. Korea, Republic of. Office of Labour Affairs. *Labour Law of Korea.* Seoul: 1969. An English translation of Korean labor laws.

13-068. OGLE, George Erving. "Labor Unions in Rapid Economic Development: The Case of the Republic of Korea in the 1960's." PhD dissertation, University of Wisconsin at Madison, 1973. 423 pp. Abstracted in *DAI* 34(10)(April 1974):6213-A; UM 74-3539. A historical analysis of the development of labor unions in Korea and the meaning of "guided capitalism" in Korea in the 1960s.

13-069. PARK, Yong-ki. "Trade Unionism in Korea." *Free Labor World* 41(January 1963):11–15. A brief history and status of Korean trade unionism.

13-070. United States. Department of Labor. *Labor Law and Practice in the Republic of Korea.* BLS Report 361 (1969). Can be used as an introductory guide to Korean labor legislation and practices.

Criminal Law

This field has been effectively treated in the following five works.

13-071. PAK, Dong Hie. "Raub und Erpressung im koreanischen Strafgesetzbuch: Zur Geschichte des europaischen Einflusses auf das ostasiatische Strafrecht." Unpublished dissertation, University of Berlin, 1971. Discusses Korean law of robbery and extortion.

13-072. RYU, Paul Kichyun. *The Korean Criminal Code.* American Series of Foreign Penal Code, no. 2. South Hackensack: Fred B. Rothman & Co., 1960. Gives an English translation of the Korean Criminal Code of 3 October 1953 and, by way of introduction, an essay analyzing the ideologies embodied in this code.

13-073. _____. "The Korean Culture and Criminal Responsibility: An Application of a Scientific Approach to Law." JSD dissertation, Yale University, 1958. Presents an analysis of cultural pattern and legal significance in Korean culture with specific reference to criminal responsibility; also contains an English translation of the 1953 Korean Criminal Code.

13-074. _____. *Das koreanische Strafgesetzbuch.* Sammlung ausserdeutscher Strafgesetzbücher in deutscher Übersetzung, no. 89. Berlin: De Gruyter, 1968. Offers German translation of the South Korean Penal Code of 3 October 1953 with a brief survey of features of the code.

13-075. _____. "The New Korean Criminal Code of October 3, 1953: An Analysis of Ideologies Embedded in It." *Journal of Criminal Law, Criminology and Political Science* 47(1957–1958):275–295. Gives a brief historical survey and main features of the 1953 code followed by an analysis of ideologies behind important problems treated in the code.

There is no noteworthy treatise on the Law of Criminal Procedure or the Law of Civil Procedure. However, writings related to these two fields are examined in the subsection on Judicial Proceedings.

Public International Law

South Korea's relations with Japan are the subject of numerous works in this field of law.

13-076. CHAI, Nam-Yearl. "Asian Attitudes toward International Law: A Case Study of Korea." PhD dissertation, University of Pennsylvania, 1967. 303 pp. Abstracted in *DA* 28 (June 1968):5125–26–A; UM 68-9189. Explores the state practice of the First Republic of Korea (1948–1960) as revealed in three international legal disputes: (1) the dispute concerning Korea's sovereignty over the adjacent seas; (2) the dispute regarding Japanese claim to property in Korea; and (3) the jurisdictional dispute over Dokto (Tok Island).

13-077. IRIE, Keishirō. "Treaty on Basic Relations between Japan and the Republic of Korea." *Japanese Annual of International Law* 10(1966):9–15. Briefly outlines the Korea–Japan basic treaty of 1965.

13-078. KIM, Dong Hi. "Accord entre la Corée du sud et le Japon sur le developpement commun de la partie sud du plateau continental adjacent aux deux pays." *Korean Journal of Comparative Law* 2(1974):103–129. Considers the 1974 accord between Japan and the Republic of Korea on the development of the adjacent continental shelf.

13-079. KOH, Kwang-lim. "The Continental Shelf: An Analytical Study of the Draft Articles on the Continental Shelf Adopted by the International Law Commission." JSD dissertation, Harvard University, 1954. Contains a commentary on the Syngman Rhee line.

13-080. LEE, Byung Joe. "'Title to Dokdo' in International Law." *Korean Journal of Comparative Law* 2(1974):85–102. Examines the question of the legal status of Dokdo (Tokto) Island in Korean perspective. A similar article appears in Byung Joe Lee, "Legal Status of Dokdo," *Korean Journal of International Law* 8(2)(1963):389–412.

13-081. ODA, Shigeru. "The Normalization of Relations between Japan and the Republic of Korea." *American Journal of International Law* 61(1967):35–56. Analyzes the 1965 treaty on basic relations between Japan and the Republic of Korea with a brief historical background note on Korea–Japan diplomatic relations until 1965.

13-082. TAKABAYASHI, Hideo. "Normalization of Relations between Japan and the Republic of Korea: Agreement on Fisheries." *Japanese Annual of International Law* 10(1966):16–22. Discusses the vexing question of fisheries under the 1965 agreement between South Korea and Japan with reference to contents of this agreement and unresolved issues.

13-083. WEISSBERG, Guenter. *Recent Developments in the Law of the Sea and the Japanese Fishery Dispute.* The Hague: M. Nijhoff, 1966. 135 pp. Discusses fishery disputes between the Republic of Korea and Japan.

The following three studies go beyond the subject of ROK–Japan relations.

13-084. "Due Process Challenge to the Korean Status of Forces Agreement." *Georgetown Law Journal* 57(5)(1969):1097–1107. Discusses background of the Status of Forces Agreement between the United States and the Republic of Korea.

13-085. PARK, Choon-ho. "Fishing under Troubled Waters: The Northeast Asia Fisheries Controversy." *Ocean Development and International Law Journal* 2(2)(1974): 93–135. Advocates regional control based on multilateral treaty agreement over the Yellow and East China Seas by coastal states, including Korea.

13-086. _____. "The Sino-Japanese-Korean Sea Resources Controversy and the Hypothesis of a 200-Mile Economic Zone." *Harvard International Law Journal* 16(1)(1975): 27–46. Reviews, among other topics, the position of the two Koreas as it relates to the regime of a 200-mile economic zone.

The following two publications can serve as a basic source of information.

13-087. Korean Association of International Law. *Korean Journal of International Law.* 1956–. Contains the English text of international legal materials related to Korea.

13-088. United States. Department of State. *Treaties in Force.* Annual since 1941. Lists treaties and other international agreements to which the United States has become a party; includes the Republic of Korea.

Civil Law

No introductory treatise on civil law based on the Civil Code and its ancillary laws has been published in a Western language, although there have been a number of works written on family law.

13-089. BERGMAN, Alexander (ed.). *Internationales Ehe- und Kindschaftsrecht: Süd-Korea.* Vol. 7. 4th ed. Frankfurt: Verlag für Standesamtswesen, 1969–. Loose-leaf. Treats laws related to marriage, parent, and child.

13-090. CHO, Key-cab. "Problems Arising from the Legal

Doctrines and Practices of the Korean Marital Law." JSD dissertation, Yale University, 1963. An exposition of problems arising from the legal doctrines and practices of marriage and divorce with a historical note on Korean marital law.

13-091. KAL, Bong Kun. "Die Neugestaltung des koreanischen Familien- und Erbrechts." *Das Standesamt* 15(5) (1962):135–140. Commentary on family and succession with an introductory note on the history of this field of law.

13-092. KIM, Chin. "Les Articles concernant la famille (parenté), Code civil de la Republique de Corée." *Seoul Law Journal* 3(1)(1961):176–224. A French translation of Book 4 (The Relatives) of the Korean Civil Code.

13-093. _____. "Les Articles concernant la famille (parenté)." *Annuario di Diritto Comparato e di Studi Legislativi* 43(1969): 141–147. An analysis of the Book on Relatives (Family) of the Korean Civil Code in French with summaries in Italian and English.

13-094. _____. "Parental Power under the Civil Code of the Republic of Korea." *Recueils de la Société Jean Brodin* 35(1975):637–644. Investigates the subject of parental power in relation to traditional Korean faiths and legislative programs concerning the protection of minors that have been adopted since 1945.

13-095. KIM, Cho-Soo. "The Marriage System in Korea." *Korea Journal* 16(7)(1976):17–29. Analyzes problems involved with marriage under the 1960 Civil Code.

13-096. _____. "A Study of Marriage and Divorce in the New Civil Code of Korea." *Bulletin of the Korean Research Center* 10(1959):35–49. Treats features of marriage and divorce law.

13-097. KIM, Chung Han. "Real Action in Korea and Japan." *Tulane Law Review* 29(4)(1955):713–737. Comments upon petitory remedies and possessory actions in relation to real actions.

13-098. KWACK, Yoon-Chick. "The Korean New Civil Code." *Bulletin of the Korean Research Center* 17(1962): 11–23. A brief summary of the 1960 Civil Code.

13-099. LEE, Hang-Nyung. "Civil Law and Korean Family System." *Korea Journal* 3(October 1963):20–21. Discusses the Korean family in terms of the Civil Code.

13-100. LIM, Jung-Pyung. "Das gegenwärtige Familienrecht Südkoreas zwischen deutscher Rechtsdogmatik und fernöstlicher Sozialdoktrin." Unpublished dissertation, Johannes-Gutenberg Universität, Mainz. Printed in Augsburg by D. W. Blasaditsch, 1973. Compares Korean family law with that of Germany.

13-101. SIGWORTH, Heather. "Adoption of South Korean Orphans in the United States." Paper prepared for the Wilson Foundation, Tucson, Arizona, 1973. Includes the English translation of relevant laws on adoption.

13-102. YANG, Byung-Hui. "Grundlagen und Gestalt des koreanischen Familien, insbesondere Ehescheidungrecht: Eine rechtsvergleichende Untersuchung." Unpublished dissertation, Universität Bochum, 1971. Discusses domestic relations and divorce in the Republic of Korea.

Commercial Law

The need for a revision of corporation law has been felt for some time in light of Korean experience with foreign investors and has prompted a number of interesting writings on the subject.

13-103. AUFRICHT, Hans (ed.). *Central Banking Legislation: Korea.* Vol. 1. Washington: International Monetary Fund, 1961. Includes the English text of the act establishing the Bank of Korea and related legal measures.

13-104. CHUN, Bong Duck. "The Commercial Laws in Korea." In National Association of Credit Management (ed.), *Digest of Commercial Laws of the World.* Vol. 3. Dobbs Ferry, N.Y.: Oceana Publications, 1966–. Looseleaf. Provides updating service of abstracts of commercial laws.

13-105. Foreign Tax Law Association. *Commercial Laws of the World: Korea.* Ormond Beach, Fla.: Foreign Tax Law Association, [1962?–]. Provides the English translation of relevant South Korean business laws and regulations for foreign business people and is occasionally updated through loose-leaf supplements.

13-106. KWACK, Y. C., David E. ALLAN, and others. *Credit and Security in Korea.* New York: Crane, Russak & Co., 1973. 197 pp. Discusses the legal aspects of development financing through loans and the various relevant legal forms of security.

13-107. LEE, Young June. "Das japanische und koreanische Gewahrleistungsrecht in seiner gesetzlichen Entwicklung und in den Formulargedingungen der Praxis unter dem Einfluss des deutschen Rechts." Unpublished dissertation, Frankfurt, 1968. Compares the Korean law of warranty to that of Germany.

13-108. LIEW, Song Kun. "Commercial Arbitration in Korea with Special Reference to the UNCITRAL Rules." *Korean Journal of Comparative Law* 5(1977):69–88. Presents legal problems involved with Korean commercial arbitration in light of international and foreign arbitration rules.

13-109. MEYER, Donald R. "Control of a Korean Stock

Corporation.'' *Seoul Law Journal* 12(1)(1971):114–124. Provides a general orientation to the pertinent statutory provisions related to control of a Korean stock corporation.

13-110. MIN, Byoung-Kook. ''Court Review of Corporate Elections.'' *Korean Journal of Comparative Law* 1(1973): 158–183. Urges revision of that article of commercial law having to do with corporation elections.

13-111. SHIN, Woong Shik. ''Section 341: Commercial Code of Korea.'' *Seoul Law Journal* 12(1)(1971):37–69. Provides revision of the section of the Commercial Code dealing with acquisition of a company's own shares.

13-112. SONG, Sang Hyun. ''A Few Notes on Korean Admiralty.'' *Korean Journal of Comparative Law* 5(1977): 114–122. Presents vexing problems of interpreting the admiralty rules under the Korean Commercial Code.

13-113. SONN, Ju-Chan and Kiljun PARK. ''Some Proposals for Amendment of Korean Stock Company Law.'' *Korean Journal of Comparative Law* 2(1974):1–29. Advocates the revision of Korean Stock Company Law by reason of various conditions of corporate finance and business in Korea.

13-114. TSCHE, Kiuon. ''Die Verfassung der Aktiengesellschaft nach koreanischem Recht im Vergleich mit dem deutschen Aktiengesetz.'' Dissertation, University of Bonn, 1965. A comparative study of Korean and German corporation law focusing on functions of the head of the company, the supervisory board, and the general membership.

13-115. YOO, Hyun. ''To Form a Stock Corporation in Korea: A Comparative Study with the American Law.'' *Korean Journal of Comparative Law* 1(1973):101–157. Explores legal problems related to the function of business corporations in Korea with a comparison to similar American law.

Private International Law

The West is well acquainted with this field of law because of the following thirteen publications.

13-116. BEITZKE, Günther. ''Zur Gültigkeit von Ehen in Deutschland lebender Japaner und Koreaner.'' *Das Standesamt* 17(1)(1964):25–26. Treats the validity of marriage of Koreans performed in Germany.

13-117. CHOE, Kong-Woong. ''Jurisdiction in Korean Conflict of Laws.'' *Korean Journal of Comparative Law* 5(1977):89–113. Inquires into principles involved with the jurisdictional aspect of Korean conflict of laws.

13-118. KIM, Chin. ''International Marriage and Divorce with Reference to the Korean Conflict Rules.'' *Bulletin of the Korean Research Center: Journal of Social Sciences and Humanities* 18(June 1963):45–57. Considers marriage and divorce in terms of Korean conflict of laws.

13-119. _____. ''The Korean Choice-of-Law Rules.'' *LAWASIA* 2(1971):96–106. Describes characteristics of the Korean Code of Private International law (otherwise known as Private Law Involving Foreign Elements). Includes an English translation of the text of the code.

13-120. _____. ''The Legal Status of Aliens in Korea.'' *Columbia Journal of Transnational Law* 8(2)(1969):220–245. Reviews legal status and economic rights of aliens under numerous Korean laws; the revised version of this article appears in Kim's ''Legal Status of Aliens in the Republic of Korea,'' *Korea Journal* 11(11)(1971):10–17, and ''Le Statut légal des étrangers en Corée,'' *Revue de Corée* 3(3)(1971):49–56.

13-121. _____. ''Renvoi and Characterization in Korean Conflict of Law.'' JSD dissertation, Yale University, 1958. Presents a theoretical exposition of questions of renvoi and characterization as related to Korean conflict of laws. A partial reproduction of this dissertation appears in Kim's ''Renvoi Clause in the Korean Private International Law,'' *Bulletin of the Korean Research Center: Journal of Social Sciences and Humanities* 24(1966):43–50.

13-122. KIM, Chin and Timothy G. CARROLL. ''Intercountry Adoption of South Korean Orphans: A Lawyer's Guide.'' *Journal of Family Law* 14(2)(1975):223–253. Discusses the difficulty and confusion in adopting South Korean orphans in the United States.

13-123. Korea, Republic of. Ministry of Foreign Affairs. *Extracts of Laws and Regulations Governing Aliens and Alien Activities in the Republic of Korea.* Seoul: 1959. Presents an unofficial translation of relevant laws and regulations that affect aliens in South Korea.

13-124. ROE, M. J. ''Problems of Proving Foreign Law in Korean Court: A Comparative Study.'' *Indian Yearbook of International Affairs* 13(1)(1964):151–173. Takes up proof of foreign law as a question of law in comparison to the approach of courts in common law countries.

13-125. SCHURIG, Klaus. ''Zur Gültigkeit 'diplomatischer' Ehen zwischen Koreanern oder Japanern in Deutschland.'' *Das Standesamt* 24(4)(1971). Discusses the validity of consular marriage between Koreans in Germany.

13-126. TOMSON, Edgar. ''Das Staatsangehörigkeitsrecht der ostasiatischen Staaten: China-Japan-Korea-Mongolei.'' *Sammlung geltender Staatsangehörigkeitsgesetze* 32(1971):271–283. Analyzes the 1948 Nationality Law, as amended, and also includes the German text of the 1948 law and the 1951 presidential decree on the Nationality Law.

13-127. TSCHE, Chong Kil. "Die Schleidung im koreanischen materiellen und internationalen Privatrecht." Unpublished dissertation, University of Cologne, 1961. Investigates the subject of divorce as related to South Korean substantive law and private international law (conflict of laws).

13-128. United Nations. *Laws Concerning Nationality.* United Nations Legislative Series, 1954. Contains the English text of the Nationality Law of 20 December 1948 and the presidential decree of 18 November 1951 concerning the Nationality Law.

Laws Governing Industrial Property and Copyright

Through increasing interest of American commercial publishers, the English summary and translation of currently effective laws related particularly to industrial property rights are readily available. Notable publications in this field of law include the following.

13-129. BAXTER, J. W. (ed.). *World Patent Law and Practice: South Korea.* Vol. 2. New York: Matthew Bender, 1975–. Loose-leaf. Contains features of South Korean patent law.

13-130. CHA, Soon Yung. "Korean Trademark Law." *Trademark Reporter* 45(6)(1955):647–652. Gives a brief summary of Korean trademark law.

13-131. CHUN, Bong Duck. "Korea (South)." In National Association of Credit Management (ed.), *Digest of Commercial Laws of the World: Patent Law and Practice—Trademark Law and Practice.* Dobbs Ferry, N.Y.: Oceana Publications, 1970–. Loose-leaf. Provides guidelines and preliminary orientation on relevant areas of patent and trademark law.

13-132. LEE, Byong Ho. *Korean Patent and Trademark.* Seoul: Hollym Corporation, 1968. 248 pp. Examines the patent, utility model, design, and trademark as conventional forms of industrial property and attempts to distinguish Korean laws of industrial property from Japanese and American laws.

13-133. _____. "Report on Current Trademark Practices in Korea." *Trademark Reporter* 47(1)(1977):46–53. Discusses the trademark license problem as well as a number of other developments subsequent to implementation of the 1974 Trademark Law.

13-134. PARK, Youngshik. "A Comparative Study of the American 'Shop Right Rule' and the Korean 'Service Invention.'" MCL thesis, University of Illinois, 1970. 137

pp. Considers the status of rights to an invention when the invention is conceived and developed by an employee who is not contractually bound to assign right, title, and interest in the invention to the employer.

13-135. SINNOTT, John P. (ed.). *World Patent Law and Practice: Korea.* Vol. 2C. New York: Matthew Bender, 1974–. Loose-leaf. Contains the English translation of Industrial Property Law, Utility Model Law, and Design Law.

13-136. WHITE, William W. and Byfleet G. RAVENSCROFT (eds.). *Trademarks throughout the World: Korea.* New York: Trade Activities, 1974–. Loose-leaf. Summarizes new laws and changes in trademark laws as they are promulgated.

JUDICIAL ADMINISTRATION IN SOUTH KOREA

What is the raison d'être of the judiciary in a modern democratic society? Can this question be answered positively in the case of South Korean society? What are the characteristics of the current South Korean justice system, which ostensibly derives from the 1894 reforms? What do ordinary South Korean citizens expect and demand from this system? Satisfactory answers to these basic questions have not yet been found. The following eight items may serve as pertinent background reading.

13-137. COHEN, Jerome Alan. "Lawyers, Politics, and Despotism in Korea." *American Bar Association Journal* 61(June 1975):730–732. Denounces the "Yushin Constitution" and emergency decrees which enable political crimes to be tried by military courts. Urges lawyers and the organized bar to lead the struggle against political repression.

13-138. HAHM, Pyong-Choon. "Decision-Process in Korea." In Glendon Schuber and David J. Danelski (eds.), *Comparative Judicial Behavior.* London: Oxford University Press, 1969. Examines the Korean judicial decision-making process in the context of its interaction with community perspective of authority.

13-139. KIM, Y. H. and S. I. KIM. "A Proposal to Facilitate the Uniform Administration of Justice in Korea through the Use of Mathematical Model." *Rutgers Journal of Computers and the Law* 4(1)(1975):284–301. Proposes sentencing by computer—one model and its implications.

13-140. Korea, Republic of. Supreme Court. *Civil Procedure of Korea.* Seoul: 1972. 15 pp. Gives an English outline of civil proceedings.

13-141. _____. _____. *Criminal Procedure of Korea.* Seoul: 1972. 31 pp. Presents an English outline of criminal proceedings.

13-142. SHAFROTH, Will. "Judicial Administration in Korea." *Journal of the American Judicature Society* 50(1) (1966):12–15. Evaluates the Korean court system based on the author's survey of the function of Korean courts. This article develops an earlier study: Shafroth's "Report on Judicial Administration in Korea," *Seoul Law Journal* 7(1)(1965):129–166.

13-143. STEINBERG, David I. "Law, Development and Korean Society." *Journal of Comparative Administration* 3(2) (1971): 215–256. Discusses the role of law as a factor in the process of Korean development.

13-144. United States. Department of Army. *Country Law Study for Korea.* Prepared by Headquarters, US Forces, Korea/Eighth US Army Office of the Judge Advocate (1971). 115 pp. Presents an outline of Korean legal systems with special emphasis on criminal procedure.

Sociological inquiries into the legal profession have recently been undertaken, and similar investigations could be made of legal aid programs and paralegal professionals. At least the following five items are worth listing.

13-145. Committee on Legal Services to the Poor in the Developing Countries. *Legal Aid and World Poverty: A Survey of Asia, Africa, and Latin America.* New York: Praeger, 1974. Reviews legal services for the poor in South Korea.

13-146. LEE, Jang-Hyun. "Social Background and Career Development of the Korean Jurists." *Korea Journal* 14(6) (1974):11–20. Makes a sociological inquiry into the social background of lawyers and their membership in the legal profession; footnote citation lists a number of sociological studies made on the subject of the Korean legal profession.

13-147. MURPHY, Jay and others. *Legal Profession in Korea: The Judicial Scrivener and Others.* Seoul: Korea Law Research Institute, 1967. Presents a study of judicial scriveners by examining their qualifications, activities, and court supervision. Includes an analysis of the functions of the notary public, patent specialist, and others engaged in the administration of justice.

13-148. WON, George, Jang-Hyun LEE, and In-Hwan OH. "Korean Lawyers: Self-Evaluation and Occupational Satisfaction." *Korea Journal* 14(11)(1974):33–39. A sociological analysis based on data collected from Korean lawyers to learn their self-evaluation of professional satisfaction.

13-149. YANG, Sŭng-du. "Comment les Coréens considèrent-ils la justice?" *Revue de Corée* 8(4)(1976):22–32. Investigates the people's attitude toward the law.

Improvement of legal education was once a key issue which culminated in the establishment of the Graduate School of Law at Seoul National University. As a result of the creation of the Institute of Judicial Training which took over the function of the Graduate School of Law in 1970, this issue has subsided.

13-150. KIM, Chin. "The Role of the Law Schools in Developing Nations: The Graduate School of Law in Korea." In Charles S. Rhyne (ed.), *Bangkok World Conference on World Peace Through Law.* Geneva: World Peace Through Law Center, 1971. Explores the role of the Graduate School of Law. A similar article appears in Kim's "The Graduate School of Law in Korea," *Associations of American Law Schools Foreign Exchange Bulletin* 1(1970):7–9.

13-151. MURPHY, Jay. "Legal Education and the Development of Law in Traditional Culture: Learning from the Korean Experience." *Journal of Legal Education* 27(2) (1975):234–245. Inquires whether South Korea has the resources for education for law.

13-152. _____. *Legal Education in a Developing Nation: The Korean Experience.* Seoul: Korea Law Research Institute, Seoul National University, 1965. Surveys Korean legal education, covering such areas as faculty, curriculum, students, teaching and examination methods, as well as class, library publications, and research facilities. Also treats the bar examination, the legal profession, law professors, and the Graduate School of Law.

13-153. PHILLIPS, David M. "The Role of the Law School in the Developing Nation." In Charles S. Rhyne (ed.), *Bangkok World Conference on World Peace Through Law.* Geneva: World Peace Through Law Center, 1971. Discusses the significance of the Graduate School of Law as the most promising avenue for legal reform and educational advancement.

13-154. RYU, Paul K. "Legal Education in the Far East." *Seoul Law Journal* 7(1)(1965):117–128. Interprets the social meaning of the present status of legal education in East Asia and relates conclusions to the creation of the Graduate School of Law in Korea. A similar article appears in Ryu's "Legal Education in Korea," *Seoul Law Journal* 6(1)(1964):155–162.

COURTS AND PROCURACY IN NORTH KOREA

Paucity of original source materials on the North Korean judicial system and the lack of actual knowledge of the function of North Korean legal institutions are notable barriers to the pursuit of research projects on this subject. The following eight studies may offer background reading.

13-155. BARINKA, Jaroslav. "Democratic People's Republic of Korea." In Vikto Knapp (ed.), *International Encyclopedia of Comparative Law: National Reports.* Vol. 1. D Series. Tübingen: J. C. B. Mohr, [1970?]. Provides a brief outline of basic principles of the North Korean legal system, including its constitutional system based on the constitution of 9 September 1948 as amended on 22 October 1962. Also reviews the arbitration court system, established in 1954.

13-156. CHO, Sung Yoon. "Judicial System of North Korea." *Asian Survey* 11(December 1971):1167–1181.

13-157. _____. "Law and Justice in North Korea." *Journal of Korean Affairs* 2(1973):3–23. Deals primarily with North Korean law and justice as affected by Russia and Communist China. Discusses important aspects of North Korean legal institutions and the guiding principles by which justice was administered from 1945 to 1948 and from 1948 to 1958. Also surveys the workings of the court system itself and examines the period after 1958. Related topics appear in 13-156 and 13-158.

13-158. _____. "The Structure and Functions of the North Korean Court System." *Quarterly Journal of the Library of Congress* 26(4)(1969):216–225.

13-159. KANG, Koo-Chin. "Law in North Korea: An Analysis of Soviet and Chinese Influences Thereupon." JSD dissertation, Harvard University Law School, 1969. Presents a study of the North Korean legal system in light of socialist ideology and tries to assess the influence of Russian and Chinese socialist legal institutions. This work is partially reproduced in: (1) Kang's "Comparison of the Legal System between North and South Korea," *Seoul Law Journal* 12(2)(1971):5–23 and 13(1)(1972):69–94; (2) Kang's "Comparison of the Legal System between North and South Korea," in C. I. Eugene Kim (ed.), *Korean Unification: Problems and Prospects* (Kalamazoo: Korean Research and Publications, 1973); and (3) Kang's "Important Aspects of Criminal Procedure in North Korea," *Korean Journal of Comparative Law* 1(1973):184–211. This dissertation also includes an English translation of the Code of Criminal Procedure, the Penal Code, and the Law on Court Organization; these legislative pieces are reproduced in Kang's "North Korean Criminal Code," *Seoul Law Journal* 11(2)(1969):151–201, and "North Korean Penal Code," *Justice* 11(1)(1973):235–279.

13-160. _____. "Machinery of Justice in North Korea." *Korean Journal of Comparative Law* 5(1977):123–155. Examines courts, procuracies, and bar and tries to characterize the North Korean approach to the "justice delivery machinery."

13-161. KIM, Ilpyong J. "The Judicial and Administrative Structure in North Korea." In R. A. Scalapino (ed.), *North Korea Today.* New York: Praeger, 1963. A brief survey of the North Korean judicial structure. This article first appeared in *China Quarterly* 14(1963):94–104.

13-162. United States. Department of Commerce. Office of Technical Services. Joint Publications Research Service. *Development of Laws in North Korea.* JPRS: 15,662 (1962). Gives the English translation of selected parts of the Korean-language book entitled *Uri nara pŏpŭi palchŏn* (Pyongyang: 1960).

For the study of the 1972 constitution, the following five items are relevant. Among them item 13-164 also deals with the courts and procuracy.

13-163. GUREEVA, N. P. "Sotsialistcheskaia Konstitutsiia KNDR." *Sovetskoe Gosudarstvo i Pravo* 43(10)(1973): 84–91. Offers a brief introduction to the 1972 constitution in Russian.

13-164. KIM, Chin and Timothy G. KEARLEY. "The 1972 Socialist Constitution of North Korea." *Texas International Law Journal* 11(1)(1976):113–135. Comprehensive analysis of the 1972 constitution of North Korea with specific reference to the courts and procuracy.

13-165. KIM, Youn-Soo. "Korea—Die Staatsrechtliche Problematik eines Geteilten Staates im Vergliech zur Bundesrepublik Deutschland." *Verfassung und Recht in Übersee* 7(4)(1974):427–441. Discusses the North Korean state structure under the 1972 constitution.

13-166. _____. "The 1972 Socialist Constitution of the Korean Democratic People's Republic." *Review of Socialist Law* 3(3)(1977):281–296. Analysis of the 1972 constitution.

13-167. SEYMOUR, James. "Korean People's Democratic Republic." In Albert P. Blaustein and Gisbert H. Flanz (eds.), *Constitutions of the Countries of the World.* Vol. 5 supplement. New York: Oceana Publications, 1973. Contains constitutional chronology, the English text of the 1972 constitution, and an annotated bibliography.

For the history of North Korean constitutional law, the next three works are helpful.

13-168. GUDOSHNIKOV, L. M. "Koreiskoi Narodno-Demokraticheskoi Respublike." In V. F. Kotak (ed.), *Gosudarstvennoe pravo stran narodnoi demokratii.* Moscow: Gos Izd-vo iurid lit-ry, 1961. A Russian author's analysis of the North Korean constitution based on the original constitution. Similar writings appear also in (1) D. L. Zlatopol'skiĭ, "Osnovy gosudarstvennogo prava Koreiskoi narodno-demokraticheskoi respubliki," in Leonid D. Voevodin (ed.), *Gosudarstvennoe pravo stran narodnoi demokratii* (Moscow: Izd-vo in-ta mezhdunarodnyx otnoshenii, 1960), and (2) V. S. Pozdniakov, "Grazhdanskoe pravo koreiskoi narodno-demokratischeskoi respubliki," in Dmitri M. Genkin (ed.), *Grazhdanskoe pravo stran narodnoi demokratii* (Moscow: Vneshtorgizdat, 1958).

13-169. KIM, Youn-Soo. "Die Verfassung der koreanischen Demokratischen Volksrepublik." *Osteuropa Recht* 18(1) (1971): 13–23. Examines the ideological background of the North Korean constitution and presents several features of the original constitution.

13-170. United States. Department of Commerce. Office of Technical Services. Joint Publications Research Service. *Draft Lecture on the Constitution of the Korean Democratic People's Republic.* JPRS: 15,824 (1962). Translates selected chapters from the Korean-language monographs *Chosŏn minju chuŭi inmin konghwaguk hŏnpŏp kangŭian* by Chong-sok Im (Nagoya, Japan: 1957).

English and French translations of the original constitution may be found in the following publications: Jan F. Triska (ed.), *Constitutions of the Communist Party-States* (Stanford: Hoover Institution, 1968); Asian-African Legal Consultative Committee, *Constitutions of Asian Countries* (Bombay: N. M. Tripathi Private Ltd., 1968); Henry Puget (ed.), *Les Constitutions d'Asie et Australasie* (Paris: Editions de L'Epargne, 1965). Item 13-171 is also valuable.

13-171. PEASLEE, Amos J. (ed.). *Constitutions of Nations.* Vol. 2. Rev. 3rd ed. The Hague: Martinus Nijhoff, 1966.

Legal fields other than constitutional law are discussed in the following seven articles and monographs.

13-172. HAHM, P. C. "Ideology and Criminal Law in North Korea." *American Journal of Comparative Law* 17(1) (1969):77–93. Explores the ideological perspective of North Korean criminal law by raising such issues as law as means of edification, the merger of law and morality, and collectivism and informalism.

13-173. HAYATA, Yoshiro. "The Lex Patrie of Chinese and Koreans." *Japanese Annual of International Law* 9(1965): 57–68. Treats the interpretation of the North Korean law of nationality under the Japanese choice of law rules.

13-174. KIM, Chin. "Law of Marriage and Divorce in North Korea." *International Lawyer* 7(4)(1973):906–917. Discusses the law of marriage and divorce in light of relevant legal measures that have been enforced since 1945 in North Korea. This article has also been reproduced in Kim's "Law of Marriage and Divorce in North Korea," *Osteuropa Recht* 20(1)(1974):53–62.

13-175. _____. "North Korean Nationality Law." *International Lawyer* 6(2)(1972):324–329. Translates the 1963 Nationality Law into English and presents special features of this statute. A German version of this article appears in Kim's "Das Staatsangehörigkeitsgesetz der Koreanischen Demokratischen Volksrepublik." *Osteuropa Recht* 20(1) (1971): 7–12.

13-176. KIM, Doo Yong. "Labor Legislation in North Korea." *Amerasia* 11(5)(1947):156–160. Contains an English translation of the full text of the 1946 North Korean Labor Law.

13-177. TOMSON, Edgar. "Das Staatsangehörigkeitsrecht der ostasiatischen Staaten: China-Japan-Korea-Mongolei." *Sammlung geltender Staatsangehörigkeitsgesetze* 32(1971):257–270. Analyzes the 1963 Nationality Law and the 1957 dual citizenship convention between North Korea and the USSR. Includes German texts of the 1963 law and the 1957 convention.

13-178. United States. Department of Commerce. Office of Technical Services. Joint Publications Research Service. *Criminal Legislation in the People's Democratic Republic of Korea.* JPRS: DC-406 (1958). 49 pp. Provides an English translation of the North Korean criminal legislation originally published in Russian as *Kitaiskaia Narodnaia Respublika Koreiskaia Narodno-Demokratischenskaia Respublika.*

CHAPTER 14
International Relations and National Reunification

B. C. Koh

with contribution by
Young Whan Kihl

INTRODUCTION

INTERNATIONAL RELATIONS

SEVERAL FACTORS have combined to make international relations a matter of utmost importance to Korea. One of them is the peculiar geopolitical position of the Korean peninsula as a strategic crossroad in East Asia. Physically surrounded by three of the world's great powers—China, Russia, and Japan—Korea has historically served as both an object and an arena of international conflict. It served as a battleground once between China and Japan in 1894–1895 and twice between Russia and Japan—first in 1904–1905 and then during the final days of World War II. The Korean War of 1950–1953 witnessed a direct military clash between the People's Republic of China (PRC) and the United States and an indirect confrontation between the Soviet Union and the United States.

The continuing strategic importance of the Korean peninsula is underlined by the apparent uneasiness with which all its powerful neighbors contemplate the possibility of any of their rivals gaining hegemony over it. Neither the Soviet Union nor the PRC is likely to feel secure should North Korea align itself with their adversary in the event of conventional warfare between the two—a possibility which neither seems prepared to rule out, given the resilience and acrimony of their dispute. No less alarming to Moscow and Peking alike is the pos-

sibility of Japanese hegemony over Korea. Indeed, their concern, fueled as it is by bitter memories, has been publicly articulated on a number of occasions. For its part, Japan has gone on record as directly linking the security of South Korea—hence the preservation of at least a partially noncommunist Korea—to its own security, a position which has been explicitly endorsed by the United States.

Closely related to Korea's geopolitical position is a set of unique circumstances which have served to magnify its international dimensions, thus accentuating the importance of its international relations in the contemporary setting. To begin with, Korea is the only country in the world which has successively experienced centuries of Chinese suzerainty, four decades of Japanese colonial rule, and several years of military occupation by both the United States and the Soviet Union. Moreover, not only Korea's liberation from Japanese rule but, more important, its simultaneous partition were eminently international affairs over which the Korean people had little or no control. The emergence of two rival regimes in Korea in 1948 was due in no small measure to the vagaries of international politics. It was due to the inability of Washington and Moscow to agree on the political future of the Korean people that the question was turned over to the United Nations. The UN, under American leadership, in turn supervised elections in the American occupation zone, thus paving the way for the establishment of the Republic of Korea (ROK). Meanwhile, the formation of the Democratic People's Republic of Korea (DPRK) in the northern half of the peninsula was heavily influenced, if not wholly controlled, by the Soviet Union.

The Korean War was not simply a fratricidal civil war but a veritable international conflict in which seventeen nations from around the globe participated as belligerents—sixteen on the UN side and the PRC on the communist side. It also provided the fledgling world organization with the opportunity to engage in a collective security action for the first time. Significantly, the UN's experiment in Korea has not been replicated elsewhere, notwithstanding the persistence of violent international conflicts. The world body has since confined its role to mediation and peacekeeping. On the other hand, it has yet to extricate itself from the Korean quagmire, for the Korean question has remained a perennial item on the agenda of the UN General Assembly. Not until 1973, moreover, was the UN Commission on the Unification and Reconstruction of Korea (UNCURK) formally disbanded at its own initiative.

The inconclusive manner in which the Korean War was terminated left animosity and a reciprocal sense of insecurity on the part of the two Korean regimes; this state of affairs in turn spawned an entangling network of international military alliances. The mutual defense treaty between South Korea and the United States is thus matched by similar pacts between North Korea on the one hand and the Soviet Union and PRC on the other. The US commitment to Seoul's security, which was pointedly reaffirmed in the wake of the communist victory in Indochina in 1975, is both symbolized and reinforced by the presence of forty thousand American troops in South Korea. Add to all this Japan's professed stake in the peace and stability of the Korean peninsula. Nowhere else in the world do the interests and commitments of the four great powers intersect so vividly, and so precariously, as they do in Korea.

One should not overlook the fact that the Korean people themselves help to inflate the international dimensions of their national vicissitudes. Apart from their understandable propensity to attribute much of their current difficulties to the misdeeds and blunders of foreign powers, their (or their leaders') apotheosis of *chuch'e* (self-reliance) is substantially undercut by their

actual behavior. To cite but one example, the two Korean regimes not only fail to manifest any qualms about vilifying each other in international forums, notably the United Nations, but continue to stage an all-out battle, which is as expensive as it is sterile, to drum up support for their respective positions among foreign countries. What is more, they lean so heavily on their alien friends that negotiation and bargaining at the UN take place not in face-to-face talks but through double mediation by their respective foreign spokesmen. It should be noted, however, that direct talks of sorts have taken place 'n the context of the Red Cross negotiations and the North-South Coordinating Committee meetings. Nor are the Koreans alone in their reliance on foreign intermediaries—witness the role of Secretary of State Kissinger in the Arab-Israeli negotiations.

Finally, the goal of economic modernization, to which both Seoul and Pyongyang are firmly committed, necessitates the conduct of international trade on a sizable scale, which in turn calls for special attention to international relations. To be sure, this problem is by no means unique to Korea, but the idiosyncrasies of natural resource distribution in Korea, coupled with the developmental strategies adopted by both regimes, help to make foreign trade a matter of pivotal importance.

NATIONAL REUNIFICATION

If the preceding factors underscore the importance of international relations for Korea, do they also buttress the need for national reunification? The answer, in my view, is yes. But it can be amplified by stressing, *inter alia,* the emotional, practical, and political aspects of the reunification question. First of all, reunification is a manifestly emotion-charged issue in Korea. It is part of national lore in North and South Korea alike that the Koreans are a homogeneous people sharing a common history, race, and language. It is simply unnatural that they should remain divided; for the partition at the 38th parallel is an aberration in Korean history, artificially devised and alien-imposed, so the reasoning goes.

There are, moreover, pressing practical reasons why reunification is highly desirable. The partition unquestionably is the root of continuing tragedy, hardship, and suffering for great numbers of the Korean people. If the people who have suffered the loss or incapacitation of their family members, relatives, and friends on account of the partition—via the Korean War, anticommunist and national security laws, and so forth—are in the minority, those who must labor under stifling political controls and a chronic sense of insecurity, engendered in part by the frequently inflated danger of invasion from North or South, are legion. What is more, there are literally millions of people whose families have been broken up by the partition and who anxiously await the opportunity for family reunion. Additionally, it is almost certain that reunification would enhance the economic capability of Korea—not only through the integration of the two economic systems but also through the diversion of resources from defense to more productive projects—and that would conceivably make higher standards of living possible for the Korean people.

Finally, there are certain political considerations which help to keep the goal of national reunification in the limelight of public attention. Reunification has been used and will probably continue to be used as a ready-made political symbol, a rallying point, and even a subterfuge for mobilizing the efforts of the people for the arduous tasks of economic and military construction, for stepping up ideological indoctrination, and for extending the tenure and powers of the incumbent political leaders in both parts of Korea. To the extent that reunification is pursued as a genuine goal, its appeal to the leaders in both Seoul and Pyongyang may be in direct proportion to the perceived likelihood of their own personal aggrandizement. That is to say, it is most likely to be sought only if the leader's prepotent position remains intact. Neither Kim Il Sung nor Park Chung Hee is likely to relinquish his unprecedented powers in the interest of reunification alone. Be that as it may, the symbolic value of national reunification all but ensures that it will remain a supreme national goal on the political landscape of Korea for some time to come.

AN OVERVIEW OF MAJOR DEVELOPMENTS

Enough has been said to indicate the extraordinary degree to which both international relations and national reunification take on significance in the Korean scheme of things. Before presenting an overview of the literature, it may be useful to make a cursory survey of the major developments pertaining to the two topics.

No attempt will be made in the following survey to maintain a strict dichotomy between developments bearing on international relations and those bearing on national reunification. They are inseparably intertwined.

Chronologically, the military occupation of Korea by American and Soviet forces can be viewed as the first major development in Korea's international relations. As previously noted, the occupation led to the emergence of two rival regimes in the peninsula and, more important, to the formation of two sets of patron-client relationship—the US–South Korea and the USSR–North Korea. This alignment was to have a lasting impact on the international behavior of both South and North Korea. Then came the Korean War—a struggle which was pregnant with international implications. The war altered Korea's international situation in a major way: it spawned a new set of patron-client relationships: the PRC–North Korea. With its massive intervention of "volunteers" in the war, the PRC was largely instrumental in saving North Korea at the brink of defeat. Peking also offered a generous helping hand in North Korea's postwar recovery efforts. Meanwhile, the American commitment to South Korea was strengthened, not only in a military-economic sense but also in a psychological sense: with the expenditure of so much treasure and so many lives, Korea became more of an American problem. Finally, the UN also became deeply enmeshed in the Korean question.

The next major development in Korea's international relations was the Sino-Soviet dispute. With their two patron states embroiled in acrimonious quarrel, North Korea at first tried to strike a posture of neutrality (1956–1961) but soon found itself aligned with Peking (1962–1964). Driven by the imperatives of economic and military modernization at home and taking advantage of a transfer of power in the Kremlin, North Korea achieved a rapprochement with Moscow in early 1965. By late 1969 and early 1970, Pyongyang and Peking once again became close allies, but North Korean-Soviet relations did not suffer any noticeable setback. Economic, technical, and military aid continued to flow from Moscow to Pyongyang, notwithstanding the latter's growing ideological solidarity with the PRC. This anomalous state of affairs appeared to be related not merely to the finesse with which North Korea played Moscow off against Peking but also to the strategic importance of North Korea as perceived by Moscow and Peking alike.

The military coup that toppled the Chang Myŏn regime in South Korea in May 1961, although an obviously domestic upheaval, generated international repercussions. It had a tangible effect on all four major powers as well as North Korea. First, it created a temporary strain in ROK–US relations. The United States strongly denounced the coup and exerted considerable pressure on the coup leaders to restore civilian rule. Second, the fiercely anticommunist rhetoric and actions of the coup leaders so alarmed North Korea that, within two months of the coup, Pyongyang concluded separate mutual defense treaties with both Moscow and Peking. Finally, the coup leaders, after legitimating their seizure of power through a national referendum on constitutional amendments and national elections, decided to normalize relations with Japan. Amid considerable domestic opposition, the Park Chung Hee government signed a normalization treaty with Japan in June 1965. Later in the year, after heated battles over its ratification in the legislative assemblies of both countries, the treaty went into force. The treaty turned out to be one of the most impressive diplomatic coups of the Park regime, for it paved the way for the inflow of Japanese capital and technology, which played a pivotal role in launching South Korea on the path to spectacular economic development.

Another international development which produced tangible payoffs for South Korea was the Vietnam conflict. Seoul's controversial decision to send troops to Vietnam in early 1965 helped South Korea in two major ways. First, it enormously strengthened Seoul's bonds with Washington; the latter not only began publicly to support the Park regime but also stepped up its military aid to Seoul. Second, South Korea's military intervention in Vietnam opened up a significant source of foreign exchange earnings for Seoul. This, coupled with the influx of Japanese capital, contributed measurably to the rejuvenation of the South Korean economy.

The next noteworthy development was North Korea's forcible seizure of the USS *Pueblo* and its 83-man crew in Wŏnsan Bay in January 1968. The incident, which re-

presented a bold challenge to American power, momentarily thrust North Korea to the center of the world stage and served as a grim reminder that, nearly two decades after the outbreak of the Korean War, the peninsula remained a tinderbox capable of igniting an international conflagration. While the incident apparently served a host of political and psychological needs for Kim Il Sung, it also led to a significant expansion of South Korea's military capability and preparedness. North Korea's attack on an American intelligence plane EC-121 fifteen months later further helped to strengthen the American commitment to South Korea.

The most signal development in the international environment of East Asia in the past two decades has been the Sino-American detente. The historic rapprochement between the two Pacific powers could not help but have a profound impact in East Asia. It is no accident that DPRK Premier Kim Il Sung made known a significant change in his posture toward South Korea within three weeks of President Nixon's stunning announcement of his proposed visit to the PRC. Kim declared on 6 August 1971 that North Korea would be willing to negotiate with "all political parties, including the [ruling] Democratic-Republican party, all social organizations, and all individuals." Six days later, Choi Doo Sun (Ch'oe Tu-sŏn), president of the ROK National Red Cross, proposed that talks be held between representatives of the Red Cross organizations in North and South Korea for the "humanitarian" purpose of reuniting separated families. When North Korea accepted the proposal two days later, a new era dawned on the Korean peninsula—the era of dialogue. It should be pointed out, however, that the groundwork for dialogue had been laid nearly two years before the beginning of the Sino-American detente. In August 1970, ROK President Park Chung Hee adumbrated Seoul's willingness to improve relations with Pyongyang under certain conditions, and, in April 1971, North Korea countered by slightly relaxing its terms for negotiations with South Korea. For the first time, Pyongyang indicated that it would not insist on the withdrawal of American troops from South Korea as a precondition for North-South negotiations. The fact nevertheless remains that a breakthrough occurred on the heels of the Nixon announcement.

Although the mere initiation of a dialogue between Seoul and Pyongyang marked a new watershed in North-South relations, it did not necessarily usher in a period of unmitigated amity between the two. For the dialogue was neither preceded nor accompanied by any appreciable reduction of mutual distrust. Symptomatic of the depth and persistence of mistrust was the ominous fact that it required an astounding total of thirty-four negotiating sessions—twenty-one sessions of "preliminary talks" and thirteen "working-level meetings" *(silmuja hoeŭi)*—spanning a period of ten months simply to map out an agenda for the full-dress talks between representatives of the North and South Korean Red Cross organizations. Even after the agenda had been set, the two sides had to hold four more negotiating sessions in order to work out procedural details. It needs to be stressed that, even though the talks were being held ostensibly between Red Cross personnel, they were tantamount to de facto government-level negotiations. The nature of the political systems in the two Koreas made it unlikely that the decisions pertaining to the talks, including their initiation and conduct, were being made by anybody other than their top political leaders.

The full-dress Red Cross talks opened in Pyongyang on 30 August 1972 amid a palpably euphoric atmosphere. For, on 4 July 1972, a momentous breakthrough had been unveiled: a North-South joint statement encompassing broad principles of reunification was published simultaneously in Seoul and Pyongyang. The statement, which was the product of secret top-level political negotiations, declared that the two sides had agreed to seek national reunification (1) independently (that is, free from interference by "external forces") (2) peacefully, and (3) in disregard of "differences in ideology, ideas, and social systems." The statement further embodied the solemn commitment of both sides to refrain from slandering and defaming each other as well as from committing armed provocations, great or small. It also disclosed the plan to install a "hot line" between Seoul and Pyongyang and to establish a "North-South Coordinating Committee" (NSCC), a body designed to promote the implementation of the various points contained in the joint statement.

The subsequent record of both the Red Cross and NSCC negotiations, however, serves to confirm the suspicion of skeptical observers that the 4 July 1972 joint statement was both misleading and premature. Simply stated, the document was too good to be true. That two parties which would neither recognize each other's existence nor call each other by their proper names should have been able to agree on the principles and procedures to their eventual political integration was an anomaly *par excellence.* The harsh reality was that the joint statement epitomized not the meeting of minds between Seoul and Pyongyang but the convergence of the perceived self-interests of their respective power elites. To judge from the uses to which the Park regime has put its dialogue with North Korea, one cannot preclude the possibility that it may have been a shrewdly calculated maneuver to generate, *inter alia,* a rationale for the drastic restructuring of the South Korean polity that was carried out in the name of "revitalizing reforms" *(yusin)* in October 1972. The prime beneficiary of the "reforms" was Park Chung Hee himself, who was all but assured of indefinite tenure as South Korea's supreme ruler, practically unencumbered by any checks and balances. On the other hand, Kim Il Sung appears to have anticipated the emergence of conditions under which one of the major stumbling blocks to his reunification plan would be removed: namely, the withdrawal of American troops from South Korea. In fact, the dialogue's principal payoff to North Korea proved to be a marked increase in its international stature.

This brings us to the next noteworthy development in Korea's international situation. In 1973 North Korea scored diplomatic gains on two fronts. First, for the first time since its inception, it established diplomatic relations with several Western European nations—Denmark, Finland, Iceland, Norway, and Sweden. Second, it gained entry into the UN system: in May it was admitted to the World Health Organization (WHO), thus acquiring the customary privilege to set up a permanent observer mission at the UN headquarters. Pyongyang proceeded to set up two such missions, one in Geneva and another in New York City. Equally important, for the first time in the annals of the UN, North Korea was invited to participate as an observer in the annual debate on the Korean question. All in all, the erstwhile gap in the relative international standing of the two Koreas, as measured by the number of diplomatic partners and membership in international organizations, was being unmistakably narrowed.

Finally, we should note the effect on Korea of the stunning communist takeovers of Cambodia and South Vietnam in early 1975. Predictably, it appeared to stimulate and encourage Kim Il Sung, who may have perceived an opportunity to replicate in Korea the feats of his Indochinese comrades. His widely publicized trip to the PRC in April 1975 was viewed in both Seoul and Washington as an attempt to sound out the Chinese leaders on the possibility of military action against South Korea. Seoul responded to the new stimuli by placing itself on a war footing. Park Chung Hee once again proclaimed a state of emergency and imposed further restrictions on what was left of civil liberties in South Korea. He also reinstated compulsory military training in secondary schools, vastly expanded the militia, and introduced a new defense surtax. Meanwhile, Washington began to echo Seoul's alarm over the possibility of North Korean attack and reaffirmed its treaty commitments to South Korea. Secretary of Defense Schlesinger's visit to Seoul in August 1975 was the latest in a long series of public pronouncements and gestures aimed at reassuring South Korea and deterring North Korea.

FOREIGN POLICY GOALS OF THE TWO KOREAS

The foregoing survey of major developments in Korea's international relations suggests that the two Koreas have pursued a set of three interrelated and partially overlapping goals in the world arena. They may be summed up as (1) unity, (2) legitimacy, and (3) autonomy. While such a neat characterization of the complex and changing foreign policy goals of North and South Korea obviously entails the risks of oversimplification and distortion, it may nonetheless serve a heuristic purpose.

The goal of unity manifests itself in a variety of ways in the international and domestic conduct of both Seoul and Pyongyang. What needs to be stressed, however, is that the concept of "unity" or "unification" evokes divergent images in the two Koreas. To Pyongyang, it means a Korea united under the Red banner of Marxism-Leninism and the "revolutionary thought" of

Kim Il Sung. To Seoul, it conjures up an image of a Korea liberated from the communist menace and crippling burdens of national defense. Divergent images of the goal itself naturally spell divergent approaches to its attainment. North Korea's path to unity thus consists of efforts to enhance its economic and military capabilities at home, to foster an anti-Park and anti-American revolutionary movement in South Korea, and to forge links with "revolutionary forces" in the world arena. Its deep-seated antagonism toward the Park regime and the United States, however, does not inhibit Pyongyang from making conciliatory overtures when opportunities to optimize its strategic objectives loom on the horizon. The Red Cross talks, the North-South joint statement of 4 July 1972, and repeated overtures to Washington for direct negotiations may be appreciated in this light. In addition to countermeasures against North Korean actions, Seoul's approaches to unity embrace the maintenance of its military alliance with Washington and the consolidation of economic and political bonds with Tokyo. There is an apparent gap between Seoul and Pyongyang in the priority assigned to the goal of unity and the vigor with which it is pursued. Even in terms of official rhetoric, Seoul appears to be markedly more reserved than Pyongyang.

In contrast, the two regimes have shown an almost identical degree of sensitivity toward the goal of legitimacy. That is, each side has insisted time and again that it is the only lawful government in the whole Korean peninsula. This claim was a major bottleneck in the negotiations for the ROK–Japan normalization treaty in 1965, and it helps to explain the intensity of diplomatic offensives waged by the two Koreas in the UN and in the Third World. Their pointed refusal to refer to each other by their official names even at the height of their dialogue bespeaks the rigidity of their posture toward legitimacy. The return of the pejorative term *koeroe* (puppet) in the official vocabulary of the two regimes within one year of the publication of the 4 July 1972 joint statement is a poignant reminder of the obsessive quest for legitimacy.

Indeed, the use of the word *koeroe* by both sides displays not only bad taste and vindictiveness unbecoming of putatively sovereign nations but also an appalling lack of realism and candor. For the third goal of North and South Korea alike is the quest for autonomy, and both have made impressive headway in their endeavors. This also happens to be the only goal which both Seoul and Pyongyang can pursue without necessarily undercutting each other's international position. To be sure, neither side has yet become sufficiently autonomous to shoulder its own defense and economic burdens. Their reliance on their respective patron states for military hardware is likely to continue for some time to come—unless, of course, the perceived need for military preparedness either evaporates or recedes drastically. On the economic front, however, both sides appear to have come a long way; both have registered impressive rates of growth in industrial output. More important, neither can be viewed as a "puppet" of its patron state. In sum, there is some ground for subsuming the seemingly divergent foreign policy goals of the two Koreas under the rubrics of unity, legitimacy, and autonomy.

AN OVERVIEW OF THE LITERATURE

We have thus far delineated the main contours of the international relations of the two Koreas during the last three decades as well as the record of their respective quest for national reunification. A brief outline of the literature on these two broad topics is now in order. As the following bibliographic entries make plain, the sheer quantity of English-language works on the topics is staggering. This becomes clear if one keeps in mind that what is presented in the following pages is not an exhaustive but a selected listing, even though it is designed to be reasonably comprehensive. I am under no illusion that I have succeeded in examining the universe of the relevant literature. It is therefore entirely possible that I may have overlooked some significant works.

It is axiomatic that quantity and quality do not necessarily go hand in hand. Unfortunately, I must concur in the sagacity of that axiom insofar as the literature I have surveyed is concerned. The quality of scholarship, the level of discourse, and the clarity of expression vary widely, and my selections inevitably reflect this fact of life. While I have taken pains to weed out most of what strike me as substandard works, I am not prepared to vouch for the caliber of scholarship reflected in the following publications. I would recommend that, for any given subfield, the would-be researcher examine all the

works listed here and make a personal appraisal of their utility.

Another striking characteristic of the literature I have encountered is the noncumulative nature of scholarship or, to put it differently, the redundancy of scholarship. This phenomenon is neither unique to Korean studies nor particularly puzzling. There is such a diverse array of outlets for scholarly works that it is virtually impossible for one individual to keep track of all relevant works on a topic. One must also bear in mind that there are quite a few commissioned studies—articles commissioned by journals and magazines, conference papers, texts or public lectures, and the like. Then, too, there are the usual incentives for publication—such as the "publish or perish" syndrome in the academic community and the psychological and monetary rewards of authorship. Finally, it could be argued that a certain amount of redundancy may be conducive to learning. Most of the works in international relations and national reunification are not hyperfactual narratives but contain a fair amount of interpretation, evaluation, and speculation. Redundancy, then, serves the function of generating a wide range of perspectives on a subject; in so doing, it may help to narrow the gap between scholarly discourse and the underlying reality.

As far as the methodology of the literature is concerned, the most common approach is what may be called a journalistic approach—a loose combination of factual narrative and speculative interpretation. Given such an approach, the author's assumptions frequently remain unarticulated and the basis for inference is not spelled out. There is also a tendency to mix description with prescription. Given the nature of the topics under consideration, one need not frown upon the latter practice, since making explicit the policy implications of one's analysis is not only a scholar's prerogative but, perhaps, one's duty as well.

From the standpoint of promoting Korean studies in a qualitative way, the most serious lacuna in the literature of international relations and national reunification appears to be the paucity of theoretically oriented studies. Closely related to this shortcoming is the virtual absence of systematic—that is, methodologically rigorous —studies. Nor is there an abundance of comparatively oriented works. The comparative approach, if executed with a modicum of rigor, would not only generate more balanced descriptions and appraisals of matters Korean; it would also contribute to the task of theory-building. Fruitful comparisons can be made along a variety of dimensions—for example, between North and South Korea, across national boundaries, or between different time periods within the same political system.

Finally, a few words about the classification of bibliographic entries are in order. Of the numerous possible ways of arranging the works on international relations, I have chosen the country-oriented scheme, largely because the four great powers surrounding Korea—China, Japan, and the Soviet Union in a geographic sense and the United States in a functional sense—have been the most frequent foci of scholarly attention. The United Nations is included because of its special relationship to Korea. Most of the works listed under the heading "General and Theoretical" belong to the "general" category. The works on national reunification are organized more or less chronologically on the premise that the initiation of dialogue between Seoul and Pyongyang in 1971 marked a significant watershed in inter-Korean relations, although its actual accomplishments thus far have been painfully meager. The existence of a modest number of theoretically oriented works on reunification appears to be related to the availability of theoretical propositions on political integration and game theory.

BIBLIOGRAPHY

GENERAL AND THEORETICAL

14-001. ABRAMOWITZ, Morton. *Moving the Glacier: The Two Koreas and the Powers*. Adelphi Papers, no. 80. London: International Institute for Strategic Studies, 1971. A perceptive, policy-oriented study of the Korean problem by a top US government analyst. Assesses the implications of major changes in Korea's internal and external situation. After reviewing three policy options, the author recommends that Seoul and Washington launch a major diplomatic effort "to supplement military means to prevent North-South hostilities."

14-002. *Asian Survey*. Berkeley: University of California Press, quarterly. In addition to frequent articles on Korea, this journal publishes short annual surveys of the two Koreas in January. These surveys typically contain reviews of the foreign relations of the two Koreas in the preceding year.

4-003. FISHER, Charles A. "The Role of Korea in the Far East." *Geographical Journal* 120(1954):282–298. A largely historical study of Korea's geopolitical position as a focus and an arena of big-power rivalries.

14-004. HAGGARD, M. T. "North Korea's International Position." *Asian Survey* 5(8)(August 1965):375–388. A good general survey of North Korea's international relations up to early 1965.

14-005. HAHM, Pyong-Choon. "Korea and the Emerging Asian Power Balance." *Foreign Affairs* 50(2)(January 1972):339–350. The author, who was special assistant to President Park of South Korea when he wrote this article, argues that only American presence in Korea can preserve peace in that part of the world. In his words: "The strategic importance of an independent and stable Korea for Asian peace cannot be overemphasized. A peaceful Korea is a linchpin for a stable Asian balance of power. The Asian powers are all too preoccupied with relative power advantages on the Korean peninsula to leave the linchpin alone. Only the United States has enough detached interest in South Korea to help keep the linchpin functioning properly."

14-006. HAN, Sungjoo. "The Interrelationship between External and Internal Goals of the South Korean Government." In Jae Kyu Park and Sungjoo Han (eds.), *East Asia and the Major Powers: From Confrontation to Accommodation*. Seoul: Kyung Nam University, 1975. A theoretically oriented analysis of the linkage between domestic goals and foreign relations. Argues that "in formulating their major goals, small Asian nations are faced with many conflicting demands and . . . have to deal with serious dilemmas in maximizing the chances of achieving these goals."

14-007. HU, Hung-lick. *Le Problème coréen*. Paris: A. Pedone, 1953. Originally a doctoral thesis submitted to the University of Paris in 1951. Parts 3 and 4 deal with Korea's international situation in the Post–World War II period. The problem of unification and the UN's role in Korea are stressed.

14-008. HUDSON, G. F. "Korea and Asia." *International Affairs* (London), 27(1)(January 1951):18–24. An assessment of the international implications of the Korean War. The author sees the strategic importance of Korea in terms of its effect on the security of Japan.

14-009. *International Affairs*. Moscow: All-Union Society "Znaniye," monthly. This is a useful source of information about Soviet foreign policy, particularly Soviet perceptions of the Korean situation and Soviet–North Korean relations. Published in Russian, English, and French.

14-010. *Journal of Korean Affairs.* Silver Spring, Md.: Research Institute on Korean Affairs, quarterly. Published in 1971–1976. A useful source of information on the international relations of the two Koreas. Accent is on North Korea. A typical issue contains "background articles," "current development," "chronicle of events," "source material," and "book review."

14-011. KIM, Il Sung. *Juche! The Speeches and Writings of Kim Il Sung.* Edited and introduced by Li Yuk-sa. New York: Grossman, 1972. A collection of ten speeches and writings by DPRK President Kim Il Sung. At least four of them have direct relevance for Pyongyang's foreign policy. The caliber of translation is superior to that found in the publications of North Korea's Foreign Languages Publishing House.

14-012. KIM, Ok Yul. "The American Role in Korean-Japanese Relations." PhD dissertation, Bryn Mawr College, 1967. 235 pp. Abstracted in *DA* 28(April 1968):4239-A; UM 68-4695. Primarily a study of the Japan–ROK normalization treaty of 1965 and the US role therein.

14-013. KIM, Young C. (ed.). *Foreign Policies of Korea.* Washington: Institute for Asian Studies, 1973. A collection of papers read at a conference held in April 1973 under the joint sponsorship of the Institute for Asian Studies and Kyung Nam University, Korea. Most of the papers are individually listed in the appropriate sections of the chapter.

14-014. _____ (ed.). *Major Powers and Korea.* Silver Spring, Md.: Research Institute on Korean Affairs, 1973. A collection of papers originally presented to a conference held in Silver Spring, Maryland, in April 1972. Most of the papers are individually annotated in this chapter.

14-015. KIM, Young C. and Abraham M. HALPERN (eds.). *The Future of the Korean Peninsula.* New York: Praeger, 1977. A collection of papers originally presented to a conference on Korea and the major powers held in Arlington, Virginia, in April 1975. In addition to essays on the foreign policies of South and North Korea, the volume contains analyses of the policies of the four Pacific powers toward the Korean peninsula. The contributors include Abraham M. Halpern, Harold C. Hinton, Gari Ledyard, Chong-Sik Lee, James W. Morley, Thomas W. Robinson, and Donald S. Zagoria.

14-016. KOH, Byung Chul. *The Foreign Policy of North Korea.* New York: Praeger, 1969. A comprehensive study

of the rhetoric and behavior of North Korea in the world arena. Relies heavily on North Korean sources. Topics discussed include "North Korea and the Sino-Soviet Rift," "North Korea and Korean Unification," and "North Korea's Relations with the Third World and Beyond."

14-017. KOH, B. C. "The Korean Workers' Party and Detente." *Journal of International Affairs* 29(1)(1975): 175–187. Argues that "the mode of response by the Korean Workers' Party to detente can best be characterized as a grudging accommodation to a *fait accompli.*" While detente among the great powers provided an impetus for Seoul-Pyongyang dialogue, the actual evolution of the dialogue has hinged more on internal political considerations of the two sides than on external stimuli.

14-018. _____. "North Korea and Its Quest for Autonomy." *Pacific Affairs* 38(3/4)(Fall/Winter 1965–1966):294–306. An overview of North Korea's domestic and foreign policies with emphasis on Kim Il Sung's *"chuch'e"* idea and its practice.

14-019. *Korea Week.* Washington: Po Sung Philip Kim, biweekly. A good source of information and opinion on Korea's international relations. Presents summaries of events, commentaries in the American press, and documentary materials. Ceased publication in 1978.

14-020. *Korean Journal of International Studies.* Seoul: Korean Institute of International Studies, quarterly. Contains both articles and materials relating to Korea's international relations. Frequently publishes proceedings of international conferences on Korea organized by the institute.

14-021. LEE, Chae-Jin. "The Development of Sino-Japanese Competition over Korea." In Young C. Kim (ed.), *Foreign Policies of Korea.* Washington: Institute of Asian Studies, 1973. A discussion of "the nature and direction of Sino-Japanese competition over Korea and the difficulties and options faced by South and North Korea in regard to evolving Sino-Japanese relations." Suggests the possibility that "both North and South Korea could use these competitive external forces as an instrument for promoting a peaceful, mutually beneficial relationship between themselves."

14-022. *Major Speeches by President Park Chung Hee, Republic of Korea.* Seoul: Samhwa Publishing Co., n.d. A collection of speeches made during the period 1970–1973. A substantial proportion of them deal with either the unification question or Korea's international relations.

14-023. MIN, Benjamin H. "North Korea's Foreign Policy: A Survey." *Journal of Korean Affairs* 1(1)(April 1971):

3.-13. An overview of the machinery, objectives, and performance of North Korea's foreign policy, with emphasis on its unification policy and posture toward the Sino-Soviet dispute.

14-024. MIN, Benjamin Byung-Hui. "North Korea's Foreign Policy in the Post-war Decade 1953–1963: Its Strategy of Korean Unification and Relations with Moscow and Peking." PhD dissertation, University of Massachusetts, 1967. 235 pp. Abstracted in *DA* 28(April 1968):4240-A; UM 68-4455. The lengthy title and subtitle accurately suggest the focus of the study. Draws on a wide array of sources, including North Korean and Japanese publications.

14-025. NAM, Il. "The Foreign Policy of the Korean People's Democratic Republic." *International Affairs* (Moscow), (September 1958):24–29. A statement by the DPRK foreign minister regarding the official foreign policy goals of his government.

14-026. PARK, Chung Hee. *Our Nation's Path: Ideology of Social Reconstruction.* A translation of Park's 1962 book setting forth his perceptions of Korea's internal and international environment.

14-027. _____. *To Build a Nation.* Washington: Acropolis Books, 1971. ROK President Park states his perceptions of the world situation as it relates to Korea as well as the basic foreign policy goals of his government.

14-028. PARK, Jae Kyu and Sungjoo HAN. *East Asia and the Major Powers: From Confrontation to Accommodation.* Seoul: Institute for Far Eastern Studies, Kyung Nam University, 1975. A collection of nine papers presented to the International Symposium on Peace and Security in East Asia, held in Seoul in January 1974. Some of the papers are individually annotated in this chapter.

14-029. REEVE, W. D. *The Republic of Korea: A Political and Economic Study.* London: Oxford University Press, 1963. The author, who served as an adviser to the ROK government from 1952 to 1957, presents a balanced study of Korea's political and economic situation up to 1962. He has separate chapters on Syngman Rhee's foreign policy and on foreign economic aid to Korea.

14-030. REISCHAUER, Edwin O. and Gregory HENDERSON. "There's Danger in Korea Still." *New York Times Magazine* (20 May 1973):42–56. A former American ambassador to Japan and a former American diplomat who served in Korea for over seven years present a highly critical analysis of the political situation in Korea, particularly Park's suppression of civil liberties, and its policy implications for both Washington and Tokyo. They urge the lat-

ter two to coordinate their policies with a view to moderating Park's repressive measures.

14-031. SCALAPINO, Robert A. "Changing Relations between the United States and the Chinese People's Republic and the Impact upon the Republic of Korea." *Journal of Korean Affairs* 2(1)(April 1972):22–30. This is the text of a statement the author made on 4 May 1972 before the Subcommittee on Asian and Pacific Affairs, the Committee on Foreign Affairs, US House of Representatives. The author foresees Pyongyang's continuing efforts to remove or weaken the commitments of the US and Japan to South Korea and recommends that Seoul adopt multifaceted countermeasures, including reversal of its policy of downgrading democratic institutions and procedures.

14-032. _____. "The Foreign Policy of North Korea." In Robert A. Scalapino (ed.), *North Korea Today.* New York: Praeger, 1963. A discussion of the "main lines of North Korean foreign policy as expressed by the most authoritative voice of the regime"—that is, Premier Kim Il Sung. This is one of the first studies of North Korean foreign policy to appear in the English language.

14-033. SHINN, Rinn-Sup et al. *Area Handbook for North Korea.* Washington: Government Printing Office, 1969. A comprehensive survey of North Korea, including its foreign relations. Carefully researched and documented. Contains an extensive bibliography.

14-034. SHINN, Rinn-Sup. "Foreign and Reunification Policies." *Problems of Communism* 22(1)(January/February 1973):55–71. An excellent overview and appraisal of recent developments in North Korea's international relations and reunification.

14-035. SIMON, Sheldon W. "The *'Pueblo'* Incident and the South Korean 'Revolution' in North Korea's Foreign Policy: A Propaganda Analysis." *Asian Forum* 2(3)(July/ September 1970):201–214. A content analysis of North Korean propaganda. Concludes that the "*Pueblo* incident and its related propaganda themes have revealed an increasingly insecure North Korean regime, concerned about the reliability of its allies' support for its goals as well as the growing ability of its Southern adversary to deter its basic unification policy."

14-036. STEINBERG, David I. *Korea: Nexus of East Asia.* Rev. ed. New York: American Asian Educational Exchange, 1970. 60 pp. One of the best short surveys of the politics and international relations of Korea in the English language. Contains a useful bibliographic guide with brief annotations.

14-037. WHITE, Nathan. "Search for Peace: The Four Powers and Korea." *Korean Journal of International Studies* 6(1)(Winter 1974/1975):37–47. Stresses the role of the big powers in the solution of the Korean impasse. Calls for big-power initiatives in breaking the deadlock of the North-South Korean talks.

KOREA AND THE UNITED STATES
The Korean War

14-038. APPLEMAN, Roy E. *United States Army in the Korean War: South to Naktong, North to Yalu (June–November 1950)*. Washington: Department of Army, Office of the Chief of Military History, 1961. A massive account (813 pp.) of the Korean War as viewed and interpreted by US military historians.

14-039. BIDERMAN, Albert D. *March to Calumny: The Story of American POW's in the Korean War*. New York: Macmillan, 1963. A study of the treatment and behavior of US prisoners of war in Korea. The author submitted a PhD thesis on the same subject to the University of Chicago in 1964.

14-040. BLANCHARD, Carroll Henry. *Korean War Bibliography and Maps of Korea*. Albany, N.Y.: Korean Conflict Research Foundation, [1964?]. 181 pp. An extensive bibliography of Western-language materials. Includes non-US publications as well as articles in popular periodicals and magazines.

14-041. CLARK, Mark W. *From the Danube to the Yalu*. New York: Harper, 1954. Contains an autobiographical account of the Korean War. The author served as commander of the UN Forces during the closing days of the Korean War.

14-042. COLLINS, Joseph L. *War in Peacetime: The History and Lessons of Korea*. Boston: Houghton Mifflin, 1969. An insider's view of the Korean War, with emphasis on the US role. The author was chief of staff of the US Army and a member of the Joint Chiefs of Staff throughout the Korean War.

14-043. GARDNER, Lloyd C. (ed.). *The Korean War*. New York: Quadrangle Books, 1972. A collection of twenty-two essays originally published in the *New York Times Magazine*. Nearly all the essays were written during the Korean War. The contributors include Dean Acheson, John Foster Dulles, John K. Galbraith, George F. Kennan, Arthur Krock, James Reston, and Barbara Ward. A long introduction by the editor is illuminating.

14-044. GEORGE, Alexander L. "American Policy-Making and the North Korean Aggression." *World Politics* 7(1)(January 1955):210–232. A study of "the effect of

strategic planning and estimates of Communist intentions and behavior on the decision to commit American forces to the defense of South Korea."

14-045. HERMES, Walter G. *Truce Tent and Fighting Front*. Washington: U.S. Department of the Army, 1966. An official history of the armistice negotiations in Korea by a US army historian.

14-046. JOY, C. Turner. *How Communists Negotiate*. New York: Macmillan, 1955. A retired admiral of the US Navy who served as senior delegate and chief of the UN Command Delegation to the Korean Armistice Conference recounts his experience.

14-047. KIM, Myong Whai. "Prisoners of War as a Major Problem of the Korean Armistice, 1953." PhD dissertation, New York University, 1960. 323 pp. Abstracted in *DA* 23(July 1962):291–292; UM 61-702. A study of the question of repatriation of POWs in the Korean armistice negotiations. Argues that POWs should not be repatriated by force.

14-048. LAI, Nathan Yu-Jen. "United States Policy and the Diplomacy of Limited War in Korea: 1950–1951." PhD dissertation, University of Massachusetts, 1974. 345 pp. Abstracted in *DAI* 35(March 1975):6221-A; UM 75-604B. An attempt to explain how and why a set of policy decisions was made by the US regarding the Korean War.

14-049. LOFGREN, Charles A. "Congress and the Korean Conflict." PhD dissertation, Stanford University, 1966. 250 pp. Abstracted in *DA* 27(October 1966):1017-A; UM 66-8629. A study of the various views held by members of Congress regarding the Korean War.

14-050. LYONS, Gene M. *Military Policy and Economic Aid: The Korean Case, 1950–1953*. Columbus: Ohio State University Press, 1961. A "case study of one aspect of American policy during the Korean conflict—the economic aid program." Utilizes, *inter alia,* personal papers of Dr. J. Donald Kingsley, first agent general of the UN Korean Reconstruction Agency (UNKRA). Focuses on the interaction between the UN and the conduct of US foreign policy. Based on a PhD dissertation submitted to Columbia University in 1958.

14-051. MUELLER, Hon E. *War, Presidents, and Public Opinion*. New York: Wiley, 1973. Contains a good analysis of public opinion data on the American people's attitude toward US participation in the Korean War.

14-052. NOBLE, Harold Joyce. *Embassy at War*. Edited with an introduction by Frank Baldwin, Jr. Seattle: University of Washington Press, 1975. An insider's view of the early stage of the Korean War and US relations with President

Syngman Rhee of South Korea. The author, a Korean-born American, served as a first secretary in the US Embassy in Seoul during this period.

14-053. OLIVER, Robert T. *Verdict in Korea.* State College, Pa.: Bald Eagle Press, 1952. A "close friend and counsellor of Syngman Rhee" discusses the ramifications of the Korean War. Presents Rhee's perceptions of the issues involved.

14-054. _____. *Why War Came in Korea.* New York: Fordham University Press, 1950. Argues that the Soviets launched the Korean War for the following reasons: "(1) Korea is of great strategic military value in north Asia, providing a good base from which to launch an attack upon Japan and Southeast Asia; (2) Russian foreign policy has long aimed to secure possession of Korea; (3) the puppet regime in North Korea was militarily strong and well propagandized; (4) the Republic of Korea seemed too weak militarily to be able to resist an attack; (5) American authoritative statements indicated that we would not defend Korea; and (6) the success of democracy in South Korea constituted an intolerable refutation of the Communist propaganda line in Asia."

14-055. PAIGE, Glenn D. *The Korean Decision, June 24–30, 1950.* New York: Free Press, 1968. A meticulous reconstruction of America's decision to intervene in the Korean War. A path-breaking study in foreign-policy decision-making, this book also illuminates the background and implications of a major event in US-Korean relations.

14-056. PARK, Hong-Kyu. *The Korean War: An Annotated Bibliography.* Marshall, Texas: Demmer Co., 1971. A useful annotated bibliography of (1) bibliographic guide, (2) official publications, (3) semiofficial sources, (4) memoirs, autobiographies, biographies, and personal records, (5) secondary works, (6) articles and essays, and (7) non-English sources. The bulk of the entries consist of English-language materials.

14-057. RAITT, Walton A. "American Ideology and the United Nations: A Study in Ambivalence." PhD dissertation, Claremont Graduate School and University Center, 1968. 301 pp. Abstracted in *DA* 29(August 1968):660-661-A; UM 68-10,536. Chapter 12 presents a case study of the US, the UN, and the Korean War.

14-058. REES, David. *Korea: The Limited War.* New York: St. Martin's Press, 1964. One of the best books of the Korean War, complete with an extensive bibliography, major documents, and statistics.

14-059. RILEY, John W. and Wilbur SCHRAMM. *The Reds Take a City: The Communist Occupation of Seoul, with*

Eyewitness Accounts. New Brunswick, N.J.: Rutgers University Press, 1951. A scholarly analysis of the North Korean occupation of Seoul in 1950 by a communications expert and a sociologist utilizing the views of participants. Narratives by eminent Koreans translated by Hugh Heungwoo Cynn.

14-060. SIMMONS, Robert R. "The Korean Civil War." In Frank Baldwin (ed.), *Without Parallel: The American-Korean Relationship Since 1945.* New York: Pantheon Books, 1974. The author argues that "the P'yongyang government was neither a passive gun for an itchy Soviet trigger finger nor a monolithic political system totally subservient to Moscow that lacked its own dynamics." The conflict, he adds, "was not a pure unprovoked aggression and it was not a complete surprise to Washington and Seoul. It was the Korean civil war."

14-061. SMITH, Gaddis. "After 25 Years—The Parallel." *New York Times Magazine* (22 June 1975):15–25. A diplomatic historian looks at the origins and consequences of the Korean War on its twenty-fifth anniversary. Urges Washington to "reconsider its attitude toward Kim Il Sung as it has toward Mao Tse-tung."

14-062. SPANIER, John W. *The Truman-MacArthur Controversy and the Korean War.* Cambridge, Mass.: Belknap Press, 1959. An excellent study of a major controversy in the American political arena during the Korean War. Contains a general survey of America's role in that war.

14-063. STEVENSON, Adlai E. "Korea in Perspective." *Foreign Affairs* 30(3)(April 1952):349–350. Places America's decision to intervene in Korea in a larger historical and strategic perspective. Argues that the US has "made historic progress toward the establishment of a viable system of collective security."

14-064. STONE, Isidor F. *The Hidden History of the Korean War.* New York: Monthly Review Press, 1952. In this controversial and highly polemical study of the Korean War, the author argues that the North Korean "invasion was encouraged politically by silence, invited militarily by defensive formations, and finally set off by some minor lunges across the border by the South Korean troops." Although Stone cites only UN and US government documents, and articles in American and British newspapers, many of his arguments are based on the inferences he makes from these sources.

14-065. United States Congress. Senate. *Military Situation in the Far East.* Hearings before the Committee on Armed Services and the Committee on Foreign Relations, 82nd Cong. 1st sess., pts. 1–5. Washington: Government Printing Office, 1951. These voluminous documents chronicle the celebrated congressional hearings on the dismissal of General MacArthur as commander of UN Forces in Korea. They are a gold mine of information about the various phases of the Korean War.

14-066. VATCHER, William H. *Panmunjom: The Story of the Korean Military Armistice Negotiations.* New York: Praeger, 1958. A participant's view of the Korean armistice negotiations. The author served as psychological warfare adviser to the Senior United Nations Delegate at the Korean Armistice Conference.

Other Aspects of Korean-American Relations

14-067. BALDWIN, Frank (ed.). *Without Parallel: The American-Korean Relationship Since 1945.* New York: Pantheon Books, 1974. A provocative reappraisal of the conventional wisdom on America's role in Korea. Contributions by eight scholars, of whom seven are American and one is German. The editor's introductory essay presents an excellent overview of the general orientations and themes of the contributors.

14-068. BERGER, Carl. *The Korean Knot: A Military-Political History.* Philadelphia: University of Pennsylvania Press, 1964. A balanced general survey of Korea, with emphasis on American-Korean relations and the Korean War. A good bibliography of English-language materials is appended.

14-069. BIX, Herbert P. "Regional Integration: Japan and South Korea in America's Asian Policy." In Frank Baldwin (ed.), *Without Parallel: The American-Korean Relationship Since 1945.* New York: Pantheon Books, 1974. A study of the genesis and evolution of America's "regional integration strategy." The latter is defined as the policy of using "the southern half of the Korean peninsula and Japan to create a configuration of military and economic power that would enable the United States to contain the might of both China and the Soviet Union, while simultaneously ensuring its own hegemony over Pacific Asia." Relies heavily on Japanese sources.

14-070. BUCHER, Lloyd M. *Bucher: My Story.* Garden City, N.Y.: Doubleday, 1970. As told by Commander Bucher, skipper of the USS *Pueblo* captured by North Koreans in 1968.

14-071. CHANG, Paul Timothy. "Political Effect of World War II on Korea: With Special Reference to the Policies of the United States." PhD dissertation, University of Notre Dame, 1953. 270 pp. Abstracted in *DA* 15(February

1955):285; UM 10,722. A study focusing on the early stage of American military occupation of Korea.

14-072. CHO, Soon Sung. *Korea in World Politics, 1940–1950: An Evaluation of American Responsibility.* Berkeley: University of California Press, 1967. A definitive study of Korean-American relations in the period 1940–1950. In addition to offering an incisive analysis of US policy toward Korea, the book contains what may be regarded as the best discussion of the origins of the Korean partition. Argues that American foreign policy was a major factor "frustrating the original plan for the independence and unification of Korea." The bibliography of English, Korean, and Japanese sources used in the study runs to thirty-one pages. Based on a PhD dissertation submitted to the University of Michigan in 1960.

14-073. CUMINGS, Bruce. "American Policy and Korean Liberation." In Frank Baldwin (ed.), *Without Parallel: The American-Korean Relationship Since 1945.* New York: Pantheon Books, 1974. One of the best studies of American policy and performance during the pre–Korean War period. Attributes much of the failure of American policy to ignorance and ethnocentrism on the part of the makers and administrators of that policy. Documentation is impressive—twenty full pages of notes.

14-074. DODGE, Herbert Wesley. "A History of U.S. Assistance to Korean Education: 1953–1966." EdD dissertation, George Washington University, 1971. 326 pp. Abstracted in *DAI* 32(6)(December 1971):3067-A; UM 72-456. A critical examination of America's effort "to help upgrade Korean education" based on "all available documentary evidence."

14-075. GOODRICH, Leland M. *Korea: A Study of U.S. Policy in the United Nations.* New York: Council on Foreign Relations, 1956. A useful study not only of US policy toward Korea in the UN but also of the relations between Korea on the one hand and the US and the UN on the other.

14-076. GORDON, Bernard K. "Korea in the Changing East Asia Policy of the United States." In Young C. Kim (ed.), *Major Powers and Korea.* Silver Spring, Md.: Research Institute on Korean Affairs, 1973. A discussion of US policy toward Korea "from the perspective of overall American foreign policy." Argues that US policy must adapt to the changing international environment in East Asia and that it should be geared to the goal of peaceful Korean unification.

14-077. HAHM, Pyong-Choon. "From a Client-State to an Ally: The U.S.-Korean Relations." *Journal of Korean*

Affairs 3(3)(October 1973):39–46. The author, who was special assistant to President Park of South Korea when he wrote this article, subsequently became Park's ambassador to the US. Presents a justification for Park's tightening up of political controls in terms of the requirements for national security and economic modernization.

14-078. _____. "Korea's 'Mendicant Mentality'? A Critique of U.S. Policy." *Foreign Affairs* 43(1)(October 1964): 165–174. A pungent critique of US policy toward South Korea. Refutes the argument that American aid to Korea is a handout to a beggar nation, asserting that it is, in effect, a token of appreciation as well as a compensation for services being rendered by the Korean people for the entire free world and, particularly, for the United States. The author concludes with a plea for "patience" and "confidence"—"The patience of our allies and their confidence in our ability to achieve finally a viable democracy in our corner of the world."

14-079. HENDERSON, Gregory. *Korea: The Politics of the Vortex*. Cambridge, Mass.: Harvard University Press, 1968. While this thought-provoking study deals primarily with Korea's internal political dynamics, it nonetheless contains an excellent discussion of American military government and other facets of American-Korean relations.

14-080. HENTHORN, W. E. *Korean Views of America, 1954–1964: An Annotated Bibliography*. Honolulu: Center for Cultural and Technical Interchange between East and West, 1965. Annotated bibliography of two types of materials that appeared in leading Korean periodicals in 1954–1964: (1) articles, editorials, and features on various aspects of American life and actions and (2) translations of American articles and books. The compiler notes: "In general, the Korean view of America is a favorable one but this view is . . . presently undergoing a process of change."

14-081. JUNG, Yong Suk. "The Rise of American National Interest in Korea: 1845–1950." PhD dissertation, Claremont Graduate School and University Center, 1970. 272 pp. Abstracted in *DAI* 31(12)(June 1971):6689-A; UM 71-13,704. Argues that "American foreign policy for the period of 1845–1950 underwent two separate stages: the first, 1845–1942, and the second, 1943–1950. The first period was marked by interests in Korea subordinate to that in Japan and China. The second stage, however, mirrored a revolutionary period in American-Korean relations. The traditionally subordinate interest in Korea was transformed to a core interest."

14-082. KANG, Han Mu. "The United States Military Gov-

ernment in Korea, 1945–1948: An Analysis and Evaluation of Its Policy." PhD dissertation, University of Cincinnati, 1970. 301 pp. Abstracted in *DAI* 31(8)(February 1971): 4242-A; UM 71-1527. A generally critical study of American military government in Korea. The study underlines "the inherent contradictions implicit in the ideals of the wartime conferences at Cairo, Yalta, and Potsdam and actual political realities faced by the Commander of American occupation forces, General John R. Hodge."

14-083. KOH, B. C. "The *Pueblo* Incident in Perspective." *Asian Survey* 9(4)(April 1969):264–280. North Korea's forcible seizure of the USS *Pueblo* and its 83-man crew in Wonsan Bay on 23 January 1968 is examined from the perspective of Pyongyang's strategic objectives and internal political dynamics.

14-084. KWAK, Tae-Hwan. "The Role of the United States and Korean Reunification." *Korean Journal of International Studies* 6(3)(Summer 1975):23–38. Applies the concept of "core interest" to analysis of US-Korean relations. Suggests a "block-building" approach to Korean reunification.

14-085. _____. "United States–Korean Relations: A Core Interest Analysis Prior to U.S. Intervention in the Korean War." PhD dissertation, Claremont Graduate School and University Center, 1969. 306 pp. Abstracted in *DAI* 30(12) (June 1970):5507-A; UM 70-8924. Relying on "American leaders' statements and actions," the author attempts to analyze to what extent the US asserted its geopolitical and ideological core interests in Korea. Among other things, he concludes that "US Korea policy was characterized as a policy of 'indecision' which led to American failure in Korea" and that "Korea served as a strategic interest to the US, defending American core interests in Japan and its strategic bases in the Pacific."

14-086. LEE, U-Gene. "American Policy towards Korea, 1942–1947: Formulation and Execution." PhD dissertation, Georgetown University, 1973. 460 pp. Abstracted in *DAI* 34(10)(April 1974):6569-A; UM 74-6424. This study is highly laudatory of Lt. Gen. John R. Hodge, commander of American occupation forces in Korea. It argues that much of the American failure could have been averted had Washington heeded Hodge's recommendations.

14-087. LEE, Won Sul. "The Impact of the United States Occupation Policy on the Socio-Political Structure of South Korea, 1945–1948." PhD dissertation, Western Reserve University, 1962. An attempt to delineate the impact of US policy on Korea with special reference to the actions of the American military government, the trusteeship controversy, the establishment of the Korean interim government, and, finally, the establishment of the Republic of Korea.

14-088. LIMB, Ben C. "The Pacific Pact: Looking Forward or Backward." *Foreign Affairs* 29(4)(July 1951):539–549. South Korea's wartime ambassador to the UN (and former foreign minister) sets forth Seoul's perceptions of the requirements for its security. He favors a Pacific collective security system patterned after the Atlantic pact (NATO).

14-089. MEADE, E. Grant. *American Military Government in Korea.* New York: King's Crown Press, 1951. A study of "the American military government operation in Korea during 1945–46, the crucial first year of occupation." The author relied on the technique of participant observation, using Chŏlla Namdo as an "experimental laboratory."

14-090. MORRIS, William G. "The Korean Trusteeship, 1941–1947: The United States, Russia, and the Cold War." PhD dissertation, University of Texas at Austin, 1974. 245 pp. Abstracted in *DAI* 35(8)(February 1975): 5312-A; UM 75-4429. In contrast to the thesis by U-Gene Lee (14-086), this study, covering the same period, argues that General Hodge's incompetence and blunders contributed greatly to American failure in Korea.

14-091. OH, John K. C. "Korean-American Relations in the 1970's." In Young C. Kim (ed.), *Foreign Policies of Korea.* Washington: Institute for Asian Studies, 1973. A discussion of the major factors impinging on the international posture of both the US and Korea as well as "some general trends in US-Korean relations in the 1970's."

14-092. _____. "Role of the United States in South Korea's Democratization." *Pacific Affairs* 43(2)(Summer 1969): 164–177. A study of an important but neglected aspect of US-Korean relations. Argues that the "United States exercised its influence quietly and judiciously as a protector of a democratic system in Korea."

14-093. OLIVER, Robert T. *Syngman Rhee: The Man behind the Myth.* New York: Dodd, Mead, 1954. This laudatory biography of the first president of South Korea by a close personal friend and adviser contains an account of Rhee's often strained relations with the US, particularly during the Korean War.

14-094. RENICK, Roderick Dhu, Jr. "Political Communication: A Case Study of United States Propaganda in North and South Korea." PhD dissertation, Tulane University, 1971. 256 pp. Abstracted in *DAI* 32(11)(May 1972):6523-24-A; UM 72-14,200. A "content analysis of the propaganda directed toward North and South Korea by the United States Army during the period 1964 to 1966."

14-095. SCALAPINO, Robert A. *Asia and the Road Ahead: Issues for the Major Powers.* Berkeley: University of California Press, 1975. The author devotes fourteen pages to a discussion of US policy toward Korea, including the moral implications of supporting an authoritarian regime and the costs and benefits of keeping US troops in South Korea. Of the latter, Scalapino concludes: "On balance, the risks of withdrawal outweigh those of retaining some American forces in Korea."

14-096. SHIN, Roy W. "The Politics of Foreign Aid: A Study of the Impact of United States Aid in Korea from 1945 to 1966." PhD dissertation, University of Minnesota, 1969. 313 pp. Abstracted in *DAI* 30(6)(December 1969):2588-A; UM 69-20,094. Examines the effect of US foreign aid on South Korea's economic and political development. Finds that US aid has had salutary effects not only on Seoul's economic growth but also on its "democratization" process.

14-097. United States Congress. House. *Inquiry into the U.S.S. Pueblo and EC-121 Plane Incidents.* Hearing before the Special Subcommittee on the U.S.S. *Pueblo* of the Committee on Armed Services, 91st Cong., 1st sess., 4, 5, 6, 10, 14, 17, 19, 20 March and 25 and 28 April 1969. Washington: Government Printing Office, 1969. Two key events in the annals of US–North Korean relations are scrutinized in this informative document.

14-098. United States Congress. Senate. *United States Security Agreements and Commitments Abroad: Republic of Korea.* Hearings before the Subcommitte on United States Security Agreements and Commitments Abroad of the Committee on Foreign Relations, 91st Cong., 2nd sess., pt. 6, 24–26 February 1970. Washington: Government Printing Office, 1970. Contains valuable information not only on US–South Korean relations but also on the military capabilities and foreign policies of the two Koreas.

14-099. United States. Department of State. *A Historical Summary of United States–Korean Relations, with a Chronology of Important Developments, 1834–1962.* Department of State Publication 7446, Far Eastern Series 115. Washington: Government Printing Office, 1962. Its lengthy title correctly explains the nature of this publication. A highly useful source book for gaining a historical perspective on Korean-American relations.

14-100. WAGNER, Edward W. "Failure in Korea." *Foreign Affairs* 40(1)(October 1961):128–135. A leading American historian of Korea takes a critical look at US policy toward Korea in the wake of the military coup in Seoul in May 1961. He attributes the "failure" of US policy to three factors: (1) The "United States has followed a policy of drift, shirking the responsibilities thrust upon it first as an occupying power and then as the mainstay of the young Republic of Korea''; (2) the "twin watchwords of internal stability and militant anti-Communism have blinded us to the overriding necessity of fostering a social order that will repel out of its own strength the Communist effort to subvert it''; and (3) "the United States has not taken an intelligent approach to the basic problem of seeking an understanding of the land and its people.''

KOREA AND JAPAN

14-101. BAERWALD, Hans H. "The Diet and the Japan-Korea Treaty." *Asian Survey* 8(12)(December 1968):951–959. Although this is primarily a study in the Japanese legislative process, it nonetheless throws light on Japanese perceptions of Japanese-Korean relations. The focus of the study is the parliamentary struggle on the ratification of the historic treaty normalizing relations between South Korea and Japan.

14-102. CHEE, Chong Il. "National Regulation of Fisheries in International Law." PhD dissertation, New York University, 1964. 327 pp. Abstracted in *DA* 27(September 1966):812-A; UM 65-6624. Includes a detailed discussion of the dispute between Japan and South Korea regarding fishing in the Sea of Japan.

14-103. CHO, Soon Sung. "Japan's Two Koreas Policy and the Problems of Korean Unification." *Asian Survey* 7(10)(October 1967):703–725. A balanced and informative analysis of Japan's policy toward North and South Korea and its implications for Korean unification. Especially useful is the author's extensive discussion of Japanese perceptions of the problem. Cho relies heavily on Japanese periodicals. He concludes that "Japan's two Koreas policy itself is not and will not be an important determinant for the unification of Korea, although it may have some effect upon it.'' What is more important, he argues, is the manner in which the newly invigorated economic relations between Japan and South Korea will be damaged by the political leaders of both countries.

14-104. _____. "North Korea's Relations with Japan." In Young C. Kim (ed.), *Foreign Policies of Korea*. Washington: Institute for Asian Studies, 1973. An "evaluation of the changing pattern of Japanese–North Korean relations." Examines "the reasons why North Korea and Japan are searching for a new policy," "the changing nature of Asian international relations and the possible unification of Korea."

14-105. CHO, Sung Yoon. "South Korea's Relations with Japan as Seen in the Normalization Treaty-Making Pro-

cess, 1964–1965. In Young C. Kim (ed.), *Japan in World Politics*. Washington: Institute for Asian Studies, 1972. A well-documented study of the landmark event in Seoul-Tokyo relations. As a legal scholar, the author provides special insight into the various legal aspects of the treaty.

14-106. CHUNG, Kiwon. "Japanese–North Korean Relations." *Asian Survey* 4(4)(April 1964):788–803. A useful survey of Tokyo-Pyongyang relations from the Korean armistice to 1963. Draws heavily on Japanese sources, although North Korean sources are not overlooked.

14-107. HAH, Chong-Do. "The Dynamics of Japanese-Korean Relations, 1945–1963: An Interpretation of International Conflict." PhD dissertation, Indiana University, 1967. 372 pp. Abstracted in *DA* 28(May 1968):4677-A; UM 68-7234. A competent analysis of the sources of conflict between Tokyo and Seoul, with emphasis on the period 1951–1960. Contains a good discussion of the Korean minority in Japan.

14-108. HELLMANN, Donald C. *Japan and East Asia: The New International Order*. New York: Praeger, 1972. Contains a discussion of Japanese-Korean relations, with special emphasis on Korea's impact on Japanese defense policies. Stresses the asymmetric nature of Seoul-Tokyo relations, with the former becoming increasingly dependent on the latter in the economic and, possibly, security fields.

14-109. JO, Yung-hwan. "Japanese-Korean Relations and Asian Diplomacy." *Orbis* 11(2)(Summer 1967):582–592. A study of the problems, motives, and terms of the 1965 normalization treaty between South Korea and Japan.

14-110. KANG, Young Hoon. "North Korean Policy Objectives towards Japan." *Journal of Korean Affairs* 4(3)(October 1974):33–38. A useful summary of North Korean-Japanese relations in the period 1972–1974. Asserts that North Korea pursues three basic goals in its policy toward Japan: "(1) promotion of trade; (2) establishment of diplomatic relations; and (3) strengthening of pro-Communist Korean residents' organizations in Japan.''

14-111. KIM, C. I. Eugene and Han-Kyo KIM. *Korea and the Politics of Imperialism, 1876–1910*. Berkeley: University of California Press, 1967. A definitive study of Japanese annexation of Korea. Relies on an impressive array of primary and secondary sources in Korean, Japanese, Chinese, and English. Essential reading for anyone who wishes to gain a historical perspective on Japanese-Korean relations.

14-112. KIM, Hong N. "South Korea's Relations with Japan." In Young C. Kim (ed.), *Foreign Policies of Korea*. Washington: Institute for Asian Studies, 1973. A review of Seoul-Tokyo relations since the signing of the normalization treaty in 1965. Identifies two major sources of "stress and strain" in the relations: "(1) the problem of trade imbalance; and (2) Japan's North Korea policy."

14-113. KIM, Kwan Bong. *The Korea-Japan Treaty Crisis and the Instability of the Korean Political System.* New York: Praeger, 1971. Although its primary focus is on South Korea's domestic political process, this study contains an excellent overview of South Korean–Japanese relations in the post–World War II period. Based on a doctoral thesis submitted to the University of London.

14-114. KIM, Young C. "Japanese Policy toward Korea." In Young C. Kim (ed.), *Major Powers and Korea.* Silver Spring, Md.: Research Institute on Korean Affairs, 1973. A brief but informative analysis of the various factors impinging on Japan's Korea policy. Foresees the continuation and acceleration of the Two Koreas policy.

14-115. KO, Seung-Kyun. "Domestic Political Process and Foreign Policy Making in the Republic of Korea: A Study of the Korean-Japanese Normalization Pacts." PhD dissertation, University of Pennsylvania, 1969. 241 pp. Abstracted in *DAI* 31(3)(September 1970):1348-A; UM 70-16,175. Primarily a study of South Korea's foreign policymaking process, this work nonetheless has relevance for understanding ROK–Japan relations. Contains a historical survey of South Korea's policy toward Japan.

14-116. KOH, B. C. "South Korea, North Korea, and Japan." *Pacific Community* (Tokyo), 6(2)(January 1975): 205–219. A discussion of the attempted assassination of South Korean President Park and the murder of Mrs. Park on 15 August 1974 and its implications for the triangular relationship among Seoul, Pyongyang, and Tokyo.

14-117. LEE, Changsoo. "Chosoren: An Analysis of the Korean Communist Movement in Japan." *Journal of Korean Affairs* 3(2)(July 1973):3–32. An informative study of the North Korea–oriented Korean residents' organization in Japan.

14-118. _____. "The Politics of the Korean Minority in Japan." PhD dissertation, University of Maryland, 1971. 288 pp. Abstracted in *DAI* 32(8)(February 1972):4694-A; UM 72-4141. Contains a discussion of the Japanese government's policy toward Korean residents as well as a comparison of the South Korea–oriented Mindan and the North Korea–oriented Chosoren.

14-119. LEE, Soon-won Stewart. "Korean-Japanese Discord, 1945–1965: A Case Study of International Conflict." PhD dissertation, Rutgers University, 1967. 304 pp. Abstracted in *DA* 28(August 1967):752-53-A; UM 67-9253. A study of the major issues in Korean-Japanese relations, the politics

of normalization, and US involvement in the Seoul-Tokyo controversy.

14-120. MITCHELL, Richard H. *The Korean Minority in Japan.* Berkeley: University of California Press, 1967. A well-documented study of an important problem in Korean-Japanese relations. Makes extensive use of Japanese materials.

14-121. NOGAMI, Tadashi. "The Korean Caper." *Japan Quarterly* (Tokyo), 21(2)(April–June 1974):160–167. A discussion of Korea's international situation with emphasis on its implications for Japan.

14-122. WAGNER, Edward W. *The Korean Minority in Japan.* New York: Institute of Pacific Relations, 1951. A pioneer study of discord in Korean-Japanese relations.

14-123. WELFIELD, John. "Japan-Korean Relations during the Cold War and After." *Korean Journal of International Studies* 4(2)(Spring 1973):39–57. An examination of "Japan's political and military relations with Korea during the Cold War decades" coupled with speculation "on the impact current power realignments in the Far East are likely to have on Japan's Korea policy."

KOREA AND THE COMMUNIST WORLD
General

14-124. KIM, Ilpyong J. "A New Approach to the Soviet Union and China: Korea's Strategy for Survival." In Young C. Kim (ed.), *Foreign Policies of Korea.* Washington: Institute for Asian Studies, 1973. A discussion of the policy implications of the changing relationship among the big powers surrounding Korea. Urges Seoul to "develop imaginative and bold policy alternatives towards approaching the Soviet Union and the People's Republic of China in order to solve the problem of Korean reunification."

14-125. KIM, Roy U. T. "North Korea's Relations with Moscow and Peking: Big Influence of a Small Ally." In Young C. Kim (ed.), *Foreign Policies of Korea.* Washington: Institute for Asian Studies, 1973. As the subtitle suggests, the author argues that the dispute between the two communist powers has enabled North Korea to gain an inordinate amount of influence and advantage.

14-126. KIM, Uoong-Tack. "Sino-Soviet Dispute and North Korea." PhD dissertation, University of Pennsylvania, 1967. 385 pp. Abstracted in *DA* 28(November 1967): 1879-A; UM 67-12,766.

14-127. KOH, B. C. "North Korea and the Sino-Soviet Schism." *Western Political Quarterly* 22(4)(December 1969):940–962. This study of Pyongyang's response to the Sino-Soviet dispute relies heavily on the North Korean party newspaper, *Nodong sinmun.* Argues that North Korea has skillfully exploited the dispute. "If its posture has oscillated between Moscow and Peking, its determination to maximize its gains by playing one off against the other has never wavered. In its precarious voyage through the stormy waters of international Communist politics, Pyongyang has consistently sought guidance from that ancient compass of national policy—self-interest."

14-128. KUN, Joseph C. "North Korea: Between Moscow and Peking." *China Quarterly* 31(July–September 1967): 48–58. An informative survey of major developments in North Korea's relations with its two communist neighbors. Includes some new information based on the Soviet press.

14-129. LEE, Chong-Sik. "North Korea between Dogmatism and Revisionism." *Journal of Korean Affairs* 1(1)(April 1971):14–24. A perceptive appraisal of North Korea's position in the Sino-Soviet dispute.

14-130. _____. "Stalinism in the East: Communism in North Korea." In Robert A. Scalapino (ed.), *The Communist Revolution in Asia: Tactics, Goals, and Achievements.* Englewood Cliffs, N.J.: Prentice-Hall, 1965. This general survey of North Korea contains an informative discussion of North Korea's relations with Moscow and Peking.

14-131. PAIGE, Glenn D. *The Korean People's Democratic Republic.* Stanford: Hoover Institution, 1966. An insightful analysis of North Korea utilizing the concept of political integration and community formation and maintenance. Discusses North Korea's relations with Peking and Moscow up to 1964.

14-132. _____. "North Korea and the Emulation of Russian and Chinese Behavior." In A. Doak Barnett (ed.), *Communist Strategies in Asia.* New York: Praeger, 1963. A thought-provoking analysis of the relative impact of Moscow and Peking on North Korean behavior. Argues that "the Korean Communists seem to have moved from a period of heavy initial reliance upon Soviet experience, through a period of noticeable experimentation with Chinese policies, into a period of a more self-oriented search for 'Korean' solutions to their developmental problems."

14-133. SCALAPINO, Robert A. "Moscow, Peking and the Communist Parties of Asia." *Foreign Affairs* 40(1)(January 1963):323–343. Contains a discussion of North Korea's relations with the two feuding communist powers.

14-134. SCALAPINO, Robert A. and Chong-Sik LEE. *Communism in Korea.* 2 vols. Berkeley: University of California Press, 1972. This two-volume study, which represents a decade of research by the authors, contains much valuable information and analysis on various aspects of North

Korea's international relations—particularly its relations with the PRC and the Soviet Union. The study won the Woodrow Wilson Foundation award from the American Political Science Association as the best political science book in 1972.

14-135. SIMMONS, Robert. *The Strained Alliance: Peking, Pyongyang, Moscow, and the Politics of the Korean Civil War.* New York: Free Press, 1975. The author presents an analysis of the relations among the three communist allies. Significantly, he argues that both the initiation and the conclusion of the Korean War were more heavily influenced by North Korea than by the Soviet Union. He concludes that the "strains created by the three Communist allies by the War go a long way toward explaining both the 'Sino-Soviet split' and North Korea's growing independent stance in the 1950's and 1960's."

14-136. YIU, Myung Kun. "Sino-Soviet Rivalry in North Korea since 1954." PhD dissertation, University of Maryland, 1969. 388 pp. Abstracted in *DAI* 31(3)(September 1970): 1352-A; UM 70-14,953. An attempt to explain the "causes" of North Korea's shifting posture toward Moscow and Peking.

Korea and the Soviet Union

14-137. BELOFF, Max. *Soviet Policy in the Far East, 1944–1951.* New York: Oxford University Press, 1953. Contains a long chapter on "The Soviet Union and Korea." Relies heavily on Russian sources.

14-138. KIM, Joungwon Alexander. "Soviet Policy in North Korea." *World Politics* 22(2)(January 1970):237–254. North Korea's assertion of independence from Moscow is traced through three stages: "(1) the satellite stage, from 1945 to 1950, (2) the transitional stage, from 1951 to 1958, and (3) the autonomous stage, from 1959 to the present." The author concludes that "North Korea appears bent on proving that the tail can wag the dog, and its defiance of Soviet controls illustrates the failure of Soviet policy in this small Asian satellite regime."

14-139. LEE, Chong-Sik and Ki-Wan OH. "The Russian Faction in North Korea." *Asian Survey* 8(4)(April 1968): 270–288. Relying on a wide array of sources, including Russian materials and firsthand experience of one of the coauthors (Oh), this article provides valuable insights into the role of the Russian faction in the formative stage of the North Korean regime. The authors show that the Russian faction played multiple roles—"the architect and builder of the party and the regime" as well as "an important link between Moscow and Pyongyang."

14-140. McLANE, Charles. "Korea in Russia's East Asian

Policy." In Young C. Kim (ed.), *Major Powers and Korea*. Silver Spring, Md.: Research Institute on Korean Affairs, 1973. Argues that "Russia's approach to the Korean question, which is essentially the question of unification, will shift as a result of recent developments in world politics and in the inter-relations of Great Powers." States that "Korea is not critical to Russia's [future]" and that "Russia's containment of China" will be the key factor influencing Russia's Korea policy.

14-141. SEJNA, Jan. "Russia Plotted the *Pueblo* Affair." *Reader's Digest* (July 1969):73–76. A former Czechoslovak general asserts that the Soviets both planned and assisted in the seizure of the USS *Pueblo* in January 1968. He bases his argument on remarks he allegedly heard from two high-ranking Soviet officials in Prague on two separate occasions.

14-142. SOH, Jin Chull. "The Role of the Soviet Union in Preparation for the Korean War." *Journal of Korean Affairs* 3(4)(January 1974):3–14. The author, who is director of research at the Institute of Foreign Affairs of the ROK Foreign Ministry, provides a descriptive summary of the Soviet role in the preparation for the Korean War. Presents the conventional view that the Soviets participated in every phase of the planning and preparation for the war.

14-143. _____. "Some Causes of the Korean War of 1950: A Case Study of Soviet Foreign Policy in Korea (1945–1950), with Emphasis on Sino-Soviet Collaboration." PhD dissertation, University of Oklahoma, 1963. 266 pp. Abstracted in *DA* 24(December 1963):2551-52; UM 64-126. A study of "the role of Soviet foreign policy in the period 1945–1950 as a causative factor in the Korean conflict. Particular emphasis is placed on Sino-Soviet collaboration and the failure of America's Korean policy in the same period."

14-144. SPAHR, William. "The Military Security Aspects of Soviet Relations with North Korea." *Journal of Korean Affairs* 4(1)(April 1974):1–8. The author, an analyst with the US Central Intelligence Agency and a specialist in Soviet military affairs, looks at Moscow's policy toward North Korea from the perspective of the former's security interests. Notes an apparent change "in Soviet attitudes toward nuclear weapons and renewed doctrinal interest in North Korea in the 1970's." North Korea, he adds, will become an important factor in the event of a conventional war between Moscow and Peking. "Neither side could tolerate even token North Korean participation on the side of the other," he asserts.

14-145. STELMACH, Daniel S. "The Influence of Russian Armored Tactics on the North Korean Invasion of 1950."

PhD dissertation, St. Louis University, 1973. 348 pp. Abstracted in *DAI* 34(9)(March 1974):5887-88-A; UM 74-4577. Utilizing classified US military documents and other sources, the author examines the impact of Soviet military aid on North Korea's conduct of the Korean War.

14-146. SUH, Dae-Sook. *The Korean Communist Movement, 1918–1948*. Princeton: Princeton University Press, 1967. A pioneering study of the Korean communist movement, this book offers an invaluable insight into the relationship between the Soviet Union and the rise of Kim Il Sung. Based on the author's PhD dissertation at Columbia University.

14-147. _____. "A Preconceived Formula for Sovietization: The Communist Takeover of North Korea." *Studies on the Soviet Union* 11(4)(1971):428–442. A highly informative study of Kim Il Sung's seizure of power in North Korea under Soviet auspices. Contains perceptive comparisons with communist takeovers in Eastern Europe. The author explains the takeover of North Korea "in terms of three stages of sovietization, evolving from (1) the formation of a genuine coalition through (2) the establishment of a bogus, Communist-dominated coalition, to (3) the creation of a monolithic Communist regime."

14-148. United States. Department of State. *North Korea: A Study in the Techniques of Takeover*. Department of State Publication 7118, Far Eastern Series 103. Washington: Government Printing Office, 1961. A report on "the findings of a State Department Research Mission sent to Korea on October 28, 1950." "Based on information obtained from interrogations of former North Korean government and party officials, farmers, and other private individuals, conducted by the Mission [in North Korea]; extensive North Korean and Russian documents captured by the U.N. forces; and data previously available in departmental files," the report details the techniques by which the Soviets controlled North Korea. It concludes that, given the nature of Soviet controls in North Korea, "the decision to attack South Korea could never have been taken without Soviet approval if not inspiration."

14-149. WASHBURN, John N. "Russia Looks at North Korea." *Pacific Affairs* 20(2)(June 1947):152–160. A study of Soviet perceptions of North Korea, based primarily on the Soviet press and radio coverage of events in that area.

Korea and the People's Republic of China

14-150. DEAN, Arthur H. "What It's Like to Negotiate with the Chinese." *New York Times Magazine* (30 October 1966):44–59. An intimate account of the abortive postarmistice Panmunjŏm talks that were intended to set up a political conference. The author served as special ambassador and chief negotiator for the UN Command at the talks. He provides rare glimpses into Sino–North Korean relations at the personal level. He says that "the Chinese Communists . . . generally pointedly ignored the North Koreans (who were always 'me, too')."

14-151. GEORGE, Alexander L. *The Chinese Communist Army in Action: The Korean War and its Aftermath.* New York: Columbia University Press, 1967. Although this is primarily a study of the social organization and dynamics of the People's Liberation Army, it nonetheless illuminates an important facet of Sino-Korean relations—the Chinese intervention in the Korean War. The study is based on interviews with Chinese POWs.

14-152. HINTON, Harold C. "Chinese Policy toward Korea." In Young C. Kim (ed.), *Major Powers and Korea.* Silver Spring, Md.: Research Institute on Korean Affairs, 1973. A survey of Sino–North Korean relations. Particularly useful is the author's analysis of the motives behind Chou En-lai's "current Korea policy."

14-153. KANG, Young Hoon. "Kim Il Sung's Trip to Peking." *Journal of Korean Affairs* 5(1)(April 1975):47–52. A brief assessment of DPRK President Kim Il Sung's trip to the PRC in April 1975. Concludes that Kim's trip "appears to have served Peking's foreign policy objectives more than those of North Korea." Particularly useful is the author's comparison of the Kim–Chou communiqué of 7 April 1970, issued in Pyongyang, and the new joint communiqué issued at the end of Kim's visit on 26 April 1975.

14-154. KIM, Ilpyong J. "Korea and China's Foreign Policy." In Jae Kyu Park and Sungjoo Han (eds.), *East Asia and the Major Powers: From Confrontation to Accommodation.* Seoul: Kyung Nam University, 1975. A discussion of the foreign policymaking process in Peking, China's current policy toward Korea, and its options. Argues that China's Korea policy can be characterized as a "united front strategy."

14-155. KIM, Roy U. T. "Sino–North Korean Relations." *Asian Survey* 8(8)(August 1968):708–722. A review of Sino–North Korean relations from the Korean armistice in 1953 to early 1968. Underlines Pyongyang's increasing assertion of independence and speculates that the *Pueblo* seizure and the abortive commando raid on the South Korean Presidential Mansion were probably carried out at Pyongyang's own initiative.

14-156. SCALAPINO, Robert A. "China and the North-South (Korea) Negotiations." *Korean Journal of Interna-*

tional Studies 4(3/4)(October 1973):73–86. Argues that Peking prefers a reduction of tension and hence the removal of any possible threat of another Sino-American confrontation on the Korean peninsula. This attitude is linked to the Sino-Soviet rivalry and Peking's wish to avoid the opening up of a "second front." The author speculates that Peking would probably oppose either a unified Korea under Kim Il Sung's domination or a unified noncommunist Korea.

14-157. SIMMONS, Robert R. "China's Cautious Relations with North Korea and Indochina." *Asian Survey* 11(7)(July 1971):629–644. Tests the conventional idea of a "cautious, low-risk" Chinese foreign policy against the record of Peking's recent relations with North Korea and Indochina. "Over the past decades," the author states, "China's relations with these countries have developed a pattern, one of martial words uncomplemented by military deeds."

14-158. THOMAS, S. B. "Chinese Communists' Economic and Cultural Agreement with North Korea." *Pacific Affairs* 27(1954):61–65. A short analysis of the nature and importance of the economic and cultural agreements of November 1953 between the PRC and North Korea.

14-159. WHITING, Allen S. *China Crosses the Yalu: The Decision to Enter the Korean War.* New York: Macmillan, 1960. In this penetrating study, "developments attending the Korean War are viewed from the perspective of decision makers in Peking, in so far as that perspective can be reconstructed from Chinese Communist statements and behavior." The author stresses "the political importance of Chinese intervention in relation to its expected effect on US-Japanese relations, China's role in Asia, and the security of the regime against subversion or attack from domestic anti-Communist groups assisted by American or Nationalist forces, or both."

KOREA AND THE THIRD WORLD

14-160. DAYAL, Shiv. *India's Role in the Korean Question: A Study in the Settlement of International Disputes under the United Nations.* Delhi: S. Chand, 1959. Originally a JSD dissertation submitted to the University of Michigan Law School. Examines not only India's role in the UN's handling of the Korean question but also the role of the UN itself in the settlement of the Korean conflict.

14-161. GUPTA, Karunakar. *Indian Foreign Policy in Defence of National Interest.* Calcutta: World Press, 1956. Contains a discussion of India's role in the UN's handling of the Korean War. Originally a PhD dissertation submitted to the University of London in 1954.

14-162. HEIMSATH, Charles H., IV. "India's Role in the Korean War." PhD dissertation, Yale University, 1957. 342 pp. Abstracted in *DA* 26(January 1966):4055; UM 66-36. A study of "Indian participation in the diplomacy of the Korean War and in the prisoner of war exchange following the armistice."

14-163. KIM, Chonghan. "Korea's Diplomacy toward Africa." *Orbis* 11(3)(Fall 1967):885–896. A rare study of South Korea's relations with Africa based largely on the author's firsthand experience as a senior diplomat in the ROK Foreign Ministry.

14-164. KO, Seung K. "South Korea's Policy toward the Non-aligned Countries." *Asian Forum* 3(2)(April/June 1971):111–118. An overview of the objectives and performance of Seoul's policy toward the nonaligned nations.

14-165. PLOTKIN, Arieh L. "Israel's Role in the United Nations: An Analytical Study." PhD dissertation, Princeton University, 1955. 317 pp. Abstracted in *DA* 15(November 1955):2280-81; UM 13,722. Includes a detailed examination of Israel's "stand and vote on the Korean conflict when it was brought before the U.N. General Assembly."

KOREA AND THE UNITED NATIONS

14-166. ALEXANDRIDES, Costas G. "The United Nations Economic Assistance to the Republic of Korea: A Case Study of Economic Reconstruction and Development." PhD dissertation, New York University, 1960. 359 pp. Abstracted in *DA* 27(November 1966):1148-50-A; UM 66-9659. A study of UN involvement in the economic rehabilitation of South Korea.

14-167. ATTIA, Gamal el-Din. *Les Forces Armées des Nations Unies en Corée et au Moyen-Orient.* Geneva: Droz, 1963. A legally oriented study of the operations of UN troops in Korea and the Middle East.

14-168. EVERETT, John Thomas, Jr. "The United Nations and the Korean Situation, 1947–1950: A Study of International Techniques of Pacific Settlement." PhD dissertation, University of Cincinnati, 1955. 312 pp. Abstracted in *DA* 15(August 1965):1433-34; UM 12,937. Focuses on the various mechanisms created by the UN to deal with the Korean question.

14-169. FRANKENSTEIN, Marc. *L'organisation des Nations Unies devant le Conflit Coréen.* Paris: Pedone, 1952. A legal and political study of the UN's role in the Korean War. Contains a useful bibliography of works in French as well as in English.

14-170. GOODRICH, Leland M. "Korea: Collective Measures against Aggression." *International Conciliation* 494 (October 1953):129–192. A succinct review of the UN's role in the Korean War.

14-171. GORDENKER, Leon. *The United Nations and the Peaceful Unification of Korea: The Politics of Field Operations, 1947–1950.* The Hague: M. Nijhoff, 1959. An excellent study of the operations of the various UN commissions on Korea, with emphasis on political dynamics and contexts. Based on the author's PhD dissertation submitted to Columbia University in 1958.

14-172. HALLIDAY, Jon. "The United Nations and Korea." In Frank Baldwin (ed.), *Without Parallel.* New York: Pantheon Books, 1974. An exceedingly critical examination of the role of the US and the UN in Korea. Although well documented, the study suffers from dubious inferences which the author makes from his sources. From Dae-Sook Suh's *Korean Communist Movement,* for example, the author infers that "a heroic left-wing revolutionary movement . . . had the support of the overwhelming majority of the population" in liberated Korea in 1945.

14-173. KAHNG, Tae Jin. *Law, Politics, and the Security Council: An Inquiry into the Handling of Legal Questions Involved in International Disputes and Situations.* 2nd enlarged ed. The Hague: M. Nijhoff, 1969. Although this is primarily a study of the interplay of law and politics in the Security Council, it contains an informative analysis of the role of that body in the Korean War. Based on the author's PhD dissertation submitted to Columbia University in 1962.

14-174. KIM, Chong Han. "The Korean Reunification Issue in the United Nations." In Se-Jin Kim and Chang-Hyun Cho (eds.), *Government and Politics of Korea.* Silver Spring, Md.: Research Institute on Korean Affairs, 1972. A survey of the various aspects of the Korean question in the UN—its origins, substantive and procedural aspects, and the attitudes of Seoul and Pyongyang toward it.

14-175. KIM, Joungwon Alexander and Carolyn Campbell KIM. "The Divided Nations in the International System." *World Politics* 25(4)(July 1973):479–507. The authors discuss the problem of membership of divided nations in the UN and its affiliated agencies. Although heavily legalistic, the article may illuminate the issues surrounding the joint or separate admission of the two Koreas to the UN.

14-176. KOH, B. C. "The United Nations and the Politics of Korean Reunification." *Journal of Korean Affairs* 3(4) (January 1974):37–56. Based in part on the author's firsthand observation of the Korean debate in the First Committee of the UN General Assembly in November 1973, this article examines the manner in which the Korean question was handled by the 28th session of the UN General Assembly. The session marked the first time that representatives of both North and South Korea participated as observers in the debate on the Korean question.

14-177. PERRIN, Kwan Sok. "The Problem of Korean Unification and the United Nations, 1945–1955." PhD dissertation, University of Utah, 1971. 189 pp. Abstracted in *DAI* 32(October 1971):2164-A; UM 71-24,999. Focuses on the roles of the US and the Soviet Union in the UN's handling of the Korean question.

14-178. RUCKER, Arthur. "Korea—The Next Stage." *International Affairs* (London), 30(3)(July 1954):313–319. A discussion of the need for Korea's economic recovery after the armistice, with emphasis on the role of the UN Korea Reconstruction Agency.

14-179. YOO, Tae-ho. *The Korean War and the United Nations: A Legal and Diplomatic Historical Study.* Louvain: Librairie Desbarax, 1965. Originally a doctoral thesis submitted to the Catholic University of Louvain in Belgium. Examines "the policies of the U.N. intervention in the Korean conflict," "its legal basis," and "the influence of power politics on U.N. collective security."

14-180. YOON, Young Kyo. "United Nations Participation in Korean Affairs: 1945–1954." PhD dissertation, American University, 1959. 271 pp. Abstracted in *DA* 20(January 1960):2880; UM 59-3642. Focuses on "the achievement of the U.N. in the establishment and recognition of the Republic of Korea" and "the U.N. collective activities against Communist aggression in the Korean War."

MISCELLANEOUS

14-181. CHAI, Nam Yearl. "Asian Attitudes toward International Law: A Case Study of Korea." PhD dissertation, University of Pennsylvania, 1967. 303 pp. Abstracted in *DA* 28(June 1968):5125-26-A; UM 68-9189. A study of the "state practice of the First Republic of Korea (1948–1960) as revealed in three legal disputes: (1) the dispute over Korea's sovereignty over the adjacent seas, (2) the dispute over Japanese claim to property in Korea, and (3) the jurisdictional dispute over Dokto island."

14-182. FREYMOND, Jacques. "Supervising Agreements: The Korean Experience." *Foreign Affairs* 37(3)(April 1959):496–503. A study of "the Neutral Nations Supervisory Commission set up under the terms of the Armistice Agreement in Korea." The author argues that "the differences in the concepts held by each side [to the armistice agreement] as to proper dealings among nations" greatly impeded the functioning of the Supervisory Commission.

14-183. KIM, Se-Jin. "South Korea's Involvement in Viet-

nam and Its Economic and Political Impact." *Asian Survey* 10(6)(June 1970):519–532. Discusses the various consequences of South Korea's massive participation in the Vietnam War—some 49,000 troops and 15,000 civilians were in Vietnam as of late 1969. The author concludes that "the Vietnam conflict served as a principal catalyst in stimulating [Seoul's] economic growth, enhancing the prestige of Chung-hee Park and his government, and raising the international position of South Korea." He asserts that it was a major ingredient in cementing ties between Seoul and Washington.

14-184. LYMAN, Princeton N. "Korea's Involvement in Vietnam." *Orbis* 12(2)(Summer 1968):563–581. A study of the origins and consequences of South Korea's participation in the Vietnam conflict.

14-185. STAIRS, Denis. *The Diplomacy of Constraint: Canada, the Korean War, and the United States.* Toronto: University of Toronto Press, 1974. In this excellent study of Canada's role in the Korean War, the author argues that the "general pattern of Canadian behavior" was one "in which initiatives were taken on a multilateral basis through the United Nations with a view to moderating the exercise of American power." In addition to a good bibliography on the Korean War, the book has a chapter on "analytical alternatives" which students of foreign policy in general may find very useful.

NATIONAL REUNIFICATION
General and Theoretical
General

14-186. BURCHETT, Wilfred G. *Again Korea.* New York: International Publishers, 1968. The author, an Australian journalist who covered the Korean War from the communist side, revisited North Korea in the spring of 1967. This is a glowing account of that visit, combined with a general discussion of the Korean unification problem as viewed from the North Korean perspective. A good PR job for Pyongyang.

14-187. GRAJDANZEV, Andrew J. "Korea Divided." *Far Eastern Survey* 14(20)(October 1945):281–283. A brief statistical comparison of the American and Soviet occupation zones in Korea. The author sees "serious dangers hidden in the social differences of policies as practiced by the respective forces of occupation." These dangers, he warns prophetically, "are of such character than an accidental division of the country along the 38th parallel may result in creation of two Koreas.

14-188. GREY, Arthur L., Jr. "The Thirty-Eighth Parallel." *Foreign Affairs* 29(3)(April 1951):482–487. A refutation of "the erroneous but widespread impression that Korea's future was decided at Yalta." The author contends that "the real significance of the Yalta conference, as far as Korea was concerned, was that it secured Russian entry into the war and thereby made Russian activity in Korea virtually inevitable." The author states that the American "decision to occupy Korea south of the thirty-eighth parallel with American troops originated with Joint Chiefs and more specifically in the War Department" in order to forestall the Soviets from occupying all of Korea.

14-189. KIM, Byong Sik. *Modern Korea: The Socialist North, Revolutionary Perspectives in the South, and Unification.* New York: International Publishers, 1970. A translation of a book originally written in Japanese, this is Pyongyang's official exposition of the thought of Kim Il Sung. Part 2 deals with Kim Il Sung's ideas on Korean reunification; pt. 3 deals with his ideas on international relations.

14-190. KIM, C. I. Eugene (ed.). *Korean Unification: Problems and Prospects.* Kalamazoo: Korea Research and Publications, 1973. A collection of ten papers, all but one of which were originally presented to a conference on Korean unification held in Seoul in 1970. The emphasis is placed on comparative analysis of the two Koreas in terms of various functional domains such as industry, science and technology, military, law, administration, parties, and local government.

14-191. KIM, Hak-Joon. "Korean Unification in the Asian Balance of Power." PhD dissertation, University of Pittsburgh, 1972. 395 pp. Abstracted in *DAI* 33(February 1973):4484-A; UM 73-1642. A study of the origins of Korean partition and the unification policies of North and South Korea during the period 1945-1972. Argues that Toynbee's concept of "challenge and response" best explains the two governments' policies.

14-192. KIM, Han K. (ed.). *Reunification of Korea: 50 Basic Documents.* Washington: Institute for Asian Studies, 1972. A collection of key documents bearing on Korean reunification, beginning with the Cairo Declaration of 1 December 1943 and ending with South Korean President Park's statement of 15 August 1971 reaffirming his policy of peaceful unification and supporting the North-South Red Cross talks. An invaluable source book.

14-193. KIM, Han-Kyo. "South Korean Policy toward North Korea." In Young C. Kim (ed.), *Major Powers and Korea.* Silver Spring, Md.: Research Institute on Korean Affairs, 1973. A thought-provoking analysis of South Korea's unification policies, with emphasis on their intel-

lectual, political, and psychological dimensions. Explores policy alternatives which may facilitate unification. Specifically, three areas are considered: "(1) establishment of stable democratic rule at home, (2) realism and flexibility in foreign relations, and (3) closing of an 'information gap.' " The author, however, remains rather pessimistic about the prospects of an early reunification.

14-194. KIM, Il Sung. *For the Independent Unification of Korea.* Pyongyang: Foreign Languages Publishing House, 1967. Collection of speeches and reports.

14-195. KIM, Kwang. "Approaches to the Problem of Korean Unification: A Study in Linkage Politics." PhD dissertation, New York University, 1974. 391 pp. Abstracted in *DAI* 35(December 1974):3822-33-A; UM 74-18,173. A study of the "linkage" between "external factors such as the international system, the foreign policies of the major powers involved in the Korean question, and North Korea's policy and strategy toward the South" on the one hand and South Korea's decision-making process on the other.

14-196. Korea University. *Report: International Conference on the Problems of Korean Unificaction.* Seoul: Korea University, Asiatic Research Center, 1971. Proceedings of an international conference held in Seoul in 1970. A total of sixty-two papers are assembled in the volume. The themes of the conference range from a consideration of the international environment to an examination of various unification plans. The quality of the works is uneven, although some important conceptual breakthrough seems to have been made. For instance, Zbigniew Brzezinski argues that Korean reunification should be examined not as "the end result of a long historical process . . . but [as] the stages of reaching that end result"—that is, as a process of reassociation.

14-197. LEDYARD, Gari K. "The Historical Necessity of Korean Unification—Past History—Present Imperatives —Future Prospects—." *Korean Journal of International Studies* 6(2)(Spring 1975):39-51. Arguing that the Korean and German divisions are basically dissimilar, the author surveys "some of the divisions and unifications that have occurred in Korean history" and then recommends a ten-point plan for peaceful unification. A provocative analysis.

14-198. MCCUNE, Shannon. "The Thirty-eighth Parallel in Korea." *World Politics* 1(1950):223-232. The author's penultimate sentence proved to be prophetic: "Therefore, the 38th parallel, originating as a hasty military expedient and functioning as a rigid barrier despite its handicaps as a natural boundary, will probably continue as a critical boundary where friction exists and where a serious world struggle might be precipitated at any time."

14-199. RHEE, Sang-Woo. "Themes of North Korea's Unification Messages: A Study on Pattern Shifts, 1948–68." *Korean Journal of International Studies* 4(2)(Spring 1973):7–36. An impressive "thematic content analysis" of a "sample of forty-nine official messages pertaining to unification sent to South Korea by North Korea or Korean unification employing systematic quantitative techniques. Among other things, the study generates empirical support for Soon Sung Cho's earlier impressionistic analysis.

14-200. ROE, Myong-joon. "Republic of Korea's Foreign Policy for Unification, 1954–1974. *Korean Journal of International Studies* 5(2–3)(Spring/Summer 1974):27–41. A somewhat legalistic survey of South Korea's unification policy and UN involvement in Korea.

14-201. SHINN, Rinn-Sup. "North Korean Policy toward South Korea." In Young C. Kim (ed.), *Major Powers and Korea.* Silver Spring, Md.: Research Institute on Korean Affairs, 1973. An excellent study of North Korean policy toward South Korea during the period 1953–1972. Highlights "continuity and change, causes and effects of a given foreign policy situation, and the question of national unification."

14-202. United States. Department of State. *The Record on Korean Unification, 1943–1960: Narrative Summary with Principal Documents.* Department of State Publication 7084, Far Eastern Series 101. Washington: Government Printing Office, 1960. An invaluable source book containing over ninety documents.

Theoretical

14-203. GALTUNG, Johan. "Divided Nations as Process: One State, Two States, and In-between: The Case of Korea." *Journal of Peace Research* 9(1972):345–360. As director of the International Peace Research Institute at the University of Oslo, the author considers the two Koreas to be in a fortunate situation of learning from the opportunity for creative process of interaction. "Far from being a tragedy," he argues, "divided nations are actually better off"—"because of the diversity at their disposal" and [because] "free competition between the systems may enrich both." He argues that the unification of the two Koreas will have to be a proccss with many stages in- between, not a jump from two states to one, and that such a process model is realistic, flexible, and pluralistic at the same time. Galtung's model suffers from the bias of grad-

ualist and functional theory of association. He nevertheless makes many valuable observations on Korea which have policy implications. He asserts, for instance, that "double seating in the U.N. and separate recognition of the two Korean states should be avoided," that "there should be a policy of non-intervention and non-aggression" by the two Koreas toward each other, and that "neither party must exploit the weakness of the other."

14-204. HENDERSON, Gregory, Richard N. LEBOW, and John G. STOESSINGER (eds.). *Divided Nations in a Divided World.* New York: McKay, 1974. A collection of twelve case studies of the divided nations and partitioned countries. The chapter on Korea is written by Henderson. The papers were originally presented to a seminar organized by the Institute on the United Nations of the City University of New York in 1967–1968. The concluding chapter attempts to derive a series of empirical generalizations applicable to the process of partition and unification. It argues, for instance, that "as divided nations develop internal strength and hostility between their respective superpower backers decreases, they are likely to possess greater freedom of action and seek improved relations with each other."

14-205. HENNESSY, John Russel. "Partition as an Alternative to Great Power Conflict: The Case Studies of Germany and Korea." PhD dissertation, Georgetown University, 1971. 447 pp. Abstracted in *DAI* 32(November 1971): 2772-A; UM 71-30,348. A comparative study of partition resulting from "disagreements between the great powers." The author argues that "the success" of partition in both Germany and Korea may be attributable to: "the mutual possession of an aggregate of military power capable of deterring the other side from challenging the partition settlement; a realistic and clearly drawn boundary line capable of being defended; a clear intention adequately promulgated to the other side, that the line of partition would be defended by force."

14-206. JO, Yung-hwan and Stephen WALKER. "Divided Nations and Reunification Strategies." *Journal of Peace Research* 9(1972):247–159. The authors advocate "an evolutionary strategy of symmetrical growth toward pluralistic reunification" of divided Korea. In doing so, they assume that the divided nations today significantly resemble nations that have never been united before and that "symmetrical growth strategy does not require the cooperation of either the Great Powers or both fragments." From various studies on international integration, they derive insights that could be employed as reunification strategies. For instance, they note that "political and cultural homogeneity [is] not necessary as a base for progress through the initial phases of reunification."

14-207. JOHNSTON, Ray E. "Partition as a Political Instrument." *Journal of International Affairs* 27(2)(1973):159–174. The author argues that to understand the phenomena of divided nations, one must first study the process of partitioning political units at different levels, be they cities, countries or states. He suggests that "a partition and unification may be two sides of the same coin" and that peaceful reunification of such divided nations as Germany, Korea, and Vietnam appears unlikely. He concludes that divided nations have two choices: (1) reunite by conflict and conquest or (2) peacefully coexist and permit the slow process of social mobilization and integration of new nations to occur.

14-208. KIHL, Young W. *Conflict Issues in North-South Korea Negotiations: An Analysis of Expert Generated Data.* CISS Divided Nations Internet Working Papers, no. 34. Pittsburgh: International Studies Association, 1975. Some twenty-five experts on Korea in the United States were surveyed as to their assessment of the progress of the North-South Korea negotiations in February and March of 1973. Experts were asked to assign scores on the intensity of the position of each Korea on a total of ten conflict issues. It was found that, as perceived by the experts, the positions of the two Koreas are widely apart on issues of high saliency—such as the abolition of anticommunist laws in South Korea, the joint admission of the two Koreas to the UN, mutual reduction of arms, establishment of nongovernmental relationship between political parties in the two Koreas. Less deviation was noted on issues of low saliency—such measures as helping unite dispersed families, establishing mail services between the two Koreas, cultural exchanges, and fishery agreements. In only about one of three instances did the experts consider that the two Koreas differ considerably in their issue positions.

14-209. KIM, Yong Soon. "Politics of Korean Unification: A Comparative Study of Systemic Outputs in Two Different Political Systems." PhD dissertation, Rutgers University, 1974. 115 pp. Abstracted in *DAI* 35(8)(February 1975): 4840-A; UM 75-3934. Studies the "politics of Korean unification" during the period 1954–1965 in order to test certain propositions derived from Rosenau's theory of system transformation and Almond's theory of system capability.

14-210. MUSHAKOJI, Kinhide. "Unification and External Powers: A Game Theoretical Model." In Korea University (ed.), *Report: International Conference on the Problem of Korean Unification.* Seoul: Korea University, Asiatic Research Center, 1971. A leading Japanese scholar of international relations develops a game theory model and applies it to the process of reunifying divided Korea. He assumes (1) that the two Koreas are confronted with a prisoner's dilemma, (2) that neither Korea can unify the country "under the hegemonic domination" unless supported by their respective allies, and (3) that neither can independently from their respective allies. The conclusion is rather dismal as far as the prospects for reunification are concerned. The author stresses that his model has neither normative nor predictive value but only a heuristic one.

14-211. RHEE, Yong-pil. "The Gradual Search for the Sequential Steps toward Korean Unification." *Korean Journal of International Studies* 6(3)(Summer 1975):39–48. An examination of the unification strategies of North and South Korea from the perspective of game theory. Suggests a three-step approach to unification: "(1) Each actor unilaterally takes some symbolic steps to reduce tension and hostility. (2) After a number of these, it makes some concessions, expecting the other actor to reciprocate. . . . (3) Finally, when unilateral symbolic moves and reciprocated concessions have markedly reduced tension and hostility, each or both actors suggest a further step at negotiation."

14-212. SUHRKE, Astri. "Gratuity or Tyranny: The Korean Alliances." *World Politics* 25(4)(July 1973):508–532. The author argues that what is described as "tyranny of the weak"—such as each of the two Koreas vis-à-vis their respective allies—may simultaneously be viewed as a gratuity extended by the larger power (the US and USSR, respectively) to its smaller client state. She supplements the argument by undertaking case studies which describe how both South and North Korea vis-à-vis their patron states have utilized bargaining power, obtained rewards, and even restricted unwanted interference and control from them.

The Pre-Dialogue Period: 1945–1970

14-213. CHO, Soon Sung. "The Politics of North Korea's Unification Policies, 1950-1965." *World Politics* 19(1) (January 1967):218–241. A penetrating analysis of North Korea's unification policies in the period 1950–1965. The author sees three major phases—the Korean War phase (1950–1953), the "peaceful unification" phase (1953–1960), and, finally, the post-1960 phase stressing North-South contacts leading to an all-Korean confederation. He argues that "from 1950 until 1960 the unification propaganda emanating from North Korea was influenced primarily by the internal economic problems and policies of North Korea itself, although the prevailing Communist ideological line and the world situation also affected the propaganda to a considerable extent." In the 1960–1965 period, however, Pyongyang's "unification propaganda has become more frequently influenced by changes from outside Korea, especially by the fluid political situation in Seoul and by the Communist Chinese ideology of the war of national liberation."

14-214. HAN, Pyo Wook. "The Problem of Korean Unification: A Study of the Unification Policy of the Republic of Korea, 1946–1960." PhD dissertation, University of Michigan, 1963. 241 pp. Abstracted in *DA* 26(February 1966):4776-77; UM 64-12,607. A detailed historical study by one of South Korea's top diplomats. The author served as South Korean ambassador to the UN after completion of his study.

14-215. HENDERSON, Gregory. "Korea: Can Cold War Ground Thaw?" *War/Peace Report* (August–September 1970):3–7. A noted specialist on Korea, who served as an American diplomat there, argues that Korea remains a neglected powderkeg, far more dangerous in 1970 than it was in 1950. He argues that the UN should "end its partisan position in Korea" (by disbanding UNCURK) and that South Korea should, *inter alia,* make some unilateral reduction of troops.

14-216. KIM, Joungwon Alexander. "North Korea's New Offensive." *Foreign Affairs* 48(1)(October 1969): 166–179. A discussion of North Korea's increasing reliance on violence against South Korea. The author's prediction that Kim Il Sung would attempt forcibly to unify Korea by his sixtieth birthday, however, proved to be erroneous.

14-217. KIM, Sam-kyu. "The Korea Question." *Japan Quarterly* (Tokyo), 17(1)(January–March 1970):37–44. After reviewing recent trends in North and South Korea, the author, a longtime advocate of Korean neutralization, argues that the Korean peninsula "will present the likeliest scene for an explosion once the Vietnam war is over."

14-218. KOH, B. C. "Dilemmas of Korean Reunification." *Asian Survey* 11(5)(May 1971):475–495. An overview of the question of Korean reunification in terms of its historical origins, the unification strategies of the two Koreas, and future prospects. A major dilemma facing the Korean people, according to the author, is the following: "Unless they succeed in reunifying their land, they must live under the perennial shadow of a fratricidal war. But, barring radical changes in the strategies of the two regimes, the more eagerly they pursue the goal of unity, the more irre-

concilably divergent they will become." He urges Seoul to initiate a dialogue and to take calculated risks in its relations with Pyongyang.

14-219. _____. "The Revolutionary Strategy of North Korea." *Pacific Community* (Tokyo), 2(2)(January 1971): 354–364. Analysis of Pyongyang's strategy of "triple revolutions" as articulated by Kim Il Sung. Also includes an evaluation of that strategy in terms of the actual performance record.

14-220. LEE, Chong-Sik. "Korean Partition and Reunification." *Journal of International Affairs* 18(2)(1964): 221–233. A thought-provoking discussion of the origins of Korean partition and the prospects for reunification. The author argues that a strong sense of national identity on the part of the Korean people is the major factor sustaining the goal of reunification but sees the fundamental conflict in the goals of the two Korean regimes as the major stumbling block to unity. He concludes on a generally pessimistic note, saying that "the only available alternative for the Koreans aspiring for eventual unification is to open some channels of contacts between the two parts of Korea by means of limited programs of exchange and trade."

14-221. PAIGE, Glenn D. "Korea." In Cyril E. Black and Thomas P. Thornton (eds.), *Communism and Revolution.* Princeton: Princeton University Press, 1964. An illuminating analysis of "Communist experience with political violence in Korea since 1945." Four main periods are identified: "A period of demonstrations, strikes, and terrorism, 1945–48; a period of armed guerrila war, 1948–50; a period of regular war, 1950–53; and a period of 'peaceful' psychological war combined with underground infiltration since 1953."

14-222. United States. Department of State. *The Korean Problem at the Geneva Conference, April 26–June 15, 1954.* Washington: Government Printing Office, 1954. A valuable source of basic information on the Korean phase of the Geneva Conference. In addition to a narrative account, this publication contains forty-eight documents.

The Post-Dialogue Period: 1971–1975

14-223. CHO, Soon Sung. "The Changing Pattern of Asian International Relations: Prospects for the Unification of Korea." *Journal of International Affairs* 27(2)(1973): 213–231. The process of North-South dialogue in 1972, the author argues, is a direct result of external influences including (1) the US-USSR and the US-China detente, (2) the end of the Vietnam War, and (3) the Ostpolitik of West

Germany. The opportunity for Korean unification, he contends, is affected by the changing pattern of international politics in Asia. Reunification of the divided Korea should be achieved, if at all, before the power relations in East Asia become consolidated.

14-224. CLEMENS, Walter C., Jr. "GRIT at Panmunjom: Conflict and Cooperation in a Divided Korea." *Asian Survey* 13(6)(June 1973):531–559. A thought-provoking analysis of North Korean–South Korean relations through analytic models developed for studying the US-Soviet cold war and other conflict dyads. GRIT—"graduated reciprocation in tension reduction"—is used both to describe the patterns of Seoul-Pyongyang detente and to prescribe a desirable strategy.

14-225. HARRISON, Selig. "One Korea?" *Foreign Policy* 17(Winter 1974–1975):35–67. The author, a former correspondent for the *Washington Post* who visited North Korea in 1972, gives a rather unorthodox view on the Korean situation. In his words: "Both critics and defenders of American policy toward Korea have framed the issues in a relatively short-range perspective by ignoring the changes in the Korean political environment in 1970's from the situation of 1950's." He claims that Kim Il Sung of North Korea has earned his nationalist credentials, while Park Chung Hee of South Korea is more "nativistic" than "nationalistic" and is heavily dependent on Japan. He concludes that a disengagement policy would serve American interests best in the long run.

14-226. HENDERSON, Gregory. "Korea: The Preposterous Division." *Journal of International Affairs* 27(2)(1973):204–212. The author examines the feasibility of Korean reunification in terms of internal and external factors which affect the process. He argues that homogeneity (ethnic and linguistic) and common history have a negligible impact on the prospects for Korean integration and that symbols of the Cold War played a greater role in militarizing and rigidifying the political life of the two Koreas. He advances an interesting hypothesis that homogeneity may increase rather than decrease interunit hostility once a split occurs.

14-227. KANG, Young Hoon. "The Military-Security Implications of the North-South Korean Dialogue." *Journal of Korean Affairs* 4(2)(July 1974):1–7. The author, former general in the ROK Army, probes the military-security aspects of the divergent positions taken by Seoul and Pyongyang in their dialogue. He foresees continuing difficulty in the talks as long as both sides perceive each other as a serious threat to their respective security.

14-228. KIHL, Young Whan. "Korean Response to Major Power Rapprochement." In Young C. Kim (ed.), *Major Powers and Korea*. Silver Spring, Md.: Research Institute on Korean Affairs, 1973. An analysis of the response of the two Koreas to the Sino-American detente and the normalization of Sino-Japanese relations.

14-229. _____. "Nixon Doctrine and South-North Korean Relations." *Korean Journal of International Studies* 4(3–4)(October 1973):105–120. The author examines the altered foreign policy of the US in Asia early in the 1970s and its impact on the Korean dialogue. The Nixon doctrine, designed to reduce America's security commitments in Asia, is an integral part of the US global strategy vis-à-vis the USSR and the PRC. The doctrine provided a stimulus for the subsequent changes in the pattern of power relations in Asia, including the Sino-American, Sino-Japanese, and North-South Korean relations. Under the circumstances, both Seoul and Pyongyang must exercise utmost discretion on matters of unifying the divided Korea and rely on self-restraint. The author argues that detente, not deterrence, seems the only credible and rational posture the two Koreas may take toward each other.

14-230. KIM, Hak-joon. "An Analysis of the Current Issues in the North-South Dialogue: The South Korean Perspective." *Korean Journal of International Studies* 6(2)(Spring 1975):17–38. A detailed review of the major issues in the Korean dialogue. Concludes that the positions of the two sides are irreconcilable.

14-231. KIM, Sam Kyu. "Peaceful Unification of Korea." *Japan Quarterly* (Tokyo), 19(4)(October–December 1972):415–421. A review of the factors surrounding the North-South Joint communiqué of 4 July 1972 and an exposition of his long-standing proposal for neutralization of Korea.

14-232. KIM, Young C. "North Korea in 1974." *Asian Survey* 15(1)(January 1975):43–52. A survey of major developments in North Korea in 1974. More than half the article deals with foreign policy and North-South relations.

14-233. _____. "North Korea's Reunification Policy: A Magnificent Obsession?" *Journal of Korean Affairs* 3(4)(January 1974):15–24. Relying primarily on "interviews the author held with officials and scholars during his visit to North Korea in the Summer of 1973," this article examines North Korean perceptions of the reunification problem and strategies and tactics for dealing with it. "After two weeks of intense discussion with North Korean leaders in Pyongyang," he writes, "I came away immensely impressed with the seriousness and sense of urgency evoked in the North by the issue of reunification of Korea."

14-234. KOH, B. C. "Convergence and Conflict in the Two Koreas." *Current History* (November 1973):205–208. The author asserts that the convergence of the two Koreas at the end of 1972, in terms of political structure and even of the ideology of self-reliance, remains superficial. The North-South dialogue has been used, he argues, "to legitimize the extension *ad infinitum* of the tenure and powers" of the top leaders on both sides.

14-235. _____. "Korea's Policy Options in the New Era." *Korean Journal of International Studies* 3(3-4)(October 1972):117-133. The author examines the emerging detente among major powers surrounding the Korean peninsula and its implications for Korea. He outlines and advocates a set of foreign and domestic policy options for South Korea, including a more flexible posture toward Moscow and Peking, cessation of "protest diplomacy" vis-à-vis Japan, stepped-up contacts with North Korea, and liberalization of political controls at home. The article was written before the publication of the 4 July 1972 joint communiqué.

14-236. _____. "North Korea: A Breakthrough in the Quest for Unity." *Asian Survey* 13(1)(January 1973):83-93. Presents North Korean perspectives on the joint North-South Korean communiqué of 4 July 1972. Also discusses Pyongyang's foreign relations in 1972.

14-237. _____. "North Korea: Old Goals and New Realities." *Asian Survey* 14(1)(January 1974):36-42. The bulk of the article deals with the evolution of the North-South dialogue and North Korea's diplomatic gains in 1973.

14-238. LEE, Chae-Jin. "South Korea: The Politics of Domestic-Foreign Linkage." *Asian Survey* 13(1)(January 1973):94-101. Discusses Seoul's perceptions of the joint North-South communiqué of 4 July 1972 and sees Seoul's new approach to Pyongyang as a symptom of its accommodation to external forces.

14-239. LEE, Chong-Sik. "Impact of the Sino-American Detente on Korea." In Gene T. Hsiao (ed.), *Sino-American Detente and Its Policy Implications*. New York: Praeger, 1974. An incisive analysis of the impact of detente on the two Koreas. The bulk of the paper deals with the Seoul-Pyongyang dialogue, its background, problems, and prospects. The author argues that the major stumbling block in the dialogue is the failure of both sides to come to grips with reality. Recognition of the existence of two states in one nation and efforts to promote a peaceful coexistence, he asserts, would be more beneficial to the cause of reunification than the largely rhetorical pursuit of reunification as an immediate goal.

14-240. "The North and South Korean Accord." *Journal of Korean Affairs* 2(2)(July 1972):35-40. A brief discussion of the historic North-South joint communiqué of 4 July 1972. The full text of the communiqué and related materials are found in the same issue of the journal.

14-241. SHAPLEN, Robert. "New Chapters in Korea, I and II." *New Yorker* (25 November 1972):116-147 and (2 December 1972):128-155. An excellent discussion of the Seoul-Pyongyang dialogue by a veteran American journalist. The two-part article is based on the author's interviews with numerous Korean officials, newsmen, and scholars as well as American diplomats. The author provides a historical perspective on the Korean situation as well.

CHAPTER 15
North Korea

Dae-Sook Suh

INTRODUCTION

THE TERM *North Korea* is more a geographic designation than an academic category. As a consequence of the partition of the Korean peninsula and the subsequent development of a socialist society in the North, however, the study of North Korea has acquired a distinct identity of its own as a subfield of Korean studies. As such, it should be treated in sections similar to those appearing elsewhere in this guide, such as history, politics, languages, literature, and other areas of academic concentration. There are practical reasons, however, why such a treatment of North Korea is not possible at this time.

A major reason is the scarcity of materials in the West. Except for highly propagandistic publications and a few standard works on the North Korean political system and the works of its leader, general research materials emanating from the North are indeed scarce.

Another reason is the formidable linguistic background required for studying the North—one must have at least a command of English and Korean and preferably a reading knowledge of Japanese, Russian, and Chinese. The North Korean tradition itself encompasses Japanese domination, Russian liberation, and the Chinese participation in the Korean War. Moreover, because of their pivotal geographical location, Koreans have long valued mastery of the languages of their powerful neighbors.

Perhaps the most important reason is the nature of the communist regime itself. The North Koreans publish little, and the majority of the material published is designed to be propaganda more than academic exposition. Publications that might help explain their system are not publicly available even in North Korea; still fewer materials filter through to the West. Except for its dealings with other communist countries, the North has been isolated from the international community, and most of the basic materials are circulated only to party members or bureaucrats to strengthen their understanding of their system.

This short bibliographic guide is a preliminary survey to introduce the North and does not provide comprehensive coverage of materials. It is a descriptive guide to the North Korean communist system. Excluded are many North Korean studies on subjects not directly related to explaining the system (for example, the North Korean interpretation of Korean history or anthropology). Except for the first two sections dealing with reference works and periodicals, the bulk of the materials discussed here deal with the communist order and aspects of the North Korean communist system. The emphasis is on general works describing the North, the works of their leader Kim Il Sung, the all-powerful party, and the state system, including foreign relations and the economic system. Individual articles appearing in North Korean journals are not listed separately except to introduce the journals. Even the articles appearing in

English in Western journals are not listed individually except for a few representative ones.

This bibliographic guide on North Korea contains mostly books and book-length monographs in Western languages. A few non-Western materials that are important to the study of the North are mentioned in the text for researchers who can make use of them, but they are omitted from the bibliography. There is a general lack of materials on humanistic studies, as opposed to social studies, and this guide reflects the imbalance. One note of caution in reading North Korean materials: One must simply endure what seems to be a repetitious and endlessly propagandistic style of writing, for in the prolixity of speeches and essays there are things to be learned and discerned about the North.

BIBLIOGRAPHY AND REFERENCE MATERIALS
BIBLIOGRAPHY

There are only a few bibliographies of North Korean sources, and even those few that have appeared recently are mostly inadequate. Perhaps the only one in English devoted to an examination of the bibliographic materials on the North is the bibliographic survey on North Korea made by the Department of the Army in 1971 (15-007). The materials presented are annotated, but the work falls short of the coverage necessary to make it a comprehensive bibliography. More detailed in its treatment, but confined to two subjects, is the study made by three scholars at Peabody College who produced a partially annotated bibliography on North Korean education and society in 1972 (15-002). There is also a good list of North Korean periodicals compiled by K. P. Yang (15-009). This unpublished list shows the American holdings of North Korean periodicals and newspapers up to 1970. There is also a short annotated listing by C. S. Lee of some 120 items on North Korea as part of a bibliographic survey of world communism.

More important than these are those bibliographies attached to major studies of communism and the communist movement in Korea. There are impressive bibliographic sections in R. A. Scalapino and C. S. Lee's study on communism in Korea (15-056) and other studies such as Vreeland's area handbook (15-093), B. C. Koh's study on foreign policy (15-171), J. S. Chung's study on economy (15-187), and D. S. Suh's studies on

the communist movement and documents (15-059, 016).

There are several bibliographies of Russian studies on Korea, and there are numerous listings of items relating to North Korea. The official Russian version is by I. S. Kazakevich, who reviewed fifty years of Soviet studies on Korea (15-004). The first attempt by an American group was the Russian supplement to the Korean studies guide compiled by R. L. Backus (15-001). The latest is the 1973 publication by G. Ginsburgs on Soviet works on Korea (15-003) covering the period from 1945 to 1970.

REFERENCE

The most comprehensive work on North Korea is the yearbook published in Korean by the Central News Agency of North Korea: *Korean Central Yearbook (Chosŏn chungang yŏn'gam).* This annual publication was begun in 1949 and has been published continuously since that year. Except for an interruption during and after the Korean War, this publication has been consistent in providing basic reference materials each year. There is no yearbook for 1953, and there are three combined issues—for the years 1951–1952 (published in 1953), 1954–1955, and 1966–1967. The Joint Publication Research Service (JPRS) began to translate portions or entire yearbooks beginning with the 1958 issue, and the citations for the JPRS numbers are listed for all issues translated (15-017).

In addition, the Joint Publications Research Service has translated many North Korean materials under various titles, such as "Economic and Statistical Information on North Korea" and "Political and Sociological Information on North Korea." These are translations from selected materials appearing in North Korean newspapers and journals that the JPRS has consolidated and published since 1966 under the title of *Translations on North Korea* (15-018).

The best reference for a decade after the liberation is a chronicle of daily events compiled in a form of ten-year diary entitled *Haebang simnyŏnji* (available only in Korean). North Korean scholars have distorted many events and dates for political purposes to justify their position today. For the years 1964 to 1968, there is a three-volume yearbook, *One Korea Yearbook (Tōitsu chōsen nenkan),* published in Japanese by a Korean newspaper company in Japan, but the information on North Korea compiled in these volumes is basically from the North Korean yearbooks.

There are good reference books in Korean published in the South—*Pukhan ch'onggam* [General yearbook of North Korea] was published in 1968 and updated in 1974 and published as *Pukhan chŏnsŏ* [Compendium of North Korea]. There are also a few informative handbooks in Japanese published by a Japanese newspaper firm in 1973, *Chōsen yōran,* covering both the North and the South. Reference books in English are published only in the North. These include such books as *Facts about Korea* (15-069) and the *Democratic People's Republic of Korea, 1948-1958* (15-011), but these works were published in the late fifties and early sixties. The latest, *Korean Review,* was published in 1974. There are brief sections on North Korea in various reference books, encyclopedias, and information books on Communist Party organizations that give basic information on the North, but these are, in general, inadequate for scholarly inquiry.

There is no biographical dictionary of North Korean leaders available in English except a rough translation by the JPRS of a short article which appeared in the popular South Korean magazine *Sedae* [Generation], but the information in it is difficult to verify and mostly unreliable (15-019). This is due in part to the unavailability of information and in part to the secretive nature of the communist leaders concerning their past. There are several unofficial and unpublished files on the leaders by both South Korean and United States intelligence agencies, but these are not widely available for public use. There are several informative biographical dictionaries on North Korean leaders in Japanese; one was compiled by Kasumigaseki-kai in 1962 and another by Sekai seikei chōsakai in 1968.

Topical reference works are published mostly in Korean by both North and South Koreans but are only occasionally translated into English. A pamphlet on North Korean economic statistics from 1946 to 1963, for example, was translated and published in Chinese, Japanese, and English in 1964 (15-013). Important reference works—such as the dictionaries of historical, political, and philosophical terms, an index to Kim Il Sung's writings, and a dictionary of North Korea—are available in Korean only.

Most of the documentary collections of any import by the North are, in general, not available. A few reports by Kim Il Sung at the regularly scheduled party congresses are published separately in pamphlet form, but all are reproduced in his selected works. Here again most documentary collections are available in Korean compiled by researchers in South Korea on various topics including laws, decrees, and policies, but none are translated into English. Documents by communist leaders other than Kim Il Sung are rare. Despite North Korea's suppression, there is, for example, the manifesto of the Workers' Party of South Korea (15-015) by Pak Hŏn-yŏng in *For a Lasting Peace, for a People's Democracy,* an organ of the Cominform. For the study of Korean communism prior to the establishment of the North Korean government, there is a collection of documents translated into English and compiled with commentary (15-016).

PERIODICALS AND NEWSPAPERS

There are numerous academic journals and interdisciplinary periodicals in the United States that carry one or two articles relating to the affairs of North Korea. These are well known to students in the United States, but they have carried so few articles over the years that it is not worthwhile to list them separately here. A few articles on the North, mostly in the social sciences, have appeared in *Asian Survey, Journal of Asian Studies, Pacific Affairs, World Politics, Atlas,* and similar journals published in the United States. There is no journal in the United States devoted solely to the affairs of North Korea. *The Journal of Korean Affairs* (15-024), which ceased publication in 1976, frequently carried articles relating to North Korea.

There are only two journals outside Korea that are devoted to North Korean affairs. One, *North Korea Quarterly* (15-034), is published in English by the Institute of Asian Affairs in Hamburg. Its first issue appeared in the third quarter of 1974. This journal, edited by M. Y. Cho, is for the most part a chronicle of events and not a regular academic journal. Another journal is published in Japanese by former Japanese ambassador to South Korea M. Kanayama: *Kita Chōsen kenkyū* [North Korean research]. This monthly began in June 1974.

In general, the most comprehensive journals that treat various segments of the North Korean scene are published by the North Koreans—most of them in Korean but a few in English as well as other languages. The most widely available ones are the monthly news magazine *Korea Today* (15-028) and a pictorial entitled *Democratic People's Republic of Korea* (15-021). There are other less-known journals in English on foreign trade (15-023), on youth and students (15-031), and on nature (15-029).

The serious journals on various academic endeavors are all published in Korean: the *Bulletin of the Academy of Sciences [Kwahagwŏn t'ongbo],* journals on history *[Yŏksa kwahak],* on economics *[Kyŏngje yŏn'gu],* on archaeology and ethnology *[Kogo minsok],* on linguistics *[Ŏmun yŏn'gu],* on education *[Inmin kyoyuk, Kodŭng kyoyuk],* and on literature *[Chosŏn munhak].* Selected items from serious political journals, such as the party organ *Kŭlloja* [Worker], are translated into English by the JPRS.

Certain journals and magazines in the South examine affairs in the North. The *East Asian Review* (15-022) perhaps best represents the South Korean treatment of the North. This quarterly, published by the Institute for East Asian Studies, frequently carries critical articles on the development of the North. A few journals support the North and condemn the South. One of them, *Korea Focus* (15-026), is published in the United States by the American-Korean Friendship and Information Center of New York. More sophisticated is the journal published in Japan by the Korean Affairs Research Institute of Tokyo, but it is available only in Japanese.

Like those of the United States, journals in the Soviet Union carry articles on the North, but so infrequently that none can be said to deal with the affairs of the North. There are five journals in which one can find materials on not only the communist North but also communism in Korea: *Tikhii Okean* [The Pacific] (15-041), *Revolyutsionny vostok* [Revolutionary East] (15-039), *Kommunist* (15-025), *Sovremennyi vostok* [Contemporary East] (15-040), and *Voprosy istorii* [Problems of history] (15-042). As can be expected, most of the materials appearing in these journals from the twenties up to the mid-sixties are articles of encouragement for the cause of communism in Korea. More analytical and sophisticated studies of the North do not appear until the late 1950s.

North Korean newspapers are few, even if one were to include all municipal and provincial papers. Each municipality, for example Kaesŏng, and each province has its own paper. The availability of these local papers in countries outside the North is extremely limited. The best-known newspapers of the North are *Nodong sinmun,* the organ of the party, and *Minju chosŏn,* the organ of the state. These two papers are similar in content to *Pravda* and *Izvestia* of the Soviet Union. Selected articles from these papers are translated into English by the JPRS in their translation series. The only English-language newspaper is the *Pyongyang Times* (15-038). The most informative on the daily affairs of Pyongyang is the Korean paper *Pyongyang sinmun.* Glimpses of the life-style of the people of the North Korean capital can be discerned by careful and continuous reading of this paper.

Both North and South Korean authorities have launched a campaign to inform the world on each other in the form of a newsletter. Although they are propagandistic in nature they are also informative in the treatment of various events. The South Koreans publish *North Korea Newsletter* (15-033); the North Koreans have published what is known as *Chollima Korea* (15-020). From the Office of Permanent Observers to the United Nations in New York, North Korea issues periodic news releases in English (15-037).

KOREAN COMMUNISM
THE MOVEMENT

For anyone who undertakes to examine the North Korean communist system, it is wise to review the development of the communist movement prior to the division of Korea and the establishment of a separate government in the North. Since the movement began during the Japanese occupation of Korea, the communists struggled to bring about not only a haven for the proletariat but also independence and the expulsion of the Japanese imperialists from Korea. It was an underground movement and records are scarce. As a result of the Japanese defeat in World War II the records of the police and the courts that tried and convicted the communists are more abundantly available. There are several studies in English that analyze and document the communist heritage in Korea. Some of the outstanding ones are pt. 1 of the work by R. A. Scalapino and C. S. Lee in 1974 (15-056) and D. S. Suh's work on the movement in 1967 (15-059). There is a five-volume study in Korean of the history of the Korean communist movement by J. Y. Kim and C. S. Kim of the Asiatic Research Center of Korean University.

The North Korean version of the development of the communist movement is, of course, quite different from Western accounts. North Korean scholars have rewritten history by putting their leader, Kim Il Sung, in the central role leading the victorious communist revolution. Most of these accounts are written by those, such as Yim Ch'un-ch'u, who serve Kim in the North today. But these are in sharp contrast to articles on Korean communist activities that appeared in the 1930s, for example, in *Inprecorr,* the organ of the Communist International. There is a Russian translation of a North Korean account, translated by M. N. Pak and edited by V. V. Lezin, of the Korean people's struggle for liberation (15-051).

For the period from 1918 to 1945, there is an excellent study in Russian by F. I. Shabshina (15-057). For the armed struggle against the Japanese, Mazurov wrote an account covering the period of the 1930s (15-052). A communist analysis of the role played by the Korean bourgeois in the movement has been written by Shipaev (15-058).

There are only a few random accounts of communist activities, such as the story narrated by Kim San and written by Nym Wales (15-048), and C. S. Lee's study of the Korean communists in Yenan (15-050). More numerous are the North Korean accounts of the activities of Kim Il Sung and his partisans in Manchuria during the late 1930s. There is a twelve-volume account of reminiscences by former partisans in Manchuria and four volumes of essays by former participants in the guerrilla struggle. Some of these accounts have been translated into English and have appeared in the English journal *Korea Today.* The North Korean accounts grossly exaggerate partisan activities. More North Korean accounts of Kim Il Sung's partisan activities are discussed in the following section on biographical accounts of Kim.

Secret Japanese accounts of communist activities in Manchuria in the archives of the army, navy, justice, and foreign ministries have been thoroughly scrutinized in studies by Scalapino and Lee, Kim and Kim, and Suh.

THE DEVELOPMENT IN THE NORTH

An attempt to cover comprehensively the communist system of the North is made by Scalapino and Lee (15-056). This study contains an impressive analysis of the North, and the compiled information covers approximately three decades of development in the North since the division. Less impressive attempts have been made by others—for example, the first decade after the liberation was studied by S. Tsuboe in Japanese, and the first fifteen-year history was written by C. S. Kim in Korean and later translated into English by the JPRS (15-073). The first twenty years of communist rule in the North were recorded in the South (15-086), and a thirty-year history of the North has also been published in Korean in the South, but the South Korean accounts tend to be heavily biased.

There are works in English that give factual information and some analysis of the North. These include the brief introductory account by G. D. Paige (15-084); articles in a volume edited by R. A. Scalapino (15-087); Vreeland and Shinn's area handbook, first published in 1964, updated in 1969, and revised in 1976 (15-093); and the recent accounts by I. J. Kim (15-077) and K. W. Nam (15-081). The official North Korean version of their development is hopelessly outdated; for example, their English version of facts about the North (15-069) and a book entitled *Democratic People's Republic of Korea* (15-067) were published in the late 1950s and early 1960s.

There are a few good analyses of certain aspects of communism in the North. For the period immediately after the liberation of Korea, F. I. Shabshina has made a good study in Russian (15-088). An account of the Russian takeover of the North was published by the United States government (15-091). A comparative analysis of the Russian sovietization of the North appears in D. S. Suh's account in *The Anatomy of Communist Takeovers* (15-089). On the evaluation of the character of the North Korean regime, there are two good articles by G. D. Paige (15-083 and 15-085) and another by C. S. Lee (15-080).

International Publishers have brought out an English version of B. S. Kim's work in Japanese, which reflects the position of North Korea in Japan (15-072). There are several works of journalistic description and analysis of the North—for example, the book by Wilfred Burchett (15-063). The North is fairly isolated, and most of the travel accounts are biased. Naturally most of them tend to be laudatory; therefore, these journalistic accounts should be used, if they are to be used at all, with care. More impressive than these are the Russian publications such as the works of G. F. Kim (15-074 and 15-075), G. D. Tyagai (15-090), and the edited work by N. K. Vaintsvaig and V. V. Lezin (15-092). Russian scholars seem to have turned their attention away from Korea, however, beginning in the early 1960s, and there is no tangible evidence of solid study of the problems of the North in the late sixties or early seventies. Nevertheless, there is an excellent theoretical study, published in 1967, of the proletarian internationalism and revolution in the East by G. F. Kim and F. I. Shabshina (15-076).

KIM IL SUNG
WORKS BY KIM

It is common to find in materials emanating from the communist countries excessive references to the writings of a major thinker or revolutionary. This tendency can be easily seen in the Russian materials attributing great credit to Marx and Lenin or in the Chinese writings quoting from the thoughts of Mao Tse-tung. In this practice, North Korea is no exception. Indeed, the recent trend in the North is to exceed the practice of other communist countries by quoting more and more of Kim Il Sung's writings, speeches, interviews, and directives. Not only simple references to Kim's words but also long verbatim quotations appear in almost every piece of writing published in the North in recent years. It seems reasonable to conjecture that there are fewer references to Marx or Lenin in North Korean writings than there are in Chinese Communist writings. The North Koreans seem to have equaled, if not excelled, the Chinese in quoting their leader. This practice and the boundless adulation of Kim by the people make it important to scrutinize and document the writings of Kim.

The present official version of Kim Il Sung's selected works is in six volumes. The work contains writings, speeches, directives, and other materials numbering 129 items covering the period from 13 October 1945 to 31 August 1973. This work is available in English (15-099)

and other languages in addition to the original Korean. The English version of the sixth volume, published in 1975, excluded two items from the original version in Korean. The publication of Kim's work will no doubt continue in several more volumes as time passes.

This official version is the third revised edition of his selected works to be published by the North. The first edition of the selected works of Kim appeared in four volumes in 1953–1954 with 134 items covering the period from 7 December 1945 to 11 May 1953. There is a wealth of material here that was not included in subsequent editions; about half the materials in the first edition were thus discarded. However, this first edition is not readily available. A Japanese translation of Kim's writings appeared in 1952 with thirty-four items covering the period from 1 March 1946 to 15 August 1952. This Japanese version is not a translation of the entire first edition of the selected works of Kim but a separate collection of his works in Japanese.

The second edition of the selected works of Kim appeared in 1960–1964 in six volumes; the first three volumes cover the selections from the first edition and the last three add more material. This edition, with some 154 items, covers the period from 13 October 1945 to 4 December 1959. Only 53 of the 154 items were carried over to the third and current edition. It is interesting to study the items excluded from the present edition. Volume 3 of the 1960–1964 (or second) edition is generally not available and contains several items of sharp criticism of party leaders by Kim during the latter part of the Korean War. Thirty-seven items were selected from the second edition, and their English translations, in two volumes, appeared in 1965 (15-098). The Russian edition (15-100) contains only twenty-four items covering the period from 5 August 1953 to 11 September 1961. The Chinese translation of the third edition is available, and there is a verbatim translation of the entire second edition. The relatively few items from the first two editions are found in the first two volumes of the third edition.

Kim's first speech in the North was delivered on 13 October 1945 and is recorded correctly in various editions of his selected works. In recent years, however, North Korean historians have introduced many speeches and writings of Kim prior to this date. The

North Koreans trace the founding congress of the Workers' Party of Korea to 10 October 1945, for example, and a speech given by Kim on this date appeared in 1975 (15-104). There are others extending to as early as 20 May 1931, when Kim was merely nineteen years of age (15-102). Several more—allegedly dated 1931 (15-106), 1937 (15-110), and 1943 (15-101)—appeared in the early 1970s for the first time. Their authenticity is questionable, to say the least, but it is probable that more materials of this nature will appear in the future.

There are several books, both in English and Korean, that collect different portions of Kim's writings. Some are indiscriminate collections of what are considered important items (such as 15-097 and 15-109); others are selected on a topical basis. There are several volumes of topical collections—on the South Korean revolution and unification, on the problems of economic management, on ideology, on the Korean War, on the military—but these are available only in Korean. There are single-volume English editions of the major reports of Kim such as the theses on socialist rural questions and on *chuch'e*. Many pamphlets of his speeches, reports, interviews, and other items are available in English, but they are not listed separately because almost all of them are collected in his selected works. The Social Science Institute of the Academy of Sciences published in 1970, in commemoration of the fifth party congress, an index of the works of Kim which is extremely useful in research. This index, available only in Korean, covers material in his selected works and some thirty-five other volumes, some of which are unavailable in the United States.

WORKS ON KIM

Much like Kim's own writings, biographical accounts of him have undergone several versions. The first to appear officially was on 10 April 1952 in a special issue of *Nodong sinmun;* the most comprehensive version is the account of Baik Bong (Paek Pong), reportedly a Korean resident in Japan, available in English (15-112). There are other short biographies of Kim published by the party (15-119 and 15-120). There are also studies on him in several volumes praising his benevolence in the North. In general, these accounts are in Korean and relate the stories on Kim and his work.

In contrast to these, there are many other versions of Kim's biography, some portraying him as a complete fake or a despicable puppet put up by the Russians. These are primarily from South Korea. Perhaps more objective are the English-language accounts by C. S. Lee (15-121 and 15-056) and D. S. Suh (15-059).

There are a number of studies on Kim's ideology and politics, mostly by Japanese and North Koreans. More important are the recent publications in the North on his ideology.

Kim's writings and biographical accounts of him have undergone considerable changes during the past thirty years of his reign in the North. No doubt, there will be more changes and more volumes of his teachings and writings, since the current accounts cover only up to 1973. The editions that were published during or shortly after the period under examination are especially significant. To study the writings and ideology of Kim up to the end of the Korean War, for example, it is more important to use the first edition (1953–1954) than the current version of his selected works; to study the decade from the early 1950s to the early 1960s, it is important to examine the second edition (1960–1964). A fascinating subject for research is the trend of revision and the contents of the discarded materials.

Excluded from the following bibliography are accounts of Kim's family, his father, mother, brothers, his first wife, the present wife, and his son, all of whom figure prominently in North Korean politics.

THE WORKERS' PARTY OF KOREA

The pervasive power of the Workers' Party of Korea is second only to that of Kim's personal leadership. The party was organized in 1946 as two separate parties: the Workers' Party of North Korea in August 1946 in Pyongyang and the Workers' Party of South Korea in November 1946 in Seoul. These two parties were united on 13 June 1949 to become the Workers' Party of Korea. However, the present official version of North Korean history claims that the party was founded on 10 October 1945, and that date is commemorated as the founding day of the party. The first meeting of the communists in the North was held on this date after the liberation, but the meeting was held under the auspices of the North Korean Branch Bureau of the Korean Communist Party, which was headquartered in Seoul. Kim Il Sung and his partisans played only a minor role, if any, in the meeting. It was not until well into the 1960s that the party backdated its founding.

The party has held five congresses and two conferences during the past thirty years. Except for the first two congresses, which were held in August 1946 and March 1948, the most accurate records of the party congresses are the daily reports made in *Nodong sinmun* at the time of each congress. The newspaper is not available for the period of the first two congresses, but a pamphlet published shortly after the first congress recorded its proceedings and major speeches delivered there. The minutes of the second congress were also published shortly after the congress. These two documents are indispensable in the study of the party, but they are available only in Korean. In sharp contrast to present North Korean accounts of the congresses, they record the events and speeches of the time. Records and documents of the subsequent third congress in April 1956 (15-135), the fourth congress in September 1961 (15-127), and the fifth congress in November 1970 are readily available in many languages, including English and the original Korean. Two party conferences were held, one in March 1958 and another in October 1966. A book in Chinese was published in Peking covering the first party conference, and several English versions are available for the second (15-136).

As for the official history of the party, the best ones are those written by the party. There is a massive study, in thirty-seven volumes, of the policies of the Workers' Party of Korea, *Chosŏn nodongdang chŏngch'aeksa* [History of the policies of the Workers' Party of Korea], but this study is not available in the United States in any language. Abridged portions of this study began to appear in 1973; for example, the book on the party's revolutionary experiences was published in two volumes. There are a widely circulated text on the history of the party and a three-volume narrative of some of the party's achievements. The bylaws of the party, all three amended versions, are available, and a commentary which explains the bylaws has been published in Korean.

There are many articles and essays by many individuals in *Kŭlloja* [Worker], the official party organ, on various aspects of the party. Recent important ones are translated into English by the JPRS. A journal exclusively devoted to the affairs of the party for party cadres was entitled *Tang kanbu* [Party cadre], later changed to *Tang kanbu ege chunŭn ch'amgo charyo* [Reference materials for party cadres]. There are only a few monographs on the party written by individual scholars in the North, however. Many works published by the party—such as the one on party policy or the one on strengthening the party—do not identify any individual author.

Articles and essays on all aspects of the party written by Kim Il Sung are found abundantly in his selected works and are not repeated here.

Some aspects of the party have been treated in short articles by scholars in the United States. Representative of these are works by B. C. Koh on the party and detente (15-133), Lee and Oh on the Russian faction (15-134), J. S. Sohn on party control of the military (15-138), and D. S. Suh on the elite group (15-141).

THE STATE SYSTEM

Materials relating to three broad topics are discussed in this section: the political system (including the legal system), the foreign relations of the North (including its relation with the South), and the economic system. For those who must rely only on English-language materials, it is useful to research the journals cited here, because only representative articles are listed.

THE POLITICAL PROCESS

The best one-volume study of the North Korean state system is the one published in 1963 by the Academy of Sciences of the North on their state and social system. This is the standard work on the subject, but it is available only in Korean and Japanese. That state system underwent a change with the amendment of the constitution in 1972 at the fifth Supreme People's Assembly, but there is as yet no study of comparable importance covering these recent changes. Many essays on the political process of the state can be found in the official government journals, as well as in the selected works of Kim Il Sung. Here again, there are only a few monographs of any import by individual writers. There are several collections of essays, some of which were written for academic degrees at an institution of higher learning or for commemoration of certain anniversaries—for example, Kim Il Sung's birthday.

In an effort to ascertain the political process of the North, scholars in the South have published a few important works including those by H. M. Yang and T. U. Pak and two 1972 publications on the structure and process of the government by the Asiatic Research Center of Korea University. Most of the serious work on the North is in Korean, however.

The text of the new constitution of the North adopted in 1972 is available in English in *Korea Today* (15-159). The text of the first constitution is available in many languages. There is an informative book recently published in English on the analysis of the socialist constitution of the North (15-154). The laws passed by the Supreme People's Assembly are published, but it is not easy to acquire this material. There are only a few published collections of the laws of the Democratic People's Republic of Korea for example, and the documents of the first Supreme People's Assembly.

A study on the legal structure of the North has been published in Korean by the Asiatic Research Center of Korea University in Seoul, and P. C. Hahm has written a good article on the ideology and the system of criminal law in North Korea (15-146). Russian and Chinese influences on the legal system of the North are the subject of an unpublished doctoral dissertation by K. C. Kang (15-148).

FOREIGN POLICY

Even with the recent diplomatic offensive by the North, there are few materials published in the North examining its foreign policy. North Korean publications are generally limited to the official proclamations and speeches of Kim Il Sung, which can be found in his selected works. Collections of materials relating to international affairs of the North appear from time to time, but these have limited usage. The scrutiny of Kim's selected work is more productive. Another type of publication is the books and pamphlets that report and document the official friendship missions and state visits by government officials of the North. There are also many pamphlets published by the bilateral friendship associations between North Korea and foreign

countries (most often with China and the Soviet Union) that emphasize mutual friendship.

The conduct of North Korean foreign policy is a subject studied more by Westerners than by the North Koreans. There is a one-volume study by B. C. Koh (15-171) which examines North Korean relations with other countries to the end of the 1960s. One may also be interested in examining the unpublished doctoral dissertation by B. Min on a decade of North Korean foreign policy from 1953 (15-176). North Korean policies in the Sino-Soviet dispute have been the subject of many articles. Among these articles, one by J. Bradbury in 1961 (15-160), two articles by B. C. Koh in *Pacific Affairs* (15-172) and *Western Political Quarterly* (15-173), one by J. C. Kun in *China Quarterly* (15-175), and one on Sino–North Korean relations by R. U. T. Kim (15-170) are representative. The North Korean attitude in the dispute is also the subject of an unpublished doctoral dissertation by C. O. Chung (15-163).

Going back to an earlier period, the strained alliance between Peking, Pyongyang, and Moscow in the Korean War is the topic of a study by R. R. Simmons (15-183). As for the war itself, the North Koreans have consistently maintained that it was a case of aggression by the United States in collusion with the South from which the North emerged victorious after three years of the war of national liberation. There are many articles and books in the West to refute this claim. The Western materials on the Korean War are treated elsewhere in this guide and thus omitted here. (See Chapter 14: 14-038 through 14-066.) The North Koreans have written many articles in support of their claim, but the official account is a book written on the war by Kim Il Sung in Korean. There is also an official history of the war by the North in English entitled *History of the Just Fatherland Liberation War of the Korean People* (15-168). Many North Korean publications contain allegations that the United States started the war; what they consider the correct facts of the war are illustrated in an official account (15-164).

There are plenty of Korean materials describing the North Korean view of the South and the unification policy directed toward the South. Many of the materials describing the South are so far removed from the realities known to the West, however, that their attempt to denigrate the South is lost amid the obvious propaganda. The standard work on North Korea's unification policy is the book by Kim Il Sung on the South Korean revolution and the unification of Korea, but this book is available only in Korean. In English, there is a one-volume collection of materials relating to policies for the unification of Korea (15-165). Many articles on unification, particularly in recent years, that have appeared in North Korean journals are not listed here, but there is a good discussion of North Korea's unification policies from 1950 to 1965 by S. S. Cho in *World Politics* (15-162).

THE ECONOMIC SYSTEM

There are more materials available on the North Korean economy than, for example, on their foreign policy. This abundance is due in part to what they regard as the successes in the industrial and agrarian sectors of their economy. Much of the material relates to the achievements resulting from the economic plans. On the other hand, it is difficult to obtain the hard facts and figures which economists need for rigorous analysis.

In the face of these difficulties, J. S. Chung analyzes the structure and development of the economy in the North and discusses the problems of studying that economy (15-187). Aside from Kim Il Sung's writings on the economic development of the North, there is a good study in Korean made by C. S. Cho on the North's economic system. There are several other North Korean accounts on the development of the economy, and there are also two studies on economic structure and development by scholars in the South under the auspices of the Asiatic Research Center, but all are available only in Korean.

Several writers have published monographs on the economic policies of the party or the government of the North which are informative and helpful in understanding economic plans and campaigns. There is, of course, the official publication by the Academy of Sciences on basic economic policy; and one journal, *Kyŏngje yŏn'gu,* is devoted solely to the economy. Portions of these are translated into English and appear frequently in translation series of the JPRS.

In the agrarian sector, there are many materials published by the North, some in English, that boast of the agrarian reform (15-190) or the successful completion of agricultural cooperativization (15-185). The North Koreans have produced two important books on their accomplishments in agriculture: one in 1971 and another in 1974. These books are not directly authored by their leader, Kim Il Sung, but they discuss the creative application of Kim's views and policies. For an analysis comparing the North Korean land reforms and collectivization with those of the Chinese and Russians, see J. M. Ha's unpublished doctoral dissertation on the subject (15-189).

Other writings include a collection of essays on economy, a topical treatment of a specific campaign or movement, and a theoretical explanation of self-reliance in economic endeavors and the building of an independent economy. However, in all these materials one finds few reliable empirical data that are required to analyze the North Korean economy. Most of the studies done in Russia on the North Korean economy are in the form of short articles and monographs. Book-length studies have appeared in general translations of North Korean publications. In addition to the statistics book already cited (15-013), important statistical information and indicators of the North Korean economy are translated into English by the JPRS. Each scholar must go through the translation series on North Korea to find the relevant information.

BIBLIOGRAPHY

BIBLIOGRAPHY AND REFERENCE MATERIALS
Bibliography

15-001. BACKUS, Robert L. *Russian Supplement to the Korean Studies Guide.* Berkeley: Institute of International Studies, University of California, 1958.

15-002. FRASER, Stewart E., Hyung-chan KIM, and Sun Ho KIM. *North Korean Education and Society: A Selected and Partially Annotated Bibliography Pertaining to the Democratic People's Republic of Korea.* London: University of London Institute of Education, 1972.

15-003. GINSBURGS, George. *Soviet Works on Korea, 1945–70.* Los Angeles: University of Southern California Press, 1973.

15-004. KAZAKEVICH, I. S. *Fifty Years of Soviet Oriental*

Studies: Korean Studies. Moscow: Nauka Publishing House, 1968.

15-005. KYRIAK, Theodore E. (comp.). *North Korea, 1957–1961: A Bibliography and Guide to Contents of a Collection of United States Joint Publications Research Service Translations on Microfilm.* Annapolis: Research and Microfilm Publications, n.d. 29 pp.

15-006. LEE, Chong-Sik (ed.). "Korea and the Korean War." In Thomas T. Hammond (ed.), *Soviet Foreign Relations and World Communism.* Princeton: Princeton University Press, 1965.

15-007. United States. Department of the Army. *Communist North Korea: A Bibliographical Survey.* DA Pamphlet 550-11. Washington: 1971.

15-008. United States. Department of Commerce. *Bibliography of Social Science Periodicals and Monograph Series: North Korea, 1945–1961.* Foreign Social Science Bibliographies Series P-92, no. 8. Washington: Department of Commerce, Bureau of the Census, 1962.

15-009. YANG, Key P. (comp.). "North Korean Serials and Newspapers." Unpublished union list of North Korean periodicals in five US libraries, 1971.

Reference

15-010. CHO, M. Y. *Die nordkoreanische Führung: Namenverzeichnis mit Einführung.* Hamburg: Mitteilungen des Instituts für Asienkunde Hamburg, 1967.

15-011. *Democratic People's Republic of Korea, 1948–1958.* Pyongyang: Foreign Languages Publishing House, 1958.

15-012. *Documents of the Fourth Congress of the Workers' Party of Korea.* Pyongyang: Foreign Languages Publishing House, 1961. Documents are also available for the third and fifth congresses and can be found in Kim's selected works. Documents relating to the first and second party congresses are available only in Korean.

15-013. Korea, Democratic People's Republic of. Central Statistics Bureau, National Planning Committee. *Statistical Returns of National Economy of the Democratic People's Republic of Korea.* Pyongyang: Foreign Languages Publishing House, 1964.

15-014. *Korean Review.* Pyongyang: Foreign Languages Publishing House, 1974. Latest handbook of North Korea. General overview of the situation as described by the North.

15-015. PAK, Hŏn-yŏng. "Manifesto of the South Korean Workers' Party." *For a Lasting Peace, for a People's Democracy* 12(72)(24 March 1950):3–4.

15-016. SUH, Dae-Sook. *Documents of Korean Communism, 1918–1948.* Princeton: Princeton University Press, 1970.

15-017. United States. Department of Commerce. Office of Technical Services. Joint Publications Research Service. *North Korean Central Yearbook.* Washington: annual. Title varies from year to year: *Excerpts from North Korean Central Yearbook, Information from North Korean Central Yearbook,* and so on. Some portions of the following yearbooks are translated:

1958 (JPRS 901-D)
1959 (JPRS 2691, 21 May 1960)
1960 (JPRS 16611, 21 May 1960)
1961 (JPRS 17890, 28 February 1963)
1962 (JPRS 21631, 28 October 1963)
1963 (JPRS 26186, 28 August 1964)
1964 (JPRS 35218, 27 April 1966)
1965 (JPRS 35146, 22 April 1966)
1966–1967 (JPRS 50942, 15 July 1970)
1968 (JPRS 50370, 22 April 1970)
1969 (JPRS 53693, April 1973)
1970 (JPRS 58775, 18 April 1973)
1971 (JPRS 58979, 9 May 1973)
1972 (JPRS 63967, 28 January 1975)
1973 (JPRS 66145)
1974 (JPRS 67117)
1975 (JPRS 67406)

15-018. United States. Department of Commerce. Office of Technical Services. Joint Publications Research Service. *Translations on North Korea.* Washington: 1966–.

15-019. United States. Department of Commerce. Office of Technical Services. Joint Publications Research Service. *Translations on North Korea No. 42,* JPRS 40950 (TT67-31592). Washington: 1967. Translations of biographies of North Korean Leaders in the popular South Korean magazine *Sedae.*

PERIODICALS AND NEWSPAPERS

15-020. *Chollima Korea.* Published by Information Bureau of the Democratic People's Republic of Korea in Stockholm from about 1974.

15-021. *Democratic People's Republic of Korea.* Illustrated monthly published by the Foreign Languages Publishing House of Pyongyang from January 1957. This publication is available in Japanese, Chinese, Korean, Russian, French, and Spanish.

15-022. *East Asian Review.* Published quarterly by the Institute for East Asian Studies of Seoul from Spring 1974.

15-023. *Foreign Trade of the Democratic People's Republic of Korea.* Published monthly by the Committee for the Promotion of International Trade of the Democratic People's Republic of Korea from about 1963.

15-024. *Journal of Korean Affairs.* Published quarterly by the Research Institute on Korean Affairs in Silver Spring, Maryland, from Fall 1970. Ceased publication in 1976.

15-025. *Kommunist.* Organ of the Central Committee of the Communist Party of the Soviet Union. Published since 1924. Eighteen issues per year.

15-026. *Korea Focus.* Published periodically by the American-Korean Friendship Information Center of New York from 1971.

15-027. *Korea News.* Trimonthly published by the Korean Central News Agency from the 1950s. Superseded by *Pyongyang Times* in April 1965.

15-028. *Korea Today.* Published monthly by the Foreign Languages Publishing House of Pyongyang. Formerly *New Korea* (1947-1958). This series available from January 1959.

15-029. *Korean Nature.* Published quarterly by the Association for Nature Conservation of the Democratic People's Republic of Korea. Available from mid-1960s.

15-030. *Korean Trade Unions.* Monthly published by the Central Committee of the General Federation of Trade Unions of Korea. Available from 1960.

15-031. *Korean Youth and Students.* Published monthly by the League of Socialist Working Youth of Korea and the Korean Student Committee. Available from about 1956.

15-032. *Kwahagwŏn t'ongbo* [Bulletin of the Academy of Sciences]. Published quarterly by the Academy of Sciences of the Democratic People's Republic of Korea of Pyongyang from 1954. Title and frequency vary: *Chosŏn minjujuŭi inmin konghwaguk kwahagwŏn t'ongbo, Chosŏn minjujuŭi inmin konghwaguk kwahagwŏn hakpo, Chosŏn kwahagwŏn t'ongbo;* 1954-1957 quarterly, 1958 bimonthly, and at times irregular. Each article has an English summary and in most cases a Western-language bibliography.

15-033. *North Korea Newsletter.* Published by Naewoe Press (Seoul). Began publication in 1976.

15-034. *North Korea Quarterly.* Published quarterly by the Institute of Asian Affairs, Hamburg. First issued in third quarter of 1974.

15-035. *Novaia Koreia.* Russian edition of the monthly magazine *Saechosŏn.* Available from 1950s.

15-036. *Novosti Koreia.* Russian edition of the monthly magazine *Chosŏn sosik.* Began publication in January 1958.

15-037. *Press Release.* Office of the Permanent Observer to the United Nations (Democratic People's Republic of Korea) in New York. From 1974.

15-038. *Pyongyang Times.* Published weekly by the Pyongyang Times in English. First published on 6 May 1965.

15-039. *Revolyutsionny vostok* [Revolutionary East]. Published as an organ of Nauchno-issled. Assotsiatsiia po izucheniiu natsional'nykh i kolonial'nykh problem. Published in 1927 as a monthly, changed to bimonthly in 1933, and ended with single issue in 1937.

15-040. *Sovremenyyi vostok* [Contemporary East]. Monthly publication from 1957 to 1961. This is the predecessor of the present journal *Aziya i Afrika segodnya.*

15-041. *Tikhii Okean* [The Pacific]. Published by Tikhookeanskii kabinet of Institut mirovogo khoziaistva i mirovoi politik as a quarterly during 1934-1937. The journal was absorbed by *Mirovoe khoziaaistvo i mirovaia politika,* which was continued as a monthly to 1947 and was in turn superseded in 1948 by *Voprosy ekonomiki.*

15-042. *Voprosy istorii* [Problems of history]. Published monthly by the Institute of History of the Academy of Sciences of the USSR since 1945.

15-043. *Women of Korea.* Published by the Central Committee of the Korean Democratic Women's Union. Bimonthly publication available from 1960s.

KOREAN COMMUNISM
The Movement

15-044. FOKIN, N. "The Vengeful Judgement upon the Korean Revolutionaries." *Inprecorr* 8(11)(March 1928): 244-245.

15-045. JUN, Moon-sup. "Reminiscences of Anti-Japanese Partisan Struggle." *Korea Today* 44(January 1960): 29-31.

15-046. KIM, Ch'ŏl-hŭi. "Glorious Anti-Japanese Armed Struggle, Thirtieth Anniversary of the Foundation of the Anti-Japanese Partisan." *Korea Today* 71(April 1962): 1-5.

15-047. KIM, G. F. "Velikii oktiabr i natsional'no osvoboditel'naia bol'ba koreiskogo naroda, 1917-1945 [Great October and national liberation struggle of the Korean people, 1917-1945]." In *Velikii Oktiabr i Narody Vostoka* [Great October and Eastern People]. Moscow: Izd vost. lit., 1957.

15-048. KIM, San and Nym WALES. *Song of Ariran: The Life Story of a Korean Rebel.* New York: John Day, 1941.

15-049. KONDO, H. "The Manchurian Bandits." *Contemporary Manchuria* 3(1)(January 1939):80-104.

15-050. LEE, Chong-Sik. "Korean Communists and Yen-an." *China Quarterly* 9(January/March 1962):182–192.

15-051. LEZIN, V. V. (ed.). *Ocherki po istorii osvobodi-telnoi borby koreiskogo naroda* [Essays on the history of the liberation struggle of the Korean people]. Translated by M. N. Pak. Moscow: Izd. vost. lit., 1953.

15-052. MAZUROV, V. M. *Antiyaponskaya vooruzhennaya borba koreiskogo naroda, 1931–40* [The anti-Japanese armed struggle of the Korean people, 1931–40]. Moscow: Izd. vost. lit., 1958.

15-053. PAK, Dinshoon. "The Revolutionary East and the Next Task of the Communist International." *Communist International* 11–12(June–July 1920):2315–2320.

15-054. PAK, Mikhail N. *Iz istorii osvoboditel'nogo dvizheniia koreiskogo naroda* [From the history of the liberation movement of the Korean people]. Moscow: Zhanie, 1955.

15-055. PIGULEVSKAYA, E. A. *Koreiskii narod v bor'be za nezavisimost'i democratiiu* [The Korean people in the fight for independence and democracy]. Moscow: Izd-vo. Akademii Nauk, 1952.

15-056. SCALAPINO, Robert A. and Chong-Sik LEE. *Communism in Korea*. 2 vols. Berkeley: University of California Press, 1974.

15-057. SHABSHINA, F. I. *Ocherki noveishei istorii Korei, 1918–1945gg.* [Essays on the contemporary history of Korea, 1918–1945]. Moscow: Izd. vost. lit., 1959.

15-058. SHIPAEV, V. I. *Koreiskaya burzhuaziya v natsionalno osvoboditelnom dvizhenii* [The Korean bourgeoisie in the national liberation movement]. Moscow: "Nauka," 1966.

15-059. SUH, Dae-Sook. *The Korean Communist Movement, 1918–1948*. Princeton: Princeton University Press, 1967.

15-060. TANG, Shin She. "The Partisan Movement in Manchuria." *Inprecorr* 17(54)(December 1937):1324.

15-061. YIM, Ch'un-ch'u. "Great Plan for Fatherland Restoration." *Democratic People's Republic of Korea* 5(1962):4–7.

The Development in the North

15-062. BRUN, Ellen. "North Korea: A Case of Real Development." *Monthly Review* 22(2)(June 1970):25–37.

15-063. BURCHETT, Wilfred G. *Again Korea*. New York: International Publishers, 1968.

15-064. CARRIER, Fred J. *North Korean Journey: The Revolution against Colonialism*. New York: International Publishers, 1975.

15-065. CHAN, Yun-Den. "Der sozialistische Aufbau in der Koreanischen Volksrepublik." *Deutsche Aussenpolitik* 5(1960):424–431.

15-066. Democratic People's Republic of Korea. *Our Modern Socialist Countryside*. Pyongyang: Foreign Languages Publishing House, 1974.

15-067. *Democratic People's Republic of Korea*. Pyongyang: Foreign Languages Publishing House, 1958.

15-068. Democratic People's Republic of Korea. *Socialist Constitution of the Democratic People's Republic of Korea*. Pyongyang: Foreign Languages Publishing House, 1972.

15-069. *Facts about Korea*. Pyongyang: Foreign Languages Publishing House, 1961.

15-070. *Impressions of Korea*. Pyongyang: Foreign Languages Publishing House, 1961.

15-071. *Inside North Korea: Three Decades of Duplicity*. Seoul: Institute for Internal and External Affairs, 1975.

15-072. KIM, Byong Sik. *Modern Korea: The Socialist North, Revolutionary Perspectives in the South and Unification*. New York: International Publishers, 1970.

15-073. KIM, Ch'ang-sun. *Fifteen-year History of North Korea*. JPRS: 18,925 (26 April 1963).

15-074. KIM, G. F. *Rabochii Klass novoi Korei* [The working class of New Korea]. Moscow: Profizdat, 1960.

15-075. ———. *Rabochii Klass Korei* [The working class of Korea]. Moscow: 1962.

15-076. KIM, G. F. and F. I. SHABSHINA. *Proletarskii internationalizm i revoliutsii v strankakh vostoka* [Proletarian internationalism and revolution in the socialist East]. Moscow: Izd. Nauka., 1967.

15-077. KIM, Ilpyong J. *Communist Politics in North Korea*. New York: Praeger Special Studies, 1975.

15-078. KIM, Young C. "North Korea in 1974." *Asian Survey* 15(1)(January 1975):43–52.

15-079. KURNITZKY, Horst and K. D. WOLFF. "Volksrepublik Nordkorea." *Kursbuch* 30(1972).

15-080. LEE, Chong-Sik. "Stalinism in the East: Communism in North Korea." In Robert A. Scalapino (ed.), *The Communist Revolution in Asia*. Englewood Cliffs, N.J.: Prentice-Hall, 1965.

15-081. NAM, Koon Woo. *The North Korean Communist Leadership, 1945–1965*. University: University of Alabama Press, 1974.

15-082. *North Korea Seen from Abroad*. Seoul: Korea Information Service Inc., 1976.

15-083. PAIGE, Glenn D. "Korea." In Cyril E. Black and Thomas P. Thornton (eds.), *Communism and Revolution: Strategic Uses of Political Violence*. Princeton, N.J.: Princeton University Press, 1964.

15-084. _____. *The Korean People's Democratic Republic.* Stanford: Hoover Institution Press, 1966.

15-085. _____. "North Korea and the Emulation of Russian and Chinese Behavior." In A. Doak Barnett (ed.), *Communist Strategies in Asia.* New York: Praeger, 1963.

15-086. RYU, Hun. *Study of North Korea.* Seoul: Research Institute of Internal and External Affairs, 1966.

15-087. SCALAPINO, Robert A. (ed.). *North Korea Today.* New York: Praeger, 1963.

15-088. SHABSHINA, F. I. *Ocherki noveishei istorii Koreii, 1945–1953gg.* [Essays on the contemporary history of Korea, 1945–1953]. Moscow: Gospolitizdat, 1958.

15-089. SUH, Dae-Sook. "A Preconceived Formula for Sovietization: The Communist Takeover of North Korea." In Thomas T. Hammond (ed.), *The Anatomy of Communist Takeovers.* New Haven: Yale University Press, 1975.

15-090. TYAGAI, G. D. *Ocherk novoi istorii Korei* [Essay on the modern history of Korea]. Moscow: 1961.

15-091. United States. Department of State. *North Korea: A Case Study in the Techniques of Takeover.* Department of State Publication 7118. Far Eastern Series 103. Washington: 1961.

15-092. VAINTSVAIG, N. K. and V. V. LEZIN (eds.). *Koreiskaya Narodno-Demokraticheskaya Respublika* [Democratic People's Republic of Korea]. Moscow: Izd. Akad. Nauk, 1954.

15-093. VREELAND, Nena and Rinn-Sup SHINN. *Area Handbook for North Korea.* DA Pamphlet 550-81. Washington: Government Printing Office, 1976.

15-094. WASHBURN, John N. "Soviet Russia and the Korean Communist Party." *Pacific Affairs* 23(March 1950):59–63.

KIM IL SUNG
Works by Kim

15-095. KIM, Il Sung. *For the Independent Peaceful Unification of Korea.* Rev. ed. New York: Guardian Associates, 1976.

15-096. _____. *For the Independent, Peaceful Reunification of the Country.* Pyongyang: Foreign Languages Publishing House, 1976.

15-097. _____. *Juche: The Speeches and Writings of Kim Il Sung.* Edited by Yuk-sa Li. New York: Grossman Publishers, 1972.

15-098. _____. *Kim Il Sung: Selected Works.* 2 vols. Compiled by the Party History Institute of the Central Committee of the Workers' Party of Korea. Vol. 1: 23 items covering from 23 March 1946 to 5 January 1959; 497 pp.

Vol. 2: 14 items covering from 26 February 1959 to 10 October 1965; 609 pp. Pyongyang: Foreign Languages Publishing House, 1965.

15-099. _____. *Kim Il Sung: Selected Works.* 6 vols. Compiled by the Party History Institute of the Central Committee of the Workers' Party of Korea. Pyongyang: Foreign Languages Publishing House, 1970–1975.

15-100. _____. *Kim Ir sen: Izbrannve statii rechi* [Kim Il Sung: selected articles and speeches]. Moscow: Gos. Iz. Politicheskoi Literaturi, 1962.

15-101. _____. *The Korean Revolutionaries Must Know Korea Well.* Speech addressed to the political cadres and political instructors of the Korean People's Revolutionary Army on 15 September 1943. Pyongyang: Foreign Languages Publishing House, 1973.

15-102. _____. *Let Us Repudiate the "Left" Adventurist Line and Follow the Revolutionary Organizational Line.* Speech delivered at the Meeting of Party and Young Communist League Cadres held at Mingyuehkou, Yenchi County, 20 May 1931. Pyongyang: Foreign Languages Publishing House, 1973.

15-103. _____. *The Non-Alignment Movement Is a Mighty Anti-Imperialist Revolutionary Force of Our Time.* Pyongyang: Foreign Languages Publishing House, 1976.

15-104. _____. "On Building a Marxist-Leninist Party in Our Country and Its Immediate Tasks." *Korea Today* 10(October 1975):2–14. Speech delivered at the Founding Congress of the North Korean Branch Bureau of the Korean Communist Party on 10 October 1945.

15-105. _____. *On Juche in Our Revolution.* 2 vols. Pyongyang: Foreign Languages Publishing House, 1975. Collection of speeches and articles on Kim's political thoughts.

15-106. _____. *On Organizing and Waging Armed Struggle Against Japanese Imperialism.* Speech delivered at the meeting of Party and Young Communist League Cadres held at Mingyuehkou, Yenchi County, on 16 December 1931. Appeared in Korean in *Nodong sinmun* (16 December 1972). Pyongyang: Foreign Languages Publishing House, 1973.

15-107. _____. *On the Founding of Anti-Japanese People's Guerrilla Army.* Pyongyang: Foreign Languages Publishing House, 1976.

15-108. _____. *On Preparing for the Great Event of National Liberation.* Pyongyang: Foreign Languages Publishing House, 1976.

15-109. _____. *Revolution and Socialist Construction in Korea.* New York: International Publishers, 1971.

15-110. _____. *The Tasks of Korean Communists.* Treatise published in *Sŏgwang,* organ of the Korean People's Revolutionary Army, 10 November 1937. Also appeared in *Nodong sinmun* on 10 November 1972. Pyongyang: Foreign Languages Publishing House, 1972.

15-111. _____. *The Youth Must Take Over the Revolution and Carry It Forward*. Pyongyang: Foreign Languages Publishing House, 1976.

Works on Kim

15-112. BAIK, Bong. *Kim Il Sung: Biography*. 3 vols. Tokyo: Miraisha, 1970. Published in Korean as *Minjok ŭi t'aeyang Kim Il-sŏng changgun* [The sun of the nation, Marshall Kim Il Sung] (Pyongyang: Inmun Kwahaksa, 1968).

15-113. CHECA, Genaro Carnero. *Korea: Rice and Steel*. 2nd ed. Pyongyang: Foreign Languages Publishing House, 1977. A Peruvian admirer glorifies Kim. A chapter has been added to the first edition of 1974.

15-114. *Comrade Kim Il Sung: An Ingenious Thinker and Theoretician*. Pyongyang: Foreign Languages Publishing House, 1975. Collection of articles and essays on Kim by foreigners who visited North Korea.

15-115. HWANG, Soon-hi. "He Is Our Father." *Korea Today* 71(April 1962):20–23. There are many articles of this nature in North Korean journals. This article is listed here as a representative.

15-116. *In the Revolutionary Spirit of Self-Reliance*. Pyongyang: Foreign Languages Publishing House, 1976. Collection of essays by North Koreans of Kim's activities in the North. This is a translation of the Korean book series entitled "Among the People" (Inmindŭl sogesŏ).

15-117. *Juche Idea: The Current of Thought in the Present Time*. Pyongyang: Foreign Languages Publishing House, 1977. A collection of thirteen essays by foreign journalists about Kim and his ideas.

15-118. *Kim Il Sung: Great Leader of People*. Pyongyang: Foreign Languages Publishing House, 1977. A collection of thirty-two essays about Kim by foreign visitors to the North.

15-119. *Kim Il Sung: Short Biography*. 2 vols. Pyongyang: Foreign Languages Publishing House, 1973.

15-120. Korea, Democratic People's Republic of. Party History Institute of the Central Committee of the Workers' Party of Korea. *Brief History of the Revolutionary Activities of Comrade Kim Il Sung*. Pyongyang: Foreign Languages Publishing House, 1969. Published in Korean as *Kim Il-sŏng tongjiŭi hyŏngmyŏng hwaltong yangyŏk* [Brief history of the revolutionary activities of Comrade Kim Il Sung] (Pyongyang: Nodongdang ch'ulp'ansa, 1969).

15-121. LEE, Chong-Sik. "Kim Il Sung of North Korea." *Asian Survey* 7(6)(June 1967):374–382.

15-122. *President Kim Il Sung Moves Asia and the World*. Pyongyang: Foreign Languages Publishing House, 1976. Collection of articles on Kim by foreign correspondents and writers.

15-123. *The World Historic Significance of the Juche Idea*. Pyongyang: Foreign Languages Publishing House, 1975. Collection of articles by Japanese newsmen and others in English.

THE WORKERS' PARTY OF KOREA

15-124. AHN, Byung-young. "Political Leadership in North Korea." *Social Science Journal* 3(1975):135–152.

15-125. BAGMET, N. S. *Borba koreiskogo naroda za postroenie sotsializma 1945-1960gg.* [Struggle of the Korean people for the construction of socialism, 1945-1960]. Kiev: Izd. Kievskogo un-ta, 1960.

15-126. "Boundless Loyalty to the Leader as the Most Basic Quality of the Chuch'e Type Communist Revolutionary." *Kŭlloja* (May 1974). JPRS: 63478, no. 383 (20 November 1974).

15-127. *Documents of the Fourth Congress of the Workers' Party of Korea*. Pyongyang: Foreign Languages Publishing House, 1961. Available in Korean, Japanese, Chinese, and Russian.

15-128. "The Great Leader Comrade Kim Il Sung: Founder of the Workers' Party Korea." *Korea Today* 10(October 1975):15–25.

15-129. IVANOV, T. "Blizhe k zhizni, k massam, o zadachakh Trudovoi partii Korei [Closer to life, to the masses, on the tasks of the Workers' Party of Korea]." *Partiinaya zhizn* 14(1961):63–66.

15-130. KIM, Chang-soon. "The North Korean Communist Party." *Korean Affairs* 2(2)(1963):130–140.

15-131. KIM, G. F. "Vedushchya rol Trudovoi partii Korei v narodno-demokraticheskoi revolyutsii, 1945-1950gg [Leading role of the Workers' Party of Korea in the People's Democratic Revolution, 1945-1950]." *Sovetskoe vostokovedenie* 2(1955):47–60.

15-132. KIM, Ir Sen. "Otchenyi doklad tsentralnogo komiteta Trudovoi Partii Korei IV s'ezdu partii [Report of the Central Committee of the Workers' Party of Korea to the Fourth Party Congress]." *Kommunist* 14(1961):93–156.

15-133. KOH, B. C. "The Korean Workers' Party and Detente." *Journal of International Affairs* 29(1)(1975):175–187.

15-134. LEE, Chong-Sik and Ki-wan OH. "The Russian Faction in North Korea.'' *Asian Survey* 8(4)(April 1968): 270–288.

15-135. *Materialy III sëzda Trudovoi partii Korei 23–29 Aprelya 1956g* [Materials of the Third Congress of the Workers' Party of Korea, 23–29 April 1956]. Pyongyang: Foreign Languages Publishing House, 1956. Published in Korean as *Chosŏn nodongdang chesamhoe taehoe munhŏn* [Documents of the Third Congress of the Workers' Party of Korea] (Pyongyang: Chosŏn Nodongdang Ch'ulp'ansa, 1956).

25-136. *The Present Situation and the Task of Our Party.* Pyongyang: Foreign Languages Publishing House, 1968.

15-137. SHIN, Sang-cho. ''North Korean Workers' Party in the Span of a Generation.'' *East Asian Review* 2(4)(Winter 1975):367–378.

15-138. SOHN, Jae-souk. ''Factionalism and Party Control of the Military in Communist North Korea.'' In Jacques Van Doorn (ed.), *Military Profession and Military Regimes.* The Hague: Mouton, 1969.

15-139. ''Strengthening the Party Cells Is the Basic Guarantee for Strengthening the Entire Party.'' *Kŭlloja* (July 1972). JPRS: 57932, no. 280 (8 January 1973).

15-140. SUH, Dae-Sook. ''Communist Party Leadership.'' In Dae-Sook Suh and Chae-Jin Lee, *Political Leadership in Korea.* Seattle: University of Washington Press, 1976.

15-141. _____. ''North Korea: Emergence of an Elite Group.'' In Richard F. Staar (ed.), *Aspects of Modern Communism.* Columbia: University of South Carolina Press, 1968.

15-142. VAINTSVAIG, N. K. (ed.). *Ocherki sotsialisticheskogo stroitelstva v Koreiskoi Narodno-Demokraticheskoi Respublike* [Essays on socialist construction in the Korean People's Democratic Republic]. Moscow: Izd. vost. lit., 1963.

THE STATE SYSTEM
The Political Process

15-143. CARRIER, Fred J. ''Democratic Republic of Korea: Socialism and Modernization in One Generation.'' *Korea Focus* 1(2)(Spring 1972):3–16. Highly biased for the North.

15-144. Democratic People's Republic of Korea. Ministry of Justice. *Criminal Legislation in the People's Democratic Republic of Korea.* JPRS: DC-406 (2 December 1958).

15-145. DUBIN, Wilbert B. ''The Political Evolution of the Pyongyang Government.'' *Pacific Affairs* 23(4)(December 1950): 381–392.

15-146. HAHM, Pyong Choon. ''Ideology and Criminal Law in North Korea.'' *American Journal of Comparative Law* 17(1)(1969):78–93.

15-147. ''The Invincible Power of the People's Political Regime.'' *Kŭlloja* (30 October 1967). JPRS: 44250, no. 72 (6 February 1968).

15-148. KANG, Koo-chin. ''Law in North Korea: An Analysis of Soviet-Chinese Influences Thereupon.'' JSD dissertation, Harvard University, 1969.

15-149. KOH, B. C. ''Ideology and Political Control in North Korea.'' *Journal of Politics* 32(3)(August 1970): 655–674.

15-150. LEE, Chong-Sik. ''The 1972 Constitution and Top Communist Leaders.'' In Dae-Sook Suh and Chae-Jin Lee (eds.), *Political Leadership in Korea.* Seattle: University of Washington Press, 1976.

15-151. Lee, Chong-Sik and Nam-sik KIM. ''Control and Administrative Mechanisms in the North Korean Countryside.'' *Journal of Asian Studies* 29(2)(February 1970): 309–326.

15-152. LEE, Mun Woong. *Rural North Korea under Communism: A Study of Socio-Cultural Change.* Rice University Studies, vol. 62, no. 1. Houston: Rice University, 1976.

15-153. ''A New State Organ System Which Reflects the Practical Demands of the Revolution and Construction.'' *Kŭlloja* (September 1973). JPRS: 61248, no. 340 (February 1970), pp. 309–326.

15-154. *On the Socialist Constitution of the Democratic People's Republic of Korea.* Pyongyang: Foreign Languages Publishing House, 1975. This is an informative book explaining the 1972 constitution of the North. The appendix contains many documents.

15-155. PAK, M. N. *Koreiskaia Narodo-Demokraticheskaia Respublika na putiakh k sotsializmu* [Democratic People's Republic of Korea in her fight for socialism]. Moscow: Znanie, 1958.

15-156. Party History Institute of the Central Committee of the Workers' Party of Korea. *Establishing the People's Revolutionary Government: A Genuine People's Power.* Pyongyang: Foreign Languages Publishing House, 1974. This publication, one of the series ''For the Freedom and Liberation of the People,'' is a collection of articles written by the leaders of the North. There are several issues in English.

15-157. Research Institute for Internal and External Affairs. *North Korea under Communism: A Study of Suppression.* Seoul: Research Institute of Internal and External Affairs, 1963. Biased against the North.

15-158. SCALAPINO, Robert A. ''The Nature of the North

Korean Regime: An Assessment." *China Report* 8(1/2) (January/April 1972):63–71.

15-159. "Socialist Constitution of the Democratic People's Republic of Korea." *Korea Today* 196(1973):24–30.

Foreign Policy

15-160. BRADBURY, John. "Sino-Soviet Competition in North Korea." *China Quarterly* 6(April–June 1961): 15–28.

15-161. CHO, M. Y. *Die Entwicklung der Beziehungen zwischen Peking und P'yongyang, 1949–1967: Analyse und Dokumente.* Wiesbaden: Otto Harrassowitz, 1967.

15-162. CHO, Soon Sung. "The Politics of North Korea's Unification Policies: 1950–65." *World Politics* 19(2)(January 1967):218–241.

15-163. CHUNG, Chin Owyee. "North Korea's Attitude in the Sino-Soviet Dispute, 1958–67." PhD dissertation, University of Nebraska, 1969. 303 pp. Abstracted in *DAI* 30(7)(January 1970):3073-A; UM 69-22,259.

15-164. *Facts Tell.* Pyongyang: Foreign Languages Publishing House, 1960.

15-165. *For Korea's Peaceful Unification.* Pyongyang: Foreign Languages Publishing House, 1961.

15-166. HARRARD, M. T. "North Korea's International Position." *Asian Survey* 5(August 1965):375–388.

15-167. HARRISON, Selig S. "One Korea?" *Foreign Policy* 17(Winter 1974–1975):35–62.

15-168. *History of the Just Fatherland Liberation War of the Korean People.* Pyongyang: Foreign Languages Publishing House, 1961.

15-169. KIM, J. Alexander. "Soviet Policy in North Korea." *World Politics* 22(2)(January 1970):237–254.

15-170. KIM, Roy U. T. "Sino-North Korean Relations." *Asian Survey* 8(August 1968):708–722.

15-171. KOH, B. C. *The Foreign Policy of North Korea.* New York: Praeger, 1969.

15-172. _____. "North Korea and Its Quest for Autonomy." *Pacific Affairs* 38(3/4)(Fall/Winter 1965/1966):294–306.

15-173. _____. "North Korea and the Sino-Soviet Schism." *Western Political Quarterly* 22(4)(December 1969):940–962.

15-174. *Korea Must Be Reunified Independently.* Pyongyang: Foreign Languages Publishing House, 1975. Collection of articles written by foreign correspondents in favor of North Korea's position.

15-175. KUN, Joseph C. "North Korea: Between Moscow and Peking." *China Quarterly* 31(July–September 1967): 48–58.

15-176. MIN, Benjamin Byung-Hui. "North Korea's Foreign Policy in the Post-war Decade, 1953–63." PhD dissertation, University of Massachusetts, 1967. 235 pp. Abstracted in *DA* 28(April 1968):4240-41-A; UM 68-4455.

15-177. *On the Question of Korea.* Pyongyang: Foreign Languages Publishing House, 1975. Collection of speeches of representatives at the twenty-ninth session of the UN General Assembly. This collection presents only speeches favorable to the North.

15-178. PAIGE, Glenn D. "North Korea and the Emulation of Russian and Chinese Behavior." In A. Doak Barnett (ed.), *Communist Strategies in Asia: A Comparative Analysis of Governments and Parties.* New York: Praeger, 1963.

15-179. PAK, Yun Baik. *The Struggle of Korean People for Peaceful Unification of the Country.* Pyongyang: Foreign Languages Publishing House, 1959.

15-180. REES, David. "North Korea: Undermining the Truce." *Conflict Studies* 69(March 1976):1–14.

15-181. ROMASHKIN, P. *Za mirnoe razreshenie koreiskogo voprosa* [For the peaceful, democratic solution of the Korean question]. Moscow: Gospolitizdat, 1954.

15-182. SAMSONOV, G. E. *Borba za mirnoe demokraticheskoe reshenie koreiskogo voprosa* [Struggle for a peaceful, democratic solution of the Korean question]. Moscow: Izd. vost. lit., 1960.

15-183. SIMMONS, Robert R. *The Strained Alliance: Peking, Pyongyang, Moscow and the Politics of the Korean Civil War.* New York: Free Press, 1975.

15-184. YIU, Myung Kun. "Sino-Soviet Rivalry in North Korea since 1954." PhD dissertation, University of Maryland, 1969. Abstracted in *DAI* 31(3)(September 1970): 1353-A; UM 70-14,953.

The Economic System

15-185. *Agricultural Cooperativization in DPRK.* Pyongyang: Foreign Languages Publishing House, 1958.

15-186. CHUNG, Joseph S. H. "North Korea's Seven Year Plan: Economic Performance and Reforms." *Asian Survey* 12(6)(June 1972):527–545.

15-187. _____. *The North Korean Economy: Structure and Development.* Stanford: Hoover Institution Press, 1974.

15-188. GRYAZNOV, G. V. *Sotsialisticheskaya industrializatsiya v KNDR, 1945–1960gg* [Socialist industrialization in the DPRK, 1945–1960]. Moscow: "Nauka," 1966.

15-189. HA, Joseph Man-Kyung. "Politics of Korean Peasantry: A Study of Land Reform and Collectivization with Reference to Sino-Soviet Experiences." PhD dissertation, Columbia University, 1971. 498 pp. Abstracted in *DAI* 34(10)(April 1974):6714-15-A; UM 74-8182.

15-190. *Historical Experience of the Agrarian Reform in Our Country.* Pyongyang: Foreign Languages Publishing House, 1974.

15-191. KARSHINOV, L. N. *Koreiskaya Narodno-Demokraticheskaya Respublika, ekonomika i vneshnyaya torgovlya* [Economy and foreign trade of the Democratic People's Republic of Korea]. Moscow: Vneshtorgizdat, 1958.

15-192. KIM, Han-joo. *Great Victory in Agricultural Cooperativization in DPRK.* Pyongyang: Foreign Languages Publishing House, 1959.

15-193. KIM, Il Sung. *All Efforts to Attain the Goal of Eight Million Tons of Grain.* Pyongyang: Foreign Languages Publishing House, 1975. Speech delivered at the National Agricultural Congress, 15 January 1975.

15-194. _____. *Let Us Further Consolidate and Develop the Great Successes Achieved in the Building of a Socialist Countryside.* Pyongyang: Foreign Languages Publishing House, 1974. Speech delivered at the National Agricultural Congress, 10 January 1974.

15-195. _____. *On Our Party's Policy for the Future Development of Agriculture.* Pyongyang: Foreign Languages Publishing House, 1964.

15-196. _____. *On the Victory of Socialist Agricultural Collectivization and the Further Development of Agriculture in Our Country.* Pyongyang: Foreign Languages Publishing House, 1972.

15-197. _____. *Results of the Agrarian Reform and Future Tasks.* Pyongyang: Foreign Languages Publishing House, 1974.

15-198. "Kim Il Sung Urges a New Upsurge in Socialist Construction." *Kŭlloja* (March 1974). JPRS: 62610, no. 367 (31 July 1974).

15-199. KIM, Yoon-Hwan. "Tasks and Prospect of North Korean Economy in the 70's." *East Asian Review* 1(1)(Spring 1974):12–36.

15-200. KUARK, John Yoon Tai. "A Comparative Study of Economic Development in North and South Korea during the Post–Korean War Period." PhD dissertation, University of Minnesota, 1966. 327 pp. *DA* 27(May 1967):3558-59-A; UM 67-5211.

15-201. LEE, Joong-Koon. "North Korean Foreign Trade in Recent Years and the Prospects for North-South Korean Trade." *Journal of Korean Affairs* 4(3)(October 1974): 18–32.

15-202. LEE, Pong S. "An Estimate of North Korea's National Income." *Asian Survey* 12(6)(June 1972):518–526.

15-203. PAK, Ki Hyuk. "A Comparative Study of the Agrarian Systems of North and South Korea." In W. A. Douglas Jackson (ed.), *Agrarian Policies and Problems in Communist Countries.* Seattle: University of Washington Press, 1971.

15-204. ROBINSON, Joan. "Korean Miracle." *Monthly Review* 16(9)(January 1965):541–549.

15-205. *Self-Reliance and the Building of the Independent Economy.* Pyongyang: Foreign Languages Publishing House, 1965.

CHAPTER 16
Russian-Language Materials

George Ginsburgs

INTRODUCTION

KOREAN STUDIES in the Soviet Union emerged as a separate field only after World War II. Prior to that, Soviet research and writing on Korean themes had been treated essentially as an appendage of Japanese studies and specialists on Korea proper devoting full time to that country and its problems were a rather rare breed in Soviet scholarly circles. The emergence of a communist regime in North Korea after the defeat of Japan, the USSR's enhanced role in the North Pacific sector following Japan's downfall, the Korean War—all conspired to promote renewed interest in Korean affairs in Soviet quarters and to focus attention on the historical and contemporary record of the Korean people. To be sure, the foregoing factors also stamped the character of the end product. The analysis of the Korean scene has unfolded within the framework of the Marxist canon. Fortunately, this framework itself managed to evolve to a considerable degree from the early coarseness and rigidity of the Stalinist outlook to a markedly more relaxed and sophisticated approach to various domestic and foreign issues which colors the Soviet attitude today. Some topics have continued to attract a disproportionate share of attention on the part of Soviet authors out of ideological considerations. Nevertheless, here too the tone, style, and sometimes even substance of the comments evince a subtle, yet unmistakable, shift from the relatively crude categorizations of the past to a more nu-anced appreciation of reality that is the current norm at certain levels of the Soviet establishment.

The same reasons have operated to further the growth of a corps of professional experts in the field of Korean studies. As a partner in the "Socialist Commonwealth," the Democratic People's Republic of Korea (DPRK) requires regular and sustained coverage in publications dealing with the political, economic, and cultural life of each member of the fraternity and the club as a whole and therefore fuels the need for people with an intimate knowledge of local conditions. Increased Soviet involvement in the complicated diplomatic maneuvers between Japan, the United States, and the People's Republic of China (PRC) in the northeast Pacific basin has intensified its awareness of the strategic geopolitical role of the entire Korean peninsula at the crossroads of these competing ambitions and calculations as well as of the deft balancing act maintained by the Kim Il Sung regime between Moscow and Peking in pursuit of its own autonomous objectives. This diversified picture has elicited a wider range of commentary and a more critical assessment of the raw data than had been the case when bipolarity prevailed, friends and foes were clearly identified, the lines separating the rival camps were neatly drawn, and divergences within each phalanx went unnoticed or were dismissed as insignificant. The current complexity of political phenomena within the former "bloc" and in the matrix of relations across old alliance lines has proved a boon for the scholarly community in the USSR just as elsewhere and has in turn served to attract fresh talent which sees the possibility of venturing into hitherto unexplored terrain and the prospect that the efforts will be duly rewarded because of their practical relevance for the USSR's present policy agenda.

At any rate, there is no denying that Soviet scholarship on Korea has made impressive strides in the course of the last thirty years, both quantitatively and qualitatively. The progression has not been uniformly steady, however. On occasion, political difficulties (especially during chilly spells in the relations between Moscow and Pyongyang) have intruded to curb drastically the amount of space devoted to the treatment of questions connected with Korea in the scholarly and mass-consumption literature produced in the Soviet Union. At other times, a dramatic event like the Korean War preempts the scene and reduces virtually everything said on the subject to the crass level of ad hoc propaganda. But the device can also work in the opposite direction. The Soviet preoccupation with its dispute with the PRC, for example, has had the effect of bringing to light a lot of additional information on the inside history of Soviet experience with its Far Eastern neighbors, Korea included, of which next to nothing was either known or suspected until now. Be that as it may, although the route traversed by Soviet studies on Korea since the end of World War II has been tortuous, uneven, and less than lineal in its forward thrust, the fact remains that it has, on balance, moved ahead persistently and at a fairly rapid pace. At this juncture it has reached a plateau from which it can safely aspire to general recognition of its scholarly achievements and the intellectual excellence of its recent performance and of its future potential—provided the political climate stays comparatively propitious to such an endeavor.

The accompanying bibliographic manual is only a small sample of the Soviet published output in this area. The items have been selected on the basis of their typicality—that is, with an eye to how accurately they represent the prevailing caliber of Soviet scholarship in their respective sectors at a given time, so that the best specimens of the worst kind of Stalinist lore are cited along with superior examples of the current crop which have no trouble fulfilling the established standards of academic respectability. The following paragraphs offer a brief survey of how each of these branches of Soviet Koreanology has fared between 1945 and 1975, what specific elements determined its growth pattern, at what point it stands at this stage of the game, and what immediate outlook it faces. I conclude with an attempt to draw up an overall balance sheet.

BIBLIOGRAPHIC GUIDES AND SURVEYS

A rather striking feature of Soviet literature on Korea is the absence of a comprehensive bibliography of Soviet books and periodical items dealing in whole or in part with Korean affairs. Yet the bibliographic business has, as a rule, flourished in the USSR; both China and Japan, for instance, have been the object of masterly bibliographic inventorying. Korea, for some unknown reason, has not been so favored up till now.[1]

True, the cupboard is not entirely bare and a few examples of such stocktaking may be found. Most of these, however, were produced with some special occasion in mind and were content to list a limited number of pieces which had a bearing on the specific event being commemorated. (Thus an anniversary of the liberation of Korea by the Red Army might prompt an exercise in compiling a skeleton outline of around a dozen titles which shed light on the subject.) None of these works is very satisfactory. Far better and much more useful are a handful of surveys that have recently been published in the USSR which chart a particular area from the point of view of the resources available in that domain, the substantive profile of the investigations conducted in that field, or the organizational evolution of research activities on a designated front. The three pieces cited under this heading all fall into that class and have been picked because of their scholarly value, albeit for rather narrow concrete purposes. The first title (16-001) is an authoritative discussion of Soviet plans in the realm of publication of assorted rare "classics" of ancient Oriental literature originals or authenticated copies in Soviet archival and museum collections. It is an ambitious program which has already several achievements to its credit and which meets the most rigorous technical standards. Korea is adequately represented and, if present expectations materialize, more monuments of traditional Korean literature will eventually be added to the roster.

The second item in the list (16-002) is of interest because it amounts to a pocket tour of Russian and Soviet writings on Korea led by a scholar who has been closely associated with the field in both a personal and a professional capacity. The emphasis, though, is on the highlights of the record. No attempt is made to provide either a comprehensive or a systematic assessment of the total *oeuvre*. The essay is further skewed by the author's insistence on trying to demonstrate the major contribution of the Soviet complement of Korea watchers to the cause of Soviet-Korean friendship through their efforts at dissemination of an "accurate conception" of the past and present of the Korean people. Still, the article offers a worthwhile bird's-eye view of the salient features of the landscape.

The last entry (16-003) here is a reconstruction of the process of institutional growth of Soviet Oriental studies since their inception and allows one to trace the organizational format of research on Korea during the first forty years of the Soviet system. The picture is, of course, one of emancipation and growth and a constant search for an optimal structural setting in which to promote this enterprise, fluctuating between experiments with versions of the horizontal area principle and different designs of the vertical branch/discipline model. Despite a certain sense of repetitiveness and excess attention to minor detail, the monograph constitutes a unique source of information on the internal shifts in institute and department arrangements and of the turnover in the personnel in charge of the assorted subdivisions. As such, it is well worth consulting to get an inkling of how Korean studies, *inter alia,* have been handled through this period in operational terms at the research level.

GENERAL

The omnibus description "general" fits a broad range of Soviet writing on Korea—from the almanac-type sketch of the country (or countries—DPRK and ROK) to the encyclopedia-reference article. It even comprehends a travelogue account which can stretch from a slight vignette to a quite perceptive firsthand description of the local scene. Serious scholarly studies which lack a specific focus or profile and which treat of various disparate aspects of the situation in North or South Korea

or both by stringing together between a single set of covers a half-dozen or so essays on a diversity of topics also end up in this pigeonhole, simply for lack of a better solution. For instance, Item 16-004 consists of eight chapters by different authors and addressed, respectively, to: the working class as the leading force of socialist construction in the DPRK; economic construction in the DPRK; the formation of a technical intelligentsia in the DPRK; the struggle of the Soviet Union and other socialist countries for the peaceful democratic solution of the Korean question; the economy of South Korea in the grip of American "aid"; deepening of the crisis of the South Korean regime; anticommunism as a doctrinal-political weapon of South Korean reaction; some lessons of the past two decades (1945–1965).

The random collection can, despite its lack of a central theme, have scholarly merit, and, indeed, this particular work at times does. The bulk of such literature, however, consists of an ephemeral and marginal genre of reporting which has a first-person intimacy, a human-interest flavor, but often very little hard data. Sometimes, though, a passing observation can offer an unusual glimpse behind the stolid official facade and convey an impression of ordinary people and the tenor of their daily lives that is never to be found in the academic brand of prose. In that respect, the "general" piece can on occasion serve a significant function by projecting a different, and usually neglected, dimension of the routine aspects of the individual's existence which rarely gets notice in the more scholarly scripts.

Apart from these few incidental benefits, it must be said that the quality of Soviet work in this sector has improved markedly as of late. To be sure, the journalistic essay which gives a breezy and chatty synopsis of a tourist's visit to the DPRK—the buildings, the factories, the conversations—still represents a big slice of the Soviet Union's annual output of publications on Korea. Other works of a "general" nature have recently been added to the repertory, however, and a few of them have real merit. For instance, the reference volume on modern Korea (16-006) is a fine handbook of the country as a whole and its northern and southern halves. It contains a mass of information (including statistical indices) on geography, administrative apportionment, population, religion, language and writing, history, the state structure, political parties and civic organizations, foreign relations, economy, culture, the arts, libraries, museums, press and radio broadcasting, public hygiene and physical culture, and sports. Granted, the evidence has to be used cautiously and sparingly, and the interpretation is often politically tendentious; but the sweep of the coverage and the array of factual data are nonetheless impressive and the project is far superior in conception and execution to anything analogous attempted earlier by the Russian scholarly community. The very ability to tackle a job of such scope amply attests to the growth of that community's resources and the expansion of its ranks to comprise enough specialists to deal with the entire spectrum of themes crowding a canvas of this size.

Items 16-005 and 16-007 are a novelty too in that they are harbingers of a promising trend in Soviet "social science" literature—a bid to mine the memoirs, diaries, and recollections of the second- and third-echelon participants in certain events which now seem worth recalling and discussing in print. Hitherto, only a few select figures in the Soviet hierarchy enjoyed that privilege, except in connection with saccharine eulogies of Lenin by anyone who had had the privilege of coming into contact with the great man, no matter how briefly or inconsequentially, and eyewitness accounts of certain critical moments in the nation's history (military reminiscences, for instance, or tales of guerrilla derring-do from the era of the revolution and civil war). Now subordinate personnel are being given the opportunity to provide a worm's-eye view of history's underbelly. As glimpses of the inner working of microdiplomacy, these cameos are fascinating in their own fashion. They let us see how the mechanism ticked at the middle and lower levels of the bureaucracy which was charged with administering policy, coping with quotidian problems, and maintaining a fixed routine, and not with formulating big decisions. The *coup d'oeil* backstage is a valuable corrective to the common obsession with the behavior of the "stars" clustered under the official spotlight. At least the inside view makes one realize how vast a number of people are involved in keeping the show running, how many crisscrossing bonds of loyalty there are in these huge networks, how thick a layer of connective tissue this web of shared self-interest, professional solidarity, and associational congruence can produce, and what

potent influence this inner structure can then exert over the whole apparatus. It is to be hoped that the experiment will catch on and more of these "notes from the scrapbooks of petty officials" will be forthcoming to supply us with a bit of badly needed insight into the ancillary political processes and logistical infrastructure of public management in the communist world.

GEOGRAPHY

Geography is a rather straightforward science, and the performance of Soviet scholars in this domain readily compares with the activities of their Western colleagues. The Soviet record here to date invites three general observations.

To begin with, the most ambitious, solid, and successful piece of work in this field so far is still a treatise written back in 1947 and reissued in 1951 (16-012). For all its excellence, which is undeniable, the volume is in large part hopelessly out of date by now. No attempt has been made to upgrade it or replace it with something executed on the same scale. A more recent study (16-009) is a fine, well-researched monograph, based on current data and adequately documented, but it is much narrower in scope, less systematic in approach, and strikes one more as an introductory text than the kind of synthesis that its predecessor sought to achieve.

Next, Soviet geographers tend to focus on physical geography. The latest concepts and techniques of political geography do not seem to have penetrated yet into their universe or at least to have been sufficiently accepted to generate important analytical studies fit for publication. In this respect, Soviet geography resembles Soviet anthropology, which also is heavily preoccupied with the "ethnography of material indicia" and ignores the new currents and theories which have stimulated contemporary anthropological inquiry in the West.

Finally, Soviet scholars are determined to win due recognition for the important contribution of Russian scientists to the common fund of knowledge about Korea. To that end, several works by Russian travelers of the previous century have been republished, appropriately cleansed to eliminate any material that might prove offensive to present-day sensitivities and intended to illustrate the primacy of Russian ventures into this field. The desire and the claim are, in fact, quite legitimate and valid since competent Russian explorers did visit Korea at a time when access to the country by foreigners entailed great difficulties and then reported intelligently and critically on what they had seen. To that extent, their reports constitute a primary source of considerable value which ought to be incorporated into the data bank of any serious investigator of the history of Korean social mores and cultural environment. Unfortunately, these logs have hitherto enjoyed only limited circulation and, moreover, Russian was for long a more exotic language than it is today. Consequently, the use of these data has been sparse, a situation which the current efforts to revive interest in these old documents may yet succeed in correcting, to the benefit of all concerned.

HISTORY

History is one area of Koreanology in the USSR which has prospered, and the fruits of that affluence can be seen both in the quality and the quantity of the output. To be sure, conditions here are still by no means perfect, gaps continue to exist, certain barnacles of the past have not been completely stripped and occasionally manage to hinder progress, but on the whole the historian's trade is undergoing a modest, but visible, boom. Just a few of the more prominent features of that process can be noted in this context.

Their Marxist orientation has fueled in Soviet historical circles an abiding interest in the phenomena of mass movements as a manifestation of the inevitable class struggle splitting all presocialist societies. In the case of Korea, this has found expression in the recurrence of the theme of peasant uprisings at various stages of Korea's feudal experience. The technical caliber of the initial treatment of the subject was low. The political overtones of the topic, coupled with the lack of recognized expertise on the part of those who addressed themselves to these questions at the outset, led to excessive reliance on the pronouncements of the "classics" of Marxism-Leninism-Stalinism and a great deal of a priori theorizing. Moreover, one runs across ludicrously doctrinaire interpretations of even that small sample of original data which was tapped for the purpose of reaching conclusions effectively dictated by ideological preconceptions. This fascination persists, but the quality of the

script has improved dramatically: primary sources are regularly consulted; familiarity with the secondary literature is taken for granted; the analysis is more sophisticated, reflects more accurately the complexity of those events, and so approximates better the multiplicity of the forces and motives involved in these confrontations. Instead of a flat, monochromatic picture we now have a richly textured tapestry—essentially still couched in Marxist terms, of course, but no longer compressed into the shallow and simpleminded schematics of the Stalinist canon.

The pattern is repeated on a number of issues which seem to represent perennial landmarks in Soviet scholarly explorations of Korea: the national liberation struggle against Japanese rule; the role of the native bourgeoisie in that struggle; imperialist aggression against the Korean people throughout the centuries, including incidents implicating the United States either in an active capacity or in silent collusion with the nefarious plans of other powers, finally culminating in America's alleged acquiescence in and even overt encouragement of the Japanese seizure of Korea. All these themes pop up again and again in Soviet literature on Korea, inspiring a steady stream of articles, pamphlets, and monographs dealing with various aspects of those problems. But whereas once it was all right for Soviet scholars to spin out lurid scenarios on these subjects, generously larded with quotations from the Marxist gospels and only occasionally spiced up with some carefully selected facts in a belated bid to sustain a vague scholarly claim, things are not done that way any more. Marxist dicta may predetermine the outcome of the analysis, may establish the parameters of the inquiry, may set the tone and decide well in advance what thesis will be propounded; but the manner in which the operation will be conducted will outwardly strive to observe the norms of scholarly propriety and thereby will indeed create an impression of relative academic credibility. Different viewpoints and divergent readings of the evidence are, after all, the essence of Western scholarly tradition. If the Soviets now speak in measured and reasonable tones, show an apparent respect for minimal standards of factual accuracy, argue their case instead of just loudly asserting it, and try to cite empirical data in support of their contentions instead of merely disregarding what did not suit their requirements, they will get a fair hearing and will be judged accordingly on the merits of their commodity. This offers grounds for a modicum of communication and dialogue, much of which was formerly precluded by Soviet adherence to crass dogma, and constitutes a significant step forward for the advancement of knowledge.

A sector in which the Soviets have always invested heavily—and their efforts have, on the whole, paid off quite satisfactorily—is economic history, again perhaps because of the influence of Marxist thought and the precedence it has consistently assigned to economic forces in the shaping of human history. It is also an area that has largely been ignored by the profession in the non-communist countries and so meets with little competition abroad and incurs less invidious comparison than many other fields. Be that as it may, economic history is a well-developed craft in the USSR. Granted, it too has its quota of shibboleths: an exaggerated accent on class stratification and conflicts in Korean society in the earlier periods; the mandatory mythologizing of the proletariat; the overemphasis on the importance of the embryo of capitalist elements in modern Korean experience in order to justify an accelerated pace of transition to "socialism" and promote the proletariat to top billing in connection with that enterprise. Yet there are real pluses to compensate for these obvious defects. And until Western historians tackle the job themselves, their Soviet counterparts will continue to enjoy an edge in an area for which they have a natural affinity anyway.

A criticism that can be leveled at the products of Soviet scholarship in this department is the absence of a sound sociological framework for their analysis of the mechanics of economic history. Without putting the inquiry into a broader communal setting, the recording of economic history can turn into a pretty sterile exercise. Soviet historians do not seem to be aware of the void—perhaps because in their mind the Marxist frame of reference provides an authoritative classificatory scheme for all social phenomena and operating automatically within this conceptual grid prevents Soviet authors from realizing that they are in fact functioning in an empirical vacuum. What is needed, of course, is to establish the organic link between economic practices and social structures in those days as it was, rather than as Marx postulated it must be in order to fit into his philosophical system. Whether Soviet writers will be allowed (or themselves even wish) to venture into this ideologically booby-trapped terrain is highly problematic.

In closing, let me reiterate that, whatever shortcomings still afflict Soviet historical studies in this domain (and many do exist), the verdict must nonetheless be that dramatic progress has been achieved in the discipline. A new generation of Soviet historians has emerged in the last three decades and joined the ranks of the profession—well trained, skilled in the use of the tools of the trade, familiar with the documentary materials, linguistically adept and eager to engage in serious research work on important subjects that heretofore had not been adequately examined. A major testimonial to what resources the Soviet community of Korea watchers can mobilize today is the recently published two-volume set on the history of Korea (16-016) from ancient times to the present day, a seminal work of Marxian synthesis in this domain which required a quantum of energy and talent not previously available in the USSR and probably not available in most countries even now. Sizable investment and careful cultivation have at last reached the payoff stage.

ECONOMICS

Similar observations can be made about the record in the field of economics. On this front also the picture is one of increased analytical aptitude, a broadening of the horizon, and improved technical artifacts—except that the Russians, like the rest of us, suffer from the recent drought of hard data on the performance of the DPRK's economic apparatus.

The bulk of Soviet writings in the field has, quite naturally, been concerned with the economic career of the DPRK and specifically with the emergence and growth of a socialist economic system in the northern half of the peninsula and such ancillary developments as the evolution and expansion of the working class, the new peasant class, and so forth.

Paradoxically, good studies on the land reform and collectivization experiments are more numerous and of higher grade than the literature on the process of industrialization. Perhaps the rural sector was perceived as the crucial test for socialism's viability in the DPRK (as

in the other people's democracies of Asia) and hence attracted greater attention. Or perhaps the topic lent itself
to deeper and more creative analysis because of its immediate and profound impact on the social fabric of the
community thereby inviting a discussion that called for
a mix of economic and sociological evaluation, albeit
the latter was content to operate with rather primitive
conceptual gear. At any rate, the sweeping changes engineered in the countryside have been the object of some
interesting and worthwhile dissection by Soviet scholars. The common Soviet predilection for reciting statistics and assuming that quantity equals quality and more
means better has been tempered somewhat by awareness
of the close relationship between these measures and the
life-style of the human beings drastically affected by
these innovations. Abstract juggling of figures was not
felt to be wholly adequate in these circumstances, and a
whiff of the people who bore the brunt of the onslaught
occasionally creeps into the picture to impart it with a
little taste of blood and flesh.

Most encouraging, too, is the fact that a recent monograph on the subject of the DPRK's rural economy
(16-043) has departed from the usual practice in the past
of focusing solely on the conditions encountered in
whatever country was then being scrutinized. Instead, it
attempts to use a comparative approach—juxtaposing
and contrasting salient features of the DPRK's record in
this regard with that of sister socialist states and seeking
to offer concrete explanations for at least some of the
divergences thus uncovered and the objective reasons
which prompted resort to solutions specially adjusted to
local exigencies. This is a promising start although this
particular piece is certainly not the last word on the subject—requiring, *inter alia,* a more detailed look at what
the respective statutes prescribed and how their provisions were actually implemented in order to get a more
complete diagnosis. It nevertheless marks what one
hopes will be the beginning of a new trend which could
shed more light on this important contribution by Marxist draftsmen and architects to the art of organizing
humankind's economic activity.

The lone title in the subdivision on industry (16-044)
is not an accurate reflection of the volume of publication on the subject, but it is, I think, a true index to the
quality of the stock. The rest of the merchandise in this
section consists of the standard statistic-laden vignette,
long on enumeration and quotation of gross amounts
and percentiles and short on "live" analysis. The present study is far better than most in that it at least contains faint echoes of the principles of political economy
and suggests that maybe more of this can be expected in
the future—an attractive prospect and a desirable goal
since it would humanize and infuse a sense of reality into a field too long dominated by abstract arithmetical
computations. Should the Soviets go even further some
day and address themselves squarely to some of the
problems of the interplay of their economic experiments
and the target human environment, we will then have a
major breakthrough in this realm and witness a bid to
fuse sociology and economics in a way that would cast
the data in a fresh and far more revealing perspective.

Meantime, on a more modest scale, one must note the
steady increase in Soviet scholarly work on the economic problems of South Korea. Undertaken with the obvious purpose of making invidious comparisons between North and South and demonstrating the "tragic
position" of South Korea's economy, these studies still
manage to exhibit considerable familiarity with the relevant sources. They display, moreover, an ability to admit and ingenuity to explain away such "anomalies" as
the apparent successes scored by the "bourgeois economic machinery" in some areas, its flexibility, and its
resilience in the face of successive terminal pronouncements by a large coterie of doom-sayers both in the
communist world and elsewhere. Despite the frank political motives, the style and substance of the performance is not unimpressive and with time might even get
better. If one discounts judgments or premises which
blatantly parrot ideological imperatives, one can learn
something from this alternative appreciation of the
scenery and enrich one's own vision with whatever valid
insights this critique from the opposite angle might furnish.

POLITICS

Political science has never been a Soviet forte. Most
local ventures into this arena follow the same format
and deal with the following principal themes: the key
leadership role of the Communist Party, the organizational, economic, and social transformations wrought

under its direction, and the drive to complete the building of socialism. Or something to that effect. The tone is uniformly positive and optimistic: the Party is always right; its program is correct and is being implemented successfully and enthusiastically; the masses are in full agreement with the agenda and labor devotedly to consummate the transition to full socialism before tackling the business of pushing on to communism. Couched in popular or pseudoscholarly language, these publications offer a pretty, cosmetized picture of the political landscape, stick mostly to generalities, quote lavishly from official speeches, statements, programs, and manifestos, and avoid originality like the plague.

Two recent occurrences, however, point to a possible revival. One is a monograph (16-054) which tries to apply the comparative test to the DPRK's portfolio: identifying the elements which it shares in common with its fellow members in the socialist fraternity and those which are unique to it, supplying reasons for this phenomenon, and attempting to distinguish between the core ingredients which feature in all the recipes for concocting socialism and the extra, marginal, or optional components which can be varied or modified to suit a particular milieu or a congeries of deviant ad hoc conditions. To be sure, the spotlight is still firmly fixed on the universal aspects of the socialist experience—that is, the design pioneered by the USSR. But as compared to the earlier situation where it was automatically assumed that the Soviet blueprint applied in full to all states wishing to travel the road to socialism, the present acknowledgment that slavish imitation is neither desirable in this connection, nor possible, nor, indeed, corroborated by the historical record, is a substantial boost for the concept of polycentric communism or the primacy of national models in the building of socialist polities. The change entails a commensurate downgrading of the older thesis that concentrated exclusively on the Soviet stereotype and took it for granted that its lessons would be faithfully repeated by all countries which gravitated into the USSR's orbit.

The novelty of the second example (16-055) resides chiefly in its status as memoir literature, for the book in question is identified as a diary kept by the author while stationed in Seoul as the wife of the Soviet consul-general to Korea. In substantive terms, the account contains nothing very startling, but the literary genre is sufficiently unusual for the Soviet repertory to warrant attention and whet one's appetite for more. Compared to the run-of-the-mill Soviet academic treatise on political science themes, this piece at least has the virtue of sounding alive, curious, and excited and has a light touch of personality in contrast with the deadpan monotone affected by the other scribes working in this department.

LAW

The Soviets acquit themselves much better in the legal field. They have produced excellent documentary compilations (for example, 16-063) not matched by anything in the West. Though by no means exhaustive, these compendia covering broad areas or particular sectors nevertheless make it infinitely easier to engage in legal research work or even to analyze the highlights of legal developments on various subjects without enjoying access to the original DPRK statutory sources. Several treatises in this realm are likewise of very high quality—for instance, the monograph on the state structure of the DPRK (16-059) and the companion study on the role of state and law in promoting the transformation of legal relations in North Korea's rural sector, both by the same author. Neither of these books has a competitor in Western literature on the legal experience of the DPRK, which, in fact, is extremely sparse, patchy, and often of depressingly low caliber. On this score, then, Soviet scholarship has a net advantage over ours.

The trouble is that the best Soviet work in this field dates from the fifties and early sixties and the gratifying level of these academic investigations has not been kept up since. Either the Russians too now suffer from lack of enough information about North Korea's legal universe, especially its practical *modus operandi,* or Soviet scholars have let themselves be seduced by more glamorous pastures. Whatever the reasons, work on the DPRK's legal system has stagnated or even registered a decline during the last decade. The only bright spot on the horizon is the appearance of some personal recollections by a gentleman who sports the title of lieutenant-colonel and who served as legal adviser to the Red Army's command staff in North Korea following Japan's capitulation. As such, he was closely associated with the organization and consolidation of a new indigenous administrative apparatus in North Korea which eventually emerged as the government of the DPRK and his reminiscences shed some interesting light on the process (16-062).

Otherwise, the current state of affairs here is rather disquieting. Even the adoption of the new constitution and the ensuing institutional changes in the governing mechanism have failed to elicit serious analytical assessment of the important innovations effected by these moves, apart from a few random pieces offering a superficial commentary on the more obvious aspects of the incident. It is to be hoped that conditions on this front will soon improve since so little is known of the DPRK's legal mores. Even when the Soviets contributed to the meager fund of knowledge, only the tip of the iceberg had been explored to any extent. Should the recent trend of benign neglect continue, the whole area could easily recede into darkness.

INTERNATIONAL RELATIONS

A lot of what has already been said about Soviet writings on history also applies to the published output relating to foreign affairs. The initial samples of "scholarly" endeavor in this area were marked by the worst kind of Stalinist cliché-ism: rabid in tone, crude in substance, and oblivious of any need to observe academic decorum with respect to minimal standards of factual accuracy or elementary truthfulness. The situation has appreciably improved, at least in the sense that partisan contentions are now presented in a more civilized manner and with a better chance of earning a hearing instead of being dismissed outright as gross propaganda.

There has, as of late, been a noticeable increase in Soviet research on South Korea, with emphasis, as might be expected, on its international difficulties and its manhandling by the great imperialist powers, primarily the United States. The "enslavement" of South Korea, the imposition of a succession of autocratic and unpopular regimes on the country with US military and financial blessing and support—these are the themes that exercise a growing contingent of Soviet scholars today. All in all, a goodly proportion of the emphasis in Soviet Korean studies, whether in the field of politics, economics, or international relations, has shifted to

South Korea in recent years, either because of the urge to know one's enemy or to weigh a potential target or to reconnoiter a likely arena of future confrontation which would also involve Japan—or, more innocuously, perhaps because the skill and talent are in stock and North Korea cannot absorb the accumulated scholarly resources. Whatever the reasons, South Korea receives a considerable amount of attention, principally as an object of external imperialist ambitions and, consequently, as a prospective hot spot in this corner of Asia.

By contrast, few major items are written about the diplomatic ties of the DPRK or, for that matter, about Soviet policies toward the two Koreas. Apart from the standard disquisitions about Moscow's peace-loving aspirations in connection with the perennial subject of Korean reunification, the Soviets seem to wish to remain in the background, leave the initiative to the DPRK, and not hog the scene. This is true even on the academic plane. It very well may be that the Russians prefer to maintain a certain distance between themselves and the North Koreans lest they get themselves identified with any reckless moves by the latter. Or perhaps the North Koreans have proved so prickly that Soviet spokesmen would rather not comment on anything that might be taken amiss by their hypersensitive allies. Quite clearly, Soviet scholars do not appear to want to venture into this terrain except to write little congratulatory bonbons to commemorate special occasions which could not conceivably ruffle anyone's feathers. The result is a curiously lopsided inventory, dominated by the conspicuous absence of any major treatment of the record of Soviet–North Korean association over the past thirty years, leading one to wonder whether the current situation is not so good as to warrant the usual gushy account and yet not so bad as to call for a tirade—a state of affairs that is indeterminate enough to counsel prudent silence.

As for the Korean War, that tragic event could not be disregarded in any bibliographic survey. Let me point out, however, that Soviet writings on the subject fall under either of two headings: raw propaganda or legal-like indictments of the behavior of the US and UN forces in Korea on charges of aggression, waging bacteriological warfare, mistreatment of prisoners of war, and systematic violations of the rules pertaining to the status of civilians and combatants. The legal briefs illustrate Soviet views on various facets of the international law of war, but Korea features in them only passively, as the place where these alleged transgressions occurred: another geographic forum could have inspired exactly the same script. Ironically, it is the marathon Sino-Soviet polemic that has prompted a number of curious revelations about the USSR's reported role in the Korean War which the Soviets had never seen fit to disclose before—such as the acknowledgment that Soviet forces participated in combat operations on the Korean front, the claim that the USSR was preparing in 1950 to dispatch five divisions to Korea if the military position of the DPRK showed signs of further deterioration, and so forth. How much of this can be believed is, of course, open to argument, but the fact remains that the Soviets had not hitherto found it necessary to cite these alibis vis-à-vis the North Koreans and constant Chinese criticism alone finally forced them to resort to these defenses. The phenomenon does say something about the state of Sino-Soviet relations as compared with Soviet–North Korean relations, though the latter too have gone through periods of serious strain and a few less than frankly effusive opinions of each other were exchanged by Moscow and Pyongyang in the midst of these chilly spells.

Just a few words in conclusion will suffice. When I wrote the bibliographic guide to Soviet publications on Korea (*Soviet Works on Korea, 1945–1970;* Item 15-003), I suggested in the introductory essay that Soviet Koreanology had become sufficiently professionalized and diversified that even the onset of political coolness between the USSR and the DPRK would no longer have the drastic impact on the volume of Soviet writings on Korea that it seemed to have had at earlier stages of the game. Then, so much of Soviet work on Korea consisted of ad hoc political reportage and monitoring of current events that it was extremely vulnerable to any change in temperature between the two partners. As Soviet research branched out into more routinely academic fields, it would, in my estimate, acquire greater immunity from transient shocks of this kind. I still think the prognosis is valid.

I also noted that the pace of Soviet writing on Korea appeared to be slowing down and attributed this to the persistence of tensions between the USSR and the DPRK, Soviet unhappiness with Kim Il Sung's flirtation with Peking, his reckless behavior, his unabating cult of the personality, and the like. When I visited Moscow in the summer of 1974 and had a chance to talk at length with the people at the Institute of Oriental Studies, I was told that the so-called decline had a very simple explanation: the community of Soviet Koreanists had at last decided to pool its efforts in turning out a series of major treatises on Korea (the two-volume set on the history of Korea, the reference tome on contemporary Korea, and the like) which consumed both time and energy. Presumably, a point had been reached when it was felt that the churning out of smaller pieces, articles and pamphlets, was not productive any more and had ceased to meet the profession's requirements. Synthesizing tomes which put together all that had been learned so far and would serve as a launching pad for the ascent to the next plateau were given priority. Some of these projects have, as previously indicated, already borne fruit, but at the expense of "regular production" as it were. Once the foundations are laid, the tempo may well pick up again.

NOTE

1. The oversight is being corrected. The Institute for Oriental Studies of the USSR Academy of Sciences is now preparing a comprehensive bibliography of Soviet writings on Korea since 1917. The volume is likely to come out around the same time as the present guide.

BIBLIOGRAPHY

BIBLIOGRAPHIC GUIDES AND SURVEYS

16-001. DREYER, O. K. "Publication of Orientalist Literature in the U.S.S.R. and Its Trends." In B. G. Gafurov (ed.), *Asia in Soviet Studies.* Moscow: "Nauka," 1969.

16-002. KAZAKEVICH, I. S. "Internatsionalnyi dolg Koreevedov [The international debt of the Koreanists]." In *Nerushimaya druzhba* [Indestructible friendship]. Moscow: "Nauka," 1971.

16-003. KUZNETSOVA, N. A. and L. M. KULAGINA. *Iz istorii Sovetskogo vostokovedeniya 1917–1967* [From the history of Soviet Oriental studies 1917–1967]. Moscow: "Nauka," 1970.

GENERAL

16-004. *Koreya: Sever i Yug* [Korea: north and south]. Moscow: "Nauka," 1965. 262 pp.

16-005. *Nerushimaya druzhba: sbornik statei* [Indestructible friendship: collection of articles]. Moscow: "Nauka," 1971. 190 pp.

16-006. *Sovremennaya Koreya: spravochnoe izdanie* [Modern Korea: reference volume]. Moscow: "Nauka," 1971. 418 pp.

16-007. *Vo imya druzhby s narodom Korei: vospominaniya i stat'i* [In the name of friendship with the people of Korea: recollections and articles]. Moscow: "Nauka," 1965. 229 pp.

GEOGRAPHY

16-008. GARIN, N. G. [N. G. MIKHAILOVSKII]. *Iz dnevnikov krugosvetnogo puteshestviya po Koree, Manchzhurii i Lyaodunskomu poluostrovu* [From diaries of a round-the-world voyage through Korea, Manchuria and the Liaotung peninsula]. Abridged edition with introductory article and commentaries by V. T. Zaichikov. Moscow: Geografgiz, 1949. 404 pp.

16-009. MARTYNOV, V. V. *Koreya: ekonomiko-geograficheskaya kharakteristika KNDR i Yuzhnoi Korei* [Korea: economic-geographic description of the DPRK and South Korea]. Moscow: "Mysl," 1970. 215 pp.

16-010. *Opisanie Korei* [Description of Korea]. Sokr. pereizd., pod. red. I. S. Kazakevicha i dr., Moscow: Izd. vost. lit., 1960. 662 pp.

16-011. *Po Koree: Puteshestviya 1885–1896 gg.* [Through Korea: travels 1885–1896]. Anthology compiled with introduction and commentaries by G. D. Tyagai. Moscow: Izd. vost. lit., 1958. 292 pp. (Russkie puteshestvenniki v stranakh Vostoka.)

16-012. ZAICHIKOV, V. T. *Koreya* [Korea]. 2nd ed. Moscow: Geografgiz, 1951. 480 pp.

16-013. _____. "Vklad russkikh uchenykh v issledovanie Korei [Contribution of Russian scientists to the exploration of Korea]." *Voprosy geografii* 8(1948):37–60.

HISTORY

16-014. DZHARYLGASINOVA, R. Sh. *Drevnie kogurestsy (k etnicheskoi istorii koreitsev)* [The ancient Koguryŏs: on the ethnic history of Koreans]. Moscow: "Nauka," 1972. 201 pp.

16-015. IONOVA, Yu. V. "Koreiskaya derevnya v kontse XIX–nachale XXvv. (Ist.-etnogr. ocherk) [The Korean village at the end of the 19th–beginning of the 20th century: a historical-ethnographic essay]." *Trudy in-ta etnografii im. Miklukho-Maklaya* 60(1960):3–118.

16-016. *Istoriya Korei* [History of Korea]. 2 vols. Moscow: "Nauka," 1974.

16-017. KAZAKEVICH, I. S. *Agrarnye otnosheniya v Koree nakanune vtoroi mirovoi voiny* [Agrarian relations in Korea on the eve of the Second World War]. Moscow: Izd. vost. lit., 1958. 127 pp.

16-018. KHAN, M. *Osvoboditelnaya borba koreiskogo naroda v gody yaponskogo protektorata (1905–1910 gg)* [The liberation struggle of the Korean people in the years of the Japanese Protectorate: 1905–1910]. Moscow: Izd. vost. lit., 1961. 71 pp.

16-019. KIM, G. F. and F. I. SHABSHINA. *Proletarskii internatsionalizm i revolyutsii v stranakh vostoka* [Proletarian internationalism and revolutions in the countries of the East]. Moscow: "Nauka," 1967. 399 pp.

16-020. KIM, Syn Khva. *Ocherki po istorii sovetskikh koreitsev* [Essays on the history of Soviet Koreans]. Alma-Ata: "Nauka," 1965. 251 pp.

16-021. MAZUROV, V. M. *Antiyaponskaya vooruzhennaya borba koreiskogo naroda (1931–1940)* [The anti-Japanese armed struggle of the Korean people: 1931–1940]. Moscow: Izd. vost. lit., 1958. 104 pp.

16-022. PAK, B. D. *Osvoboditelnaya borba koreiskogo naroda nakanune pervoi mirovoi voiny* [The liberation struggle of the Korean people on the eve of the First World War]. Moscow: "Nauka," 1967. 167 pp.

16-023. PAK, M. N. "O kharaktere sotsialno-ekonomicheskikh otnoshenii v gosudarstve Silla (III–VIvv.) [On the character of social-economic relations in the Silla Kingdom: 3rd–6th centuries]." *Voprosy istorii* 7(1956): 49–65.

16-024. SHABSHINA, F. I. *Narodnoe vosstanie 1919 g. v Koree* [Popular uprising of 1919 in Korea]. Moscow: Izd. AN SSSR, 1952. 280 pp.

16-025. SHIPAEV, V. I. *Kolonialnoe zakabalenie Korei yaponskim imperializmom (1895–1917)* [The colonial enslavement of Korea by Japanese imperialism: 1895–1917]. Moscow: "Nauka," 1964. 242 pp.

16-026. _____. *Koreiskaya burzhuaziya v natsionalno-osvoboditelnom dvizhenii* [The Korean bourgeoisie in the national liberation movement]. Moscow: "Nauka," 1966. 299 pp.

16-027. TYAGAI, G. D. *Krestyanskoe vosstanie v Koree 1893–1895 gg.* [Peasant uprising of 1893–1895 in Korea]. Moscow: Izd. AN SSSR, 1953. 208 pp.

16-028. _____. "Materialy arkhivov Moskvy i Leningrada

kak istochnik dlya izucheniya istorii Korei XIXv. [Materials of the archives of Moscow and Leningrad as a source for the study of the history of Korea of the 19th century]." *Kratkie soobsch. In-ta narodov Azii* 64(1963): 115–124.

16-029. _____. *Narodnoe dvizhenie v Koree vo vtoroi polovine XIX veka* [Popular movement in Korea in the second half of the 19th century]. Moscow: Izd. AN SSSR, 1958. 191 pp.

16-030. _____. *Obshchestvennaya mysl Korei v epokhu pozdnego feodalizma* [Social thought in Korea in the period of late feudalism]. Moscow: "Nauka," 1971. 256 pp.

16-031. VANIN, Yu. V. *Ekonomicheskoe razvitie Korei v XVII–XVIII. vekakh* [The economic development of Korea in the 17th–18th centuries]. Moscow: "Nauka," 1968. 285 pp.

16-032. _____. *Feodalnaya Koreya v XIII–XIV vekakh* [Feudal Korea in the 13th–14th centuries]. Moscow: Izd. vost. lit., 1962. 198 pp.

ECONOMICS
General

16-033. GLEBOVA, M. E. *Razvitie ekonomiki Koreiskoi Narodno-Demokraticheskoi Respubliki: kratkii ekon. obzor* [Development of thc economy of the Democratic People's Republic of Korea: concise economic survey]. Moscow: 1959. 90 pp.

16-034. KARSHINOV, L. N. "Koreiskaya Narodno-Demokraticheskaya Respublika [The Korean People's Democratic Republic]." In *Razvitie ekonomiki stran narodnoi demokratii Azii (obzor za 1956g.)* [Development of the economy of the countries of People's Democracy of Asia: survey for 1956]. Moscow: Vneshtorgizdat, 1957.

16-035. _____. "Koreiskaya Narodno-Demokraticheskaya Respublika [The Democratic People's Republic of Korea]." In *Razvitie ekonomiki stran narodnoi demokratii Evropy i Azii (statisticheskii sbornik)* [Development of the economy of the countries of People's Democracy of Europe and Asia: statistical collection]. Moscow: Vneshtorgizdat, 1961.

16-036. KIM, G. F. "Ekonomicheskoe i kulturnoe stroitelstvo v Koreiskoi Narodno-Demokraticheskoi Respublike (1945–1950gg) [Economic and cultural construction in the Democratic People's Republic of Korea: 1945–1950]." *Voprosy istorii* 6(1954):27–42.

16-037. _____. *Rabochii klass novoi Korei* [The working class of new Korea]. Moscow: Profizdat, 1960. 111 pp.

16-038. *Koreya: Istoriya i ekonomika: sbornik statei* [Korea: history and economy: collection of articles]. Edited by I. S. Kazakevich. Moscow: Izd. vost. lit., 1958. 236 pp.

16-039. SEMENOVA, N. P. "Razvitie vnutrennei torgovli v Koreiskoi Narodno-Demokraticheskoi Respublike [Development of internal trade in the Democratic People's Republic of Korea]." *Uchenye zapiski kafedry geografii i ekonomiki stran Vostoka* (In-t mezhdunarodnykh otnoshenii) 3(1960):31–50.

16-040. TRIGUBENKO, M. E. "Koreiskaya Narodno-Demokraticheskaya Respublika [The Democratic People's Republic of Korea]." In *Mirovaya sotsialisticheskaya sistema khozyaistva* [The world socialist economic system]. Vol. 4. Moscow: "Mysl," 1967.

Agriculture

16-041. KIM, N. S. "Agrarnye preobrazovaniya v Koreiskoi Narodno-Demokraticheskoi Respublike [Agrarian transformations in the Democratic People's Republic of Korea]." In E. F. Kovalev (ed.), *Agrarnye preobrazovaniya v narodno-demokraticheskikh stranakh Azii* [Agrarian transformations in the people's democratic countries of Asia]. Moscow: Gospolitizdat, 1957.

16-042. KOROLEV, P. G. "Nekotorye voprosy sotsialisticheskogo stroitelstva v selskom khozyaistve KNDR (1953–1961gg.) [Some questions of socialist construction in the rural economy of the Democratic People's Republic of Korea: 1953–1961]." *Kratkie soobshch. In-ta narodov Azii* 59(1961):46–57.

16-043. TRIGUBENKO, M. E. *Selskoe khozyaistvo KNDR: Put sotsialisticheskogo razvitiya* [The rural economy of the DPRK: path of socialist development]. Moscow: "Nauka," 1973. 135 pp.

Industry

16-044. GRYAZNOV, G. V. *Sotsialisticheskaya industrializatsiya v KNDR (1945–1960gg.)* [Socialist industrialization in the DPRK: 1945–1960]. Moscow: "Nauka," 1966. 216 pp.

Foreign Trade and Aid

16-045. KARSHINOV, L. N. *Koreiskaya Narodno-Demokraticheskaya Respublika: ekonomika i vneshnyaya torgovlya* [The Democratic People's Republic of Korea: economy and foreign trade]. Moscow: Vneshtorgizdat, 1958. 94 pp.

16-046. SEMENOVA, N. P. "Znachenie vneshnetorgovykh svyazei dlya razvitiya narodnogo khozyaistva Koreiskoi Narodno-Demokraticheskoi Respubliki [The significance of foreign trade ties for the development of the national economy of the Democratic People's Republic of Korea]." *Uchenye zapiski In-ta mezhdunarodnykh otnoshenii* (Moscow), 9(1962):43-65.

16-047. SUSLINA, S. S. "Nekotorye voprosy razvitiya ekonomicheskogo sotrudnichestva mezhdu SSSR i KNDR [Some questions of development of economic cooperation between the USSR and the DPRK]." In *Dalnii Vostok: istoriya, ekonomika* [Far East: history, economy]. Moscow: "Nauka," 1974.

South Korea

16-048. KAZAKEVICH, I. S. *Agrarnyi vopros v Yuzhnoi Korei* [The agrarian question in South Korea]. Moscow: "Nauka," 1964. 157 pp.

16-049. SINITSYN, B. V. *Ocherki ekonomiki Yuzhnoi Korei (1953-1964)* [Essays on the economy of South Korea: 1953-1964]. Moscow: "Nauka," 1967. 171 pp.

16-050. _____. *Promyshlennost i polozhenie rabochego klassa Yuzhnoi Korei (1945-1959gg.)* [Industry and the situation of the working class of South Korea: 1945-1959]. Moscow: Izd. vost. lit., 1961. 152 pp.

POLITICS

16-051. BAGMET, N. S. *Borba koreiskogo naroda za postroenie sotsializma 1945-1960gg.* [Struggle of the Korean people for the construction of socialism: 1945-1960]. Kiev: Izd. Kievskogo un-ta, 1960. 227 pp.

16-052. BAYANOV, B. *Narodnaya Koreya na puti k sotsializmu* [People's Korea on the path to socialism]. Moscow: Gospolitizdat, 1959. 144 pp.

16-053. *15 let osvobozhdeniya Korei: sbornik statei* [Fifteen years of the liberation of Korea: collection of articles]. Moscow: Izd. IMO, 1960. 154 pp.

16-054. SHABSHINA, F. I. *Sotsialisticheskaya Koreya (O formakh proyavleniya v Koreiskoi Narodno-Demokraticheskoi Respublike obshchikh zakonomernostei stroitelstva sotsializma)* [Socialist Korea: on the forms of manifestation in the Democratic People's Republic of Korea of the general laws of building socialism]. Moscow: Izd. vost. lit., 1963. 199 pp.

16-055. _____. *Yuzhnaya Koreya 1945-1946gg.: Zapiski ochevidtsa* [South Korea 1945-1946: notes of an eyewitness]. Moscow: "Nauka," 1974. 271 pp.

16-056. VAINTSVAIG, N. K. and V. V. LEZIN (eds.). *Koreiskaya Narodno-Demokraticheskaya Respublika: sbornik statei* [The Democratic People's Republic of Korea: collection of articles]. Moscow: Izd. AN SSSR, 1954. 448 pp.

16-057. VAINTSVAIG, N. K., V. V. LEZEN, et al. (eds.).

Ocherki sotsialisticheskogo stroitelstva v Koreiskoi Narodno-Demokraticheskoi Respublike [Essays on socialist construction in the Democratic People's Republic of Korea]. Moscow: Izd. vost. lit., 1963. 290 pp.

LAW

16-058. GUDOSHNIKOV, L. M. "Perestroika upravleniya narodnym khozyaistvom v Koreiskoi Narodno-Demokraticheskoi Respublike [Reorganization of the management of the national economy in the Democratic People's Republic of Korea]." *Sovetskoe gosudarstvo i pravo* 3(1961): 73-77.

16-059. KIM, V. A. *Gosudarstvennyi stroi Koreiskoi Narodno-Demokraticheskoi Respubliki* [State structure of the Democratic People's Republic of Korea]. Moscow: Gosyurizdat, 1955. 203 pp.

16-060. _____. *Rol narodno-demokraticheskogo gosudarstva i prava v sotsialisticheskom preobrazovanii selskogo khozyaistva (na opyte Koreiskoi Narodno-Demokraticheskoi Respubliki)* [Role of the people's democratic state and law in the socialist transformation of the rural economy: on the experience of the Democratic People's Republic of Korea]. Alma-Ata: Izd. AN KazSSR, 1962. 312 pp.

16-061. SHCHETININ, B. V. "Vlast—narodu [Power to the people]." In *Vo imya druzhby s narodom Korei: vospominaniya i stat'i* [In the name of friendship with the people of Korea: recollections and articles]. Moscow: "Nauka," 1965.

16-062. _____. "Vozniknovenie narodnykh komitetov v Severnoi Koree [Inception of people's committees in North Korea]." *Sovetskoe gosudarstvo i pravo* 4(1947): 67-72.

16-063. TAVROV, G. [G. I. TUNKIN] (ed.). *Konstitutsiya i osnovnye zakonodatelnye akty Koreiskoi Narodno-Demokraticheskoi Respubliki* [Constitution and basic legislative acts of the Democratic People's Republic of Korea]. Moscow: Izd. inostr. lit., 1952. 396 pp.

INTERNATIONAL RELATIONS

16-064. KIM, G. F. (ed.). *Yuzhnaya Koreya: Ekonomicheskoe i politicheskoe polozhenie (1945-1958gg.)* [South Korea: economic and political position: 1945-1958]. Moscow: Izd. vost. lit., 1959. 272 pp.

16-065. MAZUROV, V. M. *Sozdanie antinarodnogo rezhima v Yuzhnoi Koree (1945-1950gg.)* [Creation of an antipopular regime in South Korea: 1945-1950]. Moscow: Izd. vost. lit., 1963. 195 pp.

16-066. _____. *Yuzhnaya Koreya i SShA (1950-1970 gody)* [South Korea and the USA: 1950-1970]. Moscow: "Nauka," 1971. 267 pp.

16-067. MAZUROV, V. M. and B. V. SINITSYN. *Yuzhnaya Koreya: Dramaticheskoe perep$u$tie* [South Korea: dramatic crossroads]. Moscow: Izd. vost. lit., 1963. 152 pp.

16-068. NOVIKOV, I. T. "Chetvert veka druzhby i sotrudnichestva (K 25-letiyu Soglasheniya ob ekonomicheskom i kulturnom sotrudnichestve mezhdu SSSR i KNDR) [A quarter century of friendship and cooperation: on the occasion of the 25th anniversary of the agreement on economic and cultural cooperation between the USSR and the DPRK]." *Problemy Dalnego Vostoka* 1(1974):3–12.

16-069. PIGULEVSKAYA, E. A. *Koreiskii narod v borbe za nezavisimost i demokratiyu* [The Korean people in the struggle for independence and democracy]. Moscow: Izd. AN SSSR, 1952. 362 pp.

16-070. ROMASHKIN, P. *Za mirnoe razreshenie koreiskogo voprosa* [For the peaceful solution of the Korean question]. Moscow: Gospolitizdat, 1954. 100 pp.

16-071. SAMSONOV, G. E. *Borba za mirnoe demokraticheskoe reshenie koreiskogo voprosa* [Struggle for a peaceful, democratic solution of the Korean question]. Moscow: Izd. vost. lit., 1960. 143 pp.

16-072. TAVROV, G. [G. I. TUNKIN]. "Koreiskii vopros posle vtoroi mirovoi voiny [The Korean question after the Second World War]." *Sovetskoe gosudarstvo i pravo* 7(1950):27–42.

16-073. VORONTSOV, V. B. *Koreya v planakh SShA v gody vtoroi mirovoi voiny* [Korea in the plans of the USA in the years of the Second World War]. Moscow: Izd. vost. lit., 1962. 140 pp.

KOREAN WAR

16-074. "Bakteriologicheskaya voina—prestupnoe orudie amerikanskikh imperialistov [Bacteriological warfare—criminal weapon of American imperialists]." *Izvestiya AN SSSR, ot-d ekonomiki i prava* 2(1952):89–97.

16-075. KOROVIN, E. A. *Chudovishchnye zlodeyaniya amerikanskikh agressorov v Koree* [Monstrous crimes of the American aggressors in Korea]. Moscow: "Znanie," 1952. 24 pp.

16-076. KRAVTSOV, I. *Agressiya amerikanskogo imperializma v Koree, 1945-1951gg.* [Aggression of American imperialism in Korea: 1945-1951]. Moscow: Gospolitizdat, 1951. 440 pp.

16-077. MOLODTSOV, S. "Prestupnoe narushenie amerikanskimi interventami v Koree zakonov i obychaev voiny [Criminal violation by American interventionists in Korea of the laws and customs of war]." *Sotsialisticheskaya zakonnost* 12(1952):26–35.

16-078. RAGINSKII, M. Yu., S. Ya ROZENBLIT, and L. N. SMIRNOV. *Bakteriologicheskaya voina—prestupnoe orudie imperialisticheskoi agressii* [Bacteriological warfare—criminal weapon of imperialist aggression]. Moscow: Izd. AN SSSR, 1950. 136 pp.

16-079. ROMASHKIN, P. S. *Chudovishchnye prestupleniya amerikanskikh agressorov v Koree* [Monstrous crimes of American aggressors in Korea]. Moscow: Gospolitizdat, 1953. 207 pp.

16-080. TAVROV, G. [G. I. TUNKIN]. "Prestupnaya voina amerikanskikh imperialistov protiv koreiskogo naroda [Criminal war of the American imperialists against the Korean people]." *Trudy Instituta prava AN SSSR* (Moscow), 1(1951):85–111.

16-081. VASIL'EV, A., I. VOLK, and V. KORNILOV. *Koreya v borbe: zametki zhurnalistov* [Korea in the struggle: notes of journalists]. Moscow: "Sovetskii pisatel," 1951. 112 pp.

16-082. ZASLAVSKII, D. *Peremirie v Koree—vazhnyi vklad v delo mira* [Armistice in Korea—important contribution to the cause of peace]. Moscow: Gospolitizdat, 1953. 40 pp.

MILITARIA

16-083. MATSULENKO, V. *Koreiskaya Narodnaya Armiya* [The Korean People's Army]. Moscow: Voenizdat, 1959. 126 pp.

16-084. TOLCHENOV, M. P. *Vooruzhennaya borba koreiskogo naroda za svoyu svobodu i nezavisimost: obzor voennykh deistvii* [The armed struggle of the Korean people for its freedom and independence: a survey of military actions]. Moscow: Voenizdat, 1952. 112 pp.

16-085. YURZHONOV, V. *V geroicheskoi Koree: zapiski sovetskogo zhurnalista* [In heroic Korea: notes of a Soviet journalist]. Moscow: Voenizdat, 1958. 164 pp.

ARTS

16-086. DZHARYLGASINOVA, R. Sh. "Monumentalnaya zhivopis drevne-koguresskikh grobnits (iz istorii koreiskogo izobrazitelnogo iskusstva) [Monumental painting on ancient Koguryŏ tombs: from the history of Korean pictorial art]." *Problemy vostokovedeniya* 4(1959):35–40.

16-087. KYUNER, N. V. and E. T. DUBROVINA. "Drevnii koreiskii farfor iz kollektsii Muzeya antropologii i etnografii [Ancient Korean porcelain from the collection of the Museum of Anthropology and Ethnography]." *Sbornik Muzeya antropologii i etnografii* (In-t etnografii im. Miklukho-Maklaya), 15(1953):332–356.

CULTURE AND EDUCATION

16-088. KOVALENKO, S. S. "Razvitie narodnogo obrazovaniya v Koreiskoi Narodno-Demokraticheskoi Respublike [Development of public education in the Democratic People's Republic of Korea]." *Sovetskaya pedagogika* 10(1960):126–137.

16-089. NAM, S. G. *Formirovanie narodnoi intelligentsii v KNDR (1945–1962gg.)* [Formation of a people's intelligentsia in the DPRK: 1945–1962]. Moscow: "Nauka," 1970. 110 pp.

16-090. _____. "Politekhnicheskoe obuchenie v uchebnykh zavedeniyakh KNDR (1945–1960) [Polytechnical instruction in the educational institutions of the DPRK: 1945–1960]." In *Strany Dalnego Vostoka: Istoriya i ekonomika* [Countries of the Far East: history and economy]. Moscow: "Nauka," 1973.

16-091. _____. "Trudovoe vospitanie molodezhi v KNDR [Labor education of youth in the DPRK]." In *Strany Dalnego Vostoka: Istoriya i ekonomika* [Countries of the Far East: history and economy]. Moscow: "Nauka," 1973.

THE PRESS

16-092. PAK, B. D. "Iz istorii koreiskoi emigrantskoi pechati (1910–1914) [From the history of the Korean emigré press: 1910–1914]." *Narody Azii i Afriki* 3(1965):172–178.

LINGUISTICS

16-093. GUSEVA, E. K. *Sistema vidov v sovremennom koreiskom yazyke* [The system of aspects in the contemporary Korean language]. Moscow: Izd. vost. lit., 1961. 119 pp.

16-094. KHOLODOVICH, A. A. *Koreisko-russkii slovar* [Korean-Russian dictionary]. Moscow: Gos. izd. inostrannykh i natsionalnykh slovarei, 1951. 664 pp.

16-095. _____. *Ocherk grammatiki koreiskogo yazyka* [Essay on the grammar of the Korean language]. Moscow: Gosinlitizdat, 1954. 324 pp.

16-096. MAZUR, Yu. N. *Koreiskii yazyk* [Korean language]. Moscow: Izd. vost. lit., 1960. 117 pp.

16-097. _____. *Sklonenie v koreiskom yazyke* [Declension in the Korean language]. Moscow: Izd. Moskovskogo un-ta, 1962. 112 pp.

16-098. NIKOLSKII, L. B. "Formirovanie natsionalnogo literaturnogo yazyka v Koree [Formation of the national literary language in Korea]." In Akademiya Nauk SSSR, Institut narodov Azii, *Sovremennye literaturnye yazyki stran Azii* [Contemporary literary languages of the countries of Asia]. Moscow: 1965.

16-099. _____. *Sluzhebnye slova v koreiskom yazyke* [Service words in the Korean language]. Moscow: Izd. vost. lit., 1962. 179 pp.

16-100. USATOV, D. M. et al. *Russko-koreiskii slovar* [Russian-Korean dictionary]. Moscow: Gos. izd. inostrannykh i natsionalnykh slovarei, 1951. 1056 pp. Approximately 30,000 words; includes a concise grammatical outline of the Korean language by Yu. N. Mazur.

LITERATURE

16-101. *Ch'unhyang chon: Chkunkhyan Kvonzhitan: kratkaya povest o Chkhunkhyan* [*Ch'unhyang chŏn:* The Tale of Ch'unhyang]. Translation, introduction, and commentary by A. F. Trotsevich. Moscow: "Nauka," 1968. Facsimiles. (Pamyatniki pismennosti Vostoka.)

16-102. ELISEEV, D. D. *Koreiskaya srednevekovaya literatura pkhesol (Nekotorye problemy proiskhozhdeniya i zhanra)* [The Korean medieval literature P'aesŏl: some problems of origins and genre]. Moscow: "Nauka," 1968. 136 pp.

16-103. EREMENKO, L. E. and V. I. IVANOVA. *Koreiskaya literatura: kratkii ocherk* [Korean literature: brief outline]. Moscow: "Nauka," 1964. 154 pp. (Literatura Vostoka.)

16-104. IVANOVA, V. I. "Iz istorii proletarskogo literaturnogo dvizheniya v Koree (1924–1934gg.) [From the history of the proletarian literary movement in Korea: 1924–1934]." *Kratkie soobshch. In-ta vostokovedeniya* (Moscow), 24(1958):38–50.

16-105. _____. *Li Gi En: Zhizn i tvorchestvo* [Yi Kiyŏng: Life and Work]. Moscow: izd. vost. lit., 1962. 103 pp.

16-106. KIM, Busik. *Samguk sagi (istoricheskie zapiski trekh gosudarstv, v 3-kh tomakh)* [*Samguk sagi:* historical notes of the Three Kingdoms, in 3 vols.]. Facsimile of Korean manuscript. Translation and commentary by M. N. Pak. Moscow: Izd. vost. lit., 1959. Vol. 1: *Letopisi Silla* [The chronicles of Silla].

16-107. KONTSEVICH, L. R. "Pervyi pamyatnik koreiskoi pismennosti [The first monument of Korean writing]." *Narody Azii i Afriki* 4(1965):160–173. Also published in English as "The First Monument of Korean Writing (Essay in Critical Translation)" in B. G. Gafurov (ed.), *Asia in Soviet Studies* (Moscow: "Nauka," 1969).

16-108. NIKITINA, M. I. and A. F. TROTSEVICH. *Ocherki istorii koreiskoi literatury do XIVv.* [Essays on the history of Korean literature prior to the 14th century]. Moscow: "Nauka," 1969. 238 pp.

16-109. TROTSEVICH, A. F. "Ideal cheloveka v koreiskoi srednevekovoi povesti [The ideal of man in the Korean medieval novel]." *Kratkie soobshch. In-ta narodov Azii* 63(1963):93–100.

NATURAL SCIENCES

16-110. GRIGOR'EV, V. M., S. I. GROSHIN, and Sen Uk PAK. "Osnovnye cherty geologicheskogo stroeniya Korei [Basic traits of the geological structure of Korea]." *Izvestiya vyssh. uchebnykh zavedenii, Geologiya i razvedka* 1(1960):3–17.

16-111. PUTINTSEV, V. K. and S. E. SINITSKII. "Kratkii ocherk geologii severno-vostochnoi chasti KNDR [Brief essay on the geology of the northeastern part of the DPRK]." *Trudy Vsesoyuznogo nauch.-issled. geol. in-ta* 100(1963):33–57.

16-112. RUSTANOVICH, D. N., V. L. MASAITIS, and Khen Suk CHON. "Seismichnost i voprosy seismicheskogo raionirovaniya Korei [Seismism and questions of seismic regionalization of Korea]." *Izvestiya Akademii nauk SSSR, seriya geofiz.* 10(1961):1441–1463.

Major Korean Dynasties and Rulers

Koguryŏ　高句麗　고구려　(?37 BC–AD 668)
1. Tongmyŏng Wang　東明王　동명왕　(37 BC–19 BC)
2. Yuri Wang　琉璃王　유리왕　(19 BC–AD 18)
3. Taemusin Wang　大武神王　대무신왕　(18–44)
4. Minjung Wang　閔中王　민중왕　(44–48)
5. Mobon Wang　慕本王　모본왕　(48–53)
6. T'aejo Wang　太祖王　태조왕　(53–146)
7. Ch'adae Wang　次大王　차대왕　(146–165)
8. Sindae Wang　新大王　신대왕　(165–179)
9. Kogukch'ŏn Wang　故國川王　고국천왕　(179–197)
10. Sansang Wang　山上王　산상왕　(197–227)
11. Tongch'ŏn Wang　東川王　동천왕　(227–248)
12. Chungch'ŏn Wang　中川王　중천왕　(248–270)
13. Sŏch'ŏn Wang　西川王　서천왕　(270–292)
14. Pongsang Wang　烽上王　봉상왕　(292–300)
15. Mich'ŏn Wang　美川王　미천왕　(300–331)
16. Kogug'wŏn Wang　故國原王　고국원왕　(331–371)
17. Sosurim Wang　小獸林王　소수림왕　(371–384)
18. Kogug'yang Wang　故國壤王　고국양왕　(384–391)
19. Kwanggaet'o Wang　廣開土王　광개토왕　(391–413)
20. Changsu Wang　長壽王　장수왕　(413–491)
21. Munja Wang　文咨王　문자왕　(491–519)
22. Anjang Wang　安藏王　안장왕　(519–531)
23. Anwŏn Wang　安原王　안원왕　(531–545)
24. Yangwŏn Wang　陽原王　양원왕　(545–559)
25. P'yŏngwŏn Wang　平原王　평원왕　(559–590)
26. Yŏngyang Wang　嬰陽王　영양왕　(590–618)
27. Yŏngnyu Wang　榮留王　영류왕　(618–642)
28. Pojang Wang　寶藏王　보장왕　(642–668)

Paekche　百濟　백제　(?18 BC–AD 660)
1. Onjo Wang　溫祚王　온조왕　(18 BC–AD 28)
2. Taru Wang　多婁王　다루왕　(28–77)
3. Kiru Wang　己婁王　기루왕　(77–128)
4. Kaeru Wang　盖婁王　개루왕　(128–166)
5. Ch'ogo Wang　肖古王　초고왕　(166–214)
6. Kusu Wang　仇首王　구수왕　(214–234)
7. Saban Wang　沙伴王　사반왕　(234)
8. Koi Wang　古爾王　고이왕　(234–286)
9. Ch'aekkye Wang　責稽王　책계왕　(286–298)
10. Punsŏ Wang　汾西王　분서왕　(298–304)
11. Piryu Wang　比流王　비류왕　(304–344)
12. Kye Wang　契王　계왕　(344–346)
13. Kŭnch'ogo Wang　近肖古王　근초고왕　(346–375)
14. Kŭngusu Wang　近仇首王　근구수왕　(375–384)
15. Ch'imnyu Wang　枕流王　침류왕　(384–385)
16. Chinsa Wang　辰斯王　진사왕　(385–392)
17. Asin Wang　阿莘王　아신왕　(392–405)
18. Chŏnji Wang　腆支王　전지왕　(405–420)
19. Kuisin Wang　久爾辛王　구이신왕　(420–427)
20. Piyu Wang　毗有王　비유왕　(427–455)
21. Kaero Wang　盖鹵王　개로왕　(455–475)
22. Munju Wang　文周王　문주왕　(475–477)
23. Samgŭn Wang　三斤王　삼근왕　(477–479)
24. Tongsŏng Wang　東城王　동성왕　(479–501)
25. Muryŏng Wang　武寧王　무령왕　(501–523)
26. Sŏng Wang　聖王　성왕　(523–554)
27. Widŏk Wang　威德王　위덕왕　(554–598)
28. Hye Wang　惠王　혜왕　(598–599)

29. Pŏp Wang　法王　법왕　(599–600)
30. Mu Wang　武王　무왕　(600–641)
31. Ŭija Wang　義慈王　의자왕　(641–660)
32. P'ung Wang　豊王　풍왕　(660–663)

Silla　新羅　신라　(57 BC–AD 935)
1. Hyŏkkŏse Kŏsŏgan　赫居世居西于　혁거세거서간
   (57 BC–AD 4)
2. Namhae Ch'ach'aung　南海次次雄　남해차차웅
   (4–24)
3. Yuri Nisagŭm　儒理尼師今　유리니사금　(24–57)
4. T'alhae Nisagŭm　脫解尼師今　탈해니사금　(57–80)
5. P'asa Nisagŭm　婆娑尼師今　파사니사금　(80–112)
6. Chima Nisagŭm　祇摩尼師今　지마니사금　(112–134)
7. Ilsŏng Nisagŭm　逸聖尼師今　일성니사금　(134–154)
8. Adalla Nisagŭm　阿達羅尼師今　아달라니사금
   (154–184)
9. Pŏrhyu Nisagŭm　伐休尼師今　벌휴니사금　(184–195)
10. Naehae Nisagŭm　奈解尼師今　내해니사금
    (195–230)
11. Chobun Nisagŭm　助賁尼師今　조분니사금
    (230–247)
12. Ch'ŏmhae Nisagŭm　沾解尼師今　첨해니사금
    (247–261)
13. Mich'u Nisagŭm　味鄒尼師今　미추니사금　(261–284)
14. Yurye Nisagŭm　儒禮尼師今　유례니사금　(284–298)
15. Kirim Nisagŭm　基臨尼師今　기림니사금　(298–310)
16. Hŭlhae Nisagŭm　訖解尼師今　흘해니사금　(310–356)
17. Naemul Maripkan　奈勿麻立干　내물마립간
    (356–402)
18. Silsŏng Maripkan　實聖麻立干　실성마립간
    (402–417)
19. Nulchi Maripkan　訥祇麻立干　눌지마립간
    (417–458)
20. Chabi Maripkan　慈悲麻立干　자비마립간　(458–479)
21. Soji Maripkan　炤知麻立干　소지마립간　(479–500)
22. Chijŭng Wang　智證王　지증왕　(500–514)
23. Pŏphŭng Wang　法興王　법흥왕　(514–540)
24. Chinhŭng Wang　眞興王　진흥왕　(540–576)
25. Chinji Wang　眞智王　진지왕　(576–579)
26. Chinp'yŏng Wang　眞平王　진평왕　(579–632)
27. Sŏndŏk Yŏwang　善德女王　선덕여왕
    (632–647)(queen)
28. Chindŏk Yŏwang　眞德女王　진덕여왕
    (647–654) (queen)
29. Muyŏl Wang　武烈王　무열왕　(654–661)
30. Munmu Wang　文武王　문무왕　(661–681)
31. Sinmun Wang　神文王　신문왕　(681–692)

32. Hyoso Wang　孝昭王　효소왕　(692–702)
33. Sŏngdŏk Wang　聖德王　성덕왕　(702–737)
34. Hyosŏng Wang　孝成王　효성왕　(737–742)
35. Kyŏngdŏk Wang　景德王　경덕왕　(742–765)
36. Hyegong Wang　惠恭王　혜공왕　(765–780)
37. Sŏndŏk Wang　宣德王　선덕왕　(780–785)
38. Wŏnsŏng Wang　元聖王　원성왕　(785–798)
39. Sosŏng Wang　昭聖王　소성왕　(798–800)
40. Aejang Wang　哀莊王　애장왕　(800–809)
41. Hŏndŏk Wang　憲德王　헌덕왕　(809–826)
42. Hŭngdŏk Wang　興德王　흥덕왕　(826–836)
43. Hŭigang Wang　僖康王　희강왕　(836–838)
44. Minae Wang　閔哀王　민애왕　(838–839)
45. Sinmu Wang　神武王　신무왕　(839)
46. Munsŏng Wang　文聖王　문성왕　(839–857)
47. Hŏnan Wang　憲安王　헌안왕　(857–861)
48. Kyŏngmun Wang　景文王　경문왕　(861–875)
49. Hŏn'gang Wang　憲康王　헌강왕　(875–886)
50. Chŏnggang Wang　定康王　정강왕　(886–887)
51. Chinsŏng Yŏwang　眞聖女王　진성여왕　(887–897)
    (queen)
52. Hyogong Wang　孝恭王　효공왕　(897–912)
53. Sindŏk Wang　神德王　신덕왕　(912–917)
54. Kyŏngmyŏng Wang　景明王　경명왕　(917–924)
55. Kyŏng'ae Wang　景哀王　경애왕　(924–927)
56. Kyŏngsun Wang　敬順王　경순왕　(927–935)

Karak (Kaya)　駕洛(伽倻)　가락(가야)　(?AD 42–532)
1. Suro Wang　首露王　수로왕　(42–199)
2. Kŏdŭng Wang　居登王　거등왕　(199–259)
3. Map'um Wang　麻品王　마품왕　(259–291)
4. Kŏjilmi Wang　居叱彌王　거질미왕　(291–346)
5. Isip'um Wang　伊尸品王　이시품왕　(346–407)
6. Chwaji Wang　坐知王　좌지왕　(407–421)
7. Ch'wihi Wang　吹希王　취히왕　(421–451)
8. Chilchi Wang　銍知王　질지왕　(451–492)
9. Kyŏmji Wang　鉗知王　겸지왕　(492–521)
10. Kuhyŏng Wang　仇衡王　구형왕　(521–532)

Parhae　渤海　발해　(699–926)
1. Ko Wang (Taejoyŏng)　高王(大祚榮)　고왕(대조영)
   (699–719)
2. Mu Wang　武王　무왕　(719–737)
3. Mun Wang　文王　문왕　(737–793)
4. Wang Wŏnŭi　王元義　왕원의　(793–794)
5. Sŏng Wang　成王　성왕　(794–795)
6. Kang Wang　康王　강왕　(795–809)
7. Chŏng Wang　定王　정왕　(809–813)

8. Hŭi Wang 僖王 회왕 (813–817)
9. Kan Wang 簡王 간왕 (817–818)
10. Sŏn Wang 宣王 선왕 (818–830)
11. Wang Ichin 王彝震 왕이진 (830–858)
12. Wang Kŏnhwang 王虔晃 왕건황 (858–870)
13. Kyŏng Wang 景王 경왕 (870–901)
14. Ae Wang 哀王 애왕 (901–926)

Koryŏ 高麗 고려 (918–1392)
1. T'aejo 太祖 태조 (918–943)
2. Hyejong 惠宗 혜종 (943–945)
3. Chŏngjong 定宗 정종 (945–949)
4. Kwangjong 光宗 광종 (949–975)
5. Kyŏngjong 景宗 경종 (975–981)
6. Sŏngjong 成宗 성종 (981–997)
7. Mokchong 穆宗 목종 (997–1009)
8. Hyŏnjong 顯宗 현종 (1009–1031)
9. Tŏkjong 德宗 덕종 (1031–1034)
10. Chŏngjong 靖宗 정종 (1034–1046)
11. Munjong 文宗 문종 (1046–1083)
12. Sunjong 順宗 순종 (1083)
13. Sŏnjong 宣宗 선종 (1083–1094)
14. Hŏnjong 獻宗 헌종 (1094–1095)
15. Sukjong 肅宗 숙종 (1095–1105)
16. Yejong 睿宗 예종 (1105–1122)
17. Injong 仁宗 인종 (1122–1146)
18. Ŭijong 毅宗 의종 (1146–1170)
19. Myŏngjong 明宗 명종 (1170–1197)
20. Sinjong 神宗 신종 (1197–1204)
21. Hŭijong 熙宗 희종 (1204–1211)
22. Kangjong 康宗 강종 (1211–1213)
23. Kojong 高宗 고종 (1213–1259)
24. Wŏnjong 元宗 원종 (1259–1274)
25. Ch'ungnyŏl Wang 忠烈王 충열왕 (1274–1308)
26. Ch'ungsŏn Wang 忠宣王 충선왕 (1308–1313)
27. Ch'ungsuk Wang 忠肅王 충숙왕 (1313–1330)
28. Ch'unghye Wang 忠惠王 충혜왕 (1330–1332)
29. Ch'ungsuk Wang 忠肅王 충숙왕 (1332–1339)
    (restored to throne)
30. Ch'unghye Wang 忠惠王 충혜왕 (1339–1344)
    (restored to throne)
31. Ch'ungmok Wang 忠穆王 충목왕 (1344–1348)
32. Ch'ungjŏng Wang 忠定王 충정왕 (1348–1351)
33. Kongmin Wang 恭愍王 공민왕 (1351–1374)
34. Sin'u 辛禑 신우 (1374–1388) (considered a usurper)
35. Sinch'ang 辛昌 신창 (1388–1389) (considered a usurper)
36. Kong'yang Wang 恭讓王 공양왕 (1389–1392)

Chosŏn 朝鮮 조선 (1392–1910)
1. T'aejo 太祖 태조 (1392–1398)
2. Chŏngjong 定宗 정종 (1398–1400)
3. T'aejong 太宗 태종 (1400–1418)
4. Sejong 世宗 세종 (1418–1450)
5. Munjong 文宗 문종 (1450–1452)
6. Tanjong 端宗 단종 (1452–1455)
7. Sejo 世祖 세조 (1455–1468)
8. Yejong 睿宗 예종 (1468–1469)
9. Sŏngjong 成宗 성종 (1469–1494)
10. Yŏnsan-gun 燕山君 연산군 (1494–1506)
11. Chungjong 中宗 중종 (1506–1544)
12. Injong 仁宗 인종 (1544–1545)
13. Myŏngjong 明宗 명종 (1545–1567)
14. Sŏnjo 宣祖 선조 (1567–1608)
15. Kwanghae-gun 光海君 광해군 (1608–1623)
16. Injo 仁祖 인조 (1623–1649)
17. Hyojong 孝宗 효종 (1649–1659)
18. Hyŏnjong 顯宗 현종 (1659–1674)
19. Sukjong 肅宗 숙종 (1674–1720)
20. Kyŏngjong 景宗 경종 (1720–1724)
21. Yŏngjo 英祖 영조 (1724–1776)
22. Chŏngjo 正祖 정조 (1776–1800)
23. Sunjo 純祖 순조 (1800–1834)
24. Hŏnjong 憲宗 헌종 (1834–1849)
25. Ch'ŏljong 哲宗 철종 (1849–1863)
26. Kojong 高宗 고종 (1863–1907)
27. Sunjong 純宗 순종 (1907–1910)

Japanese Government-General of Chōsen (1910–1945)
1. Terauchi Masatake 寺内正毅 (1910–1916)
2. Hasegawa Yoshimichi 長谷川好道 (1916–1919)
3. Saitō Makoto 齋藤實 (1919–1927)
4. Ugaki Kazushige 宇垣一成 (1927) (acting governor-general)
5. Yamanashi Hanzō 山梨半造 (1927–1929)
6. Saitō Makoto 齋藤實 (1929–1931)
7. Ugaki Kazushige 宇垣一成 (1931–1936)
8. Minami Jirō 南次郎 (1936–1942)
9. Koiso Kuniaki 小磯國昭 (1942–1944)
10. Abe Nobuyuki 阿部信行 (1944–1945)

Republic of Korea (1948–)
1. Yi, Sŭng-man (Syngman Rhee) 李承晚 이승만 (1948–1960)
   President: first elected 1948; reelected 1952, 1956, 1960
2. Hŏ, Chŏng 許政 허정 (1960)
   Acting president, interim government

3. Yun, Po-sŏn 尹譜善 윤보선 (1960–1961)
   President
4. Pak, Chŏng-hŭi (Chung Hee Park) 朴正熙 박정희
   (1961–)
   Chairman, Supreme Council for National Reconstruction
   (1961–1963)
   President: first elected 1963; reelected 1967, 1971, 1972,
   1978

Democratic People's Republic of Korea (1948–)
1. Kim, Tu-bong 金枓奉 김두봉 (1948–1957)
   Chairman of the Presidium of the Supreme People's
   Assembly
2. Ch'oe, Yong-gŏn 崔鏞健 최용건 (1957–1972)
   Chairman of the Presidium of the Supreme People's
   Assembly: first elected 1957; reelected 1962, 1967
3. Kim Il-sŏng (Kim Il Sung) 金日成 김일성
   (1948–)
   Premier: 1948–1972
   President: 1972–

AUTHOR INDEX

1. Authors are arranged in alphabetical order. Family names appear first (in capital letters) followed by the personal names.

2. The numerals that follow the authors' names are the bibliographic item numbers used throughout the guide; the first two digits indicate the chapter.

3. When more than one work by the same author is cited, the first two digits of the item number are not repeated if they are identical. Semicolons are used between items appearing in different chapters. For example: 03-123, 258; 08-037.

4. When there is more than one citation for the same work, subsequent citations are given in parentheses. For example: MOOSE, J. Robert. 03-312 (=04-152; 10-083).

5. When the identity of the author of a work cannot be determined, the name of the publisher is listed. In cases where journals or other periodicals are involved, their names are italicized.

6. Occasionally the name of an author is given in different forms in the original publications we have examined. We list all different "names" for the author, but the bibliographic item numbers appear only after the name shown in the most frequently encountered spelling or in the more recent publications. Cross-references are given in these cases.

7. Hyphenated personal (first) names of Korean authors are treated as if the hyphen were absent. For example: "SUH, Sang-Chul" precedes "SUH, Sang Mok."

8. The Korean diacritical mark (˘) is ignored in alphabetizing. But the apostrophe (') used for aspirated sounds is recognized. For example: "CHŎN, Haejong" precedes "CHON, Munam," "CHŎN, Sang-un," and "CH'ON, Kwan-u" in the order shown here.

9. The use of capital letters for Korean names is highly irregular, especially for the two-part hyphenated personal (first) names. We honor the spelling used in the original publications. Whenever inconsistencies arise in the name of the same individual, however, we have opted for lowercase letters. For example: "CHŎN, Sang-un" rather than "CHŎN, Sang-Un."

A

AALTO, P. 05-105
ABASOLO, Rafael, O.F.M. 05-159
ABBERTON, Evelyn. 05-039
ABE, Hiroshi. 03-550
ABRAMOWITZ, Morton. 14-001
ABRAMSON, Arthur S. 05-040
Academy of Korean Studies. 01-085
ADAMS, Don. 08-014, 015, 016, 045, 046, 111; 10-014
ADAMS, Donald Kendrick. See ADAMS, Don.

ADAMS, Edward B. 07-018
ADELMAN, Irma. 11-064, 065 (=12-286), 083
AHN, Byong Man. 12-177
AHN, Byung-young. 15-124
AHN, Chang-Shick. 11-178
AHN, Cook-chin. 12-178
AHN, Ho-Sam. 05-309
AHN, Hwi-Joon. 07-041, 049
AHN, In-sik. 04-034
AHN, Kenneth K. 12-179
AHN, Kye-Hyŏn. 04-055
AHN, Seung Chul. 11-176

AHN, Yong Choon. 04-112
ALEXANDRIDES, Costas G. 14-166
ALLAN, David E. 13-106
ALLEN, Clark. 05-333
ALLEN, Horace Newton. 03-278, 299, 300; 04-018; 06-032
ALLEN, Richard C. 12-121
ALLOCCO, Vincent Anello. 05-315
American Council of Learned Societies. 01-004
American-Korean Friendship and Information Center. 01-104 (=15-026)
American University. 01-062

AMIRAULT, Jacques. 03-481, 496
AN, Ho-sang. 04-019
AN, Pyŏng-ju. 03-204
AN, Pyong-uk. 03-344
AN, Rosario Lee. 12-064
AN, Thomas. 12-405
ANDERSON, P. S. 05-275
ANDERSON, Sara May. 07-155
ANSELMO, Valerio. 03-060, 121, 134;
 05-100, 246, 310
APPLEMAN, Roy E. 14-038
AQUA, Ronald. 10-075
ARAKAWA, H. 09-085
ARNOLD, Dean Alexander. 03-372
Art Council of Great Britain. 07-013
Asea Munje Yŏn'guso. 05-001
ASH, James K. 03-122, 345
Asian-African Legal Consultative Commit-
 tee. 13-036
Asian Survey. 14-002
Asian Writers' Translation Bureau. 06-006,
 040, 041
Association for Asian Studies. 01-020
ASTON, W. G. 05-257
ATTIA, Gamal el-Din. 14-167
AUFRICHT, Hans. 13-103
AUH, Paul (Ch'ŏn-Sŏk). 08-112
AVISON, O. R. 03-590
AWE, Chulho. 04-113

B

BACKUS, Robert L. 01-001 (=15-001)
BACON, Wilbur D. 03-148; 07-019
BAEK, Se Myung. 04-090
BAELZ, E. 03-061
BAERWALD, Hans H. 14-101
BAGMET, N. S. 15-125; 16-051
BAIK, Bong. 03-505 (=12-430; 15-112)
BALDWIN, Frank. 03-497, 498; 14-067
BAN, Sung Hwan. 10-076
BANG, Hung-Kyu. 08-113
Bank of Korea. 01-120 (=11-002), 121
 (=11-035); 11-001, 015
BARINKA, Jaroslav. 07-001; 13-155
BARK, Dong-Suh. 01-002; 12-287 (=513),
 288, 289, 290 (=10-165), 309; 10-164
BARNES, Elaine Milam. 08-114
BARRINGER, Herbert R. 10-048, 121
 (=12-234), 138, 146
BARTZ, Carl F., Jr. 08-047
BARTZ, Fritz. 09-095
BARTZ, Patricia McBride. 09-024
BATEMAN, Doris. 04-114
BAXTER, J. W. 13-129
BAYANOV, B. 16-052
BECKER, Anne-Katrein. 05-106, 358, 359
BEGUIN, O. 04-115
BEITZKE, Günther. 13-116
BELIAEV, Iu N. 01-122
BELOFF, Max. 14-137

BENBEN, John. 08-017
BERGER, Carl. 14-068
BERGMAN, Alexander. 13-089
BERGMAN, Stan. 03-538 (=09-034)
BERTHIER, Francois. 07-028
BIDERMAN, Albert D. 14-039
BIERNATZKI, William Eugene, S.J.
 10-067
BISHOP, Donald M. 03-373
BISHOP, Isabella Lucy Bird. 03-301
 (=04-116); 09-035
BIX, Herbert P. 14-069
BLAIR, Herbert E. 04-117
BLAIR, William Newton. 04-184
BLANCHARD, Carroll Henry. 01-003
 (=14-040)
BLEECKER, Theodore. 13-064
BOOTS, John L. 03-608
BORTON, Hugh. 03-441
BOSCARO, Andriana. 03-001
BOUCHEZ, Daniel. 06-064
BOURDARET, Émile. 03-317
BOWEN, Genevieve. 08-018
BOWMAN, Newton H. 03-591
BRADBURY, John. 15-160
BRANDT, Vincent S. R. 09-058 (=10-077,
 12-065); 10-125
BREIDENSTEIN, Gerhard. 11-058, 059
BREZETTE, Majel C. 07-156
BRIGGS, Walter. 12-122
BROWN, Arthur Judson. 03-442 (=04-186),
 443 (=04-187); 04-185
BROWN, George Thompson. 04-188, 189
BROWN, Gilbert T. 11-196
BRUDNOY, David. 03-444
BRUN Ellen. 11-226 (=12-514, 15-062), 227
 (=12-350, 515)
BRUNNER, Edmund de S. 03-539; 10-089
BUCHER, Lloyd M. 12-351 (=14-070)
BUNCE, Arthur C. 03-519
BURCHETT, Wilfred G. 12-516 (=14-186,
 15-063)
BUSTEED, J. B. 03-592
BUTLER, Lucius A. 01-005
BUTLER, Sir Paul. 03-445
BUTTERFIELD, Kenyon L. 04-118
BYON, Douglas. 04-172
BYUN, Hyung-yoon. 11-124

C

CABLE, E. M. 07-094
CALDWELL, John Cope. 12-180
CALHOUN, Alexander D. 13-041
California, University of. Institute of East
 Asiatic Studies. See MARCUS, Richard.
CAMPBELL, Arch. 04-119
CAMPBELL, Colin D. 11-178, 179
Canada. Department of Mines and Techni-
 cal Surveys. 09-050
CANANOWICZ, I. M. 04-020

CARLES, William R. 03-312 (=09-036)
Carnegie Endowment for International
 Peace. 03-295
CARPENTER, Frances. 06-033
CARRIER, Fred J. 15-064, 143
CARROLL, Timothy G. 13-122
CAVENDISH, Alfred Edward John. 09-037
Center for East Asian Cultural Studies
 (Tokyo). 03-002
Center for Korean Studies. See University
 of Hawaii.
CHA, Byung-Kwon. 11-125
CHA, Marn J. 12-291
CHA, Soon Yung. 13-130
CHAI, Alice Y. 10-068
CHAI, Jae Yung. 12-123
CHAI, Nam-Yearl. 13-076 (=14-181)
CHAN, Yun-Den. 15-065
CHANDRA, Vipan. 03-325, 326, 327
CHANG, Choo-Un. 05-334
CHANG, Chung-oung. 06-065
CHANG, Dae Hong. 03-190; 10-050
 (=13-009), 069; 12-101
CHANG, David W. 12-124
CHANG, Oh-Hyun. 11-094
CHANG, Paul Timothy. 14-071
CHANG, Pyŏng Gil. 04-001
CHANG, S.-U. 05-322
CHANG, Sa-hun. 07-116, 117, 118
CHANG, Suk G. 10-023
CHANG, Suk-Jin. 05-135, 160, 161, 162
CHANG, Sun. 05-163
CHANG, Sung-Un. 05-335, 336, 337
CHANG, Tok-sun. 05-287; 06-034; 13-010
CHANG, Yun-shik. 03-446; 10-126
 (=12-066)
CHAPIN, Emerson. 11-197; 12-001
CHAPIN, Helen B. 07-020, 021, 022, 023
CHARD, Chester S. 02-001, 002
CHASE, David. 02-003
CHAVANNES, Edouard. 03-138
CHAY, Jongsuk. 03-374, 375
CHECA, Genaro Carnero. 15-113
CHEE, C. B. See CHEE, Chang-Boh.
CHEE, Chang-Boh. 08-043 (=12-428, 512);
 12-078
CHEE, Chong Il. 14-102
CHEN, Cheng-siang. 09-096
CHEN, Edward I-te. 03-447, 448, 449
CHEN, Ta. 03-520
CHEONG, Ji Woong. 10-090
CHEUN, Sang-Buom. 05-247
CHEVALIER, Henri. 03-521
CHEY, Soon-Ju. 08-115
CHI, Chul Young. 07-157
CHIEN, Frederick Foo. 03-401
China. Imperial Maritime Customs. 03-296
China. Inspectorate General of Customs.
 03-287
CHINN, Dennis Leslie. 11-198

CHO, Byung-hwa. 06-007
CHO, Chang-Hyun. 12-025 (=12-280, 370, 504), 263, 498
CHO, Choon-Hak. 05-164, 364
CHO, Dong Kyu. 09-097, 098
CHO, Hyoung. 10-055
CHO, Hyo-won. 12-181
CHO, J. H. 10-106
CHO, Jaekwan. 12-475
CHO, Ji-hoon. 04-091
CHO, Key-cab. 13-090
CHO, M. Y. 15-010, 161
CHO, Myung-ki. 04-057
CHO, Oh Kon. 06-066; 07-215
CHO, S. B. 05-066
CHO, Sek Yen K. 05-288
CHO, Seung-Hak. 08-116
CHO, Soon Sung. 03-557 (=12-354; 14-072; 15-162); 12-002 (=12-353), 182 (=12-352); 14-103, 104, 213, 223
CHO, Suk Choon. 10-147; 12-264 (=12-292)
CHO, Sun. 11-066
CHO, Sung-Yoon. 12-499 (=13-156); 13-157, 158; 14-105
CHO, Timothy Hyo-Hoon. 04-190
CHO, Won-Kyung. 07-190
CHO, Yong Sam. 11-242
CHOE, Andreas. 03-205
CHOE, Byung-Sook. 08-117
CHOE, Chae-Sŏk. 08-088; 10-056, 057, 078
CHOE, Ching Young. 03-149, 187
CHOE, Choon. 03-376
CHOE, Ehn-hyun. 11-243
CHOE, Jae-Sok. See CHOE, Chae-Sŏk.
CHOE, Kong-Woong. 13-117
CHOE, Sae-Hyun. 08-118
CHOE, Sang-Su. 07-191, 192, 205, 206
CHOE, Suk-hee. 07-216
CHOE, W. P. 08-048
CH'OE, Ch'ang-gyu. 03-150
CH'OE, Dong-hul. 04-092
CH'OE, Jae-sok. See CHOE, Chae-Sŏk.
CH'OE, Sŏk-U. 04-173
CH'OE, Sŭng-hi. 03-151
CH'OE, Yŏng-ho. 03-054, 152, 191, 241
CHOI, Choong-shik. 11-199
CHOI, Den Khu. 05-025
CHOI, Dong-hi. 04-083
CHOI, Dong Hoon. 03-377
CHOI, Ho-Chin. 11-041, 042, 043, 044
CHOI, Hong-gi. 10-024
CHOI, Jae-sok. See CHOE, Chae-Sŏk
CHOI, Kwang-sok. 04-093
CHOI, Min-hong. 04-035
CHOI, Suk. 03-153
CHOI, Sung-il. 12-003, 125, 265
CHOI, Sung-Pyo. 08-119
CHOI, Woonsang. 03-408
CHOI, Yearn H. 12-126
CHOI, Young-soon Park. 05-279

CHOI, Yung. 12-406
CH'OI, Jin Ho. 10-139
CHŎN, Haejong. See CHUN, Hae-jong.
CHON, Khen Suk. 16-112
CHŎN, Munam. 01-006
CHŎN, Sang-un. See JEON, Sang-woon.
CH'ŎN, Hye-bong. 03-610.
CH'ŎN, Kwan-u. 03-123, 217 (=03-573)
CHŎNG, Bŏm-Mo. 08-071, 089
CHŎNG, Chong-bok. 03-206
CHŎNG, Hyŏng-u. 03-598
CHŎNG, In-kook. 07-024
CHONG, Key Ray. 03-233, 234
CHŎNG, Pyŏng-uk. 06-001; 07-193
CHŎNG, T'ae-Si. 08-019, 020, 021, 049
CHŎNG, To-Yong. 03-522 (=11-044)
CHOO, Hackchung John. 11-067
CHOO, Young Ha. 03-213
Chŏson Shimpŏsha, Tokyo. 01-115
Chosŏn Chung'ang T'ongsinsa, Pyongyang. 01-118
CHOY, Bong Y. See CHOY, Bong-youn.
CHOY, Bong-youn. 03-003 (=13-055); 05-338
CHOY, Young-Ho. 08-120
CHU, Shao-hsien. 12-183, 293
CHUN, Bong Duck. 13-104, 131
CHUN, Hae-jong. 03-032, 033, 055, 216, 242, 328
CHUN, Shin-yong. 03-097
CHUN, Sung-chun. 04-191
CHUNG, Bŏm-Mo. See CHŎNG, Bŏm-Mo.
CHUNG, Chai Sik. 03-207, 235, 346
CHUNG, Chin O. See CHUNG, Chin Owyee.
CHUNG, Chin Owyee. 12-431 (=500); 15-163
CHUNG, Chong-shik. 12-184
CHUNG, David Tae-wi. 04-002, 036
CHUNG, Doock-kyu. 12-212
CHUNG, Henry. 03-297, 450; 12-355
CHUNG, Joong-Gun. 12-294
CHUNG, Joseph Sang-hoon. 11-039, 060, 061, 086 (=11-229), 087 (=15-186), 088, 141, 170, 180, 195, 228, 230 (=12-518; 15-187); 12-517; 15-186
CHUNG, Kae H. 11-126
CHUNG, Kiwon. 12-432 (=12-476); 14-106
CHUNG, Kuang-Hsung. 13-042
CHUNG, Kyung Cho. 12-004, 005
CHUNG, Sae-Gyu. 08-121 (=12-067)
CHUNG, T'ai-Si. See CHŎNG, T'ae-Si.
CHUNG, Won-Si. 07-207
CHUNG, Yong Sun. 01-007
CHUNG, Young-Hwan. 08-122
CHUNG, Young-iob. 03-176, 523 (=11-045)
Chung-Ang University. 11-244
Chungang Chido Munhwasa. 09-146, 147
CHWAE, Seung-Pyung. 05-165

CLARE, Kenneth G. 01-063
CLARK, Allen D. 03-546 (=04-120); 04-121; 09-059
CLARK, Charles Allen. 03-028 (=03-347; 04-003); 04-122, 123, 124, 192
CLARK, Donald N. 03-431;09-059
CLARK, Mark Wayne. 14-041
CLEMENS, Walter C., Jr. 14-224
CLIPPINGER, Morgan E. 03-540
CODECASA, Maria Silvia. 03-249
COHEN, Jerome Alan. 13-137
COHN, William. 07-029
COLE, David Chamberlin. 12-006 (=12-295)
COLHOUN, E. R. 05-131
COLLINS, Joseph L. 14-042
Committee for Solidarity with the Korean People. 01-103
Committee on Legal Services to the Poor in the Developing Countries. 13-145
Comparative and International Education Society. 08-010
CONROY, Hilary. 03-409
COOK, Eung-Do. 05-067, 166, 167
COOK, Harold Francis. 03-329, 432
COOPER, S. Kate. 04-193
CORDIER, Henri. 01-008; 09-129
CORFE, C. J. 04-194
COURANT, Maurice. 01-009 (=09-001); 03-124; 07-130
COX, Susan. 07-042
COZIN, Mark L. 10-176
CRAIG, Albert M. 03-005
CRANE, Paul S. 10-001
CRÉMAZY, Laurent. 13-019, 020
CUMINGS, Bruce. 10-015; 12-185, 407; 14-073
CUMMINGS, Malcolm Stanley. 04-195
CURZON, George Nathaniel. 03-303

D

DALLET, Charles. 03-154 (=04-004; 10-002; 11-046), 348 (=04-174)
DAUGNY, J. 03-410
DAVIDSON, J. Le Roy. 07-043
DAYAL, Shiv. 14-160
DE LAGUÉRIE, Villetard. 03-362, 411
DE ROSNY, Léon. 03-062
DEGE, Eckart. 09-025, 099, 100
DEMENT'EV, V. A. 09-009
DENNETT, Tyler. 03-378, 379, 380, 381, 558
DENNY, Owen N. 03-304
DESTOMBES, Paul. 04-175
DEUCHLER, Martina. 03-208, 330; 07-131
DIAMOND, Walter H. 13-043
Disques Vogue. 07-170
DIX, Griffin. 10-177
DMITRIEVA, V. N. 05-136
DODGE, Herbert Wesley. 08-123 (=14-074)

DONG, Chon. 03-363, 412, 413
DONG, Wonmo. 03-452, 453
Dongguk University Press. 04-056
DORWART, Jeffery M. 03-382
DOUGLAS, William A. 04-049 (=12-119); 12-127, 186
DRAKE, H[enry] B[urgess]. 03-541
DREDGE, Paul. 05-280; 10-178
DREYER, O. K. 16-001
DUBIN, Wilbert B. 15-145
DUBROVINA, E. T. 16-087
DULL, Paul S. 13-029
DUMOULIN, Heinrich. 04-058
DUSTIN, Frederick H. 03-402
DZHARYLGASINOVA, R. Sh. 16-014, 086

E

EARL, David M. 12-187
East-West Center. 07-171
ECKARDT, André. 03-004; 05-137, 138, 139, 238, 258, 289, 329, 330, 339, 340
ECKARDT, P. Andreas. 04-059; 07-002, 119, 120
EDDY, Sherwood. 04-125
EDMAN, Marion L. 08-050
EIDMANN, P. K. 04-060
EIKEMEIER, Dieter. 03-034, 098, 218; 13-011
ELISEEV, D. D. 16-102
ELISSEEFF, Vadime. 07-014
ELROD, Jefferson McRee. 01-010; 04-101
ELLO, Paul Stephen. 12-477 (=12-519)
EREMENKO, L. E. 16-103
ESMAN, M. J. 10-087
ESTHUS, Raymond A. 03-383
Evangelical Missions of Korea. 01-091 (=03-293)
EVERETT, John Thomas, Jr. 14-168
EVERSULL, Frank L. 08-051

F

FABRE, André. 05-107
FAIRBANK, John K. 03-005, 243
FANG, Chaoying. 01-011 (=09-002)
Far Eastern Association. 01-012
Federal Council of the Churches of Christ in America. 03-499
Federal Council of Missions in Korea. 04-126
FENWICK, Malcolm C. 4-127
FIGGESS, John. 07-095
FIGULLA, H. H. 05-140
First Korean Congress, Philadelphia. 03-482
First National City Bank, Seoul Branch. 11-181
FISHER, Charles A. 09-125 (=14-003)
FISHER, James Earnest. 03-551 (=08-124)
FITCH, Geraldine T. 03-483
FLANZ, Gisbert H. 13-027, 030

FOGG, Helen. 08-022
FOKIN, N. 15-044
Folkways Records and Service Corp. 07-172, 173, 174, 175
FONTEIN, Von Jan. 07-004, 096, 097
Foreign Tax Law Association, Inc. 13-058, 059, 105
FOULK, George C. 03-279, 280
FRANKENSTEIN, Marc. 14-169
FRASER, Mowart G. 08-023
FRASER, Stewart E. 08-001 (=15-002), 024
FRAZER, Everett. 03-305
FREEDLEY, George. 07-194
FREYMOND, Jacques. 14-182
FULTON, C. Darby. 04-128

G

GALE, James S. 03-006, 306; 04-021, 129
GALLAGHER, David. 09-075, 076
GALTUNG, Johan. 14-203
GAMBLE, Sidney D. 09-062
GARDINER, K. H. J. 02-004 (=03-063); 03-064, 065, 139, 140
GARDNER, Arthur L. 03-042
GARDNER, Lloyd C. 14-043
GARIN, N. G. [N. G. MIKHAILOVSKII]. 16-008
GARVER, R. A. 12-188
GASSNER, John. 07-195
GAZZARD, Barry. 07-044
GEHMAN, Richard. 04-130
GEORGE, Alexander L. 14-044, 151
George Peabody College for Teachers. 08-012
Georgetown Law Journal. 13-084
Geuthner. 04-052
GIBNEY, Frank. 12-128
GIFFORD, Daniel L. 03-307; 04-022
GILMORE, George W. 03-308
GINSBURGS, George. 01-013 (=15-003)
GLEBOVA, M. E. 16-033
GOFORTH, Jonathan. 04-131
GOLDBERG, Charles N. 10-179
GOMPERTZ, G. St. G. M. 01-014 (=09-003); 03-433; 07-050, 051, 052, 056, 067, 068, 069, 070, 071, 072, 073, 074, 075, 076, 077
GOOD, Sister Alice Maria. 09-093
GOODRICH, L. Carrington. 03-244, 245
GOODRICH, Leland Matthew. 14-075, 170
GOOLD-ADAMS, Henry E. 09-037
GORDENKER, Leon. 12-189; 14-171
GORDON, Bernard K. 14-076
GORDON, E. A. 04-061
GORRINI, G. 03-364
GRAF, Olaf. 04-005
GRAFFSHAGEN, Stephan. 04-132
GRAJDANZEV, Andrew J. 03-454, 455, 456 (=11-047; 13-022), 457; 14-187
GRAVES, Louis. 03-384

GRAY, Basil. 07-098
Great Britain. Foreign Office. 03-270
Great Britain. Parliamentary Papers. 03-272
Great Britain. Public Record Office. 03-271
GREY, Arthur L., Jr. 14-188
GRIFFING, Robert P., Jr. 07-059, 078
GRIFFIS, William Elliot. 03-007, 281, 434; 06-035
GRIGORÉV, V. M. 16-110
GRISWOLD, Alexander. 07-005
GROSHIN, S. I. 16-110
GRYAZNOV, G. V. 15-188 (=16-044)
GUDOSHNIKOV, L. M. 13-168 (=16-058)
GUILLEMOZ, Alexandre. 10-025, 180
GUNDERT, Wilhelm. 04-006
GUPTA, Karunakar. 14-161
GUREEVA, N. P. 13-163
GURLEY, John G. 11-182
GUSEVA, E. K. 05-141 (=16-093), 142

H

HA, Chong-on. 05-068
HA, Hyon-Kang. 03-192, 349
HA, Joseph Man-Kyung. 10-107; 12-478 (=15-189)
HAFNER, Ambrosius. 04-037, 176
HAGGARD, M. T. 14-004
HAGUENAUER, Charles. 03-066, 067, 068, 069, 099, 100, 101, 250; 05-013, 101, 102, 311
HAH, Chong-Do. 14-107
HAHM, Pyong-Choon. 03-155, 174 (=12-068; 13-005), 331; 10-026, 148; 12-408 (=13-172; 15-146); 13-138; 14-005, 077, 078
HAHN, Bae-ho. 12-007 (=12-357, 501), 129 (=12-190), 191 (=12-479), 356
HAHN, Man-young. 07-132
HAHN, Sung-joe. 12-069
HAHN, Youngki. 11-201
Hakwon-sa. 01-064 (=04-007; 09-012; 10-005)
HALL, Captain Basil. 03-258; 09-038
HALL, Budd L. 08-026
HALLIDAY, Jon. 14-172
HALPERN, Abraham M. 14-015
HAM, Eui-Yong. 12-224
HAMEL, Hendrik. 03-259
HAMILTON, A. W. 03-424
HAN, Chungnim. 10-108
HAN, Hae-Bok. 11-095
HAN, Jong-il. 12-131
HAN, Kee-chun. 11-105, 127, 150
HAN, Ki-Shik. 04-133; 12-132, 192
HAN, Kiuk. 12-296
HAN, Ki-Un. 08-025
HAN, Mieko S. 05-041, 042
HAN, Nae Bok. 10-091, 092
HAN, Ponghum. 06-067
HAN, Pyo Wook. 14-214

HAN, Pyŏng-sam. 02-005
HAN, Sang-Bok. 10-079, 093, 109
HAN, Sun Nam. 04-196
HAN, Sung-joo. 11-062 (=12-010); 12-009
  (=12-133), 011; 14-006, 028
HAN, Tae-Soo. 12-193 (=12-267), 194
  (=12-266), 195
HAN, Tai-yon. 12-268
HAN, Wan-sang. 10-027; 12-070
HAN, Woo-keun. 03-008
HAN, Y[ung] C[hul]. 12-071 (=12-198),
  196, 197, 269.
HAN, Yŏng-u. 03-156, 219
HAN, Young-hie. 05-043, 168
HAN, Young-un. 06-008
HANAYAMA, Shinsho. 04-053
Han'gong Chido Kongŏpsa. 09-148
Hapdong News Agency. 01-119 (=01-129;
  12-008, 270, 297)
HARDCASTLE, W. J. 05-044
HARRARD, M. T. 15-166
HARRINGTON, Fred Harvey. 03-385
HARRIS, Sue Ann. 08-125
HARRISON, John A. 03-275
HARRISON, Selig S. 14-225 (=15-167)
Harvard University. 01-015, 016
HARVEY, Youngsook. 10-064
HASAN, Paryez. 11-202
HATADA, Takashi. 03-009
HATTORI, Sh. 05-259
HAYATA, Yoshiro. 13-173
HAYDEN, Ralston. 03-458
HAZARD, Benjamin Harrison, Jr. 03-090,
  125, 126
HEIMSATH, Charles H[erman], IV. 14-162
HELLMANN, Donald C. 14-108
HEMPEL, Rose. 07-004
HENDERSON, Gregory. 03-019 (=03-460;
  12-012, 072, 134, 199; 13-031; 14-079),
  030, 031 (=04-048), 070, 220; 07-060, 061,
  079, 080, 081; 12-013 (=14-204); 14-030,
  215, 226
HENNESSEY, John Russel. 14-205
HENTHORN, William E. 01-017, 018
  (=14-080); 02-006; 03-010, 096, 132;
  06-061
HENTZE, Carl. 03-102
HERLIHY, Francis. 04-177
HERMES, Walter G. 14-045
HERSH, Jacques. 11-227 (=12-350, 515)
HETT, G. V. 04-039; 09-039
HEUKEN, Adolf. 04-178
HEWES, Gordon. 02-007
HEYMAN, Alan C. 04-062; 07-196
HILL, R. 10-051
HINTON, Harold C. 14-152
HIROSE, H. 05-045
HOANG, Hee Young. 05-046
HOBSON, R. L. 07-062, 082
HOCHINS, Chang-su. 03-043

HOCHINS, Lee. 03-043
HONEY, William Bowyer. 07-053, 054,
  055, 083, 084
HONG, I-Sŏp. 02-032 (=03-017); 03-221
  (=09-016), 569; 04-040
HONG, Kyung-hi. 09-113, 114, 115
HONG, Myoung-hee. 06-042
HONG, Soon C. 03-386
HONG, Soon-ho. 03-365
HONG, Suhn-Kyoung. 10-181
HONG, Sung-chick. 10-028 (=12-073), 029,
  030, 031, 094, 149; 11-203; 12-074, 075
HONG, Woong-Sun. 08-052
HONG, Yi-sup. See HONG, I-Sŏp.
HOOPER, James Leon. 04-197
Hoover Institution. See Stanford Univer-
  sity.
HOPE, E. R. 05-290
HORNE, Elianor C. 05-341
HOYT, James. 06-068
HSIANG, P. S. 05-014
HSU, Shuhsi. 03-035
HU, Bom. 12-298
HU, Hung-lick. 14-007
HUANG, Sung-Mo. See HWANG, Sŏng-
  Mo.
HUDSON, G. F. 14-008
HUH, Woo Kung. 09-086
HUH, Woong. 05-020
HULBERT, Homer B. 03-011 (=04-008),
  157, 318, 599 (=09-017), 600, 601
  (=04-023), 611; 04-084; 05-260
HUNT, C. 12-079
HUNT, Walter E. 12-076
HWANG, Chul-Su. 08-053
HWANG, Eung-yun. 10-032
HWANG, Juck-ryoon. 05-281
HWANG, Sŏng-Mo. 04-198; 12-200
HWANG, Soon-hi. 15-115
HWANG, Su-yŏng. 07-030
HWANG, Tong-gon. 10-150
HWANG, Wŏn-gu. 03-222
HYUN, Soong-Jong. 13-006
HYUNG, Kie Ju. 09-116, 117, 131

I

IKEUCHI, Hiroshi. 03-118
ILYON. 03-071
IM, Duck-Soon. 09-126, 127
IM, H. J. 02-026
IM, Pang. 06-036
The Independent. 03-290
Institute of Asian Affairs, Hamburg. 01-097
  (=15-034)
Institute for Asian Studies. 01-075
Institute for East Asian Studies. 01-077
  (=15-022)
Institute for Internal and External Affairs.
  15-071 (See also Research Institute for In-
  ternal and External Affairs)

International Affairs. 14-009
International Centre for Settlement of In-
  vestment Dispute. 13-044
International Cultural Foundation. 03-200
  (=10-145); 10-003, 004
International Research Center. 01-096
IONOVA, Yu. V. 16-015
IRELAND, Alleyne. 03-461
IRIE, Keishiro. 13-077
ITO, Akio. 03-081
IVANOV, T. 15-129
INVANOVA, V. I. 16-103, 104, 105
Izd. IMO. 16-053
Izd. Vost. Lit. 16-010
Izvestiya AN SSSR. 16-074

J

JAISOHN, Muriel. 03-435
JAMIESON, John Charles. 03-082, 141
JANATA, Alfred. 07-037
JANELLI, Roger. 10-033, 070
JANG, Woo Tai. 12-359
JANSEN, Marius B. 03-319
Japan. Bureau of Customs. 03-289
Japan. Government-General of Chōsen.
  03-462 (=11-048; 13-023), 463; 09-063,
  149
Japan. Residency General of Korea. 03-288
Japan. Rikugun Sambo Hombu (Army
  General Staff). 09-150
Japan Chronicle. 03-464, 500
Japan Weekly Mail. 03-291
JEON, Sang-woon. 03-570 (=09-018), 571,
  574, 575, 576, 609
JEONG, Changyoung. 11-128
JEWELL, Malcom E. 12-077 (=12-201)
JHO, Sung-do. 03-251
JI, Myung Kwan. 04-094
JI, Won-Yong. 04-134, 135
JIN, Hyung Ki. 11-183
JO, Mi-Jeung. 05-282
JO, Yung-hwan. 03-350; 12-014, 360;
  14-109, 206
JOHNSTON, Ray E. 14-207
Joint Committee on Korean Studies, SSRC-
  ACLS. 01-099
Joint Publications Research Service (JPRS).
  See United States. Department of Com-
  merce, Joint Publications Research Ser-
  vice.
JONES, George Heber. 04-024, 199
JONES, Helen Dudenbostel. 01-019
  (=09-004)
JONES, P. H. M. 11-231
Journal of Korean Affairs. 14-240
JOY, Charles Turner. 12-433; 14-046
JUHN, Daniel Sungil. 03-524 (=11-049),
  525; 11-143 (=12-520)
JUN, Jong-sup. 12-299
JUN, Moon-sup. 15-045

JUNG, Insub. See ZŎNG, In-Sŏb.
JUNG, Yong Suk. 14-081
JUNKER, Heinrich F. J. 05-008, 069, 070, 071, 108, 143, 291

K

KAGAYA, R. 05-047, 048
KAHNG, Tae Jin. 14-173
KAKHUN. 04-063
KAL, Bong-Keun. 12-271; 13-091
KAL, Bong Kun. See KAL, Bong-Keun
KALTON, Michael C. 03-223
KANAZAWA, Shosaburo. 05-239
KANESA-THASAN, S. 11-204
KANG, Chinch'ol. 03-020 (=10-095)
KANG, Chul Won. 03-526 (=11-050)
KANG, Dae Hyeon. 09-080
KANG, Han Mu. 12-202 (=14-082)
KANG, Hi-Woong. See KANG, Hugh H. W.
KANG, Hugh H. W. 03-021, 056, 091, 092, 093
KANG, Hui-Su. 08-101
KANG, Kil-Soo. 08-002, 102
KANG, Koo-chin. 12-502; 13-159 (=15-148), 160
KANG, Man-gil. 03-177, 224
KANG, Man-Kil. See KANG, Man-gil.
KANG, Pyung-Kun. 12-015, 300, 301
KANG, Sangwoon. 01-021
KANG, Shin-Pyo. 10-016
KANG, Thomas Hosuck. 01-022; 03-351
KANG, Wi Jo. 03-547, 548; 04-085
KANG, Won Yong. 04-136, 137
KANG, Younghill. 03-561 (=06-043; 09-040)
KANG, Young-Hoon. 12-434; 14-110, 153, 227
KARDOSS, John. 07-197
KARSHINOV, L. N. 05-325; 11-232; 16-034, 035, 045 (=15-191)
KASSA, T. 05-021
KATZ, Herman M. 03-436
KAUFMANN, Walter. 07-121
KAUH, Kwang-Man. 08-072, 090, 091
KAWASAKI, S. 09-077
KAWASHIMA, Fujiya. 03-057, 158 (=10-071), 193
KAY, Il Seung. 04-138
KAZAKEVICH, I. S. 01-023 (=15-004); 16-002, 017, 038, 048
KEARLEY, Timothy G. 13-164
KEH, Chung-sik. 07-122, 158
KEH, Young-He. 08-054
KEIM, Willard D. 10-096 (=11-096; 12-203)
KENDALL, Carlton Waldo. 03-484
KENNEDY, Gerald F. 10-133
KENYON, Albert. 04-009
KEON, Michael. 12-016(=12-135)
KERNER, Robert Joseph. 01-024
KHAN, M. 16-018

KHEGAI, M. A. 05-132
KHOLODOVICH, A. A. 05-009, 144, 145 (=16-095), 146, 292, 324 (=16-094)
KICKMAN, Bert G. 11-068
KIHL, Young Whan. 10-140; 12-017, 136, 204, 205, 206 (=12-302), 211 (=12-480), 212; 14-208, 228, 229
KIM, Bernice B. H. 03-044
KIM, Bo-gyŏm. 05-109, 240
KIM, Bong-gi. 03-022
KIM, Busik. 16-106
KIM, Byong Sik. 12-435 (=12-521; 14-189; 15-072)
KIM, Byoung Kuk. 11-192
KIM, Byoung Wook. 05-049
KIM, Byung-ha. 03-178, 179
KIM, C. I. Eugene. 03-320 (=14-111), 414, 465, 552; 10-141; 12-018, 019 (=12-361), 020 (=12-363), 078, 079, 080, 137, 138, 139, 207, 208, 209, 210, 211 (=12-480), 212, 272, 273, 274, 362 (=14-190)
KIM, C. L. See KIM, Chong Lim.
KIM, Chae-Kwang. 12-275
KIM, Chan-Jin. 11-151; 13-045, 046
KIM, Chang-hoon. 03-366
KIM, Ch'ang-Mun. 04-179
KIM, Chang Soon. See KIM, Ch'ang-sun.
KIM, Ch'ang-sun. 12-364 (=15-073), 481 (=15-130)
KIM, Changyup Daniel. 04-201
KIM, Chewon. 02-008; 03-072; 07-005, 006, 007, 031, 056, 085, 099, 100, 101
KIM, Chi-ha. 06-009
KIM, Chi Sun. 12-213 (=13-065); 13-066
KIM, Chin. 01-025 (13-007); 13-008, 047, 092, 093, 094, 118, 119, 120, 121, 122, 150, 164, 174, 175
KIM, Chin-gyun. 07-159
KIM, Chin-man. 12-081
KIM, Chin-W. 05-022, 026, 050, 051, 072, 073, 074, 075, 076, 077, 078
KIM, Chin Wu. See KIM, Chin-W.
KIM, Cho-Soo. 13-095, 096
KIM, Chol-choon. 02-032 (=03-017)
KIM, Ch'ŏl-hŭi. 15-046
KIM, Chŏng-bae. 03-073, 074
KIM, Chong-Chol. 08-055, 073
KIM, Chong Han. 14-163, 174
KIM, Chong Ik Eugene. See KIM, C. I. Eugene.
KIM, Chong-ki. 02-009
KIM, Chong-guk. 03-214
KIM, Chong Lim. 10-127; 12-077 (=12-201), 082 (=12-214), 140 (=12-216), 141, 142, 174, 215, 217
KIM, Chong-shin. 12-143
KIM, Chongsoon. 05-356
KIM, Chong-Sun. 03-083, 084, 085, 086
KIM, Chong-un. 06-057
KIM, Choong-Bae. 05-079

KIM, Chulsu. 12-218
KIM, Chung-Choon. 04-139
KIM, Chung Han. 13-097
KIM, Dae-Hwan. 10-151, 152
KIM, Dae-Kwan. 08-074
KIM, Dalchoong. 03-403
KIM, Dong Hi. 11-097; 13-078
KIM, Dong Su. 12-436
KIM, Dong-uk. 03-023
KIM, Doo Hun. 03-103 (=04-041)
KIM, Doo Yong. 13-176
KIM, Doo Yung. 12-482
KIM, Du-chong. 03-593
KIM, Eui Whan. 04-140
KIM, F. Z. 05-293, 294, 295, 296
KIM, G. F. 03-506; 15-047, 074 (=16-037), 075, 076 (=16-019), 131; 16-036, 064
KIM, Gaab Chol. 12-409
KIM, Gi Yun. 05-325
KIM, H. Edward. 09-041
KIM, Ha-tai. 03-252; 04-042
KIM, Hak-joon. 14-191, 230
KIM, Han-ju. 12-522 (=15-192)
KIM, Han K. See Kim, Han-Kyo.
KIM, Han Keyn. 11-245
KIM, Han-Kon. 05-110, 169, 364
KIM, Han-Kyo. 03-320 (=14-111), 466; 14-192, 193
KIM, Helen Kiteuk. 03-553 (=08-126)
KIM, Ho-Gwon. 08-103
KIM, Ho-soon. 07-217
KIM, Hong Han. 13-048
KIM, Hong N. 14-112
KIM, Hwang Joe. 11-246
KIM, Hyon-cho. 11-069
KIM, Hyŏng Ch'an. See KIM, Hyung-chan.
KIM, Hyong-hio. 03-209
KIM, Hyŏng-Kyu. 05-015, 316
KIM, Hyoung Yul. 11-098 (=12-303)
KIM, Hyun-Chul. 08-127
KIM, Hyung-chan. 03-045, 046, 047, 352; 08-092 (=12-410), 093, 104, 105, 128
KIM, Hyung Tae. 04-141
KIM, Il-Chul. 10-097
KIM, Il-sŏng. See KIM, Il Sung.
KIM, Il Sung. 03-507; 11-026, 027, 028 (=12-411, 439, 15-098), 063, 090, 112 (=15-193), 113 (=15-194), 114 (=15-196), 115 (=15-197), 116 (=12-525), 233; 12-365, 437, 438 (=15-095), 523, 524; 14-011 (=15-097), 194; 15-096, 099, 100, 101, 102, 103, 104, 105, 106, 107, 108, 109, 110, 111, 195
KIM, Ilpyong J. 11-234; 12-366 (=12-412, 440, 483; 15-077), 413, 484, 503 (=12-526); 13-161; 14-124, 154
KIM, In Kie. 11-184
KIM, Ir Sen. 15-132. See also KIM, Il Sung.
KIM, Jae-On. 12-219

KIM, Jae-Un. 10-058
KIM, Jaihiun. 06-010
KIM, Jai-hyup. 12-144
KIM, Jeong-hak. 02-010
KIM, Jin-Eun. 08-129
KIM, Jong Gil. 06-011
KIM, Jong-pil. 12-145 (=12-276), 146
KIM, Jong Yule. 05-170
KIM, Joungwon Alexander. 11-089; 12-021
   (=12-147, 367, 441, 527), 022, 023, 148,
   368, 369 (=14-138; 15-169), 442, 443, 528;
   13-049; 14-175, 216
KIM, Jung-bae. 02-011
KIM, Jung-sae. 11-185
KIM, K. H. 03-367
KIM, K. W. See KIM, Kyung-won.
KIM, Kay H. 06-002
KIM, Ki-Bŏm. 12-277 (=13-028), 278
KIM, Ki-hong. 10-017
KIM, Kong-On. 05-052, 053, 080, 111
KIM, Kwan Bong. 12-220 (=14-113)
KIM, Kwan Suk. 03-527 (=11-051); 11-129
KIM, Kwang. 14-195
KIM, Kwang-il. 03-594 (=10-034); 10-035
KIM, Kyong Dong. 10-036, 049, 153;
   12-221
KIM, Kyu-sik. 03-559
KIM, Kyu Sung. 12-279
KIM, Kyu-taik. 12-130, 149, 222
KIM, Kyung-won. 10-018; 12-083
KIM, Man-Hee. 07-113, 114, 115
KIM, Min-su. 05-027, 276
KIM, Myong-Whai. 12-223, 224; 14-047
KIM, Myung-Han. 08-130
KIM, N. S. 16-041
KIM, Nam-Kil. 05-171, 172
KIM, Nam-shik. See KIM, Nam-sik.
KIM, Nam-sik. 12-444, 530 (=15-151)
KIM, Ok Yul. 14-012
KIM, Po Sung Philip. 01-110
KIM, Pyung-ku. 12-084
KIM, Quee-Young. 10-172
KIM, Ran-Soo. 08-131
KIM, Richard E. 03-562 (=06-046); 06-045,
   047
KIM, Roy U. T. 12-372 (=14-126), 445
   (=14-155; 15-170); 14-125
KIM, S. I. 13-139
KIM, Sam-kyu. 14-217, 231
KIM, San. 03-515 (=15-048)
KIM, San-O. 11-247
KIM, Se-jin. 10-037 (=10-154; 12-085, 225);
   11-205 (=12-304; 14-183); 12-024, 025
   (=12-280, 370, 504)
KIM, Seung-hee. 11-186, 206, 207, 208
KIM, Seyeul. 10-134 (=11-099)
KIM, Shin-Bok. 08-132
KIM, So-un. 06-037
KIM, So-wŏl. 06-012, 013
KIM, Song-Hui. 12-226

KIM, Sŏng-jong. 03-188
KIM, Soo-Gon. 05-081
KIM, Soon-ae. 07-160
KIM, Soon-Ham Park. 05-173, 174
KIM, Soon Tae. 09-087
KIM, Sun Ho. 08-133 (=12-414)
KIM, Sun Jai. 05-360
KIM, Sung-Il. 08-134
KIM, Sung-sik. 12-227
KIM, Sung Tae. 11-187
KIM, Sungwoo. 10-128
KIM, Swang Iel. 10-023
KIM, Syn Khva. 16-020
KIM, T. W. 05-131
KIM, T'ae-Gil. 04-095; 08-056; 12-086, 087
KIM, T'ae-gon. 10-038
KIM, Tae Han. 05-175
KIM, Tae-Ho. 12-446 (=12-505)
KIM, Tae-Kil. See KIM, T'ae-Gil.
KIM, Tae-suh. 12-447 (=12-506)
KIM, Taek Kyoo. 10-052 (=080)
KIM, Tong-hwa. 04-064, 065
KIM, Tschong Dae. 03-159
KIM, Tuk-Yul (Andrew). 08-135
KIM, U-chang. 06-014
KIM, Ui-hwan. 03-415
KIM, Uk-Hwan. 08-136
KIM, Uoong Tack. See KIM, Roy U. T.
KIM, V. A. 16-059, 060
KIM, Warren Y. 03-048
KIM, Wha-Chun. 05-176
KIM, Won-mo. 03-387
KIM, Won-yong. 02-012, 013, 014, 015;
   07-006, 032, 057
KIM, Y. H. 13-139
KIM, Yang Sun. 04-142
KIM, Yong Choon. 04-086
KIM, Yong-dŏk. 03-225
KIM, Yŏng-ho. 03-180
KIM, Yong-jin. 02-016
KIM, Yong-joon. 07-038
KIM, Yŏng-mo. 03-160, 542
KIM, Yong-Shik. 08-027
KIM, Yong Soon. 14-209
KIM, Yong-sŏp. 03-226, 332
KIM, Yong-woon. 03-577, 578, 579, 580
KIM, Yoon H. 12-088
KIM, Yoon-Hwan. 15-199
KIM, Youn-Soo. 13-032, 165, 166, 169
KIM, Young C[hin]. 11-130; 12-371
   (=15-078), 415; 14-013, 014, 015, 114,
   232, 233
KIM, Young Choon. 03-236, 237, 238, 239
KIM, Young-geun. 12-247
KIM, Young-Ho. 03-353
KIM, Young Ik. 06-048, 049
KIM, Young Il. 03-602 (=09-142)
KIM, Young Jeh. 12-448
KIM, Youngjeung. 12-026
KIM, Young Kun. 12-474

KIM, Young-mo. 12-089
KIM, Young Moo. 13-050
KIM, Young-Shik. 08-137
KIM, Yu-nam. 12-449
KIM, Yun Kuk. 04-143
KIM, Yun-kyung. 05-297, 298
KIM, Yung Chung. 03-425
KIM, Yung Sam. 12-305
KIM, Zhen Tser. 05-325
KIM-RENAUD, Young-Key. 05-082, 083,
   084, 085, 086, 283
King Seijong Memorial Society. 03-161
   (=03-572)
KIYOSAKI, Wayne S. 12-457
KLEPPER, Montes R. 09-075
KLOTH, Edward W. 11-144
KNEZ, Eugene I. 01-026; 02-017; 10-110
KO, Byung-ik. See KOH, Byong-ik
KO, Hwang-Kyong. 08-094
KO, Hyun Bong. 04-144
KO, Seung-K[yun]. 03-501; 14-115, 164
KO, Won. 06-015
KO, Yŏng-Bok. 10-019, 155; 12-090, 228
KOBAYASHI, Teiichi. 09-064, 065
KOH, B. C. See KOH, Byung Chul.
KOH, Byong-ik. 03-036, 135, 227
   (=04-043), 260, 368
KOH, B[yung] C[hul]. 12-027, 091
   (=12-417), 219, 306, 373 (=14-127;
   15-173), 374 (=14-236), 375, 416
   (=12-450; 14-016; 15-171), 418 (=12-452;
   15-149), 419 (=14-018; 15-172), 451
   (=12-485), 453, 454 (=14-083), 455
   (=14-219); 14-017 (=15-133), 116, 176,
   218, 234, 235, 237
KOH, Byung-ik. See KOH, Byong-ik.
KOH, Hesung Chun. 01-027, 028; 03-194
KOH, Kwang Il. 12-150
KOH, Kwang-lim. 13-051, 079
KOH, Seung-Jae. See KOH, Sung-Jae.
KOH, Soo Kohn. 11-152
KOH, Sung-Jae. 03-049, 528, 529, 530
   (=11-052)
KOH, Young Bok. See KO, Yŏng-Bok.
KOLB, Albert. 09-026
KONDO, H. 15-049
KONTSEVICH, L. R. 05-003, 028, 087,
   299 (=16-107), 312
KOPPELMANN, D. H. 05-261
Korea, Democratic People's Republic of.
   Association for Nature Conservation.
   15-029
Korea, Democratic People's Republic of.
   Central Statistical Bureau. 01-123
   (=15-013); 11-040
Korea, Democratic People's Republic of.
   Committee for the Promotion of Interna-
   tional Trade. 15-023
Korea, Democratic People's Republic of.
   Foreign Languages Publishing House.

01-065 (=11-025; 15-069), 102 (=15-021), 109 (=15-028); 09-032; 11-021 (=15-011, 067), 022 (=15-135), 023 (=15-012, 127), 024, 110 (=15-185), 111 (=15-190); 15-014, 066, 068, 070, 114, 116, 117, 118, 119, 122, 123, 136, 154, 164, 165, 168, 174, 177, 205

Korea, Democratic People's Republic of. General Federation of Trade Unions. 15-030

Korea, Democratic People's Republic of. Information Bureau in Stockholm. 15-020

Korea, Democratic People's Republic of. Korean Central News Agency. 01-106 (=15-027)

Korea, Democratic People's Republic of. Korean Democratic Women's Union. 15-043

Korea, Democratic People's Republic of. Kwahagwŏn. 15-032

Korea, Democratic People's Republic of. League of Socialist Working Youth of Korea. 15-031

Korea, Democratic People's Republic of. Ministry of Justice. 15-144

Korea, Democratic People's Republic of. Party History Institute. 12-456 (=15-120); 15-156

Korea, Democratic People's Republic of. Permanent Observer to the United Nations. 15-037

Korea, Republic of. 09-066, 067; 11-071, 072, 073, 074, 075

Korea, Republic of. Central Election Management Committee. 13-037

Korea, Republic of. Central Meteorological Office. 09-155

Korea, Republic of. Economic Planning Board. 01-124 (=11-007, 12-028, 307), 125 (=11-038); 11-004, 005, 006, 016, 017a, 017b, 036, 037, 070, 153, 209, 210, 211

Korea, Republic of. Heavy and Chemical Industry Promotion Council. 11-133, 134

Korea, Republic of. Kukka Chaegŏn Ch'oego Hoeŭi. See Korea, Republic of. Supreme Council for National Reconstruction.

Korea, Republic of. Ministry of Agriculture and Fisheries. 01-126

Korea, Republic of. Ministry of Agriculture and Forestry. 11-008

Korea, Republic of. Ministry of Construction. 09-061

Korea, Republic of. Ministry of Culture and Information. 01-066, 067; 06-063; 07-008

Korea, Republic of. Ministry of Education. 08-005, 006; 09-143

Korea, Republic of. Ministry of Finance. 11-189

Korea, Republic of. Ministry of Foreign Affairs. 12-281; 13-123

Korea, Republic of. Ministry of Health and Social Affairs. 11-009

Korea, Republic of. Ministry of Home Affairs. 01-127

Korea, Republic of. Ministry of Public Information. 11-075

Korea, Republic of. National Academy of Fine Arts. 07-009, 010, 104, 198

Korea, Republic of. Oemubu. See Korea, Republic of. Ministry of Foreign Affairs.

Korea, Republic of. Office of Fisheries. 09-101

Korea, Republic of. Office of Forestry. 09-094

Korea, Republic of. Office of Labour Affairs. 13-067

Korea, Republic of. Office of National Tax Administration. 13-060

Korea, Republic of. Office of the President. 10-118

Korea, Republic of. Office of Public Information. 01-128

Korea, Republic of. Office of Rural Development. 09-156; 10-116, 117

Korea, Republic of. Supreme Council for National Reconstruction. 12-029, 282

Korea, Republic of. Supreme Court. 13-001, 140, 141

Korea Development Bank. 11-131

Korea Development Research Institute. 11-132

Korea Herald. 01-105

Korea Information Service. 15-082

Korea Institute of Agricultural Economics. 11-100

Korea Land Economics Research Center. 11-101

Korea Times. 01-108

Korea Today. 01-109

Korea University. 01-079; 03-273; 10-175 (=12-031, 308); 11-102; 12-030 (=12-376; 14-196)

Korea Week. 01-110 (=14-019)

Korean Affairs Institute, Washington, D.C. 01-117

Korean Agricultural Sector Study Team, East Lansing, Mich. 10-081 (=11-103)

Korean-American Cultural Association. 01-094

Korean-American Educational Commission. 01-095

Korean Commission to America and Europe. 03-486

Korean Development Association. 11-135

Korean Economic Society, Arlington, Va. 01-089

Korean Federation of Education Associations. 08-057

Korean Geographical Society. 09-008, 013

Korean Information Bureau, Philadelphia. 01-088

Korean Information Office. 01-112

Korean Information Service. 01-111

Korean Institute of Geographical Research. 09-007

Korean Institute of International Studies. 01-090 (=14-020)

Korean Legal Center. 13-026

Korean Musicological Society. 07-123

Korean National Commission for UNESCO. 01-068 (=08-031; 09-014), 084, 100; 06-051; 07-039, 199; 08-030; 10-053, 144

Korean National Committee of Historical Sciences. 03-058

Korean Overseas Information Service. 01-086

Korean Pacific Press. 01-113

Korean PEN, 06-018

Korean Poets Association. 06-016, 017

Korean Research Center. 01-076, 082

Korean Research Council. 01-093

Korean Studies Society, Seattle. 01-081

Korean Traders Association. 13-052

KORNILOV, V. 16-081

KOROLEV, P. G. 16-042

KOROVIN, E. A. 16-075

Koryŏ taehakkyo. See Korea University.

KOTO, Bunjiro. 09-068, 069

KOVALENKO, S. S. 16-088

Krasnyi Archiv [Red Archives]. 03-274

KRAVTSOV, I. 16-076

KRAZKIEWICZ, T. Mark. 11-154

KUARK, J. Y. T. See KUARK, John Yoon Tai.

KUARK, John Yoon Tai. 11-091, 117, 145; 15-200

Kukche Sŏjŏm, Pyongyang. 01-029

KULAGINA, L. M. 16-003

KUN, Joseph C. 14-128 (=15-174)

KUNO, Yoshi S. 03-037

KURNITZKY, H. 15-079

KUZNETS, Paul W. 11-136, 212, 213, 248

KUZNETSOVA, N. A. 16-003

KWACK, Y. C. See KWACK, Yoon Chick.

KWACK, Yoon Chick. 11-190 (=13-106); 13-098

KWAK, Soon-Il. 08-138

KWAK, Tae-Hwan. 14-084, 085

KWON, Chan. 12-151, 152

KWON, Hyogmyon. 05-262

KWON, Ik Whan. 03-531, 532

KWON, Jane K. 11-130

KWON, O-Sik. 08-058

KWON, Sang-no. 04-066

KWON, Tai Hwan. 10-119, 139

KYE, Chŏng-sik. See KEH, Chung-sik.

KYRIAK, Theodore E. 01-030 (=15-005)

KYUNER, N. V. 16-087

L

LADD, George Trumbull. 03-309
LAI, Nathan Yu-Jen. 14-048
LAMBUTH, David Kelly. 04-025
LANDIS, Eli Barr. 03-595, 603 (=04-026);
  04-027, 028, 067, 087
LANDOR, Arnold Henry Savage. 09-042
LASSITER, D. 10-072
LATOURETTE, Kenneth. 04-146, 147, 180
LAUTENSACH, Hermann. 09-005, 027,
  028, 102, 103
LEBOW, Richard N. 14-204
LEDYARD, Gari Keith. 03-024, 133, 246,
  261 (=09-043); 04-068; 05-300; 14-197
LEE, Bae-yong. 03-369
LEE, Bok-Soo. 10-094
LEE, Byong Ho. 13-132, 133
LEE, Byong-Sul. 09-088, 089
LEE, Byong-Won. 07-133, 134, 161, 162
LEE, Byung-Choon. 10-098
LEE, Byung-Gun. 05-088
LEE, Byung Joe. 13-080
LEE, C. J. See LEE, Chae-Jin.
LEE, C. S. See LEE, Chong-Sik.
LEE, C. Y. 05-045
LEE, Chae-Jin. 12-033, 034 (=14-238), 171
  (=12-467, 536), 229, 230, 309; 14-021
LEE, Ch'an. 03-604 (=09-134); 09-132, 133
LEE, Chang Hei. 05-342
LEE, Changsoo. 14-117, 118
LEE, Chong-Sik. 01-031 (=15-006), 044;
  03-488, 489, 508 (=15-050), 509, 511
  (=11-030; 12-394, 426, 464, 492, 510, 534;
  14-134; 15-056), 512; 11-118, 171; 12-035
  (=12-378), 377, 379, 380, 381 (=12-487),
  382 (=14-130; 15-080), 420 (=14-129), 421
  (=12-488), 458 (=15-121), 459, 460
  (=14-139; 15-134), 486 (=12-529), 507
  (=15-150), 530 (=15-151); 14-220, 239
LEE, Chul-hyun. 12-092
LEE, Chung-Min. 05-089, 177, 178, 179,
  180
LEE, Chung Myun. 09-104, 105
LEE, Dae Sung. 11-155
LEE, Dong Jun. 12-388
LEE, Du-Hyun. 06-062; 07-208, 209, 210,
  211, 212
LEE, Eric Youngkoo. 11-191
LEE, Eun Ho. 12-153
LEE, Gabriel Gab-Soo. 04-148
LEE, George J. 07-086, 087
LEE, Hae Young. 10-059
LEE, Hahn-Been. 12-310, 311, 312
LEE, Han Soon. 09-111
LEE, Hang-Nyung. 04-096; 13-099
LEE, Hey-Sook. 05-054
LEE, Hi-Seung. 03-490; 05-301
LEE, Hong-Bae. 05-147, 181, 182, 183,
  184, 185, 186

LEE, Hong-Koo. 10-156
LEE, Hoon K[oo]. 03-533 (=09-106; 11-053)
LEE, Hwa-Soo. 08-095; 12-093, 094
LEE, Hy Sang. 11-156
LEE, Hye-Ku. 07-124, 125, 135, 136
LEE, Hye-Sook. 05-090
LEE, Hyo-chai. 10-054, 060, 061, 062, 066,
  120; 12-095
LEE, Hyo-Jae. See LEE, Hyo-chai.
LEE, Hyon-jong. 03-333
LEE, Hyun Bok. 05-187
LEE, Hyun-jae. 11-214
LEE, Ick-whan. 12-096
LEE, Ik-Hwan. 05-091
LEE, Ik-Mo. 05-056
LEE, Jae-Ho. 05-055
LEE, Jang-Hyun. 10-169, 170; 12-231;
  13-146, 148
LEE, Jeong-Ho. 05-302, 303
LEE, Joong-Koon. 11-172 (=15-201), 173
LEE, Joung-sik. 12-036, 097 (=12-154),
  155, 232, 233
LEE, Kang-O. 04-029
LEE, Kang-sook. 07-137, 163
LEE, Keedong. 05-092, 188, 189, 190
LEE, Ke-Soon. 05-364
LEE, Ki-baik. 03-025, 075, 104, 491, 502
LEE, Ki-Moon. 05-023, 029, 030, 031, 133,
  241, 248, 263, 304
LEE, Kie Wook. 11-076
LEE, Kwang Kyu. 10-063, 064
LEE, Kwang-rin. 03-162, 334, 354, 355,
  356
LEE, Kyu. 07-025
LEE, Kyu-Hwan. 08-075
LEE, Kyu-tae. 12-037
LEE, Kyung-Sook Chang. 11-215
LEE, Lena Kim. 07-007, 036, 045
LEE, Maeng-Sung. 05-191, 343
LEE, Man-Gap. 10-082, 099, 100, 121
  (=12-234), 129; 12-118, 156
LEE, Moon-chong. 09-081
LEE, Mun Woong. 15-152
LEE, Ou Young. 10-006
LEE, Peter H. 03-105, 106 (=04-069), 107,
  163, 164; 06-003 (=07-200), 019, 020, 021,
  022, 023, 052
LEE, Pong S. 11-146, 235, 236 (=15-202),
  237
LEE, Pyong-geun. 05-270
LEE, Samuel Sang-ok. 13-061
LEE, Sang-beck. 05-305; 10-157
LEE, Sang-eun. 04-044
LEE, Sang-min. 12-461
LEE, Sang Oak. 05-249
LEE, Seung Yun. 10-086; 11-192
LEE, Soon Hi. 01-032
LEE, Soon-won Stewart. 14-119
LEE, Sun-keun. 03-416
LEE, Sung-Hwa. 08-139

LEE, Sung-nyǒng. 01-033 (=02-018);
  05-032, 306
LEE, Tai Ro. 13-062
LEE, Taikwhi. 12-235
LEE, Takyun. 11-216
LEE, U-Gene. 14-086
LEE, Won-chul. 03-587
LEE, Won Sul. 03-560; 12-313; 14-087
LEE, Woosung. 03-228
LEE, Y. H. 05-322
LEE, Y.-S. C. 05-346
LEE, Yong-Kul. 08-106
LEE, Yong Sun. 12-157 (=12-314)
LEE, Young Bum. 03-417
LEE, Young-ho. 09-118; 10-039 (=12-315),
  040, 041 (=10-158), 160 (=12-159);
  12-098, 099, 100, 158
LEE, Young June. 13-107
LEE, Yung Dug. 08-096
LEE, Yur-bok. 03-388, 389
LENSEN, George Alexander. 03-310
LEW, Young Ick. 01-034; 03-335, 336, 357,
  418, 419
LEWIN, Bruno. 05-112
LEWIS, David M. 12-101
LEWIS, John P. 11-077
LEZIN, V. V. 15-051, 092
LI, Kang-Jong. 08-059
LI, Kitak. 03-426
LI, Mirok. 03-563 (=06-053; 09-044)
LI, Ogg. 01-035; 03-013, 076, 077, 078, 108,
  109, 110, 111, 112, 113, 142, 467
LI, Yuk-sa. 12-422
LIEM, Channing. 03-437
LIEROP, Peter Van. 04-208
LIEW, Song Kun. 13-108
LIM, Bang-Hyun. 12-102
LIM, Hy-Sop. 10-042, 043, 159
LIM, Jung-Pyung. 13-100
LIM, Sang-un. 12-236
LIM, Youngil. 10-020 (=11-219); 11-157,
  217, 218
LIMB, Ben C. 14-088
LIN, T. C. 03-404
LISKER, Leigh. 05-040
LOEHR, Max. 07-046
LOFGREN, Charles A. 14-049
LOH, Keie-hyun. 03-026
LONG, Charles Chaillé. 04-070
LONGFORD, Joseph H. 03-014
LOO, Robert Kalei Wah Kit. 12-237
  (=12-489)
LOVELL, John P. 10-160 (=12-159); 12-158
LOWELL, Percival. 03-311 (=09-045)
LOWENBERG, Gerhard. 12-082 (=12-214)
LUCY, L. W. Wilson. 03-468
LUKOFF, Fred. 05-033, 148, 344
LYMAN, Albert. 13-024, 025
LYMAN, Princeton N. 11-200 (=12-006,
  295), 220 (=12-316); 12-103; 14-184

LYONS, Gene Martin. 11-158 (=12-317; 14-050)
Lyrichord Discs Inc. 07-176, 177
LYU, Kingsley K. 03-050

M

MALKOV, F. V. 05-149, 150
MALOZEMOFF, Andrew. 03-427
MARCH, Arthur C. 04-054
MARCUS, Richard. 01-036 (=05-002); 09-006
MARTIN, Samuel Elmo. 05-093, 094, 113, 264, 265, 277, 284, 322, 336, 345, 346
MÁRTONFI, F. 05-250, 317
MARTYNOV, V. V. 09-029; 16-009
MASAITIS, V. L. 16-112
MATSULENKO, V. 16-083
MAXWELL, Murray. 04-181
MAZUR, Yu. N. 05-034, 114, 115 (=16-097), 151 (=16-096), 271
MAZUROV, V. M. 15-052 (=16-021); 16-065, 066, 067
McBRIAN, Charles D. 10-111
McCANN, David R. 06-025, 026, 069
McCUNE, Evelyn. 02-019 (=07-011)
McCUNE, George McAfee. 03-253, 254, 263, 275, 469; 05-313; 11-054 (=12-038)
McCUNE, Shannon. 03-503; 09-030 (=12-039), 031, 090, 107, 135, 136, 137, 138; 14-198
McGRANE, George A. 03-321
McKEE, Thomas. 04-149
McKENZIE, Frederick Arthur. 03-322, 492
McLANE, Charles B. 14-140
McVOY, Edgar C. 11-249
MEADE, Edward Grant. 12-040 (=14-089)
Medium Industry Bank (Seoul). 11-137
MEDLEY, Margaret. 07-063, 088
MEER, K. Van der. 09-082
MERRILL, Henry F. 03-282
MERRILL, John Espy. 03-390
MESKILL, John. 03-165
MESLER, David P. 03-493
Methodist Publishing House, Seoul. 01-087 (=03-292)
METZGER, Berta. 06-038
MEYER, Donald R. 13-109
Michigan State University. Agricultural Economics Research Institute. 10-085
MIDDLETON, Dorothy H. 09-060
MIDDLETON, William D. 09-060
MILLER, Frederick S. 04-150
MILLER, Robert P. 05-337
MILLER, Roy A. 05-266, 267
MILLS, Edwin W. 03-612
MILLS, John E. 10-083
MIN, Benjamin B. H. 14-024 (=15-176)
MIN, Byong-Gi. 12-238
MIN, Byong-tae. 12-041
MIN, Byoung-Kook. 13-110

MIN, Leo Yoon-Gee. 08-140
MIN, Pyong-chon. 12-318
MIN, Pyŏng-ha. 03-094
MIN, Pyung Kun. 10-044
MIN, Suk-Hong. 12-104
MINN, Young-gyu. 03-210
MITCHELL, Charles Clyde, Jr. 13-056
MITCHELL, Richard H. 03-544 (=14-120)
M'LEOD, John. 09-046
MOAK, Samuel K. 11-119, 120 (=12-531)
MOBIUS, J. Mark. 12-239, 240
MOFFETT, Samuel Hugh. 04-151
MOHR, A. 02-029
MOK, Yung-man. 09-139
MOLODTSOV, S. 16-077
MOON, Chang-joo. 12-042
MOON, Pal Yong. 11-104
MOON, Seung Gyu. 10-101, 122
MOON, Won-Taik. 11-250 (=12-241, 319)
MOON, Yang-Soo. 05-251
MOORE, S. F. 04-071
MOOS, Felix. 10-045
MOOSE, J. Robert. 03-312 (=14-152; 10-084)
MORGAN, Robert M. 08-076
MORLEY, James William. 12-043
MORRIS, William G. 14-090
MORTIMORE, Doretha E. 03-465
MOSCOWITZ, Karl. 03-470 (=11-055)
MOST, Amicus. 11-159, 160, 161
MOTT, John R. 04-153
MOZDYKOV, V. M. 05-326, 328
MUELLER, Hon E. 14-051
MUN, Hui-Sok. 10-160; 12-158, 159
MURPHY, Jay. 13-147, 151, 152
Museum of Far Eastern Antiquities, Stockholm. 07-064
Museum of Fine Arts of Boston. 07-065
MUSHAKOJI, Kinhide. 14-210
MUTEL, Gustave. 04-182

N

Naewoe Press, Seoul. 01-114 (=15-033)
NAHM, Andrew Chang-woo. 01-037; 03-337, 338, 391, 420 (=03-471; 10-142); 10-143 (=12-044, 383)
NAKAMURA, Hiroshi. 03-605 (=09-140), 606
NAKAMURA, James I. 03-534
NAM, Byung-Hun. 08-141
NAM, Duck Woo. 11-078
NAM, Il. 14-025
NAM, Ki Shim. 05-192
NAM, Koon Woo. 12-462 (=12-490; 15-081), 463
NAM, S. G. 16-089, 090, 091
NAM, Won-suh. 10-161
National Agricultural Cooperative Federation (Seoul). 10-115; 11-010
National Construction Research Institute (Seoul). 09-130

National Museum of Korea. 07-015, 016
Nauchno-issled. 15-039
Nauka (Moscow). 16-004, 005, 006, 007, 016
NEEDHAM, Joseph, 03-581 (=09-019), 582, 613, 614
NELSON, Melvin Frederick. 03-038
NELSON, Sarah Milledge. 02-020
NEVIUS, John L. 04-209
NEW, Ilhan. 03-564
NIKITINA, M. I. 16-108
NIKOLSKII, L. B. 05-116, 117 (=16-099), 118, 119, 278, 327; 16-098
NISBET, Anabel Major. 04-210
NO, Chong-u. 03-596, 597
NOBLE, G. A. 08-107
NOBLE, Harold Joyce. 03-392, 393, 394, 472; 12-384; 14-052
NOBLE, Mattie Wilcox. 04-155
NOGAMI, Tadashi. 14-121
Nonesuch Records Inc. 07-178
NORTH, Eric M. 04-156
NORTH, Richard. 08-032
NORTON, Roger D. 11-079
Novaia Koreia. 15-035
NOVIKOV, I. T. 16-068
Novosti Koreia. 15-036
NUNN, G. Raymond. 01-038

O

O, Kap Hwan. 10-162
O'BRIEN, B. Thomas. 04-157
ODA, Shigeru. 13-081
OGLE, George Ewing. 11-251 (=12-242; 13-068)
OGURA, Shimpei. 05-004, 272
OGURA, Tautoma. 09-079
OH, Bonnie Bongwan. 03-370, 421
OH, Byung Hun. 10-163
OH, Chae-gyong. 01-069 (=08-033)
OH, Chae-Kyong. See OH, Chae-gyong.
OH, Choon-Kyu. 05-193, 194, 195, 196
OH, Chung Hwan. 12-321
OH, In-hwan. 10-169, 170; 12-244, 245; 13-148
OH, Jin Hwan. 12-246, 247
OH, John Kie-chiang. 12-045, 046, 106 (=14-092), 160; 14-091
OH, Ki-Hyong. 08-108
OH, Ki-Wan. 12-460 (=14-139; 15-134)
OH, Kwan Chi. 11-193
OH, Suck Hong. 12-320
OH, Young-Kyun. 10-102
OHLINGER, F. 04-072
OKADA, Takematsu. 09-091
OLIVER, Egbert S. 04-045
OLIVER, Robert T. 03-438 (=03-565; 12-161; 14-093), 473; 04-046; 14-053, 054
OLMSTEDT, David Lockwood. 05-347
OOE, Takao. 05-120
OPPERT, Ernest. 03-313

ORANGE, Marc. 03-262, 428; 06-070
O'ROURKE, Kevin. 06-054
OSGOOD, Cornelius. 01-070 (=04-011; 10-007; 12-047)
OTAM-METRA International. 10-135
OTT, Alfons. 04-097
OUM, Ky-moon. 12-248
OVERSTREET, William. 09-075

P

PAE, Sung-moun. 12-294, 322
PAE, Yang-Seo. See PAI, Yang-Seo.
PAGE, Ben. 12-423
PAHK, Induk. 03-566
PAI, Edward W. 05-348
PAI, Man-sill. 07-111
PAI, Paul. 04-030
PAI, Seong-tong. 10-127
PAI, Yang-Seo. 05-134, 361
PAIGE, Glenn D. 01-039, 040; 03-510; 12-048, 049, 323, 385 (=12-508; 14-131; 15-084), 386 (=14-221; 15-083), 387 (=14-132; 15-085, 178), 388; 14-055
PAIK, Hyŏn-Ki. 08-034, 077, 078, 079, 098, 099, 109, 142
PAIK, Keum-ju. 05-273
PAIK, L. George. 03-114, 358 (=04-211); 08-080; 09-047
PAIK, Lak-Geoon George. See PAIK, L. George.
PAIK, Nak Choon. See PAIK, L. George.
PAIK, Sang-ki. 12-162
PAIK, Wanki. 12-324
PAINE, Robert Treat, Jr. 07-017
PAK, B. D. 16-022, 092
PAK, Chan-kirl. 02-021
PAK, Chi-Young. 12-283 (=13-033)
PAK, Dinshoon. 15-053
PAK, Dong Hie. 13-071
PAK, G. A. 05-121, 122
PAK, Hŏn-yŏng. 15-015
PAK, Ki Hyok. 09-062; 10-086, 112; 11-092 (=15-203), 105
PAK, Ki-Hyuk. See PAK, Ki Hyok.
PAK, Kwon-sang. 12-249
PAK, Mikhail N. 15-054, 155; 16-023
PAK, N. S. 05-123
PAK, No-ch'un. 03-229
PAK, Pyŏng-Ho. See PARK, Byong Ho.
PAK, Sen Uk. 16-110
PAK, Tu-jin. 06-027
PAK, Young-Sook. 07-047
PAK, Yun Baik. 15-179
PALAIS, James B. 01-099; 03-166, 189, 264, 323; 12-050
PALMER, Spencer J. 03-029, 275, 395; 04-012 (=10-046), 158, 212
PARDE, Maurice. 09-083
PARK, Bong Bae. 04-159
PARK, Bong-Mok. 08-143
PARK, Bong-Nam. 05-349

PARK, Byong Ho. 03-181 (=13-014); 13-012, 013, 015, 016
PARK, Byung Ho. 09-119
PARK, Byung-Soo. 05-197, 198, 199
PARK, C. J. 12-168
PARK, Chang-Hai. 05-350
PARK, Chin Keun. 11-194
PARK, Chong Gil. 07-164
PARK, Chong-hong. 03-230; 04-047, 073, 098, 099, 100
PARK, Chong Kee. 10-008
PARK, Choon-Ho. 09-128; 13-085, 086
PARK, Chung Hee. 12-107 (=12-165), 108 (=12-164; 14-026), 109 (=12-166), 110 (=12-163; 14-027), 167; 14-022
PARK, Dong Suh. See BARK, Dong-Suh.
PARK, Dong-Wa. 08-035
PARK, Han-shik. 12-250
PARK, Hee-bum. 12-251
PARK, Hong-Kyu. 01-041 (=14-056)
PARK, Hun. 08-144
PARK, Hyoung Cho. 10-073
PARK, Jae Kyu. 14-028
PARK, Kiljun. 13-113
PARK, Moon Ok. 12-325
PARK, N. Y. 12-111
PARK, Nei Hei. 12-326
PARK, No-Sik. 09-070
PARK, Pong Nang. 04-213
PARK, Sang-Yol. 10-103
PARK, Seong Ho. 11-162
PARK, Seong-Rae. 03-422
PARK, Soon Ham. See KIM, Soon-Ham Park.
PARK, Tai-Sun. 08-081
PARK, Thomas Choonbai. 08-145
PARK, Won-Son. 03-182
PARK, Yong-ki. 12-252 (=13-069)
PARK, Young-Han. 09-120
PARK, Young-horm. 12-424
PARK, Young June. 11-106
PARK, Young-Youl. 08-146
PARK, Youngshik. 13-134
PARRY, Albert. 01-042
PARSONS, Howard L. 08-036
Party History Institute of the Central Committee of the Workers' Party of Korea. See Korea, Democratic People's Republic of. Party History Institute.
PASKOV, B. K. 05-035
PASSIN, Herbert. 03-195
PATRICK, Hugh T. 11-182
PATTERSON, Betty Soon-Ju. 05-200
PATTERSON, Wayne. 03-047, 396
PAULLIN, Charles Oscar. 03-397
PAWLOSKI, Auguste. 09-141
PEARSON, Richard J. 02-022, 023, 024, 025, 026
PEASLEE, Amos J. 13-038, 039, 171
PERLO, Ellen. 08-060
PERRIN, Kwan Sok. 14-177

PERRY, Jean. 04-160
PETERSON, Mark. 03-196 (=10-065)
PETROVA, O. P. 05-005, 006
Philips. 07-179
PHILLIPS, David M. 13-153
PIGULEVSKAYA, E. A. 15-055 (=16-069)
PIHL, Marshall R., Jr. 05-152; 06-055 (=10-009), 071
PITTS, Forrest R. 09-108, 121
PLOTKIN, Arieh Leopold. 14-165
POLIVANOV, E. D. 05-242
POLLARD, Robert T. 03-398
POTT, Peter H. 07-005
Presbyterian Church in Korea. 04-110, 111
Presbyterian Church in the USA. Board of Foreign Missions. 04-102, 103, 109
Presbyterian Church, USA. Korea Mission. 04-108, 205
Protestant Evangelical Missions in Korea. 04-104, 105, 106, 107
PROVINE, Robert C., Jr. 07-126, 138, 139, 140
Public Relations Association of Korea. 01-043, 107
PUCEK, V. 05-307
PUGET, Henry. 13-040
PULTR, Alois. 05-307, 331, 351
PUTINTSEV, V. K. 16-111
Pyongyang Times. 01-116 (=15-038)
PYUN, Y. T. 04-161

Q

QUINONES, Carlos Kenneth. 03-339, 340

R

RACHKOV, G. E. 05-057, 153, 154, 155
RACKHAM, Bernard. 07-066
RAGINSKII, M. Yu. 16-078
RAHDER, Johannes. 05-103
RAITT, Walton A. 14-057
RAMSEY, S. Robert. 05-252, 253
RAMSTEDT, Gustav John. 05-017, 104, 105, 124, 125, 126, 156, 243
RAVENSCROFT, Byfleet G. 13-136
REE, J. J. See REE, Joe Jungno.
REE, Joe Jungno. 05-127, 201, 202, 203
REEDMAN, Anthony John. 09-071
REES, David. 14-058; 15-180
REEVE, W. D. 11-020; 12-052 (=12-327; 13-034; 14-029)
REISCHAUER, Edwin. 04-031, 032, 033
REISCHAUER, Edwin O. 03-005, 119; 05-313; 14-030
RENAUD, Bertrand M. 09-122; 11-138, 139, 221
RENAUDE, Young-Key Kim. See KIM-RENAUD, Young-Key.
RENICK, Roderick Dhu, Jr. 14-094
REORDAN, Robert Edwin. 03-399
Research Center for Peace and Unification 01-083

Research Institute for Internal and External Affairs. 15-157
Research Institute of Asian Economies. 01-074
Research Institute on Korean Affairs. 01-080 (=14-010; 15-024)
REUBENS, Edwin P. 11-163
REW, Joung Yole. 03-474
RHEE, Chongik. 12-328
RHEE, Jae Han. 11-107
RHEE, Sang-Woo. 14-199
RHEE, Syngman. 03-475; 12-112 (=12-169)
RHEE, T. C. 11-222 (=12-329)
RHEE, Yong-pil. 12-051 (=12-330); 14-211
RHEE, Yu-Sang. 08-037
RHI, Ki-Yŏng. 03-115; 04-074
RHI, Sang-Kyu. 12-284
RHIE, Tschang-boum. 06-056
RHO, Do Yang. 09-020
RHODES, Harry A. 04-214, 215
RIEKEL, A. 05-011
RILEY, John W. 12-389 (=14-059), 395
RIM, Han-Young. 08-147
RO, Bong Rin. 04-216
RO, Chung-Hyun. 10-124, 130; 12-331 (=12-532)
RO, Kil-myong. 10-149
ROBINSON, Joan. 11-238 (=12-533; 15-204)
ROBINSON, Michael E. 03-494
ROCCO, Kenneth. 12-139
ROCKHILL, William W. 03-247, 283, 298; 10-021
ROCKWELL, Coralie. 07-127, 141, 142, 165
ROE, Chungil Han. 08-148
ROE, Myong-Joon. 13-124; 14-200
ROGERS, Michael C. 03-120, 136, 137, 143, 144, 145; 05-157
ROGIER, Robert H. 13-047
ROH, Chang Shub. 10-074
ROH, Do-yang. 03-607
ROMASHKIN, P. S. 15-181 (=16-070); 16-079
ROSÉN, Staffan. 05-007, 254
ROSS, John. 03-015
Royal Asiatic Society. Korea Branch. 01-101
ROZENBLIT, S. Ya. 16-078
RUCKER, Arthur N. 14-178
RUDNEV, A. 05-244
RUDOLPH, Philip. 11-239 (=12-390, 425, 509), 240
RUFUS, W. Carl. 03-583, 584, 585, 586, 587
RUSTANOVICH, D. N. 16-112
RUTT, Richard. 03-016, 087, 439; 04-013 (=10-047), 162, 163; 06-028, 029, 030, 031, 057
RYANG, J. S. 04-217

RYU, Hun. 11-029 (=15-086); 12-391
RYU, Jai Poong. 10-173
RYU, Paul Kichyun. 13-002, 072, 073, 074, 075, 154

S

SAISON, Camille. 03-146
SAITO, Makoto. 03-476
SALISBURY, Harrison E. 12-392
SAMPLE, Lillie Laetitia. 02-027, 028, 029
SAMPLE, Raymond C. 09-075
SAMSONOV, G. E. 15-182 (=16-071)
SANDS, William F. 03-314
SANSOM, George. 03-255
SANTANGELO, Paolo. 03-039, 429
SAUER, Charles A. 04-218
SAWYER, Robert. 12-053
SCALAPINO, Robert A. 01-044; 03-511 (=11-030, 147; 12-394, 426, 464, 492, 510, 534; 14-134; 15-056), 512; 12-054, 393 (=15-087); 14-031, 032, 095, 133, 156; 15-158
SCHERZER, M. F. 03-167
SCHOFIELD, Frank W. 03-504
SCHRAMM, Wilbur. 12-389, 395, 493; 14-059
SCHROEDER, Peter Brett. 01-045
SCHULMAN, Frank Joseph. 01-046, 047, 048
SCHUMACHER, F. Carl, Jr. 12-396
SCHUMPETER, S. B. 03-535
SCHURIG, Klaus. 13-125
SECKEL, Dietrich. 07-033
SEJNA, Jan. 14-141
SEMENOVA, N. P. 16-039, 046
SEO, Kyung Bo. 04-075
SEOH, M. S. See SEOH, Munsang.
SEOH, Munsang. 03-127, 211
SESSION, Eldred Steed. 08-149
SEYMOUR, James. 13-167
SHABAD, Theodore. 12-535
SHABSHINA, F. I. 15-057, 076 (=16-019), 088; 16-024, 054, 055
SHAPLEN, Robert. 14-241
SHAW, E. S. 11-182
SHAW, William. 03-175 (=13-017)
SHCHETININ, B. V. 16-061, 062
SHEARER, Roy E. 03-549 (=04-164); 04-165
SHELDON, Robert Lewis. 04-166
SHIBATANI, M. 05-080, 204, 205, 206
SHIM, Sang P'il. 10-022
SHIN, Bong Ju. 11-223
SHIN, Doh Chull. 12-332
SHIN, Doo Bum. 12-323
SHIN, Il-ch'ol. 12-113
SHIN, Linda. 03-051
SHIN, Myŏng-sŏp. 04-014
SHIN, Roy W. 12-333 (=14-096)
SHIN, Sang-cho. 15-137

SHIN, Suk-ho. 03-265, 266, 267
SHIN, Susan Sandler. 03-183, 184, 197 (=10-166), 198 (=10-104; 11-056); 10-113
SHIN, Woong Shik. 13-003, 111
SHIN, Yong-ha. 03-536
SHINN, Rinn-Sup. 01-071 (=09-051), 073(=11-031; 12-060, 402; 15-093); 14-034, 201
SHIPAEV, V. I. 15-058 (=16-026); 16-025
SHIRATORI, Kurakichi. 03-079
SHUFELDT, Robert W. 03-284
SHULTZ, Edward J. 03-095
SIBATA, Takesi. 05-128
SIGWORTH, Heather. 13-101
SILBERMAN, Bernard S. 01-049
SIMMONS, Robert R. 12-397, 398; 14-060, 135 (=15-183), 157
SIMON, Sheldon W. 14-035
SIN, Yong-ha. 03-359
SINITSKII, S. E. 16-111
SINITSYN, B. V. 16-049, 050, 067
SINNOTT, John P. 13-135
SITLER, Lydia Arlene. 08-150
SKALIČKOVÁ, A. 05-058, 059, 060, 061
SKILLEND, W. E. 01-050 (=06-058); 06-004, 059
SLOBODA, John. 10-131, 182
SMIRNOV, L. N. 16-078
SMITH, Gaddis. 14-061
SMITH, Lenore K. 07-166
SMITH, Warren William, Jr. 03-215
SOBEL, Bernard. 07-201
SOCHUREK, Howard. 09-048
SOH, Jin Chull. 14-142, 143
SOHN, Han. 05-063, 095
SOHN, Ho-min. 05-012, 207, 208, 209, 210, 211, 212, 213, 214
SOHN, Jae-souk. 12-170, 468 (=12-494); 15-138
SOHN, John Young. 05-268
SOHN, Pow-Key. 01-130; 02-030, 031, 032 (=03-017); 03-168, 268, 360, 615, 616, 617
SOHN, Yun-Mok. 12-253
SOK, Do-Ryun. 04-015, 076, 077
SOLBERG, Sammy Edward. 06-072
SOMERVILLE, John N. 03-199 (=10-174)
SONG, Bang-song. 01-051 (=07-128); 07-129, 143, 144, 145, 146, 147, 148, 149, 150, 151, 152, 167
SONG, Byung Nak. 11-224
SONG, Byung-Soon. 08-151 (=12-114, 427)
SONG, Chu-yŏng. 03-231, 232
SONG, June-ho. 03-169
SONG, Kyong-nin. 07-153
SONG, Sang Hyun. 13-112
SONG, Seok-Choong. 05-036, 215, 216, 217, 218, 219, 220, 221, 255
SONG, Yo-In. 05-285, 286, 362
SONG, Yoon Keun. 11-019

SONN, Ju-Chan. 13-113
SOPER, Alexander. 07-027
Sovremennyi vostok. 15-040
SPAHR, William. 14-144
SPANIER, John W. 14-062
SPRINGER, John Frederick. 12-115 (=12-334)
STAIRS, Denis. 14-185
Stanford University. 12-358
STANLEY, John W. 10-011
STARR, Frederick. 04-079, 080; 07-112
STEINBERG, David I. 12-055 (=14-036); 13-143
STELCHEN, M. 03-256
STELMACH, Daniel S. 14-145
STEPHAN, John J. 03-052
STERN, Harold P. 07-089
STEVENSON, Adlai E. 14-063
STEVENSON, Frederick Boyd. 03-477
STINE, James H. 09-123
STODDARD, George D. 08-061
STOESSINGER, John G. 14-204
STOKES, Charles Davis. 04-219
STONE, Isidore F. 14-064
STRAIGHT, Willard D. 03-285
SUDZUKI, Osamu. 03-588
SUEMATSU, Yasukazu. 03-128, 269
SUH, Chan-ki. 09-110
SUH, Cheong-soo. 05-018
SUH, Cho-soon. 05-363
SUH, Dae-Sook. 03-495, 513 (=15-016), 514 (=12-399, 465); 14-146; 15-059); 12-171 (=12-467, 536), 400, 466 (=15-141); 14-147; 15-089, 140
SUH, Doo-Soo. 05-037, 352 (=07-202)
SUH, In-jung. 07-168
SUH, Sang-Chul. 03-537 (=11-057)
SUH, Sang Mok. 11-252
SUHRKE, Astri. 14-212
SUK, Kyoung-Jing. 05-222
SUNG, Ok Ryen. 06-073
SUNOO, Harold Hag-Won. 03-423; 05-158
SUR, Donald. 07-154
SURET-CANALE, Jean. 09-124
SUSLINA, S. S. 16-047
SWANN, Peter. 07-012
SWANSON, Chang-su. 01-026 (=02-016)
SWISHER, Ralph Blakeslee. 10-114; 12-116 (=12-335)
SYNN, Seung Kwon. 03-430
SZCZESNIAK, Boleslaw. 03-129, 147

T

TAGASHIRA, Yoshiko. 05-223
TAKABAYASHI, Hideo. 13-082
TANG, Shin She. 15-060
TATEIWA, Iwao. 09-072
TAVROV, G. [G. I. TUNKIN]. 16-063, 072
TCHEU, Soc-Kiou. 05-064, 096, 318
TENG, Ssü-yu. 03-243

TEWKSBURY, Donald G. 03-059 (=12-056)
THAYER, Nathaniel B. 03-130
THOMAS, S. B. 11-174 (=14-158)
THORPE, Norman. 06-060
THROWER, Norman J. W. 03-602 (=09-142)
TIANEN, Walter. 07-169
Tikhii Okean. 15-041
TJONG, Zong Uk. 13-018
TOBY, Ronald T. 03-257, 554
TOH, Soo-Hee. 05-256
TOLCHENOV, M. P. 16-084
TOMITA, Kōjiro. 07-034, 102, 103
TOMSON, Edgar. 13-126, 177
TOWNSEND, Alexander. 02-033
TRAGER, George L. 05-097
TREAT, Payson J. 03-405
TREWARTHA, Glenn T. 09-112
TRIGUBENKO, M. E. 16-040, 043
Trilingual Press, Seoul. 03-294
TROLLOPE, Mark Napier. 04-081
TROSTSEVICH, A. F. 16-101, 108, 109
TSCHE, Chong Kil. 13-127
TSCHE, Djon Chu. 05-245
TSCHE, Kiuon. 13-114
TSCHÖ, Hyŏnbä. 03-131
TSCHŎN, Pongdŏk. See CHUN, Bong Duck.
TSIANG, T. F. 03-371
TSUKAMOTO, Zenryu. 04-082
TSURUTANI, Taketsugu. 01-052
TULLOCK, Gordon. 11-179
TUNKIN, G. I. See TAVROV, G.
TYAGAI, G. D. 15-090; 16-027, 028, 029, 030

U

UM, Sangho. 09-071
UMEDA, Hiroyuki. 05-098, 274, 332
UMEHARA, Sueji. 07-048
UNDERWOOD, Horace G. 04-167; 08-062
UNDERWOOD, Horace Horton. 01-053; 03-555 (=08-038), 618; 06-005, 060; 08-152
UNDERWOOD, Joan V. 05-323
UNDERWOOD, Lillias Horton. 03-315
Union of Soviet Socialist Republics. Academy of Sciences. Institute of History. 15-042
Union of Soviet Socialist Republics. Communist Party. 15-025
Union of Soviet Socialist Republics. Geological Institute. 09-073
United Korean Committee in America. 03-485, 487
United Nations. 11-011, 012, 080, 081; 12-057; 13-128
United Nations. Asian Institute for Economic Development and Planning. 08-003

United Nations. Educational, Scientific, and Cultural Organization. 08-004, 007, 008, 009, 039, 040, 063, 064, 065, 066, 067, 068, 082, 083, 084, 085, 086
United Nations. Food and Agricultural Organization. 11-108
United States. Comptroller General. 11-164
United States. Congress. 12-059; 14-065, 097, 098
United States. Department of Army. 01-056 (=15-007); 09-052; 12-058, 469 (=12-495); 13-144
United States. Department of Army. Army Language School. 05-353, 354, 355
United States. Department of Army. Army Map Service. 09-144, 145, 151, 152, 153, 154
United States. Department of Commerce. Bureau of the Census. 01-054 (=15-008), 055
United States. Department of Commerce. Bureau of International Commerce. 11-165
United States. Department of Commerce. Joint Publications Research Service. 01-078 (=15-018); 11-013, 014, 032, 148, 175; 13-162, 170, 178; 15-017, 019, 126, 139, 147, 153, 198
United States. Department of Interior. Bureau of Mines. 11-140, 149
United States. Department of Interior. Bureau of Reclamation. 09-084
United States. Department of Labor. 11-253, 254 (=13-070)
United States. Department of State. 03-276; 09-053, 054, 055, 056, 057; 11-033, 121; 12-401 (=14-148; 15-091); 13-088; 14-099, 202, 222
United States. Department of State. Bureau of Intelligence and Research. 11-122
United States. Library of Congress. 01-057, 058
United States. Operations Mission to Korea. 08-069, 087; 10-136
United States. Weather Bureau. 09-092
University of Hawaii. Center for Korean Studies. 01-098
UNRUH, Ellen S. 03-088
UPHOFF, N. T. 10-087
USATOV, D. M. 05-326, 328 (=16-100)
USHIJIMA, T. 05-045

V

VAINTSVAIG, N. K. 15-092 (=16-056), 142 (=16-057)
VALENCE, D. 12-254
VAN BUSKIRK, James Dale. 04-168
VANIN, Yu V. 16-031, 032
VASIL'EV, A. G. 05-129, 130; 16-081
VASIL'EV, I. V. 05-065

VATCHER, William Henry. 14-066
VIESSMAN, Warren. 03-619 (=07-026)
VINACKE, Harold M. 04-016
VINOCOUR, Seymour Murray. 12-172
VOIVODAS, Constantin. 11-166
VOLK, I. 16-081
VORONTSOV, V. B. 16-073
VOS, Frits. 03-116; 05-019, 024, 038, 269,
    319, 320
VREELAND, Nena. 01-072, 073 (=12-060,
    402; 15-093)

W

WADA, Yuji. 03-589
WAGNER, Edward W. 03-027, 170, 171,
    201, 202, 203 (=10-167), 545 (=14-122);
    05-356; 12-061 (=14-100)
WAGNER, Ellasue. 03-543
WALES, Nym. 03-515 (=15-048)
WALKER, Hugh Dyson. 03-040, 041, 248
WALKER, Stephen. 14-206
WALTER, Gary D. 03-400
WANG, In Keun. 10-105
WANGERIN, Theodora S. 04-169
WARNER, Lorraine d'O. 07-090, 091
WASHBURN, John N. 03-516 (=12-496;
    15-094); 12-511 (=14-149)
WASSON, Alfred W. 04-170, 171
WATANABE, Susumu. 11-167
WATSON, Burton. 03-080
WATSON, William. 07-035
WEEMS, Benjamin B. 03-240 (=04-089);
    04-088
WEEMS, Clarence Norwood, Jr. 03-018,
    341, 361, 440; 12-062
WEISSBERG, Guenter. 13-083
WEITZMAN, R. S. 05-042
WELFIELD, John. 14-123
WELLINGTON, Donald. 11-173
WERTH, Richard. 08-041
WESTPHAL, Larry Edward. 11-082, 083
WHANG, Byung-Joon. 11-225
WHANG, Chan-Ho. 05-364
WHANG, Hichul Henry. 08-153
WHANG, In-Joung. 10-168; 11-084; 12-173
    (=12-336), 312, 337, 338
WHANG, Won-Koo. 05-308
WHELAN, J. B. 04-220
WHITE, D. G. 12-403
WHITE, Gordon. 11-241
WHITE, Nathan. 14-037
WHITE, Oswald. 03-478
WHITE, Peter T. 09-049
WHITE, William W. 13-136
WHITING, Allen S. 14-159
WIDEMAN, Bernard F. 11-109 (=12-339);
    12-255 (=12-340)
WIDEMAN, Bernie. See WIDEMAN, Ber-
    nard F.
WILKINSON, Thomas O. 10-132

WILKINSON, William H. 03-316 (=13-021)
WILLIAMS, F. W. 12-395, 493
WILSON, Elizabeth C. 08-154
WILSON, George. 12-396
WINKLER, Robin L. 01-019
WOLF, Charles, Jr. 11-085 (=12-341)
WOLFF, K. D. 15-079
WON, George. 10-169 (=13-148), 170
WON, Yu-han. 03-172, 173, 185, 186, 342
    (=03-620)
WOO, Byung-Kyu. 12-140, 141 (=12-216),
    142, 174, 217, 256
WOO, Ki-do. 11-255
WOO, Nak-Ki. 09-021
WOO, Philip Myungsup. 03-343
WOOD, C. W. 08-042
WOOD, Robert S. 01-059
World Peace Through Law Center. 13-004
WRIGHT, Edward R. 12-063 (=12-342)
WRIGHT, Mary C. 03-406

Y

YANAGI, Sōetsu. 07-058, 092, 093
YANAIHARA, Tadao. 03-479
YANG, Byung-Hui. 13-102
YANG, Dong Whee. 05-224, 225, 226, 227,
    228, 229, 230, 231
YANG, Ho-min. 12-470
YANG, In-Seok. 05-232, 233, 234, 235,
    236, 237
YANG, K. P. See YANG, Key Paik.
YANG, Key Paik. 01-060; 03-030, 031
    (=04-048); 08-043 (=12-428, 512); 11-034;
    15-009
YANG, Kyung-rin. 02-021, 034, 035
YANG, Sung-Chul. 12-117, 257
YANG, Sŭng-du. 13-149
YANG, Yung Yong. 11-168
YE, Yun Ho. 04-017
YI, Ch'un-yŏng. 03-621
YI, Gouzea. 12-258
YI, Hu-Rak. 12-259
YI, Hyo-jae. See LEE, Hyo-chai.
YI, Kyu-tae. 03-324 (=10-012)
YI, Man-gap. See LEE, Man Gap.
YI, Myonggu. 04-049 (=12-119)
YI, Pangja. 03-567
YI, Pyŏng-do. 03-089; 09-022
YI, Tu-hyon. See LEE, Du-Hyun.
YI, Yuk. 06-036
YIM, Ch'un-ch'u. 15-061
YIM, Dong Jae. 03-407
YIM, Han-yong. 03-556
YIM, Louise. 03-568
YIM, Yong Soon. 12-175 (=12-471), 343
    (=12-537)
YIU, Myung Kun. 12-429 (=12-472; 15-184)
YOH, Suk-kee. 07-213, 214
Yonsei University. 10-123, 137
YOO, Hoon. 12-344, 348

YOO, Hyong Jin. 08-044, 100, 155; 12-080
YOO, Hyun. 13-115
YOO, Hyung-chin. See YOO, Hyong Jin.
YOO, Jong Hae. 03-480; 12-345
YOO, Ki Hong. 12-473
YOO, Se Hee. 03-517, 518
YOO, Stanley-Sung Soon. 08-156
YOO, Tae-ho. 14-179
YOO, Tai-Yong. 08-110
YOO, Young-Dae. 08-157
YOO, Young Hyun. 01-061
YOON, Chun-joo. 12-260
YOON, Ho Il. 13-053, 054
YOON, Hong-key. 09-023
YOON, Hyoung-sup. 12-224
YOON, Jai-Poong. 01-002
YOON, Jong-Joo. 10-088
YOON, Matheous. 04-183
YOON, Suk Bum. 11-169
YOON, Woo-kon. 10-171 (=12-346); 12-347
YOON, Young Kyo. 14-180
YOSHIKAWA, Tarao. 09-074
YOU, In-Jong. 08-158
YOU, Young-June. 12-120 (=12-176)
YOUN, Eul-sou. 04-050
YOUN, Laurent E. 03-212
YOUN, Moo-Byong. 02-008
YOUNG, John. 05-357
YOUNGS, Chaesoon T. 01-005
YU, Chang-Kyun. 05-321
YU, Chin-o. 12-285
YU, Hoon. See YOO, Hoon.
YU, Hyung-Jin. See YOO, Hyong Jin.
YU, Joon-young. 07-040
YU, Suk Ryul. 12-261
YU, Tal-Young. 12-349
YUM, Ki Sup. 08-159
YUN, Ch'i-ho. 03-286
YUN, Ki-bong. 12-404 (=12-497)
YUN, Kun-Sik. 13-035
YUN, Sang Soon. 05-341
YUN, Seung-Young. 13-063
YUN, Sŏng-sun. 04-051
YUN, Soon Young. 10-183
YUN, Yŏ-jun. 03-053
YURZHONOV, V. 16-085

Z

ZABOROWSKI, Hans-Jurgen. 03-117
ZAGORIA, Donald S. 12-474
ZAICHIKOV, V. T. 09-033 (=16-012);
    16-013
ZASLAVSKII, D. 16-082
ZELINSKY, Wilbur. 09-112
ZEON, Young-cheol. 12-262 (=13-057)
ZINDER, L. R. 05-099
ZIRING, Lawrence. 12-020 (=12-363)
ZO, Zayong. 07-105, 106, 107, 108, 109, 110
ZŎNG, In-Sŏb. 05-314; 06-039; 07-203,
    204; 10-013

Production Notes

This book was typeset on the Unified Composing System by The University Press of Hawaii.

The text typeface is Compugraphic Times Roman and the display typeface is Univers.

Offset presswork and binding were done by Halliday Lithograph. Text paper is Glatfelter P & S Offset Vellum, basis 45.